78.99

Mac OS X Internals

Mac OS X Internals

A Systems Approach

Amit Singh

✦Addison-Wesley

Upper Saddle River, NJ • Boston • Indianapolis • San Francisco
New York • Toronto • Montreal • London • Munich • Paris • Madrid
Capetown • Sydney • Tokyo • Singapore • Mexico City

Many of the designations used by manufacturers and sellers to distinguish their products are claimed as trademarks. Where those designations appear in this book, and the publisher was aware of a trademark claim, the designations have been printed with initial capital letters or in all capitals.

The author and publisher have taken care in the preparation of this book, but make no expressed or implied warranty of any kind and assume no responsibility for errors or omissions. No liability is assumed for incidental or consequential damages in connection with or arising out of the use of the information or programs contained herein.

The publisher offers excellent discounts on this book when ordered in quantity for bulk purchases or special sales, which may include electronic versions and/or custom covers and content particular to your business, training goals, marketing focus, and branding interests. For more information, please contact:

U.S. Corporate and Government Sales, (800) 382-3419, corpsales@pearsontechgroup.com

For sales outside the United States, please contact:

International Sales, international@pearsoned.com

FREE 45-day online access

A searchable electronic version of this book's content is available for a limited time through Safari Bookshelf.

Safari Bookshelf is an electronic reference library that lets you easily search thousands of technical books, find code samples, download chapters, and access technical information whenever and wherever you need it.

To gain 45-day FREE Safari access to this book:

- Go to http://www.awprofessional.com/safarienabled
- Complete the brief registration form
- Enter the coupon code EUMQ-IH3L-XVUX-T1L6-E6JZ

If you have difficulty registering on Safari Bookshelf or accessing the online edition, please e-mail customer-service@safaribooksonline.com.

Visit us on the Web: www.awprofessional.com

Library of Congress Cataloging-in-Publication Data

Singh, Amit.
    Mac OS X internals : a systems approach / Amit Singh.
        p. cm.
    Includes bibliographical references and index.
    ISBN 0-321-27854-2 (hardback : alk. paper)
    1. Mac OS. 2. Operating systems (Computers) 3. Macintosh (Computer)--Programming. I. Title.
    QA76.76.O63S5645 2006
    005.4'4682—dc22

                                                                    2006014901

    Pearson Education, Inc.
    Rights and Contracts Department
    75 Arlington Street, Suite 300
    Boston, MA 02116
    Fax: (617) 848-7047
ISBN 0321278542

Text printed in the United States on recyled paper at Courier Westford in Westford, Massachusetts.

3rd Printing   December 2006

To my parents, Sharda and Amar Singh,
for teaching me everything I know about learning,
for giving me everything that I ever needed (or wanted) from them,
and for always being in my way without becoming an obstacle.

Contents

Preface

Although Mac OS X is a relatively new operating system, its lineage is rather colorful, and the history of most of its components is much older. Mac OS X, and Apple in general, has attracted a lot of attention in recent years. Given Apple's "cult-like" status, and the unique cultural and technical composition of Mac OS X, it is not surprising that people with vastly different backgrounds and interests—both users and non-users of Mac OS X—are curious about the system.

After working on, programming on, and extending several operating systems over the years, I was introduced to Mac OS X on April 1, 2003.[1] I was soon curious about the structure of the system. Despite the availability of several good books on Mac OS X, I was dismayed to find that I could not learn the details of Mac OS X internals from a book—*no such book existed*. There are books describing how to perform various tasks on Mac OS X; how to configure, customize, and tweak the system; and how certain user-visible aspects differ between Mac OS X and Windows. There are also books covering specific Mac OS X programming topics, such as the Cocoa and Carbon APIs. Other books make life easier for a Unix[2] user migrating to Mac OS X—such books typically discuss the command-line interface to the operating system. Although these books play important roles in making Mac OS X accessible, the core architecture and implementation of Mac OS X and its components have remained mysteries. To make matters worse, besides the lack of information, it is common to find misinformation on the composition of

---

1. The date is interesting because coincidentally, Apple was founded on April 1, 1976.

2. I use the term "Unix" to represent one of a UNIX system, a UNIX-derived system, or a UNIX-like system.

Mac OS X. Consequently, the system is often misunderstood because of long-standing myths and stereotypes, or is perceived as a black box.

The purpose of this book is to deconstruct and demystify Mac OS X by describing it from a system-design perspective. It takes an implementation-oriented approach to understanding the system. Consider the example of interprocess communication (IPC). Mac OS X has numerous user-level and kernel-level IPC mechanisms, some of which are well known and documented. Rather than just showing how to use these mechanisms, the book explains the design and implementation of the most fundamental mechanism (Mach IPC), and then discusses how the other mechanisms are layered on top of one another. My goal is not to teach you how to do something specific—my goal is to provide you with enough knowledge and examples so that after reading the book, depending on your interests and background, you can build upon your newly gained knowledge and do what you choose.

Along with text, the book uses detailed illustrations, function call graphs, annotated code excerpts, and programming examples to present a detailed examination of Mac OS X. To keep the subject matter interesting and accessible—even to the casual reader—the book contains relevant trivia, digressions, and other tidbits.[3]

Who This Book Is For

I hope the book will be useful to anyone curious about the composition and working of Mac OS X.

Application programmers can gain a deeper understanding of how their applications interact with the system. System programmers can use the book as a reference and to construct a better picture of how the core system works. In my experience as a programmer, a solid understanding of system internals is immensely useful in design, development, and debugging. For example, you know what the system is capable of, what is feasible and what is not, what the "best" option is in a given situation, and what the plausible reasons are for certain program behavior. This book's primary goal is to build a strong foundation for anyone who programs on Mac OS X.

Mac OS X users can read the book to better understand how the system is designed and how it comes together. System administrators and technical support staff will also find value in the book.

---

3. And a healthy dose of footnotes, too!

Besides those who use Mac OS X, the intended audience includes members of other technical communities, such as the BSD, Linux, and Windows communities. Given that many internal aspects of Mac OS X are radically different from these systems (for example, how the Mach kernel is used), the book will help such readers broaden their knowledge, and will assist them in comparing and contrasting Mac OS X with other operating systems.

The book will also be useful in an advanced operating systems course, particularly if you wish to do a case study on Mac OS X. The book is not suitable, however, as an introductory text. Most of the material is not presented at an introductory level, although I introduce many of the advanced topics with at least some background information.

The Book's Structure

Modern operating systems have become so large and complex that it is impossible to reasonably describe an entire system in a book. This book is somewhat ambitious in that it attempts to cover Mac OS X in substantial breadth *and* depth. The most important contributors to the book's depth are the carefully selected programming examples. The book is organized into twelve chapters. Although much of the book's content is rather technical, each chapter has sections that should be accessible to non-programmers.

Chapter 1, "Origins of Mac OS X," describes the technical history of Mac OS X and the systems it derives from. An unabridged version of Chapter 1, which covers all of Apple's past and present operating systems, is available on this book's accompanying web site.

Chapter 2, "An Overview of Mac OS X," is an eclectic tour of Mac OS X and its important features. It contains brief overviews of various layers that constitute the system.

Chapter 3, "Inside an Apple," describes the PowerPC architecture, using the PowerPC 970 ("G5") processor line as a specific example. It also discusses the PowerPC assembly language and calling conventions.

Chapter 4, "The Firmware and the Bootloader," describes both Open Firmware and the Extensible Firmware Interface (EFI), along with their respective bootloaders. It discusses the roles the firmware and the bootloader play in the system's operation, usage scenarios, and events that occur during early bootstrapping.

Chapter 5, "Kernel and User-Level Startup," describes the sequence of events—including initializations of kernel subsystems—from where the kernel starts executing to the point where the first user-space program (launchd) is run by the kernel. The discussion includes launchd's function and implementation.

Chapter 6, "The xnu Kernel," describes the core kernel architecture of Mac OS X. The discussion includes system call families and their implementation, low-level tracing and debugging mechanisms, and special features such as the virtual machine monitor in the PowerPC version of the kernel.

Chapter 7, "Processes," describes abstractions such as tasks, threads, and processes, the various forms in which they exist in Mac OS X subsystems, and processor scheduling. The discussion includes using various kernel-level and user-level interfaces for manipulating the aforementioned abstractions.

Chapter 8, "Memory," describes the Mac OS X memory subsystem's architecture, including discussions of the Mach virtual memory architecture, paging, the unified buffer cache, the working-set detection mechanism, kernel-level and user-level memory allocators, and support for 64-bit addressing.

Chapter 9, "Interprocess Communication," describes various IPC and synchronization mechanisms available in Mac OS X. In particular, it discusses the implementation and usage of Mach IPC.

Chapter 10, "Extending the Kernel," describes the I/O Kit, the object-oriented driver subsystem in Mac OS X.

Chapter 11, "File Systems," describes the overall file system layer in Mac OS X, including brief discussions of each file system type. The discussion also covers partitioning schemes, disk management, and the Spotlight search technology.

Chapter 12, "The HFS Plus File System," describes the internals of the HFS Plus file system. The discussion is aided by the use of a custom file system debugger written for this chapter.

Appendix A, "Mac OS X on x86-Based Macintosh Computers," highlights the key differences between the x86-based and PowerPC-based versions of Mac OS X. Besides this appendix, the book covers the details of several key x86-specific topics, such as EFI, GUID-based partitioning, and Universal Binaries. *Most of Mac OS X is architecture-independent, and consequently, the majority of the book is architecture-independent.*

Given the book's length, I chose to exclude several topics that are well covered in other texts. The TCP/IP stack is an example—there is no "networking" chapter in the book since the Mac OS X TCP/IP stack is largely a derivative of the FreeBSD stack, which is already well documented. In general, information that is generic across Unix variants and can be found in standard texts is not included in this book.

How to Read This Book

Since the first two chapters provide the background and overall picture of Mac OS X, respectively, I recommend that you read these chapters first. The subsequent chapters are best read sequentially, although, depending on your interests and familiarity with the topics, you can skip certain sections (and perhaps even chapters) and still gain value from the book.

It will help if you have some familiarity with operating system concepts and have used a Unix operating system.

Given that the book has a large number of C programs and program excerpts, you should have some programming experience, and in particular, knowledge of the C programming language. I sometimes use code not only to demonstrate the working of a concept, but also to *describe* the concept. I realize that it is usually considered "difficult" to "read" code, and authors often expect that many readers will simply skip the code. My belief is that reading the code (as opposed to only running it) in this book will be particularly helpful to programmers.

Despite the book's technical nature, several parts of the book can be read casually by both programmers and non programmers.

I hope that as a reference on Mac OS X internals, the book and its examples will be useful to its readers for a long time to come.

How to Use the Examples

I have included a number of self-contained examples in the book. Many of these examples are non-trivial in that they do something that is both useful and interesting. I hope that these examples will serve as food for thought and building blocks for other projects. Almost all of the examples in the book are shown along with the command lines used to compile and run them.

The examples were tested on both PowerPC-based and x86-based Macintosh computers where applicable. It is interesting to note that in the cases where the code is PowerPC-only, say, in a PowerPC assembly language example, it can usually be both compiled and run on an x86-based Macintosh—such code will run under the Rosetta binary translation software. However, a small number of examples in the book require a PowerPC Macintosh—they will not run under Rosetta.

Related Material

Technology moves so fast these days that it is almost impossible to publish a fully up-to-date book. Thankfully, Internet access allows the author and publisher to make various materials available to readers after the book is published. The most useful resource for this book is its accompanying web site, www.osxbook.com, which provides the following resources:

- Errata and updates
- Source code from the book
- The book's blog, with news and announcements about the availability of new material
- A set of discussion forums where topics related to the book (and to Mac OS X in general) can be discussed
- A bonus content section, which contains additional articles, presentations, binaries, and source code relevant to the book
- Sample content from the book, including a detailed table of contents

Acknowledgments

This book was the most arduous, time-consuming, and energy-sapping project I have ever done. The only reason I could get through this was the love and support I received from my wife, Gowri. Around the same time as I decided to write this book, we learned that we were expecting a baby. As all of my free time went to the book, Gowri's responsibilities increased exponentially, especially after little Arjun arrived. With her seemingly infinite strength and patience, Gowri made it all work eventually. My greatest thanks go to her. Arjun continually gave me energy through his wonderful smile and antics. I also thank our families for their love and support, and especially Gowri's mom and her sister, Gayethri, for traveling halfway across the world—several times during the two years I spent on the book—to help us when we needed family support.

Very special thanks to Steve Welch, my manager at IBM Research, who was incredibly supportive and put up with my erratic schedule at work.

I can't thank Snorri Gylfason enough. He is single-handedly responsible for introducing me to the Macintosh. Had it not been for him, I would not have begun to use Mac OS X, would not have been curious about the system, and would not have written this book. Snorri was also the most prolific and hard-working reviewer for the book he meticulously went through each page, each illustration, and each example, using his rather easy flowing red markers to great effect. We had countless all-night reviewing sessions. On many other occasions (essentially every day), Snorri patiently listened to the frustrated whining of an overworked author. Even after he moved back to his native Iceland, Snorri fulfilled all his reviewing commitments.

Thanks to Mark A. Smith for reviewing almost the entire book despite having no initial interest in Mac OS X. Mark provided valuable feedback, often reading at a bewildering pace but catching errors so subtle that it defied logic. Thanks to Ted Bonkenburg, Úlfar Erlingsson, and Anurag Sharma for reviewing several chapters with uncompromising scrutiny. Ted graciously had numerous discussions with me, as I stole time from his extremely busy schedule.

Thanks to Anita Holmgren of Tenon Systems for sending me a copy of Mach^{Ten}.

Thanks to the team at Addison-Wesley for all their hard work and dedication. In particular, thanks to my editor Catherine Nolan for managing this project (and for dealing with me). Thanks to Mark Taub, John Wait, Denise Mickelsen, Stephane Nakib, Kim Spilker, Beth Wickenhiser, Lara Wysong, and all others whose names I do not know for the roles they played in the making of this book.

Finally, thanks to my copy editor, Chrysta Meadowbrooke, for her top-notch work.

About the Author

Amit Singh is an operating systems researcher currently working at Google. Amit was formerly with the IBM Almaden Research Center. Previously, he worked for a Silicon Valley startup that did cutting-edge work in the virtualization of operating systems. Amit also was a member of technical staff in the Information Sciences Research Center at Bell Laboratories, where he worked on operating systems and networking. He created and maintains www.osxbook.com and www.kernelthread.com.

CHAPTER 1

Origins of Mac OS X

"Most ideas come from previous ideas." —Alan Curtis Kay

The Mac OS X operating system represents a rather successful coming together of paradigms, ideologies, and technologies that have often resisted each other in the past. A good example is the cordial relationship that exists between the command-line and graphical interfaces in Mac OS X. The system is a result of the trials and tribulations of Apple and NeXT, as well as their user and developer communities. Mac OS X exemplifies how a capable system can result from the direct or indirect efforts of corporations, academic and research communities, the Open Source and Free Software movements, and, of course, individuals.

Apple has been around since 1976, and many accounts of its history have been told. If the story of Apple as a company is fascinating, so is the *technical* history of Apple's operating systems. In this chapter,[1] we will trace the history of Mac OS X, discussing several technologies whose confluence eventually led to the modern-day Apple operating system.

---

1. This book's accompanying web site (www.osxbook.com) provides a more detailed technical history of all of Apple's operating systems.

1.1 Apple's Quest for *the*[2] Operating System

It was March 1988. The Macintosh had been around for four years. Some Apple engineers and managers had an offsite meeting. As they brainstormed to come up with future operating system strategies, they noted down their ideas on three sets of index cards that were colored blue, pink, and red.

Blue would be the project for improving the existing Macintosh operating system. It would eventually form the core of System 7.

Pink would soon become a revolutionary operating system project at Apple. The operating system was planned to be object-oriented. It would have full memory protection, multitasking with lightweight threads, a large number of protected address spaces, and several other modern features. After languishing for many years at Apple, Pink would move out to Taligent, a company jointly run by Apple and IBM.

Since the color red is "pinker than pink," ideas considered too advanced even for Pink were made part of the *Red* project.

As the 1980s drew to an end, the Macintosh system software was at major version 6. System 7, a result of the Blue project, would be Apple's most significant system yet. However, that would not appear until 1991.

Meanwhile, Microsoft had developed its Windows 3.x operating system, which became extremely successful after its release in 1990. Microsoft had also been working on a new operating system codenamed *Chicago*. Initially slated for release in 1993, Chicago kept slipping. It was eventually released as Windows 95. However, Microsoft did release another Windows operating system—Windows NT—in 1993 (Figure 1–1). NT was an advanced operating system meant for high-end client-server applications. It had various important features such as symmetric multiprocessing support, a preemptive scheduler, integrated networking, subsystems for OS/2 and POSIX, virtual machines for DOS and 16-bit Windows, a new file system called NTFS, and support for the Win32 API.

Apple needed an answer to Microsoft's onslaught, particularly in the face of the upcoming Windows 95, which was to be an end-user operating system.

The Pink and Red projects would turn out to be rather unsuccessful. Apple would continue to attempt to solve the "OS problem" one way or another.

---

2. Whereas the word "the" is used here to designate prominence and desirability, it is an interesting coincidence that "THE" was the name of a multiprogramming system described by Edsger W. Dijkstra in a 1968 paper.

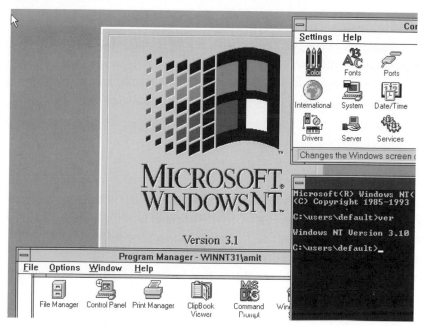

FIGURE 1–1 Microsoft Windows NT 3.1

1.1.1 Star Trek

Star Trek was a bold project that Apple ran jointly with Novell to port Mac OS to run on the x86 platform. A team consisting of engineers from both Apple and Novell succeeded in creating a very reasonable prototype in an incredibly short amount of time. The project was canceled, however, for various reasons: Apple had already committed to the PowerPC; many within and outside of Apple thought that adding support for the x86 platform would disrupt Apple's existing business model; and vendor feedback was not encouraging.

Many years later, Darwin—the core of Apple's far more successful Mac OS X—runs on both the PowerPC and the x86. Whereas the Star Trek prototype showed the "Happy Mac" logo while booting up, Darwin/x86 prints the message "Welcome to Macintosh" during boot.

Star Trek was finally vindicated with Apple's mid-2005 announcement of transitioning Mac OS X to the x86 platform. The first x86-based Macintosh computers—the iMac and the MacBook Pro (the successor to the PowerBook)—were unveiled at the San Francisco Macworld Conference & Expo in January 2006.

1.1.2 Raptor

Raptor was, in many respects, the Red project. It was supposed to provide Apple with a next-generation microkernel that would run on any architecture. As the Star Trek project was being canceled, it was considered for absorption by Raptor, which itself died later due to budgetary limitations and employee attrition, among other reasons.

1.1.3 NuKernel

NuKernel was a kernel project at Apple that was meant to result in a modern operating system kernel on more than one occasion. NuKernel was meant to be an efficient microkernel that would facilitate features such as preemptive multitasking, protected memory, an efficient memory model, a high degree of system extensibility, and most significantly, a hardware abstraction layer (HAL) that was expected to allow any computer vendor to easily design Mac OS–compatible systems.

1.1.4 TalOS

Apple and IBM formed a company called *Taligent* in early 1992 to continue work on the Pink project. Pink originally aimed to be an object-oriented operating system but later morphed into an object-oriented environment called *CommonPoint* that ran on many modern operating systems such as AIX, HP-UX, OS/2, Windows 95, and Windows NT. It was also meant to run on Apple's NuKernel. *Taligent Object Services* (TalOS) was the name given to a set of lower-level technologies to be built around version 3.0 of the Mach kernel. TalOS was meant to be an extensible and portable operating system, with a small footprint and good performance.

TalOS was object-oriented from the kernel up, with even device drivers and network protocols implemented in an object-oriented fashion. Taligent's object-oriented libraries were known as *frameworks*. There were frameworks for user interfaces, text, documents, graphics, multimedia, fonts, printing, and low-level services such as drivers. These, along with the TalOS development tools, explicitly strived to shift the burden of programming from application developers to application system engineers.

Note that even though there existed other commercial systems such as NEXTSTEP that had object-oriented *application frameworks*, Taligent aimed to build its entire programming model around objects. In NEXTSTEP, the developers who created frameworks had to map object behavior to the underlying libraries, Unix system calls, Display PostScript, and so on—all of which had procedural APIs. In contrast, Taligent's CommonPoint applications were not meant to use the host operating system APIs *at all*.

In 1995, Taligent became a wholly owned subsidiary of IBM. The Pink project did not give Apple the next-generation operating system that Apple had been seeking.

1.1.5 Copland

Apple made an announcement in early 1994 that it would channel more than a decade of experience into the next major release of the Macintosh operating system: Mac OS 8. The project was codenamed *Copland*. It was expected that Copland would be Apple's *real* response to Microsoft Windows. With Copland, Apple hoped to achieve several goals, many of which had been long elusive.

- Adopt RISC[3] as a key foundation technology by making the system fully PowerPC-native.
- Integrate, improve, and leverage existing Apple technologies such as ColorSync, OpenDoc, PowerShare, PowerTalk, QuickDraw 3D, and QuickDraw GX.
- Retain and improve the Mac OS interface's ease of use while making it multi-user and fully customizable. In particular, Copland's implementation of themes allowed customization of most user-interface elements on a per-user basis.
- Extend interoperability with DOS and Windows.
- Make Mac OS systems the best network clients.
- Incorporate active assistance that works across applications and networks—that is, make it very easy to automate a wide variety of tasks.
- Release Copland as a system that may be openly licensed to foster development of Mac OS–compatible clones by third parties.

To achieve these goals, Copland was supposed to have a comprehensive set of system-level features, for example:

- A hardware abstraction layer that would also help vendors in creating compatible systems

---

3. Reduced instruction-set computing.

- A microkernel (the NuKernel) at its core
- Symmetric multiprocessing with preemptive multitasking
- Improved virtual memory with memory protection
- A flexible and powerful system extension mechanism
- Critical subsystems such as I/O, networking, and file systems running as services on top of the kernel
- Built-in low-level networking facilities such as X/Open Transport Interface (OTI), System V STREAMS, and Data Link Provider Interface (DLPI)
- File searching based on both metadata and content
- The ability to perform "live upgrades" on a system without affecting the performance of other running programs

Figure 1–2 shows a conceptual view of Copland.

Work on Copland gained momentum during the early 1990s, and by the mid-1990s, Copland was heavily counted on to do wonders for the company. Apple dubbed it as "The Mac OS Foundation for the Next Generation of Personal Computers." However, the project kept slipping. A few prototypical Driver Development Kit (DDK) releases went out, but a 1996 release—as had been planned and hoped for—did not seem feasible. Due to numerous pressures, full memory protection had not been included after all. Apple's CEO Gil Amelio described the state of Copland as "just a collection of separate pieces, each being worked on by a different team . . . that were expected to magically come together somehow. . . ."[4]

Apple eventually decided to cancel Copland in May 1996. Amelio announced that Copland's best pieces would be shipped with future releases of their existing system, beginning with the upcoming System 7.6, whose name was formally changed to *Mac* OS 7.6.

1.1.6 Gershwin

After the Copland debacle, Apple's need for a new operating system was direr than ever. Focus shifted briefly to a project named *Gershwin*, which was to include the painfully elusive memory protection, among other things. However, it

---

4. *On the Firing Line*, by Gil Amelio and William L. Simon (New York: Harper Business, 1998).

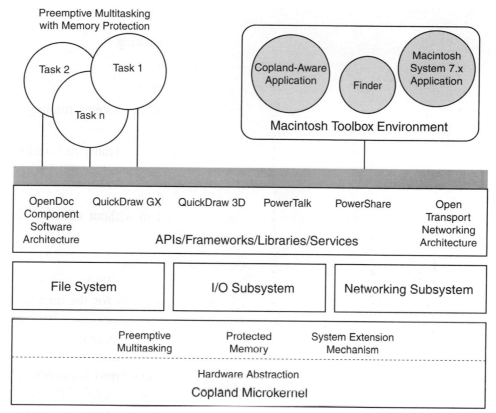

FIGURE 1–2 Copland architecture

was apparently nothing more than a codename, and it is believed that nobody ever worked on Gershwin.

1.1.7 BeOS

Apple briefly considered partnering with Microsoft to create an Apple OS based on Windows NT. Other systems under consideration were Solaris from Sun Microsystems and BeOS from Be. In fact, Apple's acquisition of Be came rather close to materializing.

Be was founded in 1990 by Jean-Louis Gassée, Apple's former head of product development. Be's capable engineering team had created an impressive operating system in BeOS (Figure 1–3). It had memory protection, preemptive

FIGURE 1–3 BeOS

multitasking, and symmetric multiprocessing. It even ran on the PowerPC,[5] thus fitting with Apple's hardware agenda. BeOS was designed to be especially adept at handling multimedia. It had a metadata-rich file system called BeFS that allowed files to be accessed via multiple attributes. However, BeOS was still an unfinished and unproven product. For example, it did not yet support file sharing or printing, and only a few applications had been written for it.

Gassée and Apple negotiated back and forth over Be's acquisition. The total investment in Be at that time was estimated at about $20 million, and Apple valued Be at $50 million. Gassée sought over $500 million, confident that Apple would buy Be. Apple negotiated up to $125 million, and Be negotiated down to

---

5. BeOS initially ran on Be's own PowerPC-based machine called the BeBox. It was later ported to the x86 platform.

$300 million. When things still did not work out, Apple offered $200 million, and even though it is rumored that Gassée was actually willing to accept this offer, it is also said that he came back with a "final price" of $275 million, hoping Apple would bite the bullet. The deal did not happen. In any case, Be had a tough contender in NeXT, a company founded and run by another one-time Apple employee: Steve Jobs.

Be eventually failed as a company—its technological assets were acquired by Palm, Inc., in 2001.

1.1.8 Plan A

Unlike Be, NeXT's operating systems had at least been proven in the market, despite NeXT not having any resounding successes. In particular, the OPEN-STEP system had been well received in the enterprise market. Moreover, Steve Jobs pitched NeXT's technology very strongly to Apple, asserting that OPEN-STEP was many years ahead of the market. The deal with NeXT did go through: Apple acquired NeXT in February 1997 for over $400 million. Amelio later quipped that they picked "plan A" instead of "plan Be."[6]

NeXT's acquisition would prove pivotal to Apple, as NeXT's operating system technology would be the basis for what would become Mac OS X. Let us now look at the background of NeXT's systems.

1.2 The NeXT Chapter

All of Steve Jobs' operational responsibilities at Apple were "taken away" on May 31, 1985. Around this time, Jobs had come up with an idea for a startup for which he pulled in five other Apple employees. The idea was to create the perfect research computer for universities, colleges, and research labs. Jobs had even attempted to seek the opinion of Nobel laureate biochemist Paul Berg on using such a computer for simulations. Although interested in investing in Jobs' startup, Apple sued Jobs upon finding out about the Apple employees who joined him. After some mutual agreements, Apple dropped the suit a year after. The startup was NeXT Computer, Inc.

---

6. *Apple: The Inside Story of Intrigue, Egomania, and Business Blunders*, by Jim Carlton (New York: HarperPerennial, 1998).

NeXT's beginnings were promising. Jobs initially used $7 million of his personal money. Several larger investments were made in NeXT, such as $20 million from Ross Perot and $100 million from Canon a few years later. True to its original goal, NeXT strived to create a computer that would be perfect in form and function. The result was the NeXT cube.

The cube's motherboard had a clever, visually appealing design. Its magnesium case was painted black with a matte finish. The monitor stand required an astonishing amount of engineering (for a monitor stand). An onboard digital signal-processing chip allowed the cube to play stereo-quality music—an exceptional feature for that time. The machines were manufactured in NeXT's own state-of-the-art factory.

1.2.1 NEXTSTEP

Jobs unveiled the NeXT cube on October 12, 1988, at the Davies Symphony Hall in San Francisco. The computer ran an operating system called NEXTSTEP, which used as its kernel a port of CMU[7] Mach 2.0[8] with a 4.3BSD environment. NEXTSTEP's window server was based on Display PostScript—a marriage of the PostScript page-description language and window system technologies.

> In 1986, Sun Microsystems had announced its own Display PostScript Window System called NeWS.

NEXTSTEP offered both a graphical user interface and a Unix-style command-line interface. The NEXTSTEP graphical user interface had multilevel menus, windows whose contents were shown while being dragged, and smooth scrolling. A *dock* application always stayed on top and held frequently used applications. Other NEXTSTEP features included the following:

- The ability to "hide" applications instead of quitting them
- CD-quality sound
- A versatile mail application that supported voice annotation of messages, inline graphics, and dynamic lookup of email addresses over the network

---

7. Carnegie Mellon University.

8. The Mach implementation in NEXTSTEP included NeXT-specific features, as well as some features from later versions of CMU Mach.

- Drag and drop of complex objects between applications
- A *services* menu that could be accessed from various applications to provide services such as dictionary and thesaurus
- A *Digital Librarian* application that could build searchable indexes of content dragged to it
- A file viewer that extended across the network
- An object-oriented device driver framework called the *Driver Kit*

NEXTSTEP used drag and drop as a fundamental, powerful operation. It was possible to drag an image from, say, the mail application to a document editing application such as WordPerfect. Conversely, you could drag a spreadsheet to the mail application to attach it to a message. Since the file viewer was network capable, a remote directory could be dragged as a shortcut on the user's desktop (specifically, on the *shelf*).

NEXTSTEP's native programming language was Objective-C. The system included *Interface Builder*, a tool for designing application user interfaces graphically. Several *software kits* were provided to aid in application development. A software kit was a collection of reusable classes (or object templates). Examples include the Application Kit, the Music Kit, and the Sound Kit.

Objective-C

Objective-C is an object-oriented, compiled programming language invented by Brad Cox and Tom Love in the early 1980s. It is a superset of C, with dynamic binding and a messaging syntax inspired by Smalltalk. It aims to be a simpler language than C++. Consequently, it does not have many features of C++, such as multiple inheritance and operator overloading.

Cox and Love founded StepStone Corporation, from which NeXT licensed the language and created its own compiler. In 1995, NeXT acquired all rights to StepStone's intellectual property related to Objective-C.

Apple's Objective-C compiler used in Mac OS X is a modified version of the GNU compiler.

At the time of the cube's announcement, NEXTSTEP was at version 0.8. It would be another year before a 1.0 mature release would be made.

NEXTSTEP 2.0 was released a year after 1.0, with improvements such as support for CD-ROMs, color monitors, NFS, on-the-fly spell checking, and dynamically loadable device drivers.

In the fall of 1990, Timothy John "Tim" Berners-Lee at CERN created the first web browser. It offered WYSIWYG browsing and authoring. The browser was prototyped on a NeXT computer in the space of a few months. The speed of implementation was attributed to the qualities of the NEXTSTEP software development system.

NEXTSTEP tools allowed fast prototyping for ideas in human-interface design and navigation techniques.

At the 1992 NeXTWORLD Expo, NEXTSTEP 486—a $995 version for the x86—was announced.

NEXTSTEP ran on the 68K, x86, PA-RISC, and SPARC platforms. It was possible to create a single version of an application containing binaries for all supported architectures. Such multiple-architecture binaries are known as "fat" binaries.[9]

Canon had a personal workstation, the object.station 41, which was designed to run NEXTSTEP. The system's 100MHz Intel 486DX4 processor was upgradeable to an Intel Pentium OverDrive processor. Besides NEXTSTEP as the operating system, the machine included Insignia Solutions' SoftPC.

The last version of NEXTSTEP—3.3 (Figure 1–4)—was released in February 1995. By that time, NEXTSTEP had powerful application development facilities courtesy of tools such as the Project Builder and the Interface Builder. There existed an extensive collection of libraries for user interfaces, databases, distributed objects, multimedia, networking, and so on. NEXTSTEP's object-oriented device driver toolkit was especially helpful in driver development. Figure 1–5 shows the timeline and lineage of NeXT's operating systems.

Despite the elegance of NeXT's hardware and the virtues of NEXTSTEP, the company had proven to be economically unviable over the years. In early 1993, NeXT announced its plans to leave the hardware business but continue development of NEXTSTEP for the x86 platform.

---

9. Fat binaries are the same as the so-called Universal binaries, which are used with the advent of the x86 version of Mac OS X.

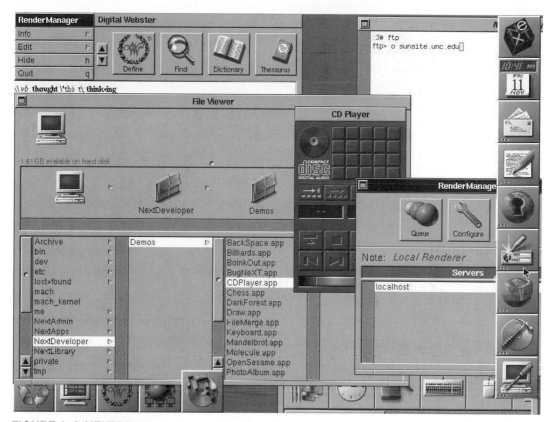

FIGURE 1–4 NEXTSTEP

1.2.2 OPENSTEP

NeXT partnered with Sun Microsystems to jointly release specifications for OpenStep, an open platform comprised of several APIs and frameworks that anybody could use to create their own implementation of an object-oriented operating system—running on any underlying core operating system. The OpenStep API was implemented on SunOS, HP-UX, and Windows NT. NeXT's own implementation, essentially an OpenStep-compliant version of NEXTSTEP, was released as OPENSTEP 4.0 (Figure 1–6) in July 1996, with 4.1 and 4.2 following shortly afterwards.

The OpenStep API and the OPENSTEP operating system did not seem to turn things around for NeXT, even though they caused some excitement in the business, enterprise, and government markets. NeXT started to shift focus to its

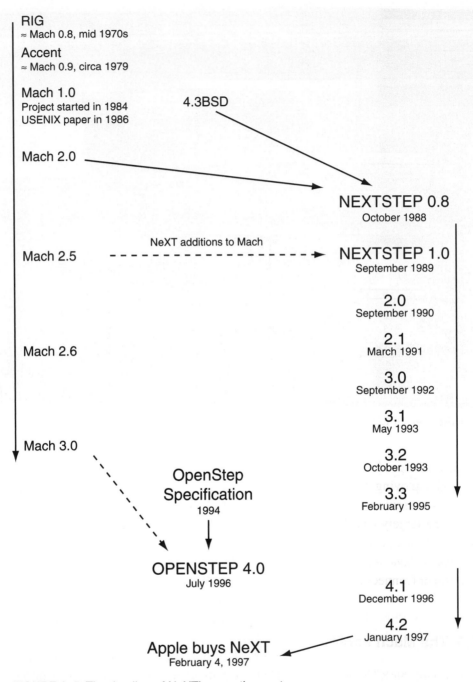

FIGURE 1–5 The timeline of NeXT's operating systems

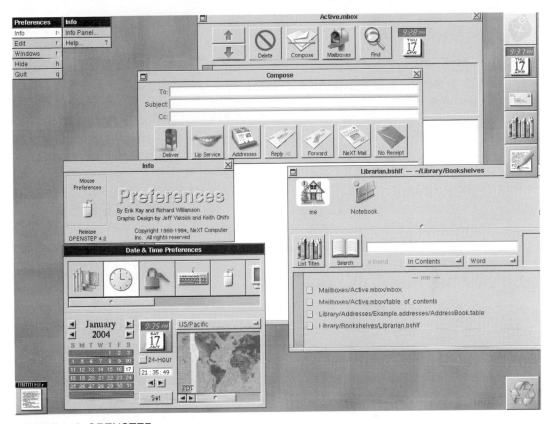

FIGURE 1–6 OPENSTEP

WebObjects product, which was a multiplatform environment for rapidly building and deploying web-based applications.

As we saw earlier, NeXT was purchased by Apple in early 1997. Mac OS X would be largely based on NeXT's technology. WebObjects would keep up with advancements in its domain, as exemplified by its support for Web Services and Enterprise Java. Apple uses WebObjects for its own web sites, such as the Apple Developer Connection (ADC) site, the online Apple Store, and the .Mac offering.

1.3 The Mach Factor

Along with NeXT's operating system came its kernel, which became the kernel foundation of Apple's future systems. Let us now briefly discuss the origins and evolution of Mach—a key component of the NEXTSTEP kernel and, in turn, of the Mac OS X kernel.

1.3.1 Rochester's Intelligent Gateway

A group of researchers at the University of Rochester, New York, began development of an "intelligent" gateway system named *RIG* (Rochester's Intelligent Gateway) in 1975. Jerry Feldman, who coined the name RIG, largely did the system's initial design. RIG was meant to provide uniform access—say, via terminals—to a variety of local and remote computing facilities. Local facilities could be locally connected disks, magnetic tapes, printers, plotters, batch-processing or timesharing computers, and so on. Remote facilities could be available through a network such as the ARPANET. RIG's operating system, called *Aleph*, ran on a Data General Eclipse minicomputer.

The Aleph kernel was structured around an interprocess communication (IPC) facility. RIG processes could send messages to each other, with a *port* specifying the destination. A port was an in-kernel message queue that was globally identified by a dotted pair of integers: a process number and a port number. A process could have several ports defined within itself, each of which could be used to wait for a message to arrive on. A process X could *shadow* or *interpose* another process Y. In the case of shadowing, X received a copy of every message sent to Y. While interposing, X intercepted all messages sent to or originating from Y. This IPC facility based on messages and ports was a basic building block of the operating system.

RIG was killed a few years later due to several fundamental shortcomings in its design or in the underlying hardware, for example:

- The lack of paged virtual memory
- A 2KB limit on the size of a message due to the limited address space provided by the underlying hardware
- Inefficient IPC due to limited message size
- No protection for ports
- No way to notify the failure of a process to a dependent process without explicit registration of such dependencies
- Networking not an area of emphasis in the original design

RIG port numbers were global, allowing any process to create or use them. Therefore, any process could send a message to any other process. However, RIG processes, which were single threaded, did have protected address spaces.

1.3.2 Accent

Richard Rashid was one of the people who worked on RIG. In 1979, Rashid moved to Carnegie Mellon University, where he would work on *Accent*, a network operating system kernel. Active development of Accent began in April 1981. Like RIG, Accent was also a communication-oriented system that used IPC as the basic system-structuring tool, or "glue." However, Accent addressed many of RIG's shortcomings.

- Processes had large (4GB), sparse virtual address spaces that were linearly addressable.
- There was flexible and powerful virtual memory management, which was integrated with IPC and file storage. The kernel itself could be paged, although certain critical parts of the kernel, such as I/O memory and the virtual memory table, were "wired" in physical memory.
- Copy-on-write (COW) memory mapping was used to facilitate large message transfers. Based on experience with RIG, it was expected that most messages would be simple. There were optimizations for the common case.
- Ports had the semantics of *capabilities*.
- Messages could be sent to processes on another machine through an intermediary process, thus providing location transparency.

Memory-related API calls in Accent included functions for creating, destroying, reading, and writing memory *segments*, with support for copy-on-write. One may think of Accent as RIG enhanced with virtual memory and network-transparent messaging.

> Accent was developed to support two distributed computing projects: SPICE (distributed personal computing) and DSN (fault-tolerant distributed sensor network). Accent was also the name of a food product (a spice) sold by Accent International, Inc. The only ingredient of this product was monosodium glutamate (MSG). In computing, one often abbreviates "message" as "msg".

Accent ran on PERQ computers, which were commercial graphics workstations. Three Rivers Corporation delivered the first PERQ in 1980. QNIX was a UNIX environment based on AT&T System V UNIX that ran under Accent on PERQ machines. Developed by Spider Systems, QNIX used its own microcode[10]

---

10. The PERQ had soft-microcode, allowing its instruction set to be extended.

but ran in an Accent window managed by Accent's *Sapphire* window manager, with other Accent programs running alongside. A LISP machine (SPICE LISP) was also available for Accent, along with other languages such as Ada, PERQ, Pascal, C, and Fortran. PERQ could interpret bytecode in hardware, akin to latter-day mechanisms for Java.

Within a few years, the future of Accent did not look promising. It needed a new hardware base, support for multiprocessors, and portability to other kinds of hardware. Accent also had difficulty supporting UNIX software.

Matchmaker

The *Matchmaker* project was started in 1981 as part of the SPICE project. Matchmaker was an interface-specification language intended for use with existing programming languages. Using the Matchmaker language, object-oriented remote procedure call (RPC) interfaces could be specified. The specification would be converted into interface code by a multitarget compiler. Matchmaker is readily comparable to the *rpcgen* protocol compiler and its language. The *Mach Interface Generator* (MIG) program, which is also used in Mac OS X, was derived from Matchmaker.

1.3.3 Mach

The sequel to Accent was called *Mach*, which was conceived as a UNIX-compatible Accent-inspired system. In retrospect, with respect to the first version (1.0) of Mach, one could consider Accent and RIG to be Mach versions 0.9 and 0.8, respectively.

When Mach was developed, UNIX had been around for over 15 years. Although the designers of Mach subscribed to the importance and usefulness of UNIX, they noted that UNIX was no longer as simple or as easy to modify as it once had been. Richard Rashid called the UNIX kernel a "dumping ground for virtually every new feature or facility."[11] Mach's design goals were partially a response to the inexorably increasing complexity of UNIX.

The Mach project started in 1984 with an overall goal of creating a micro-kernel that would be the operating system foundation for other operating systems. The project had several specific goals.

---

11. "Threads of a New System," by Richard Rashid (*Unix Review*, August 1986, pp. 37–49).

- Provide full support for multiprocessing.

- Exploit other features of modern hardware architectures that were emerging at that time. Mach aimed to support diverse architectures, including shared memory access schemes such as Non-Uniform Memory Access (NUMA) and No-Remote Memory Access (NORMA).

- Support transparent and seamless distributed operation.

- Reduce the number of features in the kernel to make it less complex, while giving the programmer a very small number of abstractions to work with. Nevertheless, the abstractions would be general enough to allow several operating systems to be implemented on top of Mach.

- Provide compatibility with UNIX.

- Address the shortcomings of previous systems such as Accent.

Mach was intended to primarily implement processor and memory management, but no file system, networking, or I/O. The "real" operating system was to run as a user-level Mach task. Written in C, the Mach kernel was also meant to be highly portable.

Mach's implementation used 4.3BSD as the starting code base. Its designers had RIG and Accent as references in the area of message-passing kernels. DEC's TOPS-20[12] operating system provided some ideas for Mach's virtual memory subsystem. As Mach evolved, portions of the BSD kernel were replaced by their Mach equivalents, and various new components were added.

When published in 1986, the original Mach paper hailed Mach as "A New Kernel Foundation for UNIX Development."[13] While not everybody saw or sees it that way, Mach went on to become a rather popular system. From Apple's standpoint, the paper's title might as well have been "A NuKernel Foundation. . . ."

Initially the Mach designers presented four basic abstractions in the kernel.

1. A *task* is a container for the resources of one[14] or more threads. Examples of resources include virtual memory, ports, processors, and so on.

---

12. TOPS-20 was a descendant of the TENEX operating system.

13. "Mach: A New Kernel Foundation For UNIX Development," by Mike Accetta, Robert Baron, William Bolosky, David Golub, Richard Rashid, Avadis Tevanian, and Michael Young. In *USENIX Association Conference Proceedings* (Atlanta, GA: USENIX Association, June 1986).

14. It is possible to have a Mach task with zero threads, although such a task would not be very useful.

Nomenclature

Avadis Tevanian, one of the inventors of Mach and Apple's Chief Software Technology Officer, told me the following history about how Mach was named. (Tevanian qualified the account as his best memory of an event that occurred two decades ago.) On a rainy day in Pittsburgh, Tevanian and some others were on their daily trek to lunch. As they were thinking of names for the yet unnamed Mach kernel, Tevanian, navigating around one of the numerous mud puddles, suggested the name "MUCK" in jest. MUCK was to stand for "Multi-User Communication Kernel" or "Multiprocessor Universal Communication Kernel." As a joke, Richard Rashid passed the name along to a colleague, Dario Giuse, who was Italian. Giuse inadvertently pronounced MUCK as "Mach," and Rashid liked it so much that the name stuck.

2. A *thread* is a basic unit of execution in a task. The task provides an execution environment for its threads, whereas the threads actually run. The various threads of a task share its resources, although each has its own execution state, which includes the program counter and various other registers. Thus, unlike a process in Accent, a Mach "process" is divided[15] into a task and multiple threads.

3. A *port* is similar to an Accent port—it is an in-kernel message queue with capabilities. Ports form the basis for Mach's IPC facilities. Mach implements ports as simple integral values.

4. A *message* is a collection of data that threads in different tasks, or in the same task, can send to each other using ports.

Another basic Mach abstraction is that of a *memory object*, which can be thought of as a container for data (including file data) mapped into a task's address space. Mach requires a paged memory-management unit (PMMU). Through its physical map (pmap) layer, Mach provides an excellent interface to the machine-dependent MMU facilities. Mach's virtual memory subsystem was designed to support large, sparse virtual address spaces and was integrated with IPC. In traditional UNIX, contiguous virtual memory space was implied, with the heap and the stack growing toward each other. In contrast, Mach allowed for sparse address spaces. Regions of memory could be allocated from anywhere in

---

15. Certain subsequent versions of Mach further subdivided a thread into an *activation* and a *shuttle*.

the address space. Memory could be shared for reading and writing in a structured manner. Copy-on-write techniques were used both to optimize copy operations and for sharing physical memory between tasks. The generalized memory object abstraction allowed for *external*[16] memory pagers to handle page faults and page-out data requests. The source or target data could even reside on another machine.

> FreeBSD's virtual memory architecture is based on Mach's.

One of CMU's important decisions was to provide all Mach software with unrestrictive licensing: free of distribution fees or royalties.

As noted earlier, Mach was neither meant to provide nor provided any file system, networking, or I/O capabilities. It was to be used as a *service operating system* to create other operating systems from. It was hoped that this approach would maintain simplicity and promote portability of operating systems. One or more operating systems could run on top of Mach as user-level tasks. However, real life implementations deviated from this concept. Release 2.0 of Mach, as well as the rather successful Release 2.5, had monolithic implementations in that Mach and BSD resided in the same address space.

The Open Software Foundation[17] (OSF) used Release 2.5 of Mach for providing many of the kernel services in the OSF/1 operating system. Mach 2.x was also used in Mt. Xinu, Multimax (Encore), Omron LUNA/88k, NEXTSTEP, and OPENSTEP.

The Mach 3 project was started at CMU and continued by OSF. Mach 3 was the first *true microkernel* version—BSD ran as a user-space Mach task, with only fundamental features being provided by the Mach kernel. Other changes and improvements in Mach 3 included the following:

- Kernel preemption and a real-time scheduling framework to provide real-time support
- Low-level device support wherein devices were presented as ports to which data or control messages could be sent, with support for both synchronous and asynchronous I/O

---

16. Implies external to the kernel—that is, in user space.

17. The OSF was formed in May 1988 to develop core software technologies and supply them to the entire industry on fair and reasonable terms. It went on to have several hundred members from among commercial end users, software companies, computer manufacturers, universities, research laboratories, and so on. The OSF later became the Open Group and then Silicomp.

- A completely rewritten IPC implementation
- System call redirection that allowed a set of system calls to be handled by user-space code running within the calling task
- Use of *continuations*, a kernel facility that gives a thread the option to block by specifying a function (the *continuation function*) that is called when the thread runs again

Historically, arguments in favor of "true" microkernels have emphasized a greater degree of system structure and modularity, improved software engineering, ease of debugging, robustness, software malleability (e.g., the ability to run multiple operating system personalities), and so on. The intended benefits of microkernel-based operating systems such as Mach 3 were offset by the significant real-life performance problems that occurred due to reasons such as the following:

- The cost of maintaining separate protection domains, including the cost of context switching from one domain to another (often, simple operations resulted in many software or hardware layers to be crossed)
- The cost of kernel entry and exit code
- Data copies in MIG-generated stub routines
- The use of semantically powerful but implementation-heavy IPC mechanisms, even for same-machine RPC

Many operating systems were ported to the conceptual virtual machine provided by the Mach API, and several user-mode operating system interfaces were demonstrated to execute on top of Mach. The *Mach-US* symmetric multiserver operating system contained a set of server processes that provided generic system services such as local IPC; networking; and management of devices, files, processes, and terminals. Each server typically ran in a separate Mach task. An emulation library, which was loaded into each user process, provided an operating system personality. Such libraries used generic services to emulate different operating systems by intercepting system calls and redirecting them to the appropriate handlers. Mach emulators existed for BSD, DOS, HP-UX, OS/2, OSF/1, SVR4, VMS, and even the Macintosh operating system.

> Richard Rashid went on to become the head of Microsoft Research. As noted earlier, Mach coinventor Avie Tevanian would be the Chief Software Technology Officer at Apple.

1.3.4 MkLinux

Apple and OSF began a project to port Linux to run on various Power Macintosh platforms, with Linux hosted on top of OSF's Mach implementation. The project led to a core system called *osfmk*. The overall system was known as *MkLinux*. The first version of MkLinux was based on Linux 1.3. It was released as MkLinux DR1 in early 1996. Subsequent releases moved to Linux 2.0 and beyond. One of the releases was incorporated into Apple's Reference Release.

MkLinux used a single-server approach: The monolithic Linux kernel ran as a single Mach task. Mac OS X uses a kernel base derived from osfmk and includes many MkLinux enhancements. However, all kernel components in Mac OS X, including the BSD portions, reside in the same address space.

Mach^Ten

The Mach^Ten product from Tenon Systems was introduced as an unobtrusive UNIX solution for Mac OS: It ran as an application atop Apple's operating system. Mach^Ten was based on the Mach kernel with a BSD environment. It provided preemptive multitasking for UNIX applications running within it, although the Mac OS execution environment remained cooperative multitasking.

Although the marriage of Mach, BSD, and Macintosh in Mach^Ten sounds similar to the latter-day Mac OS X, there is a critical difference in design and philosophy. Mac OS X was a continuation of NEXTSTEP technology in several ways. Apple provided legacy compatibility and ease of transition at two primary levels: through APIs such as Carbon and through the Classic virtualizer. In contrast, Mach^Ten was a logical opposite: Mac OS remained the first-class citizen, whereas UNIX ran in a virtual machine (UVM) that was implemented within a standard Macintosh application. The UVM provided a preemptive multitasking execution environment with a set of UNIX APIs (such as POSIX, including the standard C library and POSIX threads), a BSD-style networking stack, file systems such as UFS and FFS, RPC, NFS, and so on. Mach^Ten also included an implementation of the X Window System.

Although confined within a single application, Mach^Ten consisted of various subsystems similar to a full-fledged operating system. At the logically lowest level, an interface layer talked to Mac OS. The Mach kernel resided above this layer, providing services such as memory management, IPC, tasks, and threads. Other Mach^Ten subsystems that directly talked to the Mac OS interface layer included the window manager and the networking stack's ARP layer.

1.3.5 Musical Names

Apple's operating system strategy after acquiring NeXT was two-pronged: It would keep improving Mac OS for the consumer desktop market, and it would create a high-end operating system based on NeXT technology. The new system—called *Rhapsody*—would mainly be targeted toward the server and enterprise markets.

Besides chromatic aberrations such as Pink and Red, Apple had a string of musically inspired codenames for its operating system projects. Copland and Gershwin were named after Aaron Copland and George Gershwin, both American composers. *Rhapsody in Blue* is a famous work of Gershwin.[18]

1.4 Strategies

The first release of an Apple operating system after Apple announced that it would purchase NeXT was in late 1996 with version 7.6. This release represented the initial stage of Apple's new operating system roadmap. It was the first system to be called "Mac OS." Apple's plan was to release full stand-alone installations once a year, with updates in between. Many Power Macintosh and PowerBook models that were not supported by Mac OS 7.6 were supported by the 7.6.1 incremental update. The system originally slated to be version 7.7 would eventually become Mac OS 8.

Mac OS 7.6 required a compatible computer that was 32-bit clean, with at least a 68030 processor. It offered performance enhancements in several areas such as virtual memory, memory management, PowerPC Resource Manager routines, system startup, and the File Manager's caching scheme. It also integrated key Apple technologies such as Cyberdog, OpenDoc, Open Transport, and QuickTime.

Two phenomena were sweeping the computer world at that time: the Internet and Microsoft Windows 95. Apple emphasized compatibility of Mac OS 7.6 with Windows 95 and highlighted the system's Internet prowess. Mac OS 7.6 included built-in support for TCP/IP, PPP, and Apple Remote Access (ARA). Its integrated Cyberdog technology could be used to incorporate Internet features into documents that used "Live Objects." For example, live web links and email addresses could reside on the Desktop and could be activated from the Finder.

---

18. George Gershwin's brother Ira actually came up with the title *Rhapsody in Blue*.

1.4.1 Mac OS 8 and 9

As we saw earlier, Copland and Pink were potential candidates for Mac OS 8 at one time or another. Similarly, Gershwin was a candidate for Mac OS 9. Over the years, some important features that were either created or improved for Copland were added to Mac OS 8 and 9, as was originally intended. The following are examples of such features:

- A search engine that could search on local drives, network servers, and the Internet (released as Sherlock)
- The Copland API, which gradually evolved into Carbon
- The Platinum-look user interface
- Multiple users, with support for per-user preferences

Mac OS 8 had a multithreaded Finder that allowed several file-oriented operations simultaneously. Other notable features included the following:

- The Mac OS Extended file system (HFS Plus), which was introduced with Mac OS 8.1
- Contextual menus activated by a control-click
- Spring-loaded folders[19]
- Personal web hosting
- Web browsers (Microsoft Internet Explorer and Netscape Navigator) bundled with the system
- Macintosh Runtime for Java (MRJ—Apple's implementation of the Java environment) as part of the system
- Enhancements to power management, USB, and FireWire

Mac OS 8.5 (Figure 1–7) was only for PowerPCs. The system's *nanokernel*[20] was overhauled in Mac OS 8.6 to integrate multitasking and multiprocessing. It included a preemption-safe memory allocator. The multiprocessor (MP) API library could now run with virtual memory enabled, although virtual memory was still optional.

---

19. Spring-loaded folders are a feature of the Finder's user interface. If the user pauses briefly while dragging an item onto a folder icon, a window springs open, displaying the folder's contents. This allows the user to choose where to put the item. Continuing to hold the item causes a subfolder to spring open, and so on.

20. A term sometimes used to refer to a kernel that is even smaller than a microkernel.

FIGURE 1–7 Mac OS 8

Nanokernel

System 7.1.2 was the first Apple operating system to run on the PowerPC, even though much of the code was not PowerPC-native. A nanokernel was used to "drive" the PowerPC. Executing in supervisor mode, the nanokernel acted as the hardware abstraction layer. It exported low-level interfaces for interrupt management, exception handling, memory management, and so on. Only the system software, and possibly debuggers, could use the nanokernel interface.

When Mac OS 9 (Figure 1–8) was released in 1999, it was hailed by Apple as the "best Internet operating system ever."[21] It was the first Mac OS version that

---

21. As stated by Steve Jobs during a special event introducing Mac OS 9 on October 5, 1999.

FIGURE 1–8 Mac OS 9

could be updated over the Internet. It could also use the AppleTalk protocol over TCP/IP. Its useful security features included file encryption and the *Keychain* mechanism for storing passwords securely.

An important component of Mac OS 9 was a mature installation of the Carbon APIs, which at the time represented about 70% of the legacy Mac OS APIs. Carbon provided compatibility with Mac OS 8.1 and later.

The last release of Mac OS 9 occurred in late 2001 as version 9.2.2. With the advent of Mac OS X, this "old" Mac OS would eventually be referred to as *Classic*.

1.4.2 Rhapsody

We saw that after acquiring NeXT, Apple based its next-generation operating system, Rhapsody (Figure 1–9), on NeXT's OPENSTEP. Rhapsody was first demonstrated

FIGURE 1–9 Rhapsody

at the 1997 Worldwide Developers Conference (WWDC). It consisted of the following primary components:

- The kernel and related subsystems that were based on Mach and BSD
- A Mac OS–compatibility subsystem (the *Blue Box*)
- An extended OpenStep API implementation (the *Yellow Box*)
- A Java virtual machine
- A Display PostScript–based windowing system
- A user interface that was similar to Mac OS but also had features from OPENSTEP

Apple had plans to port to Rhapsody most key Mac OS frameworks: Quick-Time, QuickDraw 3D, QuickDraw GX, ColorSync, and so on. Rhapsody was also to support numerous file systems such as Apple Filing Protocol (AFP), FAT, HFS, HFS Plus, ISO9660, and UFS.

There were two developer releases of Rhapsody, dubbed DR1 and DR2. These were released for both the PowerPC and x86 platforms.

1.4.2.1 Blue Box

Shortly after Rhapsody DR1 was released, Apple extended the PowerPC version with a Mac OS–compatibility environment called the Blue Box. Implemented by a Rhapsody application (MacOS.app), the Blue Box was a virtual environment that appeared as a new Macintosh hardware model. MacOS.app loaded a Macintosh ROM file from disk and created an environment within which Mac OS ran mostly unchanged. Blue Box initially ran Mac OS 8.x, full-screen, with the ability to switch between Rhapsody and Mac OS using the **cmd-return** key combination. It placed certain restrictions on the applications that ran within it. For example, an application could neither access the hardware directly nor use undocumented Mac OS APIs. The implementers' initial goal was to achieve 90% to 115% of native Mac OS performance. Blue Box beta 1.0 used Open Transport—rather than BSD sockets—for networking. Support for newer versions of Mac OS, as well as for running the Blue Box windowed, was added later. The Blue Box environment would be known as the *Classic environment* in Mac OS X, provided by an application named Classic Startup.app.[22]

> The Blue Box environment is a virtualization layer—*not* an emulation layer. "Harmless" instructions execute natively on the processor, whereas "harmful" instructions—such as those that can affect the hardware—are trapped and handled appropriately.

1.4.2.2 Yellow Box

Rhapsody's development platform was called the Yellow Box (Figure 1–10). Besides being hosted on the Power Macintosh and x86 versions of Rhapsody, it was also available independently for Microsoft Windows.

Yellow Box included most of OPENSTEP's integrated frameworks, which were implemented as shared object libraries. These were augmented by a runtime

---

22. The application was called Classic.app in earlier versions of Mac OS X.

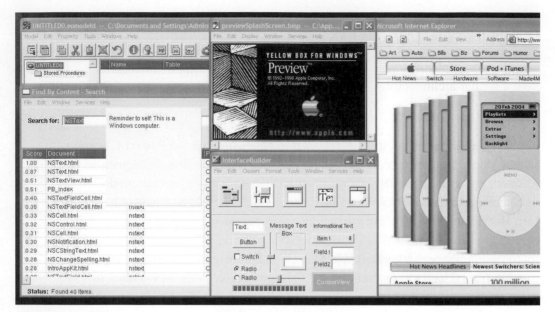

FIGURE 1–10 Yellow Box running on Microsoft Windows XP

and development environment. There were three core object frameworks whose APIs were available in Objective-C and Java.

1. *Foundation* was a collection of base classes with APIs for allocating, deallocating, examining, storing, notifying, and distributing objects.

2. *Application Kit* was a set of APIs for creating user interfaces; managing and processing events; and using services such as color and font management, printing, cut and paste, and text manipulation.

3. *Display PostScript* was a set of APIs for drawing in PostScript, compositing images, and performing other visual operations. It could be considered as a subset of Application Kit.

Yellow Box included NeXT's Project Builder integrated development environment and the Interface Builder visual tool for creating graphical user interfaces. The Windows NT implementation of Yellow Box provided a very similar environment through a combination of the following Apple-provided Windows system services and applications:

- The Mach Emulation Daemon (the `machd` service)
- The Netname Server (the `nmserver` service)

- The Window Server (the `WindowServer` application)
- The Pasteboard Server (the `pbs` application)

Earlier implementations of the OpenStep API for platforms such as Solaris used a similar architecture. Yellow Box evolved into the Mac OS X Cocoa APIs.

1.5 Toward Mac OS X

After Rhapsody's DR2 release, Apple would still alter its operating system strategy but would finally be on its way toward achieving its goal of having a *new* system. During the 1998 Worldwide Developers Conference, Adobe's Photoshop ran on what would be Mac OS X. However, the first shipping release of Mac OS X would take another three years. Figure 1–11 shows an approximation of the progression from Rhapsody toward Mac OS X.

1.5.1 Mac OS X Server 1.x

As people were expecting a DR3 release of Rhapsody, Apple announced Mac OS X Server 1.0 in March 1999. Essentially an improved version of Rhapsody, it was bundled with WebObjects, the QuickTime streaming server, a collection of developer tools, the Apache web server, and facilities for booting or administering over the network.

Apple also announced an initiative called *Darwin*: a fork of Rhapsody's developer release. Darwin would become the open source core of Apple's systems.

Over the next three years, as updates would be released for the server product, development of the desktop version would continue, with the server sharing many of the desktop improvements.

1.5.2 Mac OS X Developer Previews

There were four Developer Preview releases of Mac OS X, named DP1 through DP4. Substantial improvements were made during these DP releases.

1.5.2.1 DP1

An implementation of the Carbon API was added. Carbon represented an overhaul of the "classic" Mac OS APIs, which were pruned, extended, or modified to

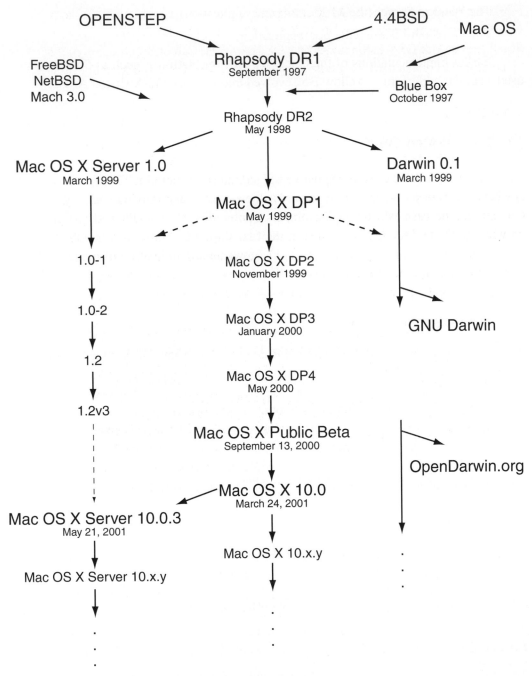

FIGURE 1–11 An approximation of the Mac OS X timeline

run in the more modern Mac OS X environment. Carbon was also meant to help Mac OS developers transition to Mac OS X. A Classic application would require an installation of Mac OS 9 to run under Mac OS X, whereas Carbon applications could be compiled to run as native applications under both Mac OS 9 and Mac OS X.

1.5.2.2 DP2

The Yellow Box evolved into Cocoa, originally alluding to the fact that besides Objective-C, the API would be available in Java. A version of the Java Development Kit (JDK) was included, along with a just-in-time (JIT) compiler. The Blue Box environment was provided via `Classic.app` (a newer version of `MacOS.app`) that ran as a process called `TruBlueEnvironment`. The Unix environment was based on 4.4BSD. DP2 thus contained a multitude of APIs: BSD, Carbon, Classic, Cocoa, and Java. There was widespread dissatisfaction with the existing user interface. The Aqua user interface had not been introduced yet, although there were rumors that Apple was keeping the "real" user interface a secret.[23]

Carbon is sometimes perceived as "the old" API. Although Carbon indeed contains modernized versions of many old APIs, it also provides functionality that may not be available through other APIs. Parts of Carbon are complementary to "new" APIs such as Cocoa. Nevertheless, Apple has been adding more functionality to Cocoa so that dependencies on Carbon can be eventually eliminated. For example, before Mac OS X 10.4, much of the QuickTime functionality was available only through Carbon. In Mac OS X 10.4, Apple introduced the QTKit Cocoa framework, which reduces or eliminates Carbon dependencies for QuickTime.

1.5.2.3 DP3

The Aqua user interface was first demonstrated during the San Francisco Macworld Expo in January 2000. Mac OS X DP3 included Aqua along with its distinctive elements: "water-like" elements, pinstripes, pulsating default buttons, "traffic-light" window buttons, drop shadows, transparency, animations, sheets, and so on. The DP3 Finder was Aqua-based as well. The *Dock* was introduced with support for photorealistic icons that were dynamically scalable up to 128×128 pixels.

---

23. Apple had referred to the Mac OS X user interface as "Advanced Mac OS Look and Feel."

1.5.2.4 DP4

The Finder was renamed the *Desktop* in DP4. The System Preferences application (`Preferences.app`—the precursor to `System Preferences.app`) made its first appearance in Mac OS X, allowing the user to view and set a multitude of system preferences such as Classic, ColorSync, Date & Time, Energy Saver, Internet, Keyboard, Login Items, Monitors, Mouse, Network, Password, and others. Prior to DP4, the Finder and the Dock were implemented within the same application. The Dock was an independent application (`Dock.app`) in DP4. It was divided into two sections: the left side for applications and the right side for the trash can, files, folders, and minimized windows. Other notable components of DP4 included an integrated development environment and OpenGL.

> The Dock's visual indication of a running application underwent several changes. In DP3, an application's Dock icon had a bottom edge a few pixels high that was color-coded to indicate whether the application was running. This was replaced by an ellipsis in DP4 and was followed by a triangle in subsequent Mac OS X versions. DP4 also introduced the smoke cloud animation that ensues after an item is dragged off the Dock.

1.5.3 Mac OS X Public Beta

Apple released a beta version of Mac OS X (Figure 1–12) at the Apple Expo in Paris on September 13, 2000. Essentially a publicly available preview release for evaluation and development purposes, the Mac OS X Public Beta was sold for $29.95 at the Apple Store. It was available in English, French, and German. The software's packaging contained a message from Apple to the beta testers: "You are holding the future of the Macintosh in your hands." Apple also created a Mac OS X tab on its web site that contained information on Mac OS X, including updates on third-party applications, tips and tricks, and technical support.

    Although the beta release was missing important features and ostensibly lacked in stability and performance, it demonstrated several important Apple technologies at work, particularly to those who had not been following the DP releases. The beta's key features were the following:

- The Darwin core with its xnu kernel that offered "true" memory protection, preemptive multitasking, and symmetric multiprocessing
- The PDF-based Quartz 2D drawing engine

FIGURE 1–12 Mac OS X Public Beta

- OpenGL support
- The Aqua interface and the Dock
- Apple's new mail client, with support for IMAP and POP
- A new version of the QuickTime player
- The Music Player application for playing MP3s and audio CDs
- A new version of the Sherlock Internet-searching tool
- A beta version of Microsoft Internet Explorer

With Darwin, Apple would continually leverage a substantial amount of existing open source software by using it for—and often integrating it with—Mac OS X. Apple and Internet Systems Consortium, Inc. (ISC), jointly founded the *OpenDarwin* project in April 2002 for fostering cooperative open source development of Darwin. *GNU-Darwin* is an open source Darwin-based operating system.

The New Kernel

Darwin's kernel is called xnu. It is unofficially an acronym for "X is Not Unix." It is also a coincidental tribute to the fact that it *is* indeed the NuKernel for Mac OS X. xnu is largely based on Mach and FreeBSD, but it includes code and concepts from various sources such as the formerly Apple-supported MkLinux project, the work done on Mach at the University of Utah, NetBSD, and OpenBSD.

1.5.4 Mac OS X 10.x

The first version of Mac OS X was released on March 24, 2001, as Mac OS X 10.0 Cheetah. Soon afterwards, the versioning scheme of the server product was revised to synchronize it with that of the desktop system. Since then, the trend has been that a new version of the desktop is released first, soon followed by the equivalent server revision.

Table 1–1 lists several major Mac OS X releases. Note that the codenames are all taken from felid taxonomy.

TABLE 1–1 Mac OS X Versions

Version	Codename	Release Date
10.0	Cheetah	March 24, 2001
10.1	Puma	September 29, 2001
10.2	Jaguar	August 23, 2002
10.3	Panther	October 24, 2003
10.4	Tiger	April 29, 2005
10.5	Leopard	2006/2007?

Let us look at some notable aspects of each major Mac OS X release.

1.5.4.1 *Mac OS X 10.0*

Apple dubbed Cheetah as "the world's most advanced operating system," which would become a frequently used tagline for Mac OS X.[24] Finally, Apple had

---

24. Mac OS X page on Apple's web site, www.apple.com/macosx/ (accessed April 26, 2006).

shipped an operating system with features that it had long sought. However, it was clear that Apple had a long way to go in terms of performance and stability. Key features of 10.0 included the following:

- The Aqua user interface, with the Dock and the Finder as the primary user-facing tools
- The PDF-based Quartz 2D graphics engine
- OpenGL for 3D graphics
- QuickTime for streaming audio and video (shipping for the first time as an integrated feature)
- Java 2 Standard Edition (J2SE)
- Integrated Kerberos
- Mac OS X versions of the three most popular Apple applications available as free downloads: iMovie 2, iTunes, and a preview version of AppleWorks
- Free IMAP service for Mac.com email accounts

> When Mac OS X 10.0 was released, there were approximately 350 applications available for it.

1.5.4.2 Mac OS X 10.1

Puma was a free update released six months after 10.0's release. It offered significant performance enhancements, as indicated by Apple's following claims:

- Up to 3× improvement in application launch speed
- Up to 5× improvement in menu performance
- Up to 3× improvement in window resizing
- Up to 2× improvement in file copying

There were substantial performance boosts in other areas such as system startup, user login, Classic startup, OpenGL, and Java. Other key features of this release included the following:

- The ability to move the Dock from its usual place at the bottom to the left or right
- System status icons on the menu bar to provide easier access to commonly used functions such as volume control, display settings, date and time, Internet connection settings, wireless network monitoring, and battery charging

- iTunes and iMovie as part of system installation, and the introduction of iDVD
- A new DVD player with a simplified interface
- Improved iDisk functionality based on WebDAV
- A built-in image-capturing application to automatically download and enhance pictures from digital cameras
- The ability to burn over 4GB of data to a DVD, with support for burning recordable DVD discs directly in the Finder
- An integrated SMB/CIFS client

The Carbon API implementation in 10.1 was complete enough to allow important third-party applications to be released. Carbonized versions of Microsoft Office, Adobe Photoshop, and Macromedia Freehand were released soon after 10.1 went public.

1.5.4.3 Mac OS X 10.2

Jaguar was released at 10:20 P.M. to emphasize its version number. Its important feature additions included the following:

- *Quartz Extreme*—an integrated hardware acceleration layer for rendering on-screen objects by compositing them using primarily the graphics processing unit (GPU) on supported graphics cards
- *iChat*—an instant-messaging client compatible with AOL Instant Messaging (AIM)
- An enhanced mail application (`Mail.app`) with built-in adaptive spam filtering
- A new Address Book application with support for vCards, Bluetooth, and iSync synchronization with .Mac servers, PDAs, certain cell phones, and other Mac OS X computers (the Address Book's information was accessible to other applications)
- QuickTime 6, with support for MPEG-4
- An improved Finder with quick file searching from the toolbar and support for spring-loaded folders
- *Inkwell*—a handwriting recognition technology integrated with the text system, allowing text input using a graphics tablet

- *Rendezvous*,[25] which was Apple's implementation of *ZeroConf*, a zero-configuration networking technology allowing enabled devices to find one another on the network
- Better compatibility with Windows networks
- Version 3 of the Sherlock Internet services tool

Hereafter, Apple introduced new applications and incorporated technologies in Mac OS X at a bewildering pace. Other notable additions to Mac OS X after the release of Jaguar included the iPhoto digital photo management application, the Safari web browser, and an optimized implementation of the X Window System.

1.5.4.4 Mac OS X 10.3

Panther added several productivity and security features to Mac OS X, besides providing general performance and usability improvements. Notable 10.3 features included the following:

- An enhanced Finder, with a sidebar and support for labels
- Audio and video conferencing through the iChat AV application
- *Exposé*—a user-interface feature that can "live shrink" each on-screen window such that no windows overlap, allowing the user to find a window visually, after which each window is restored to its original size and location
- *FileVault*—encryption of a user's home directory
- Secure deletion of files in a user's trash can via a multipass overwriting algorithm
- Fast user switching
- Built-in faxing
- Improved Windows compatibility courtesy of better support for SMB shares and Microsoft Exchange
- Support for HFSX—a case-sensitive version of the HFS Plus file system

1.5.4.5 Mac OS X 10.4

Besides providing typical evolutionary improvements, Tiger introduced several new technologies such as *Spotlight* and *Dashboard*. Spotlight is a search technology

---

25. Rendezvous was later renamed Bonjour.

consisting of an extensible set of metadata importer plug-ins and a query API for searching files based on their metadata, even immediately after new files are created. Dashboard is an environment for creating and running lightweight desktop utilities called *widgets*, which normally remain hidden and can be summoned by a key-press. Other important Tiger features include the following:

- Improved 64-bit support, with the ability to compile 64-bit binaries, and 64-bit support in the libSystem shared library
- *Automator*—a tool for automating common procedures by visually creating workflows
- *Core Image*—a media technology employing GPU-based acceleration for image processing
- *Core Video*—a media technology acting as a bridge between QuickTime and the GPU for hardware-accelerated video processing
- *Quartz 2D Extreme*—a new set of Quartz layer optimizations that use the GPU for the entire drawing path (from the application to the framebuffer)
- *Quartz Composer*—a tool for visually creating compositions using both graphical technologies (such as Quartz 2D, Core Image, OpenGL, and QuickTime) and nongraphical technologies (such as MIDI System Services and Rich Site Summary [RSS])
- Support for a resolution-independent user interface
- Improved iChat AV, with support for multiple simultaneous audio and video conferences
- *PDF Kit*—a Cocoa framework for managing and displaying PDF files from within applications
- Improved Universal Access, with support for an integrated spoken interface
- An embeddable SQL database engine (SQLite) allowing applications to use SQL databases without running a separate RDBMS[26] process
- *Core Data*—a Cocoa technology that integrates with Cocoa bindings and allows visual description of an application's data entities, whose instances can persist on a storage medium
- *Fast Logout and Autosave* for improved user experience
- Support for access control lists (ACLs)

---

26. Relational database management system.

- New formalized and stable interfaces, particularly for kernel programming
- Improvements to the Web Kit (including support for creating and editing content at the DOM level of an HTML document), the Safari web browser (including RSS support), QuickTime (including support for the H.264 code and a new QuickTime Kit Cocoa framework), the Audio subsystem (including support for OpenAL, the Open Audio Library), the Mac OS X installer application, Sync Services, the Search Kit, Xcode, and so on

> The first shipping x86-based Macintosh computers used Mac OS X 10.4.4 as the operating system.

As we have seen in this chapter, Mac OS X is a long evolution of many disparate technologies. The next version of Mac OS X is expected to continue the remarkable pace of development, especially with the transition from the PowerPC to the x86 platform.

In Chapter 2, we will take a diverse tour of Mac OS X and its features, including brief overviews of the various layers. The remaining chapters discuss specific aspects and subsystems of Mac OS X in detail.

CHAPTER 2

An Overview of Mac OS X

We saw in Chapter 1 that Mac OS X is a mix of several technologies that differ not only in what they do but also in where they came from, which philosophies they represent, and how they are implemented. Nevertheless, Mac OS X presents a cohesive and consistent picture to the end user. The fact that Apple computers have a well-defined, limited hardware base is conducive to Apple's success in maintaining a mostly positive user experience despite the underlying software eclecticism seen in Mac OS X.

From a high-level standpoint, Mac OS X may be seen as consisting of three classes of technologies: those that originated at Apple, those that originated at NeXT, and "everything else." The latter consists mostly of third-party[1] open source software. On the one hand, such confluence makes it somewhat hard to clearly visualize the structure of Mac OS X and might even be a stumbling block for the new Mac OS X programmer. On the other hand, Mac OS X programmers have a rather colorful environment to give vent to their creative fervors. The end user is the bigger beneficiary, enjoying a range of software that is not seen on any

---

1. The other two categories also contain open source components.

other single platform. In particular, Mac OS X provides the benefits of a typical Unix system, while maintaining the traditional ease of use of a Macintosh. The Mac OS X Unix environment is standard enough so that most portable Unix software—such as the GNU suite and X Window applications—runs easily. Mac OS X is often dubbed a mass-market Unix system, and yet, traditionally non-Unix, mainstream software, such as Microsoft Office and the Adobe Creative Suite, is available natively for Mac OS X. Apple's own software repertoire is wide ranging in that it includes offerings such as the following:

- Everyday applications such as those for managing email, instant messaging, and web browsing
- "Digital-lifestyle" applications such as those for managing digital photos, music, and movies
- "Office" applications for creating presentations, slide shows, and other documents
- High-end professional software for animation, movie editing and effects, music editing and generation, DVD creation, and photography postproduction

This chapter is a whirlwind tour of the high-level architecture of Mac OS X. We will identify the main technologies that constitute Mac OS X and see how they fit in the overall picture. Many—*but not all*—topics that are mentioned in this chapter will be discussed in greater detail in subsequent chapters.

Figure 2–1 shows a layered view of the important components of the Mac OS X architecture. The picture is approximate since it is impractical—if not impossible—to divide various components into cleanly separated layers. Sometimes there is overlap between the layers. For example, OpenGL is functionally the hardware abstraction layer (HAL) of the graphics subsystem and logically sits atop the graphics hardware—this is not obvious from Figure 2–1. As another example, the BSD application environment, which includes the standard C library, logically sits atop the kernel but is shown alongside other application environments in Figure 2–1. In general, the following statements apply to the layered view shown here.

- Lower layers, which are shown closer to the kernel, provide functionality that is more fundamental than that provided by higher layers. Typically, higher layers use lower layers in their implementation.
- A layer may consist of applications, libraries, and *frameworks*.[2]

---

2. In the simplest sense, a framework is a packaged dynamic shared library. We will discuss frameworks in Section 2.8.3.

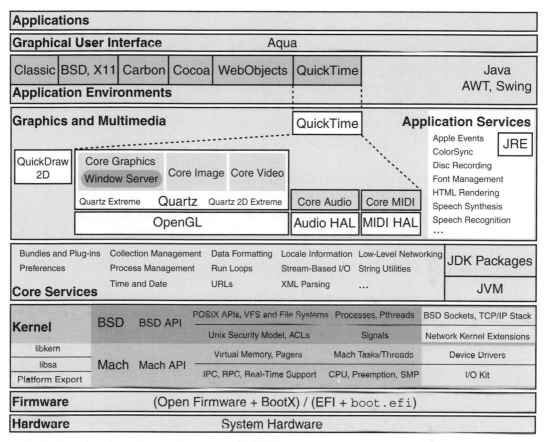

FIGURE 2–1 The high-level architecture of Mac OS X

- Entities may exist with the same (or similar) name in multiple layers. For example, QuickTime is both an application environment and an application service. Similarly, we have a layer named Core Services in Figure 2–1, but there is also a similarly named framework (`CoreServices.framework`). Moreover, many critical components of Mac OS X reside in the `/System/Library/CoreServices/` directory.

- End users interact with the highest layers, whereas developers additionally interact with one or more lower layers, depending on the kind of development they do. For example, a developer creating an end-user Cocoa application may not need[3] to go any "lower" than the Cocoa application environment.

---

3. In most cases, it would still be to a developer's advantage to understand how the system works.

2.1 Firmware

The firmware is not technically a part of Mac OS X, but it plays an important role in the operation of an Apple computer. Whereas PowerPC-based Apple computers use Open Firmware, x86-based Apple computers use the Extensible Firmware Interface (EFI).

Open Firmware is a nonproprietary, platform-independent boot firmware that lives in the boot ROM[4] of a PowerPC-based Apple computer. Its role in booting is somewhat analogous to that of the PC BIOS for x86-based computers. However, Open Firmware includes various other capabilities: It can be used for customized booting, diagnosing, debugging, and even programming. In fact, Open Firmware is a user-accessible runtime and programming environment in its own right. EFI is conceptually very similar to Open Firmware. Chapter 4 discusses Open Firmware and EFI.

2.2 Bootloader

The bootloader on the PowerPC version of Mac OS X is called *BootX*, which resides as a single file on the file system. Open Firmware loads it from a bootable device, which could be a locally attached storage device or the network.[5] BootX contains code that runs in the Open Firmware runtime environment. It performs a sequence of steps to arrange for the Mac OS X kernel to run, and it eventually launches the kernel. We will look at the structure and operation of BootX in Section 4.10.

The x86 version of Mac OS X uses a bootloader called `boot.efi`, which is an executable that runs in the EFI environment. Its purpose and operation are very similar to those of BootX.

2.3 Darwin

As we saw in Chapter 1, Darwin was released as a fork of a developer release of the Rhapsody operating system, which was an immediate precursor to Mac OS X.

---

4. In modern Apple computers, the boot ROM is an onboard flash EEPROM.

5. In the context of network booting, we treat the network as a bootable device.

An important component of Darwin is the Mac OS X kernel environment, which, together with the Darwin user environment, makes Darwin a stand-alone operating system. Until Apple announced the transition of Mac OS X to the x86 platform in mid-2005, Mac OS X had been a strictly PowerPC-only operating system. In contrast, Darwin has always been supported on both the PowerPC and the x86 platforms.

2.3.1 Darwin Packages

Darwin can be best understood as a collection of open source technologies that have been integrated by Apple to form a fundamental part of Mac OS X. It contains source code both from Apple and from third parties, including the Open Source and Free Software communities. Apple makes Darwin available as a set of *packages*, where each package is an archive containing source code of some component of Mac OS X. Darwin packages range from trivial ones such as *Liby* to gigantic ones such as *GCC* and *X11*. The exact number of packages in Darwin varies from release to release. For example, Darwin 8.6 (PowerPC)—which corresponds to Mac OS X 10.4.6—contains about 350 packages. Sources for Darwin components that originated at Apple are usually provided under the Apple Public Source License (APSL), which is a free software license.[6] The rest of the packages are provided under their respective licenses, such as the GNU General Public License (GPL), the BSD License, the Carnegie Mellon University License, and so on.

2.3.2 The Benefits of Darwin

Darwin represents a substantial amount of software that Apple has leveraged from a variety of sources: NEXTSTEP and OPENSTEP, Mach, various BSD flavors (largely FreeBSD), the GNU software suite, the XFree86 project, and so on. More importantly, Apple has integrated such "external" software rather well, making important modifications to optimize and adapt it to Mac OS X. Even though you can configure and control most of this software as you normally would, say, on a traditional Unix system, Mac OS X provides simplified and mostly consistent user interfaces that usually work well by hiding the underlying com-

---

6. The Free Software Foundation (FSF) classifies versions 1.0, 1.1, and 1.2 of the APSL as nonfree software licenses, whereas version 2.0 of the APSL is classified by the FSF as a free software license.

plexity. Such efficiency in adopting technology from diverse sources, and integrating it to create a synergistic effect, is one of the great strengths of Mac OS X.

2.3.3 Darwin and Mac OS X

It is important to note that Darwin is not Mac OS X. It can be thought of as a subset of Mac OS X—essentially the low-level foundation upon which Mac OS X is built. Darwin does not include many proprietary components that are integral parts of Mac OS X, such as the Aqua look-and-feel, Carbon, Cocoa, OpenGL, Quartz, and QuickTime. Consequently, it also does not support key Apple software such as the iLife suite, iChat AV, Safari, and the Xcode development environment.

> Although Darwin lacks the visual technologies of Mac OS X, it is possible to run Darwin with the X Window System providing the graphical user interface.

2.4 The xnu Kernel

The Mac OS X kernel is called *xnu*. In the simplest sense, xnu could be viewed as having a Mach-based core, a BSD-based operating system personality, and an object-oriented runtime environment for drivers[7] and other kernel extensions. The Mach component is based on Mach 3, whereas the BSD component is based on FreeBSD 5. A running kernel contains numerous drivers that do not reside in the xnu code base but have their own Darwin packages. In this sense, the Mac OS X kernel is "more than" xnu. However, we will usually not make distinctions based on packaging—we will use the term "xnu" to refer to the combination of the base kernel (as implemented in the xnu Darwin package) and all kernel extensions. With this understanding, we can divide the Mac OS X kernel into the following components:

- Mach—the services layer
- BSD—the primary system programming interface provider
- The I/O Kit—the runtime environment for drivers
- libkern—an in-kernel library

---

7. A driver is a specific type of kernel extension.

- libsa—an in-kernel library that is normally used only during early system startup
- The Platform Expert—the hardware abstraction module[8]
- Kernel extensions—various I/O Kit families, the majority of loadable device drivers, and some non-I/O Kit extensions

The Darwin xnu package consists of roughly a million lines of code, of which about half could be categorized under BSD and a third under Mach. The various kernel extensions, not all of which are needed (or loaded) on a given system, together constitute another million lines of code.

> The number of kernel extensions loaded at any time on a given system is significantly less than the total number of kernel extensions present on the system. The `kextstat` command can be used to list the currently loaded kernel extensions. The `/System/Library/Extensions/` directory is the standard location of kernel extensions.

Chapter 6 discusses several details of xnu. Several other chapters discuss specific areas of kernel functionality. Let us now briefly discuss the important kernel components.

2.4.1 Mach

If the xnu kernel is the core of Mac OS X, then Mach may be considered the core of xnu. Mach provides critical low-level services that are transparent to applications. System aspects that Mach is responsible for include the following:

- Hardware abstraction to some extent
- Processor management, including symmetric multiprocessing and scheduling
- Preemptive multitasking, including support for tasks and threads
- Virtual memory management, including low-level paging, memory protection, sharing, and inheritance
- Low-level IPC mechanisms that are the basis for all messaging in the kernel

---

8. The Platform Expert consists of support code in the base kernel and a platform-specific kernel extension.

- Real-time support that allows time-sensitive applications (e.g., media applications such as GarageBand and iTunes) to have latency-bounded access to processor resources
- Kernel debugging support[9]
- Console I/O

> Prior to Mac OS X 10.4, xnu already supported more than 4GB of physical memory on 64-bit hardware, although process virtual address spaces were still 32-bit. Consequently, an individual process could not address more than 4GB of virtual memory. With Mac OS X 10.4, xnu added support for 64-bit processes on 64-bit hardware, with an upper limit of 18 exabytes[10] on process virtual address spaces.

Mach is often unequivocally equated to a microkernel, but as we saw in Chapter 1, it was not until version 3 of Mach that it was used as a true microkernel. Earlier versions—including Mach 2.5, which was the basis for the Open Software Foundation's OSF/1 operating system—had monolithic implementations in which BSD and Mach resided in the same "kernel" address space. Even though Apple uses a Mach implementation that derives from Mach 3, xnu does not use Mach as a traditional microkernel. Various subsystems that would be implemented as user-space servers in a true microkernel system are part of the kernel proper in Mac OS X. In particular, the BSD portion of xnu, the I/O Kit, and Mach, all reside in the same address space. However, they have well-defined responsibilities that separate them in terms of function and implementation.

2.4.2 BSD

The xnu kernel contains a substantial amount of BSD-derived code, which is what we collectively refer to as BSD in the context of Mac OS X. However, it is not the case that a well-defined BSD kernel runs within xnu, whether as a single Mach task or otherwise. Whereas some BSD-derived portions in xnu are similar

---

9. xnu's built-in low-level kernel debugger is called KDB (or DDB). It is implemented in the Mach portion of the kernel, and so is KDP—a remote kernel debugging protocol used by the GNU debugger (GDB).

10. 10^{18} bytes.

to their original forms, other portions are quite different, since they were made to coexist with non-BSD entities such as the I/O Kit and Mach. Consequently, one can find several instances of code of different origins intertwined in the xnu kernel. Some aspects that BSD (or BSD-style code) is responsible for include the following:

- BSD-style process model
- Signals
- User IDs, permissions, and basic security policies
- POSIX APIs
- Asynchronous I/O APIs (AIO)
- BSD-style system calls
- TCP/IP stack, BSD sockets, and firewalling
- Network Kernel Extensions (NKEs), a type of kernel extension for making the BSD networking architecture fit into xnu[11]
- The virtual file system (VFS) layer and numerous file systems, including a file-system-independent VFS-level journaling mechanism
- System V and POSIX interprocess communication mechanisms
- In kernel cryptographic framework
- A system notification mechanism based on FreeBSD's *kqueue/kevent* mechanism, which is a system-wide service enabling notifications between applications, and from the kernel to applications
- The *fsevents* file system change notification mechanism that is used by the Spotlight search technology
- Access control lists (ACLs) and the *kauth* authorization framework[12]
- Various synchronization primitives

Certain kernel functionality has a lower level implementation in one portion of the kernel with higher-level abstraction layers in another portion. For example, the traditional process structure (`struct proc`), which is the primary kernel data

---

11. Before Mac OS X 10.4, an NKE was a specially designated kernel extension. Beginning with 10.4, NKE functionality is accessible to a regular kernel extension through a set of kernel programming interfaces (KPIs).

12. Beginning with Mac OS X 10.4, the kauth framework is used for the evaluation of ACLs. It is a general-purpose, extensible authorization framework.

structure that represents a UNIX process, is contained in the BSD portion, as is the *u-area*.[13] However, strictly speaking, in Mac OS X, a BSD process does not execute—it corresponds to exactly one Mach task, which contains one or more Mach threads, and it is *these threads* that execute. Consider the example of the fork() system call, which, along with variants like vfork(), is the only way to create a new process on a UNIX system. In Mac OS X, Mach tasks and threads are created and manipulated using Mach calls, which user programs typically do not use directly. The BSD-style fork() implementation in the kernel uses these Mach calls to create a task and a thread. Additionally, it allocates and initializes a process structure that is associated with the task. From the standpoint of the caller of fork(), these operations occur atomically, with the Mach and BSD-style data structures remaining in sync. Therefore, the BSD process structure acts as Unix "glue"[14] in Mac OS X.

Similarly, BSD's unified buffer cache (UBC) has a back-end that hooks into Mach's virtual memory subsystem.

> The UBC allows the file system and the virtual memory subsystem to share kernel memory buffers. Each process's virtual memory typically contains mappings from both physical memory and on-disk files. Unifying the buffer cache yields a single backing store for various entities, reducing disk accesses and the amount of "wired" memory used.

Funnels

An important synchronization abstraction in Mac OS X prior to version 10.4 is the *funnel*, which has the semantics of a mutex of large scope[15] that automatically drops when the holding thread sleeps. Funnels are used to serialize access to the BSD portion of the kernel. Beginning with version 10.4, xnu uses finer-grained locking. However, funnels still exist for the benefit of old code or code that is not performance critical.

---

13. Historically, the user area (or u-area) is the name for a data structure containing per-process or per-thread data that is swappable.

14. It simplifies the incorporation of BSD code that depends upon the process structure.

15. Such a mutex is sometimes referred to as a *giant mutex*.

In addition to BSD system calls, which include `sysctl()` and `ioctl()` calls, Mac OS X uses Mach system calls—or *Mach traps*—as necessary. There are several ways to map memory, perform block-copy operations, and otherwise exchange information between the Mac OS X user and kernel spaces.

2.4.3 The I/O Kit

xnu has an object-oriented device driver framework called the *I/O Kit*, which uses a restricted subset[16] of C++ as its programming language. C++ features that are not allowed in this subset include exceptions, multiple inheritance, templates, complicated constructors, initialization lists, and runtime type identification (RTTI). However, the I/O Kit *does* implement its own minimal RTTI system.

The I/O Kit's implementation consists of kernel-resident C++ libraries (libkern and IOKit) and a user-space framework (`IOKit.framework`). The kernel-resident libraries are available to loadable drivers (and for that matter, the kernel). Note that the Kernel framework (`Kernel.framework`) encapsulates the kernel-resident libraries in order to export their header files—the executable code for these libraries is contained in the kernel. `IOKit.framework` is a conventional framework used for writing user-space programs that communicate with the I/O Kit.

The I/O Kit's runtime architecture is modular and layered. It provides an infrastructure for capturing, representing, and maintaining relationships between the various hardware and software components that are involved in I/O connections. In this manner, the I/O Kit presents abstractions of the underlying hardware to the rest of the system. For example, the abstraction of a disk partition involves dynamic relationships between numerous I/O Kit classes: the physical disk, the disk controller, the bus that the controller is attached to, and so on. The device driver model provided by the I/O Kit has several useful features, such as the following:

- Extensive programming interfaces, including interfaces for applications and user-space drivers to communicate with the I/O Kit
- Numerous device families such as ATA/ATAPI, FireWire, Graphics, HID, Network, PCI, and USB
- Object-oriented abstractions of devices
- Plug-and-play and dynamic device management ("hot-plugging")
- Power management

---

16. The subset is based on Embedded C++.

- Preemptive multitasking, threading, symmetric multiprocessing, memory protection, and data management
- Dynamic matching and loading of drivers for multiple bus types
- A database for tracking and maintaining detailed information on instantiated objects (the *I/O Registry*)
- A database of all I/O Kit classes available on a system (the *I/O Catalog*)
- Interfaces for applications and user-space drivers to communicate with the I/O Kit
- Driver stacking

> The I/O Registry can be browsed either programmatically or by using a system utility such as `ioreg`, `IORegistryExplorer.app` (part of Apple Developer Tools), and `Mr. Registry.app` (part of the FireWire SDK).

Standard devices that conform to well-defined and well-supported specifications typically do not require custom I/O Kit drivers. For example, devices such as mice and keyboards are likely to work out of the box. Moreover, even if a device requires a custom driver, it may need only a user-space driver, provided it uses a FireWire or USB connection to the computer.

2.4.4 The libkern Library

The libkern library implements the runtime system for the restricted subset of C++ used by the I/O Kit's programming model. Besides providing commonly needed services to drivers, libkern also contains classes that are generally useful for kernel software development. In particular, it defines the `OSObject` class, which is the root base class for the Mac OS X kernel. `OSObject` implements dynamic typing and allocation features for supporting loadable kernel modules. The following are examples of the functionality provided by libkern:

- Dynamic allocation, construction, and destruction of objects, with support for a variety of built-in object types such as Arrays, Booleans, and Dictionaries
- Atomic operations and miscellaneous functions such as `bcmp()`, `memcmp()`, and `strlen()`
- Functions for byte-swapping

- Provisions for tracking the number of current instances for each class
- Mechanisms that help alleviate the C++ *fragile base-class problem*

The Fragile Base-Class Problem

The fragile base-class problem occurs when modifications to a nonleaf class "break" a derived class. A nonleaf class is one that is a base class of at least one other class. The said breakage may occur because the derived class is relying—explicitly or implicitly—on the knowledge of certain characteristics of the nonleaf class. Examples of such characteristics include the size of the base class's virtual table (vtable), offsets in the vtable, offsets to class-protected data, and offsets to public data.

libkern provides ways to create reserved slots for class data members and virtual functions to absorb future addition of these entities—up to a limit.

2.4.5 The libsa Library

libsa is an in-kernel support library—essentially an in-kernel linker—used during early system startup for loading kernel extensions. The "sa" in its name is a vestigial reference to its being a library that provides functions for use by *stand-alone* applications—in this case, the kernel.

> Stand-alone libraries exist on other operating systems—often with the name *libstand*—to provide minimal runtime environments.

Mac OS X kernel extensions are normally loaded on demand through the `kextd` user-space daemon (`/usr/libexec/kextd`). During early stages of bootstrapping, `kextd` is not yet available. libsa provides a subset of `kextd`'s capabilities to the kernel. Examples of specific functionality implemented by libsa for loading, linking, and recording kernel extension object files include the following:

- Simple memory allocation
- Binary searching
- Sorting
- Miscellaneous string-handling functions
- Symbol remangling

- A dependency graph package used while determining kernel extension dependencies
- Decompression of compressed kernels and verification of checksums

Note that libsa is not a generally available kernel library. In a typical bootstrapping scenario, libsa's code is removed from the kernel once `kextd` becomes available. Even when libsa is present, its constituent functions are not available to the kernel as part of any programming interface.[17]

2.4.6 The Platform Expert

The Platform Expert is an object—essentially a motherboard-specific driver—that knows the type of platform that the system is running on. The I/O Kit registers a *nub* for the Platform Expert at system initialization time. An instance of the `IOPlatformExpertDevice` class becomes the root of the device tree. The root nub then loads the correct platform-specific driver, which further discovers the busses present on the system, registering a nub for each bus found. The I/O Kit loads a matching driver for each bus nub, which in turn discovers the devices connected to the bus, and so on.

Nubs

In the context of the I/O Kit, a nub is an object that defines an access point and communication channel for a physical device or a logical service. A physical device could be a bus, a disk drive or partition, a graphics card, and so on. Examples of logical services include arbitration, driver matching, and power management.

The Platform Expert abstraction provides access to a wide variety of platform-specific functions and information, such as those related to:

- Constructing device trees
- Parsing certain boot arguments
- Identifying the machine, which includes determining processor and bus clock speeds

---

17. The kernel accesses libsa's extension-loading functionality through a function pointer shared between libsa and the kernel. libsa's constructor function initializes this pointer to point to a libsa function.

- Accessing power management information
- Retrieving and setting system time
- Retrieving and setting console information
- Halting and restarting the machine
- Accessing the interrupt controller
- Creating the system serial number string
- Saving kernel panic information
- Initializing a "user interface" to be used in case of kernel panics
- Reading and writing the nonvolatile memory (NVRAM)
- Reading and writing the parameter memory (PRAM)

2.4.7 Kernel Extensions

Besides the core kernel, the Mac OS X kernel environment includes kernel extensions that are dynamically loaded as needed. Most standard kernel extensions are targeted for the I/O Kit, but there are exceptions such as certain networking-related and file-system-related kernel extensions—for example, `webdav_fs.kext` and `PPP.kext`. On a typical Mac OS X installation, there may be close to a hundred kernel extensions loaded at any time. Many more reside in the `/System/Library/Extensions/` directory.

2.5 A User-Space View of the File System

The Mac OS X user space is where end users and most developers spend their computing time. The file system—or rather, its content and layout—is fundamental to how users interact with the system. The Mac OS X file system's layout is largely a superimposition of Unix-derived and NEXTSTEP-derived file systems, with many traditional Macintosh influences.

2.5.1 File System Domains

The Unix-style file system view in Mac OS X can be used to access all files and directories on a volume, including the Mac OS X–specific portions of the file system. Some Unix-specific aspects of this view include standard directories such as

`/bin/`, `/dev/`, `/etc/`, `/sbin/`, `/tmp/`, `/usr/`, `/usr/X11R6/`,[18] `/usr/include/`, `/usr/lib/`, `/usr/libexec/`, `/usr/sbin`, `/usr/share/`, and `/var/`.

Mac OS X conceptually divides the file system into four *domains*: User, Local, Network, and System.

2.5.1.1 *The User Domain*

The *User* domain contains user-specific resources. In Unix terminology, this is a user's home directory. For a user named amit, the default local home directory location is `/Users/amit/`, and the default network home directory location is `/Network/Users/amit/`. A user's home directory contains several standard directories, such as `.Trash`, `Applications`, `Desktop`, `Documents`, `Library`, `Movies`, `Music`, `Pictures`, `Public`, and `Sites`. Certain per-user directories such as `Public` and `Sites` are meant to be publicly accessible and therefore have read permissions for other users.

2.5.1.2 *The Local Domain*

The *Local* domain contains resources available to all users on a single system. It includes shared applications and documents. It is usually located on the boot volume, which, typically, is also the root volume. The `/Applications/` directory lies in the Local domain. Unlike the User domain, which can be arbitrarily manipulated by its owning user, only a user with system administrator privileges may modify the Local domain.

2.5.1.3 *The Network Domain*

The *Network* domain contains resources available to all users on a local area network—for example, applications and documents that are shared over a network. The Network domain is usually located on a file server and is locally mounted on a client machine under `/Network/`. Only a user with network administrator privileges may modify this domain. Specific directories within this domain include `Applications`, `Library`, `Servers`, and `Users`.

---

18. Some components, such as the X Window System, are optional. If they are not installed, certain directories may not be present.

2.5.1.4 *The System Domain*

The *System* domain contains resources belonging to Mac OS X. Its contents include the operating system, libraries, programs, scripts, and configuration files. Like the Local domain, the System domain resides on a boot/root volume. Its standard location is the `/System/` directory.

The system searches for resources such as fonts and plug-ins in various domains in the order of the most specific domain first and the most general domain last, that is, User, Local, Network, and System.

2.5.2 The `/System/Library/` Directory

Each file system domain contains several standard directories, some of which may exist in multiple (or all) domains. Perhaps the most interesting directory in any domain—and one that exists in all domains—is `Library`. It contains a hierarchy of several standard subdirectories. In particular, a substantial part of the operating system resides in `/System/Library/`. Let us look at examples of its contents.

- `/System/Library/Caches/` contains system-level caches for various types of data. Most notably, it contains the kernel and kernel extension (*kext*) caches. A kernel cache contains kernel code, prelinked kernel extensions, and information dictionaries of any number of kernel extensions. Kernel caches reside in `/System/Library/Caches/com.apple.kernelcaches/`.

- `/System/Library/Extensions/` contains device drivers and other kernel extensions. The multiextension (or *mkext*) cache—`/System/Library/Extensions.mkext`—contains multiple kernel extensions and their information dictionaries. An mkext cache is used during early system startup. A kext repository cache containing the information dictionaries of all kernel extensions[19] in `/System/Library/Extensions/` exists as the file `/System/Library/Extensions.kextcache`.

- `/System/Library/Frameworks/` contains those Apple-provided frameworks and shared libraries that have published APIs.

---

19. The kext repository cache also includes the information dictionaries of any plug-ins that may reside within kernel extensions.

- `/System/Library/PrivateFrameworks/` contains those Apple-provided frameworks and shared libraries that are private to Apple and not available to third-party programmers.
- `/System/Library/Filesystems/` contains loadable file systems.
- `/System/Library/LaunchAgents/` and `/System/Library/Launch-Daemons/` contain `launchd` configuration files for system-level agents and daemons. The `launchd` program (`/sbin/launchd`) is the master daemon that manages other daemons and agents beginning with Mac OS X 10.4.

The `/System/Library/CoreServices/` directory contains several system components used in the system's normal operation, such as the Dock and Finder applications. Other examples include those listed here.

- `AppleFileServer.app` is the Apple Filing Protocol (AFP) server.
- The `BezelUI` directory contains the program and images to display user-interface overlays in a variety of situations: when the user adjusts screen brightness or volume using keyboard buttons, when the user presses the eject button, when the batteries of an Apple Bluetooth mouse or keyboard are low, and so on.
- `BootX` (PowerPC) and `boot.efi` (x86) are the Mac OS X bootloaders.
- `CCacheServer.app` is the Kerberos Credentials Cache Server.
- `Classic Startup.app` is the Classic virtual environment provider.
- `Crash Reporter.app` is used for sending a problem report to Apple when an application crashes or when the system restarts after a kernel panic. It prompts the user before sending the report, which consists of system information and the crashed program's debugging information. Figure 2–2 shows the sequence of GNU debugger (GDB) commands used to generate the debugging information. These commands are part of the `gdb-generate-crash-report-script` GDB script, which resides as a resource within `Crash Reporter.app`.
- `Network Diagnostics.app` is used for solving Internet connection problems.
- `OBEXAgent.app` is the Bluetooth file exchange agent.
- `loginwindow.app` is roughly analogous to the `login` program on a UNIX system.
- `pbs` is the pasteboard server and a helper daemon for Cocoa applications.

FIGURE 2–2 Sequence of GDB commands for generating a crash report

```
# Stacks of all threads
thread apply all bt

# Local variable information
info locals

# Register values
info all-registers

# Values below stack pointer
x/64x $r1-100

# Values from stack pointer and beyond
x/64x $r1

# Shared library address information
info sharedlibrary

# Mach memory regions
info mach-regions
```

2.6 The Runtime Architecture

Given a loose enough definition of a runtime environment, one can say that modern operating systems often provide multiple runtime environments. For example, whereas the Java virtual machine on Mac OS X is a runtime environment for Java programs, the virtual machine implementation itself executes in another, "more native" runtime environment. Mac OS X has several runtime environments for applications, as we will see later in this chapter. However, an operating system typically has only a single lowest-level (or "native") runtime environment that we will refer to as *the* runtime environment. The foundation of the runtime environment is the *runtime architecture*, which has the following key aspects.

- It provides facilities for launching and executing programs.
- It specifies how code and data reside on disk—that is, it specifies the binary format. It also specifies how compilers and related tools must generate code and data.
- It specifies how code and data are loaded into memory.
- It specifies how references to external libraries are resolved.

Mac OS X has only one runtime architecture: *Mach-O*. The name refers to the Mach Object File Format, although the term "Mach" is somewhat of a misnomer in this case since Mach is not meant to understand any object file format. Neither is Mach aware of the runtime conventions of user-space programs. The Mac OS X kernel, however, does understand the Mach-O format. In fact, Mach-O is the only binary format that the kernel can load[20]—using the execve()[21] system call, which is implemented in the BSD portion of the Mac OS X kernel.

2.6.1 Mach-O Files

Mac OS X uses Mach-O files for implementing several types of system components, for example, the following:

- Bundles (programmatically loadable code)
- Dynamic shared libraries
- Frameworks
- Umbrella frameworks, which contain one or more other frameworks
- Kernel extensions
- Linkable object files
- Static archives
- Executables

We will discuss frameworks, umbrella frameworks, and bundles later in this chapter. Before we continue, let us enumerate some programs that are useful in creating, analyzing, or manipulating Mach-O files. Such programs include the following:

- as—the GNU-based assembler front-end
- dyld—the default dynamic link editor (or runtime linker)
- gcc, g++—GNU compiler front-ends
- ld—the static link editor (or static linker[22])

---

20. Note that we explicitly say *binary* format: The kernel can arrange for scripts to run.

21. The execve() system call executes the specified program, which may be a binary executable or a script, in the address space of the calling process.

22. Note that "static" in static linker refers to the fact that the program operates at compile time—and not dynamically at runtime. The static linker supports both dynamic shared libraries and static archive libraries.

- libtool—a program that creates dynamically linked shared libraries and statically linked libraries from Mach-O object files; called by the compiler driver during library creation
- nm—a program that displays the object file symbol table
- otool—a versatile program for displaying the internals of Mach-O files; has disassembling capabilities

A Mach-O file contains a fixed-size *header* (see Figure 2–3) at the very beginning, followed by typically several variable-sized *load commands*, followed by one or more *segments*. Each segment can contain one or more *sections*.

FIGURE 2–3 The structure of the Mach-O header (32-bit version)

```
struct mach_header {
    uint32_t        magic;      /* mach magic number identifier */
    cpu_type_t      cputype;    /* cpu specifier */
    cpu_subtype_t   cpusubtype; /* machine specifier */
    uint32_t        filetype;   /* type of file */
    uint32_t        ncmds;      /* number of load commands */
    uint32_t        sizeofcmds; /* the size of all the load commands */
    uint32_t        flags;      /* flags */
};
```

The Mach-O header describes the features, layout, and linking characteristics of the file. The filetype field in the Mach-O header indicates the type and, therefore, the purpose of the file. Mach-O file types include the following:

- MH_BUNDLE—plug-in code that is programmatically loaded into applications at runtime
- MH_CORE—a file that stores the address space of an aborted program, that is, a *core file* containing a "core dump"
- MH_DYLIB—a dynamic shared library; conventionally a file with a .dylib suffix if it is a stand-alone library
- MH_DYLINKER—a special shared library that is a dynamic linker
- MH_EXECUTE—a standard demand-paged executable
- MH_OBJECT—an intermediate, relocatable object file (conventionally with a .o suffix); also used for kernel extensions

For executable files, one of the load commands (LC_LOAD_DYLINKER) in the Mach-O header specifies the path to the linker to be used for loading the program.

By default, this load command specifies the standard dynamic linker, dyld (/usr/lib/dyld), which itself is a Mach-O file of type MH_DYLINKER. The kernel and dyld (or in theory, another dynamic linker, if one is specified) together prepare a Mach-O binary for execution using the following sequence of operations, which has been simplified for brevity.[23]

- The kernel examines the executable's Mach-O header and determines its file type.

- The kernel interprets the load commands contained in the Mach-O header. For example, to handle LC_SEGMENT commands, it loads program segments into memory.

- The kernel handles the LC_LOAD_DYLINKER load command by loading the specified dynamic linker into memory.

- The kernel eventually executes the dynamic linker on the program file. Note that this is the first user-space code that runs in the program's address space. The arguments passed to the linker include the program file's Mach-O header, the argument count (argc), and the argument vector (argv).

- The dynamic linker interprets load commands from the Mach-O header. It loads the shared libraries that the program depends on, and it binds external references that are required to start execution—that is, it binds the Mach-O file's *imported symbols* to their *definitions* in a shared library or framework.

- The dynamic linker calls the entry point function specified by the LC_UNIXTHREAD (or LC_THREAD) load command, which contains the initial thread state of a program's main thread. This entry point is normally a language runtime environment function, which in turn calls the program's "main" function.

Let us look at the example of a trivial executable. Figure 2–4 shows a C program that is compiled to an executable called empty.

FIGURE 2–4 A trivial C program to be compiled to an "empty" executable

```
// empty.c

int
main(void)
{
    return 0;
}
```

---

23. Further details of program execution by the kernel are discussed in Section 7.5.

Figure 2–5 shows the use of the `otool` program to list the load commands contained in `empty`.

FIGURE 2–5 Displaying the load commands in an executable's Mach-O header

```
$ otool -l ./empty
empty:
Load command 0
      cmd LC_SEGMENT
  cmdsize 56
  segname __PAGEZERO
...
Load command 4
        cmd LC_LOAD_DYLINKER
      cmdsize 28
        name /usr/lib/dyld (offset 12)
Load command 5
        cmd LC_LOAD_DYLIB
...
Load command 10
        cmd LC_UNIXTHREAD
    cmdsize 176
     flavor PPC_THREAD_STATE
      count PPC_THREAD_STATE_COUNT
     r0  0x00000000 r1  0x00000000 r2  0x00000000 r3   0x00000000 r4    0x00000000
...
ctr 0x00000000 mq  0x00000000 vrsave 0x00000000 srr0 0x000023cc srr1 0x00000000
```

The `LC_UNIXTHREAD` load command shown in Figure 2–5 contains the initial values of the program's registers. In particular, the `srr0` PowerPC register[24] contains the address of the entry point function—$0x23cc$ in this case. As we can verify by using the `nm` program, this address belongs to a function called `start()`. Consequently, `empty` begins execution in this function, which comes from the language runtime stub `/usr/lib/crt1.o`. The stub initializes the program's runtime environment state before calling the `main()` function. The compiler links in `crt1.o` during compilation.

Note that if the Mach-O file in Figure 2–5 were an x86 executable, its `LC_UNIXTHREAD` command would contain x86 register state. In particular, the `eip` register would contain the address of the `start()` function.

---

24. Chapter 3 discusses the PowerPC architecture in detail.

> Depending on aspects such as the program being compiled, the programming language, the compiler, and the operating system, more than one such stub may be linked in during compilation. For example, bundles and dynamic shared libraries on Mac OS X are linked along with `/usr/lib/bundle1.o` and `/usr/lib/dylib1.o`, respectively.

2.6.2 Fat Binaries

We came across "fat" binaries in Chapter 1, when we looked at NEXTSTEP. Since NEXTSTEP ran on multiple platforms such as Motorola 68K, x86, HP PA-RISC, and SPARC, it was rather easy to come across *multifat* binaries.

Fat binaries first became useful on Mac OS X with the advent of 64-bit user address space support, since a fat binary could contain both 32-bit and 64-bit Mach-O executables of a program. Moreover, with Apple's transition to the x86 platform, fat binaries become still more important: Apple's Universal Binary format is simply another name for fat binaries. Figure 2–6 shows an example of creating a three-architecture fat binary on Mac OS X.[25] The `lipo` command can be used to list the architecture types in a fat file. It is also possible to build a fat Darwin kernel—one that contains the kernel executables for both the PowerPC and x86 architectures in a single file.

FIGURE 2–6 Creating fat binaries

```
$ gcc -arch ppc -arch ppc64 -arch i386 -c hello.c
$ file hello.o
hello.o: Mach-O fat file with 3 architectures
hello.o (for architecture ppc):   Mach-O object ppc
hello.o (for architecture i386):  Mach-O object i386
hello.o (for architecture ppc64): Mach-O 64-bit object ppc64
$ lipo -detailed_info hello.o
Fat header in: hello.o
fat_magic 0xcafebabe
nfat_arch 3
architecture ppc
    cputype CPU_TYPE_POWERPC
    cpusubtype CPU_SUBTYPE_POWERPC_ALL
    offset 68
    size 368
    align 2^2 (4)
```

(continues)

---

25. Apple's build of GCC 4.0.0 or higher is required to create fat binaries on Mac OS X.

FIGURE 2–6 Creating fat binaries *(continued)*

```
architecture i386
    cputype CPU_TYPE_I386
    cpusubtype CPU_SUBTYPE_I386_ALL
    offset 436
    size 284
    align 2^2 (4)
architecture ppc64
    cputype CPU_TYPE_POWERPC64
    cpusubtype CPU_SUBTYPE_POWERPC_ALL
    offset 720
    size 416
    align 2^3 (8)
```

Figure 2–7 shows the structure of a fat binary containing PowerPC and x86 executables. Note that a fat binary is essentially a *wrapper*—a simple archive that concatenates Mach-O files for multiple architectures. A fat binary begins with a fat header (struct fat_header) that contains a magic number followed by an integral value representing the number of architectures whose binaries reside in the fat binary. The fat header is followed by a sequence of fat architecture specifiers (struct fat_arch)—one for each architecture contained in the fat binary. The fat_arch structure contains the offset into the fat binary at which the corresponding Mach-O file begins. It also includes the size of the Mach-O file, along with a power of 2 value that specifies the alignment of the offset. Given this information, it is straightforward for other programs—including the kernel—to locate the code for the desired architecture within a fat binary.

Note that although a platform's Mach-O file in a fat binary follows that architecture's byte ordering, the fat_header and fat_arch structures are always stored in the big-endian byte order.

2.6.3 Linking

Dynamic linking is the default on Mac OS X—all normal user-level executables are dynamically linked. In fact, Apple does not support static linking of user-space programs (Mac OS X does not come with a static C library). One reason for not supporting static linking is that the binary interface between the C library and the kernel is considered private. Consequently, system call trap instructions should not appear in normally compiled executables. Although you can statically

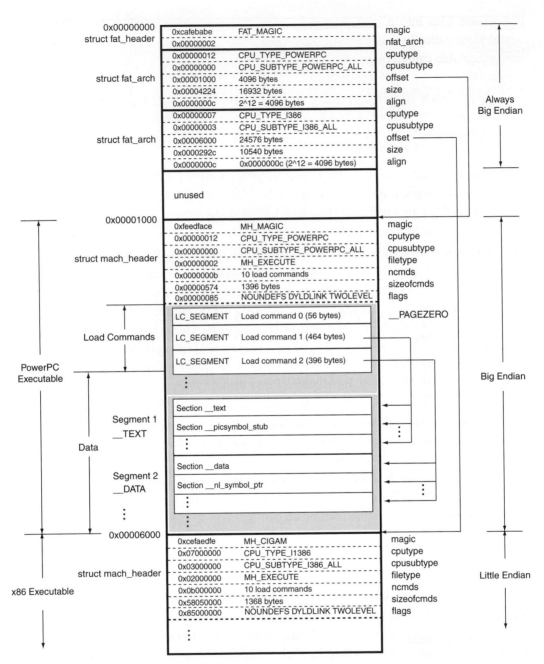

FIGURE 2–7 A Universal Binary containing PowerPC and x86 Mach-O executables

link object files into a static archive library,[26] the language runtime stub that would yield statically linked executables doesn't exist. Therefore, a statically linked user executable cannot be generated using the default tools.

> Mac OS X kernel extensions must be statically linked. However, kernel extensions are not Mach-O executables (`MH_EXECUTE`) but Mach-O object files (`MH_OBJECT`).

The `otool` command can be used to display the names and version numbers of the shared libraries used by an object file. For example, the following command determines the libraries that `launchd` depends on (`launchd`'s library dependencies are interesting because it is the first program to execute in user space—typically, such programs are statically linked on Unix systems):

```
$ otool -L /sbin/launchd # PowerPC version of Mac OS X
/sbin/launchd:
        /usr/lib/libbom.dylib (...)
        /usr/lib/libsm.dylib (...)
$ otool -L /sbin/launchd # x86 version of Mac OS X
/sbin/launchd:
        /usr/lib/libsm.dylib (...)
        /usr/lib/libgcc_s.1.dylib (...)
        /usr/lib/libSystem.B.dylib (...)
```

Figure 2–8 shows examples of compiling a dynamic shared library, compiling a static archive library, and linking with the two libraries.

FIGURE 2–8 Compiling dynamic and static libraries

```
$ cat libhello.c
#include <stdio.h>

void
hello(void)
{
    printf("Hello, World!\n");
}
$ cat main.c
extern void hello(void);
```

(continues)

---

26. Static archive libraries can be used for distributing code that is not desirable in a shared library but is otherwise usable while compiling multiple programs.

FIGURE 2–8 Compiling dynamic and static libraries *(continued)*

```
int
main(void)
{
    hello();
    return 0;
}
$ gcc -c main.c libhello.c
$ libtool -static -o libhello.a libhello.o
$ gcc -o main.static main.o libhello.a
$ otool -L main.static
main.static:
        /usr/lib/libmx.A.dylib (...)
        /usr/lib/libSystem.B.dylib (...)
$ gcc -dynamiclib -o libhello.dylib -install_name libhello.dylib libhello.o
$ gcc -o main.dynamic main.o -L. -lhello
$ otool -L main.dynamic
main.dynamic:
        libhello.dylib (...)
        /usr/lib/libmx.A.dylib (...)
        /usr/lib/libSystem.B.dylib (...)
```

When compiling a dynamic shared library, you can specify a custom initialization routine that will be called before any symbol is used from the library. Figure 2–9 shows an example.

FIGURE 2–9 Using a custom initialization routine in a dynamic shared library

```
$ cat libhello.c
#include <stdio.h>

void
my_start(void)
{
    printf("my_start\n");
}

void
hello(void)
{
    printf("Hello, World!\n");
}
$ cat main.c
extern void hello(void);

int
main(void)
```

(continues)

FIGURE 2–9 Using a custom initialization routine in a dynamic shared library *(continued)*

```
{
    hello();
    return 0;
}
$ gcc -c main.c libhello.c
$ gcc -dynamiclib -o libhello.dylib -install_name libhello.dylib \
        -init _my_start libhello.o
$ gcc -o main.dynamic main.o -L. -lhello
$ ./main.dynamic
my_start
Hello, World!
```

Other notable aspects of the Mach-O runtime architecture include multiple binding styles, two-level namespaces, and weakly linked symbols.

2.6.3.1 Multiple Binding Styles

When binding imported references in a program, Mac OS X supports *just-in-time* (lazy) binding, *load-time* binding, and *prebinding*. With lazy binding, a shared library is loaded only when a symbol from that library is used for the first time. Once the library is loaded, not all of the program's unresolved references from that library are bound immediately—references are bound upon first use. With load-time binding, the dynamic linker binds all undefined references in a program when it is launched—or, as in the case of a bundle, when it is loaded.

We will look at details of prebinding in Section 2.8.4.

2.6.3.2 Two-Level Namespaces

A two-level namespace implies that imported symbols are referenced both by the symbol's name and by the name of the library containing it. Mac OS X uses two-level namespaces by default.

When two-level namespaces are being used, it is not possible to use dyld's DYLD_INSERT_LIBRARIES environment variable[27] to preload libraries before the ones specified in a program. It is possible to ignore two-level namespace bindings at runtime by using dyld's DYLD_FORCE_FLAT_NAMESPACE environment variable, which forces all images in the program to be linked as flat-namespace images. However, doing so may be problematic when the images have multiply defined symbols.

---

27. This variable is analogous to the LD_PRELOAD environment variable supported by the runtime linker on several other platforms.

2.6.3.3 Weakly Linked Symbols

A weakly linked symbol[28] is one whose absence does not cause the dynamic linker to throw a runtime binding error—a program referencing such a symbol *will* execute. However, the dynamic linker will explicitly set the address of a non-existent weak symbol to NULL. It is the program's responsibility to ensure that a weak symbol exists (i.e., its address is not NULL) before using it. It is also possible to link to an entire framework weakly, which results in all of the framework's symbols being weakly linked. Figure 2–10 shows an example of using a weak symbol.

FIGURE 2–10 Using weak symbols on Mac OS X 10.2 and newer

```
$ cat libweakfunc.c
#include <stdio.h>

void
weakfunc(void)
{
    puts("I am a weak function.");
}
$ cat main.c
#include <stdio.h>

extern void weakfunc(void) __attribute__((weak_import));

int
main(void)
{
    if (weakfunc)
        weakfunc();
    else
        puts("Weak function not found.");

    return 0;
}

$ gcc -c libweakfunc.c
$ gcc -dynamiclib -o libweakfunc.dylib \
        -install_name libweakfunc.dylib libweakfunc.o
$ MACOSX_DEPLOYMENT_TARGET=10.4 gcc -o main main.c -L. -lweakfunc
$ ./main
I am a weak function.
$ rm libweakfunc.dylib
$ ./main
Weak function not found.
```

---

28. We use the term "symbol" interchangeably with the term "reference" in this discussion. A reference is to a symbol, which may represent code or data.

2.6.3.4 *dyld Interposing*

Beginning with Mac OS X 10.4, `dyld` does support programmatic interposing of library functions, although the corresponding source code is not included in the open source version of `dyld`. Suppose you wish to use this feature to intercept a C library function, say, `open()`, with your own function, say, `my_open()`. You can achieve the interposing by creating a dynamic shared library that implements `my_open()` and also contains a section called `__interpose` in its `__DATA` segment. The contents of the `__interpose` section are the "original" and "new" function-pointer tuples—in this case, { `my_open`, `open` }. Using the `DYLD_INSERT_LIBRARIES` variable with such a library will enable the interposing. Note that `my_open()` can call `open()` normally, without having to first look up the address of the "open" symbol. Figure 2–11 shows an example of `dyld` interposing—the programmer-provided library "takes over" the `open()` and `close()` functions.

> As a word of caution, one must note that calls to certain library functions could lead to recursive invocations of the interposer functions. For example, the implementation of `printf()` may call `malloc()`. If you are interposing `malloc()` and calling `printf()` from within your version of `malloc()`, a recursive situation can arise.

FIGURE 2–11 Interposing a library function through `dyld`

```
// libinterposers.c

#include <stdio.h>
#include <unistd.h>
#include <fcntl.h>

typedef struct interpose_s {
    void *new_func;
    void *orig_func;
} interpose_t;

int my_open(const char *, int, mode_t);
int my_close(int);

static const interpose_t interposers[] \
    __attribute__ ((section("__DATA, __interpose"))) = {
        { (void *)my_open,  (void *)open  },
        { (void *)my_close, (void *)close },
    };
```

(continues)

FIGURE 2-11 Interposing a library function through `dyld` *(continued)*

```
int
my_open(const char *path, int flags, mode_t mode)
{
    int ret = open(path, flags, mode);
    printf("--> %d = open(%s, %x, %x)\n", ret, path, flags, mode);
    return ret;
}

int
my_close(int d)
{
    int ret = close(d);
    printf("--> %d = close(%d)\n", ret, d);
    return ret;
}

$ gcc -Wall -dynamiclib -o /tmp/libinterposers.dylib libinterposers.c
$ DYLD_INSERT_LIBRARIES=/tmp/libinterposers.dylib cat /dev/null
--> 9 = open(/dev/null, 0, 0)
--> 0 = close(9)
```

2.7 The C Library

The user-level standard C library—the ubiquitous *libc*—is known as *libSystem* on Mac OS X. /usr/lib/libc.dylib is a symbolic link to /usr/lib/libSystem.dylib. libSystem could be thought of as a metalibrary, as it consists of several BSD libraries, some of which are independent libraries on a typical Unix system. Normalcy is maintained by symbolically linking such libraries to libSystem, as is the case with libc. Some of libSystem's constituent libraries are specific to Mac OS X or otherwise internal to libSystem. The following are examples of externally visible libraries contained in libSystem:

- *libc*—the standard C library
- *libdbm*—a database library
- *libdl*—a programming interface to the dynamic linking loader
- *libinfo*—a library that provides various "info" APIs, such as DNS and multicast DNS, NIS, and NetInfo
- *libkvm*—a library that provides a uniform interface for accessing kernel virtual memory images; used by programs such as ps

- *libm*—the standard math library
- *libpoll*—a wrapper library that emulates the System V poll() system call on top of BSD's select() system call
- *libpthread*—the POSIX thread[29] library
- *librpcsvc*—a miscellaneous "Sun" RPC services library

> On Mac OS X 10.3 and earlier, libdl is a wrapper library that emulates the POSIX dynamic linking loader API—the dlopen(), dlclose(), dlsym(), and dlerror() functions[30]—on top of Darwin's native dyld API. On Mac OS X 10.4 and later, the dlopen() function family is implemented natively within dyld.

Internally available functionality in libSystem includes the following:

- *libdyldapis*—provides a low-level API to the dynamic link editor
- *libkeymgr*—used for maintaining process-wide global data known to all threads across all dynamic libraries
- *liblaunch*—provides an interface to launchd, the manager of system-wide and per-user daemons and agents
- *libmacho*—provides an API for accessing segments and sections in Mach-O files
- *libnotify*—allows applications to exchange events through namespace-based[31] stateless notifications
- *libstreams*—implements an I/O streams mechanism
- *libunc*—allows creation, dispatch, and manipulation of user notifications

libSystem also includes an object file containing the *commpage* symbols. As we will see in Chapters 5 and 6, the commpage area is a region of memory that is mapped (shared and read-only) into every process's address space. It contains frequently used system-wide code and data. The commpage symbols in libSystem

---

29. POSIX threads (Pthreads) on Mac OS X are implemented using Mach kernel threads, with one Mach thread per pthread.

30. Typical libdl implementations also provide the dladdr() function, which is not defined by POSIX. dladdr() queries the dynamic linker for information about the image containing a specified address.

31. The clients of this API share a global namespace. Clients may post notifications, which are associated with names. Similarly, clients may monitor names by registering for notifications.

are placed in a special section (the __commpage section within the __DATA segment), which allows a debugger to access them.

2.8 Bundles and Frameworks

Before discussing other layers of Mac OS X, let us look at the *bundle* and *framework* abstractions, since much of the user-level functionality in Mac OS X is implemented as frameworks, and a framework is a specific type of a bundle.

2.8.1 Bundles

A bundle is a collection of related resources packaged as a directory hierarchy. Examples of resources that reside in bundles include executables, shared libraries, plug-ins, header files, images, audio files, documentation, and—recursively— other bundles. The bundle abstraction is very useful in packaging, deploying, maintaining, and using software. Consider the example of an application bundle, which is one of the most commonly used bundle types on Mac OS X. Figure 2–12 shows the hierarchical structure of the iTunes application bundle.

An application bundle is a directory with a name that conventionally has a .app suffix. Mac OS X applications are often more than just a single stand-alone executable. For example, an application may use a variety of media files—icons, splash images, and sounds—in its user interface. An application may implement much of its functionality modularly, across one or more dynamic shared libraries. An application may also support a plug-in architecture through which anybody may extend the application's functionality by writing loadable plug-ins. Bundles are well suited for such applications because they keep the various constituents of the application together in a structured manner. As shown in Figure 2–12, the iTunes application bundle contains the main iTunes executable, a loadable plug-in bundle, icons, media files, a helper application, localized documentation, and so on. Everything resides within the iTunes.app directory, rather than being strewn over many system directories. Given such bundles, application installation and removal can be as trivial as copying or deleting, respectively, a single .app directory. Applications can also be moved after installation since they are usually self-contained.

The Finder treats several types of bundles as opaque, atomic entities—as if they were files and not directories. For example, double-clicking on an application

```
iTunes.app                          Application bundle
Contents/
   Info.plist                       Information property list file
   PkgInfo
   version.plist
   MacOS/                           Could also have a MacOSClassic/
      iTunes                        Main application executable
   Frameworks/
      InternetUtilities.bundle/     Loadable bundle
         Contents/
            MacOS/
               InternetUtilities    MH_BUNDLE object file
            PkgInfo
            Resources/
   Resources/
      complete.aif
      iTunes-aac.icns               Icons, media files
      ...
      iTunes-wma.icns
      iTunes.icns
      iTunes.rsrc
      iTunesHelper.app/             Application bundle
         Contents/
            Info.plist
            MacOS/
               iTunesHelper   Main application executable for this bundle
            PkgInfo
            Resources/
            ...
            version.plist
      da.lproj/
      ...
      Dutch.lproj/
      ...
      English.lproj/                Localized resources
         InfoPlist.strings
         iTunes Help/
            gfx/
            ...
            pgs/
               500x.html
               ...
            pgs2/
            ...
            sty/
               access.css
               task_tbl_style.css
            Localized.rsrc
            locversion.plist
      fi.lproj/
      ...
      French.lproj/
      ...
      ...
      zh_TW.lproj/
      ...
```

FIGURE 2–12 Hierarchical structure of the iTunes application bundle

bundle launches the application. The user may browse the bundle's contents by using the Finder's Show Package Contents contextual-menu item. A bundle's opaqueness may be asserted in several ways, for example, through a property list file, through a `PkgInfo` file, and through the `kHasBundle` file system attribute.

Several types of Mach-O binaries exist within bundles on Mac OS X. Bundles can be programmatically accessed using the *CFBundle* and *NSBundle* APIs. Table 2–1 lists several examples of bundle types on Mac OS X.

TABLE 2–1 Examples of Bundle Types on Mac OS X

Bundle Type	Default Extension	Explanation
Automator action	`.action`	Automator actions are extensions to the default set of actions supported by the Automator workflow-based application, which allows users to graphically construct a sequence of actions by picking one or more actions from a palette of available actions. These bundles can be implemented in Objective-C or AppleScript.
Application	`.app`	Mac OS X application bundles typically contain dynamically linked executable programs along with any resources needed by the programs.
Bundle	`.bundle`	A `.bundle` package is a loadable bundle containing dynamically linked code that can be loaded by a program at runtime. The program must explicitly load such a bundle using dynamic linking functions. Several Mac OS X applications use `.bundle` plug-ins to extend their feature sets. For example, the Address Book application can load Action Plug-In bundles from specific directories, allowing programmers to populate the Address Book rollover menus with custom items. iTunes uses bundles to implement visual plug-ins, whereas iMovie uses them to implement effects, titles, and transitions.
Component	`.component`	Core Audio plug-ins, which are useful for manipulating generating, processing, or receiving audio streams, are implemented as `.component` bundles.
Dashboard widget	`.wdgt`	Dashboard is a lightweight runtime environment introduced in Mac OS X 10.4 for running small accessory programs called *widgets* in a logically separate layer atop the desktop. Dashboard widgets are packaged as `.wdgt` bundles.
Debug (application)	`.debug`	Applications with debugging symbols can be packaged as `.debug` bundles, which the Finder treats similarly to `.app` bundles.

(continues)

TABLE 2–1 Examples of Bundle Types on Mac OS X *(Continued)*

Bundle Type	Default Extension	Explanation
Framework	`.framework`	A framework is a dynamic shared library packaged with resources such as header files, API documentation, localized strings, helper programs, icons, splash images, sound files, and interface definition files. An umbrella framework is a bundle that contains one or more subframeworks in its `Frameworks` subdirectory. The Carbon and Core Services frameworks are examples of umbrella frameworks.
Kernel extension	`.kext`	Kernel extensions are dynamically loadable kernel modules. They are similar to `.bundle` bundles in that they contain code that is programmatically introduced into a running program—the program being the kernel in this case. However, kernel extensions are statically linked.
Keynote file	`.key`	Applications can use bundles as complex "file formats" to hold arbitrary data in documents. Apple's Keynote software uses bundles to store presentations. A `.key` bundle contains an XML-based representation of the presentation's structure, along with resources such as images, thumbnails, audio, and video.
Metadata importer	`.mdimporter`	Metadata importers are used by the integrated Spotlight search technology in Mac OS X. Such an importer gathers information from one or more specific file formats. Developers of applications with custom file formats can provide their own metadata importers that Spotlight can use as plug-ins while indexing a file system.
Package	`.pkg`, `.mpkg`	A `.pkg` bundle is an installation package created using the `PackageMaker.app` application. A package's contents include files and directories belonging to the installable software it represents, along with information that may be needed to install the software. A metapackage—a `.mpkg` bundle—contains a file that includes a list of packages or metapackages and any other information that might be needed to install them. Unlike a package, a metapackage does not itself contain any installable software. Double-clicking a package or a metapackage launches the Mac OS X installer application.
Palette	`.palette`	A palette is a loadable bundle that contains code and user-interface objects used by Apple's integrated development environment (IDE).
Plug-in	`.plugin`	A `.plugin` is a loadable bundle similar in concept to a `.bundle` but has more architectural and implementation requirements. Contextual-menu plug-ins, which are used to extend the list of commands on Finder contextual menus, are implemented as `.plugin` bundles. Other examples of such bundles include certain QuickTime plug-ins and extensions called *Image Units* to the Core Image and Core Video technologies.

(continues)

TABLE 2–1 Examples of Bundle Types on Mac OS X *(Continued)*

Bundle Type	Default Extension	Explanation
Preference pane	`.prefPane`	Preference panes are bundles used to manage system-wide software and hardware preferences. The System Preferences application displays the union of various `.prefPane` bundles located in `/System/Library/PreferencePanes/`, `/Library/PreferencePanes/`, and `~/Library/PreferencePanes/`.
Profile (application)	`.profile`	Applications with profiling data can be packaged as `.profile` bundles, which the Finder treats similarly to `.app` bundles.
Service	`.service`	A service is a bundle that provides generic functionality for use by other applications. Examples of services include text-to-speech conversion, (`SpeechService.service`), spell checking (`AppleSpell.service`), and Spotlight searching (`Spotlight.service`). Services can be made available on a system-wide basis through `.service` bundles. A service is usually contextual in its operation—it operates on a currently selected entity, such as a piece of text. For example, the AppleSpell service will run a spelling check on the selected text.
Screensaver	`.saver`, `.slideSaver`	Mac OS X provides APIs for creating screensavers based on program-generated content or slide shows. Such screensaver programs are packaged as `.saver` and `.slideSaver` bundles, respectively. Note that a `.slideSaver` bundle does not contain any executable code—it contains only a set of images in its `Resources` directory and an information property list file.
System Profiler reporter	`.spreporter`	The System Profiler application displays information about the system's hardware and software. It uses `.spreporter` bundles residing in `/System/Library/SystemProfiler/` to collect information. Each reporter bundle provides information about a particular area. For example, there are system reporter bundles for attached displays, FireWire devices, Serial ATA devices, USB devices, and installed software and fonts.
Web plug-in	`.webplugin`	The Safari web browser supports an Objective-C-based plug-in model for displaying new types of content in the browser through plug-ins. QuickTime support in Safari is implemented as a `.webplugin` bundle.
Xcode plug-in	`.ibplugin`, `.pbplugin`, `.xcplugin`, `.xctxtmacro`, `.xdplugin`	The functionality of Apple's Xcode development environment can be extended through several types of plug-ins.

As shown in Table 2–1, bundles are used to implement several types of plug-ins. From a generic standpoint, a plug-in is an external piece of code that runs in a *host* environment. Typically the host is an application, but it can be an operating system or perhaps even another plug-in. The host must be designed to be extensible through plug-ins—it must export an API for the plug-in to conform to. Thus, by using the host's plug-in API, a plug-in can add functionality to the host without requiring recompilation of, or even access to, the host's source.

Note that the bundle extensions listed in Table 2–1 are only conventions—it is possible to have a bundle with an arbitrary extension, as long as certain requirements are satisfied or the application using the bundle knows how to handle the extension.

2.8.2 Property List Files

You will frequently come across *property list* (plist) files on Mac OS X. They are on-disk representations of organized data. When such data is in memory, it is structured using basic data types native to the Core Foundation framework.

> The Core Foundation data types used in property lists are `CFArray`, `CFBoolean`, `CFData`, `CFDate`, `CFDictionary`, `CFNumber`, and `CFString`. An important feature of these data types is that they are readily portable across multiple Mac OS X subsystems—for example, CF data types have analogs in the I/O Kit.

An on-disk property list is a serialized version of an in-memory property list. A plist file may store information in either binary format or human-readable XML format.[32] The two most common uses of plist files on Mac OS X are by bundles and by applications.

A bundle uses a special type of plist file—an *information property list*—to specify its critical attributes, which are read by other programs while handling the bundle. The default name for an information property list file is `Info.plist`. Consider an application bundle's `Info.plist` file, whose contents may include attributes such as the following:

- The document types handled by the application
- The name of the bundle's main executable file

---

32. Many people opine that XML is hardly readable by humans. Although it is cumbersome for a normal person to parse, XML is decidedly more human-friendly than a "raw" binary format.

- The name of the file containing icons for the bundle
- The application's unique identification string
- The application's version

Applications use property list files to store user preferences or other custom configuration data. For example, the Safari web browser stores a user's bookmarks in a plist file called `Bookmarks.plist`. Numerous configuration plist files can be found in a user's `~/Library/Preferences/` directory. Typically, applications store per-user configurations or preferences in this directory using a reverse DNS naming convention. For example, the Safari web browser's preferences are stored in `com.apple.Safari.plist`.

Property list files can be created and manipulated using several tools on Mac OS X. The `plutil` command-line program can be used to convert a plist file from one format to another. It also checks plist files for syntax errors. XML-format plist files can be edited using any text editor, although it might be more convenient (and less error-prone) to use the Property List Editor graphical application, which is part of Apple Developer Tools. The Cocoa and Core Foundation frameworks provide APIs for programmatically accessing plist files. As alluded to earlier, several standard object types in these frameworks are stored, organized, and accessed as property lists.

2.8.3 Frameworks

In its simplest form, a Mac OS X framework is a bundle containing one or more shared libraries. Besides stand-alone shared libraries—such as the ones in `/usr/lib/`—Mac OS X contains a large number of frameworks. Whereas a shared library contains shared code, a framework usually contains one or more shared libraries along with other types of related resources.[33] From an implementation standpoint, a framework is a directory hierarchy encapsulating shared resources such as the following:

- Dynamic shared libraries
- Headers
- Nib (NeXT Interface Builder) files
- Localized strings

---

33. It is possible for a framework to contain no shared code but only resources.

- Images
- Documentation files
- Information property lists
- Sounds

A framework directory has a well-defined structure consisting of files and folders, some of which are mandatory; the others are optional. Figure 2–13 shows the files and folders contained in the hypothetical Foo framework.

FIGURE 2–13 Bundle structure of a Mac OS X framework

```
Foo.framework/                                   # Top-level directory
  Headers -> Versions/Current/Headers            # Symbolic link
  Foo -> Versions/Current/Foo                    # Symbolic link
  Libraries -> Versions/Current/Libraries        # Symbolic link
  Resources -> Versions/Current/Resources        # Symbolic link
  Versions/                                       # Contains framework major versions
    A/                                            # Major version A
      Foo                                         # Framework's main dynamic library
      Headers/                                    # Public headers
        Bar.h
        Foo.h
      Libraries/                                  # Secondary dynamic libraries
        libfoox.dylib
        libfooy.dylib
      Resources/
        English.lproj/                            # Language-specific resources
          Documentation/                          # API documentation
          InfoPlist.strings                       # Localized strings
        Info.plist                                # Information property list file
    B/                                            # Major version B
      Foo
      Headers/
        Bar.h
        Foo.h
      Libraries/
        libfoox.dylib
        libfooy.dylib
      Resources/
        English.lproj/
          Documentation/
          InfoPlist.strings
        Info.plist
    Current -> B                                  # Symbolic link to most recent version
```

The `Info.plist` file within the `Resources` subdirectory of a framework contains its identifying information. Frameworks support versioning: If an application depends on a particular version of a framework, either the exact version or a compatible version of that framework must exist for the application to run. Major version differences are incompatible, whereas minor version differences are compatible. A single framework bundle may contain multiple major versions. The framework shown in Figure 2–13 contains two versions, A and B. Moreover, all files and directories in the framework's top-level directory, except `Versions`, are symbolic links to entities belonging to the major version `Current`. `Foo`, the file with the same name as that of the framework directory's prefix, is the main dynamic shared library.

Figure 2–14 shows the standard Mac OS X frameworks categorized by the typical purposes they are used for.

An umbrella framework can contain other subframeworks and even other subumbrella frameworks. Umbrella frameworks are used to hide interdependencies between discrete system libraries by effectively presenting a metalibrary that is the union of all libraries within it. An umbrella framework's bundle structure is similar to that of a standard framework, but it also contains a subdirectory called `Frameworks`, which contains subframeworks. Typically, the programmer may not link directly to subframeworks.[34] In fact, the programmer need not know whether a framework is an umbrella framework or not—linking to an umbrella framework automatically provides access to its constituents. At runtime, if the dynamic linker comes across a symbol that has been recorded as "contained in an umbrella framework," the linker will search the umbrella framework's subframeworks, sublibraries, and subumbrellas. Similarly, an umbrella framework's header files automatically include any header files in the subframeworks. Figure 2–15 shows the standard umbrella frameworks on Mac OS X.

Frameworks can also be *private* in that they are unavailable for linking by user programs. Some frameworks are private because they are embedded within other bundles such as application bundles. Mac OS X contains a number of frameworks that are private to Apple. These reside in `/System/Library/PrivateFrameworks/`. Examples of private frameworks include `DiskImages.framework`, `Install.framework`, `MachineSettings.framework`, `SoftwareUpdate.framework`, and

---

34. While compiling an umbrella framework, it is possible to specify through a linker option that a given client name can link to a given subframework, even though the client is external—say, a bundle. The client name for a bundle is also set through a linker option while compiling the bundle.

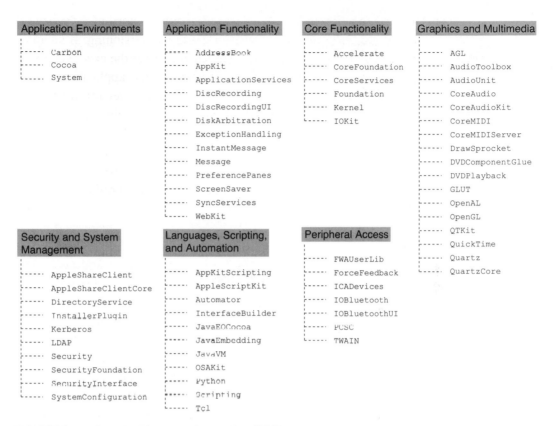

FIGURE 2–14 Standard frameworks on Mac OS X

VideoConference.framework. Their privacy is manifested in the following ways from the standpoint of a third-party programmer.

- Apple does not publish the APIs of these frameworks. Even their header files are not available.

- By default, a third-party programmer cannot link with these frameworks. However, it is possible to link with a private framework by explicitly passing the full pathname of its containing directory to the linker. Doing so is unsupported by Apple.

When a dynamically linked program is compiled, the installation paths of the libraries it links with are recorded in the program. These paths are typically absolute for system frameworks that are part of Mac OS X. Some applications, particularly third-party applications, may contain their own frameworks within their application bundles. Paths to such frameworks or libraries, when recorded in an application, can be recorded relative to the application bundle.

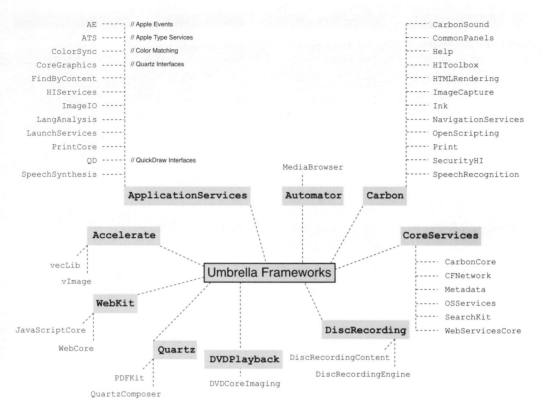

FIGURE 2–15 Standard umbrella frameworks on Mac OS X

When the dynamic link editor needs to search for frameworks, the fallback paths it uses are `~/Library/Frameworks/`, `/Library/Frameworks/`, `/Network/Library/Frameworks/`, and `/System/Library/Frameworks/`, in that order. Similarly, fallback paths for dynamic libraries are `~/lib/`, `/usr/local/lib/`, and `/usr/lib/`. Note that path searching is not performed in a user's home directory for setuid programs that are not executed by the real user.

2.8.4 Prebinding

Mac OS X uses a concept called *prebinding* to optimize Mach-O applications to launch faster by reducing the work of the runtime linker.

As we saw earlier, the dynamic link editor, `dyld`, is responsible for loading Mach-O code modules, resolving library dependencies, and preparing the code for execution. Resolving undefined symbols in executables and dynamic libraries at runtime involves mapping the dynamic code to free address ranges and computing the resultant symbol addresses. If a dynamic library is compiled with pre-binding support, it can be *predefined* at a given preferred address range.[35] This way, dyld can use predefined addresses to reference symbols in such a library. For this to work, libraries cannot have overlapping preferred addresses. To support prebinding, Apple marks several address ranges as either reserved or preferred for its own software and specifies allowable ranges for use by third-party libraries.

> dyld was optimized in Mac OS X 10.3.4 such that prebinding of applications is no longer necessary. Moreover, prebinding of applications is entirely deprecated on Mac OS X 10.4.

Let us consider an example—that of the System framework (System.framework). The shared library within this framework is actually a symbolic link to the libSystem dynamic library in /usr/lib/. In other words, System.framework is a wrapper around libSystem. Let us use otool to display the load commands in libSystem to determine its preferred load address (Figure 2–16).

FIGURE 2–16 Listing the load commands in a Mach-O file

```
$ otool -l /usr/lib/libSystem.dylib
/usr/lib/libSystem.dylib:
Load command 0
      cmd LC_SEGMENT
  cmdsize 872
  segname __TEXT
   vmaddr 0x90000000
   vmsize 0x001a7000
  fileoff 0
 filesize 1732600
  maxprot 0x00000007
 initprot 0x00000005
   nsects 12
    flags 0x0
...
```

---

35. A framework's preferred address can be specified at compile time using the segladdr linker flag.

The vmaddr value shown in Figure 2–16 is the preferred load address of libSystem. We can use the C program in Figure 2–17 to print the names and load addresses of all Mach-O object files loaded into the program's address space and to check whether libSystem is loaded at its preferred address or not.

FIGURE 2–17 Printing libraries loaded in a program

```
// printlibs.c

#include <stdio.h>
#include <mach-o/dyld.h>

int
main(void)
{
    const char *s;
    uint32_t    i, image_max;

    image_max = _dyld_image_count();
    for (i = 0; i < image_max; i++)
        if ((s = _dyld_get_image_name(i)))
            printf("%10p %s\n", _dyld_get_image_header(i), s);
        else
            printf("image at index %u (no name?)\n", i);

    return 0;
}

$ gcc -Wall -o printlibs printlibs.c
$ ./printlibs
   0x1000 /private/tmp/./printlibs
0x91d33000 /usr/lib/libmx.A.dylib
0x90000000 /usr/lib/libSystem.B.dylib
0x901fe000 /usr/lib/system/libmathCommon.A.dylib
```

The update_prebinding program is run to attempt to synchronize pre-binding information when new files are added to a system. This can be a time-consuming process even if you add or change only a single file. For example, all libraries and executables that might dynamically load the new file must be found. Package information is used to expedite this process. A dependency graph is also built. Eventually redo_prebinding is run to prebind files appropriately.

> After a software update or installation, while the installer program displays the "Optimizing..." status message, it is running the update_ prebinding and redo_prebinding (if necessary) programs.

As shown in Figure 2–18, `otool` can be used to determine whether a binary is prebound.

FIGURE 2–18 Determining whether a Mach-O file is prebound

```
$ otool -hv /usr/lib/libc.dylib
/usr/lib/libc.dylib:
Mach header
  magic    cputype cpusubtype filetype ncmds sizeofcmds flags
  MH_MAGIC PPC     ALL        DYLIB    10    2008       NOUNDEFS DYLDLINK
                                                        PREBOUND SPLIT_SEGS
                                                        TWOLEVEL
```

2.9 Core Services

The Core Services layer implements various low-level features for use by higher layers. It can be visualized as sitting atop the kernel. Its most important constituents are the Core Foundation framework (`CoreFoundation.framework`) and the Core Services umbrella framework (`CoreServices.framework`). These frameworks contain critical nongraphical system services and APIs. For example, the Core Foundation framework includes APIs for basic data management. These APIs are C-based and are primarily meant for use by Carbon applications. However, other types of applications can indirectly use them. For example, the Cocoa framework links to the Foundation framework, which in turn links to the Core Foundation framework. In any case, Core Foundation data types may be seamlessly used with the Cocoa Foundation interfaces: Many Foundation classes are based on equivalent Core Foundation opaque types, allowing *cast-conversion* between compatible types.[36]

> Much of the exported kernel functionality—roughly equivalent to what is provided by commonly used BSD and Mach system calls—can be accessed via the Core Services layer.

---

36. Such cast-conversion between Foundation classes and Core Foundation opaque types is sometimes referred to as toll-free bridging.

Examples of functionality contained in the Core Services layer include the following:

- Core parts of Carbon, including legacy Carbon Managers[37] (`CarbonCore. framework`)

- APIs for user-level networking, including support for various protocols and mechanisms such as HTTP, FTP, LDAP, SMTP, sockets, and Bonjour (`CFNetwork.framework`)

- APIs for Open Transport, various hardware-related Carbon Managers, and access to system-related components such as disk partitions, power management information, sound, and system keychain (`OSServices.framework`)

- APIs for indexing and searching text in multiple languages (`SearchKit. framework`)

- APIs for using Web Services via SOAP[38] and XML-RPC (`WebServicesCore. framework`)

- APIs for the Spotlight search technology, including support for importing and querying metadata from the Spotlight metadata store (`Metadata. framework`)

- Facilities for applications to access URLs, parse XML, create and manage a variety of data structures, and maintain property lists (`CoreFoundation. framework`).

> The roots of searching technology in Mac OS X lie in Apple's Information Access Toolkit—or V-Twin, as it was codenamed earlier. Various Apple applications that implement searching, such as the Address Book, Apple Help, the Finder, the Mail application, and Spotlight, all use the Search Kit framework in some way.

2.10 Application Services

This layer could be perceived as providing two types of services: those specialized for graphics and multimedia applications and those usable by any kind of an application.

---

37. A Manager in Carbon is a set of one or more libraries defining a programming interface.

38. Simple Object Access Protocol.

2.10.1 Graphics and Multimedia Services

The graphics and multimedia services layer provides APIs for using 2D graphics, 3D graphics, video, and audio. Figure 2–19 shows how this layer fits in the overall graphics and multimedia architecture.

2.10.1.1 Quartz

The core of the Mac OS X imaging model is called *Quartz*, which provides support for rendering 2D shapes and text. Its graphics-rendering functionality is exported via the Quartz 2D client API, which is implemented in the Core Graphics framework (`CoreGraphics.framework`)—a subframework of the Application Services umbrella framework. Quartz is also used for window management.

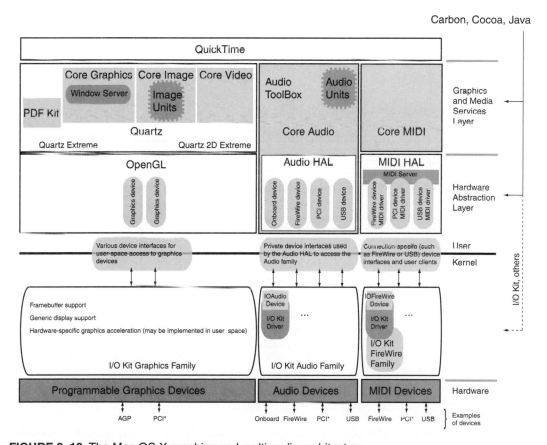

FIGURE 2–19 The Mac OS X graphics and multimedia architecture

It provides a lightweight window server, the Quartz Compositor, which is implemented partly in the `WindowServer` application[39] and partly in the Core Graphics framework. Figure 2–20 shows a conceptual view of Quartz's constituents.

Quartz 2D

Quartz 2D uses the Portable Document Format (PDF) as the native format for its drawing model.[40] In other words, Quartz stores rendered content internally as PDF. This facilitates features such as automatically generating PDF files (so you can save a screenshot "directly" to PDF), importing PDF data into native applications, and rasterizing PDF data (including PostScript and Encapsulated PostScript

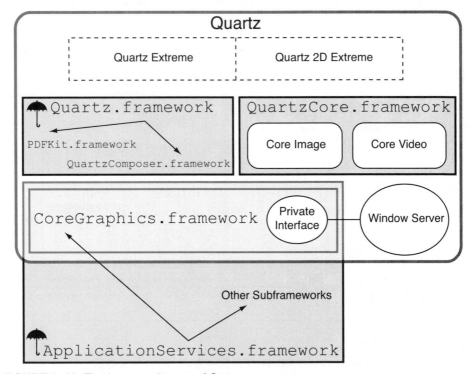

FIGURE 2–20 The key constituents of Quartz

---

39. The `WindowServer` application resides in the `Resources` subdirectory of the Core Graphics framework.

40. We saw in Chapter 1 that the windowing system in NEXTSTEP and OPENSTEP used Display PostScript for its imaging model.

conversion). Quartz 2D is also responsible for device- and resolution-independent rendering of bitmap images, vector graphics, and anti-aliased text.

Vector and Raster Graphics

PDF is a *vector* image file type. PDF images—and vector graphics in general—can be created through a sequence of mathematical statements that specify placement of geometric objects in a 2D or 3D vector space. Starting from a simple image (say, one consisting only of a straight line), a complex image can be drawn by adding more shapes—much like how one would draw such a picture on a piece of paper. Moreover, the various elements of the picture are stored as individual objects. This makes it easy to alter the picture without loss of information.

Another approach to digital imaging is known as *raster* graphics. When a digital camera or a scanner is used to capture a picture, the resulting image is a raster image. A raster is a coordinate grid that resides in the display space. A raster image is a set of samples of this space. The image file's contents contain color (or monochrome) values that apply to each of the coordinates. Since the file's "bits" map to the display grid, raster images are commonly known as bitmap images. Unlike a vector image, it is difficult to alter a raster image without loss of information. One could think of a vector image as "the formula to generate image data," whereas a raster image would be "image data." Consequently, vector image files are typically smaller in size than raster images.

Examples of vector image formats include PDF, EPS (Encapsulated Post-Script), and SVG (Scalable Vector Graphics). Examples of raster image formats include BMP (Windows Bitmap), GIF (Graphics Interchange Format), JPEG (Joint Photographic Experts Group), and TIFF (Tagged Image File Format).

Beginning with Mac OS X 10.4, Quartz includes the PDF Kit (`PDFKit. framework`)—a Cocoa framework containing classes and methods for accessing, manipulating, and displaying PDF files.

Quartz Compositor

The Quartz Compositor is so called because of how it operates. Compositing refers to the process of overlaying independently rendered images into a single final image, while taking into account aspects such as transparency. Quartz implements layered compositing whereby an on-screen pixel can be shared between multiple windows in real time. The Quartz Compositor can composite pixels belonging to content from sources such as Quartz 2D, OpenGL, and QuickTime. In this sense, it follows a video-mixer model. Its implementation consists of the `WindowServer` program, which is an OpenGL application, and some private Apple libraries. Note that the Compositor does not perform any rendering itself—rendering is OpenGL's responsibility and is hardware accelerated when possible.

Quartz Services

Whereas the window server APIs are private, certain low-level features of the window server are exposed through the Quartz Services API. In particular, the API provides functions for accessing and manipulating display hardware. It also provides functions to access low-level window server events, thus allowing a program to "drive" the system remotely.

Quartz Extreme

Quartz has an integrated hardware acceleration layer called *Quartz Extreme*, which automatically becomes active if suitable hardware is available. Specific hardware features required for Quartz Extreme include a minimum of 16MB video memory and a graphics card that supports arbitrary texture sizes, multitexturing, and pixel formats used by Quartz.

Quartz Extreme is an implementation technique that uses OpenGL support in the graphics card so that the graphics processing unit (GPU)—rather than the CPU—does the compositing of window backing-stores[41] to the framebuffer. Consequently, the CPU is freer, leading to improvements in system responsiveness and performance. Figure 2–21 shows an overview of Quartz Extreme.

As Figure 2–21 shows, even when Quartz Extreme is active, the CPU is used to place pixels into window backing-stores, which reside in main memory. The GPU uses direct memory access (DMA) to asynchronously transfer the backing stores. It was not until Mac OS X 10.4 that Quartz 2D gained the capability to use the GPU for the *entire* drawing path—from the application to the framebuffer. This feature, called *Quartz Extreme with Accelerated 2D* (QE2D), is an evolution of Quartz Extreme. It can move data from an application to a window backing-store using DMA, while keeping track of frequently used data sets in an adaptively purged in-memory cache. QE2D strives to make rendering much faster than software rendering, while maintaining almost software-like quality. Common operations such as drawing glyphs, images, lines, and rectangles are implemented

---

41. A window backing-store is essentially a bitmap for the window. It contains information saved by the window system to track the window's contents.

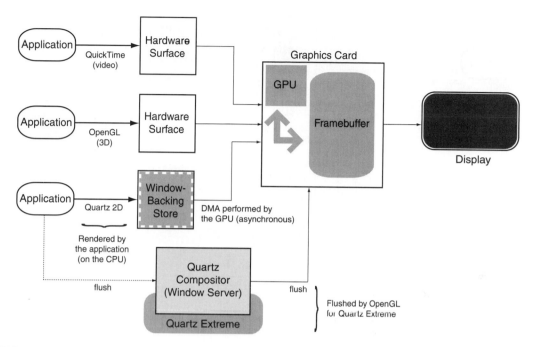

FIGURE 2–21 An overview of Quartz Extreme

using OpenGL. Uncommon drawing operations, or those that cannot be handled well without software rendering,[42] are handled through an optimized CPU drawing path. QE2D requires a GPU with the `ARB_fragment_program` OpenGL extension. Figure 2–22 shows an overview of QE2D. Note that backing stores are now cached in video memory. Moreover, graphics resources such as colors, images, layers, and patterns are also cached. For this scheme to work well, the programmer must judiciously retain references to resources.

Quartz also uses hardware vector processing, when available on the CPU, to enhance performance.

2.10.1.2 QuickDraw 2D

QuickDraw 2D is a deprecated API for creating, manipulating, and displaying 2D shapes, text, and pictures. QuickDraw on Mac OS X is a reimplementation of the legacy QuickDraw API. It exists for the benefit of older projects as they transition

---

42. Drawing a complex path with shading or stroking is an example of such an operation.

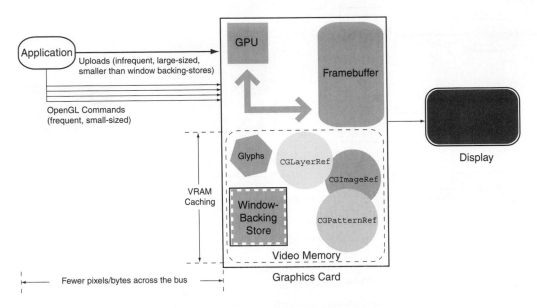

FIGURE 2–22 An overview of Quartz Extreme with Accelerated 2D

to Quartz. QuickDraw makes use of the Velocity Engine but does not use graphics hardware acceleration like Quartz 2D.

You can also make Quartz rendering calls from within QuickDraw, but mixing QuickDraw and Quartz 2D code in an application will result in hardware acceleration being disabled altogether for the rendering.

2.10.1.3 OpenGL

Mac OS X includes an implementation of OpenGL—a cross-platform graphics API standard for creating 3D and 2D graphics. OpenGL works with Quartz 2D and the Quartz Compositor, enabling system-wide visual effects and the graphical aspects of features such as Exposé and Dashboard.

As Figure 2–23 shows, there are several interfaces to OpenGL in Mac OS X.

2.10.1.4 Core Image and Core Video

Core Image is a high-level image-processing interface to a GPU-based media technology. Using Core Image, application developers can harness the GPU without needing to resort to low-level programming. Depending on available hardware,

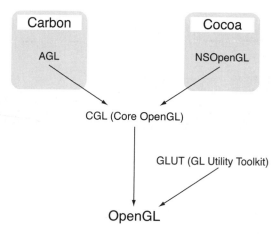

FIGURE 2–23 Interfaces to OpenGL in Mac OS X

Core Image uses GPU-based acceleration and vector processing to improve performance. It supports 32-bit floating-point pixels for enhanced accuracy. It also uses other, more fundamental graphical technologies such as OpenGL,[43] Quartz, and QuickTime for optimal image processing.

Core Image uses a plug-in architecture[44] for accessing *filters, transitions,* and *effects* packages— these are called *Image Units*. Developers can use the various Image Units shipped with Core Image or create their own by describing filters and effects using dynamically compiled expressions. Examples of bundled Image Units include filters for blurring and sharpening, color adjustment, compositing, distortion, gradients, halftones, tiling, and transitions. Figure 2–24 shows a conceptual view of image processing with Core Image. The key components of Core Image include the following:

- Context (`CIContext`)—a destination for images to be drawn, say, one created from an OpenGL context

- Image (`CIImage`)—an image that theoretically extends to infinity, with a subrectangle as the region of interest

- Filter (`CIFilter`)—an object that encapsulates an image-processing kernel and represents an effect or transition, with a parameter-passing interface

---

43. Even when you use Core Image, it is OpenGL that eventually rasterizes the data.

44. The Core Image plug-in architecture is inspired by the Core Audio plug-in architecture.

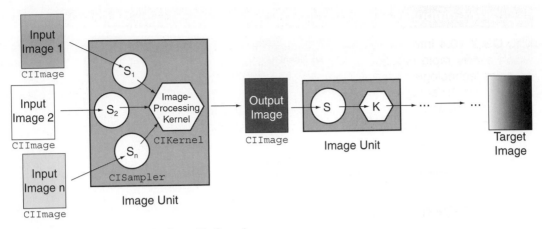

FIGURE 2–24 Image processing with Core Image

- Sampler (`CISampler`)—an accessor object that is used (typically by a kernel) to retrieve samples (pixels) from an image
- Kernel (`CIKernel`)—an object that lives within a filter and contains the per-pixel instructions that actually apply the filter's image-processing effect

Core Video applies concepts similar to Core Image to video, allowing video filters and effects to benefit from hardware acceleration. It could be seen as a bridge between QuickTime and the graphics hardware for processing video data by enhancing performance and lowering CPU requirements. Figure 2–25 shows a conceptual overview of using both Core Image and Core Video in an instance of the QuickTime video-rendering pipeline.

Core Image and Core Video are both parts of the Quartz Core framework.

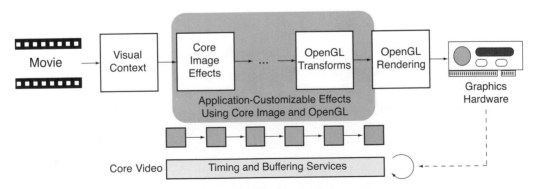

FIGURE 2–25 Core Image and Core Video in the QuickTime video-rendering pipeline

> ### Quartz Composer
>
> Mac OS X 10.4 introduced a visual development tool called Quartz Composer, which allows rapid creation of graphical applications using several Mac OS X graphics technologies such as Core Image, OpenGL, Quartz 2D, and QuickTime. Besides graphical content, Quartz Composer can also use Rich Site Summary (RSS) content and MIDI System Services. For example, by simply dragging and dropping graphical building blocks into a grid, and "connecting" the blocks appropriately, you can rapidly create, say, a rotating cube with a different image rendered onto each of its faces, with custom lighting effects.

2.10.1.5 QuickTime

QuickTime is both a graphics environment and an application environment. It provides features for working with interactive multimedia. Depending on the media type, QuickTime allows you to manipulate media in several ways, such as:

- Accessing media (open, play, or display)
- Capturing media from an external device
- Compressing media
- Creating certain types of media—for example, author panorama movies, object movies, and scenes using QuickTime Virtual Reality (QTVR)
- Editing and enhancing media, including synchronizing multiple media to a single timeline
- Streaming media over a local network or the Internet using protocols such as HTTP, RTP (Real-Time Transport Protocol), and RTSP (Real-Time Streaming Protocol)
- Translating between media formats

QuickTime works with several types of media such as video, graphics, animation, virtual reality, audio, and text—in a variety of file and streaming formats. The media could reside on a local disk, be accessed over the network in its entirety, or be streamed in real time.

The QuickTime architecture is modular and extensible. QuickTime components can be written to implement support for new media types, to implement a new codec, and to interact with custom media capture hardware. As indicated in Figure 2–25, beginning with Mac OS X 10.4, QuickTime cooperates with Core Image and Core Video to improve performance.

Besides being an integrated technology in Mac OS X, QuickTime is available for other platforms such as Java, Mac OS 9, and several versions of Microsoft Windows.

2.10.1.6 Core Audio

The Core Audio layer (see Figure 2–19) allows management of audio software and hardware. It uses a plug-in architecture in which a plug-in can perform software operations on audio data or interact with audio hardware. Core Audio's hardware abstraction layer hides unnecessary details of the underlying hardware from applications. Core Audio APIs provide functionality for performing operations such as the following:

- Accessing and manipulating audio files
- Aggregating multiple audio devices into a single "virtual" device, which can be seamlessly made available to all applications
- Working with multichannel audio, including channel mixing
- Converting audio data between various formats
- Developing audio codecs
- Providing low-level access to audio hardware, including device sharing between multiple applications
- Synthesizing audio using software
- Using MIDI hardware and software

Apple's AU Lab digital mixing application (`AULab.app`) allows blending audio from multiple sources: the input of an audio device, audio generated by an Audio Unit Instrument, and audio generated from an Audio Unit Generator. It supports multiple outputs.

OpenAL

The Open Audio Library (OpenAL) is a cross-platform 3D audio API for use in games or other applications that require high-quality spatialized audio. It is available for systems such as BSD, IRIX, Linux, Solaris, Microsoft Windows, Mac OS 8, Mac OS 9, Sony PlayStation 2, Microsoft Xbox/Xbox360, and Nintendo GameCube. On Mac OS X, OpenAL is implemented using Core Audio as the underlying device. In the OpenAL specification, which is inspired by the OpenGL specification for graphics, a *device* is defined as an implementation-dependent entity that can be a hardware device, a daemon, or a system service.

2.10.2 Other Application Services

The Application Services umbrella framework contains subframeworks that facilitate development of many types of applications—hence the name. The following are examples of this framework's subframeworks.

- *AE* allows creation and manipulation of events in the Apple Events mechanism for interapplication communication.

- *ATS* allows font layout and management using Apple Type Services.

- *ColorSync* is used for color matching using Apple's integrated color management system, which is also called ColorSync.

- *CoreGraphics* provides the Core Graphics API.

- *FindByContent* provides an interface for searching specific volumes or directories for files containing specified content.

- *HIServices* provides human-interface services such as Accessibility, Icon Management, Copy and Paste, Process Management, Translation Management, and Internet Configuration.

- *LangAnalysis* provides an interface to the Language Analysis Manager that lets you analyze morphemes[45] in text.

- *LaunchServices* provides an interface for opening URLs and starting applications, including opening documents with either a specified application or the default.

- *PrintCore* provides an interface to the printing subsystem.

- *QD* provides the QuickDraw API.

- *SpeechSynthesis* provides an interface for generating synthesized speech.

2.11 Application Environments

Most of the typical application development occurs in the Application Environments layer. Mac OS X has multiple application environments, each providing features that may appeal to certain types of developers. For example, those interested in programming using "plain old" Unix APIs are equally well served on

---

45. A morpheme is a meaningful linguistic unit—a distinctive collection of phonemes having no smaller meaningful parts. A phoneme is an indivisible phonetic unit in a language.

Mac OS X as those who wish to use visual tools for rapid prototyping, creation of complex graphical user interfaces, and object-oriented development. Of the vast number of portable programming language implementations in existence, many are readily accessible on Mac OS X, and some are bundled by Apple. In particular, Apple's own programming environment offers rich APIs for Mac OS X–specific development. Although it would be impractical to enumerate all types of applications that can run on or be developed on Mac OS X, let us consider the following examples:

- Unix-style command-line tools and X Window applications written entirely using portable interfaces such as POSIX
- Carbon-based GUI and command-line applications written in C
- Cocoa-based GUI and command-line applications written in Objective-C, Java, or AppleScript
- AWT-based and Swing-based applications[46] written in Java
- Generic command-line applications—or *tools*—written in C++ or C that may link with one or more frameworks such as Core Foundation, Core Services, Foundation, and I/O Kit

We saw earlier that the Mac OS X kernel understands only the Mach-O binary executable format. Although Mach-O is the preferred runtime architecture, it is possible to run certain legacy format binaries on Mac OS X.

> The Mac OS X kernel could be seen as an application environment for specialized applications—dynamically loadable kernel extensions—that execute in the kernel's address space.

2.11.1 BSD

The BSD application environment in Mac OS X is similar to, but not the same as, a traditional user-level environment on a BSD-based Unix system. It provides POSIX APIs, BSD-specific APIs, and some Unix-flavored APIs that export Mac OS X–specific functionality. You can use the BSD environment for writing Unix tools, daemons, and shell scripts. In many cases, programs targeted for the Mac OS X BSD environment would be readily portable to other Unix systems and vice

---

46. Java's Abstract Windowing Toolkit (AWT) provides facilities for creating GUIs and for drawing graphics. Swing is a relatively more modern GUI toolkit that evolved from AWT.

versa. The standard libraries and headers for the BSD environment reside in their traditional Unix locations: /usr/lib/ and /usr/include/, respectively.

> Technically, many header files in /usr/include/ are part of the System framework. However, the System.framework directory neither contains nor links to these headers since the C compiler searches in /usr/include/ by default.

2.11.2 The X Window System

The X Window System could be seen as a graphical extension to the BSD environment. Mac OS X includes an optimized X Window server (/usr/X11R6/bin/Xquartz) along with a modern X Window environment. The X server is integrated with the Mac OS X Quartz subsystem. It conceptually sits atop the native Core Graphics APIs, tying into the native Mac OS X event system. Through this architecture, the X server enjoys hardware acceleration.

The environment includes quartz-wm—an X Window manager with the native Mac OS X look-and-feel that allows X applications to run alongside native Mac OS X programs. quartz-wm provides Aqua window controls, drop shadows, integration with the Dock, and so on. Although the X server's default operating mode is rootless, it can also be run in full-screen mode.

> Even though the Mac OS X user interface does not use *focus-follows-mouse* mode, it is possible to configure quartz-wm to enable this mode for X Window applications. With this mode, X application windows can be focused by simply moving the mouse pointer over them. To enable this mode, the wm_ffm Boolean property must be set to true in the com.apple.x11.plist file.

Because of the availability of the BSD and X Window environments, it is usually straightforward to port existing Unix applications to Mac OS X simply by recompiling them, with little or no source modification.

2.11.3 Carbon

The Carbon application environment contains APIs based on the original Mac OS 9 APIs. In fact, some of Carbon's constituent interfaces date back to Mac OS 8.1. The Carbon interfaces are procedural in nature and are implemented in the C programming language. Carbon was originally designed to provide an easy development migration path from Mac OS 8 and Mac OS 9 to newer systems. It allows a compliant application, one that uses only features supported on both Mac OS 9 and Mac OS X, to run natively on both systems. It is implemented as a framework (`Carbon.framework`) on Mac OS X, whereas it is implemented as a system extension (`CarbonLib`) on Mac OS 9.

2.11.3.1 Support for CFM Binaries

The Code Fragment Manager (CFM) was a part of older Mac OS versions. It loaded *fragments* of PowerPC code from Preferred Executable Format (PEF) files into memory and prepared them for execution. A fragment is an arbitrarily sized basic unit of executable code and its associated data. It has certain well-defined properties and a method of addressing its contents. The following are examples of fragments:

- An application
- A system extension
- A shared library, which could be an import library or a plug-in
- Any other block of code and associated data

Besides mapping fragments into memory, the CFM's responsibilities included releasing fragments when they were no longer needed, resolving references to symbols imported from other fragments, and providing support for special initialization and termination routines.

The Mac OS X native runtime architecture (`dyld`/Mach-O) is *not* the same as that on Mac OS 9 (CFM/PEF). All Mac OS X libraries, including those that are part of Carbon, use the Mach-O format. However, Carbon supports the CFM on Mac OS X for Mac OS 9 compatibility—it is possible to create and run CFM applications on Mac OS X. In fact, an application that must run on both systems either must be compiled separately for the two systems or must be a CFM application. Carbon uses the `LaunchCFMApp` helper application[47] to run programs created for the CFM. `LaunchCFMApp` can run only native PowerPC code. It does not support resource-based fragments. Moreover, Carbon provides a one-way bridge to CFM applications to link to Mach-O code. Using this bridge, a CFM application can call a Mach-O library, but not vice versa.

---

47. `LaunchCFMApp` resides in the `Support` subdirectory of the Carbon framework.

2.11.3.2 Carbon APIs

Carbon does not include all of the old APIs, but it contains a subset (about 70%) that covers most of the functionality used by typical applications. APIs that are not critical, or are no longer applicable due to radical differences between Mac OS X and earlier systems, have been dropped in Carbon. These include APIs that were specific to the 68K architecture, those that accessed the hardware directly, and those that were replaced by improved APIs. The following are noteworthy features of Carbon.

- Some of the APIs included in Carbon have been modified or extended to benefit from the more modern nature of Mac OS X, which uses preemptive multitasking and protected memory as fundamental features. In contrast, such features were retrofitted—with limited applicability—in Mac OS 9.

- Some new APIs were added to Carbon and made available on Mac OS 9. Several new APIs in Carbon are available only on Mac OS X.

- Carbon applications running on Mac OS X have the system's native look-and-feel.

The New "Old" API

Although Carbon is best understood as an overhaul of several older APIs that were pruned, extended, modified, and supplemented with new APIs to run in the modern Mac OS X environment, it does not represent an obsolete set of interfaces. Not only does Carbon support standard Aqua user-interface elements, but Carbon user interfaces can even be designed using the Interface Builder—similar to Cocoa applications. Carbon functionality is widely used in Mac OS X and is critical for C-based development. Some parts of Carbon are complementary to object-oriented APIs such as Cocoa.

The following are examples of Carbon's subframeworks.

- *CarbonSound* provides Carbon Sound Manager interfaces.

- *CommonPanels* provides interfaces for displaying commonly used GUI panels,[48] such as the Color window and the Font window.

- *Help* provides interfaces for using Apple Help in applications.

---

48. A panel is a special kind of window that usually serves an auxiliary function in an application.

- *HIToolbox*[49] provides interfaces for the `HIToolbox` object, the Carbon Event Manager, and others. This framework provides various objects (such as `HIObject` and `HIView`) for organizing windows, controls, and menus in Carbon applications. The "view" objects provided by the HIToolbox framework benefit from native Quartz rendering (with automatic layering), the ability to be hidden, and the ability to be attached or detached from windows.

- *HTMLRendering* provides interfaces for rendering HTML content. However, the Web Kit framework has superseded it.

- *ImageCapture* provides interfaces for capturing images from digital cameras.

- *Ink* provides interfaces for handwriting recognition based on input from pen-based devices. Features provided by this framework include programmatic enabling or disabling of handwriting recognition, direct access to Ink data, the ability to toggle between deferred and on-demand recognition, and the ability to manipulate text directly through gestures. Moreover, a programmer can incorporate custom correction models that allow incoming handwriting data to be interpreted in alternative ways.

- *NavigationServices* provides interfaces for file navigation.

- *OpenScripting* contains AppleScript and Open Scripting Architecture (OSA) interfaces.

- *Print* provides print dialog interfaces.

- *SecurityHI* provides security dialog interfaces.

- *SpeechRecognition* provides Speech Recognition Manager interfaces.

There are several frameworks that, although usable from other environments, are primarily for use by Carbon applications and are considered part of the Carbon environment. These include the Application Services, Core Foundation, and Core Services frameworks. Thus, Carbon provides procedural interfaces both for GUI development and for lower-level development involving manipulation of system resources, event handling, and data management.

From a programmer's standpoint, it is generally easier to create an application from scratch using Cocoa (see Section 2.11.4) rather than Carbon, since Cocoa automatically provides several features that would require explicit coding in Carbon. For example, Cocoa objects by default provide many aspects of a well-behaved Mac OS X application: document management, window manage-

---

49. HIToolbox stands for Human Interface Toolbox.

ment, opening and saving of documents, pasteboard behavior, and so on. Similarly, the Core Data framework (see Section 2.11.4.2), which allows modeling and lifecycle management of data, is accessible only to Cocoa programs.

2.11.4 Cocoa

The Cocoa environment provides object-oriented APIs for rapid application development in the Objective-C and Java programming languages.[50] Cocoa is both a collection of APIs and a set of visual tools that are particularly useful for rapid prototyping, data modeling, and overall reduction in design and development efforts. Examples of such tools include the Interface Builder and Xcode's class- and data-modeling tools. Interface Builder allows a programmer to create most (and often all) of an application's user interface graphically rather than programmatically. The class-modeling tool allows the programmer to visualize, browse, and annotate classes in terms of class relationships and the protocols they implement. The data-modeling tool allows the programmer to visually design a schema for application data in terms of entities that constitute the data and the relationships between them.

> Apple recommends Cocoa as the preferred way to develop typical applications on Mac OS X. Between Cocoa and Carbon, you should use Cocoa unless your desired functionality is available only through Carbon, you must have legacy compatibility, or you must use C-based procedural interfaces.
>
> A Cocoa application can call Carbon APIs. It is possible, and common, for an application to be linked against both the Carbon and Cocoa frameworks. iDVD, iMovie, and Safari are examples of such applications.

Cocoa is an important inheritance from NeXT, as indicated by the various names with the "NS" prefix in Cocoa APIs. Many of the Cocoa APIs are largely based on OpenStep frameworks. Cocoa primarily consists of two object-oriented frameworks: Foundation (`Foundation.framework`) and Application Kit (`AppKit.framework`). Several other frameworks add specific functionality to Cocoa, such as Core Data, PDF Kit, and QuickTime Kit.

---

50. It is possible for other programming or scripting languages to have bindings to Cocoa. For example, it is possible to use Cocoa interfaces from AppleScript.

The Foundation framework provides fundamental classes and methods for bundle access, data management, file access, interprocess communication, memory management, network communication, process notification, and various low-level features.

The Application Kit provides classes that implement user-interface elements such as windows, dialogs, controls, menus, and event handling.

Core Data makes object lifecycle management easier by providing classes and methods for data management.

> Cocoa is effectively an umbrella framework consisting of the Foundation, Application Kit, and Core Data subframeworks. The dynamic library inside `Cocoa.framework` is a wrapper that links to these frameworks. Consequently, linking with `Cocoa.framework` links in these (effective) subframeworks. However, in this particular case, the subframeworks are also available for individual linking. This is not the case with most umbrella frameworks, where it is illegal to attempt to link to a specific subframework.

2.11.4.1 Nib Files

When creating user interfaces with the Interface Builder, you will often come across *nib* files. As we saw earlier, the term stands for NeXT Interface Builder. A nib file contains descriptions of some or all of an application's user interface along with references to any resources (e.g., images and audio) that the interface may use. It is essentially an archive. Usually there is a "main" nib file that contains an application's main menu and other user-interface elements intended to appear when the application starts. During an application's execution, its nib files are opened and user-interface objects are unarchived. From the standpoint of the Model-View-Controller (MVC) design pattern, nib files define the view part of an application, while also defining connections into controller instances.

The `nibtool` command-line program can be used to print, update, and verify the contents of a nib file. Figure 2–26 shows an example.

2.11.4.2 Core Data

Core Data is a Cocoa framework that facilitates data-model-driven application development through fine-grained management of data objects.

FIGURE 2–26 Using `nibtool` to view the contents of a nib file

```
$ nibtool -a /Applications/Utilities/Terminal.app/Contents/\
Resources/English.lproj/Terminal.nib
/* Objects */
Objects = {

    "Object 1" = {
        Class = "NSCustomObject";
        CustomClass = "TerminalApp";
        Name = "File's Owner";
        className = "TerminalApp";
    };

    ...
}; /* End Objects */

/* Object Hierarchy */
Hierarchy = {
    "Object 1 <NSCustomObject> (File's Owner)" = {
        "Object -1 <IBFirstResponder> (First Responder)";
        "Object 37 <NSMenu> (MainMenu)" = {
            "Object 12 <NSMenuItem> (Windows)" = {
...
}; /* End Hierarchy */

/* Connections */
Connections = {
    "Connection 89" = {
        Action = "cut:";
        Class = "NSNibControlConnector";
        Source = "3";
    };
...
}; /* End Connections */

/* Classes */
Classes = {
    IBClasses = (
        {
            ACTIONS = {enterSelection = id; findNext = id; findPanel = id;
                    findPrevious = id; };
            CLASS = FindPanel;
            LANGUAGE = ObjC;
            OUTLETS = {findPanel = id; };
            SUPERCLASS = NSObject;
        },
...
```

Core Data's primary benefits are for applications that have a highly structured data model to begin with.[51] In such cases, the data model can be represented by a schema, which in turn can be built using graphical tools in Xcode. Therefore, instead of defining data structures programmatically, developers can create visual descriptions—or *models*—of data objects.[52] The application accesses the data through the Core Data framework, which is responsible for creating and managing instances of the data model.

> Examples of applications that are good candidates for Core Data include Mail, iTunes, and Xcode. Each of these applications uses highly structured data: mailbox files, music libraries, and project files, respectively.

Core Data offers several benefits to the developer, such as those listed here.

- It manages data objects in memory and on disk. It can automatically serialize data to disk, while supporting multiple formats for persistent storage of data, namely, Binary, SQLite, and XML.

- It supports validation of property values. For example, properties in a data model can be validated for minimum values, maximum values, string lengths, and so on.

- It supports automatic undo and redo of data manipulations by tracking changes in the application's *object graph*,[53] relieving the developer of this responsibility.[54]

- It supports synchronizing data changes with user-interface elements. It uses integration with Cocoa Bindings for this purpose. Moreover, it can group and filter in-memory changes.

- It enhances scalability by efficiently managing object lifecycles—data objects that are not currently needed by the application do not reside in memory. For objects that are not memory-resident, placeholder objects are

---

51. Core Data is ideally suited for managing the data model of an MVC application.

52. It is still possible to create models programmatically.

53. In this context, an object graph is a collection of data objects (entities) with references to one another (relationships).

54. Even without Core Data, Cocoa applications can use the NSUndoManager class to record operations for undo and redo. However, doing so requires additional work from the developer.

maintained with appropriate reference counting. Accessing a placeholder object results in Core Data fetching the actual object. This is similar to page-faulting in a virtual memory implementation.

> The file formats supported by Core Data vary in several properties: atomic access, human readability, performance, and scalability. For example, SQLite offers the best performance and is the most scalable. However, it is not human readable. XML is slower but is human readable.

Since Core Data's essence is model-driven development, the most critical abstraction from the developer's standpoint in Core Data is the *model*, which is akin to an entity-relationship (ER) diagram. A model contains the following key elements.

- *Entities* are roughly equivalent to classes in that they represent types of objects. The developer may specify a class name to represent an entity at runtime. Like classes, entities support inheritance.[55] Each entity can have certain properties: *attributes*, *relationships*, and *fetched properties*. An attribute is similar to class data. Attributes can have associated validation rules and default values. They can be optional or even transient.[56] Relationships are references from one entity to another. A relationship can be one-to-one or one-to-many. A fetched property is a reference from an entity to a query.

- *Predefined queries* are essentially query templates that can be instantiated at runtime.

- *Configurations* allow for advanced file management by mapping entities to persistent stores. A single entity can exist in multiple configurations.

Core Data applications typically use Core Data APIs to load models from storage into memory. The generic data object in Core Data is an instance of the NSManagedObject class. It is also a required superclass for any custom data object classes. As shown in Figure 2–27, the following primary components of the Core Data architecture interact in a logical "stack"[57] at runtime.

---

55. Entity inheritance in Core Data is independent of class inheritance.

56. A transient attribute is maintained in memory for convenience or performance reasons.

57. Each document in a document-based application has its own Core Data stack.

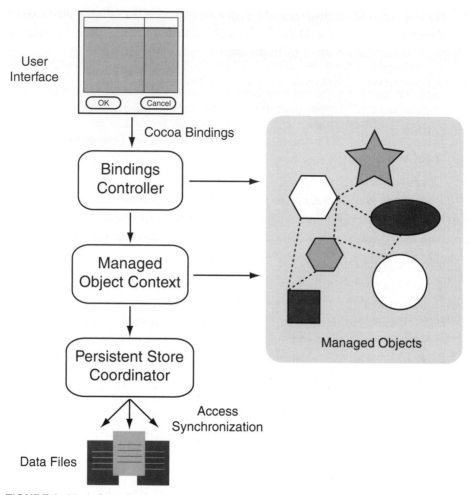

FIGURE 2–27 A Core Data stack

- A *Bindings Controller* is responsible for transferring in-memory data changes to the user interface through Cocoa Bindings.

- A *Managed Object Context* sits atop the Persistent Store Coordinator. It provides in-memory scratch space for loading data objects from disk, making changes to the objects, and either rejecting or saving those changes. It tracks all such changes and provides undo/redo support.

- A *Persistent Store Coordinator* exists for each Managed Object Context and, in turn, for each Core Data stack. It presents a unified view of one or more underlying persistent stores. For example, it can merge the contents of multiple data files to present them as a single store to its Managed Object Context.

If Core Data is used judiciously, it can significantly reduce the amount of code that a developer would have to otherwise write.

2.11.5 WebObjects

WebObjects is an independent Apple product—it is not a part of Mac OS X. It provides an application environment for developing and deploying Java server applications and Web Services. Using WebObjects frameworks and tools, developers can also create user interfaces for various types of web content, including database-driven and dynamically generated content. As we noted in Chapter 1, several Apple web sites are implemented using WebObjects.

2.11.6 Java

The Java environment is a core component of Mac OS X. It includes the Java runtime and the Java Development Kit (JDK), which are accessible both through the command line and through Xcode. The Java runtime includes the HotSpot Java virtual machine (JVM) with just-in-time (JIT) bytecode compilation. It can also treat Java archives—or *jar files*—as shared libraries. The Java Virtual Machine framework (`JavaVM.framework`) contains Java classes in jar files, command-line programs such as `java` and `javac`,[58] headers, documentation, Java Native Interface (JNI) libraries, and support libraries.

Cocoa includes Java packages corresponding to the Foundation and the Application Kit frameworks. Therefore, Cocoa applications can be created using Java as the programming language instead of Objective-C. Moreover, Java programs can call Carbon and other frameworks via JNI—a standard programming interface for writing Java native methods and embedding the Java virtual machine into native applications. In particular, Java applications can use Mac OS X native technologies such as QuickTime and Carbon. Since the Swing implementation on Mac OS X generates native Mac OS X user-interface elements, Swing-based Java applications have the same look-and-feel as Cocoa applications written using Objective-C.

---

58. Besides `javac`, Mac OS X includes the Jikes open source Java compiler from IBM.

> The Cocoa-Java programming interface is deprecated in Mac OS X versions later than 10.4. Apple announced in mid-2005 that Cocoa features introduced in newer versions of Mac OS X will not be added to the Cocoa-Java API, requiring the Objective-C Cocoa API to employ the new features.

Although Java is considered an application environment, the Java subsystem can itself be represented as different layers, as depicted in Figure 2–1. For example, the JVM along with the core JDK packages are analogous to the Core Services layer. In fact, the JVM conceptually provides the combined functionality of a computer system's hardware and the operating system kernel.

2.11.7 QuickTime

QuickTime's functionality is available to applications through various APIs such as those listed here.

- The Carbon QuickTime API provides an extensive procedural C-based interface.

- Higher-level Cocoa classes such as `NSMovie` and `NSMovieView` provide a limited subset of QuickTime's functionality.

- The QuickTime Kit (`QTKit.framework`) Cocoa framework was introduced in Mac OS X 10.4 to provide more comprehensive native access to QuickTime from Cocoa programs.

2.11.8 Classic

Classic is a binary compatibility environment for running unmodified Mac OS 9 applications on the PowerPC version of Mac OS X. Classic functionality is provided through a combination of the following components.

- A core service resides as the `Classic Startup.app` application bundle in `/System/Library/CoreServices/`. The bundle contains a virtualizer program called `TruBlueEnvironment`.

- A Mac OS 9 installation resides in `/System Folder/` by default.

- Special support exists in the Mac OS X kernel for the Classic environment.

Classic Startup is a Mach-O application that runs Mac OS 9 within its address space. It provides a hardware abstraction layer between Mac OS 9 and Mac OS X by virtualizing traps, system calls, and interrupts. It runs in a protected memory environment, with multiple Mac OS 9 processes within it layered on top of a single Mac OS X BSD process. Each Carbon application in Mac OS 9 has its own Carbon Process Manager process. In this sense, Classic support in Mac OS X is essentially "Mac OS 9 in a process." However, note that the Classic Startup application itself is multithreaded.

In certain ways, Classic is "more" than Mac OS 9, since its integration with Mac OS X allows sharing of resources, as illustrated by the following examples.

- Fonts stored in the Classic system folder's `Fonts` subdirectory are shared with Mac OS X, but Mac OS X fonts are not available to Classic.

- AppleScript running within Classic can communicate with Mac OS X applications.

- Classic support is fully integrated with the Finder and other Mac OS X application environments. In particular, you can copy and paste as well as drag and drop between Classic and Mac OS X. However, Mac OS 9 applications retain their original look-and-feel—their user-interface elements *do not* look like Mac OS X's.

- Classic can use volumes of any file system type that is supported by Mac OS X, since it shares files through the host operating system.

- Classic networking is largely integrated with Mac OS X networking, allowing various types of networking devices, IP addresses, and IP ports to be shared between Mac OS X and Classic. Whereas Carbon provides a limited Open Transport implementation built atop BSD sockets, Classic provides a complete Open Transport protocol stack implementation.

> Classic Startup is *not an emulator*—it is a *virtualizer*. Nevertheless, it allows both 68K-based Mac OS 9 applications and PowerPC-based CFM applications[59] to run under Mac OS X. There is emulation involved in running 68K code, but that emulation was part of Mac OS 9 and remains unchanged.

---

59. Classic does not support CFM-68K—the 68K version of CFM.

As we saw in Section 2.11.3.1, another legacy runtime environment is provided by the CFM, which uses PEF binaries.

Many APIs

Depending on the particular application environment you program in, you may often have to use different, environment-specific APIs for performing similar tasks. In some cases, it may also be possible to use some APIs from multiple environments in a single application. Let us consider the example of launching an application.

At the lowest level, a process is tied to a Mach task, which should not be directly created by user programs. At the Unix system-call level, a `fork()` and `exec()` sequence is normally used to run an application in a new process. However, typical Mac OS X applications do not use `fork()` and `exec()` directly but use the Launch Services framework to launch applications or to "open" documents. In particular, the Finder uses Launch Services to map document types to applications that can handle those types. Launch Services itself calls `fork()` and `exec()` to run applications. Cocoa applications can launch applications using the `NSWorkspace` class, which in turn calls Launch Services.

2.11.9 Rosetta

The x86 version of Mac OS X uses a binary translation process called Rosetta that allows PowerPC executables—both CFM and Mach-O—to run on x86-based Macintosh computers.

Like Classic, Rosetta is meant as a technology devised to help transition from one platform to another. It is limited in the type of executables it supports. Examples of PowerPC executables it does *not* support include the following:

- G5-specific executables
- Kernel extensions
- Programs that communicate with one or more kernel extensions that are available only on PowerPC systems
- Java applications that use the JNI
- The Classic virtualizer and the applications that run within it
- PowerPC-specific screensavers

For an application to run successfully under Rosetta, all components of the application, including loadable plug-ins, must be PowerPC-based.

Rosetta is launched by the kernel to handle a file that is one of the supported PowerPC executable types. Rosetta code resides in the same Mach task as the "guest" executable. It dynamically translates—with optimizations—blocks of PowerPC code to x86 code, while alternating between code translation and code execution. To improve translation performance, Rosetta caches blocks of translated code.

2.12 User Interface

Aqua is the cornerstone of visual user experience in Mac OS X. It is not one or more specific applications, libraries, or APIs but a set of guidelines that describe the look-and-feel, behavior, and integration of GUI elements. Besides user-interface guidelines, the Mac OS X user experience also depends on applications using recommended technologies in their implementations. Mac OS X application environments that support GUI-based applications—Carbon, Cocoa, and Java—all provide the Aqua look-and-feel.[60] The Interface Builder assists programmers in laying out user-interface elements in accordance with interface guidelines.

The X Window System and Aqua

In the X Window System, the window manager is an X application that is a client of the X Window server. We saw earlier in this chapter that the Mac OS X implementation of the X Window System includes a window manager (`quartz-wm`) that provides the Aqua look-and-feel.

However, only certain visual and behavioral aspects of an X Window application—specifically those controlled by the window manager—will benefit from Aqua. The application's own look and feel will depend on the specific widget set being used.

The Mac OS X user interface has several distinctive features, many of which depend on the features of the available graphics hardware. Let us look at the important user-interface features.

---

60. As we saw earlier, Mac OS 9 applications running under Classic retain their original look-and-feel because Classic does not conform to Aqua.

2.12.1 Visual Effects

Aqua uses animation, color, depth, translucence, textures, and photorealistic icons rendered at various sizes up to 256×256 pixels,[61] making possible a visually appealing interface. Icon images at various sizes are contained in .icns files.

> You can use the Icon Browser application (icns Browser.app), which is installed as part of Apple Developer Tools, to view the contents of .icns files. Use the Icon Composer application (Icon Composer.app) to create .icns files—for example, from arbitrarily sized images in various formats—by simply dragging the images[62] to the Icon Composer window.

2.12.2 Resolution-Independent User Interface

Beginning with Mac OS X 10.4, Aqua is resolution-independent. The system supports multiple scaling modes: *framework scaling mode*, *application scaling mode*, and *magnified mode*. Each mode provides support in applying scaling factors to rendered graphics.

In framework scaling mode, the graphics subsystem in use—such as the Application Kit (Cocoa) or HIView (Carbon)—automatically handles most of the scaling. For example, the relevant frameworks will automatically scale user-interface elements, apply scaling transforms to rendered content, increase the size of window buffers, and so on.

In application scaling mode, the application must handle scaling of rendered content. The frameworks will still scale system-defined user-interface elements, such as menus and title bars.

In magnified mode, the window server will simply create a magnified view of the image by applying a scaling factor to the window buffer. This is essentially a digital zoom—there is no gain in image detail while zooming in since pixel data is simply being interpolated to a new size.

---

61. Mac OS X 10.4 added support for 256×256 pixel icons.

62. An icon usually has an associated "mask" used to designate certain parts of the icon as transparent, allowing arbitrarily shaped icons to be generated. You can specify the data and mask components of the icon by dragging an image for each, or Icon Composer can automatically calculate the mask based on the data image.

> You can experiment with user-interface resolution scaling by using the Quartz Debug application (`Quartz Debug.app`), which allows you to vary the scaling factor from its default value of 1. Quartz Debug is a part of Apple Developer Tools.

2.12.3 Productivity Features

Mac OS X includes several user-interface features that enhance user experience, for example: in-place document preview, in-icon status indication,[63] instant access to any open window with a single keystroke (*Exposé*), fast user switching, *Dashboard*, and the user interface to *Spotlight*.

2.12.3.1 Fast User Switching

Newer versions of Mac OS X include support for switching between users rapidly through the fast user-switching feature. With this feature, a user's session remains active "behind the scenes" while another user accesses the computer in an independent GUI session using the mouse, keyboard, and display. Multiple users can switch in this manner—only one user remains the "current" user, and everybody else's session remains intact in the background. Note that if there is an application that does not run correctly when multiple instances of that application are run, and multiple users attempt to run such an application, fast user-switching may cause problems. Mac OS X 10.4 added support for making operations such as logging out, shutting down, and restarting the system faster and less cumbersome.

2.12.3.2 Dashboard

Dashboard—introduced in Mac OS X 10.4—is an environment for running lightweight desktop utilities called *widgets*.[64] Dashboard widgets are confined to a special layer of the Mac OS X desktop that is hidden from view until activated by the user. When activated—for example, through a predefined key combination[65]—the Dashboard layer is overlaid on top of the normal Desktop, providing

---

63. Applications can superimpose information on their icons to convey it to the user. For example, Apple's Mail application uses a status indicator in its icon to display the number of unread messages.

64. Technically, Dashboard is an application environment, the "applications" being widgets.

65. The default key assigned to Dashboard is **F12**.

rapid access to the currently selected widgets. Deactivating Dashboard hides the widget layer.

2.12.3.3 Spotlight

Although it is a file system technology, Spotlight is an important addition to the Mac OS X user interface since it fundamentally changes how users access files. The Spotlight metadata search technology roughly encompasses three distinct pieces of functionality:

1. An in-kernel notification mechanism that can inform user-space subscribers of file system changes as they occur

2. A database of various types of file-related information—in particular, of *harvested* metadata

3. The programmer and end-user interfaces to Spotlight

A user-space Spotlight server subscribes to receive file system changes from the kernel. It can gather metadata from documents and other relevant user files, both dynamically (as files are created or modified) and statically (by scanning for files). It incorporates the harvested metadata into a searchable lightweight database. Spotlight's integration with the Finder provides a powerful search mechanism to the user. Moreover, the Finder can use file metadata to display additional relevant information about files.[66] The Spotlight search API allows searching for files programmatically by using database-style queries. Spotlight is extensible by third-party developers: If an application uses a custom file format, it can provide a Spotlight importer plug-in that will parse the application's documents and gather metadata.

2.12.4 Universal Access Support

Mac OS X supports several accessibility technologies and features, such as those listed here.

- *Enhanced Contrast* can be varied through the **ctrl-cmd-option-,** and **ctrl-cmd-option-.** key combinations.

---

66. For example, in the case of a PDF document, the PDF file's metadata may contain attributes such as the document's title, author, number of pages, page dimensions, creator application, and summary. The Finder and Spotlight search results window can display these attributes.

- *Full Keyboard Access* allows the keyboard to be used for navigating and interacting with on-screen items.
- *Grayscale Mode* can be toggled through a checkbox in the Seeing pane of the Universal Access system preference.
- *Inverted Colors Mode* can be toggled through the **ctrl-cmd-option-8** key combination.
- *Mouse Keys* allows controlling the mouse pointer using the numeric keypad.
- *Screen Zooming* allows increasing the size of on-screen elements. It can be turned on or off through the **cmd-option-8** key combination. Once the feature is enabled, you can zoom in and zoom out using **cmd-option-+** and **cmd-option--**, respectively.
- *Speech Recognition* allows the user to speak commands rather than type them. When this feature is enabled, the computer will listen for commands and, if recognized, act on them.
- *Sticky Keys* allows the user to press a set of modifier keys as a sequence, rather than having to press several keys at once.
- *Text-to-Speech* enables the computer to speak the text in dialogs and alert messages.
- *VoiceOver* provides spoken user-interface features—that is, it describes what is happening on the screen. It can be turned on or off through the **cmd-F5** key combination.

> Accessibility features can be controlled through the Universal Access pane in the System Preferences application.

Two of the most important Mac OS X frameworks, Carbon and Cocoa, automatically provide several accessibility features to applications.

2.13 Programming

Mac OS X includes an integrated development environment (IDE) called *Xcode*, numerous general-purpose and special-purpose libraries, compilers and interpreters for various programming languages, and a rich set of debugging and optimization tools.

2.13.1 Xcode

The development environment provided by Xcode has the following noteworthy features:

- Support for creating Universal Binaries
- A file browser and organizer
- Support for project window configurations called *workspaces*,[67] which let you choose a preferred layout for Xcode's on-screen components
- A source code editor with code completion, syntax highlighting, symbol indexing, and embedded editors in most windows, allowing source viewing and modification without switching windows
- A class browser
- Background indexing of project files to improve the performance of features such as class browsing and code completion
- A documentation viewer that can link symbols in the code to documentation and otherwise allows viewing and searching Apple documentation
- The Interface Builder application, which provides a graphical user interface for laying out interface objects, customizing them (resizing, setting, and modifying attributes), connecting objects, and so on
- A built-in visual design tool that lets you create persistence models (for use with the Core Data framework) and class models (for C++, Java, and Objective-C classes)
- Distributed builds—for example, across several machines on a network—via integration with the `distcc` open source distributed front-end to the GNU C compiler
- GDB-based graphical and command-line debugging, including remote graphical debugging[68]
- *Predictive compilation*, which runs the compiler in the background as you edit a single source file, with the expectation that once you are ready to build, most of the building may already have been done

---

67. Xcode comes with multiple preconfigured project workspaces, such as *Default*, *Condensed*, and *All-In-One*.

68. Remote debugging uses SSH public-key authentication while connecting to the remote computer. Xcode can use the `ssh-agent` helper application for this purpose.

- *Precompiled headers*, a feature that improves compilation speed (Figure 2–28 shows an example)
- *ZeroLink*, a feature that causes linking to occur at runtime instead of compile time, whereby only code needed to run the application is linked and loaded

> When ZeroLink is used, Xcode generates an application stub containing the full paths to the relevant object files, which are linked, as needed, at runtime. Note that ZeroLink is intended for use only during development—it requires you to run the application from within Xcode. In other words, applications compiled with ZeroLink enabled cannot be deployed.

- *Fix and Continue*, a feature that allows you to make a minor change to your code, have the code compiled, and have it inserted into a running program through in-memory patching[69]
- *Dead-Code Stripping*, a feature that makes the static linker strip unused code and data from executables, thereby potentially reducing their sizes and memory footprints

FIGURE 2–28 Using precompiled headers

```
$ cat foo.h
#define FOO 10
$ cat foo.c
#include "foo.h"
#include <stdio.h>
int
main(void)
{
    printf("%d\n", FOO);
    return 0;
}
$ gcc -x c-header -c foo.h
$ ls foo*
foo.c           foo.h           foo.h.gch
$ file foo.h.gch
foo.h.gch: GCC precompiled header (version 012) for C
$ rm foo.h
$ gcc -o foo foo.c
$ ./foo
10
```

---

69. There are several restrictions on the types of changes accommodated under Fix and Continue.

- Support for browsing memory and global variables in the debugger
- Support for launching software performance analysis tools
- Support for automating the build process using AppleScript
- Support for multiple version control systems such as CVS, Perforce, and Subversion

A new Xcode project can be instantiated from a large number of templates, depending on the type of application, programming language, target environment, and so on. Supported languages include AppleScript, C, C++, Java, Objective-C, and Objective-C++. Examples of supported templates include those for Automator Actions, Image Unit Plug-ins, Metadata Importers, Preference Panes, Screen Savers, and Sherlock Channels.

Although Xcode is normally used through its graphical user interface, you can also work with existing Xcode projects from the command line. The `xcodebuild` command-line program can be used to build one or more targets contained in an Xcode project, optionally with a specific build style such as Development or Deployment. The `pbprojectdump` command-line program can be used to dump an Xcode project dictionary in a human-readable format, thus allowing you to view the project structure. If you must avoid Xcode altogether, you can manage your projects "manually"—for example, by creating makefiles and tracking dependencies. Mac OS X includes the BSD and GNU versions of the make program: `bsdmake` and `gnumake`, respectively.

> The back-end of the Xcode build system is based on the Jam product (`/Developer/Private/jam`) from Perforce Software, Inc.

2.13.2 Compilers and Libraries

Apple provides a customized and optimized version of the GNU C compiler with back-ends for multiple languages. As we saw earlier in this chapter, two Java compilers are included. Other compilers for a variety of languages are available both commercially[70] and freely.[71] The situation is similar for libraries: Several are

---

70. Commercially available compilers include those from Intel and Absoft Corporation.

71. Numerous open source compilers, interpreters, and libraries can be readily compiled from source on Mac OS X. In general, the difficulty of doing so is roughly on par with that on systems such as Linux and FreeBSD.

included with Mac OS X and several can be compiled from source. In particular, Mac OS X includes some optimized, special-purpose libraries, for example, BLAS, LAPACK, vBigNum, vDSP, vImage, and vMathLib. All these libraries, which are meant for image processing or numerical and scientific computing, are accessible through the Accelerate umbrella framework (`Accelerate.framework`).

2.13.3 Interpreters

Several scripting languages are included in Mac OS X: AppleScript, Perl, PHP, Python,[72] Ruby, and Tcl. Multiple Unix shells are also included, such as bash, ksh, tcsh, and zsh. Mac OS X supports the *Open Scripting Architecture* (OSA), with AppleScript as the default (and only) installed language. Other languages for the OSA are available from third parties.

2.13.3.1 AppleScript

AppleScript is the preferred scripting language on Mac OS X, providing direct control of many parts of the system as well as applications. For example, using AppleScript, you can write scripts to automate operations, exchange data with applications, or send commands to applications. AppleScript can be used in—and across—all application environments. For application-specific actions to be performed using AppleScript, the application must explicitly support AppleScript. Such support typically requires a data model that lends itself well to being manipulated externally. However, generic operations (such as launching an application) are supported automatically. Figure 2–29 shows a trivial AppleScript program that speaks the operating system version. You can use either the osascript command-line tool or the AppleScript editor (/Applications/AppleScript/ Script Editor.app) to run this program.

FIGURE 2–29 A trivial AppleScript program

```
-- osversion.scpt
tell application "Finder"
    set system_version to (get the version)
    say "[[emph +]]Cool. This is Mac OS Ten" & system_version
end tell
```

---

72. Python on Mac OS X includes bindings to Core Graphics.

`osascript` executes a script file, which may be either a textual version or a compiled version of an AppleScript program. The `osacompile` command[73] can be used to compile source files, the standard input, or other compiled scripts into a single script.

2.13.3.2 Automator

The Automator application is a visual tool for automating repetitive operations on Mac OS X. An Automator *action* is a modular unit—an indivisible task from Automator's standpoint. For example, a task can create a directory, open a file, capture a screenshot, send an email message, or run a shell script. Multiple actions can be connected in a particular sequence to construct a workflow, which in turn is executed to perform the arbitrarily complex set of tasks that the workflow represents. An action may or may not require additional information—or arguments—when it executes as part of a workflow. If additional information is required, the action displays a user interface consisting of text fields, checkboxes, buttons, pop-up menus, and so on. Automator includes a large number of predefined actions, but users can create their own actions using either AppleScript or Objective-C. A workflow is created visually by dragging or adding actions to a construction area. Finally, workflows can be saved for running later.

2.13.3.3 Command-Line Support

With each major release of Mac OS X, Apple has improved the system's command-line support by exposing more aspects of the system to be driven from the command line. In some cases, Apple has made command-line tools behave correctly and consistently. For example, in Mac OS X versions prior to 10.4, Unix-derived commands such as `cp`, `mv`, `tar`, and `rsync` did not handle certain aspects of Apple's HFS Plus file system correctly.[74] As still newer file system features such as metadata-based searching and access control lists (ACLs) were added in Mac OS X 10.4, the aforementioned commands were updated to behave consistently.

Let us consider a few other examples of using the command line in Mac OS X.

---

73. The `osascript` and `osacompile` commands will work with any installed scripting language that conforms to the OSA.

74. These commands were not aware of HFS Plus resource forks until Mac OS X 10.4. We will look at details of HFS Plus in Chapter 12.

The `drutil` command can be used to interact with the Disc Recording framework (`DiscRecording.framework`), which manages CD and DVD burners. Figure 2–30 shows an example of its use.

FIGURE 2–30 Command-line interaction with the Disc Recording framework

```
$ drutil list
    Vendor    Product              Rev    Bus      SupportLevel
1   HL-DT-ST DVD-RW GWA-4082B      C03D   ATAPI    Apple Shipping

$ drutil getconfig current
...
GetConfiguration returned 128 bytes.

  00>  00 00 00 80 00 00 00 00 00 00 03 28 00 11 00 00
  10>  00 14 00 00 00 13 00 00 00 1A 00 00 00 1B 00 00
  20>  00 10 00 00 00 09 00 00 00 0A 00 00 00 08 00 00
...
      001Ah      DVD+RW                DVD ReWritable
      001Bh      DVD+R                 DVD Recordable
      0010h      DVD-ROM               Read only DVD
...
```

The `hdiutil` command interacts with the Disk Images framework (`DiskImages.framework`), which is used for accessing and manipulating disk images. Figure 2–31 shows an example of its use.

FIGURE 2–31 Command-line interaction with the Disk Images framework

```
$ hdiutil plugins       # Print information about plug-ins
...
<dictionary> {
   "plugin-key" = "CEncryptedEncoding"
   "plugin-name" = "AES-128 (recommended)"
   "plugin-class" = "CFileEncoding"
   "plugin-type" = "builtin"
   "plugin-encryption" = Yes
}
...
$ hdiutil burn foo.dmg # Burn image to an attached burning device
...
```

The say command uses the Speech Synthesis Manager to convert input text to audible speech. The resultant speech data may be either played back or saved to an AIFF file.

The sips[75] command provides basic image-processing functionality from the command line. It supports several image formats. Its goal is to allow quick and convenient desktop automation of common queries and operations on images. Figure 2–32 shows an example of using sips.

FIGURE 2–32 Using the sips command to resample an image and convert its format

```
$ sips -g all image.gif
/private/tmp/image.gif
pixelWidth: 1024
  pixelHeight: 768
  typeIdentifier: com.compuserve.gif
  format: gif
  formatOptions: default
  dpiWidth: 72.000
  dpiHeight: 72.000
  samplesPerPixel: 4
  bitsPerSample: 8
  hasAlpha: yes
  space: RGB
  profile: Generic RGB Profile
$ sips --resampleHeightWidth 640 480 -s format jpeg\
       --out image.jpg /private/tmp/image.gif
  /private/tmp/image.jpg
```

The Spotlight metadata search functionality is accessible from the command line. The mdls command lists the names and values of all metadata attributes associated with the specified files. The mdfind command can be used to find files matching a given query, optionally limiting the search to a specified directory. Moreover, mdfind can operate in "live" mode: It will continue to run until interrupted, while updating the number of matches. Figure 2–33 shows an example of using mdfind.

---

75. sips stands for Scriptable Image Processing System.

FIGURE 2–33 Using the `mdfind` command to find files matching a given query

```
$ mdfind -live "kMDItemFSName == 'foo.txt'"
[type ctrl-C to exit]
Query update: 1 matches # foo.txt created
Query update: 0 matches # foo.txt deleted
...
^C
$ mdfind "kMDItemContentType == 'com.adobe.pdf'"
/Developer/About Xcode Tools.pdf
...
```

2.13.4 Tools

In addition to the development tools that are accessible through Xcode, Mac OS X provides a wide range of tools for analyzing, debugging, monitoring, profiling, and understanding both hardware and software.

> Apple's general philosophy is to encourage programmers to use the highest possible level of abstraction as far as possible and to let the platform handle low-level details. This way, programmers can avoid using interfaces or system aspects that are likely to change during the evolution of Mac OS X. This approach—particularly when followed for end-user software—is conducive to overall stability and a consistent user experience.

2.13.4.1 Debugging and Analysis Tools

The following are examples of debugging and analysis tools available on Mac OS X.

- `fs_usage` reports system calls and page faults related to file system activity.
- `heap` lists all `malloc()`-allocated buffers in a process's heap.
- `install_name_tool` changes the dynamic shared library names installed in a Mach-O file.
- `ktrace` enables kernel process tracing. `kdump` is used to view the resultant trace dump.
- `leaks` searches a process's memory for unreferenced `malloc()` buffers.
- `lipo` can create a multiple-architecture fat executable from one or more input files, list the architectures in a fat file, extract a single architecture file

from a fat file, or create a fat file from an existing one, with the new file containing a subset of the architectures contained in the original.

- `lsof` lists information about open files, where a file could be a regular file, a directory, a device file, a socket, and so on.
- `MallocDebug.app` tracks and analyzes allocated memory.
- `malloc_history` shows a process's `malloc()`-based allocations.
- `MergePef` merges two or more PEF files into a single file.
- `ObjectAlloc.app` tracks Objective-C and Core Foundation object allocations and deallocations.
- `OpenGL Profiler.app` is used for profiling OpenGL applications.
- `otool`, as we have seen earlier, displays various parts of an object file.
- `pagestuff` displays information on specified pages of a Mach-O file.
- `PEFViewer` displays the contents of a PEF binary.
- `QuartzDebug.app` is a visualizer for an application's screen-drawing behavior—it briefly flashes the areas that are being redrawn. It also allows you to alter the user interface's scale factor and enable or disable graphics hardware acceleration.
- `sample` profiles a process during a given time interval.
- `Sampler.app` is a viewer for a program's execution behavior.
- `sc_usage` shows system call usage statistics.
- `Spin Control.app` samples applications that fail to respond quickly enough, causing the spinning cursor to appear.
- `Thread Viewer.app` is a viewer for threads and thread activity.
- `vmmap` displays virtual memory regions in a process.
- `vm_stat` displays Mach virtual memory statistics.

2.13.4.2 *Computer Hardware Understanding Development Tools*

The Computer Hardware Understanding Development (CHUD) package is a set of low-level tools that can be optionally installed on Mac OS X. CHUD tools include the following specific programs.

- `BigTop.app` is a graphical equivalent to command-line tools such as `top` and `vm_stat`. It displays a variety of system statistics.
- `CacheBasher.app` is a tool for measuring cache performance.

- MONster.app is a tool for collecting and visualizing hardware-level performance data.

- PMC Index.app is a tool for searching Performance Monitoring Counter (PMC) events.

- Reggie SE.app is a viewer and editor for CPU and PCI configuration registers.

- Saturn.app is a tool for profiling applications at the function-call level. It is also used for visualizing the profile data.

- Shark.app performs system-wide sampling and profiling to create a profile of a program's execution behavior. This helps the programmer understand where time is being spent as the code runs.

- Skidmarks GT.app is a processor-performance benchmarking tool. It supports integer, floating-point, and vector benchmarks.

- SpindownHD.app is a utility for displaying the sleep/active status of attached drives.

- amber traces all threads of execution in a process, recording every instruction and data access to a trace file. acid analyzes traces generated by amber.

- simg4 is a cycle-accurate core simulator of the Motorola PowerPC G4 processor.

- simg5 is a cycle-accurate core simulator of the IBM PowerPC 970 (G5) processor.

2.13.4.3 Visual Tools

Mac OS X also provides several visual design and programming tools, most of which we came across earlier in this chapter, for example, AppleScript Studio, Automator, AU Lab, Interface Builder, Quartz Composer, and Xcode class- and data-modeling tools.

2.14 Security

We could informally define computer security as a condition wherein all computer resources are always used "as intended." However, it is impossible to exhaustively enumerate all of one's intentions, which will differ in any case from one person—or one scenario—to another.[76] We could express the notion of computer

---

76. Surely, there could be situations that neither the designers of a system nor its users have thought of yet.

security in somewhat more concrete terms as follows: Security is the union of software, hardware, policies, and practices that allows a system and its users to achieve the following:

- Verify identities of users and system services
- Safeguard sensitive information (such as personal data, cryptographic keys, and passwords) during storage, transmission, and use

A definition of security could be reinforced by describing the absence of security, that is, *insecurity*. A computer system's resources—including external, shared resources such as the network—are all vulnerable to attacks: from outside and often from within. We can think of a *vulnerability* as a potential for unintended use—a result of a software bug, a design oversight or error, a misconfiguration, and so on. When exploited via *attacks*, vulnerabilities could lead to tangible or intangible damage. The following are examples of common types of potential damage:

- Leaking of sensitive data
- Modification of sensitive data
- Destruction of sensitive data
- Unauthorized use of a system service
- Denial of a system service so that its legitimate users cannot use it
- Disruption or degradation of any system operation in general

A system's resources could be misused without denying service to legitimate users or without causing any *apparent* damage to the system itself. For example, if a system's resources are lying idle, it can still be misused as a stepping-stone to infiltrate another system.

Now that we have an informal understanding of computer security, let us look at important security-related aspects and features in Mac OS X. Figure 2–34 depicts many of these features.

Figure 2–34 does not show some daemons that play security-related roles in the operating system. For example, `lookupd` caches and makes available a variety of information such as user accounts, groups, computer names, and printers. Another daemon, `memberd`, resolves group memberships and responds to membership API calls made by clients. Examples of these calls include `mbr_uid_to_uuid()` and `mbr_uuid_to_id()`.

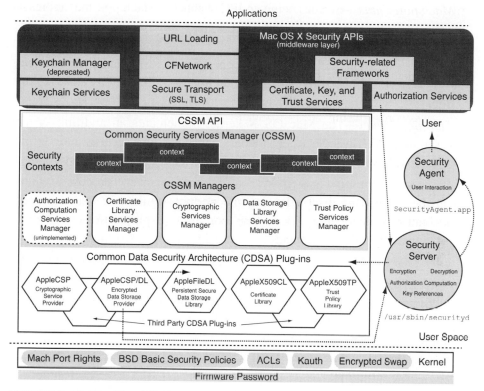

FIGURE 2–34 The Mac OS X security architecture

Mac OS X security features can be divided between those provided by the kernel-level and user-level security models. Additionally, a firmware password may be used on Apple computers in a potentially hardware- or model-dependent manner. We will look at Open Firmware password protection in Chapter 4.

2.14.1 Kernel-Space Security

The Mac OS X kernel security model consists of both Mac OS X–specific and typical Unix-style features. The following are examples of the kernel's security-related features.

- *BSD user and group identifiers (UIDs and GIDs)*—Traditional UIDs and GIDs form the kernel's most basic and least flexible means of security enforcement. Examples of BSD security policies based on UIDs and GIDs include ownership of file system objects; read/write/execute permissions on file system objects; operations restricted to processes with an effective UID of 0 (*root euid policy*); and operations on an object restricted to a process belonging to the object's owner or to a process with an effective UID of 0 (*owner or root euid policy*).

- *Mach port rights*—Besides being an IPC channel, a Mach port may represent a variety of resources, examples of which include tasks, threads, memory ranges, processors, and other devices. Moreover, Mach is a capability-based system in which port rights determine which operations a task may or may not perform on a port. The kernel manages and protects ports, thereby ensuring that only tasks with the required rights can perform privileged operations.

- *Auditing system*—The Mac OS X kernel implements an auditing system based on BSM (Basic Security Module), which is both a security audit format and an API used to track security-related events in the operating system.

- *Process accounting*—System-level accounting for every process executed can be enabled or disabled using the `accton` command. When process accounting is enabled, the `lastcomm` command displays information about previously executed commands.

- *Encrypted virtual memory*—The kernel can optionally use the AES algorithm to encrypt virtual memory pages that are swapped out to secondary storage.

- *ACLs*—File system ACLs are supported for finer-grained and flexible admission control when using on-disk information. Per-file ACLs are implemented as extended attributes in the file system.

- *Kauth*—Kauth is an in-kernel mechanism for the evaluation of ACLs. It is flexible and extensible, allowing kernel programmers to install their own callbacks—or *listeners*—for authorization requests in the kernel. When an entity wishes to perform an operation on an object, all registered listeners are invoked and provided with contextual information about the requester's credentials and the requested operation. A listener may allow, deny, or defer the request. The latter essentially lets the listener opt out from decision making—it is up to the remaining listeners, and eventually the default listener, to allow or deny the request.

2.14.2 User-Space Security

Mac OS X provides a flexible user-space security model that is largely based on the Common Data Security Architecture (CDSA). CDSA is an open source security architecture adopted as a technical standard[77] by the Open Group. It consists of a cryptographic framework and several layers of security services. Apple uses its own CDSA implementation, which is depicted in Figure 2–34.

CDSA helps in the implementation of security features such as encryption, fine-grained access permissions and user authentication, and secure data storage.

---

77. The CDSA Specification was initiated by Intel Architecture Labs. The current standard is a cooperative work of many organizations and companies, including Apple and IBM.

2.14.2.1 CDSA Plug-ins

The lowest layer of CDSA consists of plug-ins called by the layer above. CDSA plug-ins are allowed to call each other as well. Apple-provided CDSA plug-ins are shown in Figure 2–34. CDSA allows additional plug-ins to exist.

2.14.2.2 CSSM API

CDSA's core is a set of modules called the Common Security Services Manager (CSSM). The CSSM modules shown in the CSSM Managers block in Figure 2–34 together provide the CSSM API. The Authorization Computation Services Manager module shown within a dotted outline is not present in Apple's CDSA implementation.

2.14.2.3 Mac OS X Security APIs

Mac OS X applications normally use Apple's middleware security APIs that are built atop the CSSM API to access CDSA functionality. However, it is possible for an application to use the CSSM API directly. Examples of services provided by the middleware APIs include the following.

- *Keychain Services* provides secure storage for certificates, keys, passwords, and arbitrary information.
- *Secure Transport* provides secure network communication through implementations of the Secure Socket Layer (SSL) and Transport Layer Security (TLS) protocols.
- *Certificate, Key, and Trust Services*, respectively, create, access, and manipulate certificates; create encryption keys; and manage trust policies.
- *Authorization Services* is used as the primary API by applications to authorize access to specific actions[78] (e.g., creating a file in a restricted directory) or data.

2.14.2.4 Security Server and Security Agent

As shown in Figure 2–34, Authorization Services communicate with the Security Server, which then uses the CDSA APIs. Besides authorization, the Authorization Services API also handles authentication if required.

---

78. Applications can use Authorization Services to implement fine-grained authorization.

> *Authorization* involves asking whether a given entity is allowed to perform a given operation. Before the question may be answered, the requester is typically required to *authenticate*—that is, to prove his or her identity. Then it is determined whether the entity in question has the appropriate permissions.

The Security Server[79] (`/usr/sbin/securityd`) acts as an arbiter of many types of security-related operations and accesses. For example, fine-grained authorization of arbitrary operations by applications is based on rules contained in the `/etc/authorization` policy database. The Authorization Services API includes functions to add, delete, edit, and read policy database items. When an application requests a right—for example, `com.osxbook.Test.DoSomething`[80]—it makes an authorization call. The call is routed to `securityd`, which consults the policy database. `securityd` attempts to find a rule that exactly matches the requested right. If none is found, `securityd` looks for wildcard rules that may match, in the order of the longest match first. If there are no matches at all, `securityd` uses the generic rule, which is used for rights that do not have any specific rules. If the user authenticates successfully, `securityd` creates a credential with an expiration period of 5 minutes.[81]

The Security Agent application (`/System/Library/CoreServices/SecurityAgent.app`) is the user-interface handler for `securityd`—the latter does not interact with the user directly but launches Security Agent as a separate process, which in turn displays a username and password request dialog. Thus, Security Agent enforces GUI interaction, which normally warrants physical presence.[82]

2.14.2.5 Using Authorization Services

Figure 2–35 shows a program that requests a right named `com.osxbook.Test.DoSomething`. If the right doesn't exist in the policy database—which should

---

79. The Security Server is not part of CDSA.

80. Rules and rights are conventionally named in the policy database using a reverse DNS naming scheme.

81. The expiration period is specified through the `timeout` key in the policy database.

82. Physical presence is warranted unless the system is being driven remotely through a product such as Apple Remote Desktop. Beginning with Mac OS X 10.4, an application can authorize a user by passing in a username and password to the authorization function—without displaying the authentication dialog box.

be the case when the program is run for the first time—it sets up the right based on an existing standard rule called kAuthorizationAuthenticateAsSessionUser. The latter requires the user to authenticate as the session owner—that is, the currently logged-in user.

FIGURE 2–35 Using Authorization Services

```c
// testright.c

#include <stdio.h>
#include <stdlib.h>
#include <CoreFoundation/CoreFoundation.h>
#include <Security/Authorization.h>
#include <Security/AuthorizationDB.h>

const char kTestActionRightName[] = "com.osxbook.Test.DoSomething";

int
main(int argc, char **argv)
{
    OSStatus            err;
    AuthorizationRef    authRef;
    AuthorizationItem   authorization = { 0, 0, 0, 0 };
    AuthorizationRights rights = { 1, &authorization };
    AuthorizationFlags  flags = kAuthorizationFlagInteractionAllowed |\
                                kAuthorizationFlagExtendRights;

    // Create a new authorization reference
    err = AuthorizationCreate(NULL, NULL, 0, &authRef);
    if (err != noErr) {
        fprintf(stderr, "failed to connect to Authorization Services\n");
        return err;
    }

    // Check if the right is defined
    err = AuthorizationRightGet(kTestActionRightName, NULL);
    if (err != noErr) {
        if (err == errAuthorizationDenied) {
            // Create right in the policy database
            err = AuthorizationRightSet(
                    authRef,
                    kTestActionRightName,
                    CFSTR(kAuthorizationRuleAuthenticateAsSessionUser),
                    CFSTR("You must be authorized to perform DoSomething."),
                    NULL,
                    NULL
                );
```

(continues)

FIGURE 2–35 Using Authorization Services *(continued)*

```
            if (err != noErr) {
                fprintf(stderr, "failed to set up right\n");
                return err;
            }
        }
        else {
            // Give up
            fprintf(stderr, "failed to check right definition (%ld)\n", err);
            return err;
        }
    }

    // Authorize right
    authorization.name = kTestActionRightName;
    err = AuthorizationCopyRights(authRef, &rights, NULL, flags, NULL);
    if (err != noErr)
        fprintf(stderr, "failed to acquire right (%s)\n", kTestActionRightName);
    else
        fprintf(stderr, "right acquired (%s)\n", kTestActionRightName);

    // Free the memory associated with the authorization reference
    AuthorizationFree(authRef, kAuthorizationFlagDefaults);

    exit(0);
}


$ gcc -Wall -o testright testright.c -framework Security\
        -framework CoreFoundation
$ ./testright
...
$ less /etc/authorization
...
<key>com.osxbook.Test.DoSomething</key>
<dict>
    <key>default-prompt</key>
    <dict>
        <key></key>
        <string>You must be authorized to perform DoSomething.</string>
    </dict>
    <key>rule</key>
    <string>authenticate-session-user</string>
</dict>
...
```

2.14.2.6 Miscellaneous Security-Related Features

Other Mac OS X security features readily available to end users, or otherwise controllable by them, include the following.

- Mac OS X provides a feature called *FileVault*, wherein an AES-encrypted disk image is used to hold the contents of a user's home directory. For example, if FileVault is enabled for an existing user amit, then amit's home directory— /Users/amit/—will contain a disk image file called amit.sparseimage. This file contains an HFS Plus volume and is visible—say, from an administrator account—when amit is not logged in. Once amit logs in, the volume within the disk image is mounted on /Users/amit/, whereas the previous contents of /Users/amit/ (in particular, the image file itself) are moved to /Users/.amit/.

- Mac OS X provides secure file deletion through the Finder's Secure Empty Trash menu item and through the srm command-line program. The Disk Utility application (Disk Utility.app) allows disks and volumes to be securely erased using one of many schemes: write zeros over all data on disk (zero-out data), write data over the entire disk 7 times (7-pass erase), and write data over the entire disk 35 times (35-pass erase). Moreover, recovery of already deleted files can be made difficult by securely erasing existing free space on a volume.

- We earlier looked at encrypted virtual memory as a kernel feature. It can be enabled or disabled through the Security pane of the System Preferences application. At boot time, the operating system checks for the ENCRYPTSWAP shell variable to determine whether virtual memory should be encrypted. The variable's value is set to -YES- or -NO- in /etc/hostconfig depending on the setting selected in System Preferences.

2.14.3 System Administration

Mac OS X can be effectively administered through either graphical user interfaces or the command line. Let us look at some examples of using the command line to control Mac OS X–specific aspects of system administration.

2.14.3.1 Interacting with the Security Framework

The security command provides access to the functionality in the Security framework (Security.framework). In particular, it can be used to access and manipulate certificates, keys, keychains, and password items, as shown in Figure 2–36.

FIGURE 2–36 Examining keychains using the `security` command

```
$ security list-keychains
"/Users/amit/Library/Keychains/login.keychain"
    "/Library/Keychains/System.keychain"
$ security dump-keychain login.keychain
...
keychain: "/Users/amit/Library/Keychains/login.keychain"
class: "genp"
attributes:
    0x00000007 <blob>="AirPort Express"
    0x00000008 <blob>=<NULL>
...
```

2.14.3.2 Interacting with Directory Services

The server version of Mac OS X uses the LDAP-based[83] Open Directory software to provide directory and authentication services for Mac OS X, Unix, and Windows clients. A directory service is simply a central repository for storing and vending information about users, computers, printers, and other network resources in an organization. Application and system software can access such information for a variety of purposes: authenticating logins, locating user home directories, enforcing resource quotas, controlling accesses to file systems, and so on. Traditionally, Unix systems store such information in flat text files, such as those in the /etc directory. In fact, the Unix /etc directory could be seen as a primitive directory service. Other examples of directory services include Sun's Network Information Service (NIS)[84] and Microsoft's Active Directory.[85] The legacy directory service in Mac OS X Server is called *NetInfo*. Although no longer used for shared directories, NetInfo is still the directory service for the *local* directory domain on Mac OS X—that is, for users and resources on the local system.

---

83. LDAP stands for Lightweight Directory Access Protocol. It is a widely deployed open standard.

84. An old name for NIS is Yellow Pages (yp). The successor to NIS is called NIS+. Recent versions of Solaris have deprecated NIS and NIS+ in favor of LDAP-based directory services.

85. Active Directory is LDAP-based as well.

The `dscl` command can be used for operating on data sources, which can be directory node names or hosts that are running directory services. Similarly, the `niutil` command utility can be used for operating on NetInfo domains. However, note that Open Directory includes a NetInfo plug-in that allows interoperation with NetInfo. Figure 2–37 shows examples of using `dscl` and `niutil`.

FIGURE 2–37 Interacting with Directory Services by using command-line tools

```
$ niutil -list . / # List directories in the path '/' in the local domain '/'
1       users
2       groups
3       machines
4       networks
...
$ dscl /NetInfo/root -list / # List subdirectories of the path '/'
                             # using the data source /Netinfo/root
AFPUserAliases
Aliases
Groups
Machines
Networks
...
# dscl sorts by directory names, niutil sorts by directory IDs
$ dscl . -read /Users/amit # Read record for user amit
...
NFSHomeDirectory: /Users/amit
Password: ********
Picture: /Library/User Pictures/Nature/Lightning.tif
PrimaryGroupID: 501
RealName: Amit Singh
RecordName: amit
...
$ niutil -read . /users/amit # Read record for user amit
...
$ niutil -read . /users/uid=501 # Read record for user with UID 501
...
$ dscl . -passwd /Users/amit # Change amit's password
...
$ dscl . -search /Users UserShell "/usr/bin/false"
# Search for users with the specified shell
nobody          UserShell = ("/usr/bin/false")
daemon          UserShell = ("/usr/bin/false")
unknown         UserShell = ("/usr/bin/false")
...
```

2.14.3.3 *Managing System Configuration*

The `scutil` command can be used to access and manipulate various configuration aspects of the local system. The System Configuration daemon (`/usr/sbin/configd`) stores relevant configuration data in a dynamic store that is accessible via `scutil`. It uses several *configuration agents*—each of which is a plug-in that handles a particular configuration management area—to form an overall view of system configuration. The agents reside in `/System/Library/SystemConfiguration/` as bundles. For example, the `IPConfiguration` agent is responsible for establishing (say, via DHCP) and maintaining IPv4 addresses.

Figure 2–38 shows an example of accessing the system configuration dynamic store using `scutil`.

FIGURE 2–38 Using the `scutil` command to access the System Configuration dynamic store

```
$ scutil
> list
subKey [0] = DirectoryService:PID
subKey [1] = Plugin:IPConfiguration
subKey [2] = Setup:
subKey [3] = Setup:/
...
subKey [26] = State:/Network/Interface/en1/AirPort
subKey [27] = State:/Network/Interface/en1/IPv4
...
> show State:/Network/Interface/en1/AirPort
<dictionary> {
  Power Status : 1
  BSSID : <data> 0x00aabbccdd
  Card Mode : 1
  Link Status : 4
  SSID : dummyssid
}
> show State:/Network/Interface/en1/IPv4
<dictionary> {
  Addresses : <array> {
    0 : 10.0.0.1
  }
  BroadcastAddresses : <array> {
    0 : 10.0.0.255
  }
  SubnetMasks : <array> {
    0 : 255.255.255.0
  }
}
```

2.14.4 The Auditing System

The Mac OS X auditing system consists of kernel support and a suite of user-space programs.[86] The kernel records audit events to a log file—an *audit trail* file—based on several types of criteria. A user-space daemon—auditd—listens to *trigger events* from the kernel and *control events* from user programs (the audit command-line utility by default). Trigger events inform auditd if the current log file has become full or if the file system free space has fallen below a configured threshold; if so, auditd will attempt to rectify the situation. For example, it may attempt to rotate the log. In this sense, auditd is a log management daemon. Control events are used to instruct auditd to switch to a new log file, reread the configuration file, or terminate the auditing system.

Table 2–2 lists the key executables and configuration files in the auditing system.

TABLE 2–2 Auditing System Components

File/Directory	Description
/usr/sbin/auditd	Audit log management daemon—receives "trigger" messages from the kernel and "control" messages from the audit management utility
/usr/sbin/audit	Audit management utility—used to control the audit daemon by sending it control messages
/usr/sbin/auditreduce	Utility that selects records from the audit trail files based on the specified criteria and prints matching records in raw form—either to a file or to the standard output
/usr/sbin/praudit	Utility that prints selected records in human-readable format
/var/audit/	Directory for storing audit trail files
/etc/security/rc.audit	Script executed during system startup by the /etc/rc master script to start the audit daemon
/etc/security/audit_control	Default audit policy file—contains global audit parameters
/etc/security/audit_class	File containing descriptions of audit event classes
/etc/security/audit_event	File containing descriptions of audit events
/etc/security/audit_user	File specifying event classes that are to be audited on a per-user basis
/etc/security/audit_warn	Administrator-configurable script run when the audit daemon generates a warning

---

86. In Mac OS X 10.4, user-space auditing programs and configuration files are provided by the Common Criteria Tools package, which is not installed by default.

Auditing can be enabled or disabled by setting the AUDIT variable to -YES- or -NO-, respectively, in the /etc/hostconfig file. The variable can also be set to -FAILSTOP- or -FAILHALT-, both of which enable auditing with additional conditions. The former runs auditd with the -s argument, which specifies that individual processes will stop if the audit log becomes full and running the processes will result in loss of audit records. The latter runs auditd with the -h argument, which specifies that the system should halt in case of an auditing failure.

The kernel logs to only one audit trail file at a time. Trail filenames use a specific format: a string consisting of the file's creation time, followed by a period, followed by the termination time. The name of the active trail file—that is, the one that has not been terminated yet—contains the string not_terminated instead of the termination time. Both time substrings are constructed by using the %Y%m%d%H%M%S format specifier with the strftime() function.

The audit_control, audit_user, and audit_warn files are typically modified to configure the auditing system. Figure 2–39 shows the representative contents of an audit_control file.

FIGURE 2–39 An audit control file

```
# /etc/security/audit_control

# Directory/directories where audit logs are stored
#
dir:/var/audit

# Event classes that are to be audited system-wide for all users
# (Per-user specifications are in /etc/security/audit_user)
#
# This is a comma-separated list of audit event classes, where each class
# may have one of the following prefixes:
#
#     +  Record successful events
#     -  Record failed events
#     ^  Record both successful and failed events
#     ^+ Do not record successful events
#     ^- Do not record failed events
#
# The class specifiers are listed in audit_class(5)
# Examples:
#
#     all All events
#     ad  Administrative events
#     cl  File close events
#     fa  File attribute access events
```

(continues)

FIGURE 2–39 An audit control file *(continued)*

```
#     fc  File create events
#     lo  Login/logout events
#
flags:lo,ad,-all,^-fa,^-fc,^-cl

# Minimum free space required on the file system where audit logs are stored
# When free space falls below this limit, a warning will be issued
#
minfree:20

# Event classes that are to be audited even when an action cannot be
# attributed to a specific user
#
naflags:lo
```

2.15 Mac OS X Server

The Mac OS X Server operating system is architecturally identical to Mac OS X. In fact, for a given processor architecture, Apple uses the same kernel binary on every system, whether it is a Mac mini or the highest-end Xserve.[87] The key differences between the server and desktop versions of Mac OS X lie in bundled software and the underlying hardware.[88] Examples of server-specific features include the following:

- Integrated management tools—for example, Server Admin and Workgroup Manager—that aid in configuring and deploying network services for multi-platform clients
- The NetBoot service, which allows multiple Macintosh clients to boot from a single disk image on the server
- The Network Install service, which allows installation of Mac OS X from a single installation image to multiple clients
- Support for automatic reboot (say, after a crash) courtesy of a hardware watchdog timer, if one is available on the system
- A virtual private network (VPN) server

---

87. Xserve is Apple's line of 1U servers. A U, or unit, refers to a standard way of defining the height of a rack-mountable piece of equipment.

88. Although Mac OS X Server is primarily targeted to run on Xserve hardware, it is also supported on other Macintosh hardware.

- Support for hosting a software update proxy/cache server, allowing clients to obtain updates from that server instead of from Apple
- An iChat- and Jabber-compatible instant-messaging server with support for SSL-based encryption
- A weblog server for publishing and syndicating weblogs
- Software for adaptive junk mail filtering (SpamAssassin) and virus detection and quarantine (ClamAV)
- The ability to be an Xgrid controller

Let us look at two Apple technologies—*Xgrid* and *Xsan*—that are typically used in the context of server computing.

2.15.1 Xgrid

The abundance of computing and networking resources, along with the fact that such resources are often not fully used, has led to the harnessing of these resources to solve a variety of problems. An early example of this concept is the Xerox worm experiments, wherein programs ran multimachine computations across several Ethernet-connected Alto computers.

Xerox Worms

In 1975, science fiction writer John Brunner wrote about worm programs in his book *The Shockwave Rider*. Xerox PARC researchers John F. Shoch and Jon A. Hupp experimented with worm programs in the early 1980s. The experimental environment consisted of over a hundred Ethernet-connected Altos. Each machine held a segment of the worm. Segments on various machines could communicate with each other. If a segment was lost, say, because its machine went down, the remaining segments would search for an idle Alto on which to load a new copy—self-repairing software! It is important to note that mischief was not the idea behind the worm experiments. The researchers intended to create useful programs that would use otherwise idle machines—essentially a form of distributed computing.[89] Nevertheless, the aberrant potential of worms was clearly identified, although worms were still not perceived as a real security risk. Comparatively, viruses and self-replicating Trojan horse programs were considered bigger threats to security.

---

89. The Alto worms were conceptually similar, in some aspects, to the controller and agent programs in a modern grid-computing environment such as Apple's Xgrid.

In general, multiple computers can be combined to do a computing-intensive task,[90] provided the task can be broken into subtasks that each computer can handle independently. Such a group of computers is called a *computational grid*. One may distinguish between a *grid* and a *cluster* based on how tightly coupled the constituent computers are. A grid is usually a group of loosely coupled systems that are often not even geographically close.[91] Moreover, the systems may have any platform and may run any operating system that supports the grid software. In contrast, a cluster typically contains tightly coupled systems that are centrally managed, collocated, and interconnected through a high-performance network, and they often run the same operating system on the same platform.

2.15.1.1 Xgrid Architecture

Apple's Xgrid technology provides a mechanism for deploying and managing Mac OS X–based computational grids.[92] Figure 2–40 shows a simplified view of the Xgrid architecture. Xgrid has the following key components and abstractions.

- A *job* represents the overall problem to be worked on. When a job is submitted to the grid, it will be divided into pieces that individual computers in the grid can handle. A job consists of one or more programs and relevant data.

- A *task* is an indivisible piece of a job. It is given to a grid participant to perform. A task must be large enough to justify the cost of distributing tasks.

- The *controller* is the grid manager. Mac OS X Server includes software necessary for a system to act as the Xgrid controller.

- A *client* is a system that submits jobs to the controller. Xgrid client software can run on both Mac OS X and Mac OS X Server.

- An *agent* is a grid participant system that is willing to perform tasks the controller sends. An agent system can run one task at a time for each CPU in the system. Xgrid agent software can run on both Mac OS X and Mac OS X Server. Moreover, agents can be *dedicated* or *part-time*. A dedicated

---

90. There are other varieties of "big" computing, such as High Performance Computing (HPC) and High Throughput Computing (HTC). The discussion of these is beyond the scope of this book.

91. An example of such a grid is the SETI@home project, which is a scientific experiment that uses participating computers on the Internet in the Search for Extraterrestrial Intelligence (SETI).

92. It is possible for Linux systems to participate as agents in an Xgrid. Apple officially supports only Mac OS X and Mac OS X Server agents.

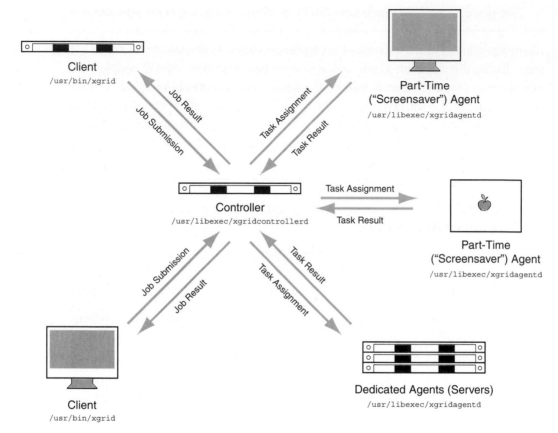

FIGURE 2–40 Xgrid architecture

agent is always available to Xgrid, whereas a part-time agent is available only when the system is idle.[93]

Thus, clients submit jobs to the controller, which maintains most of the Xgrid logic, and the agents perform tasks. The controller's specific responsibilities include the following.

- It can advertise its presence through multicast DNS (mDNS), allowing clients to discover the controller using *Bonjour*—without having to know the controller's hostname or IP address.

---

93. The Mac OS X Server Xgrid agent is dedicated by default, whereas the agent on Mac OS X will not accept tasks by default unless the system has been idle—as determined by the lack of user input—for at least 15 minutes. The process of using desktop systems in this manner is sometimes referred to as *desktop recovery*.

- It accepts connections from agents. An agent can connect to only one controller at a time.[94] If a system is enabled to be an Xgrid agent, it will—by default—attempt to connect to the first available controller on the local network, although it can be bound to a specific controller. Xgrid may be configured to require authentication between agents and controllers.

- It accepts connections from clients. A user on an Xgrid client system submits jobs to the controller, optionally after authenticating—for example, through single sign-on or passwords. The Xgrid client software allows creation of plug-ins—essentially predefined jobs—that the controller can store and later instantiate.

- It divides client-submitted jobs into tasks, which it then dispatches to the agents. Dispatching involves the controller sending an archive—a tar file, for example—containing binary executables, scripts, and data files to the client. The client copies the received files into a temporary working directory. Programs that execute on the client as part of the task are run as the user *nobody*. Moreover, these programs must not require any GUI interaction.

- It receives task results from agents in the form of archives. Once all task results are collected, it returns the job result to the submitting client.

- If an agent fails to finish a task, it reassigns the failed task to another agent.

An Xgrid may be classified into the following categories based on the type of participating systems:

- *Distributed*—unmanaged, geographically distributed systems; high job-failure rate; low performance; low cost

- *Local*—managed systems, usually geographically close; systems that accept jobs when idle; varying performance; medium cost

- *Cluster-based*—strictly managed, collocated systems; dedicated agents; very low job-failure rate; highest performance; highest cost

2.15.1.2 Xgrid Software

Xgrid provides GUI-based tools for monitoring grids and submitting jobs. It can also be managed from the command line: The `xgrid` command can be used to submit and monitor jobs, whereas the `xgridctl` command can be used to query,

---

94. Multiple logical grids can exist on a subnetwork, but each logical grid has exactly one controller.

start, stop, or restart Xgrid daemons. The Xgrid agent and controller daemons reside as `/usr/libexec/xgrid/xgridagentd` and `/usr/libexec/xgrid/xgridcontrollerd`, respectively. The `/etc/xgrid/agent/` and `/etc/xgrid/controller/` directories contain the daemons' configuration files.

The Xgrid public API (`XgridFoundation.framework`) provides interfaces for connecting to and managing Xgrid instances.[95] Custom Cocoa applications can be written with Xgrid integration.

2.15.2 Xsan

Apple's Xsan product is a storage area network (SAN) file system along with a graphical management application—the Xsan Admin. Xsan is based on the StorNext multiplatform file system from Advanced Digital Information Corporation (ADIC). In fact, Macintosh clients can be added to an existing StorNext SAN. Conversely, Xserve and Xserve RAID systems can act as controllers and storage, respectively, for client computers running StorNext software on platforms such as AIX, HP-UX, Irix, Linux, Solaris, UNICOS/mp, and Microsoft Windows.

As is the case with a typical SAN, Xsan connects computer systems and storage devices using high-speed communication channels, providing fast access to users and on-demand, nondisruptive expandability to administrators. Figure 2–41 shows Xsan's high-level architecture.

An Xsan consists of the following constituents:

- Storage devices
- One or more computers acting as metadata controllers
- Client computers that use storage
- Communication infrastructure consisting of Ethernet and Fibre Channel networks, along with associated hardware such as Fibre Channel switches and adapters

2.15.2.1 Storage in Xsan

The logical, user-facing view of storage in Xsan is a *volume*, which represents shared storage. Figure 2–41 shows how an Xsan volume is constructed.

The smallest physical building block in Xsan is a *disk*, whereas the smallest logical building block is a *logical unit number* (LUN). A LUN can be an Xserve

---

95. Another Xgrid framework—`XgridInterface.framework`—is a private framework.

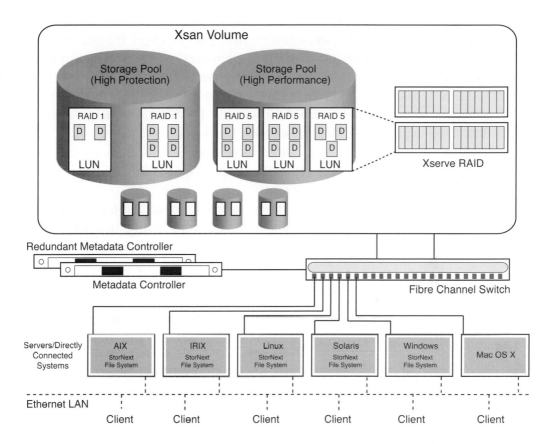

FIGURE 2–41 Xsan architecture

RAID array or slice. It can also be a JBOD.[96] LUNs are combined to form *storage pools*, which can have different characteristics for data loss protection or performance. For example, Figure 2–41 shows two storage pools: one that contains RAID 1 arrays for high recoverability through redundancy, and another that contains RAID 5 arrays for high performance.[97] At the file system level, Xsan allows assigning directories to storage pools through *affinities*, wherein users can have one directory for storing files that must have high recoverability and another for

96. JBOD stands for Just a Bunch of Disks. A JBOD LUN is a virtual disk drive created from the concatenation of multiple physical disks. There is no redundancy in a JBOD configuration.

97. A RAID 1 configuration mirrors data on two or more disks. A RAID 5 configuration stripes data blocks across three or more disks. RAID 5 intersperses parity information across the drive array. Parity is used to recover lost data in the case of a drive failure.

storing files that must have fast access. Storage pools are combined to form user-visible volumes. Once an Xsan volume is mounted by a client, the latter can use it as a local disk. It is more than a local disk, however, because its capacity can be increased dynamically, and it can be shared in the SAN.

Xsan volumes support permissions and quotas. Xsan also allows different allocation strategies to be specified for volumes. The *balance* strategy causes new data to be written to the storage pool that has the largest amount of free space. The *fill* strategy causes Xsan to fill available storage pools in sequence, starting with the first. The *round-robin* strategy causes Xsan to circularly iterate over all available pools while writing new data.

An Xsan's storage capacity can be increased by adding new volumes, by adding new storage pools to existing volumes, or by adding new LUNs to an existing storage pool.[98]

2.15.2.2 Metadata Controllers

An Xsan metadata controller's primary functions are the following:

- Managing volume metadata[99]
- Coordinating access to shared volumes, including controlling concurrent access to files
- Maintaining a file system journal

There must be at least one metadata controller—usually an Xserve system—in an Xsan. Additional controllers may be added as standby controllers, which take over if the primary controller fails. Note that the metadata controller manages only the metadata and the journal; it does not store them on its local storage. By default, a volume's metadata and journal reside on the first storage pool added to the volume.

2.15.2.3 Client Systems

Xsan clients can range from single-user desktop computers to multiuser servers. A metadata controller can be a client as well. As we saw earlier, Xsan can support other client platforms that run the StorNext software.

---

98. The existing storage pool cannot be the one that holds the volume's metadata or journal data.

99. Xsan volume metadata includes the actual physical locations of files.

2.15.2.4 Communication Infrastructure

Xsan clients use Fibre Channel for file data (i.e., while communicating with Xserve RAID systems) and Ethernet for metadata[100] (i.e., while communicating with the metadata controller).

Xsan supports *Fibre Channel Multipathing*: If multiple physical connections are available, Xsan can either use dedicated connections[101] to certain LUNs in a volume, or it can use separate connections for read and write traffic.

> On a system with Xsan software installed, the Xsan command-line utilities reside in `/Library/Filesystems/Xsan/bin/`.

2.16 Networking

Most of the Mac OS X networking subsystem is derived from that of 4.4BSD, although there are some important differences, such as in the handling of timers and the interaction of network devices with the higher layers of the networking stack.

The I/O Kit's Network family provides various classes that together constitute the low-level layers of the Mac OS X networking subsystem. For example, if you wish to create a network controller driver, you use the framework defined by the Network family. Moreover, the networking subsystem has a *data link interface layer* (DLIL) that connects the Network family with the BSD networking code. Specifically, the DLIL is used for communication between the Network family's `IONetworkInterface` class and higher-level components such as the protocols.

A notable feature of the Mac OS X implementation is the Network Kernel Extensions (NKE) mechanism, which provides ways to extend the system's networking architecture through loadable kernel modules that interact with the networking stack. Examples of applications of NKEs include implementation of new protocols, modification of existing protocols, creation of link-layer encryption mechanisms, and attachment of filters at various layers of the stack.

Before Mac OS X 10.4, a kernel extension had to be explicitly designated as an NKE. Beginning with version 10.4, the kernel exports several kernel programming

---

100. Xsan administration traffic also goes over Ethernet.

101. Such dedicated connections are assigned at volume-mount time.

interfaces (KPIs) that make NKE functionality available to kernel extensions. The following are examples of header files that correspond to these KPIs:

- `kpi_interface.h`—for interacting with network interfaces
- `kpi_mbuf.h`—for interacting with mbufs
- `kpi_protocol.h`—for interacting with network protocols
- `kpi_socket.h`—for manipulating and using sockets in the kernel
- `kpi_socketfilter.h`—for implementing filters at the socket layer
- `kpi_ipfilter.h`—for implementing filters at the IP layer
- `kpi_interfacefilter.h`—for implementing filters at the interface layer

CHAPTER 3

Inside an Apple

Apple initiated its transition from the 68K hardware platform to the PowerPC in 1994. Within the next two years, Apple's entire line of computers moved to the PowerPC. The various PowerPC-based Apple computer families available at any given time have often differed in system architecture,[1] the specific processor used, and the processor vendor. For example, before the G4 iBook was introduced in October 2003, Apple's then current systems included three generations of the PowerPC: the G3, the G4, and the G5. Whereas the G4 processor line is supplied by Motorola, the G3 and the G5 are from IBM. Table 3–1 lists the various PowerPC processors[2] used by Apple.

On June 6, 2005, at the Worldwide Developers Conference in San Francisco, Apple announced its plans to base future models of Macintosh computers on Intel processors. The move was presented as a two-year transition: Apple stated that

---

1. System architecture refers to the type and interconnection of a system's hardware components, including—but not limited to—the processor type.

2. The list does not account for minor differences between processor models—for example, differences based solely on processor clock frequencies.

TABLE 3–1 Processors Used in PowerPC-Based Apple Systems

Processor	Introduced	Discontinued
PowerPC 601	March 1994	June 1996
PowerPC 603	April 1995	May 1996
PowerPC 603e	April 1996	August 1998
PowerPC 604	August 1995	April 1998
PowerPC 604e	August 1996	September 1998
PowerPC G3	November 1997	October 2003
PowerPC G4	October 1999	—
PowerPC G5	June 2003	—
PowerPC G5 (dual-core)	October 2005	—

although x86-based Macintosh models would become available by mid-2006, all Apple computers would transition to the x86 platform only by the end of 2007. The transition was faster than expected, with the first x86 Macintosh computers appearing in January 2006. These systems—the iMac and the MacBook Pro—were based on the Intel Core Duo[3] dual-core processor line, which is built on 65 nm process technology.

In this chapter, we will look at the system architecture of a specific type of Apple computer: a G5-based dual-processor Power Mac. Moreover, we will discuss a specific PowerPC processor used in these systems: the 970FX. We focus on a G5-based system because the 970FX is more advanced, more powerful, and more interesting in general than its predecessors. It is also the basis for the first 64-bit dual-core PowerPC processor: the 970MP.

3.1 The Power Mac G5

Apple announced the Power Mac G5—its first 64-bit desktop system—in June 2003. Initial G5-based Apple computers used IBM's PowerPC 970 processors. These were followed by systems based on the 970FX processor. In late 2005, Apple revamped the Power Mac line by moving to the dual-core 970MP proces-

---

3. This processor was originally codenamed *Yonah*.

sor. The 970, 970FX, and 970MP are all derived from the execution core of the POWER4 processor family, which was designed for IBM's high-end servers. G5 is Apple's marketing term for the 970 and its variants.

IBM's Other G5

There was another G5 from IBM—the microprocessor used in the S/390 G5 system, which was announced in May 1998. The S/390 G5 was a member of IBM's CMOS[4] mainframe family. Unlike the 970 family processors, the S/390 G5 had a Complex Instruction-Set Computer (CISC) architecture.

Before we examine the architecture of any particular Power Mac G5, note that various Power Mac G5 models may have slightly different system architectures. In the following discussion, we will refer to the system shown in Figure 3–1.

3.1.1 The U3H System Controller

The U3H system controller combines the functionality of a memory controller[5] and a PCI bus bridge.[6] It is a custom integrated chip (IC) that is the meeting point of key system components: processors, the Double Data Rate (DDR) memory system, the Accelerated Graphics Port (AGP)[7] slot, and the HyperTransport bus that runs into a PCI-X bridge. The U3H provides bridging functionality by performing point-to-point routing between these components. It supports a Graphics Address Remapping Table (GART) that allows the AGP bridge to translate linear addresses used in AGP transactions into physical addresses. This improves the performance of direct memory access (DMA) transactions involving multiple pages that would typically be noncontiguous in virtual memory. Another table supported by the U3H is the Device Address Resolution Table (DART),[8] which translates linear addresses to physical addresses for devices attached to the

---

4. CMOS stands for Complementary Metal Oxide Semiconductor—a type of integrated circuit technology. CMOS chips use metal oxide semiconductor field effect transistors (MOSFETs), which differ greatly from the bipolar transistors that were prevalent before CMOS. Most modern processors are manufactured in CMOS technology.

5. A memory controller controls processor and I/O interactions with the memory system.

6. The G5 processors use the PCI bus bridge to execute operations on the PCI bus. The bridge also provides an interface through which PCI devices can access system memory.

7. AGP extends the PCI standard by adding functionality optimized for video devices.

8. DART is sometimes expanded as DMA Address Relocation Table.

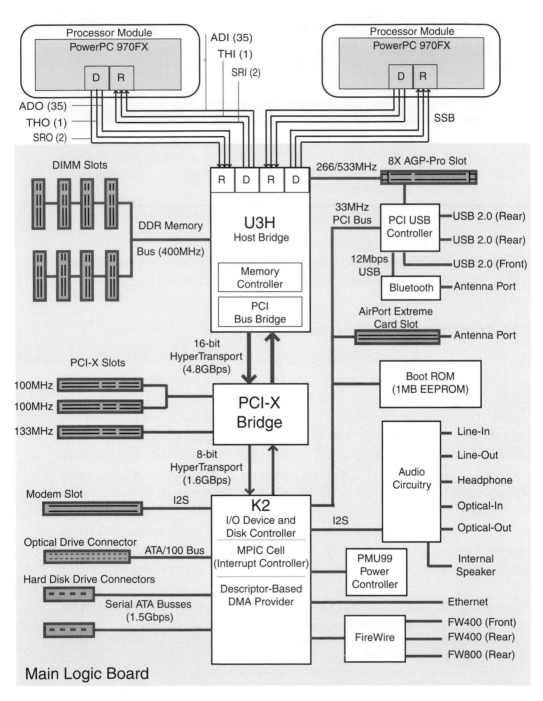

FIGURE 3–1 Architecture of a dual-processor Power Mac G5 system

HyperTransport bus. We will come across the DART in Chapter 10, when we discuss the I/O Kit.

3.1.2 The K2 I/O Device Controller

The U3H is connected to a PCI-X bridge via a 16-bit HyperTransport bus. The PCI-X bridge is further connected to the K2 custom IC via an 8-bit HyperTransport bus. The K2 is a custom integrated I/O device controller. In particular, it provides disk and multiprocessor interrupt controller (MPIC) functionality.

3.1.3 PCI-X and PCI Express

The Power Mac system shown in Figure 3–1 provides three PCI-X 1.0 slots. Power Mac G5 systems with dual-core processors use PCI Express.

3.1.3.1 PCI-X

PCI-X was developed to increase the bus speed and reduce the latency of PCI (see the sidebar "A Primer on Local Busses"). PCI-X 1.0 was based on the existing PCI architecture. In particular, it is also a shared bus. It solves many—but not all—of the problems with PCI. For example, its split-transaction protocol improves bus bandwidth utilization, resulting in far greater throughput rates than PCI. It is fully backward compatible in that PCI-X cards can be used in Conventional PCI slots, and conversely, Conventional PCI cards—both 33MHz and 66MHz—can be used in PCI-X slots. However, PCI-X is not electrically compatible with 5V-only cards or 5V-only slots.

PCI-X 1.0 uses 64-bit slots. It provides two speed grades: PCI-X 66 (66MHz signaling speed, up to 533MBps peak throughput) and PCI-X 133 (133MHz signaling speed, up to 1GBps peak throughput).

PCI-X 2.0 provides enhancements such as the following:

- An error correction code (ECC) mechanism for providing automatic 1-bit error recovery and 2-bit error detection
- New speed grades: PCI-X 266 (266MHz signaling speed, up to 2.13GBps peak throughput) and PCI-X 533 (533MHz signaling speed, up to 4.26GBps peak throughput)
- A new 16-bit interface for embedded or portable applications

Note how the slots are connected to the PCI-X bridge in Figure 3–1: Whereas one of them is "individually" connected (a *point-to-point* load), the other two "share" a connection (a *multidrop* load). A PCI-X speed limitation is that *its highest speed grades are supported only if the load is point-to-point.* Specifically, two PCI-X 133 loads will each operate at a maximum of 100MHz.[9] Correspondingly, two of this Power Mac's slots are 100MHz each, whereas the third is a 133MHz slot.

> The next revision of PCI-X—3.0—provides a 1066MHz data rate with a peak throughput of 8.5GBps.

3.1.3.2 PCI Express

An alternative to using a shared bus is to use point-to-point links to connect devices. PCI Express[10] uses a high-speed, point-to-point architecture. It provides PCI compatibility using established PCI driver programming models. Software-generated I/O requests are transported to I/O devices through a split-transaction, packet-based protocol. In other words, PCI Express essentially serializes and packetizes PCI. It supports multiple interconnect widths—a link's bandwidth can be linearly scaled by adding signal pairs to form *lanes*. There can be up to 32 separate lanes.

A Primer on Local Busses

As CPU speeds have increased greatly over the years, other computer subsystems have not managed to keep pace. Perhaps an exception is the main memory, which has fared better than I/O bandwidth. In 1991,[11] Intel introduced the *Peripheral Component Interconnect* (PCI) local bus standard. In the simplest terms, a bus is a shared communications link. In a computer system, a bus is implemented as a set of wires that connect some of the computer's subsystems. Multiple busses are typically used as building blocks to construct complex com-

---

9. Four PCI-X 133 loads in a multidrop configuration will operate at a maximum speed of 66MHz each.

10. The PCI Express standard was approved by the PCI-SIG Board of Directors in July 2002. PCI Express was formerly called 3GIO.

11. This was also the year that Macintosh System 7 was released, the Apple-IBM-Motorola (AIM) alliance was formed, and the Personal Computer Memory Card International Association (PCMCIA) was established, among other things.

puter systems. The "local" in local bus implies its proximity to the processor.[12] The PCI bus has proven to be an extremely popular interconnect mechanism (also called simply an interconnect), particularly in the so-called North Bridge/South Bridge implementation. A *North Bridge* typically takes care of communication between the processor, main memory, AGP, and the South Bridge. Note, however, that modern system designs are moving the memory controller to the processor die, thus making AGP obsolete and rendering the traditional North Bridge unnecessary.

A typical *South Bridge* controls various busses and devices, including the PCI bus. It is common to have the PCI bus work both as a plug-in bus for peripherals and as an interconnect allowing devices connected directly or indirectly to it to communicate with memory.

The PCI bus uses a shared, parallel multidrop architecture in which address, data, and control signals are multiplexed on the bus. When one PCI bus master[13] uses the bus, other connected devices must either wait for it to become free or use a contention protocol to request control of the bus. Several *sideband* signals[14] are required to keep track of communication directions, types of bus transactions, indications of bus-mastering requests, and so on. Moreover, a shared bus runs at limited clock speeds, and since the PCI bus can support a wide variety of devices with greatly varying requirements (in terms of bandwidth, transfer sizes, latency ranges, and so on), bus arbitration can be rather complicated. PCI has several other limitations that are beyond the scope of this chapter.

PCI has evolved into multiple variants that differ in backward compatibility, forward planning, bandwidth supported, and so on.

- **Conventional PCI**—The original PCI Local Bus Specification has evolved into what is now called *Conventional PCI*. The PCI Special Interest Group (PCI-SIG) introduced PCI 2.01 in 1993, followed by revisions 2.1 (1995), 2.2 (1998), and 2.3 (2002). Depending on the revision, PCI bus characteristics include the following: 5V or 3.3V signaling, 32-bit or 64-bit bus width, operation at 33MHz or 66MHz, and a peak throughput of 133MBps, 266MBps, or 533MBps. Conventional PCI 3.0—the current standard—finishes the migration of the PCI bus from being a 5.0V signaling bus to a 3.3V signaling bus.

- **MiniPCI**—MiniPCI defines a smaller form factor PCI card based on PCI 2.2. It is meant for use in products where space is a premium—such as notebook computers, docking stations, and set-top boxes. Apple's AirPort Extreme wireless card is based on MiniPCI.

---

12. The first local bus was the VESA local bus (VLB).

13. A bus master is a device that can initiate a read or write transaction—for example, a processor.

14. In the context of PCI, a sideband signal is any signal that is not part of the PCI specification but is used to connect two or more PCI-compliant devices. Sideband signals can be used for product-specific extensions to the bus, provided they do not interfere with the specification's implementation.

- **CardBus**—CardBus is a member of the PC Card family that provides a 32-bit, 33MHz PCI-like interface that operates at 3.3V. The PC Card Standard is maintained by the PCMCIA.[15]

PCI-X (Section 3.1.3.1) and PCI Express (Section 3.1.3.2) represent further advancements in I/O bus architecture.

3.1.4 HyperTransport

HyperTransport (HT) is a high-speed, point-to-point, chip interconnect technology. Formerly known as Lightning Data Transport (LDT), it was developed in the late 1990s at Advanced Micro Devices (AMD) in collaboration with industry partners. The technology was formally introduced in July 2001. Apple Computer was one of the founding members of the HyperTransport Technology Consortium. The HyperTransport architecture is open and nonproprietary.

HyperTransport aims to simplify complex chip-to-chip and board-to-board interconnections in a system by replacing multilevel busses. Each connection in the HyperTransport protocol is between two devices. Instead of using a single bidirectional bus, each connection consists of *two unidirectional links*. Hyper-Transport point-to-point interconnects (Figure 3–2 shows an example) can be extended to support a variety of devices, including tunnels, bridges, and end-point devices. HyperTransport connections are especially well suited for devices on the main logic board—that is, those devices that require the lowest latency and the highest performance. Chains of HyperTransport links can also be used as I/O channels, connecting I/O devices and bridges to a host system.

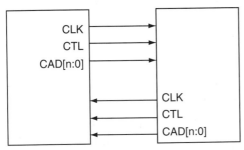

FIGURE 3–2 HyperTransport I/O link

---

15. The PCMCIA was established to standardize certain types of add-in memory cards for mobile computers.

Some important HyperTransport features include the following.

- HyperTransport uses a packet-based data protocol in which narrow and fast unidirectional point-to-point links carry *command*, *address*, and *data* (CAD) information encoded as packets.

- The electrical characteristics of the links help in cleaner signal transmission, higher clock rates, and lower power consumption. Consequently, considerably fewer sideband signals are required.

- Widths of various links do not need to be equal. An 8-bit-wide link can easily connect to a 32-bit-wide link. Links can scale from 2 bits to 4, 8, 16, or 32 bits in width. As shown in Figure 3–1, the HyperTransport bus between the U3H and the PCI-X bridge is 16 bits wide, whereas the PCI-X bridge and the K2 are connected by an 8-bit-wide HyperTransport bus.

- Clock speeds of various links do not need to be equal and can scale across a wide spectrum. Thus, it is possible to scale links in both *width* and *speed* to suit specific needs.

- HyperTransport supports *split transactions*, eliminating the need for inefficient retries, disconnects by targets, and insertion of wait states.

- HyperTransport combines many benefits of serial and parallel bus architectures.

- HyperTransport has comprehensive legacy support for PCI.

Split Transactions

When split transactions are used, a *request* (which requires a response) and *completion* of that request—the *response*[16]—are separate transactions on the bus. From the standpoint of operations that are performed as split transactions, the link is free after the request is sent and before the response is received. Moreover, depending on a chipset's implementation, multiple transactions could be pending[17] at the same time. It is also easier to route such transactions across larger fabrics.

HyperTransport was designed to work with the widely used PCI bus standard—it is software compatible with PCI, PCI-X, and PCI Express. In fact, it could be viewed as a superset of PCI, since it can offer complete PCI transparency by preserving

---

16. The response may also have data associated with it, as in the case of a read operation.
17. This is analogous to tagged queuing in the SCSI protocol.

PCI definitions and register formats. It can conform to PCI ordering and configuration specifications. It can also use Plug-and-Play so that compliant operating systems can recognize and configure HyperTransport-enabled devices. It is designed to support both CPU-to-CPU communications and CPU-to-I/O transfers, while emphasizing low latency.

A HyperTransport tunnel device can be used to provide connection to other busses such as PCI-X. A system can use additional HyperTransport busses by using an HT-to-HT bridge.

Apple uses HyperTransport in G5-based systems to connect PCI, PCI-X, USB, FireWire, Audio, and Video links. The U3H acts as a North Bridge in this scenario.

System Architecture and Platform

From the standpoint of Mac OS X, we can define a system's *architecture* to be primarily a combination of its processor type, the North Bridge (including the memory controller), and the I/O controller. For example, the AppleMacRISC4PE system architecture consists of one or more G5-based processors, a U3-based North Bridge, and a K2-based I/O controller. The combination of a G3- or G4-based processor, a UniNorth-based host bridge, and a KeyLargo-based I/O controller is referred to as the AppleMacRISC2PE system architecture.

A more model-specific concept is that of a *platform*, which usually depends on the specific motherboard and is likely to change more frequently than system architecture. An example of a platform is PowerMac11,2, which corresponds to a 2.5GHz quad-processor (dual dual-core) Power Mac G5.

3.1.5 Elastic I/O Interconnect

The PowerPC 970 was introduced along with Elastic I/O, a high-bandwidth and high-frequency processor-interconnect (PI) mechanism that requires no bus-level arbitration.[18] Elastic I/O consists of two 32-bit logical busses, each a high-speed source-synchronous bus (SSB) that represents a unidirectional point-to-point connection. As shown in Figure 3–1, one travels from the processor to the U3H companion chip, and the other travels from the U3H to the processor. In a dual-processor system, each processor gets its own dual-SSB bus. Note that the SSBs also support cache-coherency "snooping" protocols for use in multiprocessor systems.

---

18. In colloquial terms, arbitration is the mechanism that answers the question, "Who gets the bus?"

A *synchronous* bus is one that includes a clock signal in its control lines. Its communication protocol functions with respect to the clock. A *source-synchronous* bus uses a timing scheme in which a clock signal is forwarded along with the data, allowing data to be sampled precisely when the clock signal goes high or low.

Whereas the logical width of each SSB is 32 bits, the physical width is greater. Each SSB consists of 50 signal lines that are used as follows:

- 2 signals for the differential bus clock lines
- 44 signals for data, to transmit 35 bits of address and data or control information (AD), along with 1 bit for transfer-handshake (TH) packets for acknowledging such command or data packets received on the bus
- 4 signals for the differential snoop response (SR) bus to carry snoop-coherency responses, allowing global snooping activities to maintain cache coherency

Using 44 physical bits to transmit 36 logical bits of information allows 8 bits to be used for parity. Another supported format for redundant data transmission uses a balanced coding method (BCM) in which there are exactly 22 high signals and 22 low signals if the bus state is valid.

The overall processor interconnect is shown in Figure 3–1 as logically consisting of three inbound segments (ADI, THI, SRI) and three outbound segments (ADO, THO, SRO). The direction of transmission is from a driver side (D), or master, to a receive side (R), or slave. The unit of data transmission is a packet.

Each SSB runs at a frequency that is an integer fraction of the processor frequency. The 970FX design allows several such ratios. For example, Apple's dual-processor 2.7GHz system has an SSB frequency of 1.35GHz (a PI bus ratio of 2:1), whereas one of the single-processor 1.8GHz models has an SSB frequency of 600MHz (a PI bus ratio of 3:1).

The bidirectional nature of the channel between a 970FX processor and the U3H means there are dedicated data paths for reading and writing. Consequently, throughput will be highest in a workload containing an equal number of reads and writes. Conventional bus architectures that are shared and unidirectional-at-a-time will offer higher peak throughput for workloads that are mostly reads or mostly writes. In other words, Elastic I/O leads to higher bus utilization for balanced workloads.

> The Bus Interface Unit (BIU) is capable of self-tuning during startup to ensure optimal signal quality.

3.2 The G5: Lineage and Roadmap

As we saw earlier, the G5 is a derivative of IBM's POWER4 processor. In this section, we will briefly look at how the G5 is similar to and different from the POWER4 and some of the POWER4's successors. This will help us understand the position of the G5 in the POWER/PowerPC roadmap. Table 3–2 provides a high-level summary of some key features of the POWER4 and POWER5 lines.

TABLE 3–2 POWER4 and Newer Processors

	POWER4	POWER4+	POWER5	POWER5+
Year introduced	2001	2002	2004	2005
Lithography	180 nm	130 nm	130 nm	90 nm
Cores/chip	2	2	2	2
Transistors	174 million	184 million	276 million/chip[a]	276 million/chip
Die size	415 mm^2	267 mm^2	389 mm^2/chip	243 mm^2/chip
LPAR[b]	Yes	Yes	Yes	Yes
SMT[c]	No	No	Yes	Yes
Memory controller	Off-chip	Off-chip	On-chip	On-chip
Fast Path	No	No	Yes	Yes
L1 I-cache	2×64KB	2×64KB	2×64KB	2×64KB
L1 D-cache	2×32KB	2×32KB	2×32KB	2×32KB
L2 cache	1.41MB	1.5MB	1.875MB	1.875MB
L3 cache	32MB+	32MB+	36MB+	36MB+

a. A chip includes two processor cores and L2 cache. A multichip module (MCM) contains multiple chips and usually L3 cache. A four-chip POWER5 MCM with four L3 cache modules is 95 mm^2.
b. LPAR stands for (processor-level) Logical Partitioning.
c. SMT stands for simultaneous multithreading.

Transcribing Transistors

In light of the technical specifications of modern processors, it is interesting to see how they compare with some of the most important processors in the history of personal computing.

- **Intel 4004**—1971, 750kHz clock frequency, 2,300 transistors, 4-bit accumulator architecture, 8 μm pMOS, 3×4 mm^2, 8–16 cycles/instruction, designed for a desktop printing calculator
- **Intel 8086**—1978, 8MHz clock frequency, 29,000 transistors, 16-bit extended accumulator architecture, assembly-compatible with the 8080, 20-bit addressing through a segmented addressing scheme
- **Intel 8088**—1979 (prototyped), 8-bit bus version of the 8086, used in the IBM PC in 1981
- **Motorola 68000**—1979, 8MHz clock frequency, 68,000 transistors, 32-bit general-purpose register architecture (with 24 address pins), heavily microcoded (even nanocoded), eight address registers, eight data registers, used in the original Macintosh in 1984

3.2.1 Fundamental Aspects of the G5

All POWER processors listed in Table 3–2, as well as the G5 derivatives, share some fundamental architectural features. They are all *64-bit* and *superscalar*, and they perform *speculative*, *out-of-order* execution. Let us briefly discuss each of these terms.

3.2.1.1 64-bit Processor

Although there is no formal definition of what constitutes a *64-bit* processor, the following attributes are shared by all 64-bit processors:

- 64-bit-wide general-purpose registers
- Support for 64-bit virtual addressing, although the physical or virtual address spaces may not use all 64 bits
- Integer arithmetic and logical operations performed on all 64 bits of a 64-bit operand—without being broken down into, say, two operations on two 32-bit quantities

The PowerPC architecture was designed to support both 32-bit and 64-bit computation modes—an implementation is free to implement only the 32-bit subset.

The G5 supports both computation modes. In fact, the POWER4 supports multiple processor architectures: the 32-bit and 64-bit POWER; the 32-bit and 64-bit PowerPC; and the 64-bit Amazon architecture. We will use the term PowerPC to refer to both the *processor* and the *processor architecture*. We will discuss the 64-bit capabilities of the 970FX in Section 3.3.12.1.

Amazon

The Amazon architecture was defined in 1991 by a group of IBM researchers and developers as they collaborated to create an architecture that could be used for both the RS/6000 and the AS/400. Amazon is a 64-bit-only architecture.

3.2.1.2 Superscalar

If we define *scalar* to be a processor design in which one instruction is issued per clock cycle, then a *superscalar* processor would be one that issues a variable number of instructions per clock cycle, allowing a clock-cycle-per-instruction (CPI) ratio of less than 1. It is important to note that even though a superscalar processor can issue multiple instructions in a clock cycle, it can do so only with several caveats, such as whether the instructions depend on each other and which specific functional units they use. Superscalar processors typically have multiple functional units, including multiple units of the same type.

VLIW

Another type of multiple-issue processor is a *very-large instruction-word* (VLIW) processor, which packages multiple operations into one very long instruction. The compiler—rather than the processor's instruction dispatcher—plays a critical role in selecting which instructions are to be issued simultaneously in a VLIW processor. It may schedule operations by using heuristics, traces, and profiles to guess branch directions.

3.2.1.3 Speculative Execution

A *speculative* processor can execute instructions before it is determined whether those instructions will need to be executed (instructions may not need to be executed because of a branch that bypasses them, for example). Therefore, instruction execution does not wait for *control* dependencies to resolve—it waits only for the instruction's operands (*data*) to become available. Such speculation can be done by the compiler, the processor, or both. The processors in Table 3–2 employ in-hardware dynamic branch prediction (with multiple branches "in flight"), speculation, and dynamic scheduling of instruction groups to achieve substantial instruction-level parallelism.

3.2.1.4 Out-of-Order Execution

A processor that performs *out-of-order execution* includes additional hardware that can bypass instructions whose operands are not available—say, due to a cache miss that occurred during register loading. Thus, rather than always executing instructions in the order they appear in the programs being run, the processor may execute instructions whose operands are ready, deferring the bypassed instructions for execution at a more appropriate time.

3.2.2 New POWER Generations

The POWER4 contains two processor cores in a single chip. Moreover, the POWER4 architecture has features that help in virtualization. Examples include a special hypervisor mode in the processor, the ability to include an address offset when using nonvirtual memory addressing, and support for multiple global interrupt queues in the interrupt controller. IBM's Logical Partitioning (LPAR) allows multiple independent operating system images (such as AIX and Linux) to be run on a single POWER4-based system simultaneously. Dynamic LPAR (DLPAR), introduced in AIX 5L Version 5.2, allows dynamic addition and removal of resources from active partitions.

The POWER4+ improves upon the POWER4 by reducing its size, consuming less power, providing a larger L2 cache, and allowing more DLPAR partitions.

The POWER5 introduces simultaneous multithreading (SMT), wherein a single processor supports multiple instruction streams—in this case, two—simultaneously.

Many Processors . . . Simultaneously

IBM's RS 64 IV, a 64-bit member of the PowerPC family, was the first mainstream processor to support processor-level multithreading (the *processor* holds the states of multiple threads). The RS 64 IV implemented coarse-grained two-way multithreading—a single thread (the foreground thread) executed until a high-latency event, such as a cache miss, occurred. Thereafter, execution switched to the background thread. This was essentially a very fast hardware-based context-switching implementation. Additional hardware resources allowed two threads to have their state in hardware at the same time. Switching between the two states was extremely fast, consuming only three "dead" cycles.

The POWER5 implements two-way SMT, which is far more fine-grained. The processor fetches instructions from two active instruction streams. Each instruction includes a thread indicator. The processor can issue instructions from both streams simultaneously to the various functional units. In fact, an instruction pipeline can simultaneously contain instructions from both streams in its various stages.

A two-way SMT implementation does not provide a factor-of-two performance improvement—the processor effectively behaves as if it were more than one processor, but not quite two processors. Nevertheless, the operating system sees a symmetric-multiprocessing (SMP) programming mode. Typical improvement factors range between 1.2 and 1.3, with a best case of about 1.6. In some pathological cases, the performance could even degrade.

A single POWER5 chip contains two cores, each of which is capable of two-way SMT. A multichip module (MCM) can contain multiple such chips. For example, a four-chip POWER5 module has eight cores. When each core is running in SMT mode, the operating system will see *sixteen* processors. Note that the operating system will be able to utilize the "real" processors first before resorting to SMT.

The POWER5 supports other important features such as the following:

- 64-way multiprocessing.
- Subprocessor partitioning (or *micropartitioning*), wherein multiple LPAR partitions can share a single processor.[19] Micropartitioned LPARs support automatic CPU load balancing.
- *Virtual Inter-partition Ethernet*, which enables a VLAN connection between LPARs—at gigabit or even higher speeds—without requiring physical network interface cards. Virtual Ethernet devices can be defined through the management console. Multiple virtual adapters are supported per partition, depending on the operating system.
- *Virtual I/O Server Partition*,[20] which provides virtual disk storage and Ethernet adapter sharing. Ethernet sharing connects virtual Ethernet to external networks.

---

19. A single processor may be shared by up to 10 partitions, with support for up to 160 partitions total.

20. The Virtual I/O Server Partition must run in either a dedicated partition or a micropartition.

- An on-chip memory controller.

- Dynamic firmware updates.

- Detection and correction of errors in transmitting data courtesy of specialized circuitry.

- *Fast Path*, the ability to execute some common software operations directly within the processor. For example, certain parts of TCP/IP processing that are traditionally handled within the operating system using a sequence of processor instructions could be performed via a single instruction. Such silicon acceleration could be applied to other operating system areas such as message passing and virtual memory.

Besides using 90-nm technology, the POWER5+ adds several features to the POWER5's feature set, for example: 16GB page sizes, 1TB segments, multiple page sizes per segment, a larger (2048-entry) translation lookaside buffer (TLB), and a larger number of memory controller read queues.

The POWER6 is expected to add evolutionary improvements and to extend the Fast Path concept even further, allowing functions of higher-level software—for example, databases and application servers—to be performed in silicon.[21] It is likely to be based on a 65-nm process and is expected to have multiple ultra-high-frequency cores and multiple L2 caches.

3.2.3 The PowerPC 970, 970FX, and 970MP

The PowerPC 970 was introduced in October 2002 as a 64-bit high-performance processor for desktops, entry-level servers, and embedded systems. The 970 can be thought of as a stripped-down POWER4+. Apple used the 970—followed by the 970FX and the 970MP—in its G5-based systems. Table 3–3 contains a brief comparison of the specifications of these processors. Figure 3–3 shows a pictorial comparison. Note that unlike the POWER4+, whose L2 cache is shared between cores, each core in the 970MP has its own L2 cache, which is twice as large as the L2 cache in the 970 or the 970FX.

Another noteworthy point about the 970MP is that both its cores share the same input and output busses. In particular, the output bus is shared "fairly" between cores using a simple round-robin algorithm.

---

21. The "reduced" in RISC becomes not quite reduced!

TABLE 3–3 POWER4+ and the PowerPC 9xx

	POWER4+	PowerPC 970	PowerPC 970FX	PowerPC 970MP
Year introduced	2002	2002	2004	2005
Lithography	130 nm	130 nm	90 nm[a]	90 nm
Cores/chip	2	1	1	2
Transistors	184 million	55 million	58 million	183 million
Die size	267 mm^2	121 mm^2	66 mm^2	154 mm^2
LPAR	Yes	No	No	No
SMT	No	No	No	No
Memory controller	Off-chip	Off-chip	Off-chip	Off-chip
Fast Path	No	No	No	No
L1 I-cache	2×64KB	64KB	64KB	2×64KB
L1 D-cache	2×32KB	32KB	32KB	2×32KB
L2 cache	1.41MB shared[b]	512KB	512KB	2×1MB
L3 cache	32MB+	None	None	None
VMX (AltiVec[c])	No	Yes	Yes	Yes
PowerTune[d]	No	No	Yes	Yes

a. The 970FX and 970MP use 90 nm lithography, in which copper wiring, strained silicon, and silicon-on-insulator (SOI) are fused into the same manufacturing process. This technique accelerates electron flow through transistors and provides an insulating layer in silicon. The result is increased performance, transistor isolation, and lower power consumption. Controlling power dissipation is particularly critical for chips with low process geometries, where subthreshold leakage current can cause problems.

b. The L2 cache is shared between the two processor cores.

c. Although jointly developed by Motorola, Apple, and IBM, AltiVec is a trademark of Motorola, or more precisely, Freescale. In early 2004, Motorola spun out its semiconductor products sector as Freescale Semiconductor, Inc.

d. PowerTune is a clock-frequency and voltage-scaling technology.

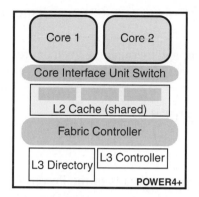

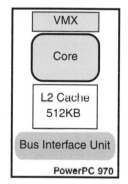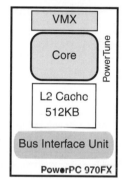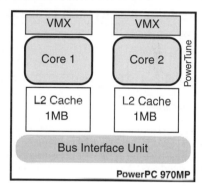

FIGURE 3–3 The PowerPC 9xx family and the POWER4+

3.2.4 The Intel Core Duo

In contrast, the Intel Core Duo processor line used in the first x86-based Macintosh computers (the iMac and the MacBook Pro) has the following key characteristics:

- Two cores per chip
- Manufactured using 65-nm process technology
- 90.3 mm² die size
- 151.6 million transistors
- Up to 2.16GHz frequency (along with a 667MHz processor system bus)
- 32KB on-die I-cache and 32KB on-die D-cache (write-back)
- 2MB on-die L2 cache (shared between the two cores)
- Data prefetch logic

- Streaming SIMD[22] Extensions 2 (SSE2) and Streaming SIMD Extensions 3 (SSE3)
- Sophisticated power and thermal management features

3.3 The PowerPC 970FX

3.3.1 At a Glance

In this section, we will look at details of the PowerPC 970FX. Although several parts of the discussion could apply to other PowerPC processors, we will not attempt to identify such cases. Table 3–4 lists the important technical specifications of the 970FX.

TABLE 3–4 The PowerPC 970FX at a Glance

Feature	Details
Architecture	64-bit PowerPC AS,[a] with support for 32-bit operating system bridge facility
Extensions	Vector/SIMD Multimedia extension (VMX[b])
Processor clock frequency	Up to 2.7GHz[c]
Front-side bus frequency	Integer fraction of processor clock frequency
Data-bus width	128 bits
Address-bus width	42 bits
Maximum addressable physical memory	4TB (2^{42} bytes)
Address translation	65-bit virtual addresses, 42-bit real addresses, support for large (16MB) virtual memory pages, a 1024-entry translation lookaside buffer (TLB), and a 64-entry segment lookaside buffer (SLB)
Endianness	Big-endian; optional little-endian facility *not* implemented
L1 I-cache	64KB, direct-mapped, with parity
L1 D-cache	32KB, two-way set-associative, with parity

(continues)

---

22. Section 3.3.10.1 defines SIMD.

TABLE 3–4 The PowerPC 970FX at a Glance *(Continued)*

Feature	Details
L2 cache	512KB, eight-way set-associative, with ECC, fully inclusive of L1 D-cache
L3 cache	None
Cache line width	128 bytes for all caches
Instruction buffer	32 entries
Instructions/cycle	Up to five (up to four nonbranch + up to one branch)
General-purpose registers	32×64-bit
Floating-point registers	32×64-bit
Vector registers	32×128-bit
Load/Store Units	Two units, with 64-bit data paths
Fixed-Point Units	Two asymmetrical[d] 64-bit units
Floating-Point Units	Two 64-bit units, with support for IEEE-754 double-precision floating-point, hardware fused multiply-add, and square root
Vector units	A 128-bit unit
Condition Register Unit	For performing logical operations on the Condition Register (CR)
Execution pipeline	Ten execution pipelines, with up to 25 stages in a pipeline, and up to 215 instructions in various stages of execution at a time
Power management	Multiple software-initialized power-saving modes, PowerTune frequency and voltage scaling

a. AS stands for Advanced Series.

b. VMX is interchangeable with AltiVec. Apple markets the PowerPC's vector functionality as Velocity Engine.

c. As of 2005.

d. The two fixed-point (integer) units of the 970FX are not symmetrical. Only one of them can perform division, and only one can be used for special-purpose register (SPR) operations.

3.3.2 Caches

A multilevel cache hierarchy is a common aspect of modern processors. A cache can be defined as a small chunk of very fast memory that stores recently used data, instructions, or both. Information is typically added and removed from a cache in aligned quanta called *cache lines*. The 970FX contains several caches and other special-purpose buffers to improve memory performance. Figure 3–4 shows a conceptual diagram of these caches and buffers.

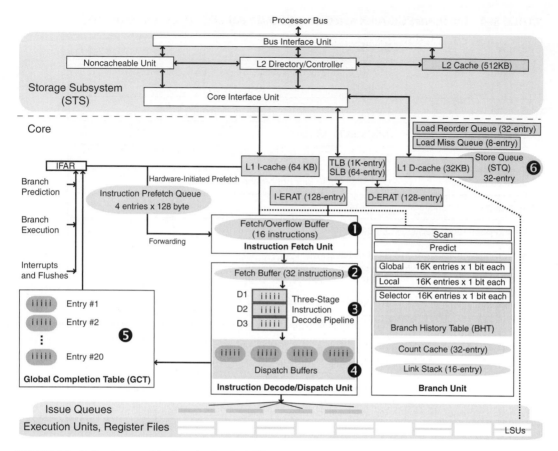

FIGURE 3–4 Caches and buffers in the 970FX

3.3.2.1 L1 and L2 Caches

The level 1 (L1) cache is closest to the processor. Memory-resident information must be loaded into this cache before the processor can use it, unless that portion of memory is marked noncacheable. For example, when a load instruction is being executed, the processor refers to the L1 cache to see if the data in question is already held by a currently resident cache line. If so, the data is simply loaded from the L1 cache—an L1 cache *hit*. This operation takes only a few processor cycles as compared to a few hundred cycles for accessing main memory.[23] If there is an L1 *miss*, the processor checks the next level in the cache hierarchy: the level 2 (L2) cache. An L2 hit would cause the cache line containing the data to be loaded into the

---

23. Main memory refers to the system's installed and available dynamic memory (DRAM).

L1 cache and then into the appropriate register. The 970FX does not have level 3 (L3) caches, but if it did, similar steps would be repeated for the L3 cache. If none of the caches contains the requested data, the processor must access main memory.

As a cache line's worth of data is loaded into L1, a resident cache line must be flushed to make room for the new cache line. The 970FX uses a pseudo-least-recently-used (LRU) algorithm[24] to determine which cache line to evict. Unless instructed otherwise, the evicted cache line is sent to the L2 cache, which makes L2 a *victim* cache. Table 3–5 shows the important properties of the 970FX's caches.

TABLE 3–5 970FX Caches

Property	L1 I-cache	L1 D-cache	L2 Cache
Size	64KB	32KB	512KB
Type	Instructions	Data	Data and instructions
Associativity	Direct-mapped	Two-way set-associative	Eight-way set-associative
Line size	128 bytes	128 bytes	128 bytes
Sector size	32 bytes	—	—
Number of cache lines	512	256	4096
Number of sets	512	128	512
Granularity	1 cache line	1 cache line	1 cache line
Replacement policy	—	LRU	LRU
Store policy	—	Write-through, with no allocate-on-store-miss	Write-back, with allocate-on-store-miss
Index	Effective address	Effective address	Physical address
Tags	Physical address	Physical address	Physical address
Inclusivity	—	—	Inclusive of L1 D-cache
Hardware coherency	No	Yes	Yes, standard MERSI cache-coherency protocol
Enable bit	Yes	Yes	No

(continues)

---

24. The 970FX allows the data-cache replacement algorithm to be changed from LRU to FIFO through a bit in a hardware-dependent register.

TABLE 3–5 970FX Caches *(Continued)*

Property	L1 I-cache	L1 D-cache	L2 Cache
Reliability, availability, and serviceability (RAS)	Parity, with invalidate-on-error for data and tags	Parity, with invalidate-on-error for data and tags	ECC on data, parity on tags
Cache locking	No	No	No
Demand load latencies (typical)	—	3, 5, 4, 5 cycles for GPRs, FPRs, VPERM, and VALU, respectively[a]	11, 12, 11, 11 cycles for GPRs, FPRs, VPERM, and VALU, respectively[a]

a. Section 3.3.6.1 discusses GPRs and FPRs. Section 3.3.10.2 discusses VPERM and VALU.

Harvard Architecture

The 970FX's L1 cache is split into separate caches for instructions and data. This design aspect is referred to as the *Harvard Architecture*, alluding to the separate memories for instructions and data in the Mark-III and Mark-IV vacuum tube machines that originated at Harvard University in the 1940s.

You can retrieve processor cache information using the sysctl command on Mac OS X as shown in Figure 3–5. Note that the hwprefs command is part of Apple's CHUD Tools package.

FIGURE 3–5 Retrieving processor cache information using the sysctl command

```
$ sudo hwprefs machine_type # Power Mac G5 Dual 2.5GHz
PowerMac7,3
$ sysctl -a hw
...
hw.cachelinesize: 128
hw.l1icachesize: 65536
hw.l1dcachesize: 32768
hw.l2settings = 2147483648
hw.l2cachesize: 524288
...
$ sudo hwprefs machine_type # Power Mac G5 Quad 2.5GHz
PowerMac11,2
$ sysctl -a hw
...
hw.cachelinesize = 128
hw.l1icachesize = 65536
hw.l1dcachesize = 32768
hw.l2settings = 2147483648
hw.l2cachesize = 1048576
...
```

3.3.2.2 Cache Properties

Let us look more closely at some of the cache-related terminology used in Table 3–5.

Associativity

As we saw earlier, the granularity of operation for a cache—that is, the unit of memory transfers in and out of a cache—is a cache line (also called a *block*). The cache line size on the 970FX is 128 bytes for both the L1 and L2 caches. The *associativity* of a cache is used to determine where to place a cache line's worth of memory in the cache.

If a cache is *m-way set-associative*, then the total space in the cache is conceptually divided into *sets*, with each set containing *m* cache lines. In a set-associative cache, a block of memory can be placed only in certain locations in the cache: It is first mapped to a set in the cache, after which it can be stored in any of the cache lines within that set. Typically, given a memory block with address B, the target set is calculated using the following modulo operation:

```
target set = B MOD {number of sets in cache}
```

A *direct-mapped* cache is equivalent to a one-way set-associative cache. It has the same number of sets as cache lines. This means a memory block with address B can exist only in one cache line, which is calculated as the following:

```
target cache line = B MOD {number of cache lines in cache}
```

Store Policy

A cache's store policy defines what happens when an instruction writes to memory. In a *write-through* design, such as the 970FX L1 D-cache, information is written to both the cache line and to the corresponding block in memory. There is no L1 D-cache allocation on write misses—the affected block is modified only in the lower level of the cache hierarchy and is not loaded into L1. In a *write-back* design, such as the 970FX L2 cache, information is written only to the cache line—the affected block is written to memory only when the cache line is replaced.

> Memory pages that are contiguous in virtual memory will normally not be contiguous in physical memory. Similarly, given a set of virtual addresses, it is not possible to predict how they will fit in the cache. A related point is that if you take a block of contiguous virtual memory the same size as a cache, say, a 512KB block (the size of the entire L2 cache), there is little chance that it will fit in the L2 cache.

MERSI

Only the L2 cache is physically mapped, although all caches use physical address tags. Stores are always sent to the L2 cache in addition to the L1 cache, as the L2 cache is the data *coherency* point. Coherent memory systems aim to provide the same view of all devices accessing the memory. For example, it must be ensured that processors in a multiprocessor system access the correct data—whether the most up-to-date data resides in main memory or in another processor's cache. Maintaining such coherency in hardware introduces a protocol that requires the processor to "remember" the state of the sharing of cache lines.[25] The L2 cache implements the MERSI cache-coherency protocol, which has the following five states.

1. **M**odified—This cache line is modified with respect to the rest of the memory subsystem.
2. **E**xclusive—This cache line is not cached in any other cache.
3. **R**ecent—The current processor is the most recent reader of this shared cache line.
4. **S**hared—This cache line was cached by multiple processors.
5. **I**nvalid—This cache line is invalid.

RAS

The caches incorporate parity-based error detection and correction mechanisms. *Parity bits* are additional bits used along with normal information to detect and correct errors in the transmission of that information. In the simplest case, a single parity bit is used to detect an error. The basic idea in such parity checking is to add an extra bit to each unit of information—say, to make the number of 1s in each unit either odd or even. Now, if a single error (actually, an odd number of errors) occurs during information transfer, the parity-protected information unit would be invalid. In the 970FX's L1 cache, parity errors are reported as cache misses and therefore are implicitly handled by refetching the cache line from the L2 cache. Besides parity, the L2 cache implements an error detection and correction scheme that can detect double errors and correct single errors by using a *Hamming code*.[26] When a single error is detected during an L2 fetch request, the

---

25. Cache-coherency protocols are primarily either directory-based or snooping-based.

26. A Hamming code is an *error-correcting code*. It is an algorithm in which a sequence of numbers can be expressed such that any errors that appear in certain numbers (say, on the receiving side after the sequence was transmitted by one party to another) can be detected, and corrected, subject to certain limits, based on the remaining numbers.

bad data is corrected and actually written back to the L2 cache. Thereafter, the good data is refetched from the L2 cache.

3.3.3 Memory Management Unit (MMU)

During virtual memory operation, software-visible memory addresses must be *translated* to real (or physical) addresses, both for instruction accesses and for data accesses generated by load/store instructions. The 970FX uses a two-step address translation mechanism[27] based on *segments* and *pages*. In the first step, a software-generated 64-bit *effective address* (EA) is translated to a 65-bit *virtual address* (VA) using the segment table, which lives in memory. *Segment table entries* (STEs) contain *segment descriptors* that define virtual addresses of segments. In the second step, the virtual address is translated to a 42-bit *real address* (RA) using the hashed *page table*, which also lives in memory.

The 32-bit PowerPC architecture provides 16 segment registers through which the 4GB virtual address space can be divided into 16 segments of 256MB each. The 32-bit PowerPC implementations use these segment registers to generate VAs from EAs. The 970FX includes a transitional bridge facility that allows a 32-bit operating system to continue using the 32-bit PowerPC implementation's segment register manipulation instructions. Specifically, the 970FX allows software to associate segments 0 through 15 with any of the 2^{37} available virtual segments. In this case, the first 16 entries of the segment lookaside buffer (SLB), which is discussed next, act as the 16 segment registers.

3.3.3.1 SLB and TLB

We saw that the segment table and the page table are memory-resident. It would be prohibitively expensive if the processor were to go to main memory not only for data fetching but also for address translation. Caching exploits the principle of locality of memory. If caching is effective, then address translations will also have the same locality as memory. The 970FX includes two on-chip buffers for caching recently used segment table entries and page address translations: the *segment lookaside buffer* (SLB) and the *translation lookaside buffer* (TLB), respectively. The SLB is a 64-entry, fully associative cache. The TLB is a 1024-entry,

---

27. The 970FX also supports a real addressing mode, in which physical translation can be effectively disabled.

four-way set-associative cache with parity protection. It also supports large pages (see Section 3.3.3.4).

3.3.3.2 Address Translation

Figure 3–6 depicts address translation in the 970FX MMU, including the roles of the SLB and the TLB. The 970FX MMU uses 64-bit or 32-bit effective addresses, 65-bit virtual addresses, and 42-bit physical addresses. The presence of the DART introduces another address flavor, the I/O address, which is an address in a 32-bit address space that maps to a larger physical address space.

> Technically, a computer architecture has three (and perhaps more) types of memory addresses: the processor-visible *physical address*, the software-visible *virtual address*, and the *bus address*, which is visible to an I/O device. In most cases (especially on 32-bit hardware), the physical and bus addresses are identical and therefore not differentiated.

The 65-bit extended address space is divided into pages. Each page is mapped to a physical page. A 970FX page table can be as large as 2^{31} bytes (2GB), containing up to 2^{24} (16 million) page table entry groups (PTEGs), where each PTEG is 128 bytes.

As Figure 3–6 shows, during address translation, the MMU converts program-visible effective addresses to real addresses in physical memory. It uses a part of the effective address (the effective segment ID) to locate an entry in the segment table. It first checks the SLB to see if it contains the desired STE. If there is an SLB miss, the MMU searches for the STE in the memory-resident segment table. If the STE is still not found, a memory access fault occurs. If the STE is found, a new SLB entry is allocated for it. The STE represents a segment descriptor, which is used to generate the 65-bit virtual address. The virtual address has a 37-bit virtual segment ID (VSID). Note that the page index and the byte offset in the virtual address are the same as in the effective address. The concatenation of the VSID and the page index forms the virtual page number (VPN), which is used for looking up in the TLB. If there is a TLB miss, the memory-resident page table is looked up to retrieve a page table entry (PTE), which contains a real page number (RPN). The RPN, along with the byte offset carried over from the effective address, forms the physical address.

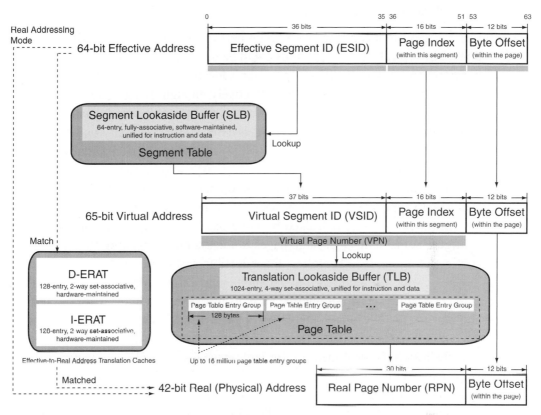

FIGURE 3–6 Address translation in the 970FX MMU

> The 970FX allows setting up the TLB to be direct-mapped by setting a particular bit of a hardware-implementation-dependent register.

3.3.3.3 Caching the Caches: ERATs

Information from the SLB and the TLB may be cached in two *effective-to-real address translation* caches (ERATs)—one for instructions (I-ERAT) and another for data (D-ERAT). Both ERATs are 128-entry, two-way set-associative caches. Each ERAT entry contains effective-to-real address translation information for a 4KB block of storage. Both ERATs contain invalid information upon power-on. As shown in Figure 3–6, the ERATs represent a shortcut path to the physical address when there is a match for the effective address in the ERATs.

3.3.3.4 Large Pages

Large pages are meant for use by high-performance computing (HPC) applications. The typical page size of 4KB could be detrimental to memory performance in certain circumstances. If an application's locality of reference is too wide, 4KB pages may not capture the locality effectively enough. If too many TLB misses occur, the consequent TLB entry allocations and the associated delays would be undesirable. Since a large page represents a much larger memory range, the number of TLB hits should increase, as the TLB would now cache translations for larger virtual memory ranges.

It is an interesting problem for the operating system to make large pages available to applications. Linux provides large-page support through a pseudo file system (*hugetlbfs*) that is backed by large pages. The superuser must explicitly configure some number of large pages in the system by preallocating physically contiguous memory. Thereafter, the hugetlbfs instance can be mounted on a directory, which is required if applications intend to use the mmap() system call to access large pages. An alternative is to use shared memory calls—shmat() and shmget(). Files may be created, deleted, mmap()'ed, and munmap()'ed on hugetlbfs. It does not support reads or writes, however. AIX also requires separate, dedicated physical memory for large-page use. An AIX application can use large pages either via shared memory, as on Linux, or by requesting that the application's data and heap segments be backed by large pages.

Note that whereas the 970FX TLB supports large pages, the ERATs do not; large pages require multiple entries—corresponding to each referenced 4KB block of a large page—in the ERATs. Cache-inhibited accesses to addresses in large pages are not permitted.

3.3.3.5 No Support for Block Address Translation Mechanism

The 970FX does not support the Block Address Translation (BAT) mechanism that is supported in earlier PowerPC processors such as the G4. BAT is a software-controlled array used for mapping large—often much larger than a page—virtual address ranges into contiguous areas of physical memory. The entire map will have the same attributes, including access protection. Thus, the BAT mechanism is meant to reduce address translation overhead for large, contiguous regions of special-purpose virtual address spaces. Since BAT does not use pages, such memory cannot be paged normally. A good example of a scenario where BAT is useful is that of a region of framebuffer memory, which could be memory-mapped effectively via BAT. Software can select block sizes ranging from 128KB to 256MB.

On PowerPC processors that implement BAT, there are four BAT registers each for data (DBATs) and instructions (IBATs). A BAT register is actually a pair of *upper* and *lower* registers, which are accessible from supervisor mode. The eight pairs are named DBAT0U-DBAT3U, DBAT0L-DBAT3L, IBAT0U-IBAT3U, and IBAT0L-IBAT3L. The contents of a BAT register include a block effective page index (BEPI), a block length (BL), and a block real page number (BRPN). During BAT translation, a certain number of high-order bits of the EA—as specified by BL—are matched against each BAT register. If there is a match, the BRPN value is used to yield the RA from the EA. Note that BAT translation is used over page table translation for storage locations that have mappings in both a BAT register and the page table.

3.3.4 Miscellaneous Internal Buffers and Queues

The 970FX contains several miscellaneous buffers and queues internal to the processor, most of which are not visible to software. Examples include the following:

- A 4-entry (128 bytes per entry) Instruction Prefetch Queue logically above the L1 I-cache
- Fetch buffers in the Instruction Fetch Unit and the Instruction Decode Unit
- An 8-entry Load Miss Queue (LMQ) that tracks loads that missed the L1 cache and are waiting to receive data from the processor's storage subsystem
- A 32-entry Store Queue (STQ)[28] for holding stores that can be written to cache or memory later
- A 32-entry Load Reorder Queue (LRQ) in the Load/Store Unit (LSU) that holds physical addresses for tracking the order of loads and watching for hazards
- A 32-entry Store Reorder Queue (SRQ) in the LSU that holds physical addresses and tracks all active stores
- A 32-entry Store Data Queue (SDQ) in the LSU that holds a double word of data
- A 12-entry Prefetch Filter Queue (PFQ) for detecting data streams for prefetching
- An 8-entry (64 bytes per entry) fully associative Store Queue for the L2 cache controller

---

28. The STQ supports forwarding.

3.3.5 Prefetching

Cache miss rates can be reduced through a technique called *prefetching*—that is, fetching information before the processor requests it. The 970FX prefetches instructions and data to hide memory latency. It also supports software-initiated prefetching of up to eight data streams called *hardware streams*, four of which can optionally be vector streams. A stream is defined as a sequence of loads that reference more than one contiguous cache line.

The prefetch engine is a functionality of the Load/Store Unit. It can detect sequential access patterns in ascending or descending order by monitoring loads and recording cache line addresses when there are cache misses. The 970FX does not prefetch store misses.

Let us look at an example of the prefetch engine's operation. Assuming no prefetch streams are active, the prefetch engine will act when there is an L1 D-cache miss. Suppose the miss was for a cache line with address A; then the engine will create an entry in the Prefetch Filter Queue (PFQ)[29] with the address of either the next or the previous cache line—that is, either A + 1 or A − 1. It guesses the direction (up or down) based on whether the memory access was located in the top 25% of the cache line (guesses down) or the bottom 75% of the cache line (guesses up). If there is another L1 D-cache miss, the engine will compare the line address with the entries in the PFQ. If the access is indeed sequential, the line address now being compared must be either A + 1 or A − 1. Alternatively, the engine could have incorrectly guessed the direction, in which case it would create another filter entry for the opposite direction. If the guessed direction was correct (say, up), the engine deems it a sequential access and allocates a stream entry in the Prefetch Request Queue (PRQ)[30] using the next available stream identifier. Moreover, the engine will initiate prefetching for cache line A + 2 to L1 and cache line A + 3 to L2. If A + 2 is read, the engine will cause A + 3 to be fetched to L1 from L2, and A + 4, A + 5, and A + 6 to be fetched to L2. If further sequential demand-reads occur (for A + 3 next), this pattern will continue until all streams are assigned. The PFQ is updated using an LRU algorithm.

The 970FX allows software to manipulate the prefetch mechanism. This is useful if the programmer knows data access patterns ahead of time. A version of the *data-cache-block-touch* (dcbt) instruction, which is one of the storage con-

---

29. The PFQ is a 12-entry queue for detecting data streams for prefetching.

30. The PRQ is a queue of eight streams that will be prefetched.

trol instructions, can be used by a program to provide hints that it intends to read from a specified address or data stream in the near future. Consequently, the processor would initiate a data stream prefetch from a particular address.

Note that if you attempt to access unmapped or protected memory via software-initiated prefetching, no page faults will occur. Moreover, these instructions are not guaranteed to succeed and can fail silently for a variety of reasons. In the case of success, no result is returned in any register—only the cache block is fetched. In the case of failure, no cache block is fetched, and again, no result is returned in any register. In particular, failure does not affect program correctness; it simply means that the program will not benefit from prefetching.

Prefetching continues until a page boundary is reached, at which point the stream will have to be reinitialized. This is so because the prefetch engine does not know about the effective-to-real address mapping and can prefetch only within a real page. This is an example of a situation in which large pages—with page boundaries that are 16MB apart—will fare better than 4KB pages.

On a Mac OS X system with AltiVec hardware, you can use the vec_dst() AltiVec function to initiate data read of a line into cache, as shown in the pseudocode in Figure 3–7.

FIGURE 3–7 Data prefetching in AltiVec

```
while (/* data processing loop */) {

    /* prefetch */
    vec_dst(address + prefetch_lead, control, stream_id);

    /* do some processing */

    /* advance address pointer */
}

/* stop the stream */
vec_dss(stream_id);
```

The address argument to vec_dst() is a pointer to a byte that lies within the first cache line to be fetched; the control argument is a word whose bits specify the block size, the block count, and the distance between the blocks; and the stream_id specifies the stream to use.

3.3.6 Registers

The 970FX has two *privilege modes* of operation: a user mode (*problem state*) and a supervisor mode (*privileged state*). The former is used by user-space applications, whereas the latter is used by the Mac OS X kernel. When the processor is first initialized, it comes up in supervisor mode, after which it can be switched to user mode via the Machine State Register (MSR).

The set of architected registers can be divided into three levels (or models) in the PowerPC architecture:

1. User Instruction Set Architecture (UISA)
2. Virtual Environment Architecture (VEA)
3. Operating Environment Architecture (OEA)

The UISA and VEA registers can be accessed by software through either user-level or supervisor-level privileges, although there are VEA registers that cannot be written to by user-level instructions. OEA registers can be accessed only by supervisor-level instructions.

3.3.6.1 UISA and VEA Registers

Figure 3–8 shows the UISA and VEA registers of the 970FX. Their purpose is summarized in Table 3–6. Note that whereas the general-purpose registers are all 64-bit wide, the set of supervisor-level registers contains both 32-bit and 64-bit registers.

Processor registers are used with all normal instructions that access memory. In fact, there are no computational instructions in the PowerPC architecture that modify storage. For a computational instruction to use a storage operand, it must first load the operand into a register. Similarly, if a computational instruction writes a value to a storage operand, the value must go to the target location via a register. The PowerPC architecture supports the following addressing modes for such instructions.

- *Register Indirect*—The effective address EA is given by (rA | 0).
- *Register Indirect with Immediate Index*—EA is given by (rA | 0) + offset, where offset can be zero.
- *Register Indirect with Index*—EA is given by (rA | 0) + rB.

User Model   UISA

General-Purpose
| GPR0 |
| GPR1 |
| ... |
| GPR31 |

Floating-Point
| FPR0 |
| FPR1 |
| ... |
| FPR31 |

VMX
| VR0 |
| VR1 |
| ... |
| VR31 |

Condition Register
| CR |

Floating-Point Status and Control Register
| FPSCR |

Vector Status and Control Register
| VSCR |

Fixed-Point Exception Register
| XER | SPR1

Vector Save/Restore Register
| VRSAVE | SPR256

Link Register
| LR | SPR8

Count Register
| CTR | SPR9

Performance-Monitoring Registers (read-only)

Performance Counters
| UPMC1 | SPR771
| UPMC2 | SPR772
| UPMC3 | SPR773
| UPMC4 | SPR774
| UPMC5 | SPR775
| UPMC6 | SPR776
| UPMC7 | SPR777
| UPMC8 | SPR778

Monitor Control Registers
| UMMCR0 | SPR779
| UMMCR1 | SPR782
| UMMCRA | SPR770

Sampled Address Registers
| USIAR | SPR780
| USDAR | SPR781

Instruction Match CAM Register
| UIMC | SPR799

Timebase Facility (read-only, read as a 64-bit value)
| TBL | | TBU |
TBR268   TBR269

User Model   VEA

| 32-bit | | 64-bit | | 128-bit |

FIGURE 3–8 PowerPC UISA and VEA registers

TABLE 3–6 UISA and VEA Registers

Name	Width	Count	Notes
General-Purpose Registers (GPRs)	64-bit	32	GPRs are used as source or destination registers for fixed-point operations—e.g., by fixed-point load/store instructions. You also use GPRs while accessing special-purpose registers (SPRs). Note that GPR0 is not hardwired to the value 0, as is the case on several RISC architectures.
Floating-Point Registers (FPRs)	64-bit	32	FPRs are used as source or destination registers for floating-point instructions. You also use FPRs to access the Floating-Point Status and Control Register (FPSCR). An FPR can hold integer, single-precision floating-point, or double-precision floating-point values.
Vector Registers (VRs)	128-bit	32	VRs are used as vector source or destination registers for vector instructions.
Integer Exception Register (XER)	32-bit	1	The XER is used to indicate carry conditions and overflows for integer operations. It is also used to specify the number of bytes to be transferred by a *load-string-word-indexed* (`lswx`) or *store-string-word-indexed* (`stswx`) instruction.
Floating-Point Status and Control Register (FPSCR)	32-bit	1	The FPSCR is used to record floating-point exceptions and the result type of a floating-point operation. It is also used to toggle the reporting of floating-point exceptions and to control the floating-point rounding mode.
Vector Status and Control Register (VSCR)	32-bit	1	Only two bits of the VSCR are defined: the saturate (SAT) bit and the non-Java mode (NJ) bit. The SAT bit indicates that a vector saturating-type instruction generated a saturated result. The NJ bit, if cleared, enables a Java-IEEE-C9X-compliant mode for vector floating-point operations that handles denormalized values in accordance with these standards. When the NJ bit is set, a potentially faster mode is selected, in which the value 0 is used in place of denormalized values in source or result vectors.
Condition Register (CR)	32-bit	1	The CR is conceptually divided into eight 4-bit fields (CR0–CR7). These fields store results of certain fixed-point and floating-point operations. Some branch instructions can test individual CR bits.
Vector Save/Restore Register (VRSAVE)	32-bit	1	The VRSAVE is used by software while saving and restoring VRs across context-switching events. Each bit of the VRSAVE corresponds to a VR and specifies whether that VR is in use or not.

(continues)

TABLE 3–6 UISA and VEA Registers *(Continued)*

Name	Width	Count	Notes
Link Register (LR)	64-bit	1	The LR can be used to return from a subroutine—it holds the return address after a branch instruction if the link (LK) bit in that branch instruction's encoding is 1. It is also used to hold the target address for the *branch-conditional-to-Link-Register* (bclrx) instruction. Some instructions can automatically load the LR to the instruction following the branch.
Count Register (CTR)	64-bit	1	The CTR can be used to hold a loop count that is decremented during execution of branch instructions. The *branch-conditional-to-Count-Register* (bcctrx) instruction branches to the target address held in this register.
Timebase Registers (TBL, TBU)	32-bit	2	The Timebase (TB) Register, which is the concatenation of the 32-bit TBU and TBL registers, contains a periodically incrementing 64-bit unsigned integer.

> rA and rB represent register contents. The notation (rA | 0) means the contents of register rA unless rA is GPR0, in which case (rA | 0) is taken to be the value 0.

The UISA-level performance-monitoring registers provide user-level read access to the 970FX's performance-monitoring facility. They can be written only by a supervisor-level program such as the kernel or a kernel extension.

> Apple's Computer Hardware Understanding Development (CHUD) is a suite of programs (the "CHUD Tools") for measuring and optimizing performance on Mac OS X. The software in the CHUD Tools package makes use of the processor's performance-monitoring counters.

The Timebase Register

The Timebase (TB) provides a long-period counter driven by an implementation-dependent frequency. The TB is a 64-bit register containing an unsigned 64-bit integer that is incremented periodically. Each increment adds 1 to bit 63 (the lowest-order bit) of the TB. The maximum value that the TB can hold is $2^{64} - 1$, after which it resets to zero without generating any exception. The TB can either be incremented at a frequency that is a function of the processor clock frequency, or it can be driven by the rising edge of the signal on the TB enable (TBEN) input pin.[31] In the former case, the 970FX increments the TB once every eight full frequency processor clocks. It is the operating system's responsibility to initialize the TB. The TB can be read—but not written to—from user space. The program shown in Figure 3–9 retrieves and prints the TB.

FIGURE 3–9 Retrieving and displaying the Timebase Register

```
// timebase.c

#include <stdio.h>
#include <stdlib.h>
#include <sys/types.h>

u_int64_t mftb64(void);
void mftb32(u_int32_t *, u_int32_t *);

int
main(void)
{
    u_int64_t tb64;
    u_int32_t tb32u, tb32l;

    tb64 = mftb64();
    mftb32(&tb32u, &tb32l);

    printf("%llx %x%08x\n", tb64, tb32l, tb32u);
    exit(0);
}

// Requires a 64-bit processor
// The TBR can be read in a single instruction (TBU || TBL)
u_int64_t
mftb64(void)
{
    u_int64_t tb64;

    __asm("mftb %0\n\t"
          : "=r" (tb64)
          :
    );

    return tb64;
}
```

(continues)

---

31. In this case, the TB frequency may change at any time.

FIGURE 3–9 Retrieving and displaying the Timebase Register *(continued)*

```
// 32-bit or 64-bit
void
mftb32(u_int32_t *u, u_int32_t *l)
{
    u_int32_t tmp;

    __asm(
    "loop:              \n\t"
        "mftbu    %0    \n\t"
        "mftb     %1    \n\t"
        "mftbu    %2    \n\t"
        "cmpw     %2,%0 \n\t"
        "bne      loop  \n\t"
        : "=r"(*u), "=r"(*l), "=r"(tmp)
        :
    );
}
```

```
$ gcc -Wall -o timebase timebase.c
$ ./timebase; ./timebase; ./timebase; ./timebase; ./timebase
b6d10de300000001 b6d10de4000002d3
b6d4db7100000001 b6d4db72000002d3
b6d795f700000001 b6d795f8000002d3
b6da5a3000000001 b6da5a31000002d3
b6dd538c00000001 b6dd538d000002d3
```

Note in Figure 3–9 that we use inline assembly rather than create a separate
assembly source file. The GNU assembler inline syntax is based on the template
shown in Figure 3–10.

FIGURE 3–10 Code template for inline assembly in the GNU assembler

```
__asm__ volatile(
        "assembly statement 1\n"
        "assembly statement 2\n"
        ...
        "assembly statement N\n"
    :   outputs, if any
    :   inputs, if any
    :   clobbered registers, if any
);
```

We will come across other examples of inline assembly in this book.

Viewing Register Contents: The Mac OS X Way

The contents of the TBR, along with those of several configuration registers, memory management registers, performance-monitoring registers, and miscellaneous registers can be viewed using the Reggie SE graphical application (`Reggie SE.app`), which is part of the CHUD Tools package. Reggie SE can also display physical memory contents and details of PCI devices.

3.3.6.2 OEA Registers

The OEA registers are shown in Figure 3–11. Examples of their use include the following.

- The bit-fields of the *Machine State Register* (MSR) are used to define the processor's state. For example, MSR bits are used to specify the processor's computation mode (32-bit or 64-bit), to enable or disable power management, to determine whether the processor is in *privileged* (supervisor) or *nonprivileged* (user) mode, to enable single-step tracing, and to enable or disable address translation. The MSR can be explicitly accessed via the *move-to-MSR* (`mtmsr`), *move-to-MSR-double* (`mtmsrd`), and *move-from-MSR* (`mfmsr`) instructions. It is also modified by the *system-call* (`sc`) and *return-from-interrupt-double* (`rfid`) instructions.

- The *Hardware-Implementation-Dependent* (HID) registers allow very fine-grained control of the processor's features. Bit-fields in the various HID registers can be used to enable, disable, or alter the behavior of processor features such as branch prediction mode, data prefetching, instruction cache, and instruction prefetch mode and also to specify which data cache replacement algorithm to use (LRU or first-in first-out [FIFO]), whether the Timebase is externally clocked, and whether large pages are disabled.

- The *Storage Description Register* (SDR1) is used to hold the page table base address.

3.3.7 Rename Registers

The 970FX implements a substantial number of *rename registers*, which are used to handle register-name dependencies. Instructions can depend on one another from the point of view of *control*, *data*, or *name*. Consider two instructions, say, `I1` and `I2`, in a program, where `I2` comes after `I1`.

```
                                                          User Model   UISA
      ...
      ...                                                 User Model   VEA

                          Configuration Registers

Hardware-Implementation-Dependent Registers        Processor Version Register
 HID0    SPR1008     HID4    SPR1012                 PVR     SPR287
 HID1    SPR1009     HID5    SPR1014                Machine State Register
                                                    MSR

                     Memory Management Registers

Address Space Register                             Storage Description Register
 ASR          SPR280                                SDR1         SPR25

                     Exception-Handling Registers

Special-Purpose Registers    Data Address Register    Save and Restore Registers
 SPRG0    SPR272             DAR         SPR19         SRR0         SPR26
 SPRG1    SPR273                                       SRR1         SPR27
 SPRG2    SPR274
 SPRG3    SPR275     Data Storage Interrupt Status Register
                     DSISR   SPR18

                        Miscellaneous Registers

Scan Communications     Trigger Registers         Timebase Facility (writing)
 SCOMC    SPR276         TRIG0      SPR976          TBL    SPR284
 SCOMD    SPR277         TRIG1      SPR977          TBU    SPR285
Data Address Breakpoint  TRIG2      SPR978
 DABR     SPR1013                                 Decrementer
 DABRX    SPR1015                                  DEC    SPR22

Hardware Interrupt Offset   IMC Array Address      Processor Identification Register
 HIOR        SPR311         UIMC       SPR783       PIR    SPR1023

                    Performance-Monitoring Registers

Performance Counters     Monitor Control
 PMC1   SPR787           MMCR0      SPR795
 PMC2   SPR788           MMCR1      SPR798
 PMC3   SPR789           MMCRA      SPR786
 PMC4   SPR790
 PMC5   SPR791           Sampled Address Registers
 PMC6   SPR792           SIAR       SPR796
 PMC7   SPR793           SDAR       SPR797
 PMC8   SPR794
                                      Supervisor Model   OEA

  32-bit              64-bit                    128-bit
```

FIGURE 3–11 PowerPC OEA registers

```
I1
...
Ix
...
I2
```

In a data dependency, I2 either uses a result produced by I1, or I2 has a data dependency on an instruction Ix, which in turn has a data dependency on I1. In both cases, a value is effectively transmitted from I1 to I2.

In a name dependency, I1 and I2 use the same logical resource or *name*, such as a register or a memory location. In particular, if I2 writes to the same register that is either read from or written to by I1, then I2 would have to wait for I1 to execute before it can execute. These are known as *write-after-read* (WAR) and *write-after-write* (WAW) hazards.

```
I1 reads (or writes) <REGISTER X>
...
I2 writes <REGISTER X>
```

In this case, the dependency is not "real" in that I2 does not *need* I1's result. One solution to handle register-name dependencies is to *rename* the conflicting register used in the instructions so that they become independent. Such renaming could be done in software (statically, by the compiler) or in hardware (dynamically, by logic in the processor). The 970FX uses pools of physical *rename registers* that are assigned to instructions during the *mapping* stage in the processor pipeline and released when they are no longer needed. In other words, the processor internally renames *architected* registers used by instructions to *physical* registers. This makes sense only when the number of physical registers is (substantially) larger than the number of architected registers. For example, the PowerPC architecture has 32 GPRs, but the 970FX implementation has a pool of 80 physical GPRs, from which the 32 architected GPRs are assigned. Let us consider a specific example, say, of a WAW hazard, where renaming is helpful.

```
; before renaming
r20 ← r21 + r22 ; r20 is written to
...
r20 ← r23 + r24 ; r20 is written to... WAW hazard here
r25 ← r20 + r26 ; r20 is read from

; after renaming
r20 ← r21 + r22 ; r20 is written to
...
r64 ← r23 + 424 ; r20 is renamed to r64... no WAW hazard now
r25 ← r64 + r26 ; r20 is renamed to r64
```

Renaming is also beneficial to speculative execution, since the processor can use the extra physical registers to reduce the amount of architected register state it must save to recover from incorrectly speculated execution.

Table 3–7 lists the available renamed registers in the 970FX. The table also mentions *emulation* registers, which are available to cracked and microcoded instructions, which, as we will see in Section 3.3.9.1, are processes by which complex instructions are broken down into simpler instructions.

TABLE 3–7 Rename Register Resources

Resource	Architected (Logical Resource)	Emulation (Logical Resource)	Rename Pool (Physical Resource)
GPRs	32×64-bit	4×64-bit	80×64-bit.
VRSAVE	1×32-bit	—	Shared with the GPR rename pool.
FPRs	32×64-bit	1×64-bit	80×64-bit.
FPSCR	1×32-bit	—	One rename per active instruction group using a 20-entry buffer.
LR	1×64-bit	—	16×64-bit.
CTR	1×64-bit	—	LR and CTR share the same rename pool.
CR	8×4-bit	1×4-bit	32×4-bit.
XER	1×32-bit	—	24×2-bit. Only two bits—the overflow bit OV and the carry bit CA—are renamed from a pool of 24 2-bit registers.
VRs	32×128-bit	—	80×128-bit.
VSCR	1×32-bit	—	20×1-bit. Of the VSCR's two defined bits, only the SAT bit is renamed from a pool of 20 1-bit registers.

3.3.8 Instruction Set

All PowerPC instructions are 32 bits wide regardless of whether the processor is in 32-bit or 64-bit computation mode. All instructions are *word aligned*, which means that the two lowest-order bits of an instruction address are irrelevant from the processor's standpoint. There are several instruction formats, but bits 0 through 5 of an instruction word always specify the *major opcode*. PowerPC instructions typically have three operands: two source operands and one result.

One of the source operands may be a constant or a register, but the other operands are usually registers.

We can broadly divide the instruction set implemented by the 970FX into the following instruction categories: fixed-point, floating-point, vector, control flow, and everything else.

3.3.8.1 Fixed-Point Instructions

Operands of fixed-point instructions can be bytes (8-bit), half words (16-bit), words (32-bit), or double words (64-bit). This category includes the following instruction types:

- Fixed-point load and store instructions for moving values between the GPRs and storage
- Fixed-point *load-multiple-word* (lmw) and *store-multiple-word* (stmw), which can be used for restoring or saving up to 32 GPRs in a single instruction
- Fixed-point *load-string-word-immediate* (lswi), *load-string-word-indexed* (lswx), *store-string-word-immediate* (stswi), and *store-string-word-indexed* (stswx), which can be used to fetch and store fixed- and variable-length strings, with arbitrary alignments
- Fixed-point arithmetic instructions, such as *add, divide, multiply, negate,* and *subtract*
- Fixed-point compare instructions, such as *compare-algebraic, compare-algebraic-immediate, compare-algebraic-logical,* and *compare-algebraic-logical-immediate*
- Fixed-point logical instructions, such as *and, and-with-complement, equivalent, or, or-with-complement, nor, xor, sign-extend,* and *count-leading-zeros* (cntlzw and variants)
- Fixed-point rotate and shift instructions, such as *rotate, rotate-and-mask, shift-left,* and *shift-right*
- Fixed-point *move-to-system-register* (mtspr), *move-from-system-register* (mfspr), *move-to-MSR* (mtmsr), and *move-from-MSR* (mfmsr), which allow GPRs to be used to access system registers

> Most load/store instructions can optionally update the base register with the effective address of the data operated on by the instruction.

3.3.8.2 Floating-Point Instructions

Floating-point operands can be single-precision (32-bit) or double-precision (64-bit) floating-point quantities. However, floating-point data is always stored in the FPRs in double-precision format. Loading a single-precision value from storage converts it to double precision, and storing a single-precision value to storage actually rounds the FPR-resident double-precision value to single precision. The 970FX complies with the IEEE 754 standard[32] for floating-point arithmetic. This instruction category includes the following types:

- Floating-point load and store instructions for moving values between the FPRs and storage
- Floating-point comparison instructions
- Floating-point arithmetic instructions, such as *add*, *divide*, *multiply*, *multiply-add*, *multiply-subtract*, *negative-multiply-add*, *negative-multiply-subtract*, *negate*, *square-root*, and *subtract*
- Instructions for manipulating the FPSCR, such as *move-to-FPSCR*, *move-from-FPSCR*, *set-FPSCR-bit*, *clear-FPSCR-bit*, and *copy-FPSCR-field-to-CR*
- PowerPC optional floating-point instructions, namely: *floating-square-root* (`fsqrt`), *floating-square-root-single* (`fsqrts`), *floating-reciprocal-estimate-single* (`fres`), *floating-reciprocal-square-root-estimate* (`frsqrte`), and *floating-point-select* (`fsel`)

> The precision of floating-point-estimate instructions (`fres` and `frsqrte`) is less on the 970FX than on the G4. Although the 970FX is at least as accurate as the IEEE 754 standard requires, the G4 is more accurate than required. Figure 3–12 shows a program that can be executed on a G4 and a G5 to illustrate this difference.

3.3.8.3 Vector Instructions

Vector instructions execute in the 128-bit VMX execution unit. We will look at some of the VMX details in Section 3.3.10. The 970FX VMX implementation contains 162 vector instructions in various categories.

---

32. The IEEE 754 standard governs binary floating-point arithmetic. The standard's primary architect was William Velvel Kahan, who received the Turing Award in 1989 for his fundamental contributions to numerical analysis.

FIGURE 3–12 Precision of the floating-point-estimate instruction on the G4 and the G5

```
// frsqrte.c

#include <stdio.h>
#include <stdlib.h>

double
frsqrte(double n)
{
    double s;

    asm(
        "frsqrte %0, %1"
        : "=f" (s)   /* out */
        : "f"  (n)   /* in */
    );

    return s;
}

int
main(int argc, char **argv)
{
    printf("%8.8f\n", frsqrte(strtod(argv[1], NULL)));
    return 0;
}

$ machine
ppc7450
$ gcc -Wall -o frsqrte frsqrte.c
$ ./frsqrte 0.5
1.39062500

$ machine
ppc970
$ gcc -Wall -o frsqrte frsqrte.c
$ ./frsqrte 0.5
1.37500000
```

3.3.8.4 Control-Flow Instructions

A program's control flow is sequential—that is, its instructions logically execute in the order they appear—until a control-flow change occurs either explicitly (because of an instruction that modifies the control flow of a program) or as a side effect of another event. The following are examples of control-flow changes:

- An explicit *branch* instruction, after which execution continues at the target address specified by the branch

- An *exception*, which could represent an error, a signal external to the processor core, or an unusual condition that sets a status bit but may or may not cause an *interrupt*[33]

- A *trap*, which is an interrupt caused by a trap instruction

- A *system call*, which is a form of software-only interrupt caused by the *system-call* (sc) instruction

Each of these events could have *handlers*—pieces of code that handle them. For example, a trap handler may be executed when the conditions specified in the trap instruction are satisfied. When a user-space program executes an sc instruction with a valid system call identifier, a function in the operating system kernel is invoked to provide the service corresponding to that system call. Similarly, control flow also changes when the program is returning from such handlers. For example, after a system call finishes in the kernel, execution continues in user space—in a different piece of code.

The 970FX supports *absolute* and *relative* branching. A branch could be *conditional* or *unconditional*. A conditional branch can be based on any of the bits in the CR being 1 or 0. We earlier came across the special-purpose registers LR and CTR. LR can hold the return address on a procedure call. A leaf procedure—one that does not call another procedure—does not need to save LR and therefore can return faster. CTR is used for loops with a fixed iteration limit. It can be used to branch based on its contents—the *loop counter*—being zero or nonzero, while decrementing the counter automatically. LR and CTR are also used to hold target addresses of conditional branches for use with the bclr and bcctr instructions, respectively.

> Besides performing aggressive dynamic branch prediction, the 970FX allows *hints* to be provided along with many types of branch instructions to improve branch prediction accuracy.

3.3.8.5 Miscellaneous Instructions

The 970FX includes various other types of instructions, many of which are used by the operating system for low-level manipulation of the processor. Examples include the following types:

---

33. When machine state changes in response to an exception, an interrupt is said to have occurred.

- Instructions for processor management, including direct manipulation of some SPRs

- Instructions for controlling caches, such as for touching, zeroing, and flushing a cache; requesting a store; and requesting a prefetch stream to be initiated—for example: *instruction-cache-block-invalidate* (icbi), *data-cache-block-touch* (dcbt), *data-cache-block-touch-for-store* (dcbtst), *data-cache-block-set-to-zero* (dcbz), *data-cache-block-store* (dcbst), and *data-cache-block-flush* (dcbf)

- Instructions for loading and storing conditionally, such as *load-word-and-reserve-indexed* (lwarx), *load-double-word-and-reserve-indexed* (ldarx), *store-word-conditional-indexed* (stwcx.), and *store-double-word-conditional-indexed* (stdcx.)

> The lwarx (or ldarx) instruction performs a load and sets a reservation bit internal to the processor. This bit is hidden from the programming model. The corresponding store instruction—stwcx. (or stdcx.)—performs a conditional store if the reservation bit is set and clears the reservation bit.

- Instructions for memory synchronization,[34] such as *enforce-in-order-execution-of-i/o* (eieio), *synchronize* (sync), and special forms of sync (lwsync and ptesync)

- Instructions for manipulating SLB and TLB entries, such as *slb-invalidate-all* (slbia), *slb-invalidate-entry* (slbie), *tlb-invalidate-entry* (tlbie), and *tlb-synchronize* (tlbsync)

3.3.9 The 970FX Core

The 970FX core is depicted in Figure 3–13. We have come across several of the core's major components earlier in this chapter, such as the L1 caches, the ERATs, the TLB, the SLB, register files, and register-renaming resources.

The 970FX core is designed to achieve a high degree of instruction parallelism. Some of its noteworthy features include the following.

---

34. During memory synchronization, bit 2 of the CR—the EQ bit—is set to record the successful completion of a store operation.

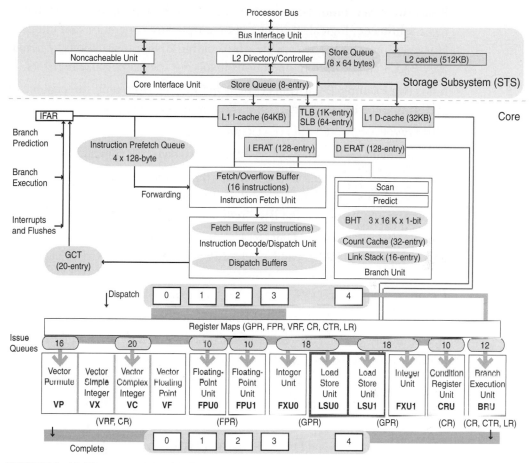

FIGURE 3–13 The core of the 970FX

- It has a highly superscalar 64-bit design, with support for the 32-bit operating-system-bridge[35] facility.
- It performs dynamic "cracking" of certain instructions into two or more simpler instructions.
- It performs highly speculative execution of instructions along with aggressive branch prediction and dynamic instruction scheduling.
- It has twelve logically separate functional units and ten execution pipelines.

---

35. The "bridge" refers to a set of optional features defined to simplify the migration of 32-bit operating systems to 64-bit implementations.

- It has two Fixed-Point Units (FXU0 and FXU1). Both units are capable of basic arithmetic, logical, shifting, and multiplicative operations on integers. However, only FXU0 is capable of executing divide instructions, whereas only FXU1 can be used in operations involving special purpose registers.

- It has two Floating-Point Units (FPU0 and FPU1). Both units are capable of performing the full supported set of floating-point operations.

- It has two Load/Store Units (LSU0 and LSU1).

- It has a Condition Register Unit (CRU) that executes CR logical instructions.

- It has a Branch Execution Unit (BRU) that computes branch address and branch direction. The latter is compared with the predicted direction. If the prediction was incorrect, the BRU redirects instruction fetching.

- It has a Vector Processing Unit (VPU) with two subunits: a Vector Arithmetic and Logical Unit (VALU) and a Vector Permute Unit (VPERM). The VALU has three subunits of its own: a Vector Simple-Integer[36] Unit (VX), a Vector Complex-Integer Unit (VC), and a Vector Floating-Point Unit (VF).

- It can perform 64-bit integer or floating-point operations in one clock cycle.

- It has deeply pipelined execution units, with pipeline depths of up to 25 stages.

- It has reordering issue queues that allow for out-of-order execution.

- Up to 8 instructions can be fetched in each cycle from the L1 instruction cache.

- Up to 8 instructions can be issued in each cycle.

- Up to 5 instructions can complete in each cycle.

- Up to 215 instructions can be *in flight*—that is, in various stages of execution (partially executed)—at any time.

> The processor uses a large number of its resources such as reorder queues, rename register pools, and other logic to track in-flight instructions and their dependencies.

---

36. Simple integers (non-floating-point) are also referred to as fixed-point. The "X" in "VX" indicates "fixed."

3.3.9.1 Instruction Pipeline

In this section, we will discuss how the 970FX processes instructions. The overall instruction pipeline is shown in Figure 3–14. Let us look at the important stages of this pipeline.

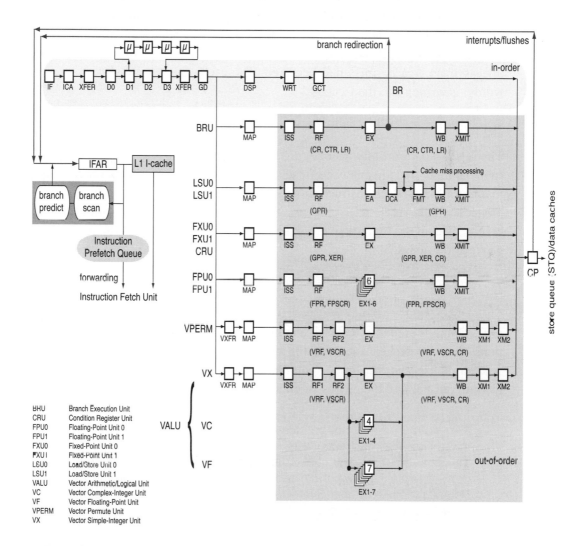

FIGURE 3–14 The 970FX instruction pipeline

IFAR, ICA[37]

Based on the address in the Instruction Fetch Address Register (IFAR), the instruction-fetch-logic fetches eight instructions every cycle from the L1 I-cache into a 32-entry instruction buffer. The eight-instruction block, so fetched, is 32-byte aligned. Besides performing IFAR-based demand fetching, the 970FX prefetches cache lines into a 4×128-byte Instruction Prefetch Queue. If a demand fetch results in an I-cache miss, the 970FX checks whether the instructions are in the prefetch queue. If the instructions are found, they are inserted into the pipeline as if no I-cache miss had occurred. The cache line's critical sector (eight words) is written into the I-cache.

D0

There is logic to partially decode (predecode) instructions after they leave the L2 cache and before they enter the I-cache or the prefetch queue. This process adds five extra bits to each instruction to yield a 37-bit instruction. An instruction's predecode bits mark it as illegal, microcoded, conditional or unconditional branch, and so on. In particular, the bits also specify how the instruction is to be grouped for dispatching.

D1, D2, D3

The 970FX splits complex instructions into two or more internal operations, or *iops*. The iops are more RISC-like than the instructions they are part of. Instructions that are broken into exactly two iops are called *cracked* instructions, whereas those that are broken into three or more iops are called *microcoded* instructions because the processor emulates them using microcode.

> An instruction may not be atomic because the atomicity of cracked or microcoded instructions is at the iop level. Moreover, it is the iops, and not programmer-visible instructions, that are executed out-of-order. This approach allows the processor more flexibility in parallelizing execution. Note that AltiVec instructions are neither cracked nor microcoded.

Fetched instructions go to a 32-instruction fetch buffer. Every cycle, up to five instructions are taken from this buffer and sent through a decode pipeline that

---

37. Instruction Cache Access.

is either *inline* (consisting of three stages, namely, D1, D2, and D3), or *template-based* if the instruction needs to be microcoded. The template-based decode pipeline generates up to four iops per cycle that emulate the original instruction. In any case, the decode pipeline leads to the formation of an instruction *dispatch group*.

Given the out-of-order execution of instructions, the processor needs to keep track of the program order of all instructions in various stages of execution. Rather than tracking individual instructions, the 970FX tracks instructions in dispatch groups. The 970FX forms such groups containing one to five iops, each occupying an instruction slot (0 through 4) in the group. Dispatch group formation[38] is subject to a long list of rules and conditions such as the following.

- The iops in a group must be in program order, with the oldest instruction being in slot 0.
- A group may contain up to four nonbranch instructions and optionally a branch instruction. When a branch is encountered, it is the last instruction in the current group, and a new group is started.
- Slot 4 can contain only branch instructions. In fact, *no-op* (no-operation) instructions may have to be inserted in the other slots to force a branch instruction to fall in slot 4.
- An instruction that is a branch target is always at the start of a group.
- A cracked instruction takes two slots in a group.
- A microcoded instruction takes an entire group by itself.
- An instruction that modifies an SPR with no associated rename register terminates a group.
- No more than two instructions that modify the CR may be in a group.

XFER

The iops wait for resources to become free in the XFER stage.

GD, DSP, WRT, GCT, MAP

After group formation, the execution pipeline divides into multiple pipelines for the various execution units. Every cycle, one group of instructions can be sent (or dispatched) to the issue queues. Note that instructions in a group remain together from dispatch to completion.

---

38. The instruction grouping performed by the 970FX has similarities to a VLIW processor.

As a group is dispatched, several operations occur before the instructions actually execute. Internal group instruction dependencies are determined (GD). Various internal resources are assigned, such as issue queue slots, rename registers and mappers, and entries in the load/store reorder queues. In particular, each iop in the group that returns a result must be assigned a register to hold the result. Rename registers are allocated in the dispatch phase before the instructions enter the issue queues (DSP, MAP).

To track the groups themselves, the 970FX uses a *global completion table* (GCT) that stores up to 20 entries in program order—that is, up to 20 dispatch groups can be in flight concurrently. Since each group can have up to 5 iops, as many as 100 iops can be tracked in this manner. The WRT stage represents the writes to the GCT.

ISS, RF

After all the resources that are required to execute the instructions are available, the instructions are sent (ISS) to appropriate issue queues. Once their operands appear, the instructions start to execute. Each slot in a group feeds separate issue queues for various execution units. For example, the FXU/LSU and the FPU draw their instructions from slots { 0, 3 } and { 1, 2 }, respectively, of an instruction group. If one pair goes to the FXU/LSU, the other pair goes to the FPU. The CRU draws its instructions from the CR logical issue queue that is fed from instruction slots 0 and 1. As we saw earlier, slot 4 of an instruction group is dedicated to branch instructions. AltiVec instructions can be issued to the VALU and the VPERM issue queues from any slot except slot 4. Table 3–8 shows the 970FX issue queue sizes—each execution unit listed has one issue queue.

The FXU/LSU and FPU issue queues have odd and even halves that are hardwired to receive instructions only from certain slots of a dispatch group, as shown in Figure 3–15.

As long as an issue queue contains instructions that have all their data dependencies resolved, an instruction moves every cycle from the queue into the appropriate execution unit. However, there are likely to be instructions whose operands are not ready; such instructions block in the queue. Although the 970FX will attempt to execute the oldest instruction first, it will reorder instructions within a queue's context to avoid stalling. Ready-to-execute instructions access their source operands by reading the corresponding register file (RF), after which they enter the execution unit pipelines. Up to ten operations can be issued in a cycle—one to each of the ten execution pipelines. Note that different execution units may have varying numbers of pipeline stages.

TABLE 3–8 Sizes of the Various 970FX Issue Queues

Execution Unit	Queue Size (Instructions)
LSU0/FXU0[a]	18
LSU1/FXU1[b]	18
FPU0	10
FPU1	10
BRU	12
CRU	10
VALU	20
VPERM	16

a. LSU0 and FXU0 share an 18-entry issue queue.
b. LSU1 and FXU1 share an 18-entry issue queue.

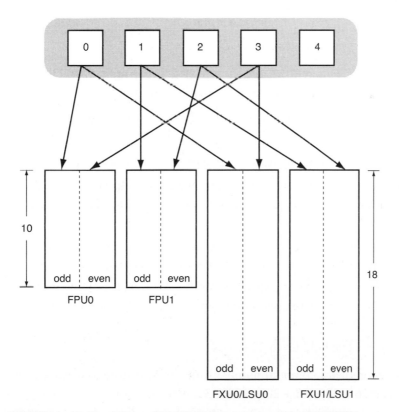

FIGURE 3–15 The FPU and FXU/LSU issue queues in the 970FX

We have seen that instructions both issue and execute out of order. However, if an instruction has finished execution, it does not mean that the program will "know" about it. After all, from the program's standpoint, instructions must execute in program order. The 970FX differentiates between an instruction finishing execution and an instruction *completing*. An instruction may finish execution (speculatively, say), but unless it completes, its effect is not visible to the program. All pipelines terminate in a common stage: the group completion stage (CP). When groups complete, many of their resources are released, such as load reorder queue entries, mappers, and global completion table entries. One dispatch group may be "retired" per cycle.

> When a branch instruction completes, the resultant target address is compared with a predicted address. Depending on whether the prediction is correct or incorrect, either all instructions in the pipeline that were fetched after the branch in question are flushed, or the processor waits for all remaining instructions in the branch's group to complete.

Accounting for 215 In-Flight Instructions

We can account for the theoretical maximum of 215 in-flight instructions by looking at Figure 3–4—specifically, the areas marked 1 through 6.

1. The Instruction Fetch Unit has a fetch/overflow buffer that can hold 16 instructions.

2. The instruction fetch buffer in the decode/dispatch unit can hold 32 instructions.

3. Every cycle, up to 5 instructions are taken from the instruction fetch buffer and sent through a three-stage instruction decode pipeline. Therefore, up to 15 instructions can be in this pipeline.

4. There are four dispatch buffers, each holding a dispatch group of up to five operations. Therefore, up to 20 instructions can be held in these buffers.

5. The global completion table can track up to 20 dispatch groups after they have been dispatched, corresponding to up to 100 instructions in the 970FX core.

6. The store queue can hold up to 32 stores.

Thus, the theoretical maximum number of in-flight instructions can be calculated as the sum $16 + 32 + 15 + 20 + 100 + 32$, which is 215.

3.3.9.2 Branch Prediction

Branch prediction is a mechanism wherein the processor attempts to keep the pipeline full, and therefore improve overall performance, by fetching instructions in the hope that they will be executed. In this context, a branch is a decision point for the processor: It must predict the outcome of the branch—whether it will be *taken* or not—and accordingly prefetch instructions. As shown in Figure 3–14, the 970FX scans fetched instructions for branches. It looks for up to two branches per cycle and uses multistrategy branch prediction logic to predict their target addresses, directions, or both. Consequently, up to 2 branches are predicted per cycle, and up to 16 predicted branches can be in flight.

All conditional branches are predicted, based on whether the 970FX fetches instructions beyond a branch and speculatively executes them. Once the branch instruction itself executes in the BRU, its actual outcome is compared with its predicted outcome. If the prediction was incorrect, there is a severe penalty: Any instructions that may have speculatively executed are discarded, and instructions in the correct control-flow path are fetched.

The 970FX's dynamic branch prediction hardware includes three branch history tables (BHTs), a link stack, and a count cache. Each BHT has 16K 1-bit entries.

> The 970FX's hardware branch prediction can be overridden by software.

The first BHT is the *local predictor table*. Its 16K entries are indexed by branch instruction addresses. Each 1-bit entry indicates whether the branch should be taken or not. This scheme is "local" because each branch is tracked in isolation.

The second BHT is the *global predictor table*. It is used by a prediction scheme that takes into account the execution path taken to reach the branch. An 11-bit vector—the *global history vector*—represents the execution path. The bits of this vector represent the previous 11 instruction groups fetched. A particular bit is 1 if the next group was fetched sequentially and is 0 otherwise. A given branch's entry in the global predictor table is at a location calculated by performing an XOR operation between the global history vector and the branch instruction address.

The third BHT is the *selector table*. It tracks which of the two prediction schemes is to be favored for a given branch. The BHTs are kept up to date with the actual outcomes of executed branch instructions.

The link stack and the count cache are used by the 970FX to predict branch target addresses of *branch-conditional-to-link-register* (bclr, bclrl) and *branch-conditional-to-count-register* (bcctr, bcctrl) instructions, respectively.

So far, we have looked at *dynamic* branch prediction. The 970FX also supports static prediction wherein the programmer can use certain bits in a conditional branch operand to statically override dynamic prediction. Specifically, two bits called the "a" and "t" bits are used to provide hints regarding the branch's direction, as shown in Table 3–9.

TABLE 3–9 Static Branch Prediction Hints

"a" Bit	"t" Bit	Hint
0	0	Dynamic branch prediction is used.
0	1	Dynamic branch prediction is used.
1	0	Dynamic branch prediction is disabled; static prediction is "not taken"; specified by a "-" suffix to a branch conditional mnemonic.
1	1	Dynamic branch prediction is disabled; static prediction is "taken"; specified by a "+" suffix to a branch conditional mnemonic.

3.3.9.3 Summary

Let us summarize the instruction parallelism achieved by the 970FX. In every cycle of the 970FX, the following events occur.

- Up to eight instructions are fetched.
- Up to two branches are predicted.
- Up to five iops (one group) are dispatched.
- Up to five iops are renamed.
- Up to ten iops are issued from the issue queues.
- Up to five iops are completed.

3.3.10 AltiVec

The 970FX includes a dedicated vector-processing unit and implements the VMX instruction set, which is an AltiVec[39] interchangeable extension to the PowerPC architecture. AltiVec provides a SIMD-style 128-bit[40] vector-processing unit.

---

39. AltiVec was first introduced in Motorola's e600 PowerPC core—the G4.

40. All AltiVec execution units and data paths are 128 bits wide.

3.3.10.1 *Vector Computing*

SIMD stands for *single-instruction, multiple-data*. It refers to a set of operations that can efficiently handle large quantities of data in parallel. SIMD operations do not necessarily require more or wider registers, although more *is* better. SIMD essentially better uses registers and data paths. For example, a non-SIMD computation would typically use a hardware register for each data element, even if the register could hold multiple such elements. In contrast, SIMD would use a register to hold multiple data elements—as many as would fit—and would perform the *same operation on all elements* through a *single instruction*. Thus, any operation that can be parallelized in this manner stands to benefit from SIMD. In AltiVec's case, a vector instruction can perform the same operation on all constituents of a vector. Note that AltiVec instructions work on fixed-length vectors.

> SIMD-based optimization does not come for free. A problem must lend itself well to vectorization, and the programmer must usually perform extra work. Some compilers—such as IBM's XL suite of compilers and GCC 4.0 or above—also support auto-vectorization, an optimization that auto-generates vector instructions based on the compiler's analysis of the source code.[41] Auto-vectorization may or may not work well depending on the nature and structure of the code.

Several processor architectures have similar extensions. Table 3–10 lists some well-known examples.

AltiVec can greatly improve the performance of data movement, benefiting applications that do processing of vectors, matrices, arrays, signals, and so on. As we saw in Chapter 2, Apple provides portable APIs—through the Accelerate framework (`Accelerate.framework`)—for performing vector-optimized operations.[42] Accelerate is an umbrella framework that contains the vecLib and vImage[43] subframeworks. vecLib is targeted for performing numerical and scientific computing—it

---

41. For example, the compiler may attempt to detect patterns of code that are known to be well suited for vectorization.

42.   The Accelerate framework automatically uses the best available code that it implements, depending on the hardware it is running on. For example, it will use vectorized code for AltiVec if AltiVec is available. On the x86 platform, it will use MMX, SSE, SSE2, and SSE3 if these features are available.

43.   vImage is also available as a stand-alone framework.

TABLE 3–10 Examples of Processor Multimedia-Extensions

Processor Family	Manufacturers	Multimedia Extension Sets
Alpha	Hewlett-Packard (Digital Equipment Corporation)	MVI
AMD	Advanced Micro Devices (AMD)	3DNow!
MIPS	Silicon Graphics Incorporated (SGI)	MDMX, MIPS-3D
PA-RISC	Hewlett-Packard	MAX, MAX2
PowerPC	IBM, Motorola	VMX/AltiVec
SPARC V9	Sun Microsystems	VIS
x86	Intel, AMD, Cyrix	MMX, SSE, SSE2, SSE3

provides functionality such as BLAS, LAPACK, digital signal processing, dot products, linear algebra, and matrix operations. vImage provides vector-optimized APIs for working with image data. For example, it provides functions for alpha compositing, convolutions, format conversion, geometric transformations, histograms operations, and morphological operations.

> Although a vector instruction performs work that would typically require many times more nonvector instructions, vector instructions are not simply instructions that deal with "many scalars" or "more memory" at a time. The fact that a vector's members are related is critical, and so is the fact that the same operation is performed on all members. Vector operations certainly play better with memory accesses—they lead to *amortization*. The semantic difference between performing a vector operation and a sequence of scalar operations on the same data set is that you are implicitly providing more information to the processor about your intentions. Vector operations—by their nature—alleviate both data and control hazards.

AltiVec has wide-ranging applications since areas such as high-fidelity audio, video, videoconferencing, graphics, medical imaging, handwriting analysis, data encryption, speech recognition, image processing, and communications all use algorithms that can benefit from vector processing.

Figure 3–16 shows a trivial AltiVec C program.

As also shown in Figure 3–16, the `-faltivec` option to GCC enables AltiVec language extensions.

FIGURE 3–16 A trivial AltiVec program

```
// altivec.c

#include <stdio.h>
#include <stdlib.h>

int
main(void)
{
    // "vector" is an AltiVec keyword
    vector float v1, v2, v3;

    v1 = (vector float)(1.0, 2.0, 3.0, 4.0);
    v2 = (vector float)(2.0, 3.0, 4.0, 5.0);

    // vec_add() is a compiler built-in function
    v3 = vec_add(v1, v2);

    // "%vf" is a vector-formatting string for printf()
    printf("%vf\n", v3);

    exit(0);
}

$ gcc -Wall -faltivec -o altivec altivec.c
$ ./altivec
3.000000 5.000000 7.000000 9.000000
```

3.3.10.2 The 970FX AltiVec Implementation

The 970FX AltiVec implementation consists of the following components:

- A vector register file (VRF) consisting of 32 128-bit architected vector registers (VR0–VR31)

- 48 128-bit rename registers for allocation in the dispatch phase

- A 32-bit Vector Status and Control Register (VSCR)

- A 32-bit Vector Save/Restore Register (VRSAVE)

- A Vector Permute Unit (VPERM) that benefits the implementation of operations such as arbitrary byte-wise data organization, table lookups, and packing/unpacking of data

- A Vector Arithmetic and Logical Unit (VALU) that contains three parallel subunits: the Vector Simple-Integer Unit (VX), the Vector Complex-Integer Unit (VC), and the Vector Floating-Point Unit (VF)

The CR is also modified as a result of certain vector instructions.

> The VALU and the VPERM are both dispatchable units that receive predecoded instructions via the issue queues.

The 32-bit VRSAVE serves a special purpose: Each of its bits indicates whether the corresponding vector register is in use or not. The processor maintains this register so that it does not have to save and restore every vector register every time there is an exception or a context switch. Frequently saving or restoring 32 128-bit registers, which together constitute 512 bytes, would be severely detrimental to cache performance, as other, perhaps more critical data would need to be evicted from cache.

Let us extend our example program from Figure 3–16 to examine the value in the VRSAVE. Figure 3–17 shows the extended program.

FIGURE 3–17 Displaying the contents of the VRSAVE

```
// vrsave.c

#include <stdio.h>
#include <stdlib.h>
#include <sys/types.h>

void prbits(u_int32_t);
u_int32_t read_vrsave(void);

// Print the bits of a 32-bit number
void
prbits32(u_int32_t u)
{
    u_int32_t i = 32;

    for (; i--; putchar(u & 1 << i ? '1' : '0'));

    printf("\n");
}

// Retrieve the contents of the VRSAVE
u_int32_t
read_vrsave(void)
{
    u_int32_t v;
```

(continues)

FIGURE 3–17 Displaying the contents of the VRSAVE *(continued)*

```
    __asm("mfspr %0,VRsave\n\t"
        : "=r"(v)
        :
    );

    return v;
}

int
main()
{
    vector float v1, v2, v3;

    v1 = (vector float)(1.0, 2.0, 3.0, 4.0);
    v2 = (vector float)(2.0, 3.0, 4.0, 5.0);

    v3 = vec_add(v1, v2);

    prbits32(read_vrsave());

    exit(0);
}


$ gcc -Wall -faltivec -o vrsave vrsave.c
$ ./vrsave
11000000000000000000000000000000
```

We see in Figure 3–17 that two high-order bits of the VRSAVE are set and the rest are cleared. This means the program uses two VRs: VR0 and VR1. You can verify this by looking at the assembly listing for the program.

The VPERM execution unit can do merge, permute, and splat operations on vectors. Having a separate permute unit allows data-reorganization instructions to proceed in parallel with vector arithmetic and logical instructions. The VPERM and VALU both maintain *their own copies of the VRF* that are synchronized on the half cycle. Thus, each receives its operands from its own VRF. Note that vector loads, stores, and data stream instructions are handled in the usual LSU pipes. Although no AltiVec instructions are cracked or microcoded, vector store instructions logically break down into two components: a vector part and an LSU part. In the group formation stage, a vector store is a single entity occupying one slot. However, once the instruction is issued, it occupies two issue queue slots: one in the vector store unit and another in the LSU. Address generation takes place in the LSU. There is a slot for moving the data out of the VRF in the vector unit.

This is not any different from scalar (integer and floating-point) stores, in whose case address generation still takes place in the LSU, and the respective execution unit—integer or floating-point—is used for accessing the GPR file (GPRF) or the FPR file (FPRF).

AltiVec instructions were designed to be pipelined easily. The 970FX can dispatch up to four vector instructions every cycle—regardless of type—to the issue queues. Any vector instruction can be dispatched from any slot of the dispatch group except the dedicated branch slot 4.

> It is usually very inefficient to pass data between the scalar units and the vector unit because data transfer between register files is not direct but goes through the caches.

3.3.10.3 AltiVec Instructions

AltiVec adds 162 vector instructions to the PowerPC architecture. Like all other PowerPC instructions, AltiVec instructions have 32-bit-wide encodings. To use AltiVec, no context switching is required. There is no special AltiVec operating mode—AltiVec instructions can be used along with regular PowerPC instructions in a program. AltiVec also does not interfere with floating-point registers.

> AltiVec instructions should be used at the UISA and VEA levels of the PowerPC architecture but not at the OEA level (the kernel). The same holds for floating-point arithmetic. Nevertheless, it is possible to use AltiVec and floating-point in the Mac OS X kernel beginning with a revision of Mac OS X 10.3. However, doing so would be at the cost of performance overhead in the kernel, since using AltiVec or floating-point will lead to a larger number of exceptions and register save/restore operations. Moreover, AltiVec data stream instructions cannot be used in the kernel. High-speed video scrolling on the system console is an example of the Floating-Point Unit being used by the kernel—the scrolling routines use floating-point registers for fast copying. The audio subsystem also uses floating-point in the kernel.

The following points are noteworthy regarding AltiVec vectors.

- A vector is 128 bits wide.
- A vector can be comprised of one of the following: 16 bytes, 8 half words, 4 words (integers), or 4 single-precision floating-point numbers.

- The largest vector element size is hardware-limited to 32 bits; the largest adder in the VALU is 32 bits wide. Moreover, the largest multiplier array is 24 bits wide, which is good enough for only a single-precision floating-point mantissa.[44]

- A given vector's members can be all unsigned or all signed quantities.

- The VALU behaves as multiple ALUs based on the vector element size.

Instructions in the AltiVec instruction set can be broadly classified into the following categories:

- Vector load and store instructions

- Instructions for reading from or writing to the VSCR

- Data stream manipulation instructions, such as *data-stream-touch* (dst), *data-stream-stop* (dss), and *data-stream-stop-all* (dssall)

- Vector fixed-point arithmetic and comparison instructions

- Vector logical, rotate, and shift instructions

- Vector pack, unpack, merge, splat, and permute instructions

- Vector floating-point instructions

> Vector single-element loads are implemented as lvx, with undefined fields not zeroed explicitly. Care should be taken while dealing with such cases as this could lead to denormals[45] in floating-point calculations.

3.3.11 Power Management

The 970FX supports power management features such as the following.

- It can dynamically stop the clocks of some of its constituents when they are idle.

- It can be programmatically put into predefined power-saving modes such as *doze*, *nap*, and *deep nap*.

---

44. The IEEE 754 standard defines the 32 bits of a single-precision floating-point number to consist of a sign (1 bit), an exponent (8 bits), and a mantissa (23 bits).

45. Denormal numbers—also called subnormal numbers—are numbers that are so small they cannot be represented with full precision.

- It includes *PowerTune*, a processor-level power management technology that supports scaling of processor and bus clock frequencies and voltage.

3.3.11.1 *PowerTune*

PowerTune allows clock frequencies to be dynamically controlled and even synchronized across multiple processors. PowerTune frequency scaling occurs in the processor core, the busses, the bridge, and the memory controller. Allowed frequencies range from f—the full nominal frequency—to $f/2$, $f/4$, and $f/64$. The latter corresponds to the deep nap power-saving mode. If an application does not require the processor's maximum available performance, frequency and voltage can be changed system-wide—without stopping the core execution units and without disabling interrupts or bus snooping. All processor logic, except the bus clocks, remains active. Moreover, the frequency change is very rapid. Since power has a quadratic dependency on voltage, reducing voltage has a desirable effect on power dissipation. Consequently, the 970FX has much lower typical power consumption than the 970, which did not have PowerTune.

3.3.11.2 *Power Mac G5 Thermal and Power Management*

In the Power Mac G5, Apple combines the power management capabilities of the 970FX/970MP with a network of fans and sensors to contain heat generation, power consumption, and noise levels. Examples of hardware sensors include those for fan speed, temperature, current, and voltage. The system is divided into discrete cooling zones with independently controlled fans. Some Power Mac G5 models additionally contain a liquid cooling system that circulates a thermally conductive fluid to transfer heat away from the processors into a radiant grille. As air passes over the grille's cooling fins, the fluid's temperature decreases.[46]

The Liquid in Liquid Cooling

The heat transfer fluid used in the liquid cooling system consists of mostly water mixed with antifreeze. A deionized form of water called DI water is used. The low concentration of ions in such water prevents mineral deposits and electric arcing, which may occur because the circulating coolant can cause static charge to build up.

---

46. Similar to how an automobile radiator works.

Operating system support is required to make the Power Mac G5's thermal management work properly. Mac OS X regularly monitors various temperatures and power consumption. It also communicates with the fan control unit (FCU). If the FCU does not receive feedback from the operating system, it will spin the fans at maximum speed.

A liquid-cooled dual-processor 2.5GHz Power Mac has the following fans:

- CPU A PUMP
- CPU A INTAKE
- CPU A EXHAUST
- CPU B PUMP
- CPU B INTAKE
- CPU B EXHAUST
- BACKSIDE
- DRIVE BAY
- SLOT

Additionally, the Power Mac has sensors for current, voltage, and temperature, as listed in Table 3–11.

TABLE 3–11 Power Mac G5 Sensors: An Example

Sensor Type	Sensor Location/Name
Ammeter	CPU A AD7417[a] AD2
Ammeter	CPU A AD7417 AD4
Ammeter	CPU B AD7417 AD2
Ammeter	CPU B AD7417 AD4
Switch	Power Button
Thermometer	BACKSIDE
Thermometer	U3 HEATSINK
Thermometer	DRIVE BAY
Thermometer	CPU A AD7417 AMB

(continues)

TABLE 3–11 Power Mac G5 Sensors: An Example *(Continued)*

Sensor Type	Sensor Location/Name
Thermometer	CPU A AD7417 AD1
Thermometer	CPU B AD7417 AMB
Thermometer	CPU B AD7417 AD1
Thermometer	MLB INLET AMB
Voltmeter	CPU A AD7417 AD3
Voltmeter	CPU B AD7417 AD3

a. The AD7417 is a type of analog-to-digital converter with an on-chip temperature sensor.

We will see in Chapter 10 how to programmatically retrieve the values of various sensors from the kernel.

3.3.12 64-bit Architecture

We saw earlier that the PowerPC architecture was designed with explicit support for 64- and 32-bit computing. PowerPC is, in fact, a 64-bit architecture with a 32-bit subset. A particular PowerPC implementation may choose to implement only the 32-bit subset, as is the case with the G3 and G4 processor families used by Apple. The 970FX implements both the 64-bit and 32-bit forms[47]—*dynamic computation modes*[48]—of the PowerPC architecture. The modes are dynamic in that you can switch between the two dynamically by setting or clearing bit 0 of the MSR.

3.3.12.1 64-bit Features

The key aspects of the 970FX's 64-bit mode are as follows:

- 64-bit registers:[49] the GPRs, CTR, LR, and XER
- 64-bit addressing, including 64-bit pointers, which allow one program's address space to be larger than 4GB
- 32-bit and 64-bit programs, which can execute side by side

---

47. A 64-bit PowerPC implementation must implement the 32-bit subset.

48. The computation mode encompasses addressing mode.

49. Several registers are defined to be 32-bit in the 64-bit PowerPC architecture, such as CR, FP-SCR, VRSAVE, and VSCR.

- 64-bit integer and logical operations, with fewer instructions required to load and store 64-bit quantities[50]
- Fixed instruction size—32 bits—in both 32- and 64-bit modes
- 64-bit-only instructions such as *load-word-algebraic* (`lwa`), *load-word-algebraic-indexed* (`lwax`), and "double-word" versions of several instructions

Although a Mac OS X process must be 64-bit itself to be able to directly access more than 4GB of virtual memory, having support in the processor for more than 4GB of physical memory benefits both 64-bit and 32-bit applications. After all, physical memory *backs* virtual memory. Recall that the 970FX can track a large amount of physical memory—42 bits worth, or 4TB. Therefore, as long as there is enough RAM, much greater amounts of it can be kept "alive" than is possible with only 32 bits of physical addressing. This is beneficial to 32-bit applications because the operating system can now keep more working sets in RAM, reducing the number of page-outs—even though a single 32-bit application will still "see" only a 4GB address space.

3.3.12.2 *The 970FX as a 32-bit Processor*

Just as the 64-bit PowerPC is not an extension of the 32-bit PowerPC, the latter is not a performance-limited version of the former—there is no penalty for executing in 32-bit-only mode on the 970FX. There are, however, some differences. Important aspects of running the 970FX in 32-bit mode include the following.

- The sizes of the floating-point and AltiVec registers are the same across 32-bit and 64-bit implementations. For example, an FPR is 64 bits wide and a VR is 128 bits wide on both the G4 and the G5.
- The 970FX uses the same resources—registers, execution units, data paths, caches, and busses—in 64- and 32-bit modes.
- Fixed point logical, rotate, and shift instructions behave the same in both modes.
- Fixed-point arithmetic instructions (except the negate instruction) actually produce the same result in 64- and 32-bit modes. However, the carry (CA)

---

50. One way to use 64-bit integers on a 32-bit processor is to have the programming language maintain 64-bit integers as two 32-bit integers. Doing so would consume more registers and would require more load/store instructions.

and overflow (OV) fields of the XER register are set in a 32-bit-compatible way in 32-bit mode.

- Load/store instructions ignore the upper 32 bits of an effective address in 32-bit mode. Similarly, branch instructions deal with only the lower 32 bits of an effective address in 32-bit mode.

3.3.13 Softpatch Facility

The 970FX provides a facility called *softpatch*, which is a mechanism that allows software to work around bugs in the processor core and to otherwise debug the core. This is achieved either by replacing an instruction with a substitute micro-coded instruction sequence or by making an instruction cause a trap to software through a softpatch exception.

The 970FX's Instruction Fetch Unit contains a seven-entry array with content-addressable memory (CAM). This array is called the Instruction Match CAM (IMC). Additionally, the 970FX's instruction decode unit contains a microcode *softpatch table*. The IMC array has eight rows. The first six IMC entries occupy one row each, whereas the seventh entry occupies two rows. Of the seven entries, the first six are used to match partially (17 bits) over an instruction's major opcode (bits 0 through 5) and extended opcode (bits 21 through 31). The seventh entry matches in its entirety: a 32-bit full instruction match. As instructions are fetched from storage, they are matched against the IMC entries by the Instruction Fetch Unit's matching facility. If matched, the instruction's processing can be altered based on other information in the matched entry. For example, the instruction can be replaced with microcode from the instruction decode unit's softpatch table.

The 970FX provides various other tracing and performance-monitoring facilities that are beyond the scope of this chapter.

3.4 Software Conventions

An application binary interface (ABI) defines a system interface for compiled programs, allowing compilers, linkers, debuggers, executables, libraries, other object files, and the operating system to work with each other. In a simplistic sense, an ABI is a low-level, "binary" API. A program conforming to an API *should* be compilable from source on different systems supporting that API, whereas a binary executable conforming to an ABI *should* operate on different systems supporting that ABI.[51]

An ABI usually includes a set of rules specifying how hardware and software resources are to be used for a given architecture. Besides interoperability, the conventions laid down by an ABI may have performance-related goals too, such as minimizing average subroutine-call overhead, branch latencies, and memory accesses. The scope of an ABI could be extensive, covering a wide variety of areas such as the following:

- Byte ordering (endianness)
- Alignment and padding
- Register usage
- Stack usage
- Subroutine parameter passing and value returning
- Subroutine prologues and epilogues
- System calls
- Object files
- Dynamic code generation
- Program loading and dynamic linking

The PowerPC version of Mac OS X uses the Darwin PowerPC ABI in its 32-bit and 64-bit versions, whereas the 32-bit x86 version uses the System V IA-32 ABI. The Darwin PowerPC ABI is similar to—but not the same as—the popular IBM AIX ABI for the PowerPC. In this section, we look at some aspects of the Darwin PowerPC ABI without analyzing its differences from the AIX ABI.

3.4.1 Byte Ordering

The PowerPC architecture natively supports 8-bit (byte), 16-bit (half word), 32-bit (word), and 64-bit (double word) data types. It uses a flat-address-space model with byte-addressable storage. Although the PowerPC architecture provides an optional little-endian facility, the 970FX does not implement it—it implements only the big-endian addressing mode. Big-endian refers to storing the "big" end of a multibyte value at the lowest memory address. In the PowerPC

---

51. ABIs vary in whether they strictly enforce cross-operating-system compatibility or not.

architecture, the leftmost bit—bit 0—is defined to be the *most significant bit*, whereas the rightmost bit is the *least significant bit*. For example, if a 64-bit register is being used as a 32-bit register in 32-bit computation mode, then bits 32 through 63 of the 64-bit register represent the 32-bit register; bits 0 through 31 are to be ignored. By corollary, the leftmost byte—byte 0—is the most significant byte, and so on.

> In PowerPC implementations that support both the big-endian and little-endian[52] addressing modes, the LE bit of the Machine State Register can be set to 1 to specify little-endian mode. Another bit— the ILE bit—is used to specify the mode for exception handlers. The default value of both bits is 0 (big-endian) on such processors.

3.4.2 Register Usage

The Darwin ABI defines a register to be dedicated, volatile, or nonvolatile. A *dedicated* register has a predefined or standard purpose; it should not be arbitrarily modified by the compiler. A *volatile* register is available for use at all times, but its contents may change if the context changes—for example, because of calling a subroutine. Since the caller must save volatile registers in such cases, such registers are also called *caller-save* registers. A *nonvolatile* register is available for use in a local context, but the user of such registers must save their original contents before use and must restore the contents before returning to the calling context. Therefore, it is the *callee*—and not the caller—who must save nonvolatile registers. Correspondingly, such registers are also called *callee-save* registers.

> In some cases, a register may be available for general use in one runtime environment but may have a special purpose in some other runtime environment. For example, GPR12 has a predefined purpose on Mac OS X when used for indirect function calls.

Table 3–12 lists common PowerPC registers along with their usage conventions as defined by the 32-bit Darwin ABI.

---

52. The use of little-endian mode on such processors is subject to several caveats as compared to big-endian mode. For example, certain instructions—such as load/store multiple and load/store string—are not supported in little-endian mode.

TABLE 3–12 Register Conventions in the 32-bit Darwin PowerPC ABI

Register(s)	Volatility	Purpose/Comments
GPR0	Volatile	Cannot be a base register.
GPR1	Dedicated	Used as the stack pointer to allow access to parameters and other temporary data.
GPR2	Volatile	Available on Darwin as a local register but used as the Table of Contents (TOC) pointer in the AIX ABI. Darwin does not use the TOC.
GPR3	Volatile	Contains the first argument word when calling a subroutine; contains the first word of a subroutine's return value. Objective-C uses GPR3 to pass a pointer to the object being messaged (i.e., "self") as an implicit parameter.
GPR4	Volatile	Contains the second argument word when calling a subroutine; contains the second word of a subroutine's return value. Objective-C uses GPR4 to pass the method selector as an implicit parameter.
GPR5–GPR10	Volatile	GPRn contains the $(n-2)$th argument word when calling a subroutine.
GPR11	Varies	In the case of a nested function, used by the caller to pass its stack frame to the nested function—register is nonvolatile. In the case of a leaf function, the register is available and is volatile.
GPR12	Volatile	Used in an optimization for dynamic code generation, wherein a routine that branches indirectly to another routine must store the target of the call in GPR12. No special purpose for a routine that has been called directly.
GPR13–GPR29	Nonvolatile	Available for general use. Note that GPR13 is reserved for thread-specific storage in the 64-bit Darwin PowerPC ABI.
GPR30	Nonvolatile	Used as the frame pointer register—i.e., as the base register for access to a subroutine's local variables.
GPR31	Nonvolatile	Used as the PIC-offset table register.
FPR0	Volatile	Scratch register.
FPR1–FPR4	Volatile	FPRn contains the nth floating-point argument when calling a subroutine; FPR1 contains the subroutine's single-precision floating-point return value; a double-precision floating-point value is returned in FPR1 and FPR2.
FPR5–FPR13	Volatile	FPRn contains the nth floating-point argument when calling a subroutine.
FPR14–FPR31	Nonvolatile	Available for general use.
CR0	Volatile	Used for holding condition codes during arithmetic operations.
CR1	Volatile	Used for holding condition codes during floating-point operations.
CR2–CR4	Nonvolatile	Various condition codes.

(continues)

TABLE 3–12 Register Conventions in the 32-bit Darwin PowerPC ABI *(Continued)*

Register(s)	Volatility	Purpose/Comments
CR5	Volatile	Various condition codes.
CR6	Volatile	Various condition codes; can be used by AltiVec.
CR7	Volatile	Various condition codes.
CTR	Volatile	Contains a branch target address (for the `bcctr` instruction); contains counter value for a loop.
FPSCR	Volatile	Floating-Point Status and Control Register.
LR	Volatile	Contains a branch target address (for the `bclr` instruction); contains subroutine return address.
XER	Volatile	Fixed-point exception register.
VR0, VR1	Volatile	Scratch registers.
VR2	Volatile	Contains the first vector argument when calling a subroutine; contains the vector returned by a subroutine.
VR3–VR19	Volatile	VRn contains the $(n-1)$th vector argument when calling a subroutine.
VR20–VR31	Nonvolatile	Available for general use.
VRSAVE	Nonvolatile	If bit n of the VRSAVE is set, then VRn must be saved during any kind of a context switch.
VSCR	Volatile	Vector Status and Control Register.

3.4.2.1 Indirect Calls

We noted in Table 3–12 that a function that branches indirectly to another function stores the target of the call in GPR12. Indirect calls are, in fact, the default scenario for dynamically compiled Mac OS X user-level code. Since the target address would need to be stored in a register in any case, using a standardized register allows for potential optimizations. Consider the code fragment shown in Figure 3–18.

FIGURE 3–18 A simple C function that calls another function

```
void
f1(void)
{
    f2();
}
```

By default, the assembly code generated by GCC on Mac OS X for the function shown in Figure 3–18 will be similar to that shown in Figure 3–19, which has been annotated and trimmed down to relevant parts. In particular, note the use of GPR12, which is referred to as r12 in the GNU assembler syntax.

FIGURE 3–19 Assembly code depicting an indirect function call

```
...
_f1:
        mflr r0            ; prologue
        stmw r30,-8(r1)    ; prologue
        stw r0,8(r1)       ; prologue
        stwu r1,-80(r1)    ; prologue
        mr r30,r1          ; prologue
        bl L_f2$stub       ; indirect call
        lwz r1,0(r1)       ; epilogue
        lwz r0,8(r1)       ; epilogue
        mtlr r0            ; epilogue
        lmw r30,-8(r1)     ; epilogue
        blr                ; epilogue
...
L_f2$stub:
        .indirect_symbol _f2
        mflr r0
        bcl 20,31,L0$_f2
L0$_f2:
        mflr r11

        ; lazy pointer contains our desired branch target
        ; copy that value to r12 (the 'addis' and the 'lwzu')
        addis r11,r11,ha16(L_f2$lazy_ptr-L0$_f2)
        mtlr r0
        lwzu r12,lo16(L_f2$lazy_ptr-L0$_f2)(r11)

        ; copy branch target to CTR
        mtctr r12

        ; branch through CTR
        bctr
.data
.lazy_symbol_pointer
L_f2$lazy_ptr:
        .indirect_symbol _f2
        .long dyld_stub_binding_helper
```

3.4.2.2 Direct Calls

If GCC is instructed to statically compile the code in Figure 3–18, we can verify in the resultant assembly that there is a direct call to f2 from f1, with no use of GPR12. This case is shown in Figure 3–20.

FIGURE 3–20 Assembly code depicting a direct function call

```
        .machine ppc
        .text
        .align 2
        .globl _f1
_f1:
        mflr r0
        stmw r30,-8(r1)
        stw r0,8(r1)
        stwu r1,-80(r1)
        mr r30,r1
        bl _f2
        lwz r1,0(r1)
        lwz r0,8(r1)
        mtlr r0
        lmw r30,-8(r1)
        blr
```

3.4.3 Stack Usage

On most processor architectures, a stack is used to hold automatic variables, temporary variables, and return information for each invocation of a subroutine. The PowerPC architecture does not explicitly define a stack for local storage: There is neither a dedicated stack pointer nor any push or pop instructions. However, it is conventional for operating systems running on the PowerPC—including Mac OS X—to designate (per the ABI) an area of memory as the stack and grow it from a high memory address to a low memory address. If the stack is arranged as in Figure 3–21, we say that it grows *upward*. GPR1, which is used as the stack pointer, points to the top of the stack.

Both the stack and the registers play important roles in the working of subroutines. As listed in Table 3–12, registers are used to hold subroutine arguments, up to a certain number.

Functional Subtleties

The terms *function*, *procedure*, and *subroutine* are sometimes used in programming language literature to denote similar but slightly differing entities. For example, a function is a procedure that always returns a result, but a "pure" procedure does not return a result. *Subroutine* is often used as a general term for either a function or a procedure. The C language does not make such fine distinctions, but some languages do. We use these terms synonymously to represent the fundamental programmer-visible unit of callable execution in a high-level language like C.

Similarly, the terms *argument* and *parameter* are used synonymously in informal contexts. In general, when you declare a function that "takes arguments," you use *formal parameters* in its declaration. These are placeholders for *actual parameters*, which are what you specify when you call the function. Actual parameters are often called *arguments*.

The mechanism whereby actual parameters are matched with (or *bound* to) formal parameters is called *parameter passing*, which could be performed in various ways, such as *call-by-value* (actual parameter represents its value), *call-by-reference* (actual parameter represents its location), *call-by-name* (actual parameter represents its program text), and variants.

If a function f1 calls another function f2, which calls yet another function f3, and so on in a program, the program's stack grows per the ABI's conventions. Each function in the call chain owns part of the stack. A representative runtime stack for the 32-bit Darwin ABI is shown in Figure 3–21.

In Figure 3–21, f1 calls f2, which calls f3. f1's stack frame contains a *parameter area* and a *linkage area*.

The parameter area must be large enough to hold the largest parameter list of all functions that f1 calls. f1 typically will pass arguments in registers as long as there are registers available. Once registers are exhausted, f1 will place arguments in its parameter area, from where f2 will pick them up. However, f1 must reserve space for all arguments of f2 in any case—even if it is able to pass all arguments in registers. f2 is free to use f1's parameter area for storing arguments if it wants to free up the corresponding registers for other use. Thus, in a subroutine call, the caller sets up a parameter area in its own stack portion, and the callee can access the caller's parameter area for loading or storing arguments.

The linkage area begins after the parameter area and is at the top of the stack—adjacent to the stack pointer. The adjacency to the stack pointer is important: The linkage area has a fixed size, and therefore the callee can find the

stack pointer before call to f3 →	back chain to f1	low address
	saved CR (saved by f3)	
	saved LR (saved by f3)	
	reserved	f2's linkage area
	reserved	
	saved TOC pointer	
	argument word 1 for f3	
	...	arguments set by f2
	argument word M for f3	parameters used by f3
	f2's local variables	f2's local stack
	(padding)	padding for alignment (if needed)
	first GPR to save	
	...	f2 saves f1's nonvolatile GPRs
	last GPR to save	(up to 19 words maximum)
	first FPR to save	
	...	f2 saves f1's nonvolatile FPRs
	last FPR to save	(up to 19 words maximum)
stack pointer before call to f2 →	back chain to main	
	saved CR (saved by f2)	
	saved LR (saved by f2)	
	reserved	f1's linkage area
	reserved	
	saved TOC pointer	
	argument word 1 for f2	
	...	arguments set by f1
	argument word N for f2	parameters used by f2
	f1's local variables	f1's local stack

stack grows ↑

high address

FIGURE 3–21 Darwin 32-bit ABI runtime stack

caller's parameter area deterministically. The callee can save the CR and the LR in the caller's linkage area if it needs to. The stack pointer is always saved by the caller as a back chain to its caller.

In Figure 3–21, f2's portion of the stack shows space for saving nonvolatile registers that f2 changes. These must be restored by f2 before it returns to its caller.

Space for each function's local variables is reserved by growing the stack appropriately. This space lies below the parameter area and above the saved registers.

The fact that a called function is responsible for allocating its own stack frame does not mean the programmer has to write code to do so. When you compile a function, the compiler inserts code fragments called the *prologue* and the *epilogue* before and after the function body, respectively. The prologue sets up the stack frame for the function. The epilogue undoes the prologue's work, restoring any saved registers (including CR and LR), incrementing the stack pointer to its previous value (that the prologue saved in its linkage area), and finally returning to the caller.

> A 32-bit Darwin ABI stack frame is 16-byte aligned.

Consider the trivial function shown in Figure 3–22, along with the corresponding annotated assembly code.

FIGURE 3–22 Assembly listing for a C function with no arguments and an empty body

```
$ cat function.c
void
function(void)
{
}
$ gcc -S function.c
$ cat function.s
...
_function:
      stmw r30,-8(r1) ; Prologue: save r30 and r31
      stwu r1,-48(r1) ; Prologue: grow the stack 48 bytes
      mr r30,r1       ; Prologue: copy stack pointer to r30
      lwz r1,0(r1)    ; Epilogue: pop the stack (restore frame)
      lmw r30,-8(r1)  ; Epilogue: restore r30 and r31
      blr             ; Epilogue: return to caller (through LR)
```

The Red Zone

Just after a function is called, the function's prologue will decrement the stack pointer from its existing location to reserve space for the function's needs. The area above the stack pointer, where the newly called function's stack frame would reside, is called the *Red Zone*.

In the 32-bit Darwin ABI, the Red Zone has space for 19 GPRs (amounts to $19 \times 4 = 76$ bytes) and 18 FPRs (amounts to $18 \times 8 = 144$ bytes), for a total of 220 bytes. Rounded up to the nearest 16-byte boundary, this becomes 224 bytes, which is the size of the Red Zone.

Normally, the Red Zone is indeed occupied by the callee's stack frame. However, if the callee does not call any other function—that is, it is a *leaf function*—then it does not need a parameter area. It may also not need space for local variables on the stack if it can fit all of them in registers. It may need space for saving the nonvolatile registers it uses (recall that if a callee needs to save the CR and LR, it can save them in the caller's linkage area). As long as it can fit the registers to save in the Red Zone, it does not need to allocate a stack frame or decrement the stack pointer. Note that by definition, there is only one leaf function active at one time.

3.4.3.1 *Stack Usage Examples*

Figures 3–23 and 3–24 show examples of how the compiler sets up a function's stack depending on the number of local variables a function has, the number of parameters it has, the number of arguments it passes to a function it calls, and so on.

f1 is identical to the "null" function that we encountered in Figure 3–22, where we saw that the compiler reserves 48 bytes for the function's stack. The portions shown as shaded in the stacks are present either for alignment padding or for some current or future purpose not necessarily exposed through the ABI. Note that GPR30 and GPR31 are always saved, GPR30 being the designated frame pointer.

f2 uses a single 32-bit local variable. Its stack is 64 bytes.

f3 calls a function that takes no arguments. Nevertheless, this introduces a parameter area on f3's stack. A parameter area is at least eight words (32 bytes) in size. f3's stack is 80 bytes.

f4 takes eight arguments, has no local variables, and calls no functions. Its stack area is the same size as that of the null function because space for its arguments is reserved in the parameter area of its caller.

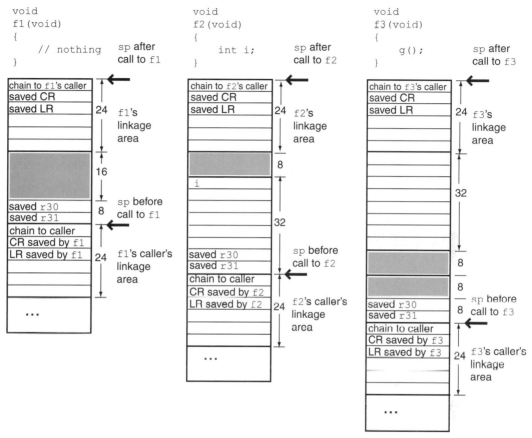

FIGURE 3–23 Examples of stack usage in functions

f5 takes no arguments, has eight word-size local variables, and calls no functions. Its stack is 64 bytes.

3.4.3.2 Printing Stack Frames

GCC provides built-in functions that may be used by a function to retrieve information about its callers. The current function's return address can be retrieved by calling the `__builtin_return_address()` function, which takes a single argument—the *level*, an integer specifying the number of stack frames to walk. A level of 0 results in the return address of the current function. Similarly, the `__builtin_frame_address()` function may be used to retrieve the frame

```
void                                          void
f4(int a1, int a2, int a3, int a4             f5(void)
   int a5, int a6, int a7, int a8)            {
{                                                 int 11, 12, 13, 14,
    /* no local variables */                        15, 16, 17, 18;
    /* no functions called */                     /* no functions called */
}                                             }
```

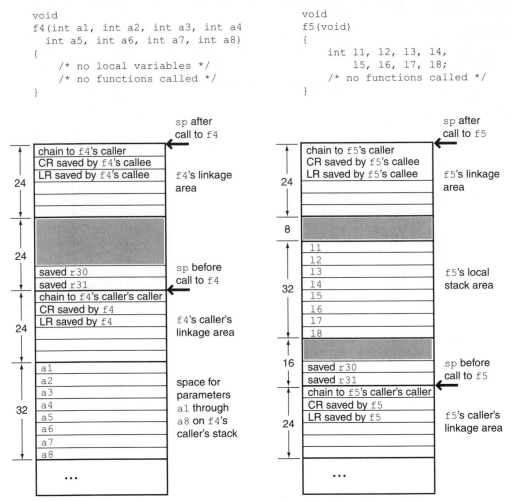

FIGURE 3–24 Examples of stack usage in functions (continued from Figure 3–23)

address of a function in the call stack. Both functions return a NULL pointer when the top of the stack has been reached.[53] Figure 3–25 shows a program that uses these functions to display a stack trace. The program also uses the dladdr() function in the dyld API to find the various function addresses corresponding to return addresses in the call stack.

---

53. For __builtin_frame_address() to return a NULL pointer upon reaching the top of the stack, the first frame pointer must have been set up correctly.

FIGURE 3–25 Printing a function call stack trace[54]

```c
// stacktrace.c

#include <stdio.h>
#include <dlfcn.h>

void
printframeinfo(unsigned int level, void *fp, void *ra)
{
    int     ret;
    Dl_info info;

    // Find the image containing the given address
    ret = dladdr(ra, &info);
    printf("#%u %s%s in %s, fp = %p, pc = %p\n",
           level,
           (ret) ? info.dli_sname : "?",      // symbol name
           (ret) ? "()" : "",                 // show as a function
           (ret) ? info.dli_fname : "?", fp, ra); // shared object name
}

void
stacktrace()
{
    unsigned int level = 0;
    void    *saved_ra = __builtin_return_address(0);
    void    **fp       = (void **)__builtin_frame_address(0);
    void    *saved_fp = __builtin_frame_address(1);

    printframeinfo(level, saved_fp, saved_ra);
    level++;
    fp = saved_fp;
    while (fp) {
        saved_fp = *fp;
        fp = saved_fp;
        if (*fp == NULL)
            break;
        saved_ra = *(fp + 2);
        printframeinfo(level, saved_fp, saved_ra);
        level++;
    }
}
```

(continues)

---

54. Note in the program's output that the function name in frames #5 and #6 is `tart`. The `dladdr()` function strips leading underscores from the symbols it returns—even if there is no leading underscore (in which case it removes the first character). In this case, the symbol's name is `start`.

FIGURE 3–25 Printing a function call stack trace *(continued)*

```
void f4() { stacktrace(); }
void f3() { f4(); }
void f2() { f3(); }
void f1() { f2(); }

int
main()
{
    f1();
    return 0;
}

$ gcc -Wall -o stacktrace stacktrace.c
$ ./stacktrace
#0 f4() in /private/tmp/./stacktrace, fp = 0xbffff850, pc = 0x2a3c
#1 f3() in /private/tmp/./stacktrace, fp = 0xbffff8a0, pc = 0x2a68
#2 f2() in /private/tmp/./stacktrace, fp = 0xbffff8f0, pc = 0x2a94
#3 f1() in /private/tmp/./stacktrace, fp = 0xbffff940, pc = 0x2ac0
#4 main() in /private/tmp/./stacktrace, fp = 0xbffff990, pc = 0x2aec
#5 tart() in /private/tmp/./stacktrace, fp = 0xbffff9e0, pc = 0x20c8
#6 tart() in /private/tmp/./stacktrace, fp = 0xbffffa40, pc = 0x1f6c
```

3.4.4 Function Parameters and Return Values

We saw earlier that when a function calls another with arguments, the parameter area in the caller's stack frame is large enough to hold all parameters passed to the called function, regardless of the number of parameters actually passed in registers. Doing so has benefits such as the following.

- The called function might want to call further functions that take arguments or might want to use registers containing its arguments for other purposes. Having a dedicated parameter area allows the callee to store an argument from a register to the argument's "home location" on the stack, thus freeing up a register.

- It may be useful to have all arguments in the parameter area for debugging purposes.

- If a function has a variable-length parameter list, it will typically access its arguments from memory.

3.4.4.1 *Passing Parameters*

Parameter-passing rules may depend on the type of programming language used—for example, procedural or object-oriented. Let us look at parameter-passing rules for C and C-like languages. Even for such languages, the rules further depend on whether a function has a fixed-length or a variable-length parameter list. The rules for fixed-length parameter lists are as follows.

- The first eight parameter words (i.e., the first 32 bytes, not necessarily the first eight arguments) are passed in GPR3 through GPR10, unless a floating-point parameter appears.

- Floating-point parameters are passed in FPR1 through FPR13.

- If a floating-point parameter appears, but GPRs are still available, then the parameter is placed in an FPR, as expected. However, the next available GPRs that together sum up to the floating-point parameter's size are skipped and not considered for allocation. Therefore, a single-precision floating-point parameter (4 bytes) causes the next available GPR (4 bytes) to be skipped. A double-precision floating-point parameter (8 bytes) causes the next two available GPRs (8 bytes total) to be skipped.

- If not all parameters can fit within the available registers in accordance with the skipping rules, the caller passes the excess parameters by storing them in the parameter area of its stack frame.

- Vector parameters are passed in VR2 through VR13.

- Unlike floating-point parameters, vector parameters do not cause GPRs—or FPRs, for that matter—to be skipped.

- Unless there are more vector parameters than can fit in available vector registers, no space is allocated for vector parameters in the caller's stack frame. Only when the registers are exhausted does the caller reserve any vector parameter space.

Let us look at the case of functions with variable-length parameter lists. Note that a function may have some number of required parameters preceding a variable number of parameters.

- Parameters in the variable portion of the parameter list are passed in both GPRs and FPRs. Consequently, floating-point parameters are always *shadowed* in GPRs instead of causing GPRs to be skipped.

- If there are vector parameters in the fixed portion of the parameter list, 16-byte-aligned space is reserved for such parameters in the caller's parameter area, even if there are available vector registers.

- If there are vector parameters in the variable portion of the parameter list, such parameters are also shadowed in GPRs.

- The called routine accesses arguments from the fixed portion of the parameter list similarly to the fixed-length parameter list case.

- The called routine accesses arguments from the variable portion of the parameter list by copying GPRs to the callee's parameter area and accessing values from there.

3.4.4.2 Returning Values

Functions return values according to the following rules.

- Values less than one word (32 bits) in size are returned in the least significant byte(s) of GPR3, with the remaining byte(s) being undefined.

- Values exactly one word in size are returned in GPR3.

- 64-bit fixed-point values are returned in GPR3 (the 4 low-order bytes) and GPR4 (the 4 high-order bytes).

- Structures up to a word in size are returned in GPR3.

- Single-precision floating-point values are returned in FPR1.

- Double-precision floating-point values are returned in FPR1.

- A 16-byte long double value is returned in FPR1 (the 8 low-order bytes) and FPR2 (the 8 high-order bytes).

- A composite value (such as an array, a structure, or a union) that is more than one word in size is returned via an implicit pointer that the caller must pass. Such functions require the caller to pass a pointer to a memory location that is large enough to hold the return value. The pointer is passed as an "invisible" argument in GPR3. Actual user-visible arguments, if any, are passed in GPR4 onward.

3.5 Examples

Let us now look at several miscellaneous examples to put some of the concepts we have learned into practice. We will discuss the following specific examples:

- Assembly code corresponding to a recursive factorial function
- Implementation of an atomic compare-and-store function

- Rerouting function calls
- Using a cycle-accurate 970FX simulator

3.5.1 A Recursive Factorial Function

In this example, we will understand how the assembly code corresponding to a simple, high-level C function works. The function is shown in Figure 3–26. It recursively computes the factorial of its integer argument.

FIGURE 3–26 A recursive function to compute factorials

```
// factorial.c

int
factorial(int n)
{
    if (n > 0)
        return n * factorial(n - 1);
    else
        return 1;
}

$ gcc -Wall -S factorial.c
```

The GCC command line shown in Figure 3–26 generates an assembly file named factorial.s. Figure 3–27 shows an annotated version of the contents of this file.

Noting Annotations

Whereas the listing in Figure 3–27 is hand-annotated, GCC can produce certain types of annotated output that may be useful in some debugging scenarios. For example, the -dA option annotates the assembler output with some minimal debugging information; the -dp option annotates each assembly mnemonic with a comment indicating which pattern and alternative were used; the -dP option intersperses assembly-language lines with transcripts of the register transfer language (RTL); and so on.

FIGURE 3–27 Annotated assembly listing for the function shown in Figure 3–26

```
; factorial.s

.section __TEXT,__text
    .globl _factorial
_factorial:

    ; LR contains the return address, copy LR to r0.
    mflr r0

    ; Store multiple words (the registers r30 and r31) to the address starting
    ; at [-8 + r1]. An stmw instruction is of the form "stmw rS,d(rA)" -- it
    ; stores n consecutive words starting at the effective address (rA|0)+d.
    ; The words come from the low-order 32 bits of GPRs rS through r31. In
    ; this case, rS is r30, so two words are stored.
    stmw r30,-8(r1)

    ; Save LR in the "saved LR" word of the linkage area of our caller.
    stw r0,8(r1)

    ; Grow the stack by 96 bytes:
    ;
    ; * 24 bytes for our linkage area
    ; * 32 bytes for 8 words' worth of arguments to functions we will call
    ;    (we actually use only one word)
    ; * 8 bytes of padding
    ; * 16 bytes for local variables (we actually use only one word)
    ; * 16 bytes for saving GPRs (such as r30 and r31)
    ;
    ; An stwu instruction is of the form "stwu rS, d(rA)" -- it stores the
    ; contents of the low-order 32 bits of rS into the memory word addressed
    ; by (rA)+d. The latter (the effective address) is also placed into rA.
    ; In this case, the contents of r1 are stored at (r1)-96, and the address
    ; (r1)-96 is placed into r1. In other words, the old stack pointer is
    ; stored and r1 gets the new stack pointer.
    stwu r1,-96(r1)

    ; Copy current stack pointer to r30, which will be our frame pointer --
    ; that is, the base register for accessing local variables, etc.
    mr r30,r1

    ; r3 contains our first parameter
    ;
    ; Our caller contains space for the corresponding argument just below its
    ; linkage area, 24 bytes away from the original stack pointer (before we
    ; grew the stack): 96 + 24 = 120
    ; store the parameter word in the caller's space.
    stw r3,120(r30)
```

(continues)

FIGURE 3–27 Annotated assembly listing for the function shown in Figure 3–26 *(continued)*

```
; Now access n, the first parameter, from the caller's parameter area.
; Copy n into r0.
; We could also use "mr" to copy from r3 to r0.
lwz r0,120(r30)

; Compare n with 0, placing result in cr7 (corresponds to the C line
; "if (n > 0)").
cmpwi cr7,r0,0

; n is less than or equal to 0: we are done. Branch to factorial0.
ble cr7,factorial0

; Copy n to r2 (this is Darwin, so r2 is available).
lwz r2,120(r30)

; Decrement n by 1, and place the result in r0.
addi r0,r2,-1

; Copy r0 (that is, n - 1) to r3.
; r3 is the first argument to the function that we will call: ourselves.
mr r3,r0

; Recurse.
bl _factorial

; r3 contains the return value.
; Copy r3 to r2
mr r2,r3

; Retrieve n (the original value, before we decremented it by 1), placing
; it in r0.
lwz r0,120(r30)

; Multiply n and the return value (factorial(n - 1)), placing the result
; in r0.
mullw r0,r2,r0

; Store the result in a temporary variable on the stack.
stw r0,64(r30)

; We are all done: get out of here.
b done

factorial0:
; We need to return 1 for factorial(n), if n <= 0.
li r0,1
```

(continues)

FIGURE 3–27 Annotated assembly listing for the function shown in Figure 3–26 *(continued)*

```
    ; Store the return value in a temporary variable on the stack.
    stw r0,64(r30)

done:
    ; Load the return value from its temporary location into r3.
    lwz r3,64(r30)

    ; Restore the frame ("pop" the stack) by placing the first word in the
    ; linkage area into r1.
    ;
    ; The first word is the back chain to our caller.
    lwz r1,0(r1)

    ; Retrieve the LR value we placed in the caller's linkage area and place
    ; it in r0.
    lwz r0,8(r1)

    ; Load LR with the value in r0.
    mtlr r0

    ; Load multiple words from the address starting at [-8 + r1] into r30
    ; and r31.
    lmw r30,-8(r1)

    ; Go back to the caller.
        blr
```

3.5.2 An Atomic Compare-and-Store Function

We came across the *load-and-reserve-conditional* (lwarx, ldarx) and *store-conditional* (stwcx., stdcx.) instructions earlier in this chapter. These instructions can be used to enforce storage ordering of I/O accesses. For example, we can use lwarx and stcwx. to implement an atomic compare-and-store function. Executing lwarx loads a word from a word-aligned location but also performs the following two actions *atomically* with the load.

- It creates a reservation that can be used by a subsequent stwcx. instruction. Note that a processor cannot have more than one reservation at a time.

- It notifies the processor's storage coherence mechanism that there is now a reservation for the specified memory location.

`stwcx.` stores a word to the specified word-aligned location. Its behavior depends on whether the location is the same as the one specified to `lwarx` to create a reservation. If the two locations are the same, `stwcx.` will perform the store *only if* there has been no other store to that location since the reservation's creation—one or more other stores, if any, could be by another processor, cache operations, or through any other mechanism. If the location specified to `stwcx.` is different from the one used with `lwarx`, the store may or may not succeed, but the reservation will be lost. A reservation may be lost in various other scenarios, and `stwcx.` will fail in all such cases. Figure 3–28 shows an implementation of a compare-and-store function. The Mac OS X kernel includes a similar function. We will use this function in our next example to implement function rerouting.

FIGURE 3–28 A hardware-based compare-and-store function for the 970FX

```
// hw_cs.s
//
// hw_compare_and_store(u_int32_t old,
//                      u_int32_t new,
//                      u_int32_t *address,
//                      u_int32_t *dummyaddress)
//
// Performs the following atomically:
//
// Compares old value to the one at address, and if they are equal, stores new
// value, returning true (1). On store failure, returns false (0). dummyaddress
// points to a valid, trashable u_int32_t location, which is written to for
// canceling the reservation in case of a failure.

        .align  5
        .globl  hw_compare_and_store

_hw_compare_and_store:
        // Arguments:
        //     r3      old
        //     r4      new
        //     r5      address
        //     r6      dummyaddress

        // Save the old value to a free register.
        mr      r7,r3

looptry:
        // Retrieve current value at address.
        // A reservation will also be created.
        lwarx   r9,0,r5
```

(continues)

FIGURE 3–28 A hardware-based compare-and-store function for the 970FX *(continued)*

```
        // Set return value to true, hoping we will succeed.
        li      r3,1

        // Do old value and current value at address match?
        cmplw   cr0,r9,r7

        // No! Somebody changed the value at address.
        bne--   fail

        // Try to store the new value at address.
        stwcx.  r4,0,r5

        // Failed! Reservation was lost for some reason.
        // Try again.
        bne--   looptry

        // If we use hw_compare_and_store to patch/instrument code dynamically,
        // without stopping already running code, the first instruction in the
        // newly created code must be isync. isync will prevent the execution
        // of instructions following itself until all preceding instructions
        // have completed, discarding prefetched instructions. Thus, execution
        // will be consistent with the newly created code. An instruction cache
        // miss will occur when fetching our instruction, resulting in fetching
        // of the modified instruction from storage.
        isync

        // return
        blr

fail:
        // We want to execute a stwcx. that specifies a dummy writable aligned
        // location. This will "clean up" (kill) the outstanding reservation.
        mr      r3,r6
        stwcx.  r3,0,r3

        // set return value to false.
        li      r3,0

        // return
        blr
```

3.5.3 Function Rerouting

Our goal in this example is to intercept a function in a C program by substituting a new function in its place, with the ability to call the original function from the new function. Let us assume that there is a function function(int, char *), which we wish to replace with `function_new(int, char *)`. The replacement must meet the following requirements.

- After replacement, when `function()` is called from anywhere within the program, `function_new()` is called instead.

- `function_new()` can use `function()`, perhaps because `function_new()` is meant to be a wrapper for the original function.

- The rerouting can be programmatically installed or removed.

- `function_new()` is a normal C function, with the only requirement being that it has the exact same prototype as `function()`.

3.5.3.1 Instruction Patching

Assume that `function()`'s implementation is the instruction sequence $i_0, i_1, \ldots, i_M$, whereas `function_new()`'s implementation is the instruction sequence $j_0, j_1, \ldots, j_N$, where M and N are some integers. A caller of `function()` executes i_0 first because it is the first instruction of `function()`. If our goal is to arrange for all invocations of `function()` to actually call `function_new()`, we could overwrite i_0 in memory with an unconditional branch instruction to j_0, the first instruction of `function_new()`. Doing so would leave `function()` out of the picture entirely. Since we also wish to call `function()` from within `function_new()`, we cannot clobber `function()`. Moreover, we also wish to be able to turn off the rerouting and restore `function()` as it originally was.

Rather than clobber i_0, we save it somewhere in memory. Then, we allocate a memory region large enough to hold a few instructions and mark it executable. A convenient way to preallocate such a region is to declare a dummy function: one that takes the exact same number and type of arguments as `function()`. The dummy function will simply act as a stub; let us call it `function_stub()`. We copy i_0 to the beginning of `function_stub()`. We craft an instruction—an unconditional jump to i_1—that we write as the second instruction of `function_stub()`.

We see that we need to craft two branch instructions: one from `function()` to `function_new()`, and another from `function_stub()` to `function()`.

3.5.3.2 Constructing Branch Instructions

PowerPC unconditional branch instructions are self-contained in that they encode their target addresses within the instruction word itself. Recall from the previous example that it is possible to update a word—a single instruction—atomically on the 970FX using a compare-and-store (also called compare-and-*update*) function. It would be more complicated in general to overwrite multiple instructions. Therefore, we will use unconditional branches to implement rerouting. The overall concept is shown in Figure 3–29.

The encoding of an unconditional branch instruction on the PowerPC is shown in Figure 3–30. It has a 24-bit address field (LI). Since all instructions are 4 bytes long, the PowerPC refers to words instead of bytes when it comes to branch target addresses. Since a word is 4 bytes, the 24 bits of LI are as good as 26 bits for our purposes. Given a 26-bit-wide effective branch address, the branch's maximum *reachability* is 64MB total,[55] or 32MB in either direction.

The Reach of a Branch

The "reachability" of a branch is processor-specific. A jump on MIPS uses 6 bits for the operand field and 26 bits for the address field. The effective addressable jump distance is actually 28 bits—four times more—because MIPS, like PowerPC, refers to the number of words instead of the number of bytes. All instructions in MIPS are 4 bytes long; 28 bits give you 256MB (±128MB) of total leeway. SPARC uses a 22-bit signed integer for branch addresses, but again, it has two zero bits appended, effectively providing a 24-bit program counter relative jump reachability. This amounts to reachability of 16MB (±8MB).

The AA field specifies whether the specified branch target address is absolute or relative to the current instruction (AA = 0 for relative, AA = 1 for absolute). If LK is 1, the effective address of the instruction following the branch instruction is placed in the LR. We do not wish to clobber the LR, so we are left with relative and absolute branches. We know now that to use a relative branch, the branch target must be within 32MB of the current instruction, but more importantly, we need to retrieve the address of the current instruction. Since the PowerPC does not have a program counter[56] register, we choose to use an unconditional branch with AA = 1 and LK = 0. However, this means the absolute address must be ±32MB relative to *zero*. In other words, function_new and

---

55. 2^{26} bytes.

56. The conceptual Instruction Address Register (IAR) is not directly accessible without involving the LR.

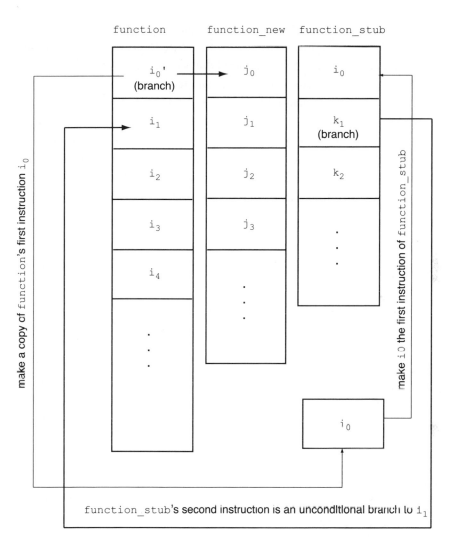

FIGURE 3–29 Overview of function rerouting by instruction patching

| major opcode (18) | LI | AA | LK |

0   5 6   30   31

FIGURE 3–30 Unconditional branch instruction on the PowerPC

function_stub must reside in virtual memory *within the first 32MB or the last 32MB of the process's virtual address space!* In a simple program such as ours, this condition is actually likely to be satisfied due to the way Mac OS X sets up process address spaces. Thus, in our example, we simply "hope" for function_new() (our own declared function) and function_stub() (a buffer allocated through the malloc() function) to have virtual addresses that are less than 32MB. This makes our "technique" eminently unsuitable for production use. However, there is almost certainly free memory available in the first or last 32MB of any process's address space. As we will see in Chapter 8, Mach allows you to allocate memory at specified virtual addresses, so the technique can also be improved.

Figure 3–31 shows the code for the function-rerouting demo program. Note that the program is 32-bit only—it will behave incorrectly when compiled for the 64-bit architecture.

FIGURE 3–31 Implementation of function rerouting by instruction patching

```
// frr.c

#include <stdio.h>
#include <fcntl.h>
#include <stdlib.h>
#include <string.h>
#include <unistd.h>
#include <sys/types.h>
#include <sys/mman.h>

// Constant on the PowerPC
#define BYTES_PER_INSTRUCTION 4

// Branch instruction's major opcode
#define BRANCH_MOPCODE 0x12

// Large enough size for a function stub
#define DEFAULT_STUBSZ 128

// Atomic update function
//
int hw_compare_and_store(u_int32_t  old,
                         u_int32_t  new,
                         u_int32_t *address,
                         u_int32_t *dummy_address);
```

(continues)

FIGURE 3–31 Implementation of function rerouting by instruction patching *(continued)*

```c
// Structure corresponding to a branch instruction
//
typedef struct branch_s {
    u_int32_t OP: 6;  // bits 0 - 5, primary opcode
    u_int32_t LI: 24; // bits 6 - 29, LI
    u_int32_t AA: 1;  // bit 30, absolute address
    u_int32_t LK: 1;  // bit 31, link or not
} branch_t;

// Each instance of rerouting has the following data structure associated with
// it. A pointer to a frr_data_t is returned by the "install" function. The
// "remove" function takes the same pointer as argument.
//
typedef struct frr_data_s {
    void *f_orig; // "original" function
    void *f_new;  // user-provided "new" function
    void *f_stub; // stub to call "original" inside "new"
    char  f_bytes[BYTES_PER_INSTRUCTION]; // bytes from f_orig
} frr_data_t;

// Given an "original" function and a "new" function, frr_install() reroutes
// so that anybody calling "original" will actually be calling "new". Inside
// "new", it is possible to call "original" through a stub.
//
frr_data_t *
frr_install(void *original, void *new)
{
    int        ret = -1;
    branch_t   branch;
    frr_data_t *FRR = (frr_data_t *)0;
    u_int32_t  target_address, dummy_address;

    // Check new's address
    if ((u_int32_t)new >> 25) {
        fprintf(stderr, "This demo is out of luck. \"new\" too far.\n");
        goto ERROR;
    } else
        printf("    FRR: \"new\" is at address %#x.\n", (u_int32_t)new);

    // Allocate space for FRR metadata
    FRR = (frr_data_t *)malloc(sizeof(frr_data_t));
    if (!FRR)
        return FRR;

    FRR->f_orig = original;
    FRR->f_new = new;
```

(continues)

FIGURE 3–31 Implementation of function rerouting by instruction patching *(continued)*

```
// Allocate space for the stub to call the original function
FRR->f_stub = (char *)malloc(DEFAULT_STUBSZ);
if (!FRR->f_stub) {
    free(FRR);
    FRR = (frr_data_t *)0;
    return FRR;
}


// Prepare to write to the first 4 bytes of "original"
ret = mprotect(FRR->f_orig, 4, PROT_READ|PROT_WRITE|PROT_EXEC);
if (ret != 0)
    goto ERROR;


// Prepare to populate the stub and make it executable
ret = mprotect(FRR->f_stub, DEFAULT_STUBSZ, PROT_READ|PROT_WRITE|PROT_EXEC);
if (ret != 0)
    goto ERROR;


memcpy(FRR->f_bytes, (char *)FRR->f_orig, BYTES_PER_INSTRUCTION);


// Unconditional branch (relative)
branch.OP = BRANCH_MOPCODE;
branch.AA = 1;
branch.LK = 0;


// Create unconditional branch from "stub" to "original"
target_address = (u_int32_t)(FRR->f_orig + 4) >> 2;
if (target_address >> 25) {
    fprintf(stderr, "This demo is out of luck. Target address too far.\n");
    goto ERROR;
} else
    printf("   FRR: target_address for stub -> original is %#x.\n",
           target_address);
branch.LI = target_address;
memcpy((char *)FRR->f_stub, (char *)FRR->f_bytes, BYTES_PER_INSTRUCTION);
memcpy((char *)FRR->f_stub + BYTES_PER_INSTRUCTION, (char *)&branch, 4);


// Create unconditional branch from "original" to "new"
target_address = (u_int32_t)FRR->f_new >> 2;
if (target_address >> 25) {
    fprintf(stderr, "This demo is out of luck. Target address too far.\n");
    goto ERROR;
} else
    printf("   FRR: target_address for original -> new is %#x.\n",
           target_address);
branch.LI = target_address;
```

(continues)

FIGURE 3–31 Implementation of function rerouting by instruction patching *(continued)*

```
    ret = hw_compare_and_store(*((u_int32_t *)FRR->f_orig),
                               *((u_int32_t *)&branch),
                               (u_int32_t *)FRR->f_orig,
                               &dummy_address);
    if (ret != 1) {
        fprintf(stderr, "Atomic store failed.\n");
        goto ERROR;
    } else
        printf("    FRR: Atomically updated instruction.\n");

    return FRR;

    ERROR:
    if (FRR && FRR->f_stub)
        free(FRR->f_stub);
    if (FRR)
        free(FRR);
    return FRR;
}

int
frr_remove(frr_data_t *FRR)
{
    int        ret;
    u_int32_t dummy_address;

    if (!FRR)
        return 0;

    ret = mprotect(FRR->f_orig, 4, PROT_READ|PROT_WRITE|PROT_EXEC);
    if (ret != 0)
        return -1;

    ret = hw_compare_and_store(*((u_int32_t *)FRR->f_orig),
                               *((u_int32_t *)FRR->f_bytes),
                               (u_int32_t *)FRR->f_orig,
                               &dummy_address);

    if (FRR && FRR->f_stub)
        free(FRR->f_stub);

    if (FRR)
        free(FRR);

    FRR = (frr_data_t *)0;

    return 0;
}
```

(continues)

FIGURE 3–31 Implementation of function rerouting by instruction patching *(continued)*

```c
int
function(int i, char *s)
{
    int   ret;
    char *m = s;

    if (!s)
        m = "(null)";

    printf(" CALLED: function(%d, %s).\n", i, m);
    ret = i + 1;
    printf(" RETURN: %d = function(%d, %s).\n", ret, i, m);

    return ret;
}


int (* function_stub)(int, char *);

int
function_new(int i, char *s)
{
    int   ret = -1;
    char *m = s;

    if (!s)
        m = "(null)";

    printf(" CALLED: function_new(%d, %s).\n", i, m);

    if (function_stub) {
        printf("CALLING: function_new() --> function_stub().\n");
        ret = function_stub(i, s);
    } else {
        printf("function_new(): function_stub missing.\n");
    }

    printf(" RETURN: %d = function_new(%d, %s).\n", ret, i, m);

    return ret;
}

int
main(int argc, char **argv)
{
    int        ret;
    int        arg_i = 2;
    char       *arg_s = "Hello, World!";
    frr_data_t *FRR;
```

(continues)

FIGURE 3–31 Implementation of function rerouting by instruction patching *(continued)*

```
    function_stub = (int(*)(int, char *))0;

    printf("[Clean State]\n");
        printf("CALLING: main() --> function().\n");
    ret = function(arg_i, arg_s);

    printf("\n[Installing Rerouting]\n");
    printf("Maximum branch target address is %#x (32MB).\n", (1 << 25));
    FRR = frr_install(function, function_new);
    if (FRR)
        function_stub = FRR->f_stub;
    else {
        fprintf(stderr, "main(): frr_install failed.\n");
        return 1;
    }

    printf("\n[Rerouting installed]\n");
    printf("CALLING: main() --> function().\n");
    ret = function(arg_i, arg_s);

    ret = frr_remove(FRR);
    if (ret != 0) {
        fprintf(stderr, "main(): frr_remove failed.\n");
        return 1;
    }

    printf("\n[Rerouting removed]\n");
    printf("CALLING: main() --> function().\n");
    ret = function(arg_i, arg_s);

    return 0;
}
```

Figure 3–32 shows a sample run of the function-rerouting demonstration program.

FIGURE 3–32 Function rerouting in action

```
$ gcc -Wall -o frr frr.c
$ ./frr
[Clean State]
CALLING: main() --> function().
CALLED: function(2, Hello, World!).
RETURN: 3 = function(2, Hello, World!).
```

(continues)

FIGURE 3–32 Function rerouting in action *(continued)*

```
[Installing Rerouting]
Maximum branch target address is 0x2000000 (32MB).
FRR: "new" is at address 0x272c.
FRR: target_address for stub -> original is 0x9a6.
FRR: target_address for original -> new is 0x9cb.
FRR: Atomically updated instruction.

[Rerouting installed]
CALLING: main() --> function().
CALLED: function_new(2, Hello, World!).
CALLING: function_new() --> function_stub().
CALLED: function(2, Hello, World!).
RETURN: 3 = function(2, Hello, World!).
RETURN: 3 = function_new(2, Hello, World!).

[Rerouting removed]
CALLING: main() --> function().
CALLED: function(2, Hello, World!).
RETURN: 3 = function(2, Hello, World!).
```

3.5.4 Cycle-Accurate Simulation of the 970FX

Apple's CHUD Tools package includes the `amber` and `simg5` command-line programs that were briefly mentioned in Chapter 2. `amber` is a tool for tracing all threads in a process, recording every instruction and data access to a trace file. `simg5`[57] is a cycle-accurate core simulator for the 970/970FX. With these tools, it is possible to analyze the execution of a program at the processor-cycle level. You can see how instructions are broken down into iops, how the iops are grouped, how the groups are dispatched, and so on. In this example, we will use `amber` and `simg5` to analyze a simple program.

The first step is to use `amber` to generate a trace of a program's execution. `amber` supports a few trace file formats. We will use the TT6E format with `simg5`.

Tracing the execution of an entire application—even a trivial program—will result in the execution of an extremely large number of instructions. Execution of the "empty" C program in Figure 3–33 causes over 90,000 instructions to be traced. This is so because although the program does not have any programmer-provided code (besides the empty function body), it still contains the runtime environment's startup and teardown routines.

---

57. `simg5` was developed by IBM.

FIGURE 3–33 Tracing an "empty" C program using amber

```
$ cat null.c
main()
{
}
$ gcc -o null null.c
$ amber ./null
...
Session Instructions Traced:  91353
Session Trace Time:           0.46 sec [0.20 million inst/sec]
...
```

Typically, you would not be interested in analyzing the execution of the language runtime environment. In fact, even within your own code, you may want to analyze only small portions at a time. It becomes impractical to deal with a large number—say, more than a few thousand—of instructions using these tools. When used with the -i or -I arguments, amber can toggle tracing for an application upon encountering a privileged instruction. A readily usable example of such an instruction is one that accesses an OEA register from user space. Thus, you can instrument your code by surrounding the portion of interest with two such illegal instructions. The first occurrence will cause amber to turn tracing on, and the second will cause tracing to stop. Figure 3–34 shows the program we will trace with amber.

FIGURE 3–34 A C program with instructions that are illegal in user space

```
// traceme.c

#include <stdlib.h>

#if defined(__GNUC__)
#include <ppc_intrinsics.h>
#endif

int
main(void)
{
    int i, a = 0;

    // supervisor-level instruction as a trigger
    // start tracing
    (void)__mfspr(1023);
```

(continues)

FIGURE 3–34 A C program with instructions that are illegal in user space *(continued)*

```
for (i = 0; i < 16; i++) {
    a += 3 * i;
}

// supervisor-level instruction as a trigger
// stop tracing
(void)__mfspr(1023);

exit(0);
}
```

We trace the program in Figure 3–34 using amber with the -I option, which directs amber to trace only the instrumented thread. The -i option would cause all threads in the target process to be traced. As shown in Figure 3–35, the executable will not run stand-alone because of the presence of illegal instructions in the machine code.

FIGURE 3–35 Tracing program execution with amber

```
$ gcc -S traceme.c # GCC 4.x
$ gcc -o traceme traceme.c
$ ./traceme
zsh: illegal hardware instruction  ./traceme
$ amber -I ./traceme
...
* Targeting process 'traceme' [1570]
* Recording TT6E trace
* Instrumented executable - tracing will start/stop for thread automatically
* Ctrl-Esc to quit

* Tracing session #1 started *

Session Instructions Traced: 214
Session Traced Time:          0.00 sec [0.09 million inst/sec]

* Tracing session #1 stopped *

* Exiting... *
```

---

amber creates a subdirectory called trace_xxx in the current directory, where xxx is a three-digit numerical string: 001 if this is the first trace in the directory. The trace_xxx directory contains further subdirectories, one per thread in your program, containing TT6E traces of the program's threads. A trace provides information such as what instructions were issued, what order they were issued in, what were the load and store addresses, and so on. Our program has only one thread, so the subdirectory is called `thread_001.tt6e`. As shown in Figure 3–35, `amber` reports that 214 instructions were traced. Let us account for these instructions by examining the generated assembly `traceme.s`, whose partial contents (annotated) are shown in Figure 3–36. Note that we are interested only in the portion between the pair of `mfspr` instructions. However, it is noteworthy that the instruction immediately following the first `mfspr` instruction is not included in `amber`'s trace.

FIGURE 3–36 Accounting for instructions traced by `amber`

```
; traceme.s (compiled with GCC 4.x)
        mfspr r0, 1023              ←
        stw    r0,60(r30)   ; not traced
        ; instructions of interest begin here
        li     r0,0
        stw    r0,68(r30)
        b      L2
L3:
        lwz    r2,68(r30)    ; i[n]
        mr     r0,r2         ; i[n + 1]
        slwi   r0,r0,1       ; i[n + 2]
        add    r2,r0,r2      ; i[n + 3]
        lwz    r0,64(r30)    ; i[n + 4]
        add    r0,r0,r2      ; i[n + 5]
        stw    r0,64(r30)    ; i[n + 6]
        lwz    r2,68(r30)    ; i[n + 7]
        addi   r0,r2,1       ; i[n + 8]
        stw    r0,68(r30)    ; i[n + 9]
L2:
        lwz    r0,68(r30)    ; i[n + 10]
        cmpwi  cr7,r0,15     ; i[n + 11]
        ble    cr7,L3        ; i[n + 12]
        mfspr r0, 1023              ←
```

Each of the 3 instructions before the `L3` loop label are executed only once, whereas the rest of the instructions that lie between the `L3` loop label and the second `mfspr` instruction are executed during one or all iterations of the loop. Instructions `i[n]` through `i[n + 9]` (10 instructions) are executed exactly 16 times, as the C variable `i` is incremented. The assembly implementation of the loop begins by jumping to the `L2` label and checks whether `i` has attained the value 16, in which case the loop terminates. Since i is initially zero, instructions i[n + 10] through i[n + 12] (3 instructions) will be executed exactly 17 times. Thus, the total number of instructions executed can be calculated as follows:

$$3 + (10 \times 16) + (3 \times 17) = 214$$

Let us now run simg5 on this trace. simg5 allows you to change certain characteristics of the simulated processor, for example, by making the L1 I-cache, the L1 D-cache, the TLBs, or the L2 cache infinite. There also exists a Java viewer for viewing simg5's output. simg5 can automatically run the viewer upon finishing if the auto_load option is specified.

```
$ simg5 trace_001/thread_001.tt6e 214 1 1 test_run1 -p 1 -b 1 -e 214 -auto_load
...
```

Figure 3–37 shows simg5's output as displayed by the Java viewer. The left side of the screen contains a cycle-by-cycle sequence of processor events. These are denoted by labels, examples of which are shown in Table 3–13.

TABLE 3–13 Processor Event Labels

Label	Event	Notes
FVB	Fetch	Instruction fetched into the instruction buffer
D	Decode	Decode group formed
M	Dispatch	Dispatch group dispatched
su	Issue	Instruction issued
E	Execute	Instruction executing
f	Finish	Instruction finished execution
C	Completion	Instruction group completed

In the simg5 output, we can see the breaking down of architected instructions into iops. For example, the second instruction of interest in Figure 3–36 has two corresponding iops.

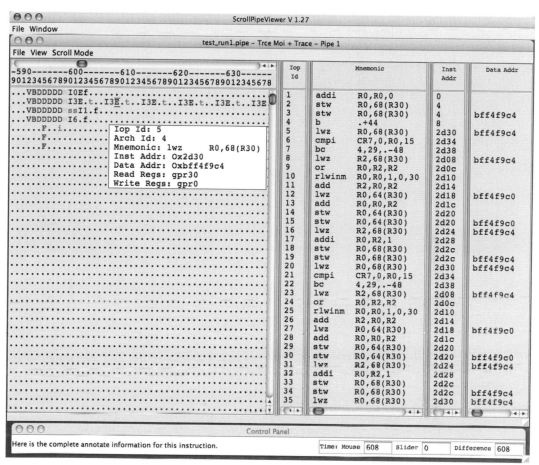

FIGURE 3–37 `simg5` output

CHAPTER 4

The Firmware and the Bootloader

When a computer system's power is turned on, or the system is reset, the process of its "coming up" is called *bootstrapping*, or simply *booting*.[1] A modern Apple computer presents a capable and interesting firmware environment even before an operating system runs on it. In this chapter, we will explore this environment on a PowerPC-based Macintosh computer. We will also look at the sequence of events that happens during booting—up to the point where the Mac OS X kernel gains control. Finally, we will briefly discuss an equally interesting firmware environment (EFI) for x86-based Macintosh computers.

4.1 Introduction

As we saw in Chapter 3, a representative computer system consists of a main logic board (or the motherboard), one or more CPUs, busses, memory, storage devices, and so on. The computer's operating system resides on a storage device

---

1. The term is an allusion to the expression "lifting oneself up by the bootstraps."

that is either locally attached or is accessible over a network connection. The operating system must somehow be loaded into memory as the computer boots. In the most commonly used approach, the master CPU[2] has access to some read-only memory (ROM) from which it executes an initial piece of code. This code is commonly called the *Basic Input/Output System* (BIOS), particularly in the context of x86-based computers. Modern BIOSs usually reside in *programmable* read-only memory (PROM) or one of its variants, such as *flash* memory, to allow easy upgrades. This "software embedded in hardware" represents a middle ground between hardware and software and is therefore called *firmware*. A typical BIOS is also firmware, but not every piece of firmware is considered a BIOS. The BIOS's analog is called *Open Firmware* on modern PowerPC-based Apple computers and *Extensible Firmware Interface* (EFI) on x86-based Apple computers. It must be noted that the roles and capabilities of both Open Firmware and EFI far exceed those of a typical PC BIOS.

> The PC BIOS is as old as the PC itself, whereas the acronym *BIOS* is even older, dating back to the CP/M operating system. BIOS was one of the three primary components of CP/M, the other two being BDOS (Basic Disk Operating System) and CCP (Console Command Processor).

In a typical booting scenario, after the system is powered on, the CPU, or the designated master CPU in a multiprocessor system, finds and executes firmware-resident code. The firmware performs a *power-on self-test* (POST), which is a series of initialization and testing routines for various hardware components. The firmware then loads a *bootloader*, a program that can load a more complex program such as an operating system or perhaps the next-stage bootloader in what could be a multistage bootloading mechanism. A bootloader may provide a user interface for selecting one of many operating systems to boot and may also prompt for arguments to be passed to the selected operating system.

4.1.1 Varieties of Firmware

Specific firmware implementations may differ from—or may have details in addition to—the generic discussion so far. In most cases, a platform-dependent

---

2. In a multiprocessor system, one CPU is usually designated as a master (or main) CPU using some platform-specific algorithm.

entity, such as an even lower-level firmware than the BIOS or Open Firmware, may be the very first stored program to gain control of the machine. This firmware may perform some fundamental initialization and tests before passing control to the main user-visible firmware, which is often called the *CPU* or *system* firmware. Installed hardware cards such as SCSI, network, and video adapter cards may contain their own firmware in their own ROMs. During boot, the main firmware passes control to these ancillary firmware modules.

In this chapter, we will discuss only user-visible firmware, which, for the sake of simplicity, may be visualized as sitting directly atop the hardware. Typically, both the bootloader and the operating system interact with the firmware. Moreover, we will use the term *firmware* by itself generically, to denote a BIOS, Open Firmware, EFI, or any other variant.

> Note that although modern operating systems typically do not use the BIOS once they finish booting, older systems such as MS-DOS and CP/M made heavy use of BIOS services for implementing large parts of their functionality.
>
> Entire operating systems may also reside in firmware, as is the case with many embedded systems that use a PROM as a boot device. It is even possible—and arguably useful—to use a conventional operating system *as* a computer's firmware. The LinuxBIOS project is one such example.

4.1.2 Preferential Storage

User-configurable settings that are referenced during boot by the BIOS—and in some cases by the operating system—are stored in a low-power, battery-backed memory such as a CMOS-based device. A reserved area on a disk drive may also be used to store such settings.

Modern Apple computers have a *power management unit* (PMU), a microcontroller chip that controls the power consumption behavior of various devices. Still newer models have a more advanced *system management unit* (SMU) instead of the PMU. The SMU also is an onboard microcontroller that controls the computer's power functions.

The PMU takes care of spinning down hard disks and adjusting the backlight. It handles the machine's sleep, wake-up, idle, turn-on, and turn-off behaviors, including deciding when *not* to put the machine to sleep—for example, in the case of an active modem connection. The PMU also manages the onboard real-time clock and maintains the *parameter memory* (PRAM). The SMU performs many similar functions. Apple's SMU-related kernel extensions (such as `AppleSMU.kext`, `AppleSMUMonitor.kext`, and `IOI2CControllerSMU.kext`) provide internal APIs for accessing battery information, controlling fans, managing date and time, controlling the power supply, maintaining the PRAM, and so on.

The PRAM is a battery-backed memory used to store miscellaneous system configuration information such as startup chime volume, time zone, speaker volume, DVD region setting, and the text corresponding to a kernel panic. The PRAM's exact contents depend on the specific computer system and its configuration. On a system running Mac OS X, less information is stored in the PRAM as compared to the same computer running an earlier Apple operating system. The Mac OS X kernel accesses PRAM contents through the Platform Expert.

The Reset Set

The PMU and the SMU can be reset in a model-dependent manner. For example, whereas a notebook computer model may allow you to reset the PMU using a combination of the power button and one or more keys, a Power Mac model may require a button to be pressed on the logic board. The SMU on certain models can be reset by simply unplugging the power for a few seconds.

Note that resetting the PMU or the SMU does not reset the PRAM. You can reset a computer's PRAM by pressing and holding the **-option-p-r** key combination as you turn the computer on. You must press the keys before the gray screen appears and must keep them pressed until the computer restarts and you hear the startup chime for the second time.

Open Firmware uses another nonvolatile memory—the NVRAM—for storing its user-configurable variables and some other startup information. The NVRAM is accessed by Open Firmware during system startup. EFI similarly uses and accesses its own NVRAM. A typical NVRAM is based on flash memory.

4.2 A Whole New World

The Macintosh was not designed to run multiple operating systems. The Macintosh ROM contained both low-level and high-level code. The low-level code was for hardware initialization, diagnostics, drivers, and so on. The higher-level *Toolbox* was a collection of software routines meant for use by applications, quite like a shared library. Toolbox functionality included the following:

- Management of dialog boxes, fonts, icons, pull-down menus, scroll bars, and windows
- Event handling
- Text entry and editing
- Arithmetic and logical operations

Before the iMac was introduced, Apple computers used a large, monolithic ROM—also called the Toolbox ROM—that contained a substantial part of the system software as both low-level and high-level code. Examples of low-level, hardware-specific code included hardware initialization code, drivers, feature tables, and diagnostics. Examples of higher-level code included the 68K emulator, the nanokernel, Toolbox managers, SCSI Manager, and QuickDraw. Note that the ROM contained not only code that was needed by the computer at power-up time but also code that provided application-level APIs.

As Macintosh system software increased in functionality and complexity, it became increasingly difficult to maintain the ROM. Apple attempted to ameliorate the situation by redirecting modifications and changes to disk-resident files instead of changing the ROM itself. For example, the *System File*, which was loaded early on during the boot process, contained portions of the Toolbox, ROM extensions and patches, fonts, sounds, and other resources. The System File was loaded into RAM, after which its contents were available to the operating system and applications. The concept of a *System Enabler* was introduced in 1992 along with System 7.1. System Enablers allowed Apple to introduce new Macintoshes without revising the base system software. For example, the Macintosh 32-bit System Enabler was a system software extension and a replacement for the MODE32 software, which provided access to memory-addressing features of System 7.1.

MODE32 Software

Certain machines such as the Macintosh II, IIx, IIcx, and SE/30 could have 32-bit support and a larger virtual memory capability through a 32-bit System Enabler program (called `MODE32`) on System 7. The standard ROMs of these machines were not 32-bit clean and therefore were compatible only with 24-bit addressing. `MODE32` allowed selecting and changing between 24-bit and 32-bit addressing modes. With 32-bit addressing, it was possible to use more than 8MB of contiguous physical memory. With virtual memory, it was possible to use hard disk space as "swap" space to run programs.

4.2.1 "New" Is Good News

With the introduction of the iMac, Apple reached a far cleaner separation between the hardware-specific and generic (across various Apple computers) parts of the system software. The new approach used a small *Boot ROM* that contained only the code needed to boot the computer, with the remaining components of the system software residing as files on disk—effectively, a *software ROM*. The Boot ROM has the ability to load the software ROM into a portion of physical memory (RAM). This portion, which is marked read-only, is unavailable for other use. Apple used the term *New World* to refer to this architecture. This was also called the *ROM-in-RAM* design. Another important feature of the New World machines was the extensive use of Open Firmware. Although it had been introduced in earlier Apple computers, Open Firmware's use was minimal in the so-called Old World machines. Table 4–1 summarizes the temporal worldliness of the Macintosh family.

> The iMac's ROM image resided in a file called Mac OS ROM in the System Folder. It contained the Toolbox, kernel, and the 68K emulator. Once loaded, the ROM consumed approximately 3MB of physical memory.

TABLE 4–1 The Macintosh Family: New and Old Worlds

CPU	Bus	ROM	Software ROM	World
68K	NuBus	Mac OS ROM (68K)	—	—
PowerPC	NuBus,[a] PCI	System ROM (PowerPC) Mac OS ROM (68K)[b]	—	—
PowerPC	PCI	Open Firmware 1.x Mac OS ROM	—	Old
PowerPC	PCI	Open Firmware 2.x Mac OS ROM	—	Old
PowerPC	PCI	Open Firmware 3.x	Mac OS ROM	New
PowerPC	PCI	Open Firmware 4.x	BootX (Mac OS X)	New

a. Some of the earliest PowerPC-based Macintosh computers (the x100 generation) used NuBus.

b. The PowerPC System ROM started the nanokernel, on which the 68K Mac OS ROM ran largely unmodified.

NuBus

NuBus—specified by the IEEE 1196 standard—was a simple 32-pin bus originally developed at the Laboratory for Computer Science (LCS), Massachusetts Institute of Technology (MIT). It was used in Apple computers beginning with the Macintosh II, until Apple switched to the PCI bus. NeXT computers also used NuBus.

4.2.2 Modern Boot ROM (PowerPC)

The Boot ROM of a modern PowerPC-based Macintosh is stored in up to 2MB[3] of flash EEPROM.[4] Over time, and especially with the advent of Mac OS X, the composition of the ROM has changed greatly. For example, the modern ROM does not contain a 68K emulator or the nanokernel. The firmware-resident code in the Boot ROM includes POST functionality for hardware initialization and diagnostics. The firmware also contains Open Firmware, which completes hardware initialization,[5] incrementally builds a description of the system's hardware, loads initial operating system software (the bootloader), and eventually transfers control to the latter. Several properties of the Boot ROM can be viewed on Mac OS X using the `ioreg` command-line utility.

```
$ ioreg -p IODeviceTree -n boot-rom -w 0 | less
...
| +-o boot-rom@fff00000  <class IOService, !registered, !matched, active,
                          busy 0, retain count 4>
   | |  {
   | |    "reg" = <fff0000000100000>
   | |    "has-config-block" = <>
   | |    "image" = <00080000>
   | |    "AAPL,phandle" = <ff8935b8>
   | |    "security-modes" = <"none, full, command, no-password">
   | |    "write-characteristic" = <"flash">
   | |    "BootROM-build-date" = <"10/26/04 at 16:30:32">
   | |    "model" = <"Apple PowerMac7,3 5.1.8f7 BootROM built on ...">
   | |    "info" = <fff000...000>
   | |    "name" = <"boot-rom">
   | |    "BootROM-version" = <"$0005.18f7">
   | |    "hwi-flags" = <48fdd37e>
   | |  }
...
```

---

3. A dual-processor 2.7GHz Power Mac G5 contains 1MB of onboard flash EEPROM.

4. The "EE" in EEPROM stands for electrically eraseable.

5. Open Firmware automatically assigns interrupts to PCI devices.

> The Boot ROM also contains device drivers for certain fundamental devices, such as the USB hub, Apple USB keyboard and mouse, and Apple Bluetooth keyboard and mouse. Therefore, even with a wireless (Bluetooth) keyboard and mouse, you can drop into the firmware before the operating system boots and interact with the system.

The file type of Apple's software ROM file is `tbxi`, which stands for *Toolbox image*—a remnant of the Old World. The Toolbox image file is also called a *bootinfo* file. It resides on the boot device and has a localizable name. Therefore, it is searched for based on file *type*—not filename. Its default location is in the directory marked as the "blessed folder" in the HFS Plus volume header.[6] If you perform a file search using the Finder on Mac OS X and specify `tbxi` as the file type to search for, you should get one result on a computer with a single Mac OS X installation: `/System/Library/CoreServices/BootX`, which is the Mac OS X bootloader. The same search under Mac OS 9 or Mac OS 8 would yield the file `/System Folder/Mac OS ROM`. On a Mac OS X 10.4 or newer system, such a search could be performed through Spotlight. The four-character file type is converted to a four-byte (32-bit) integer, each of whose bytes is the ASCII value of the corresponding file type character. The ASCII values of "t", "b", "x", and "i" are `0x74`, `0x62`, `0x78`, and `0x69`, respectively. Therefore, the file type to use while searching with Spotlight is `0x74627869`.

```
$ mdfind 'kMDItemFSTypeCode == 0x74627869'
/System/Library/CoreServices/BootX
/System Folder/Mac OS ROM
$
```

The specifier for Open Firmware's default boot device contains `\\:tbxi` as the filename component, which tells the firmware to look for a file of type `tbxi` in the boot directory. The volume header of an HFS Plus file system contains an eight-element array called `finderInfo`. Each element of this array is a 32-bit unsigned integer. The first element contains the ID of the blessed folder, which contains `BootX` on Mac OS X, and `Mac OS ROM` under Mac OS 9. This way, Open Firmware can easily find a bootable system—if one exists. You can use `bless(8)` to set volume bootability and startup disk options. The `-info` argument of `bless` displays relevant elements of the `finderInfo` array.

---

6. We will look at details of HFS Plus in Chapter 12.

```
$ bless -info /
finderinfo[0]:   3317 => Blessed System Folder is /System/Library/CoreServices
finderinfo[1]:      0 => No Startup App folder (ignored anyway)
finderinfo[2]:      0 => Open-folder linked list empty
finderinfo[3]: 877875 => OS 9 blessed folder is /System Folder
finderinfo[4]:      0 => Unused field unset
finderinfo[5]:   3317 => OS X blessed folder is /System/Library/CoreServices
64-bit VSDB volume id:   0x79A955B7E0610F64
```

Note that on an x86-based Macintosh computer, the second element of the `finderInfo` array contains the ID of the blessed system file, which is the EFI bootloader in its case.

```
$ hostinfo
...
2 processors are physically available.
2 processors are logically available.
Processor type: i486 (Intel 80486)
...
$ bless -info /
findcrinfo[0]: 3050 -> Blessed System Folder is /System/Library/CoreServices
finderinfo[1]: 6484 => Blessed System File is /System/Library/CoreServices/boot.efi
...
```

4.3 Power-On Reset

When a PowerPC-based Apple computer system is powered on, a power-on reset (POR) unit handles the "coming to life" of a processor. On the 970FX, the POR sequence consists of seven phases tracked by hardware state machines. The sequence involves communication between the processor core, the North Bridge (the U3H), and a custom microcontroller. During the sequence, the processor is initialized by a hardcoded set of instructions, which also run certain tests and synchronize the processor interconnect interfaces. In the third phase of the POR sequence, the *hardware interrupt offset register* (HIOR) is initialized. The HIOR is used for interrupt vector relocation: It defines the base physical address for the interrupt vectors. In the last phase, the processor's storage subsystem clock is started and the storage interface is reset. At this point, the processor starts fetching instructions at the *system reset exception* vector. The system reset exception is a nonmaskable, asynchronous exception that has the highest priority of all exceptions. It causes the processor's interrupt mechanism to ignore all other exceptions and generate a non-context-synchronizing interrupt—the *system reset interrupt* (SRI).

Machine Check Exception

Another example of a nonmaskable, asynchronous exception is the *machine check exception* (MCE). It can only be delayed by a system reset exception.

The handler for the SRI is the first entry in the PowerPC interrupt vector table. Its effective address is calculated by combining its vector offset, which is 0x100, with certain bits of the HIOR. Thus, the processor core resumes execution at HIOR + 0x0000_0000_0000_0100. At power-on, the SRI handler, and any others in the table, all belong to Open Firmware, which is in control of the processor. At this point, the processor is in real address mode—that is, memory translation is disabled (an effective address is the same as a physical address). Moreover, the processor caches are disabled.

Note that a system reset exception could be due to a hard or a soft reset. A hard reset—such as one due to a real POR—is seen only by Open Firmware. In contrast, the Mac OS X kernel will see only a soft reset—regardless of whether the processor is being brought up after a POR or is waking up from sleep.

> On a multiprocessor system, Open Firmware selects one processor, using a suitable algorithm, to be the master processor, which is then responsible for booting the client and providing the Open Firmware user interface. The other processors are typically stopped so they do not interfere with the master processor.

4.4 Open Firmware

Open Firmware originated at Sun Microsystems in 1988. The "pizza-box" SPARCstation 1 was released in 1989 with *OpenBoot 1.0*, the first shipping implementation of Open Firmware. The firmware standard was later adopted by Apple, IBM, and other vendors such as those creating ARM-based[7] and PowerPC-based embedded systems. Sun's implementation is trademarked as OpenBoot, whereas Apple simply calls it Open Firmware. The Open Firmware Working Group was formed in 1991, with one of its goals being to publish relevant information on Open Firmware, including recommended practices.

---

7. ARM originally stood for Acorn RISC Machine and later stood for Advanced RISC Machine.

Open Firmware is a nonproprietary, platform-independent, programmable, and extensible environment for use in boot ROMs. Its key features include the following:

- The Open Firmware software architecture is defined by the IEEE Standard for Boot (Initialization Configuration) Firmware standard, which is also known as IEEE 1275. The standard is open and anybody may create an implementation. However, note that the IEEE withdrew the standard in 1999.[8]

- Open Firmware's architecture is independent of the underlying instruction set, busses, other hardware, and operating system. However, the core requirements and practices specified by the standard *are* augmented by platform-specific requirements. For example, processors such as PowerPC and SPARC, or busses such as PCI and Sun's SBus, all have their own requirements and bindings. The union of the core and platform-specific requirements provides a complete firmware specification for a given platform.

- Open Firmware exposes various interfaces such as one for interaction with the end user, another for use by operating systems, and yet another for use by developers of plug-in devices. It presents a machine's various hardware components and their interconnections in the form of a hierarchical data structure: the *device tree*.

- An Open Firmware implementation is based on the Forth programming language, in particular, the *FCode* dialect. FCode is an ANS-compliant[9] dialect that supports compilation of source to machine-independent bytecode. This allows FCode drivers to be used on different platforms. Moreover, FCode bytecodes need less storage space than Forth textual strings do. They are also evaluated faster than Forth text. An FCode evaluator is part of a ROM-resident Open Firmware implementation.

- Open Firmware is modular in the sense that many features of the architecture are optional for an implementation. Moreover, if certain plug-in devices are required at boot time, the expansion ROMs on the cards for such devices can contain FCode-based drivers. As an Open Firmware–equipped machine is turned on, the main ROM begins execution. It probes both onboard and

---

8. The IEEE's withdrawal of the standard does not mean that the standard has been abandoned. It means only that the standard is no longer supported or made available by the IEEE. Vendors such as IBM, Sun, and Apple continue to use and improve Open Firmware.

9. ANS stands for American National Standards.

plug-in devices, as part of which the FCode programs on the plug-in ROMs are also executed. Consequently, such plug-in device drivers become part of the Open Firmware environment. A plug-in FCode driver's references to procedures in the main firmware are resolved in a linking process similar to one involving shared libraries in a traditional execution environment. Note that FCode is *position-independent*.

- Open Firmware provides useful facilities for diagnosing hardware and for debugging its own programs as well as the operating system.

4.4.1 Interacting with Open Firmware

In the rest of the discussion, we will use the term *Open Firmware* to refer to Apple's implementation, unless otherwise stated.

You can enter Open Firmware by keeping the key combination -**option-o-f** pressed for a few seconds just as you power-on or reset the machine. After seeing a welcome message and other verbiage, you will be dropped into a prompt like the following:

```
ok
0 >
```

At this point, you may continue booting the machine by typing mac-boot, reinitialize the hardware—including Open Firmware's data structures—by typing reset-all, or shut the machine down by typing shut-down.

Let us now look at several ways of interacting with Open Firmware.

4.4.1.1 Forth Shell

Open Firmware's ok prompt represents a Forth command interpreter: a *shell*. Apple's implementation includes the optional command-line editor extensions that provide some powerful editing features, most of which should be familiar to users of the EMACS editor. Table 4–2 lists some examples of commonly used key combinations. The ^ character represents the **control** key.

Despite the command-line editing extensions, the Open Firmware "shell" might not be suitable for an edit-run-debug cycle, particularly if nontrivial code is involved. Let us look at other alternatives that are likely to be better for serious Open Firmware programming endeavors.

TABLE 4–2 Key Combinations for Open Firmware Command-Line Editing

Keys	Purpose
^<space>	Complete the preceding word.[a]
^/	Show all possible matches.[b]
^a	Go to the beginning of the line.
^b	Go backward one character.[c]
esc-b	Go backward one word.
^d	Erase the character over the cursor.
esc-d	Erase the word beginning at the character over the cursor, to the end of the word.
^e	Go to the end of the line.
^f	Go forward one character.[c]
esc-f	Go forward one word.
^h	Erase the previous character.
esc-h	Erase from the beginning of the word to the character before the cursor.
^k	Erase from the cursor to the end of the line.
^l	Display the command-line history.[d]
^n	Go to the next line.[c]
^p	Go to the previous line.[c]
^u	Erase the entire line.
^y	Insert the contents of the save buffer before the cursor.[e]

a. Does not show all possible matches.
b. Does not complete the preceding word.
c. You can also use the arrow keys to move up (**^p**), down (**^n**), left (**^b**), and right (**^f**).
d. The command h _N_ executes the contents of history line number _N_.
e. Commands that erase more than one character cause the erased characters to be stored in a save buffer.

4.4.1.2 TELNET

Open Firmware includes the `telnet` support package,[10] which you can use to access the Forth prompt over the network—from an arbitrary computer using a TELNET client. You can verify the presence of the `telnet` package as follows:

```
0 > dev /packages/telnet ok
```

---

10. An Open Firmware package is the combination of a device node's properties, methods, and private data. It may be roughly equated to a class in the object-oriented sense. See also Section 4.6.3.

If you did get an ok response, start a TELNET server in Open Firmware as follows:

```
0 > " enet:telnet,10.0.0.2" io
```

The TELNET server will use 10.0.0.2 as the IP address on the default Ethernet device. You can and *should* choose an appropriate local IP address. Note that although the firmware prints ok after the successful completion of most commands, hitting **<ENTER>** after typing the telnet command line will *not* result in ok being printed.

Once the TELNET server is running, you should be able to connect to Open Firmware on IP address 10.0.0.2 using a TELNET client, say, from a Windows computer. You do need to connect the two machines over Ethernet.[11]

With the TELNET solution, you can write a Forth program in your favorite text editor on a client machine, copy it, and paste it into your TELNET session. This works well, especially since operations that cannot be performed inside the TELNET session—such as graphics operations—will still be performed appropriately (on the Open Firmware "server").

4.4.1.3 TFTP

It is possible to download programs from a remote machine using the trivial file transfer protocol (TFTP) and to execute them within Open Firmware. Technically, in doing this, you are simply *loading* a program from a boot device, which happens to be the network in this case. Similarly, programs can also be accessed from a local boot device such as a locally attached disk. However, it may be rather inconvenient to boot into the operating system to edit programs and then reboot into Open Firmware to run them.

As with the TELNET scenario, you need two machines for TFTP. We refer to the machine running Open Firmware as the *client* and the one running the TFTP daemon as the *server*. The following description assumes that the server is also running Mac OS X, although this is not a requirement.

We enable tftpd, the TFTP daemon, on the server machine by using the service command-line script.

---

11. Ethernet ports on many modern computers, and those on all newer Apple computers, are auto-sensing and auto-configuring. Therefore, a cross-over cable is not required to connect such a computer to another computer directly.

```
$ service --list
smtp
fax-receive
...
tftp
$ service --test-if-available tftp
$ echo $?
0
$ service --test-if-configured-on tftp
$ echo $?
1
$ sudo service tftp start
$ service --test-if-configured-on tftp
$ echo ?
0
```

> Beginning with Mac OS X 10.4, the TFTP service is managed by the `launchd` super daemon. The `service` script acts as a simple wrapper: It modifies the TFTP configuration file (`/System/Library/LaunchDaemons/tftp.plist`) by adding or removing the `Disabled` Boolean property, as appropriate. Thereafter, it calls the `launchctl` command to load or unload the TFTP job. We will discuss `launchd` in Chapter 5.
>
> On older systems, `service` modifies `/etc/xinetd.d/tftp`, the TFTP configuration file for the extended Internet services daemon, by setting the `disable` keyword to value "no".

You can verify whether the TFTP service is indeed running by using the `netstat` command-line utility to display whether the default TFTP daemon port—UDP port 69—is being listened on.

```
$ netstat -na | grep \*.69
udp4       0      0  *.69                    *.*
udp6       0      0  *.69                    *.*
```

By default, `tftpd` uses `/private/tftpboot/` as the directory that contains files that may be downloaded by TFTP clients. If desired, a different directory may be specified in the TFTP daemon's configuration file. You should test your setup by creating a file called, say, `/private/tftpboot/hello.of`. The file's contents could be a trivial Forth program:

```
\ TFTP demo
\ Some commentary is required to make Open Firmware happy.

." Hello, World!" cr
```

Ensure that the file is readable by everybody:

```
$ sudo chmod 644 /private/tftpboot/hello.of
```

Again, the two machines need to be on the same Ethernet. Let us assume that the IP address of the client (running Open Firmware) is 10.0.0.2 and that of the server (running tftpd) is 10.0.0.1. Next, we instruct Open Firmware to boot using TFTP—that is, to download the specified file from the specified remote machine and execute it.

```
0 > boot enet:10.0.0.1,hello.of,10.0.0.2;255.255.255.0,;10.0.0.1
```

In general, the format of the boot command for booting using TFTP is:

```
boot enet:<my ip>,<file>,<server ip>;<netmask>,;<gateway ip>
```

> If you connect the two machines directly with an Ethernet cable, you must use the server's IP address as the gateway address as well.

If all goes well, the boot command line should result in the message "Hello, World!" being printed, followed by the ok prompt.

4.4.1.4 Serial Download

Open Firmware supports downloading Forth code over a serial port—if one is present—and executing it. The dl command can be used for this purpose.

4.4.2 Open Firmware Emulators

Serious Open Firmware developers, such as those writing device drivers, should consider using an Open Firmware emulator that runs on a standard host operating system. A good emulator may implement a comprehensive Open Firmware environment along with a set of peripheral devices—perhaps even including the graphics extensions. The details and availability of such emulators are beyond the scope of this book.

4.5 Forth

Open Firmware is based on the Forth programming language. All programming examples that follow are also written in Forth. Therefore, let us take a whirlwind tour of the language before we continue our discussion of Open Firmware.

Forth is an interactive, extensible, high-level programming language developed by Charles "Chuck" Moore in the early 1970s while he was working at the National Radio Astronomy Observatory (NRAO) in Arizona. Moore was using a third-generation minicomputer, the IBM 1130. The language he created was meant for the next—*fourth*—generation computers, and Moore would have called it *Fourth*, except that the 1130 permitted only five-character identifiers. Hence, the "u" was dropped, and Fourth became *Forth*. Moore's most important goals in developing the language were *extensibility* and *simplicity*. Forth provides a rich vocabulary of built-in commands or *words*. The language can be extended by defining one's own words,[12] either by using existing words as building blocks or by defining words directly in Forth assembly. Forth combines the properties of a high-level language, an assembly language, an operating environment, an interactive command interpreter, and a set of development tools.

4.5.1 Cells

A *cell* is the primary unit of information in a Forth system. As a data type, a cell consists of a certain number of bits depending on the underlying instruction set architecture. A *byte* is defined to contain one address unit, whereas a cell usually contains multiple address units. A typical cell size is 32 bits.

4.5.2 Stacks

Forth is a *stack-based* language that uses reverse Polish notation (RPN), also known as *postfix notation*. You can interact with Forth at Open Firmware's ok prompt:

```
 ok
0 > 3 ok
1 > 5 ok
2 > + ok
1 > . 8 ok
0 >
```

---

12. A key point to understand is that the language itself can be extended: Forth allows you to define words that can be used in subsequent word definitions as keywords, if you will. Similarly, you can define new words that are used while compiling Forth words.

The number before the > indicates the number of items on the stack; initially there are zero items. Typing a number pushes it on the stack. Thus, after typing 3 and 5, the stack has two items. Next, we type +, an operator that consumes two numbers and yields one: the sum. The top two items on the stack are replaced by their sum, leaving a single item on the stack. Typing . displays the topmost item *and* pops it from the stack.

Sometimes, you might find it useful to have Open Firmware display the entire contents of the stack instead of only the number of items. The showstack command achieves this by including the stack's contents in the prompt:

```
0 > showstack  ok
-> <- Empty 1  ok
-> 1 <- Top 2  ok
-> 1 2 <- Top 3  ok
-> 1 2 3 <- Top + ok
-> 1 5 <- Top
```

The noshowstack command turns off this behavior. You can use the .s command to display the entire contents of the stack without any side effects:

```
0 > 1 2 3 4  ok
4 > .s -> 1 2 3 4 <- Top  ok
4 >
```

The stack, or more precisely the *data* or *parameter* stack, is simply a region of last-in first-out (LIFO) memory whose primary use is to pass parameters to commands. The size of a single element (cell) on the stack is determined by the word size of the underlying processor.

> Note that a *processor word* (e.g., 32 bits of addressable information) is different from a Forth word, which is Forth parlance for *command*. We shall use the term *word* to mean a Forth word, unless stated otherwise.

Forth also has a *return stack* that the system uses to pass control between words, and for programming-constructs such as looping. Although the programmer *can* access the return stack and can use it to store data temporarily, such use may have caveats, and the Forth standard discourages it.

4.5.3 Words

Forth *words* are essentially commands—typically analogous to procedures in many high-level languages. Forth provides a variety of standard, built-in words. New ones can be easily defined. For example, a word to compute the square of a number can be defined as follows:

```
: mysquare
    dup *
;
```

mysquare expects to be called with at least one item—a number—on the stack. It will "consume" the number, which would be the top item on the stack, without referring to any other items that may be present on the stack. dup, a built-in word, duplicates the top item. The multiplication operator (*) multiplies the top two items, replacing them with their product.

Forth is a rather terse language, and it is beneficial to comment your code as much as possible. Consider mysquare again, commented this time:

```
\ mysquare - compute the square of a number
: mysquare ( x -- square )
    dup    ( x x )
    *      ( square )
;
```

Figure 4–1 shows the structure of a typical word definition.

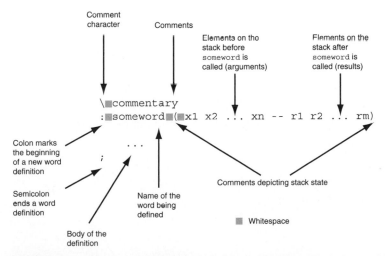

FIGURE 4–1 Defining a Forth word: syntactic requirements and conventions

The \ character is conventionally used for descriptive comments, whereas comments that show the stack state are usually placed between (and). It is often sufficient to describe a Forth word by simply specifying its stack notation that shows "before" and "after" stack contents.

> In the context of Forth programming in the Open Firmware environment, we will use the term *word* interchangeably with the terms *function* and *method*, except in places where such use is likely to cause confusion.

4.5.4 Dictionary

The region of memory where Forth stores its word definitions is called the *dictionary*. It is prepopulated with a built-in set of Forth words: the *base set*, as defined by the ANSI X3.215-1994 standard. When a new word is defined, Forth compiles it—that is, translates it into an internal format—and stores it in the dictionary, which stores new words in a last-come first-used fashion. Let us consider an example.

```
0 > : times2 ( x -- ) 2 * . ;  ok \ Double the input number, display it, and pop it
0 > 2 times2 4  ok
0 > : times2 ( x -- ) 3 * . ;  ok \ Define the same word differently
0 > 2 times2 6  ok                \ New definition is used
0 > forget times2  ok             \ Forget the last definition
0 > 2 times2 4  ok                \ Original definition is used
0 > forget times2  ok             \ Forget that definition too
0 > 2 times2                      \ Try using the word
times2, unknown word
 ok
0 > forget times2
times2, unknown word
```

forget removes the topmost instance of a word, if any, from the dictionary. You can view the definition of an existing word by using the see word:

```
0 > : times2 ( x -- ) 2 * . ;  ok
0 > see times2
: times2
  2 * . ; ok
```

4.5.4.1 A Sampling of Built-in Words

Open Firmware's Forth environment contains built-in words belonging to various categories. Let us look at some of these categories. Note that words are "described" through their stack notations.

Stacks

This category includes words for duplication, removal, and rearrangement of stack elements.

```
dup     ( x -- x x )
?dup    ( x -- x x ) if x is not 0, ( x -- x ) if x is 0
clear   ( x1 x2 ... xn -- )
depth   ( x1 x2 ... xn -- n )
drop    ( x -- )
rot     ( x1 x2 x3 -- x2 x3 x1 )
-rot    ( x1 x2 x3 -- x3 x1 x2 )
swap    ( x1 x2 -- x2 x1 )
```

The return stack is shown with an R: prefix in the stack notation. There exist words to move and copy items between the data and return stacks:

```
\ move from data stack to return stack
>r      ( x -- ) ( R: -- x )

\ move from return stack to data stack
r>      ( -- x ) ( R: x -- )

\ copy from return stack to data stack
r@      ( -- x ) ( R: x -- x )
```

Memory

This category includes words for memory access, allocation, and deallocation.

```
\ fetch the number of address units in a byte
/c                  ( -- n )

\ fetch the number of address units in a cell
/n                  ( -- n )

\ fetch the item stored at address addr
addr @              ( addr -- x )

\ store item x at address addr
x addr !            ( x addr -- )
```

```
\ add v to the value stored at address addr
v addr +!              ( v addr -- )

\ fetch the byte stored at address addr
addr c@               ( addr -- b )

\ store byte b at address addr
b addr c!              ( b addr -- )

\ display len bytes of memory starting at address addr
addr len dump          ( addr len -- )

\ set n bytes beginning at address addr to value b
addr len b fill        ( addr len b -- )

\ set len bytes beginning at address addr to 0
addr len erase         ( addr len -- )

\ allocate len bytes of general-purpose memory
len alloc-mem          ( len -- addr )

\ free len bytes of memory starting at address addr
addr len free-mem      ( addr len -- )

\ allocate len bytes of general-purpose memory, where
\ mybuffer names the address of the allocated region
len buffer: mybuffer ( len -- )
```

Creating and accessing named data are very common operations in a programming endeavor. The following are some examples of doing so.

```
0 > 1 constant myone   ok    \ Create a constant with value 1
0 > myone . 1  ok            \ Verify its value
0 > 2 value mytwo  ok        \ Set value of mytwo to 2
0 > mytwo . 2  ok            \ Verify value of mytwo
0 > 3 to mytwo  ok           \ Set value of mytwo to 3
0 > mytwo . 3  ok            \ Verify value of mytwo
0 > 2 to myone               \ Try to modify value of a constant
invalid use of TO

0 > variable mythree  ok     \ Create a variable called mythree
0 > mythree . ff9d0800  ok   \ Address of mythree
0 > 3 mythree !  ok          \ Store 3 in mythree
0 > mythree @  ok            \ Fetch the contents of mythree
1 > . 3  ok

0 > 4 buffer: mybuffer  ok     \ get a 4-byte buffer
0 > mybuffer . ffbd2c00  ok    \ allocation address
0 > mybuffer 4 dump            \ dump memory contents
ffbd2c00: ff ff fb b0 |....| ok
```

```
0 > mybuffer 4 erase   ok          \ erase memory contents
0 > mybuffer 4 dump                \ dump memory contents
ffbd2c00: 00 00 00 00 |....| ok
0 > mybuffer 4 1 fill   ok         \ fill memory with 1's
0 > mybuffer 4 dump                \ dump memory contents
ffbd2c00: 01 01 01 01 |....| ok
0 > 4 mybuffer 2 + c!   ok         \ store 4 at third byte
0 > mybuffer 4 dump                \ dump memory contents
ffbd2c00: 01 01 04 01 |....| ok
```

Operators

This category includes words for single-precision integer arithmetic operations, double-number arithmetic operations, bitwise logical operations, and comparison.

```
1+       ( n -- n+1 )
2+       ( n -- n+2 )
1-       ( n -- n-1 )
2-       ( n -- n-2 )
2*       ( n -- 2*n )
2/       ( n -- n/2 )
abs      ( n -- |n| )
max      ( n1 n2 -- greater of n1 and n2 )
min      ( n1 n2 -- smaller of n1 and n2 )
negate   ( n -- -n )
and      ( n1 n2 -- n1&n2 )
or       ( n1 n2 -- n1|n2 )
decimal  ( -- change base to 10 )
hex      ( -- change base to 16 )
octal    ( -- change base to 8 )
```

> One double number uses two items on the stack, with the most significant part being the topmost item.

The variable called base stores the current number base. Besides using the built-in words for changing the base to a commonly used value, you can set the base to an arbitrary number by "manually" storing the desired value in the base variable.

```
0 > base @   ok
1 > . 10   ok
0 > 123456   ok
1 > 2 base !   ok
1 > . 11110001001000000   ok
0 > 11111111   ok
1 > hex   ok
1 > . f   ok
0 >
```

Console I/O

This category includes words for console input and output, reading of characters and edited input lines from the console input device, formatting, and string manipulation.

```
key           ( -- c )          waits for a character to be typed
ascii x       ( x -- c )        ascii code for x
c emit        ( c -- )          prints character with ascii code c
cr            ( -- )            carriage return
space         ( -- )            single space
u.r           ( u width -- )    prints u right-justified within width
." text"      ( -- )            prints the string
.( text)      ( -- )            prints the string
```

> A literal string is specified with a leading space after the opening quote, for example: `" hello"`.

Control Flow

This category includes words for conditional and iterative loops, the if-then-else clause, and the case statement. Many of these words refer to a Boolean flag that can be either `true` (−1) or `false` (0). Such a flag is often a result of a comparison operator:

```
0 > 1 2 <  ok         \ is 1 < 2 ?
1 > . ffffffff  ok    \ true
0 > 2 1 <  ok         \ is 2 < 1 ?
1 > . 0  ok           \ false
```

Following are some common control-flow constructs used in Forth programs.

```
\ Unconditional infinite loop
begin
    \ do some processing
again

\ Conditional "while" loop
begin
    <C> \ some condition
    while
        … \ do some processing
    repeat

\ Conditional branch
<C> \ some condition
```

```
if
    … \ condition <C> is true
else
    … \ condition <C> is false
then


\ Iterative loop with a unitary increment
<limit> <start> \ maximum and initial values of loop counter
do
    … \ do some processing
    … \ the variable i contains current value of the counter
loop


\ Iterative loop with a specified increment
<limit> <start> \ maximum and initial values of loop counter
do
    … \ do some processing
    … \ the variable i contains current value of the counter
<delta> \ value to be added to loop counter
+loop
```

Other commonly used Forth words include the following:

- Words for converting data types and address types
- Words for error handling, including an exception mechanism that supports catch and throw
- Words for creating and executing machine-level code definitions

This BootROM Is Brought to You By . . .

The built-in word `kudos` shows a list of credits containing names of those who contributed to the hardware initialization, Open Firmware, and diagnostics aspects of the Boot ROM.

4.5.4.2 Searching the Dictionary

Open Firmware's Forth dictionary may contain thousands of words. The `sifting` word allows you to search for words containing a specified string:

```
0 > sifting get-time
get-time
in /pci@f2000000/mac-io@17/via-pmu@16000/rtc
get-time ok
```

A search could also yield multiple matches:

```
0 > sifting buffer
frame-buffer-addr          buffer:          alloc-buffer:s
in /packages/deblocker
empty-buffers
in /pci@f0000000/ATY,JasperParent@10/ATY,Jasper_A@0
frame-buffer-adr
in /pci@f0000000/ATY,JasperParent@10/ATY,Jasper_B@1
frame-buffer-adr   ok
```

An unsuccessful search fails silently:

```
0 > sifting nonsense   ok
0 >
```

4.5.5 Debugging

Open Firmware includes a source-level debugger for single-stepping and tracing
Forth programs. Some of the relevant words include the following:

```
debug      ( command -- )  mark command for debugging
resume     ( -- )          exit from the debugger's subinterpreter
                           and go back into the debugger
stepping   ( -- )          set single-stepping mode for debugging
tracing    ( -- )          set trace mode for debugging
```

Let us trace the execution of the following simple Forth program.

```
: factorial ( n -- n! )
   dup 0 >
   if
     dup 1 - recurse *
   else
     drop 1
   then
;

0 > showstack   ok
-> <- Empty debug factorial   ok
-> <- Empty tracing   ok
-> <- Empty 3 factorial
debug:
factorial  type ? for help
at ffa22bd0 -- -> 3 <- Top --> dup
at ffa22bd4 -- -> 3 3 <- Top --> 0
at ffa22bd8 -- -> 3 3 0 <- Top --> >
at ffa22bdc -- -> 3 ffffffff <- Top --> if
```

```
at ffa22be4 -- -> 3 <- Top --> dup
at ffa22be8 -- -> 3 3 <- Top --> 1
at ffa22bec -- -> 3 3 1 <- Top --> -
at ffa22bf0 -- -> 3 2 <- Top --> factorial
at ffa22bf4 -- -> 3 2 <- Top --> *
at ffa22bf8 -- -> 6 <- Top --> branch+
at ffa22c04 -- -> 6 <- Top --> exit ok
-> 6 <- Top
```

Alternatively, single-stepping through the program will prompt the user for a keystroke at every Forth word—that is, the single-stepping is at Forth word level. Valid keystrokes that the user may type to control the execution of the program include the following.

- **<space>** executes the current word and goes to the next word.
- **c** continues the program without prompting any further; the program is traced, however.
- **f** suspends debugging and starts a secondary Forth shell, which can be exited through the resume command, after which debugging continues from the point it was suspended.
- **q** aborts execution of the current word and all its callers; control goes back to the Open Firmware prompt.

> Depending on the Open Firmware version and the underlying processor architecture, contents of processor registers can be viewed, and in some cases modified, through implementation-specific words.

4.6 The Device Tree

From the standpoint of system initialization and booting, Open Firmware's core data structure is the *device tree*, which is referred to by all interfaces supported by Open Firmware.

The device tree is a representation of various hardware components in the system and their interconnections. It also contains *pseudo-devices* that have no corresponding physical devices.

The root node of the device tree is / (as in a Unix file system):

```
0 > dev /   ok
0 > ls
ff88feb0: /cpus
```

```
ff890118:   /PowerPC,G5@0
ff8905c8:     /l2-cache
ff891550:   /PowerPC,G5@1
ff891a00:     /l2-cache
ff891bf0: /chosen
ff891d98: /memory@0,0
ff891fa8: /openprom
ff892108:   /client-services
ff8933f8: /rom@0,ff800000
ff8935b8:   /boot-rom@fff00000
ff8937a8:   /macos
ff893840: /options
ff8938d8: /packages
ff893cc8:   /deblocker
ff894618:   /disk-label
ff895098:   /obp-tftp
ff89fc68:   /telnet
...
ff9a7610:   /temperatures
ffa1bb70:     /drive-bay@4
ffa1f370:     /backside@6
...
ff9a77a8:   /audible-alarm
ff9a7940:   /thermostats
ffa1cfb8:     /overtemp*-signal@5800
ok
0 >
```

In the device tree, an individual node represents a bus, a physical device, or a pseudo-device. A node with children—visually indicated by indentations in the output of ls—is often a bus. You can use the dev command to go to a certain node in the tree.

```
0 > dev /pseudo-hid  ok      \ Go to node /pseudo-hid
0 > ls                       \ List children of current node
ff943ff0: /keyboard
ff944788: /mouse
ff944d50: /eject-key
0 > dev mouse  ok            \ Go to a child
0 > pwd /pseudo-hid/mouse ok \ Tell us where we are
0 > dev ..  ok               \ Go one level "up"
0 > pwd /pseudo-hid ok
0 > dev /cpus ok             \ Go to node /cpus
0 > ls
ff890118: /PowerPC,G5@0
ff8905c8:   /l2-cache
ff891550: /PowerPC,G5@1
ff891a00:   /l2-cache
 ok
```

Since the complete *pathname* of a device could be rather long and inconvenient to use, commonly used devices have shorthand representations, or *aliases*. `devalias` shows the current list of aliases:

```
0 > devalias
keyboard            /pseudo-hid/keyboard
mouse               /pseudo-hid/mouse
eject-key           /pseudo-hid/eject-key
pci0                /pci@0,f0000000
ipc                 /ipc
scca                /ht/pci@3/mac-io/escc/ch-a
nvram               /nvram
uni-n               /u3
u3                  /u3
dart                /u3/dart
...
first-boot          /ht@0,f2000000/pci@7/k2-sata-root@c/k2-sata
second-boot         /ht@0,f2000000/pci@5/ata-6@d/disk
last-boot           /ht@0,f2000000/pci@6/ethernet
screen              /pci@0,f0000000/ATY,WhelkParent@10/ATY,Whelk_A@0
ok
```

`devalias` followed by an alias shows the latter's expansion (note that the / separator is not used when specifying an alias):

```
0 > devalias hd /ht/pci@7/k2-sata-root/k2-sata@0/disk@0 ok
0 > devalias wireless /ht@0,f2000000/pci@4/pci80211@1 ok
```

The `dir` command can be used to list files on an HFS Plus or HFS volume. Its argument is a device path that represents a volume and a path within that volume. The device path can be an alias or a complete path.

```
0 > dir hd:\
```

Size/	GMT			File/Dir
bytes	date	time	TYPE CRTR	Name
12292	6/18/ 5	15:23:14		.DS_Store
131072	5/25/ 5	10: 1:30		.hotfiles.btree
16777216	5/12/ 5	1:57:11	jrnl hfs+	.journal
4096	5/12/ 5	1:57:10	jrnl hfs+	.journal_info_block
	6/18/ 5	1:32:14		.Spotlight-V100
...				
	5/12/ 5	1:57:12		%00%00%00%00HFS+%20Private%20Data

```
ok
0 > dir hd:\System\Library\CoreServices
```

Size/	GMT			File/Dir
bytes	date	time	TYPE CRTR	Name

```
    869  5/12/ 5  2:28:21  tbxj chrp   .disk_label
     12  5/12/ 5  2:28:21              .disk_label.contentDetails
          6/ 9/ 5  4: 8:44              AppleFileServer.app
          3/28/ 5  4:53:13             Automator%20Launcher.app
          3/28/ 5  4:42:25             BezelUI
          3/28/ 5  4:51:51             Bluetooth%20Setup%20Assistant.app
  14804  3/26/ 5 22:47: 0              bluetoothlauncher
          3/28/ 5  4:51:51             BluetoothUIServer.app
          3/21/ 5  3:12:59             BOMArchiveHelper.app
 174276  5/19/ 5  3:46:35  tbxi chrp   BootX
...
```

Each node in the device tree may have *properties*, *methods*, and *data*.

4.6.1 Properties

A node's properties are externally visible data structures that describe the node and possibly its associated devices, which may further have their own specific properties. Open Firmware's client programs, as well as its own procedures, may inspect and modify properties. Access to properties is also available from the Open Firmware user interface. The .properties word shows the names and values of the current node's properties.

```
0 > dev enet   ok
0 > .properties
vendor-id
                         0000106b
device-id                0000004c
revision-id              00000000
class-code               00020000
interrupts               00000029 00000001
min-grant                00000040
...
name                     ethernet
device_type              network
network-type             ethernet
...
local-mac-address        ...
gbit-phy

 ok
0 > dev /cpus/PowerPC,G5@0   ok
0 > .properties
name                     PowerPC,G5

device_type              cpu
reg                      00000000
```

```
cpu-version          003c0300
cpu#                 00000000
soft-reset           00000071
state                running
clock-frequency      9502f900
bus-frequency        4a817c80
config-bus-frequency 4a817c80
timebase-frequency   01fca055
reservation-granule-size00000080
tlb-sets             00000100
tlb-size             00001000
d-cache-size         00008000
i-cache-size         00010000
d-cache-sets         00000080
i-cache-sets         00000200
i-cache-block-size   00000080
d-cache-block-size   00000080
graphics
performance-monitor
altivec
data-streams
dcbz                 00000080
general-purpose
64-bit
32-64-bridge
...
```

The `dump-properties` word can be used to show properties of all nodes in the device tree.

```
0 > dump-properties
/
PROPERTIES:
model                PowerMac7,3
compatible           PowerMac7,3
                     MacRISC4
                     Power Macintosh
...
/cpus/PowerPC,G5@0/l2-cache
PROPERTIES:
name                 l2-cache
device_type          cache
i-cache-size         00080000
...
/sep/thermostats/overtemp*-signal@5800
PROPERTIES:
name                 overtemp*-signal
...
```

Properties are represented as collections of names and their corresponding values. Property names are human-readable text strings, and property values are variable-length—possibly zero-length—byte arrays representing encoded information. Standard property names found in a package include the following:

- `name`—the name of the package
- `reg`—the package's "registers"
- `device_type`—the characteristics the package's device is expected to have, such as `block`, `byte`, `display`, `memory`, `network`, `pci`, and `serial`

A package's registers can represent very different information depending on the nature of the package. For example, the registers of the `memory` package contain the physical memory addresses installed in the system. Details of installed memory can be examined through the `.properties` command.

The machine in Figure 4–2 has two PC2700 DDR SDRAM memory modules installed. The two pairs of numbers shown against `reg` specify the starting address and size of the module. The first RAM module starts at address `0x00000000` and has a size `0x10000000` (256MB). The second module starts at `0x10000000` (256MB) and has a size 256MB. The total RAM is therefore 512MB.

FIGURE 4–2 Physical memory properties in the device tree of a PowerBook G4

```
0 > dev /memory .properties ok
name                    memory
device_type             memory
reg                     00000000   10000000
                        10000000   10000000
slot-names              00000003
                        SODIMM0/J25LOWER
                        SODIMM1/J25UPPER

...
dimm-types              DDR SDRAM
                        DDR SDRAM
dimm-speeds             PC2700U-25330
                        PC2700U-25330

...
```

It is possible to delete certain properties and specify your own. In the case of memory, this would be useful if you need to reduce the installed RAM size seen by Mac OS X without physically removing a RAM module. This way, you could simulate an arbitrary memory size that is less than the total memory installed.

The following command sequence disables the second of the two memory modules installed in the machine from Figure 4–2. The change is not permanent in that it is *not* written to NVRAM—once the system is rebooted, the "disabled" module will be detected and used as before.

```
0 > dev /memory
0 > " reg" delete-property  ok
0 > 0 encode-int 10000000 encode-int encode+ " reg" property  ok
```

It must be noted that the reg properties may change from machine to machine, or more likely, with architectural changes. For example, the format of memory properties changed with the Power Mac G5. Figure 4–3 shows the memory properties on a quad-processor Power Mac G5 with six of its eight RAM slots filled, each with a 512MB DDR2 module.

FIGURE 4–3 Physical memory properties in the device tree of a Power Mac G5

```
0 > dev /memory   ok
0 > .properties
name                    memory
device_type             memory
reg                     00000000 00000000  20000000
                        00000000 20000000  20000000
                        00000000 40000000  20000000
                        00000000 60000000  20000000
                        00000001 00000000  20000000
                        00000001 20000000  20000000
                        00000000 00000000  00000000
                        00000000 00000000  00000000
slot-names              000000ff
                        DIMM0/J6700
                        DIMM1/J6800
                        DIMM2/J6900
                        DIMM3/J7000
                        DIMM4/J7100
                        DIMM5/J7200
                        DIMM6/J7300
                        DIMM7/J7400
available               00003000 1f5ed000
ram-map                 ...
bank-names              000000ff
                        64 bit Bank0/J6700/J6800/front
                        64 bit Bank1/J6700/J6800/back
                        64 bit Bank2/J6900/J7000/front
                        64 bit Bank3/J6900/J7000/back
                        64 bit Bank4/J7100/J7200/front
```

(continues)

FIGURE 4–3 Physical memory properties in the device tree of a Power Mac G5 *(continued)*

```
                         64 bit Bank5/J7100/J7200/back
                         64 bit Bank6/J7300/J7400/front
                         64 bit Bank7/J7300/J7400/back
...
dimm-types               DDR2 SDRAM
                         DDR2 SDRAM
                         DDR2 SDRAM
                         DDR2 SDRAM
                         DDR2 SDRAM
                         DDR2 SDRAM


dimm-speeds              PC2-4200U-444
                         PC2-4200U-444
                         PC2-4200U-444
                         PC2-4200U-444
                         PC2-4200U-444
                         PC2-4200U-444
...
```

A less adventurous and more appropriate way to limit visible RAM is to use the kernel's maxmem boot argument. You can use the nvram command-line program from within Mac OS X to get and set Open Firmware NVRAM variables. For example, the following command executed at a shell prompt in Mac OS X would limit available memory size to 128MB:

```
$ sudo nvram boot-args="maxmem=128"
```

> A package that defines a physical address space usually contains the #address-cells and #size-cells standard properties. The value of #address-cells defines the number of cells required to encode a physical address within the address space defined by the package. The #size-cells property defines the number of cells required to represent the length of a physical address range. For example, the value of #address-cells for the root node of the device tree is 2 on the G5 and 1 on the G4.

4.6.2 Methods

A node's methods are simply software procedures supported by the device it represents. The words Forth word shows the current node's methods:

```
0 > dev enet   ok
0 > words

power-down      ((open))        max-transfer    block-size      #blocks
dma-free        dma-alloc       load            write           flush
read            close           (open)          open            enet-quiesce
...
show-enet-debug?                enet-base       my_space   ok
```

As we noted earlier, a word's definition may be viewed using see:

```
0 > see flush
: flush
    " enet: Flush" 1 .enet-debug restart-rxdma ; ok
```

The dump-device-tree word walks the entire device tree, showing each node's methods and properties.

4.6.3 Data

A node may also have private data used by its methods. Such data could be either instance-specific or static. Static data, which is seen by all instances, persists across instances.

There is a related abstraction called a *package* that we referred to earlier. Usually, a package is synonymous with a device. A distinction is made for pseudo-devices, which have no corresponding physical device. Pseudo-devices are said to have *software-only* packages. Here is a simple way to look at this.

- The device tree has device nodes, some of which represent software-only devices.

- A package is the combination of a device node's properties, methods, and data.

- Multiple packages may implement the same interface. For example, two distinct network device driver packages—say, for two different network cards—may each implement the same network device interface.

There is a special category of packages: the *support packages*. These do not correspond to any specific devices but implement general-purpose utility methods. They live under the /packages node in the device tree.

```
0 > dev /packages
0 > ls
ff893cc8: /deblocker
```

```
ff894618: /disk-label
ff895098: /obp-tftp
ff89fc68: /telnet
ff8a0520: /mac-parts
ff8a1e48: /mac-files
ff8a4fc0: /hfs-plus-files
ff8aa268: /fat-files
ff8ad008: /iso-9660-files
ff8ade20: /bootinfo-loader
ff8afa88: /xcoff-loader
ff8b0560: /macho-loader
ff8b33d0: /pe-loader
ff8b3dd8: /elf-loader
ff8b5d20: /usb-hid-class
ff8b8870: /usb-ms-class
ff8bb540: /usb-audio-class
ff929048: /ata-disk
ff92b610: /atapi-disk
ff92daf0: /sbp2-disk
ff931508: /bootpath-search
ff9380f8: /terminal-emulator
ok
0 >
```

We came across the `telnet` support package earlier when we used it to connect to Open Firmware from another computer. `obp-tftp` implements a TFTP client for use in network booting. `atapi-disk` lets you communicate with an ATAPI device using the ATAPI protocol.

ATAPI

ATAPI stands for *ATA Packet Interface*, where ATA, in turn, stands for *AT Attachment*. AT (advanced technology) refers to the IBM PC/AT of 1984. ATA is a device interface for mass-storage devices. It is colloquially referred to as IDE (integrated device electronics) or EIDE (extended IDE). ATAPI can be viewed as an ATA extension used by a variety of non-hard-disk storage devices.

4.7 Open Firmware Interfaces

When we enumerated Open Firmware's key features, we noted that it provides multiple interfaces: for end users, for client programs, and for device vendors.

4.7.1 The User Interface

In this chapter, we have so far used Open Firmware's user interface to interact with it. We likened the Forth interpreter's command-line feature to a Unix shell. The user interface provides a set of words for interactively performing various Open Firmware functions such as managing configurations; debugging hardware, firmware, and software; and controlling aspects of booting.

4.7.2 The Client Interface

Open Firmware provides a client interface that its clients may use. A client is a program—such as a bootloader or an operating system—that is loaded and executed by Open Firmware. As we will see shortly, in the case of Mac OS X, Open Firmware's primary client is BootX, the bootloader. Examples of important services provided through the client interface include the following.

- It provides access to the device tree: walking and searching the tree, opening and closing devices, performing I/O on devices, and so on. In particular, a client uses this interface to access devices that may be critical for booting, such as console, network, and storage devices.
- It provides capabilities for allocating, deallocating, and mapping memory.
- It facilitates transfer of control during the boot process.

The device tree contains standard *system nodes* such as /chosen, /openprom, and /options. These nodes play important roles in the client interface. We will take a look at them when we discuss the bootloader.

Typically, you need to *open* a device and get an *instance handle* before you can call the device's methods. This can be achieved by using a method such as open-dev, although there are other approaches, including shortcut methods that open a device, call a specified method in it, and close it—all in a single invocation. Opening a device using open-dev causes all devices in the chain to be opened. We will frequently use the following idiom for calling device methods in our programming examples:

```
0 value mydevice
" devicename" open-dev to mydevice
arg1 arg2 … argN " methodname" mydevice $call-method
```

4.7.3 The Device Interface

Open Firmware's third interface is the device interface, which exists between Open Firmware and a developer's device. The expansion ROM in a plug-in device contains an FCode program that uses the device interface. This allows Open Firmware to identify the device during probing, to characterize it, and to possibly use it during booting.

4.8 Programming Examples

In this section, we will look at examples of programming in the Open Firmware environment. While doing so, we will also come across several device support extensions implemented by Apple's version of Open Firmware. These device-specific extensions allow programs to access the keyboard, mouse, real-time clock (RTC), NVRAM, and so on.

4.8.1 Dumping NVRAM Contents

In the example shown in Figure 4–4, we dump the entire contents—in a raw format—of the NVRAM device. The following relevant methods are provided by the NVRAM device:

```
size ( -- <size in bytes> )
seek ( position.low position.high -- <boolean status> )
read ( <buffer address> <bytes to read> -- <bytes read> )
```

We first open the NVRAM device and query its size, which is reported to be 8KB (0x2000 bytes). We allocate an 8KB buffer to pass to the read method. Before we read from the device, we seek to its beginning. We use the dump word to display the contents of the buffer in a meaningful format. Among the NVRAM's contents, you can see the computer's serial number and the various Open Firmware variables.

FIGURE 4–4 Dumping NVRAM contents

```
0 > 0 value mynvram   ok
0 > " nvram" open-dev to mynvram   ok
0 > " size" mynvram $call-method   ok
1 > . 2000   ok
```

(continues)

FIGURE 4–4 Dumping NVRAM contents *(continued)*

```
0 > 2000 buffer: mybuffer   ok
0 >   0 0 " seek" mynvram $call-method   ok
1 > . ffffffff   ok
0 > mybuffer 2000 " read" mynvram $call-method   ok
1 >   . 2000   ok
0 > mybuffer 2000 dump
ffbba000: 5a 82 00 02 6e 76 72 61 6d 00 00 00 00 00 00 00 |Z...nvram.......|
ffbba010: bb f1 64 59 00 00 03 3c 00 00 00 00 00 00 00 00 |..dY...<........|
ffbba020: 5f 45 00 3e 73 79 73 74 65 6d 00 00 00 00 00 00 |_E.>system......|
ffbba030: 00 02 00 00 64 61 79 74 00 06 00 00 00 00 00 00 |....dayt........|
...
ffbba400: 70 bd 00 c1 63 6f 6d 6d 6f 6e 00 00 00 00 00 00 |p...common......|
ffbba410: 6c 69 74 74 6c 65 2d 65 6e 64 69 61 6e 3f 3d 66 |little-endian?=f|
ffbba420: 61 6c 73 65 00 72 65 61 6c 2d 6d 6f 64 65 3f 3d |alse.real-mode?=|
ffbba430: 66 61 6c 73 65 00 61 75 74 6f 2d 62 6f 6f 74 3f |false.auto-boot?|
ffbba440: 3d 74 72 75 65 00 64 69 61 67 2d 73 77 69 74 63 |=true.diag-switc|
ffbba450: 68 3f 3d 66 61 6c 73 65 00 66 63 6f 64 65 2d 64 |h?=false.fcode-d|
ffbba460: 65 62 75 67 3f 3d 66 61 6c 73 65 00 6f 65 6d 2d |ebug?=false.oem-|
ffbba470: 62 61 6e 6e 65 72 3f 3d 66 61 6c 73 65 00 6f 65 |banner?=false.oe|
ffbba480: 6d 2d 6c 6f 67 6f 3f 3d 66 61 6c 73 65 00 75 73 |m-logo?=false.us|
ffbba490: 65 2d 6e 76 72 61 6d 72 63 3f 3d 66 61 6c 73 65 |e-nvramrc?=false|
ffbba4a0: 00 75 73 65 2d 67 65 6e 65 72 69 63 3f 3d 66 61 |.use-generic?=fa|
ffbba4b0: 6c 73 65 00 64 65 66 61 75 6c 74 2d 6d 61 63 2d |lse.default-mac-|
ffbba4c0: 61 64 64 72 65 73 73 3f 3d 66 61 6c 73 65 00 73 |address?=false.s|
ffbba4d0: 6b 69 70 2d 6e 65 74 62 6f 6f 74 3f 3d 66 61 6c |kip-netboot?=fal|
ffbba4e0: 73 65 00 72 65 61 6c 2d 62 61 73 65 3d 2d 31 00 |se.real-base=-1.|
ffbba4f0: 72 65 61 6c 2d 73 69 7a 65 3d 2d 31 00 6c 6f 61 |real-size=-1.loa|
ffbba500: 64 2d 62 61 73 65 3d 30 78 38 30 30 30 30 30 00 |d-base=0x800000.|
ffbba510: 76 69 72 74 2d 62 61 73 65 3d 2d 31 00 76 69 72 |virt-base=-1.vir|
ffbba520: 74 2d 73 69 7a 65 3d 2d 31 00 6c 6f 67 67 65 72 |t-size=-1.logger|
ffbba530: 2d 62 61 73 65 3d 2d 31 00 6c 6f 67 67 65 72 2d |-base=-1.logger-|
...
```

4.8.2 Determining Screen Dimensions

In this example, we call the `dimensions` method of the `screen` device to retrieve the horizontal and vertical pixel counts of the display associated with the device. Alternatively, the `screen-width` and `screen-height` words can be used to query this information.

```
0 > showstack   ok
-> <- Empty 0 value myscreen   ok
-> <- Empty " screen" open-dev to myscreen   ok
```

```
-> <- Empty " dimensions" myscreen $call-method  ok
-> 1280 854 <- Top 2drop  ok
-> <- Empty
```

4.8.3 Working with Colors

In Open Firmware's default (8-bit) graphics model, each pixel is represented by an 8-bit value that defines the pixel's color. This value—the color number—maps to one of 256 colors according to entries in a color lookup table (CLUT). Each entry is a triplet of red, green, and blue (RGB) values. For example, the default CLUT defines color number 0 to be black—corresponding to the (0, 0, 0) RGB triplet—and defines color number 255 to be white—corresponding to the (255, 255, 255) RGB triplet. The color! and color@ methods of the display device allow individual CLUT entries to be set and retrieved, respectively.

```
color@      ( color# -- red blue green )
color!      ( red blue green color# -- )
get-colors ( clut-dest-address starting# count -- )
set-colors ( clut-src-address starting# count -- )
```

get-colors and set-colors, respectively, can be used to retrieve or set a range of consecutive colors, including an entire CLUT.

```
0 > showstack  ok
-> <- Empty 0 value myscreen  ok
-> <- Empty " screen" open-dev to myscreen  ok
-> <- Empty 0 " color@" myscreen $call-method  ok
-> 0 0 0 <- Top 3drop  ok
-> <- Empty 255 " color@" myscreen $call-method  ok
-> 255 255 255 <- Top 3drop  ok
-> <- Empty foreground-color  ok
-> 0 <- Top drop  ok
-> <- Empty background-color  ok
-> 15 <- Top " color@" myscreen $call-method  ok
-> 255 255 255 <- Top 3drop  ok
-> <- Empty 256 3 * buffer: myclut  ok
-> <- Empty myclut 0 256 " get-colors" myscreen $call-method  ok
-> <- Empty myclut 256 3 * dump
ffbbc000: 00 00 00 00 aa 00 aa 00 00 ...
...
ffbbd2e0: d5 fd 68 ... ff ff ff
-> <- Empty
```

The foreground-color and background-color words, respectively, fetch the color numbers of the foreground colors—defined to be 0 (black)—and background colors—defined to be 15 (white). Note that color number 15 also maps to the white color in the default CLUT. This is in accordance with Open Firmware's 16-color text extension, which states that the display driver shall initialize the first 16 colors per a predefined list.

4.8.4 Drawing a Color-Filled Rectangle

Open Firmware's graphics extension standard provides a method to draw a color-filled rectangle (`fill-rectangle`), a method to draw a rectangle using a specified pixel map (`draw-rectangle`), and a method to read a rectangular pixel map from the display buffer (`read-rectangle`). Using these methods as primitives, more sophisticated drawing routines can be constructed.

```
draw-rectangle ( src-pixmap x y width height -- )
fill-rectangle ( color# x y width height -- )
read-rectangle ( dest-pixmap x y width height -- )
```

The following program draws a black rectangle that is 100 pixels wide and 100 pixels tall, with its top-left corner at the center of the screen.

```
\ fill-rectangle-demo
\ fill-rectangle usage example

0 value myscreen
" screen" open-dev to myscreen

0 value mycolor

\ color x y width height
mycolor screen-width 2 / screen-height 2 / 100 100
        " fill-rectangle" myscreen $call-method
```

Running the `fill-rectangle-demo` program, say, by "booting" it using the TFTP method, should draw the desired black rectangle. Note that the screen's origin, that is, position (0, 0), is located at the top left of the physical display.

4.8.5 Creating an Animated Solution to the "Towers of Hanoi" Problem

Given the ability to draw a rectangle at a specified location on the screen, let us look at a more complex example: an animated solution to the Towers of Hanoi problem.[13] We will use the ms word, which sleeps for a specified number of milli-seconds, to control the rate of animation. Figure 4–5 shows the layout and relative dimensions of the objects we will draw on the screen.

The code for the program can be conveniently divided into two parts: the code for animating and the code for generating moves for the Towers of Hanoi problem. We will use the stack-based algorithm shown as pseudocode in Figure 4–6 for solving an N-disk Towers of Hanoi problem.

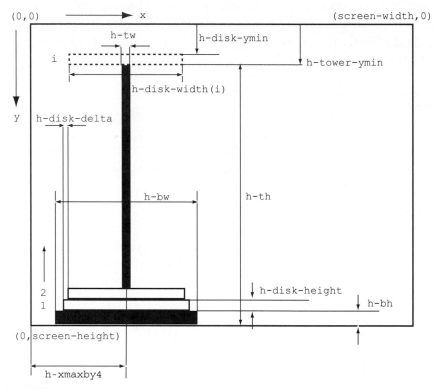

FIGURE 4–5 The Towers of Hanoi: layout and relative dimensions of on-screen objects

---

13. There are three towers arranged left to right. The leftmost tower contains some number of un-equally sized disks, arranged such that a smaller disk is never below a larger disk. The objective is to move all the disks to the rightmost tower, one at a time, while using the middle tower as temporary storage. At no time during the transfer may a larger disk be on top of a smaller one.

FIGURE 4–6 The Towers of Hanoi: simulating recursion using a stack

```
stack = (); /* empty */
push(stack, N, 1, 3, 0);
while (notempty(stack)) {
    processed = pop(stack);
    to = pop(stack);
    from = pop(stack);
    n = pop(stack);
    left = 6 - from - to;
    if (processed == 0) {
        if (n == 1)
            movedisk(from, to);
        else
            push(stack, n, from, to, 1, n - 1, from, left, 0);
    } else {
        movedisk(from, to);
        push(stack, n - 1, left, to, 0);
    }
}
```

The `movedisk` function in Figure 4–6 is required to graphically move a disk from one tower to another. It could be broken down into distinct steps from an animation standpoint, corresponding to the horizontal and vertical motion of the disk. For example, moving a disk from the left tower to the right tower requires us to first move the disk up on the source tower, move it to the right so that it reaches the destination tower, and finally move it down until it comes to rest in its appropriate position on the destination tower. The code shown in Figure 4–7 is the first part of the program that provides the following key functionality:

- Initializes and draws all static graphical objects on the screen—that is, the tower bases, the tower poles, and the specified number of disks on the source tower (`hanoi-init`)
- Implements a function to animate the upward motion of a disk (`hanoi-disk-move-up`)
- Implements a function to animate the horizontal (left or right—based on a function argument) motion of a disk (`hanoi-disk-move-lr`)
- Implements a function to animate the downward motion of a disk (`hanoi-disk-move-down`)

The functions are subdivided into smaller functions. The `hanoi-disk-move` function is a harness function that is equivalent to `movedisk` in Figure 4–6.

FIGURE 4–7 The Towers of Hanoi: Forth code for animation

```
\ Towers of Hanoi Demo
\ Commentary required for "booting" this program.

\ Configurable values
variable h-delay 1 h-delay !
variable h-maxdisks 8 h-maxdisks !

: hanoi-about ( -- ) cr ." The Towers of Hanoi in Open Firmware" cr ;
: hanoi-usage ( -- ) cr ." usage: n hanoi, 1 <= n <= " h-maxdisks @  . cr ;

decimal \ Switch base to decimal

\ Open primary display
0 value myscreen
" screen" open-dev to myscreen

\ Convenience wrapper function
: hanoi-fillrect ( color x y w h -- ) " fill-rectangle" myscreen $call-method ;

\ Calculate display constants

screen-height 100 / 3 *      value h-bh          \ 3% of screen height
screen-width 100 / 12 *      value h-bw          \ 12% of screen width
screen-width 4 /             value h-xmaxby4     \ 25% of screen width
screen-height 100 / 75 *     value h-th          \ 75% of screen height
h-bh 2 /                     value h-tw
screen-height h-th h-bh + -  value h-tower-ymin
screen-height 100 / 2 *      value h-disk-height \ 2% of screen height
screen-width 100 / 1 *       value h-disk-delta
h-tower-ymin h-disk-height - value h-disk-ymin

\ Colors
2   value h-color-base
15 value h-color-bg
50 value h-color-disk
4   value h-color-tower

\ Miscellaneous variables
variable h-dx \ A disk's x-coordinate
variable h-dy \ A disk's y-coordinate
variable h-dw \ A disk's width
variable h-dh \ A disk's height
variable h-tx \ A tower's x-coordinate
variable h-N  \ Number of disks to solve for
variable h-dcolor
variable h-delta

3 buffer: h-tower-disks
```

(continues)

FIGURE 4–7 The Towers of Hanoi: Forth code for animation *(continued)*

```
: hanoi-draw-tower-base ( n -- )
    h-color-base swap
    h-xmaxby4 * h-bw -
    screen-height h-bh -
    h-bw 2 *
    h-bh
    hanoi-fillrect
;

: hanoi-draw-tower-pole ( tid -- )
    dup 1 - 0 swap h-tower-disks + c!
    h-color-tower swap
    h-xmaxby4 * h-tw -
    screen-height h-th h-bh + -
    h-tw 2 *
    h-th
    hanoi-fillrect
;

: hanoi-disk-width ( did -- cdw )
    h-bw swap h-disk-delta * -
;

: hanoi-disk-x          ( tid did -- x )
    hanoi-disk-width    ( tid cdw )
    swap                ( cdw tid )
    h-xmaxby4 * swap    ( [tid * h-xmaxby4] cdw )
    -                   ( [tid * h-xmaxby4] - cdw )
;

: hanoi-disk-y ( tn -- y )
    screen-height swap ( screen-height tn )
    1 +                ( screen-height [tn + 1] )
    h-disk-height *    ( screen-height [[tn + 1] * h-disk-height] )
    h-bh +             ( screen-height [[[tn + 1] * h-disk-height] + h-bh] )
    -                  ( screen-height - [[[tn + 1] * h-disk-height] + h-bh] )
;

: hanoi-tower-disks-inc    ( tid -- tn )
    dup                    ( tid tid )
    1 - h-tower-disks + c@ \ fetch cn, current number of disks
    dup                    ( tid cn cn )
    1 +                    ( tid cn [cn + 1] )
    rot                    ( cn [cn + 1] tid )
    1 - h-tower-disks + c!
;
```

(continues)

FIGURE 4–7 The Towers of Hanoi: Forth code for animation *(continued)*

```
: hanoi-tower-disks-dec    ( tid -- tn )
    dup                    ( tid tid )
    1 - h-tower-disks + c@ \ fetch cn, current number of disks
    dup                    ( tid cn cn )
    1 -                    ( tid cn [cn - 1] )
    rot                    ( cn [cn + 1] tid )
    1 - h-tower-disks + c!
;


: hanoi-tower-disk-add    ( tid did -- )
    h-color-disk          ( tid did color )
    -rot                  ( color tid did )
    2dup                  ( color tid did tid did )
    hanoi-disk-x          ( color tid did x )
    -rot                  ( color x tid did )
    over                  ( color x tid did tid )
    hanoi-tower-disks-inc ( color x tid did tn )
    hanoi-disk-y          ( color x tid did y )
    -rot                  ( color x y tid did )
    hanoi-disk-width 2 *  ( color x y tid w )
    swap                  ( color x y w tid )
    drop                  ( color x y w )
    h-disk-height         ( color x y w h )
    hanoi-fillrect
;


: hanoi-init ( n -- )

    \ Initialize variables
    0 h-dx !
    0 h-dy !
    0 h-tower-disks c!
    0 h-tower-disks 1 + c!
    0 h-tower-disks 2 + c!

    \ Draw tower bases
    1 hanoi-draw-tower-base
    2 hanoi-draw-tower-base
    3 hanoi-draw-tower-base

    \ Draw tower poles
    1 hanoi-draw-tower-pole
    2 hanoi-draw-tower-pole
    3 hanoi-draw-tower-pole

    \ Add disks to source tower
    1 +
    1
```

(continues)

FIGURE 4–7 The Towers of Hanoi: Forth code for animation *(continued)*

```
    do
        1 i hanoi-tower-disk-add
    loop
;

: hanoi-sleep ( msec -- )
    ms
;

: hanoi-drawloop-up ( limit start -- )
do
    h-color-bg
    h-dx @
    h-dy @ i - h-dh @ + 1 -
    h-dw @
    1
    hanoi-fillrect

    h-color-disk
    h-dx @
    h-dy @ i - 1 -
    h-dw @
    1
    hanoi-fillrect

    h-dy @ i - h-disk-ymin >
    if
        h-color-tower
        h-tx @
        h-dy @ i - h-dh @ + 1 -
        h-tw 2 *
        1
        hanoi-fillrect
    then

    h-delay @ hanoi-sleep
loop
;

: hanoi-drawloop-down ( limit start -- )
do
    h-color-bg
    h-dx @
    h-disk-ymin i +
    h-dw @
    1
    hanoi-fillrect
```

(continues)

FIGURE 4–7 The Towers of Hanoi: Forth code for animation *(continued)*

```
    h-color-disk
    h-dx @
    h-disk-ymin i + 1 + h-dh @ +
    h-dw @
    1
    hanoi-fillrect

    i h-dh @ >
    if
        h-color-tower
        h-tx @
        h-disk-ymin i +
        h-tw 2 *
        1
        hanoi-fillrect
    then

    h-delay @ hanoi-sleep
loop
;

: hanoi-drawloop-lr ( limit start -- )
do
    h-color-bg
    h-dx @ i +
    h-disk-ymin
    h-dw @
    h-dh @
    hanoi-fillrect

    h-color-disk
    h-dx @ i + h-delta @ +
    h-disk-ymin
    h-dw @
    h-dh @
    hanoi-fillrect

    h-delay @ hanoi-sleep

h-delta @
+loop
;

: hanoi-disk-move-up      ( tid did -- )
    h-color-disk          ( tid did color )
    -rot                  ( color tid did )
    2dup                  ( color tid did tid did )
```

(continues)

FIGURE 4–7 The Towers of Hanoi: Forth code for animation *(continued)*

```
    hanoi-disk-x           ( color tid did x )
    -rot                   ( color x tid did )
    over                   ( color x tid did tid )
    hanoi-tower-disks-dec  ( color x tid did tn )
    1 -                    ( color x tid tid [tn - 1] )
    hanoi-disk-y           ( color x tid did y )
    -rot                   ( color x y tid did )
    hanoi-disk-width       ( color x y tid w )
    swap                   ( color x y w tid )
    drop                   ( color x y w )
    h-disk-height          ( color x y w h )
    h-dh !
    2 * h-dw !
    h-dy !
    h-dx !
    h-dcolor !
    h-dx @ h-dw @ 2 / + h-tw - h-tx !
    h-dy @ h-disk-ymin -
    0
    hanoi-drawloop-up
;

: hanoi-disk-move-down     ( tid did -- )
    h-color-disk           ( tid did color )
    -rot                   ( color tid did )
    2dup                   ( color tid did tid did )
    hanoi-disk-x           ( color tid did x )
    -rot                   ( color x tid did )
    over                   ( color x tid did tid )
    hanoi-tower-disks-inc  ( color x tid did tn )
    hanoi-disk-y           ( color x tid did y )
    -rot                   ( color x y tid did )
    hanoi-disk-width 2 *   ( color x y tid w )
    swap                   ( color x y w tid )
    drop                   ( color x y w )
    h-disk-height          ( color x y w h )
    h-dh !
    h-dw !
    h-dy !
    h-dx !
    h-dcolor !
    h-dx @ h-dw @ 2 / + h-tw - h-tx !
    h-dy @ h-disk-ymin -
    0
    hanoi-drawloop-down
;
```

(continues)

FIGURE 4–7 The Towers of Hanoi: Forth code for animation *(continued)*

```
: hanoi-disk-move-lr ( tto tfrom -- )
    2dup <
    if
        \ We are moving left
        1 negate h-delta !
        - h-xmaxby4 * h-delta @ -
        0
    else
        \ We are moving right
        1 h-delta !
        - h-xmaxby4 *
        0
    then

    hanoi-drawloop-lr
;

: hanoi-disk-move ( totid fromtid did -- )
    h-N @ 1 + swap -
    1 pick 1 pick hanoi-disk-move-up
    2 pick 2 pick hanoi-disk-move-lr
    2 pick 1 pick hanoi-disk-move-down
    3drop
;
```

Now that we have an implementation of movedisk, we can implement the algorithm in Figure 4–6, which will give us a complete implementation. Figure 4–8 shows the remaining part of the overall program. Note that we will provide the end user with a simple Forth word called hanoi, which requires one argument—the number of disks—on the stack. Figure 4–9 shows a screenshot of the running program.

FIGURE 4–8 The Towers of Hanoi: Forth code for the program's core logic

```
: hanoi-solve
begin
depth
    0 >
    while
        6 3 pick 3 pick + -      ( n from to processed left )
        1 pick
        0 =
        if
            4 pick
```

(continues)

FIGURE 4–8 The Towers of Hanoi: Forth code for the program's core logic *(continued)*

```
            1 =
            if
                2 pick
                4 pick
                6 pick
                hanoi-disk-move
                2drop 2drop drop
            else
                                ( n from to processed left )
                1 -rot          ( n from to 1 processed left )
                swap drop       ( n from to 1 left )
                4 pick 1 - swap ( n from to 1 [n - 1] left )
                4 pick swap 0   ( n from to 1 [n - 1] from left 0 )
            then
        else
                                ( n from to processed left )
            swap drop           ( n from to left )
            1 pick
            3 pick
            5 pick
            hanoi-disk-move
                                ( n from to left )
            swap                ( n from left to )
            rot drop            ( n left to )
            rot 1 -             ( left to [n - 1] )
            -rot 0              ( [n - 1] left to 0 )
        then
    repeat
;

: hanoi-validate ( n -- n true|false )
    depth
    1 < \ assert that the stack has exactly one value
    if
        cr ." usage: n hanoi, where 1 <= n <= " h-maxdisks @ . cr
        false
    else
        dup 1 h-maxdisks @ between
        if
            true
        else
            cr ." usage: n hanoi, where 1 <= n <= " h-maxdisks @ . cr
            drop
            false
        then
    then
;
```

(continues)

FIGURE 4–8 The Towers of Hanoi: Forth code for the program's core logic *(continued)*

```
: hanoi ( n -- )
   hanoi-validate
   if
       erase-screen cr
       ." Press control-z to quit the animation." cr
       dup h-N !
       dup hanoi-init
       1 3 0 hanoi-solve
   then
;
```

FIGURE 4–9 Actual photo of the Towers of Hanoi program in Open Firmware

4.8.6 Fabricating and Using a Mouse Pointer

In this example, we will write a program to move a "pointer"—one that we will fabricate—on the screen using the mouse. Moreover, clicking a mouse button will print the coordinates of the click on the screen. We will use the `fill-rectangle` method to draw, erase, and redraw the pointer, which will be a small square. Opening the mouse device gives us access to its `get-event` method.

get-event (ms -- pos.x pos.y buttons true|false)

get-event is called with one argument: the time in milliseconds to wait for an event before returning failure. It returns four values: the coordinates of the mouse event, a bit mask containing information about any buttons pressed, and a Boolean value indicating whether an event happened in that interval. An interval of zero milliseconds causes get-event to wait until an event occurs.

The event coordinates returned by get-event may be *absolute* (for a device such as a tablet), or they may be *relative* to the *last event*, as in the case of a mouse. This implies that the pos.x and pos.y values should be treated as signed or unsigned depending on the type of device. This may be programmatically determined by checking for the presence of the absolute-position property.

The mouse demonstration program is shown in Figure 4–10. It starts by drawing a pointer at position (0, 0) and then goes into an infinite loop, waiting for get-event to return. Note that this program—and Open Firmware programs in general—can be interrupted by typing **control-z**.

Because we are using a mouse, get-event will give us the new position relative to the old one. Therefore, we need to remember the old coordinates. Once we get the new position, we will erase the old pointer and draw one in the new position. For the sake of simplicity, we will not handle the case when the pointer is moved "outside" one of the edges of the screen. Moreover, our mouse pointer is essentially an *eraser* in the drawing sense too: Since we will not save the region under the pointer, anything that the pointer moves over will be erased as we will simply redraw the newly uncovered region using the background color.

FIGURE 4–10 Fabricating and using a mouse pointer in Open Firmware

```
\ Mouse Pointer Demo
\ Commentary required for "booting" this program.

decimal

\ Our mouse pointer's dimensions in pixels
8 value m-ptrwidth
8 value m-ptrheight

\ Colors
foreground-color value m-color-ptr
background-color value m-color-bg

\ Variables for saving pointer position
variable m-oldx 0 m-oldx !
variable m-oldy 0 m-oldy !
```

(continues)

```
0 value myscreen
" screen" open-dev to myscreen

0 value mymouse
" mouse" open-dev to mymouse

: mouse-fillrect ( color x y w h -- )
    " fill-rectangle" myscreen $call-method ;

: mouse-get-event ( ms -- pos.x pos.y buttons true|false )
    " get-event" mymouse $call-method ;

: mouse-demo ( -- )
    cr ." Press control-z to quit the mouse demo." cr
begin
    0
    mouse-get-event
    if
        \ Check for button presses
        0 =              ( pos.x pos.y buttons 0 = )
        if
                            \ no buttons pressed
        else
                            ( pos.x pos.y )
            2dup m-oldy @ + swap m-oldx @ +
            ." button pressed ( " . ." , " . ." )" cr
        then

        m-color-bg      ( pos.x pos.y m-color-bg )
        m-oldx @        ( pos.x pos.y m-color-bg m-oldx )
        m-oldy @        ( pos.x pos.y m-color-bg m-oldx m-oldy )
        m-ptrwidth      ( pos.x pos.y m-color-bg m-oldx m-oldy )
        m-ptrheight     ( pos.x pos.y m-color-bg m-oldx m-oldy )
        mouse-fillrect  ( pos.x pos.y )
        m-color-ptr     ( pos.x pos.y m-color-ptr )
        -rot            ( m-color-ptr pos.x pos.y )
        m-oldy @        ( m-color-ptr pos.x pos.y m-oldy )
        +               ( m_color pos.x newy )
        swap            ( m-color-ptr newy pos.x )
        m-oldx @        ( m-color-ptr newy pos.x m-oldx )
        +               ( m-color-ptr newy newx )
        swap            ( m-color-ptr newx newy )
        2dup            ( m-color-ptr newx newy newx newy )
        m-oldy !        ( m-color-ptr newx newy newx )
        m-oldx !        ( m-color-ptr newx newy )
        m-ptrwidth      ( m-color-ptr newx newy m-ptrwidth )
        m-ptrheight     ( m-color-ptr newx newy m-ptrwidth )
        mouse-fillrect
    then
again
;
```

We can also create an arbitrarily shaped mouse pointer, including a familiar arrow-shaped one that is partially transparent, by using a well-known masking technique. Suppose we wish to create a 5×5 pointer in the shape of an X. If C is the pointer's color and S is the screen background color, then the 5×5 square containing the pointer would look like the following when displayed on the screen:

```
C S S S C
S C S C S
S S C S S
S C S C S
C S S S C
```

We can achieve this effect by having two masks: an AND mask and an XOR mask, as shown in Figure 4–11.

FIGURE 4–11 AND and XOR masks for an X-shaped pointer

```
0 1 1 1 0      C 0 0 0 C      S S S S S
1 0 1 0 1      0 C 0 C 0      S S S S S
1 1 0 1 1      0 0 C 0 0      S S S S S
1 0 1 0 1      0 C 0 C 0      S S S S S
0 1 1 1 0      C 0 0 0 C      S S S S S


AND mask (A)    XOR mask (X)    Screen (S)
```

While displaying the cursor on the screen, we use the following sequence of operations, which yields the desired 5×5 square:

$$S_{new} = (S_{current} \textbf{ AND } A) \textbf{ XOR } X$$

We now need to maintain in-memory bitmaps for the pointer and the region underneath it. Before drawing the contents of the pointer's bitmap on the screen (using `draw-rectangle` instead of `fill-rectangle`), we need to perform the masking operation, which will give us the desired partially transparent mouse pointer.

4.8.7 Stealing a Font

Apple's Open Firmware includes the `terminal-emulator` support package, which presents a display framebuffer device as a *cursor-addressable* text terminal. Another support package, fb8, provides generic framebuffer routines that can be used by display device drivers to perform low-level operations. Thus, there are several ways to display characters on the screen in Open Firmware. We shall devise yet another—rather contrived—way in this example.

We will create a function called `font-print` that takes an input ASCII string and draws it on the screen, starting at a specified pixel location. To achieve this, we will use the display device's `draw-rectangle` method, which requires a memory address containing data for the rectangle to be drawn. We can consider each character in a font to be contained in an imaginary rectangle. Our program will perform the following operations.

- Create a font containing ASCII characters.
- Allocate a font buffer.
- For each character in the font, store its font data in the font buffer at an offset that either is the same as or is a function of the character's ASCII code.
- For each character in the input string, calculate the address of its font data in the font buffer and call `draw-rectangle` to draw the character at an appropriate position on the screen.

Although these steps appear straightforward, the first step of creating a font is rather arduous—at least in our context. We will *bypass* this step in our example by stealing Open Firmware's default font.

As our program is booted by Open Firmware, we will output on the screen a template string containing all ASCII characters of interest. Open Firmware provides Forth words to determine the height and width of a character: `char-height` and `char-width`, respectively. Since we have a priori knowledge that our string will appear on the first line of the screen, we know the *position* and *dimensions* of the screen region containing the template string that we print. We will simply copy this region using `read-rectangle`, which will give us a ready-made font buffer. Figure 4–12 shows the implementation of the `font-print` word.

FIGURE 4–12 Pixel-addressable printing in Open Firmware made possible by stealing a font

```
\ Font Demo
\ Commentary required for "booting" this program.

decimal

0 value myscreen
" screen" open-dev to myscreen
```

(continues)

FIGURE 4–12 Pixel-addressable printing in Open Firmware made possible by stealing a font *(continued)*

```
: font-drawrect ( adr x y w h -- )   " draw-rectangle" myscreen $call-method ;
: font-readrect ( adr x y w h -- )   " read-rectangle" myscreen $call-method ;

\ Starts from (x, y) = (4 * 6, 6 + 6 + 11) = (24, 23)
\ =
\ _ok
\ =
\ 0_>_0123...
\
\ ASCII 32 (space) to 126 (~) decimal
\
." ! #$%&'()*+,-./0123456789:;<=>?@ABCDEFGHIJKLMNOPQRSTUVWXYZ[\]^_`abcdefghijklmno
pqrstuvwxyz{|}~"
cr cr
32  value f-ascii-min
126 value f-ascii-max
f-ascii-max f-ascii-min - 1 + value f-nchars

char-height char-width * value f-size

\ Steal the default font
variable f-buffer
f-nchars f-size * alloc mem
f-buffer !
f-nchars
0
do
    f-buffer @ f-size i * +
    i char-width *
    4
    char-width
    char-height
    font-readrect
loop
erase screen

variable f-string
variable f-x
variable f-y

\ If character is not within the supported range, replace it
: font-validate-char ( char -- char )
    dup
    f-ascii-min f-ascii-max between
    if
        \ ok
```

(continues)

FIGURE 4–12 Pixel-addressable printing in Open Firmware made possible by stealing a font *(continued)*

```
    else
        drop
        f-ascii-min
    then
;

\ Print a string starting at a specified position
: font-print ( string x y -- )
    f-y !
    f-x !
    0
    rot
    f-string !
    do
        f-string @ i + c@
        font-validate-char
        f-ascii-min -
        f-size *
        f-buffer @ +
        f-x @ i char-width * +
        f-y @
        char-width
        char-height
        font-drawrect
    loop
;
```

4.8.8 Implementing a Clock

Given the functionality of font-print from Figure 4–12, we can make a clock appear, say, in a corner of the screen. We will use two additional functions for this: one to retrieve the current time and another that will allow us to update the clock every second.

Open Firmware provides the get-time function, which retrieves the current time. Calling the function results in six items being pushed on the stack:

```
0 > decimal get-time .s -> 32 16 12 20 3 2004 <- Top  ok
```

The items are (from the bottom to the top on the stack): *seconds, minutes, hours, day of the month, month,* and *year.* For our clock, we will discard the date-related items.

The `alarm` function allows us to periodically invoke another function. Thus, we can arrange for a clock-drawing function to be invoked every second. `alarm` takes two arguments: an *execution token* of the function to be periodically invoked and the period in milliseconds.

> The method to be periodically invoked through `alarm` must neither consume any stack items nor leave any items on the stack once it has finished. In other words, this function's stack notation must be (`--`).

A function's execution token is its *identification*. `[']` returns the execution token of the function name that follows it, as shown by the following example:

```
0 > : myhello ( -- ) ." Hello!" ;  ok
0 > myhello Hello ok
0 > ['] myhello . ff9d0a30  ok
0 > ff9d0a30 execute Hello ok
```

Given an execution token of a function, the `execute` word can be used to execute the corresponding function. Note that retrieving a function's execution token is context-specific; `[']` is not a valid way to get a method's execution token inside a word definition, for example.

The code shown in Figure 4–13 creates a clock that updates every second. It is displayed at the top-right corner of the screen. Note that `(u.)` converts an unsigned number into a text string, which is what `font-print` requires as one of the arguments.

FIGURE 4–13 A clock implemented in the Open Firmware environment

```
: mytime ( -- )
   get-time ( seconds minutes hour day month year )
   3drop    ( seconds minutes hour )
   swap     ( seconds hour minutes )
   rot      ( hour minutes seconds )
   (u.) screen-width 2 char-width * - 0 font-print
   " :" screen-width 3 char-width * - 0 font-print
   (u.) screen-width 5 char-width * - 0 font-print
   " :" screen-width 6 char-width * - 0 font-print
   (u.) screen-width 8 char-width * - 0 font-print
;

' mytime 1000 alarm
```

4.8.9 Drawing Images

In this example, let us examine how to draw images in Open Firmware. In fact, we have already encountered all the functionality required to do so: The draw-rectangle function can draw a memory buffer's contents to screen. The buffer requires the image data to be in an appropriate format. We can make the task easier by choosing to draw the Apple logo drawn during booting, since we can find the corresponding data in the correct format in the bootloader's source code.

Drawing the Apple logo—or any image in general—will require the logo data and the custom CLUT (if one is needed) to be in memory. The Apple logo data can be found in a C header file called appleboot.h in BootX's source (bootx.tproj/sl.subproj/appleboot.h). The custom CLUT can be found in another header file—clut.h—in the same directory as appleboot.h. Both files contain byte arrays that can be readily used with Open Firmware. For example, the CLUT data can be simply passed to set-colors. Thus, we can draw the Apple logo using the following steps.

- Open the screen device.
- Call set-colors to set up the custom CLUT.
- Load the logo data in memory.
- Call draw-rectangle to draw the logo at the desired position.

If you wish to draw an arbitrary image, you could do so by converting the image to a format that makes it easy to view the RGB values for each pixel. The ASCII-based *portable pixmap* (PPM) is such a format. Given a PPM file, we could write a script that reads the file and generates Forth versions of both the CLUT and the image data. Consider the example of a 4×4-pixel image, whose PPM file looks like the one in Figure 4–14.

FIGURE 4–14 PPM image data for a 4×4-pixel image

```
P3
4 4
15
0   0   0     0   0   0     0   0   0    15   0  15
0   0   0     0  15   7     0   0   0     0   0   0
0   0   0     0   0   0     0  15   7     0   0   0
15  0  15     0   0   0     0   0   0     0   0   0
```

The first line shown in Figure 4–14 is a *magic number.*[14] The second line contains the image's width and height. The value 15 on the third line specifies the maximum decimal value that a color component has. The last four lines contain RGB values for each of the 16 pixels of the image. Since this image has only three *distinct* RGB triplets, our custom CLUT needs only three entries:

```
decimal
0 0 0 0 color!   \ CLUT entry with index 0
15 0 15 1 color! \ CLUT entry with index 1
0 15 7 2 color!  \ CLUT entry with index 2
```

> Since Open Firmware's 8-bits-per-pixel model means a CLUT can have at most 256 entries, you may need to reduce the number of colors in an image before you draw it using the approach described in this example.

4.8.10 Creating Windows

Given the various examples discussed so far, we are now in a position to create a window that can be dragged around using the mouse. Doing so may be a worthwhile exercise for those interested in learning how to create graphical environments from scratch. We could combine multiple techniques in the following way.

- Create a "true" mouse pointer using the AND/XOR mask technique.
- Create a window with a title bar. This is tantamount to creating a *related* set of rectangles and lines, along with some textual or perhaps graphical window content.
- Create backing stores for repairing damage to the portions of the screen under the window and the pointer.
- Move the window, if necessary, in the mouse event handler function.

Figure 4–15 shows a rudimentary implementation in Open Firmware of a window that can be dragged.[15]

---

14. A constant entity (often a number) used to identify some aspect of another entity. For example, the byte sequence 0xcafebabe, which is used as the beginning of a Universal Binary file, serves as a magic number identifying the file's type.

15. The source code for the implementation pictured here is available on this book's accompanying web site (www.osxbook.com).

```
ok
0 > ofwindows
Press control-z to quit the OF Windows Demo.
```

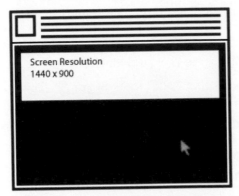

Screen Resolution
1440 x 900

FIGURE 4–15 A window created using Open Firmware primitives

> Open Firmware provides various other types of functionality that is beyond the scope of this book. For example, you can "talk" to IDE, SATA, and SCSI drives *directly* in Open Firmware, thus allowing you to fabricate your own command packets to such devices and perform I/O.

4.9 Firmware Boot Sequence

Recall from our discussion in Section 4.1 that at power-on time, a typical computer performs low-level initialization followed by a self-test that sanity-checks the processor and closely connected hardware. In the case of a PowerPC-based Apple computer, Open Firmware is passed control next. As Open Firmware begins initializing itself, it performs the following sequence of operations.

- It determines the memory configuration of the machine. It then allocates and initializes memory for its internal data structures, memory pools, the device tree, and the Forth runtime environment.

- It initializes devices that are necessary for a basic Forth environment: the memory management unit, interrupt controllers, timers, and so on.

- It verifies its NVRAM. If the NVRAM's contents are invalid, it resets the NVRAM variables to their default values.

- If the `use-nvramrc?` NVRAM variable contains a `true` value, Open Firmware evaluates the `nvramrc` script (see Section 4.9.1).

- After handling `nvramrc`, Open Firmware probes for plug-in devices. It evaluates the FCodes residing on the ROMs of discovered devices. In this manner, the device tree incrementally grows as each device is found.

- Next, Open Firmware installs a console[16] and prints a banner. You could also arrange for your own banner to be printed. For example, the following command causes your email address to be printed as the banner by Open Firmware:

```
0 > setenv oem-banner you@your.email.address   ok
0 > setenv oem-banner? true   ok
```

- It then performs some secondary diagnostics and any platform-dependent initialization.

- If the variable `auto-boot?` is `false`, Open Firmware drops into a prompt; otherwise it looks for a boot device, unless one was explicitly specified through boot arguments. The variable `boot-device` contains the default boot device. A typical device specification includes not just the containing device of the appropriate client program—the bootloader—but also the client program's location on that device. Note that whether booting continues automatically also depends on the configured firmware security mode, as we will see in Section 4.12.

- Open Firmware is capable of reliably reading files from block devices. It invokes the boot device's `load` method to read the client program from that device into memory. This is done using a device-dependent protocol. For example, in the case of a local disk, Open Firmware reads the bootloader from disk. Alternatively, it can use TFTP for booting over the network, in which case it downloads three files: the bootloader, the kernel, and a kernel extensions cache.

- If Open Firmware fails to find a boot device, it displays a blinking folder.

- If all steps were completed successfully, Open Firmware eventually executes the bootloader.

---

16. The console may be a plug-in device, which is why Open Firmware installs a console after probing for devices.

Specifying Boot Devices

A boot device could be a locally attached hard disk or optical disc, a network interface, a ROM device, a serial line, and so on. A typical value of the `boot-device` variable is `hd:,\\:tbxi`, which specifies the boot device to be a file of type `tbxi` on the device referred to by the `hd` alias. This normally resolves to the Mac OS X bootloader. Note that the default definition of the `hd` alias may not contain a partition specifier, for example:

```
0 > devalias hd /pci@f4000000/ata-6@d/disk@0   ok
0 >
```

In such a case, Open Firmware will attempt to boot from the first bootable partition on the device. If you have multiple bootable partitions, `boot-device` can be set to be more specific. For example, `hd:3,\\:tbxi` refers to the third partition on the device specified by `hd`. Similarly, `/ht/pci@7/k2-sata-root/k2-sata@0/disk@0:9,\\:tbxi` refers to the ninth partition on an explicitly specified device path. A file can be referred to by its full pathname instead of file type, as in `hd:3,\System\Library\CoreServices\MegaBootLoader`.

Open Firmware can directly load ELF, XCOFF, and bootinfo files as client programs, although it cannot load Mach-O binaries. BootX, which *can* load Mach-O binaries, is presented to Open Firmware as a file with a bootinfo header and an XCOFF trailer.

4.9.1 The Script

The user may create a script, usually simply called *the script*, which is also stored in NVRAM. The script's contents are user-defined commands that can be executed during startup, depending on the value of the `use-nvramrc?` firmware variable. The script is initially empty. You can start editing the (intended) contents of the script by calling `nvedit` from Open Firmware. Doing so runs the script editor, which supports rudimentary text editing. Table 4–3 lists some useful key combinations available in `nvedit`.

The text you edit using `nvedit` is stored in a temporary buffer. Once you exit the editor, you may discard the buffer's contents using `nvquit` or copy them to NVRAM using `nvstore`. You may also execute the contents using `nvrun`.

> **Warning:** An erroneous script can render the system unbootable and may even cause permanent damage that would necessitate hardware repair. Use extreme caution while experimenting with this feature of Open Firmware.

TABLE 4–3 Key Combinations for `nvedit` Command-Line Editing

Keys	Purpose
^c	Exit the script editor and return to the Open Firmware prompt.
^k	Delete from the current position to the end of the line. If the cursor is at the end of the line, then join the current line with the next line—that is, kill the newline.
^l	Display the entire contents of the editing buffer.
^n	Go to the next line.
^o	Open another line at the current cursor position.
^p	Go to the previous line.

4.9.2 Snag Keys

Open Firmware supports *snag keys* that you can press as the computer is started to redirect the boot sequence to various boot devices. Table 4–4 shows some examples of such keys.

TABLE 4–4 Boot-Time Snag Keys

Snag Keys	Description
c	Use the first bootable partition on the `cd` alias—normally a CD-ROM drive.
d	Use the first bootable partition on the `hd` alias—normally a disk drive.
n	Attempt to force boot over the network using BOOTP[a]/TFTP on the `enet` alias—normally a network device.
t	Boot into target disk mode.
x	Boot a Mac OS X system (as opposed to Mac OS 9) if a bootable installation exists. This key is deprecated.
z	Use the first bootable partition on the `zip` alias—normally a ZIP drive.
option	Interrupt Open Firmware's boot device selection and invoke the OS Picker application, which allows the user to choose an alternate boot device or system installation.
shift	Boot in safe mode.
⌘-option-o-f	Boot into Open Firmware.

(continues)

TABLE 4–4 Boot-Time Snag Keys *(Continued)*

-option-p-r	Zap the parameter memory.
-option-shift-delete	Attempt to force boot from any device *other than* the one specified by the `boot-device` firmware variable.
-v	Boot in verbose mode.

a. Bootstrap Protocol.

Target Disk Mode

Pressing the **t** key as an Apple computer powers on will boot it into the FireWire target disk mode. Essentially, your machine becomes an external FireWire disk drive that can be connected to another computer through a FireWire cable. This mode is implemented by an Open Firmware package called `firewire-disk-mode`. You can also enter this mode from the Open Firmware prompt by using the `target-mode` word. Beginning with Mac OS X 10.4, the Startup Disk preference pane provides a button for restarting the computer in the target disk mode. Clicking this button is equivalent to setting the `boot-command` firmware variable (whose usual value is `mac-boot`) as follows. The *first* reboot after setting this variable will result in the computer entering the target disk mode, after which `boot-command` will be reset to `mac-boot`.

```
$ sudo nvram boot-command='" mac-boot" " boot-command" $setenv target-mode'
```

4.10 BootX

BootX is the default bootloader on PowerPC-based Mac OS X systems.[17] As the first software that runs during system startup, it prepares an initial execution environment for the kernel, to which it passes control eventually.

4.10.1 File Format

The BootX file is in the *bootinfo* format: It contains an XML header, various types of data (such as icons), Forth source, FCode bytecodes, and machine code.

---

17. BootX is also the name of a third-party open source bootloader—unrelated to Apple's BootX—that allows dual-booting Mac OS and Linux on Old World machines.

Figure 4–16 shows an example of a bootinfo file. The OS-BADGE-ICONS element can contain icons to be displayed in the Open Firmware boot selector.

FIGURE 4–16 A bootinfo file

```
<CHRP-BOOT>
<COMPATIBLE>
MacRISC MacRISC3 MacRISC4
</COMPATIBLE>
<DESCRIPTION>
Boot Loader for Mac OS X.
</DESCRIPTION>
<OS-BADGE-ICONS>
1010
...
</OS-BADGE-ICONS>
<BOOT-SCRIPT>
load-base
begin
...
until
( xcoff-base )
load-size over load-base - -
( xcoff-base xcoff-size )
load-base swap move
init-program go
</BOOT SCRIPT>
</CHRP-BOOT>
^D
... machine code
```

BootX is compiled from source into a Mach-O executable, which is then converted to XCOFF format. The XCOFF file is appended to a bootinfo header to yield the BootX file that resides in /System/Library/CoreServices/. The /usr/standalone/ppc/ directory contains the XCOFF file (bootx.xcoff), along with a copy of BootX in bootinfo format (bootx.bootinfo). Recall that Open Firmware can load both the bootinfo file and the XCOFF binary.

It is possible to create your own bootloader—rather, a boot *chooser*—by creating a bootinfo file with a Forth script (the BOOT-SCRIPT element) that displays various booting options such as the following:

- Boot from a disk drive (specified by variations of the hd alias).
- Boot from an optical drive (specified by the cd alias).

- Boot from a FireWire drive (specified by a device tree path).
- Boot over the network (using the `enet` alias).
- Enter the target disk mode (using the `target-mode` word).
- Power cycle the computer (using the `reset-all` word).
- Shut down the computer (using the `shut-down` word).
- Eject an optical disc (using the `eject` word).

Each of these options can be served by existing Open Firmware words. Such a bootloader could even be graphical, where you use the framebuffer to display a menu and use the mouse to make a selection. Pressing the **option** key during startup launches a similar Open Firmware application, the OS Picker.

4.10.2 Structure

BootX can be functionally divided into a client interface, a file system interface, a secondary loader, and a utility library. These components are implemented in the `ci.subproj`, `fs.subproj`, `sl.subproj`, and `libclite.subproj` subdirectories, respectively, in the BootX source.

BootX implements a plug-in interface for file systems that it supports. Apple's default implementation of BootX can load kernels from the HFS, HFS Plus, UFS, and Ext2 file systems. BootX also includes a file system abstraction for the Network file system—essentially a wrapper around a TFTP client implementation. Besides kernel binaries in the Mach-O format, BootX can also load ELF kernels.

ELF Support

Mac OS X does not use the ELF support in BootX. Old World Macintosh computers had various issues with the implementation of Open Firmware. This caused many booting problems for Apple engineers and even more problems for third parties porting Linux to the PowerPC. Having access to the firmware's source, Apple solved most of the problems either via NVRAM patches or by integrating the required changes into BootX itself. The latter was done in the instances where the changes could not be implemented as patches. As BootX matured, Apple added support for Ext2 and ELF with the goal of making the platform more amenable to PowerPC Linux.

4.10.3 Operation

Let us look at the sequence of events that occur when BootX starts executing after being handed control by Open Firmware.

- The entry point of the BootX executable is a symbol called `StartTVector`, which points to a function called `Start()`. BootX is called with a pointer to the Open Firmware client interface. `Start()` moves the stack pointer 256 bytes from the end of a 32K chunk of BootX's heap, from where it will grow upward during use. `Start()` then calls `Main()`.

```
const unsigned long StartTVector[2] = {(unsigned long)Start, 0};

char gStackBaseAddr[0x8000];
...
static void
Start(void *unused1, void *unused2, ClientInterfacePtr ciPtr)
{
    long newSP;

    // Move the Stack to a chunk of the BSS
    newSP = (long)gStackBaseAddr + sizeof(gStackBaseAddr) - 0x100;
    __asm__ volatile("mr r1, %0" : : "r" (newSP));

    Main(ciPtr);
}
```

- `Main()` calls `InitEverything()`, which, as its name suggests, performs a variety of initialization steps. It initializes the Open Firmware client interface that BootX uses to talk to the firmware. It also retrieves the firmware version.

- BootX then creates an Open Firmware pseudo-device called `sl_words` (`sl` stands for *secondary loader*) and defines various Forth words in it. For example, the code for the spinning cursor seen during booting is set up here.

- BootX uses the firmware's client interface to look up the `options` device, which contains various system configuration variables that may be viewed and set using the `printenv` and `setenv` words in Open Firmware.

```
0 > dev /options .properties
name                options
little-endian?      false
real-mode?          false
auto-boot?          true
diag-switch?        false
...
boot-command        mac-boot
...
```

You can also examine the properties of the `options` device and even browse a representation of the device tree from Mac OS X. Tools such as `IORegistryExplorer.app` and `ioreg` can be used for this purpose.

```
$ ioreg -p IODeviceTree -l 0 -w | less
...
+-o options  <class IODTNVRAM, registered, matched, ...
|   {
|     "fcode-debug?" = No
|     "skip-netboot?" = <"false">
...
```

- BootX looks up the `chosen` device, which contains system parameters chosen or specified at runtime: instance handles for entities such as memory, the console input and output devices, the MMU, the PMU, the CPU, the programmable interrupt controller (PIC), and so on. If the keyboard cannot be initialized based on `chosen`'s contents, BootX attempts to obtain an instance handle to the keyboard device by explicitly trying to open the `keyboard` and `kbd` devices. It then initializes the keymap by calling `slw_init_keymap`, which is one of the `sl` words.

```
0 > dev /chosen .properties
name            chosen
stdin           ffbc6e40
stdout          ffbc6600
memory          ffbdd600
mmu             ...
...
```

- BootX checks the value of the `security-mode` firmware variable. If this variable is set and has a value other than `none`, BootX sets the "secure" bit in its boot mode variable. It also checks whether the *verbose mode* (the -v key combination) or *single-user mode* (the -s key combination) were specified, enabling verbose messages to be printed during booting if either were specified. Note that no messages are printed in the secure boot mode, regardless of the verbosity flags.

- By default, BootX is compiled to display a failure screen if booting fails. Alternatively, BootX can be compiled to go back to Open Firmware on failure.

- BootX checks whether the system is booting in *safe mode*. If so, it sets the corresponding bit in its boot mode variable.

- BootX claims memory for various purposes. A typical memory map assumed by BootX occupies 96MB of physical memory starting at address `0x0`. The beginning of this physical range contains the PowerPC exception vectors. The end of this range contains the Open Firmware image. The hole in the middle is free memory, which is claimed by BootX. Table 4–5 shows a breakdown of the memory map normally used by BootX.[18]

TABLE 4–5 BootX Logical Memory Map

Starting Address	Ending Address	Purpose
0x00000000	0x00003FFF	Exception vectors.
0x00004000	0x03FFFFFF	Kernel image, boot structures, and drivers.
0x04000000	0x04FFFFFF	File load area.
0x05000000	0x053FFFFF	Simple read-time cache for file system metadata. Cache hits are serviced from memory, whereas cache misses result in disk access.
0x05400000	0x055FFFFF	Malloc zone: a simple memory allocator is implemented in BootX's `libclite` subproject. The starting and ending addresses of this range define the block of memory used by the allocator.
0x05600000	0x057FFFFF	BootX image.
0x05800000	0x05FFFFFF	Unused (occupied by the Open Firmware image).

- BootX allocates 0x4000 bytes for the *vector save area*.
- BootX finds all displays and sets them up. It does this by searching for nodes of type display in the device tree. The primary display is referred to by the screen alias.

```
0 > dev screen .properties
name            ATY,Bee_A
compatible      ATY,Bee
width           00000400
height          00000300
linebytes       00000400
depth           00000008
display-type    4c434400
device_type     display
character-set   ISO859-1
...
```

---

18. The memory map may change across BootX versions.

- While setting up one or more displays, BootX calls the Open Firmware `set-colors` word to initialize the CLUT for the display if its depth is 8 bit. It also sets the screen color of each display to a 75% gray color by calling the Open Firmware `fill-rectangle` word. At this point, `InitEverything` returns to `Main`.

- BootX looks up the boot device and boot arguments to determine the location of the kernel.

- The default name of the kernel file is `mach_kernel`. BootX refers to several pieces of information while constructing the path to the kernel file. It first attempts to use the path contained in the `bootpath` property of the `chosen` node. If that fails, it looks at the `boot-device` property of the `options` node. It also looks for a file called `com.apple.Boot.plist`, which, if found, is loaded and its contents are parsed.

- Just as Open Firmware can fetch the bootloader from either a local disk or a remote computer, BootX can load locally or remotely resident kernels. Consequently, the kernel path constructed by BootX depends on whether it is booting from a block device or a network device. In the usual case of a block device, BootX also calculates paths for loading kernel caches.

- Eventually, BootX sets the `rootpath` and `boot-uuid` properties of the `chosen` node. The `boot-uuid` property contains a file system UUID[19] that BootX calculates for the boot volume. These and other properties of `chosen` can be seen on a running system through the `ioreg` utility (Figure 4–17).

FIGURE 4–17 Properties of the `chosen` device node as seen from Mac OS X

```
$ ioreg -p IODeviceTree -n chosen
+-o Root  <class IORegistryEntry, retain count 12>
  +-o device-tree  <class IOPlatformExpertDevice, registered, matched, ...>
    +-o chosen  <class IOService, !registered, !matched, active, busy 0, ...>
    | | {
    | |   "nvram" = <ffb6f200>
    | |   "stdin" = <ffb44000>
    | |   "bootpath" = <"/ht/pci@7/k2-sata-root/k2-sata@0/disk@0:3,\\:tbxi">
    | |   "memory" = <ffb7c980>
    | |   "cpu" = <ffb7ca00>
    | |   "name" = <"chosen">
    | |   "pmu" = <ffb6f080>
```

(continues)

---

19. Universally unique identifier.

FIGURE 4–17 Properties of the `chosen` device node as seen from Mac OS X *(continued)*

```
| |    "boot-uuid" = <"B229E7FA-E0BA-XXXX-XXXX-XXXXXXXXXXXX">
| |    "rootpath" = <"/ht/pci@7/k2-sata-root/k2-sata@0/disk@0:3,\mach_kernel">
| |    "BootXCacheHits" = <000000a6>
| |    "mmu" = <ffb7ca00>
| |    "uni-interrupt-controller" = <ff981ee0>
| |    "bootargs" = <00>
| |    "stdout" = <00000000>
| |    "BootXCacheMisses" = <0000000f>
| |    "platform" = <ff9a6c38>
| |    "AAPL,phandle" = <ff891bf0>
| |    "BootXCacheEvicts" = <00000000>
| | }
...
```

Kernel Extension Caches

There may be close to a hundred kernel extensions loaded on a typical Mac OS X installation, and perhaps twice as many residing in the system's designated directories for such extensions. A kernel extension can have dependencies on other extensions. Rather than scan all extensions every time the system boots (or worse, every time an extension is to be loaded), Mac OS X uses caching for kernel extensions. It also caches a version of the kernel that is prelinked with the necessary kernel extensions. The general name for such a cache is a *kext cache*. Mac OS X uses three types of kext caches: a *kernel cache*, an *mkext cache*, and a *kext repository cache*.

A kernel cache contains the kernel code prelinked with several kernel extensions—typically those deemed essential to early system startup. This cache can also contain the information dictionaries of any number of kernel extensions. The default cache directory for kernel caches is `/System/Library/Caches/com.apple.kernelcaches/`. Files in this directory are named `kernelcache.XXXXXXXX`, where the suffix is a 32-bit Adler checksum.[20]

An mkext—or multiextension—cache contains multiple kernel extensions and their information dictionaries. Such caches are used during early system startup as BootX attempts to load a previously cached list of device drivers. If an mkext cache is corrupt or missing, BootX looks in the `/System/Library/Extensions/` directory for extensions needed in that boot scenario—as determined by the value of the `OSBundleRequired` property in the `Info.plist` file of an extension's bundle. The default mkext cache exists as `/System/Library/Extensions.mkext`.

---

20. The checksum algorithm is named after its inventor, Mark Adler, who also wrote parts of the popular gzip compression program.

Note that the system will *not* regenerate this cache unless the /System/ Library/Extensions/ directory is newer than /mach_kernel: a caveat that is especially noteworthy if a new extension is to be installed for auto-loading at boot time. An mkext cache can be created or updated through the kextcache program. You can use the mkextunpack program to extract the contents of an mkext archive.

```
$ mkextunpack -v /System/Library/Extensions.mkext
Found 148 kexts:
ATTOExpressPCIPlus - com.ATTO.driver.ATTOExpressPCIPlus (2.0.4)
CMD646ATA - com.apple.driver.CMD646ATA (1.0.7f1)
...
IOSCSIFamily - com.apple.iokit.IOSCSIFamily (1.4.0)
IOCDStorageFamily - com.apple.iokit.IOCDStorageFamily (1.4)
```

The kext repository cache contains the information dictionaries for all kernel extensions—including their plug-ins—residing in a single repository directory. This cache exists by default as /System/Library/Extensions.kextcache, which is simply a large, XML-based, gzip-compressed property list file.

- Next, by default, if BootX fails to construct or use the boot paths, it draws a failed boot picture and goes into an infinite loop.

- BootX draws the Apple logo splash screen. If booting from a network device, it draws a spinning globe instead.

- BootX attempts to retrieve and load the kernel cache file. For a kernel cache file to be used, several conditions must be satisfied. For example, the file's name must match the kernel that BootX has found, the cache must not be expired, and the current booting mode must not be safe or network. If BootX determines that the kernel cache cannot be used, it uses its file system abstraction layer to access the kernel binary.

Making the Globe Go Round

The process for drawing the spinning globe is similar to the Apple logo example we discussed in Section 4.8.9. The globe data is contained in the netboot.h file in the BootX source. It contains 18 animation frames, each a 32×32 image, in contiguous memory. The secondary loader words slw_spin_init and slw_spin are responsible for setting up and performing, respectively, the animation, which occurs at a rate of 10 frames per second.

- BootX "decodes" the kernel. If the kernel header indicates a compressed[21] kernel, BootX attempts to decompress it. If the kernel binary is fat, BootX "thins" it—that is, it locates the Mach-O binary for the architecture it is running on.

- BootX attempts to decode the file—possibly "thinned"—as a Mach-O binary. The Mach-O header's magic number must be the constant MH_MAGIC (0xfeedface). As decoding proceeds, BootX iterates through Mach-O load commands, handling them as appropriate. Note that BootX processes only the LC_SEGMENT, LC_SYMTAB, and LC_UNIXTHREAD Mach-O commands, ignoring any other types found in the executable.

- If decoding the kernel as a Mach-O binary fails, BootX tries to decode it as an ELF binary. If that too fails, BootX gives up. It then draws a designated failed boot picture and goes into an infinite loop.

The Kernel's Mach-O Load Commands

The LC_SEGMENT command defines a segment of the executable to be mapped into the address space of the process that loads the file. The command also includes all of the sections contained in the segment. When BootX comes across the __VECTORS segment, it copies the segment's data—up to a maximum of 16KB—to a special vector save area whose address is contained in the gVectorSaveAddr BootX variable. The __VECTORS segment contains the kernel's exception vectors, such as the low-level system call and interrupt handlers.

The LC_SYMTAB command specifies the symbol table for the executable. BootX handles this command by decoding the symbol table and copying it to a range in the kernel's memory map.

The LC_UNIXTHREAD command defines the initial thread state of the main thread of the process. On the PowerPC, the flavor of the thread data structure specified by the Mac OS X kernel's LC_UNIXTHREAD command is PPC_THREAD_STATE. This flavor includes a PowerPC register state consisting of GPRs 0 through 31 along with the CR, CTR, LR, XER, SRR0, SRR1, and VRSAVE registers. SRR0 contains the entry point of the kernel: the address of the first instruction in the kernel to be executed.

---

21. A compressed kernel uses typical LZSS compression, which is suitable for data that is compressed once but expanded many times. LZSS stands for Lempel-Ziv-Storer-Szymanski. Published in 1982 by J. A. Storer and T. G. Szymanski, LZSS is a compression algorithm based on the earlier LZ77 algorithm.

- If BootX is successful thus far, it performs its last set of actions in preparation of launching the kernel. It saves BootX file system cache hits, misses, and evicts as `BootXCacheHits`, `BootXCacheMisses`, and `BootXCacheEvicts`, respectively, in the `chosen` node.

- It sets up various boot arguments and values that it will communicate to the kernel.

- It calls a recursive function to flatten the device tree.

- Shortly before handing over control to the kernel, BootX *quiesces* Open Firmware, an operation that causes any asynchronous tasks in the firmware, timers, and DMA to be stopped.

- Next, BootX saves the MSR and SPRs G0 through G3; turns off data address translation by setting the DR bit of the MSR to 0; moves Open Firmware's exception vectors from `0x0` to a vector save address (`gOFVectorSave`); and copies the kernel's exception vectors from `gVectorSaveAddr` to `0x0`. At this point, all preparations for launching the kernel have been completed.

- BootX finally calls the kernel's entry point. If this succeeds, BootX's job is done, and it exists no more. If calling the kernel fails, BootX restores Open Firmware's exception vectors, restores the registers it saved prior to calling the kernel, restores data address translations, and returns a `-1` value as an error.

BootX passes control to the kernel along with a signature[22] and a set of boot arguments, which it packs into a boot arguments structure (`struct boot_args`). The structure contains critical information needed at boot time and is propagated throughout the initial kernel startup. The kernel and BootX share this structure's type definition.

```
// pexpert/pexpert/ppc/boot.h
// x86-specific structures are in pexpert/pexpert/i386/boot.h

struct Boot_Video {
    unsigned long v_baseAddr;  // Base address of video memory
    unsigned long v_display;   // Display code (if applicable)
    unsigned long v_rowBytes;  // # of bytes per pixel row
    unsigned long v_width;     // Width
    unsigned long v_height;    // Height
    unsigned long v_depth;     // Pixel depth
};
...
```

---

22. The signature is the number `0x4D4F5358`, which corresponds to the string `"MOSX"`.

```
struct DRAMBank {
    unsigned long base; // physical base of DRAM bank
    unsigned long size; // size of DRAM bank
};
...
struct boot_args {
    // Revision of boot_args structure
    unsigned short Revision;

    // Version of boot_args structure
    unsigned short Version;

    // Passed in the command line (256 bytes maximum)
    char CommandLine[BOOT_LINE_LENGTH];

    // Base/range pairs for DRAM banks (26 maximum)
    DRAMBank PhysicalDRAM[kMaxDRAMBanks];

    // Video information
    Boot_Video Video;

    // Machine type (Gestalt)
    unsigned long machineType;

    // Base of the flattened device tree
    void *deviceTreeP;

    // Length of the flattened device tree
    unsigned long deviceTreeLength;

    // Last (highest) address of kernel data area
    unsigned long topOfKernelData;
};
```

BootX populates the boot_args structure as follows.

- It sets the Revision field to 1.
- The value of the Version field can be either 1 or 2. Version 2 of the boot_args structure contains page numbers in the physical memory banks, whereas version 1 contains byte addresses. BootX determines the version to pass based on the #address-cells and #size-cells properties of the device tree's root node: If either of these two values is greater than 1, BootX uses page numbers for bank ranges and marks the boot_args structure as being version 2.
- The CommandLine string consists of the contents of the Open Firmware boot-args variable. If a special booting mode—such as safe, single user,

or verbose—was specified via snag keys, BootX adds the corresponding characters to the string.

- It queries the `reg` property of the `/memory` node in the device tree. It breaks down the contents of `reg` into pairs of base and size values, and it populates the `PhysicalDRAM` array.

- It retrieves various display properties using the Open Firmware client interface. For example, the `v_baseAddr` field of `boot_args` is assigned the address returned by the `frame-buffer-adr` Open Firmware word.

- It sets the `machineType` field to 0.

- It recursively flattens the device tree in kernel memory. At the end of the flattening operation, it sets the `deviceTreeP` and `deviceTreeLength` fields appropriately.

- The last step of the boot argument setup is the assignment of the `topOfKernelData` field. BootX maintains a pointer to the "last" kernel address throughout its operation. It uses this pointer as the basis for a simple-minded memory allocation scheme: "kernel" memory is allocated by incrementing the pointer by the requested memory size, rounded up to a page size multiple. BootX sets the final value of this pointer as the value of `topOfKernelData`.

Closed After Boot

The Open Firmware standard does not require the user interface to operate correctly after a client program—for example, the operating system—has begun execution. Nevertheless, some implementations do allow the firmware to be accessed by the end user from a running operating system. For example, on a SPARC machine, you can access the OpenBoot monitor through the **STOP-A** key combination by "suspending" a normally running operating system. In contrast, Apple's Open Firmware is not available once the operating system has booted.

4.11 Alternate Booting Scenarios

In this section, we look at the following examples of booting in alternate ways: booting a user-specified kernel, booting from a software RAID device, and booting over the network.

4.11.1 Booting an Alternate Kernel

A kernel other than the default can be booted by appropriately setting Open Firmware's boot-file variable, which is empty on a typical Mac OS X installation. BootX explicitly looks for the kernel by its default name (mach_kernel) in the root directory of the boot device. Setting boot-file overrides this behavior.

Suppose the alternate kernel you wish to boot also resides in the root directory of the file system containing the default kernel. Let the alternate kernel's name be mach_kernel.debug. First, we determine the BSD name of the disk device containing these kernels.

```
$ mount
/dev/disk0s3 on / (local, journaled)
...
```

We see that the root file system is on the third partition of disk 0. Although we can use the complete Open Firmware pathname of the disk while setting boot-file, in this case it is simpler to use the hd alias, which expands to the complete pathname of the primary disk. Figure 4–18 shows an example of retrieving an Open Firmware path for a given BSD device node.[23]

FIGURE 4–18 Retrieving a BSD device node's Open Firmware path

```
// getfwpath.c

#include <stdio.h>
#include <fcntl.h>
#include <stdlib.h>
#include <unistd.h>
#include <sys/disk.h>

#define PROGNAME "getfwpath"

int
main(int argc, char **argv)
{
    int fd;
    dk_firmware_path_t path = { { 0 } };

    if (argc != 2) {
        fprintf(stderr, "usage: %s <path>\n", PROGNAME);
        exit(1);
    }
```

(continues)

---

23. There may be multiple Open Firmware pathnames for a given device.

FIGURE 4–18 Retrieving a BSD device node's Open Firmware path *(continued)*

```
    if ((fd = open(argv[1], O_RDONLY)) < 0) {
        perror("open");
        exit(1);
    }

    if (ioctl(fd, DKIOCGETFIRMWAREPATH, &path) < 0) {
        perror("ioctl");
        close(fd);
        exit(1);
    }

    printf("%s\n", path.path);

    close(fd);
    exit(0);
}

$ gcc -Wall -o getfwpath getfwpath.c

$ machine # PowerPC-based Macintosh
ppc970
$ sudo ./getfwpath /dev/rdisk0
first-boot/@0:0
$ sudo ./getfwpath /dev/rdisk0s3
first-boot/@0:3
$ sudo ./getfwpath /dev/rdisk1
sata/k2-sata@1/@:0

$ machine # x86-based Macintosh
i486
$ sudo ./getfwpath /dev/rdisk0
/PCI0@0/SATA@1F,2/@0:0
```

In the context of the current example, the following setting for `boot-file` will result in /`mach_kernel.debug` being booted instead of /`mach_kernel`.

```
$ sudo nvram boot-file
boot-file
$ sudo nvram boot-file="hd:3,mach_kernel.debug"
```

If booting the alternate kernel fails, or if you otherwise wish to revert to the previous kernel, you can edit the value of `boot-file` appropriately. In particular, if `boot-file` previously had a custom value, you can restore it to its original value. Alternatively, you can reset all Open Firmware variables, which will result in /mach_kernel being used by default. The following sequence of Open Firmware commands will achieve this:

```
0 > set-defaults
0 > sync-nvram
0 > reset-nvram
0 > mac-boot
```

set-defaults resets most configuration variables to their default values. However, it does not alter any user-created configuration variables. It also does not affect security-related variables.

4.11.1.1 NVRAM Caveats

There are certain noteworthy caveats regarding the manipulation of NVRAM variables from Mac OS X. Most importantly, it must be realized that making any changes to the NVRAM variables does not result in the NVRAM controller committing those changes to flash memory immediately. The changes are only stored in the I/O Kit, which maintains them under the options node. When the system goes through a proper shutdown—say, due to a halt or a reboot—the Platform Expert makes a call to the NVRAM controller, which commits the in-memory NVRAM image to nonvolatile storage. Therefore, if you change the value of an NVRAM variable using the nvram command-line program and simply power off the system without a proper shutdown, the change will be lost.

When a kernel panic occurs, a panic log may be saved to NVRAM under certain circumstances. In particular, it is *not* saved if panic debugging is enabled. When the log is present, it is contained in NVRAM as the value of a firmware variable called aapl,panic-info. The kernel attempts to compress the log before saving it to NVRAM. If the panic log is too large,[24] it is truncated before it is saved.

Moreover, it is possible for certain NVRAM variables to be altered or reset as a side effect of using a system application. For example, the boot-args variable is reset, and the boot-device variable is modified, as side effects of choosing a different system to boot in the Startup Disk preference pane. Specifically, the Startup Disk bundle (StartupDisk.prefPane) resets boot-args to prevent potential interference by arguments that might be inappropriate in the new boot scenario.

---

24. The kernel uses a hardcoded value of 2040 bytes as the upper limit on the size of the panic log—compressed or otherwise—that can be saved to NVRAM.

4.11.2 Booting from a Software RAID Device

Newer versions of BootX support booting from a RAID device configured using Apple's software RAID implementation (AppleRAID). AppleRAID may be visualized as a type of partitioning scheme—one that spans multiple disks but presents a single virtual disk. Let us consider a specific example of an AppleRAID configuration and see how a Mac OS X installation is booted. Figure 4–19 shows a RAID 0 configuration with two disks.

Each disk in Figure 4–19 has a small auxiliary partition of type `Apple_Boot`, which is conventionally named *eXternal booter*. This partition contains an HFS Plus file system, which in turn contains BootX, a boot property list (plist) file (`com.apple.Boot.plist`), and a few other files. The plist file lists the RAID set's members.

```
$ cat com.apple.Boot.plist
...
<plist version="1.0">
<array>
        <dict>
                <key>IOBootDevicePath</key>
                <string>IODeviceTree:sata/k2-sata@1/@0:4</string>
                <key>IOBootDeviceSize</key>
                <integer>159898714112</integer>
        </dict>
        <dict>
                <key>IOBootDevicePath</key>
                <string>IODeviceTree:first-boot/@0:4</string>
                <key>IOBootDeviceSize</key>
                <integer>159898714112</integer>
        </dict>
</array>
</plist>
```

The `boot-device` NVRAM variable in this setup refers to one of the `Apple_Boot` partitions.

```
$ nvram boot-device
boot-device      sata/k2-sata@1/@0:3,\\:tbxi
$ sudo ./getfwpath /dev/rdisk0s3
sata/k2-sata@1/@0:3
```

When a RAID-capable BootX looks for boot paths, it checks for the existence of a boot plist file on the boot device. If one is found, its contents are parsed and entered into a dictionary. It then iterates over the list of potential RAID set

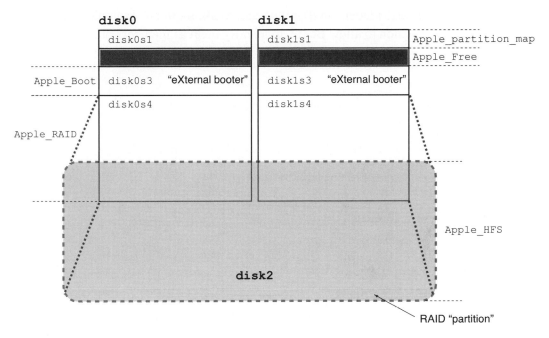

FIGURE 4–19 An AppleRAID software RAID configuration

members, examining the RAID header of each. An Apple RAID header[25] resides
on an `Apple_RAID` partition at an offset that is a function of the partition's size:

```
enum {
    kAppleRAIDHeaderSize      = 0x1000,
    kAppleRAIDDefaultChunkSize = 0x8000
};

#define ARHEADER_OFFSET(s) ((UInt64) \
    (s) / kAppleRAIDHeaderSize * kAppleRAIDHeaderSize - kAppleRAIDHeaderSize)
...
struct AppleRAIDHeaderV2 {
    char      raidSignature[16];
    char      raidUUID[64];
    char      memberUUID[64];
    UInt64    size;
    char      plist[];
};
```

---

25. This example uses version 2 of the AppleRAID header.

The RAID headers on `disk0s4` and `disk1s4` in our example contain sufficient information to allow BootX to identify them as members of a RAID set.

```
/* disk0s4 RAID header */
...
<key>AppleRAID-MemberUUID</key>
<string ID="3">4C7D4187-5A3A-4711-A283-844730B5041B</string>
...
<key>AppleRAID-SetUUID</key>
<string ID="9">2D10F9DB-1E42-497A-920C-F318AD446518</string>
...
<key>AppleRAID-Members</key>
<array ID="13">
    <string ID="14">77360F81-72F4-4FB5-B9DD-BE134556A253</string>
    <string IDREF="3"/>
</array>
...

/* disk1s4 RAID header */
...
<key>AppleRAID-MemberUUID</key>
<string ID="3">77360F81-72F4-4FB5-B9DD-BE134556A253</string>
...
<key>AppleRAID-SetUUID</key>
<string ID="9">2D10F9DB-1E42-497A-920C-F318AD446518</string>
...
<key>AppleRAID-Members</key>
<array ID="13">
    <string IDREF="3"/>
    <string ID="15">4C7D4187-5A3A-4711-A283-844730B5041B</string>
</array>
...
```

If BootX determines that all members of a RAID set that are required to make the set complete have been found, it proceeds with booting. BootX itself implements a library for performing I/O on RAID devices. The library provides *open*, *close*, *read*, *write*,[26] and *seek* functions for RAID device I/O.

4.11.3 Booting over a Network

We saw earlier how to "boot" Forth programs by downloading them using TFTP from a remote computer. Mac OS X itself can be both booted and "rooted" over the network. The easiest way to configure and manage network booting for one or

---

26. Writing to a RAID device is not supported by BootX. This function simply returns an error.

more Mac OS X computers is through the NetBoot service in Mac OS X Server. Such managed network booting offers several benefits.

- Several client systems can boot from a single server-based disk image. Consequently, the administrator has to manage only one image.

- Groups of client systems can boot from images customized for the respective groups.

- Large clusters of computers, whether they are computational clusters or computers within a data center, can be identically configured, booted, and managed.

- Computers can be booted in "diskless" mode for simplified administration in controlled computing environments such as kiosks and quality assurance (QA) installations. Another use of diskless booting is for diagnosing and fixing problems on a client computer, especially if a problem involves the client's local disks. Disk images for such booting can be served over NFS or HTTP.

> Mac OS X can automatically discover a network boot image on the server using a BOOTP/DHCP extension: the *Boot Server Discovery Protocol* (BSDP).

If you have at least two machines, network booting can be quite useful while debugging a kernel or a kernel extension. One machine hosts the kernel, and the other is the test machine that runs the kernel. It is especially convenient if the host machine is also the build machine.

Although Apple's NetBoot service makes it easier to configure network booting, it is not required to boot Mac OS X over the network. Let us look at an example of network booting a client "manually." We will assume a simple setup suitable for the aforementioned kernel-debugging scenario: The test machine—the booting client—will use the root file system on its local disk.

Let us call the booting system CLIENT. The other machine—call it SERVER—can be any system capable of running the TFTP service. However, we will assume that both CLIENT and SERVER are running Mac OS X. We will explicitly assign an IP address to CLIENT for network booting. If it must get an IP address dynamically, a DHCP server would also be required.

CLIENT would need to download three items from SERVER: BootX, the kernel, and an mkext cache.

First we must ensure that the TFTP service is enabled on SERVER. Recall from our earlier examples that we can use the `service` command to enable or disable services.

```
$ sudo service tftp start
```

Next, we copy BootX and the kernel to the TFTP directory. If SERVER is also the build machine, a symbolic link pointing to the kernel's build location could be created in the TFTP directory.

```
$ sudo cp /usr/standalone/ppc/bootx.xcoff /private/tftpboot/bootx.xcoff
$ sudo cp /path/to/kernel /private/tftpboot/mach_kernel.debug
$ sudo chmod 0644 /private/tftpboot/bootx.xcoff /private/tftpboot/mach_kernel.debug
```

The mkext cache must be created on CLIENT. Doing so avoids problems that may arise from CLIENT and SERVER having different kernel extension requirements.

```
$ kextcache -l -n -a ppc -m /tmp/mach_kernel.debug.mkext /System/Library/Extensions
```

The `-l` option in the `kextcache` command line instructs `kextcache` to include the extensions required for local disk boot, and the `-n` option specifies extensions for network boot. The resultant mkext file is transferred to SERVER and copied to the TFTP directory. Note that the name of the mkext file is not arbitrary—for a kernel file named `foo`, BootX will look for an mkext file called `foo.mkext`.

Next, we need to set the values of three Open Firmware variables on CLIENT: `boot-device`, `boot-file`, and `boot-args`. Let us assume that the IP addresses of SERVER and CLIENT are `10.0.0.1` and `10.0.0.2`, respectively. We set the values of `boot-device` and `boot-file` using the network booting syntax we came across in previous examples.

```
0 > setenv boot-device enet:10.0.0.1,bootx.xcoff,10.0.0.2;255.255.255.0,;10.0.0.1
0 > setenv boot-file enet:10.0.0.1,mach_kernel.debug,10.0.0.2;255.255.255.0,;10.0.0.1
```

> We noted that the names of the kernel and the mkext cache must be related. However, there is a caveat due to the way certain versions of BootX parse the `boot-file` variable. For computing the mkext file's name, BootX assumes the kernel's name to be the string after the last comma in the contents of `boot-file`. In our current example, the kernel's name, as computed by BootX, would be

> ;10.0.0.1. In a typical network booting configuration, where we do not need to specify CLIENT's IP address, this issue will not arise because boot-file is of the form enet:<TFTP server's IP address>,<kernel filename>. If the BootX implementation you are using exhibits this behavior, you can get around the issue by creating a symbolic link named ;10.0.0.1.mkext to mach_kernel. debug.mkext in SERVER's TFTP directory.

The remaining configuration step is to set the value of boot-args:

```
0 > setenv boot-args -s -v rd=*<root device specification>
```

The -s and -v arguments specify single-user and verbose boot modes, respectively. The rd argument specifies CLIENT's root device prefixed with an asterisk character, which forces the root file system to be local. Here is a specific example:

```
0 > setenv boot-args -s -v rd=*/pci@f4000000/ata-6@d/disk@0:3
```

Finally, we can flush the NVRAM and reboot.

```
0 > sync-nvram
...
0 > mac-boot
```

If everything is set up correctly, the network boot process will start. You might see a flashing globe briefly, followed by the Apple logo with a spinning globe below it. CLIENT should boot into a single user shell.

4.12 Firmware Security

Open Firmware includes a security feature that allows you to set a password that is required to access most commands from the firmware prompt, and optionally, to even boot the system. Open Firmware security settings can be changed either from the firmware prompt or through Apple's Open Firmware Password application. The latter is available for newer versions of Mac OS X on the installation media.

4.12.1 Managing Firmware Security

The password command prompts the user—twice—to type a newline-terminated security password string. The password, which is not echoed on the screen, can contain only ASCII characters. If both user-typed password strings match, Apple's implementation of Open Firmware encodes the password using a simple scheme and stores the encoded version in the `security-password` variable. The scheme is shown in Table 4–6.

Note that setting the password alone does not enable password protection; a security mode must also be set through the `security-mode` variable. The security mode defines the level of access protection. The following levels are supported.

- none—This sets no security; even though a password may be set, it will not be required.

TABLE 4–6 Open Firmware Encoding of an ASCII Password

ASCII	Encoded	ASCII	Encoded	ASCII	Encoded	ASCII	Encoded	ASCII	Encoded
sp	%8a	3	%99	F	%ec	Y	%f3	l	%c6
!	%8b	4	%9e	G	%ed	Z	%f0	m	%c7
"	%88	5	%9f	H	%e2	[	%f1	n	%c4
#	%89	6	%9c	I	%e3	\	%f6	o	%c5
$	%8e	7	%9d	J	%e0	]	%f7	p	%da
%	%8f	8	%92	K	%e1	^	%f4	q	%db
&	%8c	9	%93	L	%e6	_	%f5	r	%d8
'	%8d	:	%90	M	%e7	`	%ca	s	%d9
(	%82	;	%91	N	%e4	a	%cb	t	%de
)	%83	<	%96	O	%e5	b	%c8	u	%df
*	%80	=	%97	P	%fa	c	%c9	v	%dc
+	%81	>	%94	Q	%fb	d	%ce	w	%dd
,	%86	?	%95	R	%f8	e	%cf	x	%d2
-	%87	@	%ea	S	%f9	f	%cc	y	%d3
.	%84	A	%eb	T	%fe	g	%cd	z	%d0
/	%85	B	%e8	U	%ff	h	%c2	{	%d1
0	%9a	C	%e9	V	%fc	i	%c3			%d6
1	%9b	D	%ee	W	%fd	j	%c0	}	%d7
2	%98	E	%ef	X	%f2	k	%c1	~	%d4

- command—A password is required for all firmware commands except for booting the system using default settings. The system can automatically boot in this mode after power-on.

- full—A password is required for all firmware commands, *including* for booting the system with default settings. The system will not automatically boot without a password.

- no-password—Access to Open Firmware is entirely disabled. The system will simply boot into the operating system regardless of any keys pressed at boot time. Note that this is not a standard Open Firmware mode.

The following is an example of enabling Open Firmware password protection.

```
0 > password
Enter a new password: ********
Enter password again: ********
Password will be in place on the next boot! ok
0 > setenv security-mode full   ok
0 >
```

> When the security mode is set to either command or full, the ability to use snag keys is blocked: pressing keys such as **c**, **n**, or **t** will not alter booting behavior. Similarly, pressing **-v**, **-s**, or -option-p-r will not result in a verbose boot, single-user boot, or PRAM-reset, respectively.

The security-#badlogins firmware variable contains a total count of failed access attempts while the security mode was set to command or full. Each time an incorrect password is entered at the Open Firmware prompt, this counter is incremented by one.

The values of the security-related firmware variables can be examined or set from within Mac OS X by using the nvram utility. However, setting security-password through nvram is not recommended, as the encoding scheme shown in Table 4–6 is not guaranteed to remain unchanged across firmware revisions. Note that superuser access is required to view the contents of security-password.

```
$ sudo nvram -p | grep security
security-#badlogins     1
security-password       %c4%c5%c4%cf
security-mode   none
```

4.12.2 Recovering the Open Firmware Password

Open Firmware security is not foolproof—it is meant to be only a deterrent. It is possible to reset, change, and perhaps even recover the firmware password. The superuser can disable firmware security by using the `nvram` utility to change the value of security-mode to `none`. The password may also be reset via physical access to the inside of the computer.[27]

4.13 Launching the Kernel

In Chapter 5, we will discuss system startup from the point where the kernel begins to execute. Let us briefly examine the kernel binary to determine the starting point of the kernel—that is, the point at which BootX transfers control.

The Mac OS X kernel is a Mach-O executable. Recall from Chapter 2 that we can use the `otool` command-line program to view a Mach-O executable's header and load commands.

```
$ file /mach_kernel
/mach_kernel: Mach-O executable ppc
$ otool -hv /mach_kernel
/mach_kernel:
Mach header
      magic cputype cpusubtype    filetype ncmds sizeofcmds      flags
  MH_MAGIC      PPC        ALL     EXECUTE     9       2360    NOUNDEFS
$ otool -l /mach_kernel
/mach_kernel:
Load command 0
      cmd LC_SEGMENT
  cmdsize 532
  segname __TEXT
   vmaddr 0x0000e000
   vmsize 0x0034f000
...
Load command 2
      cmd LC_SEGMENT
  cmdsize 124
  segname __VECTORS
   vmaddr 0x00000000
   vmsize 0x00007000
   fileoff 3624960
```

---

27. The password may be reset by altering the memory configuration of the computer and then resetting the PRAM.

```
     filesize 28672
      maxprot 0x00000007
     initprot 0x00000003
       nsects 1
        flags 0x0
Section
      sectname __interrupts
      segname __VECTORS
         addr 0x00000000
         size 0x00007000
       offset 3624960
        align 2^12 (4096)
       reloff 0
       nreloc 0
        flags 0x00000000
    reserved1 0
    reserved2 0
...
Load command 8
          cmd LC_UNIXTHREAD
      cmdsize 176
       flavor PPC_THREAD_STATE
        count PPC_THREAD_STATE_COUNT
... srr0 0x00092340 srr1 0x00000000
```

The SRR0 register contains the value 0x00092340 in the initial thread state of this particular kernel. The code at this address is the entry point of the kernel. We can use nm to determine the symbol, if any, that has this address.

```
$ nm /mach_kernel | grep 00092340
00092340 T __start
```

4.14 The BootCache Optimization

Mac OS X uses a boot-time optimization called *BootCache* —effectively a smart read-ahead scheme—that monitors the pattern of incoming read requests to a block device and sorts the pattern into a *play list*, which is then used to cluster reads into a private cache. Each play-list entry represents a disk region to be cached and is specified as a { block address, length } pair. This "boot cache" is thereafter used to satisfy incoming read requests if possible. The scheme also measures the cache-hit rate. The request pattern is stored in a *history list* to allow the scheme to be adaptive. If the hit rate is too low, the caching is disabled.

BootCache is only supported on the root device. It requires at least 128MB of physical RAM to be automatically enabled. The BootCache kernel extension (BootCache.kext) registers a callback named mountroot_post_hook() with the kernel to request notification of the mounting of the root file system. The kernel extension has the OSBundleRequired property set to Local-Root, which marks it as a requirement for mounting root on a local volume. Therefore, before a local root file system is mounted, the kernel will ensure that the BootCache kernel extension is loaded.

BootCache's loadable read pattern is sorted and stored in the /var/db/ BootCache.playlist file. Once this pattern is loaded, the cache comes into effect. When a recorded read pattern is fetched, the cache is disabled and the associated memory is freed. The entire process is invisible from the user and requires no action on the latter's part. A user-level control utility called BootCacheControl can be used to start or stop the cache, manipulate play lists, and view cache statistics.

```
$ sudo BootCacheControl -f /var/db/BootCache.playlist print
512-byte blocks
143360      4096
2932736     4096
3416064     4096

...
122967457792 512    prefetch
122967576576 4096
122967666688 4096
122967826432 4096
122968137728 4096
94562816 blocks
$ sudo BootCacheControl statistics
block size                512
initiated reads           2823
blocks read               176412
...
extents in cache          1887
extent lookups            4867
extent hits               4557
extent hit ratio          93.63%
hits not fulfilled        0
blocks requested          167305
blocks hit                158456
blocks discarded by write 0
block hit ratio           94.71%
...
```

4.15 Boot-Time Kernel Arguments

Arguments can be passed to the Mac OS X kernel through the `boot-args` NVRAM variable. The kernel parses these arguments as it boots, and in some cases, kernel extensions refer to boot arguments too. In this section, a large number of kernel arguments are tabulated. We will come across some of the arguments, and the contexts in which they are used, in subsequent chapters. Only brief explanations are provided in this section for the rest. Note the following points about the use of these arguments.

- The set of available kernel arguments may change across kernel revisions. Therefore, some arguments listed here may not be available on certain kernel versions. Conversely, some kernels may support arguments that are not listed here.

- Many of these arguments are intended for debugging or developmental purposes only. However, classifying them as appropriate or inappropriate for production use is an exercise in subjectivity—consequently, the arguments are listed *as is*.

- The arguments are roughly classified based on the purposes they serve. However, there may be some overlap between these categories.

- The value of the `boot-args` variable can be programmatically obtained on Mac OS X through the I/O Kit or the Mach user-level APIs. Moreover, as we saw earlier, the `nvram` utility displays the contents of `boot-args` from the command line.

Table 4–7 lists arguments that affect the overall booting behavior of the system. Note that most of these arguments are deprecated in Mac OS X 10.4 or newer.

TABLE 4–7 Kernel Arguments for Boot Behavior

Argument	Description
-b	The kernel sets `RB_NOBOOTRC` in its reboot flags variable to indicate that `/etc/rc.boot` should not be run. Deprecated.
-D	`mach_init` starts in normal mode. Core dumps are not taken for launched servers. Deprecated.

(continues)

TABLE 4–7 Kernel Arguments for Boot Behavior *(Continued)*

Argument	Description
-d	`mach_init` starts in debug mode, with extensive logging. Core dumps are taken for any launched servers that crash. On Mac OS X 10.4 or newer, this argument causes the `launchd` program to daemonize early during its initialization.
-F	`mach_init` forks during initialization. Note that it always forks if its process ID is 1. Deprecated.
-f	This argument is passed to the init program to indicate that a fast boot is desired. Deprecated.
-r	`mach_init` registers itself in a previously running copy of itself. Deprecated.
-s	This specifies single-user mode.
-v	This specifies a verbose boot.
-x	The system attempts to boot conservatively in safe mode.

Table 4–8 lists arguments that can be used to alter the kernel's allocation of key data structures.

TABLE 4–8 Kernel Arguments for Resource Allocation

Argument	Description
ht_shift	This argument is used to scale the hash table size during system page table allocation. By default, the kernel uses one page table entry group (PTEG) per four physical pages. Positive values of `ht_shift` make the hash table larger, and negative values make it smaller.
initmcl	This specifies the number of mbuf clusters to allocate during mbuf initialization.
mseg	This sets the maximum descriptor-based DMA (DBDMA) segment size.
nbuf	This specifies the number of I/O buffers to allocate. It defaults to 1% of physical memory pages, up to a maximum of 8192 and a minimum of 256.
ncl	This indicates the number of mbuf clusters used to calculate the `nmbclusters` value, which is the number of mapped clusters.
zsize	This sets the target zone size used while allocating address space for zones during virtual memory subsystem initialization. It defaults to 25% of physical memory, with 12MB and 768MB being the minimum and maximum values, respectively.

Table 4–9 lists arguments that affect the behavior of the kernel's locking mechanisms.

TABLE 4–9 Kernel Arguments for Locking Behavior

Argument	Description
dfnl	Setting `dfnl=1` disables the split funnel. Removed in Mac OS X 10.4.
lcks	This argument specifies various locking options found in `osfmk/ppc/locks.h` and `osfmk/i386/locks.h`.
mtxspin	This sets the lock timeout in microseconds.
refunn	This enables the "refunnel" hint. Removed in Mac OS X 10.4.

Table 4–10 lists arguments that can be used either by themselves or in conjunction with other arguments to specify the root device.

TABLE 4–10 Kernel Arguments for Root Devices

Argument	Description
boot-uuid	This argument specifies a root device by its UUID. Used along with `rd=uuid`.
rd, rootdev	This specifies the root device as a device string. A string of the form `/dev/diskY` specifies a disk, where `Y` is the slice. Similarly, a string of the form `/dev/mdx` specifies a RAM disk, where `x` is a single-digit hexadecimal number. Other alternatives include `cdrom`, `enet`, and `uuid`.
rp, rootpath	This indicates the booter-specified root path.
vndevice	Setting `vndevice=1` causes the kernel to use the vnode disk driver instead of the disk image controller (hdix) while accessing an image remotely. Note that HTTP can be used only with hdix.

Table 4–11 lists arguments that affect the kernel's scheduling behavior.

TABLE 4–11 Kernel Arguments for Scheduling Behavior

Argument	Description
idlehalt	Setting `idlehalt=1` causes the kernel to halt a CPU core if no other thread in that core is active, causing the core to go into a low-power mode. An x86-only argument.

(continues)

TABLE 4–11 Kernel Arguments for Scheduling Behavior *(Continued)*

Argument	Description
poll	This argument sets the maximum poll quanta. Default value is 2.
preempt	This specifies the preemption rate in hertz. Default value is 100.
unsafe	This identifies the maximum unsafe quanta. Default value is 800.
yield	This is used to set the sched_poll_yield_shift scheduling variable, which is used while computing the time value for a polled depress thread yield. Default value is 4.

Table 4–12 lists arguments that can be used to enable or disable certain hardware and software features. It also lists arguments that are useful for various types of debugging.

TABLE 4–12 Kernel Arguments for Modifying Hardware/Software Properties and Debugging

Argument	Description
artsize	Specifies the number of pages to be used for the address resolution table (ART).
BootCacheOverride	The BootCache driver is loaded—but does not run—in the case of a network boot. Setting BootCacheOverride=1 overrides this behavior.
cpus	Specifying cpus=N limits the number of CPUs to N, which must be a number less than or equal to the number of physically available CPUs.
ctrc	Limits tracing to a specific processor (see the tb argument).
dart	Setting dart=0 turns off the system PCI address mapper (DART) on 64-bit hardware. DART is required on machines with more than 2GB of physical memory but is enabled by default on all machines, regardless of their memory sizes.
debug	Specifies a variety of debug flags including those for kernel-debugging behavior. See Table 4–13 for details of these flags.
diag	Enables the kernel's built-in diagnostics API and its specific features.
fhrdl1	Setting fhrdl1=1 forces hardware recovery of data cache level 1 (L1 D-cache) errors. Deprecated (see the mcksoft argument).
fill	Specifies an integer value that is used to fill all memory pages at boot time.

(continues)

TABLE 4–12 Kernel Arguments for Modifying Hardware/Software Properties and Debugging *(Continued)*

Argument	Description
fn	Alters the processor's force-nap behavior. Setting `fn=1` turns force-nap off; setting `fn=2` turns force-nap on.
_fpu	Disables FPU features on the x86. A string value of `387` disables FXSR/SSE/SSE2, whereas a string value of `sse` disables SSE2.
hfile	Name of the hibernate file (also stored in the `kern.hibernatefile` sysctl variable).
io	Specifies I/O Kit debugging flags. In particular, setting the `kIOLogSynchronous` bit (the value `0x00200000`) ensures that the `IOLog()` function will complete synchronously. Normally, `IOLog()` output goes to a circular buffer that is emptied periodically.
kdp_match_mac	Specifies a MAC address that is to be used by the remote kernel-debugging protocol.
kdp_match_name	Specifies a BSD network interface name that is to be used by the remote kernel-debugging protocol.
maxmem	Setting `maxmem=N` limits the available physical memory to `N` (in megabytes). `N` must be less than or equal to the actual amount of physical memory installed.
mcklog	Specifies machine check flags.
mcksoft	Setting `mcksoft=1` enables machine check software recovery.
novmx	Setting `novmx=1` disables AltiVec.
_panicd_ip	Specifies the IP address of a remote kernel-core-dump server machine, which is expected to be running the `kdumpd` daemon on UDP port 1069.
pcata	Setting `pcata=0` disables the onboard PC ATA driver. This may be useful during development—for example, if a polled-mode driver is to be loaded.
platform	Specifies a string to be used as the platform name in the fake device tree on the x86. The default platform name used is `ACPI`.
pmsx	Setting `pmsx=1` enables the experimental Power Management Stepper (PMS) mode introduced in Mac OS X 10.4.3.
romndrv	Setting `romndrv=1` allows a native graphics driver (ndrv) to be used even if its creation date is older than a predefined minimum date, which is March 1, 2001.
_router_ip	Specifies the router through which the remote kernel-debugging protocol is to be routed while transmitting kernel core dumps to a remote machine.
serial	Setting `serial=1` enables the serial console.

(continues)

TABLE 4–12 Kernel Arguments for Modifying Hardware/Software Properties and Debugging *(Continued)*

Argument	Description
serialbaud	Specifies the baud rate for the serial port. The initialization routine for the `kprintf()` function checks this argument.
smbios	Setting `smbios=1` enables detailed log messages in the SMBIOS driver. An x86-only argument.
srv	Setting `srv=1` indicates a server boot. The kernel may check the value of this variable to alter its behavior.
tb	The kernel supports event tracing to a circular in-memory buffer. A non-default trace buffer size can be specified through the `tb` argument. By default, the kernel uses 32 pages in debug mode and 8 pages in nondebug mode. The minimum and maximum values are 1 and 256 pages, respectively.
vmdx, pmdx	Cause the kernel to attempt to create a memory disk at boot time. Used as `vmdx=base.size`, where x is a single-digit hexadecimal number (0–f), `base` is a page-aligned memory address, and `size` is a multiple of the page size. The v specifies virtual memory. A p can be used instead to specify physical memory. If the creation is successful, device nodes `/dev/mdx` and `/dev/rmdx` will appear after boot.
vmmforce	Specifies virtual machine monitor (VMM) features as a logical OR of feature bits. The features so specified are enforced for all virtual machine instances.
wcte	Setting `wcte=1` enables the write combine timer (or store gather timer) in the PowerPC noncacheable unit (NCU). By default, this timer is disabled.

Table 4–13 lists the various bits that can be set in the kernel's `debug` argument, which is perhaps the most versatile and useful argument available for kernel-level debugging.

TABLE 4–13 Details of the `debug` Kernel Argument

Bit	Name	Description
0x1	DB_HALT	Halt at boot time and wait for a debugger connection.
0x2	DB_PRT	Send kernel-debugging output generated by the kernel's `printf()` function to the console.

(continues)

TABLE 4–13 Details of the `debug` Kernel Argument *(Continued)*

Bit	Name	Description
0x4	DB_NMI	Enable the kernel-debugging facility, including support for generating a nonmaskable interrupt (NMI) without a physical programmer's switch. On a Power Mac, an NMI can be generated by briefly pressing the power button. On a notebook computer, the **command** key must be held down while pressing the power button. If the power button is held down for more than five seconds, the system will power off. The DB_NMI bit is cleared if you use System Preferences to change the startup disk.
0x8	DB_KPRT	Send kernel-debugging output generated by `kprintf()` to the remote output device, which is typically a serial port (if one is available). Note that `kprintf()` output is synchronous.
0x10	DB_KDB	Use KDB instead of GDB as the default kernel debugger. Unlike GDB, KDB must be explicitly compiled into the kernel. Moreover, KDB-based debugging requires native serial port hardware (as opposed to, say, USB-based serial port adapters).
0x20	DB_SLOG	Enable logging of miscellaneous diagnostics to the system log. For example, the `load_shared_file()` kernel function logs extra information if this bit is set.
0x40	DB_ARP	Allow the kernel debugger nub to use ARP, allowing debugging across subnets.
0x80	DB_KDP_BP_DIS	Deprecated. Used for supporting old versions of GDB.
0x100	DB_LOG_PI_SCRN	Disable the graphical panic screen so that panic data can be logged to the screen. It is also useful for monitoring the progress of a kernel core dump transmission.
0x200	DB_KDP_GETC_ENA	Prompt for one of the `c`, `r`, and `k` characters to continue, reboot, or enter KDB, respectively, after a kernel panic.
0x400	DB_KERN_DUMP_ON_PANIC	Trigger core dump on panic.
0x800	DB_KERN_DUMP_ON_NMI	Trigger core dump on NMI.
0x1000	DB_DBG_POST_CORE	Wait for a debugger connection (if using GDB) or wait in the debugger (if using KDB) after an NMI-induced core dump. If DB_DBG_POST_CORE is not set, the kernel continues after the core dump.
0x2000	DB_PANICLOG_DUMP	Send only a panic log—not a full core dump—on panic.

4.16 The Extensible Firmware Interface

In this section, we look at the Extensible Firmware Interface (EFI), which is a specification for an interface between operating systems and platform firmware. x86-based Macintosh computers use EFI instead of Open Firmware. EFI is conceptually very similar to Open Firmware. Although it is platform independent in theory, EFI is primarily intended for the IA-32 and IA-64 architectures.

4.16.1 Legacy Pains

The primitive nature of the PC BIOS had long been an industry-wide problem even as the twenty-first century arrived. One reason for the longevity of the BIOS, and for its sustained primitivity, is the extremely successful MS-DOS (and clones), which was built on top of the BIOS. DOS programs call BIOS routines via software interrupts. For example, the BIOS disk routine corresponds to interrupt number `0x13` (`INT 0x13`). This is similar to many erstwhile Apple systems where the Macintosh ROM contained both low-level code and the higher-level Toolbox.

Although the BIOS has seen numerous tweaks, improvements, extensions, and additions over the years, a traditional BIOS in a modern environment still has numerous severe limitations, such as the following.

- x86 computers always come up in the IA-32 *real mode*—an emulation of the ancient 8086/8088 Intel processors. The BIOS executes in this mode, which is severely limited, especially for an ambitious BIOS—say, one that wishes to provide a powerful preboot environment. Effective memory addresses in the x86 real mode are calculated by multiplying the *segment* (a 16-bit number) by 16 and adding an *offset* (another 16-bit number) to it. Thus, a segment is 16 bits wide—restricted to 65,536 bytes (64KB)—and a memory address is 20 bits wide—restricted to 1,048,576 bytes (1MB). In particular, the instruction pointer (the IP register) is also 16 bits wide, which places a 64KB size limit on the code segment. Memory is a *very* limited resource in real mode. Moreover, a BIOS may require static reservation of resources—especially memory ranges.

- The BIOS is inefficient at providing detailed information about the system hardware to its client programs (such as bootloaders).[28]

---

28. Modern BIOSs support a mechanism called E820 to report any memory present in the system at POST. The report is in the form of a table of memory segments along with the purpose each segment is used for.

Extended Memory

A small range of extended memory addresses can be accessed in real mode.[29] The 386 and higher x86 processors can be switched from protected mode to real mode without a reset, which allows them to operate in the *big real mode*: a modified real mode in which the processor can access up to 4GB of memory. BIOSs can put the processor in this mode during POST to make access to extended memory easier.

- A BIOS usually has hardcoded knowledge of supported boot devices. Support for booting from newer devices typically is added to most BIOSs very slowly, if at all.

- An *option ROM* is firmware typically residing on a plug-in card. It may also live on the system board. Option ROMs are executed by the BIOS during platform initialization. The legacy option ROM space is limited to 128KB, which is shared by all option ROMs. An option ROM typically compacts itself by jettisoning some initialization code, leaving behind a smaller runtime code. Nevertheless, this is a severe limitation.

- Legacy BIOSs depend on VGA, which is a legacy standard and is unnecessarily complicated to program for.

- The traditional PC partitioning scheme, which is the de facto scheme used with the BIOS, is rather inadequate, particularly when it comes to multibooting or having a large number of partitions. PC partitions may be *primary*, *extended*, or *logical*, with at most four primary partitions allowed on a disk. The first 512-byte sector of a PC disk—the *master boot record* (MBR)—has its 512 bytes divided as follows: 446 bytes for bootstrap code, 64 bytes for four partition table entries of 16 bytes each, and 2 bytes for a signature. The rather limited size of a PC partition table limits the number of primary partitions. However, one of the primary partitions may be an extended partition. An arbitrary number of logical partitions may be defined within an extended partition.

- Even with standard network boot protocols such as Preboot Execution Environment (PXE) and related security enhancements such as Boot Integrity Services (BIS), it is rather difficult, and often impossible, to deploy and

---

29. This is known as the Gate A20 option.

manage computers in a "zero-touch" fashion. In particular, the BIOS is extremely difficult to work with when it comes to remote management at the system firmware level or management of the system firmware itself.

> Regardless of their nature, modern operating systems running on the x86 platform must interact with the BIOS via legacy interfaces at system startup. The processor starts up in real mode and typically remains in real mode even as an operating system kernel gains control, after which the kernel eventually switches the processor into protected mode.

A representative legacy BIOS could be visualized as containing three sets of procedures: those that are the same on all BIOSs (the *core* procedures), those that are specific to chips on the platform (the *silicon support* procedures), and those that are specific to a system board. There are many "secret-sauce" elements in the BIOS. The BIOS APIs are very limited, and in general it is very hard to extend the BIOS—it is a black box both to end users and to those wishing to develop preboot applications. Even if such developers license the BIOS source, the environment is expensive to develop for and deploy in.

Preeminence of Preboot

As PC hardware and software vendors attempt to differentiate their offerings, the preboot environment is becoming increasingly important. A computer with preboot functionality for backup and restore, disk maintenance, data recovery, virus scanning, and so on is expected to have more value than one without. In some cases, an application must be prebooted because it cannot rely on the operating system. Examples of such applications include those for performing low-level diagnostics, for recovering the operating system, and for updating certain firmware. In some other cases, an application may not need the full operating system and may explicitly wish to run without the operating system, perhaps to make the computer behave like an appliance—for example, as a DVD or MP3 player, mail client, or web browser.

With legacy BIOS, such preboot applications are rather expensive to develop, deploy, and run. EFI strives to simplify this domain greatly and includes specifications for creating preboot software. Even a high-level application developer could create a preboot application using familiar development tools.

4.16.2 A New Beginning

The PC world was rather late to adopt 64-bit computing. With the advent of 64-bit PCs—those based on Intel's Itanium Processor Family, or IA-64, for example—a better solution to the BIOS problem was sought. Even though the x86 real mode can be emulated in the IA-64 architecture, 64-bit PCs were introduced *without* the legacy BIOS. The IA-64 firmware was divided into three primary components: the *Processor Abstraction Layer* (PAL), the *System Abstraction Layer* (SAL), and the *Extensible Firmware Interface* (EFI).

PAL abstracts the processor hardware implementation from the point of view of SAL and the operating system. Different processor models with potential implementation differences appear uniformly via PAL. Examples of the PAL layer's functionality include the following:

- Interruption entry points including those invoked by hardware events such as processor reset, processor initialization, and machine checks

- Procedures that can be invoked by the operating system or higher-level firmware, such as procedures for obtaining processor identification, configuration, and capability information; for initializing the cache; and for enabling or disabling processor features

PAL has no knowledge of platform implementation details. Note, however, that PAL is part of the IA-64 architecture. The processor vendor supplies the firmware implementation of PAL, which resides in OEM flash memory.

SAL provides an abstraction for the platform implementation, without any knowledge of processor implementation details. SAL is not part of the IA-64 architecture—it is part of the Developer's Interface Guide for 64-bit Intel Architecture (DIG64). The OEM provides the firmware implementation of PAL.

> As on IA-32 systems, Advanced Configuration and Power Interface (ACPI) exists on IA-64 as an interface for allowing the operating system to direct configuration and power management on the computer. ACPI is also a part of the firmware—it could be listed as the fourth primary component besides PAL, SAL, and EFI. Note that since EFI also exists for IA-32, only PAL and SAL are the parts of IA-64 firmware that are specific to IA-64.

The remaining component—EFI—could be thought of as the *grand solution* to the PC BIOS problem.

4.16.3 EFI

EFI can be traced back to the Intel Boot Initiative (IBI) program that started in 1998, based on a white paper by Intel engineer Andrew Fish. The EFI specification—developed and maintained by a consortium of companies—defines a set of APIs and data structures that are exported by a system's firmware and used by clients such as the following:

- EFI device drivers
- EFI system and diagnostic utilities
- EFI shell
- Operating system loaders
- Operating systems

In a representative EFI system, a thin Pre-EFI Initialization Layer (PEI) might do most of the POST-related work traditionally done by the BIOS POST. This includes operations such as chipset initialization, memory initialization, and bus enumeration. EFI prepares a Driver Execution Environment (DXE) to provide generic platform functions that EFI drivers may use. The drivers themselves provide specific platform capabilities and customizations.

4.16.3.1 EFI Services

There are two classes of services available in the EFI environment: *boot services* and *runtime services*.

Boot Services

Applications that run only within the preboot environment make use of boot services, which include services for the following:

- Events, timers, and task priority
- Memory allocation
- Handling of EFI protocols
- Loading of various types of images such as EFI applications, EFI boot services drivers, and EFI runtime drivers
- Miscellaneous purposes such as setting a hardware watchdog timer, stalling execution on the processor, copying or filling memory, manipulating EFI System Table entries, and computing data-buffer checksums

An operating system loader also uses boot services to determine and access the boot device, to allocate memory, and to create a functional environment for the operating system to start loading. At this point, an operating system loader could call the `ExitBootServices()` function, after which boot services are not available. Alternatively, an operating system kernel could call this function.

Runtime Services

Runtime services are available both before and after `ExitBootServices()` is called. This category includes the following types of services:

- Management of variables (key-value pairs) used for sharing information between the EFI environment and the applications that run within it
- Management of hardware time devices
- Virtual memory—for example, to allow an operating system loader or an operating system to invoke runtime services with virtual memory addressing instead of physical addressing
- Retrieval of the platform's monotonic counter
- Resets of the platform

> Although EFI was designed for IA-64-based computers, its scope was widened to include the next generation of IA-32 computers, with provisions for legacy BIOS compatibility through a *Compatibility Support Module* (CSM). The CSM consists of a series of drivers that cooperate with a legacy BIOS runtime component. It loads into memory in well-known legacy areas (below 1MB). Standard BIOS memory areas such as the BIOS Data Area (BDA) and the Extended BDA are initialized. The Boot Device Selection (BDS) mechanism appropriately selects either EFI or legacy BIOS.

Figure 4–20 shows a conceptual view of the EFI architecture.

4.16.3.2 EFI Drivers

EFI drivers can be built into the EFI implementation. Alternatively, they can come from the option ROM of a card or from a device supported natively by EFI. Most EFI drivers would conform to the EFI Driver Model. Such drivers are written in C and operate in a flat memory model. Driver images, which may be converted to EFI Byte Code (EBC), are typically compressed using *Deflate*—a

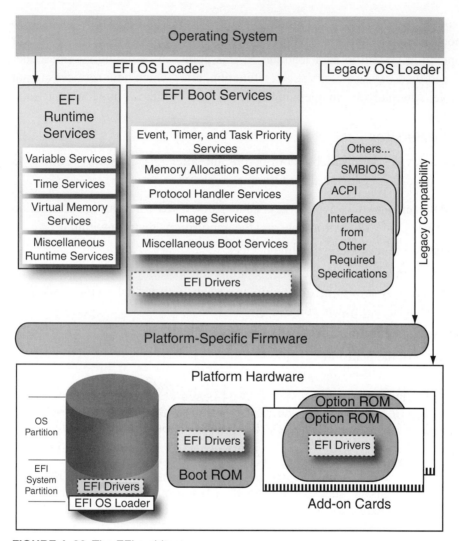

FIGURE 4–20 The EFI architecture

combination of LZ77[30] compression and Huffman coding. Examples of EFI driver types include the following:

- *Bus drivers*, which manage and enumerate bus controllers (such as a PCI network interface controller) installed onto the bus's controller handle

---

30. LZ77 is a lossless data compression algorithm that was originally published by A. Lempel and J. Ziv in 1977.

- *Hybrid drivers*, which manage and enumerate bus controllers (such as a SCSI host controller) installed onto the bus's controller handle *and* the bus's child handles
- *Device drivers*, which manage controllers or peripheral devices such as a PS/2 or USB keyboard

EFI also supports drivers that may not conform to the EFI Driver Model. Examples of such drivers include the following:

- Initializing drivers that perform one-time initialization functions
- Root bridge drivers that manage part of the core chipset
- Service drivers that provide services such as the decompression protocol and the EBC Virtual Machine to other EFI drivers
- Older EFI drivers

An EFI *protocol* is a set of related interfaces. EFI drivers consume various protocols such as PCI I/O, Device Path, USB I/O, and USB Path. They also produce several protocols such as Simple Input, Simple Pointer, Block I/O, UGA Draw, UGA I/O, Simple Text Output, SCSI Block I/O, SCSI Pass-through, Network Interface Identification, Serial I/O, Debug Port, and Load File.

EFI drivers are typically needed only for devices that must be used before the operating system starts running. The primary example is that of a storage device on which the operating system resides. The EFI driver for a storage device allows EFI to export block I/O services, which the bootloader uses to load the operating system kernel.

4.16.4 A Sampling of EFI

Let us now look at a few specific aspects of EFI, including examples of interacting with the EFI environment.

4.16.4.1 EFI NVRAM

EFI defines an area of nonvolatile memory, or NVRAM, which is used to store both global and application-specific data in the form of variables. The NVRAM store can be programmatically accessed—for retrieval or storage—using the EFI API. Variables are stored using a two-level namespace: a globally unique ID (GUID) as the first level and variable names as the second level. Thus, it is possible for two variables with the same name to exist in two GUIDs without namespace collision. All architecturally defined global variables use a reserved GUID such as the following:

```
#define EFI_GLOBAL_VARIABLE \
    {8BE4DF61-93CA-11d2-AA0D-00E098032B8C}
```

Examples of global variables include the currently configured language code (`Lang`), the ordered boot-option load list (`BootOrder`), the ordered driver-load option list (`DriverOrder`), and the device paths of the default input and output consoles (`ConIn` and `ConOut`, respectively).

Application-specific variables, which are passed directly to EFI applications, are also stored in the NVRAM. Moreover, the NVRAM may be used for storing diagnostic data or other information that may be useful in failover and recovery scenarios, as long as the NVRAM has enough space to hold such information.

4.16.4.2 The Boot Manager

The EFI firmware includes an application called the *boot manager*, which can load EFI bootloaders, EFI drivers, and other EFI applications. The boot manager consults global NVRAM variables to determine what to boot. It accesses bootable files from an EFI-defined file system or via an EFI-defined image-loading service.

Figure 4–21 depicts a representative sequence of actions that occur after an EFI-based system is powered on. The core EFI firmware passes control to the boot manager, which uses the NVRAM facility to display a menu of installed bootable applications. In Figure 4–21, the user has selected an operating system bootloader for Mac OS X as the application to boot, which is launched by the boot manager. While executing in the EFI environment, the bootloader loads the kernel, collects any parameters that may exist in the NVRAM, and eventually hands off control to the kernel. If a boot application exits, control returns to the boot manager.

4.16.4.3 The EFI Shell

The EFI environment optionally includes an interactive shell that allows a user to perform tasks such as the following:

- Launch other EFI programs
- Load, test, and debug drivers manually

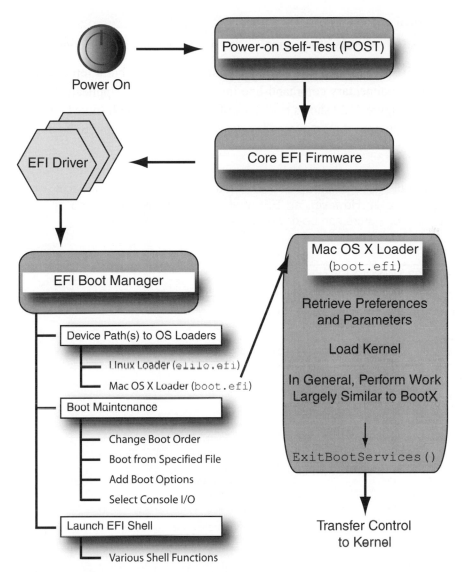

FIGURE 4–21 Booting an operating system through EFI

- Load ROM images
- View or manipulate memory and hardware state
- Manage system variables
- Manage files
- Edit text

- Run shell scripts
- Access the network—for example, via an Ethernet or a dial-up connection

The EFI specification does not cover a shell *interface*, but a representative EFI shell is a rudimentary command-line interpreter—an EFI application implemented in C. Figure 4–22 shows examples of using an EFI shell (note that specifying the -b option to most commands causes the displayed output to break after one screen).

> Apple did not include an EFI shell with the first x86-based Macintosh models. However, an EFI shell implementation that runs on these computers can be downloaded from Intel's web site.

FIGURE 4–22 Using the EFI shell

```
fs0:\> ver
EFI Specification Revision : 1.10
EFI Vendor             : Apple
EFI Revision           : 8192.1


fs0:\> ls
Directory of: fs0:\
...
  02/28/06  02:15p              172,032  tcpipv4.efi
  02/28/06  02:15p               14,336  rtunload.efi
  02/28/06  02:15p               15,360  rtdriver.efi
  02/28/06  02:15p              126,976  route.efi
  02/28/06  02:15p               16,384  ramdisk.efi
  02/28/06  02:15p              339,968  python.efi
  02/28/06  02:15p              172,032  pppd.efi
  02/28/06  02:15p               16,896  pktxmit.efi
  02/28/06  02:15p               19,968  pktsnoop.efi
  02/28/06  02:15p              126,976  ping.efi
...
        40 File(s)   2,960,866 bytes
         2 Dir(s)


fs0:\> drivers -b
          T  D
D         Y C I
R         P F A
V  VERSION E G G #D #C DRIVER NAME                          IMAGE NAME
== ======== = = = == == ==================================== ====================
```

(continues)

FIGURE 4–22 Using the EFI shell *(continued)*

```
4E 00000010 D - -  4  - Usb Uhci Driver                   Uhci
...
54 00000010 D - -  2  - Usb Keyboard Driver               UsbKb
55 00000010 D - -  2  - Usb Mouse Driver                  UsbMouse
71 00000010 D - -  1  - <UNKNOWN>                         AppleBootBeep
74 00000001 D - -  1  - ICH7M IDE Controller Init Driver  IdeController
75 00000001 D - -  1  - ICH7M Serial ATA Controller       InitialSataController
...
AE 0010003F D - -  1  - ATI Radeon UGA Driver 01.00.063   Radeon350
AF 00000010 D - -  1  - Apple Airport Driver              AppleAirport
...


fs0:\> dh -b
  Handle Dump
    1: Image(DxeMain)
...
   80: Image(AppleHidInterface) DriverBinding ComponentName
   81: Image(AppleRemote) DriverBinding ComponentName
   82: Image(FireWireOhci) DriverBinding ComponentName
   83: Image(FireWireDevice) DriverBinding ComponentName
   84: Image(HfsPlus) DriverBinding ComponentName
   85: Image(AppleSmc)
...


fs0:\> load tcpipv4.efi
Interface attached to lo0
Interface attached to sni0
Interface attached to ppp0
Timecounter "TcpIpv4" frequency 4027 Hz
Network protocol loaded and initialized
load: Image fs0:\tcpipv4.efi loaded at 1FCF4000 - Success


fs0:\> ifconfig sni0 inet 10.0.0.2 netmask 255.255.255.0 up
fs0:\> ifconfig -a
lo0: flags=8008<LOOPBACK,MULTICAST> mtu 16384
sni0: flags=8802<BROADCAST,SIMPLEX,MULTICAST> mtu 1500
        inet 10.0.0.2 netmask 0xffffff00 broadcast 10.0.0.255
        ether 00:16:cb:xx:xx:xx
ppp0: flags=8010<POINTTOPOINT,MULTICAST> mtu 1500


fs0:\> ping 10.0.0.1
PING 10.0.0.1 (10.0.0.1): 56 data bytes
64 bytes from 10.0.0.1: icmp_seq=0 ttl=255 time<1 ms
```

(continues)

FIGURE 4–22 Using the EFI shell *(continued)*

```
...
fs0:\> ftp 10.0.0.1
Connected to 10.0.0.1.
220 g5x8.local FTP server (tnftpd 20040810) ready.
Name (10.0.1.1):
...


fs0:\> help
    ...
    Use 'help -b' to display commands one screen at a time.
```

Note in Figure 4–22 that it is possible to have network connectivity within EFI's user-visible environment.

4.16.4.4 *The GUID-Based Partitioning Scheme*

EFI defines a new partitioning scheme called the *GUID Partition Table* (GPT), which must be supported by an EFI firmware implementation. GPT uses GUIDs to tag partitions. Each disk is also identified by a GUID. This scheme includes several features that make it far superior to the legacy MBR-based partitioning scheme. Examples of such features include the following:

- 64-bit logical block access (LBA), and consequently, 64-bit disk offsets
- An arbitrary number of partitions without resorting to nesting schemes like extended partitioning
- Version number and size fields for future expansion
- CRC32 checksum fields for higher data integrity
- A 36-character, human-readable, Unicode name per partition
- Partition content type defined using a GUID and other attributes
- Primary and backup partition tables for redundancy

Figure 4–23 shows a GPT-partitioned disk. A dummy MBR is stored at logical block 0 for legacy compatibility. The primary header structure of a GPT is stored at logical block 1, whereas a backup is stored at the last logical block. A GPT header may never span more than one block on the device. Moreover, although GPT does not support nesting of partitions, it is legal to have a legacy MBR nested *inside* a GPT partition. However, EFI firmware does not execute the boot code on a legacy MBR.

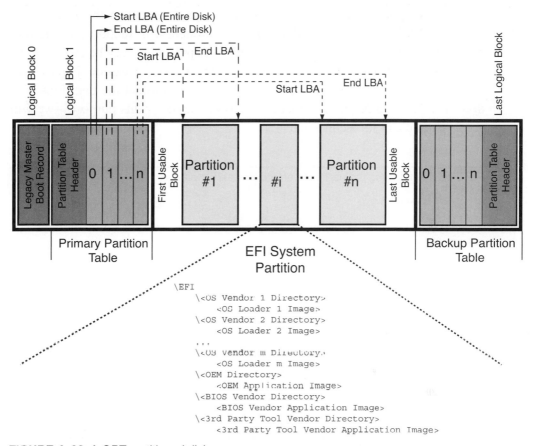

FIGURE 4–23 A GPT-partitioned disk

GUIDs

A GUID (also called UUID, for universally unique identifier) is specified to be 128 bits long in Intel's *Wired for Management* (WfM) specification. It is unique across time (e.g., until 3400 A.D. per a specific GUID-generation algorithm) and space (relative to other GUIDs). A key to generating a GUID without requiring a centralized authority is the use of a globally unique value—a *node identifier*—that is available to each GUID generator. For networked systems, the node identifier is a 48-bit IEEE 802 address, which is usually a host address, or *the* host address if there is only one network interface. For a host without an IEEE 802 address, this value is chosen in a probabilistically unique fashion. However, this alone is not sufficient for uniqueness. Other values involved in GUID generation include a timestamp, a clock sequence, and a version number.

EFI supports a dedicated on-disk system partition called the *EFI System Partition* (ESP). The ESP uses the FAT-32 file system with support for long file-names. EFI drivers,[31] bootloaders, and other EFI applications can be stored on the ESP. The boot manager can run boot applications from this partition. Figure 4–24 shows the use of a GPT disk utility (`diskpart.efi`) to list the partitions on a disk. The Mac OS X `gpt` command can also be used for this purpose—we will see an example of its use in Chapter 11.

FIGURE 4–24 Listing the partitions on a GPT-partitioned disk

```
fs0:\> diskpart
...
DiskPart> select 0
Selected Disk =     0
DiskPart> inspect
Selected Disk =     0
  ###  BlkSize          BlkCount
  ---  -------  ----------------
*   0      200           12A19EB0
  0: EFI system partition
     C12A7328-F81F-11D2 = EFISYS
     34D22C00-1DD2-1000 @              0
                 28 -          64027
  1: Customer
     48465300-0000-11AA
     00004904-06B7-0000 @              0
               64028 -       129D9E87
```

4.16.4.5 *Universal Graphics Adapter*

Given the needs of modern preboot applications, VGA-based graphics support in a legacy BIOS environment is both very limited and hard to program with for several reasons—for example, a maximum resolution of 640×480, a small frame-buffer, and the use of palette modes. EFI defines the Universal Graphics Adapter (UGA) specification as a replacement for VGA and VESA. Any graphics device with UGA firmware can be considered a UGA device. It may also contain VGA firmware for compatibility. The EFI execution environment interprets UGA firmware, which is implemented in a high-level language. In particular, programming

---

31. In general, drivers that are not required to access the ESP are good candidates for residing on the ESP.

a UGA device does not require the programmer to deal with low-level details such as hardware registers.

In the UGA model, the UGA firmware does not necessarily have to reside *on* a graphics device—it may be part of the system firmware if the graphics device is onboard, or it may even reside on a regular storage device.

UGA provides a *draw protocol*[32] for drawing on a video screen and an *I/O protocol* for creating a device-independent, operating system–specific driver, which is simply a "lowest common denominator" driver in that it is not meant to replace a high-performance device-specific driver that would normally be part of an operating system. Nevertheless, a generic UGA driver may be used in the post-boot environment in scenarios such as the following:

- As a fallback driver when the regular driver is corrupt or missing from the operating system

- As the primary driver in machines—such as servers—where graphics performance is irrelevant

- In special operating system modes such as during "safe" booting or when the kernel has panicked

- For displaying graphical elements when the primary driver may not be available temporarily—for example, during operating system installation, early startup, and hibernation

> Unlike VGA, the UGA firmware does not access the graphics hardware directly. It operates within a virtual machine. A vendor may provide a library that implements a thin logical layer above EFI, encapsulating a specific UGA firmware implementation.

4.16.4.6 EFI Byte Code

Option ROMs require different executable images for different processors and platforms. EFI defines an EFI Byte Code (EBC) Virtual Machine to abstract such differences. The firmware includes an EBC interpreter so that EFI images compiled to EBC are guaranteed to function on all EFI-compliant systems. C language source can be compiled into EBC and linked to yield drivers that run under the interpreter.

---

32. The basic graphics operation in the draw protocol is the *block transfer* (BLT) operation.

The EBC Virtual Machine uses two sets of 64-bit registers: eight general-purpose registers and two dedicated registers. For data offsets, it uses natural indexing relative to a base address—instead of a fixed number of bytes as an offset unit, it uses a *natural unit* defined as the operation `sizeof(void *)`, rather than being a constant. This allows EBC to execute seamlessly on 64-bit and 32-bit systems.

> Programs targeted for EBC must follow several restrictions. For example, they must not use floating-point, inline assembly, or C++.

4.16.4.7 Binary Format

EFI uses the PE32 binary format. The executable and object file formats under Microsoft Windows are called *Portable Executable* (PE) and *Common Object File Format* (COFF), respectively. A PE file is essentially a COFF file with a header that's compatible with MS-DOS 2.0. An optional header contains a magic number that further designates a PE file as PE32 or PE32+. The header also specifies the entry point for image execution.[33]

The *subsystem ID* in an EFI PE image header is either `0xa`, `0xb`, or `0xc`, depending on whether an image is an EFI application, an EFI boot service driver, or an EFI runtime driver, respectively.

4.16.5 The Benefits of EFI

EFI aims to be a powerful and modular firmware that is readily extensible, even by (power) users. The following list is a summary of key EFI benefits.

- It is modular and extensible. It is written in C, which makes it portable.
- It is implementation agnostic and is compatible between architectures. It provides a consistent view of the underlying platform to the operating system.
- It is backward compatible and can be used to complement existing interfaces.
- It does not require the x86 real mode. It runs in a flat memory model, with the entire address space being addressable.
- It does not place a restriction on the total size of option ROMs. EFI drivers can be loaded anywhere in the EFI address space.

---

33. An EBC file contains EBC instructions—rather than native processor instructions—at its entry point.

- It aims to replace the legacy VGA over time with simple graphics primitives courtesy of the UGA.

- It includes an optional shell that gives the user considerable freedom and flexibility.

- It represents a system's hardware topology as a hierarchical structure consisting of device pathnames.

- Its preboot environment supports a network interface compatible with BSD sockets, along with a port of the FreeBSD TCP/IPv4 protocol stack.

- It provides versatile booting options. Given the appropriate drivers, an EFI-based system can boot from a floppy disk, a hard disk, an optical disc, a USB storage device, a wired or wireless network, and so on. Network booting is a fundamental capability in EFI, rather than being dependent on the network card.

- It replaces ancient MBR-based disk partitioning with a much better scheme.

Despite having several features found in operating systems, EFI is not meant to be a replacement for a "real" operating system. Despite all its capabilities, EFI is a limited execution environment. Moreover, it is single-threaded and nonpreemptive. Nevertheless, EFI's preboot environment can facilitate robust solutions for secure network booting, secure network resetting, and remote system management. The latter employs bootable EFI programs—or *agents*—that allow remote firmware management, provisioning, and setup.

CHAPTER 5

Kernel and User-Level Startup

We saw in Chapter 4 that Open Firmware hands control over to BootX, the Mac OS X bootloader, which performs various operations before the Mac OS X kernel can begin to execute. In this chapter, we continue discussion from the point where the kernel takes over from BootX. We will look at the important events that occur during kernel startup, visit various kernel subsystems, see how they are initialized, see how the kernel launches the first user-space program, and look at the details of user-level startup—up to the point where the system is ready for the user. In doing so, we will come across numerous concepts and terms that have not been introduced so far in this book. In this sense, this chapter makes a number of implicit or explicit forward references.

Perhaps the most fruitful approach to understanding system startup would be to refer to Darwin source—especially the xnu package—in conjunction with this chapter. It is important to realize that the Mac OS X kernel is an evolving entity: Its internal details are subject to change, and sometimes change greatly, across revisions.

> In this chapter, we associate names of kernel functions with the pathnames of the files that implement them. For example, _start() [osfmk/ppc/start.s] means that the function _start() is implemented in the file osfmk/ppc/start.s in the kernel source tree. Unless stated otherwise, all pathnames are relative to the kernel source tree's root directory, which is usually named xnu-x.y.z, where x, y, and z are components of the kernel's version number. An important purpose of referring to functions along with their implementation files is to allow easy lookups of further information. Moreover, you can see which portions of the kernel the caller and the callee belong to. Examples of path prefixes are osfmk (Mach), bsd (BSD), iokit (the I/O Kit), libkern (the I/O Kit kernel library), libsa (the stand-alone library), and pexpert (the Platform Expert).

5.1 Arranging for the Kernel to Execute

The Mac OS X kernel is a Mach-O executable that resides as /mach_kernel by default on a boot volume. Recall that in Chapter 4, we examined the kernel executable using the otool program to determine the kernel's entry point. When the kernel is compiled, the final linking stage arranges several aspects of the executable, such as the following:

- The executable's entry point is set to _start [osfmk/ppc/start.s]. The LC_UNIXTHREAD load command in the Mach-O header contains the entry point's value in the SRR0 register of the thread state.
- The address of the __VECTORS segment is set to 0x0.
- The address of the __HIB segment, which is used to implement hibernation, is set to 0x7000.
- The address of the __TEXT segment is set to 0xe000.
- The __text section in the __TEXT segment has its alignment set to 0x1000 (4096 bytes).
- The __common section in the __DATA segment has its alignment set to 0x1000 (4096 bytes).
- The __bss section in the __DATA segment has its alignment set to 0x1000 (4096 bytes).
- A __text section is created (with the contents of /dev/null—i.e., with no contents) in the __PRELINK segment. Similarly, sections __symtab and __info are created from /dev/null in the __PRELINK segment.

5.1.1 Exceptions and Exception Vectors

The __VECTORS segment contains the kernel's exception vectors. As we saw in Chapter 4, BootX copies these to their designated locations—starting at address 0x0—before calling the kernel. These vectors are implemented in osfmk/ppc/ lowmem_vectors.s. Table 5–1 contains an overview of PowerPC exceptions, most of which are subject to one or more conditions. For example, exceptions caused by failed effective-to-virtual address translations occur only if address translation is enabled. Moreover, most exceptions can occur only when no higher-priority exception exists.

TABLE 5–1 PowerPC Exceptions

Vector Offset	Exception	xnu Interrupt ("rupt") Code	Cause/Comments
0x0100	System reset	T_RESET	A hard or soft processor reset. This exception is nonmaskable and asynchronous.
0x0200	Machine check	T_MACHINE_CHECK	Various causes: parity error detection in the L1 cache, the TLB, or the SLB; uncorrectable ECC error detection in the L2 cache; etc. May be recoverable or unrecoverable.
0x0300	Data access	T_DATA_ACCESS	A page fault or erroneous data memory access, such as an operation with invalid memory rights.
0x0380	Data segment	T_DATA_SEGMENT	Effective address of a storage location failed to be translated to a virtual address.
0x0400	Instruction access	T_INSTRUCTION_ACCESS	Similar to data access exception, but for instructions.
0x0480	Instruction segment	T_INSTRUCTION_SEGMENT	Effective address of the next instruction to be executed failed to translate to a virtual address.
0x0500	External interrupt	T_INTERRUPT	Asserted by an external interrupt input signal.
0x0600	Alignment	T_ALIGNMENT	Various alignment-related causes: e.g., certain load/store instructions encountered misaligned operands.
0x0700	Program	T_PROGRAM	Various causes: e.g., floating-point exception, or exception due to the execution of an illegal or privileged instruction.
0x0800	Floating-point unavailable	T_FP_UNAVAILABLE	Floating-point unit unavailable or disabled.

(continues)

TABLE 5–1 PowerPC Exceptions *(Continued)*

Vector Offset	Exception	xnu Interrupt ("rupt") Code	Cause/Comments
0x0900	Decrementer	T_DECREMENTER	The decrementer is negative.
0x0a00	I/O controller interface error	T_IO_ERROR	Unused on Mac OS X.
0x0b00	Reserved	T_RESERVED	—
0x0c00	System call	T_SYSTEM_CALL	The system call (sc) instruction is executed.
0x0d00	Trace	T_TRACE	Single-step tracing or branch tracing is enabled and an instruction successfully completed.
0x0e00	Floating-point assist	T_FP_ASSIST	A floating-point operation needs software assistance.
0x0f00	Performance monitor	T_PERF_MON	Various performance-monitoring exception conditions.
0x0f20	Vector processing unit unavailable	T_VMX	VMX is unavailable or disabled.
0x1000	Instruction translation miss	T_INVALID_EXCP0	Unused on Mac OS X.
0x1100	Data-load translation miss	T_INVALID_EXCP1	Unused on Mac OS X.
0x1200	Data-store translation miss	T_INVALID_EXCP2	Unused on Mac OS X.
0x1300	Instruction address break-point	T_INSTRUCTION_BKPT	The 970FX only supports this feature through a support-processor interface.
0x1400	System management	T_SYSTEM_MANAGEMENT	Implementation-dependent.
0x1500	Soft Patch	T_SOFT_PATCH	Implementation-dependent softpatch facility emitted a special exception-causing internal operation. Used for working around defective instructions and for debugging.
0x1600	AltiVec Java Mode assist/ maintenance	T_ALTIVEC_ASSIST	Implementation-dependent maintenance exception. Can be signaled by various internal events and by explicit commands.

(continues)

TABLE 5–1 PowerPC Exceptions *(Continued)*

Vector Offset	Exception	xnu Interrupt ("rupt") Code	Cause/Comments
0x1700	AltiVec Java Mode assist/ thermal	T_THERMAL	An input operand or the result of an operation was denormalized while operating in AltiVec Java Mode.
0x1800	Thermal (64-bit)	T_ARCHDEP0	Signaled by assertion of a thermal interrupt input signal.
0x2000	Instrumentation	T_INSTRUMENTATION	Unused on Mac OS X.
0x2100	VMM ultra-fast path	—	Filter ultra-fast path system calls for the virtual machine monitor (VMM)[a] facility in the Mac OS X kernel. Not used in Mac OS X 10.4.

a. We will discuss the VMM facility in Section 6.9.

Most hardware exceptions in the Mac OS X kernel are channeled through a common exception-handling routine: exception_entry() [osfmk/ppc/lowmem_vectors.s]. The designated exception handler saves GPR13 and GPR11, sets a "rupt" code in GPR11, and jumps to exception_entry. For example, the following is the exception handler for T_INSTRUCTION_ACCESS:

```
            . = 0x400
.L_handler400:
            mtsprg  2,r13                    ; Save R13
            mtsprg  3,r11                    ; Save R11
            li      r11,T_INSTRUCTION_ACCESS ; Set rupt code
            b       .L_exception_entry       ; Join common
```

Note that several exceptions in Table 5–1 may do "nothing," depending on the hardware being used, whether the kernel is being debugged, and other factors.

5.1.2 Kernel Symbols

Two other related files are usually present on the root volume: /mach.sym and /mach. The /mach.sym file contains symbols from the currently running kernel. It is meant for use by programs that need to access kernel data structures. In some cases, the on-disk kernel executable may not correspond to the running kernel— for example, in the case of a network boot. In fact, there may not even be a kernel executable present on the root file system. To address this issue, the kernel can generate a dump of its own symbols and write it to a designated file. This file's pathname can be retrieved using the KERN_SYMFILE sysctl, which provides read access to the kern.symfile sysctl variable.

```
$ sysctl kern.symfile
kern.symfile = \mach.sym
```

The kernel implementation of the KERNEL_SYMFILE sysctl checks whether /mach.sym is open by looking at a global Boolean variable. If it is not open, the kernel outputs kernel symbols to /mach.sym and marks it as open. The kernel does not dump symbols to /mach.sym if the root device is being accessed over the network, if /mach.sym exists as a nonregular file, or if it exists as a file with a link count of more than one. This symbol-file creation is triggered during user-level system startup from /etc/rc, which uses the sysctl command to retrieve the value of the kern.symfile variable.

```
# /etc/rc
...
# Create mach symbol file
sysctl -n kern.symfile
if [ -f /mach.sym ]; then
        ln -sf /mach.sym /mach
else
        ln -sf /mach_kernel /mach
fi
```

We see that if /mach.sym exists, /mach is created as a symbolic link to it, otherwise /mach is a symbolic link to /mach_kernel. Moreover, since /mach.sym is useful only if it corresponds to the running kernel, it is deleted and recreated during every boot.

```
$ ls -l /mach*
lrwxr-xr-x  1 root  admin        9 Mar 10 16:07 /mach -> /mach.sym
-r--r--r--  1 root  admin   598865 Mar 10 16:07 /mach.sym
-rw-r--r--  1 root  wheel  4330320 Feb  3 20:51 /mach_kernel
```

Note that the kernel supports dumping symbols only once per boot—if you delete /mach.sym, running the sysctl command will not regenerate it unless you reboot.

The symbols in /mach.sym are the same as in the running kernel's executable, although section references in the symbol table are converted to absolute references. In fact, /mach.sym is a Mach-O executable containing a load command for the __TEXT segment, a load command for the __DATA segment, and an

LC_SYMTAB load command for the symbol table. Only the __const section of the __TEXT segment is nonempty, containing the kernel vtables.

```
$ otool -hv /mach.sym
/mach.sym:
Mach header
      magic cputype cpusubtype    filetype ncmds sizeofcmds     flags
   MH_MAGIC     PPC        ALL     EXECUTE     3        816   NOUNDEFS
$ otool -l /mach.sym
...
Load command 2
      cmd LC_SYMTAB
 cmdsize 24
  symoff 184320
   nsyms 11778
   stroff 325656
  strsize 273208
$ nm -j /mach_kernel > /tmp/mach_kernel.sym
$ nm -j /mach.sym > /tmp/mach.sym.sym
$ ls -l /tmp/mach_kernel.sym /tmp/mach.sym.sym
-rw-r--r--   1 amit  wheel  273204 Mar 10 19:22 /tmp/mach.sym.sym
-rw-r--r--   1 amit  wheel  273204 Mar 10 19:22 /tmp/mach_kernel.sym
$ diff /tmp/mach_kernel.sym /tmp/mach.sym.sym
# no output produced by diff
$ nm /mach_kernel | grep __start_cpu
00092380 T __start_cpu
$ nm /mach.sym | grep __start_cpu
00092380 A __start_cpu
```

5.1.3 Run Kernel Run

Figure 5–1 shows a very high level overview of Mac OS X system startup. In the rest of this chapter, we will look at details of the steps listed in the "Kernel" and "User" boxes.

> The qualifications *low-level* and *high-level* are subjective and approximate. For example, the I/O Kit—specifically the platform driver, such as AppleMacRISC4PE—handles certain low-level aspects of processor initialization, but the I/O Kit is not active during very early kernel startup.

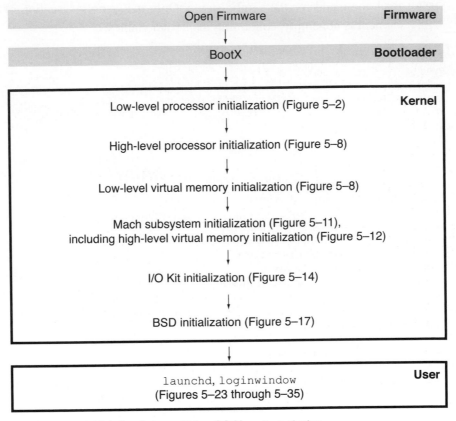

FIGURE 5–1 A high-level view of Mac OS X system startup

5.2 Low-Level Processor Initialization

As shown in Figure 5–2, BootX launches the kernel by calling the `_start` symbol in the kernel. In a multiprocessor system, the kernel begins execution on one processor that was chosen by Open Firmware. For the purposes of kernel startup, we consider this the *master processor* and the rest, if any, as *slave processors*.

> We will use the terms *CPU* and *processor* interchangeably unless the terms have specific meanings in some context. In Mach parlance, a processor is typically a hardware-independent entity, whereas a CPU represents the underlying hardware entity.

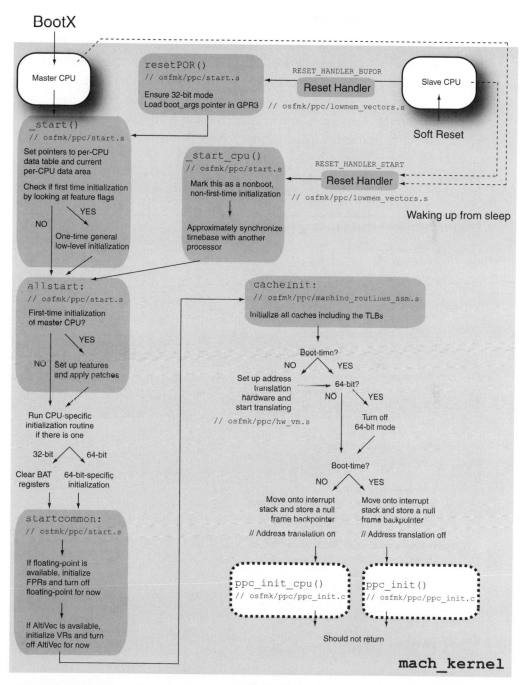

FIGURE 5–2 Low-level processor initialization

5.2.1 Per-Processor Data

_start() first initializes a pointer to the current *per-processor data area*. The kernel maintains a table of such per-processor data structures. The table—PerProcTable—is an array of per_proc_entry structures. A per_proc_entry structure consists of a per_proc_info structure, which holds data for one processor. The per_proc_info structure for the master processor is specially labeled as BootProcInfo. These structures reside in aligned memory. Note that a thread's machine-specific context includes a pointer to the current per_proc_info structure. Figure 5–3 shows an excerpt from the declaration of the per_proc_info structure.

FIGURE 5–3 The kernel's per-processor data table

```
// osfmk/ppc/exception.h

struct per_proc_info {
    // This processor's number
    unsigned short          cpu_number;

    // Various low-level flags
    unsigned short          cpu_flags;

    // Interrupt stack
    vm_offset_t             istackptr;
    vm_offset_t             intstack_top_ss;
    ...

    // Special thread flags
    unsigned int            spcFlags;
    ...

    // Owner of the FPU on this processor
    struct facility_context *FPU_owner

    // VRSave associated with live vector registers
    unsigned int            liveVRSave;

    // Owner of the VMX on this processor
    struct facility_context *VMX_owner;
    ...

    // Interrupt related
    boolean_t               interrupts_enabled;
    IOInterruptHandler      interrupt_handler;
    void                    *interrupt_nub;
    unsigned                interrupt_source;
    ...
```

(continues)

FIGURE 5–3 The kernel's per-processor data table *(continued)*

```
    // Processor features
    procFeatures            pf;
    ...


    // Copies of general-purpose registers used for temporary save area
    uint64_t                tempr0;
    ...
    uint64_t                tempr31;
    ...


    // Copies of floating-point registers used for floating-point emulation
    double                  emfp0;
    ...
    double                  emfp31;
    ...


    // Copies of vector registers used both for full vector emulation or
    // save areas while assisting denormals
    unsigned int            emvr0[4];
    ...
    unsigned int            emvr31[4];
    ...


    // Hardware exception counters
    hwCtrs                  hwCtr;


    // Processor structure
    unsigned int            processor[384];
};

extern struct per_proc_info BootProcInfo;

#define MAX_CPUS 256

struct per_proc_entry {
    addr64_t                ppe_paddr;
    unsigned int            ppe_pad4[1];
    struct per_proc_info *ppe_vaddr;
};

extern struct per_proc_entry PerProcTable[MAX_CPUS-1];
```

The `pf` member of the `per_proc_info` structure is a structure of type `procFeatures`. It holds per-processor features such as the reported processor type, which processor facilities are available, various cache sizes, supported power-saving modes, and the maximum physical address supported.

```
// osfmk/ppc/exception.h

struct procFeatures {
        unsigned int    Available;          /* 0x000 */
#define pfFloat         0x80000000
#define pfFloatb        0
#define pfAltivec       0x40000000
#define pfAltivecb      1
...
#define pfValid         0x00000001
#define pfValidb        31
        unsigned short  rptdProc;           /* 0x004 */
        unsigned short  lineSize;           /* 0x006 */
        unsigned int    l1iSize;            /* 0x008 */
        unsigned int    l1dSize;            /* 0x00C */
...
        unsigned int    pfPowerTune0;       /* 0x080 */
        unsigned int    pfPowerTune1;       /* 0x084 */
        unsigned int    rsrvd88[6];         /* 0x088 */
};
...
typedef struct procFeatures procFeatures;
```

5.2.2 Reset Types

Several types of processor initializations can be performed by Mac OS X. The kernel distinguishes between these by setting or clearing certain bits of the Condition Register (CR). For example, if it is the first processor coming up in a given context, the CR bit specified by the bootCPU variable is set. If it is the first time that particular processor is being initialized, the CR bit specified by the firstInit variable is set. The logical AND of bootCPU and firstInit is called firstBoot. It will be nonzero if it is the first processor starting up during kernel initialization (as opposed to a processor waking up from sleep, say). If the processor indeed is in a first-ever initialization, _start() performs one-time general low-level initialization before control flows to the allstart label in osfmk/ppc/start.s. As Figure 5–2 shows, other code paths also lead to this point in the code, depending on the type of reset the processor is going through. Unlike in the case when BootX directly calls _start(), other reset operations are handled by a designated *reset handler*.

Recall from Table 5–1 that 0x0100 is the vector offset for the system reset exception, which could be a result of a hard or soft processor reset. A structure variable called ResetHandler, which is of type resethandler_t, resides in memory at offset 0xF0—just before the 0x0100 exception handler.

```
// osfmk/ppc/exception.h

typedef struct resethandler {
    unsigned int type;
    vm_offset_t  call_paddr;
    vm_offset_t  arg__paddr;
} resethandler_t;
...
extern resethandler_t ResetHandler;
...
#define RESET_HANDLER_NULL     0x0
#define RESET_HANDLER_START    0x1
#define RESET_HANDLER_BUPOR    0x2
#define RESET_HANDLER_IGNORE   0x3
...
```

```
// osfmk/ppc/lowmem_vectors.s

                        . = 0xf0
                        .globl  EXT(ResetHandler)
EXT(ResetHandler):
                        .long   0x0
                        .long   0x0
                        .long   0x0

                        . = 0x100
.L_handler100:
                        mtsprg  2,r13    /* Save R13 */
                        mtsprg  3,r11    /* Save R11 */
                        /*
                         * Examine the ResetHandler structure
                         * and take appropriate action.
                         */
                        ...
```

When the 0x0100 handler runs to handle a reset exception, it examines the ResetHandler structure to determine the type of reset. Note that the 0x0100 handler will never be run because of a true *hard reset*—such a reset will be seen only by Open Firmware. For other types of resets, namely *start*, *BUPOR*,[1] and *ignore*, the kernel will set up the ResetHandler structure appropriately before a reset exception is generated.

A RESET_HANDLER_START is generated when the system is waking up from sleep. In this case, the 0x0100 handler clears the reset type by setting it to RESET_HANDLER_NULL, loads the arg__paddr field of the ResetHandler

---

1. BUPOR stands for bring-up power-on reset.

structure to GPR3, loads the `call_paddr` field to LR, and finally branches through LR to call the function pointed to by `call_paddr`. The `cpu_start()` [osfmk/ppc/cpu.c] and `cpu_sleep()` [osfmk/ppc/cpu.c] functions use this mechanism by setting `ResetHandler` fields. Specifically, they set `call_paddr` to point to `_start_cpu()` [osfmk/ppc/start.s]. `_start_cpu()` clears the `bootCPU` and `firstInit` fields, sets the current per-processor data pointer, sets the processor's Timebase Register using values from another processor, and branches to the `allstart` label. In doing so, it bypasses some initial instructions that only the boot processor executes.

A `RESET_HANDLER_BUPOR` is used to bring up a processor when starting directly from a power-on reset (POR). For example, the `startCPU()` method of the platform-dependent processor driver can generate a soft reset. In the specific case of the 970FX, the `startCPU()` method implemented in the `MacRISC4CPU` class (which inherits from the `IOCPU` class) performs a reset by strobing the processor's reset line. The `0x0100` handler calls `resetPOR()` [osfmk/ppc/start.s] to handle this type of reset. `resetPOR()` sets the type field of `ResetHandler` to `RESET_HANDLER_NULL`, ensures that the processor is in 32-bit mode, loads GPR3 with a pointer to the boot arguments structure, and branches to `_start()`.

> In a multiprocessor system, each CPU's Processor ID Register (PIR) is set to a unique value during a POR.

Finally, if the reset type is `RESET_HANDLER_IGNORE`, the kernel ignores the reset. This is used for *software debouncing*—for example, when a nonmaskable interrupt (NMI) is used to enter a debugger.

> Both `ResetHandler` and the exception routines reside in physically addressed memory. The kernel uses special machine-dependent routines—implemented in `osfmk/ppc/machine_routines_asm.s`—to read from and write to such locations. These routines handle the necessary preprocessing and postprocessing while performing I/O to physical addresses. For example, on the 970FX, this preprocessing makes the floating-point and vector-processing units unavailable, delays recognition of external exceptions and decrementer exception conditions, and disables data translation. Postprocessing reverses the changes made by preprocessing.

5.2.3 Processor Types

The initial kernel code in `osfmk/ppc/start.s` uses a table of processor types—`processor_types`—that maps specific processor types to their relevant features. The table contains entries for numerous PowerPC processor models: 750CX (version 2.x), 750 (generic), 750FX (version 1.x and generic), 7400 (versions 2.0 through 2.7 and generic), 7410 (version 1.1 and generic), 7450 (versions 1.xx, 2.0, and 2.1), 7455 (versions 1.xx, 2.0, and 2.1), 7457, 7447A, 970, and 970FX.[2] The entries in this table are ordered: A more specific entry appears before a less restrictive entry. Figure 5–4 shows an annotated version of the table entry for the 970FX processor.

FIGURE 5–4 The entry for the PowerPC 970FX in the processor-type table

```
; osfmk/ppc/start.s
; 970FX

; Always on word boundary
.align 2

; ptFilter
; Mask of significant bits in the processor Version/Revision code
; 0xFFFF0000 would match all versions
.long   0xFFFF0000

; ptVersion
; Version bits from the Processor Version Register (PVR)
; PROCESSOR_VERSION_970FX is 0x003C
.short PROCESSOR_VERSION_970FX

; ptRevision
; Revision bits from the PVR. A zero value denotes generic attributes
.short 0

; ptFeatures
; Processor features that are available (defined in osfmk/ppc/exception.h)
.long  pfFloat    |\ ; FPU
       pfAltivec  |\ ; VMX
       pfSMPcap   |\ ; symmetric multiprocessing capable
       pfCanSleep |\ ; can go to sleep
       pfCanNap   |\ ; can nap
```

(continues)

---

2. The 970MP and the 970FX are considered identical processor types. Unless otherwise noted, the discussion in this chapter applies to the 970FX and the 970MP alike.

FIGURE 5–4 The entry for the PowerPC 970FX in the processor-type table *(continued)*

```
        pf128Byte  |\ ; has 128-byte cache lines
        pf64Bit    |\ ; GPRs are 64-bit
        pfL2          ; has L2 cache

; ptCPUCap
; Default value for _cpu_capabilities (defined in osfmk/ppc/cpu_capabilities.h)
.long                          \
        ; has VMX
        kHasAltivec            |\

        ; GPRs are 64-bit
        k64Bit                 |\

        ; has 128-byte cache lines
        kCache128                 |\

        ; dst, dstt, dstst, dss, and dssall available, but not recommended,
        ; unless the "Recommended" flag is present too
        kDataStreamsAvailable  |\

        ; enhanced dcbt instruction available and recommended
        kDcbtStreamsRecommended |\

        ; enhanced dcbt instruction available (but may or may not be recommended)
        kDcbtStreamsAvailable  |\

        ; has fres, frsqrt, and fsel instructions
        kHasGraphicsOps         |\

        ; has stfiwx instruction
        kHasStfiwx             |\

        ; has fsqrt and fsqrts instructions
        kHasFsqrt

; ptPwrModes
; Available power management features. The 970FX is the first processor used by
; Apple to support IBM's PowerTune Technology
.long  pmPowerTune

; ptPatch
; Patch features
.long  PatchLwsync

; ptInitRout
; Initialization routine for this processor. Can modify any of the other
; attributes.
.long  init970
```

(continues)

FIGURE 5–4 The entry for the PowerPC 970FX in the processor-type table *(continued)*

```
; ptRptdProc
; Processor type reported. CPU_SUBTYPE_POWERPC_970 is defined to be
; ((cpu_subtype_t)100). In contrast, note that CPU_SUBTYPE_POWERPC_7450
; is defined to be ((cpu_subtype_t)11)!
.long CPU_SUBTYPE_POWERPC_970

; ptLineSize
; L1 cache line size in bytes
.long  128

; ptl1iSize
; L1 I-cache size in bytes (64KB for the 970FX)
.long  64*1024

; ptl1dSize
; L1 D-cache size in bytes (32KB for the 970FX)
.long  32*1024

; ptPTEG
; Number of entries in a page table entry group (PTEG)
.long  128

; ptMaxVAddr
; Maximum virtual address (bits)
.long  65

; ptMaxPAddr
; Maximum physical address (bits)
.long  42
```

The kernel uses the contents of the current CPU's Processor Version Register (PVR) to find a matching entry in `processor_table` by looping through the table and examining the `ptFilter` and `ptVersion` fields of each candidate entry. Once a matching entry is found, a pointer to `ptInitRout()`, the processor-specific initialization routine, is also saved.

At this point, if the master processor is booting for the first time, a variety of processor features and capabilities are set in the CPU capabilities vector, which is an integer variable called `_cpu_capabilities` [osfmk/ppc/commpage/commpage.c] and whose bits represent CPU capabilities. Since the processors in a multiprocessor system have identical features, this step is bypassed for a secondary processor—the master's feature information is simply copied for the others.

5.2.4 Memory Patching

Although a given version of Mac OS X uses the same kernel executable regardless of the computer model, the kernel may alter itself at boot time, based on the underlying hardware. During an initial boot, the master processor consults one or more *patch tables* built into the kernel and examines their entries to determine whether any of them are applicable. Figure 5–5 shows the structure of a patch-table entry.

FIGURE 5–5 Data structure and related definitions of a patch-table entry

```
// osfmk/ppc/exception.h

struct patch_entry {
    unsigned int        *addr; // address to patch
    unsigned int        data;  // data to patch with
    unsigned int        type;  // patch type
    unsigned int        value; // patch value (for matching)
};

#define PATCH_INVALID       0
#define PATCH_PROCESSOR     1
#define PATCH_FEATURE       2
#define PATCH_END_OF_TABLE  3

#define PatchExt32          0x80000000
#define PatchExt32b         0
#define PatchLwsync         0x40000000
#define PatchLwsyncb        1
...
```

The kernel's patch table is defined in osfmk/ppc/ppc_init.c. Figure 5–6 shows an annotated excerpt from this table.

As the kernel examines each entry in the patch table, it checks the entry's type. If the type is PATCH_FEATURE, the kernel compares the patch value with the ptPatch field from the current processor's processor_types table entry. If there is a match, the kernel applies the patch by writing the patch data to the location specified by the patch address. If the entry is of type PATCH_PROCESSOR instead, the kernel compares it with the ptRptdProc field (processor type reported) of its processor_types table entry to check for a potential match. Let us look at specific examples.

FIGURE 5–6 The kernel's patch table

// osfmk/ppc/ppc_init.c

```
patch_entry_t patch_table[] = {

    // Patch entry 0
    {
        &extPatch32,          // address to patch
        0x60000000,           // data to patch with
        PATCH_FEATURE,        // patch type
        PatchExt32,           // patch value (for matching)
    }

    // Patch entry 1
    {
        &extPatchMCK,
        0x60000000,
        PATCH_PROCESSOR,
        CPU_SUBTYPE_POWERPC 970,
    }
    ...
    // Patch entry N
    {
        &suickPatch_eieio,
        0x7c2004ac,
        PATCH_FEATURE,
        PatchLwsync,
    }
    ...
    {
        NULL,
        0x00000000,
        PATCH_END_OF_TABLE,
        0
    }
};
```

The first patch entry shown in Figure 5–6 has a patch value `PatchExt32`. This value appears as the `ptPatch` value in the `processor_types` entries of all 32-bit processors that Mac OS X supports. Therefore, it will match on all 32-bit processors but will not match on 64-bit processors such as the 970 and the 970FX. The address to patch, `extPatch32`, is in the `osfmk/ppc/lowmem_vectors.s` file:

```
.L_exception_entry:
...
            .globl EXT(extPatch32)
```

```
LEXT(extPatch32)
               b           extEntry64
...
               /* 32-bit context saving */
...
               /* 64-bit context saving */
extEntry64:
...
```

Since the patch value will not match on 64-bit processors, the code fragment will remain as shown on these processors. On a 32-bit processor, however, the instruction that branches to extEntry64 will be replaced by the patch entry's data, 0x60000000, which is the PowerPC no-op instruction (nop).

Patch entry 1 in Figure 5–6 will match on a 970 or a 970FX, causing the instruction at address extPatchMCK to be turned into a no-op instruction. By default, the instruction at extPatchMCK is a branch that bypasses 64-bit-specific code in the Machine Check Exception (MCE) handler [osfmk/ppc/lowmem_vectors.s].

Patch entry N in Figure 5–6 replaces an eieio instruction with an lwsync instruction on matching systems.

Uniprocessor Patch Table

There is another patch table (patch_up_table[] [osfmk/ppc/machine_routines.c]) used only on a uniprocessor system. When the CPU interrupt controller is initialized, it calls ml_init_cpu_max() [osfmk/ppc/machine_routines.c], which applies the patches contained in this table if there is only one *logical* processor on the system. The patches convert isync and eieio instructions in several synchronization routines to no-op instructions.

5.2.5 Processor-Specific Initialization

The ptInitRout field of a processor_types table entry, if valid, points to a function for model-specific initialization of the processor. This field points to init970() [osfmk/ppc/start.s] for both the 970 and the 970FX. init970() clears the "deep nap" bit of HID0[3] during all types of processor initialization:

---

3. Recall from Chapter 3 that the 970FX contains four Hardware-Implementation-Dependent (HID) registers: HID0, HID1, HID4, and HID5.

during the boot processor's first initialization, when a slave processor is started, or when a processor wakes up from sleep. In the case of the boot processor initializing for the first time, `init970()` synthesizes a dummy L2 cache register (L2CR), with its value set to the actual L2 cache size on the 970FX (512KB).

At this point, the kernel sets the valid bit (`pfValid`) in the `Available` field of the processor features member (pF) of the `per_proc_info` structure.

Next, the kernel performs initialization based on whether the processor is 32-bit or 64-bit. For example, on a 32-bit processor, the BAT registers are cleared and the contents of the HID0 register are adjusted to clear any sleep-related bits. Thereafter, the code branches to `startcommon()` [osfmk/ppc/start.s]. On a 64-bit processor, the kernel sets the value of HID0 appropriately, prepares a machine status value in the SRR1 register, and loads the continuation point (the `startcommon()` routine) in SRR0. It then executes an `rfid` instruction, which results in the machine state in SRR1 to be restored to the Machine State Register (MSR). Execution then continues in `startcommon()`.

5.2.6 Other Early Initialization

The kernel checks whether the floating-point facility is available on the processor, and if so, it loads FPR0 with a known floating-point initialization value, which is then copied to the rest of the FPRs. Floating-point is then turned off for the time being. The initialization value is defined in `osfmk/ppc/aligned_data.s`:

```
.globl  EXT(FloatInit)
            .align   3

EXT(FloatInit):
            .long    0xC24BC195
    /* Initial value */
            .long    0x87859393
    /* of floating-point registers */
            .long    0xE681A2C8
    /* and others */
            .long    0x8599855A
```

After booting, the value can be seen in an FPR as long as that FPR has not been used. For example, you can debug a simple program using GDB and view the contents of the FPRs.

```
$ cat test.c
main() { }
$ gcc -g -o test test.c
```

```
$ gdb ./test
...
(gdb) break main
Breakpoint 1 at 0x2d34: file test.c, line 1.
(gdb) run
...
Breakpoint 1, main () at test.c:1
1              main() { }
(gdb) info all-registers
...
f14            -238423838475.15292        (raw 0xc24bc19587859393)
f15            -238423838475.15292        (raw 0xc24bc19587859393)
f16            -238423838475.15292        (raw 0xc24bc19587859393)
...
```

Similarly, the kernel checks whether AltiVec is available—if it is, the kernel sets the VRSAVE register to zero, indicating that no VRs have been used yet. It sets the non-Java (NJ) bit and clears the saturate (SAT) bit in the VSCR—we discussed these bits in Chapter 3. A special vector initialization value is loaded into VR0, which is then copied to the other VRs. AltiVec is then turned off for the time being. The initialization value, labeled QNaNbarbarian, is defined in osfmk/ppc/aligned_data.s. It is a sequence of long integers, each with a value of 0x7FFFDEAD. Again, you can potentially see this value in untouched VRs while debugging a program.

```
(gdb) info all-registers
...
v0             {
  uint128 = 0x7fffdead7fffdead7fffdead7fffdead,
  v4_float = {nan(0x7fdead), nan(0x7fdead), nan(0x7fdead), nan(0x7fdead)},
  v4_int32 = {2147475117, 2147475117, 2147475117, 2147475117},
  v8_int16 = {32767, -8531, 32767, -8531, 32767, -8531, 32767, -8531},
  v16_int8 = "\177??\177??\177??\177??"
}        (raw 0x7fffdead7fffdead7fffdead7fffdead)
...
```

Quiet NaNs

A floating-point number's value is considered a "Not a Number" (NaN) if the number's exponent is 255 and its fraction is nonzero. Moreover, the NaN is a signaling NaN (SNaN) or a quiet NaN (QNaN) depending on whether the most significant bit of its fraction field is zero or nonzero, respectively. Whereas a signaling NaN signals exceptions when it is specified as an arithmetic operand, a quiet NaN is propagated through most floating-point operations.

The kernel then initializes all caches by calling `cacheInit()` [osfmk/ ppc/machine_routines_asm.s], which first ensures that a variety of features are turned off.[4] For example, it turns off data and instruction address translation, external interrupts, floating-point, and AltiVec. It also initializes various caches via steps such as the following:

- It stops all data streams using the `dssall` instruction.
- It purges and syncs the TLBs using the `tlbie` and `tlbsync` instructions, respectively.
- On the 64-bit PowerPC, it syncs the page table entries using `ptesync`.
- On the 32-bit PowerPC, it initializes the L1, L2, and L3 caches. If a cache was enabled earlier, its contents are first flushed to memory. Hardware-assisted cache flush is used when available. Thereafter, the caches are invalidated and eventually turned on.

On 64-bit processors, cache management is rather different than on 32-bit processors. For example, the L2 cache cannot be disabled on the 970FX. Consequently, the kernel performs a different set of operations to initialize the caches.

- It disables instruction prefetching by clearing bits 7 and 8 of HID1.
- It disables data prefetching by setting bit 25 of HID4.
- It enables L1 D-cache[5] *flash invalidation* by setting bit 28 of HID4. Flash invalidation is a special mode that allows complete invalidation of the L1 D-cache by simply setting a bit and executing the `sync` instruction.
- It disables the L1 D-cache by setting bits 37 and 38 of HID4.
- It manipulates the L2 cache to use direct-mapped mode instead of set-associative mode. It uses the processor's Scan Communications facility (see the sidebar "The SCOM Facility") to make this change. Thereafter, victims to evict from the cache are selected based on a simple address decode of real address bits 42 through 44.
- It performs a memory flush of the entire L2 cache through a sequence of loads of 4MB cacheable regions of memory from addresses that increment according to the algorithm shown in Figure 5–7.

---

4. Many of these features are likely to be turned off already.

5. Recall from Chapter 3 that the L1 D-cache on the 970FX is a store-through cache—it never stores modified data. There may be pending stores in the store queue above the L1 D-cache, which may require the `sync` instruction to be executed to ensure global coherency.

FIGURE 5–7 Flushing the L2 cache on the PowerPC 970FX

```
// pseudocode

offset = 0;

do {
    addr = 0x400000; // 4MB cacheable memory region
    addr = addr | offset;

    load_to_register_from_address(addr);

    for (i = 1; i < 8; i++) {

        // increment the direct map field (bits [42:44]) of the load address
        addr += 0x80000;

        // load a line
        load_to_register_from_address(addr);
    }

    // increment the congruence address field (bits [48:56]) of the load address
    offset += 128;

} while (offset < 0x10000);
```

The SCOM Facility

The 970FX provides a Scan Communications (SCOM) facility that is accessible through a special-purpose register interface consisting of the SCOMC (control) and SCOMD (data) registers. Internally, SCOM designates address ranges to registers representing processor functionality. Examples of such SCOM registers include an Instruction Address Breakpoint Register, a Power Management Control Register, and the Storage Subsystem Mode Register. The kernel sets a bit in the latter to enable L2 cache direct-mapped mode.

After cache initialization, the kernel configures and starts address translation, unless the underlying processor is the boot processor, in which case it is not yet time for virtual memory. Address translation is configured by calling hw_setup_trans() [osfmk/ppc/hw_vm.s], which first marks the segment registers (SRs) and segment table entries (STEs) invalid by appropriately setting the validSegs field of the per-processor structure (struct per_proc_info). It further sets the structure's ppInvSeg field to 1 to force the complete invalidation of SRs and the segment lookaside buffer (SLB). It also sets the ppCurSeg field to 0 to specify that the current segment is a kernel segment.

If running on 32-bit hardware, the kernel invalidates BAT mappings by loading the data and instruction BAT register with zeros. Next, it retrieves the base address (hash_table_base) and size (hash_table_size) of the page hash table and loads it into the SDR1 register. Note that these variables are not initialized yet during the initial boot of the master processor. However, they are defined for a slave processor, which is the scenario in which the kernel calls hw_setup_trans() at this point. The kernel then loads each SR with the predefined invalid segment value of 1.

If running on 64-bit hardware, the setup is somewhat simpler, since there are no BAT registers. The kernel sets up the page hash table as in the 32-bit case and invalidates all SLB entries via the slbia instruction. It also ensures that 64-bit mode is turned off.

After configuring address translation, the kernel starts address translation by calling hw_start_trans() [osfmk/ppc/hw_vm.s], which sets the data relocate (DR) and instruction relocate (IR) bits of the MSR to enable data and instruction address translation, respectively.

At this point, the kernel is almost ready to continue execution in higher-level code; the boot processor will execute the ppc_init() [osfmk/ppc/ppc_init.c] function, whereas a nonboot processor will execute the ppc_init_cpu() [osfmk/ppc/ppc_init.c] function. Both these functions do not return. Before calling either of these functions, the kernel fabricates a C language call frame. It initializes GPR1 with a pointer to an interrupt stack, stores a zero as a null frame backpointer on the stack, and loads GPR3 with a pointer to the boot arguments. Thereafter, it calls ppc_init() or ppc_init_cpu() as appropriate. The kernel guards the calls to these functions by placing a breakpoint trap—a tw instruction—after each call. Consequently, in the unlikely case that either call returns, a trap will be generated.

5.3 High-Level Processor Initialization

Figure 5–8 shows an overview of the control flow of the ppc_init() function, including other notable functions it calls. Note that ppc_init() also marks the transition from assembly-language code to C code.

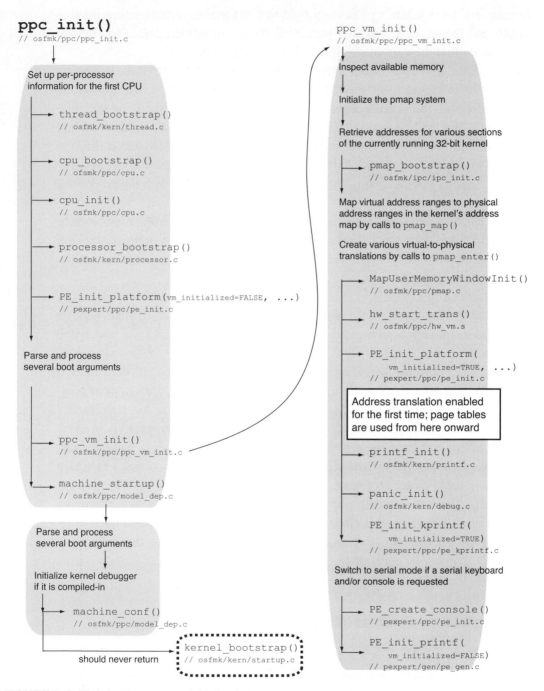

FIGURE 5–8 High-level processor initialization

ppc_init() first sets up various fields in the per-processor data area of the boot processor. One of the fields is pp_cbfr [osfmk/console/ppc/serial_console.c], a pointer to a per-processor console buffer used by the kernel to handle multiprocessor console output. Let us look at the key operations performed by each function in the sequence depicted in Figure 5–8.

5.3.1 Before Virtual Memory

thread_bootstrap() [osfmk/kern/thread.c] populates a static thread structure (thread_template) used as a template for fast initialization of newly created threads. It then uses this template to initialize init_thread, another static thread structure. thread_bootstrap() finishes by setting init_thread as the current thread, which in turn loads the SPRG1 register[6] with init_thread. Upon return from thread_bootstrap(), ppc_init() initializes certain aspects of the current thread's machine-dependent state.

cpu_bootstrap() [osfmk/ppc/cpu.c] initializes certain locking data structures.

cpu_init() [osfmk/ppc/cpu.c] restores the Timebase Register from values saved in the per_proc_info structure. It also sets the values of some informational fields in the per_proc_info structure.

```
// osfmk/ppc/cpu.c

void
cpu_init(void)
{
    // Restore the Timebase
    ...
    proc_info->cpu_type = CPU_TYPE_POWERPC;
    proc_info->cpu_subtype = (cpu_subtype_t)proc_info->pf.rptdProc;
    proc_info->cpu_threadtype = CPU_THREADTYPE_NONE;
    proc_info->running = TRUE;
}
```

processor_bootstrap() [osfmk/kern/processor.c] is a Mach function that sets the value of the global variable master_processor from the value of the global variable master_cpu, which is set to 0 before this function is called. It calls the cpu_to_processor() [osfmk/ppc/cpu.c] function to convert a cpu (an integer) to a processor (a processor_t).

---

6. SPRG1 holds the active thread.

```
// osfmk/ppc/cpu.c

processor_t
cpu_to_processor(int cpu)
{
    return ((processor_t)PerProcTable[cpu].ppe_vaddr->processor);
}
```

As we saw in Figure 5–3, the `ppe_vaddr` field points to a `per_proc_info` structure. Its processor field, shown as a character array in Figure 5–3, houses a `processor_t` data type, which is Mach's abstraction for a processor.[7] Its contents include several data structures related to scheduling. `processor_bootstrap()` calls `processor_init()` [osfmk/kern/processor.c], which initializes a `processor_t`'s scheduling-related fields, and sets up a timer for quantum expiration.

`ppc_init()` then sets the `static_memory_end` global variable to the highest address used in the kernel's data area, rounded off to the nearest page. Recall from Chapter 4 that the `topOfKernelData` field of the `boot_args` structure contains this value. `ppc_init()` calls `PE_init_platform()` [pexpert/ppc/pe_init.c] to initialize some aspects of the Platform Expert. The call is made with the first argument (`vm_initialized`) set to `FALSE`, indicating that the virtual memory (VM) subsystem is not yet initialized. `PE_init_platform()` copies the boot arguments pointer, the pointer to the device tree, and the display properties to a global structure variable called `PE_state`, which is of type `PE_state_t`.

```
// pexpert/pexpert/pexpert.h

typedef struct PE_state {
    boolean_t   initialized;
    PE_Video    video;
    void        *deviceTreeHead;
    void        *bootArgs;
#if __i386__
    void        *fakePPCBootArgs;
#endif
} PE_state_t;

extern PE_state_t PE_state;

// pexpert/ppc/pe_init.c

PE_state_t PE_state;
```

---

7. We will look at details of Mach's processor abstraction in Chapter 7.

PE_init_platform() then calls DTInit() [pexpert/gen/device_ tree.c] to initialize the Open Firmware device tree routines. DTInit() simply initializes a pointer to the device tree's root node. Finally, PE_init_platform() calls pe_identify_machine() [pexpert/ppc/pe_identify_machine.c], which populates a clock_frequency_info_t variable (gPEClockFrequencyInfo) with various frequencies such as that of the Timebase, the processor, and the bus.

// pexpert/pexpert/pexpert.h

```
struct clock_frequency_info_t {
  unsigned long        bus_clock_rate_hz;
  unsigned long        cpu_clock_rate_hz;
  unsigned long        dec_clock_rate_hz;
  ...
  unsigned long long cpu_frequency_hz;
  unsigned long long cpu_frequency_min_hz;
  unsigned long long cpu_frequency_max_hz;
};

typedef struct clock_frequency_info_t clock_frequency_info_t;

extern clock_frequency_info_t gPEClockFrequencyInfo;
```

ppc_init() parses several boot arguments at this point, such as novmx, fn, pmsx, lcks, diag, ctrc, tb, maxmem, wcte, mcklog, and ht_shift. We came across all these in Chapter 4. However, not all arguments are processed immediately—in the case of some arguments, ppc_init() sets the values of only certain kernel variables for later referral.

5.3.2 Low-Level Virtual Memory Initialization

ppc_init() calls ppc_vm_init() [osfmk/ppc/ppc_vm_init.c] to initialize hardware-dependent aspects of the virtual memory subsystem. The key actions performed by ppc_vm_init() are shown in Figure 5–8.

5.3.2.1 Sizing Memory

ppc_vm_init() first invalidates the in-memory shadow BATs by loading them with zeros. It then retrieves information about physical memory banks from the boot arguments. This information is used to calculate the total amount of memory on the machine. For each available bank that is usable, ppc_vm_init() initializes a memory region structure (mem_region_t).

```
// osfmk/ppc/mappings.h

typedef struct mem_region {
    phys_entry  *mrPhysTab;  // Base of region table
    ppnum_t      mrStart;    // Start of region
    ppnum_t      mrEnd;      // Last page in region
    ppnum_t      mrAStart;   // Next page in region to allocate
    ppnum_t      mrAEnd;     // Last page in region to allocate
} mem_region_t;
...
#define PMAP_MEM_REGION_MAX 11
extern mem_region_t \
    pmap_mem_regions[PMAP_MEM_REGION_MAX + 1];
extern int pmap_mem_regions_count;
...
```

Note that it is possible for physical memory to be noncontiguous. The kernel maps the potentially noncontiguous physical space into contiguous physical-to-virtual mapping tables. `pmap_vm_init()` creates an entry in the `pmap_mem_regions` array for each DRAM bank it uses, while incrementing `pmap_mem_regions_count`. The kernel calculates several maximum values for memory size. For example, on machines with more than 2GB of physical memory, one of the maximum memory values is pinned at 2GB for compatibility. Certain data structures must also reside within the first 2GB of physical memory. The following are specific examples of memory limits established by `ppc_vm_init()`.

- `mem_size` is the 32-bit physical memory size, minus any performance buffer. It is pinned at 2GB on machines with more than 2GB of physical memory. It can be limited by the `maxmem` boot-time argument.

- `max_mem` is the 64-bit memory size. It can also be limited by `maxmem`.

- `mem_actual` is the 64-bit physical memory size that equals the highest physical address plus 1. It cannot be limited by `maxmem`.

- `sane_size` is the same as `max_mem`, unless `max_mem` exceeds `VM_MAX_KERNEL_ADDRESS`, in which case `sane_size` is pinned at `VM_MAX_KERNEL_ADDRESS`, which is defined to be `0xDFFFFFFF` (3.5GB) in `osfmk/mach/ppc/vm_param.h`.

`ppc_vm_init()` sets the `first_avail` variable, which represents the first available virtual address, to `static_memory_end` (note that virtual memory is not operational yet). Next, it computes `kmapsize`—the size of kernel text and data—by retrieving segment addresses from the kernel's Mach-O headers. It then calls `pmap_bootstrap()` [`osfmk/ppc/pmap.c`] with three arguments: `max_mem`, `first_avail`, and `kmapsize`. Next, `pmap_bootstrap()` prepares the system for running with virtual memory.

5.3.2.2 Pmap Initialization

The physical map (*pmap*) layer[8] is the machine-dependent portion of Mach's virtual memory subsystem. `pmap_bootstrap()` first initializes the kernel's physical map (`kernel_pmap`). It then finds space for the page table entry group (PTEG) hash table and the PTEG Control Area (PCA). The in-memory hash table has the following characteristics.

- The kernel allocates one PTEG per four physical pages.[9] As we saw in Chapter 4, the `ht_shift` boot argument allows the hash table's size to be altered.

- The table is allocated in physical memory in the highest available range of physically contiguous memory.

- The PCA resides immediately before the hash table. Its size is calculated from the hash table size.

The PCA's structure is declared in `osfmk/ppc/mappings.h`.

`// osfmk/ppc/mappings.h`

```
typedef struct PCA {
    union flgs {
        unsigned int PCAallo;       // Allocation controls
        struct PCAalflgs {
            unsigned char PCAfree;  // Indicates the slot is free
            unsigned char PCAsteal; // Steal scan start position
            unsigned char PCAauto;  // Indicates that the PTE was autogenned
            unsigned char PCAmisc;  // Miscellaneous flags
#define PCAlock 1                   // This locks up the associated PTEG
#define PCAlockb 31
        } PCAalflgs;
    } flgs;
} PCA_t;
```

The program in Figure 5–9 performs the same calculations as the kernel to calculate the page hash table size on a machine. You can use it to determine the

---

8. We will discuss the pmap layer in Chapter 8.

9. The IBM-recommended hash table size is one PTEG per two physical pages.

amount of memory used by the page table given the amount of physical memory on the machine and the size of a PTEG. Note the use of the `cntlzw` PowerPC instruction to count the number of leading zeros.

FIGURE 5–9 Calculating the PowerPC PTEG hash table size used by the kernel

```
$ cat hash_table_size.c
// hash_table_size.c

#define PROGNAME "hash_table_size"

#include <stdio.h>
#include <stdlib.h>
#include <sys/types.h>
#include <mach/vm_region.h>

typedef unsigned int uint_t;

#define PTEG_SIZE_G4 64
#define PTEG_SIZE_G5 128

extern unsigned int cntlzw(unsigned int num);

vm_size_t
calculate_hash_table_size(uint64_t msize, int pfPTEG, int hash_table_shift)
{
    unsigned int nbits;
    uint64_t     tmemsize;
    vm_size_t    hash_table_size;

    // Get first bit in upper half
    nbits = cntlzw(((msize << 1) - 1) >> 32);

    // If upper half is empty, find bit in lower half
    if (nbits == 32)
        nbits = nbits + cntlzw((uint_t)((msize << 1) - 1));

    // Get memory size rounded up to a power of 2
    tmemsize = 0x8000000000000000ULL >> nbits;

    // Ensure 32-bit arithmetic doesn't overflow
    if (tmemsize > 0x0000002000000000ULL)
        tmemsize = 0x0000002000000000ULL;

    // IBM-recommended hash table size (1 PTEG per 2 physical pages)
    hash_table_size = (uint_t)(tmemsize >> (12 + 1)) * pfPTEG;
```

(continues)

FIGURE 5–9 Calculating the PowerPC PTEG hash table size used by the kernel *(continued)*

```c
    // Mac OS X uses half of the IBM-recommended size
    hash_table_size >>= 1;

    // Apply ht_shift, if necessary
    if (hash_table_shift >= 0) // make size bigger
        hash_table_size <<= hash_table_shift;
    else // Make size smaller
        hash_table_size >>= (-hash_table_shift);

    // Ensure minimum size
    if (hash_table_size < (256 * 1024))
        hash_table_size = (256 * 1024);

    return hash_table_size;
}

int
main(int argc, char **argv)
{
    vm_size_t htsize;
    uint64_t msize;

    if (argc != 2) {
        fprintf(stderr, "%s <memory in MB>\n", PROGNAME);
        exit(1);
    }

    msize = ((uint64_t)(atoi(argv[1])) << 20);
    htsize = calculate_hash_table_size(msize, PTEG_SIZE_G5, 0);

    printf("%d bytes (%dMB)\n", htsize, htsize >> 20);

    exit(0);
}
```
```
$ cat cntlzw.s
; cntlzw.s
; count leading zeros in a 32-bit word
;
        .text
        .align 4
        .globl _cntlzw
_cntlzw:
        cntlzw r3,r3
        blr
$ gcc -Wall -o hash_table_size hash_table_size.c cntlzw.s
$ ./hash_table_size 4096
33554432 bytes (32MB)
$ ./hash_table_size 2048
16777216 bytes (16MB)
```

pmap_bootstrap() calls hw_hash_init() [osfmk/ppc/hw_vm.s] to initialize the hash table and the PCA. It then calls hw_setup_trans() [osfmk/ppc/hw_vm.s], which we came across earlier in this chapter. Recall that hw_setup_trans() only configures the hardware registers required for address translation—it does not actually start address translation.

pmap_bootstrap() calculates the amount of memory that needs to be designated as "allocated" (i.e., it cannot be marked free). This includes memory for the initial context save areas, trace tables, physical entries (phys_entry_t), the kernel text, the logical pages (struct vm_page) needed to map physical memory, and the address-mapping structures (struct vm_map_entry). It then allocates the initial context save areas by calling savearea_init() [osfmk/ppc/savearea.c]. This allows the processor to take an interrupt.

Save Areas

Save areas are used to store process control blocks (PCBs). Depending on its type, a save area can contain a general processor context, a floating-point context, a vector context, and so on. Various save area structures are declared in osfmk/ppc/savearea.h. A save area never spans a page boundary. Moreover, besides referring to a save area by its virtual address, the kernel may also reference it by its physical address, such as from within an interrupt vector, where exceptions must not occur. The kernel maintains two global save area free lists: the save area *free pool* and the save area *free list*. There is one local list for each processor.

pmap_bootstrap() initializes the mapping tables by calling mapping_init() [osfmk/ppc/mappings.c]. It then calls pmap_map() [osfmk/ppc/pmap.c] to map memory for page tables in the kernel's map. The page tables are mapped V=R—that is, with virtual address being equal to the real address. On 64-bit machines, pmap_bootstrap() calls pmap_map_physical() [osfmk/ppc/pmap.c] to block-map physical memory regions—in units of up to 256MB—into the kernel's address map. Physical memory is mapped at virtual addresses starting from PHYS_MEM_WINDOW_VADDR, which is defined to be 0x100000000ULL (4GB) in osfmk/ppc/pmap.h. Moreover, in this physical memory window, an I/O hole of size IO_MEM_WINDOW_SIZE (defined to be 2GB in osfmk/ppc/pmap.h) is mapped at an offset IO_MEM_WINDOW_VADDR (defined to be 2GB in osfmk/ppc/pmap.h). The pmap_map_iohole() [osfmk/ppc/pmap.c] function is called on a 64-bit machine to map the I/O hole.

Finally, pmap_bootstrap() sets the next available page pointer (first_avail) and the first free virtual address pointer (first_free_virt). The rest of the memory is marked free and is added to the free regions, from where it can be allocated by pmap_steal_memory() [osfmk/vm/vm_resident.c].

ppc_vm_init() now calls pmap_map() to map (again, V=R) exception vectors in the kernel's address map, starting from the address exception_entry through the address exception_end—both addresses are defined in osfmk/ppc/lowmem_vectors.s. Other pmap_map() calls that are made include those for the kernel's text (__TEXT) and data (__DATA) segments. The __KLD and __LINKEDIT segments are mapped (wired) through pmap_enter() [osfmk/ppc/pmap.c], page by page. These segments are unloaded by the I/O Kit in their entirety, to reclaim that memory, after booting completes.

ppc_vm_init() next calls MapUserMemoryWindowInit() [osfmk/ppc/pmap.c] to initialize a mechanism the kernel uses for mapping portions of user-space memory into the kernel. The copyin() and copyout() functions, both of which are implemented in osfmk/ppc/movc.s, primarily use this facility by calling MapUserMemoryWindow() [osfmk/ppc/pmap.c], which maps a user address range into a predefined kernel range. The range is 512MB in size and starts at USER_MEM_WINDOW_VADDR, which is defined to be 0xE0000000ULL (3.5GB) in osfmk/ppc/pmap.h.

5.3.2.3 Starting Address-Translation

Now that the memory management hardware has been configured and virtual memory subsystem data structures have been allocated and initialized, ppc_vm_init() calls hw_start_trans() [osfmk/ppc/hw_vm.s] to start address translation. Note that this is the *first time* in the boot process that address translation is enabled.

5.3.3 After Virtual Memory

ppc_vm_init() makes a call to PE_init_platform(), but with the vm_initialized Boolean argument set to TRUE (unlike the earlier call made by ppc_init()). As a result, PE_init_platform() calls pe_init_debug() [pexpert/gen/pe_gen.c], which copies the debug flags, if any, from the boot arguments to the kernel variable DEBUGFlag.

printf_init() [osfmk/kern/printf.c] initializes locks used by the printf() and sprintf() kernel functions. It also calls bsd_log_init() [bsd/kern/subr_log.c] to initialize a message buffer for kernel logging. The buffer structure is declared in bsd/sys/msgbuf.h.

// bsd/sys/msgbuf.h

```
#define MSG_BSIZE (4096 - 3 * sizeof(long))

struct msgbuf {
#define MSG_MAGIC 0x063061

    long msg_magic;
    long msg_bufx;              // write pointer
    long msg_bufr;              // read pointer
    char msg_bufc[MSG_BSIZE];   // buffer
};
#ifdef KERNEL
extern struct msgbuf *msgbufp;
...
```

Since logs may be written at interrupt level, it is possible for a log manipulation to affect another processor at interrupt level. Therefore, printf_init() also initializes a log spinlock to serialize access to log buffers.

panic_init() [osfmk/kern/debug.c] initializes a lock used to serialize modifications by multiple processors to the global panic string. printf() and panic() are required if a debugger needs to run.

5.3.3.1 Console Initialization

PE_init_kprintf() [pexpert/ppc/pe_kprintf.c] determines which console character output method to use. It checks the /options node in the device tree for the presence of input-device and output-device properties. If either property's value is a string of the format scca:x, where x is a number with six or fewer digits, PE_init_kprintf() attempts to use a serial port, with x being the baud rate. However, if the serialbaud boot argument is present, its value is used as the baud rate instead. PE_init_kprintf() then attempts to find an onboard serial port.

Figure 5–10 shows an excerpt from kprintf() initialization.

FIGURE 5–10 Initialization of the `kprintf()` function

// pexpert/ppc/pe_kprintf.c

```
void serial_putc(char c);
void (* PE_kputc)(char c) = 0;
...
vm_offset_t scc = 0;

void
PE_init_kprintf(boolean_t vm_initialized)
{
    ...
    // See if "/options" has "input-device" or "output-device"
    ...
    if ((scc = PE_find_scc())) { // Can we find a serial port?
        scc = io_map_spec(scc, 0x1000); // Map the serial port
        initialize_serial((void *)scc, gPESerialBaud); // Start serial driver
        PE_kputc = serial_putc;
        simple_lock_init(&kprintf_lock, 0);
    } else
        PE_kputc = cnputc;
    ...
}
```

PE_find_scc() [pexpert/ppc/pe_identify_machine.c] looks for a serial port[10] in the device tree. If one is found, PE_find_scc() returns the physical I/O address of the port, which is then passed to io_map_spec() [osfmk/ppc/io_map.c] to be mapped into the kernel's virtual address space. Since virtual memory is enabled at this point, io_map_spec() calls io_map() [osfmk/ppc/io_map.c] to allocate pageable kernel memory in which the desired mapping is created. initialize_serial() [osfmk/ppc/serial.c] configures the serial hardware by performing I/O to the appropriate registers. Finally, PE_init_kprintf() sets the PE_kputc function pointer to serial_putc() [osfmk/ppc/ke_printf.c], which in turn calls scc_putc() [osfmk/ppc/serial_io.c] to output a character to a serial line.

If no serial ports could be found, PE_init_kprintf() sets PE_kprintf to cnputc() [osfmk/console/ppc/serial_console.c], which calls the putc member of the appropriate entry[11] of the cons_ops structure to perform console output.

---

10. A legacy serial port is named escc-legacy, whereas a new-style serial port is named escc in the device tree.

11. Depending on whether the serial console or the graphics console is the default, the appropriate entry is set to SCC_CONS_OPS or VC_CONS_OPS, respectively, at compile time.

```
// osfmk/console/ppc/serial_console.c

#define OPS(putc, getc, nosplputc, nosplgetc) putc, getc

const struct console_ops {
    int (* putc)(int, int, int);
    int (* getc)(int, int, boolean_t, boolean_t);
} cons_ops[] = {

#define SCC_CONS_OPS 0
    { OPS(scc_putc, scc_getc, no_spl_scputc, no_spl_scgetc) },

#define VC_CONS_OPS 1
    { OPS(vcputc, vcgetc, no_spl_vcputc, no_spl_vcgetc) },
};
#define NCONSOPS (sizeof cons_ops / sizeof cons_ops[0])
```

> `osfmk/console/ppc/serial_console.c` contains a console opera-
> tions table with entries for both a serial console and a video console.

vcputc() [osfmk/console/video_console.c] outputs to the graphical
console by drawing characters directly to the framebuffer.

ppc_vm_init() now checks whether a serial console was requested at boot
time, and if so, it calls switch_to_serial_console() [osfmk/console/ppc/
serial_console.c] to set the SCC_CONS_OPS entry of console_ops as the
default for console output.

ppc_vm_init() calls PE_create_console() [pexpert/ppc/pe_init.c]
to create either the graphical or the textual console, depending on the type of
video set in the PE_state.video.v_display field, which was initialized earlier by PE_init_platform().

```
// pexpert/ppc/pe_init.c

void
PE_init_platform(boolean_t vm_initialized, void *_args)
{
    ...
    boot_args *args = (boot_args *)_args;

    if (PE_state.initialized == FALSE) {
        PE_state.initialized = TRUE;
        ...
        PE_state.video.v_display = args->Video.v_display;
        ...
    }
    ...
}
```

```
...

void
PE_create_console(void)
{
    if (PE_state.video.v_display)
        PE_initialize_console(&PE_state.video, kPEGraphicsMode);
    else
        PE_initialize_console(&PE_state.video, kPETextMode);
}
```

PE_initialize_console() [pexpert/ppc/pe_init.c] supports disabling the screen (switching to the serial console), enabling the screen (switching to the "last" console), or simply initializing the screen. All three operations involve calling initialize_screen() [osfmk/console/video_console.c], which is responsible for retrieving the graphical framebuffer address. osfmk/console/video_console.c also implements functions used while displaying boot progress during a graphical boot.

ppc_vm_init() finally calls PE_init_printf() [pexpert/gen/pe_gen.c].

After ppc_vm_init() returns, ppc_init() processes the wcte and mcksoft boot arguments (see Table 4–12) on 64-bit hardware.

5.3.3.2 *Preparing for the Bootstrapping of Kernel Subsystems*

Finally, ppc_init() calls machine_startup() [osfmk/ppc/model_dep.c], which never returns.

machine_startup() processes several boot arguments. In particular, it checks whether the kernel must halt in the debugger. It initializes locks used by the debugger (debugger_lock) and the backtrace print mechanism (pbtlock). debugger_lock is used to ensure that there is only one processor in the debugger at a time. pbtlock is used by print_backtrace() [osfmk/ppc/model_dep.c] to ensure that only one backtrace can occur at a time. If the built-in kernel debugger—KDB—has been compiled into the kernel, machine_startup() calls ddb_init() [osfmk/ddb/db_sym.c] to initialize KDB. Moreover, if the kernel has been instructed to halt in KDB, machine_startup() calls Debugger() [osfmk/ppc/model_dep.c] to enter the debugger.

// osfmk/ppc/model_dep.c

```
#define TRAP_DEBUGGER __asm__ volatile("tw 4,r3,r3");
...
```

```
void
machine_startup(boot_args *args)
{
    ...
#if MACH_KDB
    ...
    ddb_init();

    if (boot_arg & DDB_KDB)
        current_debugger = KDB_CUR_DB;

    if (halt_in_debugger && (current_debugger == KDB_CUR_DB)) {
        Debugger("inline call to debugger(machine_startup)");
        ...
    }
    ...
}
...

void
Debugger(const char *message)
{
    ...
    if ((current_debugger != NO_CUR_DB)) { // debugger configured
        printf("Debugger(%s)\n", message);
        TRAP_DEBUGGER; // enter the debugger
        splx(spl);
        return;
    }
    ...
}
```

machine_startup() calls machine_conf() [osfmk/ppc/model_dep.c], which manipulates Mach's machine_info structure [osfmk/mach/machine.h]. The host_info() Mach call[12] retrieves information from this structure. Note that the memory_size field is pinned to 2GB on machines with more than 2GB of physical memory.

// osfmk/mach/machine.h

```
struct machine_info {
    integer_t major_version;    // kernel major version ID
    integer_t minor_version;    // kernel minor version ID
    integer_t max_cpus;         // maximum number of CPUs possible
    integer_t avail_cpus;       // number of CPUs now available
    uint32_t  memory_size;      // memory size in bytes, capped at 2GB
```

---

12. We will see an example of using this call in Chapter 6.

```
    uint64_t  max_mem;          // actual physical memory size
    integer_t physical_cpu;     // number of physical CPUs now available
    integer_t physical_cpu_max; // maximum number of physical CPUs possible
    integer_t logical_cpu;      // number of logical CPUs now available
    integer_t logical_cpu_max;  // maximum number of logical CPUs possible
};

typedef struct machine_info *machine_info_t;
typedef struct machine_info machine_info_data_t;

extern struct machine_info machine_info;
...
```

> On older kernels, `machine_startup()` also initializes thermal moni-
> toring for the processor by calling `ml_thrm_init()` [`osfmk/ppc/`
> `machine_routines_asm.s`]. Newer kernels handle thermal initial-
> ization entirely in the I/O Kit—`ml_thrm_init()` performs no work
> on these kernels.

Finally, `machine_conf()` calls `kernel_bootstrap()` [`osfmk/kern/`
`startup.c`], which never returns.

5.4 Mach Subsystem Initialization

`kernel_bootstrap()` performs much of the higher-level kernel startup. In fact,
it eventually launches BSD initialization, which in turn ends by initiating user-
level system startup. Figure 5–11 shows the key steps performed by `kernel_`
`bootstrap()`.

`lck_mod_init()` [`osfmk/kern/locks.c`] initializes data structures that
are used by Mach's locking primitives.

5.4.1 Scheduler Initialization

`sched_init()` [`osfmk/kern/sched_prim.c`] initializes the processor scheduler. It sets the default preemption rate to `DEFAULT_PREEMPTION_RATE` (defined
to be 100 per second in `osfmk/kern/sched_prim.c`), unless a boot argument
was used to set it to some other value. `sched_init()` calculates the values of
fundamental scheduling constants. For example, it calculates the standard
timeslicing quantum in microseconds as the number 1,000,000 divided by the

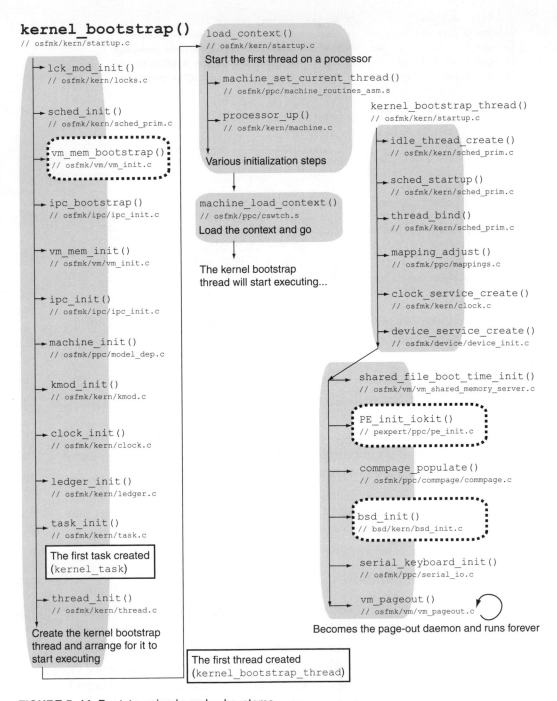

FIGURE 5–11 Bootstrapping kernel subsystems

default preemption rate. It then prints a message advertising the value so calculated. In a verbose boot (PowerPC), this is the first kernel message seen by the user:

```
standard timeslicing quantum is 10000 us
```

sched_init() also performs the following specific operations.

- It calls wait_queues_init() [osfmk/kern/sched_prim.c] to initialize the event wait queues used by the scheduler APIs. The hash of wait
  queue structures—consisting of NUMQUEUES (59) buckets—is statically
  allocated in osfmk/kern/sched_prim.c. Each bucket contains a queue
  of threads that have the same hash function value. All wait queues are initialized with a synchronizer wait ordering policy of SYNC_POLICY_FIFO.

- It calls load_shift_init() [osfmk/kern/sched_prim.c] to initialize the
  timeshare loading factors contained in the sched_load_shifts array. The
  array contains a per-run-queue factor, which is used as the dynamic, load-
  based component in the computation of the timeshare priority conversion
  factor.

- It calls pset_init() [osfmk/kern/processor.c] to initialize the default
  processor set. Mach scheduling uses processor sets,[13] hence this is necessary
  for the scheduler to run. pset_init() initializes the components of the
  specified processor-set data structure, including its various queues.

- Finally, sched_init() sets the *scheduler tick*—the sched_tick variable—
  to 0.

5.4.2 High-Level Virtual Memory Subsystem Initialization

kernel_bootstrap() calls vm_mem_bootstrap() [osfmk/vm/vm_init.c] to
initialize the platform-independent virtual memory subsystem—a major step in
bootstrapping. Figure 5–12 shows the sequence of actions performed by vm_
mem_bootstrap().

vm_page_bootstrap() [osfmk/vm/vm_resident.c] initializes the resident memory module.[14] It allocates memory for VM management data structures, initializes the page queues, "steals" memory for Mach's map and zone
subsystems, allocates and initializes the virtual-to-physical table hash buckets,

---

13. We will look at Mach processor sets and scheduling in Chapter 7.

14. We will look at Mach VM details in Chapter 8.

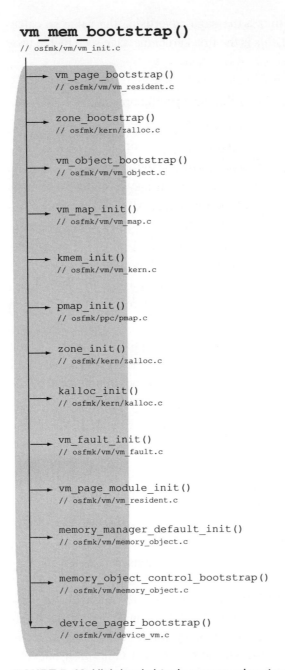

FIGURE 5–12 High-level virtual memory subsystem initialization

allocates the resident page table by calling pmap_startup() [osfmk/vm/vm_resident.c], and computes the number of pages that must be marked as "wired" because they cannot be moved. pmap_startup() calculates the amount of free memory and allocates space for all page frames that would be needed. It then iterates over available physical pages, calling vm_page_init() [osfmk/vm/vm_resident.c] to initialize page frames. Figure 5–13 depicts this operation.

FIGURE 5–13 Initializing page frames during VM subsystem initialization

```
// osfmk/vm/vm_resident.c

struct vm_page vm_page_template;
...
void
vm_page_bootstrap(vm_offset_t *startp, vm_offset_t *endp)
{

    register vm_page_t m;
    ...

    // Initialize the vm_page_template
    m = &vm_page_template;
    m->object = VM_OBJECT_NULL;
    m->offset = (vm_object_offset_t)-1;
    ...

    // Set various fields of m
    ...
    m->phys_page = 0;
    ...

    // "Steal" memory for Mach's map and zone subsystems
    vm_map_steal_memory();
    zone_steal_memory();

    ...
    pmap_startup(&virtual_space_start, &virtual_space_end);
    ...
}
...
void
pmap_startup(vm_offset_t *startp, vm_offset_t *endp)
{
    unsigned int i, npages, pages_initialized, fill, fillval;

    vm_page_t pages;
    ppnum_t   phys_page;
```

(continues)

FIGURE 5–13 Initializing page frames during VM subsystem initialization *(continued)*

```
addr64_t  tmpaddr;
...

// We calculate (in npages) how many page frames we will have, and then
// allocate the page structures in one chunk

// Get the amount of memory left
tmpaddr = (addr64_t)pmap_free_pages() * (addr64_t)PAGE_SIZE;

// Account for any slack
tmpaddr = tmpaddr + \
    (addr64_t)(round_page_32(virtual_space_start) - (virtual_space_start);

npages = (unsigned int)(tmpaddr / (addr64_t)(PAGE_SIZE + sizeof(*pages)));

pages = (vm_page_t)pmap_steal_memory(npages * sizeof(*pages));

// Initialize the page frames
for (i = 0, pages_initialized = 0; i < npages; i++) {

    // Allocate a physical page
    if (!pmap_next_page(&phys_page))
        break;

    // Initialize the fields in a new page
    vm_page_init(&pages[i], phys_page);

    vm_page_pages++;
    pages_initialized++;
}
    ...
}
...
void
vm_page_init(vm_page_t mem, ppnum_t phys_page)
{
    assert(phys_page);
    *mem = vm_page_template;
    mem->phys_page = phys_page;
}
```

Once `vm_page_bootstrap()` returns, all physical memory is accounted for, and the kernel can explicitly use virtual addresses. As Figure 5–12 shows, `vm_mem_bootstrap()` then initializes various other components of the VM subsystem.

zone_bootstrap() [osfmk/kern/zalloc.c] initializes zone_zone, the "zone of zones,"[15] which uses fixed memory allocated earlier during memory subsystem initialization.

vm_object_bootstrap() [osfmk/vm/vm_object.c] initializes Mach's VM objects module. This includes initializing zones for VM objects (vm_object_zone) and VM object hash entries (vm_object_hash_zone). The kernel object (kernel_object) and the submap object (vm_submap_object) are also initialized here. Mach's external page management hint technology,[16] which maintains a (potentially incomplete) map of pages written to external storage for a range of virtual memory, is initialized via a call to vm_external_module_initialize() [osfmk/vm/vm_external.c].

vm_map_init() [osfmk/vm/vm_map.c] initializes a zone for allocating vm_map structures (vm_map_zone), a zone for allocating nonkernel vm_map_entry structures (vm_map_entry_zone), a special zone for allocating kernel-only vm_map_entry structures (vm_map_kentry_zone), and a zone for vm_map_copy structures (vm_map_copy_zone).

kmem_init() [osfmk/vm/vm_kern.c] initializes the kernel's virtual memory map (kernel_map). Moreover, any virtual memory that may have been allocated so far—as determined by the difference between the constant VM_MIN_KERNEL_ADDRESS and the lower address bound passed to kmem_init()—is reserved by entering it into the kernel's map. kmem_init() also sets the value of the vm_page_wire_count global variable, which, at this point, represents all kernel memory used.

```
vm_page_wire_count = (atop_64(max_mem)
                     - (vm_page_free_count
                     + vm_page_active_count
                     + vm_page_inactive_count));
```

pmap_init() [osfmk/ppc/pmap.c] finishes the initialization of the physical map module by allocating the remaining data structures that the module needs to map virtual memory. It initializes a zone of pmap structures (pmap_zone) from which new physical maps are allocated, marks pmap as initialized, and sets the free pmap count to zero.

---

15. We will look at Mach's zone-based memory allocator in Chapter 8.

16. This should not be confused with Mach's external (to the kernel) memory management, which is not available in Mac OS X.

vm_mem_bootstrap() then checks for the presence of the zsize boot argument, which, if present, specifies the maximum amount of address space allocated for zones—that is, the zone map size. By default, the kernel uses 25% of the physical memory size (sane_size). Regardless of whether zsize is specified or not, the kernel clamps the maximum and minimum values of the zone map size to 768MB and 12MB, respectively. vm_mem_bootstrap() now calls zone_init() [osfmk/kern/zalloc.c] to allocate address space for zones.

kalloc_init() [osfmk/kern/kalloc.c] initializes the kernel memory allocator, which uses multiple power-of-2-sized zones and a 16MB submap allocated from kernel_map. The latter is used in conjunction with kmem_alloc() [osfmk/vm/vm_kern.c] for allocations that are too large for a zone. kalloc_init() determines the value for kalloc_max, which represents the first power of 2 for which no zone exists. By default, kalloc_max is set to 16KB, unless the page size is more than 16KB, in which case it is set to the page size. kalloc_init() then iterates over supported allocation sizes—starting from 1 and going up to kalloc_max in powers of two. It initializes a zone for sizes KALLOC_MIN-SIZE (16 bytes) and higher by calling zinit(). The zones are named kalloc.16, kalloc.32, kalloc.64, and so on. The maximum number of elements in a zone depends on the size that the zone handles.

- kalloc.16 has 1024 elements.
- kalloc.32 through kalloc.256 have 4096 elements.
- kalloc.512 through kalloc.4096 have 1024 elements.
- kalloc.8192 has 4096 elements.

vm_fault_init() [osfmk/vm/vm_fault.c] initializes any private data structures that the kernel might have in the page-fault-handling module.

vm_page_module_init() [osfmk/vm/vm_resident.c] initializes a zone for "fictitious" resident page structures that do not actually refer to any physical pages but are used for holding important page information. The physical page address for such pages is set to -1.

memory_manager_default_init() [osfmk/vm/memory_object.c] initializes a mutex that is used while getting or setting the default memory manager Mach port. memory_object_control_bootstrap() [osfmk/vm/memory_object.c] initializes a zone (mem_obj_control_zone) used for allocating pager[17] request ports. device_pager_bootstrap() [osfmk/vm/device_vm.c] initializes a zone for device node pager structures (device_pager_zone).

---

17. As we will see in Chapter 8, a pager in Mach's VM subsystem represents a data source.

5.4.3 IPC Initialization

`kernel_bootstrap()` calls `ipc_bootstrap()` [osfmk/ipc/ipc_init.c] to set up the IPC subsystem[18] enough for the kernel task to be created. `ipc_bootstrap()` performs the following actions.

- It initializes zones for IPC capability spaces (`ipc_space_zone`), IPC tree entries (`ipc_tree_entry_zone`), IPC ports and port sets (`ipc_object_zones[IOT_PORT]` and `ipc_object_zones[IOT_PORT_SET]`, respectively), and IPC kernel messages (`ipc_kmsg_zone`).

- It calls `mig_init()` [osfmk/kern/ipc_kobject.c] to initialize the Mach Interface Generator (MIG). As part of this initialization, various standard MIG subsystems, such as those for tasks and threads, are examined as the MIG hash table is populated. When an IPC message is sent to the kernel, the message ID is used to search for a matching entry in the hash table. The entry specifies the size of the message's reply and contains a pointer to the routine that performs the corresponding kernel function.

- It calls `ipc_table_init()` [osfmk/ipc/ipc_table.c] to allocate and initialize a table of IPC capabilities (`ipc_table_entries`) and another for dead-name requests (`ipc_table_dnrequests`).

- It calls `ipc_hash_init()` [osfmk/ipc/ipc_hash.c] to allocate and initialize a reverse hash global table for IPC entries.

- It calls `semaphore_init()` [osfmk/kern/sync_sema.c] to initialize the zone from which semaphores are allocated (`semaphore_zone`).

- It calls `lock_set_init()` [osfmk/kern/sync_lock.c] to initialize the lock set subsystem.

- It calls `mk_timer_init()` [osfmk/kern/mk_timer.c] to initialize the zone from which Mach timers are allocated (`mk_timer_zone`).

- It calls `host_notify_init()` [osfmk/kern/host_notify.c] to initialize the zone from which host notification request entries are allocated (`host_notify_zone`).

---

18. Chapter 9 discusses the Mac OS X IPC subsystem.

5.4.4 Finishing VM and IPC Initialization

`kernel_bootstrap()` next calls `vm_mem_init()` [osfmk/vm/vm_init.c], which in turn calls `vm_object_init()` [osfmk/vm/vm_object.c] to finish initializing the kernel object.

`ipc_init()` [osfmk/ipc/ipc_init.c] performs the final initialization of the IPC subsystem. It allocates two pageable maps: the `ipc_kernel_map` map to manage memory allocations made during Mach IPC calls and the `ipc_kernel_copy_map` map in which space is allocated during Mach IPC for out-of-line data that is to be physically copied. `ipc_init()` finally calls `ipc_host_init()` [osfmk/kern/ipc_host.c], which performs the following actions.

- It allocates some of the special host ports, such as the `HOST_PORT`, the `HOST_PRIV_PORT`, and the `HOST_SECURITY_PORT`. Moreover, it sets the special ports by calling `kernel_set_special_port()` [osfmk/kern/host.c].

- It sets all the host-level exception ports to `IP_NULL`.

- It calls `ipc_pset_init()` [osfmk/kern/ipc_host.c] to allocate the control and name ports for the default processor set. Next, it calls `ipc_pset_enable()` [osfmk/kern/ipc_host.c] to set these ports, which in turn calls `ipc_kobject_set()` [osfmk/kern/ipc_kobject.c] to make the ports represent the processor set and its name, respectively.

- It calls `ipc_processor_init()` [osfmk/kern/ipc_host.c] to allocate the master processor's control port. Next, it calls `ipc_processor_enable()` [osfmk/kern/ipc_host.c], which calls `ipc_kobject_set()` to make the port represent the processor.

5.4.5 Initializing Miscellaneous Subsystems

`machine_init()` [osfmk/ppc/model_dep.c] calls `clock_config()` [osfmk/kern/clock.c] to configure the clock subsystem. `clock_config()` calls the configuration (but not initialization) functions of all available clock devices, such as the calendar and the system clocks. It also calls `timer_call_initialize()` [osfmk/kern/timer_call.c], which registers `timer_call_interrupt()` [osfmk/kern/timer_call.c] as the function to be called from the real-time clock device interrupt handler whenever the real-time clock timer expires (in other words, `timer_call_interrupt()` services the timer callout queue for a processor).

`machine_init()` also calls `perfmon_init()` [osfmk/ppc/hw_perfmon.c], which initializes a lock used by the performance-monitoring facility.

kmod_init() [osfmk/kern/kmod.c] initializes locks and a command queue used by the kernel module subsystem. The kernel enqueues data packets containing module load requests in this queue, which is serviced by the kextd user-space daemon.

clock_init() [osfmk/kern/clock.c] calls the initialization functions of all available clock devices. Note that unlike clock_config(), which is called only once on the master processor at boot time, clock_init() is called every time a processor is started.

ledger_init() [osfmk/kern/ledger.c] initializes Mach ledgers. A ledger is a kernel abstraction used for resource accounting. It can be used to limit consumption of other resources. Ledgers are not used in Mac OS X, and xnu's implementation of ledgers is not functional.

5.4.6 Tasks and Threads

task_init() [osfmk/kern/task.c] initializes a zone (task_zone) from which new task structures are allocated. The built-in limit on the number of tasks is defined as TASK_MAX in osfmk/kern/mach_param.h, with a typical value of 1024. task_init() calls task_create_internal() [osfmk/kern/task.c] to create the first task—the kernel task (kernel_task). The kernel task's default address space map is deallocated—kernel_map is assigned as its address space instead. Note that since the kernel task's parent task is TASK_NULL, it does not inherit any memory.

thread_init() [osfmk/kern/thread.c] initializes a zone (thread_zone) from which new thread structures are allocated. The built-in limit on the number of threads is defined as THREAD_MAX (2560) in osfmk/kern/mach_param.h. thread_init() also calls stack_init() [osfmk/kern/stack.c], which allocates a map (stack_map) for kernel stacks. A kernel stack is 16KB in size and resides in nonpageable memory. thread_init() also calls machine_thread_init() [osfmk/ppc/pcb.c], which may perform machine-specific initializations.

5.4.7 Launching the Kernel Bootstrap Thread

kernel_bootstrap() now creates a kernel thread, with kernel_bootstrap_thread() [osfmk/kern/startup.c] as the continuation function,[19] for com-

---

19. We will look at continuations in Chapter 7.

pleting the remaining kernel startup operations. This will be the first kernel thread to run on the processor. The thread's resources are deallocated before it is handed over to `load_context()` [osfmk/kern/startup.c] for execution. `load_context()` calls `machine_set_current_thread()` [osfmk/ppc/machine_routines_asm.s], which loads the SPRG1 register with the current thread pointer.[20] It then calls `processor_up()` [osfmk/kern/machine.c], the machine-independent Mach-level CPU enabler routine that adds the specified processor to the default processor set. The processor's state is set as `PROCESSOR_RUNNING`. The global `machine_info` structure's `avail_cpus` field is atomically incremented by one. `processor_up()` also calls the `ml_cpu_up()` [osfmk/ppc/machine_routines.c] machine-dependent routine. `ml_cpu_up()` atomically increments the `physical_cpu` and `logical_cpu` fields of `machine_info` by one each. Finally, `load_context()` calls `machine_load_context()` [osfmk/ppc/cswtch.s] to load the thread's hardware context and set it running.

5.5 The First Thread

`kernel_bootstrap_thread()` [osfmk/kern/startup.c] performs the following operations.

- It calls `idle_thread_create()` [osfmk/kern/sched_prim.c] to create the idle kernel thread for the processor. An idle thread, which is bound to a processor, runs at the idle priority (`IDLEPRI`), looking for other threads to execute. It is marked as being in the `TH_RUN` and `TH_IDLE` states simultaneously.

- It calls `sched_startup()` [osfmk/kern/sched_prim.c], which starts scheduler services. In particular, it creates the scheduler tick thread (`sched_tick_thread`), which sets a scheduler variable (`sched_tick_deadline`) to the Timebase Register's contents, which have been retrieved via `mach_absolute_time()` [osfmk/ppc/machine_routines_asm.s]. The scheduler tick thread performs periodic scheduler-related bookkeeping, such as aging processor usage, scanning the run queues for timesharing threads that may need to have their priorities recalculated, and computing the Mach Factor. `sched_startup()` then calls `thread_daemon_init()`

---

20. The Mac OS X kernel conventionally uses SPRG1 for this purpose.

[osfmk/kern/thread.c], which creates kernel threads for running the "terminate" and "stack" daemons. The former deals with terminating threads that have been enqueued for final clean up. The latter allocates stacks for threads that have been enqueued on the stack allocation queue.[21] Finally, sched_startup() calls thread_call_initialize() [osfmk/kern/thread_call.c] to initialize the thread-based callout module. This includes initializing the relevant locks, initializing wait and callout queues, initializing a delayed timer callout, and creating the activate thread that executes callout threads. Callouts are used by various kernel subsystems[22] to register functions to be invoked at some time in the future.

- It calls thread_bind() [osfmk/kern/sched_prim.c] to force itself to continue executing on the current (master) processor as additional processors come online.

- It calls mapping_adjust() [osfmk/ppc/mappings.c] to perform bookkeeping of virtual-to-physical mappings. In this first invocation, mapping_adjust() also initializes a callout for itself, which is used indirectly by the pageout daemon when it attempts to trigger garbage collection.

- It calls clock_service_create() [osfmk/kern/clock.c] to initialize the clock IPC service facility. clock_service_create() initializes IPC control of clocks by allocating each clock's service and control ports. Moreover, it enables IPC access to each clock by calling ipc_kobject_set() [osfmk/kern/ipc_kobject.c] to make the ports represent that clock kernel object. clock_service_create() also initializes a zone (alarm_zone) for allocating user alarm structures (alarm_t).

- It calls device_service_create() [osfmk/device/device_init.c] to initialize the device service. This allocates the master device port (master_device_port), which is the host's master privileged I/O object (HOST_IO_MASTER_PORT). Recall that other host special ports were created earlier.

- It calls shared_file_boot_time_init() [osfmk/vm/vm_shared_memory_server.c], which calls shared_file_init() [osfmk/vm/vm_shared_memory_server.c] to allocate two 256MB regions that are later mapped

---

21. The thread_invoke() function enqueues threads on the stack allocation queue if it fails to allocate a kernel stack for the thread.

22. For example, the kernel uses a callout to display the gearwheel progress animation during a graphical boot.

into address spaces of tasks, allowing them to share the contents of these regions. We will come across these functions again in Section 5.7.8. `shared_region_mapping_create()` [osfmk/vm/vm_shared_memory_ server.c] is called to allocate and initialize data structures for this shared region mapping. `shared_com_boot_time_init()` [osfmk/vm/vm_shared_ memory_server.c] is called to initialize the "comm" region (or the comm-page area)[23]—a range of pages meant to contain data and text shared between all processes on the system—the region is mapped read-only into every task's address space. There are separate 32-bit and 64-bit comm regions, each being `_COMM_PAGE_AREA_LENGTH` (defined to be seven 4KB pages in osfmk/ppc/cpu_capabilities.h) in size. Note that a task structure contains a pointer to the system shared region (`system_shared_ region`). `shared_file_boot_time_init()` finally calls `vm_set_shared_ region()` [osfmk/vm/vm_shared_memory_server.c] to set this pointer in the current task.

- It calls `PE_init_iokit()` [pexpert/ppc/pe_init.c] to initialize the I/O Kit. We will look at details of `PE_init_iokit()` in Section 5.6.

- It calls `commpage_populate()` [osfmk/ppc/commpage/commpage.c] to populate the 32-bit and 64-bit comm regions. A comm region resides in wired memory. Its contents include information about processor capabilities and features, a mapping of the Timebase Register, and frequently used routines.

- It calls `bsd_init()` [bsd/kern/bsd_init.c] to initialize the BSD portion of the kernel and to initiate user-level startup. We will look at details of `bsd_init()` in Section 5.7.

- It calls `serial_keyboard_init()` [osfmk/ppc/serial_io.c], which checks whether the system console is on the serial port. If not, it simply returns; otherwise it starts a kernel thread running `serial_keyboard_ start()` [osfmk/ppc/serial_io.c], which hands control to `serial_ keyboard_poll()` [osfmk/ppc/serial_io.c]. The latter runs forever, calling `scc_getc()` [osfmk/ppc/serial_io.c] to retrieve any characters that may be available in the serial port's buffer. The retrieved characters are fed to the keyboard monitor module by calling `cons_cinput()` [bsd/ dev/ppc/km.c]. `cons_cinput()` uses the console's `tty` structure to fetch the corresponding entry in the line-discipline switch table (the `linesw` structure) and calls the receiver interrupt function pointer (`l_rint`).

---

23. We will discuss the commpage area in Chapter 6.

- It unbinds the current thread from the master processor by calling `thread_bind()` with a `PROCESSOR_NULL` argument.

- Finally, `kernel_bootstrap_thread()` becomes the pageout daemon by calling `vm_pageout()` [osfmk/vm/vm_pageout.c]. `vm_pageout()` sets its thread's `vm_privilege` field to `TRUE`, which allows it to use reserved memory if necessary. It then adjusts its thread's priority, initializes paging parameters, adjusts some other relevant information, and runs forever in `vm_pageout_scan()` [osfmk/vm/vm_pageout.c], which implements the pageout daemon's core functionality.

5.6 I/O Kit Initialization

`PE_init_iokit()` [pexpert/ppc/pe_init.c] initializes the I/O Kit. Figure 5–14 shows its sequence of operations.

`PE_init_iokit()` first calls `PE_init_kprintf()` [pexpert/ppc/pe_kprintf.c], which was also called by `ppc_vm_init()` earlier in the startup sequence. We saw that `PE_init_kprintf()` initializes the serial port if it is present. It then calls `PE_init_printf()` [pexpert/gen/pe_gen.c], which was also called earlier during the startup, but `PE_init_iokit()` calls it with the `vm_initialized` Boolean argument set to `TRUE`. `PE_init_printf()` calls `vcattach()` [osfmk/console/video_console.c] to arrange for acquiring the screen if the bootstrap is proceeding in nongraphical mode, in which case it also uses `vcputc()` [osfmk/console/video_console.c] to print messages in the kernel's log buffer for kernel `printf()` calls.

`PE_init_iokit()` uses `DTLookupEntry()` [pexpert/gen/device_tree.c] to look up the /chosen/memory-map entry in the device tree. If the lookup succeeds, the `BootCLUT` and `Pict-FailedBoot` properties are retrieved from the entry. `BootCLUT` is the 8-bit boot-time color lookup table that was passed to the kernel by BootX. `Pict-FailedBoot`—also passed to the kernel by BootX—is the picture shown if booting fails. You can examine this portion of the device tree by using one of the I/O Registry tools:

```
$ ioreg -S -p IODeviceTree -n memory-map | less
+-o Root  <class IORegistryEntry>
  +-o device-tree  <class IOPlatformExpertDevice>
    +-o chosen  <class IOService>
    | +-o memory-map  <class IOService>
    |     "Kernel-__VECTORS" = <0000000000007000>
```

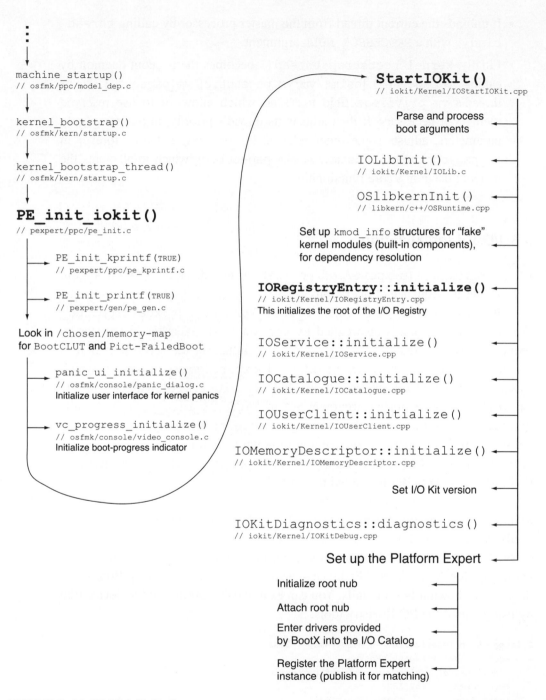

FIGURE 5–14 I/O Kit initialization

```
    |        "Kernel-__PRELINK" = <0043700000874000>
    |        "AAPL,phandle" = <ffa26f00>
    |        "Pict-FailedBoot" = <00d7a00000004020>
    |        "BootArgs" = <00d78000000001fc>
    |        "Kernel-__DATA" = <0035d000000a0000>
    |        "BootCLUT" = <00d7900000000300>
    |        "Kernel-__HIB" = <0000700000007000>
    |        "name" = <"memory-map">
    |        "Kernel-__TEXT" = <0000e0000034f000>
    |    }
    |
...
```

If BootCLUT is found, PE_init_iokit() copies its contents to appleClut8, the default Mac OS X color lookup table. It then calls panic_ui_initialize() [osfmk/console/panic_dialog.c], which sets the active CLUT pointer.

It is possible to replace the default panic picture either by recompiling the kernel with another picture or by dynamically loading a new picture through a sysctl interface. Moreover, the kernel also allows the panic user interface to be tested without inducing an actual panic. An image to be used as the panic picture must be converted either to a C structure that can be compiled into the kernel or to a kernel-loadable file. The genimage.c and qtif2kraw.c files in osfmk/console/panic_ui/ contain sources for utilities that convert an uncompressed Quick-Time RAW image file into a C structure and a loadable RAW file, respectively. Arbitrary image formats can be converted to QuickTime RAW—a .qtif file—using QuickTime facilities, among other tools. Figure 5–15 shows an example of replacing the kernel's default panic image by loading a new one from user space.

FIGURE 5–15 Loading a replacement panic user interface image into the kernel

```
$ sips -g all image.qtif
...
  typeIdentifier: com.apple.quicktime-image
  format: qtif
  ...
  bitsPerSample: 8
  hasAlpha: no
  space: RGB
  profile: Generic RGB Profile
$ qtif2kraw -i image.qtif -o image.kraw
Verifying image file...
Image info: width: 640 height: 480 depth: 8...
Converting image file to 8 bit raw...
Converted 307200 pixels...
```

(continues)

FIGURE 5–15 Loading a replacement panic user interface image into the kernel *(continued)*

```
Found 307200 color matches in CLUT...
Encoding image file...
Writing to binary panic dialog file image.kraw, which is suitable for loading into
kernel...
$ cat load_panic_image.c
// load_panic_image.c

#define PROGNAME "load_panic_image"

#include <stdio.h>
#include <stdlib.h>
#include <unistd.h>
#include <fcntl.h>
#include <sys/types.h>
#include <sys/stat.h>
#include <sys/sysctl.h>

int
main(int argc, char **argv)
{
    int     ret, fd;
    char    *buf;
    size_t  oldlen = 0, newlen;
    struct  stat sb;
    int     mib[3] = { CTL_KERN, KERN_PANICINFO, KERN_PANICINFO_IMAGE };

    if (argc != 2) {
        fprintf(stderr, "usage: %s <kraw image file path>\n", PROGNAME);
        exit(1);
    }

    if (stat(argv[1], &sb) < 0) {
        perror("stat");
        exit(1);
    }

    newlen = sb.st_size;
    buf = (char *)malloc(newlen); // assume success

    fd = open(argv[1], O_RDONLY); // assume success
    ret = read(fd, buf, sb.st_size); // assume success
    close(fd);

    if (sysctl(mib, 3, NULL, (void *)&oldlen, buf, newlen))
        perror("sysctl");

    exit(ret);
}
$ gcc -Wall -o load_panic_image load_panic_image.c
$ sudo ./load_panic_image ./image.kraw
```

You can cause the kernel to display the panic user interface through another sysctl, as shown in Figure 5–16.

FIGURE 5–16 Testing the panic user interface

```
// panic_test.c

#include <stdlib.h>
#include <sys/types.h>
#include <sys/sysctl.h>


#define KERN_PANICINFO_TEST (KERN_PANICINFO_IMAGE + 2)

int
main(void)
{
    int ret;
    size_t oldnewlen = 0;
    int mib[3] = { CTL_KERN, KERN_PANICINFO, KERN_PANICINFO_TEST };

    ret = sysctl(mib, 3, NULL, (void *)&oldnewlen, NULL, oldnewlen);

    exit(ret);
}
```

Next, `PE_init_iokit()` calls `vc_progress_initialize()` [osfmk/ console/video_console.c] to initialize the rotating gearwheel boot-progress indicator. The image for the wheel is 32×32 pixels in size. It animates at 24 frames per second. Image data for the animation frames resides in `pexpert/pexpert/ GearImage.h`. The kernel calls `vc_progress_set()` [osfmk/console/ video_console.c] to toggle the animation on or off. When enabled, it arranges for `vc_progress_task()` [osfmk/console/video_console.c] to be scheduled to run via a callout.

`PE_init_ioikit()` finally calls `StartIOKit()` [iokit/Kernel/ IOStartIOKit.cpp], passing it pointers to the device tree's root and the boot arguments.

`StartIOKit()` calls `IOLibInit()` [iokit/Kernel/IOLib.c] to initialize the I/O Kit's basic runtime environment. `IOLibInit()` creates a submap of the kernel map for use as the I/O Kit pageable space map. The size of this allocation is `kIOPageableMapSize` (96MB). A structure of type `gIOKitPageableSpace` and a queue of contiguous malloc entries are also initialized. The `IOMalloc- Contiguous()` [iokit/Kernel/IOLib.c] function uses the latter.

StartIOKit() calls OSlibkernInit() [libkern/c++/OSRuntime.cpp]
to initialize the I/O Kit C++ runtime environment. OSlibkernInit() calls
getmachheaders() [osfmk/mach-o/mach_header.c] to fetch the address of
the link-editor-defined _mh_execute_header symbol as the first element of an
array of mach_header structures. The address so retrieved is set as the starting
address of the libkern library's kmod_info structure [osfmk/mach/kmod.h].

> While linking a Mach-O file, the link editor defines a symbol called
> _MH_EXECUTE_SYM, which is defined to be the string "__mh_
> execute_header". This symbol, which appears only in a Mach-O
> executable, is the address of the Mach header in the executable.
> Moreover, the symbol is absolute and is not part of any section.

OSlibkernInit() then provides a pointer to the kmod_info structure as an
argument to OSRuntimeInitializeCPP() [libkern/c++/OSRuntime.cpp],
which scans all segments listed in the kernel's Mach header, looking for sections
named __constructor. Upon finding such sections, it invokes the constructors.
If it fails, it calls OSRuntimeUnloadCPPForSegment() [libkern/c++/
OSRuntime.cpp], which looks for sections named __destructor in the segment and invokes the corresponding destructors.

```
$ otool -l /mach_kernel
...
Section
  sectname __constructor
   segname __TEXT
      addr 0x0035c858
      size 0x000000f4
    offset 3467352
     align 2^2 (4)
    reloff 0
    nreloc 0
     flags 0x00000000
 reserved1 0
 reserved2 0
Section
  sectname __destructor
   segname __TEXT
      addr 0x0035c94c
      size 0x000000f0
    offset 3467596
     align 2^2 (4)
    reloff 0
    nreloc 0
```

```
    flags 0x00000000
reserved1 0
reserved2 0
...
```

Kernel extensions explicitly declare their dependencies on other kernel components,[24] which may be other kernel extensions, or abstract "extensions" such as the Mach component, the BSD component, the I/O Kit, and so on. StartIOKit() fabricates kmod_info structures for such fictitious extensions, examples of which include the following ones defined by the gIOKernelMods string in iokit/KernelConfigTables.cpp:

```
const char *gIOKernelKmods =
"{"
    "'com.apple.kernel'                      = '';"
    "'com.apple.kpi.bsd'                     = '';"
    "'com.apple.kpi.iokit'                   = '';"
    "'com.apple.kpi.libkern'                 = '';"
    "'com.apple.kpi.mach'                    = '';"
    "'com.apple.kpi.unsupported'             = '';"
    "'com.apple.iokit.IONVRAMFamily'         = '';"
    "'com.apple.driver.AppleNMI'             = '';"
    "'com.apple.iokit.IOSystemManagementFamily' = '';"
    "'com.apple.iokit.ApplePlatformFamily'   = '';"
    "'com.apple.kernel.6.0'                  = '7.9.9';"
    "'com.apple.kernel.bsd'                  = '7.9.9';"
    "'com.apple.kernel.iokit'                = '7.9.9';"
    "'com.apple.kernel.libkern'              = '7.9.9';"
    "'com.apple.kernel.mach'                 = '7.9.9';"
"}";
```

> The gIOKernelMods string represents a serialized data structure consisting of key-value pairs (i.e., an OSDictionary). StartIOKit() unserializes it to iterate over the list of fictitious extensions.

> The fictitious extensions (also called *pseudo-extensions*) are implemented as plug-ins within the System kernel extension (System.kext), which contains no executable code for any of the extensions—each plug-in extension contains an information property list file (Info.plist), a version property list file (version.plist), and for some extensions, a Mach-O object file containing only a table of exported symbols.

---

24. We will look at details of kernel extensions in Chapter 10.

StartIOKit() initializes the IORegistry class by calling IORegistry-Entry::initialize() [iokit/Kernel/IORegistryEntry.cpp], which returns a pointer to the root of the I/O Registry. It also initializes the IOService, IOCatalogue, IOUserClient, and IOMemoryDescriptor classes by calling their initialize() methods, which allocate and set up locks, queues, and other class-specific data structures.

StartIOKit() calls IOKitDiagnostics::diagnostics() [iokit/Kernel/IOKitDebug.cpp] to instantiate the IOKitDiagnostics class, which provides I/O Kit debugging functionality such as the ability to print dumps of I/O Kit planes[25] and memory. A serialized version of this class resides in the I/O Registry as the IOKitDiagnostics property.

Finally, StartIOKit() instantiates the IOPlatformExpertDevice class [iokit/Kernel/IOPlatformExpert.cpp]. The resultant instance is the I/O Kit's root nub, which is then initialized by a call to the initWithArgs() method, followed by a call to the attach() method. initWithArgs() creates and initializes a new IOWorkLoop object for the Platform Expert. It also saves the arguments it received as the root nub's IOPlatformArgs property.

```
// iokit/Kernel/IOPlatformExpert.cpp

bool
IOPlatformExpertDevice::initWithArgs(void *dtTop, void *p2, void *p3, void *p4)
{
    IORegistryEntry *dt = 0;
    void            *argsData[4];
    bool             ok;

    if (dtTop && (dt = IODeviceTreeAlloc(dtTop)))
        ok = super::init(dt, gIODTplane);
    else
        ok = super::init();

    if (!ok)
        return false;

    workLoop = IOWorkLoop::workLoop();
    if (!workLoop)
        return false;

    argsData[ 0 ] = dtTop;
    argsData[ 1 ] = p2;
```

---

25. We will discuss I/O Kit planes and several other aspects of the I/O Kit in Chapter 10.

```
    argsData[ 2 ] = p3;
    argsData[ 3 ] = p4;

    setProperty("IOPlatformArgs", (void *)argsData, sizeof(argsData));

    return true;
}
...
```

Note that the `IOPlatformExpertDevice` class inherits from `IOService`, which inherits from `IORegistryEntry`. The latter implements the `setProperty()` method.

`StartIOKit()` calls the `recordStartupExtensions()` [iokit/Kernel/ IOCatalogue.cpp] method of the `IOCatalogue` class instance to build dictionaries for the startup extensions put into memory by BootX. The dictionaries are recorded in a startup extensions dictionary. The recording is performed by calling the function pointed to by the `record_startup_extensions_function` pointer, which points to the `recordStartupExtensions()` function implemented in `libsa/catalogue.cpp`. The resultant dictionary has the following format:

```
{
    "plist" = /* extension's Info.plist file as an OSDictionary */
    "code"  = /* extension's executable file as an OSData */
}
```

`StartIOKit()` finally calls the root nub's `registerService()` method, which is implemented in the `IOService` class. Consequently, the I/O Kit matching process starts as the root nub is published for matching.

5.7 BSD Initialization

As we saw in Figure 5–11, before becoming the pageout daemon, the kernel bootstrap thread calls `bsd_init()` [bsd/kern/bsd_init.c], which initializes the BSD portion of the Mac OS X kernel and eventually passes control to user space. Figure 5–17 shows `bsd_init()`'s sequence of actions.

5.7.1 Miscellaneous BSD Initialization (Part 1)

bsd_init() allocates the kernel funnel using funnel_alloc() [bsd/kern/thread.c]. It then acquires the kernel funnel. Although the funnel mechanism is deprecated in Mac OS X 10.4, it is still present for backward compatibility.[26]

bsd_init() next prints the well-known BSD copyright message, which is defined in bsd/kern/bsd_init.c.

```
char copyright[] =
"Copyright (c) 1982, 1986, 1989, 1991, 1993\n\t"
"The Regents of the University of California. "
"All rights reserved.\n\n";
```

kmeminit() [bsd/kern/kern_malloc.c] initializes the BSD-specific kernel memory allocator. This allocator designates each type of memory with a numerical value, where "type" represents the purpose of the memory as specified by the caller. Some types have their own Mach allocator zones from which that type of memory is allocated. Other types either share another type's Mach zone or use an appropriate power-of-2-sized kalloc zone.

parse_bsd_args() [bsd/kern/bsd_init.c] retrieves BSD-related arguments from the boot command line. Some of these arguments affect allocation sizes of certain BSD data structures, whereas the others are eventually forwarded to the "init" program started by the kernel.

kauth_init() [bsd/kern/kern_authorization.c] initializes the kauth centralized authorization subsystem. It initializes its constituent modules by calling kauth_cred_init() [bsd/kern/kern_credential.c], kauth_identity_init() [bsd/kern/kern_credential.c], kauth_groups_init() [bsd/kern/kern_credential.c], kauth_scope_init() [bsd/kern/kern_authorization.c], and kauth_resolver_init() [bsd/kern/kern_credential.c].

procinit() [bsd/kern/kern_proc.c] initializes the following global process-related data structures: the list of all processes (allproc); the list of zombie processes (zombproc); and hash tables for process identifiers (pidhashtbl), process groups (pgrphashtbl), and user identifiers (uihashtbl).

bsd_init() then initializes various aspects of process 0. Unlike subsequent processes, the data structures of process 0—such as structures related to its credentials, open files, accounting, statistics, process limits, and signal actions—are statically allocated and never freed. Moreover, process 0 is handcrafted—

---

26. We will look at funnels in Chapter 9.

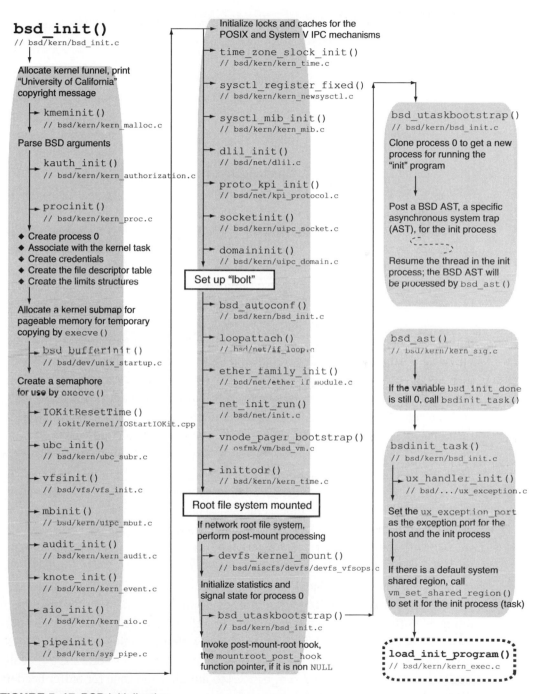

FIGURE 5–17 BSD initialization

> Prior to Mac OS X 10.4, `bsd_init()` also allocates the network fun-
> nel, which is not used in 10.4.

`bsd_init()` associates it with the already existent kernel task (`kernel_task`). Its name is explicitly set to `kernel_task`, and its process ID is set to 0. It is placed at the head of the `allproc` list. The `chgproccnt()` [bsd/kern/kern_proc.c] function is called to increment the count of processes owned by root (user ID 0).

`bsd_init()` allocates a submap from the kernel map to use for BSD-related pageable memory. The size of this map is `BSD_PAGABLE_MAP_SIZE` (defined to be 8MB in `bsd/kern/bsd_init.c`). The map is used by `execve()` [bsd/kern/kern_exec.c] to allocate a buffer into which it copies in (from user space) the first argument of `execve()`—that is, the path, which is used in the kernel's working set caching mechanism and for supporting the launching of `.app` applications. `bsd_init()` also initializes the `execve()` semaphore, which is used while allocating and freeing space for saved arguments.

`bsd_init()` calls `bsd_bufferinit()` [bsd/dev/unix_startup.c], which calls `bsd_startupearly()` [bsd/dev/unix_startup.c]. The latter allocates a submap of the kernel map and then allocates kernel memory into this map using the kernel object (`kernel_object`). `bsd_startupearly()` also computes the values of parameters related to buffer management for networking and cluster I/O, making additional adjustments unless the machine's physical memory is less than 64MB. For example, it attempts to scale the values of `tcp_sendspace` and `tcp_recvspace`, the default send and receive window sizes for TCP, respectively, up to a maximum.

`bsd_bufferinit()` allocates another submap (`mb_map`) of the kernel map that is used for allocating mbuf clusters. This map's size is the product of `nmbclusters` and `MCLBYTES`, which are initialized to 2048 and 512, respectively, in `bsd/ppc/param.h` but may be adjusted during kernel startup. Finally, `bsd_bufferinit()` calls `bufinit()` [bsd/vfs/vfs_bio.c] to initialize file system buffers and related data structures. `bufinit()` also initializes `bcleanbuf_thread` [bsd/vfs/vfs_bio.c], the buffer laundry thread, which removes buffers from the queue containing buffers that need cleaning and performs asynchronous blocking write operations with their contents. This initialization allows the BSD layer to read disk labels. Moreover, `bufinit()` calls `bufzoneinit()` [bsd/vfs/vfs_bio.c] to initialize the zone for buffer headers (`buf_hdr_zone`).

IOKitResetTime() [iokit/Kernel/IOStartIOKit.cpp] calls
IOService::waitForService() [iokit/Kernel/IOService.cpp] to wait
for the IORTC (real-time clock) and IONVRAM (Open Firmware nonvolatile
memory) services to be matched and published. It then calls clock_
initialize_calendar() [osfmk/ppc/rtclock.c] to initialize the calendar
clock based on the platform clock.

5.7.2 File System Initialization

At this point, bsd_init() starts file-system-related initialization. It calls ubc_
init() [bsd/kern/ubc_subr.c] to initialize the zone (ubc_info_zone) for
the unified buffer cache (UBC), which unifies buffering of vnodes with virtual
memory (Mach VM objects, specifically). The zone has 10,000 elements, the size
of each being the size of the ubc_info structure [bsd/sys/ubc.h].

bsd_init() then calls vfsinit() [bsd/vfs/vfs_init.c], which initializes the vnode structures and each built-in file system type. The specific
actions performed by vfs_init() include the following.

- It allocates various file system locks—for example, the lock for the list of
  mounted file systems.

- It sets the *console user* to have the user ID 0. The console user, whose identity is used for access purposes, is the owner of files and directories whose
  on-disk permissions are ignored. Typically, the console user is the currently
  logged-in user.

- It calls vntblinit() [bsd/vfs/vfs_subr.c] to initialize the lists of free
  vnodes (vnode_free_list), inactive vnodes (vnode_inactive_list),
  and mounted file systems (mountlist). It also initializes the vnodetarget
  variable, which represents the number of vnodes the kernel expects to get
  back from the inactive vnode list and VM object cache. When the number of
  free vnodes falls below VNODE_FREE_MIN (defined to be 300 in bsd/vfs/
  vfs_subr.c), vnreclaim() [bsd/vfs/vfs_subr.c] is called to reclaim
  some—desirably vnodetarget—vnodes from the inactive list and the VM
  object cache. vntblinit() calls adjust_vm_object_cache() [osfmk/
  vm/vm_object.c] to scale the size of the VM object cache to accommodate the number of vnodes the kernel wants to cache, which is the difference
  between desiredvnodes and VNODE_FREE_MIN. The formula for computing desiredvnodes is defined in bsd/conf/param.c.

- It calls `vfs_event_init()` [bsd/vfs/vfs_subr.c] to initialize a list of `knote` structures [bsd/sys/event.h] that will be used for the file system event mechanism.

- It calls `nchinit()` [bsd/vfs/vfs_cache.c] to initialize data structures used for vnode name caching—for example, a hash table of strings and a table of 32-bit checksum remainders.

- It calls `journal_init()` [bsd/vfs/vfs_journal.c] to initialize locks used by the VFS journaling mechanism.

- It calls `vfs_op_init()` [bsd/vfs/vfs_init.c], which initializes known vnode operations vectors by setting them to `NULL`. `vfs_op_init()` calculates the number of operations that exist by counting the contents of the `vfs_op_descs` table, which is defined in bsd/vfs/vnode_if.c. This is followed by a call to `vfs_opv_init()` [bsd/vfs/vfs_init.c], which allocates and populates the operations vectors.[27]

- It iterates over the static list (`vfsconf`) of defined file system types and invokes each file system's initialization function—that is, the `vfs_init()` member of the `vfc_vfsops` field of the `vfsconf` structure.

- It calls `vnode_authorize_init()` [bsd/vfs/vfs_subr.c], which registers the vnode scope—KAUTH_SCOPE_VNODE, defined to be the string "com.apple.kauth.vnode"—with the kauth authorization mechanism.[28] This scope is used for all authorizations within the VFS layer. The listener callback function for the scope is `vnode_authorize_callback()` [bsd/vfs/vfs_subr.c].

5.7.3 Miscellaneous BSD Initialization (Part 2)

`bsd_init()` calls `mbinit()` [bsd/kern/uipc_mbuf.c] to initialize mbufs, the memory buffers typically used by the networking subsystem. `mbinit()` allocates memory and initializes locks, statistics, reference counts, and so on. It also calls `IOMapperIOVMAlloc()` [iokit/Kernel/IOMapper.cpp], which determines whether the system-wide I/O bus mapper exists and, if it does, registers the number of memory pages assigned to the mbuf cluster pool with it. Moreover, `mbinit()` starts a kernel thread running `mbuf_expand_thread()` [bsd/kern/

---

27. We will look at details of these data structures in Chapter 11.

28. We will look at details of this mechanism in Chapter 11.

uipc_mbuf.c] in the kernel task, with the purpose of growing the cluster pool if the number of free clusters becomes low.

audit_init() [bsd/kern/kern_audit.c] initializes the kernel's audit event table, audit memory zone, associated data structures, and the BSM audit subsystem.[29] It calls kau_init() [bsd/kern/kern_bsm_audit.c] to initialize the latter, which, among other things, calls au_evclassmap_init() [bsd/kern/kern_bsm_klib.c] to set up the initial audit-event-to-event-class mapping for system calls. For example, an event called AUE_OPEN_R (defined in bsd/bsm/audit_kevents.h) is mapped to an event class called AU_FREAD (defined in bsd/sys/audit.h). audit_init() also initializes a zone (audit_zone) for audit records. Note that audit logging is not initiated until the user-space audit daemon—auditd—is started.

knote_init() [bsd/kern/kern_event.c] initializes a zone (knote_zone) for the kqueue kernel event notification mechanism. It also allocates kqueue-related locks.

aio_init() [bsd/kern/kern_aio.c] initializes the asynchronous I/O (AIO) subsystem. This includes initialization of locks, queues, statistics, and an AIO work queue zone (aio_workq_zonep) for AIO work queue entries. aio_init() creates AIO worker threads by calling _aio_create_worker_threads() [bsd/kern/kern_aio.c]. The number of threads created is contained in the variable aio_worker_threads [bsd/conf/param.c], which is initialized to the constant AIO_THREAD_COUNT (defined to be 4 in bsd/conf/param.c). An AIO worker thread runs the function aio_work_thread() [bsd/kern/kern_aio.c].

pipeinit() [bsd/kern/sys_pipe.c] initializes a zone (pipe_zone) for pipe data structures and allocates locking data structures.

bsd_init() now initializes locks for the POSIX and System V IPC mechanisms. Moreover, it calls pshm_cache_init() [bsd/kern/posix_shm.c] and psem_cache_init() [bsd/kern/posix_sem.c] to initialize hash tables for storing hash values of looked-up names of POSIX shared memory and semaphores, respectively.

bsd_init() then calls time_zone_slock_init() [bsd/kern/kern_time.c] to initialize tz_slock, a simple lock used for accessing the global time zone structure, tz, which is defined in bsd/conf/param.c. The lock is used by the gettimeofday() and settimeofday() calls.

---

29. BSM stands for Basic Security Module. We will look at the implementation details of the audit subsystem in Chapter 6.

Next, `bsd_init()` calls `sysctl_register_fixed()` [bsd/kern/kern_newsysctl.c] to register sysctl object IDs from the statically defined sysctl lists, such as `newsysctl_list` [bsd/kern/sysctl_init.c] and `machdep_sysctl_list` (bsd/dev/ppc/sysctl.c). This includes creating and populating top-level sysctl nodes such as `kern`, `hw`, `machdep`, `net`, `debug`, and `vfs`. `bsd_init()` then calls `sysctl_mib_init()` [bsd/kern/kern_mib.c] to populate optional sysctls.

5.7.4 Networking Subsystem Initialization

At this point, `bsd_init()` starts initialization of the networking subsystem. `dlil_init()` [bsd/net/dlil.c] initializes the data link interface layer (DLIL). This includes initializing queues for data link interfaces, interface families, and protocol families. `dlil_init()` also starts the DLIL input thread (`dlil_input_thread()` [bsd/net/dlil.c]) and another thread for invoking delayed detachment[30] of protocols, protocols filters, and interface filters (`dlil_call_delayed_detach_thread()` [bsd/net/dlil.c]).

The input thread services two input queues of mbufs: one for the loopback[31] interface and the other for nonloopback interfaces. For each packet, it invokes `dlil_input_packet()` [bsd/net/dlil.c] with three arguments: the interface the packet was received on, an mbuf pointer for the packet, and a pointer to the packet header. Finally, the input thread calls `proto_input_run()` [bsd/net/kpi_protocol.c], which first handles any pending attachment or detachment[32] of protocol input handler functions and then iterates over all existing protocol input entries, looking for those with a nonempty chain of packets. It calls `proto_delayed_inject()` [bsd/net/kpi_protocol.c] on entries that have packets to input.

`proto_kpi_init()` [bsd/net/kpi_protocol.c] allocates locking data structures used by the protocol code in bsd/net/kpi_protocol.c.

`socketinit()` [bsd/kern/uipc_socket.c] allocates locking data structures and initializes a zone (`so_cache_zone`) for the kernel's socket-caching mechanism. It also arranges for `so_cache_timer()` [bsd/kern/uipc_socket.c] to run periodically. The latter frees cached socket structures whose timestamps are older than the current timestamp by `SO_CACHE_TIME_LIMIT`

---

30. The detachment is delayed if it is not safe to detach.

31. Mac OS X supports only one loopback interface.

32. If an input handler is already registered, it is detached.

[bsd/sys/socketvar.h] or more. This caching mechanism allows process control blocks to be reused for sockets cached in the socket layer.

domaininit() [bsd/kern/uipc_domain.c] first creates a list of all available communications domains. It then calls init_domain() [bsd/kern/uipc_domain.c] on each available domain. Figure 5–18 depicts the domain and protocol initialization performed by these functions.

FIGURE 5–18 Domain and protocol initialization

```
// bsd/sys/domain.h

struct domain {
    int             dom_family;     // AF_xxx
    char            *dom_name;      // string name
    void            (*dom_init)__P((void)); // initialization routine
    ...
    struct protosw *dom_protosw;    // chain of protosw structures
    struct domain  *dom_next;       // next domain on chain
    ...
};

// bsd/kern/uipc_domain.c

void
domaininit()
{
    register struct domain *dp;
    ...
    extern struct domain localdomain, routedomain, ndrvdo-main, ...;
    ...

    // Initialize locking data structures
    ...

    // Put them all on the global domain list
    concat_domain(&localdomain);
    concat_domain(&routedomain);
    ...

    // Initialize each domain
    for (dp = domains; dp; dp = dp->dom_next)
        init_domain(dp);
    ...
    timeout(pffasttimo, NULL, 1);
    timeout(pfslowtimo, NULL, 1);
}
...
```

(continues)

FIGURE 5–18 Domain and protocol initialization *(continued)*

```
void
init_domain(register struct domain *dp)
{
    ...

    // Call domain's initialization function
    if (dp->dom_init)
        (*dp->dom_init)();

    // Initialize the currently installed protocols in this domain
    for (pr = dp->dom_protosw; pr; pr = pr->pr_next) {
        if (pr->pr_usrreqs == 0)
            panic("domaininit: %ssw[%d] has no usrreqs!",
                    dp->dom_name, (int)(pr - dp->dom_protosw));

        if (pr->pr_init)
            (*pr->pr_init)();
    }
    ...
}
...


void
pfslowtimo(void *arg)
{
    // For each protocol within each domain, if the protocol has a
    // pr_slowtimo() function, call it.
    //
    // Moreover, if do_reclaim is TRUE, also call each protocol's
    // pr_drain() if it has one.
    ...
    timeout(pfslowtimo, NULL, hz/2);
}

void
pffasttimo(void *arg)
{
    // For each protocol within each domain, if the protocol has a
    // pr_fasttimo() function, call it.
    ...
    timeout(pffasttimo, NULL, hz/5);


}
```

---

init_domain() calls the initialization routine—if one exists—for the domain. It then uses the domain structure's dom_protosw field to retrieve the chain of protocol switch structures supported for the address family represented by the domain. It iterates over the list of protosw structures [bsd/sys/protosw.h], calling each installed protocol's initialization routine (the pr_init field of the protosw structure). init_domain() also looks at the domain's protocol header length (the dom_protohdrlen field of the domain structure), and, if needed, updates the values of the following global variables: max_linkhdr (largest link-level header systemwide), max_protohdr (largest protocol header systemwide), max_hdr (largest system/protocol pair systemwide), and max_datalen (the difference of MHLEN and max_hdr, where MHLEN is computed in bsd/sys/mbuf.h).

5.7.5 Miscellaneous BSD Initialization (Part 3)

bsd_init() sets process 0's root directory and current directory pointers to NULL. Note that the root device has not been mounted yet.

bsd_init() then calls thread_wakeup() to wake threads sleeping on lbolt, the global once-a-second sleep address. Next, it calls timeout() [bsd/kern/kern_clock.c] to start running lightning_bolt() [bsd/kern/bsd_init.c], which will continue to call thread_wakeup() on lbolt every second. lightning_bolt() also calls klogwakeup() [bsd/kern/subr_log.c], which checks whether any log entries are pending, and if so, it calls logwakeup() [bsd/kern/subr_log.c] to notify any processes (such as system loggers) that may be waiting for log output.

```
// bsd/kern/bsd_init.c

void
lightning_bolt()
{
    boolean_t   funnel_state;
    extern void klogwakeup(void);

    funnel_state = thread_funnel_set(kernel_flock, TRUE);

    thread_wakeup(&lbolt);
    timeout(lightning_bolt, 0, hz);
    klogwakeup();

    (void)thread_funnel_set(kernel_flock, FALSE);
}
```

bsd_init() calls bsd_autoconf() [bsd/kern/bsd_init.c], which first calls kminit() [bsd/dev/ppc/km.c] to tell BSD's keyboard (input) and monitor (output) module to flag itself initialized. It then initializes the pseudo-devices by iterating over the `pseudo_inits` array of `pseudo_init` structures [`bsd/dev/busvar.h`] and calling each element's `ps_func` function. The `pseudo_inits` array is generated at compile time by the `config` utility:

```
// build/obj/RELEASE_PPC/bsd/RELEASE/ioconf.c

#include <dev/busvar.h>

extern pty_init();
extern vndevice_init();
extern mdevinit();
extern bpf_init();
extern fsevents_init();
extern random_init();

struct pseudo_init pseudo_inits[] = {
        128,    pty_init,
        4,      vndevice_init,
        1,      mdevinit,
        4,      bpf_init,
        1,      fsevents_init,
        1,      random_init,
        0,      0,
};
```

   `bsd_autoconf()` finally calls `IOKitBSDInit()` [`iokit/bsddev/ IOKitBSDInit.cpp`], which publishes the BSD kernel as a resource named "IOBSD".

   `bsd_init()` attaches the loopback interface by calling `loopattach()` [`bsd/net/if_loop.c`], which calls `lo_reg_if_mods()` [`bsd/net/if_ loop.c`] to register the `PF_INET` and `PF_INET6` protocol families by calling `dlil_reg_proto_module()` [`bsd/net/dlil.c`]. `loopattach()` then calls `dlil_if_attach()` [`bsd/net/dlil.c`] to attach the loopback interface, followed by a call to `bpfattach()` [`bsd/net/bpf.c`], which attaches the loopback interface to the Berkeley Packet Filter (BPF)[33] mechanism. The link layer type used in this attachment is `DLT_NULL`.

   `ether_family_init()` [`bsd/net/ether_if_module.c`] initializes the Ethernet interface family by calling `dlil_reg_if_modules()` [`bsd/net/dlil.c`]. This is followed by calls to `dlil_reg_proto_module()` [`bsd/net/dlil.c`] to

---

33. BPF provides a raw interface to data link layers independently of protocols.

register the `PF_INET` and `PF_INET6` protocol families for the Ethernet interface family. `ether_family_init()` also initializes support for IEEE 802.Q Virtual LANs (VLANs) by calling `vlan_family_init()` [bsd/net/if_vlan.c]. This creates a VLAN pseudo-device—a device in software—that uses much of the Ethernet interface family's functionality. Finally, `ether_family_init()` calls `bond_family_init()` [bsd/net/if_bond.c] to initialize support for IEEE 802.3ad Link Aggregation, which allows multiple Ethernet ports to be *bonded*, or aggregated, into a single virtual interface, with automatic load balancing across the ports.

The kernel provides an interface—the `net_init_add()` function—to register functions that will be called when the network stack is being initialized. This is useful for kernel extensions that wish to register network filters before any sockets are created or any network activity occurs in the kernel. After initializing the Ethernet interface family, `bsd_init()` calls `net_init_run()` [bsd/net/init.c] to run any such registered functions.

`vnode_pager_bootstrap()` [osfmk/vm/bsd_vm.c] initializes a zone (vnode_pager_zone) for the vnode pager's data structures. This zone has an allocation size of one page and an element size the same as that of a vnode_pager structure [osfmk/vm/bsd_vm.c]. The zone can use a maximum memory that allows for as many as `MAX_VNODE` such structures. `MAX_VNODE` is defined to be 10,000 in osfmk/vm/bsd_vm.c.

`inittodr()` [bsd/kern/kern_time.c] calls `microtime()` [bsd/kern/kern_time.c] to retrieve the calendar time value in a timeval structure [bsd/sys/time.h]. If either of the seconds or microseconds components of the structure is negative, `inittodr()` resets the calendar clock by calling `setthetime()` [bsd/kern/kern_time.c].

5.7.6 Mounting the Root File System

`bsd_init()` now initiates mounting of the root file system. As shown in Figure 5–19, it goes into an infinite loop that breaks when the root file system is successfully mounted. Within the loop, `bsd_init()` calls `setconf()` [bsd/kern/bsd_init.c], which determines the root device, including whether it is to be accessed over the network. `bsd_init()` then calls `vfs_mountroot()` [bsd/vfs/vfs_subr.c] to attempt to mount the root device.

FIGURE 5–19 Mounting the root file system

```
// bsd/kern/bsd_init.c

void
bsd_init()
{
    ...

    // Mount the root file system
    while (TRUE) {
        int err;

        setconf();
        ...
        if (0 == (err = vfs_mountroot()))
            break;
#if NFSCLIENT
        if (mountroot == netboot_mountroot) {
            printf("cannot mount network root, errno = %d\n", err);
            mountroot = NULL;
            if (0 == (err = vfs_mountroot()))
                break;
        }
#endif
        printf("cannot mount root, errno = %d\n", err);
        boothowto |= RB_ASKNAME;
    }
    ...
}
```

As shown in Figure 5–20, setconf() calls IOFindBSDRoot() [iokit/bsddev/IOKitBSDInit.cpp]—an I/O Kit function—to determine the root device. On success, IOFindBSDRoot() populates the rootdev variable that is passed to it as an argument. If IOFindBSDRoot() fails, setconf() may explicitly set the root device to /dev/sd0a as a debugging aid. setconf() also checks the value of the flags variable, because IOFindBSDRoot() sets its lowest bit in the case of the root being a network boot device. If so, setconf() sets a global function pointer—mountroot [bsd/vfs/vfs_conf.c]—to point to the function netboot_mountroot() [bsd/kern/netboot.c]. If the value of flags is 0, the mountroot pointer is set to NULL. Later, vfs_mountroot() checks whether mountroot is a valid pointer; if so, it invokes the corresponding function to attempt to mount the root file system.

FIGURE 5–20 Finding the root device with help from the I/O Kit

`// bsd/kern/bsd_init.c`

```
dev_t rootdev;        // root device major/minor number
char rootdevice[16]; // root device name
...
extern int (*mountroot) __P((void));
...
setconf()
{
    u_int32_t flags;
    ...
    err = IOFindBSDRoot(rootdevice, &rootdev, &flags);
    ...
    if (err) {
        // debugging: set root device to /dev/sd0a
        flags = 0;
    }

    if (flags & 1) {
        // root will be mounted over the network
        mountroot = netboot_mountroot;
    } else {
        // the VFS layer will query each file system to
        // determine if it can provide the root
        mountroot = NULL;
    }
}
```

Let us look at the working of `IOFindBSDRoot()`. Since `setconf()` is called in a loop, `IOFindBSDRoot()` may be called more than once. As Figure 5–21 shows, `IOFindBSDRoot()` keeps track of the number of times it has been called and sleeps for 5 seconds on the second and subsequent invocations. It checks for the presence of the `rd` and `rootdev` (in that order) boot arguments. If it finds either, it retrieves its value.

FIGURE 5–21 Doing the core work of finding the root device

`// iokit/bsddev/IOKitBSDInit.cpp`

```
kern_return_t
IOFindBSDRoot(char *rootName, dev_t *root, u_int32_t *oflags)
{
    ...
```

(continues)

FIGURE 5–21 Doing the core work of finding the root device *(continued)*

```
IOService       *service;
IORegistryEntry *regEntry;
OSDictionary    *matching = 0;
...
OSData          *data = 0;
...
UInt32           flags = 0;
int              minor, major;
bool             findHFSChild = false;
char            *mediaProperty = 0;
char            *rdBootVar;
char            *str;
const char      *look = 0;
...
bool             forceNet = false;
...
const char      *uuidStr = NULL;
static int       mountAttempts = 0;
enum { kMaxPathBuf = 512, kMaxBootVar = 128 };
...

if (mountAttempts++)
    IOSleep(5 * 1000);

// allocate memory for holding the root device path
str = (char *)IOMalloc(kMaxPathBuf + kMaxBootVar);
if (!str)
    return (kIOReturnNoMemory);
rdBootVar = str + kMaxPathBuf;

if (!PE_parse_boot_arg("rd", rdBootVar )
 && !PE_parse_boot_arg("rootdev", rdBootVar ))
    rdBootVar[0] = 0;
...
}
```

Next, `IOFindBSDRoot()` queries the I/O Registry as follows.

- It checks whether the `/chosen` node contains the `boot-uuid` property. If so, it sets the `matching` dictionary to that of the `boot-uuid-media` property of the `IOResources` class.

- If the previous step failed, it looks for the `rootpath` property of `/chosen`. If the property is found, it sets the `look` variable to point to the property's data.

- If the previous step failed, it looks for the boot-file property of /options. If the property is found, it sets the look variable to point to the property's data.

- If the first character of the user-specified root device, if any, is the asterisk character, it indicates that the root device should not be network-based. It sets the forceNet variable to false and increments the look pointer by one character. Consequently, it will attempt to parse the specified root device from the next character onward. Moreover, it will not consider the value it may have retrieved from /chosen or /options in the previous steps.

- If there is no asterisk character in the user-specified root device, it looks for the /net-boot property in the device tree. If the property is found, forceNet is set to true.

IOFindBSDRoot() then checks for the property named RAMDisk in the /chosen/memory-map node. If the property is found, its data specifies the base address and size of a RAM disk. IOFindBSDRoot() calls mdevadd() [bsd/dev/memdev.c] to find a free RAM disk slot and add a pseudo disk device whose path is of the form /dev/mdx, where x is a single-digit hexadecimal number. Note that if IOFindBSDRoot() is called multiple times, it builds the RAM disk only once—the first time it is called. For a RAM disk to be used as the root device, the root device specification in the boot arguments must contain the BSD name of the RAM disk device to use. IOFindBSDRoot() then checks whether the contents of rdBootVar are of the form /dev/mdx, and if so, it calls mdevlookup() [bsd/dev/memdev.c] to retrieve the device number—a dev_t data type that encodes the major and minor numbers—from the device ID (the x in mdx). If a RAM disk device is found, IOFindBSDRoot() sets the outgoing flags (oflags) value to 0, indicating that this is not a network root device, and returns success.

If the look pointer is nonzero, that is, if IOFindBSDRoot() had previously found content in either rootpath (/chosen) or boot-file (/options), IOFindBSDRoot() checks the content to see if it begins with the string "enet". If so, it deems the root as a network device; otherwise, it defaults to a disk device. However, if forceNet is true, IOFindBSDRoot() also treats the content as a network device.

In the case of a network device, IOFindBSDRoot() calls IONetwork-NamePrefixMatching() [iokit/bsddev/IOKitBSDInit.cpp] to retrieve the matching dictionary for the device. In the case of a disk, it calls IODiskMatching() [iokit/bsddev/IOKitBSDInit.cpp] instead. If this retrieval fails, it tries a few other alternatives—such as the following—to construct a matching dictionary for the root device.

- If the first two characters of the root specifier are `'e'` and `'n'`, it calls `IONetworkNamePrefixMatching()` [iokit/bsddev/IOKitBSDInit.cpp] on the less restrictive prefix `"en"`.

- If the root specifier contains the prefix `"cdrom"`, it calls `IOCDMatching()` [iokit/bsddev/IOKitBSDInit.cpp]. Note that in the case of a CD-ROM, `IOFindBSDRoot()` later attempts to look for an `Apple_HFS` partition type on the device.

- If the root specifier is the string `"uuid"`, it looks for the `boot-uuid` boot argument, which must specify the UUID of the boot volume.

- In the absence of a more specific root device, it calls `IOBSDNameMatching()` [iokit/bsddev/IOKitBSDInit.cpp] to look for a device of any kind with the specified BSD name.

- If all else fails, it calls `IOService::serviceMatching()` [iokit/Kernel/IOService.cpp] to match any type of storage media device with the content type `Apple_HFS`.

`IOFindBSDRoot()` then goes into a loop, calling `IOService::wait-ForService()` with the matching dictionary it has constructed. It waits for the matching service to be published with a timeout of `ROOTDEVICETIMEOUT` (60 seconds). If the service fails to get published, or if this is the tenth time `IOFindBSDRoot()` is being called, a failed boot icon is displayed, followed by a "Still waiting for root device" log message.

If an `Apple_HFS` "child" was explicitly requested, such as in the case of a CD-ROM device, `IOFindBSDRoot()` waits for child services to finish registering and calls `IOFindMatchingChild()` [iokit/bsddev/IOKitBSDInit.cpp] on the parent service to look for a child service whose `Content` property is `Apple_HFS`. Alternatively, if the boot volume was specified via its UUID, `IOFindBSDRoot()` looks for the `boot-uuid-media` property of the service it has found.

`IOFindBSDRoot()` checks whether the matched service corresponds to a network interface—that is, whether it is a subclass of `IONetworkInterface`. If so, it calls `IORegisterNetworkInterface()` [iokit/bsddev/IOKitBSDInit.cpp] on the service to name and register the interface with the BSD portion of the kernel. Specifically, the `IONetworkStack` service is published, and the network device's unit number and path are set as properties of this service. In the case of a non-network root device, such device registration is done later and is triggered from user space.

At this point, if IOFindBSDRoot() has a successfully matched service, it retrieves the BSD name, the BSD major number, and the BSD minor number from the service. If there is no service, IOFindBSDRoot() falls back to using en0—the primary network interface—as the root device and sets the oflags (outgoing flags) parameter's lowest bit to 1, indicating a network root device.

As shown in Figure 5–20, before setconf() returns to bsd_init(), it sets the mountroot function pointer to netboot_mountroot if a network root device was indicated, and to NULL otherwise. bsd_init() calls vfs_mountroot() [bsd/vfs/vfs_subr.c] to actually mount the root file system.

```
// bsd_init() in bsd/kern/bsd_init.c
        ...
        setconf();
        ...
        if (0 = (err = vfs_mountroot()))
            break;
#if NFSCLIENT
        if (mountroot == netboot_mountroot) {
            printf("cannot mount network root, errno - %d\n", err);
            mountroot = NULL;
            if (0 = (err = vfs_mountroot()))
                break;
        }
#endif
        ...
```

vfs_mountroot() first calls the function pointed to by the mountroot function pointer (if the pointer is not NULL) and returns the result.

```
// vfs_mountroot()
        ...
        if (mountroot != NULL) {
            error = (*mountroot)();
            return (error);
        }
        ...
```

vfs_mountroot() creates a vnode for the root file system's block device. It then iterates over the entries in vfsconf [bsd/vfs/vfs_conf.c]—the global list of configured file systems.

```
// bsd/vfs/vfs_conf.c
        ...
        static struct vfsconf vfsconflist[] = {
```

```
                    // 0: HFS/HFS Plus
                    { &hfs_vfsops, ... },

                    // 1: FFS
                    { &ufs_vfsops, ... },

                    // 2: CD9660
                    { &cd9660_vfsops, ... },

                    ...
                };
                ...
                struct vfsconf *vfsconf = vfsconflist;
                ...
```

vfs_mountroot() looks at each entry of the vfsconflist array and checks whether that vfsconf structure has a valid vfc_mountroot field, which is a pointer to a function that mounts the root file system for that file system type. Since vfs_mountroot() goes through the list starting from the beginning, it attempts the HFS/HFS Plus file system first, followed by FFS,[34] and so on. In particular, for the typical case of a local, HFS Plus root file system, vfs_mountroot() will call hfs_mountroot() [bsd/hfs/hfs_vfsops.c].

```
// vfs_mountroot() in bsd/vfs/vfs_subr.c
    ...
    for (vfsp = vfsconf; vfsp; vfsp = vfsp->vfc_next) {
        if (vfsp->vfc_mountroot == NULL)
            continue;
        ...
        if ((error = (*vfsp->vfc_mountroot)(...)) == 0) {
            ...
            return (0);
        }
        vfs_rootmountfailed(mp);

        if (error != EINVAL)
         printf("%s_mountroot failed: %d\n", vfsp>vfc_name, error);
    }
    ...
```

In the case of a network root device, netboot_mountroot() [bsd/kern/netboot.c] is called. It first determines the root device—the network interface to use—by calling find_interface() [bsd/kern/netboot.c]. Unless the rootdevice global variable contains a valid network interface name, the list of

---

34. Berkeley Fast File System.

all network interfaces is searched for the first device that is not a loopback or a point-to-point device. If such a device is found, netboot_mountroot() brings it up. It then calls get_ip_parameters() [bsd/kern/netboot.c], which looks for the dhcp-response and bootp-response properties—in that order—of the /chosen entry in the I/O Registry. If one of these properties has any data, get_ip_parameters() calls dhcpol_parse_packet() [bsd/netinet/dhcp_options.c] to parse it as a DHCP or BOOTP packet and to retrieve the corresponding options. If successful, this provides the IP address, netmask, and router's IP address to be used for the boot. If no data was retrieved from the I/O Registry, netboot_mountroot() calls bootp() [bsd/netinet/in_bootp.c] to retrieve these parameters using BOOTP. If there is no router, netboot_mountroot() enables proxy ARP.

netboot_mountroot() then calls netboot_info_init() [bsd/kern/netboot.c] to set up root file system information, which must come from one of the following sources (in the given order):

- The rp boot argument
- The rootpath boot argument
- The bsdp-response property of /chosen
- The bootp response property of /chosen

If none of these sources provides valid information, booting fails.

A root file system for network booting can be a traditional NFS mount, or it can be a remote disk image mounted locally. The latter can use one of two mechanisms: the BSD vndevice interface (a software disk driver for vnodes) and Apple's Disk Image Controller (also called hdix). Even when a remote disk image is mounted locally, the image must still be accessed remotely, either using NFS (both vndevice and hdix) or HTTP (hdix only). The kernel prefers to use hdix, but you can force it to use vndevice by specifying vndevice=1 as a boot argument. The following are some examples of root file system specifiers for network booting (note that a literal colon character in the specifier must be escaped using a backslash character):

nfs:<IP>:<MOUNT>[:<IMAGE PATH>]

```
nfs:10.0.0.1:/Library/NetBoot/NetBootSP0:Tiger/Tiger.dmg
nfs:10.0.0.1:/Volumes/SomeVolume\:/Library/NetBoot/NetBootSP0:Tiger/Tiger.dmg
```

http://<HOST><IMAGE URL>

```
http://10.0.0.1/Images/Tiger/Tiger.dmg
```

BSD uses an I/O Kit hook—`di_root_image()` [`iokit/bsddev/DINetBootHook.cpp`]—to use the services of the Apple Disk Image Controller driver. This hook causes the `com.apple.AppleDisk-ImageController` resource to explicitly load by setting its `load` property to `true`.

Once the root file system is successfully mounted, there is exactly one entry on the list of mounted file systems. `bsd_init()` sets the `MNT_ROOTFS` bit (defined in `bsd/sys/mount.h`) of this entry to mark it as the root file system. `bsd_init()` also calls the file system's `VFS_ROOT` operation to retrieve its root vnode, a pointer to which is thereafter held in the global variable `rootvnode`. If the `VFS_ROOT` operation fails, there is a kernel panic. An additional reference to this vnode is added so that it is always busy, and consequently, cannot be normally unmounted. `bsd_init()` sets process 0's current directory vnode pointer to `rootvnode`.

If the root file system is being mounted over the network, additional setup may be required at this point in certain scenarios. The `netboot_setup()` [`bsd/kern/netboot.c`] function is called for this purpose. For example, if the root file system image is being mounted using vndevice, `netboot_mountroot()` does not actually mount the file system contained in the vndevice node—`netboot_setup()` mounts it.

5.7.7 Creating Process 1

`bsd_init()` performs the following actions after mounting the root file system.

- It sets process 0's start time and the kernel's boot time to the current time.
- It initializes process 0's running time (the `p_rtime` field of the `proc` structure) to zero.
- It calls `devfs_kernel_mount()` [`bsd/miscfs/devfs/devfs_vfsops.c`] to "manually" mount the device file system on `/dev/`.
- It calls `siginit()` [`bsd/kern/kern_sig.c`] to initialize process 0's signal state, which includes marking signals that are to be ignored.
- It calls `bsd_utaskbootstrap()` [`bsd/kern/bsd_init.c`], which arranges for the first user-space program to run.
- If there is a post-mount-root hook function—`mountroot_post_hook()`—registered with the kernel, `bsd_init()` invokes it. We saw in Chapter 4 that the BootCache kernel extension uses this hook.
- It drops the kernel funnel.

bsd_utaskbootstrap() clones a new process from process 0 by calling cloneproc() [bsd/kern/kern_fork.c], which in turn calls procdup() [bsd/kern/kern_fork.c]. Since procdup() is a BSD-level call, creating a new process results in the creation of a new Mach task with a single thread. The new process, which has a process ID of 1, is marked runnable by cloneproc(). bsd_utaskbootstrap() points the initproc global variable to this process. It then calls act_set_astbsd() [osfmk/kern/thread_act.c] on the new thread to post an asynchronous system trap (AST), with the "reason" for the trap being AST_BSD (defined in osfmk/kern/ast.h). An AST is a trap delivered to a thread when it is about to return from an interrupt context, which could have been due to an interrupt, a system call, or another trap. act_set_astbsd() calls thread_ast_set() [osfmk/kern/ast.h] to set the AST by atomically OR'ing the reason bits with the thread structure's one or more pending ASTs [osfmk/kern/thread.h]. bsd_utaskbootstrap() finishes by calling thread_resume() [osfmk/kern/thread_act.c] on the new thread, which awakens the thread.

ast_check() [osfmk/kern/ast.c] is called to check for pending ASTs—for example, in thread_quantum_expire() [osfmk/kern/priority.c], after the quantum and priority for a thread are recomputed. It propagates the thread's ASTs to the processor. Before the thread can execute, a pending AST causes ast_taken() [osfmk/kern/ast.c]—the AST handler—to be called. It handles AST_BSD as a special case by clearing the AST_BSD bit from the thread's pending ASTs and calling bsd_ast() [bsd/kern/kern_sig.c]. AST_BSD is used for other purposes besides kernel startup; therefore, bsd_ast() is called in other scenarios too. bsd_ast() maintains a Boolean flag to remember whether BSD initialization has completed and calls bsdinit_task() [bsd/kern/bsd_init.c] the first time it is called.

```
// bsd/kern/kern_sig.c

void
bsd_ast(thread_act_t thr_act)
{
    ...
    static bsd_init_done = 0;
    ...
    if (!bsd_init_done) {
        extern void bsdinit_task(void);

        bsd_init_done = 1;
        bsdinit_task();
    }
    ...
}
```

`bsdinit_task()` [`bsd/kern/bsd_init.c`] performs the following key operations in the given order.

- It sets the current process's name to `init`.

- It calls `ux_handler_init()` [`bsd/uxkern/ux_exception.c`] to initialize the Unix exception handler.[35] This creates a kernel thread that runs `ux_handler()` [`bsd/uxkern/ux_exception.c`]. Its job is to translate Mach exceptions to Unix signals. Both the host exception port and the task special port are set to the `ux_exception_port` global Mach port.

- It calls `get_user_regs()` [`osfmk/ppc/status.c`] to create a new, default user state context. It then sets the per-thread `uthread` structure's `uu_ar0` pointer—the address of the saved user-state GPR0—to the newly created context.

- It sets the `bsd_hardclockinit` global variable to 1, which starts the BSD "hardware" clock—that is, the `bsd_hardclock()` [`bsd/kern/kern_clock.c`] function starts performing work instead of simply returning.

- It sets the global variable `bsd_init_task` to the current task. This may be used later—say, in a debug build—to identify whether a task is the init task. For example, if `trap()` [`osfmk/ppc/trap.c`], the high-level trap handler, detects that there has been an exception in the init task, it treats it seriously and provides a detailed debugging dump containing the exception code, subcode, contents of general-purpose and several special-purpose registers, and a stack trace. This debugging data is stored in a special global buffer, `init_task_failure_data` [`osfmk/kern/bsd_kern.c`], whose contents are zeroed by `bsdinit_task()`.

- It sets up the system shared region (see Section 5.7.8).

- It calls `load_init_program()` [`bsd/kern/kern_exec.c`] to launch the first user-space program (see Section 5.8).

- It sets the `app_profile` global variable to 1, which enables application profiling as part of the kernel's working set detection subsystem.[36]

5.7.8 Shared Memory Regions

The kernel can maintain one or more shared memory regions that can be mapped into each user task's address space. The `shared_region_task_mappings`

---

35. We will discuss exception handling in Chapter 9.

36. We will discuss this subsystem in Chapter 8.

structure [osfmk/vm/vm_shared_memory_server.h] is used for tracking a shared-region task mapping. The kernel keeps track of these regions by *environment*, where an environment is a combination of a file system base (the fs_base field), and a system identifier (the system field). The global variable that holds the default environment's shared regions is defined in osfmk/vm/vm_shared_memory_server.c.

// osfmk/vm/vm_shared_memory_server.h

```
struct shared_region_task_mappings {
    mach_port_t  text_region;
    vm_size_t    text_size;
    mach_port_t  data_region;
    vm_size_t    data_size;
    vm_offset_t  region_mappings;
    vm_offset_t  client_base;
    vm_offset_t  alternate_base;
    vm_offset_t  alternate_next;
    unsigned int fs_base;
    unsigned int system;
    int          flags;
    vm_offset_t  self;
};
...
typedef struct shared_region_task_mappings *shared_region_task_mappings_t;
typedef struct shared_region_mapping *shared_region_mapping_t;
...
// Default environment for system and fs_root
#define SHARED_REGION_SYSTEM    0x1
...
#define ENV DEFAULT_ROOT    0
...
```

// osfmk/vm/vm_shared_memory_server.c

```
shared_region_mapping_t default_environment_shared_regions = NULL;
...
```

bsdinit_task() defines the *system region* to be the one whose fs_base and system fields are equal to ENV_DEFAULT_ROOT and the processor type, respectively. The processor type—as contained in the cpu_type field of the per-processor structure—is retrieved by calling cpu_type() [osfmk/ppc/cpu.c]. bsdinit_task() looks for the system region on the list of default environment shared regions. If it fails to find the region, it calls shared_file_boot_time_init() [osfmk/vm/vm_shared_memory_server.c] to initialize the default system region. Recall that shared_file_boot_time_init() would previously have been called by `kernel_bootstrap_thread()`. We saw that `shared_file_boot_time_init()` calls `shared_file_init()` [osfmk/vm/vm_shared_memory_server.c] to allocate two 256MB shared regions—one for text and the other for data—for mapping into task address spaces. `shared_file_init()` also sets up data structures for keeping track of virtual address mappings of loaded shared files. `osfmk/mach/shared_memory_server.h` defines the addresses of the shared text and data regions in a client task's address space.[37]

// osfmk/mach/shared_memory_server.h

```
#define SHARED_LIBRARY_SERVER_SUPPORTED
#define GLOBAL_SHARED_TEXT_SEGMENT 0x90000000
#define GLOBAL_SHARED_DATA_SEGMENT 0xA0000000
#define GLOBAL_SHARED_SEGMENT_MASK 0xF0000000

#define SHARED_TEXT_REGION_SIZE      0x10000000
#define SHARED_DATA_REGION_SIZE      0x10000000
#define SHARED_ALTERNATE_LOAD_BASE 0x90000000
```

You can use the `vmmap` command to display the virtual memory regions allocated in a process and thus see the entities that may be mapped at the shared addresses.

```
$ vmmap -interleaved $$
...
__TEXT     90000000-901a7000 [ 1692K] r-x/r-x SM=COW  ...libSystem.B.dylib
__LINKEDIT 901a7000-901fe000 [  348K] r--/r-- SM=COW  ...libSystem.B.dylib
__TEXT     901fe000-90203000 [   20K] r-x/r-x SM=COW  ...libmathCommon.A.dylib
__LINKEDIT 90203000-90204000 [    4K] r--/r-- SM=COW  ...libmathCommon.A.dylib
__TEXT     92c9b000-92d8a000 [  956K] r-x/r-x SM=COW  ...libiconv.2.dylib
__LINKEDIT 92d8a000-92d8c000 [    8K] r--/r-- SM=COW  ...libiconv.2.dylib
__TEXT     9680f000-9683e000 [  188K] r-x/r-x SM=COW  ...libncurses.5.4.dylib
__LINKEDIT 9683e000-96852000 [   80K] r--/r-- SM=COW  ...libncurses.5.4.dylib
__DATA     a0000000-a000b000 [   44K] rw-/rw- SM=COW  ...libSystem.B.dylib
__DATA     a000b000-a0012000 [   28K] rw-/rw- SM=COW  ...libSystem.B.dylib
__DATA     a01fe000-a01ff000 [    4K] r--/r-- SM=COW  ...ibmathCommon.A.dylib
__DATA     a2c9b000-a2c9c000 [    4K] r--/r-- SM=COW  ...libiconv.2.dylib
__DATA     a680f000-a6817000 [   32K] rw-/rw- SM=COW  ...libncurses.5.4.dylib
__DATA     a6817000-a6818000 [    4K] rw-/rw- SM=COW  ...libncurses.5.4.dylib
...
```

---

37. In this context, the kernel is the shared memory server and a task is the client.

5.8 Launching the First User-Space Program

As BSD initialization concludes, `load_init_program()` [bsd/kern/kern_
exec.c] is called to launch the first user program, which is traditionally /sbin/
init on Unix systems but is another init program on Mac OS X.[38] The function
first attempts to execute /sbin/launchd. If that fails, it attempts /sbin/mach_
init. If that too fails, it prompts the user for a pathname to the program to run.
The kernel uses `getchar()` [bsd/dev/ppc/machdep.c] to read the name character by character, echoing each character read. `getchar()` uses `cngetc()` and
`cnputc()` [osfmk/console/ppc/serial_console.c], which are wrappers
around the now established console I/O operations.

   `load_init_program()` allocates a page of memory in the current task's
map. It populates the page with a null-terminated list of arguments that have been
collected so far in a string variable. `argv[0]` contains the init program's null-terminated name (e.g., /sbin/launchd), `argv[1]` contains an argument string
that has a maximum size of 128 bytes (including the terminating NUL character),
and `argv[2]` is NULL. Examples of arguments passed to the init program include
those indicating safe (-x), single-user (-s), and verbose (-v) booting modes. An
`execve_args` structure [bsd/sys/exec.h] is populated so that `execve()` can
be called from within the kernel, while pretending as if it were called from user
space. Consequently, these arguments are first copied out to user space, since the
`execve()` system call expects its arguments to be there.

```
// bsd/kern/kern_exec.c

static char *init_program_name[128] = "/sbin/launchd";
static const char *other_init = "/sbin/mach_init";

char init_args[128] = "";

struct execve_args init_exec_args;
int init_attempts = 0;

void
load_init_program(struct proc *p)
{
    vm_offset_t  init_addr;
    char         *argv[3];
    int          error;
    register_t   retval[2];
    error = 0;
```

---

38. /sbin/launchd is the default init program beginning with Mac OS X 10.4.

```
    do {
        ...

        // struct execve_args {
        //     char *fname;
        //     char **argp;
        //     char **envp;
        // };
        init_exec_args.fname = /* user space init_program_name */
        init_exec_args.argp  = /* user space init arguments */
        init_exec.args.envp  = /* user space NULL */

        // need init to run with uid and gid 0
        set_security_token(p);

        error = execve(p, &init_exec_args, retval);
    } while (error);
}
```

Finally, the first user-space program begins to execute.

5.9 Slave Processors

Before we discuss user-level startup, let us look at the `ppc_init_cpu()` [`osfmk/ppc/ppc_init.c`] function. Recall from Figure 5–2 that at boot time, a slave processor calls `ppc_init_cpu()` instead of `ppc_init()`. The execution journey of a slave processor is much shorter than that of the master processor. Figure 5–22 shows the execution path of `ppc_init_cpu()`.

   `ppc_init_cpu()` clears the `SleepState` bit in the `cpu_flags` field of the processor's `per_proc_info` structure. On 64-bit hardware, `ppc_init_cpu()` checks whether the `wcte` global variable is set to `0`; if so, it disables the noncacheable unit's store gather timer through an SCOM command. The value of the `wcte` variable can be set through the `wcte` boot argument (see Table 4–12).

   Next, `ppc_init_cpu()` calls `cpu_init()` [`osfmk/ppc/cpu.c`], which we came across earlier in this chapter. `cpu_init()` restores the Timebase Register from values saved in the CPU's `per_proc_info` structure. It also sets the values of some fields in the `per_proc_info` structure. Finally, `ppc_init_cpu()` calls `slave_main()` [`osfmk/kern/startup.c`], which never returns.

   Recall how the `kernel_bootstrap()` function, while running on the master processor, arranged—through `load_context()`—for `kernel_bootstrap_thread()` to start executing. Similarly, `slave_main()` arranges for `processor_`

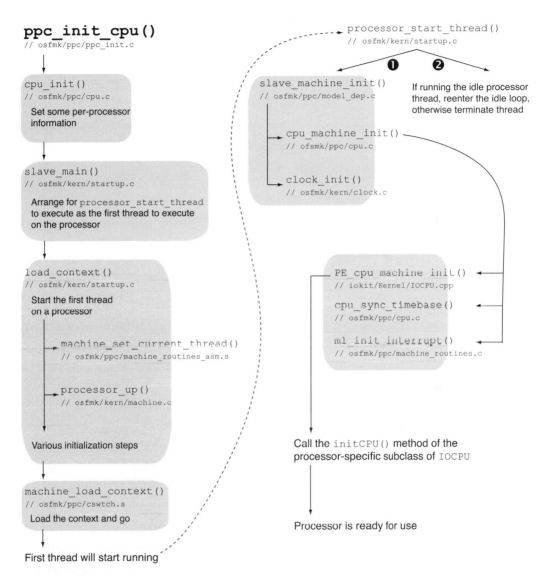

FIGURE 5–22 Slave processor initialization

start_thread() [osfmk/kern/startup.c] to start executing. processor_
start_thread() calls slave_machine_init() [osfmk/ppc/model_dep.c].
    slave_machine_init() initializes the processor by calling cpu_
machine_init() [osfmk/ppc/cpu.c] and the clock by calling clock_

init() [osfmk/kern/clock.c]. We earlier noted the operation of clock_init(), which calls the initialization functions of all available clock devices. cpu_machine_init() calls PE_cpu_machine_init() [iokit/Kernel/IOCPU.cpp], synchronizes the Timebase Register with the master processor, and enables interrupts.

```
// iokit/Kernel/IOCPU.cpp

void
PE_cpu_machine_init(cpu_id_t target, boolean_t boot)
{
    IOCPU *targetCPU = OSDynamicCast(IOCPU, (OSObject *)target);

    if (targetCPU)
        targetCPU->initCPU(boot);
}
```

5.10 User-Level Startup

As Section 5.8 described, user-level startup is initiated when the kernel executes /sbin/launchd as the first user process. We will now look at the implementation and operation of launchd.

5.10.1 launchd

launchd is the master bootstrap daemon beginning with Mac OS X 10.4. It subsumes the functionality of the traditional init program and the erstwhile Mac OS X mach_init program. The following are notable features of launchd.

- It manages both system-wide *daemons* and per-user *agents*. An agent is a type of daemon that runs while a user is logged in. Unless the distinction is necessary, we will use the term *daemons* in this discussion to refer to both daemons and agents.
- As the first user process, it performs user-level system bootstrap.
- It handles both single-user and multiuser booting modes. In a multiuser boot, it runs the traditional BSD-style command script (/etc/rc) and sets up daemons whose configuration files are located in designated directories such as /System/Library/LaunchDaemons/, /Library/LaunchDaemons/,

`/System/Library/LaunchAgents/`, `/Library/LaunchAgents/`, and `~/Library/LaunchAgents/`.

- It supports daemons that are designed to run under the `inetd` superserver on Unix systems.
- It can run jobs periodically. A `launchd` job is an abstraction that consists of a runnable entity (a program) along with the entity's configuration.
- It allows several aspects of a daemon to be configured through a property list file, rather than the daemon having to programmatically configure itself.
- It can start daemons on demand, based on a variety of conditions.

`launchd` simplifies the configuration, management, and, in many cases, even creation of daemons.

5.10.1.1 Daemon Configuration and Management

`launchd` provides a set of predefined keys that can be used in a daemon's property list file to specify various runtime aspects of the daemon. The following are examples of such aspects:

- User and group names (or identifiers)
- Root and working directories
- Umask value
- Environment variables
- Standard error and standard output redirections
- Soft and hard resource limits
- Scheduling priority alterations
- I/O priority alterations

An important ability of `launchd` is that it can launch daemons when they are needed, rather than having "always on" processes. Such on-demand launching can be based on criteria such as the following:

- A given periodic interval
- An incoming connection request on a given TCP port number
- An incoming connection request on a given `AF_UNIX` path
- Modification of a given file system path
- Appearance or modification of file system entities in a given queue directory

The `launchd` configuration file for a daemon is an XML property list file. Let us look at some examples. Figure 5–23 shows the configuration file for the SSH daemon.

FIGURE 5–23 A `launchd` configuration file

```
$ ls -1 /System/Library/LaunchDaemons
bootps.plist
com.apple.KernelEventAgent.plist
com.apple.atrun.plist
com.apple.mDNSResponder.plist
...
ssh.plist
swat.plist
telnet.plist
tftp.plist
$ cat /System/Library/LaunchDaemons/ssh.plist
...
<plist version="1.0">
<dict>
    <key>Label</key>
    <string>com.openssh.sshd</string>
    <key>Program</key>
    <string>/usr/libexec/sshd-keygen-wrapper</string>
    <key>ProgramArguments</key>
    <array>
        <string>/usr/sbin/sshd</string>
        <string>-i</string>
    </array>
    <key>Sockets</key>
    <dict>
        <key>Listeners</key>
        <dict>
            <key>SockServiceName</key>
            <string>ssh</string>
            <key>Bonjour</key>
            <array>
                <string>ssh</string>
                <string>sftp-ssh</string>
            </array>
        </dict>
    </dict>
    <key>inetdCompatibility</key>
    <dict>
        <key>Wait</key>
        <false/>
    </dict>
    <key>SessionCreate</key>
```

(continues)

FIGURE 5–23 A `launchd` configuration file *(continued)*

```
    <true/>
    <key>StandardErrorPath</key>
    <string>/dev/null</string>
</dict>
</plist>
```

The meanings of keys shown in Figure 5–23 are as follows.

- The `Label` key uniquely identifies the job to `launchd`. This key is mandatory.

- The `Program` key is used as the first argument of `execvp()` by `launchd`.

- The `ProgramArguments` key is used as the second argument of `execvp()` by `launchd`. Note that if the `Program` key is absent, the first element of the `ProgramArguments` key's array value is used instead.

- The `Sockets` key specifies launch-on-demand sockets that allow `launchd` to determine when to run the job. The `SockServiceName` key specifies the service name that can be used by the `getaddrinfo(3)` function to determine the well-known port for this service.

- The `Bonjour` key requests registration of the service with the `mDNSResponder` program. Its value is either a list of names to advertise or a Boolean, in which case the name to advertise is inferred from `SockServiceName`.

- The `inetdCompatibility` key specifies that the daemon expects to run under `inetd`, and an appropriate compatibility environment should be provided by `launchd`. The `Wait` Boolean key specifies the `wait` or `nowait` options of `inetd`.

- The `SessionCreate` Boolean key, if set to `true`, causes `launchd` to use the `dlopen` interface to call the `SessionCreate()` function from the Security framework (`/System/Library/Frameworks/Security.framework`). `SessionCreate()` creates a security session, wherein a new bootstrap sub-set port[39] is created for the calling process.

- The `StandardErrorPath` key causes `launchd` to open the specified path and duplicate the resultant descriptor to the standard error descriptor.

Consider another example—that of the `cron` daemon. Its `launchd` configuration file (`com.vix.cron.plist`) specifies that `/usr/sbin/cron` is to be run

---

39. We will look at bootstrap ports in Chapter 9.

whenever either the /etc/crontab file or the /var/cron/tabs/ directory is modified. For example, creating a crontab file in /var/cron/tabs/ will cause launchd to run cron.

```
$ cat /System/Library/LaunchDaemons/com.vix.cron.plist
...
<dict>
        <key>Label</key>
        <string>com.vix.cron</string>
        <key>ProgramArguments</key>
        <array>
                <string>/usr/sbin/cron</string>
        </array>
        <key>RunAtLoad</key>
        <true/>
        <key>WatchPaths</key>
        <array>
                <string>/etc/crontab</string>
        </array>
        <key>QueueDirectories</key>
        <array>
                <string>/var/cron/tabs</string>
        </array>
</dict>
...
```

5.10.1.2 Daemon Creation

Figure 5–24 shows an example of creating a trivial launchd job that runs every 10 seconds. The job uses the logger command-line program to write a "hello" message to the system log.

FIGURE 5–24 Creating a periodic launchd job

```
$ whoami
amit
$ launchctl list
$ sudo launchctl list
com.apple.KernelEventAgent
...
com.apple.ftpd
com.openssh.sshd
$ cat com.osxbook.periodic.plist
<?xml version="1.0" encoding="UTF-8"?>
<!DOCTYPE plist PUBLIC "-//Apple Computer//DTD PLIST 1.0//EN" "http://www.apple.com/
DTDs/PropertyList-1.0.dtd">
<plist version="1.0">
```

(continues)

FIGURE 5–24 Creating a periodic `launchd` job *(continued)*

```
<dict>
    <key>Label</key>
    <string>com.osxbook.periodic</string>
    <key>ProgramArguments</key>
    <array>
        <string>/usr/bin/logger</string>
        <string>-p</string>
        <string>crit</string>
        <string>hello</string>
    </array>
    <key>StartInterval</key>
    <integer>10</integer>
</dict>
</plist>
$ launchctl load com.osxbook.periodic.plist
$ launchctl list
com.osxbook.periodic
$ tail -f /var/log/system.log
Jul  4 13:43:15 g5x2 amit: hello
Jul  4 13:43:25 g5x2 amit: hello
Jul  4 13:43:35 g5x2 amit: hello
^c
$ launchctl unload com.osxbook.periodic.plist
```

Let us also look at how `launchd` simplifies the programmatic creation of a daemon. Since `launchd` handles several aspects of a daemon's operation, certain guidelines must be followed while writing a `launchd`-compliant daemon. Figure 5–25 shows some examples of relevant guidelines and caveats.

We will now create a trivial network daemon called `dummyd`, which echos back lines of text sent to it by a client. We can avoid writing any network code by using `launchd`'s `inetd`-compatibility mode. However, we will take a somewhat longer route in order to demonstrate how a daemon participates in advanced communication with `launchd`: We will arrange for `launchd` to provide our daemon a socket file descriptor to call `accept()` on when there is an incoming client connection.

In dummyd's `launchd` configuration file, we will also specify a variety of settings and then verify from within dummyd that they were set as expected by `launchd`. Our implementation of dummyd will perform the following primary actions.

- Install a handler for `SIGTERM`.
- Display the settings that we requested `launchd` to set. We will print the settings on the standard error, which, as specified in dummyd's configuration file, will be sent to a custom log file.

MUST

▶ Must provide a property list file containing at least the mandatory properties.

MUST NOT

▶ Must not call `fork(2)` or `vfork(2)`.

▶ Must not call `daemon(3)`.

SHOULD

▶ Should provide a `SIGTERM` handler.

▶ Should "check in" with `launchd` during daemon initialization. Use the `launch(3)` API for this purpose.

▶ Retrieve the daemon's launch dictionary during check in. Save a daemon-local copy of the contents for performance reasons.

▶ Should specify the sockets or file paths used by the daemon in the property list file.

▶ Should consider shutting the daemon down when idle for a certain amount of time. It will be relaunched by `launchd` when required.

SHOULD NOT

▶ Should not close stray file descriptors.

▶ Should not call `chroot(2)`: use the `RootDirectory` key.

▶ Should not call `setsid(2)`: let `launchd` deal with session creation.

▶ Should not call `chdir(2)` or `fchdir(2)`: use the `WorkingDirectory` key.

▶ Should not call `setuid(2)`, `setgid(2)`, `seteuid(2)`, or `setgid(2)`: use keys such as `UserName`, `UID`, `GroupName`, and `GID`.

▶ Should not programmatically redirect standard I/O streams: use the `StandardOutPath` and `StandardErrorPath` keys.

▶ Should not call `setrlimit(2)`: use the `SoftResourceLimits` and `HardResourceLimits` keys.

▶ Should not call `setpriority(2)`: use the `Nice` and `LowPriorityIO` keys.

FIGURE 5–25 Guidelines and caveats for creating `launchd`-compliant daemons

- Check in with `launchd` using the `launch(3)` interface.
- Use the `kqueue(2)` mechanism[40] to arrange to be notified about incoming connections.

---

40. We will discuss the `kqueue(2)` mechanism in Chapter 9.

- Enter a loop that accepts an incoming connection and creates a thread to process the connection. The processing involves reading a newline-terminated string from the client and writing it back to the client.

Figure 5–26 shows the code for dummyd.

FIGURE 5–26 A trivial echo server called dummyd

```c
// dummyd.c

#include <stdio.h>
#include <stdlib.h>
#include <unistd.h>
#include <errno.h>
#include <sys/param.h>
#include <sys/socket.h>
#include <sys/event.h>
#include <launch.h>
#include <pthread.h>

#define MY_LAUNCH_JOBKEY_LISTENERS "Listeners"

// error-handling convenience
#define DO_RETURN(retval, fmt, ...) { \
    fprintf(stderr, fmt, ## __VA_ARGS__); \
    return retval; \
}

int
SIGTERM_handler(int s)
{
    fprintf(stderr, "SIGTERM handled\n"), // primitive SIGTERM handler
    exit(s);
}

ssize_t
readline(int fd, void *buffer, size_t maxlen)
{
    ssize_t n, bytesread;
    char c, *bp = buffer;

    for (n = 1; n < maxlen; n++) {
        bytesread = read(fd, &c, 1);
        if (bytesread == 1) {
            *bp++ = c;
            if (c == '\n')
                break;
```

(continues)

FIGURE 5–26 A trivial echo server called `dummyd` *(continued)*

```
        } else if (bytesread == 0) {
            if (n == 1)
                return 0;
            break;
        } else {
            if (errno == EINTR)
                continue;
            return -1;
        }
    }

    *bp = 0;

    return n;
}


void *
daemon_loop(void *fd)
{
    ssize_t ret;
    char    buf[512];

    for (;;) { // a simple echo loop
        if ((ret = readline((int)fd, buf, 512)) > 0)
            write((int)fd, buf, ret);
        else {
            close((int)fd);
            return (void *)0;
        }
    }
}


int
main(void)
{
    char            path[MAXPATHLEN + 1];
    char            *val;
    int             fd, kq;
    size_t          i;
    pthread_t       thread;
    struct kevent   kev_init, kev_listener;
    struct          sockaddr_storage ss;
    socklen_t       slen;
    launch_data_t   checkin_response, checkin_request;
    launch_data_t   sockets_dict, listening_fd_array;

    setbuf(stderr, NULL); // make stderr unbuffered
```

(continues)

FIGURE 5–26 A trivial echo server called dummyd *(continued)*

```
// launchd will send us a SIGTERM while terminating
signal(SIGTERM, (sig_t)SIGTERM_handler);


// print our cwd: our configuration file specified this
if (getcwd(path, MAXPATHLEN))
    fprintf(stderr, "Working directory: %s\n", path);


// print $DUMMY_VARIABLE: our configuration file specified this
fprintf(stderr, "Special enivronment variables: ");
if ((val = getenv("DUMMY_VARIABLE")))
    fprintf(stderr, "DUMMY_VARIABLE=%s\n", val);


if ((kq = kqueue()) == -1) // create a kernel event queue for notification
    DO_RETURN(EXIT_FAILURE, "kqueue() failed\n");


// prepare to check in with launchd
checkin_request = launch_data_new_string(LAUNCH_KEY_CHECKIN);
if (checkin_request == NULL)
    DO_RETURN(EXIT_FAILURE, "launch_data_new_string(%s) failed (errno = %d)"
              "\n", LAUNCH_KEY_CHECKIN, errno);


checkin_response = launch_msg(checkin_request); // check in with launchd
if (checkin_response == NULL)
    DO_RETURN(EXIT_FAILURE, "launch_msg(%s) failed (errno = %d)\n",
              LAUNCH_KEY_CHECKIN, errno);
if (launch_data_get_type(checkin_response) == LAUNCH_DATA_ERRNO)
    DO_RETURN(EXIT_FAILURE, "failed to check in with launchd (errno = %d)"
              "\n", launch_data_get_errno(checkin_response));


// retrieve the contents of the <Sockets> dictionary
sockets_dict = launch_data_dict_lookup(checkin_response,
                                       LAUNCH_JOBKEY_SOCKETS);
if (sockets_dict == NULL)
    DO_RETURN(EXIT_FAILURE, "no sockets\n");


// retrieve the value of the MY_LAUNCH_JOBKEY_LISTENERS key
listening_fd_array = launch_data_dict_lookup(sockets_dict,
                                             MY_LAUNCH_JOBKEY_LISTENERS);
if (listening_fd_array == NULL)
    DO_RETURN(EXIT_FAILURE, "no listening socket descriptors\n");


for (i = 0; i < launch_data_array_get_count(listening_fd_array); i++) {

    launch_data_t fd_i = launch_data_array_get_index(listening_fd_array, i);

    EV_SET(&kev_init,                    // the structure to populate
           launch_data_get_fd(fd_i),     // identifier for this event
           EVFILT_READ,                  // return on incoming connection
```

(continues)

FIGURE 5–26 A trivial echo server called dummyd *(continued)*

```
                EV_ADD,                 // flags: add the event to the kqueue
                0,                      // filter-specific flags (none)
                0,                      // filter-specific data (none)
                NULL);                  // opaque user-defined value (none)
        if (kevent(kq,                  // the kernel queue
                &kev_init,              // changelist
                1,                      // nchanges
                NULL,                   // eventlist
                0,                      // nevents
                NULL) == -1)            // timeout
            DO_RETURN(EXIT_FAILURE, "kevent(/* register */) failed\n");
    }

    launch_data_free(checkin_response);

    while (1) {

        if ((fd = kevent(kq, NULL, 0, &kev_listener, 1, NULL)) == -1)
            DO_RETURN(EXIT_FAILURE, "kevent(/* get events */) failed\n");

        if (fd == 0)
            return EXIT_SUCCESS;

        slen = sizeof(ss);
        fd = accept(kev_listener.ident, (struct sockaddr *)&ss, &slen);
        if (fd == -1)
            continue;

        if (pthread_create(&thread, (pthread_attr_t *)0, daemon_loop,
                           (void *)fd) != 0) {
            close(fd);
            DO_RETURN(EXIT_FAILURE, "pthread_create() failed\n");
        }

        pthread_detach(thread);
    }

    return EXIT_SUCCESS;
}
```

The launchd configuration file for dummyd is shown in Figure 5–27. Note that we specify to launchd that dummyd be run as an inetd-based server listening on TCP port 12345. Moreover, if we need to have IPC communication with launchd, the ServiceIPC Boolean key must be set to true.

FIGURE 5–27 The contents of the `com.osxbook.dummyd.plist` configuration file

```xml
<?xml version="1.0" encoding="UTF-8"?>
<!DOCTYPE plist PUBLIC "-//Apple Computer//DTD PLIST 1.0//EN" "http://www.apple.com/
DTDs/PropertyList-1.0.dtd">
<plist version="1.0">
<dict>
<key>Label</key>
        <string>com.osxbook.dummyd</string>

        <key>ProgramArguments</key>
        <array>
                <string>/tmp/dummyd</string>
                <string>Dummy Daemon</string>
        </array>

        <key>OnDemand</key>
        <true/>

        <key>WorkingDirectory</key>
        <string>/tmp</string>

        <key>EnvironmentVariables</key>
        <dict>
            <key>DUMMY_VARIABLE</key>
            <string>dummyvalue</string>
        </dict>

        <key>ServiceIPC</key>
        <true/>

        <key>StandardErrorPath</key>
        <string>/tmp/dummyd.log</string>

        <key>Sockets</key>
        <dict>
            <key>Listeners</key>
            <dict>
                <key>Socktype</key>
                <string>stream</string>
                <key>SockFamily</key>
                <string>IPv4</string>
                <key>SockProtocol</key>
                <string>TCP</string>
                <key>SockServiceName</key>
                <string>12345</string>
            </dict>
        </dict>
</dict>
</plist>
```

Let us now test dummyd by loading its configuration into launchd using the launchctl command.

```
$ gcc -Wall -o /tmp/dummyd dummyd.c
$ launchctl load com.osxbook.dummyd.plist
$ launchctl list
com.osxbook.dummyd
$ ls /tmp/dummyd.log
ls: /tmp/dummyd.log: No such file or directory
$ ps -axw | grep dummyd | grep -v grep
$ netstat -na | grep 12345
tcp4       0      0  *.12345              *.*              LISTEN
$ telnet 127.0.0.1 12345
Trying 127.0.0.1...
Connected to localhost.
Escape character is '^]'.
hello
hello
world
world
^]
telnet> quit
Connection closed.
$ cat /tmp/dummyd.log
Working directory: /private/tmp
Special enivronment variables: DUMMY_VARIABLE=dummyvalue
$ launchctl unload com.osxbook.dummyd.plist
$
```

5.10.1.3 `launchd` *Operation*

Figure 5–28 shows the high-level operation of launchd, whose own initialization consists of the following primary operations.

- It creates kernel event queues (kqueues) and registers callbacks with them for various types of events. Examples of callbacks are kqasync_callback(), kqsignal_callback(), and kqfs_callback(), which are for EVFILT_READ, EVFILT_SIGNAL, and EVFILT_FS events, respectively.

- It initializes several data structures, especially in the conceive_firstborn() internal function.

- It loads the /etc/launchd.conf configuration file, if it exists. When running in the context of a user, it also looks for the ~/.launchd.conf per-user configuration file. It runs subcommands contained in these files using the launchctl command.

- It eventually goes into a server loop in which it receives and processes events.

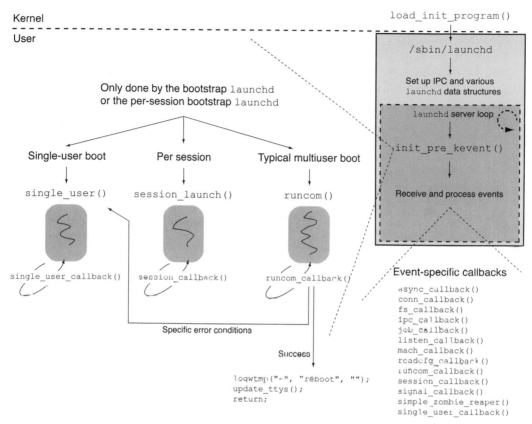

FIGURE 5–28 A high-level depiction of `launchd`'s operation

- The first time the server loop runs in a given context—for example, during system startup—the `init_pre_kevent()` function is called to perform critical initialization such as single-user system startup, session creation, and the normal multiuser system startup.

5.10.2 Multiuser Startup

In a multiuser startup, `launchd` runs the command script contained in `/etc/rc`, which in turn follows different execution paths depending on the kind of booting being performed: whether it is a normal boot, whether it is a network boot, or whether the system is booting from a CD-ROM for installation purposes.

Figures 5–29. and 5–30 show the chain of important events that occur during a local or network-based multiuser boot. Note that in the case of a nonverbose (graphical) boot, `/etc/rc` eventually runs the `/usr/libexec/WaitingForLoginWindow`

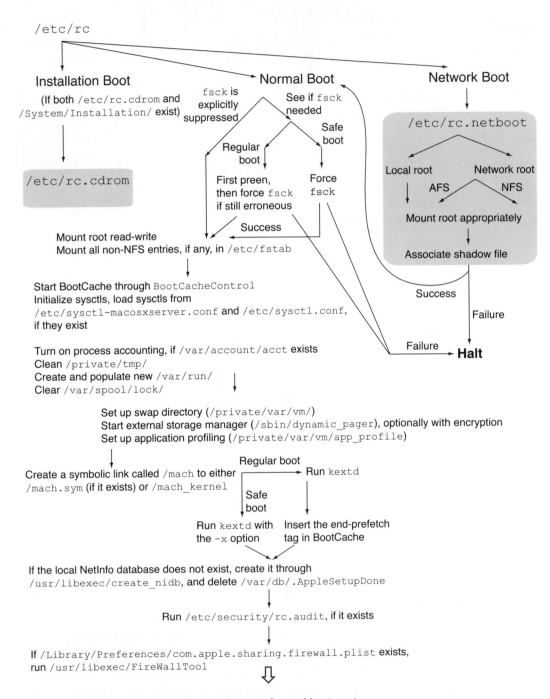

FIGURE 5–29 The sequence of operations performed by /etc/rc

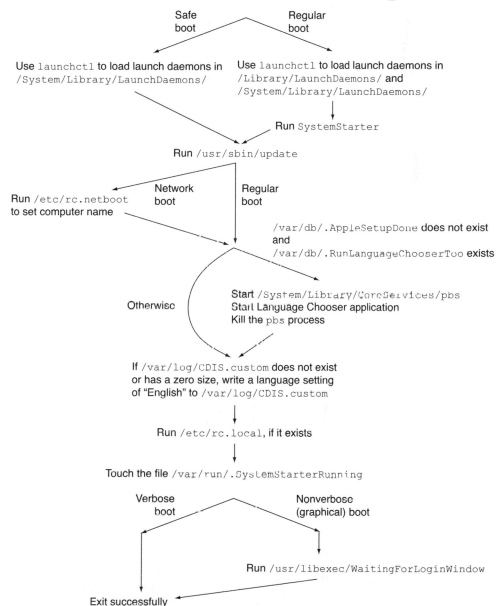

FIGURE 5–30 The sequence of operations performed by /etc/rc (continued from Figure 5–29)

program. This program displays the "Starting Mac OS X . . ." panel with a progress bar. The latter is a dummy progress bar whose rate of progress is based on the contents of the file /var/db/loginwindow.boottime. The file is updated by WaitingForLoginWindow upon every boot, so that upon the next boot WaitingForLoginWindow can use the saved time duration. This way, the program attempts to match the displayed rate of progress with the actual time taken to boot. WaitingForLoginWindow exits when it receives a notification that the loginwindow program (/System/Library/CoreServices/loginwindow.app) is ready to display the login panel. loginwindow is run by launchd too as part of its session launching, which is shown in Figure 5–31.

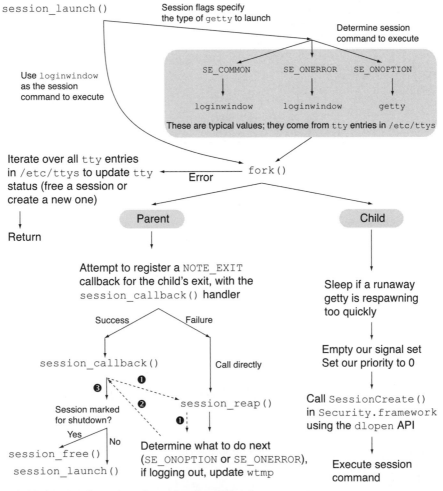

FIGURE 5–31 Overview of session launching by launchd

launchd maintains a global list of sessions. As shown in Figure 5–32, the init_pre_kevent() function launches these sessions. The session list is populated by update_ttys(), which calls getttyent(3) to read entries from /etc/ttys. After /etc/rc exits successfully, update_ttys() is called by runcom_callback(). update_ttys() can also be triggered by sending a hangup (HUP) signal to launchd.

FIGURE 5–32 Implementation of session creation and launching by launchd

```
// launchd/src/init.c

void
init_pre_kevent(void)
{
    session_t s;

    if (single_user_mode && single_user_pid == 0)
        single_user();

    if (run_runcom)
        runcom();

    if (!single_user_mode && !run_runcom && runcom_pid == 0) {
        ...
        // Go through the global list of sessions
        TAILQ_FOREACH(s, &sessions, tqe) {
            if (s->se_process == 0)
                session_launch(s);
        }
    }
}
...

static void
runcom_callback(...)
{
    ...
    if (/* /etc/rc exited successfully */) {
        logwtmp("~", "reboot", "");
        update_ttys();
        return;
    } else ...
    ...
}

static void
session_launch(session_t s)
```

(continues)

FIGURE 5–32 Implementation of session creation and launching by `launchd` *(continued)*

```
{
    ...
}
...

void
update_ttys(void)
{
    session_t sp;
    struct ttyent *ttyp;
    int session_index = 0;
    ...

    while ((ttyp = getttyent())) {
        ++session_index;

        // Check all existing sessions to see if ttyp->ty_name
        // matches any session's device

        // If no session matches, create new session by calling
        // session_new()

        // session_new() adds the session to the global list
        // of sessions
        ...
    }
    ...
}
```

5.10.2.1 *User Login*

The login panel displayed by the `loginwindow` program contains fields for the user to provide login information, which is then used by `loginwindow` to authenticate the user. The following points are noteworthy about the graphical login provided by `loginwindow`.

- You can switch to a text-based login prompt at the console by providing >console as the username, which results in /usr/libexec/getty being run to handle user login. In this case, upon a successful login, the user's shell will be a child of the login process (/usr/bin/login).

- Similarly, you can cause the system to sleep, restart, or shut down by providing >sleep, >restart, or >shutdown, respectively, as the username.

- You can configure the system so that a designated user is automatically logged in after system startup, bypassing the `loginwindow` prompt. This is achieved by saving that user's password in the `/etc/kcpassword` file, which stores the password in an obfuscated format. The obfuscation scheme uses a position-based mapping of characters—that is, the ASCII value of a given character in a password is statically mapped to different values based on the character's position in the password string.

- During software installation, `loginwindow` can be bypassed after system startup because the installer program is launched automatically.

Figure 5–33 shows the important steps performed by `loginwindow`. Note that an authenticated user session encapsulates the user's processes, which are typically the children of either the `loginwindow` or the `WindowServer` processes. The operating context, or *scope*, of these processes is different from that of system processes that start before the user logs in—such processes (typically daemons) are started by `launchd` in the *root* context. Consequently, they are available to all user sessions. In contrast, an agent, although similar to a daemon in that it too is a background program, runs in the context of a user session. Therefore, in general, daemons are systemwide and agents are user-specific. Moreover, since the `WindowServer` process runs in a user context, daemons cannot draw graphical user interfaces, whereas agents can.

To Each Its Own

When multiple users are logged in simultaneously through the fast user-switching feature, each user gets an individual graphical login—that is, there is a per-user `loginwindow` process, along with the associated processes that `loginwindow` creates. For example, each login has its own pasteboard server, Finder, and Dock.

A remote login—say, through SSH—does not launch `loginwindow`. It involves a traditional Unix-style invocation of the login program (`/usr/bin/login`), which results in a separate session for that login. However, a remotely logged-in user *can* communicate with the window server from outside of the console session, provided the user ID is that of either the superuser or the active console user. This enables a remotely logged-in user to launch graphical applications—for example, using the `open` command-line program.

The Mac OS X login mechanism supports running a custom script with superuser privileges when a user logs in. This script—a *login hook*—is executed by `loginwindow`. It is enabled on a system-wide basis, but it receives the short

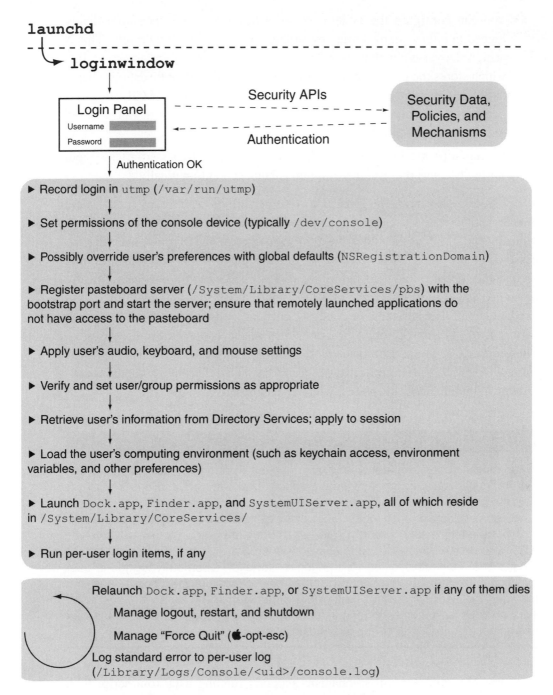

FIGURE 5–33 Important steps performed by the `loginwindow` application

name of the logging-in user as its first argument. A login hook can be registered either by editing the /etc/ttys file or by setting a property for loginwindow in the Mac OS X defaults system. In the former case, the line containing the path to loginwindow in /etc/ttys is modified to include the -LoginHook argument, whose value is the login hook's path.

```
# /etc/ttys
...
# Before login hook:
#
# console "/System/Library/CoreServices/loginwindow.app/Contents/MacOS/loginwindow"
vt100 on secure onoption="/usr/libexec/getty std.9600"
#
# After login hook:
console "/System/Library/CoreServices/loginwindow.app/Contents/MacOS/loginwindow
-LoginHook /path/to/login/hook/script" vt100 on secure onoption="/usr/libexec/getty
std.9600"
...
```

Alternatively, the defaults command can be used to set the LoginHook property for loginwindow.

```
$ sudo defaults write com.apple.loginwindow LoginHook /path/to/login/hook/script
```

5.10.2.2 User Logout, System Restart, and System Shutdown

Figure 5–34 shows how loginwindow handles the procedures for logging out, restarting, or shutting down the system. Selecting an action from the Apple menu causes the foreground process to send the appropriate Apple Event to loginwindow. An application can also send these events programmatically. For example, the following AppleScript code fragment sends the kAELogOut event to loginwindow:

```
tell application "loginwindow"
     «event aevtlogo»
end tell
```

> With reference to Figure 5–34, when loginwindow sends a kAEQuitApplication to a Cocoa application, the event is not seen as is by the application. Instead, the Application Kit framework calls the applicationShouldTerminate: delegate method of the application. If the application wishes to cancel the termination sequence, it must implement this delegate and return NSTerminateCancel from it.

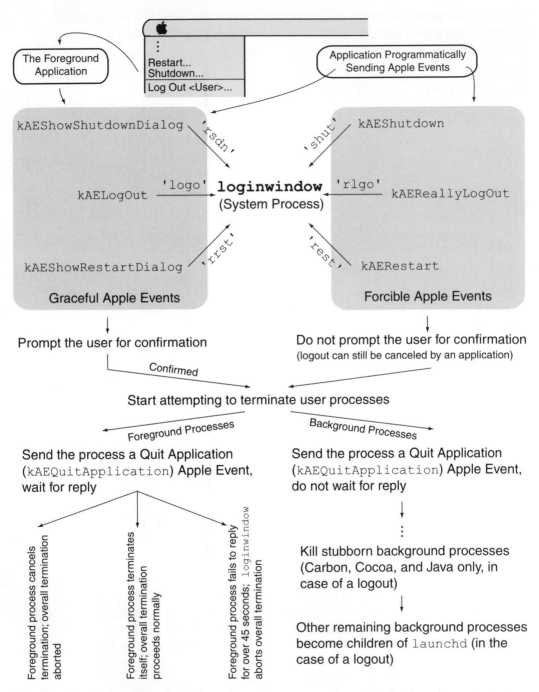

FIGURE 5–34 The handling of user logout, system restart, and system shutdown by loginwindow

In a graceful termination sequence, `loginwindow` displays a dialog requesting confirmation from the user. Typically, the dialog has a two-minute countdown timer, after which `loginwindow` proceeds with the termination sequence.

Note that when system shutdown is initiated, `launchd` will stop each job by sending it a `SIGTERM` signal. Moreover, `launchd` sets the `SE_SHUTDOWN` bit in each session's "flags" variable, which prevents the session from being restarted. Further user logins are also disabled.

5.10.3 Single-User Startup

Figure 5–35 shows the sequence of events that occurs during single-user startup. `launchd` skips running `/etc/rc` and creating any sessions, and simply runs the shell defined by the `_PATH_BSHELL` macro in `<paths.h>`. Note that a single-user

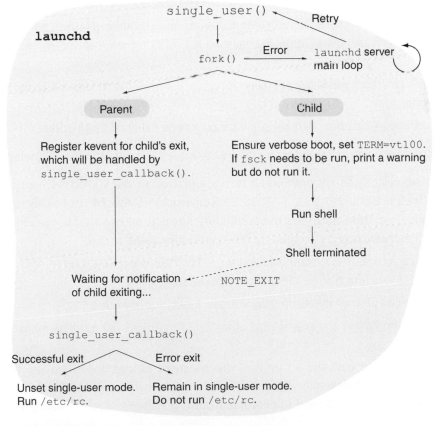

FIGURE 5–35 Single-user bootstrap through `launchd`

boot implies verbose mode. It is also possible to boot the system and stay in single-user mode by manually executing /etc/rc from the single-user shell prompt.

5.10.4 Installation Startup

An installation boot is triggered when /etc/rc detects the presence of both the /etc/rc.cdrom file and the /System/Installation/ directory. Neither of these two exists on an installed Mac OS X system. The contents of /System/ Installation/ on an installation CD-ROM include the following.

- CDIS/Installation Log.app is an installation log viewer that can show detailed installation progress. It provides options such as Show Errors Only, Show Errors and Progress, and Show Everything.

- CDIS/LCA.app is the Language Chooser Application. It also contains support for Bluetooth device discovery and setup, along with instructions for setting up Bluetooth peripherals before commencing installation.

- CDIS/instlogd is a daemon that maintains an external log buffer, which is shared with the installation log viewer. It listens on a local socket on the 127.0.0.1 address.

- CDIS/preheat.sh is a script that—if present—can be run to reduce CD-ROM booting time.

- Packages/ contains various software packages—that is, "pkg" files.

  Important operations performed by /etc/rc.cdrom include the following.

- It disables on-the-fly prebinding for the duration of the CD-ROM boot by setting the DYLD_NO_FIX_PREBINDING environment variable to 1. This prevents dyld from notifying the prebinding agent if an executable could not be launched using its prebinding information for some reason.

- It sanity-checks the system date and time. The date is explicitly set to April 1, 1976, if it is found to be "less" than that date.

- It sets the value of the kern.maxvnodes sysctl variable to 2500.

- It runs the /System/Installation/CDIS/preheat.sh preheat script if it exists.

- It runs kextd with the -j option, which causes kextd not to jettison the kernel linker. Consequently, kextd loads native drivers in the kernel and exits, allowing the kernel to continue handling all load requests. Using this option along with an appropriate mkext cache improves startup time from a CD-ROM.

- It brings the loopback interface up with an address of `127.0.0.1` and a netmask of `255.0.0.0`. This allows local NetInfo communication.

- It creates a 512KB RAM disk using the `hdik` program for in-kernel disk image mounting. This RAM disk is used for `/Volumes/`.

```
dev=`hdik -drivekey system-image=yes -nomount ram://1024`  # 512KB
if [ $? -eq 0 ] ; then
  newfs $dev
  mount -o union -o nobrowse $dev /Volumes
fi
```

- It checks for the presence of the Installation Log application. If present, the application is used as a graphical crash catcher, and the `CatchExit` environment variable is set to `GUI`. If the application is absent, the variable is set to `CLI`.

- It creates a 128KB RAM disk for use by `securityd`.

```
dev=`hdik -drivekey system-image=yes -nomount ram://256` # 128KB
newfs $dev
mount -o union -o nobrowse $dev /var/tmp
mkdir -m 1777 /var/tmp/mds
```

- It creates a 128KB RAM disk that is mounted on `/var/run/`. The system log daemon (`syslogd`) needs it to create the `/var/run/syslog` pipe.

- It starts the external log buffer daemon (`instlogd`), the system log daemon (`syslogd`), and the NetInfo binder daemon (`nibindd`).

- It logs the system boot time to the system log for potential debugging or profiling of the installation process.

```
/usr/sbin/sysctl kern.boottime | head -1 | /usr/bin/logger -p install.debug -t ""
```

- It calls `/usr/libexec/register_mach_bootstrap_servers` to start services whose configuration files are located in `/etc/mach_init.d/`.

- It calls `/usr/bin/pmset` to disable sleeping of the display, the disk, and the system. It also prevents the machine from sleeping upon pressing of the power button. Moreover, it tells the power management subsystem to reduce processor speed if necessary.

- It starts the Crash Reporter daemon (`/usr/libexec/crashreporterd`). If the `CatchExit` environment variable is set to `CLI`, it creates a 1MB RAM disk, creates a file system on it, and mounts it on `/Library/Logs/`.

- It runs `/etc/rc.cdrom.local` if it exists.

Deprecated Ways to Bootstrap Servers

In Mac OS X 10.4, not all boot-time daemons have been migrated to `launchd`. Therefore, the system continues to support multiple boot-time daemon startup mechanisms.

The `/etc/mach_init.d/` and `/etc/mach_init_per_user.d/` directories contain property list files for system-wide and per-user daemons, respectively. These daemons can be launched using a bootstrapping mechanism similar to `launchd`. The mechanism is deprecated beginning with Mac OS X 10.4. In this mechanism, the `/usr/libexec/register_mach_bootstrap_servers` program parses the daemons' property list files and makes RPC calls to either `launchd` or `mach_init` (on Mac OS X 10.3) to create the corresponding services. In particular, the mechanism supports on-demand launching of daemons.

The SystemStarter program (`/sbin/SystemStarter`) handles daemons whose property list files are located in `/System/Library/StartupItems/` (system-provided startup items) and `/Library/StartupItems/` (user-installed startup items).

As we saw in Figure 5–30, `launchd` executes the `/etc/rc` startup script, which calls upon all supported daemon startup mechanisms.

- It starts Apple Type Services by running `StartATSServer`, which resides in the `Support/` subdirectory of the ATS subframework within the Application Services umbrella framework.

- It starts the pasteboard server (`/System/Library/CoreServices/pbs`).

Finally, `/etc/rc.cdrom` prepares to launch the installer application (`/Application/Utilities/Installer.app`) with the appropriate arguments, depending on whether it is an automated installation (the `/etc/minstallconfig.xml` file exists), a custom installation—say, of an application (the `/etc/rc.cdrom.packagePath` file exists)—or a typical operating system installation. In the latter case, installation begins with the `/System/Installation/Packages/OSInstall.mpkg` metapackage, which includes `BaseSystem.pkg`, `Essentials.pkg`, `BSD.pkg`, and others as its contents. It also contains the configuration migratory program (`ConfMigrator`) as a resource.

Unless it is an automated installation, the installer program is run through LCA, which displays the installation progress bar.

```
# /etc/rc.cdrom
...
LAUNCH=/System/Installation/CDIS/LCA.app/Contents/MacOS/LCA
```

```
if [ ! -x ${LAUNCH} ]; then
    LAUNCH=/System/Installation/CDIS/splash
fi

INSTALLER=/Applications/Utilities/Installer.app/Contents/MacOS/Installer

STDARGS="-ExternalLog YES -NSDisabledCharacterPaletteMenuItem YES"
EXTRAARGS=`cat /System/Installation/CDIS/AdditionalInstallerArgs 2>/dev/null`
...

${LAUNCH} ${INSTALLER}                                   \
          -ReadVerifyMedia YES                           \
          ${STDARGS}                                     \
          ${EXTRAARGS}                                   \
          /System/Installation/Packages/OSInstall.mpkg \
          2>&1 | /usr/bin/logger -t "" -p install.warn
```

CHAPTER 6

The xnu Kernel

W e saw in previous chapters that the Mac OS X kernel environment consists of Mach and BSD derivatives, the I/O Kit driver framework, in-kernel libraries, loadable I/O Kit drivers, and other loadable extensions. Although the Darwin xnu package contains only about half the code that potentially runs in the kernel environment, we will consider xnu to be *the* kernel. In this chapter, we will look at several abstractions and mechanisms in xnu, while deferring subsystem-specific details to later chapters.

6.1 xnu Source

In Chapter 5, we visited various parts of the kernel as we traced the execution of kernel code during system startup. Let us now take a brief tour of the xnu kernel source to better understand how the source is organized. Since the xnu package contains close to 3000 files, it is impractical to visit each file. We will only look at major directories in the xnu source tree to enumerate the components implemented within.

> In this section, file and directory names are listed relative to the top-level directory in the xnu source archive. For example, given that the `xnu-<version>.tar.gz` Darwin package will unpack into a top-level directory called `xnu-<version>`, we refer to a file `xnu-<version>/foo/bar` as `foo/bar`.

At the topmost level, xnu contains the directories listed in Table 6–1. Besides these, there exist a few other miscellaneous files and directories that are not important in the current discussion. We will look at some of them later in this chapter in the context of kernel compilation (Section 6.10).

TABLE 6–1 Primary Components of the xnu Kernel Source

Directory	Component
`bsd/`	The BSD kernel
`config/`	Lists of per-subsystem exported functions, property list files for pseudo-extensions
`iokit/`	The I/O Kit kernel runtime
`libkern/`	The kernel library
`libsa/`	The stand-alone library
`osfmk/`	The Mach kernel
`pexpert/`	The Platform Expert

Table 6–2 lists some contents of the `bsd/` directory. Section 2.4.2 provides an overview of the functionality implemented in the kernel's BSD portion.

TABLE 6–2 Primary Contents of the `bsd/` Directory

Directory	Description
`bsd/bsm/`	Basic Security Module (BSM) headers used by the kernel's auditing mechanism. BSM is both a security audit format and an API used to track security-related events in the operating system.
`bsd/crypto/`	Various cipher and hash implementations: AES (Rijndael), Blowfish, CAST-128, DES, MD5, RC4, SHA-1, and SHA-2.
`bsd/dev/memdev.c`	A RAM disk driver (for `/dev/mdX` devices).

(continues)

TABLE 6–2 Primary Contents of the `bsd/` Directory *(Continued)*

Directory	Description
`bsd/dev/ppc/`	BSD drivers for entities such as `/dev/console`, `/dev/mem`, `/dev/kmem`, `/dev/null`, `/dev/zero`, and a BSD driver wrapper for the NVRAM. The latter calls Platform Expert functions to perform the actual work. The BSD device switch tables for block and character devices are also initialized here. Also present are some machine-dependent functions used in the BSD subsystem, such as `unix_syscall()`, `unix_syscall_return()`, `ppc_gettimeofday()`, and signal-handling functions.
`bsd/dev/random/`	An implementation of the Yarrow[a] pseudorandom number generator (PRNG) and the `/dev/random` device.
`bsd/dev/unix_startup.c`	Functions that initialize various BSD-related data structures during system startup.
`bsd/dev/vn/`	The vnode disk driver, which provides block and character interfaces to a vnode, allowing files to be treated as disks. The `/usr/libexec/vndevice` utility is used to control the driver.
`bsd/hfs/`	The HFS and HFS Plus file systems.
`bsd/isofs/`	The ISO 9660 file system for read-only optical discs.
`bsd/kern/`	The core of xnu's BSD component. It contains implementations of asynchronous I/O calls, the kauth mechanism, the audit mechanism, process-related system calls, sysctl calls, POSIX IPC, System V IPC, the unified buffer cache, sockets, mbufs, and various other system calls.
`bsd/libkern/`	Utility routines such as `bcd()`, `bcmp()`, `inet_ntoa()`, `rindex()`, and `strtol()`.
`bsd/miscfs/`	Miscellaneous file systems: the dead file system for vnodes whose underlying file system has been dissociated (deadfs), the device file system (devfs), the file descriptor file system (fdesc), the fifo file system (fifofs), the null mount file system (nullfs), the file system for device-special files (specfs), the in-memory synthfs used for synthesizing mount points, the union mount file system (union), and the volume ID file system (volfs).
`bsd/net/`	Networking: the Berkeley packet filter (BPF), bridging, data link interface layer (DLIL), Ethernet, ARP, PPP, routing, IEEE 802.1q (VLAN), IEEE 802.3ad (Link Aggregation), etc.
`bsd/netat/`	AppleTalk Networking.
`bsd/netinet/`	IPv4 Networking: BOOTP, DHCP, ICMP, TCP, UDP, IP, the "dummynet" bandwidth limiter, and divert sockets.
`bsd/netinet6/`	IPv6 Networking.

(continues)

TABLE 6–2 Primary Contents of the `bsd/` Directory *(Continued)*

Directory	Description
bsd/netkey/	PF_KEY Key Management API (RFC 2367).
bsd/nfs/	NFS client and the kernel portion of the NFS server.
bsd/ufs/	An implementation of UFS based on the fast file system (ffs).
bsd/uxkern/	A Mach exception handler that translates Mach exceptions into Unix signals.
bsd/vfs/	The BSD virtual file system layer.
bsd/vm/	Vnode pager (swap to/from vnodes, demand paging from files), shared memory server calls.

a. Yarrow gets its name from a flowering plant with distinctive flat flower heads and lacy leaves. In China, its stalks have been used as a randomizer in divination since the second millennium B.C.

Table 6–3 lists some contents of the `iokit/` directory. Section 2.4.3 provides an overview of the I/O Kit's functionality.

TABLE 6–3 Primary Contents of the `iokit/` Directory

Directory	Description
iokit/Drivers/platform/	Implementations of I/O Kit classes listed in the KernelConfigTables array—e.g., AppleCPU, AppleNMI, and AppleNVRAM. As we will see in Chapter 10, the I/O Catalog is initialized with the contents of this array.
iokit/Families/IONVRAM/	Subclass of the NVRAM controller class—simply calls the Platform Expert to register the NVRAM controller, which publishes the "IONVRAM" resource in the I/O Kit.
iokit/Families/ IOSystemManagement/	Watchdog timer.
iokit/IOKit/	I/O Kit header files.
iokit/Kernel/	Implementations of core I/O Kit classes and utility functions.
iokit/KernelConfigTables.cpp	Declarations of the list of "fake" kernel extensions and the KernelConfigTables array.
iokit/bsddev/	Support functions for BSD—e.g., the di_root_image() net-boot hook called by BSD to mount a disk image as the root device, and several other functions used by BSD while searching for a root device.

Table 6–4 lists some contents of the `libkern/` directory. Section 2.4.4 provides an overview of libkern's functionality.

TABLE 6–4 Primary Contents of the `libkern/` Directory

Directory	Description
`libkern/c++/`	Implementations of various libkern classes (see Table 6–5).
`libkern/gen/`	High-level-language wrappers around assembly functions for atomic operations, miscellaneous debugging functions.
`libkern/kmod/`	Start and stop routines for the kernel's C++ and C language runtime environments.
`libkern/libkern/`	libkern header files.
`libkern/mach-o/`	A header describing the format of Mach-O files (`loader.h`), and another header containing definitions for accessing Mach-O headers (`mach_header.h`).
`libkern/ppc/`	Implementations of PowerPC-specific `bcmp()`, `memcmp()`, `strlen()`, and atomic increment/decrement functions.
`libkern/stdio/`	An implementation of `scanf()`.
`libkern/uuid/`	Routines for parsing and generating universally unique identifiers (UUIDs) based on the first Ethernet device's hardware address and the current time.

libkern is part of the Kernel framework (`Kernel.framework`), which is exposed to the developer. Its headers are located in `/System/Library/Frameworks/Kernel.framework/Headers/libkern/`. Table 6–5 shows the important classes contained in this library.

TABLE 6–5 libkern Classes and Routines

Base and Abstract Classes	
`OSObject`	The abstract base class for the Mac OS X kernel. It derives from the true root class `OSMetaClassBase`. It implements basic functionality such as allocation primitives, reference counting, and type-safe object casting.
`OSMetaClass`	A peer class to `OSObject`. It derives from the true root class `OSMetaClassBase`. An instance of this class represents one class that is known by the I/O Kit's RTTI system.

(continues)

TABLE 6–5 libkern Classes and Routines *(Continued)*

OSCollection	The abstract superclass for all collections.
OSIterator	The abstract superclass for iterator classes.
Collection Classes	
OSArray	A class for maintaining lists of object references.
OSDictionary	A class for maintaining dictionaries of object references.
OSOrderedSet	A class for maintaining and sorting sets of OSMetaClassBase-derived objects.
OSSet	A class for storing OSMetaClassBase-derived objects.
OSCollectionIterator	A class that provides a mechanism to iterate over OSCollection-derived collections.
Container Classes	
OSBoolean	A class for Boolean values.
OSData	A class for managing byte arrays.
OSNumber	A class for numeric values.
OSString	A class for managing strings.
OSSymbol	A class for representing unique string values.
OSSerialize	A class used by the container classes to serialize their instance data.
OSUnserializeXML	A class that recreates a container object from its serialized instance data in an XML buffer.

Table 6–6 lists some contents of the libsa/ directory. Section 2.4.5 provides an overview of libsa's functionality.

TABLE 6–6 Primary Contents of the libsa/ Directory

File	Description
libsa/bootstrap.cpp	Constructor and destructor functions for libsa.
libsa/bsearch.c, libsa/dgraph.c, libsa/sort.c	Functions for binary searching, directed graphs, and heap sort—used for supporting kernel extension loading.

(continues)

TABLE 6–6 Primary Contents of the `libsa/` Directory *(Continued)*

File	Description
`libsa/c++rem3.c`	Symbol remangler for code compiled with version 2.95 of the GNU C++ compiler—invoked during symbol table parsing when a Mach-O object file (typically a kernel extension) is mapped.
`libsa/catalogue.cpp`	I/O Catalog routines, such as those for accessing and manipulating kernel extension dictionaries, accessing mkext caches, and recording boot-time kernel extensions into dictionaries.
`libsa/kext.cpp, libsa/kld_patch.c, libsa/kmod.cpp, libsa/load.c`	The core of libsa's functionality: routines for resolving kernel extension dependencies, retrieving kernel extension versions, loading kernel extensions, patching vtables, etc.
`libsa/malloc.c`	Simple implementations of `malloc()` and `realloc()`.
`libsa/mkext.c`	Routines for LZSS compression/decompression, and for computing 32-bit Adler checksums.
`libsa/strrchr.c, libsa/strstr.c`	String functions.
`libsa/vers_rsrc.c`	Routines for parsing and generating version strings.

Recall from Chapter 2 that the libsa stand-alone library is used only for loading kernel extensions during system startup. In a typical booting scenario, when the kernel extension daemon (`kextd`) is started, it sends a `kIOCatalogRemoveKernelLinker` message to the I/O Catalog in the kernel. This message notifies the I/O Catalog that `kextd` is ready to handle the loading of kernel extensions from user space. Moreover, the message triggers the I/O Catalog to invoke destructors for the kernel's `__KLD` segment and to deallocate it. The `__KLD` segment contains libsa's code. The kernel's `__LINKEDIT` segment is also deallocated.

Section 2.4.1 provides an overview of the functionality implemented in the Mach portion of xnu. Table 6–7 lists the important components of the `osfmk/` directory.

TABLE 6–7 Primary Contents of the `osfmk`/Directory

Directory or File	Description
`osfmk/UserNotification/`	Kernel portion of the Kernel User Notification Center (KUNC) mechanism, which can be used by software running in the kernel to execute user-space programs and to display notices or alert messages. The `/usr/libexec/kuncd` daemon is the user-space agent that processes such requests from the kernel.
`osfmk/console/i386/`	VGA text console, x86 serial console.
`osfmk/console/iso_font.c`	Data for the ISO Latin-1 font.
`osfmk/console/panic_dialog.c`	Panic user-interface routines, including routines for drawing, managing, and testing the panic dialog.
`osfmk/console/panic_image.c`	Pixel data for the default panic image—an 8-bit, 472×255 image.
`osfmk/console/panic_ui/`	Panic image files and utilities to convert them into a kernel-usable format.
`osfmk/console/ppc/`	Fast video scrolling, PowerPC serial console.
`osfmk/console/rendered_numbers.c`	Pixel data for hexadecimal digits 0 through F and the colon character.
`osfmk/console/video_console.c`	Hardware-independent portion of the video console.
`osfmk/ddb/`	Built-in kernel debugger.
`osfmk/default_pager/`	Default pager, including the back-end for managing swap files.
`osfmk/device/`	Mach support for the I/O Kit, including device representation through Mach ports. The I/O Kit master port is also set here.
`osfmk/ipc/`	The core of Mach's IPC facility implementation.
`osfmk/kdp/`	A kernel debugging protocol called KDP that uses a TFTP-like UDP-based transfer mechanism.
`osfmk/kern/`	The core Mach kernel: implementations of abstractions such as processors, processor sets, tasks, threads, memory allocation, and timers. IPC interfaces are also implemented here.
`osfmk/mach/`	Mach headers and MIG definition files.
`osfmk/mach-o/`	Functions for accessing Mach-O headers.

(continues)

TABLE 6–7 Primary Contents of the `osfmk`/Directory *(Continued)*

Directory or File	Description
`osfmk/mach_debug/`	Mach debugging headers and MIG definition files.
`osfmk/machine/`	Headers that are wrappers for machine-dependent headers.
`osfmk/ppc/`	PowerPC-specific code: machine startup, exception vectors, trap handling, low-level context-switching code, low-level memory management, diagnostic calls, Classic support functions, machine-dependent debugger components, virtual machine monitor, kernel components for Apple's CHUD Tools, etc.
`osfmk/profiling/`	Kernel profiling support, which must be explicitly compiled in. The `kgmon` utility is used to control the profiling mechanism: It can stop or start the collection of kernel profiling data, dump the contents of the profile buffers, reset all the profile buffers, and retrieve specific named values from the kernel.
`osfmk/sys/`	Miscellaneous headers.
`osfmk/vm/`	Mach virtual memory subsystem, including the in-kernel shared memory server.

Section 2.4.6 provides an overview of the functionality of the Platform Expert. Table 6–8 lists the important components of the `pexpert/` directory.

TABLE 6–8 Primary Contents of the `pexpert/` Directory

Directory or File	Description
`pexpert/gen/bootargs.c`	Boot-argument parsing routines.
`pexpert/gen/device_tree.c`	Routines for accessing device tree entries and their properties.
`pexpert/gen/pe_gen.c`	Miscellaneous functions, including an 8-bit color lookup table used during bootstrapping.
`pexpert/i386/`	Machine identification, debugging output support, keyboard driver, generic interrupt handler, polled-mode serial port driver, and other platform-dependent routines such as for reading the timestamp counter, setting and clearing interrupts, generating a fake device tree, etc.

(continues)

TABLE 6–8 Primary Contents of the `pexpert/` Directory *(Continued)*

Directory or File	Description
`pexpert/pexpert/`	Miscellaneous platform headers, including those containing image data for the rotating gearwheel image shown at startup to indicate boot progress.
`pexpert/ppc/`	Machine identification, debugging output support, clock speed determination by running timed loops, timebase value retrieval, and other platform functions.

6.2 Mach

Let us briefly review our discussion of Mach from Chapters 1 and 2. Mach was designed as a communications-oriented operating system kernel with full multiprocessing support. Various types of operating systems could be built upon Mach. It aimed to be a microkernel in which traditional operating system services such as file systems, I/O, memory managers, networking stacks, and even operating system personalities were meant to reside in user space, with a clean logical and modular separation between them and the kernel. In practice, releases of Mach prior to release 3 had monolithic implementations. Release 3—a project started at Carnegie Mellon University and continued by the Open Software Foundation— was the first true microkernel version of Mach: BSD ran as a user-space task in this version.

The Mach portions of xnu were originally based on Open Group's Mach Mk 7.3 system, which in turn was based on Mach 3. xnu's Mach contains enhancements from MkLinux and work done on Mach at the University of Utah. Examples of the latter include the *migrating thread model*, wherein the thread abstraction is further decoupled into an execution context and a schedulable thread of control with an associated chain of contexts.

xnu Is Not a Microkernel

All kernel components reside in a single kernel address space in Mac OS X. Although the kernel is modular and extensible, it is still monolithic. Nevertheless, note that the kernel closely works with a few user-space daemons such as `dynamic_pager`, `kextd`, and `kuncd`.

In this chapter, we will discuss basic Mach concepts and programming abstractions. We will look at some of these concepts in more detail in the next three chapters in the context of process management, memory management, and interprocess communication (IPC).

> In this book, Mach-related programming examples are presented to demonstrate the internal working of certain aspects of Mac OS X. However, Apple does not support the direct use of most Mach-level APIs by third-party programs. Consequently, you are advised against using such APIs in software you distribute.

6.2.1 Kernel Fundamentals

Mach provides a *virtual machine* interface to higher layers by abstracting system hardware—a scenario that is common among many operating systems. The core Mach kernel is designed to be simple and extensible: It provides an IPC mechanism that is the building block for many services offered by the kernel. In particular, Mach's IPC features are unified with its virtual memory subsystem, which leads to various optimizations and simplifications.

> The 4.4BSD virtual memory system was based on the Mach 2.0 virtual memory system, with updates from newer versions of Mach.

Mach has five basic abstractions from a programmer's standpoint:

- Task
- Thread
- Port
- Message
- Memory object

Besides providing the basic kernel abstractions, Mach represents various other hardware and software resources as port objects, allowing manipulation of such resources through its IPC mechanism. For example, Mach represents the overall computer system as a *host* object, a single physical CPU as a *processor* object, and one or more groups of CPUs in a multiprocessor system as *processor set* objects.

6.2.1.1 *Tasks and Threads*

Mach divides the traditional Unix abstraction of a process into two parts: a task and a thread. As we will see in Chapter 7, the terms *thread* and *process* have context-specific connotations in the Mac OS X user space, depending on the environment. Within the kernel, a BSD process, which is analogous to a traditional Unix process, is a data structure with a one-to-one mapping with a Mach task. A Mach task has the following key features.

- It is an execution environment and a *static* entity. A task does not execute—that is, it performs no computation—by itself. It provides a framework within which other entities (threads) execute.

- It is the basic unit of resource allocation and can be thought of as a *resource container*. A task contains a collection of resources such as access to processors, paged virtual address space (virtual memory), IPC space, exception handlers, credentials, file descriptors, protection state, signal management state, and statistics. Note that a task's resources include Unix items too, which on Mac OS X are contained in a task through its one-to-one association with a BSD process structure.

- It represents the protection boundary of a program. One task cannot access another task's resources unless the former has obtained explicit access using some well-defined interface.

A thread is the actual executing entity in Mach—it is a point of control flow in a task. It has the following features.

- It executes within the context of a task, representing an independent program counter—a stream of instructions—within the task. A thread is also the fundamental schedulable entity, with associated scheduling priority and attributes. Each thread is scheduled preemptively and independently of other threads, whether they are in the same task or in any other task.

- The code that a thread executes resides within the address space of its task.

- Each task may contain zero or more threads, but each thread belongs to exactly one task. A task with no threads—although legitimate—cannot run.

- All threads within a task share all the task's resources. In particular, since all threads share the same memory, a thread can overwrite another thread's memory within the same task, without requiring any additional privileges. Since there may be several concurrently executing threads in one task, threads within a task must cooperate.

- A thread may have its own exception handlers.

- Each thread has its own computation state, which includes processor registers, a program counter, and a stack. Note that while a thread's stack is designated as private, it resides in the same address space as other threads within the same task. As noted earlier, threads within a task can access each other's stacks if they choose to.

- A thread uses a kernel stack for handling system calls. A kernel stack's size is 16KB.

To sum up, a task is passive, owns resources, and is a basic unit of protection. Threads within a task are active, execute instructions, and are basic units of control flow.

A single-threaded traditional Unix process is analogous to a Mach task with only one thread, whereas a multithreaded Unix process is analogous to a Mach task with many threads.

> A task is considerably more expensive to create or destroy than a thread.

Whereas every thread has a containing task, a Mach task is *not* related to its creating task, unlike Unix processes. However, the kernel maintains process-level parent-child relationships in the BSD process structures. Nevertheless, we may consider a task that creates another task to be the parent task and the newly created task to be the child task. During creation, the child inherits certain aspects of the parent, such as registered ports, exception and bootstrap ports, audit and security tokens, shared mapping regions, and the processor set. Note that if the parent's processor set has been marked inactive, the child is assigned to the default processor set.

The Kernel Task

As we saw in our discussion of kernel startup in Chapter 5, the kernel uses the task and thread abstractions to divide its functionality into various execution flows. The kernel uses a single task—the *kernel task*—with multiple threads that perform kernel operations such as scheduling, thread reaping, callout management, paging, and Unix exception handling. Thus, xnu is a monolithic kernel containing markedly different components such as Mach, BSD, and the I/O Kit, all running as groups of threads in a single task in the same address space.

Once a task is created, anyone with a valid task identifier (and thus the appropriate rights to a Mach IPC port) can perform operations on the task. A task can send its identifier to other tasks in an IPC message, if it so desires.

6.2.1.2 Ports

A Mach port is a multifaceted abstraction. It is a kernel-protected unidirectional IPC channel, a capability, and a name. Traditionally in Mach, a port is implemented as a message queue with a finite length.

> Besides Mach ports, Mac OS X provides many other types of IPC mechanisms, both within the kernel and in user space. Examples of such mechanisms include POSIX and System V IPC, multiple notification mechanisms, descriptor passing, and Apple Events. We will examine several IPC mechanisms in Chapter 9.

The port abstraction, along with associated operations (the most fundamental being send and receive), is the basis for communication in Mach. A port has kernel-managed *capabilities*—or *rights*—associated with it. A task must hold the appropriate rights to manipulate a port. For example, rights determine which task can send messages to a given port or which task may receive messages destined for it. Several tasks can have *send rights* to a particular port, but only one task can hold *receive rights* to a given port.

In the object-oriented sense, a port is an object reference. Various abstractions in Mach, including data structures and services, are represented by ports. In this sense, a port acts as a protected access provider to a system resource. You access objects such as tasks, threads, or memory objects[1] through their respective ports. For example, each task has a *task port* that represents that task in calls to the kernel. Similarly, a thread's point of control is accessible to user programs through a *thread port*. Any such access requires a port capability, which is the right to send or receive messages to that port, or rather, to the object the port represents. In particular, you perform operations on an object by sending messages to one of its ports.[2] The object holding receive rights to the port can then receive

---

1. With the exception of virtual memory, all Mach system resources are accessed through ports.

2. Objects may have multiple ports representing different types of functionality or access level. For example, a privileged resource may have a control port accessible only to the superuser and an information port accessible to all users.

the message, process it, and possibly perform an operation requested in the message. The following are two examples of this mechanism.

- A window manager can represent each window it manages by a port. Its client tasks can perform window operations by sending messages to the appropriate *window ports*. The window manager task receives and processes these operations.

- Each task, and each thread within the task, has an *exception port*. An error handler can register one of its ports as a thread's exception port. When an exception occurs, a message will be sent to this port. The handler can receive and process this message. Similarly, a debugger can register one of its ports as the task's exception port. Thereafter, unless a thread has explicitly registered its own thread exception port, exceptions in all of the task's threads will be communicated to the debugger.

Since a port is a per-task resource, all threads within a task automatically have access to the task's ports. A task can allow other tasks to access one or more of its ports. It does so by passing port rights in IPC messages to other tasks. Moreover, a thread can access a port only if the port is known to the containing task—there is no global, system-wide port namespace.

Several ports may be grouped together in a *port set*. All ports in a set share the same queue. Although there still is a single receiver, each message contains an identifier for the specific port within the port set on which the message was received. This functionality is similar to the Unix select() system call.

Network-Transparent Ports

Mach ports were designed to be network transparent, allowing tasks on network-connected machines to communicate with each other without worrying about where other tasks were located. A *network message server* (netmsgserver) was typically used in such scenarios as a trusted intermediary. Tasks could advertise their services by checking in with the netmsgserver. A check-in operation registered a unique name with the netmsgserver. Other tasks, including tasks on other machines, could look up service names on the netmsgserver, which itself used a port available to all tasks. This way, the netmsgserver could propagate port rights across networks. Mac OS X does not support this distributed IPC feature of Mach, and as such does not have any internal or external network message servers. Distributed IPC is, however, possible on Mac OS X using higher-level mechanisms such as the Cocoa API's *Distributed Objects* feature.

Note that a port can be used to send messages in only one direction. Therefore, unlike a BSD socket, a port does not represent an end point of a bidirectional communication channel. If a request message is sent on a certain port and the sender needs to receive a reply, another port must be used for the reply.

As we will see in Chapter 9, a task's IPC space includes mappings from port names to the kernel's internal port objects, along with rights for these names. A Mach port's name is an integer—conceptually similar to a Unix file descriptor. However, Mach ports differ from file descriptors in several ways. For example, a file descriptor may be duplicated multiple times, with each descriptor being a different number referring to the same open file. If multiple port rights are similarly opened for a particular port, the port names will coalesce into a single name, which would be reference-counted for the number of rights it represents. Moreover, other than certain standard ports such as registered, bootstrap, and exception ports, Mach ports are not inherited implicitly across the `fork()` system call.

6.2.1.3 *Messages*

Mach IPC messages are data objects that threads exchange with each other to communicate. Typical intertask communication in Mach, including between the kernel and user tasks, occurs using messages. A message may contain actual *inline* data or a pointer to *out-of-line* (OOL) data. OOL data transfer is an optimization for large transfers, wherein the kernel allocates a memory region for the message in the receiver's virtual address space, without making a physical copy of the message. The shared memory pages are marked *copy-on-write* (COW).

A message may contain arbitrary program data, copies of memory ranges, exceptions, notifications, port capabilities, and so on. In particular, the only way to transfer port capabilities from one task to another is through messages.

Mach messages are transferred asynchronously. Even though only one task can hold receive rights to a port, multiple threads within a task may attempt to receive messages on a port. In such a case, only one of the threads will succeed in receiving a given message.

6.2.1.4 *Virtual Memory and Memory Objects*

Mach's virtual memory (VM) system can be cleanly separated into machine-independent and machine-dependent parts. For example, address maps, memory objects, share maps, and resident memory are machine-independent, whereas the physical map (*pmap*) is machine-dependent. We will discuss VM-related abstractions in detail in Chapter 8.

Features of Mach's VM design include the following.

- Mach provides per-task protected address spaces, with a sparse memory layout. A task's address space description is a linear list of memory regions (vm_map_t), where each region points to a memory object (vm_object_t).

- The machine-dependent address mappings are contained in a pmap object (pmap_t).

- A task can allocate or deallocate regions of virtual memory both within its own address space and in other tasks' address spaces.

- Tasks can specify protection and inheritance properties of memory on a per-page basis. Memory pages can be unshared between tasks or shared using either copy-on-write or read-write mode. Each group of pages—a *memory region*—has two protection values: a *current* and a *maximum*. The current protection corresponds to the actual hardware protection being used for the pages, whereas the maximum protection is the highest (most permissive) value that current protection may ever achieve. The maximum protection is an absolute upper limit in that it cannot be elevated (made more permissive), but only lowered (made more restrictive). Therefore, the maximum protection represents the most access that can be had to a memory region.

A memory object is a container for data (including file data) that is mapped into the address space of a task. It serves as a channel for providing memory to tasks. Mach traditionally allows a memory object to be managed by a user-mode *external memory manager*, wherein the handling of page faults and page-out data requests can be performed in user space. An external pager can also be used to implement networked virtual memory. This external memory management (EMM) feature of Mach is not used in Mac OS X. xnu provides basic paging services in the kernel through three pagers: the default (anonymous) pager, the vnode pager, and the device pager.

The *default pager* handles anonymous memory—that is, memory with no explicitly designated pager. It is implemented in the Mach portion of the kernel. With help from the dynamic_pager user-space application,[3] which manages on-disk

---

3. The dynamic_pager application is not involved in actual paging operations—it only creates or deletes swap files based on various criteria.

backing-store (or *swap*) files, the default pager pages to swap files on a normal file system.

> Swap files reside under the `/var/vm/` directory by default. The files are named `swapfileN`, where `N` is the swap file's number. The first swap file is called `swapfile0`.

The *vnode pager* is used for memory-mapped files. Since the Mac OS X VFS is in the BSD portion of the kernel, the vnode pager is implemented in the BSD layer.

The *device pager* is used for non-general-purpose memory. It is implemented in the Mach layer but used by the I/O Kit.

6.2.2 Exception Handling

A Mach exception is a synchronous interruption of a program's execution that occurs due to the program itself. The causes for exceptions can be erroneous conditions such as executing an illegal instruction, dividing by zero, or accessing invalid memory. Exceptions can also be caused deliberately, such as during debugging, when a debugger breakpoint is hit.

xnu's Mach implementation associates an array of exception ports with each task and another with each thread within a task. Each such array has as many slots as there are exception types defined for the implementation, with slot 0 being invalid. All of a thread's exception ports are set to the null port (IP_NULL) when the thread is created, whereas a task's exception ports are inherited from those of the parent task. The kernel allows a programmer to get or set individual exception ports for both tasks and threads. Consequently, a program can have multiple exception handlers. A single handler may also handle multiple exception types. Typical preparation for exception handling by a program involves allocation of one or more ports to which the kernel will send exception notification messages. The port can then be registered as an exception port for one or more types of exceptions for either a thread or a task. The exception handler code typically runs in a dedicated thread, waiting for notification messages from the kernel.

Exception handling in Mach can be viewed as a metaoperation consisting of several suboperations. The thread that causes an exception is called the *victim* thread, whereas the thread that runs the exception handler is called the *handler* thread. When a victim causes (raises) an exception, the kernel suspends the victim thread and sends a message to the appropriate exception port, which may be either a thread exception port (more specific) or a task exception port (if the thread has not set an exception port). Upon receiving (catching) the message, the handler thread processes the exception—an operation that may involve fixing the victim's state, arranging for it to be terminated, logging an error, and so on. The handler replies to the message, indicating whether the exception was processed successfully (cleared). Finally, the kernel either resumes the victim or terminates it.

A thread exception port is typically relevant for error handling. Each thread may have its own exception handlers that process exceptions corresponding to errors that affect only individual threads. A task exception port is typically relevant for debugging. A debugger can attach to a task by registering one of its own ports as the debugged task's exception port. Since a task inherits its exception ports from the creating task, the debugger will also be able to control child processes of the debugged program. Moreover, exception notifications for all threads that have no registered exception port will be sent to the task exception port. Recall that a thread is created with null exception ports and, correspondingly, with no default handlers. Therefore, this works well in the general case. Even when a thread does have valid exception ports, the corresponding exception handlers can forward exceptions to the task exception port.

We will look at a programming example of Mach exception handling in Chapter 9.

6.3 A Flavor of the Mach APIs

Let us look at a few simple examples of using the Mach APIs. These will serve as a prelude to more complex or subsystem-specific examples that we will see later in this chapter and in subsequent chapters.

> Documentation for most Mach calls exported by the xnu kernel is available in the `osfmk/man/` directory within the xnu package. You might find it useful to test API-based examples while referring to the API documentation.

6.3.1 Displaying Host Information

The `host_info()` Mach call retrieves information about a host, such as the type and number of processors installed, the number of processors currently available,

and the memory size. As is the case with many Mach "info" calls, host_info()
takes a *flavor* argument, which specifies the kind of information to be retrieved.
For example, host_info() accepts the HOST_BASIC_INFO, HOST_SCHED_INFO,
and HOST_PRIORITY_INFO flavors as arguments to return basic, scheduler-
related, and scheduler-priority-related information, respectively, from the kernel.
Besides host_info(), other calls such as host_kernel_version(), host_
get_boot_info(), and host_page_size() can be used to retrieve miscellaneous information. Figure 6–1 shows an example of using the host_info() call.

FIGURE 6–1 Retrieving basic host information using Mach calls

```
// host_basic_info.c

#include <stdio.h>
#include <stdlib.h>
#include <mach/mach.h>

#define EXIT_ON_MACH_ERROR(msg, retval) \
    if (kr != KERN_SUCCESS) { mach_error(msg ":" , kr); exit((retval)); }

int
main()
{
    kern_return_t           kr; // the standard return type for Mach calls
    host_name_port_t        myhost;
    kernel_version_t        kversion;
    host_basic_info_data_t  hinfo;
    mach_msg_type_number_t  count;
    char                    *cpu_type_name, *cpu_subtype_name;
    vm_size_t               page_size;

    // get send rights to the name port for the current host
    myhost = mach_host_self();

    kr = host_kernel_version(myhost, kversion);
    EXIT_ON_MACH_ERROR("host_kernel_version", kr);

    count = HOST_BASIC_INFO_COUNT;      // size of the buffer
    kr = host_info(myhost,              // the host name port
                HOST_BASIC_INFO,        // flavor
                (host_info_t)&hinfo,    // out structure
                &count);                // in/out size
    EXIT_ON_MACH_ERROR("host_info", kr);

    kr = host_page_size(myhost, &page_size);
    EXIT_ON_MACH_ERROR("host_page_size", kr);
```

(continues)

FIGURE 6–1 Retrieving basic host information using Mach calls *(continued)*

```
    printf("%s\n", kversion);

    // the slot_name() library function converts the specified
    // cpu_type/cpu_subtype pair to a human-readable form
    slot_name(hinfo.cpu_type, hinfo.cpu_subtype, &cpu_type_name,
              &cpu_subtype_name);

    printf("cpu              %s (%s, type=0x%x subtype=0x%x "
           "threadtype=0x%x)\n", cpu_type_name, cpu_subtype_name,
           hinfo.cpu_type, hinfo.cpu_subtype, hinfo.cpu_threadtype);
    printf("max_cpus         %d\n", hinfo.max_cpus);
    printf("avail_cpus       %d\n", hinfo.avail_cpus);
    printf("physical_cpu     %d\n", hinfo.physical_cpu);
    printf("physical_cpu_max %d\n", hinfo.physical_cpu_max);
    printf("logical_cpu      %d\n", hinfo.logical_cpu);
    printf("logical_cpu_max  %d\n", hinfo.logical_cpu_max);
    printf("memory_size      %u MB\n", (hinfo.memory_size >> 20));
    printf("max_mem          %llu MB\n", (hinfo.max_mem >> 20));
    printf("page_size        %u bytes\n", page_size);

    exit(0);
}


$ gcc -Wall -o host_basic_info host_basic_info.c
$ ./host_basic_info # Power Mac G5 Quad 2.5GHz
Darwin Kernel Version 8.5.0: ... root:xnu-792.6.61.obj~1/RELEASE_PPC
cpu              ppc970 (PowerPC 970, type=0x12 subtype=0x64 threadtype=0x0)
max_cpus         4
avail_cpus       4
physical_cpu     4
physical_cpu_max 4
logical_cpu      4
logical_cpu_max  4
memory_size      2040 MB
max_mem          4096 MB
page_size        4096 bytes

$ ./host_basic_info # iMac Core Duo 1.83GHz
Darwin Kernel Version 8.5.1: ... root:xnu-792.8.36.obj~1/RELEASE_I386
cpu              i486 (Intel 80486, type=0x7, subtype=0x4, threadtype=0x0)
max_cpus         2
avail_cpus       2
...
page_size        4096 bytes
```

Note in Figure 6–1 that as discussed in Chapter 5, the `memory_size` value reported by Mach is pinned to 2GB on a machine with more than 2GB of physical memory.

6.3.2 Accessing the Kernel's Clock Services

The kernel provides clock services with different clock types such as *system*, *calendar*, and *real time*. Accessing these services involves acquiring send rights to their ports and sending messages requesting the clocks' attributes or functionality. Figure 6–2 shows a program that retrieves the attributes and current time values from the kernel's various clocks.

FIGURE 6–2 Retrieving clock attributes and time values in Mach

```
// host_clock.c

#include <stdio.h>
#include <stdlib.h>
#include <sys/time.h>
#include <mach/mach.h>
#include <mach/clock.h>

#define OUT_ON_MACH_ERROR(msg, retval) \
    if (kr != KERN_SUCCESS) { mach_error(msg ":" , kr); goto out; }

int
main()
{
    kern_return_t           kr;
    host_name_port_t        myhost;
    clock_serv_t            clk_system, clk_calendar, clk_realtime;
    natural_t               attribute[4];
    mach_msg_type_number_t  count;
    mach_timespec_t         timespec;
    struct timeval          t;

    myhost = mach_host_self();

    // Get a send right to the system clock's name port
    kr = host_get_clock_service(myhost,  SYSTEM_CLOCK,
                            (clock_serv_t *)&clk_system);
    OUT_ON_MACH_ERROR("host_get_clock_service", kr);
```

(continues)

FIGURE 6–2 Retrieving clock attributes and time values in Mach *(continued)*

```
// Get a send right to the calendar clock's name port
kr = host_get_clock_service(myhost, CALENDAR_CLOCK,
                            (clock_serv_t *)&clk_calendar);
OUT_ON_MACH_ERROR("host_get_clock_service", kr);


// Get a send right to the real-time clock's name port
kr = host_get_clock_service(myhost, REALTIME_CLOCK,
                            (clock_serv_t *)&clk_realtime);
OUT_ON_MACH_ERROR("host_get_clock_service", kr);


//// System clock
count = sizeof(attribute)/sizeof(natural_t);
// Get the clock's resolution in nanoseconds
kr = clock_get_attributes(clk_system, CLOCK_GET_TIME_RES,
                          (clock_attr_t)attribute, &count);
OUT_ON_MACH_ERROR("clock_get_attributes", kr);
// Get the current time
kr = clock_get_time(clk_system, &timespec);
OUT_ON_MACH_ERROR("clock_get_time", kr);
printf("System clock  : %u s + %u ns (res %u ns)\n",
       timespec.tv_sec, timespec.tv_nsec, attribute[0]);


//// Real-time clock
count = sizeof(attribute)/sizeof(natural_t);
kr = clock_get_attributes(clk_realtime, CLOCK_GET_TIME_RES,
                          (clock_attr_t)attribute, &count);
OUT_ON_MACH_ERROR("clock_get_attributes", kr);
kr = clock_get_time(clk_realtime, &timespec);
OUT_ON_MACH_ERROR("clock_get_time", kr);
printf("Realtime clock: %u s + %u ns (res %u ns)\n",
       timespec.tv_sec, timespec.tv_nsec, attribute[0]);


//// Calendar clock
count = sizeof(attribute)/sizeof(natural_t);
kr = clock_get_attributes(clk_calendar, CLOCK_GET_TIME_RES,
                          (clock_attr_t)attribute, &count);
OUT_ON_MACH_ERROR("clock_get_attributes", kr);
kr = clock_get_time(clk_calendar, &timespec);
gettimeofday(&t, NULL);
OUT_ON_MACH_ERROR("clock_get_time", kr);
printf("Calendar clock: %u s + %u ns (res %u ns)\n",
       timespec.tv_sec, timespec.tv_nsec, attribute[0]);


printf("gettimeofday  : %ld s + %d us\n", t.tv_sec, t.tv_usec);

out:
```

(continues)

FIGURE 6–2 Retrieving clock attributes and time values in Mach *(continued)*

```
    // Should deallocate ports here for cleanliness
    mach_port_deallocate(mach_task_self(), myhost);
    mach_port_deallocate(mach_task_self(), clk_calendar);
    mach_port_deallocate(mach_task_self(), clk_system);
    mach_port_deallocate(mach_task_self(), clk_realtime);

    exit(0);
}


$ gcc -Wall -o host_clock host_clock.c
$ ./host_clock
System clock  : 134439 s + 840456243 ns (res 10000000 ns)
Realtime clock: 134439 s + 841218705 ns (res 10000000 ns)
Calendar clock: 1104235237 s + 61156000 ns (res 10000000 ns)
gettimeofday  : 1104235237 s + 61191 us
```

6.3.3 Using a Clock Service to Ring an Alarm

Having seen how to acquire send rights to a clock service's port, we can use these rights to request the service to ring an alarm at a specified time. The clock will notify us by sending an IPC message when the alarm is fired. The program shown in Figure 6–3 sets an alarm to ring after 2.05 seconds and waits for the alarm message to arrive on a port it allocated.

FIGURE 6–3 Setting an alarm using Mach calls

```
// host_alarm.c

#include <stdio.h>
#include <stdlib.h>
#include <sys/time.h>
#include <mach/mach.h>
#include <mach/clock.h>

#define OUT_ON_MACH_ERROR(msg, retval) \
    if (kr != KERN_SUCCESS) { mach_error(msg ":" , kr); goto out; }

// Structure for the IPC message we will receive from the clock
typedef struct msg_format_recv_s {
    mach_msg_header_t  header;
    int                data;
```

(continues)

FIGURE 6–3 Setting an alarm using Mach calls *(continued)*

```
    mach_msg_trailer_t trailer;
} msg_format_recv_t;

int
main()
{
    kern_return_t      kr;
    clock_serv_t       clk_system;
    mach_timespec_t    alarm_time;
    clock_reply_t      alarm_port;
    struct timeval     t1, t2;
    msg_format_recv_t message;
    mach_port_t        mytask;

    // The C library optimized this call by returning the task port's value
    // that it caches in the mach_task_self_ variable
    mytask = mach_task_self();

    kr = host_get_clock_service(mach_host_self(), SYSTEM_CLOCK,
                                (clock_serv_t *)&clk_system);
    OUT_ON_MACH_ERROR("host_get_clock_service", kr);

    // Let us set the alarm to ring after 2.05 seconds
    alarm_time.tv_sec = 2;
    alarm_time.tv_nsec = 50000000;

    // Allocate a port (specifically, get receive right for the new port)
    // We will use this port to receive the alarm message from the clock
    kr = mach_port_allocate(
            mytask,                  // the task acquiring the port right
            MACH_PORT_RIGHT_RECEIVE, // type of right
            &alarm_port);            // task's name for the port right
    OUT_ON_MACH_ERROR("mach_port_allocate", kr);

    gettimeofday(&t1, NULL);

    // Set the alarm
    kr = clock_alarm(clk_system,     // the clock to use
                     TIME_RELATIVE,  // how to interpret alarm time
                     alarm_time,     // the alarm time
                     alarm_port);    // this port will receive the alarm message
    OUT_ON_MACH_ERROR("clock_alarm", kr);

    printf("Current time %ld s + %d us\n"
           "Setting alarm to ring after %d s + %d ns\n",
           t1.tv_sec, t1.tv_usec, alarm_time.tv_sec, alarm_time.tv_nsec);
```

(continues)

FIGURE 6–3 Setting an alarm using Mach calls *(continued)*

```
// Wait to receive the alarm message (we will block here)
kr = mach_msg(&(message.header),      // the message buffer
              MACH_RCV_MSG,            // message option bits
              0,                       // send size (we are receiving, so 0)
              message.header.msgh_size,// receive limit
              alarm_port,              // receive right
              MACH_MSG_TIMEOUT_NONE,   // no timeout
              MACH_PORT_NULL);         // no timeout notification port
// We should have received an alarm message at this point
gettimeofday(&t2, NULL);
OUT_ON_MACH_ERROR("mach_msg", kr);

if (t2.tv_usec < t1.tv_usec) {
    t1.tv_sec += 1;
    t1.tv_usec -= 1000000;
}

printf("\nCurrent time %ld s + %d us\n", t2.tv_sec, t2.tv_usec);
printf("Alarm rang after %ld s + %d us\n", (t2.tv_sec - t1.tv_sec),
    (t2.tv_usec - t1.tv_usec));

out:
    mach_port_deallocate(mytask, clk_system);

    // Release user reference for the receive right we created
    mach_port_deallocate(mytask, alarm_port);

    exit(0);
}


$ gcc -Wall -o host_alarm host_alarm.c
$ ./host_alarm
Current time 1104236281 s + 361257 us
Setting alarm to ring after 2 s + 50000000 ns

Current time 1104236283 s + 412115 us
Alarm rang after 2 s + 50858 us
```

6.3.4 Displaying Host Statistics

The `host_statistics()` call can be used to retrieve statistical information about processor and virtual memory usage on a system-wide basis. Figure 6–4 shows an example of using this call.

FIGURE 6–4 Using Mach calls to retrieve scheduling and virtual memory statistics

```c
// host_statistics.c

#include <stdio.h>
#include <stdlib.h>
#include <mach/mach.h>

// Wrapper function with error checking
kern_return_t
do_host_statistics(host_name_port_t        host,
                   host_flavor_t           flavor,
                   host_info_t             info,
                   mach_msg_type_number_t  *count)
{
    kern_return_t kr;

    kr = host_statistics(host,                  // control port for the host
                         flavor,                // type of statistics desired
                         (host_info_t)info,     // out buffer
                         count);                // in/out size of buffer
    if (kr != KERN_SUCCESS) {
        (void)mach_port_deallocate(mach_task_self(), host);
        mach_error("host info:", kr);
        exit(1);
    }

    return kr;
}

int
main()
{
    kern_return_t           kr;
    host_name_port_t        host;
    mach_msg_type_number_t  count;
    vm_size_t               page_size;
    host_load_info_data_t   load_info;
    host_cpu_load_info_data_t cpu_load_info;
    vm_statistics_data_t    vm_stat;

    host = mach_host_self();

    count = HOST_LOAD_INFO_COUNT;
    // Get system loading statistics
    kr = do_host_statistics(host, HOST_LOAD_INFO, (host_info_t)&load_info,
                            &count);
```

(continues)

FIGURE 6–4 Using Mach calls to retrieve scheduling and virtual memory statistics *(continued)*

```
count = HOST_VM_INFO_COUNT;
// Get virtual memory statistics
kr = do_host_statistics(host, HOST_VM_INFO, (host_info_t)&vm_stat, &count);


count = HOST_CPU_LOAD_INFO_COUNT;
// Get CPU load statistics
kr = do_host_statistics(host, HOST_CPU_LOAD_INFO,
                          (host_info_t)&cpu_load_info, &count);


kr = host_page_size(host, &page_size);

printf("Host statistics:\n");


// (average # of runnable processes) / (# of CPUs)
printf("Host load statistics\n");
printf("  time period (sec) %5s%10s%10s\n", "5", "30", "60");
printf("  load average %10u%10u%10u\n", load_info.avenrun[0],
       load_info.avenrun[1], load_info.avenrun[2]);
printf("  Mach factor  %10u%10u%10u\n", load_info.mach_factor[0],
       load_info.mach_factor[1], load_info.mach_factor[2]);

printf("\n");

printf("Cumulative CPU load statistics\n");
printf("  User state ticks   = %u\n",
       cpu_load_info.cpu_ticks[CPU_STATE_USER]);
printf("  System state ticks = %u\n",
       cpu_load_info.cpu_ticks[CPU_STATE_SYSTEM]);
printf("  Nice state ticks   = %u\n",
       cpu_load_info.cpu_ticks[CPU_STATE_NICE]);
printf("  Idle state ticks   = %u\n",
       cpu_load_info.cpu_ticks[CPU_STATE_IDLE]);

printf("\n");

printf("Virtual memory statistics\n");
printf("  page size          = %u bytes\n", page_size);
printf("  pages free         = %u\n", vm_stat.free_count);
printf("  pages active       = %u\n", vm_stat.active_count);
printf("  pages inactive     = %u\n", vm_stat.inactive_count);
printf("  pages wired down   = %u\n", vm_stat.wire_count);
printf("  zero fill pages    = %u\n", vm_stat.zero_fill_count);
printf("  pages reactivated  = %u\n", vm_stat.reactivations);
printf("  pageins            = %u\n", vm_stat.pageins);
printf("  pageouts           = %u\n", vm_stat.pageouts);
printf("  translation faults = %u\n", vm_stat.faults);
printf("  copy-on-write faults = %u\n", vm_stat.cow_faults);
```

(continues)

FIGURE 6–4 Using Mach calls to retrieve scheduling and virtual memory statistics *(continued)*

```
    printf("  object cache lookups = %u\n", vm_stat.lookups);
    printf("  object cache hits    = %u (hit rate %2.2f %%)\n", vm_stat.hits,
           100 * (double)vm_stat.hits/(double)vm_stat.lookups);

    exit(0);
}
```

```
$ gcc -Wall -o host_statistics host_statistics.c
$ ./host_statistics
Host statistics:
Host load statistics
   time period (sec)     5        30        60
   load average        276       233       70
   Mach factor        1685      1589      1609

Cumulative CPU load statistics
  User state ticks    = 109098
  System state ticks  = 41056
  Nice state ticks    = 535
  Idle state ticks    = 1974855

Virtual memory statistics
  page size           = 4096 bytes
  pages free          = 434154
  pages active        = 70311
  pages inactive      = 236301
  pages wired down    = 45666
  zero fill pages     = 2266643
  pages reactivated   = 0
  pageins             = 55952
  pageouts            = 0
  translation faults  = 4549671
  copy-on-write faults = 83912
  object cache lookups = 36028
  object cache hits   = 19120 (hit rate 53.07 %)
```

6.4 Entering the Kernel

On a typical operating system, user processes are logically insulated from the kernel's memory by using different processor execution modes. The Mac OS X kernel executes in a higher-privileged mode (PowerPC OEA) than any user program (PowerPC UISA and VEA). Each user process—that is, each Mach task—has its own virtual address space. Similarly, the kernel has its own, distinct virtual address space that does *not* occupy a subrange of the maximum possible address space of a user process. Specifically, the Mac OS X kernel has a private 32-bit (4GB) virtual address space, and so does each 32-bit user process. Similarly, a 64-bit user process also gets a private virtual address space that is not subdivided into kernel and user parts.

> Although the Mac OS X user and kernel virtual address spaces are not subdivisions of a single virtual address space, the amounts of virtual memory usable within both are restricted due to conventional mappings. For example, kernel addresses in the 32-bit kernel virtual address space lie between `0x1000` and `0xDFFFFFFF` (3.5GB). Similarly, the amount of virtual memory a 32-bit user process can use is significantly less than 4GB, since various system libraries are mapped by default into each user address space. We will see specific examples of such mappings in Chapter 8.

We will refer to the kernel virtual address space simply as the *kernel space*. Moreover, even though each user process has its own address space, we will often use the phrase *the user space* when the specific process is not relevant. In this sense, we can think of all user processes as residing in the user space. The following are some important characteristics of the kernel and user spaces.

- The kernel space is inaccessible to user tasks. The kernel enforces this protection by using memory management hardware to create a boundary between kernel-level and user-level code.
- The user space is fully accessible to the kernel.
- The kernel normally prevents one user task from modifying, or even accessing, another task's memory. However, such protection is usually subject to task and system ownership. For example, there exist kernel-provided mechanisms through which a task T1 can access the address space of another task T2 if T1 is running with root privileges, or if T1 and T2 are both owned by the same user. Tasks can also explicitly share memory with other tasks.
- The user space cannot directly access hardware. However, it is possible to have user-space device drivers that access hardware after mediation by the kernel.

Since the kernel mediates access to physical resources, a user program must exchange information with the kernel to avail the kernel's services. Typical user-space execution requires exchange of both *control information* and *data*. In such an exchange between a Mach task and the kernel, a thread within the task transitions to kernel space from user space, transferring control to the kernel. After handling the user thread's request, the kernel returns control back to the thread, allowing it to continue normal execution. At other times, the kernel can acquire control even though the current thread was not involved in the reason for the transfer—in fact, the transfer is often not explicitly requested by the programmer. We refer to execution within the kernel and user spaces as being in the *kernel mode* and the *user mode*, respectively.

A Modal Dialog

Technically, even the Mac OS X kernel mode can be thought of as consisting of two submodes. The first mode refers to the environment in which the kernel's own threads run—that is, the kernel task and its resources. The kernel task is a proper Mach task (it is the first Mach task to be created) that runs several dozen kernel threads on a typical system.

The second mode refers to threads running in the kernel after they enter the kernel from user space through a system call—that is, threads *trap* from user space into the kernel. Kernel subsystems that need to be aware of the two modes may handle them differently.

6.4.1 Types of Control Transfer

Although such transfers of control are traditionally divided into categories based on the events that caused them, at the PowerPC processor level, all categories are handled by the same exception mechanism. Examples of events that can cause the processor to change execution mode include the following:

- External signals, such as from the interrupt controller hardware
- Abnormal conditions encountered while executing an instruction
- Expected system events such as rescheduling and page faults
- Trace exceptions caused by deliberate enabling of single-stepping (setting the SE bit of the MSR) or branch-tracing (setting the BE bit of the MSR)
- Conditions internal to the processor, such as the detection of a parity error in the L1 D-cache
- Execution of the system call instruction

Nevertheless, it is still useful to categorize control transfers in Mac OS X based on the events causing them. Let us look at some broad categories.

6.4.1.1 External Hardware Interrupts

An external hardware interrupt is a transfer of control into the kernel that is typically initiated by a hardware device to indicate an event. Such interrupts are signaled to the processor by the assertion of the processor's external interrupt input signal, which causes an external interrupt exception in the processor. External interrupts are asynchronous, and their occurrence is typically unrelated to the currently executing thread. Note that external interrupts can be masked.

An example of an external interrupt is a storage device controller causing an interrupt to signal the completion of an I/O request. On certain processors, such as the 970FX, a thermal exception—used to notify the processor of an abnormal condition—is signaled by the assertion of the thermal interrupt input signal. In this case, even though the abnormal condition is internal to the processor, the source of the interrupt is external.

6.4.1.2 Processor Traps

A processor trap is a transfer of control into the kernel that is initiated by the processor itself because of some event that needs attention. Processor traps may be synchronous or asynchronous. Although the conditions that cause traps could all be termed abnormal in that they are all exceptional (hence the exception), it is helpful to subclassify them as *expected* (such as page faults) or *unexpected* (such as a hardware failure). Other examples of reasons for traps include divide-by-zero errors, completion of a traced instruction, illegal access to memory, and the execution of an illegal instruction.

6.4.1.3 Software Traps

The Mac OS X kernel implements a mechanism called *asynchronous system traps* (ASTs), wherein one or more reason bits can be set by software for a processor or a thread. Each bit represents a particular software trap. When a processor is about to return from an interrupt context, including returns from system calls, it checks for these bits, and takes a trap if it finds one. The latter operation involves executing the corresponding interrupt-handling code. A thread checks for such traps in many cases when it is about to change its execution state, such as from being suspended to running. The kernel's clock interrupt handler also periodically checks for ASTs. We categorize ASTs on Mac OS X as software traps because they are both initiated and handled by software. Some AST implementations may use hardware support.

6.4.1.4 *System Calls*

The PowerPC system call instruction is used by programs to generate a system call exception, which causes the processor to prepare and execute the system call handler in the kernel. The system call exception is synchronous. Hundreds of system calls constitute a well-defined set of interfaces serving as entry points into the kernel for user programs.

POSIX

A standard set of system calls, along with their behavior, error handling, return values, and so on, is defined by a Portable Operating System Interface (POSIX) standard, which defines an interface and not its implementation. Mac OS X provides a large subset of the POSIX API.

The name POSIX was suggested by Richard Stallman. POSIX documentation suggests that the word should be pronounced *pahz-icks*, as in *positive*, and not *poh-six* or other variations.

To sum up, a hardware interrupt from an external device generates an external interrupt exception, a system call generates a system call exception, and other situations result in a variety of exceptions.

6.4.2 Implementing System Entry Mechanisms

PowerPC exceptions are the fundamental vehicles for propagating any kind of interrupts (other than ASTs), whether hardware- or software-generated. Before we discuss how some of these exceptions are processed, let us look at the key components of the overall PowerPC exception-processing mechanism on Mac OS X. These include the following, some of which we have come across in earlier chapters:

- The kernel's exception vectors that reside in a designated memory area starting at physical memory address 0x0
- PowerPC exception-handling registers
- The rfid (64-bit) and rfi (32-bit) system linkage instructions, which are used for returning from interrupts
- The sc system linkage instruction, which is used to cause a system call exception

- Machine-dependent thread state, including memory areas called *exception save areas*, which are used for saving various types of context during exception processing

> A *system linkage instruction* connects user-mode and supervisor-mode software. For example, by using a system linkage instruction (such as `sc`), a program can call on the operating system to perform a service. Conversely, after performing the service, the operating system can return to user-mode software by using another system linkage instruction (such as `rfid`).

6.4.2.1 Exceptions and Exception Vectors

The __VECTORS segment of the kernel executable (Figure 6–5) contains the kernel's exception vectors. As we saw in Chapter 4, BootX copies these to their designated location (starting at 0x0) before transferring control to the kernel. These vectors are implemented in osfmk/ppc/lowmem_vectors.s.

FIGURE 6–5 The Mach-O segment containing the exception vectors in the kernel executable

```
$ otool -l /mach_kernel
...
Load command 2
      cmd LC_SEGMENT
  cmdsize 124
  segname __VECTORS
   vmaddr 0x00000000
   vmsize 0x00007000
  fileoff 3624960
 filesize 28672
  maxprot 0x00000007
 initprot 0x00000003
   nsects 1
    flags 0x0
Section
  sectname __interrupts
  segname __VECTORS
      addr 0x00000000
      size 0x00007000
    offset 3624960
     align 2^12 (4096)
    reloff 0
    nreloc 0
     flags 0x00000000
```

(continues)

FIGURE 6–5   The Mach-O segment containing the exception vectors in the kernel executable *(continued)*

```
reserved1 0
 reserved2 0
...
```

Table 5–1 lists various PowerPC processor exceptions and some of their details. Recall that most exceptions are subject to one or more conditions; for example, most exceptions can occur only when no higher-priority exception exists. Similarly, exceptions caused by failed effective-to-virtual address translations can occur only if address translation is enabled. Moreover, depending on a system's specific hardware, or whether the kernel is being debugged, some exceptions listed in Table 5–1 may be inconsequential. Figure 6–6 shows an excerpt from `lowmem_vectors.s`. For example, when there is a system call exception, the processor executes the code starting at the label `.L_handlerC00` (vector offset 0xC00).

FIGURE 6–6 The kernel's exception vectors

```
; osfmk/ppc/lowmem_vectors.s
...
#define VECTOR_SEGMENT .section __VECTORS, __interrupts
          VECTOR_SEGMENT
          .globl EXT(lowGlo)
EXT(lowGlo):
          .globl EXT(ExceptionVectorsStart)
EXT(ExceptionVectorsStart):
baseR:
          ...
          . = 0x100 ; T_RESET
          .globl EXT(ResetHandler)
.L_handler100:
          ...
          . = 0x200 ; T_MACHINE_CHECK
.L_handler200:
          ...
          . = 0x300 ; T_DATA_ACCESS
.L_handler300:
          ...
          . = 0xC00 ; T_SYSTEM_CALL
.L_handlerC00:
          ...
```

The exception vectors for the x86 version of Darwin are implemented in `osfmk/i386/locore.s`.

Exception Vectors in Early UNIX

The concept of exception vectors in early UNIX was very similar to the one being discussed here, although there were far fewer vectors. The UNIX trap vectors were defined in an assembly file called `low.s` or `l.s`, representing that the vectors resided in low memory. Figure 6–7 shows an excerpt from the `low.s` file in the Third Edition UNIX source.

FIGURE 6–7 Trap vectors in Third Edition UNIX

```
/ PDP-11 Research UNIX V3 (Third Edition), circa 1973
/ ken/low.s
/ low core
...
.globl start

. = 0^.
        4
        br      1f


/ trap vectors
        trap; br7+0             / bus error
        trap; br7+1             / illegal instruction
        trap; br7+2             / bpt-trace trap
        trap; br7+3             / iot trap
        trap; br7+4             / power fail
        trap; br7+5             / emulator trap
        trap; br7+6             / system entry

. = 040^.
1:      jmp     start

. = 060^.
        klin; br4
        klou; br4
...
```

6.4.2.2 *Exception-Handling Registers*

The Machine Status Save/Restore Register 0 (SRR0) is a special branch-processing register in the PowerPC architecture. It is used to save machine status on interrupts and to restore machine status on return from interrupts. When an interrupt occurs, SRR0 is set to the current or next instruction address, depending on the nature of the interrupt. For example, if an interrupt is being caused due to an illegal instruction exception, then SRR0 will contain the address of the current instruction (the one that failed to execute).

SRR1 is used for a related purpose: It is loaded with interrupt-specific information when an interrupt occurs. It also mirrors certain bits of the Machine State Register (MSR) in the case of an interrupt.

The special-purpose registers SPRG0, SPRG1, SPRG2, and SPRG3 are used as support registers (in an implementation-dependent manner) in various stages of exception processing. For example, the Mac OS X kernel uses SPRG2 and SPRG3 to save interrupt-time general-purpose registers GPR13 and GPR11, respectively, in the implementation of the low-level exception vectors. Furthermore, it uses SPRG0 to hold a pointer to the per_proc structure.

6.4.2.3 System Linkage Instructions

System Call

When a system call is invoked from user space, GPR0 is loaded with the system call number, and the sc instruction is executed. The effective address of the instruction following the system call instruction is placed in SRR0, certain bit ranges of the MSR are placed into the corresponding bits of SRR1, certain bits of the SRR1 are cleared, and a system call exception is generated. The processor fetches the next instruction from the well-defined effective address of the system call exception handler.

Return from Interrupt

rfid (*return-from-interrupt-double-word*) is a privileged, context-altering, and context-synchronizing instruction used to continue execution after an interrupt. Upon its execution, among other things, the next instruction is fetched from the address specified by SRR0. rfid's 32-bit counterpart is the rfi instruction.

> A *context-altering* instruction is one that alters the context in which instructions are executed, data is accessed, or data and instruction addresses are interpreted in general. A *context-synchronizing* instruction is one that ensures that any address translations associated with instructions following it will be discarded if the translations were performed using the old contents of the page table entry (PTE).

6.4.2.4 Machine-Dependent Thread State

We will examine the in-kernel thread data structure [osfmk/kern/thread.h] and related structures in Chapter 7. Each thread contains a machine-dependent state, represented by a machine_thread structure [osfmk/ppc/thread.h].

Figure 6–8 shows a portion of the machine_thread structure. Its fields include the following.

- The kernel and user *save area* pointers (pcb and upcb, respectively) refer to saved kernel-state and user-state contexts. The contents of a save area in xnu are analogous to those of the *process control block* (PCB) in a traditional BSD kernel.

- The *current*, *deferred*, and *normal* facility context structures (curctx, deferctx, and facctx, respectively) encapsulate the contexts for the floating-point and AltiVec facilities. Note that the save area holds only a normal context that does not include floating-point or vector contexts.

- The vmmCEntry and vmmControl pointers point to data structures related to the kernel's virtual machine monitor (VMM) facility, which allows a user program to create, manipulate, and run virtual machine (VM) instances. A VMM instance includes a processor state and an address space. The VMM facility and its use are discussed in Section 6.9.

- The kernel stack pointer (ksp) either points to the top of the thread's kernel stack or is zero.

- The machine_thread structure also contains several data structures related to the kernel's support for the Blue Box—that is, the Classic environment.

FIGURE 6–8 Structure for a thread's machine-dependent state

```
// osfmk/kern/thread.h

struct thread {
    ...
    struct machine_thread machine;
    ...
};

// osfmk/ppc/thread.h

struct facility_context {
    savearea_fpu        *FPUsave;  // FP save area
    savearea            *FPUlevel; // FP context level
```

(continues)

FIGURE 6–8 Structure for a thread's machine-dependent state *(continued)*

```
    unsigned int              FPUcpu;    // last processor to enable FP
    unsigned int              FPUsync;   // synchronization lock
    savearea_vec             *VMXsave;   // VMX save area
    savearea                 *VMXlevel;  // VMX context level
    unsigned int              VMXcpu;    // last processor to enable VMX
    unsigned int              VMXsync;   // synchronization lock
    struct thread_activation *facAct;    // context's activation
};
typedef struct facility_context facility_context;
...

struct machine_thread {
    savearea              *pcb;         // the "normal" save area
    savearea              *upcb;        // the "normal" user save area
    facility_context      *curctx;      // current facility context pointer
    facility_context      *deferctx;    // deferred facility context pointer
    facility_context       facctx;      // "normal" facility context structure
    struct vmmCntrlEntry  *vmmCEntry;   // pointer to current emulation context
    struct vmmCntrlTable  *vmmControl;  // pointer to VMM control table
    ...
    unsigned int           ksp;         // top of stack or zero
    unsigned int           preemption_count;
    struct per_proc_info  *PerProc;     // current per-processor data
    ...
};
```

6.4.2.5 Exception Save Areas

Save areas are fundamental to xnu's exception processing. Important characteristics of the kernel's save area management include the following.

- Save areas are stored in pages, with each page logically divided into an integral number of save area slots. Consequently, a save area never spans a page boundary.

- The kernel accesses save areas using both virtual and physical addressing. A low-level interrupt vector refers to a save area using its physical address, as exceptions (including PTE misses) must not occur at that level. Certain queuing operations during save area management are also performed using physical addresses.

- Save areas can be permanent, or they can be dynamically allocated. Permanent save areas are allocated at boot time and are necessary so that interrupts can be taken. The initial save areas are allocated from physical memory. The number of initial save areas is defined in osfmk/ppc/savearea.h, as are other save area management parameters. Eight "back-pocket" save areas are also allocated at boot time for use in emergencies.

- Save areas are managed using two global free lists: the save area free list, and the save area free pool. Each processor additionally has a local list. The pool contains entire pages, with each slot within a page being marked free or otherwise. The free list gets its save areas from pool pages. The free list can be grown or shrunk as necessary. An unused save area from the free list is returned to its pool page. If all slots in a pool page are marked free, it is taken off the free pool list and entered into a pending release queue.

We can write a simple program as follows to display some save-area-related sizes used by the kernel.

```
$ cat savearea_sizes.c
// savearea_sizes.c

#include <stdio.h>
#include <stdlib.h>

#define XNU_KERNEL_PRIVATE
#define __APPLE_API_PRIVATE
#define MACH_KERNEL_PRIVATE
#include <osfmk/ppc/savearea.h>

int
main(void)
{
    printf("size of a save area structure in bytes = %ld\n", sizeof(savearea));
    printf("# of save areas per page                = %ld\n", sac_cnt);
    printf("# of save areas to make at boot time     = %ld\n", InitialSaveAreas);
    printf("# of save areas for an initial target    = %ld\n", InitialSaveTarget);
    exit(0);
}
$ gcc -I /work/xnu -Wall -o savearea_sizes savearea_sizes.c
$ ./savearea_sizes
size of a save area structure in bytes = 640
# of save areas per page               = 6
# of save areas to make at boot time   = 48
# of save areas for an initial target  = 24
```

Structure declarations for the various save area types are also contained in osfmk/ppc/savearea.h.

```
// osfmk/ppc/savearea.h

#ifdef MACH_KERNEL_PRIVATE
typedef struct savearea_comm {
```

```
    // ... fields common to all save areas
    // ... fields used to manage individual contexts
} savearea_comm;
#endif

#ifdef BSD_KERNEL_PRIVATE
typedef struct savearea_comm {
    unsigned int save_000[24];
} savearea_comm;
#endif

typedef struct savearea {

    savearea_comm save_hdr;

    // general context: exception data, all GPRs, SRR0, SRR1, XER, LR, CTR,
    // DAR, CR, DSISR, VRSAVE, VSCR, FPSCR, Performance Monitoring Counters,
    // MMCR0, MMCR1, MMCR2, and so on
    ...
} savearea;

typedef struct savearea_fpu {

    savearea_comm save_hdr;

    ...
    // floating-point context - that is, all FPRs

} savearea_fpu;

typedef struct savearea_vec {

    savearea_comm save_hdr;

    ...
    save_vrvalid; // valid VRs in saved context
    // vector context - that is, all VRs

} savearea_vec;
...
```

When a new thread is created, a save area is allocated for it by `machine_thread_create()` [`osfmk/ppc/pcb.c`]. The save area is populated with the thread's initial context. Thereafter, a user thread begins life with a *taken interrupt*—that is, it looks from an observer's standpoint that the thread is in the kernel because of an interrupt. It returns to user space through `thread_return()` [`osfmk/ppc/hw_exception.s`], retrieving its context from the save area. In the case of kernel threads, `machine_stack_attach()` [`osfmk/ppc/pcb.c`] is called to attach a kernel stack to a thread and initialize its state, including the address where the thread will continue execution.

```
// osfmk/ppc/pcb.c

kern_return_t
machine_thread_create(thread_t thread, task_t task)
{
    savearea *sv;                    // pointer to newly allocated save area
    ...
    sv = save_alloc();               // allocate a save area
    bzero((char *)((unsigned int)sv  // clear the save area
        + sizeof(savearea_comm)),
        (sizeof(savearea) - sizeof(savearea_comm)));

    sv->save_hdr.save_prev = 0;      // clear the back pointer
    ...
    sv->save_hdr.save_act = thread;  // set who owns it
    thread->machine.pcb = sv;        // point to the save area

    // initialize facility context
    thread->machine.curctx = &thread->machine.facctx;

    // initialize facility context pointer to activation
    thread->machine.facctx.facAct = thread;
    ...
    thread->machine.upcb = sv;       // set user pcb
    ...
    sv->save_fpscr = 0;              // clear all floating-point exceptions
    sv->save_vrsave = 0;             // set the vector save state
    ...
    return KERN_SUCCESS;
}
```

What's in a Context?

When a thread executes, its execution environment is described by a *context*, which in turn relates to the thread's memory state and its execution state. The memory state refers to the thread's address space, as defined by the virtual-to-real address mappings that have been set up for it. The execution state's contents depend on whether the thread is running as part of a user task, running as part of the kernel task to perform some kernel operation, or running as part of the kernel task to service an interrupt.[4]

---

4. All threads in the kernel are created within the kernel task.

6.5 Exception Processing

Figure 6–9 shows a high-level view of exception processing. Recall from earlier discussion that the vectors reside in physical memory starting at location 0x0. Consider the example of an instruction access exception, which is caused when the effective address of an instruction fails to translate to a virtual address. As listed in Table 5–1, the vector offset for this exception is 0x400. Consequently, the processor executes the code at physical address 0x400 to handle this exception. Most exception handlers simply save GPR13 and GPR11, set an interrupt code in GPR11, and jump to .L_exception_entry() [osfmk/ppc/lowmem_vectors.s] for further processing. For some exceptions, such as system reset (0x100), system call (0xC00), and trace (0xD00), the first-level exception handlers

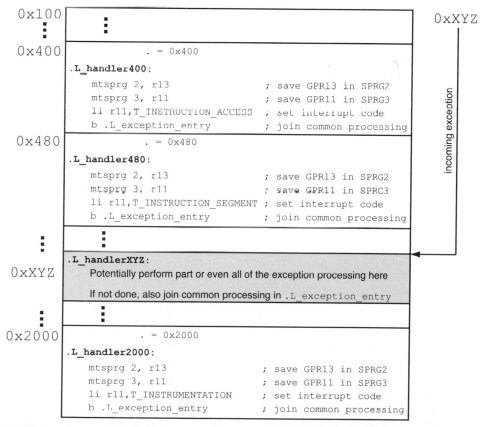

FIGURE 6–9 A high-level view of exception processing in the xnu kernel

perform more work. Nevertheless, there exists a code path from each handler to
`.L_exception_entry()`.

Figure 6–10 shows the code structure of `.L_exception_entry()`. It first
saves a variety of context—an operation whose implementation is different for
32-bit and 64-bit processors. The address labeled as `extPatch32` contains an
unconditional branch instruction to 64-bit-specific code. This branch must not be
taken on a 32-bit processor—instead, execution should continue with the 32-bit
code that follows this instruction. As we saw in Chapter 5, the kernel performs
boot-time memory patching of instructions and data. In this case, the kernel
would replace the unconditional branch with a no-op instruction at boot time on a
32-bit processor.

FIGURE 6–10 Common code for exception processing

```
; osfmk/ppc/lowmem_vectors.s

; Caller's GPR13 is saved in SPRG2
; Caller's GPR11 is saved in SPRG3
; Exception code is in GPR11
; All other registers are live
; Interrupts are off
; VM is off
; In 64-bit mode, if supported
;
.L_exception_entry:
            .globl EXT(extPatch32)
LEXT(extPatch32)
            b extEntry64 ; Patched to a no-op if 32-bit
            ...

            ; 32-bit context saving
            ...

            b xcpCommon  ; Join common interrupt processing

            ; 64-bit context saving
extEntry64:
            ...
            b xcpCommon  ; Join common interrupt processing

            ; All of the context is now saved
            ; We will now get a fresh save area
            ; Thereafter, we can take an interrupt
```

(continues)

FIGURE 6–10 Common code for exception processing *(continued)*

```
xcpCommon:
            ...
            ; Save some more aspects of the context, such as some
            ; floating-point and vector status
            ...


            ; Done saving all of the context
            ; Start filtering the interrupts
Redrive:
            ...
            ; Use the exception code to retrieve the next-level exception
            ; handler from xcpTable
            ...


            ; Load the handler in CTR
            ...


            bctr ; Go process the exception
```

Once .L_exception_entry() has saved all the context, it refers to an exception vector filter table called xcpTable, which too is defined in osfmk/ppc/lowmem_vectors.s and resides in low memory (the first 32KB of physical memory). The common exception-handling code in .L_exception_entry() uses the incoming exception code to look up the handler in the filter table, after which it branches to the handler. Table 6–9 lists the exception handlers corresponding to the various exception codes set by the exception vectors. For example, the codes T_INTERRUPT (vector offset 0x500), T_DECREMENTER (vector offset 0x900), T_SYSTEM_MANAGEMENT (vector offset 0x1400), and T_THERMAL (vector offset 0x1700) are all channeled to code labeled as PassUpRupt, which leads to a higher-level interrupt handler. Similarly, traps (various exception codes) and system calls (the T_SYSTEM_CALL exception code) are channeled to the PassUpTrap and xcpSyscall labels, respectively. Figure 6–11 depicts a simplified view of the processing of traps, interrupts, and system calls.

Table 6–9 lists some handlers with the EXT() macro, which is defined in osfmk/ppc/asm.h. This macro simply adds an underscore prefix to its argument, allowing assembly code to refer to the corresponding external symbol while maintaining the C language name (without the underscore) for visual consistency.

TABLE 6–9 Table-Driven Exception Filtering

Exception Code	Handler	Notes
T_IN_VAIN	EatRupt	Restore state, return from interrupt
T_RESET	PassUpTrap	Handled by thandler() [osfmk/ppc/hw_exception.s]
T_MACHINE_CHECK	MachineCheck	MachineCheck() implemented in osfmk/ppc/lowmem_vectors.s
T_DATA_ACCESS	EXT(handlePF)	handlePF() implemented in osfmk/ppc/hw_vm.s
T_INSTRUCTION_ACCESS	EXT(handlePF)	
T_INTERRUPT	PassUpRupt	Handled by ihandler() [osfmk/ppc/hw_exception.s]
T_ALIGNMENT	EXT(AlignAssist)	AlignAssist() implemented in osfmk/ppc/Emulate.s
T_PROGRAM	EXT(Emulate)	Emulate() implemented in osfmk/ppc/Emulate.s
T_FP_UNAVAILABLE	PassUpFPU	Handled by fpu_switch() [osfmk/ppc/cswtch.s]
T_DECREMENTER	PassUpRupt	
T_IO_ERROR	PassUpTrap	
T_RESERVED	PassUpTrap	
T_SYSTEM_CALL	xcpSyscall	Handled locally in the case of a "CutTrace" system call, by FirmwareCall() [osfmk/ppc/Firmware.s] in the case of other firmware calls, and by shandler() [bsd/dev/ppc/systemcalls.c] in the case of normal system calls
T_TRACE	PassUpTrap	
T_FP_ASSIST	PassUpTrap	
T_PERF_MON	PassUpTrap	
T_VMX	PassUpVMX	Handled by vec_switch() [osfmk/ppc/cswtch.s]
T_INVALID_EXCP0	PassUpTrap	
T_INVALID_EXCP1	PassUpTrap	
T_INVALID_EXCP2	PassUpTrap	
T_INSTRUCTION_BKPT	PassUpTrap	
T_SYSTEM_MANAGEMENT	PassUpRupt	

(continues)

TABLE 6–9 Table-Driven Exception Filtering *(Continued)*

Exception Code	Handler	Notes
T_ALTIVEC_ASSIST	EXT(AltivecAssist)	AltivecAssist() implemented in osfmk/ppc/AltiAssist.s
T_THERMAL	PassUpRupt	
T_INVALID_EXCP5	PassUpTrap	
T_INVALID_EXCP6	PassUpTrap	
T_INVALID_EXCP7	PassUpTrap	
T_INVALID_EXCP8	PassUpTrap	
T_INVALID_EXCP9	PassUpTrap	
T_INVALID_EXCP10	PassUpTrap	
T_INVALID_EXCP11	PassUpTrap	
T_INVALID_EXCP12	PassUpTrap	
T_INVALID_EXCP13	PassUpTrap	
T_RUNMODE_TRACE	PassUpTrap	
T_SIGP	PassUpRupt	
T_PREEMPT	PassUpTrap	
T_CSWITCH	conswtch	conswtch() implemented in osfmk/ppc/lowmem_vectors.s
T_SHUTDOWN	PassUpRupt	
T_CHOKE	PassUpAbend	Handled by chandler() [osfmk/ppc/hw_exception.s]
T_DATA_SEGMENT	EXT(handleDSeg)	handleDSeg() implemented in osfmk/ppc/hw_vm.s
T_INSTRUCTION_SEGMENT	EXT(handleISeg)	handleISeg() implemented in osfmk/ppc/hw_vm.s
T_SOFT_PATCH	WhoaBaby	WhoaBaby() implemented in osfmk/ppc/lowmem_vectors.s—simply an infinite loop
T_MAINTENANCE	WhoaBaby	
T_INSTRUMENTATION	WhoaBaby	
T_ARCHDEP0	WhoaBaby	
T_HDEC	EatRupt	

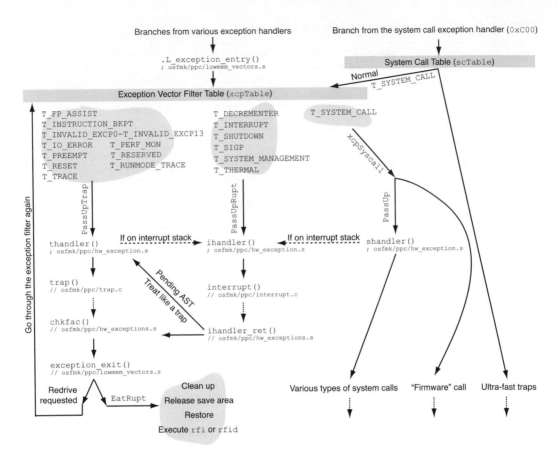

FIGURE 6–11 Processing of traps, interrupts, and system calls

Examples of exception handlers[5] shown in Figure 6–11 and Table 6–9 include `PassUpTrap`, `PassUpRupt`, `EatRupt`, `xcpSyscall`, and `WhoaBaby`. Let us briefly look at each of these.

- `PassUpTrap` loads the address of `thandler()` [osfmk/ppc/hw_exception.s] in GPR20 and branches to `PassUp`. When `thandler()` executes, virtual memory is turned on, but interrupts are turned off.

- `PassUpRupt` loads the address of `ihandler()` [osfmk/ppc/hw_exception.s] in GPR20 and branches to `PassUp`. As is the case with `thandler()`, `ihandler()` also executes with virtual memory turned on and interrupts turned off.

---

5. In many cases, the handlers are labels in assembly code.

- `EatRupt` is the main place for returning from an interrupt. It is also used if the interrupt has already been handled and nothing further needs to be done. For example, if it is found during page-fault processing that the exception has already been handled (say, due to another fault for the same page), the page-fault handler will return a `T_IN_VAIN`, which is handled by `EatRupt`. Other examples of this situation include software assistance of floating-point and VMX.

- `xcpSyscall` handles system calls depending on their types, such as whether they are normal or special system calls. In the case of normal system calls, `xcpSyscall` loads the address of `shandler()` [osfmk/ppc/hw_exception.s] in GPR20 and branches to `PassUp`. We will discuss system call types and their processing in Section 6.6.

- `WhoaBaby` is for exceptions that must not occur during the normal functioning of the operating system. Its handler is extremely simple—merely an infinite loop.

```
; osfmk/ppc/lowmem_vectors.s

WhoaBaby:    b       . ; open the hood and wait for help
```

`PassUp` [osfmk/ppc/lowmem_vectors.s] places the exception code in GPR3 and the next-level exception handler's address in SRR0. It also switches segment registers between the kernel and the user. It finally executes the `rfid` instruction (`rfi` on 32-bit processors) to launch the exception handler.

6.5.1 Hardware Interrupts

A true hardware interrupt can only occur because of a device that has a physical connection—an *interrupt line*—from itself to the system's interrupt controller. Such a connection may involve a device controller. A PCI device is a good example: An interrupt line connects a PCI device slot to the PCI controller, which connects it to the interrupt controller. When the system boots, Open Firmware assigns one or more interrupts to a PCI device. The interrupts used by the device are listed in an array called `IOInterruptSpecifiers` in the device's I/O Registry node. When the device causes a hardware interrupt, it is signaled to the processor by setting an interrupt identifier bit and asserting the processor's external interrupt input signal, causing an external interrupt exception (vector offset 0x500, exception code `T_INTERRUPT`). As we saw earlier, processing of this exception will eventually lead to the `ihandler()` function. Moreover, as shown in Figure 6–11, other exception codes such as T_DECREMENTER and T_SHUTDOWN also lead to ihandler().

> Not all devices cause true hardware interrupts. A USB device, for example, generates an "interrupt" by sending a message on the USB bus without involving the system's interrupt controller.

ihandler() ensures the integrity of the interrupt stack, marks it busy, and calls the higher-level interrupt() function [osfmk/ppc/interrupt.c], which disables preemption and performs different operations depending on the specific exception code it is called with.

```
// osfmk/ppc/interrupt.c

struct savearea *
interrupt(int type, struct savearea *ssp, unsigned int dsisr, unsigned int dar)
{
    ...
    disable_preemption();
    ...
    switch (type) {
        case T_DECREMENTER:
            ...
            break;

        case T_INTERRUPT:
            ...
            break;

        ...

        default:
#if MACH_KDP || MACH_KDB
            if (!Call_Debugger(type, ssp))
#endif
                unresolved_kernel_trap(type, ssp, dsisr, dar, NULL);
            break;
    }

    enable_preemption();
    return ssp;
}
```

In the case of a T_DECREMENTER exception code, interrupt() calls rtclock_intr() [osfmk/ppc/rtclock.c]—the real-time clock device interrupt function. `interrupt()` also checks whether the current thread has its quick-activation single-shot timer set; if so, it checks whether the timer has expired, in which case it is cleared. The kernel's virtual machine monitor facility uses this timer.

In the case of a `T_INTERRUPT` exception code, `interrupt()` increments the count of incoming interrupts and calls the platform-specific interrupt handler function referred to in the per-processor structure. The type of this handler function (`IOInterruptHandler`) is defined in `iokit/IOKit/IOInterrupts.h`.

```
typedef void (* IOInterruptHandler)(void *target,
                                    void *refCon,
                                    void *nub,
                                    int   source);
```

In the case of a `T_SHUTDOWN` exception code, which is generated by a special system call (a so-called firmware call—see Section 6.8.8.1), `interrupt()` calls `cpu_doshutdown()` [`osfmk/ppc/cpu.c`].

> If an invalid exception code is sent to `ihandler()` for processing, it will either panic the system or drop into the debugger if one is available. The panic will be accompanied by an "Unresolved kernel trap . . ." message.

6.5.2 Miscellaneous Traps

The low-level trap handler—`thandler()` [`osfmk/ppc/hw_exception.s`]—performs different operations depending on the specific trap. A system call exception may end up in the trap handler if there is nothing for the system call to do except generate a trap. The trap handler may jump to the interrupt handler if it finds that it is running on an interrupt stack. `thandler()` eventually calls the higher-level `trap()` function [`osfmk/ppc/trap.c`] to process traps.

```
// osfmk/ppc/trap.c

struct savearea *
trap(int trapno, struct savearea *ssp, unsigned int dsisr, addr64_t dar)
{
    int exception;
    ...
    exception = 0;
    ...
```

```
    if (/* kernel mode */) {
        // Handle traps originating from the kernel first
        // Examples of such traps are T_PREEMPT, T_PERF_MON, T_RESET

        // Various traps should never be seen here
        // Panic if any of these traps are encountered
        ...
    } else {
        /* user mode */

        // Handle user mode traps
        ...
    }

    // The 'exception' variable may have been set during trap processing
    if (exception) {
        doexception(exception, code, subcode);
    }

    ...
    if (/* user mode */) {
        // If an AST is needed, call ast_taken()
        // Repeat until an AST is not needed
    }

    return ssp;
}
```

There are several criteria for the invalidity of a trap's occurrence. For example, `T_IN_VAIN` should never be seen by `trap()` because it should have been disposed of by `EatRupt` in `osfmk/ppc/lowmem_vectors.s`. Note that `trap()` determines whether a trap originated from the user mode or kernel mode by looking at the contents of the SRR1 in the save area. It uses the `USER_MODE()` macro [`osfmk/ppc/proc_reg.h`] for this purpose.

```
// osfmk/ppc/proc_reg.h

#define ENDIAN_MASK(val,size) (1 << ((size-1) - val))
...
#define MASK32(PART)        ENDIAN_MASK(PART ## _BIT, 32)
...
#define MASK(PART)          MASK32(PART)
...
#define MSR_PR_BIT          17
...
#define USER_MODE(msr)      (msr & MASK(MSR_PR) ? TRUE : FALSE)
```

The Choker

In the case of fatal errors, an exception of type T_CHOKE is generated. This exception results in chandler() [osfmk/ppc/hw_exception.s]—the *choke handler*—being called. The choke handler "chokes" the system by going into an infinite loop that increments GPR31 by 1 in each iteration. If thandler() or ihandler() detects that the kernel or interrupt stack, respectively, is invalid, it invokes a special firmware system call for choking the system by setting the external interrupt value to T_CHOKE.

6.5.3 System Calls

The remaining type of exception is for system calls. As noted earlier, system calls are well-defined entry points into the kernel typically used by user-level programs. The next section covers the details of the Mac OS X system call mechanism.

6.6 System Call Processing

In traditional UNIX, a system call is one of a well-defined set of functions that allow a user process to interact with the kernel. A user process invokes a system call to request the kernel to perform one or more operations on its behalf. The kernel may perform the requested operations after validating input parameters to the system call, if any, and perhaps several other checks. A system call may involve exchange of data—typically at least a return value—between the kernel and the user process.

Our definition of a Mac OS X system call is *a function callable through the sc instruction*. Note that it is legal to use the sc instruction from within the kernel. It is also possible to directly—from within the kernel—call an internal function that implements a system call. Nevertheless, a typical invocation of a system call *is* from user space.

Since the Mac OS X kernel is an amalgamation of entities with quite different personalities and characteristics, it is interesting to ask which portions of xnu these system calls provide entry to: BSD, Mach, the I/O Kit, or something else? The answer is: all of them, and more.

Based on how they are processed, Mac OS X system calls can be categorized as *ultra-fast traps*, *firmware calls*, and *normal system calls*. Figure 6–12 shows the key code paths involved in system call processing. The figure should be followed beginning at the "Start" label.

We can also categorize Mac OS X system calls based on what they do, that is, based on their flavors. The following categorization also captures—largely—the division based on the kernel subsystems that these system calls provide access to.

- *BSD system calls* are the Unix system calls, although several system calls in this category either have Mac OS X–specific nuances or are seen only on Mac OS X. The BSD system calls substantially contribute to Mac OS X's POSIX compatibility at the system call level.

- *Mach system calls*—or Mach traps—serve as the building blocks for exporting a variety of Mach functionality through kernel calls, which are invoked from user space via Mach IPC. In particular, unlike BSD, Mach's kernel functionality is often accessed through kernel-user IPC, rather than having separate system calls for individual pieces of functionality.

- *I/O Kit traps* constitute a subset of the Mach traps.

- PowerPC-only *special system calls* include special-purpose calls for diagnostics, for performance monitoring, for access to the kernel's virtual machine monitor, and for calls related to the Blue Box.

- PowerPC-only *ultra-fast traps* are system calls that perform very little work, do not have the context save/restore overhead of regular system calls, and return very quickly. Another type of a fast system call is a *fastpath call*, which is conceptually similar to an ultra-fast call but performs somewhat more work. These calls also do not return as rapidly as the ultra-fast calls.

- Certain system calls can be optimized using the *commpage* feature on Mac OS X. The commpage area of memory contains frequently used code and data. These entities are grouped together as a set of consecutive pages that are mapped by the kernel into the address space of each process. The `gettimeofday()` system call is optimized in this manner—when a user process executes `gettimeofday()`, its commpage implementation is attempted first, failing which the actual system call is executed. We will see details of this mechanism later in this chapter.

As shown in Figure 6–12, the details of how each system call category is handled in the kernel differ. Nevertheless, all system calls are invoked from user space via the same basic mechanism. Each category uses one or more unique ranges of system call numbers. In a typical invocation of any type of system call, the calling entity in user space places the system call number in GPR0 and executes

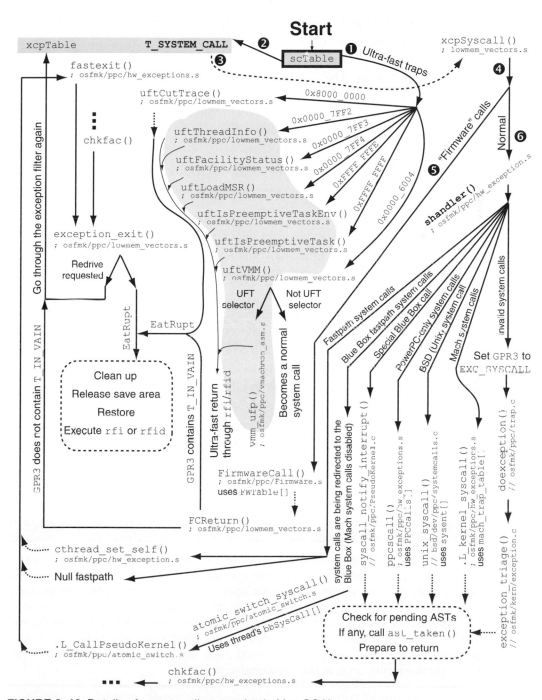

FIGURE 6–12 Details of system call processing in Mac OS X

the `sc` instruction. These statements must be qualified with the following points to avoid confusion.

- User programs normally do not call a system call directly—a library stub invokes the `sc` instruction.

- Some program invocations of system calls may never transition to the kernel because they are handled by a library entirely in user space. The commpage-optimized calls are examples of this.

- Regardless of the programmer-visible invocation mechanism, a system call that does transition to the kernel always involves execution of the `sc` instruction.

The kernel's hardware vector for the system call exception maps the system call number in GPR0 to an index into the first-level dispatch table containing handlers for various types of system calls. It then branches to the call handler. Figure 6–13 shows details of this mapping.

The first-level dispatch table—`scTable`—also resides in low memory. As Figure 6–13 shows, it can map ultra-fast system calls to their individual handlers, route all non-ultra-fast valid system calls to a normal dispatcher, and if an impossible index is encountered, it can send the call to `WhoaBaby`. The dispatcher for normal system calls sets the exception code in GPR11 to `T_SYSTEM_CALL`. Such calls, including BSD and Mach system calls, are next processed by `.L_exception_entry()`, the exception-handling code common to most exceptions. As shown in Figure 6–11, `.L_exception_entry()` branches to `xcpSyscall` to handle the `T_SYSTEM_CALL` exception code. `xcpSyscall` hands over the processing of most system calls to `shandler()` [`osfmk/ppc/hw_exception.s`].

User-Level System Call Emulation

Remnants of the Mach multiserver emulation facility can be seen in the xnu kernel. A typical multiserver configuration consisted of the Mach kernel along with one or more servers, as well as an emulation library that intercepted system calls for emulated processes, redirecting them to the appropriate emulation services. A user-process address space consisted of user code representing the application and the emulation library. xnu includes some of this code inherited from Mach, such as the `task_set_emulation()` and `task_set_emulation_vector()` functions. However, the code is *not* functional in xnu.

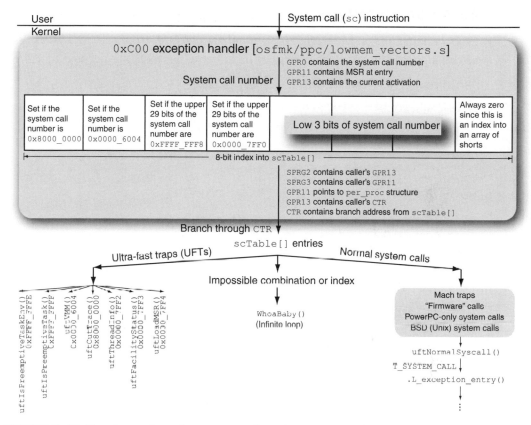

FIGURE 6–13 Mapping an incoming system call number to an index in the first-level system call dispatch table

6.7 System Call Categories

Let us now look at details and examples of the various system call categories, beginning with the most staple variety from a developer's standpoint: the BSD system calls.

6.7.1 BSD System Calls

shandler() calls unix_syscall() [bsd/dev/ppc/systemcalls.c] to handle BSD system calls. unix_syscall() receives as its argument a pointer to a save area—the *process control block*. Before we discuss unix_syscall()'s operation, let us look at some relevant data structures and mechanisms.

6.7.1.1 Data Structures

BSD system calls on Mac OS X have numbers that start from zero and go as high as the highest numbered BSD system call. These numbers are defined in <sys/syscall.h>.

```
// <sys/syscall.h>

#ifdef __APPLE_API_PRIVATE
#define SYS_syscall      0
#define SYS_exit         1
#define SYS_fork         2
#define SYS_read         3
#define SYS_write        4
#define SYS_open         5
#define SYS_close        6
...
#define SYS_MAXSYSCALL 370
#endif
```

> Several system call numbers are reserved or simply unused. In some cases, they may represent calls that have been obsoleted and removed, creating holes in the sequence of implemented system calls.

Note that the zeroth system call—syscall()—is the *indirect* system call: It allows another system call to be invoked given the latter's number, which is provided as the first argument to syscall(), followed by the actual arguments required by the target system call. The indirect system call has traditionally been used to allow testing—say, from a high-level language like C—of new system calls that do not have stubs in the C library.

```
// Normal invocation of system call number SYS_foo
ret = foo(arg1, arg2, ..., argN);

// Indirect invocation of foo using the indirect system call
ret = syscall(SYS_foo, arg1, arg2, ..., argN);
```

The syscall.h file is generated during kernel compilation by the bsd/kern/makesyscalls.sh shell script,[6] which processes the system call master file bsd/kern/syscalls.master. The master file contains a line for each sys-

---

6. The script makes heavy use of the awk and sed Unix utilities.

tem call number, with the following entities in each column within the line (in this order):

- The system call number
- The type of cancellation supported by the system call in the case of a thread cancellation: one of PRE (can be canceled on entry itself), POST (can be canceled only after the call is run), or NONE (not a cancellation point)
- The type of funnel[7] to be taken before executing the system call: one of KERN (the kernel funnel) or NONE
- The files to which an entry for the system call will be added: either ALL or a combination of T (bsd/kern/init_sysent.c—the system call table), N (bsd/kern/syscalls.c—the table of system call names), H (bsd/sys/syscall.h—system call numbers), and P (bsd/sys/sysproto.h—system call prototypes)
- The system call function's prototype
- Comments that will be copied to output files

```
; bsd/kern/syscalls.master
;
; Call# Cancel  Funnel  Files    { Name and Args }       { Comments }
;
...
0       NONE    NONE    ALL      { int nosys(void); }    { indirect syscall }
1       NONE    KERN    ALL      { void exit(int rval); }
2       NONE    KERN    ALL      { int fork(void); }
...
368     NONE    NONE    ALL      { int nosys(void); }
369     NONE    NONE    ALL      { int nosys(void); }
```

The file `bsd/kern/syscalls.c` contains an array of strings—`syscallnames[]`—that contains each system call's textual name.

```
// bsd/kern/syscalls.c

const char *syscallnames[] = {
        "syscall",      /* 0 = syscall indirect syscall */
        "exit",         /* 1 = exit */
        "fork",         /* 2 = fork */
        ...
        "#368",         /* 368 = */
        "#369",         /* 369 = */
};
```

---

7. Beginning with Mac OS X 10.4, the network funnel is not used.

We can examine the contents of the syscallnames[] array—and for that matter, other kernel data structures—from user space by reading from the kernel memory device /dev/kmem.[8]

Running nm on the kernel binary gives us the address of the symbol syscallnames, which we can dereference to access the array.

```
$ nm /mach_kernel | grep syscallnames
0037f3ac D _syscallnames
$ sudo dd if=/dev/kmem of=/dev/stdout bs=1 count=4 iseek=0x37f3ac | od -x
...
0000000     0032    a8b4
0000004
$ sudo dd if=/dev/kmem of=/dev/stdout bs=1 count=1024 iseek=0x32a8b4 | strings
syscall
exit
fork
...
```

The file bsd/kern/init_sysent.c contains the system call switch table, sysent[], which is an array of sysent structures, containing one structure for each system call number. This file is generated from the master file during kernel compilation.

```
// bsd/kern/init_sysent.c

#ifdef __ppc__
#define AC(name) (sizeof(struct name) / sizeof(uint64_t))
#else
#define AC(name) (sizeof(struct name) / sizeof(register_t))
#endif

__private_extern__ struct sysent sysent[] = {
{
        0,
        _SYSCALL_CANCEL_NONE,
        NO_FUNNEL,
        (sy_call_t *)nosys,
        NULL,
        NULL,
        _SYSCALL_RET_INT_T
    }, /* 0 = nosys indirect syscall */
```

---

8. The /dev/kmem and /dev/mem devices have been removed from the x86 version of Mac OS X. A simple kernel extension can be written to provide /dev/kmem's functionality, allowing experiments such as this one. This book's accompanying web site (www.osxbook.com) provides information about writing such a driver.

```
    {
        AC(exit_args),
        _SYSCALL_CANCEL_NONE,
        KERNEL_FUNNEL,
        (sy_call_t *)exit,
        munge_w,
        munge_d,
        _SYSCALL_RET_NONE
    }, /* 1 = exit */

    ...

    {
        0,
        _SYSCALL_CANCEL_NONE,
        NO_FUNNEL,
        (sy_call_t *)nosys,
        NULL,
        NULL,
        _SYSCALL_RET_INT_T
    }, /* 369 = nosys */
};
int nsysent = sizeof(sysent) / sizeof(sysent[0]);
```

The sysent structure is declared in bsd/sys/sysent.h.

// bsd/sys/sysent.h

```
typedef int32_t sy_call_t(struct proc *, void *, int *);
typedef void    sy_munge_t(const void *, void *);

extern struct sysent {
    int16_t    sy_narg;          // number of arguments
    int8_t     sy_cancel;        // how to cancel, if at all
    int8_t     sy_funnel;        // funnel type, if any, to take upon entry
    sy_call_t  *sy_call;         // implementing function
    sy_munge_t *sy_arg_munge32;  // arguments munger for 32-bit process
    sy_munge_t *sy_arg_munge64;  // arguments munger for 64-bit process
    int32_t    sy_return_type;   // return type
} sysent[];
```

The sysent structure's fields have the following meanings.

- sy_narg is the number of arguments—at most eight—taken by the system call. In the case of the indirect system call, the number of arguments is limited to seven since the first argument is dedicated for the target system call's number.

- As we saw earlier, a system call specifies whether it can be canceled before execution, after execution, or not at all. The `sy_cancel` field holds the cancellation type, which is one of `_SYSCALL_CANCEL_PRE`, `_SYSCALL_CANCEL_POST`, or `_SYSCALL_CANCEL_NONE` (corresponding to the `PRE`, `POST`, and `NONE` cancellation specifiers, respectively, in the master file). This feature is used in the implementation of the `pthread_cancel(3)` library call, which in turn invokes the `__pthread_markcancel()` [bsd/kern/kern_sig.c] system call to cancel a thread's execution. Most system calls cannot be canceled. Examples of those that can be canceled include `read()`, `write()`, `open()`, `close()`, `recvmsg()`, `sendmsg()`, and `select()`.

- The `sy_funnel` field may contain a funnel type that causes the system call's processing to take (lock) the corresponding funnel before the system call is executed, and drop (unlock) the funnel after it has executed. The possible values for this argument in Mac OS X 10.4 are `NO_FUNNEL` and `KERNEL_FUNNEL` (corresponding to the `KERN` and `NONE` funnel specifiers, respectively, in the master file).

- The `sy_call` field points to the kernel function that implements the system call.

- The `sy_arg_munge32` and `sy_arg_munge64` fields point to functions that are used for munging[9] system call arguments for 32-bit and 64-bit processes, respectively. We will discuss munging in Section 6.7.1.2.

- The `sy_return_type` field contains one of the following to represent the system call's return type: `_SYSCALL_RET_NONE`, `_SYSCALL_RET_INT_T`, `_SYSCALL_RET_UINT_T`, `_SYSCALL_RET_OFF_T`, `_SYSCALL_RET_ADDR_T`, `_SYSCALL_RET_SIZE_T`, and `_SYSCALL_RET_SSIZE_T`.

Recall that `unix_syscall()` receives a pointer to the process control block, which is a `savearea` structure. The system call's arguments are received as saved registers GPR3 through GPR10 in the save area. In the case of an indirect system call, the actual system call arguments start with GPR4, since GPR3 is used for the system call number. `unix_syscall()` copies these arguments to the `uu_arg` field within the `uthread` structure before passing them to the call handler.

---

9. Munging a data structure means rewriting or transforming it in some way.

```
// bsd/sys/user.h

struct uthread {
    int       *uu_ar0;    // address of user's saved GPR0
    u_int64_t uu_arg[8];  // arguments to current system call
    int       *uu_ap;     // pointer to argument list
    int       uu_rval[2]; // system call return values
    ...
};
```

> As we will see in Chapter 7, an xnu thread structure contains a pointer to the thread's *user structure*, roughly analogous to the user area in BSD. Execution within the xnu kernel refers to several structures, such as the Mach task structure, the Mach thread structure, the BSD process structure, and the BSD uthread structure. The latter contains several fields used during system call processing.

The U-Area

Historically, the UNIX kernel maintained an entry for every process in a process table, which always remained in memory. Each process was also allocated a user structure—or a *u-area*—that was an extension of the process structure. The u-area contained process-related information that needed to be accessible to the kernel only when the process was executing. Even though the kernel would not swap out a process structure, it could swap out the associated u-area. Over time, the criticality of memory as a resource has gradually lessened, but operating systems have become more complex. Correspondingly, the process structure has grown in size and the u-area has become less important, with much of its information being moved into the process structure.

6.7.1.2 Argument Munging

Note that uu_arg is an array of 64-bit unsigned integers—each element represents a 64-bit register. This is problematic since a parameter passed in a register from 32-bit user space will not map as is to the uu_arg array. For example, a long long parameter will be passed in a single GPR in a 64-bit program, but in two GPRs in a 32-bit program.

unix_syscall() addresses the issue arising from the difference depicted in Figure 6–14 by calling the system call's specified argument munger, which copies arguments from the save area to the uu_arg array while adjusting for the differences.

FIGURE 6–14 Passing a long long parameter in 32-bit and 64-bit ABIs

```
$ cat foo.c
extern void bar(long long arg);

void
foo(void)
{
    bar((long long)1);
}
$ gcc -static -S foo.c
$ cat foo.s
...
        li r3,0
        li r4,1
        bl _bar
...
$ gcc -arch ppc64 -static -S foo.c
$ cat foo.s
...
        li r3,1
        bl _bar
...
```

The munger functions are implemented in bsd/dev/ppc/munge.s. Each function takes two arguments: a pointer to the beginning of the system call parameters within the save area and a pointer to the uu_arg array. A munger function is named munge_<encoding>, where <encoding> is a string that encodes the number and types of system call parameters. <encoding> is a combination of one or more of the d, l, s, and w characters. The characters mean the following:

- d represents a 32-bit integer, a 64-bit pointer, or a 64-bit long when the calling process is 64-bit—that is, in each case, the parameter was passed in a 64-bit GPR. Such an argument is munged by copying two words from input to output.

- l represents a 64-bit long long passed in two GPRs. Such an argument is munged by skipping a word of input (the upper 32 bits of the first GPR), copying a word of input to output (the lower 32 bits of the first GPR), skipping another word of input, and copying another word from input to output.

- s represents a 32-bit signed value. Such an argument is munged by skipping a word of input, loading and sign-extending the next word of input to yield two words, and copying the two words to output.

- w represents a 32-bit unsigned value. Such an argument is munged by skipping a word of input, copying a zero word to output, and copying a word from input to output.

Moreover, multiple munger functions are aliased to a common implementation if each function, except one, is a prefix of another. For example, `munger_w`, `munger_ww`, `munger_www`, and `munger_wwww` are aliased to the same implementation—consequently, four arguments are munged in each case, regardless of the actual number of arguments. Similarly, `munger_wwwww`, `munger_wwwwww`, `munger_wwwwwww`, and `munger_wwwwwwww` are aliased to the same implementation, whose operation is shown in Figure 6–15.

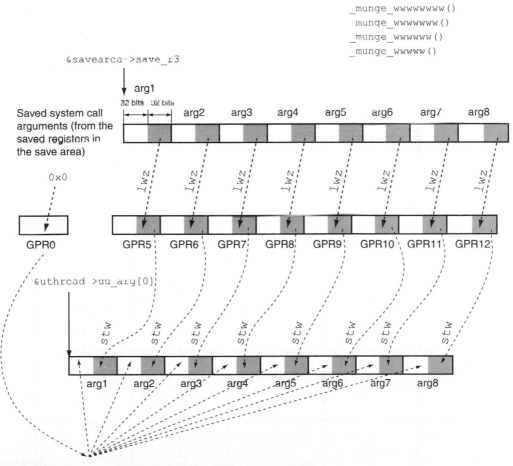

FIGURE 6–15 An example of system call argument munging

Consider the example of the `read()` system call. It takes three arguments: a file descriptor, a pointer to a buffer, and the number of bytes to read.

```
ssize_t
read(int d, void *buf, size_t nbytes);
```

The 32-bit and 64-bit mungers for the `read()` system call are `munge_www()` and `munge_ddd()`, respectively.

6.7.1.3 Kernel Processing of BSD System Calls

Figure 6–16 shows pseudocode depicting the working of `unix_syscall()`, which, as we saw earlier, is called by `shandler()` to process BSD system calls.

FIGURE 6–16 Details of the final dispatching of BSD system calls

```
// bsd/dev/ppc/systemcalls.c

void
unix_syscall(struct savearea *regs)
{
    thread_t        thread_act;
    struct uthread *uthread;
    struct proc    *proc;
    struct sysent  *callp;
    int             error;
    unsigned short  code;
    ...

    // Determine if this is a direct or indirect system call (the "flavor").
    // Set the 'code' variable to either GPR3 or GPR0, depending on flavor.
    ...

    // If kdebug tracing is enabled, log an entry indicating that a BSD
    // system call is starting, unless this system call is kdebug_trace().
    ...

    // Retrieve the current thread and the corresponding uthread structure.
    thread_act = current_thread();
    uthread = get_bsdthread_info(thread_act);
    ...

    // Ensure that the current task has a non-NULL proc structure associated
    // with it; if not, terminate the current task.
    ...
```

(continues)

FIGURE 6–16 Details of the final dispatching of BSD system calls *(continued)*

```
// uu_ar0 is the address of user's saved GPR0.
uthread->uu_ar0 = (int *)regs;

// Use the system call number to retrieve the corresponding sysent
// structure. If system call number is too large, use the number 63, which
// is an internal reserved number for a nosys().
//
// In early UNIX, the sysent array had space for 64 system calls. The last
// entry (that is, sysent[63]) was a special system call.
callp = (code >= nsysent) ? &sysent[63] : &sysent[code];

if (callp->sy_narg != 0) { // if the call takes one or more arguments
    void        *regsp;
    sy_munge_t *mungerp;

    if (/* this is a 64-bit process */) {
        if (/* this is a 64-bit unsafe call */) {
            // Turn it into a nosys() -- use system call #63 and bail out.
            ...
        }
        // 64-bit argument munger
        mungerp = callp->sy_arg_munge64;
    } else { /* 32-bit process */
        // 32-bit argument munger
        mungerp = callp->sy_arg_munge32;
    }

    // Set regsp to point to either the saved GPR3 in the save area (for a
    // direct system call), or to the saved GPR4 (for an indirect system
    // call). An indirect system call can take at most 7 arguments.
    ...

    // Call the argument munger.
    (*mungerp)(regsp, (void *)&uthread->uu_arg[0]);
}

// Evaluate call for cancellation, and cancel, if required and possible.
...

// Take the kernel funnel if the call requires so.
...

// Assume there will be no error.
error = 0;

// Increment saved SRR0 by one instruction.
regs->save_srr0 += 4;
```

(continues)

FIGURE 6–16 Details of the final dispatching of BSD system calls *(continued)*

```
    // Test if this is a kernel trace point -- that is, if system call tracing
    // through ktrace(2) is enabled for this process. If so, write a trace
    // record for this system call.
    ...

    // If auditing is enabled, set up an audit record for the system call.
    ...

    // Call the system call's specific handler.
    error = (*(callp->sy_call))(proc, (void *)uthread->uu_arg,
            &(uthread->uu_rval[0]));

    // If auditing is enabled, commit the audit record.
    ...

    // Handle return value(s)
    ...

    // If this is a ktrace(2) trace point, write a trace record for the
    // return of this system call.
    ...

    // Drop the funnel if one was taken.
    ...

    // If kdebug tracing is enabled, log an entry indicating that a BSD
    // system call is ending, unless this system call is kdebug_trace().
    ...

    thread_exception_return();
    /* NOTREACHED */
}
```

unix_syscall() potentially performs several types of tracing or logging: kdebug tracing, ktrace(2) tracing, and audit logging. We will discuss kdebug and ktrace(2) later in this chapter.

Arguments are passed packaged into a structure to the call-specific handler. Let us consider the example of the socketpair(2) system call, which takes four arguments: three integers and a pointer to a buffer for holding two integers.

```
int socketpair(int domain, int type, int protocol, int *rsv);
```

The bsd/sys/sysproto.h file, which, as noted earlier, is generated by bsd/kern/makesyscalls.sh, contains argument structure declarations for all

BSD system calls. Note also the use of left and right padding in the declaration of the `socketpair_args` structure.

// bsd/sys/sysproto.h

```
#ifdef __ppc__
#define PAD_(t) (sizeof(uint64_t) <= sizeof(t) \
                         ? 0 : sizeof(uint64_t) - sizeof(t))
#else
...
#endif
#if BYTE_ORDER == LITTLE_ENDIAN
...
#else
#define PADL_(t) PAD_(t)
#define PADR_(t) 0
#endif
...
struct socketpair_args {
    char domain_l_[PADL_(int)]; int domain; char domain_r_[PADR_(int)];
    char type_l_[PADL_(int)]; int type; char type_r_[PADR_(int)];
    char protocol_l_[PADL_(int)]; int protocol; char protocol_r_[PADR_(int)];
    char rsv_l_[PADL_(user_addr_t)]; user_addr_t rsv; \
                                        char rsv_r_[PADR_(user_addr_t)];
};
...
```

The system call handler function for `socketpair(2)` retrieves its arguments as fields of the incoming `socket_args` structure.

// bsd/kern/uipc_syscalls.c

```
// Create a pair of connected sockets
int
socketpair(struct proc          *p,
           struct socketpair_args *uap,
           __unused register_t    *retval)
{
    struct fileproc *fp1, *fp2;
    struct socket    *so1, *so2;
    int fd, error, sv[2];

    ...
    error = socreate(uap->domain, &so1, uap->type, &uap->protocol);
    ...
    error = socreate(uap->domain, &so2, uap->type, &uap->protocol);
    ...
```

```
    error = falloc(p, &fp1, &fd);
    ...
    sv[0] = fd;

    error = falloc(p, &fp2, &fd);
    ...
    sv[1] = fd;

    ...
    error = copyout((caddr_t)sv, uap->rsv, 2 * sizeof(int));
    ...

    return (error);
}
```

Note that before calling the system call handler, unix_syscall() sets the error status to zero, assuming that there will be no error. Recall that the saved SRR0 register contains the address of the instruction immediately following the system call instruction. This is where execution would resume after returning to user space from the system call. As we will shortly see, a standard user-space library stub for a BSD system call invokes the cerror() library function to set the errno variable—this should be done *only if* there is an error. unix_syscall() increments the saved SRR0 by one instruction, so that the call to cerror() will be skipped if there is no error. If the system call handler indeed does return an error, the SRR0 value is decremented by one instruction.

After returning from the handler, unix_syscall() examines the error variable to take the appropriate action.

- If error is ERESTART, this is a *restartable* system call that needs to be restarted. unix_syscall() decrements SRR0 by 8 bytes (two instructions) to cause execution to resume at the original system call instruction.

- If error is EJUSTRETURN, this system call wants to be returned to user space without any further processing of return values.

- If error is nonzero, the system call returned an error, which unix_syscall() copies to the saved GPR3 in the process control block. It also decrements SRR0 by one instruction to cause the cerror() routine to be executed upon return to user space.

- If error is 0, the system call returned success. unix_syscall() copies the return values from the uthread structure to the saved GPR3 and GPR4 in the process control block. Table 6–10 shows how the return values are handled.

TABLE 6–10 Handling of BSD System Call Return Values

Call Return Type	Source for GPR3	Source for GPR4
Erroneous return	The `error` variable	Nothing
`_SYSCALL_RET_INT_T`	`uu_rval[0]`	`uu_rval[1]`
`_SYSCALL_RET_UINT_T`	`uu_rval[0]`	`uu_rval[1]`
`_SYSCALL_RET_OFF_T` (32-bit process)	`uu_rval[0]`	`uu_rval[1]`
`_SYSCALL_RET_OFF_T` (64-bit process)	`uu_rval[0]` and `uu_rval[1]` as a single `u_int64_t` value	The value 0
`_SYSCALL_RET_ADDR_T`	`uu_rval[0]` and `uu_rval[1]` as a single `user_addr_t` value	The value 0
`_SYSCALL_RET_SIZE_T`	`uu_rval[0]` and `uu_rval[1]` as a single `user_addr_t` value	The value 0
`_SYSCALL_RET_SSIZE_T`	`uu_rval[0]` and `uu_rval[1]` as a single `user_addr_t` value	The value 0
`_SYSCALL_RET_NONE`	Nothing	Nothing

Finally, to return to user mode, `unix_syscall()` calls `thread_exception_return()` [`osfmk/ppc/hw_exception.s`], which checks for outstanding ASTs. If any ASTs are found, `ast_taken()` is called. After `ast_taken()` returns, `thread_exception_return()` checks for outstanding ASTs one more time (and so on). It then jumps to `.L_thread_syscall_return()` [`osfmk/ppc/hw_exception.s`], which branches to `chkfac()` [`osfmk/ppc/hw_exception.s`], which branches to `exception_exit()` [`osfmk/ppc/lowmem_vectors.s`]. Some of the context is restored during these calls. `exception_exit()` eventually branches to `EatRupt` [`ofsmk/ppc/lowmem_vectors.s`], which releases the save area, performs the remaining context restoration and state cleanup, and finally executes the `rfid` (`rfi` for 32-bit) instruction to return from the interrupt.

Looking Back at System Calls

The system call mechanism in early UNIX operated similarly in concept to the one we have discussed here: It allowed a user program to call on the kernel by executing the trap instruction in user mode. The low-order byte of the instruction word encoded the system call number. Therefore, in theory, there could be up to 256 system calls. Their handler functions in the kernel were contained in a `sysent` table whose first entry was the indirect system call. First Edition UNIX (circa November 1971) had fewer than 35 documented system calls. Figure 6–17 shows a code excerpt from Third Edition UNIX (circa February 1973)—note that the system call numbers for various system calls are identical to those in Mac OS X.

FIGURE 6–17 System call data structures in Third Edition UNIX

```
/* Third Edition UNIX */

/* ken/trap.c */
...
struct {
      int count;
      int (*call)();
} sysent[64];
...

/* ken/sysent.c */
int sysent[]
{
    0, &nullsys,      /* 0 = indir */
    0, &rexit,        /* 1 = exit */
    0, &fork,         /* 2 = fork */
    2, &read,         /* 3 = read */
    2, &write,        /* 4 = write */
    2, &open,         /* 5 = open */
    ...
    0, &nosys,        /* 62 = x */
    0, &prproc        /* 63 = special */
...
```

6.7.1.4 User Processing of BSD System Calls

A typical BSD system call stub in the C library is constructed using a set of macros, some of which are shown in Figure 6–18. The figure also shows an assembly-language fragment for the the `exit()` system call. Note that the assembly code is shown with a static call to `cerror()` for simplicity, as the invocation is somewhat more complicated in the case of dynamic linking.

> The `f` in the unconditional branch instruction to `1f` in Figure 6–18 specifies the direction—forward, in this case. If you have another label named `1` before the branch instruction, you can jump to it using `1b` as the operand.

FIGURE 6–18 Creating a user-space system call stub

```
$ cat testsyscall.h
// for system call numbers
#include <sys/syscall.h>

// taken from <architecture/ppc/mode_independent_asm.h>
#define MI_ENTRY_POINT(name)        \
    .globl  name                @\
    .text                       @\
    .align  2                   @\
name:

#if defined(__DYNAMIC__)
#define MI_BRANCH_EXTERNAL(var)  \
    MI_GET_ADDRESS(r12,var)     @\
    mtctr   r12                 @\
    bctr
#else /* ! __DYNAMIC__ */
#define MI_BRANCH_EXTERNAL(var)  \
    b       var
#endif

// taken from Libc/ppc/sys/SYS.h

#define kernel_trap_args_0
#define kernel_trap_args_1
#define kernel_trap_args_2
#define kernel_trap_args_3
#define kernel_trap_args_4
#define kernel_trap_args_5
#define kernel_trap_args_6
#define kernel_trap_args_7

#define SYSCALL(name, nargs)          \
        .globl  cerror              @\
    MI_ENTRY_POINT(_##name)         @\
        kernel_trap_args_##nargs    @\
        li      r0,SYS_##name       @\
        sc                          @\
        b       1f                  @\
        blr                         @\
1:      MI_BRANCH_EXTERNAL(cerror)

// let us define the stub for SYS_exit
SYSCALL(exit, 1)
$ gcc -static -E testsyscall.h | tr '@' '\n'
...
```

(continues)

FIGURE 6–18 Creating a user-space system call stub *(continued)*

```
; indented and annotated for clarity
.globl cerror
    .globl _exit
    .text
    .align 2
_exit:
    li r0,1    ; load system call number in r0
    sc         ; execute the sc instruction
    b 1f       ; jump over blr, to the cerror call
    blr        ; return
1:  b cerror   ; call cerror, which will also return to the user
```

Figure 6–18 also shows the placement of the call to cerror() in the case of an error. When the sc instruction is executed, the processor places the effective address of the instruction following the sc instruction in SRR0. Therefore, the stub is set to call the cerror() function by default after the system call returns. cerror() copies the system call's return value (contained in GPR3) to the errno variable, calls cthread_set_errno_self() to set the per-thread errno value for the current thread, and sets both GPR3 and GPR4 to -1, thereby causing the calling program to receive return values of -1 whether the expected return value is one word (in GPR3) or two words (in GPR3 and GPR4).

Let us now look at an example of directly invoking a system call using the sc instruction. Although doing so is useful for demonstration, a nonexperimental user program should not use the sc instruction directly. The only API-compliant and future-proof way to invoke system calls under Mac OS X is through user libraries. Almost all supported system calls have stubs in the system library (libSystem), of which the standard C library is a subset.

> As we noted in Chapter 2, the primary reason system calls must not be invoked directly in user programs—especially shipping products—is that the interfaces between system shared libraries and the kernel are private to Apple and are subject to change. Moreover, user programs are allowed to link with system libraries (including libSystem) only dynamically. This allows Apple flexibility in modifying and extending its private interfaces without affecting user programs.

With that caveat, let us use the sc instruction to invoke a simple BSD system call—say, getpid(). Figure 6–19 shows a program that uses both the library stub and our custom stub to call `getpid()`. We need an extra instruction—say, a no-op—immediately following the `sc` instruction, otherwise the program will behave incorrectly.

FIGURE 6–19 Directly invoking a BSD system call

```
// getpid_demo.c

#include <stdio.h>
#include <sys/types.h>
#include <unistd.h>
#include <sys/syscall.h>

pid_t
my_getpid(void)
{
    int syscallnum = SYS_getpid;

    __asm__ volatile(
        "lwz r0,%0\n"
        "sc\n"
        "nop\n" // The kernel will arrange for this to be skipped
      :
      : "g" (syscallnum)
    );

    // GPR3 already has the right return value
    // Compiler warning here because of the lack of a return statement
}

int
main(void)
{
    printf("my pid is %d\n", getpid());
    printf("my pid is %d\n", my_getpid());

    return 0;
}

$ gcc -Wall -o getpid_demo getpid_demo.c
getpid_demo.c: In function 'my_getpid':
getpid_demo.c:24: warning: control reaches end of non-void function
$ ./getpid_demo
my pid is 2345
my pid is 2345
$
```

Note that since user programs on Mac OS X can only be dynamically linked with Apple-provided libraries, one would expect a user program not to have *any* sc instructions at all—it should only have dynamically resolved symbols to system call stubs. However, dynamically linked 32-bit C and C++ programs do have a couple of embedded sc instructions that come from the language runtime startup code—specifically, the __dyld_init_check() function.

```
; dyld.s in the source for the C startup code

/*
 * At this point the dynamic linker initialization was not run so print a
 * message on stderr and exit non-zero.  Since we can't use any libraries the
 * raw system call interfaces must be used.
 *
 *       write(stderr, error_message, sizeof(error_message));
 */
        li      r5,78
        lis     r4,hi16(error_message)
        ori     r4,r4,lo16(error_message)
        li      r3,2
        li      r0,4     ; write() is system call number 4
        sc
        nop              ; return here on error
/*
 *       _exit(59);
 */
        li      r3,59
        li      r0,1     ; exit() is system call number 1
        sc
        trap             ; this call to _exit() should not fall through
        trap
```

6.7.2 Mach Traps

Although Mach traps are similar to traditional system calls in that they are entry points into the kernel, they are different in that Mach kernel services are typically not offered directly through these traps. Instead, certain Mach traps are IPC entry points through which user-space *clients*—such as the system library—access kernel services by exchanging IPC messages with the *server* that implements those services, just as if the server were in user space.

> There are almost ten times as many BSD system calls as there are Mach traps.

Consider an example of a simple Mach trap—say, `task_self_trap()`, which returns send rights to the task's kernel port. The documented `mach_task_self()` library function is redefined in `<mach/mach_init.h>` to be the value of the environment variable `mach_task_self_`, which is populated by the system library during the initialization of a user process. Specifically, the library stub for the `fork()` system call[10] sets up the child process by calling several initialization routines, including one that initializes Mach in the process. This latter step caches the return value of `task_self_trap()` in the `mach_task_self_` variable.

```
// <mach/mach_init.h>

extern mach_port_t mach_task_self_;
#define mach_task_self() mach_task_self_
...
```

The program shown in Figure 6–20 uses several apparently different ways of retrieving the same information—the current task's self port.

FIGURE 6–20 Multiple ways of retrieving a Mach task's self port

```
// mach_task_self.c

#include <stdio.h>
#include <mach/mach.h>
#include <mach/mach_traps.h>

int
main(void)
{
    printf("%#x\n", mach_task_self());
#undef mach_task_self
    printf("%#x\n", mach_task_self());
    printf("%#x\n", task_self_trap());
    printf("%#x\n", mach_task_self_);

    return 0;
}

$ gcc -Wall -o mach_task_self mach_task_self.c
$ ./mach_task_self
0x807
0x807
0x807
0x807
```

---

10. We will see how `fork()` is implemented in Chapter 7.

> The value returned by `task_self_trap()` is not a unique identifier like a Unix process ID. In fact, its value will be the same for all tasks, even on different machines, provided the machines are running identical kernels.

An example of a complex Mach trap is `mach_msg_overwrite_trap()` [osfmk/ipc/mach_msg.c], which is used for sending and receiving IPC messages. Its implementation contains over a thousand lines of C code. `mach_msg_trap()` is a simplified wrapper around `mach_msg_overwrite_trap()`. The C library provides the `mach_msg()` and `mach_msg_overwrite()` documented functions that use these traps but also can restart message sending or receiving in the case of interruptions. User programs access kernel services by performing IPC with the kernel using these "msg" traps. The paradigm used is essentially client server, wherein the clients (programs) request information from the server (the kernel) by sending messages, and usually—but not always—receiving replies. Consider the example of Mach's virtual memory services. As we will see in Chapter 8, a user program can allocate a region of virtual memory using the Mach `vm_allocate()` function. Now, although `vm_allocate()` is implemented in the kernel, it is not exported by the kernel as a regular system call. It is available as a remote procedure in the "Kernel Server" and is callable by user clients. The `vm_allocate()` function that user programs call lives in the C library, representing the client end of the remote procedure call. Various other Mach services, such as those that allow the manipulation of tasks, threads, processors, and ports, are provided similarly.

Mach Interface Generator (MIG)

Implementations of Mach services commonly use the Mach Interface Generator (MIG), which simplifies the task of creating Mach clients and servers by subsuming a considerable portion of frequently used IPC code. MIG accepts a definition file that describes IPC-related interfaces using a predefined syntax. Running the MIG program—`/usr/bin/mig`—on a definition file generates a C header, a client (user) interface module, and a server interface module. We will see an example of using MIG in Chapter 9. MIG definition files for various kernel services are located in the `/usr/include/mach/` directory. A MIG definition file conventionally has a `.def` extension.

Mach traps are maintained in an array of structures called `mach_trap_table`, which is similar to BSD's `sysent` table. Each element of this array is a structure of type `mach_trap_t`, which is declared in `osfmk/kern/syscall_sw.h`. Figure 6–21 shows the `MACH_TRAP()` macro.

FIGURE 6–21 Mach trap table data structures and definitions

```
// osfmk/kern/syscall_sw.h

typedef void mach_munge_t(const void *, void *);

typedef struct {
    int mach_trap_arg_count;
    int (* mach_trap_function)(void);

#if defined(__i386__)
    boolean_t   mach_trap_stack;
#else
    mach_munge_t *mach_trap_arg_munge32;
    mach_munge_t *mach_trap_arg_munge64;
#endif

#if !MACH_ASSERT
    int mach_trap_unused;
#else
    const char * mach_trap_name;
#endif
} mach_trap_t;

#define MACH_TRAP_TABLE_COUNT   128

extern mach_trap_t mach_trap_table[];
extern int         mach_trap_count;

...
#if !MACH_ASSERT
#define MACH_TRAP(name, arg_count, munge32, munge64) \
    { (arg_count), (int (*)(void)) (name), (munge32), (munge64), 0 }
#else
#define MACH_TRAP(name, arg_count, munge32, munge64) \
    { (arg_count), (int (*)(void)) (name), (munge32), (munge64), #name }
#endif
...
```

The `MACH_ASSERT` compile-time configuration option controls the `ASSERT()` and `assert()` macros and is used while compiling debug versions of the kernel.

The MACH_TRAP() macro shown in Figure 6–21 is used to populate the Mach trap table in osfmk/kern/syscall_sw.c—Figure 6–22 shows how this is done. Mach traps on Mac OS X have numbers that start from -10, decrease monotonically, and go as high in absolute value as the highest numbered Mach trap. Numbers 0 through -9 are reserved for Unix system calls and are unused. Note also that the argument munger functions are the same as those used in BSD system call processing.

FIGURE 6–22 Mach trap table initialization

```
// osfmk/kern/syscall_sw.c

mach_trap_t mach_trap_table[MACH_TRAP_TABLE_COUNT] = {
    MACH_TRAP(kern_invalid, 0, NULL, NULL), /* Unix */        /* 0 */
    MACH_TRAP(kern_invalid, 0, NULL, NULL), /* Unix */        /* -1 */
    ...                                       ...              ...
    MACH_TRAP(kern_invalid, 0, NULL, NULL), /* Unix */        /* -9 */
    MACH_TRAP(kern_invalid, 0, NULL, NULL),                   /* -10 */
    ...                                                        ...
    MACH_TRAP(kern_invalid, 0, NULL, NULL),                   /* -25 */
    MACH_TRAP(mach_reply_port, 0, NULL, NULL),                /* -26 */
    MACH_TRAP(thread_self_trap, 0, NULL, NULL),               /* -27 */
    ...                                                        ...
    MACH_TRAP(mach_msg_trap, 7, munge_wwwwwww, munge_ddddddd), /* -31 */
    ...                                                        ...
    MACH_TRAP(task_for_pid, 3, munge_www, munge_ddd),         /* -46 */
    MACH_TRAP(pid_for_task, 2, munge_ww, munge_dd),           /* -47 */
    ...                                                        ...
    MACH_TRAP(kern_invalid, 0, NULL, NULL),                   /* -127 */
};

int mach_trap_count = (sizeof(mach_trap_table) / \
                        sizeof(mach_trap_table[0]));
...
kern_return_t
kern_invalid(void)
{
    if (kern_invalid_debug)
        Debugger("kern_invalid mach_trap");

    return KERN_INVALID_ARGUMENT;
}
...
```

The assembly stubs for Mach traps are defined in osfmk/mach/syscall_sw.h using the machine-dependent kernel_trap() macro defined in osfmk/

`mach/ppc/syscall_sw.h`. Table 6–11 enumerates the key files used in the implementation of these traps.

TABLE 6–11 Implementing Mach Traps in xnu

File	Contents
`osfmk/kern/syscall_sw.h`	Declaration of the trap table structure
`osfmk/kern/syscall_sw.c`	Population of the trap table; definitions of default error functions
`osfmk/mach/mach_interface.h`	Master header file that includes headers for the various Mach APIs—specifically the kernel RPC functions corresponding to these APIs (the headers are generated from MIG definition files)
`osfmk/mach/mach_traps.h`	Prototypes for traps as seen from user space, including declaration of each trap's argument structure
`osfmk/mach/syscall_sw.h`	Instantiation of traps by defining assembly stubs, using the machine-dependent `kernel_trap()` macro (note that some traps may have different versions for the 32-bit and 64-bit system libraries, whereas some traps may not be available in one of the two libraries)
`osfmk/mach/ppc/syscall_sw.h`	PowerPC definitions of the `kernel_trap()` macro and associated macros; definitions of other PowerPC-only system calls

The `kernel_trap()` macro takes three arguments for a trap: its name, its index in the trap table, and its argument count.

```
// osfmk/mach/syscall_sw.h


kernel_trap(mach_reply_port, -26, 0);
kernel_trap(thread_self_trap, -27, 0);
...
kernel_trap(task_for_pid, -45, 3);
kernel_trap(pid_for_task, -46, 2);
...
```

Let us look at a specific example, say, `pid_for_task()`, and see how its stub is instantiated. `pid_for_task()` attempts to find the BSD process ID for the given Mach task. It takes two arguments: the port for a task and a pointer to an integer for holding the returned process ID. Figure 6–23 shows the implementation of this trap.

FIGURE 6–23 Setting up the `pid_for_task()` Mach trap

```
// osfmk/mach/syscall_sw.h

kernel_trap(pid_for_task, -46, 2);
...


// osfmk/mach/ppc_syscall_sw.h

#include <mach/machine/asm.h>

#define kernel_trap(trap_name, trap_number, trap_args) \
ENTRY(trap_name, TAG_NO_FRAME_USED) @\
        li      r0,     trap_number @\
        sc      @\
        blr
...


// osfmk/ppc/asm.h
// included from <mach/machine/asm.h>
#define TAG_NO_FRAME_USED 0x00000000
#define EXT(x)  _ ## x
#define LEXT(x) _ ## x ## :
#define FALIGN 4
#define MCOUNT
#define Entry(x,tag)    .text@.align FALIGN@ .globl EXT(x)@ LEXT(x)
#define ENTRY(x,tag)    Entry(x,tag)@MCOUNT
...


// osfmk/mach/mach_traps.h
#ifndef KERNEL
extern kern_return_t pid_for_task(mach_port_name_t t, int *x);
...
#else /* KERNEL */
...
struct pid_for_task_args {
    PAD_ARG_(mach_port_name_t, t);
    PAD_ARG_(user_addr_t, pid);
};
extern kern_return_t pid_for_task(struct pid_for_task_args *args);
...


// bsd/vm/vm_unix.c
kern_return_t
pid_for_task(struct pid_for_task_args *args)
{
    mach_port_name_t t = args->t;
    user_addr_t pid_addr = args->pid;
    ...
}
```

Using the information shown in Figure 6–23, the trap definition for pid_
for_task() will have the following assembly stub:

```
        .text
        .align 4
        .globl _pid_for_task
_pid_for_task:
        li r0,-46
        sc
        blr
```

Let us test the assembly stub by changing the stub's function name from
_pid_for_task to _my_pid_for_task, placing it in a file called my_pid_
for_task.S, and using it in a C program. Moreover, we can call the regular
pid_for_task() to verify the operation of our stub, as shown in Figure 6–24.

FIGURE 6–24 Testing the pid_for_task() Mach trap

```
// traptest.c

#include <stdio.h>
#include <stdlib.h>
#include <sys/types.h>
#include <unistd.h>
#include <mach/mach.h>
#include <mach/mach_error.h>

extern kern_return_t my_pid_for_task(mach_port_t, int *);

int
main(void)
{
    pid_t          pid;
    kern_return_t  kr;
    mach_port_t    myTask;

    myTask = mach_task_self();

    // call the regular trap
    kr = pid_for_task(myTask, (int *)&pid);
    if (kr != KERN_SUCCESS)
        mach_error("pid_for_task:", kr);
    else
        printf("pid_for_task says %d\n", pid);

    // call our version of the trap
    kr = my_pid_for_task(myTask, (int *)&pid);
```

(continues)

FIGURE 6–24 Testing the `pid_for_task()` Mach trap *(continued)*

```
    if (kr != KERN_SUCCESS)
        mach_error("my_pid_for_task:", kr);
    else
        printf("my_pid_for_task says %d\n", pid);

    exit(0);
}


$ gcc -Wall -o traptest traptest.c my_pid_for_task.S
$ ./traptest
pid_for_task says 20040
my_pid_for_task says 20040
```

In general, handling of Mach traps follows a similar path in the kernel as BSD system calls. `shandler()` identifies Mach traps by virtue of their call numbers being negative. It looks up the trap handler in `mach_trap_table` and performs the call.

> Mach traps in Mac OS X support up to eight parameters that are passed in GPRs 3 through 10. Nevertheless, `mach_msg_overwrite_trap()` takes nine parameters, but the ninth parameter is not used in practice. In the trap's processing, a zero is passed as the ninth parameter.

6.7.3 I/O Kit Traps

Trap numbers 100 through 107 in the Mach trap table are reserved for I/O Kit traps. In Mac OS X 10.4, only one I/O Kit trap is implemented (but not used): `iokit_user_client_trap()` [iokit/Kernel/IOUserClient.cpp]. The I/O Kit framework (`IOKit.framework`) implements the user-space stub for this trap.

6.7.4 PowerPC-Only System Calls

The Mac OS X kernel maintains yet another system call table called `PPCcalls`, which contains a few special PowerPC-only system calls. `PPCcalls` is defined in `osfmk/ppc/PPCcalls.h`. Each of its entries is a pointer to a function that takes one argument (a pointer to a save area) and returns an integer.

```
// osfmk/ppc/PPCcalls.h

typedef int (*PPCcallEnt)(struct savearea *save);

#define PPCcall(rout) rout
#define dis (PPCcallEnt)0

PPCcallEnt PPCcalls[] = {
    PPCcall(diagCall),          // 0x6000
    PPCcall(vmm_get_version),   // 0x6001
    PPCcall(vmm_get_features),  // 0x6002
    ...                         // ...
    PPCcall(dis),
    ...
};
...
```

Call numbers for the PowerPC system calls begin at 0x6000 and can go up
to 0x6FFF—that is, there can be at most 4096 such calls. The assembly stubs for
these calls are instantiated in osfmk/mach/ppc/syscall_sw.h.

```
// osfmk/mach/ppc/syscall_sw.h

#define ppc_trap(trap_name,trap_number) \
ENTRY(trap_name, TAG_NO_FRAME_USED) @\
        li      r0,     trap_number @\
        sc      @\
        blr

...
ppc_trap(diagCall, 0x6000);
ppc_trap(vmm_get_version, 0x6001);
ppc_trap(vmm_get_features, 0x6002);
...
```

Note that the ppc_trap() macro is similar to the kernel_trap() macro
used for defining assembly stubs for Mach traps. shandler() passes most of
these calls to ppcscall() [osfmk/ppc/hw_exception.s], which looks up the
appropriate handler in the PPCcalls table.

Depending on their purpose, these calls can be categorized as follows:

- Calls that are used for low-level performance monitoring, diagnostics, and
  power management (Table 6–12)
- Calls that allow a user program to instantiate and control a virtual machine
  using the kernel's virtual machine monitor (VMM) facility (Table 6–13)
- Calls that provide kernel assistance to the Blue Box (Classic) environment
  (Table 6–14)

TABLE 6–12 PowerPC-Only Calls for Performance Monitoring, Diagnostics, and Power Management

Call Number	Call Name	Purpose
0x6000	diagCall	Calls the routines implemented in the kernel's built-in diagnostics facility (see Section 6.8.8.2)
0x6009	CHUDCall	Acts as a hook for the Computer Hardware Understanding Development (CHUD) interface—disabled to begin with, but is set to a private system call callback function when such a callback is registered by CHUD
0x600A	ppcNull	Does nothing and simply returns (a null system call); used for performance testing
0x600B	perfmon_control	Allows manipulation of the PowerPC performance-monitoring facility
0x600C	ppcNullinst	Does nothing but forces various timestamps to be returned (an instrumented null system call); used for performance testing
0x600D	pmsCntrl	Controls the Power Management Stepper

TABLE 6–13 PowerPC-Only Calls for the Virtual Machine Monitor

Call Number	Call Name	Purpose
0x6001	vmm_get_version	Retrieves the VMM facility's version
0x6002	vmm_get_features	Retrieves the VMM facility's supported features
0x6003	vmm_init_context	Initializes a new VMM context
0x6004	vmm_dispatch	Used as an indirect system call for dispatching various VMM system calls—is also an ultra-fast trap (see Section 6.7.5)
0x6008	vmm_stop_vm	Stops a running virtual machine

TABLE 6–14 PowerPC-Only Calls for the Blue Box

Call Number	Call Name	Purpose
0x6005	bb_enable_bluebox	Enables a thread for use in the Blue Box virtual machine
0x6006	bb_disable_bluebox	Disables a thread for use in the Blue Box virtual machine
0x6007	bb_settaskenv	Sets the Blue Box per-thread task environment data

6.7.5 Ultra-Fast Traps

Certain traps are handled entirely by the low-level exception handlers in `osfmk/ppc/lowmem_vectors.s`, without saving or restoring much (or any) state. Such traps also return from the system call interrupt very rapidly. These are the *ultra-fast traps* (UFTs). As shown in Figure 6–13, these calls have dedicated handlers in the `scTable`, from where the exception vector at `0xC00` loads them. Table 6–15 lists the ultra-fast traps.

TABLE 6–15 Ultra-Fast Traps

Call Number	Association	Purpose
`0xFFFF_FFFE`	Blue Box only	Determines whether the given Blue Box task is preemptive, and also loads GPR0 with the shadowed task environment (`MkIsPreemptiveTaskEnv`)
`0xFFFF_FFFF`	Blue Box only	Determines whether the given Blue Box task is preemptive (`MkIsPreemptiveTask`)
`0x8000_0000`	`CutTrace` firmware call	Used for low-level tracing (see Section 6.8.9.2)
`0x6004`	`vmm_dispatch`	Treats certain calls (those belonging to a specific range of selectors supported by this dispatcher call) as ultra-fast traps—eventually handled by `vmm_ufp()` [`osfmk/ppc/vmachmon_asm.s`]
`0x7FF2`	User only	Returns the `pthread_self` value—i.e., the thread-specific pointer (Thread Info UFT)
`0x7FF3`	User only	Returns floating-point and AltiVec facility status—i.e., if they are being used by the current thread (Facility Status UFT)
`0x7FF4`	Kernel only	Loads the Machine State Register—not used on 64-bit hardware (Load MSR UFT)

A comm area (see Section 6.7.6) routine uses the Thread Info UFT for retrieving the thread-specific (self) pointer, which is also called the *per-thread cookie*. The `pthread_self(3)` library function retrieves this value. The following assembly stub, which directly uses the UFT, retrieves the same value as the `pthread_self()` function in a user program.

```
; my_pthread_self.S
        .text
        .globl _my_pthread_self
```

```
_my_pthread_self:
        li r0,0x7FF2
        sc
        blr
```

Note that on certain PowerPC processors—for example, the 970 and the 970FX—the special-purpose register SPRG3, which Mac OS X uses to hold the per-thread cookie, can be read from user space.

```
; my_pthread_self_970.S
        .text
        .globl _my_pthread_self_970
_my_pthread_self_970:
        mfspr r3,259 ; 259 is user SPRG3
        blr
```

Let us test our versions of pthread_self() by using them in a 32-bit program on both a G4 and a G5, as shown in Figure 6–25.

FIGURE 6–25 Testing the Thread Info UFT

```
$ cat main.c
#include <stdio.h>
#include <pthread.h>

extern pthread_t my_pthread_self();
extern pthread_t my_pthread_self_970();

int
main(void)
{
    printf("library: %p\n", pthread_self());        // call library function
    printf("UFT    : %p\n", my_pthread_self());     // use 0x7FF2 UFT
    printf("SPRG3  : %p\n", my_pthread_self_970()); // read from SPRG3

    return 0;
}
$ machine
ppc970
$ gcc -Wall -o my_pthread_self main.c my_pthread_self.S my_pthread_self_970.S
$ ./my_pthread_self
library: 0xa000ef98
UFT    : 0xa000ef98
SPRG3  : 0xa000ef98

$ machine
ppc7450
```

(continues)

FIGURE 6–25 Testing the Thread Info UFT *(continued)*

```
$ ./my_pthread_self
library: 0xa000ef98
UFT    : 0xa000ef98
zsh: illegal hardware instruction  ./f
```

The Facility Status UFT can be used to determine which processor facilities—such as floating-point and AltiVec—are being used by the current thread. The following function, which directly uses the UFT, will return with a word whose bits specify the processor facilities in use.

```
; my_facstat.S
        .text
        .globl _my_facstat
_my_facstat:
        li r0,0x7FF3
        sc
        blr
```

The program in Figure 6–26 initializes a vector variable only if you run it with one or more arguments on the command line. Therefore, it should report that AltiVec is being used only if you run it with an argument.

FIGURE 6–26 Testing the Facility Status UFT

```
// isvector.c

#include <stdio.h>

// defined in osfmk/ppc/thread_act.h
#define vectorUsed 0x20000000
#define floatUsed  0x40000000
#define runningVM  0x80000000

extern int my_facstat(void);

int
main(int argc, char **argv)
{
    int facstat;
    vector signed int c;

    if (argc > 1)
        c = (vector signed int){ 1, 2, 3, 4 };
```

(continues)

FIGURE 6–26 Testing the Facility Status UFT *(continued)*

```
    facstat = my_facstat();

    printf("%s\n", (facstat & vectorUsed) ? \
           "vector used" : "vector not used");

    return 0;
}

$ gcc -Wall -o isvector isvector.c my_facstat.S
$ ./isvector
vector not used
$ ./isvector usevector
vector used
```

6.7.5.1 Fast Traps

A few other traps that need somewhat more processing than ultra-fast traps, or are not as beneficial to handle so urgently, are handled by `shandler()` in `osfmk/ppc/hw_exception.s`. These are called *fast traps*, or *fastpath calls*. Table 6–16 lists the fastpath calls. Figure 6–12 shows the handling of both ultra-fast and fast traps.

TABLE 6–16 Fastpath System Calls

Call Number	Call Name	Purpose
0x7FF1	CthreadSetSelf	Sets a thread's identifier. This call is used by the Pthread library to implement `pthread_set_self()`, which is used during thread creation.
0x7FF5	Null fastpath	Does nothing. It branches straight to `exception_exit()` in `lowmem_vectors.s`.
0x7FFA	Blue Box interrupt notification	Results in the invocation of `syscall_notify_interrupt()` [osfmk/ppc/PseudoKernel.c], which queues an interrupt for the Blue Box and sets an asynchronous procedure call (APC) AST. The Blue Box interrupt handler—`bbsetRupt()` [osfmk/ppc/PseudoKernel.c]—runs asynchronously to handle the interrupt.

6.7.5.2 Blue Box Calls

The Mac OS X kernel includes support code for the Blue Box virtualizer that provides the Classic runtime environment. The support is implemented as a small layer of software called the *PseudoKernel*, whose functionality is exported via a set of fast/ultra-fast system calls. We came across these calls in Tables 6–14, 6–15, and 6–16.

> The `TruBlueEnvironment` program, which resides within the Resources subdirectory of the Classic application package (`Classic Startup.app`), directly uses the `0x6005` (bb_enable_bluebox), `0x6006` (bb_disable_bluebox), `0x6007` (bb_settaskenv), and `0x7FFA` (interrupt notification) system calls.

A specially designated thread—the *Blue thread*—runs Mac OS while handling Blue Box interrupts, traps, and system calls. Other threads can only issue system calls. The bb_enable_bluebox() [osfmk/ppc/PseudoKernel.c] PowerPC-only system call is used to enable the support code in the kernel. It receives three arguments from the user-space caller: a task identifier, a pointer to the trap table (TWI_TableStart), and a pointer to a descriptor table (Desc TableStart). bb_enable_bluebox() passes these arguments in a call to enable_bluebox() [osfmk/ppc/PseudoKernel.c], which aligns the passed-in descriptor address to a page, wires the page, and maps it into the kernel. The page holds a BlueThreadTrapDescriptor structure (BTTD_t), which is declared in osfmk/ppc/PseudoKernel.h. Thereafter, enable_bluebox() initializes several Blue Box–related fields of the thread's machine-specific state (the machine_thread structure). Figure 6–27 shows pseudocode depicting the operation of enable_bluebox().

FIGURE 6–27 Enabling the kernel's Blue Box support

```
// osfmk/ppc/thread.h

struct machine_thread {
    ...
    // Points to Blue Box Trap descriptor area in kernel (page aligned)
    unsigned int bbDescAddr;
    // Points to Blue Box Trap descriptor area in user (page aligned)
    unsigned int bbUserDA;
    unsigned int bbTableStart;// Points to Blue Box Trap dispatch area in user
```
(continues)

FIGURE 6–27 Enabling the kernel's Blue Box support *(continued)*

```
    unsigned int emPendRupts;  // Number of pending emulated interruptions
    unsigned int bbTaskID;     // Opaque task ID for Blue Box threads
    unsigned int bbTaskEnv;    // Opaque task data reference for Blue Box threads
    unsigned int specFlags;    // Special flags
    ...
    unsigned int bbTrap;       // Blue Box trap vector
    unsigned int bbSysCall;    // Blue Box syscall vector
    unsigned int bbInterrupt;  // Blue Box interrupt vector
    unsigned int bbPending;    // Blue Box pending interrupt vector
    ...
};


// osfmk/ppc/PseudoKernel.c

kern_return_t
enable_bluebox(host_t host, void *taskID, void *TWI_TableStart,
               char *Desc_TableStart)
{
    thread_t       th;
    vm_offset_t    kerndescaddr, origdescoffset;
    kern_return_t  ret;
    ppnum_t        physdescpage;
    BTTD_t         *bttd;

    th = current_thread(); // Get our thread.

    // Ensure descriptor is non-NULL.
    // Get page offset of the descriptor in 'origdescoffset'.
    // Now align descriptor to a page.
    // Kernel wire the descriptor in the user's map.

    // Map the descriptor's physical page into the kernel's virtual address
    // space, calling the resultant address 'kerndescaddr'. Set the 'bttd'
    // pointer to 'kerndescaddr'.

    // Set the thread's Blue Box machine state.

    // Kernel address of the table
    th->machine.bbDescAddr = (unsigned int)kerndescaddr + origdescoffset;

    // User address of the table
    th->machine.bbUserDA = (unsigned int)Desc_TableStart;

    // Address of the trap table
    th->machine.bbTableStart = (unsigned int)TWI_TableStart;
    ...
    // Remember trap vector.
    th->machine.bbTrap = bttd->TrapVector;
```

(continues)

FIGURE 6–27 Enabling the kernel's Blue Box support *(continued)*

```
// Remember syscall vector.
th->machine.bbSysCall = bttd->SysCallVector;

// Remember interrupt vector.
th->machine.bbPending = bttd->PendingIntVector;

// Ensure Mach system calls are enabled and we are not marked preemptive.
th->machine.specFlags &= ~(bbNoMachSC | bbPreemptive);

// Set that we are the Classic thread.
th->machine.specFlags |= bbThread;
...
}
```

Once the Blue Box trap and system call tables are established, the PseudoKernel can be invoked[11] while changing Blue Box interruption state atomically. Both thandler() and shandler() check for the Blue Box during trap and system call processing, respectively.

thandler() checks the specFlags field of the current activation's machine_thread structure to see if the bbThread bit is set. If the bit is set, thandler() calls checkassist() [osfmk/ppc/hw_exception.s], which checks whether all the following conditions hold true.

- The SRR1_PRG_TRAP_BIT bit[12] of SRR1 specifies that this is a trap.
- The trapped address is in user space.
- This is not an AST—that is, the trap type is not a T_AST.
- The trap number is not out of range—that is, it is not more than a predefined maximum.

If all of these conditions are satisfied, checkassist() branches to atomic_switch_trap() [osfmk/ppc/atomic_switch.s], which loads the trap table (the bbTrap field of the machine_thread structure) in GPR5 and jumps to .L_CallPseudoKernel() [osfmk/ppc/atomic_switch.s].

shandler() checks whether system calls are being redirected to the Blue Box by examining the value of the bbNoMachSC bit of the specFlags field. If this bit

---

11. The PseudoKernel can be invoked both from PowerPC (native) and 68K (system) contexts.

12. The kernel uses bit 24 of SRR1 for this purpose. This reserved bit can be implementation-defined.

is set, `shandler()` calls `atomic_switch_syscall()` [`osfmk/ppc/atomic_ switch.s`], which loads the system call table (the `bbSysCall` field of the `machine_thread` structure) in GPR5 and falls through to `.L_CallPseudoKernel()`.

In both cases, `.L_CallPseudoKernel()`—among other things—stores the vector contained in GPR5 in the saved SRR0 as the instruction at which execution will resume. Thereafter, it jumps to `fastexit()` [`osfmk/ppc/hw_exception.s`], which jumps to `exception_exit()` [`osfmk/ppc/lowmem_vectors.s`], thus causing a return to the caller.

> A particular Blue Box trap value (`bbMaxTrap`) is used to simulate a return-from-interrupt from the PseudoKernel to user context. Returning Blue Box traps and system calls use this trap, which results in the invocation of `.L_ExitPseudoKernel()` [`osfmk/ppc/ atomic_switch.s`].

6.7.6 The Commpage

The kernel reserves the last eight pages of every address space for the kernel-user *comm area*—also referred to as the *commpage*. Besides being wired in kernel memory, these pages are mapped (shared and read-only) into the address space of every process. Their contents include code and data that are frequently accessed systemwide. The following are examples of commpage contents:

- Specifications of processor features available on the machine, such as whether the processor is 64-bit, what the cache-line size is, and whether AltiVec is present

- Frequently used routines, such as functions for copying, moving, and zeroing memory; for using spinlocks; for flushing the data cache and invalidating the instruction cache; and for retrieving the per-thread cookie

- Various time-related values maintained by the kernel, allowing the current seconds and microseconds to be retrieved by user programs without making system calls

> There are separate comm areas for 32-bit and 64-bit address spaces, although they are conceptually similar. We will discuss only the 32-bit comm area in this section.

Using the end of the address space for the comm area has an important benefit: It is possible to access both code and data in the comm area from anywhere in the address space, without involving the dynamic link editor or requiring complex address calculations. Absolute unconditional branch instructions, such as `ba`, `bca`, and `bla`, can branch to a location in the comm area from anywhere because they have enough bits in their target address encoding fields to allow them to reach the comm area pages using a sign-extended target address specification. Similarly, absolute loads and stores can comfortably access the comm area. Consequently, accessing the comm area is both efficient and convenient.

The comm area is populated during kernel initialization in a processor-specific and platform-specific manner. `commpage_populate()` [`osfmk/ppc/commpage/commpage.c`] performs this initialization. In fact, functionality contained in the comm area can be considered as processor capabilities—a software extension to the native instruction set. Various comm-area-related constants are defined in `osfmk/ppc/cpu_capabilities.h`.

```
// osfmk/ppc/cpu_capabilities.h

// Start at page -8, ie 0xFFFF8000
#define _COMM_PAGE_BASE_ADDRESS   (-8*4096)

// Reserved length of entire comm area
#define _COMM_PAGE_AREA_LENGTH   (7*4096)

// Mac OS X uses two pages so far
#define _COMM_PAGE_AREA_USED     (2*4096)

// The Objective-C runtime fixed address page to optimize message dispatch
#define OBJC_PAGE_BASE_ADDRESS   (-20*4096)

// Data in the comm page
...

// Code in the comm page (routines)
...
// Used by gettimeofday()
#define _COMM_PAGE_GETTIMEOFDAY \
                            (_COMM_PAGE_BASE_ADDRESS+0x2e0)

...
```

> The comm area's actual maximum length is seven pages (not eight) since Mach's virtual memory subsystem does not map the last page of an address space.

Each routine in the commpage is described by a `commpage_descriptor` structure, which is declared in `osfmk/ppc/commpage/commpage.h`.

```
// osfmk/ppc/cpu_capabilities.h

typedef struct commpage_descriptor {
    short  code_offset;        // offset to code from this descriptor
    short  code_length;        // length in bytes
    short  commpage_address;   // put at this address
    short  special;            // special handling bits for DCBA, SYNC, etc.
    long   musthave;           // _cpu_capability bits we must have
    long   canthave;           // _cpu_capability bits we cannot have
} commpage_descriptor;
```

Implementations of the comm area routines are in the `osfmk/ppc/commpage/` directory. Let us look at the example of `gettimeofday()`, which is both a system call and a comm area routine. It is substantially more expensive to retrieve the current time using the system call. Besides a regular system call stub for `gettimeofday()`, the C library contains the following entry point for calling the comm area version of `gettimeofday()`.

```
        .globl __commpage_gettimeofday
        .text
        .align 2
__commpage_gettimeofday:
        ba __COMM_PAGE_GETTIMEOFDAY
```

> Note that `_COMM_PAGE_GETTIMEOFDAY` is a leaf procedure that must be jumped to, instead of being called as a returning function.

Note that comm area contents are not guaranteed to be available on all machines. Moreover, in the particular case of `gettimeofday()`, the time values are updated asynchronously by the kernel and read atomically from user space, leading to occasional failures in reading. The C library falls back to the system call version in the case of failure.

```
// <darwin>/<Libc>/sys/gettimeofday.c

int
gettimeofday(struct timeval *tp, struct timezone *tzp)
{
    ...
#if defined(__ppc__) || defined(__ppc64__)
    {
        ...
```

```
        // first try commpage
        if (__commpage_gettimeofday(tp)) {
            // if it fails, try the system call
            if (__ppc_gettimeofday(tp,tzp)) {
                return (-1);
            }
        }
    }
#else
    if (syscall(SYS_gettimeofday, tp, tzp) < 0) {
        return -1;
    }
#endif
    ...
}
```

Since the comm area is readable from within every process, let us write a program to display the information contained in it. Since the comm area API is private, you must include the required headers from the kernel source tree rather than a standard header directory. The program shown in Figure 6–28 displays the data and routine descriptors contained in the 32-bit comm area.

FIGURE 6–28 Displaying the contents of the comm area

```
// commpage32.c

#include <stdio.h>
#include <stdlib.h>
#include <inttypes.h>

#define PRIVATE
#define KERNEL_PRIVATE

#include <machine/cpu_capabilities.h>
#include <machine/commpage.h>

#define WSPACE_FMT_SZ "24"
#define WSPACE_FMT "%-" WSPACE_FMT_SZ "s = "

#define CP_CAST_TO_U_INT32(x)   (u_int32_t)(*(u_int32_t *)(x))
#define ADDR2DESC(x)            (commpage_descriptor *)&(CP_CAST_TO_U_INT32(x))

#define CP_PRINT_U_INT8_BOOL(label, item) \
    printf(WSPACE_FMT "%s\n", label, \
        ((u_int8_t)(*(u_int8_t *)(item))) ? "yes" : "no")
#define CP_PRINT_U_INT16(label, item) \
    printf(WSPACE_FMT "%hd\n", label, (u_int16_t)(*(u_int16_t *)(item)))
```

(continues)

FIGURE 6–28 Displaying the contents of the comm area *(continued)*

```
#define CP_PRINT_U_INT32(label, item) \
    printf(WSPACE_FMT "%u\n", label, (u_int32_t)(*(u_int32_t *)(item)))
#define CP_PRINT_U_INT64(label, item) \
    printf(WSPACE_FMT "%#llx\n", label, (u_int64_t)(*(u_int64_t *)(item)))
#define CP_PRINT_D_FLOAT(label, item) \
    printf(WSPACE_FMT "%lf\n", label, (double)(*(double *)(item)))

const char *
cpuCapStrings[] = {
#if defined (__ppc__)
    "kHasAltivec",              // << 0
    "k64Bit",                   // << 1
    "kCache32",                 // << 2
    "kCache64",                 // << 3
    "kCache128",                // << 4
    "kDcbaRecommended",         // << 5
    "kDcbaAvailable",           // << 6
    "kDataStreamsRecommended",  // << 7
    "kDataStreamsAvailable",    // << 8
    "kDcbtStreamsRecommended",  // << 9
    "kDcbtStreamsAvailable",    // << 10
    "kFastThreadLocalStorage",  // << 11
#else /* __i386__ */
    "kHasMMX",                  // << 0
    "kHasSSE",                  // << 1
    "kHasSSE2",                 // << 2
    "kHasSSE3",                 // << 3
    "kCache32",                 // << 4
    "kCache64",                 // << 5
    "kCache128",                // << 6
    "kFastThreadLocalStorage",  // << 7
    "NULL",                     // << 8
    "NULL",                     // << 9
    "NULL",                     // << 10
    "NULL",                     // << 11
#endif
    NULL,                       // << 12
    NULL,                       // << 13
    NULL,                       // << 14
    "kUP",                      // << 15
    NULL,                       // << 16
    NULL,                       // << 17
    NULL,                       // << 18
    NULL,                       // << 19
    NULL,                       // << 20
    NULL,                       // << 21
    NULL,                       // << 22
    NULL,                       // << 23
```

(continues)

FIGURE 6–28 Displaying the contents of the comm area *(continued)*

```
    NULL,                        // << 24
    NULL,                        // << 25
    NULL,                        // << 26
    "kHasGraphicsOps",           // << 27
    "kHasStfiwx",                // << 28
    "kHasFsqrt",                 // << 29
    NULL,                        // << 30
    NULL,                        // << 31
};

void print_bits32(u_int32_t);
void print_cpu_capabilities(u_int32_t);
void print_commpage_descriptor(const char *, u_int32_t);

void
print_bits32(u_int32_t u)
{
    u_int32_t i;

    for (i = 32; i--; putchar(u & 1 << i ? '1' : '0'));
}

void
print_cpu_capabilities(u_int32_t cap)
{
    int i;
    printf(WSPACE_FMT, "cpu capabilities (bits)");
    print_bits32(cap);
    printf("\n");
    for (i = 0; i < 31; i++)
        if (cpuCapStrings[i] && (cap & (1 << i)))
            printf("%-" WSPACE_FMT_SZ "s    + %s\n", " ", cpuCapStrings[i]);
}

void
print_commpage_descriptor(const char *label, u_int32_t addr)
{
    commpage_descriptor *d = ADDR2DESC(addr);
    printf("%s @ %08x\n", label, addr);
#if defined (__ppc__)
    printf("  code_offset      = %hd\n", d->code_offset);
    printf("  code_length      = %hd\n", d->code_length);
    printf("  commpage_address = %hx\n", d->commpage_address);
    printf("  special          = %#hx\n", d->special);
#else /* __i386__ */
    printf("  code_address     = %p\n", d->code_address);
    printf("  code_length      = %ld\n", d->code_length);
    printf("  commpage_address = %#lx\n", d->commpage_address);
```

(continues)

FIGURE 6–28 Displaying the contents of the comm area *(continued)*

```
#endif
    printf("  musthave        = %#lx\n", d->musthave);
    printf("  canthave        = %#lx\n", d->canthave);
}

int
main(void)
{
    u_int32_t u;

    printf(WSPACE_FMT "%#08x\n", "base address", _COMM_PAGE_BASE_ADDRESS);
    printf(WSPACE_FMT "%s\n", "signature", (char *)_COMM_PAGE_BASE_ADDRESS);
    CP_PRINT_U_INT16("version", _COMM_PAGE_VERSION);

    u = CP_CAST_TO_U_INT32(_COMM_PAGE_CPU_CAPABILITIES);
    printf(WSPACE_FMT "%u\n", "number of processors",
           (u & kNumCPUs) >> kNumCPUsShift);
    print_cpu_capabilities(u);
    CP_PRINT_U_INT16("cache line size", _COMM_PAGE_CACHE_LINESIZE);
#if defined (__ppc__)
    CP_PRINT_U_INT8_BOOL("AltiVec available?", _COMM_PAGE_ALTIVEC);
    CP_PRINT_U_INT8_BOOL("64-bit processor?", _COMM_PAGE_64_BIT);
#endif
    CP_PRINT_D_FLOAT("two52 (2^52)", _COMM_PAGE_2_TO_52);
    CP_PRINT_D_FLOAT("ten6 (10^6)", _COMM_PAGE_10_TO_6);
    CP_PRINT_U_INT64("timebase", _COMM_PAGE_TIMEBASE);
    CP_PRINT_U_INT32("timestamp (s)", _COMM_PAGE_TIMESTAMP);
    CP_PRINT_U_INT32("timestamp (us)", _COMM_PAGE_TIMESTAMP + 0x04);
    CP_PRINT_U_INT64("seconds per tick", _COMM_PAGE_SEC_PER_TICK);

    printf("\n");

    printf(WSPACE_FMT "%s", "descriptors", "\n");

    // example descriptor
    print_commpage_descriptor("  mach_absolute_time()",
                              _COMM_PAGE_ABSOLUTE_TIME);

    exit(0);
}


$ gcc -Wall -I /path/to/xnu/osfmk/ -o commpage32 commpage32.c
$ ./commpage32
base address            = 0xffff8000
signature               = commpage 32-bit
version                 = 2
number of processors    = 2
```

(continues)

FIGURE 6–28 Displaying the contents of the comm area *(continued)*

```
cpu capabilities (bits)  = 00111000000000100000011100010011
                         + kHasAltivec
                         + k64Bit
                         + kCache128
                         + kDataStreamsAvailable
                         + kDcbtStreamsRecommended
                         + kDcbtStreamsAvailable
                         + kFastThreadLocalStorage
                         + kHasGraphicsOps
                         + kHasStfiwx
                         + kHasFsqrt
cache line size          = 128
AltiVec available?       = yes
64-bit processor?        = yes
two52 (2^52)             = 4503599627370496.000000
ten6 (10^6)              = 1000000.000000
timebase                 = 0x18f0d27c48c
timestamp (s)            = 1104103731
timestamp (us)           = 876851
seconds per tick         = 0x3e601b8f3f3f8d9b

descriptors              =
  mach_absolute_time() @ ffff8200
  code_offset       = 31884
  code_length       = 17126
  commpage_address  = 7883
  special           = 0x22
  musthave          = 0x4e800020
  canthave          = 0
```

6.8 Kernel Support for Debugging, Diagnostics, and Tracing

In this section, we will look at various facilities in the Mac OS X kernel for both kernel-level and application-level debugging, diagnostics, and tracing. Note that we will not discuss how to actually use the kernel debuggers here—we visit that topic in Chapter 10, in the context of creating kernel extensions.

6.8.1 GDB (Network-Based or FireWire-Based Debugging)

The most convenient way to perform kernel-level debugging on Mac OS X is through the GNU debugger, GDB, which supports either a network-based or

FireWire-based kernel debugging configuration, both of which require two machines.

> The standard Mac OS X kernel includes support for two-machine network-based debugging using GDB.

In the network-based configuration, GDB running on the *debugging* machine communicates over Ethernet with a stub in the *target* machine's kernel. This remote debugger protocol is called the *Kernel Debugging Protocol* (KDP). It uses a variant of TFTP over UDP as the core transfer protocol. The default debugger-side UDP port number is 41139. The following are examples of requests in the KDP protocol:

- Connection-oriented requests (`KDP_CONNECT`, `KDP_DISCONNECT`)
- Requests for obtaining client information (`KDP_HOSTINFO`, `KDP_VERSION`, `KDP_MAXBYTES`)
- Requests for obtaining executable image information (`KDP_LOAD`, `KDP_IMAGEPATH`)
- Requests for accessing memory (`KDP_READMEM`, `KDP_WRITEMEM`)
- Requests for accessing registers (`KDP_READREGS`, `KDP_WRITEREGS`)
- Requests for manipulating breakpoints (`KDP_BREAKPOINT_SET`, `KDP_BREAKPOINT_REMOVE`)

Each KDP request—and the corresponding reply—has its own packet format. Note that the target-side in-kernel KDP implementation *does not* use the kernel's networking stack but has its own minimal UDP/IP implementation.

Two fundamental functions used by the KDP implementation are for sending and receiving protocol packets. A network driver that supports kernel debugging must provide *polled-mode* implementations of these two functions: `sendPacket()`, the transmit handler, and `receivePacket()`, the receive handler. These functions are used only when the kernel debugger is active.

> Since a network driver must explicitly support KDP, remote debugging is possible only when using network interfaces driven by such drivers. In particular, the AirPort driver does not support KDP. Hence, remote debugging cannot be done over a wireless network.

In the FireWire debugging configuration, KDP is used over a FireWire cable courtesy of a kernel extension (`AppleFireWireKDP.kext`) on the target machine and a translator program (`FireWireKDPProxy`) on the debugger machine. The translator routes data between the FireWire connection and UDP port 41139 on the debugger system—that is, it acts as a local proxy for the target machine. GDB still performs network-based debugging, except that it communicates with localhost instead of directly communicating with the shim on the target machine.

6.8.2 KDB (Serial-Line-Based Debugging)

Although GDB is typically sufficient as a kernel debugger, the Mac OS X kernel also supports a built-in kernel debugger called KDB, which is more suitable—and in some cases may be the only option—for debugging low-level kernel components. Since remote debugging with GDB uses network or FireWire hardware, it cannot be used for kernel debugging before the required hardware is operational. For example, debugging the built-in Ethernet hardware used by GDB or low-level hardware interrupt handlers requires the use of the built-in debugger.

> KDB's nature and functionality are roughly similar to that of the `kdb` debugger in BSD variants.

KDB also requires two machines for debugging, although the entire debugger is built into the kernel. You interact with KDB over a serial line, which means that both the target machine and the debugging machine must have serial ports. Whereas the debugging machine can have any type of serial port, including those provided by USB-based or PCI-based serial port adapters, the target machine must have a built-in hardware serial port—typically on the main logic board. Xserve is an example of a system model that has such a real serial port.

Recall the discussion of `kprintf()` initialization from Chapter 5. Serial output from `kprintf()` is disabled unless `DB_KPRT` is set in the debug boot argument. When debug output to a serial port is enabled, `kprintf()` requires a serial device that can be directly addressed, since `scc_putc()` performs polled I/O—it directly reads and writes serial chip registers. This allows debugging to work even with interrupts disabled. Figure 6–29 shows an excerpt from the initialization of the `kprintf()` function.

FIGURE 6–29 Initialization of the `kprintf()` function

```
// pexpert/ppc/pe_kprintf.c

void
PE_init_kprintf(boolean_t vm_initialized)
{
    ...
    if ((scc = PE_find_scc())) {          // See if we can find the serial port
        scc = io_map_spec(scc, 0x1000); // Map it in
        initialize_serial((void *)scc); // Start the serial driver
        PE_kputc = serial_putc;
        simple_lock_init(&kprintf_lock, 0);
    } else
        PE_kputc = cnputc;
    ...
}

void
serial_putc(char c)
{
    (void)scc_putc(0, 1, c);
    if (c == '\n')
        (void)scc_putc(0, 1, '\r');
}

void
kprintf(const char *fmt, ...)
{
    ...
    if (!disableSerialOutput) {
        va_start(listp, fmt);
        _doprnt(fmt, &listp, PE_kputc, 16);
        va_end(listp);
    }
    ...
}
```

Moreover, unlike GDB-based remote debugging, which works with the default Mac OS X kernel, using KDB requires building a custom kernel with the DEBUG configuration (see Section 6.10 for a discussion of kernel compilation).

6.8.3 CHUD Support

The Computer Hardware Understanding Development (CHUD) Tools software is a suite of graphical and command-line programs for measuring and optimizing software performance on Mac OS X.[13] It is also used for benchmarking and analyzing various aspects of system hardware. Besides user-space programs, the CHUD Tools suite employs kernel extensions (`CHUDProf.kext` and `CHUDUtils.kext`), which export a variety of functions to the user space through I/O Kit *user clients*.[14] Finally, the kernel implements several functions and callback hooks for use by CHUD software. The `bsd/dev/ppc/chud/` and `osfmk/ppc/chud/` directories contain the implementations of these functions and hooks. Many of the functions are analogous to functions in the Mach API. The CHUD-related functions and hooks in the kernel can be categorized as described in the following subsections.

6.8.3.1 Task-Related Functions

Examples include `chudxnu_current_task()`, `chudxnu_task_read()`, `chudxnu_task_write()`, `chudxnu_pid_for_task()`, `chudxnu_task_for_pid()`, `chudxnu_current_pid()`, and `chudxnu_is_64bit_task()`.

6.8.3.2 Thread-Related Functions

Examples include `chudxnu_bind_thread()`, `chudxnu_unbind_thread()`, `chudxnu_thread_get_state()`, `chudxnu_thread_set_state()`, `chudxnu_thread_user_state_available()`, `chudxnu_thread_get_callstack()`, `chudxnu_thread_get_callstack64()`, `chudxnu_current_thread()`, `chudxnu_task_for_thread()`, `chudxnu_all_threads()`, `chudxnu_thread_info()`, and `chudxnu_thread_last_context_switch()`.

6.8.3.3 Memory-Related Functions

Examples include `chudxnu_avail_memory_size()`, `chudxnu_phys_memory_size()`, `chudxnu_io_map()`, and `chudxnu_phys_addr_wimg()`.

6.8.3.4 CPU-Related Functions

These include functions for the following operations:

- Retrieving the numbers of available and physical CPUs

---

13. We enumerated the individual programs in the CHUD Tools suite in Chapter 2.

14. An I/O Kit user client is an in-kernel object that allows a user-space application to communicate with a device that the user client represents. We will look at user clients in Chapter 10.

- Retrieving the current CPU's index
- Starting and stopping CPUs
- Enabling, disabling, and querying napping on a CPU
- Enabling and disabling interrupts
- Checking whether the current CPU is running in an interrupt context (determined by checking whether the pointer to the interrupt stack is NULL or not)
- Generating a fake I/O interrupt
- Reading and writing special-purpose registers
- Flushing and enabling CPU caches
- Acquiring and releasing the performance-monitoring facility
- Performing SCOM facility reads and writes
- Retrieving a pointer to and the size of the branch-tracing buffer
- Retrieving and clearing interrupt counters

6.8.3.5 Callback-Related Functions

The kernel supports registration of CHUD callbacks in several kernel subsystems, such as those listed here.

- *Per-CPU timer callback*—The CPU's per_proc_info structure's pp_chud field, which is a pointer to a chudcpu_data_t structure, is used to hold timer-related data structures for this callback.
- *System-wide trap callback*—The perfTrapHook function pointer points to the callback. It is invoked from trap() [osfmk/ppc/trap.c] during trap processing.
- *System-wide interrupt callback*—The perfIntHook function pointer points to the callback. It is invoked from interrupt() [osfmk/ppc/interrupt.c] during interrupt processing.
- *System-wide AST callback*—The perfASTHook function pointer points to the callback. It is invoked from trap() [osfmk/ppc/trap.c] during trap processing.
- *System-wide CPU signal callback*—The perfCpuSigHook function pointer points to the callback. It is invoked from cpu_signal_handler() [osfmk/ppc/cpu.c] during the processing of inter-CPU signals.

- *System-wide kdebug callback*—The `kdebug_chudhook` function pointer points to the callback. It is invoked from `kernel_debug()` [`bsd/kern/kdebug.c`] and its variants, which are used (as part of `KERNEL_DEBUG` macros) throughout the kernel for fine-grained tracing of kernel events.

- *System-wide system call callback*—The PowerPC-only system call `0x6009` becomes alive—calling it from user space invokes the callback in the kernel.

- *Timer callbacks*—Multiple timers can be allocated, and thread-based callouts can be established to run the CHUD timer callbacks.

Figure 6–30 shows how the kernel invokes CHUD system-wide hooks for traps and ASTs.

FIGURE 6–30 Invocation of CHUD system-wide hooks for traps and ASTs

/ `osfmk/ppc/trap.c`

```
struct savearea *
trap(int trapno, struct savearea *ssp, unsigned int dsisr, addr64_t dar)
{
    ...
    ast_t *myast;
    ...
    myast = ast_pending();
    if (perfASTHook) {
        if (*myast & AST_PPC_CHUD_ALL) {
            perfASTHook(trapno, ssp, dsisr, (unsigned int)dar);
        }
    } else {
        *myast &= ~AST_PPC_CHUD_ALL;
    }

    if (perfTrapHook) {
        if (perfTrapHook(trapno, ssp, dsisr, (unsigned int)dar) ==
            KERN_SUCCESS)
            return ssp; // if it succeeds, we are done...
    }
    ...
}
```

Let us look at the operation of the CHUD system call hook. We noted in Table 6–12 that the PowerPC-only system call `0x6009` (`CHUDCall`) is disabled by default. Figure 6–31 shows that invoking a disabled PowerPC-only system call results in an erroneous (nonzero) return.

FIGURE 6–31 Invoking a disabled PowerPC-only system call

```
// CHUDCall.c

#include <stdio.h>

int
CHUDCall(void)
{
    int ret;

    __asm__ volatile(
        "li r0,0x6009\n"
        "sc\n"
        "mr %0,r3\n"
        : "=r" (ret) // output
        :             // no input
    );

    return ret;
}

int
main(void)
{
    int ret = CHUDCall();

    printf("%d\n", ret);

    return ret;
}

$ gcc -Wall -o CHUDCall CHUDCall.c
$ ./CHUDCall
1
```

Let us now see what is involved in registering a CHUD system call callback with the kernel. If successfully registered, the callback will be invoked in the kernel when the 0x6009 system call is executed. We can carry out such an experiment by using the following steps.

- Create a trivial loadable kernel extension that has only the start and stop entry points. We will discuss kernel extensions in Chapter 10. You can create a trivial kernel extension using the Generic Kernel Extension template in Xcode.

- Implement a wrapper function that first checks whether the callback function pointer is non-NULL, and if so, it copies the save area that the 0x6009 system call receives as an argument to a thread state structure. It then invokes the callback with a pointer to the thread state structure as an argument.

- Implement a function that copies information from a save area to a thread state structure.

- Implement a function that sets PPCcalls[9]—the table entry for system call 0x6009—to point to the wrapper. Call this function from the kernel extension's start routine.

- Implement a function that disables the 0x6009 system call by setting PPCcalls[9] to NULL. Call this function from the kernel extension's stop routine.

Figure 6–32 shows most of the code for implementing these steps. Note that the code, including the portion that is not shown, is largely identical to the code in osfmk/ppc/chud/chud_osfmk_callback.c. To create a working kernel extension for this experiment, you need to provide the missing code.

FIGURE 6–32 Implementing a kernel extension to register a PowerPC-only system call

```
// CHUDSyscallExtension.c

#include <sys/systm.h>
#include <mach/mach_types.h>

#define XNU_KERNEL_PRIVATE
#define __APPLE_API_PRIVATE
#define MACH_KERNEL_PRIVATE

// Either include the appropriate headers or provide structure declarations
// for the following:
//
// struct savearea
// struct ppc_thread_state
// struct ppc_thread_state64

// PowerPC-only system call table (from osfmk/ppc/PPCcalls.h)
typedef int (* PPCcallEnt)(struct savearea *save);
extern PPCcallEnt PPCcalls[];

// The callback function's prototype
typedef kern_return_t (* ppc_syscall_callback_func_t) \
                      (thread_flavor_t flavor, thread_state_t tstate, \
                       mach_msg_type_number_t count);
```

(continues)

FIGURE 6–32 Implementing a kernel extension to register a PowerPC-only system call *(continued)*

```
// Pointer for referring to the incoming callback function
static ppc_syscall_callback_func_t callback_func = NULL;

// Identical to chudxnu_copy_savearea_to_threadstate(), which is implemented
// in osfmk/ppc/chud/chud_osfmk_callbacks.c
kern_return_t
ppc_copy_savearea_to_threadstate(thread_flavor_t          flavor,
                                 thread_state_t           tstate,
                                 mach_msg_type_number_t   *count,
                                 struct savearea          *sv)
{
    ...
}

// PPCcalls[9] will point to this when a callback is registered
kern_return_t
callback_wrapper(struct savearea *ssp)
{
    if (ssp) {
        if (callback_func) {
            struct my_ppc_thread_state64 state;
            mach_msg_type_number_t        count = PPC_THREAD_STATE64_COUNT;

            ppc_copy_savearea_to_threadstate(PPC_THREAD_STATE64,
                                             (thread_state_t)&state,
                                             &count, ssp);

            ssp->save_r3 = (callback_func)(PPC_THREAD_STATE64,
                                           (thread_state_t)&state, count);
        } else {
            ssp->save_r3 = KERN_FAILURE;
        }
    }

    return 1; // Check for ASTs
}

// Example callback function
kern_return_t
callback_func_example(thread_flavor_t          flavor,
                      thread_state_t           tstate,
                      mach_msg_type_number_t   count)
{
    printf("Hello, CHUD!\n");
    return KERN_SUCCESS;
}
```

(continues)

FIGURE 6–32 Implementing a kernel extension to register a PowerPC-only system call *(continued)*

```
/ Callback registration
kern_return_t
ppc_syscall_callback_enter(ppc_syscall_callback_func_t func)
{
    callback_func = func;
    PPCcalls[9] = callback_wrapper;
    __asm__ volatile("eieio");
    __asm__ volatile("sync");
    return KERN_SUCCESS;
}

// Callback cancellation
kern_return_t
ppc_syscall_callback_cancel(void)
{
    callback_func = NULL;
    PPCcalls[9] = NULL;
    __asm__ volatile("eieio");
    __asm__ volatile("sync");
    return KERN_SUCCESS;
}

kern_return_t
PPCSysCallKEXT_start(kmod_info_t *ki, void *d)
{
    ppc_syscall_callback_enter(callback_func_example);
    printf("PPCSysCallKEXT_start\n");
    return KERN_SUCCESS;
}

kern_return_t
PPCSysCallKEXT_stop(kmod_info_t *ki, void *d)
{
    ppc_syscall_callback_cancel();
    printf("PPCSysCallKEXT_stop\n");
    return KERN_SUCCESS;
}
```

If you run the program from Figure 6–31 after the kernel extension shown in Figure 6–32 is loaded, you should get a zero return from the system call, and the "Hello, CHUD!" message should appear in the system log.

6.8.4 Kernel Profiling (`kgmon` and `gprof`)

The Mac OS X kernel can be compiled with support for profiling its own code. Such a compilation is achieved by selecting the PROFILE configuration before initiating a kernel build. Doing so enables several aspects of the kernel profiling mechanism, such as the following.

- The kernel is compiled with the -pg GCC option, thereby generating extra code to write profiling information for subsequent analysis.
- BSD initialization during system startup calls kmstartup() [bsd/kern/subr_prof.c] to initialize profiling data structures that reside in a global gmonparam structure [bsd/sys/gmon.h] called _gmonparam. Moreover, kmstartup() allocates kernel memory for holding profile data.
- When running on the master processor, the kernel invokes bsd_hardclock() [bsd/kern/kern_clock.c] every time hertz_tick() [osfmk/kern/mach_clock.c] is called from the real-time clock interrupt handler. When kernel profiling is enabled, bsd_hardclock() updates the information in _gmonparam.
- When kernel profiling is enabled, the code for servicing the KERN_PROF sysctl is included in kern_sysctl() [bsd/kern/kern_sysctl.c]—the dispatcher for kernel-related sysctl calls.

The kgmon command-line program is used to enable or disable profiling, reset in-kernel profile buffers, and dump the contents of the profile buffers to a gmon.out file. kgmon communicates with the kernel primarily using management information base (MIB) names of the format CTL_KERN→KERN_PROF→<terminal name>, where <terminal name> can be one of the following:

- GPROF_STATE—enable or disable profiling
- GPROF_COUNT—retrieve buffer containing profile tick counts
- GPROF_FROMS—retrieve buffer containing "from" hash buckets
- GPROF_TOS—retrieve buffer containing "to" (destination) structures
- GPROF_GMONPARAM—retrieve the state of kernel profiling

Once profiling data is dumped to the gmon.out file, the standard gprof command-line program can be used to display the execution profile. Figure 6–33 shows an example of using kgmon and gprof.

FIGURE 6–33 Using `kgmon` and `gprof` for kernel profiling

```
$ uname -v       # This kernel was compiled with profiling support
Darwin Kernel Version.../BUILD/obj/PROFILE_PPC
$ kgmon          # Profiling should be disabled to begin with
kgmon: kernel profiling is off.
$ sudo kgmon -b # Resume the collection of profile data
kgmon: kernel profiling is running.
...              # Wait for the data of interest
$ sudo kgmon -h # Stop the collection of profile data
kgmon: kernel profiling is off.
$ ls             # No output files yet
$ kgmon -p       # Dump the contents of the profile buffers
kgmon: kernel profiling is off.
$ ls             # We should have a gmon.out file now
gmon.out
$ gprof /mach_kernel.profile gmon.out
...
granularity: each sample hit covers 4 byte(s) for 0.03% of 34.23 seconds


                                 called/total     parents
index  %time   self descendents called+self   name            index
                                 called/total      children


                                              <spontaneous>
[1]    98.8   33.81       0.00              _machine_idle_ret [1]


-----------------------------------------------


                                              <spontaneous>
[2]     0.6    0.22       0.00              _ml_set_interrupts_enabled [2]

...
        0.00       0.00    6/117        _thread_setstatus [818]
        0.00       0.00    6/6          _thread_userstack [1392]
        0.00       0.00    6/6          _thread_entrypoint [1388]
        0.00       0.00    3/203        _current_map [725]
        0.00       0.00    3/3          _swap_task_map [1516]
        0.00       0.00    3/3037       _pmap_switch [436]
...
Index by function name

[1149] _BTFlushPath       [257] _fdesc_readdir      [1029] _psignal_lock
...
 [782] __ZN18IOMemoryDescr [697] _ipc_kobject_destro[1516] _swap_task_map
...
  [27] _devfs_make_link   [436] _pmap_switch        [1213] _wait_queue_member
...
$
```

6.8.4.1 *Per-Process Profiling (`profil(2)`)*

The xnu kernel implements the `profil()` system call that allows a user process to gather its own CPU-usage statistics by profiling the program counter.

```
int
profil(char *samples, size_t size, u_long offset, u_int scale)
```

   `samples` is a buffer whose length is `size` bytes. It is divided into sequential bins of 16 bits each. `offset` specifies the lowest program counter (PC) value at which the kernel will sample the PC upon every clock tick—it is the starting address of the program region to be sampled. For each sampled PC, the kernel increments the value in the bin whose number is computed based on the `scale` argument. To compute the bin number, that is, the index in the samples array, the kernel subtracts `offset` from the sampled PC and multiplies the result by `scale`. If the resultant index is within the bounds of the `samples` array, the corresponding bin's value is incremented; otherwise, profiling is turned off.

   `scale` is passed as an unsigned integer but represents 16 bits' worth of fraction, with the value 1 being in the middle. Therefore, a `scale` value of `0x10000` results in a one-to-one mapping from PC value to bins, whereas a higher value results in a many-to-one mapping. A `scale` value of `0` or `1` turns off profiling.

```
// bsd/kern/subr_prof.c

#define PC_TO_INDEX(pc, prof) \
        ((int)(((u_quad_t)((pc) - (prof)->pr_off) * \
                        (u_quad_t)((prof)->pr_scale)) >> 16) & ~1)
```

   Enabling profiling sets the `P_PROF` bit in the `p_flag` field of the BSD process structure. Moreover, the `pr_scale` field of the profiling substructure within the process structure is set to the `scale` value. Thereafter, as shown in Figure 6–34, every time there is a BSD-level clock tick (100 times a second), `bsd_hardclock()` checks whether the process is running in user mode and has a nonzero scale value. If so, it sets a flag (`P_OWEUPC`) in the process, indicating that a call to `addupc_task()` [bsd/kern/subr_prof.c] is owed to the task the next time there is an AST. It then calls `astbsd_on()` to generate an `AST_BSD`, which is serviced by `bsd_ast()`, which in turn calls `addupc_task()`. The latter updates the profiling buffer, turning off profiling in the case of an error.

FIGURE 6–34 Implementation of the `profil()` system call

`// bsd/kern/kern_clock.c`

```
void
bsd_hardclock(boolean_t usermode, caddr_t pc, int numticks)
{
    register struct proc *p;
    ...
    p = (struct proc *)current_proc();
    ...
        if (usermode) {
            if (p->p_stats && p->p_stats->p_prof.pr_scale) {
                // Owe process an addupc_task() call at next AST
                p->p_flag |= P_OWEUPC;
                astbsd_on();
            }
            ...
        }
    ...
}
```

`// bsd/kern/kern_sig.c`
`// called when there is an AST_BSD`
```
void
bsd_ast(thread_t thr_act)
{
    ...
    if ((p->p_flag & P_OWEUPC) && (p->p_flag & P_PROFIL)) {
        pc = get_useraddr();
        addupc_task(p, pc, 1);
        p->p_flag &= ~P_OWEUPC;
    }
    ...
}
```

`// bsd/kern/subr_prof.c`

```
void
addupc_task(register struct proc *p, user_addr_t pc, u_int ticks)
{
    ...
    // 64-bit or 32-bit profiling statistics collection
    if (/* 64-bit process */) {
        // calculate offset in profile buffer using PC_TO_INDEX()

        // if target location lies within the buffer, copyin() existing
        // count value from that location into the kernel
```

(continues)

FIGURE 6–34 Implementation of the `profil()` system call *(continued)*

```
    // increment the count by ticks

    // copyout() the updated information to user buffer

    // if there is any error, turn off profiling

  } else {
      // do 32-bit counterpart
  }
}
```

Another system call—`add_profil()`—can be used to profile multiple, noncontiguous areas of program memory. Multiple calls to `add_profil()` can follow a single call to `profil()`. Note that calling `profil()` removes any buffers that were allocated by one or more previous calls to `add_profil()`.

6.8.4.2 Mach Task and Thread Sampling

Mach 3 provides calls for sampling tasks and threads. The `mach_sample_thread()` call periodically samples the program counter of the specified thread, saves the sampled values in buffers, and sends the buffers to the specified reply port when the buffers become full. The `mach_sample_task()` call performs a similar function, but for all threads of a given task. The sampled values are not tagged by thread, which means that samples for various threads will typically be intermingled.

The Mac OS X kernel includes code for Mach-based task and thread sampling. The code is conditionally compiled—if `MACH_PROF` is defined during kernel compilation. However, note that the code is *not* functional.

```
kern_return_t
task_sample(task_t sample_task, mach_port_make_send_t reply_port);

kern_return_t
thread_sample(thread_act_t sample_thread, mach_port_make_send_t reply_port);

kern_return_t
receive_samples(mach_port_t sample_port, sample_array_t samples,
                mach_msg_type_number_t sample_count);
```

The `receive_samples()` call is used to receive a message containing sampled values. It is invoked by `prof_server()`—a MIG-generated library function that simplifies the work involved in processing the incoming IPC message.[15] We will discuss this style of IPC in Chapter 9 when we look at Mach exception handling.

> The `osfmk/mach/prof.defs` file contains the MIG definitions for this profiling interface.

6.8.5 Per-Process Kernel Tracing (`ktrace(2)` and `kdump`)

The `ktrace()` system call can be used on Mac OS X to enable or disable tracing of selected operations in one or more processes.

```
int
ktrace(const char *tracefile, // pathname of file in which to save trace records
       int         ops,        // ktrace operation
       int         trpoints,   // trace points of interest (what to trace)
       int         pid);       // primary process of interest
                               // a negative pid specifies a process group
```

The `ops` argument to `ktrace()` can be one of the following:

- KTROP_SET—enable trace points specified in the `trpoints` argument
- KTROP_CLEAR—disable trace points specified in `trpoints`
- KTROP_CLEARFILE—stop all tracing
- KTRFLAG_DESCEND—also apply tracing change to all children of the process specified by the `pid` argument

> The `ktrace` command uses the `ktrace()` system call, allowing trace data to be logged to a specified file (`ktrace.out` by default). The `kdump` command displays the data in human-readable format. Only the superuser may trace setuid and setgid processes, or another user's processes.

Categories of operations to trace—*trace points*—are specified by logically OR'ing respective bits and passing the resultant value as the `trpoints` argument. Each selection causes the corresponding types of events to be generated at

---

15. The `prof_server()` function does not exist in the default Mac OS X system library.

one or more locations in the kernel. The following bit values can be used to specify operation types when calling `ktrace()`.

- `KTRFAC_SYSCALL` traces BSD system calls. When this bit is set, `ktrsyscall()` is called by `unix_syscall()` before the system call handler is invoked. `ktrsyscall()` writes a "system call" trace record (`struct ktr_syscall`).

- `KTR_SYSRET` traces return from BSD system calls. When this bit is set, `ktrsysret()` is called by `unix_syscall()` after the system call handler has returned and return values have been processed. `ktrsysret()` writes a "return from system call" trace record (`struct ktr_sysret`).

- `KTRFAC_NAMEI` traces name lookup operations. When this bit is set, `ktrnamei()` is called by `namei()` [bsd/vfs/vfs_lookup], `sem_open()` [bsd/kern/posix_sem.c], and `shm_open()` [bsd/kern/posix_shm.c]. `ktrnamei()` writes a string—the relevant pathname—as the trace data.

- `KTRFAC_GENIO` traces a variety of I/O operations. When this bit is set, `ktrgenio()` is called by `recvit()` and `sendit()` [both in bsd/kern/uipc_syscalls.c], and `dofileread()`, `dofilewrite()`, `rd_uio()`, and `wr_uio()` [all in bsd/kern/sys_generic.c]. `ktrgenio()` writes a "generic process I/O" trace record (`struct ktr_genio`).

- `KTRFAC_PSIG` traces posted signals. When this bit is set, `ktrpsig()` is called by `postsig()` [bsd/kern/kern_sig.c]. `ktrpsig()` writes a "processed signal" trace record (`struct ktr_psig`).

- `KTRFAC_CSW` traces context switches. When this bit is set, `ktrcsw()` is called by `_sleep_continue()` and `_sleep()` [both in bsd/kern/kern_synch.c]. `ktrcsw()` writes a "context switch" trace record (`struct ktr_csw`).

> All ktrace event-logging functions are implemented in `bsd/kern/kern_ktrace.c`.

The `p_traceflag` field of the process structure holds the operation-related bits. This field also contains other relevant flags, such as the following.

- `KTRFAC_ACTIVE` specifies that ktrace logging is in progress.

- `KTRFAC_ROOT` specifies that the tracing status for that process was previously established by the superuser, and only the superuser can now change it further.

- `KTRFAC_INHERIT` specifies that the child process arising out of a `fork()` system call will inherit the parent's `p_traceflag` field.

Note that a record resulting from some type of tracing event consists of a generic header (`struct ktr_header`) followed by an event-specific structure.

// bsd/sys/ktrace.h

```
struct ktr_header {
    int     ktr_len;                   // length of buffer that follows this header
    short   ktr_type;                  // trace record type
    pid_t   ktr_pid;                   // process ID generating the record
    char    ktr_comm[MAXCOMLEN+1];     // command name generating the record
    struct  timeval ktr_time;          // record generation timestamp (microsecond)
    caddr_t ktr_buf;                   // buffer
}
```

Event-specific structures can vary in length even for a given event type. For example, the `ktr_syscall` structure contains a system call number, the number of arguments passed to that system call, and an array of 64-bit unsigned integers containing the arguments.

```
struct ktr_syscall {
    short     ktr_code;    // system call number
    short     ktr_narg;    // number of arguments
    u_int64_t ktr_args[1]; // a 64-bit "GPR" for each argument
};
```

6.8.6 Auditing Support

We briefly looked at the user-space aspects of the auditing system in Chapter 2. The Mac OS X kernel supports auditing of system events using the Basic Security Module (BSM) format for audit records. Figure 6–35 shows the key interactions between the user and kernel components of the auditing system.

During the initialization of the kernel's BSD portion, `audit_init()` [bsd/kern/kern_audit.c] is called to initialize the auditing system. Besides allocating the relevant data structures and initializing various parameters, `audit_init()` also calls `kau_init()` [bsd/kern/kern_bsm_audit.c] to initialize the BSM audit subsystem. In particular, `kau_init()` sets up the initial event-to-class mappings for BSD system calls, Mach system calls, and several types of open events.

Initially, BSD and Mach system call events map to the null audit class (AU_NULL). Note that at this point, auditing is initialized but not started in the kernel. When the user-space audit daemon (auditd) starts up, it establishes a log file to which the kernel will write audit records—auditing in the kernel begins as a side effect of this operation. Let us first look at auditd's operation while referring to Figure 6–35.

auditd is a simple daemon whose responsibilities are limited to managing audit log files and enabling or disabling auditing. It is *not* involved in the actual writing of the audit records to disk.[16] The following are auditd's primary initialization steps.

- It installs a signal handler for the SIGTERM and SIGCHLD signals. The handler sends a Mach IPC message to auditd's main server loop. The reason these signals are not handled in the signal handler itself is that auditd may not be at a clean point while it is in the signal handler.

- It allocates a Mach port for the aforementioned signal "reflection," and another—the *audit control port*—for communication with user programs (such as the audit utility) and the kernel.

- It registers the control port with the kernel as a special host-level port by calling host_set_audit_control_port(). Thereafter, clients of auditd can communicate with it by retrieving the control port via host_get_audit_control_port(). Note that it places both ports in a single *port set*,[17] allowing it to later wait for incoming messages on either port by using the port set alone.

- It reads the audit control file (/etc/security/audit_control), which contains system-wide audit parameters. Once it has determined the pathname of the directory for storing audit log files (/var/audit/ by default), auditd generates the pathname for the audit log file itself and invokes the auditctl() system call to convey the pathname to the kernel. auditctl()'s kernel implementation creates a kernel thread running audit_worker() [bsd/kern/kern_audit.c]—unless the thread already exists,[18] in which case it is woken up.

---

16. In this sense, the audit daemon can be likened to the dynamic_pager program, which manages swap files. We will see the operation of dynamic_pager in Chapter 8.

17. We will discuss the port set concept in Chapter 9.

18. If you enable, disable, and reenable auditing on a system, the audit_worker kernel thread will exist during the reenabling and, therefore, will be woken up.

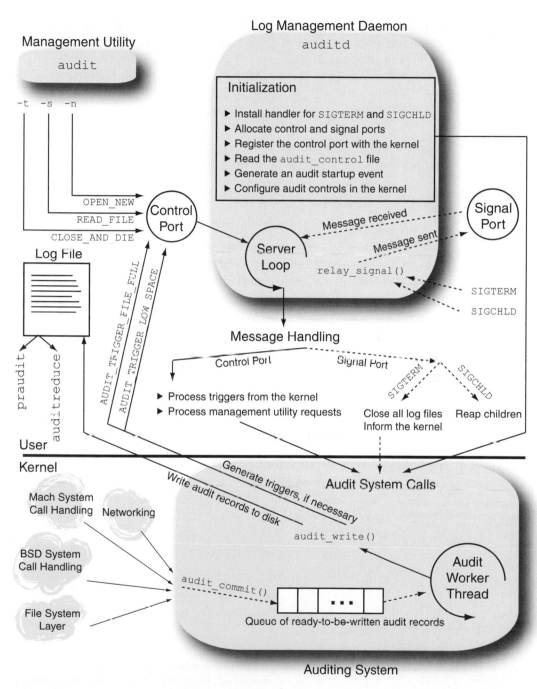

FIGURE 6–35 The Mac OS X auditing system

> Depending on the flags passed to the open() system call, it is treated as different types of open events. For example, if there are multiple invocations of the open() system call with the flags argument being O_RDONLY, O_WRONLY, and O_RDWR, the corresponding open events are AUE_OPEN_R, AUE_OPEN_W, and AUE_OPEN_RW, respectively.

- It generates an "audit startup" audit record indicating its own startup. Note that this event is "artificial" in that it is programmatically generated by auditd. It uses functions in the BSM library (libbsm.dylib) for this purpose, which in turn use the audit() system call, a function that allows user-space applications to explicitly submit audit records to the kernel for inclusion in the audit log.

- It parses the audit event file (/etc/security/audit_event), which contains descriptions of auditable events on the system, mapping an audit event number to a name (such as AUE_OPEN), a description (such as "open(2)—attr only"), and a class name (such as "fa"). The classes are described in /etc/security/audit_class—information in this file must conform with the audit class information known to the kernel. For each event line in audit_event, auditd registers the class mapping by invoking the A_SETCLASS command through the auditon() system call.

- It finally enters its server loop, waiting for messages to arrive on either of the control or signal ports.

The in-kernel audit record structure (struct kaudit_record) for a thread resides in the thread's corresponding uthread structure (struct uthread).

```
// bsd/sys/user.h

struct uthread {
    ...
    struct kaudit_record *uu_ar;
    ...
};

// bsd/bsm/audit_kernel.h

struct kaudit_record {
    struct audit_record    k_ar;        // standard audit record
    u_int32_t              k_ar_commit; // AR_COMMIT_KERNEL, AR_COMMIT_USER
    void                   *k_udata;    // opaque user data, if any
    u_int                  k_ulen;      // user data length
```

```
    struct uthread            *k_uthread;    // thread that we are auditing
    TAILQ_ENTRY(kaudit_record)  k_q;         // queue metadata
};
```

The kernel allocates and initializes a new audit record for a thread by calling audit_new() [bsd/kern/kern_audit.c] when the first auditable event occurs. This is typically when either a BSD or Mach system call is invoked. However, this can also occur during the audit() system call, which, as we saw earlier, is used by a user program to submit an audit record. Since the audit() system call itself is not audited, it is possible for a uthread structure's uu_ar field to be NULL if no auditable event has occurred so far for that thread. Various portions of the kernel code use audit macros to add information to a thread's existing audit record. These macros resolve to conditional code that operates only if auditing is currently enabled. Figure 6–36 shows an example of audit macros.

FIGURE 6–36 Audit macros in the kernel and how they are used

```
// bsd/bsm/audit_kernel.h

#define AUDIT_ARG(op, args...)  do { \
    it (audit_enabled)            \
        audit_arg_ ## op (args);   \
} while (0)

#define AUDIT_SYSCALL_ENTER(args...) do { \
    if (audit_enabled) {              \
        audit_syscall_enter(args);     \
    }                                  \
} while (0)

// Additional check for uu_ar since it is possible that an audit record
// was begun before auditing was disabled
#define AUDIT_SYSCALL_EXIT(error, proc, uthread) do { \
    if (audit_enabled || (uthread->uu_ar != NULL)) {  \
        audit_syscall_exit(error, proc, uthread);      \
    }                                                  \
} while (0)


// bsd/dev/ppc/systemcalls.c

void
unix_syscall(struct savearea *regs)
{
```

(continues)

FIGURE 6–36 Audit macros in the kernel and how they are used *(continued)*

```
    ...
    AUDIT_SYSCALL_ENTER(code, proc, uthread);
    // call the system call handler
    error = (*(callp->sy_call))(proc, (void *uthread->uu_arg,
            &(uthread->uu_rval[0]));
    AUDIT_SYSCALL_EXIT(error, proc, uthread);
    ...
}


// bsd/vfs/vfs_syscalls.c

static int
open1(...)
{
    ...
    AUDIT_ARG(fflags, oflags);
    AUDIT_ARG(mode, vap->va_mode);
    ...
}
```

When `audit_syscall_enter()` [bsd/kern/kern_audit.c] is called, the current `uthread` structure's `uu_ar` field will be NULL. If the event corresponding to the current system call and its arguments is auditable, `audit_syscall_enter()` allocates an audit record and sets `uu_ar` to point to it. As long as the system call remains in the kernel, any `audit_arg_xxx()` functions that may be called by kernel code will append information to the thread's audit record. When the system call finishes, `audit_syscall_exit()` [bsd/kern/kern_audit.c] commits the record by calling `audit_commit()` [bsd/kern/kern_audit.c] and sets the `uu_ar` field to NULL. `audit_commit()` inserts the record in a queue of audit records that are ready to be written to disk. The queue is serviced by the audit worker thread, which, as we saw earlier, is created when `auditd` first specifies a log file pathname to the kernel. The audit worker thread writes audit records to the log file by calling `audit_write()` [bsd/kern/kern_audit.c], which directly writes to the log file's vnode (the `audit_vp` variable) through the `vn_rdwr()` kernel function. Auditing is disabled by passing a NULL log file pathname, which results in the `audit_vp` variable being set to NULL. The worker thread checks for a valid `audit_vp` in each iteration of its loop—if `audit_vp` is NULL, it sets `audit_enabled` to 0, causing the various audit logger functions to be ineffective.

Other responsibilities of the worker thread include sending trigger messages to `auditd` if the log file becomes full or if the amount of free disk space on the volume containing the log file falls below a configured threshold.

6.8.7 Fine-Grained Kernel Event Tracing (kdebug)

The Mac OS X kernel provides a fine-grained kernel-tracing facility called *kdebug*, which can be enabled or disabled on a per-process basis. The `sc_usage`, `fs_usage`, and `latency` command-line tools use the kdebug facility. `sc_usage` displays ongoing system calls and various types of page faults. The output of `fs_usage` is restricted to system calls and page faults related to file system activity. `latency` monitors and displays scheduling and interrupt latency statistics. The kdebug facility also allows the CHUD toolkit to register a callback function— `kdebug_chudhook()` —that will be invoked each time kdebug logging is attempted, regardless of whether kdebug tracing is enabled or not. Finally, the kdebug facility can be enabled to collect *entropy* and therefore can be used as a source of entropy for random number generation. The Mac OS X Security Server uses the kdebug facility to sample entropy.

Specifically, the kdebug facility can be enabled to operate in modes corresponding to one or more of the following mode bits at any given time: `KDEBUG_ENABLE_TRACE`, `KDEBUG_ENABLE_ENTROPY`, and `KDEBUG_ENABLE_CHUD`. The `kdebug_enable` global variable in the kernel holds these bits.

6.8.7.1 kdebug Tracing

The kdebug facility categorizes traced operations into *classes*, *subclasses* within classes, and *codes* within subclasses. Moreover, if a traced operation marks the beginning or end of a kernel function, its trace is tagged with `DBG_FUNC_START` and `DBG_FUNC_END` function qualifiers, respectively. Nonfunction traces are tagged with `DBG_FUNC_NONE`. Figure 6–37 shows an excerpt from kdebug's hierarchy of traced operation classification. Each trace record has a 32-bit debug code whose bits represent the operation's class, subclass, code, and function qualifier. The entire hierarchy is defined in `bsd/sys/kdebug.h`.

Code throughout the kernel submits operations for kdebug tracing using macros that resolve to either `kernel_debug()` or `kernel_debug1()`, both of which are implemented in `bsd/kern/kdebug.c`.

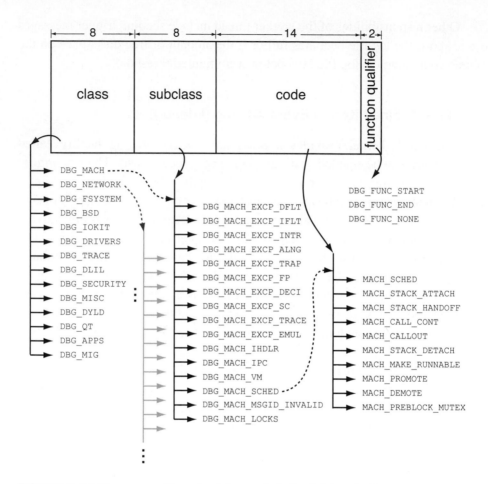

FIGURE 6–37 The composition of a debug code in the kdebug facility

```
// bsd/sys/kdebug.h

#define KERNEL_DEBUG_CONSTANT(x,a,b,c,d,e)   \
do {                                          \
    if (kdebug_enable)                        \
        kernel_debug(x,a,b,c,d,e);            \
} while(0)

#define KERNEL_DEBUG_CONSTANT1(x,a,b,c,d,e)  \
do {                                          \
    if (kdebug_enable)                        \
        kernel_debug1(x,a,b,c,d,e);           \
} while(0)
...
```

> `kernel_debug1()` is used during an `execve()` operation that fol-
> lows a `vfork()` operation—`kernel_debug1()` is a special version
> of `kernel_debug()` that receives the thread's identity as an argu-
> ment instead of calling `current_thread()`, which `kernel_debug()`
> uses. `current_thread()` cannot be used in this particular case
> since it will return the parent thread.

Let us see how the BSD system call handler uses these macros. As shown in
Figure 6–38, the handler submits trace records soon after starting and just before
finishing. Note that it skips record generation if the system call number is 180
(`SYS_kdebug_trace`), which corresponds to the `kdebug_trace()` system call.
Similar conceptually to the `audit()` system call, this call can be used by user
programs to explicitly submit a trace record to the kdebug facility. As we will
shortly see, the `BSDDBG_CODE()` macro computes a debug code given a subclass
and a code within that subclass.

FIGURE 6–38 kdebug tracing in the BSD system call handler

```
// bsd/dev/ppc/systemcalls.c

void
unix_syscall(struct savearea *regs)
{
    . . .
    unsigned int cancel_enable;

    flavor = (((unsigned int)regs->save_r0) == 0) ? 1 : 0;
    if (flavor)
        code = regs->save_r3;
    else
        code = regs->save_r0;

    if (kdebug_enable && (code != 180)) {
        if (flavor) // indirect system call
            KERNEL_DEBUG_CONSTANT(
                BSDDBG_CODE(DBG_BSD_EXCP_SC, code) | DBG_FUNC_START,
                        regs->save_r4, regs->save_r5,
                        regs->save_r6, regs->save_r7, 0);
        else        // direct system call
            KERNEL_DEBUG_CONSTANT(
                BSDDBG_CODE(DBG_BSD_EXCP_SC, code) | DBG_FUNC_START,
                        regs->save_r3, regs->save_r4, regs->save_r5,
                        regs->save_r6, 0);
    }
```

(continues)

FIGURE 6–38 kdebug tracing in the BSD system call handler *(continued)*

```
...
// call the system call handler
...
if (kdebug_enable && (code != 180)) {
    if (callp->sy_return_type == _SYSCALL_REG_SSIZE_T)
        KERNEL_DEBUG_CONSTANT(
            BSDDBG_CODE(DBG_BSD_EXCP_SC, code) | DBG_FUNC_END,
                        error, uthread->uu_rval[1], 0, 0, 0);
    else
        KERNEL_DEBUG_CONSTANT(
            BSDDBG_CODE(DBG_BSD_EXCP_SC, code) | DBG_FUNC_END,
                        error, uthread->uu_rval[0], uthread->uu_rval[1],
                        0, 0);
}

thread_exception_return();
/* NOTREACHED */
}
```

The kdebug facility is accessed from user space through `KERN_KDEBUG` sysctl operations with `CTL_KERN` as the top-level sysctl identifier. Examples of supported operations include the following:

- Enabling or disabling tracing (`KERN_KDENABLE`)
- Cleaning up the relevant trace buffers (`KERN_KDREMOVE`)
- Reinitializing the tracing facility (`KERN_KDSETUP`)
- Specifying the trace buffer size to the kernel (`KERN_KDSETBUF`)
- Specifying which process IDs to trace (`KERN_KDPIDTR`)
- Specifying which process IDs to exclude (`KERN_KDPIDEX`)
- Specifying trace points of interest to the kernel by class, by subclass, by debug code values, or by a range of debug code values (`KERN_KDSETREG`)
- Retrieving trace buffer metainformation from the kernel (`KERN_KDGETBUF`)
- Retrieving the trace buffer from the kernel (`KERN_KDREADTR`)

Note that process IDs can be either selected for or excluded from tracing. In the former case, the `KDBG_PIDCHECK` bit is set in the global kdebug-flags kernel variable (kdebug_flags), and the `P_KDEBUG` bit is set in the `p_flag` process structure field of each *selected* process. Thereafter, any process for which `P_KDEBUG` is not set is not traced. In the case of process ID exclusion, the `KDBG_PIDEXCLUDE` bit is set instead in `kdebug_flags`, and the `P_KDEBUG` bit is set for each *excluded* process.

As seen in the examples of supported kdebug operations, trace points of interest can be specified to the kernel in several ways: through a kdebug class (such as `DBG_BSD`), a subclass (such as `DBG_BSD_EXCP_SC`, which represents BSD system calls), up to four specific debug code values, or a range of such values. Figure 6–37 shows the structure of a debug code. The `bsd/sys/kdebug.h` header provides macros for constructing a debug code from its constituents.

Let us consider a specific example. Suppose we wish to use the kdebug facility to trace the use of the `chdir()` system call. The debug code for `chdir()` will have `DBG_BSD` as its class, `DBG_BSD_EXP_SC` as its subclass, and the system call's number (`SYS_chdir`) as its code. We can use the `BSDDBG_CODE()` macro to compute the code.

```
// bsd/sys/kdebug.h

#define KDBG_CODE(Class, SubClass, code) (((Class & 0xff) << 24) | \
                  ((SubClass & 0xff << 16) | ((code & 0x3fff) << 2))
...
#define MACHDBG_CODE(SubClass, code) KDBG_CODE(DBG_MACH, SubClass, code)
#define NETDBG_CODE(SubClass, code) KDBG_CODE(DBG_NETWORK, SubClass, code)
#define FSDBG_CODE(SubClass, code) KDBG_CODE(DBG_FSYSTEM, SubClass, code)
#define BSDDBG_CODE(SubClass, code) KDBG_CODE(DBG_BSD, SubClass, code)
...
```

Before we look at a programming example, let us briefly discuss the operation of `kernel_debug()`, which is the center of kdebug activity in the kernel. It performs the following primary operations.

- If the CHUD kdebug hook is registered, it calls the hook.
- If entropy is being sampled, it adds an entry to the entropy buffer unless the buffer is full. We will look at entropy sampling in Section 6.8.7.2.
- If `KDBG_PIDCHECK` is set, it returns without adding a trace record if the current process does not have `P_KDEBUG` set.
- If `KDBG_PIDEXCLUDE`, which is mutually exclusive to `KDBG_PIDCHECK`, is set, `kernel_debug()` returns if the current process does not have `P_KDEBUG` set.
- If `KDBG_RANGECHECK` is set, it checks whether the current debug code falls within the configured range of interesting trace points. If not, `kernel_debug()` returns.

- If KDBG_VALCHECK is set, it compares the debug code (minus the function qualifier bits) with the four specific values, at least one of which must have been configured. If there is no match, kernel_debug() returns.

- At this point, kernel_debug() records the trace entry, updates its book-keeping data structures, and returns.

Let us now look at an example of using the kdebug facility in a user program. We will use kdebug to trace the chdir() system call. If a process ID is passed as an argument to the program, we will configure kdebug to trace only that process; otherwise, kdebug will trace on a system-wide basis. We will use kdebug's value-checking feature to configure it to trace only one specific debug code—that corresponding to the chdir() system call. Figure 6–39 shows the program and a sample of its usage. Note that only one program can use the kdebug tracing facility at a time.

FIGURE 6–39 Using the kdebug facility in a program

```c
// kdebug.c

#define PROGNAME "kdebug"

#include <stdlib.h>
#include <stdio.h>
#include <fcntl.h>
#include <unistd.h>
#include <sys/sysctl.h>
#include <sys/ptrace.h>
#include <sys/syscall.h>

struct proc;

// Kernel Debug definitions
#define PRIVATE
#define KERNEL_PRIVATE
#include <sys/kdebug.h>
#undef KERNEL_PRIVATE
#undef PRIVATE

// Configurable parameters
enum {
    KDBG_BSD_SYSTEM_CALL_OF_INTEREST = SYS_chdir,
    KDBG_SAMPLE_SIZE                 = 16384,
    KDBG_SAMPLE_INTERVAL             = 100000, // in microseconds
};
```

(continues)

FIGURE 6–39 Using the kdebug facility in a program *(continued)*

```c
// Useful constants
enum {
    KDBG_FUNC_MASK   = 0xfffffffc, // for extracting function type
    KDBG_CLASS_MASK  = 0xff000000, // for extracting class type
    KDBG_CLASS_SHIFT = 24          // for extracting class type
};


// Global variables
int    exiting = 0; // avoid recursion in exit handlers
size_t oldlen;      // used while calling sysctl()
int    mib[8];      // used while calling sysctl()
pid_t  pid = -1;    // process ID of the traced process


// Global flags
int trace_enabled   = 0;
int set_remove_flag = 1;


// Mapping of kdebug class IDs to class names
const char *KDBG_CLASS_NAMES[256] = {
    NULL,            // 0
    "DBG_MACH",      // 1
    "DBG_NETWORK",   // 2
    "DBG_FSYSTEM",   // 3
    "DBG_BSD",       // 4
    "DBG_IOKIT",     // 5
    "DBG_DRIVERS",   // 6
    "DBG_TRACE",     // 7
    "DBG_DLIL",      // 8
    "DBG_SECURITY",  // 9
    NULL, NULL, NULL, NULL, NULL, NULL, NULL, NULL, NULL, NULL,
    "DBG_MISC",      // 20
    NULL, NULL, NULL, NULL, NULL, NULL, NULL, NULL, NULL, NULL,
    "DBG_DYLD",      // 31
    "DBG_QT",        // 32
    "DBG_APPS",      // 33
    NULL,
};


// Functions that we implement (the 'u' in ukdbg represents user space)
void ukdbg_exit_handler(int);
void ukdbg_exit(const char *);
void ukdbg_setenable(int);
void ukdbg_clear();
void ukdbg_reinit();
void ukdbg_setbuf(int);
void ukdbg_getbuf(kbufinfo_t *);
void ukdbg_setpidcheck(pid_t, int);
void ukdbg_read(char *, size_t *);
void ukdbg_setreg_valcheck(int val1, int val2, int val3, int val4);
```

(continues)

FIGURE 6–39 Using the kdebug facility in a program *(continued)*

```c
void
ukdbg_exit_handler(int s)
{
    exiting = 1;

    if (trace_enabled)
        ukdbg_setenable(0);

    if (pid > 0)
        ukdbg_setpidcheck(pid, 0);

    if (set_remove_flag)
        ukdbg_clear();

    fprintf(stderr, "cleaning up...\n");

    exit(s);
}

void
ukdbg_exit(const char *msg)
{
    if (msg)
        perror(msg);

    ukdbg_exit_handler(0);
}

// Enable or disable trace
// enable=1 enables (trace buffer must already be initialized)
// enable=0 disables
void
ukdbg_setenable(int enable)
{
    mib[0] = CTL_KERN;
    mib[1] = KERN_KDEBUG;
    mib[2] = KERN_KDENABLE;
    mib[3] = enable;
    if ((sysctl(mib, 4, NULL, &oldlen, NULL, 0) < 0) && !exiting)
        ukdbg_exit("ukdbg_setenable::sysctl");

    trace_enabled = enable;
}

// Clean up relevant buffers
void
ukdbg_clear(void)
```

(continues)

FIGURE 6–39 Using the kdebug facility in a program *(continued)*

```
{
    mib[0] = CTL_KERN;
    mib[1] = KERN_KDEBUG;
    mib[2] = KERN_KDREMOVE;
    if ((sysctl(mib, 3, NULL, &oldlen, NULL, 0) < 0) && !exiting) {
        set_remove_flag = 0;
        ukdbg_exit("ukdbg_clear::sysctl");
    }
}

// Disable any ongoing trace collection and reinitialize the facility
void
ukdbg_reinit(void)
{
    mib[0] = CTL_KERN;
    mib[1] = KERN_KDEBUG;
    mib[2] = KERN_KDSETUP;
    if (sysctl(mib, 3, NULL, &oldlen, NULL, 0) < 0)
        ukdbg_exit("ukdbg_reinit::sysctl");
}

// Set buffer for the desired number of trace entries
// Buffer size is limited to either 25% of physical memory (sane_size),
// or to the maximum mapped address, whichever is smaller
void
ukdbg_setbuf(int nbufs)
{
    mib[0] = CTL_KERN;
    mib[1] = KERN_KDEBUG;
    mib[2] = KERN_KDSETBUF;
    mib[3] = nbufs;
    if (sysctl(mib, 4, NULL, &oldlen, NULL, 0) < 0)
        ukdbg_exit("ukdbg_setbuf::sysctl");
}

// Turn pid check on or off in the trace buffer
// check=1 turns on pid check for this and all pids
// check=0 turns off pid check for this pid (but not all pids)
void
ukdbg_setpidcheck(pid_t pid, int check)
{
    kd_regtype kr;
    kr.type = KDBG_TYPENONE;
    kr.value1 = pid;
    kr.value2 = check;
    oldlen = sizeof(kd_regtype);
    mib[0] = CTL_KERN;
```

(continues)

FIGURE 6–39 Using the kdebug facility in a program *(continued)*

```
    mib[1] = KERN_KDEBUG;
    mib[2] = KERN_KDPIDTR;
    if ((sysctl(mib, 3, &kr, &oldlen, NULL, 0) < 0) && !exiting)
        ukdbg_exit("ukdbg_setpidcheck::sysctl");
}


// Set specific value checking
void
ukdbg_setreg_valcheck(int val1, int val2, int val3, int val4)
{
    kd_regtype kr;
    kr.type = KDBG_VALCHECK;
    kr.value1 = val1;
    kr.value2 = val2;
    kr.value3 = val3;
    kr.value4 = val4;
    oldlen = sizeof(kd_regtype);
    mib[0] = CTL_KERN;
    mib[1] = KERN_KDEBUG;
    mib[2] = KERN_KDSETREG;
    if (sysctl(mib, 3, &kr, &oldlen, NULL, 0) < 0)
        ukdbg_exit("ukdbg_setreg_valcheck::sysctl");
}


// Retrieve trace buffer information from the kernel
void
ukdbg_getbuf(kbufinfo_t *bufinfop)
{
    oldlen = sizeof(bufinfop);
    mib[0] = CTL_KERN;
    mib[1] = KERN_KDEBUG;
    mib[2] = KERN_KDGETBUF;
    if (sysctl(mib, 3, bufinfop, &oldlen, 0, 0) < 0)
        ukdbg_exit("ukdbg_getbuf::sysctl");
}


// Retrieve some of the trace buffer from the kernel
void
ukdbg_read(char *buf, size_t *len)
{
    mib[0] = CTL_KERN;
    mib[1] = KERN_KDEBUG;
    mib[2] = KERN_KDREADTR;
    if (sysctl(mib, 3, buf, len, NULL, 0) < 0)
        ukdbg_exit("ukdbg_read::sysctl");
}
```

(continues)

FIGURE 6–39 Using the kdebug facility in a program *(continued)*

```
int
main(int argc, char **argv)
{
    int             i, count;
    kd_buf          *kd;
    char            *kd_buf_memory;
    kbufinfo_t      bufinfo = { 0, 0, 0, 0 };
    unsigned short code;

    KDBG_CLASS_NAMES[255] = "DBG_MIG";

    if (argc > 2) {
        fprintf(stderr, "usage: %s [<pid>]\n", PROGNAME);
        exit(1);
    }

    if (argc == 2)
        pid = atoi(argv[1]);

    code = KDBG_BSD_SYSTEM_CALL_OF_INTEREST;

    // Arrange for cleanup
    signal(SIGHUP, ukdbg_exit_handler);
    signal(SIGINT, ukdbg_exit_handler);
    signal(SIGQUIT, ukdbg_exit_handler);
    signal(SIGTERM, ukdbg_exit_handler);

    kd_buf_memory = malloc(KDBG_SAMPLE_SIZE * sizeof(kd_buf));
    if (!kd_buf_memory) {
        perror("malloc");
        exit(1);
    }

    ukdbg_clear();                      // Clean up related buffers
    ukdbg_setbuf(KDBG_SAMPLE_SIZE);     // Set buffer for the desired # of entries
    ukdbg_reinit();                     // Reinitialize the facility
    if (pid > 0)
        ukdbg_setpidcheck(pid, 1);  // We want this pid
    // We want this particular BSD system call
    ukdbg_setreg_valcheck(BSDDBG_CODE(DBG_BSD_EXCP_SC, code), 0, 0, 0);
    ukdbg_setenable(1);                 // Enable tracing

    while (1) {
        ukdbg_getbuf(&bufinfo);                         // Query information
        oldlen = bufinfo.nkdbufs * sizeof(kd_buf); // How much to read?
        ukdbg_read(kd_buf_memory, &oldlen);             // Read that much
```

(continues)

FIGURE 6–39 Using the kdebug facility in a program *(continued)*

```
        count = oldlen;

        kd = (kd_buf *)kd_buf_memory;
        for (i = 0; i < count; i++) {

            char    *qual = "";
            uint64_t  cpu, now;
            int       debugid, thread, type, class;

            thread = kd[i].arg5;
            debugid = kd[i].debugid;
            type = debugid & KDBG_FUNC_MASK;
            class = (debugid & KDBG_CLASS_MASK) >> KDBG_CLASS_SHIFT;
            now = kd[i].timestamp & KDBG_TIMESTAMP_MASK;
            cpu = (kd[i].timestamp & KDBG_CPU_MASK) >> KDBG_CPU_SHIFT;

            if (debugid & DBG_FUNC_START)
                qual = "DBG_FUNC_START";
            else if (debugid & DBG_FUNC_END)
                qual = "DBG_FUNC_END";

            // Note that 'type' should be the system call we were looking for
            // (type == BSDDBG_CODE(DBG_BSD_EXCP_SC, code) is true

            printf("%lld: cpu %lld %s code %#x thread %p %s\n",
                   now,
                   cpu,
                   (KDBG_CLASS_NAMES[class]) ? KDBG_CLASS_NAMES[class] : "",
                   type,
                   (void *)thread,
                   qual);
        }

        usleep(KDBG_SAMPLE_INTERVAL);
    }
}

$ gcc -Wall -I /path/to/xnu/bsd/ -o kdebug kdebug.c
$ ./kdebug # now use the 'cd' command from another shell
9009708884894: cpu 1 DBG_BSD code 0x40c0030 thread 0x47f9948 DBG_FUNC_START
9009708885712: cpu 1 DBG_BSD code 0x40c0030 thread 0x47f9948 DBG_FUNC_END
^Ccleaning up...
```

The file /usr/share/misc/trace.codes maps kdebug codes to operation names. It is used by programs such as sc_usage and latency to display
debug codes in human-readable forms.

6.8.7.2 kdebug Entropy Collection

As we noted earlier, the kdebug facility can be enabled to sample system entropy. The samples are collected in a kernel buffer, which is then copied to user space. These steps occur within a single sysctl call. Input to this call includes a user buffer for receiving entropy entries, the buffer's size, and a timeout value. The Mac OS X Security Server (/usr/sbin/securityd) contains a system entropy management module that uses kdebug entropy collection. It performs the following operations.

- It reads the saved entropy file (/var/db/SystemEntropyCache) on startup and seeds the random number generator (RNG) for initial use.

- It periodically calls the kdebug facility to collect and retrieve system entropy, which it uses to seed the RNG.

- It periodically saves the RNG's entropy to the entropy file for use across reboots.

```
// <darwin>/<securityd>/src/entropy.cpp

void
EntropyManager::collectEntropy()
{
    int mib[4];
    mib[0] = CTL_KERN;
    mib[1] = KERN_KDEBUG;
    mib[2] = KERN_KDGETENTROPY;
    mib[3] = 1; // milliseconds of maximum delay
    mach_timespec_t timings[timingsToCollect];
    size_t size = sizeof(timings);
    int ret = sysctl(mib, 4, timings, &size, NULL, 0);
    ...
}
```

The in-kernel handler for the KERN_KDGETENTROPY sysctl calls kdbg_getentropy() [bsd/kern/kdebug.c], which performs the following operations.

- If entropy is already being sampled, it returns EBUSY. This is because there can be at most one instance of entropy collection in the kdebug facility.

- It uses kmem_alloc() to allocate a kernel buffer large enough to hold the number of entropy entries requested. If this allocation fails, it returns EINVAL.

- If the caller-specified timeout value is less than 10 ms, it alters the timeout to be 10 ms.

- It enables entropy sampling by setting the KDEBUG_ENABLE_ENTROPY bit in the kdebug_enable variable.

- It calls tsleep() [bsd/kern/kern_synch.c] to sleep for the timeout duration.

- Upon being woken up, it disables entropy sampling by clearing the KDEBUG_ENABLE_ENTROPY bit in kdebug_enable.

- It copies the kernel entropy buffer to the user buffer that was passed in the sysctl call.

- It calls kmem_free() to free the in-kernel entropy buffer.

Enabling entropy collection causes kernel_debug() to collect timestamp entries in the entropy buffer. Note that this is independent of whether kdebug tracing is enabled or the CHUD hook is installed.

```
// bsd/kern/kdebug.c

void
kernel_debug(debugid, arg1, arg2, arg3, arg4, arg5)
{
    ...
    if (kdebug_enable & KDEBUG_ENABLE_ENTROPY) {

        // collect some more entropy
        if (kd_entropy_index < kd_entropy_count) {
            kd_entropy_buffer[kd_entropy_index] = mach_absolute_time();
            kd_entropy_index++;
        }

        // do we have enough timestamp entries to fill the entropy buffer?
        if (kd_entropy_index == kd_entropy_count) {
            // disable entropy collection
            kdebug_enable &= ~KDEBUG_ENABLE_ENTROPY;
            kdebug_slowcheck &= ~SLOW_ENTROPY;
        }
    }
    ...
}
```

6.8.8 Low-Level Diagnostics and Debugging Interfaces

The Mac OS X kernel provides a low-level diagnostics and debugging interface that can be enabled at boot time by passing the diag argument to the kernel. Depending on the specific flags passed through this argument, the kernel enables specific features and behavior. The various flag bits that can be set in the diag value[19] are defined in osfmk/ppc/Diagnostics.h. Table 6–17 lists these flags and their purpose.

> The flags listed in Table 6–17 are likely to be useful only to Mac OS X core kernel developers. Enabling any of the diagnostics or low-level debugging features on production systems is not recommended.

TABLE 6–17 Flags for Enabling Diagnostic Features at Boot Time

Name	Value	Description
enaExpTrace	0x0000_0001	This bit enables ultra-low-level diagnostics tracing in the kernel. The built-in kernel debugger, KDB, can be used to view the trace records.
enaUsrFCall	0x0000_0002	This bit enables the firmware call interface to be used from user space. The interface provides hardware-dependent low-level functionality.
enaUsrPhyMp	0x0000_0004	This bit is unused.
enaDiagSCs	0x0000_0008	This bit enables the diagnostics system call interface.
enaDiagDM	0x0000_0010	If this bit is set, the driver for /dev/mem allows access to the *entire* physical memory (mem_actual), even if available physical memory has been limited through the maxmem boot-time argument.
enaDiagEM	0x0000_0020	This bit causes the special opcode 0, along with an extended opcode that is one of the X-form instructions capable of taking an alignment interrupt, to simulate an alignment exception. This is to facilitate debugging of the alignment handler.
enaDiagTrap	0x0000_0040	This bit enables the special diagnostics trap, which is of the form twi 31,r31,0xFFFX, with X being a hexadecimal digit. When enabled, the trap returns from the kernel with a return value of 1.
enaNotifyEM	0x0000_0080	Instructions that fail because of operand alignment can be emulated by low-level kernel code. This bit enables notification of such emulation—say, for logging of unaligned accesses. chudxnu_passup_alignment_exceptions() [osfmk/ppc/chud/chud_cpu.c]—a CHUD toolkit internal function—can set or clear this bit.

---

19. The diag value is passed as a logical OR of these flag bits.

6.8.8.1 Firmware Call Interface

The *firmware call interface* is so called because it provides functionality that is considered an extension of the hardware—it is *not* an interface to Open Firmware. Its functionality includes the following:

- Writing debugging information (such as register contents) to a printer or modem port (dbgDispCall)
- Storing words to physical memory and clearing physical pages (StoreRealCall and ClearRealCall, respectively)
- Loading BAT registers (LoadDBATsCall and LoadIBATsCall)
- Creating fake I/O and decrementer interrupts (CreateFakeIOCall and CreateFakeDECCall, respectively)
- Crashing the system immediately (Choke)
- Shutting down the system immediately (CreateShutdownCTXCall)
- Switching context (SwitchContextCall)
- Preempting (DoPreemptCall)

Note that the kernel uses certain firmware calls during its regular operation. For example, _ml_set_interrupts_enabled() [osfmk/ppc/machine_routines_asm.s] can conditionally invoke the DoPreemptCall() system call from within the kernel. Similarly, context-switching assembly code in osfmk/ppc/cswtch.s uses the SwitchContextCall() firmware call.

Let us look at an example of using the firmware call interface from user space. A system call is treated as a firmware call if its number has its high-order bit set to 1. As we saw in Figure 6–12, the xcpSyscall() handler tests for firmware calls early. Whereas firmware calls are always allowed from supervisor state, they must be explicitly enabled for user space, as noted in Table 6–17. If xcpSyscall() finds the high-order bit set in the system call number, and the call is allowed, it forwards the call to FirmwareCall() [xnu/osfmk/ppc/Firmware.s]. The low-order bits in the system call number represent the index of the desired call in the firmware call table (FWtable), which is declared in osfmk/ppc/Firmware.s and populated in osfmk/ppc/FirmwareCalls.h. The lowest numbered firmware call—CutTraceCall()—has the number 0x80000000. Looking at osfmk/ppc/FirmwareCalls.h, we find that the Choke() call is at index 0xa, whereas the CreateShutdownCTXCall() call is at index 0xd.

> Firmware call indices may not be the same across all kernel versions.

For example, if we make a system call with the value `0x8000000a` in GPR0, the system will crash. Similarly, a call with the value `0x8000000d` in GPR0 will cause the system to shut down instantly, as if all power to the system has been cut.

6.8.8.2 Diagnostics System Call Interface

The *diagnostics system call interface* is somewhat more generally interesting for experimentation than the firmware call interface. Its functionality includes routines for the following operations:

- Adjusting the Timebase Register—used for testing drift recovery
- Returning the physical address of a page
- Accessing physical memory (including copying physical memory pages, and reading or writing individual bytes)
- Soft-resetting the processor
- Forcing all caches, including the TLB, to be reinitialized
- Retrieving boot-screen information

A complete list of implemented diagnostics system calls can be seen in `osfmk/ppc/Diagnostics.c`. As shown in Table 6–12, the PowerPC-specific `diagCall()` system call has the number `0x6000`. This system call invokes `diagCall()` [osfmk/ppc/Diagnostics.c]—the dispatcher for these system calls. `diagCall()` uses the value in GPR3 to determine the specific diagnostics operation to perform. The available operations are defined in `osfmk/ppc/Diagnostics.h`.

```
// osfmk/ppc/Diagnostics.h

#define diagSCnum 0x00006000

#define dgAdjTB       0
#define dgLRA         1
#define dgpcpy        2
#define dgreset       3
#define dgtest        4
#define dgBMphys      5
#define dgUnMap       6
#define dgBootScreen  7
...
```

```
#define dgKfree      22
#define dgWar        23
...
```

Let us look at examples of using the diagnostics system calls. First, we create a common header file—`diagCommon.h`—containing code we will use in all examples in this section. Figure 6–40 shows `diagCommon.h`.

FIGURE 6–40 Common header file for using the diagnostics system call interface

```
// diagCommon.h

#ifndef _DIAG_COMMON_H_
#define _DIAG_COMMON_H_

#include <stdio.h>
#include <stdint.h>
#include <string.h>
#include <ppc/types.h>
#define _POSIX_C_SOURCE
#include <stdlib.h>
#include <unistd.h>

struct savearea;

// These headers are not available outside of the kernel source tree
#define KERNEL_PRIVATE
#include <ppc/Diagnostics.h>
#include <console/video_console.h>
#undef KERNEL_PRIVATE

// The diagCall() prototype in Diagnostics.h is from the kernel's standpoint
// -- having only one argument: a pointer to the caller's save area. Our user-
// space call takes a variable number of arguments.
//
// Note that diagCall() does have a stub in libSystem.
//
// Here we declare a prototype with a variable number of arguments, define
// a function pointer per that prototype, and point it to the library stub.
typedef int (*diagCall_t)(int op, ...);
diagCall_t diagCall_ = (diagCall_t)diagCall;

// Defined in osfmk/vm/pmap.h, which may not be included from user space
#define cppvPsrc      2
#define cppvNoRefSrc  32

// Arbitrary upper limit on the number of bytes of memory we will handle
#define MAXBYTES      (8 * 1024 * 1024)

#endif // _DIAG_COMMON_H_
```

Before the diagnostics system call interface can be used, it must be enabled at boot time by passing the `diag=<number>` boot argument, where `<number>` contains set bits corresponding to the `enaDiagSCs` constant (`0x8`), as noted in Table 6–17. Similarly, the firmware interface is enabled by passing set bits corresponding to the `enaUsrFCall` constant (`0x2`). For example, to enable both interfaces, pass `diag=0xa`, since `0xa` is the logical OR of `0x8` and `0x2`.

Retrieving Boot-Screen Information

In this example, we will write a program that uses the `dgBootScreen()` call to retrieve the boot-screen "video" information from the kernel. The information is maintained in a structure of type `vc_info`. The system console code in `osfmk/console/video_console.c` manages this structure. Figure 6–41 shows the output of our program on a system with a 1280×854 display attached to it. Note that the quantity labeled "physical address" shows the location of the raw frame-buffer in physical memory.

FIGURE 6–41 Retrieving boot-screen information using a diagnostics system call

```
// diagBootScreen.c

#include "diagCommon.h"

int
main(int argc, char **argv)
{
    struct vc_info vc_info;

    if (diagCall_(dgBootScreen, &vc_info) < 0)
        exit(1);

    printf("%ldx%ld pixels, %ldx%ld characters, %ld-bit\n",
            vc_info.v_width, vc_info.v_height,
            vc_info.v_columns, vc_info.v_rows,
            vc_info.v_depth);
    printf("base address %#08lx, physical address %#08lx\n",
            vc_info.v_baseaddr, vc_info.v_physaddr);
    printf("%ld bytes used for display per row\n",
            vc_info.v_rowscanbytes);

    exit(0);
}
```

(continues)

FIGURE 6–41 Retrieving boot-screen information using a diagnostics system call *(continued)*

```
$ gcc -Wall -I /path/to/xnu/osfmk/ -o diagBootScreen diagBootScreen.c
$ ./diagBootScreen
1280x854 pixels, 160x53 characters, 32-bit
base address 0x2f72c000, physical address 0xb8010000
5120 bytes used for display per row
```

Retrieving the Physical Address for a Virtual Address

In this example, we will use the dgLRA() (where LRA stands for *logical-to-real address*) call to retrieve the physical page, and therefore the physical address, for a given virtual address in the address space of the calling process. If the virtual address is not mapped in the caller's address space, the dgLRA() system call returns a nonzero value. We can verify this program by retrieving the physical address of the page beginning at virtual address 0xFFFF8000—as we saw earlier, this is the base virtual address of the comm area and should map to the same physical page in all user address spaces. Figure 6–42 shows the program.

FIGURE 6–42 Retrieving the physical address (if any) for a virtual address in the caller's address space

```
// diagLRA.c

#include "diagCommon.h"

#define PROGNAME "diagLRA"

int
main(int argc, char **argv)
{
    u_int32_t phys, virt;
    u_int64_t physaddr;

    if (argc != 2) {
        printf("usage: %s <virtual address in hex>\n", PROGNAME);
        exit(1);
    }

    // Must be in hexadecimal
    virt = strtoul(argv[1], NULL, 16);

    phys = diagCall_(dgLRA, virt);
```

(continues)

FIGURE 6–42 Retrieving the physical address (if any) for a virtual address in the caller's address space *(continued)*

```
    if (!phys) {
        printf("virtual address %08x :: physical page none\n", virt);
        exit(1);
    }

    physaddr = (u_int64_t)phys * 0x1000ULL + (u_int64_t)(virt & 0xFFF);
    printf("virtual address %#08x :: physical page %#x (address %#llx)\n",
           virt, phys, physaddr);

    exit(0);
}
```

```
$ gcc -Wall -I /path/to/xnu/osfmk/ -o diagLRA diagLRA.c
$ ./diagLRA 0x0
virtual address 00000000 :: physical page none
$ ./diagLRA 0xFFFF8000
virtual address 0xFFFF8000 :: physical page 0x1669 (address 0x1669000)
...
```

Examining Physical Memory

The dgpcpy() diagnostics system call copies physical memory into a supplied buffer. In this example, we will write a program that uses this call to fetch physical memory and dumps it on the standard output. Thereafter, we can either redirect the program's output to a file or pipe it through a utility such as hexdump to view the memory's contents in different formats. Figure 6–43 shows the program.

FIGURE 6–43 Retrieving physical memory using a diagnostics system call

```
// diagpcpy.c

#include "diagCommon.h"

#define PROGNAME "diagpcpy"

void usage(void);

int
main(int argc, char **argv)
{
    int       ret;
    u_int32_t phys;
```

(continues)

FIGURE 6–43 Retrieving physical memory using a diagnostics system call *(continued)*

```
    u_int32_t  nbytes;
    char       *buffer;

    if (argc != 3)
        usage();

    phys = strtoul(argv[1], NULL, 16);
    nbytes = strtoul(argv[2], NULL, 10);
    if ((nbytes < 0) || (phys < 0))
        usage();

    nbytes = (nbytes > MAXBYTES) ? MAXBYTES : nbytes;
    buffer = (char *)malloc(nbytes);
    if (buffer == NULL) {
        perror("malloc");
        exit(1);
    }

    // copy physical to virtual
    ret = diagCall_(dgpcpy, 0, phys, 0, buffer, nbytes, cppvPsrc|cppvNoRefSrc);

    (void)write(1, buffer, nbytes);

    free(buffer);

    exit(0);
}

void
usage(void)
{
    printf("usage: %s <physical addr> <bytes>\n", PROGNAME);
    printf("\tphysical address must be specified in hexadecimal\n");
    printf("\tnumber of bytes to copy must be specified in decimal\n");

    exit(1);
}


$ gcc -Wall -I /path/to/xnu/osfmk/ -o diagpcpy diagpcpy.c
...
```

We can test the operation of our `diagpcpy` program by examining physical memory that is known to contain specific information. Recall from Figure 6–28 that the beginning of the comm area contains a string signature. Moreover, we know that the comm area should begin at virtual address `0xFFFF8000` in every user virtual address space, and we determined the corresponding physical address using our diagLRA program in a previous example.

```
$ ./diagLRA 0xFFFF8000
virtual address 0xFFFF8000 :: physical page 0x1669 (address 0x1669000)
$ ./diagpcpy 0x1669000 16 | strings
commpage 32-bit
$
```

Let us look at another example. We know that the exception vectors reside in physical memory starting at address 0x0. We can retrieve the contents of that page and compare them with the contents of the __interrupts section in the __VECTORS segment within the kernel executable.

```
$ ./diagpcpy 0x0 4096 > /tmp/phys0.out
$ hexdump -v /tmp/phys0.out | less
...
0000100 7db2 43a6 7d73 43a6 81a0 00f0 7d60 0026
0000110 2c0d 0001 4082 001c 3960 0000 9160 00f0
0000120 8080 00f4 8060 00f8 7c88 03a6 4e80 0020
...
$ otool -s __VECTORS __interrupts /mach_kernel | less
/mach_kernel:
Contents of (__VECTORS,__interrupts) section
...
00000100 7db243a6 7d7343a6 81a000f0 7d600026
00000110 2c0d0001 4082001c 39600000 916000f0
00000120 808000f4 806000f8 7c8803a6 4e800020
...
```

Note that the hexdump output is formatted somewhat differently from otool's output. The modern-day hexdump program's output format can be configured through format strings. In this example, you can make the hexdump output identical to otool's as follows:

```
$ echo '"%07.7_Ax\\n"\n"%07.7_ax  " 4/4 "%08x " "\\n"' | \
    hexdump -v -f /dev/stdin /tmp/phys0.out
...
00000100 7db243a6 7d7343a6 81a000f0 7d600026
00000110 2c0d0001 4082001c 39600000 916000f0
00000120 808000f4 806000f8 7c8803a6 4e800020
...
```

Finally, let us retrieve a few bytes from the physical address 0x5000 and attempt to interpret them as a character string. We will see the reason for this string in Section 6.8.9.1.

```
$ ./diagpcpy 0x5000 8 | strings
Hagfish
```

Capturing a Screenshot of the Text Console

We earlier determined the physical base address of the boot display's framebuffer using the diagBootScreen program. Since diagpcpy allows us to dump physical memory, we could capture a raw screenshot of the display using these two programs. In particular, this gives us a way of capturing a screenshot of the *textual* console. Let us consider the example of the display shown in Figure 6–41; the relevant information is repeated here.

```
$ ./diagBootScreen
1280x854 pixels, 160x53 characters, 32-bit
base address 0x2f72c000, physical address 0xb8010000
5120 bytes used for display per row
```

Given the information dumped by diagBootScreen, we can see that our screenshot capturing *on this particular system* would involve copying a certain amount of physical memory starting at physical address 0xb8010000. Since this is a 32-bit framebuffer and there are 1280×854 pixels, the number of bytes we need to retrieve is $4 \times 1280 \times 854$, which is 4,372,480.

```
$ ./diagpcpy 0xb8010000 4372480 > display.dump
$ file display.dump
display.dump: data
```

> Note that diagpcpy is not the only way to read physical memory from user space. Given the appropriate privileges, a user program can read physical memory and kernel virtual memory through the /dev/mem and /dev/kmem devices, respectively. The kernel functions that serve these devices are implemented in bsd/dev/ppc/mem.c.

At this point, the display.dump file contains raw pixel data—a linear sequence of 32-bit pixel values in row-major order. When treated as big-endian, each pixel value contains a leading pad byte followed by 8-bit red, green, and blue components, in that order. We can convert this raw data to an image format—say, TIFF or JPEG—by using a variety of image-processing tools. For example, we can write a trivial Perl script to remove the padding from each pixel value to create a new raw pixel data file, which can then be converted to easily viewable image formats. The following example uses the freely available rawtoppm and ppmtojpeg command-line programs.

```
$ cat unpad.pl
#! /usr/bin/perl -w

my $PROGNAME = "unpad";

if ($#ARGV != 1) {
    die "usage: $PROGNAME <infile> <outfile>\n";
}

open(I, "<$ARGV[0]") or die "$!\n";
open(O, ">$ARGV[1]") or die "$!\n";

my $ibuf;

while (sysread(I, $buf, 4) == 4) {
    my ($pad, $r, $g, $b) = unpack('C4', $buf);
    $buf - pack('C3', $r, $g, $b);
    syswrite(O, $buf, 3);
}

close(I);
close(O);

exit(0);
$ ./unpad.pl display.dump display-rgb.raw
$ rawtoppm -rgb -interpixel 1280 854 display-rgb.raw > display.ppm
$ ppmtojpeg display.ppm > display.jpg
```

> A user program can retrieve the base address of a framebuffer using the `CGDisplayBaseAddress()` Quartz Services API call. Thereafter, the program can access and modify the framebuffer memory—say, using the `read()` and `write()` system calls. We will see an API-compliant version of the screenshot-capturing example in Chapter 10.

6.8.9 Low-Level Kernel Tracing

In addition to the various tracing facilities we have seen so far, the Mac OS X kernel contains yet another tracing facility used for low-level tracing. We have alluded to this facility earlier in this chapter in the context of the `CutTrace()` system call, which is the means by which kernel code logs low-level traces into a kernel buffer. The buffer can be examined from within KDB. Before we discuss this tracing mechanism, let us look at the low-memory global (lowglo) data structures, which also include the work area for this mechanism.

6.8.9.1 Low-Memory Global Data Structures

We have seen earlier that the first 32KB of physical memory—the *low memory*—contains critical kernel data and code. For example, the PowerPC exception vectors begin at physical address 0x0. The low-level exception filter table (xcpTable) and the first-level system call dispatch table (scTable), both of which are implemented in osfmk/ppc/lowmem_vectors.s, also reside in low memory. Another low-memory area instantiated in lowmem_vectors.s is lowGlo—a structure of type lowglo that contains global (as opposed to per-processor) constants, data areas, and pointers. These entities are accessed by kernel code directly using absolute addresses. Hence, they must reside in low physical memory. The lowGlo area starts at physical address 0x5000 and is a page long. The next physical page—starting at address 0x6000—is a shared page mapped into the kernel's address space; it can be used for low-level kernel debugging. Figure 6–44 shows the structure of the lowGlo area.

In Section 6.8.8.2, we found that memory at physical address 0x5000 contains the word *Hagfish*. To be precise, it is the string "Hagfish " (with a trailing space). It is an "eyecatcher" string used as a system verification code at the beginning of the lowGlo area. Let us use our diagpcpy program from Section 6.8.8.2 to glean some more information from this area.

Kernel Version String

As shown in Figure 6–44, physical address 0x501C contains a pointer to the kernel version string.

```
$ ./diagpcpy 0x501C 4 | hexdump
0000000 0033 1da0
0000004
$ ./diagpcpy 0x00331da0 128 | strings
Darwin Kernel Version 8.6.0: ... root:xnu-792.6.70.obj~1/RELEASE_PPC
8.6.0
Darwin
```

Per-Processor Information Areas

As shown in Figure 6–44, physical address 0x5010 points to the start of the array containing per-processor information entries. Each entry is a structure of type per_proc_entry, which contains a pointer to a structure of type per_proc_info. The latter contains a variety of static and dynamic information about a processor—for example, the hardware exception counters (struct hwCtrs). Figure 6–45 shows excerpts from these structures, some of which we came across in Chapter 5.

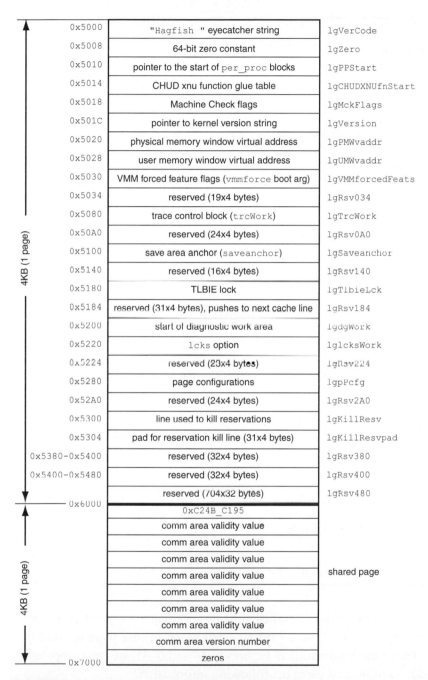

FIGURE 6–44 The low-memory global data area

FIGURE 6–45 Data structures for holding per-processor information

`// osfmk/ppc/exception.h`

```
#pragma pack(4)
struct hwCtrs {
    unsigned int hwInVains;
    unsigned int hwResets;
    unsigned int hwMachineChecks;
    unsigned int hwDSIs;
    unsigned int hwISIs;
    unsigned int hwExternals;
    unsigned int hwAlignments;
    unsigned int hwPrograms;
    ...
};
#pragma pack()

typedef struct hwCtrs hwCtrs;

...
#pragma pack(4)
struct per_proc_info {
    unsigned int cpu_number;
    ...
    hwCtrs hwCtr; // begins at offset 0x800 within the structure
    ...
}
#pragma pack()

...
#define MAX_CPUS 256

struct per_proc_entry {
    addr64_t            ppe_paddr;
    unsigned int        ppe_pad4[1];
    struct per_proc_info *ppe_vaddr;
};

extern struct per_proc_entry PerProcTable[MAX_CPUS-1];
```

Let us retrieve the value of a particular hardware counter—say, hwPrograms—using diagpcpy. We will do so for the first processor, in case there are multiple processors. Given the information in Figures 6–44 and 6–45, we can compute the physical address of interest using the following information.

- The address 0x5010 contains a pointer to PerProcTable—we are interested in the first entry of PerProcTable.

- The `ppe_paddr` field of `per_proc_entry` contains the physical address of the first page of the processor's `per_proc_info` structure. We will resolve `ppe_paddr` as a pointer to read from the corresponding memory.

- The `hwCtr` structure is at an offset `0x800` within the `per_proc_info` structure.

- The `hwPrograms` counter is at an offset of 28 bytes—seven times the size of an `unsigned int`—within the `hwCtr` structure, and therefore, at an offset of `0x81c` (`0x800` + 28) bytes within `per_proc_info`.

Let us now retrieve the value of `hwPrograms`.

```
$ ./diagpcpy 0x5010 4 | hexdump # this will give us the address of PerProcTable
00000000 0035 d000
00000004
$ ./diagpcpy 0x35d000 16 | hexdump # first 64-bit number is the first
                                   # processor's ppe_paddr
00000000 0000 0000 0035 e000 0000 0000 0035 e000
00000010
$ ./diagpcpy 0x35e81c 4 | hexdump # add 0x81c to get the address of hwPrograms
00000000 0000 0000
00000004
```

In this example, the counter's value is `0`. Let us execute a trivial program that we know *will* increment the value of this counter. For example, executing an illegal hardware instruction—say, a supervisor-only instruction in user mode—will result in a `T_PROGRAM` exception, which is counted by `hwPrograms`. Figure 6–46 shows a program that causes a `T_PROGRAM` to be generated.

FIGURE 6–46 Causing an exception and retrieving the corresponding counter from the kernel

```c
// gentprogram.c

#if defined(__GNUC__)
#include <ppc_intrinsics.h>
#endif

int
main(void)
{
    return __mfspr(1023);
}
```

(continues)

FIGURE 6–46 Causing an exception and retrieving the corresponding counter from the kernel *(continued)*

```
$ gcc -Wall -o gentprogram gentprogram.c
$ ./gentprogram
zsh: illegal hardware instruction  ./gentprogram
$ ./diagpcpy 0x35e81c 4 | hexdump
00000000 0000 0001
00000004
$ ./gentprogram; ./gentprogram; ./gentprogram
zsh: illegal hardware instruction  ./gentprogram
zsh: illegal hardware instruction  ./gentprogram
zsh: illegal hardware instruction  ./gentprogram
$ ./diagpcpy 0x35e81c 4 | hexdump
00000000 0000 0004
00000004
```

Figure 6–47 shows a portion of exception-handling code that increments various hardware exception counters. Note that the order of counter fields within the `hwCtr` structure is matched with the definition of exception numbers—an exception number is the offset of the corresponding counter within `hwCtr`. For example, T_PROGRAM is defined to be (0x07 * T_VECTOR_SIZE) in osfmk/ppc/ exception.h, with T_VECTOR_SIZE being 4.

FIGURE 6–47 Maintenance of hardware exception counters in the kernel

```
// osfmk/ppc/genassym.c

...
DECLARE("hwCounts", offsetof(struct per_proc_info *, hwCtr);
...


; osfmk/ppc/lowmem_vectors.s

.L_exception_entry:
        ...
xcpCommon:
        ...
Redrive:
        ...
        mfsprg r2,0      ; restore per_proc (SPRG0 contains per_proc ptr)
        ...
        la r12,hwCounts(r2) ; point to the exception count area
        ...
```

(continues)

FIGURE 6–47 Maintenance of hardware exception counters in the kernel *(continued)*

```
add  r12,r12,r11    ; point to the count (r11 contains T_XXX)
lwz  r25,0(r12)     ; get the old value
...
add  r25,r25,r24    ; count this one (r24 will be 1 or 0)
...
stw  r25,0(r12)     ; store it back
...
```

6.8.9.2 Low Tracing

Let us now continue our discussion of "CutTrace" low-level tracing, or simply low tracing. Figure 6–44 shows an area called lgTrcWork: This is the control block for low tracing. It is a structure of type traceWork.

```
// osfmk/ppc/low_trace.h

typedef struct traceWork {
    unsigned int traceCurr;   // Address of next slot
    unsigned int traceMask;   // Types to be traced
    unsigned int traceStart;  // Start of trace table
    unsigned int traceEnd;    // End of trace table
    unsigned int traceMsnd;   // Saved trace mask
    unsigned int traceSize;   // Size of trace table
    unsigned int traceGas[2];
} traceWork;
```

> Similarly, lgdgWork is the diagnostic work area—it is a structure of type diagWork, which is declared in osfmk/ppc/Diagnostics.h. One of this structure's fields, dgFlags, stores the diagnostic flags. The flags passed through the diag boot-time argument are stored here.

Low tracing is enabled by setting the enaExpTrace bit in the value of the diag boot-time argument. It can be limited to a specific processor by providing the processor number through the ctrc boot-time argument. Moreover, the size of the kernel buffer used for low tracing can be adjusted through the tb boot-time argument. ppc_init() [osfmk/ppc/ppc_init.c] processes these arguments during early system startup. Figure 6–48 shows this processing.

FIGURE 6–48 Processing of low-tracing-related boot-time arguments during system startup

```
// osfmk/ppc/genassym.c

...
DECLARE("trcWork", offsetof(struct lowglo *, lgTrcWork));
...


// osfmk/ppc/ppc_init.c

void
ppc_init(boot_args *args)
{
    ...
    // Set diagnostic flags
    if (!PE_parse_boot_arg("diag", &dgWork.dgFlags))
        dgWork.dgFlags = 0;
    ...
    // Enable low tracing if it is requested
    if (dgWork.dgFlags & enaExpTrace)
        trcWork.traceMask = 0xFFFFFFFF;

    // See if tracing is limited to a specific processor
    if (PE_parse_boot_arg("ctrc", &cputrace)) {
        trcWork.traceMask = (trcWork.traceMask & 0xFFFFFFF0) | (cputrace & 0xF);
    }


    // See if we have a nondefault trace-buffer size
    if (!PE_parse_boot_arg("tb", &trcWork.traceSize)) {
#if DEBUG
        trcWork.traceSize = 32;  // Default 32-page trace table for DEBUG
#else
        trcWork.traceSize = 8;   // Default 8-page trace table for RELEASE
#endif
    }


    // Adjust trace table size, if not within minimum/maximum limits
    if (trcWork.traceSize < 1)
        trcWork.traceSize = 1;    // Must be at least 1 page
    if (trcWork.traceSize > 256)
        trcWork.traceSize = 256; // Can be at most 256 pages

    // Convert from number of pages to number of bytes
    trcWork.traceSize = trcWork.traceSize * 4096;
    ...
}
```

Later during the system startup, pmap_bootstrap() [osfmk/ppc/pmap.c] reserves physical memory for the trace table.

```
// osfmk/ppc/pmap.c

void
pmap_bootstrap(uint64_t memsize, vm_offset_t *first_avail, unsigned int kmapsize)
{
    ...
    trcWork.traceCurr = (unsigned int)addr;  // set first trace slot to use
    trcWork.traceStart = (unsigned int)addr; // set start of trace table
    trcWork.traceEnd = (unsigned int)addr + trcWork.traceSize; // set end
...
}
```

As we noted earlier, low tracing is performed through the CutTrace() system call, a firmware call that is also an ultra-fast trap—it is handled in osfmk/ppc/lowmem_vectors.s (in fact, before any other ultra-fast trap). The firmware call interface provides a stub, dbgTrace() [osfmk/ppc/Firmware.s], to call CutTrace().

```
; osfmk/ppc/Firmware.s
;
; dbgTrace(traceID, item1, item2, item3, item4)
;
            .align 5
            .globl EXT(dbgTrace)
LEXT(dbgTrace)
            mr      r2,r3                  ; trace ID
            mr      r3,r4                  ; item1
            lis     r0,HIGH_ADDR(CutTrace) ; top half of firmware call number
            mr      r4,r5                  ; item2
            mr      r5,r6                  ; item3
            ori     r0,r0,LOW_ADDR(CutTrace) ; bottom half
            mr      r6,r7                  ; item4
            sc                             ; invoke the system call
            blr                            ; done
```

Various portions of the kernel add low-trace records either by calling dbgTrace() or by directly invoking the CutTrace() system call. In the latter case, the trace identifier is passed in GPR2. Figure 6–49 shows an example of kernel code creating a low-trace record.

FIGURE 6–49 An example of low-trace record generation by kernel code

`// osfmk/ipc/ipc_kmsg.c`

```
mach_msg_return_t
ipc_kmsg_get(mach_vm_address_t msg_addr,
             mach_msg_size_t size,
             ipc_kmsg_t *kmsgp)
{
    ...
#ifdef ppc
    if (trcWork.traceMask)
        dbgTrace(0x1100,
                (unsigned int)kmsg->ikm_header->msgh_id,
                (unsigned int)kmsg->ikm_header->msgh_remote_port,
                (unsigned int)kmsg->ikm_header->msgh_local_port,
                0);
#endif
    ...
}
```

A low-trace record is a structure of type `LowTraceRecord`, which is declared in `osfmk/ppc/low_trace.h`. Information contained in a `LowTraceRecord` structure includes the following:

- Processor number
- Exception code
- Upper and lower parts of the Timebase Register
- Contents of the following registers: CR, DSISR, SRR0, SRR1, DAR, LR, CTR, and GPRs 0 through 6
- Save area

A convenient way to view low-trace records is through the built-in kernel debugger KDB, whose `lt` command formats and displays these records.

```
db{0}> lt 0
...
 00ADEA80  0  00000002 FD6D0959 - 0C00
              DAR/DSR/CR: 00000000A000201C 40000000 84024A92
                 SRR0/SRR1 00000000000D6D00 1000000000001030
                 LR/CTR    00000000000D61F4 00000000000344A8
                 R0/R1/R2  FFFFFFFF80000000 000000001759BD00 0000000000004400
                 R3/R4/R5  0000000002626E60 000000000002CD38 0000000001E5791C
                 R6/sv/rsv 000000002FD78780 0000000000000000 00000000
...
```

6.9 Virtual Machine Monitor

The Mac OS X kernel (PowerPC) implements a *virtual machine monitor* (VMM) facility, which a user-space program can use to dynamically create and manipulate virtual machine (VM) contexts. Each VM instance has its own processor state and address space, both of which are controlled by the VMM. A program executing in a VM is referred to as a *guest*. The facility is primarily implemented in the `vmachmon.h`, `vmachmon.c`, and `vmachmon_asm.s` files within the `osfmk/ppc/` directory. The files `osfmk/ppc/hw_vm.s` and `osfmk/ppc/hw_exception.s` also contain support code for the VMM facility.

Let us revisit Figure 6–8, in which we saw that a thread's machine-dependent state—the `machine_thread` structure [`osfmk/ppc/thread.h`]—contains pointers to VMM control table (`vmmCntrlTable`) and VMM control table entry (`vmmCntrlEntry`) structures. `vmmCntrlTable` is non-`NULL` for a thread that is using the VMM facility. When the thread is running a VM, its `vmmCntrlEntry` points to the current emulation context but is `NULL` otherwise. Figure 6–50 shows these data structures.

FIGURE 6–50 Control data structures for the VMM facility

```
// osfmk/ppc/vmachmon.h

#define kVmmMaxContexts 32
...

typedef struct vmmCntrlEntry {
    unsigned int vmmFlags;          // Assorted control flags
    unsigned int vmmXAFlgs;         // Extended Architecture (XA) flags

    // Address of context communication area
    vmm_state_page_t *vmmContextKern; // Kernel virtual address
    ppnum_t           vmmContextPhys; // Physical address
    vmm_state_page_t *vmmContextUser; // User virtual address

    facility_context  vmmFacCtx;      // Header for VMX and FP contexts

    pmap_t            vmmPmap;        // Last dispatched pmap
    uint64_t          vmmTimer;       // Last set timer value (0 if unset)
    unsigned int      vmmFAMintercept; // FAM intercepted exceptions
} vmmCntrlEntry;

typedef struct vmmCntrlTable {
    unsigned int  vmmGFlags;          // Global flags
    addr64_t      vmmLastMap;         // Last vaddr mapping mode
```

(continues)

FIGURE 6–50 Control data structures for the VMM facility *(continued)*

```
    // An entry for each possible VMM context
    vmmCntrlEntry vmmc[kVmmMaxContexts];

    pmap_t          vmmAdsp[kVmmMaxContexts]; // Guest address space maps
} vmmCntrlTable;
...
```

For each VM, the VMM allocates a page of memory for holding the VM's *context communications area*, which is accessed both as a vmm_comm_page_t structure and a vmm_state_page_t structure—the former embeds the latter.

```
// osfmk/ppc/vmachmon.h

typedef struct vmm_comm_page_t {

    union {
        vmm_state_page_t vmcpState;     // Reserve area for state
        unsigned int     vmcpPad[768];  // Reserve state for 3/4 page state area
    } vmcpfirst;
    unsigned int vmcpComm[256];  // Last 1024 bytes used as a communications
                                 // area in a function-specific manner
} vmm_comm_page_t;
...
```

A VM's processor state is stored in a vmm_processor_state_t structure within a vmm_state_page_t structure. A vmm_processor_state_t includes the processor's general-purpose, floating-point, vector, and special-purpose registers. Note that the vmcpComm field of the vmm_comm_page_t structure is used as a general-purpose communications buffer by several VMM functions. For example, the vmm_map_list function, which maps a list of pages into a guest address space, reads the list of pages as a sequence of { host virtual address, guest virtual address } pairs from vmcpComm.

6.9.1 Features

The specific features provided by the VMM facility on a system depend on the host processor and the facility's version. The following are examples of VMM features.

- kVmmFeature_LittleEndian—The VMM supports a VM to be run in little-endian mode. This feature is available only on PowerPC processors that implement the optional little-endian facility. Therefore, it is unavailable on G5-based systems.

- kVmmFeature_Stop—The VMM supports stopping and resuming VMs.

- kVmmFeature_ExtendedMapping—The VMM supports extended protection modes for address space mappings.

- kVmmFeature_ListMapping—The VMM supports mapping a list of pages into and unmapping a list of pages from guest address spaces.

- kVmmFeature_FastAssist—The VMM supports an optimization called *fast assist mode* (FAM). In this mode, the ultra-fast-path VMM system calls are valid. As noted in Table 6–15, the calls are handled by vmm_ufp() [osfmk/ppc/vmachmon_asm.s], which ensures that the incoming system call number is within the range of calls designated as FAM calls (kVmmResumeGuest through kVmmSetGuestRegister).

- kVmmFeature_XA—The VMM supports getting and setting extended architecture (XA) flags in the control table entry of each VM context controlled by it.

- kVmmFeature_SixtyFourBit—The VMM provides 64-bit support on 64-bit host processors.

- kVmmFeature_MultAddrSpace—The VMM allows multiple address spaces, with each address space capable of handling the maximum virtual address supported by the host processor. A guest VM may be launched using any one address space.

6.9.2 Using the VMM Facility

The VMM facility exports its functionality through routines such as those for initializing a VM context (vmm_init_context), releasing a VM context (vmm_tear_down_context), and mapping a page from the host address space to a guest address space (vmm_map_page). Most of these routines do not have corresponding stubs in a user-space library; they are accessed using a dispatcher routine (vmm_dispatch), which does have a user-space stub. When the C library is compiled, it picks up assembly stubs for Mach traps—including VMM-related traps—from header files such as <mach/syscall_sw.h> and <mach/ppc/syscall_sw.h>.

```
$ nm -oj /usr/lib/libSystem.dylib | grep -i vmm
/usr/lib/libSystem.dylib:mach_traps.So:_vmm_dispatch
/usr/lib/libSystem.dylib:mach_traps.So:_vmm_get_features
/usr/lib/libSystem.dylib:mach_traps.So:_vmm_get_version
```

```
/usr/lib/libSystem.dylib:mach_traps.So:_vmm_init_context
/usr/lib/libSystem.dylib:mach_traps.So:_vmm_stop_vm
```

The `vmm_dispatch()` system call allows all exported VMM routines to be invoked from user space. The index of the desired routine is passed as the first argument to `vmm_dispatch()`, followed by arguments specific to that function. Here is an example of what using the VMM facility looks like.

```
// Get VMM version
version = vmm_dispatch(kVmmGetVersion);
...

// Get VMM features to know what we may or may not use
features = vmm_dispatch(kVmmGetFeatures);

// Allocate page-aligned memory for use with the VMM/VMs
kr = vm_allocate(myTask, &vmmCommPage, pageSize, TRUE);
...
kr = vm_allocate(...);
...

// Initialize a new VM context
kr = vmm_dispatch(kVmmInitContext, version, vmmCommPage);

// Set up the VM's initial processor state
...

// Map pages, or page lists, into the VM's address space
// Actual pages to map are in a separate "communication" page
kr = vmm_dispatch(kVmmMapList, vmmIndex, nPages, is64bit);

// Launch the VM
// Mapping a page and setting the VM running can be combined
kr = vmm_dispatch(kVmmMapExecute, vmmIndex, aPage, vAddress, protectionBits);

// Handle things when control comes back to the VMM
...

// Stop and resume the VM
...

// Tear down the VM context
kr = vmm_dispatch(kVmmTearDownContext, vmmIndex);
```

6.9.3 Example: Running Code in a Virtual Machine

Let us now look at a real programming example of using the VMM facility. In our program, `vmachmon32`, we will perform the following sequence of steps.

- Retrieve the VMM version and feature set supported by the kernel using `vmm_get_version()` and `vmm_get_features()`, respectively.

- Allocate page-aligned memory using Mach's `vm_allocate()` memory allocation function. Specifically, we will allocate a page for the VM's state, a page for the VM's stack, and a page for the VM's text (code).

- Set the VM's program counter to the beginning of the text page.

- Set the VM's stack pointer to the end of the stack page, while taking the Red Zone into account.

- Populate the text page either with a handcrafted sequence of instructions or with machine code for a function that calculates the factorial of its argument. We will obtain the function's machine code by statically compiling its C source.

- Map the stack page and the text page into the VM's address space.

- Set the VM running. When the VM runs out of code to execute, we will ensure that it returns to the VMM by making the final instruction that it executes illegal.

Moreover, we will print the contents of several VM registers at the end of the program, which will allow us to see the result of the code that the VM ran. You can run full-fledged programs (including operating systems)—rather than primitive code—within a VM provided the resources needed for the program to run are made available in the VM's address space.

Figure 6–51 shows the source for `vmachmon32`. It is liberally annotated with comments, including further description of using the VMM facility.

FIGURE 6–51 A program to run machine code within a VM using the VMM facility

```
// vmachmon32.c
// Mac OS X Virtual Machine Monitor (Vmm) facility demonstration

#define PROGNAME "vmachmon32"

#include <stdio.h>
#include <string.h>
#include <stdlib.h>
#include <sys/types.h>
#include <mach/mach.h>
#include <architecture/ppc/cframe.h>
```

(continues)

FIGURE 6–51 A program to run machine code within a VM using the VMM facility *(continued)*

```
#ifndef _VMACHMON32_KLUDGE_
// We need to include xnu/osfmk/ppc/vmachmon.h, which includes several other
// kernel headers and is not really meant for inclusion in user programs.
// We perform the following kludges to include vmachmon.h to be able to
// compile this program:
//
// 1. Provide dummy forward declarations for data types that vmachmon.h
//    needs, but we will not actually use.
// 2. Copy vmachmon.h to the current directory from the kernel source tree.
// 3. Remove or comment out "#include <ppc/exception.h>" from vmachmon.h.
//
struct  savearea;              // kludge #1
typedef int ReturnHandler;     // kludge #1
typedef int pmap_t;            // kludge #1
typedef int facility_context;  // kludge #1
#include "vmachmon.h"          // kludge #2
#endif

#define OUT_ON_MACH_ERROR(msg, retval) \
    if (kr != KERN_SUCCESS) { mach_error("*** " msg ":" , kr); goto out; }

// vmm_dispatch() is a PowerPC-only system call that allows us to invoke
// functions residing in the Vmm dispatch table. In general, Vmm routines
// are available to user space, but the C library (or another library) does
// not contain stubs to call them. Thus, we must go through vmm_dispatch(),
// using the index of the function to call as the first parameter in GPR3.
//
// Since vmachmon.h contains the kernel prototype of vmm_dispatch(), which
// is not what we want, we will declare our own function pointer and set
// it to the stub available in the C library.
//
typedef kern_return_t (* vmm_dispatch_func_t)(int, ...);
vmm_dispatch_func_t my_vmm_dispatch;

// Convenience data structure for pretty-printing Vmm features
struct VmmFeature {
    int32_t  mask;
    char     *name;
} VmmFeatures[] = {
    { kVmmFeature_LittleEndian,      "LittleEndian"     },
    { kVmmFeature_Stop,              "Stop"             },
    { kVmmFeature_ExtendedMapping,   "ExtendedMapping"  },
    { kVmmFeature_ListMapping,       "ListMapping"      },
    { kVmmFeature_FastAssist,        "FastAssist"       },
    { kVmmFeature_XA,                "XA"               },
    { kVmmFeature_SixtyFourBit,      "SixtyFourBit"     },
    { kVmmFeature_MultAddrSpace,     "MultAddrSpace"    },
```

(continues)

FIGURE 6–51 A program to run machine code within a VM using the VMM facility *(continued)*

```
    { kVmmFeature_GuestShadowAssist,   "GuestShadowAssist"   },
    { kVmmFeature_GlobalMappingAssist, "GlobalMappingAssist" },
    { kVmmFeature_HostShadowAssist,    "HostShadowAssist"    },
    { kVmmFeature_MultAddrSpaceAssist, "MultAddrSpaceAssist" },
    { -1, NULL },
};

// For Vmm messages that we print
#define Printf(fmt, ...) printf("Vmm> " fmt, ## __VA_ARGS__)

// PowerPC instruction template: add immediate, D-form
typedef struct I_addi_d_form {
    u_int32_t OP: 6;  // major opcode
    u_int32_t RT: 5;  // target register
    u_int32_t RA: 5;  // register operand
    u_int32_t SI: 16; // immediate operand
} I_addi_d_form;

// PowerPC instruction template: unconditional branch, I-form
typedef struct branch_i_form {
    u_int32_t OP: 6;  // major opcode
    u_int32_t LI: 24; // branch target (immediate)
    u_int32_t AA: 1;  // absolute or relative
    u_int32_t LK: 1;  // link or not
} I_branch_i_form;

// PowerPC instruction template: add, XO-form
typedef struct I_add_xo_form {
    u_int32_t OP: 6;  // major opcode
    u_int32_t RT: 5;  // target register
    u_int32_t RA: 5;  // register operand A
    u_int32_t RB: 5;  // register operand B
    u_int32_t OE: 1;  // alter SO, OV?
    u_int32_t XO: 9;  // extended opcode
    u_int32_t Rc: 1;  // alter CR0?
} I_add_xo_form;

// Print the bits of a 32-bit number
void
prbits32(u_int32_t u)
{
    u_int32_t i = 32;

    for (; i > 16 && i--; putchar(u & 1 << i ? '1' : '0'))
        ;
    printf(" ");
    for (; i--; putchar(u & 1 << i ? '1' : '0'))
        ;
```

(continues)

FIGURE 6–51 A program to run machine code within a VM using the VMM facility *(continued)*

```
    printf("\n");
}


// Function to initialize a memory buffer with some machine code
void
initGuestText_Dummy(u_int32_t      *text,
                    vm_address_t   guestTextAddress,
                    vmm_regs32_t  *ppcRegs32)
{
    // We will execute a stream of a few instructions in the virtual machine
    // through the Vmm (that is, us). I0 and I1 will load integer values into
    // registers GPR10 and GPR11. I3 will be an illegal instruction. I2 will
    // jump over I3 by unconditionally branching to I4, which will sum GPR10
    // and GPR11, placing their sum in GPR12.
    //
    // We will allow I5 to either be illegal, in which case control will
    // return to the Vmm, or, be a branch to itself: an infinite
    // loop. One Infinite Loop.
    //
    I_addi_d_form   *I0;
    I_addi_d_form   *I1;
    I_branch_i_form *I2;
    // I3 is illegal
    I_add_xo_form   *I4;
    I_branch_i_form *I5;

    // Guest will run the following instructions
    I0 = (I_addi_d_form   *)(text + 0);
    I1 = (I_addi_d_form   *)(text + 1);
    I2 = (I_branch_i_form *)(text + 2);
    text[3] = 0xdeadbeef; // illegal
    I4 = (I_add_xo_form   *)(text + 4);

    // Possibly overridden by an illegal instruction below
    I5 = (I_branch_i_form *)(text + 5);

    // Use an illegal instruction to be the last inserted instruction (I5)
    // in the guest's instruction stream
    text[5] = 0xfeedface;

    // Fill the instruction templates

    // addi r10,0,4      ; I0
    I0->OP = 14;
    I0->RT = 10;
    I0->RA = 0;
    I0->SI = 4; // load the value '4' in r10
```

(continues)

FIGURE 6–51 A program to run machine code within a VM using the VMM facility *(continued)*

```
    // addi r11,0,5      ; I1
    I1->OP = 14;
    I1->RT = 11;
    I1->RA = 0;
    I1->SI = 5; // load the value '5' in r11

    // ba               ; I2
    // We want to branch to the absolute address of the 5th instruction,
    // where the first instruction is at guestTextAddress. Note the shifting.
    //
    I2->OP = 18;
    I2->LI = (guestTextAddress + (4 * 4)) >> 2;
    I2->AA = 1;
    I2->LK = 0;

    // I3 is illegal; already populated in the stream

    // add  r12,r10,r11 ; I4
    I4->OP = 31;
    I4->RT = 12;
    I4->RA = 10;
    I4->RB = 11;
    I4->OE = 0;
    I4->XO = 266;
    I4->Rc = 0;

    // I5 is illegal or an infinite loop; already populated in the stream

    Printf("Fabricated instructions for executing "
           "in the guest virtual machine\n");
}

// Function to initialize a memory buffer with some machine code
void
initGuestText_Factorial(u_int32_t    *text,
                        vm_address_t  guestTextAddress,
                        vmm_regs32_t *ppcRegs32)
{
    // Machine code for the following function:
    //
    // int
    // factorial(int n)
    // {
    //     if (n <= 0)
    //         return 1;
    //     else
    //         return n * factorial(n - 1);
    // }
```

(continues)

FIGURE 6–51 A program to run machine code within a VM using the VMM facility *(continued)*

```c
    //
    // You can obtain this from the function's C source using a command-line
    // sequence like the following:
    //
    // $ gcc -static -c factorial.c
    // $ otool -tX factorial.o
    // ...
    //
    u_int32_t factorial_ppc32[] = {
        0x7c0802a6, 0xbfc1fff8, 0x90010008, 0x9421ffa0,
        0x7c3e0b78, 0x907e0078, 0x801e0078, 0x2f800000,
        0x419d0010, 0x38000001, 0x901e0040, 0x48000024,
        0x805e0078, 0x3802ffff, 0x7c030378, 0x4bfffc5,
        0x7c621b78, 0x801e0078, 0x7c0201d6, 0x901e0040,
        0x807e0040, 0x80210000, 0x80010008, 0x7c0803a6,
        0xbbc1fff8, 0x4e800020,
    };

    memcpy(text, factorial_ppc32, sizeof(factorial_ppc32)/sizeof(u_int8_t));

    // This demo takes an argument in GPR3: the number whose factorial is to
    // be computed. The result is returned in GPR3.
    //
    ppcRegs32->ppcGPRs[3] = 10; // factorial(10)

    // Set the LR to the end of the text in the guest's virtual address space.
    // Our demo will only use the LR for returning to the Vmm by placing an
    // illegal instruction's address in it.
    //
    ppcRegs32->ppcLR = guestTextAddress + vm_page_size - 4;

    Printf("Injected factorial instructions for executing "
           "in the guest virtual machine\n");
}

// Some modularity... these are the demos our program supports
typedef void (* initGuestText_Func)(u_int32_t *, vm_address_t, vmm_regs32_t *);
typedef struct {
    const char         *name;
    initGuestText_Func  textfiller;
} Demo;

Demo SupportedDemos[] = {
    {
        "executes a few hand-crafted instructions in a VM",
        initGuestText_Dummy,
    },
```

(continues)

FIGURE 6–51 A program to run machine code within a VM using the VMM facility *(continued)*

```
    {
        "executes a recursive factorial function in a VM",
        initGuestText_Factorial,
    },
};
#define MAX_DEMO_ID (sizeof(SupportedDemos)/sizeof(Demo))

static int demo_id = -1;

void
usage(int argc, char **argv)
{
    int i;

    if (argc != 2)
        goto OUT;

    demo_id = atoi(argv[1]);
    if ((demo_id >= 0) && (demo_id < MAX_DEMO_ID))
        return;

OUT:
    fprintf(stderr, "usage: %s <demo ID>\nSupported demos:\n"
            "  ID\tDescription\n", PROGNAME);
    for (i = 0; i < MAX_DEMO_ID; i++)
        fprintf(stderr, "  %d\t%s\n", i, SupportedDemos[i].name);

    exit(1);
}

int
main(int argc, char **argv)
{
    int i, j;

    kern_return_t       kr;
    mach_port_t         myTask;
    unsigned long       *return_params32;
    vmm_features_t      features;
    vmm_regs32_t        *ppcRegs32;
    vmm_version_t       version;
    vmm_thread_index_t  vmmIndex;              // The VM's index
    vm_address_t        vmmUStatePage = 0;     // Page for VM's user state
    vmm_state_page_t    *vmmUState;            // It's a vmm_comm_page_t too
    vm_address_t        guestTextPage = 0;     // Page for guest's text
    vm_address_t        guestStackPage = 0;    // Page for guest's stack
    vm_address_t        guestTextAddress = 0;
    vm_address_t        guestStackAddress = 0;
```

(continues)

FIGURE 6–51 A program to run machine code within a VM using the VMM facility *(continued)*

```
my_vmm_dispatch = (vmm_dispatch_func_t)vmm_dispatch;

// Ensure that the user chose a demo
usage(argc, argv);

// Get Vmm version implemented by this kernel
version = my_vmm_dispatch(kVmmGetVersion);
Printf("Mac OS X virtual machine monitor (version %lu.%lu)\n",
        (version >> 16), (version & 0xFFFF));

// Get features supported by this Vmm implementation
features = my_vmm_dispatch(kVmmvGetFeatures);
Printf("Vmm features:\n");
for (i = 0; VmmFeatures[i].mask != -1; i++)
    printf("  %-20s = %s\n", VmmFeatures[i].name,
            (features & VmmFeatures[i].mask) ?  "Yes" : "No");

Printf("Page size is %u bytes\n", vm_page_size);

myTask = mach_task_self(); // to save some characters (sure)

// Allocate chunks of page-sized page-aligned memory

// VM user state
kr = vm_allocate(myTask, &vmmUStatePage, vm_page_size, VM_FLAGS_ANYWHERE);
OUT_ON_MACH_ERROR("vm_allocate", kr);
Printf("Allocated page-aligned memory for virtual machine user state\n");
vmmUState = (vmm_state_page_t *)vmmUStatePage;

// Guest's text
kr = vm_allocate(myTask, &guestTextPage, vm_page_size, VM_FLAGS_ANYWHERE);
OUT_ON_MACH_ERROR("vm_allocate", kr);
Printf("Allocated page-aligned memory for guest's " "text\n");

// Guest's stack
kr = vm_allocate(myTask, &guestStackPage, vm_page_size, VM_FLAGS_ANYWHERE);
OUT_ON_MACH_ERROR("vm_allocate", kr);
Printf("Allocated page-aligned memory for guest's stack\n");

// We will lay out the text and stack pages adjacent to one another in
// the guest's virtual address space.
//
// Virtual addresses increase -->
// 0                4K                8K                12K
// +-------------------------------------------+
// | __PAGEZERO   | GUEST_TEXT  | GUEST_STACK  |
// +-------------------------------------------+
//
```

(continues)

FIGURE 6–51 A program to run machine code within a VM using the VMM facility *(continued)*

```
// We put the text page at virtual offset vm_page_size and the stack
// page at virtual offset (2 * vm_page_size).
//

guestTextAddress = vm_page_size;
guestStackAddress = 2 * vm_page_size;

// Initialize a new virtual machine context
kr = my_vmm_dispatch(kVmmInitContext, version, vmmUState);
OUT_ON_MACH_ERROR("vmm_init_context", kr);

// Fetch the index returned by vmm_init_context()
vmmIndex = vmmUState->thread_index;
Printf("New virtual machine context initialized, index = %lu\n", vmmIndex);

// Set a convenience pointer to the VM's registers
ppcRegs32 = &(vmmUState->vmm_proc_state.ppcRegs.ppcRegs32);

// Set the program counter to the beginning of the text in the guest's
// virtual address space
ppcRegs32->ppcPC = guestTextAddress;
Printf("Guest virtual machine PC set to %p\n", (void *)guestTextAddress);

// Set the stack pointer (GPR1), taking the Red Zone into account
#define PAGE2SP(x) ((void *)((x) + vm_page_size - C_RED_ZONE))
ppcRegs32->ppcGPRs[1] = (u_int32_t)PAGE2SP(guestStackAddress); // 32-bit
Printf("Guest virtual machine SP set to %p\n", PAGE2SP(guestStackAddress));

// Map the stack page into the guest's address space
kr = my_vmm_dispatch(kVmmMapPage, vmmIndex, guestStackPage,
                guestStackAddress, VM_PROT_ALL);
Printf("Mapping guest stack page\n");

// Call the chosen demo's instruction populator
(SupportedDemos[demo id].textfiller)((u_int32_t *)guestTextPage,
                                guestTextAddress, ppcRegs32);

// Finally, map the text page into the guest's address space, and set the
// VM running
//
Printf("Mapping guest text page and switching to guest virtual machine\n");
kr = my_vmm_dispatch(kVmmMapExecute, vmmIndex, guestTextPage,
                guestTextAddress, VM_PROT_ALL);

// Our demo ensures that the last instruction in the guest's text is
// either an infinite loop or illegal. The monitor will "hang" in the case
// of an infinite loop. It will have to be interrupted (^C) to gain control.
```

(continues)

FIGURE 6–51 A program to run machine code within a VM using the VMM facility *(continued)*

```
// In the case of an illegal instruction, the monitor will gain control at
// this point, and the following code will be executed. Depending on the
// exact illegal instruction, Mach's error messages may be different.
//
if (kr != KERN_SUCCESS)
    mach_error("*** vmm_map_execute32:", kr);

Printf("Returned to vmm\n");
Printf("Processor state:\n");

printf("  Distance from origin = %lu instructions\n",
        (ppcRegs32->ppcPC - vm_page_size) >> 2);

printf("  PC                   = %p (%lu)\n",
        (void *)ppcRegs32->ppcPC, ppcRegs32->ppcPC);

printf("  Instruction at PC    = %#08x\n",
        ((u_int32_t *)(guestTextPage))[(ppcRegs32->ppcPC - vm_page_size) >> 2]);

printf("  CR                   = %#08lx\n"
        "                                 ", ppcRegs32->ppcCR);
prbits32(ppcRegs32->ppcCR);

printf("  LR                   = %#08lx (%lu)\n",
        ppcRegs32->ppcLR, ppcRegs32->ppcLR);

printf("  MSR                  = %#08lx\n"
        "                                 ", ppcRegs32->ppcMSR);
prbits32(ppcRegs32->ppcMSR);

printf("  return_code          = %#08lx (%lu)\n",
        vmmUState->return_code, vmmUState->return_code);

return_params32 = vmmUState->vmmRet.vmmrp32.return_params;

for (i = 0; i < 4; i++)
    printf("  return_params32[%d]   = 0x%08lx (%lu)\n", i,
            return_params32[i], return_params32[i]);

printf("  GPRs:\n");
for (j = 0; j < 16; j++) {
    printf("  ");
    for (i = 0; i < 2; i++) {
        printf("r%-2d = %#08lx ", j * 2 + i,
                ppcRegs32->ppcGPRs[j * 2 + i]);
    }
    printf("\n");
}
```

(continues)

FIGURE 6–51 A program to run machine code within a VM using the VMM facility *(continued)*

```
    // Tear down the virtual machine ... that's all for now
    kr = my_vmm_dispatch(kVmmTearDownContext, vmmIndex);
    OUT_ON_MACH_ERROR("vmm_init_context", kr);
    Printf("Virtual machine context torn down\n");

out:
    if (vmmUStatePage)
        (void)vm_deallocate(myTask, vmmUStatePage, vm_page_size);

    if (guestTextPage)
        (void)vm_deallocate(myTask, guestTextPage, vm_page_size);

    if (guestStackPage)
        (void)vm_deallocate(myTask, guestStackPage, vm_page_size);

    exit(kr);
}
```

Virtual PC

The Virtual PC software for Mac OS X is implemented using the VMM facility. In the xnu kernel source corresponding to Mac OS X 10.0, the VMM source is copyrighted to Connectix Corporation, the developer of Virtual PC. Connectix was later acquired by Microsoft.

The code in Figure 6–51 provides two demonstrations, demo 0 and demo 1. Demo 0 calls `initGuestText_Dummy()` to populate the VM's text page with a contrived sequence of instructions terminated by an illegal instruction. The first few words of the page are as follows, assuming the page starts at virtual address `addr`:

```
addr+00 addi     r10,0,4      ; load the value '4' in r10
addr+04 addi     r11,0,5      ; load the value '5' in r11
addr+08                       ; branch to addr+16
addr+12 0xdeadbeef            ; no such instruction
addr+16 add      r12,r11,r11  ; place (r10 + r11) in r12
addr+20 0xfeedface            ; no such instruction
```

The VM bypasses the first illegal instruction in the sequence by branching over it. When execution reaches the second illegal instruction, control returns back to our host program. Alternatively, you can make the last instruction be an infinite loop, in which case the VM will run until interrupted.

When vmachmon32 finishes running demo 0, the VM's GPR10, GPR11, and GPR12 should contain the values 4, 5, and 9, respectively. Moreover, the program counter should contain addr+20, where addr is the starting address of the guest's text page. Figure 6–52 shows the result of running demo 0.

FIGURE 6–52 Result of running a sequence of machine instructions in a VM using the vmachmon32 program

```
$ gcc -Wall -o vmachmon32 vmachmon32.c
$ ./vmachmon32
usage: vmachmon32 <demo ID>
Supported demos:
  ID    Description
  0     executes a few hand-crafted instructions in a VM
  1     executes a recursive factorial function in a VM
$ ./vmachmon32 0
Vmm> Mac OS X virtual machine monitor (version 1.7)
Vmm> Vmm features:
  LittleEndian         = Yes
  Stop                 = Yes
  ExtendedMapping      = Yes
  ListMapping          = Yes
  FastAssist           = Yes
  XA                   = Yes
  SixtyFourBit         = No
  MultAddrSpace        = No
  GuestShadowAssist    = Yes
  GlobalMappingAssist  = No
  HostShadowAssist     = No
  MultAddrSpaceAssist  = No
Vmm> Page size is 4096 bytes
Vmm> Allocated page-aligned memory for virtual machine user state
Vmm> Allocated page-aligned memory for guest's text
Vmm> Allocated page-aligned memory for guest's stack
Vmm> New virtual machine context initialized, index = 1
Vmm> Guest virtual machine PC set to 0x00001000
Vmm> Guest virtual machine SP set to 0x00002f20
Vmm> Mapping guest stack page
Vmm> Fabricated instructions for executing in the guest virtual machine
Vmm> Mapping guest text page and switching to guest virtual machine
*** vmm_map_execute32 (os/kern) not receiver
Vmm> Returned to vmm
Vmm> Processor state:
  Distance from origin = 5 instructions
  PC                   = 0x00001014 (4116)
  Instruction at PC    = 0x00000060
  CR                   = 0x00000000
                         0000000000000000 0000000000000000
```

(continues)

FIGURE 6–52 Result of running a sequence of machine instructions in a VM using the vmachmon32 program *(continued)*

```
LR                       = 0x00000000  (0)
MSR                      = 0x0008d030
                           0000000000001000 1101000000110000
return_code              = 0x00000007  (7)
return_params32[0]       = 0x00001000  (4096)
return_params32[1]       = 0x40000000  (1073741824)
return_params32[2]       = 0x00000000  (0)
return_params32[3]       = 0x00000000  (0)
GPRs:
r0  = 0x00000000 r1  = 0x00002f20
r2  = 0x00000000 r3  = 0x00000000
r4  = 0x00000000 r5  = 0x00000000
r6  = 0x00000000 r7  = 0x00000000
r8  = 0x00000000 r9  = 0x00000000
r10 = 0x00000004 r11 = 0x00000005
r12 = 0x00000009 r13 = 0x00000000
r14 = 0x00000000 r15 = 0x00000000
r16 = 0x00000000 r17 = 0x00000000
r18 = 0x00000000 r19 = 0x00000000
r20 = 0x00000000 r21 = 0x00000000
r22 = 0x00000000 r23 = 0x00000000
r24 = 0x00000000 r25 = 0x00000000
r26 = 0x00000000 r27 = 0x00000000
r28 = 0x00000000 r29 = 0x00000000
r30 = 0x00000000 r31 = 0x00000000
Vmm> Virtual machine context torn down
```

> As noted in the program's comments in Figure 6–51, compiling vmachmon32.c requires that you copy osfmk/ppc/vmachmon.h from the kernel source tree to the current directory (with respect to vmachmon32.c). Additionally, the source line that includes <ppc/exception.h> must be commented out in vmachmon.h.

   Demo 1 populates the guest's text page by calling initGuestText_Factorial(), which copies machine instructions for a recursive factorial function into the page and populates the LR so that the function returns to an address containing an illegal instruction. The function takes a single argument in GPR3: the number whose factorial to compute. It returns the computed factorial in GPR3. Again, we will verify the program's working by examining the register dump at the end of the program's execution. Figure 6–53 shows the result of running demo 1. The vmachmon32 code shown in Figure 6–51 passes 10 as an argument to the factorial function. Correspondingly, GPR3 should contain 0x00375f00 as the result.

FIGURE 6–53 Result of running a recursive factorial function within a VM using the `vmachmon32` program

```
$ ./vmachmon32 1
Vmm> Mac OS X virtual machine monitor (version 1.7)
...
Vmm> Returned to vmm
Vmm> Processor state:
  Distance from origin = 1023 instructions
  PC                   = 0x00001ffc (8188)
  Instruction at PC    = 0x00000000
  CR                   = 0x00000002
                         0000000000000000 0000000000000010
  LR                   = 0x00001ffc (8188)
  MSR                  = 0x0008d030
                         0000000000001000 1101000000110000
  return_code          = 0x00000007 (7)
  return_params32[0]   = 0x00001000 (4096)
  return_params32[1]   = 0x40000000 (1073741824)
  return_params32[2]   = 0x00000000 (0)
  return_params32[3]   = 0x00000000 (0)
  GPRs:
  r0  = 0x00001ffc r1  = 0x00002f20
  r2  = 0x00058980 r3  = 0x00375f00
  r4  = 0x00000000 r5  = 0x00000000
...
Vmm> Virtual machine context torn down
```

6.10 Compiling the Kernel

In this section, we will briefly discuss the kernel compilation procedure in Mac OS X. Depending on the Darwin release, you might need the following Darwin packages to compile the xnu kernel:

- bootstrap_cmds
- cctools
- IOKitUser
- kext_tools
- Libstreams
- xnu

Mac OS X does not have a publicly well-defined kernel compilation procedure. Compiling the kernel requires certain tools and libraries that are part of Darwin but are not installed by default. These prerequisites must be compiled from source. However, they are few in number, and it is straightforward to compile them. Moreover, depending on the specific Darwin release you use, you may require more or fewer steps than the ones described in this section.

6.10.1 Retrieving Prerequisite Packages

We begin by retrieving and unpacking the required package archives.[20] Let us assume all package archives have been expanded within the /work/darwin/ directory. Each package will expand into a directory whose name includes the package's name and version. We will omit the version number in the examples in this section.

Compiler Version Dependency

Mac OS X releases have typically included two versions of the GNU C compiler: a default version (the gcc package) and another version for compiling the operating system (gcc_os). For example, on Mac OS X 10.4, the kernel is compiled using GCC 3.3, whereas the default compiler is GCC 4.0.

You can switch between compiler versions through the gcc_select command-line tool. Before compiling the kernel or the prerequisite packages, you should switch to the kernel-specific GNU C compiler for your system.

6.10.2 Compiling Prerequisite Packages

Change directory to bootstrap_cmds/relpath.tproj/, and run make to compile and install the relpath tool, which calculates the relative path from a given directory to a given path.

```
$ cd /work/darwin/bootstrap_cmds/relpath.tproj
$ sudo make install
...
$ relpath /usr/local/ /usr/local/bin/relpath
bin/relpath
```

---

20. On some Mac OS X versions, the header file ar.h may be missing from the Kernel framework's Headers/ subdirectory. If this is the case, copy /usr/include/ar.h to /System/Library/ Frameworks/Kernel.framework/Headers/.

`relpath` is used in various "doconf" shell scripts in the kernel source tree to set up build paths during the precompilation ("config") stage of the kernel build process.

> The tools and libraries that you compile and install from these support packages are installed by default in the `/usr/local/` directory hierarchy. You must ensure that `/usr/local/` is in your shell's path. A benefit of confining this software to `/usr/local/` is that you will not accidentally overwrite any standard files belonging to the operating system.

The rest of the packages are needed to satisfy the following requirements:

- Compilation of the libsa in-kernel library
- Generation of symbol sets for various kernel components after compilation finishes—this requires the `kextsymboltool` program

Figure 6–54 shows dependencies between the packages. libsa links against a static kernel link editor library (`libkld.a`), which comes from the `cctools` package. `libkld.a` in turn depends on the `Libstreams` package, the libmacho library, and the libstuff library. libmacho and libstuff come from the `cctools` package. libsa also requires a tool called `seg_hack`, which can change all segment names in a Mach-O file to the one specified on the command line. The kernel compilation process uses `seg_hack` to change segment names to __KLD while compiling libsa. We can satisfy these dependencies by appropriately traversing the graph shown in Figure 6–54.

Change directory to the `Libstreams` package, and run `make` to compile and copy the required headers and libraries to the `/usr/local/` hierarchy.

```
$ cd /work/darwin/Libstreams/
$ sudo make install
...
```

The components within the `cctools` package must be compiled in a particular sequence since they have internal dependencies.

Change directory to `cctools/libstuff/`, and run `make`. No installation is required since we need the result of this build only to compile other components in this package.

Change directory to `cctools/misc/`, and run the following commands, which compile and install `seg_hack` in `/usr/local/bin/` with the appropriate ownership and permissions.

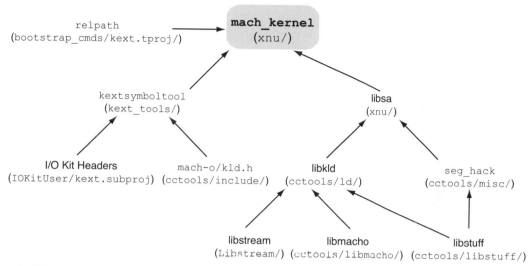

FIGURE 6–54 Software dependencies in the kernel build process

```
$ make seg_hack.NEW
$ sudo install -o root -g wheel -m 0755 seg_hack.NEW /usr/local/bin/seg_hack
```

Change directory to cctools/libmacho/, and run make. Again, no installation is required.

Change directory to cctools/ld/, and run the following commands.

```
$ make kld_build
$ sudo install -o root -g wheel -m 0755 static_kld/libkld.a /usr/local/lib/
$ sudo ranlib /usr/local/lib/libkld.a
```

Finally, we need to compile kextsymboltool, which the build process uses for generating symbol sets from compiled kernel components. BSDKernel.symbolset, IOKit.symbolset, Libkern.symbolset, and Mach.symbolset are examples of the resultant files that exist in the BUILD directory hierarchy of a compiled kernel source tree. These Mach-O relocatable object files contain nothing besides a symbol table, for example:

```
$ cd /work/darwin/xnu/BUILD/obj/DEBUG_PPC/
$ file Mach.symbolset
Mach.symbolset: Mach-O object ppc
$ otool -l Mach.symbolset
Mach.symbolset:
Load command 0
    cmd LC_SYMTAB
```

```
cmdsize 24
 symoff 52
  nsyms 2652
  stroff 31876
 strsize 49748
$ cd /work/darwin/xnu/BUILD/obj/RELEASE_PPC/
$ otool -l Mach.symbolset
Mach.symbolset:
Load command 0
      cmd LC_SYMTAB
 cmdsize 24
  symoff 52
   nsyms 52
  stroff 676
 strsize 1128
```

The source for `kextsymboltool` is in the `kext_tools` package. However, its compilation depends on header files from the `IOKitUser` and `cctools` packages. Change directory to `kext_tools/`, and run the following commands.

```
$ mkdir IOKit
$ ln -s /work/darwin/IOKitUser/kext.subproj IOKit/kext
$ gcc -I /work/darwin/cctools/include -I . -o kextsymboltool kextsymbool.c
$ sudo install -o root -g wheel -m 0755 kextsymboltool /usr/local/bin/
```

6.10.3 Compiling the xnu Package

At this point, we are ready to compile the kernel. Change directory to `xnu/`, and run the following command to initiate kernel compilation.

```
$ make exporthdrs && make all
```

This will create a standard (`RELEASE` configuration) kernel, which will be available as `xnu/BUILD/obj/RELEASE_PPC/mach_kernel` at the end of the compilation. Alternative build configurations include `DEBUG` and `PROFILE`, which yield debugging and profiling versions, respectively, of the kernel. The following command will compile a debug version, which will be available as `xnu/BUILD/obj/DEBUG_PPC/mach_kernel` at the end of the compilation:

```
$ make exporthdrs && make KERNEL_CONFIGS=DEBUG all
```

Regardless of which kernel configuration you build, a kernel object file with full symbolic information is generated as `mach_kernel.sys` in the same directory as `mach_kernel`. A typical `mach_kernel.sys` is several times larger than the corresponding `mach_kernel` and contains more symbols. Table 6–18 compares some aspects of release, profile, and debug builds for a particular kernel version.

TABLE 6–18 A Comparison of the End Products of Different Kernel Build Configurations

	RELEASE	PROFILE	DEBUG
Size of `mach_kernel`	4.06MB	4.31MB	4.57MB
Symbols in `mach_kernel`	11,677	11,679	19,611
Strings in `mach_kernel`	265KB	265KB	398KB
Size of `mach_kernel.sys`	25.37MB	25.48MB	27.04MB
Symbols in `mach_kernel.sys`	18,824	18,824	19,611
Strings in `mach_kernel.sys`	16.13MB	16.12MB	17.24MB

6.10.4 DarwinBuild

A convenient way to compile the xnu kernel (in fact, any Darwin package in general) is through DarwinBuild—a specialized open source tool that provides a build environment similar to Apple's internal build environment. DarwinBuild's usefulness is evident when building complex packages with a large number of dependencies, for example, the system library. Specifically, DarwinBuild consists of two primary harness programs: `darwinbuild`, which builds software, and `darwinxref`, which parses property list files containing project information and performs a variety of operations such as resolving dependencies, finding files, and loading indexes.

CHAPTER 7

Processes

In a typical operating system, a process represents a program in execution along with associated system resources, which may be physical (such as processor cycles and memory) or abstract[1] (such as the number of files the process can open). The kernel provides an illusion of concurrent execution by scheduling resources between ready-to-run processes. On a multiprocessor or multicore system, more than one process may execute truly concurrently.

> In their landmark 1965 paper,[2] Jack B. Dennis and Earl C. Van Horn defined a process as a "locus of control within an instruction sequence . . . an abstract entity which moves through the instructions of a procedure as the procedure is executed by a processor."

---

1. Abstract resources are often directly or indirectly limited by physical resources.

2. "Programming Semantics for Multiprogrammed Computations," by Jack B. Dennis and Earl C. Van Horn (The ACM Conference on Programming Languages and Pragmatics, San Dimas, California, August 1965).

In earlier chapters, we saw that the Mac OS X kernel divides the traditional process abstraction into multiple related abstractions. In this chapter, we will look at both kernel-level and user-level details of the Mac OS X process subsystem.

7.1 Processes: From Early UNIX to Mac OS X

The process abstraction has long been used to represent various activities in a computer system. In early UNIX, a process could be running a user program, or it could represent one or more flows of control in the kernel—for example, process 0 ran `sched()`, the process scheduler. The only way to create a new process in traditional UNIX was through the `fork()` system call, and the only way to run a new program within a process was through the `exec()` system call.

The Earliest `fork()` and `exec()` System Calls

The following are excerpts from the manual pages of the `fork()` and `exec()` system calls in First Edition Research UNIX (circa late 1971)[3]:

> *fork is the only way new processes are created. The new process's core image is a copy of that of the caller of fork; the only distinction is the return location and the fact that r0 in the old process contains the process ID of the new process.*
>
> *exec overlays the calling process with the named file, then transfers to the beginning of the core image of the file. The first argument to exec is a pointer to the name of the file to be executed. The second is the address of a list of pointers to arguments to be passed to the file. . . . There can be no return from the file; the calling core image is lost.*

As compared to modern operating systems, early UNIX had a vastly simpler process abstraction. In fact, it wasn't until UNIX was rewritten in C—and ran on a PDP-11 with an MMU—that the UNIX kernel could have more than one process in memory at a time. Consider the `proc` structure—a kernel-memory-resident process bookkeeping data structure—from Third Edition Research UNIX (circa early 1973):

---

3. *UNIX Programmers Manual*, by K. Thompson and D. M. Ritchie (Bell Laboratories, 1971).

```
struct proc {
    char p_stat;   /* (SSLEEP, SWAIT, SRUN, SIDL, SZOMB) */
    char p_flag;   /* (SLOAD, SSYS, SLOCK, SSWAP) */
    char p_pri;    /* current process priority */
    char p_sig;    /* most recent interrupt outstanding */
    char p_ndis;   /* index into priority "cookie" array */
    char p_cook;   /* cookie value */
    int  p_ttyp;   /* controlling terminal */
    int  p_pid;    /* process ID */
    int  p_ppid;   /* parent process ID */
    int  p_addr;   /* address of data segment, memory/disk */
    int  p_size;   /* size of data segment in blocks */
    int  p_wchan;  /* reason for sleeping */
    int *p_textp;  /* text segment statistics */
} proc[NPROC];
```

The value of NPROC, the number of entries in the process table, was set at compile time—a typical value was 50. Besides program text and data, each process had kernel-mode stack and a data area—the user structure or the *u-area*. There could be only one current process.

7.1.1 Mac OS X Process Limits

As is the case with modern operating systems, the Mac OS X kernel has *soft* and *hard* limits on the number of processes allowed. The hard limit is either more than or equal to the soft limit. The hard limit is set at compile time and cannot be varied. The soft limit can be varied through the sysctl interface by setting the value of the kern.maxproc variable.

```
$ sysctl -a | grep proc
kern.maxproc = 532
kern.maxfilesperproc = 10240
kern.maxprocperuid = 100
kern.aioprocmax = 16
kern.proc_low_pri_io = 0
...
```

The hard limit is computed at compile time using the following formula:

```
// bsd/conf/param.c

#define NPROC (20 + 16 * MAXUSERS)
#define HNPROC (20 + 64 * MAXUSERS)
int maxproc = NPROC;
__private_extern__ int hard_maxproc = HNPROC; /* hardcoded limit */
```

The MAXUSERS value is defined per Table 7–1 in a configuration file in the BSD portion of the kernel. The standard Mac OS X kernel is compiled in a medium configuration, with MAXUSERS being 32. The corresponding values of NPROC and HNPROC are 532 and 2068, respectively.

TABLE 7–1 System Size Configuration

Configuration	Description	MAXUSERS
xlarge	Extra-large scale	64
large	Large scale	50
medium	Medium scale	32
small	Small scale	16
xsmall	Extra-small scale	8
bsmall	Special extra-small scale (such as for boot floppies)	2

However, the difference in the number of maximum processes allowed between early UNIX and Mac OS X is insignificant compared to the differences in the respective compositions of their process subsystems. Even though modern systems are *expected* to be considerably more complicated, it would not be much of an exaggeration to say that the term *process* has more connotations in Mac OS X than there were fields in the Third Edition UNIX process structure!

7.1.2 Mac OS X Execution Flavors

Code can execute in Mac OS X in several *environments*, where environments are differentiated based on one or more of the following: machine architecture, executable format, system mode (user or kernel), miscellaneous policies,[4] and so on. Each environment has its own flavor of execution. Here are examples of such environments:

- The BSD, Mach, and I/O Kit portions of the kernel
- The BSD user-space environment

---

4. Examples of policies that affect program execution include those related to security and resource consumption.

- The Carbon environment

- The Classic environment

- The Cocoa environment

- The Java runtime environment

- The Dashboard environment for running JavaScript-based widgets

- The Rosetta binary translation environment that allows running PowerPC executables to run on x86-based Macintosh computers

Figure 7–1 shows a conceptual view of the process subsystem's composition in Mac OS X. Despite the presence of numerous process-like entities on Mac OS X, exactly one abstraction executes on a processor: the Mach thread. All other process-like entities are eventually layered atop Mach threads.

7.2 Mach Abstractions, Data Structures, and APIs

Let us examine some of the kernel data structures that play important roles in the Mac OS X process subsystem. These include the following:

- `struct processor_set` [osfmk/kern/processor.h]—the processor set structure

- `struct processor` [osfmk/kern/processor.h]—the processor structure

- `struct task` [osfmk/kern/task.h]—the Mach task structure

- `struct thread` [osfmk/kern/thread.h]—the machine-independent Mach thread structure

- `struct machine_thread` [osfmk/ppc/thread.h]—the machine-dependent thread state structure

- `struct proc` [bsd/sys/proc.h]—the BSD process structure

- `struct uthread` [bsd/sys/user.h]—the BSD per-thread user structure

- `struct run_queue` [osfmk/kern/sched.h]—the run queue structure used by the scheduler

7.2.1 Summary of Relationships

Mach groups *processors* into one or more *processor sets*. Each processor set has a *run queue* of runnable *threads*, and each processor has a local run queue. Besides

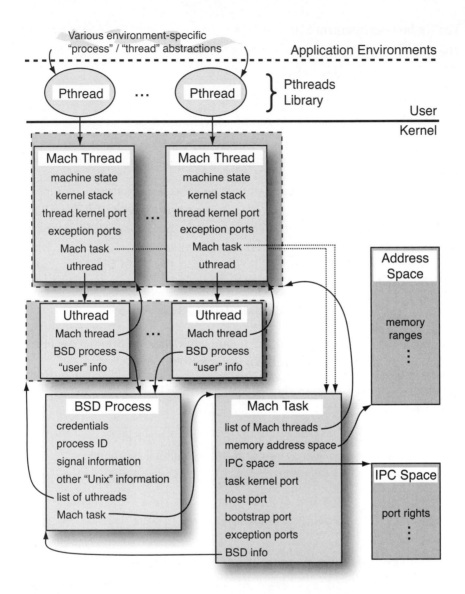

FIGURE 7–1 An overview of the Mac OS X process subsystem

the run queue, a processor set also maintains a list of all threads in the set, along with the *tasks* assigned to the set. A task contains a list of its threads. It also refers back to its assigned processor set. A thread's machine-dependent state, including the so-called *process control block* (PCB), is captured in a `machine_thread` structure. A BSD process additionally has a `proc` structure that refers to the associated task. A multithreaded process is implemented as a Mach task containing multiple Mach threads. Each thread in a BSD process contains a pointer to a `uthread` structure. Moreover, the `proc` structure contains a list of pointers to `uthread` structures—one for each thread within the process.

7.2.2 Processor Sets

Mach divides the available processors on a system into one or more processor sets. There is always a *default processor set*, which is initialized during kernel startup—before the scheduler can run. It initially contains all processors in the system. The first task created by the kernel is assigned to the default set. A processor set may be empty, except for the default set, which must contain at least one processor. A processor belongs to at most one processor set at a time.

The Purpose of Processor Sets

The original motivation behind processor sets was to group processors to allocate them to specific system activities—a coarse-grained allocation. Moreover, in early versions of Mac OS X, processor sets had associated scheduling policies and attributes, which provided a uniform control of the scheduling aspects of the threads in the set. Specific policies could be enabled and disabled at the processor set level.

7.2.2.1 Representation

As shown in Figure 7–2, a processor set object has two Mach ports representing it: a *name* port and a *control* port. The name port is only an identifier—it can be used only for retrieving information about the processor set. The control port represents the underlying object—it can be used for performing control operations, for example, to assign processors, tasks, and threads to the processor set. This scenario is representative of Mach's architecture, wherein operations on various Mach objects are performed by sending the appropriate messages to the objects' respective control ports.

FIGURE 7–2 The processor set structure in the xnu kernel

```
// osfmk/kern/processor.h

struct processor_set {
    queue_head_t      idle_queue;      // queue of idle processors
    int               idle_count;      // how many idle processors?
    queue_head_t      active_queue;    // queue of active processors
    queue_head_t      processors;      // queue of all processors
    int               processor_count; // how many processors?
    decl_simple_lock_data(,sched_lock) // scheduling lock
    struct            run_queue runq;  // run queue for this set
    queue_head_t      tasks;           // tasks assigned to this set
    int               task_count;      // how many tasks assigned?
    queue_head_t      threads;         // threads in this set
    int               thread_count;    // how many threads assigned?
    int               ref_count;       // structure reference count
    int                active;         // is this set in use?
    ...
    struct ipc_port *pset_self;        // control port (for operations)
    struct ipc_port *pset_name_self;   // name port (for information)
    uint32_t          run_count;       // threads running
    uint32_t          share_count;     // timeshare threads running
    integer_t         mach_factor;     // the Mach factor
    integer_t         load_average;    // load average
    uint32_t          pri_shift;       // scheduler load average
};

extern struct processor_set default_pset;
```

7.2.2.2 The Processor Set API

The processor set Mach API provides routines that can be called from user space to query and manipulate processor sets. Note that processor set manipulation is a privileged operation. The following are examples of routines in the processor set API.

- `host_processor_sets()` returns a list of send rights representing all processor set name ports on the host.

- `host_processor_set_priv()` translates a processor set name port into a processor set control port.

- `processor_set_default()` returns the name port for the default processor set.

- `processor_set_create()` creates a new processor set and returns the name and the control ports, whereas `processor_set_destroy()` destroys the specified processor set while reassigning its processors, tasks, and threads to the default set.[5]

- `processor_set_info()` retrieves information about the specified processor set. As we saw in Chapter 6, "info" calls in the Mach APIs typically require a flavor argument that specifies the type of information desired. This way, the same call may fetch a variety of information depending on the flavor specified. Examples of `processor_set_info()` flavors are `PROCESSOR_SET_BASIC_INFO` (the number of assigned processors to the set and the default policy[6] in effect; returned in a `processor_set_basic_info` structure), `PROCESSOR_SET_TIMESHARE_DEFAULT` (the base attributes for the timeshare scheduling policy; returned in a `policy_timeshare_base` structure), and `PROCESSOR_SET_TIMESHARE_LIMITS` (the limits on the allowed timeshare policy attributes; returned in a `policy_timeshare_limit` structure).

- `processor_set_statistics()` retrieves scheduling statistics for the specified processor set. It also requires a flavor argument. For example, the `PROCESSOR_SET_LOAD_INFO` flavor returns load statistics in a `processor_set_load_info` structure.

- `processor_set_tasks()` returns a list of send rights to the kernel ports of all tasks currently assigned to the specified processor set. Similarly, `processor_set_threads()` retrieves the processor set's assigned threads.

- `processor_set_stack_usage()` is a debugging routine that is enabled only if the kernel was compiled with the `MACH_DEBUG` option. It retrieves information on thread stack usage in a given processor set.

Note that using the list of processor sets, all tasks and threads in the system can be found.

> The processor set interface is deprecated in Mac OS X and is likely to change or disappear at some point. In fact, the xnu kernel supports only a single processor set—the interface routines operate on the default processor set.

---

5. Since the kernel supports only one processor set, the *create* and *destroy* calls always fail.

6. The default policy is hardcoded to `POLICY_TIMESHARE`.

7.2.3 Processors

The processor structure is a machine-independent description of a physical processor. Some of the processor structure's fields are similar to those of the processor_set structure, but with a per-processor (local) scope. For example, the processor structure's run queue field is used for threads bound only to that processor. Figure 7–3 shows an annotated excerpt from the processor structure's declaration. The possible states that a processor can be in are PROCESSOR_OFF_LINE (not available), PROCESSOR_RUNNING (in normal execution), PROCESSOR_IDLE (idle), PROCESSOR_DISPATCHING (transitioning from the idle state to the running state), PROCESSOR_SHUTDOWN (going offline), and PROCESSOR_START (being started).

FIGURE 7–3 The processor structure in the xnu kernel

```
// osfmk/kern/processor.h

struct processor {
    queue_chain_t      processor_queue;   // idle, active, or action queue link
    int                state;             // processor state
    struct thread      *active_thread;    // thread running on processor
    struct thread      *next_thread;      // next thread to run if dispatched
    struct thread      *idle_thread;      // this processor's idle thread
    processor_set_t    processor_set;     // the processor set that we belong to
    int                current_pri;       // current thread's priority
    timer_call_data_t  quantum_timer;     // timer for quantum expiration
    uint64_t           quantum_end;       // time when current quantum ends
    uint64_t           last_dispatch;     // time of last dispatch
    int                timeslice;         // quantum before timeslice ends
    int                deadline;          // current deadline
    struct run_queue   runq;              // local run queue for this processor
    queue_chain_t      processors;        // all processors in our processor set
    ...
    struct ipc_port    *processor_self;   // processor's control port
    processor_t        processor_list;    // all existing processors
    processor_data_t   processor_data;    // per-processor data
};

...
extern processor_t master_processor;
```

7.2.3.1 Interconnections

Figure 7–4 shows how the `processor_set` and `processor` structures are interconnected in a system with one processor set and two processors. The processors are shown to be neither on the set's idle queue nor on the active queue. The `processors` field of each processor, along with the `processors` field of the processor set, are all chained together in a circular list. In both the `processor` and the `processor_set` structures, the `processors` field is a queue element containing only two pointers: `prev` (previous) and `next`. In particular, the `next` pointer of the processor set's `processors` field points to the first (master) processor. Thus, you can traverse the list of all processors in a processor set starting from either the set or any of the processors. Similarly, you can traverse the list of all active processors in a set using the `active_queue` field of the `processor_set` structure and the `processor_queue` field of each `processor` structure in the set.

Figure 7–5 shows the situation when both processors in Figure 7–4 are on the active queue of the default processor set.

7.2.3.2 The Processor API

The following are examples of Mach routines that deal with processors.

- `host_processors()` returns an array of send rights representing all processors in the system. Note that the user-space caller receives the array as *out-of-line data* in a Mach IPC message—the memory appears implicitly allocated in the caller's virtual address space. In such a case, the caller should explicitly deallocate the memory when it is no longer needed by calling the `vm_deallocate()` or `mach_vm_deallocate()` Mach routines.

- `processor_control()` runs machine-dependent control operations, or *commands*, on the specified processor. Examples of such commands include setting performance-monitoring registers and setting or clearing performance-monitoring counters.

- `processor_info()` retrieves information about the specified processor. Examples of `processor_info()` flavors are PROCESSOR_BASIC_INFO (processor type, subtype, and slot number; whether it is running; and whether it is the master processor) and PROCESSOR_CPU_LOAD_INFO (the number of tasks and threads assigned to the processor, its load average, and its Mach factor).

- On a multiprocessor system, `processor_start()` starts the given processor if it is currently offline. The processor is assigned to the default processor

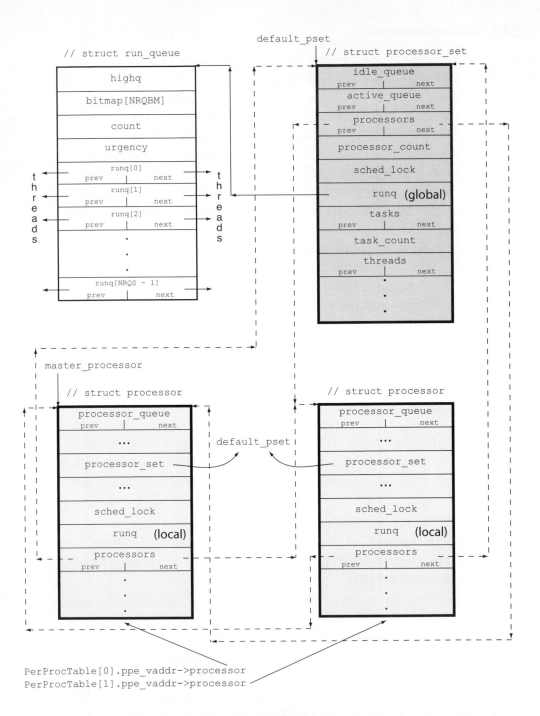

FIGURE 7–4 A processor set containing two processors

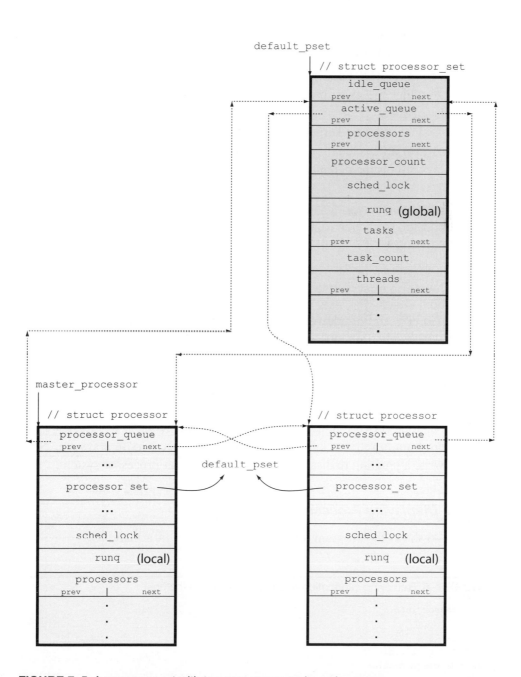

FIGURE 7–5 A processor set with two processors on its active queue

set after startup. Conversely, `processor_exit()` stops the given processor and removes it from its assigned processor set.

• `processor_get_assignment()` returns the name port for the processor set to which the given processor is currently assigned. The complementary call—`processor_assign()`—assigns a processor to a processor set. However, since the xnu kernel supports only one processor set, `processor_assign()` always returns a failure, whereas `processor_get_assignment()` always returns the default processor set.

> Several processor-related Mach routines have machine-dependent behavior. Moreover, routines that affect a processor's global behavior are privileged.

> There also exist calls to set or get the processor set affinity of tasks and threads. For example, `task_assign()` assigns a task, and optionally all threads within the task, to the given processor set. Unless all threads are included, only newly created threads will be assigned to the new processor set. As with other calls dealing with multiple processor sets, `task_assign()` always returns failure on Mac OS X.

Let us look at two examples of using the Mach processor API. First, we will write a program to retrieve information about the processors in a system. Next, we will write a program to disable a processor on a multiprocessor system.

7.2.3.3 Displaying Processor Information

Figure 7–6 shows the program for retrieving processor information.

FIGURE 7–6 Retrieving information about processors on the host

```
// processor_info.c

#include <stdio.h>
#include <stdlib.h>
#include <mach/mach.h>

void
print_basic_info(processor_basic_info_t info)
```

(continues)

FIGURE 7–6 Retrieving information about processors on the host *(continued)*

```
{
    printf("CPU: slot %d%s %s, type %d, subtype %d\n", info->slot_num,
           (info->is_master) ? " (master)," : ",",
           (info->running) ? "running" : "not running",
           info->cpu_type, info->cpu_subtype);
}

void
print_cpu_load_info(processor_cpu_load_info_t info)
{
    unsigned long ticks;

    // Total ticks do not amount to the uptime if the machine has slept
    ticks = info->cpu_ticks[CPU_STATE_USER]   +
            info->cpu_ticks[CPU_STATE_SYSTEM] +
            info->cpu_ticks[CPU_STATE_IDLE]   +
            info->cpu_ticks[CPU_STATE_NICE];
    printf("     %ld ticks "
           "(user %ld, system %ld, idle %ld, nice %ld)\n", ticks,
           info->cpu_ticks[CPU_STATE_USER],
           info->cpu_ticks[CPU_STATE_SYSTEM],
           info->cpu_ticks[CPU_STATE_IDLE],
           info->cpu_ticks[CPU_STATE_NICE]);
    printf("     cpu uptime %ld h %ld m %ld s\n",
           (ticks / 100) / 3600,          // hours
           ((ticks / 100) % 3600) / 60,   // minutes
           (ticks / 100) % 60);           // seconds
}

int
main(void)
{
    int                          i;
    kern_return_t                kr;
    host_name_port_t             myhost;
    host_priv_t                  host_priv;
    processor_port_array_t       processor_list;
    natural_t                    processor_count;
    processor_basic_info_data_t  basic_info;
    processor_cpu_load_info_data_t cpu_load_info;
    natural_t                    info_count;

    myhost = mach_host_self();
    kr = host_get_host_priv_port(myhost, &host_priv);
    if (kr != KERN_SUCCESS) {
        mach_error("host_get_host_priv_port:", kr);
        exit(1);
    }
```

(continues)

FIGURE 7–6 Retrieving information about processors on the host *(continued)*

```
kr = host_processors(host_priv, &processor_list, &processor_count);
if (kr != KERN_SUCCESS) {
    mach_error("host_processors:", kr);
    exit(1);
}

printf("%d processors total.\n", processor_count);

for (i = 0; i < processor_count; i++) {
    info_count = PROCESSOR_BASIC_INFO_COUNT;
    kr = processor_info(processor_list[i],
                        PROCESSOR_BASIC_INFO,
                        &myhost,
                        (processor_info_t)&basic_info,
                        &info_count);
    if (kr == KERN_SUCCESS)
        print_basic_info((processor_basic_info_t)&basic_info);

    info_count = PROCESSOR_CPU_LOAD_INFO_COUNT;
    kr = processor_info(processor_list[i],
                        PROCESSOR_CPU_LOAD_INFO,
                        &myhost,
                        (processor_info_t)&cpu_load_info,
                        &info_count);
    if (kr == KERN_SUCCESS)
        print_cpu_load_info((processor_cpu_load_info_t)&cpu_load_info);
}

// Other processor information flavors (may be unsupported)
//
//   PROCESSOR_PM_REGS_INFO,  // performance monitor register information
//   PROCESSOR_TEMPERATURE,    // core temperature


// This will deallocate while rounding up to page size
(void)vm_deallocate(mach_task_self(), (vm_address_t)processor_list,
                    processor_count * sizeof(processor_t *));

exit(0);
}


$ gcc -Wall -o processor_info processor_info.c
$ sudo ./processor_info
2 processors total.
CPU: slot 0 (master), running, type 18, subtype 100
    16116643 ticks (user 520750, system 338710, idle 15254867, nice 2316)
    cpu uptime 44 h 46 m 6 s
```

(continues)

FIGURE 7–6 Retrieving information about processors on the host *(continued)*

```
CPU: slot 1, running, type 18, subtype 100
    16116661 ticks (user 599531, system 331140, idle 15182087, nice 3903)
    cpu uptime 44 h 46 m 6 s
$ uptime
16:12 up 2 days, 16:13, 1 user, load averages: 0.01 0.04 0.06
```

The cpu uptime value printed by the program in Figure 7–6 is calculated based on the number of ticks reported for the processor. There is a tick every 10 ms on Mac OS X—that is, there are 100 ticks a second. Therefore, 16,116,643 ticks correspond to 161,166 seconds, which is 44 hours, 46 minutes, and 6 seconds. When we use the uptime utility to display how long the system has been running, we get a higher value: over 64 hours. This is because the *processor* uptime is not the same as the *system* uptime if the system has slept—there are no processor ticks when a processor is sleeping.

Let us modify the program in Figure 7–6 to verify that memory is indeed allocated in the calling task's address space as a side affect of receiving out-of-line data in response to the host_processors() call. We will print the process ID and the value of the processor_list pointer after the call to host_processors() and make the process sleep briefly. While the program sleeps, we will use the vmmap utility to display the virtual memory regions allocated in the process. We expect the region containing the pointer to be listed in vmmap's output. Figure 7–7 shows the modified program excerpt and the corresponding output.

FIGURE 7–7 Out-of-line data received by a process from the kernel as a result of a Mach call

```
// processor_info.c

    ...
    processor_list = (processor_port_array_t)0;
    kr = host_processors(host_priv, &processor_list, &processor_count);
    if (kr != KERN_SUCCESS) {
        mach_error("host_processors:", kr);
        exit(1);
    }
    // #include <unistd.h> for getpid(2) and sleep(3)
    printf("processor_list = %p\n", processor_list);
    printf("my process ID is %d\n", getpid());
    sleep(60);
    ...
```

(continues)

FIGURE 7–7 Out-of-line data received by a process from the kernel as a result of a Mach call *(continued)*

```
$ sudo ./processor_info
processor_list = 0x6000
my process ID is 2463
...

$ sudo vmmap 2463
Virtual Memory Map of process 2463 (processor_info)
...
==== Writable regions for process 2463
...
Mach message              00006000-00007000 [    4K] rw-/rwx SM=PRV
...
```

7.2.3.4 Stopping and Starting a Processor in a Multiprocessor System

In this example, we will programmatically stop and start one of the processors in a multiprocessor system. Figure 7–8 shows a program that calls `processor_exit()` to take the last processor offline and `processor_start()` to bring it online.

FIGURE 7–8 Starting and stopping a processor through the Mach processor interface

```c
// processor_xable.c

#include <stdio.h>
#include <stdlib.h>
#include <mach/mach.h>

#define PROGNAME "processor_xable"
#define EXIT_ON_MACH_ERROR(msg, retval) \
    if (kr != KERN_SUCCESS) { mach_error(msg, kr); exit((retval)); }

int
main(int argc, char **argv)
{
    kern_return_t          kr;
    host_priv_t            host_priv;
    processor_port_array_t processor_list;
    natural_t              processor_count;
    char                   *errmsg = PROGNAME;
```

(continues)

FIGURE 7–8 Starting and stopping a processor through the Mach processor interface *(continued)*

```
    if (argc != 2) {
        fprintf(stderr,
                "usage: %s <cmd>, where <cmd> is \"exit\" or \"start\"\n",
                PROGNAME);
        exit(1);
    }

    kr = host_get_host_priv_port(mach_host_self(), &host_priv);
    EXIT_ON_MACH_ERROR("host_get_host_priv_port:", kr);

    kr = host_processors(host_priv, &processor_list, &processor_count);
    EXIT_ON_MACH_ERROR("host_processors:", kr);

    // disable last processor on a multiprocessor system
    if (processor_count > 1) {
        if (*argv[1] == 'e') {
            kr = processor_exit(processor_list[processor_count - 1]);
            errmsg = "processor_exit:";
        } else if (*argv[1] == 's') {
            kr = processor_start(processor_list[processor_count - 1]);
            errmsg = "processor_start:";
        } else {
            kr = KERN_INVALID_ARGUMENT;
        }
    } else
        printf("Only one processor!\n");

    // this will deallocate while rounding up to page size
    (void)vm_deallocate(mach_task_self(), (vm_address_t)processor_list,
                        processor_count * sizeof(processor_t *));
    EXIT_ON_MACH_ERROR(errmsg, kr);

    fprintf(stderr, "%s successful\n", errmsg);

    exit(0);
}


$ gcc -Wall -o processor_xable processor_xable.c
$ sudo ./processor_info
2 processors total.
CPU: slot 0 (master), running, type 18, subtype 100
    88141653 ticks (user 2974228, system 2170409, idle 82953261, nice 43755)
    cpu uptime 244 h 50 m 16 s
CPU: slot 1, running, type 18, subtype 100
    88128007 ticks (user 3247822, system 2088151, idle 82741221, nice 50813)
    cpu uptime 244 h 48 m 0 s
```

(continues)

FIGURE 7–8 Starting and stopping a processor through the Mach processor interface *(continued)*

```
$ sudo ./processor_xable exit
processor_exit: successful
$ sudo ./processor_info
2 processors total.
CPU: slot 0 (master), running, type 18, subtype 100
    88151172 ticks (user 2975172, system 2170976, idle 82961265, nice 43759)
    cpu uptime 244 h 51 m 51 s
CPU: slot 1, not running, type 18, subtype 100
    88137333 ticks (user 3248807, system 2088588, idle 82749125, nice 50813)
    cpu uptime 244 h 49 m 33 s
$ sudo ./processor_xable start
processor_start: successful
$ sudo ./processor_info
2 processors total.
CPU: slot 0 (master), running, type 18, subtype 100
    88153641 ticks (user 2975752, system 2171100, idle 82963028, nice 43761)
    cpu uptime 244 h 52 m 16 s
CPU: slot 1, running, type 18, subtype 100
    88137496 ticks (user 3248812, system 2088590, idle 82749281, nice 50813)
    cpu uptime 244 h 49 m 34 s
```

7.2.4 Tasks and the Task API

A Mach task is a machine-independent abstraction of the execution environment of threads. We saw earlier that a task is a container for resources—it encapsulates protected access to a sparse virtual address space, IPC (port) space, processor resources, scheduling control, and threads that use these resources. A task has a few task-specific ports, such as the task's kernel port and task-level exception ports (corresponding to task-level exception handlers). Figure 7–9 shows an annotated excerpt from the `task` structure.

FIGURE 7–9 The `task` structure in the xnu kernel

// osfmk/kern/task.h

```
struct task {
    ...
    vm_map_t      map;          // address space description
    queue_chain_t pset_tasks;   // list of tasks in our processor set
    ...
```

(continues)

FIGURE 7–9 The `task` structure in the xnu kernel *(continued)*

```
    queue_head_t  threads;      // list of threads in this task
    int           thread_count; // number of threads in this task
    ...
    integer_t     priority;     // base priority for threads
    integer_t     max_priority; // maximum priority for threads
    ...


    // IPC structures
    ...
    struct ipc_port *itk_sself;                         // a send right
    struct exception_action  exc_actions[EXC_TYPES_COUNT]; // exception ports
    struct ipc_port          *itk_host;                 // host port
    struct ipc_port          *itk_bootstrap;            // bootstrap port
    // "registered" ports -- these are inherited across task_create()
    struct ipc_port          *itk_registered[TASK_PORT_REGISTER_MAX];
    struct ipc_space         *itk_space;                // the IPC space
    ...


    // locks and semaphores
    queue_head_t semaphore_list; // list of owned semaphores
    queue_head_t lock_set_list;  // list of owned lock sets
    int          semaphores_owned; // number of owned semaphores
    int          lock_sets_owned;  // number of owned locks
    ...

#ifdef MACH_BSD
    void         *bsd_info;       // pointer to BSD process structure
#endif

    struct shared_region_mapping *system_shared_region;
    struct tws_hash              *dynamic_working_set;
    ...
};
```

The following are examples of Mach task routines accessible through the system library.

- `mach_task_self()` is the task "identity trap"—it returns a send right to the calling task's kernel port. As we saw in Chapter 6, the system library caches the right returned by this call in a per-task variable.

- `pid_for_task()` retrieves the BSD process ID for the task specified by the given port. Note that whereas all BSD processes have a corresponding Mach task, it is technically possible to have a Mach task that is not associated with a BSD process.

- `task_for_pid()` retrieves the port for the task corresponding to the specified BSD process ID.

- `task_info()` retrieves information about the given task. Examples of `task_info()` flavors include `TASK_BASIC_INFO` (suspend count, virtual memory size, resident memory size, and so on), `TASK_THREAD_TIMES_INFO` (total times for live threads), and `TASK_EVENTS_INFO` (page faults, system calls, context switches, and so on).

- `task_threads()` returns an array of send rights to the kernel ports of all threads within the given task.

- `task_create()` creates a new Mach task that either inherits the calling task's address space or is created with an empty address space. The calling task gets access to the kernel port of the newly created task, which contains no threads. Note that this call does not create a BSD process and as such is not useful from user space.

- `task_suspend()` increments the *suspend count* for the given task, stopping all threads within the task. Newly created threads within a task cannot execute if the task's suspend count is positive.

- `task_resume()` decrements the suspend count for the given task. If the new suspend count is zero, `task_resume()` also resumes those threads within the task whose suspend counts are zero. The task suspend count cannot become negative—it is either zero (runnable task) or positive (suspended task).

- `task_terminate()` kills the given task and all threads within it. The task's resources are deallocated.

- `task_get_exception_ports()` retrieves send rights to a specified set of *exception ports* for the given task. An exception port is one to which the kernel sends messages when one or more types of exceptions occur. Note that threads can have their own exception ports, which are preferred over the task's. Only if a thread-level exception port is set to the null port (`IP_NULL`), or returns with a failure, does the task-level exception port come into play.

- `task_set_exception_ports()` sets the given task's exception ports.

- `task_swap_exception_ports()` performs the combined function of `task_get_exception_ports()` and `task_set_exception_ports()`.

- `task_get_special_port()` retrieves a send right to the given special port in a task. Examples of special ports include `TASK_KERNEL_PORT` (the same as the port returned by `mach_task_self()`—used for controlling the task), `TASK_BOOTSTRAP_PORT` (used in requests for retrieving ports representing system services), and `TASK_HOST_NAME_PORT` (the same as the port returned by `mach_host_self()`—used for retrieving host-related information).

- `task_set_special_port()` sets one of the task's special ports to the given send right.
- `task_policy_get()` retrieves scheduling policy parameters for the specified task. It can also be used to retrieve default task policy parameter values.
- `task_policy_set()` is used to set scheduling policy information for a task.

7.2.5 Threads

A Mach thread is a single flow of control in a Mach task. Depending on an application's nature and architecture, using multiple threads within the application can lead to improved performance. Examples of situations in which multiple threads could be beneficial include the following.

- When computation and I/O can be separated and are mutually independent, dedicated threads can be used to perform these two types of activities simultaneously.
- When execution contexts—threads or processes—need to be created and destroyed frequently, using threads may improve performance since a thread is substantially less expensive to create than an entire process.[7]
- On a multiprocessor system, multiple threads within the same task can run truly concurrently, which improves performance if the thread can benefit from concurrent computations.

A thread contains information such as the following:

- Scheduling priority, scheduling policy, and related attributes
- Processor usage statistics
- A few thread-specific port rights, including the thread's kernel port and thread-level exception ports (corresponding to thread-level exception handlers)

---

7. The performance improvement will typically be perceptible only if the application creates so many processes (or creates them in such a manner) that the overhead is a limiting factor in the application's performance.

- Machine state (through a machine-dependent thread-state structure), which changes as the thread executes

Figure 7–10 shows the important constituents of the thread structure in xnu.

FIGURE 7–10 The thread structure in the xnu kernel

```
// osfmk/kern/thread.h

struct thread {
    queue_chain_t       links;          // run/wait queue links
    run_queue_t         runq;           // run queue thread is on
    wait_queue_t        wait_queue;     // wait queue we are currently on
    event64_t           wait_event;     // wait queue event
    ...
    thread_continue_t   continuation;   // continue here next dispatch
    void                *parameter;     // continuation parameter
    ...
    vm_offset_t         kernel_stack;   // current kernel stack
    vm_offset_t         reserved_stack; // reserved kernel stack

    int                 state;          // state that thread is in

    // scheduling information
    ...
    // various bits of stashed machine-independent state
    ...
    // IPC data structures
    ...
    // AST/halt data structures
    ...
    // processor set information
    ...

    queue_chain_t          task_threads; // threads in our task
    struct machine_thread  machine;      // machine-dependent state
    struct task            *task;        // containing task
    vm_map_t               map;          // containing task's address map
    ...

    // mutex, suspend count, stop count, pending thread ASTs
    ...
    // other
    ...
```

(continues)

FIGURE 7–10 The `thread` structure in the xnu kernel *(continued)*

```
struct ipc_port       *ith_sself;              // a send right
struct exception_action  exc_actions[EXC_TYPES_COUNT]; // exception ports
...

#ifdef     MACH_BSD
    void *uthread; // per-thread user structure
#endif
};
```

7.2.5.1 The Thread API

A user program controls a Mach thread—normally indirectly, through the Pthreads library[8]—using the thread's kernel port. The following are examples of Mach thread routines accessible through the system library.

- `mach_thread_self()` returns send rights to the calling thread's kernel port.

- `thread_info()` retrieves information about the given thread. Examples of `thread_info()` flavors include `THREAD_BASIC_INFO` (user and system run times, scheduling policy in effect, suspend count, and so on) and obsoleted flavors for fetching scheduling policy information, such as `THREAD_SCHED_FIFO_INFO`, `THREAD_SCHED_RR_INFO`, and `THREAD_SCHED_TIMESHARE_INFO`.

- `thread_get_state()` retrieves the machine-specific user-mode execution state for the given thread, which must not be the calling thread itself. Depending on the flavor, the returned state contains different sets of machine-specific register contents. Flavor examples include `PPC_THREAD_STATE`, `PPC_FLOAT_STATE`, `PPC_EXCEPTION_STATE`, `PPC_VECTOR_STATE`, `PPC_THREAD_STATE64`, and `PPC_EXCEPTION_STATE64`.

- `thread_set_state()` is the converse of `thread_get_state()`—it takes the given user-mode execution state information and flavor type and sets the target thread's state. Again, the calling thread cannot set its own state using this routine.

- `thread_create()` creates a thread within the given task. The newly created thread has a suspend count of one. It has no machine state—its state

---

8. The Pthreads library is part of the system library (`libSystem.dylib`) on Mac OS X.

must be explicitly set by calling `thread_set_state()` before the thread can be resumed by calling `thread_resume()`.

- `thread_create_running()` combines the effect of `thread_create()`, `thread_set_state()`, and `thread_resume()`: It creates a running thread using the given machine state within the given task.

- `thread_suspend()` increments the suspend count of the given thread. As long as the suspend count is greater than zero, the thread cannot execute any more user-level instructions. If the thread was already executing within the kernel because of a trap (such as a system call or a page fault), then, depending on the trap, it may block in situ, or it may continue executing until the trap is about to return to user space. Nevertheless, the trap will return only on resumption of the thread. Note that a thread is created in the suspended state so that its machine state can be set appropriately.

- `thread_resume()` decrements the suspend count of the given thread. If the decremented count becomes zero, the thread is resumed. Note that if a task's suspend count is greater than zero, a thread within it cannot execute even if the thread's individual suspend count is zero. Similar to the task suspend count, a thread's suspend count is either zero or positive.

- `thread_terminate()` destroys the given thread. If the thread is the last thread to terminate in a task that corresponds to a BSD process, the thread termination code also performs a BSD process exit.

- `thread_switch()` instructs the scheduler to switch context directly to another thread. The caller can also specify a particular thread as a hint, in which case the scheduler will attempt to switch to the specified thread. Several conditions must hold for the hinted switch to succeed. For example, the hint thread's scheduling priority must not be real time, and it should not be bound to a processor—if at all—other than the current processor. Note that this is an example of *handoff scheduling*, as the caller's quantum is handed off to the new thread. If no hint thread is specified, `thread_switch()` forces a reschedule, and a new thread is selected to run. The caller's existing kernel stack is discarded—when it eventually resumes, it executes the continuation function[9] `thread_switch_continue()` [osfmk/kern/syscall_subr.c] on a new kernel stack. `thread_switch()` can be optionally instructed to block the calling thread for a specified time—a wait that can be canceled

---

9. We will look at continuations later in this chapter.

only by `thread_abort()`. It can also be instructed to depress the thread's priority temporarily by setting its scheduling attributes such that the scheduler provides it with the lowest possible service for the specified time, after which the scheduling depression is aborted. It is also aborted when the current thread is executed next. It can be explicitly aborted through `thread_abort()` or `thread_depress_abort()`.

- `thread_wire()` marks the given thread as privileged such that it can consume physical memory from the kernel's reserved pool when free memory is scarce. Moreover, when such a thread is to be inserted in a wait queue of threads waiting for a particular event to be posted to that queue, it is inserted at the head of the queue. This routine is meant for threads that are directly involved in the page-out mechanism—it should not be invoked by user programs.

- `thread_abort()` can be used by one thread to stop another thread—it aborts a variety of in-progress operations in the target thread, such as clock sleeps, scheduling depressions, page faults, and other Mach message primitive calls (including system calls). If the target thread is in kernel mode, a successful `thread_abort()` will result in the target appearing to have returned from the kernel. For example, in the case of a system call, the thread's execution will resume in the system call return code, with an "interrupted system call" return code. Note that `thread_abort()` works even if the target is suspended—the target will be interrupted when it resumes. In fact, `thread_abort()` should be used only on a thread that is suspended. If the target thread is executing a nonatomic operation when `thread_abort()` is called on it, the operation will be aborted at an arbitrary point and cannot be restarted. `thread_abort()` is meant for cleanly stopping the target. In the case of a call to `thread_suspend()`, if the target is executing in the kernel and the thread's state is modified (through `thread_set_state()`) when it is suspended, the state may be altered unpredictably as a side effect of the system call when the thread resumes.

- `thread_abort_safely()` is similar to `thread_abort()`. However, unlike `thread_abort()`, which aborts even nonatomic operations (at arbitrary points and in a nonrestartable manner), `thread_abort_safely()` returns an error in such cases. The thread must then be resumed, and another `thread_abort_safely()` call must be attempted.

- `thread_get_exception_ports()` retrieves send rights to one or more exception ports of a given thread. The exception types for which to retrieve the ports are specified through a flag word.

- `thread_set_exception_ports()` sets the given port—a send right—as the exception port for the specified exception types. Note that a thread's exception ports are each set to the null port (`IP_NULL`) during thread creation.

- `thread_get_special_port()` returns a send right to a specific special port for the given thread. For example, specifying `THREAD_KERNEL_PORT` returns the target thread's name port—the same as that returned by `mach_thread_self()` within the thread. Thereafter, the port can be used to perform operations on the thread.

- `thread_set_special_port()` sets a specific special port for the given thread by changing it to the caller-provided send right. The old send right is released by the kernel.

- `thread_policy_get()` retrieves scheduling policy parameters for the given thread. It can also be used to retrieve default thread-scheduling policy parameter values.

- `thread_policy_set()` is used to set scheduling policy information for a thread. Examples of thread-scheduling policy flavors include `THREAD_EXTENDED_POLICY`, `THREAD_TIME_CONSTRAINT_POLICY`, and `THREAD_PRECEDENCE_POLICY`.

> A thread can send a port right to another thread—including to a thread in another task—using Mach IPC. In particular, if a thread sends its containing task's kernel port to a thread in another task, a thread in the receiving task can control all threads in the sending task, since access to a task's kernel port implies access to the kernel ports of its threads.

7.2.5.2 Kernel Threads

We could call a Mach thread a *kernel thread* since it is the in-kernel representation of a user-space thread. As we will see in Section 7.3, all commonly available user-space thread abstractions on Mac OS X use one Mach thread per instance of the respective user threads. Another connotation of the term *kernel thread* applies to internal threads that the kernel runs for its own functioning. The following are examples of functions that the kernel runs as dedicated threads[10] to implement kernel functionality such as bootstrapping, scheduling, exception handling, networking, and file system I/O.

---

10. Such threads are created within the kernel task.

- `processor_start_thread()` [osfmk/kern/startup.c] is the first thread to execute on a processor.

- `kernel_bootstrap_thread()` [osfmk/kern/startup.c] starts various kernel services during system startup and eventually becomes the page-out daemon, running `vm_page()` [osfmk/vm/vm_pageout.c]. The latter creates other kernel threads for performing I/O and for garbage collection.

- `idle_thread()` [osfmk/kern/sched_prim.c] is the idle processor thread that runs looking for other threads to execute.

- `sched_tick_thread()` [osfmk/kern/sched_prim.c] performs scheduler-related periodic bookkeeping functions.

- `thread_terminate_daemon()` [osfmk/kern/thread.c] performs the final cleanup for terminating threads.

- `thread_stack_daemon()` [osfmk/kern/thread.c] allocates stacks for threads that have been enqueued for stack allocation.

- `serial_keyboard_poll()` [osfmk/ppc/serial_io.c] polls for input on the serial port.

- The kernel's callout mechanism runs functions supplied to it as kernel threads.

- The `IOWorkLoop` and `IOService` I/O Kit classes use `IOCreateThread()` [iokit/Kernel/IOLib.c], which is a wrapper around a Mach kernel-thread creation function, to create kernel threads.

- The kernel's asynchronous I/O (AIO) mechanism creates worker threads to handle I/O requests.

- `audit_worker()` [bsd/kern/kern_audit.c] processes the queue of audit records by writing them to the audit log file or otherwise removing them from the queue.

- `mbuf_expand_thread()` [bsd/kern/uipc_mbuf.c] runs to add more free mbufs by allocating an mbuf cluster.

- `ux_handler()` [bsd/uxkern/ux_exception.c] is the Unix exception handler that converts Mach exceptions to Unix signal and code values.

- `nfs_bind_resv_thread()` [bsd/nfs/nfs_socket.c] runs to handle bind requests on reserved ports from unprivileged processes.

- `dlil_input_thread()` [bsd/net/dlil.c] services mbuf input queues of network interfaces, including that of the loopback interface, by ingesting network packets via `dlil_input_packet()` [bsd/net/dlil.c]. It also calls `proto_input_run()` to perform protocol-level packet injection.

- `dlil_call_delayed_detach_thread()` [bsd/net/dlil.c] performs delayed (safe) detachment of protocols, filters, and interface filters.

- `bcleanbuf_thread()` [bsd/vfs/vfs_bio.c] performs file system buffer laundry—it cleans dirty buffers enqueued on a to-be-cleaned queue by writing them to disk.

- `bufqscan_thread()` [bsd/vfs/vfs_bio.c] balances a portion of the buffer queues by issuing cleanup of buffers and by releasing cleaned buffers to the queue of empty buffers.

Figure 7–11 shows the high-level kernel functions involved in kernel thread creation. Of these, `kernel_thread()` and `IOCreateThread()` should be used from Mach and the I/O Kit, respectively.

As we will see in Section 7.3, various user-space application environments in Mac OS X use their own thread abstractions, all of which are eventually layered atop Mach threads.

7.2.6 Thread-Related Abstractions

Let us now look at a few related abstractions that are relevant in the context of Mach threads as implemented in the Mac OS X kernel. In this section, we will discuss the following terms:

- Remote procedure call (RPC)
- Thread activation
- Thread shuttle
- Thread migration
- Continuations

7.2.6.1 Remote Procedure Call

Since Mach is a communication-oriented kernel, the *remote procedure call* (RPC) abstraction is fundamental to Mach's functioning. We define RPC to be the procedure call abstraction when the caller and the callee are in different tasks—that is, the procedure is remote from the caller's standpoint. Although Mac OS X uses only kernel-level RPC between local tasks, the concept is similar even if RPC participants are on different machines. In a typical RPC scenario, execution (control flow) temporarily moves to another location (that corresponding to the

```
// osfmk/kern/thread.c
thread_t
kernel_thread(task_t task,
              void (*start)(void))
{
    kern_result_t result;
    thread_t       thread;

    if (task != kernel_task)
        panic("kernel_thread");

    result = kernel_thread_start_priority(
            (thread_continue_t)start,
            NULL, -1, &thread);
    ...
    return (thread);
}
```

```
// iokit/Kernel/IOLib.c
IOThread
IOCreateThread(
    IOThreadFunc fcn, void *arg)
{
    kern_return_t result;
    thread_t       thread;

    result = kernel_thread_start(
            (thread_continue_t)fcn,
            arg, &thread);
    ...
    return (thread);
}
```

```
// osfmk/kern/thread.c
kern_return_t
kernel_thread_start(
    thread_continue_t  continuation,
    void               *parameter,
    thread_t           *new_thread)
{
    return kernel_thread_start_priority(
            continuation,
            parameter,
            -1, new_thread);
}
```

```
// osfmk/kern/thread.c
kern_return_t
kernel_thread_start_priority(
    thread_continue_t  continuation,
    void               *parameter,
    integer_t          priority,
    thread_t           *new_thread)
{
    kern_result_t result;
    thread_t       thread;

    result = kernel_thread_create(
            continuation,
            parameter,
            priority,
            &thread);
    ...
    *new_thread = thread;

    return (result);
}
```

```
// osfmk/kern/thread.c
kern_return_t
kernel_thread_create(
    thread_continue_t continuation,
    void *parameter,
    integer_t priority
    thread_t *new_thread)
{
    kern_result_t result;
    thread_t thread;
    task_t task = kernel_task;

    result = thread_create_internal(
            task, priority,
            continuation, &thread);
    ...
    *new_thread = thread;

    return (result);
}
```

```
// osfmk/kern/thread.c
static kern_return_t
thread_create_internal(
    task_t             parent_task,
    integer_t          priority,
    thread_continue_t  continuation,
    thread_t           *out_thread)
{
    /* core work of thread creation */
}
```

FIGURE 7–11 Functions for creating kernel threads

remote procedure) and later returns to the original location—akin to a system call. The caller (client) marshals any parameters together into a message and sends the message to the service provider (server). The service provider unmarshals the message—that is, separates it into its original pieces and processes it as a local operation.

7.2.6.2 Activation and Shuttle

Prior to Mac OS X 10.4, a kernel thread was divided into two logical parts: the *activation* and the *shuttle*. The motivation behind the division is to have one part that provides explicit control over the thread (the activation) and another part that is used by the scheduler (the shuttle). The thread activation represents the execution context of a thread. It remains attached to its task and thus always has a fixed, valid task pointer. Until the activation is terminated, it remains on the task's activation stack.[11] The thread shuttle is the scheduled entity corresponding to a thread. At a given time, a shuttle operates within some activation. However, a shuttle may migrate during RPC because of resource contention. It contains scheduling, accounting, and timing information. It also contains messaging support. While a shuttle uses an activation, it holds a reference on the activation.

Note that the activation is closer to the popular notion of a thread—it is the externally visible thread handle. For example, a thread's programmer-visible kernel port internally translates to a pointer to its activation. In contrast, the shuttle is the internal part of a thread. Within the kernel, `current_act()` returns a pointer to the current activation, whereas `current_thread()` returns a pointer to the shuttle.

The shuttle/activation dual abstraction has undergone implementation changes across various Mac OS X versions. In Mac OS X 10.0, a thread's implementation consisted of two primary data structures: the `thread_shuttle` structure and the `thread_activation` structure, with the thread data type (`thread_t`) being a pointer to the `thread_shuttle` structure. The activation could be accessed from the shuttle, and thus a `thread_t` represented a thread in its entirety. Figure 7–12 shows the structures in Mac OS X 10.0.

In later versions of Mac OS X, the thread data structure subsumed both the shuttle and the activation—from a syntactic standpoint—into a single structure. This is shown in Figure 7–13.

---

11. A thread, as a logical flow of control, is represented by a stack of activations in a task.

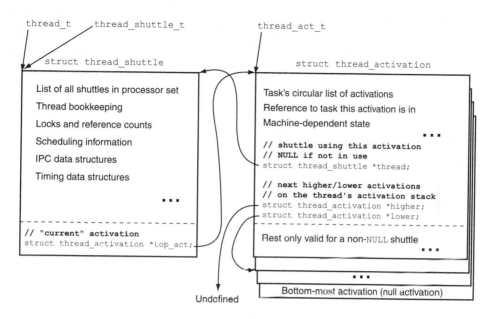

FIGURE 7–12 The shuttle and thread data structures in Mac OS X 10.0

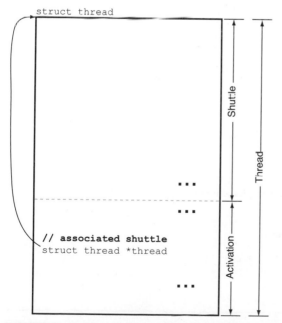

FIGURE 7–13 The shuttle and the thread within a single structure in Mac OS X 10.3

In Mac OS X 10.4, the distinction between shuttle and activation is not present. Figure 7–14 shows the implementation of `current_thread()` and `current_act()` in Mac OS X 10.3 and 10.4. In the x86 version of Mac OS X, a pointer to the current (active) thread is stored as a field of the per-cpu data structure[12] (`struct cpu_data [osfmk/i386/cpu_data.h]`).

FIGURE 7–14 Retrieving the current thread (shuttle) and the current activation on Mac OS X 10.3 and 10.4

```
// osfmk/ppc/cpu_data.h (Mac OS X 10.3)

extern __inline__ thread_act_t current_act(void)
{
    thread_act_t act;
    __asm__ volatile("mfsprg %0,1" : "=r" (act));
    return act;
};
...
#define current_thread() current_act()->thread


// osfmk/ppc/cpu_data.h (Mac OS X 10.4)

extern __inline__ thread_t current_thread(void)
{
    thread_t result;
    __asm__ volatile("mfsprg %0,1" : "=r" (result));
    return (result);
}


// osfmk/ppc/machine_routines_asm.s (Mac OS X 10.4)

/*
 * thread_t current_thread(void)
 * thread_t current_act(void)
 *
 * Return the current thread for outside components.
 */
            align   5
            .globl  EXT(current_thread)
            .globl  EXT(current_act)
LEXT(current_thread)
LEXT(current_act)
            mfsprg  r3,1
            blr
```

---

12. The GS segment register is set up such that it is based at the per-cpu data structure.

7.2.6.3 Thread Migration

In the preceding discussion of the shuttle and the activation, we alluded to the concept of thread migration. The migrating threads model was developed at the University of Utah. The term *migration* refers to the way control is transferred between a client and a server during an RPC. For example, in the case of static threads, an RPC between a client and a server involves a client thread and an unrelated, independent server thread. The sequence of events after the client initiates an RPC involves multiple context switches, among other things. With the split thread model, rather than blocking the client thread on its RPC kernel call, the kernel can migrate it so that it resumes execution in the server's code. Although some context switch is still required (in particular, that of the address space, the stack pointer, and perhaps a subset of the register state), no longer are two entire threads involved. There also is no context switch from a scheduling standpoint. Morcover, the client uses its own processor time while it executes in the server's code—in this sense, thread migration is a *priority inheritance* mechanism.

This can be compared to the Unix system call model, where a user thread (or process) migrates into the kernel during a system call, without a full-fledged context switch.

Procedural IPC

Mach's original RPC model is based on message-passing facilities, wherein distinct threads read messages and write replies. We have seen that access rights are communicated in Mach through messaging as well. Operating systems have supported procedural IPC in several forms: gates in Multics, lightweight RPC (LRPC) in TaOS, doors in Solaris, and event pairs in Windows NT are examples of cross-domain procedure call mechanisms. The thread model in Sun's Spring system had the concept of a shuttle, which was the true kernel-schedulable entity that supported a chain of application-visible threads—analogous to the activations we discussed.

7.2.6.4 Continuations

The Mac OS X kernel uses a per-thread kernel stack size of 16KB (KERNEL_STACK_SIZE, defined in osfmk/mach/ppc/vm_param.h). As the number of threads in a running system increases, the memory consumed by kernel stacks alone can become unreasonable, depending on available resources. Some operating systems multiplex several user threads onto one kernel thread, albeit at the cost of concurrency, since those user threads cannot be scheduled independently of each other. Recall that a Mach thread (or an activation, when a thread is divided into a shuttle and an activation) is bound to its task for the lifetime of the thread, and that each nontrivial task has at least one thread. Therefore, the number of threads in the system will at least be as many as the number of tasks.

Operating systems have historically used one of two models for kernel execution: the *process model* or the *interrupt model*. In the process model, the kernel maintains a stack for every thread. When a thread executes within the kernel—say, because of a system call or an exception—its dedicated kernel stack is used to track its execution state. If the thread blocks in the kernel, no explicit state saving is required, as the state is captured in the thread's kernel stack. The simplifying effect of this approach is offset by its higher resource requirement and the fact that machine state is harder to evaluate if one were to analyze it for optimizing transfer control between threads. In the interrupt model, the kernel treats system calls and exceptions as interrupts. A per-processor kernel stack is used for all threads' kernel execution. This requires kernel-blocking threads to explicitly save their execution state somewhere. When resuming the thread at a later point, the kernel will use the saved state.

The typical UNIX kernel used the process model, and so did early versions of Mach. The concept of *continuations* was used in Mach 3 as a middle-ground approach that gives a blocking thread an option to use either the interrupt or the process model. Mac OS X continues to use continuations. Consequently, a blocking thread in the Mac OS X kernel can choose how to block. The thread_block() function [osfmk/kern/sched_prim.c] takes a single argument, which can be either THREAD_CONTINUE_NULL [osfmk/kern/kern_types.h] or a continuation function.

// osfmk/kern/kern_types.h

```
typedef void (*thread_continue_t)(void *, wait_result_t);
#define THREAD_CONTINUE_NULL    ((thread_continue_t) 0)
...
```

thread_block() calls thread_block_reason() [osfmk/kern/sched_prim.c], which calls thread_invoke() [osfmk/kern/sched_prim.c] to perform a context switch and start executing a new thread selected for the current processor to run. thread_invoke() checks whether a valid continuation was specified. If so, it will attempt[13] to hand off the old thread's kernel stack to the new thread. Therefore, as the old thread blocks, its stack-based context is discarded. When the original thread resumes, it will be given a new kernel stack, on which the continuation function will execute. The `thread_block_parameter()` [`osfmk/kern/sched_prim.c`] variant accepts a single parameter that `thread_block_reason()` stores in the `thread` structure, from where it is retrieved and passed to the continuation function when the latter runs.

Threading code must be explicitly written to use continuations. Consider the example shown in Figure 7–15: `someFunc()` needs to block for some event, after which it calls `someOtherFunc()` with an argument. In the interrupt model, the thread must save the argument somewhere—perhaps in a structure that will persist as the thread blocks and resumes (the `thread` structure itself can be used for this purpose in some cases) and will block using a continuation. Note that a thread uses the `assert_wait()` primitive to declare the event it wishes to wait on and then calls `thread_block()` to actually wait.

FIGURE 7–15 Blocking with and without continuations

```
someOtherFunc(someArg)
{
    ...
    return;
}

#ifdef USE_PROCESS_MODEL

someFunc(someArg)
{
    ...
    // Assert that the current thread is about to block until the
    // specified event occurs
    assert_wait(...);

    // Pause to let whoever catch up
    // Relinquish the processor by blocking "normally"
    thread_block(THREAD_CONTINUE_NULL);

    // Call someOtherFunc() to do some more work
    someOtherFunc(someArg);
```

(continues)

---

13. A thread with a real-time scheduling policy does not hand off its stack.

FIGURE 7–15 Blocking with and without continuations *(continued)*

```
    return;
}

#else // interrupt model, use continuations

someFunc(someArg)
{
    ...
    // Assert that the current thread is about to block until the
    // specified event occurs
    assert_wait(...);

    // "someArg", and any other state that someOtherFunc() will require, must
    // be saved somewhere, since this thread's kernel stack will be discarded

    // Pause to let whoever catch up
    // Relinquish the processor using a continuation
    // someOtherFunc() will be called when the thread resumes
    thread_block(someOtherFunc);

    /* NOTREACHED */
}

#endif
```

A function specified as a continuation cannot return normally. It may call only other functions or continuations. Moreover, a thread that uses a continuation must save any state that might be needed after resuming. This state may be saved in a dedicated space that the `thread` structure or an associated structure might have, or the blocking thread may have to allocate additional memory for this purpose. The continuation function must know how the blocking thread stores this state. Let us consider two examples of continuations being used in the kernel.

The implementation of the `select()` system call on Mac OS X uses continuations. Each BSD thread—that is, a thread belonging to a task with an associated BSD `proc` structure—has an associated `uthread` structure, which is akin to the traditional u-area. The `uthread` structure stores miscellaneous information, including system call parameters and results. It also has space for storing saved state for the `select()` system call. Figure 7–16 shows this structure's relevant aspects.

FIGURE 7–16 Continuation-related aspects of the BSD `uthread` structure

```
// bsd/sys/user.h

struct uthread {
    ...
    // saved state for select()
    struct _select {
        u_int32_t *ibits, *obits; // bits to select on
        uint       nbytes;        // number of bytes in ibits and obits
        ...
    } uu_select;

    union {
        // saved state for nfsd
        int uu_nfs_myiods;

        // saved state for kevent_scan()
        struct _kevent_scan {
            kevent_callback_t call;   // per-event callback
            kevent_continue_t cont;   // whole call continuation
            uint64_t          deadline; // computed deadline for operation
            void              *data;  // caller's private data
        } ss_kevent_scan;

        // saved state for kevent()
        struct _kevent {
            ...
            int          fd;       // file descriptor for kq
            register_t   *retval;  // for storing the return value
            ...
        } ss_kevent;
    } uu_state;

    int (* uu_continuation)(int);
    ...
};
```

When a thread calls `select()` [bsd/kern/sys_generic.c] for the first time, `select()` allocates space for the descriptor set bit fields. On subsequent invocations, it may reallocate this space if it is not sufficient for the current request. It then calls `selprocess()` [bsd/kern/sys_generic.c], which, depending on the conditions, calls `tsleep1()` [bsd/kern/kern_synch.c], with `selcontinue()` [bsd/kern/sys_generic.c] specified as the continuation function. Figure 7–17 shows how the `select()` implementation uses continuations.

FIGURE 7–17 The use of continuations in the implementation of the `select()` system call

```
// bsd/kern/sys_generic.c

int
select(struct proc *p, struct select_args *uap, register_t *retval)
{
    ...
    thread_t        th_act;
    struct uthread *uth
    struct _select *sel;
    ...

    th_act = current_thread();
    uth = get_bsdthread_info(th_act);
    sel = &uth->uu_select;
    ...

    // if this is the first select by the thread, allocate space for bits
    if (sel->nbytes == 0) {
        // allocate memory for sel->ibits and sel->obits
    }

    // if the previously allocated space for the bits is smaller than
    // is requested, reallocate
    if (sel->nbytes < (3 * ni)) {
        // free and reallocate
    }

    // do select-specific processing
    ...

continuation:
    return selprocess(error, SEL_FIRSTPASS);
}

int
selcontinue(int error)
{
    return selprocess(error, SEL_SECONDPASS);
}

int
selprocess(int error, int sel_pass)
{
    // various conditions and processing
    ...
    error = tsleep(NULL, PSOCK|PCATCH, "select", sel->abstime, selcontinue);
    ...
}
```

tsleep1() [bsd/kern/kern_synch.c] calls _sleep() [bsd/kern/kern_synch.c], which saves the relevant state in the uthread structure and blocks using the _sleep_continue() continuation. The latter retrieves the saved state from the uthread structure.

// bsd/kern/kern_synch.c

```
static int
_sleep(caddr_t    chan,
     int          pri,
     char         *wmsg,
     u_int64_t  abstime,
     int (* continuation)(int),
     lck_mtx_t *mtx)
{
    ...
    if ((thread_continue_t)continuation !=
        THREAD_CONTINUE_NULL) {
        ut->uu_continuation = continuation;
        ut->uu_pri = pri;
        ut->uu_timo = abstime ? 1 : 0;
        ut->uu_mtx = mtx;
        (void)thread_block(_sleep_continue);
        /* NOTREACHED */
    }
    ...
}
```

Let us look at another example—that of nfsiod, which implements a throughput-improving optimization for NFS clients. nfsiod is a local NFS asynchronous I/O server that runs on an NFS client machine to service asynchronous I/O requests to its server. It is a user-space program, with the skeletal structure shown in Figure 7–18.

FIGURE 7–18 The skeleton of the nfsiod program

// nfsiod.c

```
int
main(argc, argv)
{
    ...
    for (i = 0; i < num_servers; i++) {
        ...
        rv = pthread_create(&thd, NULL, nfsiod_thread, (void *)i);
```

(continues)

FIGURE 7–18 The skeleton of the `nfsiod` program *(continued)*

```
        . . .
    }
}

. . .

void *
nfsiod_thread(void *arg)
{
    . . .
    if ((rv = nfssvc(NFSSVC_BIOD, NULL)) < 0) {
        . . .
    }
    . . .
}
```

`nfssvc()` [`bsd/nfs/nfs_syscalls.c`] is an NFS system call used by both `nfsiod` and `nfsd`, the NFS daemon, to enter the kernel. Thereafter, `nfsiod` and `nfsd` essentially become in-kernel servers. In the case of `nfsiod`, `nfssvc()` dispatches to `nfssvc_iod()` [`bsd/nfs/nfs_syscalls.c`].

// bsd/nfs/nfs_syscalls.c

```
int
nfssvc(proc_t p, struct nfssvc_args *uap, __unused int *retval)
{
    . . .
    if (uap->flag & NFSSVC_BIOD)
        error = nfssvc_iod(p);
    . . .
}
```

`nfssvc_iod()` determines the index of the would-be `nfsiod` in a global array of such daemons. It saves the index in the uu_nfs_myiod field of the uu_state union within the uthread structure. Thereafter, it calls nfssvc_iod_continue(), which is `nfsiod`'s continuation function.

// bsd/nfs/nfs_syscalls.c

```
static int
nfsscv_iod(__unused proc_t p)
{
    register int    i, myiod;
    struct uthread *ut,
```

```
    // assign my position or return error if too many already running
    myiod = -1;
    for (i = 0; i < NFS_MAXASYNCDAEMON; i++)
        ...

    // stuff myiod into uthread to get off local stack for continuation
    ut = (struct uthread *)get_bsdthread_info(current_thread());
    ut->uu_state.uu_nfs_myiod = myiod; // stow away for continuation

    nfssvc_iod_continue(0):
    /* NOTREACHED */
    return (0);
}
```

nfssvc_iod_continue() retrieves the daemon's index from its saved location in the uthread structure, performs the necessary processing, and blocks on the continuation—that is, on itself.

```
// bsd/nfs/nfs_syscalls.c

static int
nfssvc_iod_continue(int error)
{
    register struct nfsbuf *bp;
    register int            i, myiod;
    struct nfsmount         *nmp;
    struct uthread          *ut;
    proc_t                  p;

    // real myiod is stored in uthread, recover it
    ut = (struct uthread *)get_bsdthread_info(current_thread());
    myiod = ut->uu_state.uu_nfs_myiod;
    ...
    for (;;) {
        while (...) {
            ...
            error = msleep0((caddr_t)&nfs_iodwant[myiod],
                            nfs_iod_mutex,
                            PWAIT | PCATCH | PDROP,
                            "ntsidl",
                            0,
                            nfssvc_iod_continue);
            ...
        }
        if (error) {
            ...
            // must use this function to return to user
            unix_syscall_return(error);
        }
        ...
    }
}
```

Continuations are most useful in the cases where no or little state needs to be saved for a thread when it is blocking. Other examples of the use of continuations in the Mac OS X kernel include continuations for per-processor idle threads, the scheduler tick thread, the swap-in thread, and the page-out daemon.

7.3 Many Threads of a New System

Mac OS X was not designed from scratch by one team: It came to be as a conglomeration of vastly different technologies from numerous sources. As a commercial operating system with both legacy and new-adopter user bases to support initially, with a wide spectrum of user needs, Mac OS X includes an unusually large number of mechanisms and interfaces. The user-visible process subsystem is a good example of this phenomenon. Mac OS X has several flavors of user-level threads and processes, depending on the application environment in use. Examples include the following:

- A Mach thread created within the kernel task, for the kernel's own use
- A single-threaded BSD process created using the `fork()` system call
- A multithreaded BSD process originally created using the `fork()` system call, followed by the creation of one or more additional threads created using the Pthreads API
- Multiple Java threads in a Java application created using the `java.lang.Thread` API
- A subprocess created using the Cocoa NSTask API
- A thread created using the Cocoa NSThread API
- A Carbon Process Manager (CPM) process created by using the `LaunchApplication()` Carbon API call
- Preemptively scheduled tasks created in an application using Carbon Multiprocessing Services
- Cooperatively scheduled threads created in an application using Carbon Thread Manager
- A thread running in the Classic environment

In this section, we will look at specific examples of some of these flavors. At this juncture, the following general points can be noted regarding threads in Mac OS X.

- The kernel knows about only one type of thread: the Mach thread. Thus, any user-visible entity that runs eventually runs as a Mach thread, although a user library managing that entity may layer multiple such entities atop one Mach thread, running one of them at a time. Note that within the kernel, some threads may be specially designated, such as a Blue thread for Classic, a thread running a virtual machine, a VM-privileged thread, and so on.

- A first-class process-like entity visible to the user typically has a corresponding BSD process and, in turn, a corresponding Mach task.

- A first-class thread-like entity visible to the user typically has a corresponding pthread and, in turn, a corresponding Mach thread.

> We say "typically" and not "always" as it is technically possible to create a Mach task without a BSD process, and a Mach thread without a pthread. There may be other exceptions; for example, the entire Classic environment, along with all its Process Manager processes, corresponds to one BSD process.

7.3.1 Mach Tasks and Threads

In previous sections, we saw examples of routines in Mach's task and thread management interfaces. Let us now use these interfaces in some examples to illustrate their working.

> The Mach task and thread client APIs should not be used by user programs. Surely, unless you are implementing, say, a threading package to replace Pthreads, there is no normally justifiable reason for a program to create Mach tasks or threads directly.

7.3.1.1 Creating a Mach Task

In this example, we will create a Mach task using the `task_create()` call. The new task will have no threads and can optionally inherit memory from its parent task. Recall that Mach tasks do not have parent-child relationships. Specifically, the `task` structure does not contain information about either the parent task or the child tasks, if any, of that task. Parent-child information is maintained at the BSD level. However, in this case, since we will bypass the BSD layer, there will be no BSD `proc` structure—and correspondingly no process ID—for the new task.

Figure 7–19 shows the program. When run with no arguments, or with a single argument 0, it does not inherit the parent task's inheritable address space. In this case, the task is created with a virtual size of zero, corresponding to an empty address space.

FIGURE 7–19 Creating a Mach task

```
// task_create.c

#include <stdio.h>
#include <stdlib.h>
#include <mach/mach.h>

int
main(int argc, char **argv)
{
    kern_return_t          kr;
    pid_t                  pid;
    task_t                 child_task;
    ledger_t               ledgers;
    ledger_array_t         ledger_array;
    mach_msg_type_number_t ledger_count;
    boolean_t              inherit = TRUE;
    task_info_data_t       info;
    mach_msg_type_number_t count;
    struct task_basic_info *task_basic_info;

    if (argc == 2)
        inherit = (atoi(argv[1])) ? TRUE : FALSE;

    // have the kernel use the parent task's ledger
    ledger_count = 1;
    ledgers = (ledger_t)0;
    ledger_array = &ledgers;

    // create the new task
    kr = task_create(mach_task_self(), // prototype (parent) task
                     ledger_array,      // resource ledgers
                     ledger_count,      // number of ledger ports
                     inherit,           // inherit memory?
                     &child_task);      // port for new task
    if (kr != KERN_SUCCESS) {
        mach_error("task_create:", kr);
        exit(1);
    }
```

(continues)

FIGURE 7–19 Creating a Mach task *(continued)*

```
    // get information on the new task
    count = TASK_INFO_MAX;
    kr = task_info(child_task, TASK_BASIC_INFO, (task_info_t)info, &count);
    if (kr != KERN_SUCCESS)
        mach_error("task_info:", kr);
    else {
        // there should be no BSD process ID
        kr = pid_for_task(child_task, &pid);
        if (kr != KERN_SUCCESS)
            mach_error("pid_for_task:", kr);

        task_basic_info = (struct task_basic_info *)info;
        printf("pid %d, virtual sz %d KB, resident sz %d KB\n", pid,
                task_basic_info->virtual_size >> 10,
                task_basic_info->resident_size >> 10);
    }

    kr = task_terminate(child_task);
    if (kr != KERN_SUCCESS)
        mach_error("task_terminate:", kr);

    exit(0);
}


$ gcc -Wall -o task_create task_create.c
$ ./task_create 1
pid_for_task: (os/kern) failure
pid -1, virtual sz 551524 KB, resident sz 4 KB
$ ./task_create 0
pid_for_task: (os/kern) failure
pid -1, virtual sz 0 KB, resident sz 0 KB
```

Resource Ledgers

Note that task_create() requires an array of ports representing *resource ledgers* from which the task is supposed to draw its resources. A resource ledger is a kernel abstraction used for resource accounting—it provides a mechanism to control the use of specific resources by one or more tasks. Although the Mac OS X kernel implements the ledger interface, the mechanism is not functional.

A new Mach task is normally created during a fork() or an execve() that follows a vfork(). A user program should not call task_create().

7.3.1.2 *Creating a Mach Thread in an Existing Task*

In this example, we will use Mach thread interface functions to create a new thread, set up its machine state, and set it running. Normally, pthread_create(), which is implemented in the system library, calls thread_create() to create a Mach thread. Moreover, pthread_create() initializes or associates various Pthreads-related data items with the thread. Invocations of several functions in the system library result in these data items being referenced. Since we will directly call thread_create(), there will be no corresponding pthread. The program shown in Figure 7–20 creates a thread that executes a trivial function and exits. Depending on the Mac OS X version, the program may fail when the trivial function calls printf(), since the latter's implementation may reference the calling thread's pthread context, which would be nonexistent in this case.

FIGURE 7–20 Creating a Mach thread

```
// thread_create.c

#include <stdio.h>
#include <stdlib.h>
#include <mach/mach.h>
#include <architecture/ppc/cframe.h>

void my_thread_setup(thread_t t);
void my_thread_exit(void);
void my_thread_routine(int, char *);

static uintptr_t threadStack[PAGE_SIZE];

#define EXIT_ON_MACH_ERROR(msg, retval) \
    if (kr != KERN_SUCCESS) { mach_error(msg ":" , kr); exit((retval)); }

int
main(int argc, char **argv)
{
    thread_t        th;
    kern_return_t   kr;
    mach_port_name_t mytask, mythread;

    mytask = mach_task_self();
    mythread = mach_thread_self();

    // create new thread within our task
    kr = thread_create(mytask, &th);
    EXIT_ON_MACH_ERROR("thread_create", kr);
```

(continues)

FIGURE 7–20 Creating a Mach thread *(continued)*

```
    // set up the new thread's user mode execution state
    my_thread_setup(th);

    // run the new thread
    kr = thread_resume(th);
    EXIT_ON_MACH_ERROR("thread_resume", kr);

    // new thread will call exit
    // note that we still have an undiscarded reference on mythread
    thread_suspend(mythread);

    /* NOTREACHED */

    exit(0);
}

void
my_thread_setup(thread_t th)
{
    kern_return_t           kr;
    mach_msg_type_number_t  count;
    ppc_thread_state_t      state;
    void                    *stack = threadStack;

    // arguments to my_thread_routine() -- the function run by the new thread
    int arg1 = 16;
    char *arg2 = "Hello, Mach!";

    stack += (PAGE_SIZE - C_ARGSAVE_LEN - C_RED_ZONE);

    count = PPC_THREAD_STATE_COUNT;
    kr = thread_get_state(th,                 // target thread
                      PPC_THREAD_STATE, // flavor of thread state
                      (thread_state_t)&state, &count);
    EXIT_ON_MACH_ERROR("thread_get_state", kr);

    //// setup of machine-dependent thread state (PowerPC)

    state.srr0 = (unsigned int)my_thread_routine; // where to begin execution
    state.r1 = (uintptr_t)stack; // stack pointer
    state.r3 = arg1;             // first argument to my_thread_routine()
    state.r4 = (uintptr_t)arg2;  // second argument to my_thread_routine()
    // "return address" for my_thread_routine()
    state.lr = (unsigned int)my_thread_exit;

    kr = thread_set_state(th, PPC_THREAD_STATE, (thread_state_t)&state,
                      PPC_THREAD_STATE_COUNT);
```

(continues)

FIGURE 7–20 Creating a Mach thread *(continued)*

```
    EXIT_ON_MACH_ERROR("my_thread_setup", kr);
}

void
my_thread_routine(int arg1, char *arg2)
{
    // printf("my_thread_routine(%d, %s)\n", arg1, arg2); // likely to fail
    puts("my_thread_routine()");
}

void
my_thread_exit(void)
{
    puts("my_thread_exit(void)");
    exit(0);
}


$ gcc -Wall -o thread_create thread_create.c
$ ./thread_create
my_thread_routine()
my_thread_exit(void)
```

7.3.1.3 Displaying Task and Thread Details

Let us now write a program to display detailed information about all tasks, and all threads within those tasks, on a system. Our program—called lstasks—will use a variety of Mach task and thread routines to retrieve relevant information. The program will optionally access a process ID as an argument, in which case it will display information only for tasks and threads associated with that BSD process. Figure 7–21 shows the implementation and sample usage of lstasks.

FIGURE 7–21 Retrieving detailed task and thread information from the kernel

```
// lstasks.c

#include <getopt.h>
#include <sys/sysctl.h>
#include <mach/mach.h>
#include <Carbon/Carbon.h>

#define PROGNAME  "lstasks"
```

(continues)

FIGURE 7–21 Retrieving detailed task and thread information from the kernel *(continued)*

```
// pretty-printing macros
#define INDENT_L1 "  "
#define INDENT_L2 "    "
#define INDENT_L3 "      "
#define INDENT_L4 "        "
#define SUMMARY_HEADER \
    "task#   BSD pid program          PSN (high)   PSN (low)    #threads\n"

static const char *task_roles[] = {
    "RENICED",
    "UNSPECIFIED",
    "FOREGROUND_APPLICATION",
    "BACKGROUND_APPLICATION",
    "CONTROL_APPLICATION",
    "GRAPHICS_SERVER",
};
#define TASK_ROLES_MAX (sizeof(task_roles)/sizeof(char *))

static const char *thread_policies[] = {
    "UNKNOWN?",
    "STANDARD|EXTENDED",
    "TIME_CONSTRAINT",
    "PRECEDENCE",
};
#define THREAD_POLICIES_MAX (sizeof(thread_policies)/sizeof(char *))

static const char *thread_states[] = {
    "NONE",
    "RUNNING",
    "STOPPED",
    "WAITING",
    "UNINTERRUPTIBLE",
    "HALTED",
};
#define THREAD_STATES_MAX (sizeof(thread_states)/sizeof(char *))

#define EXIT_ON_MACH_ERROR(msg, retval) \
    if (kr != KERN_SUCCESS) { mach_error(msg ":" , kr); exit((retval)); }

// get BSD process name from process ID
static char *
getprocname(pid_t pid)
{
    size_t len = sizeof(struct kinfo_proc);
    static int name[] = { CTL_KERN, KERN_PROC, KERN_PROC_PID, 0 };
    static struct kinfo_proc kp;
```

(continues)

FIGURE 7–21 Retrieving detailed task and thread information from the kernel *(continued)*

```c
    name[3] = pid;
    kp.kp_proc.p_comm[0] = '\0';

    if (sysctl((int *)name, sizeof(name)/sizeof(*name), &kp, &len, NULL, 0))
        return "?";

    if (kp.kp_proc.p_comm[0] == '\0')
        return "exited?";

    return kp.kp_proc.p_comm;
}

void
usage()
{
    printf("usage: %s [-s|-v] [-p <pid>]\n", PROGNAME);
    exit(1);
}

// used as the printf() while printing only the summary
int
noprintf(const char *format, ...)
{
    return 0; // nothing
}

int
main(int argc, char **argv)
{
    int i, j, summary = 0, verbose = 0;
    int (* Printf)(const char *format, ...);

    pid_t pid;

    // for Carbon processes
    OSStatus            status;
    ProcessSerialNumber psn;
    CFStringRef         nameRef;
    char                name[MAXPATHLEN];

    kern_return_t kr;
    mach_port_t   myhost;                     // host port
    mach_port_t   mytask;                     // our task
    mach_port_t   onetask = 0;                // we want only one specific task
    mach_port_t   p_default_set;              // processor set name port
    mach_port_t   p_default_set_control;      // processor set control port

    //// for task-related querying
```

(continues)

FIGURE 7–21 Retrieving detailed task and thread information from the kernel *(continued)*

```
// pointer to ool buffer for processor_set_tasks(), and the size of
// the data actually returned in the ool buffer
task_array_t            task_list;
mach_msg_type_number_t task_count;

// maximum-sized buffer for task_info(), and the size of the data
// actually filled in by task_info()
task_info_data_t        tinfo;
mach_msg_type_number_t task_info_count;

// flavor-specific pointers to cast the generic tinfo buffer
task_basic_info_t          basic_info;
task_events_info_t         events_info;
task_thread_times_info_t thread_times_info;
task_absolutetime_info_t absolutetime_info;

// used for calling task_get_policy()
task_category_policy_data_t category_policy;
boolean_t get_default;

// opaque token that identifies the task as a BSM audit subject
audit_token_t      audit_token;
security_token_t security_token; // kernel's security token is { 0, 1 }

//// for thread-related querying

// pointer to ool buffer for task_threads(), and the size of the data
// actually returned in the ool buffer
thread_array_t            thread_list;
mach_msg_type_number_t thread_count;

// maximum-sized buffer for thread_info(), and the size of the data
// actually filled in by thread_info()
thread_info_data_t        thinfo;
mach_msg_type_number_t thread_info_count;

// flavor-specific pointers to cast the generic thinfo buffer
thread_basic_info_t basic_info_th;

// used for calling thread_get_policy()
thread_extended_policy_data_t          extended_policy;
thread_time_constraint_policy_data_t time_constraint_policy;
thread_precedence_policy_data_t          precedence_policy;

// to count individual types of process subsystem entities
uint32_t stat_task = 0;    // Mach tasks
uint32_t stat_proc = 0;    // BSD processes
```

(continues)

FIGURE 7–21 Retrieving detailed task and thread information from the kernel *(continued)*

```
uint32_t stat_cpm = 0;      // Carbon Process Manager processes
uint32_t stat_thread = 0;  // Mach threads

// assume we won't be silent: use the verbose version of printf() by default
Printf = printf;

myhost = mach_host_self();
mytask = mach_task_self();

while ((i = getopt(argc, argv, "p:sv")) != -1) {
    switch (i) {
        case 'p':
            pid = strtoul(optarg, NULL, 10);
            kr = task_for_pid(mytask, pid, &onetask);
            EXIT_ON_MACH_ERROR("task_for_pid", 1);
            break;
        case 's':
            summary = 1;
            Printf = noprintf;
            break;
        case 'v':
            verbose = 1;
            break;
        default:
            usage();
    }
}

// can't have both
if (summary && verbose)
    usage();

argv += optind;
argc -= optind;

kr = processor_set_default(myhost, &p_default_set);
EXIT_ON_MACH_ERROR("processor_default", 1);

// get the privileged port so that we can get all tasks
kr = host_processor_set_priv(myhost, p_default_set, &p_default_set_control);
EXIT_ON_MACH_ERROR("host_processor_set_priv", 1);

// we could check for multiple processor sets, but we know there aren't...
kr = processor_set_tasks(p_default_set_control, &task_list, &task_count);
EXIT_ON_MACH_ERROR("processor_set_tasks", 1);
```

(continues)

FIGURE 7–21 Retrieving detailed task and thread information from the kernel *(continued)*

```
if (!verbose)
    Printf(SUMMARY_HEADER);

// check out each task
for (i = 0; i < task_count; i++) {

    // ignore our own task
    if (task_list[i] == mytask)
        continue;

    if (onetask && (task_list[i] != onetask))
        continue;

    pid = 0;
    status = procNotFound;

    // note that we didn't count this task
    stat_task++;

    if (verbose)
        Printf("Task #%d\n", i);
    else
        Printf("%5d", i);

    // check for BSD process (process 0 not counted as a BSD process)
    kr = pid_for_task(task_list[i], &pid);
    if ((kr == KERN_SUCCESS) && (pid > 0)) {
        stat_proc++;

        if (verbose)
            Printf(INDENT_L1 "BSD process id (pid)   = %u (%s)\n", pid,
                    getprocname(pid));
        else
            Printf("   %6u %-16s", pid, getprocname(pid));
    } else // no BSD process
        if (verbose)
            Printf(INDENT_L1 "BSD process id (pid)   = "
                    "/* not a BSD process */\n");
        else
            Printf("   %6s %-16s", "-", "-");

    // check whether there is a process serial number
    if (pid > 0)
        status = GetProcessForPID(pid, &psn);
    if (status == noErr) {
        stat_cpm++;
        if (verbose) {
            status = CopyProcessName(&psn, &nameRef);
```

(continues)

FIGURE 7–21 Retrieving detailed task and thread information from the kernel *(continued)*

```
                CFStringGetCString(nameRef, name, MAXPATHLEN,
                                   kCFStringEncodingASCII);
                Printf(INDENT_L1 "Carbon process name    = %s\n", name);
                CFRelease(nameRef);
        } else
                Printf(" %-12d%-12d", psn.highLongOfPSN, psn.lowLongOfPSN);
    } else // no PSN
        if (verbose)
            Printf(INDENT_L1 "Carbon process name    = "
                    "/* not a Carbon process */\n");

        else
            Printf(" %-12s%-12s", "-", "-");


    if (!verbose)
        goto do_threads;

    // basic task information
    task_info_count = TASK_INFO_MAX;
    kr = task_info(task_list[i], TASK_BASIC_INFO, (task_info_t)tinfo,
                   &task_info_count);
    if (kr != KERN_SUCCESS) {
        mach_error("task_info:", kr);
        fprintf(stderr, "*** TASK_BASIC_INFO failed (task=%x)\n",
                task_list[i]);
        // skip this task
        continue;
    }
    basic_info = (task_basic_info_t)tinfo;
    Printf(INDENT_L2 "virtual size        = %u KB\n",
           basic_info->virtual_size >> 10);
    Printf(INDENT_L2 "resident size       = %u KB\n",
           basic_info->resident_size >> 10);
    if ((basic_info->policy < 0) &&
        (basic_info->policy > THREAD_POLICIES_MAX))
        basic_info->policy = 0;
    Printf(INDENT_L2 "default policy      = %u (%s)\n",
           basic_info->policy, thread_policies[basic_info->policy]);

    Printf(INDENT_L1 "Thread run times\n");

    Printf(INDENT_L2 "user (terminated)    = %u s %u us\n",
           basic_info->user_time.seconds,
           basic_info->user_time.microseconds);
    Printf(INDENT_L2 "system (terminated)  = %u s %u us\n",
           basic_info->system_time.seconds,
           basic_info->system_time.microseconds);
```

(continues)

FIGURE 7–21 Retrieving detailed task and thread information from the kernel *(continued)*

```
    // times for live threads (unreliable -- we are not suspending)
    task_info_count = TASK_INFO_MAX;
    kr = task_info(task_list[i], TASK_THREAD_TIMES_INFO,
                    (task_info_t)tinfo, &task_info_count);
    if (kr == KERN_SUCCESS) {
        thread_times_info = (task_thread_times_info_t)tinfo;
        Printf(INDENT_L2 "user (live)          = %u s %u us\n",
                thread_times_info->user_time.seconds,
                thread_times_info->user_time.microseconds);
        Printf(INDENT_L2 "system (live)        = %u s %u us\n",
                thread_times_info->system_time.seconds,
                thread_times_info->system_time.microseconds);
    }


    // absolute times for live threads, and overall absolute time
    task_info_count = TASK_INFO_MAX;
    kr = task_info(task_list[i], TASK_ABSOLUTETIME_INFO,
                    (task_info_t)tinfo, &task_info_count);
    if (kr == KERN_SUCCESS) {
        Printf(INDENT_L1 "Thread times (absolute)\n");
        absolutetime_info = (task_absolutetime_info_t)tinfo;
        Printf(INDENT_L2 "user (total)         = %lld\n",
                absolutetime_info->total_user);
        Printf(INDENT_L2 "system (total)       = %lld\n",
                absolutetime_info->total_system);
        Printf(INDENT_L2 "user (live)          = %lld\n",
                absolutetime_info->threads_user);
        Printf(INDENT_L2 "system (live)        = %lld\n",
                absolutetime_info->threads_system);
    }


    // events
    task_info_count = TASK_INFO_MAX;
    kr = task_info(task_list[i], TASK_EVENTS_INFO, (task_info_t)tinfo,
                    &task_info_count);
    if (kr == KERN_SUCCESS) {
        events_info = (task_events_info_t)tinfo;
        Printf(INDENT_L2 "page faults          = %u\n",
                events_info->faults);
        Printf(INDENT_L2 "actual pageins       = %u\n",
                events_info->pageins);
        Printf(INDENT_L2 "copy-on-write faults = %u\n",
                events_info->cow_faults);
        Printf(INDENT_L2 "messages sent        = %u\n",
                events_info->messages_sent);
        Printf(INDENT_L2 "messages received    = %u\n",
                events_info->messages_received);
```

(continues)

FIGURE 7–21 Retrieving detailed task and thread information from the kernel *(continued)*

```
        Printf(INDENT_L2 "Mach system calls    = %u\n",
               events_info->syscalls_mach);
        Printf(INDENT_L2 "Unix system calls    = %u\n",
               events_info->syscalls_unix);
        Printf(INDENT_L2 "context switches     = %u\n",
               events_info->csw);
}


// task policy information
task_info_count = TASK_CATEGORY_POLICY_COUNT;
get_default = FALSE;
kr = task_policy_get(task_list[i], TASK_CATEGORY_POLICY,
                     (task_policy_t)&category_policy,
                     &task_info_count, &get_default);
if (kr == KERN_SUCCESS) {
   if (get_default == FALSE) {
      if ((category_policy.role >= -1) &&
          (category_policy.role < (TASK_ROLES_MAX - 1)))
            Printf(INDENT_L2 "role                = %s\n",
                   task_roles[category_policy.role + 1]);
   } else // no current settings -- other parameters take precedence
         Printf(INDENT_L2 "role                = NONE\n");
}


// audit token
task_info_count = TASK_AUDIT_TOKEN_COUNT;
kr = task_info(task_list[i], TASK_AUDIT_TOKEN,
               (task_info_t)&audit_token, &task_info_count);
if (kr == KERN_SUCCESS) {
   int n;
   Printf(INDENT_L2 "audit token       = ");
   for (n = 0; n < sizeof(audit_token)/sizeof(uint32_t); n++)
       Printf("%x ", audit_token.val[n]);
   Printf("\n");
}


// security token
task_info_count = TASK_SECURITY_TOKEN_COUNT;
kr = task_info(task_list[i], TASK_SECURITY_TOKEN,
               (task_info_t)&security_token, &task_info_count);
if (kr == KERN_SUCCESS) {
   int n;
   Printf(INDENT_L2 "security token    = ");
   for (n = 0; n < sizeof(security_token)/sizeof(uint32_t); n++)
       Printf("%x ", security_token.val[n]);
   Printf("\n");
}
```

(continues)

FIGURE 7–21 Retrieving detailed task and thread information from the kernel *(continued)*

```
do_threads:

    // get threads in the task
    kr = task_threads(task_list[i], &thread_list, &thread_count);
    if (kr != KERN_SUCCESS) {
        mach_error("task_threads:", kr);
        fprintf(stderr, "task_threads() failed (task=%x)\n", task_list[i]);
        continue;
    }

    if (thread_count > 0)
        stat_thread += thread_count;

    if (!verbose) {
        Printf(" %8d\n", thread_count);
        continue;
    }

    Printf(INDENT_L1 "Threads in this task   = %u\n", thread_count);

    // check out threads
    for (j = 0; j < thread_count; j++) {

        thread_info_count = THREAD_INFO_MAX;
        kr = thread_info(thread_list[j], THREAD_BASIC_INFO,
                        (thread_info_t)thinfo, &thread_info_count);
        if (kr != KERN_SUCCESS) {
            mach_error("task_info:", kr);
            fprintf(stderr,
                    "*** thread_info() failed (task=%x thread=%x)\n",
                    task_list[i], thread_list[j]);
            continue;
        }

        basic_info_th = (thread_basic_info_t)thinfo;
        Printf(INDENT_L2 "thread %u/%u (%p) in task %u (%p)\n",
               j, thread_count - 1, thread_list[j], i, task_list[i]);

        Printf(INDENT_L3 "user run time            = %u s %u us\n",
               basic_info_th->user_time.seconds,
               basic_info_th->user_time.microseconds);
        Printf(INDENT_L3 "system run time          = %u s %u us\n",
               basic_info_th->system_time.seconds,
               basic_info_th->system_time.microseconds);
        Printf(INDENT_L3 "scaled cpu usage percentage = %u\n",
               basic_info_th->cpu_usage);
```

(continues)

```
switch (basic_info_th->policy) {

case THREAD_EXTENDED_POLICY:
    get_default = FALSE;
    thread_info_count = THREAD_EXTENDED_POLICY_COUNT;
    kr = thread_policy_get(thread_list[j], THREAD_EXTENDED_POLICY,
                           (thread_policy_t)&extended_policy,
                           &thread_info_count, &get_default);
    if (kr != KERN_SUCCESS)
        break;
    Printf(INDENT_L3 "scheduling policy          = %s\n",
           (extended_policy.timeshare == TRUE) ? \
               "STANDARD" : "EXTENDED");
    break;

case THREAD_TIME_CONSTRAINT_POLICY:
    get_default = FALSE;
    thread_info_count = THREAD_TIME_CONSTRAINT_POLICY_COUNT;
    kr = thread_policy_get(thread_list[j],
                           THREAD_TIME_CONSTRAINT_POLICY,
                           (thread_policy_t)&time_constraint_policy,
                           &thread_info_count, &get_default);
    if (kr != KERN_SUCCESS)
        break;
    Printf(INDENT_L3 "scheduling policy          = " \
           "TIME_CONSTRAINT\n");
    Printf(INDENT_L4   "period                   = %-4u\n",
           time_constraint_policy.period);
    Printf(INDENT_L4   "computation              = %-4u\n",
           time_constraint_policy.computation);
    Printf(INDENT_L4   "constraint               = %-4u\n",
           time_constraint_policy.constraint);
    Printf(INDENT_L4   "preemptible              = %s\n",
           (time_constraint_policy.preemptible == TRUE) ? \
               "TRUE" : "FALSE");
    break;

case THREAD_PRECEDENCE_POLICY:
    get_default = FALSE;
    thread_info_count = THREAD_PRECEDENCE_POLICY;
    kr = thread_policy_get(thread_list[j], THREAD_PRECEDENCE_POLICY,
                           (thread_policy_t)&precedence_policy,
                           &thread_info_count, &get_default);
    if (kr != KERN_SUCCESS)
        break;
    Printf(INDENT_L3 "scheduling policy             = PRECEDENCE\n");
    Printf(INDENT_L4 "importance                = %-4u\n",
           precedence_policy.importance);
    break;
```

(continues)

FIGURE 7–21 Retrieving detailed task and thread information from the kernel *(continued)*

```
            default:
                Printf(INDENT_L3 "scheduling policy            = UNKNOWN?\n");
                break;
            }

            Printf(INDENT_L3
                   "run state                  = %-4u (%s)\n",
                   basic_info_th->run_state,
                   (basic_info_th->run_state >= THREAD_STATES_MAX) ? \
                       "?" : thread_states[basic_info_th->run_state]);

            Printf(INDENT_L3
                   "flags                      = %-4x%s",
                   basic_info_th->flags,
                   (basic_info_th->flags & TH_FLAGS_IDLE) ? \
                       " (IDLE)\n" : "\n");

            Printf(INDENT_L3 "suspend count               = %u\n",
                   basic_info_th->suspend_count);
            Printf(INDENT_L3 "sleeping for time           = %u s\n",
                   basic_info_th->sleep_time);

        } // for each thread

        vm_deallocate(mytask, (vm_address_t)thread_list,
                   thread_count * sizeof(thread_act_t));

    } // for each task

    Printf("\n");

    fprintf(stdout, "%4d Mach tasks\n%4d Mach threads\n"
            "%4d BSD processes\n%4d CPM processes\n",
            stat_task, stat_thread, stat_proc, stat_cpm);

    vm_deallocate(mytask, (vm_address_t)task_list, task_count * sizeof(task_t));

    exit(0);
}
```

```
$ gcc -Wall -o lstasks lstasks.c -framework Carbon
$ sudo ./lstasks
task#   BSD pid program         PSN (high)   PSN (low)   #threads
  0       - -                   -            -               49
  1       1 launchd             -            -                3
  2      26 dynamic_pager       -            -                1
  3      30 kextd               -            -                2
```

(continues)

FIGURE 7–21 Retrieving detailed task and thread information from the kernel *(continued)*

```
...
    93      12149 vim                 -           -                      1

    94 Mach tasks
   336 Mach threads
    93 BSD processes
    31 CPM processes
$ sudo ./lstasks -v -p $$
Task #49
  BSD process id (pid)    = 251 (zsh)
  Carbon process name     = /* not a Carbon process */
    virtual size          = 564368 KB
    resident size         = 13272 KB
    default policy        = 1 (STANDARD|EXTENDED)
  Thread run times
    user (terminated)     = 0 s 0 us
    system (terminated)   = 0 s 0 us
    user (live)           = 19 s 501618 us
    system (live)         = 37 s 98274 us
  Thread times (absolute)
    user (total)          = 649992326
    system (total)        = 1236491913
    user (live)           = 649992326
    system (live)         = 1236491913
    page faults           = 3303963
    actual pageins        = 9
    copy-on-write faults  = 41086
    messages sent         = 257
    messages received     = 251
    Mach system calls     = 279
    Unix system calls     = 107944
    context switches      = 67653
    role                  = UNSPECIFIED
    audit token           = 0 1f5 1f5 1f5 1f5 fb 0 0
    security token        = 1f5 1f5
  Threads in this task    = 1
    thread 0/0 (0x8003) in task 49 (0x113)
      user run time                = 19 s 501618 us
      system run time              = 37 s 98274 us
      scaled cpu usage percentage  = 34
      scheduling policy            = STANDARD
      run state                    = 3     (WAITING)
      flags                        = 1
      suspend count                = 0
      sleeping for time            = 0 s
...
```

As shown in Figure 7–21, lstasks also displays the number of Mach and Unix (BSD) system calls made by the process. Let us write a test program that makes a specific number of Mach and Unix system calls and use lstasks to verify the numbers. Figure 7–22 shows the program and its usage. Note that the usage shown includes outputs of two command shells intermingled.

FIGURE 7–22 Counting the number of system calls made by a process

```c
// syscalls_test.c

#include <stdio.h>
#include <fcntl.h>>
#include <unistd.h>
#include <mach/mach.h>

int
main()
{
    int         i, fd;
    mach_port_t  p;
    kern_return_t kr;

    setbuf(stdout, NULL);
    printf("My pid is %d\n", getpid());
    printf("Note the number of Mach and Unix system calls, and press <enter>");
    (void)getchar();

    // At this point, we will have some base numbers of Mach and Unix
    // system calls made so far, say, M and U, respectively

    for (i = 0; i < 100; i++) { // 100 iterations

        // +1 Unix system call per iteration
        fd = open("/dev/null", O_RDONLY);

        // +1 Unix system call per iteration
        close(fd);

        // +1 Mach system call per iteration
        kr = mach_port_allocate(mach_task_self(), MACH_PORT_RIGHT_RECEIVE, &p);

        // +1 Mach system call per iteration
        kr = mach_port_deallocate(mach_task_self(), p);

    }
```

(continues)

FIGURE 7–22 Counting the number of system calls made by a process *(continued)*

```
// +1 Unix system call
printf("Note the number of Mach and Unix system calls again...\n"
       "Now sleeping for 60 seconds...");

// sleep(3) is implemented using nanosleep, which will call
// clock_get_time() and clock_sleep_trap() -- this is +2 Mach system calls

(int)sleep(60);

// Mach system calls = M + 2 * 100 + 2 (that is, 202 more calls)
// Unix system calls = U + 2 * 100 + 1 (that is, 201 more calls)

return 0;
}


$ gcc -Wall -o syscalls_test syscalls_test.c
$ ./syscalls_test
My pid is 12344
Note the number of Mach and Unix system calls, and press <enter>
$ sudo ./lstasks -v -p 12344
...
    Mach system calls                      = 71
    Unix system calls                      = 47
...
<enter>
Note the number of Mach and Unix system calls again...
Now sleeping for 60 seconds...
$ sudo ./lstasks -v -p 12344
...
    Mach system calls                      = 273
    Unix system calls                      = 248
...
```

7.3.2 BSD Processes

A BSD process is the representation of an application in execution on Mac OS X—all Mac OS X application environments use BSD processes. Unless otherwise stated, we will use the term *process* to mean a BSD process. As on a typical Unix system, the only way to create a process is through the fork() system call (or through the vfork() variant). A Mach task is a byproduct of the fork() system call on Mac OS X. Whereas the task encapsulates resources managed by Mach, such as address space and IPC space, a BSD process manages Unix-specific resources and abstractions, such as file descriptors, credentials, and signals. Figure 7–23 shows an excerpt from the proc structure.

FIGURE 7–23 The BSD proc structure

```
// bsd/sys/proc_internal.h

struct proc {
    LIST_ENTRY(proc)  p_list;      // list of all processes
    struct pcred      *p_cred;     // process owner's credentials
    struct filedesc   *p_fd;       // open files structure
    struct pstats     *p_stats;    // accounting/statistics
    struct plimit     *p_limits;   // process limits
    struct sigacts    *p_sigacts;  // signal actions, state
    ...
    pid_t             p_pid;       // process identifier
    LIST_ENTRY(proc)  p_pglist;    // list of processes in process group
    struct proc       *p_pptr;     // parent process
    LIST_ENTRY(proc)  p_sibling;   // list of siblings
    LIST_HEAD(, proc) p_children;  // list of children
    ...
    void              *p_wchan;    // sleep address
    ...
    struct vnode      *p_textvp;   // vnode of the executable
    ...
    // various signal-management fields
    ...
    void              *task;       // corresponding task
    ...
};
```

As we saw earlier, each Mach thread in a BSD process has an associated uthread structure to maintain thread-specific Unix information. For example, the uthread structure is used for holding system call parameters and results, miscellaneous state for system calls that use continuations, per-thread signal information, and per-thread credentials. In this sense, the uthread structure is to the thread structure what the proc structure is to the task structure. Figure 7–24 shows an excerpt from the uthread structure.

FIGURE 7–24 The BSD uthread structure

```
// bsd/sys/user.h

struct uthread {
    int *uu_ar0;      // address of user's saved R0
    int  uu_arg[8];   // arguments to the current system call
    int *uu_ap;       // pointer to the system call argument list
    int  uu_rval[2];  // system call return values

    // thread exception handling
    int  uu_code;     // exception code
    char uu_cursig;   // p_cursig for exception
    ...

    // space for continuations:
    // - saved state for select()
    // - saved state for nfsd
    // - saved state for kevent_scan()
    // - saved state for kevent()
    int (* uu_continuation)(int);
    ...

    struct proc *uu_proc; // our proc structure
    ...
    // various pieces of signal information
    sigset_t uu_siglist;  // signals pending for the thread
    sigset_t uu_sigmask;  // signal mask for the thread
    ...
    thread_act_t uu_act;  // our activation
    ...
    // list of uthreads in the process
    TAILQ_ENTRY(uthread) uu_list;
    ...
};
```

7.3.2.1 The fork() System Call: User-Space Implementation

Let us now look at the implementation of the fork() system call in Mac OS X. Figure 7–25 shows the user-space processing of fork()—that is, within the system library.

When a user program calls fork(), the system library stub invokes several internal functions in preparation for the system call. The dynamic version (which is the default) of the library also invokes fork()-time hooks implemented by the dynamic link editor. The _cthread_fork_prepare() internal function runs

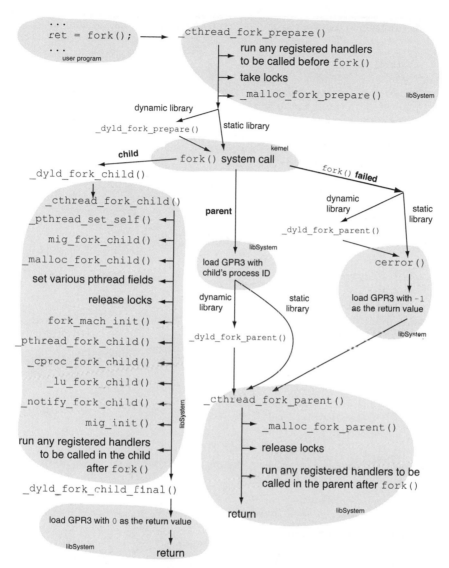

FIGURE 7–25 User-space processing of the fork() system call

any pre-fork() handlers that may have been registered through pthread_atfork(3). Figure 7–26 shows an example depicting the use of pthread_atfork(3). _cthread_fork_prepare() also acquires library-level critical section locks and prepares the malloc module for a fork() by ensuring that no thread is in a malloc critical section.

FIGURE 7–26 Registering handlers to be run before and after a `fork()` system call invocation

```
// pthread_atfork.c

#include <stdio.h>
#include <unistd.h>
#include <pthread.h>

// handler to be called before fork()
void
prepare(void)
{
    printf("prepare\n");
}

// handler to be called after fork() in the parent
void
parent(void)
{
    printf("parent\n");
}

// handler to be called after fork() in the child
void
child(void)
{
    printf("child\n");
}

int
main(void)
{
    (void)pthread_atfork(prepare, parent, child);
    (void)fork();
    _exit(0);
}

$ gcc -Wall -o pthread_atfork pthread_atfork.c
$ ./pthread_atfork
prepare
child
parent
```

Thereafter, the stub looks up the address of a pre-`fork()` prepare function—if any—implemented by `dyld`. If the function is found, the stub runs it. Next, the stub invokes the `fork()` system call. The stub handles three types of returns from the system call: a failed return to the parent, a successful return to the parent, and a successful return to the child.

If the system call returned an error, the stub looks up and calls a post-fork() parent function—if any—implemented by dyld. Then it calls cerror(), a library-internal function that sets the value of the per-thread errno variable. In the case of detached pthreads,[14] the thread-local errno variable resides as a field of the pthread data structure (struct _pthread).[15] The stub then arranges for a -1 to be returned to the caller. After this point, the processing of an erroneous return is similar to a successful return to the parent. In the latter case, on return from the system call, the stub would have arranged for the child's process ID to be returned to the caller. Both types of return to the parent finally call _cthread_fork_parent(), which releases locks taken before the system call and runs any post-fork() handlers that may be registered for running in the parent.

The stub performs substantially more work while returning to the child. It first calls a post-fork() child function—if any—implemented by dyld and then calls _cthread_fork_child(), which calls several functions to perform operations such as the following.

- Invoke the fastpath system call to set the "self" value for the pthread.
- Set various fields of the pthread structure—for example, set the kernel_thread and reply_port fields to the values returned by mach_thread_self() and mach_reply_port(), respectively.
- Release locks taken before the system call.
- Cache the values of system constants (such as the page size), and the thread's key Mach ports (such as those for the host and the containing task).
- Initialize special ports for the thread (such as the bootstrap port and the system clock's service port).
- Reserve page 0 by mapping a page of zero-filled memory at address 0x0, with a protection value of VM_PROT_NONE, which disallows all access to the memory region.
- Insert the current pthread—the only one in the process at this point—at the head of the library-maintained list of pthreads for the process, while setting the thread count to 1.
- Run any post-fork() handlers that may be registered for running in the child.

---

14. If a pthread is not detached, the global errno variable is used instead.

15. This is the per-pthread structure internally maintained by the Pthreads library.

7.3.2.2 The `fork()` System Call: Kernel Implementation

Let us now look at how the `fork()` system call is processed in the kernel. Figure 7–27 provides an overview of the kernel functions involved in `fork()`'s handling, starting from `fork()` [bsd/kern/kern_fork.c], the system call handler.

`fork1()` [bsd/kern/kern_fork.c] calls `cloneproc()` [bsd/kern/kern_fork.c], which creates a new process from the given process. `cloneproc()` first calls `forkproc()` [bsd/kern/kern_fork.c], which allocates a new `proc` structure and several of its constituent structures. `forkproc()` then finds a free process ID, wrapping around if the next available process ID is higher than `PID_MAX` (defined to be 30,000 in `bsd/sys/proc_internal.h`).

> When process IDs wrap around, the search for the next available ID starts at 100—and not 0—since low-numbered process IDs are likely to be in use by forever-running daemons.

`forkproc()` initializes various fields of the `proc` structure and implements several Unix aspects of `fork()`, such as inheriting the parent's credentials, open file descriptors, and shared memory descriptors. On return from `forkproc()`, which returns the child `proc` structure, `cloneproc()` calls `procdup()` [bsd/kern/kern_fork.c], passing it the `proc` structures of the parent and the child. `procdup()` calls `task_create_internal()` [osfmk/kern/task.c] to create a new Mach task. The new `task` structure's `bsd_info` field is set to point to the child `proc` structure. `procdup()` then calls `thread_create()` [osfmk/kern/thread.c] to create a Mach thread within the new task. `thread_create()` calls `thread_create_internal()` [osfmk/kern/thread.c], which allocates a `thread` structure and a `uthread` structure. Moreover, `thread_create_internal()` initializes various aspects of the new thread, including its machine-dependent state. `thread_create()` passes a continuation function to `thread_create_internal()`. The function is set as the thread's continuation—that is, the location where the thread will continue when dispatched. The continuation function arranges for the new thread to return to user mode as if the thread were trapping after being interrupted.

The newly created thread is returned by `procdup()` to `cloneproc()`. On return from `procdup()`, `cloneproc()` places the child's `proc` structure on various lists—the list of its parent's children, the list of all processes, and the process ID hash table. It marks the child as runnable and returns the child thread to `fork1()`, which now calls `thread_dup()` [osfmk/kern/thread_act.c]. `thread_dup()` calls `machine_thread_dup()` [osfmk/ppc/status.c] to duplicate the context of the parent (current) thread into the child thread. `fork1()` calls

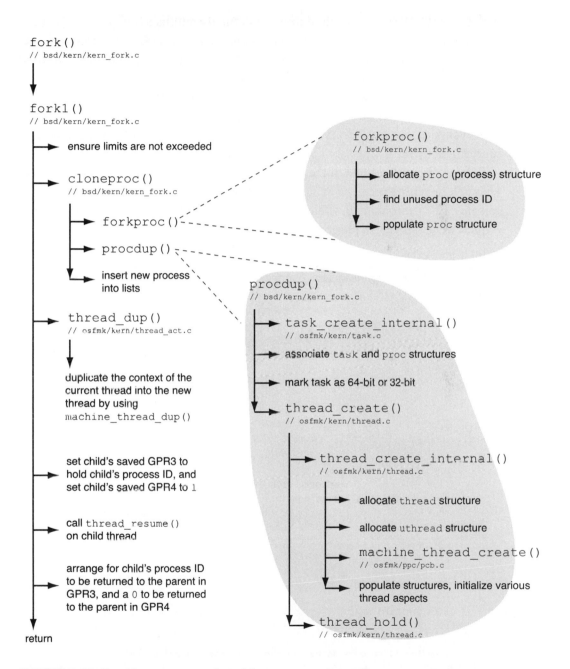

FIGURE 7–27 Kernel-space processing of the `fork()` system call

thread_resume() on the child thread and finally returns to the parent. The kernel returns 1 and 0 to the child and parent, respectively, in GPR4. Moreover, the child's process ID is returned in GPR3 in both cases. The system library returns a 0 to the child process and the child's process ID to the parent process.

Figure 7–28 shows a program that directly invokes the fork() system call, after which it writes the values of GPR3 and GPR4 to the standard output. Since we bypass the system library, none of the pre- and post-fork() work normally performed by the system library will be performed in this case. Consequently, we will be unable to use most of the system library functions in the child process. For example, even printf(3) will not work. Therefore, we will use write(2) to display raw, unformatted values of GPR3 and GPR4 on the standard output, which we can pipe to a program such as hexdump.

FIGURE 7–28 Verifying the values returned by the kernel in the case of a raw fork() system call

```
// fork_demo.c

#include <unistd.h>
#include <sys/syscall.h>

int
main(void)
{
    long r3_r4[] = { -1, -1 };
    int syscallnum = SYS_fork;

    __asm__ volatile(
        "lwz r0,%2      ; load GPR0 with SYS_fork\n"
        "sc            ; invoke fork(2)\n"
        "nop           ; this will be skipped in the case of no error\n"
        "mr %0,r3      ; save GPR3 to r3_r4[0]\n"
        "mr %1,r4      ; save GPR4 to r3_r4[1]\n"
      : "=r"(r3_r4[0]), "=r"(r3_r4[1])
      : "g"(syscallnum)
    );

    // write GPR3 and GPR4
    write(1, r3_r4, sizeof(r3_r4)/sizeof(char));

    // sleep for 30 seconds so we can check process IDs using 'ps'
    sleep(30);

    return 0;
}
```

(continues)

FIGURE 7–28 Verifying the values returned by the kernel in the case of a raw `fork()`
system call *(continued)*

```
$ gcc -Wall -o fork_demo fork_demo.c
$ ./fork_demo | hexdump -d
0000000    00000    14141    00000    00000    00000    14141    00000    00001
...
$ ps
...
14139   p9   S+     0:00.01 ./fork_demo
14140   p9   S+     0:00.00 hexdump -d
14141   p9   S+     0:00.00 ./fork_demo
```

In Figure 7–28, the first two 32-bit words in `hexdump`'s output correspond to
the GPR3 and GPR4 values returned to the parent, whereas the last two words correspond to the child. Note that GPR3 contains the child's process ID in both cases.

`fork()` and Mach Ports: Caveat

Only certain Mach ports are inherited by the child task from the parent task during a `fork()` call. These include registered ports, exception ports, the host port,
and the bootstrap port. Other than the inherited ports, any other Mach ports are
invalidated in the child. Since the child's address space is inherited from the parent, the child will have bogus port names for the invalidated ports, but no rights to
such ports. Although the system library reinitializes several key ports in the child
process after `fork()`, not every library or framework performs such cleaning. If
you run into the latter situation, one solution is to execute the same binary again
through `execve()`. The program may have to explicitly accommodate this solution.

Every BSD process begins life with one Mach task, one Mach thread, a
BSD `proc` structure associated with the `task` structure, a `uthread` structure
associated with the `thread` structure, and a pthread implemented within the user-
space system library. As we saw in Chapter 6, the `pid_for_task()` Mach routine can be used to retrieve the BSD process ID of a Mach task—provided it has
one. Conversely, `task_for_pid()` retrieves the task port for the specified BSD
process ID.

```
...
kern_return_t kr;
pid_t         pid;
mach_port_t   task;
...
```

```
// get BSD process ID for the task with the specified port
kr = pid_for_task(task, &pid);
...

// get task port for task on the same host as the given task,
// and one with the given BSD process ID
kr = task_for_pid(mach_task_self(), pid, &task);
```

7.3.2.3 The `vfork()` System Call

The `vfork()` system call is a variant of `fork()` that can be used to create a new process without fully copying the address space of the parent process. It is an optimized version of `fork()` intended for the case when the new process is being created for calling `execve()`. The following aspects describe the implementation and usage of `vfork()` on Mac OS X.

- The parent process is blocked while the child process executes using the parent's resources.
- The expected—and correct—use of `vfork()` requires the child process to either call `execve()` or to exit. Thereafter, the parent resumes execution.
- Calling `vfork()` creates a new BSD `proc` structure for the child process, but no task or thread is created. Therefore, in this case, two BSD `proc` structures refer to the same `task` structure.
- The task and the initial thread for the child process are eventually created during the processing of the `execve()` system call.
- During its execution, the child must be careful not to cause undesirable alterations to the parent's stack or other memory.

Figure 7–29 shows the processing of `vfork()` in the kernel.

Let us look at an example to show that the child process borrows the parent's resources temporarily. The program in Figure 7–30 prints the task and thread ports—as returned by `mach_task_self()` and `mach_thread_self()`, respectively—in the parent and the child. When run with no arguments, the program calls `vfork()`. Otherwise, it calls `fork()`. Moreover, the child modifies the value of an automatic variable declared in the parent. In the case of `vfork()`, the change is reflected in the parent after the parent resumes.

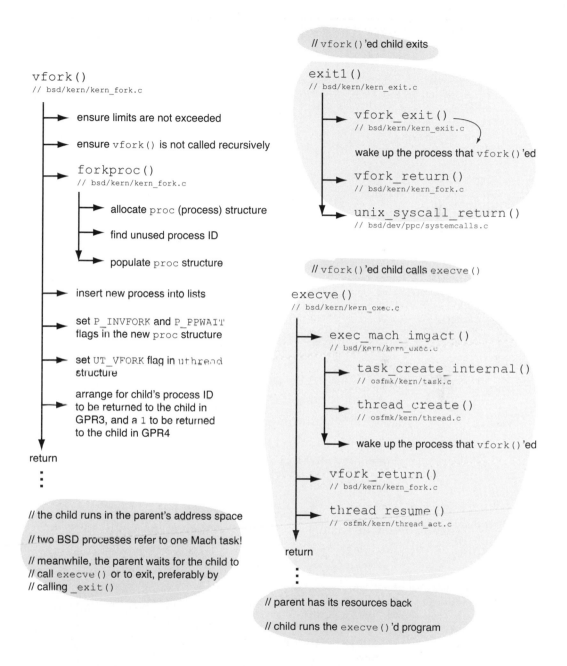

FIGURE 7–29 Kernel-space processing of the vfork() system call

---

FIGURE 7–30 Verifying that the child borrows the parent's resources during a vfork()
system call

// vfork_demo.c

```c
#include <stdio.h>
#include <unistd.h>
#include <stdlib.h>
#include <pthread.h>
#include <mach/mach.h>

int
main(int argc, char **argv)
{
    int ret, i = 0;

    printf("parent: task = %x, thread = %x\n", mach_task_self(),
           pthread_mach_thread_np(pthread_self()));

    // vfork() if no extra command-line arguments
    if (argc == 1)
        ret = vfork();
    else
        ret = fork();

    if (ret < 0)
        exit(ret);

    if (ret == 0) { // child
        i = 1;
        printf("child: task = %x, thread = %x\n", mach_task_self(),
               pthread_mach_thread_np(pthread_self()));
        _exit(0);
    } else
        printf("parent, i = %d\n", i);

    return 0;
}
```

```
$ gcc -Wall -o vfork_demo vfork_demo.c
$ ./vfork_demo
parent: task = 807, thread = d03
child: task = 807, thread = d03
parent, i = 1
$ ./vfork_demo use_vfork
parent: task = 807, thread = d03
parent, i = 0
child: task = 103, thread = 203
```

> `vfork()` cannot be called *recursively.* After a `vfork()`, calling `vfork()` again from the child process—while the parent is blocked—will return an `EINVAL` error to the caller.

7.3.3 POSIX Threads (Pthreads)

Subsequent threads can be created within a BSD process through the POSIX Threads (Pthreads) API, which is also the fundamental threading mechanism in the Mac OS X user space. Thread packages in all common application environments are built atop Pthreads.

7.3.3.1 The Pthreads API

The Pthreads library, which exists as a module within the system library, implements POSIX threads atop Mach threads by using Mach thread API functions to create, terminate, and manipulate the state of kernel threads. In particular, the library manages the program counters and stacks of threads from user space. Specific Mach routines used by the Pthreads library include the following:

- `semaphore_create()`
- `semaphore_signal()`
- `semaphore_signal_all()`
- `semaphore_signal_thread()`
- `semaphore_wait()`
- `semaphore_wait_signal()`
- `thread_create()`
- `thread_create_running()`
- `thread_get_state()`
- `thread_resume()`
- `thread_set_state()`
- `thread_terminate()`

Besides standard-conformant functions, the Mac OS X Pthreads implementation also provides a set of nonportable functions that can be used by user programs at the cost of portability. Such functions have the suffix _np in their names to indicate their nonportability. The following are examples of nonportable functions.

- `pthread_cond_signal_thread_np()` signals a condition variable, waking a specific thread.

- `pthread_cond_timedwait_relative_np()` waits on a condition variable, but in a nonstandard manner, allowing a relative time to be specified for sleeping.

- `pthread_create_suspended_np()` creates a pthread with the underlying Mach thread suspended.

- `pthread_get_stackaddr_np()` retrieves a given pthread's stack address from the corresponding pthread structure.

- `pthread_get_stacksize_np()` retrieves a given pthread's stack size from the corresponding pthread structure.

- `pthread_is_threaded_np()` returns a 1 if the current process has (or had) at least one thread in addition to the default, main thread. This function is susceptible to race conditions.

- `pthread_mach_thread_np()` returns the Mach thread corresponding to the given pthread. It is equivalent to calling `mach_thread_self()`, except that it returns an existing reference to the thread's kernel port. In contrast, `mach_thread_self()` returns a new reference that should be released by calling `mach_port_deallocate()` when not needed.

- `pthread_main_np()` returns a nonzero value if the current thread is the main thread.

- `pthread_yield_np()` invokes the `swtch_pri()` Mach trap to attempt a context switch, yielding to another runnable thread, if any. Note that `swtch_pri()` also sets the current thread's scheduling priority.

7.3.3.2 Implementation of Pthread Creation

Figure 7–31 shows how a new pthread is created in the system library. Note that the creation of the underlying Mach thread by the Pthreads library is similar to our example from Figure 7–20.

> A BSD process cannot be created on Mac OS X without an associated Mach task. Similarly, a pthread cannot be created without an associated Mach thread. Hereafter, we will not point out the implicit existence of a Mach task for every BSD process or of a Mach thread for every pthread.

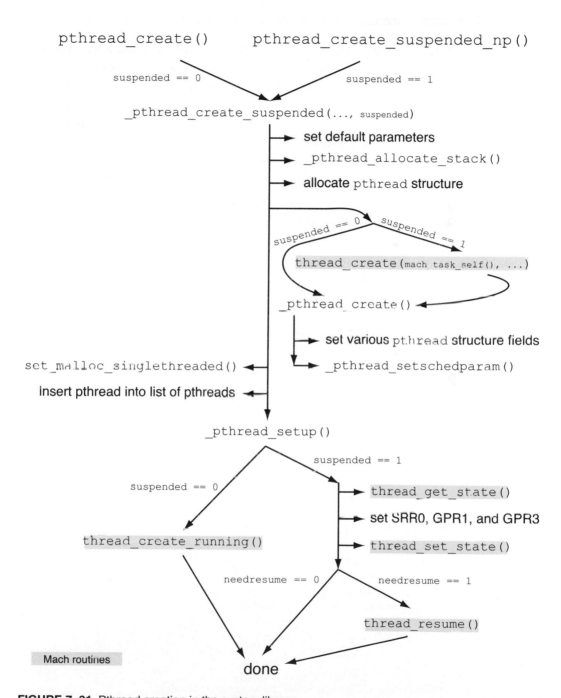

FIGURE 7–31 Pthread creation in the system library

7.3.4 Java Threads

Java's threading class (java.lang.Thread) is used to create a new thread of execution in a Java application. You can subclass java.lang.Thread and override the run() method, in which case, when the thread is started, it will execute the body of the run() method. The run() method is required by the Runnable interface (java.lang.Runnable), which java.lang.Thread implements. Alternatively, you can construct a new thread by passing it an instance of any class that implements the Runnable interface. This way, any class can provide the body of the thread without being a subclass of java.lang.Thread.

As you start a Java application on Mac OS X, one BSD process is created for the instance of the Java virtual machine (JVM). Since the JVM itself has a multithreaded implementation, this process contains several pthreads to begin with. Thereafter, each java.lang.Thread thread maps to one pthread and therefore one Mach thread. Figure 7–32 shows an example of creating and running Java threads on Mac OS X. You can use the lstasks program from Figure 7–21 to list the Mach threads in the JVM process—say, by adding one or more calls to Thread.sleep() in the Java program to prevent it from exiting too quickly to be examined.

FIGURE 7–32 Creating and running Java threads

```java
// MyThread.java

import java.lang.ThreadGroup;
import java.lang.Thread;

class MyThread extends Thread {

    MyThread(ThreadGroup group, String name) {
        super(group, name);
    }

    public void run() {
        for (int i = 0; i < 128; i++)
            System.out.print(this.getName());
    }
}

class DemoApp {
    public static void main(String[] args) {
        ThreadGroup allThreads = new ThreadGroup("Threads");
        MyThread t1 = new MyThread(allThreads, "1");
```

(continues)

FIGURE 7–32 Creating and running Java threads *(continued)*

```
        MyThread t2 = new MyThread(allThreads, "2");
        MyThread t3 = new MyThread(allThreads, "3");
        allThreads.list();
        t1.setPriority(Thread.MIN_PRIORITY);
        t2.setPriority((Thread.MAX_PRIORITY +
                        Thread.MIN_PRIORITY) / 2);
        t3.setPriority(Thread.MAX_PRIORITY);
        t1.start();
        t2.start();
        t3.start();
    }
}

$ javac MyThread.java
$ CLASSPATH=. java DemoApp
java.lang.ThreadGroup[name=Threads,maxpri=10]
    Thread[1,5,Threads]
    Thread[2,5,Threads]
    Thread[3,5,Threads]
323333333333333333333333333333333333333333333333333333333333333333333333333333
333333333333333333333333333333333333333333333222222222222222222222222222222222222
2222222222222222222222222222222222222222222222222222222222222222222222222222222222
222222211111111111111111111111111111111111111111111111111111111111111111111111
```

7.3.5 The NSTask Cocoa Class

The NSTask class in Cocoa allows the creation and launching of a task running a given executable. Using NSTask, the launched program can be treated as a subprocess from the standpoint of monitoring it. Some aspects of the program's execution can also be controlled through NSTask. Note that NSTask is built atop the Unix fork() and execve() system calls and therefore offers similar functionality. Figure 7–33 shows an example of using NSTask.

FIGURE 7–33 Using the NSTask Cocoa class

```
// NSTask.m

#import <Foundation/Foundation.h>

#define TASK_PATH "/bin/sleep"
#define TASK_ARGS "5"
```

(continues)

FIGURE 7–33 Using the NSTask Cocoa class *(continued)*

```
int
main()
{
    NSAutoreleasePool *pool = [[NSAutoreleasePool alloc] init];

    NSTask *newTask;
    int     status;

    // allocate and initialize an NSTask object
    newTask = [[NSTask alloc] init];

    // set the executable for the program to be run
    [newTask setLaunchPath:@TASK_PATH];

    // set the command arguments that will be used to launch the program
    [newTask setArguments:[NSArray arrayWithObject:@TASK_ARGS]];

    // launch the program -- a new process will be created
    [newTask launch];

    NSLog(@"waiting for new task to exit\n");
    [newTask waitUntilExit];

    // fetch the value returned by the exiting program
    status = [newTask terminationStatus];

    NSLog(@"new task exited with status %d\n", status);

    [newTask release];
    [pool release];

    exit(0);
}
```

```
$ gcc -Wall -o nstask NSTask.m -framework Foundation
$ ./nstask
2005-08-12 13:42:44.427 nstask[1227] waiting for new task to exit
2005-08-12 13:42:49.472 nstask[1227] new task exited with status 0
```

7.3.6 The NSThread Cocoa Class

The NSThread class allows for creation of multiple threads in Cocoa applications. It is particularly convenient to use NSThread for running an Objective-C method in its own thread. Each instance of the NSThread class controls one thread of execution, which maps to one pthread. Figure 7–34 shows an example of using NSThread.

FIGURE 7–34 Using the NSThread Cocoa class

// NSThread.m

```
#import <Foundation/Foundation.h>

@interface NSThreadController : NSObject

{
    unsigned long long sum1;
    unsigned long long sum2;
}

- (void)thread1:(id)arg;
- (void)thread2:(id)arg;
- (unsigned long long)get_sum1;
- (unsigned long long)get_sum2;

@end

@implementation NSThreadController

- (unsigned long long)get_sum1
{
    return sum1;
}

- (unsigned long long)get_sum2
{
    return sum2;
}

- (void)thread1:(id)arg
{
    NSAutoreleasePool *pool = [[NSAutoreleasePool alloc] init];
    [NSThread setThreadPriority:0.0];
    sum1 = 0;
    printf("thread1: running\n");
    for (;;)
        sum1++;
    [pool release];
}

- (void)thread2:(id)arg
{
    NSAutoreleasePool *pool = [[NSAutoreleasePool alloc] init];
    [NSThread setThreadPriority:1.0];
    sum2 = 0;
    printf("thread2: running\n");
```

(continues)

FIGURE 7–34 Using the NSThread Cocoa class *(continued)*

```
    for (;;)
        sum2++;
    [pool release];
}

@end

int
main()
{
    NSAutoreleasePool *pool = [[NSAutoreleasePool alloc] init];
    NSTimeInterval secs = 5;
    NSDate *sleepForDate = [NSDate dateWithTimeIntervalSinceNow:secs];

    NSThreadController *T = [[NSThreadController alloc] init];
    [NSThread detachNewThreadSelector:@selector(thread1:)
                             toTarget:T
                           withObject:nil];

    [NSThread detachNewThreadSelector:@selector(thread2:)
                             toTarget:T
                           withObject:nil];

    printf("main: sleeping for %f seconds\n", secs);
    [NSThread sleepUntilDate:sleepForDate];

    printf("sum1 = %lld\n", [T get_sum1]);
    printf("sum2 = %lld\n", [T get_sum2]);

    [T release];
    [pool release];

    exit(0);
}


$ gcc -Wall -o nsthread NSThread.m -framework Foundation
$ ./nsthread
main: sleeping for 5.000000 seconds
thread2: running
thread1: running
sum1 = 49635095
sum2 = 233587520
```

7.3.7 The Carbon Process Manager

The Process Manager provided a cooperative multitasking environment on several versions of Mac OS prior to Mac OS X. It is supported on Mac OS X as the Carbon Process Manager (CPM), but certain functionality and aspects that are not applicable in the Mac OS X environment are either unavailable or have been modified for accommodation in Mac OS X's different architecture.

Each CPM process maps to a BSD process, but not vice versa. Only those processes that are launched through the CPM are managed by Carbon. For each process that it manages, the CPM maintains certain state, including a *process serial number* (PSN) that is different from the BSD process ID. The PSN consists of a *high* part and a *low* part, both of which are unsigned long quantities.

```
struct ProcessSerialNumber {
    unsigned long highLongOfPSN;
    unsigned long lowLongOfPSN;
};
typedef struct ProcessSerialNumber ProcessSerialNumber;
typedef ProcessSerialNumber *ProcessSerialNumberPtr;
```

You can start a CPM process using the Carbon API's `LaunchApplication()` function, which launches an application from the specified file and returns the PSN on a successful launch.

As we saw in the implementation of our `lstasks` program, given a CPM process, the corresponding PSN and Carbon-specific process name can be retrieved using `GetProcessForPID()` and `CopyProcessName()`, respectively. CPM processes can be identified in the process listing generated by the `ps` command, as they are shown with an argument of the form `-psn_X_Y`, where `X` and `Y` are the high and low parts, respectively, of the PSN.

Figure 7–35 shows an example of launching a CPM process.

FIGURE 7–35 Launching an application through the Carbon Process Manager

```
// CarbonProcessManager.c

#include <Carbon/Carbon.h>

#define PROGNAME "cpmtest"
```

(continues)

FIGURE 7–35 Launching an application through the Carbon Process Manager *(continued)*

```
int
main(int argc, char **argv)
{
    OSErr              err;
    Str255             path;
    FSSpec             spec;
    LaunchParamBlockRec launchParams;

    if (argc != 2) {
        printf("usage: %s <full application path>\n", PROGNAME);
        exit(1);
    }

    c2pstrcpy(path, argv[1]);
    err = FSMakeFSSpec(0, // use the default volume
                       0, // parent directory -- determine from filename
                       path, &spec);
    if (err != noErr) {
        printf("failed to make FS spec for application (error %d).\n", err);
        exit(1);
    }

    // the extendedBlock constant specifies that we are using the fields that
    // follow this field in the structure
    launchParams.launchBlockID = extendedBlock;

    // length of the fields following this field (again, use a constant)
    launchParams.launchEPBLength = extendedBlockLen;

    // launch control flags
    // we want the existing program to continue, and not terminate
    // moreover, we want the function to determine the Finder flags itself
    launchParams.launchControlFlags = launchContinue + launchNoFileFlags;

    // FSSpec for the application to launch
    launchParams.launchAppSpec = &spec;

    // no parameters
    launchParams.launchAppParameters = NULL;

    err = LaunchApplication(&launchParams);

    if (err != noErr) {
        printf("failed to launch application (error %d).\n", err);
        exit(1);
    }
```

(continues)

FIGURE 7–35 Launching an application through the Carbon Process Manager *(continued)*

```
    printf("main: launched application, PSN = %lu_%lu\n",
           launchParams.launchProcessSN.highLongOfPSN,
           launchParams.launchProcessSN.lowLongOfPSN);
    printf("main: continuing\n");

    exit(0);
}


$ gcc -Wall -o cpmtest CarbonProcessManager.c -framework Carbon
$ ./cpmtest "Macintosh HD:Applications:Chess.app:Contents:MacOS:Chess"
main: launched application, PSN = 0_21364737
main: continuing
```

7.3.8 Carbon Multiprocessing Services

The Carbon Multiprocessing Services (MP Services) API allows you to create preemptive tasks in an application. However, an MP task is not a Mach task—it is a thread that is preemptively scheduled by MP Services, which can run tasks independently on one or more processors, dividing processor time automatically among available tasks. An MP task maps to a pthread.

Figure 7–36 shows an example of using MP Services.

FIGURE 7–36 Using Carbon Multiprocessing Services

```
// CarbonMultiprocessingServices.c

#include <pthread.h>
#include <CoreServices/CoreServices.h>

OSStatus
taskFunction(void *param)
{
    printf("taskFunction: I am an MP Services task\n");
    printf("taskFunction: my task ID is %#x\n", (int)MPCurrentTaskID());
    printf("taskFunction: my pthread ID is %p\n", pthread_self());
    return noErr;
}

int
main()
{
```

(continues)

FIGURE 7–36 Using Carbon Multiprocessing Services *(continued)*

```
MPQueueID queue;
UInt32    param1, param2;
UInt32    tParam1, tParam2;
OSStatus  status;
MPTaskID  task;

// check for availability
if (MPLibraryIsLoaded()) {
    printf("MP Services initialized\n");
    printf("MP Services version %d.%d.%d.%d\n",
            MPLibrary_MajorVersion, MPLibrary_MinorVersion,
            MPLibrary_Release, MPLibrary_DevelopmentRevision);
    printf("%d processors available\n\n", (int)MPProcessorsScheduled());
} else
    printf("MP Services not available\n");

printf("main: currently executing task is %#x\n", (int)MPCurrentTaskID());

// create a notification queue
status = MPCreateQueue(&queue);
if (status != noErr) {
    printf("failed to create MP notification queue (error %lu)\n", status);
    exit(1);
}

tParam1 = 1234;
tParam2 = 5678;

printf("main: about to create new task\n");
printf("main: my pthread ID is %p\n", pthread_self());

// create an MP Services task
status = MPCreateTask(taskFunction, // pointer to the task function
                      (void *)0,    // parameter to pass to the task
                      (ByteCount)0, // stack size (0 for default)
                      queue,        // notify this queue upon termination
                      &tParam1,     // termination parameter 1
                      &tParam2,     // termination parameter 2
                      kMPCreateTaskValidOptionsMask,
                      &task);       // ID of the newly created task
if (status != noErr) {
    printf("failed to create MP Services task (error %lu)\n", status);
    goto out;
}

printf("main: created new task %#08x, now waiting\n", (int)task);
```

(continues)

FIGURE 7–36 Using Carbon Multiprocessing Services *(continued)*

```
// wait for the task to be terminated
status = MPWaitOnQueue(queue, (void *)&param1, (void *)&param2,
                       NULL, kDurationForever);

printf("main: task terminated (param1 %lu, param2 %lu)\n",
       tParam1, tParam2);

out:
    if (queue)
        MPDeleteQueue(queue);

    exit(0);
}
```

```
$ gcc -Wall -o mps CarbonMultiprocessingServices.c -framework Carbon
$ ./mps
MP Services initialized
MP Services version 2.3.1.1
2 processors available

main: currently executing task is 0xa000ef98
main: about to create new task
main: my pthread ID is 0xa000ef98
main: created new task 0x1803200, now waiting
taskFunction: I am an MP Services task
taskFunction: my task ID is 0x1803200
taskFunction: my pthread ID is 0x1803200
main: task terminated (param1 1234, param2 5678)
```

Multitasking and Multiprocessing

Multitasking is the ability to handle several tasks simultaneously, whereas *multiprocessing* is the ability of a system to use multiple processors simultaneously. *Symmetric multiprocessing* (SMP) is a configuration in which two or more processors are managed by one kernel, with both processors sharing the same memory and having equal status for almost all purposes. In an SMP system, any thread can run on any processor, unless a thread is programmatically bound to a particular processor.

Multitasking can be either *preemptive* or *cooperative*. Preemption is the act of interrupting a currently running entity to give time to another runnable entity. In preemptive multitasking, the operating system can preempt one entity to run another, as needed. In cooperative multitasking, a running entity must give up control of the processor—cooperatively—to allow others to run. Consequently, a runnable entity can receive processing time only if another entity allows it.

7.3.9 The Carbon Thread Manager

The Carbon Thread Manager allows you to create cooperatively scheduled threads, wherein each thread must explicitly relinquish control of the processor. This is done either by calling `YieldToAnyThread()`, which invokes the Carbon Thread Manager's scheduling mechanism to run the next available thread, or by calling `YieldToThread()`, which relinquishes control to a particular thread. Even though only one Carbon Thread Manager thread runs at a time within an application, each thread maps to a pthread.

In our example program (Figure 7–37) for the Carbon Thread Manager, the main function will create several threads, mark them ready, and relinquish control to the first thread. Each thread will print its Carbon identifier, pthread identifier, and Mach port and then relinquish control to the next thread. The last thread on the list will relinquish control back to main, which will destroy all threads and exit.

FIGURE 7–37 Creating Carbon Thread Manager threads

```c
// CarbonThreadManager.c

#include <pthread.h>
#include <mach/mach.h>
#include <CoreServices/CoreServices.h>

#define MAXTHREADS 8

static ThreadID mainThread;
static ThreadID newThreads[MAXTHREADS] = { 0 };

voidPtr
threadFunction(void *threadParam)
{
    int i = (int)threadParam;

    printf("thread #%d: CTM %#08lx, pthread %p, Mach %#08x\n",
           i, newThreads[i], pthread_self(), mach_thread_self());

    if (i == MAXTHREADS)
        YieldToThread(mainThread);
    else
        YieldToThread(newThreads[i + 1]);

    /* NOTREACHED */
    printf("Whoa!\n");
```

(continues)

FIGURE 7–37 Creating Carbon Thread Manager threads *(continued)*

```
    return threadParam;
}

int
main()
{
    int    i;
    OSErr err = noErr;

    // main thread's ID
    err = GetCurrentThread(&mainThread);

    for (i = 0; i < MAXTHREADS; i++) {

        err = NewThread(
                    kCooperativeThread, // type of thread
                    threadFunction,     // thread entry function
                    (void *)i,          // function parameter
                    (Size)0,            // default stack size
                    kNewSuspend,        // options
                    NULL,               // not interested
                    &(newThreads[i]));  // newly created thread

        if (err || (newThreads[i] == kNoThreadID)) {
            printf("*** NewThread failed\n");
            goto out;
        }

        // set state of thread to "ready"
        err = SetThreadState(newThreads[i], kReadyThreadState, kNoThreadID);
    }

    printf("main: created %d new threads\n", i);

    printf("main: relinquishing control to next thread\n");
    err = YieldToThread(newThreads[0]);

    printf("main: back\n");

out:

    // destroy all threads
    for (i = 0; i < MAXTHREADS; i++)
        if (newThreads[i])
            DisposeThread(newThreads[i], NULL, false);

    exit(err);
}
```

(continues)

FIGURE 7–37 Creating Carbon Thread Manager threads *(continued)*

```
$ gcc -Wall -o ctm CarbonThreadManager.c -framework Carbon
$ ./ctm
main: created 8 new threads
main: relinquishing control to next thread
thread #0: CTM 0x1803200, pthread 0x1803200, Mach 0x001c03
thread #1: CTM 0x1803600, pthread 0x1803600, Mach 0x002e03
thread #2: CTM 0x1803a00, pthread 0x1803a00, Mach 0x003003
thread #3: CTM 0x1803e00, pthread 0x1803e00, Mach 0x003203
thread #4: CTM 0x1808400, pthread 0x1808400, Mach 0x003403
thread #5: CTM 0x1808800, pthread 0x1808800, Mach 0x003603
thread #6: CTM 0x1808c00, pthread 0x1808c00, Mach 0x003803
thread #7: CTM 0x1809000, pthread 0x1809000, Mach 0x003a03
main: back
```

7.4 Scheduling

A timesharing system provides the illusion of multiple processes running concurrently by interleaving their execution, *context switching* from one to another based on various conditions. The set of rules based on which the order of execution of threads is determined is called the *scheduling policy*. A system component called the *scheduler* implements the policy through data structures and algorithms. The implementation allows the scheduler to apply the policy while selecting threads for running from among those that are runnable. Although execution concurrency and parallelism are important goals of schedulers, especially as multiprocessor systems become commonplace, it is common for a modern operating system to support multiple scheduling policies, allowing different types of workloads to be treated differently. In its typical operation, the Mac OS X scheduler gives the processor to each thread for a brief period of time, after which it considers switching to another thread. The amount of time a scheduled thread can run before being preempted is called the thread's *timeslicing quantum*, or simply *quantum*. Once a thread's quantum expires, it can be preempted because another thread of equal or higher priority wants to run. Moreover, a running thread can be preempted regardless of its quantum if a higher-priority thread becomes runnable.

We will first look at how the Mac OS X scheduling infrastructure is initialized. Then we will discuss the scheduler's operation.

7.4.1 Scheduling Infrastructure Initialization

We saw several aspects of processor initialization during our discussion of kernel startup in Chapter 5. Figure 7–38 shows selected initializations related to scheduling. When ppc_init() starts executing on the master processor, none of the processor set structures, processor structures, and other scheduler structures have been initialized. The master processor's processor structure is initialized by processor_init() [osfmk/kern/processor.c], which sets up the processor's local run queue, sets the processor's state as PROCESSOR_OFF_LINE, marks it as belonging to no processor set, and sets other fields of the structure to their initial values.

7.4.1.1 Timeslicing Quantum

As shown in Figure 7–38, processor_init() calls timer_call_setup() [osfmk/kern/timer_call.c] to arrange for the quantum expiration function— thread_quantum_expire() [osfmk/kern/priority.c]—to be called. thread_quantum_expire() recalculates the quantum and priority for a thread. Note that timer_call_setup() only initializes a call entry structure specifying which function is to be called and with what parameters. This call entry will be placed on each processor's timer call queue. (The kernel maintains per-processor timer call queues.) Until the real-time clock subsystem is configured, these queues are not serviced.

```
// osfmk/kern/processor.c

void
processor_init(register processor_t p, int slot_num)
{
    ...
    timer_call_setup(&p->quantum_timer, thread_quantum_expire, p);
    ...
}
```

ppc_init() finally calls kernel_bootstrap() [osfmk/kern/startup.c] to start the higher-level boot process. One of the latter's first operations is scheduler initialization by calling sched_init() [osfmk/kern/sched_prim.c], which first calculates the standard timeslicing quantum. The built-in default *preemption rate*—that is, the frequency at which the kernel will preempt threads—is 100Hz. A preemption rate of 100Hz yields a timeslicing quantum of 0.01 s (10 ms). The preempt boot argument can be used to specify a custom value of the default

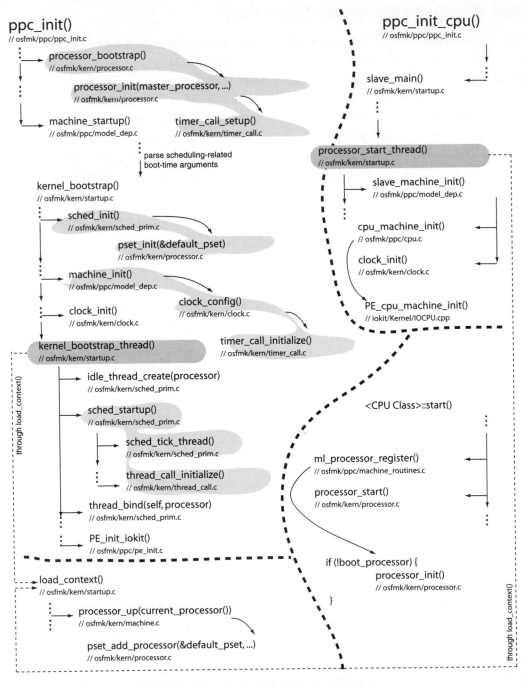

FIGURE 7–38 Scheduling-related initializations during system startup

preemption rate to the kernel. The `kern.clockrate` sysctl variable contains the values of the preemption rate and the timeslicing quantum (as microseconds).

```
$ sysctl kern.clockrate
kern.clockrate: hz = 100, tick = 10000, profhz = 100, stathz = 100
```

> The `tick` value represents the number of microseconds in a sched-uler tick. The `hz` value can be seen as the frequency of a hardware-independent system clock.

`sched_init()` then initializes the global wait queues used by threads for waiting on events, initializes the default processor set by calling `pset_init()` [osfmk/kern/processor.c], and sets the `sched_tick` global variable to 0.

7.4.1.2 Timing and Clocks

Scheduling is a clock-based activity in that several of its critical functions are driven by a periodic clock or timer interrupts. Therefore, the clock subsystem must be configured for scheduling to be started. `clock_config()` [osfmk/kern/clock.c] configures the clock subsystem.

Timer facilities on the PowerPC include the Timebase (TB) Register and the Decrementer Register (DEC). As we saw in Chapter 3, the TB Register is a 64-bit counter driven by an implementation-dependent frequency. On certain processor models, the frequency may be a function of the processor's clock frequency, whereas on some other models the TB Register is updated in accordance with an independent clock. In fact, the frequency is not even required to be constant, although a frequency change must be explicitly managed by the operating system. In any case, each increment of the TB Register adds 1 to its low-order bit. The TB Register is a volatile resource and must be initialized by the kernel during boot.

The DEC is a 32-bit counter that is updated at the same frequency as the TB Register but is decremented by 1 on every update.

> For a typical Timebase frequency, it will take thousands of years for the TB Register to attain its maximum value, but the DEC will pass zero in a few hundred seconds for the same frequency.

When the DEC's value becomes negative, that is, the sign bit of the 32-bit signed integer represented by the DEC's contents changes from 0 to 1, a decrementer interrupt is caused. As we saw in Chapter 5, the PowerPC exception vector entry for this interrupt resides at address 0x900. The low-level handler in osfmk/ppc/ lowmem_vectors.s sets the trap code as T_DECREMENTER and passes up the exception's processing to ihandler() [osfmk/ppc/hw_exception.s]—the higher-level interrupt handler. ihandler() in turn calls interrupt() [osfmk/ ppc/interrupt.c].

// **osfmk/ppc/interrupt.c**

```
struct savearea *
interrupt(int type, struct savearea *ssp, ...)
{
    ...
    switch (type) {
    case T_DECREMENTER:
        ...
        rtclock_intr(0, ssp, 0);
    break;
    }
    ...
}
```

rtclock_intr() [osfmk/ppc/rtclock.c] is the real-time clock device interrupt handler routine. The real-time clock subsystem maintains per-processor data structures such as the following:

- A real-time clock timer structure with its own, configurable deadline
- A deadline for the real-time clock tick that is driven at a frequency of HZ, which is defined to be 100, resulting in a clock tick every 10 ms

Figure 7–39 shows an overview of real-time clock interrupt processing.

FIGURE 7–39 Real-time clock interrupt processing

// **osfmk/ppc/exception.h**

```
struct per_proc_info {
    ...
    uint64_t rtclock_tick_deadline;
    struct rtclock_timer {
        uint64_t deadline;
        uint32_t is_set:1,
                 has_expired:1,
                 :0;
    } rtclock_timer;
    ...
};
```

(continues)

FIGURE 7–39 Real-time clock interrupt processing *(continued)*

// osfmk/ppc/rtclock.c

```
#define NSEC_PER_HZ (NSEC_PER_SEC / HZ)
static uint32_t rtclock_tick_interval;
...
static clock_timer_func_t rtclock_timer_expire;
...
#define DECREMENTER_MAX 0x7FFFFFFFUL
#define DECREMENTER_MIN 0XAUL
...

void
clock_set_timer_deadline(uint64_t deadline)
{
    // set deadline for the current processor's rtclock_timer
    ...
}

void
clock_set_timer_func(clock_timer_func_t func)
{
    spl_t s;

    LOCK_RTC(s);
    // global timer expiration handler
    if (rtclock_timer_expire == NULL)
        rtclock_timer_expire = func;
    UNLOCK_RTC(s);
}

...
// real-time clock device interrupt
void
rtclock_intr(__unused int device, struct savearea *ssp, __unused spl_t old_spl)
{
    uint64_t            abstime;
    int                 decr1, decr2;
    struct rtclock_timer *mytimer;
    struct per_proc_info *pp;

    decr1 = decr2 = DECREMENTER_MAX;

    pp = getPerProc();

    abstime = mach_absolute_time();
    if (pp->rtclock_tick_deadline <= abstime) {
```

(continues)

FIGURE 7-39 Real-time clock interrupt processing *(continued)*

```
        // set pp->rtclock_tick_deadline to "now" (that is, abstime) plus
        // rtclock_tick_interval

        // call the hertz_tick() function
    }

    mytimer = &pp->rtclock_timer;

    abstime = mach_absolute_time();
    if (mytimer->is_set && mytimer->deadline <= abstime) {
        mytimer->has_expired = TRUE;
        mytimer->is_set = FALSE;
        (*rtclock_timer_expire)(abstime);
        mytimer->has_expired = FALSE;
    }

    // Look at the deadlines in pp->rtclock_tick_deadline and mytimer->deadline
    // Choose the earlier one. Moreover, if a still earlier deadline is
    // specified via the special variable rtclock_decrementer_min, choose that
    // instead. None of these deadlines can be greater than DECREMENTER_MAX.

    // Now that we have a deadline, load the Decrementer Register with it.
    ...
    treqs(decr1); // sets decrementer using mtdec()
    ...
}
```

So far, we have seen the following functionality provided by the real-time clock subsystem.

- The `hertz_tick()` function is called via the `rtclock_intr()` function HZ times a second.

- The function pointed to by the `rtclock_timer_expire` function pointer is called depending on the deadline in the processor's timer structure.

A global list of clock devices is maintained by the kernel, with each entry being a clock object structure containing that particular clock's control port, service port, and a machine-dependent operations list. `clock_config()` calls the "config" function of each clock device on the list. Subsequently, `clock_init()` [osfmk/kern/clock.c] is called to initialize the clock devices—it calls the "init" function of each clock device. Note that unlike `clock_config()`, which is called only once during bootstrapping, `clock_init()` is called on a processor each time the processor is started. Consider the configuration and initialization of the system clock (Figure 7–40), whose "config" and "init" functions are `sysclk_config()` and `sysclk_init()`, respectively.

FIGURE 7–40 System clock configuration

```
// osfmk/ppc/rtclock.c

static void
timebase_callback(...)
{
    ...
    // Initialize commpage timestamp

    // Set rtclock_tick_interval, which is the global variable used by
    // rtclock_intr() to arrange for the next "tick" to occur by loading
    // the decrementer with the next deadline
    //
    nanoseconds_to_absolutetime(NSEC_PER_HZ, &abstime);
    rtclock_tick_interval = abstime;
    ...

    // This will call sched_timebase_init()
    clock_timebase_init();
}
...
int
sysclk_config(void)
{
    ...
    // The Platform Expert knows the implementation-dependent conversion factor
    // between absolute-time (Timebase-driven) and clock-time values.
    //
    // The following registration will cause the provided function --
    // timebase_callback() -- to be invoked with the Timebase frequency values
    // as parameters.
    //
    PE_register_timebase_callback(timebase_callback);
    ...
}
...
int
sysclk_init(void)
{
    ...
    // set decrementer and our next tick due
    ...
}
```

clock_config() also calls timer_call_initialize() [osfmk/kern/ timer_call.c] to initialize the timer interrupt callout mechanism, which is used by the thread-based callout mechanism.

// osfmk/kern/timer_call.c

```
void
timer_call_initialize(void)
{
    ...
    clock_set_timer_func((clock_timer_func_t)timer_call_interrupt);
    ...
}
```

As shown in Figure 7–39, clock_set_timer_func() [osfmk/ppc/ rtclock.c] merely sets its parameter (the timer_call_interrupt function pointer in this case) as the value of the rtclock_timer_expire global function pointer. Every time timer_call_interrupt() is called, it will service the timer call queue for the current processor. This way, the scheduler can arrange for thread_quantum_expire() to be invoked on a processor.

clock_timebase_init() [osfmk/kern/clock.c] is a machine-independent function that calls sched_timebase_init() [osfmk/kern/sched_prim.c] to set up various time-related values used by the scheduler, for example:

- std_quantum (10,000 µs), the standard timeslicing quantum
- min_std_quantum (250 µs), the smallest remaining quantum
- min_rt_quantum (50 µs), the smallest real-time computation
- max_rt_quantum (50 ms), the largest real-time computation
- sched_tick_interval (1000 >> SCHED_TICK_SHIFT ms)

sched_timebase_init() uses clock_interval_to_absolutetime_ interval() [osfmk/ppc/rtclock.c] to convert conventional (clock) intervals to machine-specific absolute-time intervals. SCHED_TICK_SHIFT is defined to be 3 in osfmk/kern/sched.h, yielding a value of 125 ms for sched_tick_interval.

7.4.1.3 Converting between Absolute- and Clock-Time Intervals

The kernel often needs to convert between absolute- and clock-time intervals. Absolute time is based on the machine-dependent TB Register. The Mach trap mach_absolute_time(), which is available in the commpage, retrieves the current value of the TB Register. It is the highest-resolution time-related function on

Mac OS X. To convert an absolute-time interval to a conventional clock interval (such as a value expressed in seconds), you need the implementation-dependent conversion factor, which can be retrieved by mach_timebase_info(). The conversion factor consists of a numerator and a denominator. The resultant ratio can be multiplied with an absolute-time interval to yield an equivalent clock interval in nanoseconds. Figure 7–41 shows an example of converting between the two time intervals.

FIGURE 7–41 Converting between absolute- and clock-time intervals

```
// timebase_demo.c

#include <stdio.h>
#include <stdlib.h>
#include <unistd.h>
#include <mach/mach.h>
#include <mach/mach_time.h>

#define DEFAULT_SLEEP_TIME 1
#define MAXIMUM_SLEEP_TIME 60

int
main(int argc, char **argv)
{
    kern_return_t kr;
    u_int64_t     t1, t2, diff;
    double        abs2clock;
    int           sleeptime = DEFAULT_SLEEP_TIME;

    mach_timebase_info_data_t info;

    kr = mach_timebase_info(&info);
    if (kr != KERN_SUCCESS) {
        mach_error("mach_timebase_info:", kr);
        exit(kr);
    }

    if (argc == 2) {
        sleeptime = atoi(argv[1]);
        if ((sleeptime < 0) || (sleeptime > MAXIMUM_SLEEP_TIME))
            sleeptime = DEFAULT_SLEEP_TIME;
    }

    t1 = mach_absolute_time();
    sleep(sleeptime);
    t2 = mach_absolute_time();
    diff = t2 - t1;
```

(continues)

FIGURE 7–41 Converting between absolute- and clock-time intervals *(continued)*

```
    printf("slept for %d seconds of clock time\n", sleeptime);
    printf("TB increments = %llu increments\n", diff);
    printf("absolute-to-clock conversion factor = (%u/%u) ns/increment\n",
            info.numer, info.denom);
    printf("sleeping time according to TB\n");

    abs2clock = (double)info.numer/(double)info.denom;
    abs2clock *= (double)diff;

    printf("\t= %llu increments x (%u/%u) ns/increment\n\t= %f ns\n\t= %f s\n",
            diff, info.numer, info.denom,
            abs2clock, abs2clock/(double)1000000000);

    exit(0);
}


$ gcc -Wall -o timebase_demo timebase_demo.c
$ ./timebase_demo 5
slept for 5 seconds of clock time
TB increments = 166651702 increments
absolute-to-clock conversion factor = (1000000000/33330173) ns/increment
sleeping time according to TB
        = 166651702 increments x (1000000000/33330173) ns/increment
        = 5000025112.380905 ns
        = 5.000025 s
```

7.4.1.4 *Starting the Scheduler*

The first thread to execute on the boot processor, `kernel_bootstrap_thread()` [osfmk/kern/startup.c], is started via `load_context()` [osfmk/kern/startup.c]. Besides setting up the machine-specific context of the thread, `load_context()` initializes certain aspects of the processor. In particular, it calls `processor_up()` [osfmk/kern/machine.c] to add the processor to the default processor set.

kernel_bootstrap_thread() creates an idle thread for the processor, calls `sched_startup()` [osfmk/kern/sched_prim.c] to initiate the scheduler's periodic activities, and calls `thread_bind()` [osfmk/kern/sched_prim.c] to bind the current thread to the boot processor. The latter step is required so that execution remains bound to the boot processor and does not move to any other processors as they come online. Figure 7–42 shows an overview of scheduler startup.

FIGURE 7–42 Scheduler startup

// osfmk/kern/sched_prim.c

```
void
sched_startup(void)
{
    ...
    result = kernel_thread_start_priority(
                (thread_continue_t)sched_tick_thread,
                NULL,
                MAXPRI_KERNEL,
                &thread);
    ...
    thread_call_initialize();
}

// perform periodic bookkeeping functions
void
sched_tick_continue(void)
{
    ...
}

void
sched_tick_thread(void)
{
    ...
    sched_tick_deadline = mach_absolute_time();
    sched_tick_continue();
    /* NOTREACHED */
}
```

---

sched_startup() also initializes the thread-based callout mechanism that allows functions to be recorded by the kernel for invocation later. For example, setitimer(2), which allows real, virtual, and profiling timers to be set for a process, is implemented using a thread callout.

At this point, we have the following primary scheduling-related periodic activities occurring in the kernel.

- rtclock_intr() [osfmk/ppc/rtclock.c] is called when there is a decrementer exception. This typically occurs HZ times a second, with the default value of HZ being 100. rtclock_intr() reloads the decrementer (register) with the next deadline value.
- hertz_tick() [osfmk/kern/mach_clock.c] is called by rtclock_intr().

- `timer_call_interrupt()` [osfmk/kern/timer_call.c] is called by `rtclock_intr()` if the current processor's real-time clock timer's deadline has expired. The `rtclock_timer_expire` function pointer points to `timer_call_interrupt()`—as set by `clock_set_timer_func()`.

- `sched_tick_continue()` [osfmk/kern/sched_prim.c] runs on every scheduler tick, which occurs once every 125 ms by default.

7.4.1.5 *Retrieving the Value of the Scheduler Tick*

Let us read the value of the `sched_tick` variable from kernel memory to examine the rate at which it is incremented. We can determine the address of the variable in kernel memory by running the `nm` command on the kernel executable. Thereafter, we will use the `dd` command to read its value from /dev/kmem, sleep for an integral number of seconds, and read its value again. Figure 7–43 shows a shell script that performs these steps. As seen in the output, the variable's value is incremented by 80 in 10 seconds, which is as we expected, since it should increment by 1 every 125 ms (or by 8 every second).

FIGURE 7–43 Sampling the value of the scheduler tick

```
#!/bin/sh
# sched_tick.sh

SCHED_TICK_ADDR="0x`nm /mach_kernel | grep -w _sched_tick | awk '{print $1}'`"
if [ "$SCHED_TICK_ADDR" == "0x" ]
then
    echo "address of _sched_tick not found in /mach_kernel"
    exit 1
fi

dd if=/dev/kmem bs=1 count=4 iseek=$SCHED_TICK_ADDR of=/dev/stdout | hexdump -d
sleep 10
dd if=/dev/kmem bs=1 count=4 iseek=$SCHED_TICK_ADDR of=/dev/stdout | hexdump -d

exit 0


$ sudo ./sched_tick.sh 2>/dev/null
0000000    00035   09878
0000004
0000000    00035   09958
0000004
```

7.4.1.6 Some Periodic Kernel Activities

We have already seen what `rtclock_intr()` does. Let us briefly look at the operations of `hertz_tick()`, `timer_call_interrupt()`, and `sched_tick_continue()`.

`hertz_tick()` [osfmk/kern/mach_clock.c] performs certain operations on all processors, such as gathering statistics, tracking thread states, and incrementing user-mode and kernel-mode thread timers. Examples of statistics gathered include the total number of clock ticks and profiling information (if profiling is enabled). On the master processor, `hertz_tick()` additionally calls `bsd_hardclock()`.

`bsd_hardclock()` [bsd/kern/kern_clock.c] performs several operations if there is a valid, current BSD process and the process is not exiting. If the processor was in user mode, `bsd_hardclock()` checks whether the process has a virtual interval timer—that is, an interval timer of type `ITIMER_VIRTUAL` that decrements in process-virtual time (only when the process is executing). Such a timer can be set by `setitimer(2)`. If such a timer exists and has expired, `bsd_hardclock()` arranges for a `SIGVTALRM` signal to be delivered to the process.

> As we saw in Chapter 6, the `USER_MODE()` macro—defined in osfmk/ppc/proc_reg.h—is used to examine the saved SRR1, which holds the old contents of the MSR. The `PR` (privileged) bit of the MSR distinguishes between kernel and user mode.

`bsd_hardclock()` performs other operations regardless of whether the processor was in user mode, as long as the processor was not idle. It charges the currently scheduled process with resource utilization for a tick. It then checks whether the process has exceeded its CPU time limit (as specified by the `RLIMIT_CPU` resource limit), sending it a `SIGXPU` signal if it has. Next, it checks whether the process has a profiling timer—that is, an interval timer of type `ITIMER_PROF`. Such a timer decrements both in process-virtual time and when the kernel is running on behalf of the process. It can also be set by `setitimer(2)`. If such a timer exists and has expired, `bsd_hardclock()` arranges for a `SIGPROF` signal to be delivered to the process.

`timer_call_interrupt()` [osfmk/kern/timer_call.c] traverses the timer call queue for the current processor and calls handlers for those timers whose deadlines have expired (Figure 7–44).

FIGURE 7–44 Timer call processing

`// osfmk/kern/timer_call.c`

```
#define qe(x)  ((queue_entry_t)(x))
#define TC(x)  ((timer_call_t)(x))

static void
timer_call_interrupt(uint64_t timestamp)
{
    timer_call_t  call;
    queue_t       queue;

    simple_lock(&timer_call_lock);

    queue = &PROCESSOR_DATA(current_processor(), &timer_call_queue);

    call = TC(queue_first(queue));

    while (!queue_end(queue, qe(call))) {
        if (call->deadline <= timestamp) {
            ...
            // invoke call->func(), passing it call->param0 and call->param1
            ...
        } else
            break;

        call = TC(queue_first(queue));
    }
    ...
}
```

sched_tick_continue() [osfmk/kern/sched_prim.c] performs periodic bookkeeping functions for the scheduler. As Figure 7–45 shows, it increments the sched_tick global variable by 1, calls compute_averages() [osfmk/kern/sched_average.c] to compute the load average and the Mach factor, and calls thread_update_scan() [osfmk/kern/sched_prim.c] to scan the run queues of all processor sets and processors to possibly update thread priorities.

FIGURE 7–45 The scheduler's bookkeeping function

`// osfmk/kern/sched_prim.c`

```
void
sched_tick_continue(void)
```

(continues)

FIGURE 7–45 The scheduler's bookkeeping function *(continued)*

```
{
    uint64_t abstime = mach_absolute_time();

    sched_tick++;

    // compute various averages
    compute_averages();

    // scan the run queues to account for timesharing threads that may need
    // to be updated -- the scanner runs in two passes
    thread_update_scan();

    // compute next deadline for our periodic event
    clock_deadline_for_periodic_event(sched_tick_interval,
                                      abstime, &sched_tick_deadline);

    assert_wait_deadline((event_t)sched_tick_thread, THREAD_UNINT,
                         sched_tick_deadline);

    thread_block((thread_continue_t)sched_tick_continue);

    // NOTREACHED
}
```

7.4.2 Scheduler Operation

Mac OS X is primarily a timesharing system in that threads are subject to time-sharing scheduling unless explicitly designated otherwise. Typical timesharing scheduling aims to provide—without guarantees—each competing thread a fair share of processor time, where fairness implies that the threads receive roughly equal amounts of processor resources over a reasonably long time.

Mapping the Scheduler

Figure 7–46 shows a call graph consisting of several key functions that are involved in the execution and scheduling of threads. Given the density of the graph, we will not discuss it in this chapter. However, it can be used as an accessory to further study of the Mac OS X scheduler.

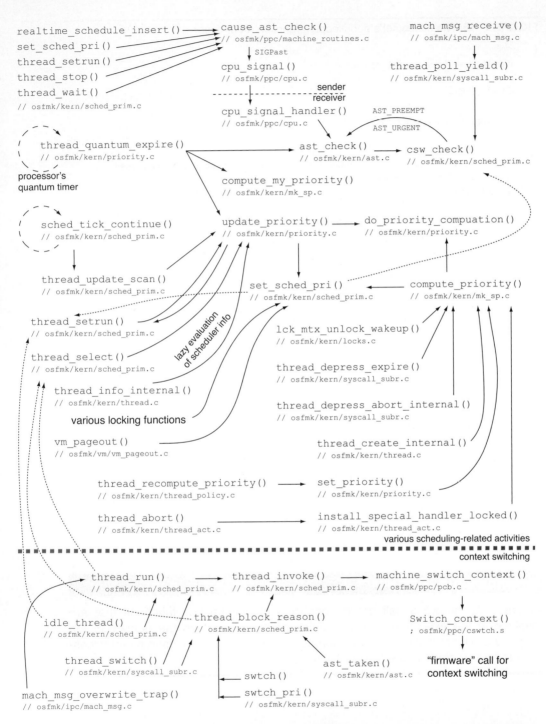

FIGURE 7–46 A nonexhaustive call graph of functions involved in thread execution and scheduling

The following general points are noteworthy about scheduling on Mac OS X.

- The scheduler schedules only Mach threads and no other higher-level entities.

- The scheduler does not use the knowledge that two or more threads may belong to the same task to select between them. In theory, such knowledge could be used to optimize intratask context switching.

- Mach uses the same scheduler for both multiprocessors and uniprocessors. In fact, Mac OS X uses the same kernel—the multiprocessor version—regardless of the number of processors on a machine.[16]

- The Mac OS X kernel supports *handoff scheduling*, wherein a thread can directly yield the processor to another thread without fully involving the scheduler. The kernel's message-passing mechanism can use handoff scheduling while sending a message—if a thread is waiting to receive a message, the sending thread can directly switch to the receiving thread. The receiver effectively inherits the sender's scheduling attributes, including the remainder of the sender's current quantum. Once this quantum expires, however, the effects of the "inheritance" disappear.

- The Mac OS X scheduler supports multiple scheduling policies, including a "soft" real-time policy. However, the scheduler does not provide an interface for loading custom policies.[17]

- Each processor has its own, dedicated idle thread that looks for other threads to execute while it runs.

7.4.2.1 Priority Ranges

The Mac OS X scheduler is priority-based. The selection of threads for running takes into account the priorities of runnable threads. Table 7-2 shows the various priority ranges in the scheduling subsystem—numerically higher values represent higher priorities. The `HOST_PRIORITY_INFO` flavor of the `host_info()` Mach routine can be used to retrieve the values of several specific priorities.

7.4.2.2 Run Queues

A fundamental data structure maintained by the Mach scheduler is a *run queue*. Each run queue structure (Figure 7–47) represents a priority queue of runnable

---

16. The multiprocessor kernel runs with some overhead on uniprocessor systems.

17. For example, the Solaris operating system supports dynamically loadable scheduling policies.

TABLE 7–2 Mac OS X Scheduler Priorities

Levels	Description
0–10	This range contains the lowest priorities (aged, idle) to lowered priorities (aged). The lowest priority (0) has several synonyms, such as MINPRI_USER, MINPRI, IDLEPRI (idle priority), and DEPRESSPRI (depress priority).
11–30	This range contains lowered priorities.
31	This is the default base priority (BASEPRI_DEFAULT) for user threads. host_info() returns this value as the *user* priority.
32–51	This range contains elevated priorities, such as those attainable through task_policy_set(). For example, BASEPRI_BACKGROUND (46), BASEPRI_FOREGROUND (47), and BASEPRI_CONTROL (48) correspond to the base priorities of tasks that have been designated as *background*, *foreground*, and *control* tasks, respectively.
52–63	This range also contains elevated priorities. MAXPRI_USER (63) is set as a new task's maximum priority when the task is created.
64–79	This range contains high priorities normally reserved for the system. The end points—64 and 79—are called MINPRI_RESERVED and MAXPRI_RESERVED, respectively. MINPRI_RESERVED is returned as the *server* priority by host_info().
80–95	This range contains kernel-only priorities. The priorities 80, 81, 93, and 95 are called MINPRI_KERNEL, BASEPRI_KERNEL, BASEPRI_PREEMPT, and MAXPRI_KERNEL, respectively. host_info() returns MINPRI_KERNEL as the value of both the *kernel* and *system* priorities.
96–127	The priorities in this range are reserved for real-time threads and are attainable through thread_policy_set(). The priorities 96, 97, and 127 are called BASEPRI_REALTIME, BASEPRI_RTQUEUES, and MAXPRI, respectively.

threads and contains an array of NRQS doubly linked lists, one corresponding to each priority level. The structure's highq member is a hint that indicates the likely location of the highest priority thread, which may be at a priority lower than the one specified by highq but *will not* be at a higher priority. Recall that each processor set has a run queue and each processor has a local run queue.

FIGURE 7–47 The run queue structure

```
// osfmk/kern/sched.h

#define NRQS      128         // 128 levels per run queue
#define NRQBM     (NRQS/32)   // number of words per bitmap
#define MAXPRI    (NRQS-1)    // maximum priority possible
#define MINPRI    IDLEPRI     // lowest legal priority schedulable
```

(continues)

FIGURE 7–47 The run queue structure *(continued)*

```
#define IDLEPRI    0         // idle thread priority
#define DEPRESSPRI MINPRI    // depress priority
...
struct run_queue {
    int highq;               // highest runnable queue
    int bitmap[NRQBM];       // run queue bitmap array
    int count;               // number of threads total
    int urgency;             // level of preemption urgency
    queue_head_t queues[NRQS]; // one for each priority
};
```

7.4.2.3 Scheduling Information in Tasks and Threads

To balance processor usage among threads, the scheduler adjusts thread priorities to account for each thread's usage. Associated with each thread and task are several priority-related limits and measurements. Let us revisit the task and thread structures to examine some of the scheduling-related information contained within them. The relevant portions of the structures are annotated in Figure 7–48.

FIGURE 7–48 Important scheduling-related fields of the task and thread structures

```
// osfmk/kern/task.h

struct task {
    ...
    // task's role in the system
    // set to TASK_UNSPECIFIED during user task creation
    task_role_t role;

    // default base priority for threads created within this task
    // set to BASEPRI_DEFAULT during user task creation
    integer_t priority;

    // no thread in this task can have priority greater than this
    // set to MAXPRI_USER during user task creation
    integer_t max_priority;
    ...
};


// osfmk/kern/thread.h
```

(continues)

FIGURE 7–48 Important scheduling-related fields of the task and thread structures *(continued)*

```
struct thread {
    ...
    // scheduling mode bits include TH_MODE_REALTIME (time-constrained thread),
    // TH_MODE_TIMESHARE (uses standard timesharing scheduling),
    // TH_MODE_PREEMPT (can preempt kernel contexts), ...
    //
    // TH_MODE_TIMESHARE is set during user thread creation
    integer_t sched_mode;

    integer_t sched_pri;      // scheduled (current) priority

    // base priority
    // set to parent_task->priority during user thread creation
    integer_t priority;

    // maximum base priority
    // set to parent_task->max_priority during user thread creation
    integer_t max_priority;

    // copy of parent task's base priority
    // set to parent_task->priority during user thread creation
    integer_t task_priority;  // copy of task's base priority


    ...

    // task-relative importance
    // set to (self->priority - self->task_priority) during user thread creation
    integer_t importance;

    // parameters for time-constrained scheduling policy
    struct {
        ...
    } realtime;

    uint32_t current_quantum; // duration of current quantum


    ...

    // last scheduler tick
    // set to the global variable sched_tick during user thread creation
    natural_t sched_stamp;

    // timesharing processor usage
    // initialized to zero in the "template" thread
    natural_t sched_usage;

    // factor for converting usage to priority
    // set to the processor set's pri_shift value during user thread creation
    natural_t pri_shift;
};
```

As shown in Figure 7–48, each thread has a *base priority*. However, the thread's *scheduled priority* is the one that the scheduler examines while selecting threads to run.[18] The scheduled priority is computed from the base priority along with an offset derived from the thread's recent processor usage. The default base priority for timesharing user threads is 31, whereas the minimum kernel priority is 80. Consequently, kernel threads are substantially favored over standard user threads.

7.4.2.4 *Processor Usage Accounting*

As a thread accumulates processor usage, its priority decreases. Since the scheduler favors higher priorities, this could lead to a situation where a thread has used so much processor time that the scheduler will assign it no further processor time owing to its greatly lowered priority. The Mach scheduler addresses this issue by *aging* processor usage—it exponentially "forgets" a thread's past processor usage, gradually increasing that thread's priority. However, this creates another problem: If the system is under such heavy load that most (or all) threads receive little processor time, the priorities of all such threads will increase. The resultant contention will deteriorate system response under heavy load. To counter this problem, the scheduler multiplies a thread's processor usage by a *conversion factor* related to system load, thereby ensuring that thread priorities do not rise because of increased system load alone. Figure 7–49 shows the calculation of a thread's timesharing priority based on its processor usage and the system's load.

FIGURE 7–49 Computation of the timesharing priority of a thread

`// osfmk/kern/priority.c`

```
#define do_priority_computation(thread, pri) \
    do { \
        (pri) = (thread->priority) /* start with base priority */ \
        - ((thread)->sched_usage >> (thread)->pri_shift); \
        if ((pri) < MINPRI_USER) \
            (pri) = MINPRI_USER; \
        else if ((pri) > MAXPRI_KERNEL) \
            (pri) = MAXPRI_KERNEL; \
    } while (FALSE);
```

---

18. This discussion applies only to timesharing threads. Real-time threads are treated specially by the scheduler.

We see in Figure 7–49 that the thread's processor usage (`thread->sched_usage`), after being lowered by a conversion factor (`thread->pri_shift`), is subtracted from its base priority (`thread->priority`) to yield the scheduled priority. Let us now see how the conversion factor is calculated and how the thread's processor usage decays over time.

> `update_priority()` [osfmk/kern/priority], which is frequently called as part of the scheduler's operation, under certain conditions updates the thread's conversion factor value by setting it to that of the processor set containing the thread.

The conversion factor consists of two components: a fixed part based on the machine-dependent absolute-time unit and a dynamic part based on system load. The global variable `sched_pri_shift` contains the fixed part, which is computed during scheduler initialization. The dynamic part is an entry in a constant array, with the array index based on the system load. Figure 7–50 shows a user-space implementation of a function to convert clock intervals to absolute-time intervals. Using this function, we can reconstruct the computation of `sched_pri_shift` in user space. The program also computes the value of `sched_tick_interval`, which corresponds to an interval of 125 ms.

FIGURE 7–50 User-space computation of `sched_pri_shift` and `sched_tick_interval`

```
// sched_pri_shift.c

#include <stdio.h>
#include <stdlib.h>
#include <mach/mach.h>
#include <mach/mach_time.h>

// defined in osfmk/kern/sched.h
#define BASEPRI_DEFAULT 31
#define SCHED_TICK_SHIFT 3

void
clock_interval_to_absolutetime_interval(uint32_t interval,
                                         uint32_t scale_factor,
                                         uint64_t *result)
{
    uint64_t t64;
    uint32_t divisor, rtclock_sec_divisor;
```

(continues)

FIGURE 7–50 User-space computation of `sched_pri_shift` and `sched_tick_interval`
(*continued*)

```
  uint64_t nanosecs = (uint64_t)interval * scale_factor;
    mach_timebase_info_data_t tbinfo;
    (void)mach_timebase_info(&tbinfo);

    // see timebase_callback() [osfmk/ppc/rtclock.c]
    rtclock_sec_divisor = tbinfo.denom / (tbinfo.numer / NSEC_PER_SEC);

    *result = (t64 = nanosecs / NSEC_PER_SEC) * (divisor = rtclock_sec_divisor);
    nanosecs -= (t64 * NSEC_PER_SEC);
    *result += (nanosecs * divisor) / NSEC_PER_SEC;
}

int
main(void)
{
    uint64_t abstime;
    uint32_t sched_pri_shift;
    uint32_t sched_tick_interval;

    clock_interval_to_absolutetime_interval(USEC_PER_SEC >> SCHED_TICK_SHIFT,
                                            NSEC_PER_USEC, &abstime);
    sched_tick_interval = abstime; // lvalue is 32-bit
    abstime = (abstime * 5) / 3;
    for (sched_pri_shift = 0; abstime > BASEPRI_DEFAULT; ++sched_pri_shift)
        abstime >>= 1;

    printf("sched_tick_interval = %u\n", sched_tick_interval);
    printf("sched_pri_shift = %u\n", sched_pri_shift);

    exit(0);
}


$ gcc -Wall -o sched_pri_shift sched_pri_shift.c
$ ./sched_pri_shift
sched_tick_interval = 4166271
sched_pri_shift = 18
```

Figure 7–51 shows a code excerpt from the computation of the conversion
factor's dynamic part.

FIGURE 7–51 Computation of the usage-to-priority conversion factor for timeshared priorities

`// osfmk/kern/sched_prim.c`

```
int8_t sched_load_shifts[NRQS];
...

// called during scheduler initialization
// initializes the array of load shift constants
static void
load_shift_init(void)
{
    int8_t   k, *p = sched_load_shifts;
    uint32_t i, j;

    *p++ = INT8_MIN; *p++ = 0;

    for (i = j = 2, k = 1; i < NRQS; ++k) {
        for (j <<= 1; i < j; ++i)
            *p++ = k;
    }
}
```

`// osfmk/kern/sched_average.c`

```
void
compute_averages(void)
{
    ...
    register int      nthreads, nshared;
    register uint32_t load_now = 0;
    ...
    if ((ncpus = pset->processor_count) > 0) {
        nthreads = pset->run_count - 1; // ignore current thread
        nshared = pset->share_count;    // so many timeshared threads
        ...
        if (nshared > nthreads)
            nshared = nthreads;          // current was timeshared!

        if (nshared > ncpus) {
            if (ncpus > 1)
                load_now = nshared / ncpus;
            else
                load_now = nshared;

            if (load_now > NRQS - 1)
                load_now = NRQS - 1;
        }
```

(continues)

FIGURE 7–51 Computation of the usage-to-priority conversion factor for timeshared priorities *(continued)*

```
        pset->pri_shift = sched_pri_shift - sched_load_shifts[load_now];

    } else {
        ...
        pset->pri_shift = INT8_MAX; // hardcoded to 127
        ...
    }

    // compute other averages
    ...
}
```

The scheduler ages processor usage of threads in a distributed manner: `update_priority()` [`osfmk/kern/priority.c`], which performs the relevant calculations, is called from several places. For example, it is called when a thread's quantum expires. The function call graph in Figure 7–46 shows several invocations of `update_priority()`. It begins by calculating the difference (`ticks`) between the current scheduler tick (`sched_tick`), which is incremented periodically, and the thread's recorded scheduler tick (`thread->sched_stamp`). The latter is brought up to date by adding `ticks` to it. If `ticks` is equal to or more than `SCHED_DECAY_TICKS` (32), the thread's processor usage is reset to zero. Otherwise, the usage is multiplied by 5/8 for each unit of difference—that is, it is multiplied by $(5/8)^{\text{ticks}}$. There were two primary reasons behind the choice of 5/8 as the exponential decay factor: It provided scheduling behavior similar to other timesharing systems, and multiplication with it can be approximated by using only shift, addition, and subtraction operations. Consider multiplying a number by 5/8, which can be written as $(4 + 1)/8$—that is, $(4/8 + 1/8)$, or $(1/2 + 1/8)$. Multiplication with $(1/2 + 1/8)$ can be performed with a right shift by 1, a right shift by 3, and an addition. To facilitate decay calculations, the kernel maintains a static array with `SCHED_DECAY_TICKS` pairs of integers—the pair at index i contains shift values to approximate $(5/8)^i$. If the value of `ticks` falls between 0 and 31, both inclusive, the pair at index `ticks` is used according to the following formula:

```
if (/* the pair's second value is positive */) {
    usage = (usage >> (first value)) + (usage >> abs(second value)));
else
    usage = (usage >> (first value)) - (usage >> abs(second value)));
```

The program in Figure 7–52 computes $(5/8)^n$, where $0 \le n < 32$, using the shift values in the kernel's decay shift array and using functions from the math library. It also calculates the percentage difference—that is, the approximation error, which is less than 15% in the worst case.

FIGURE 7–52 Approximating multiplication by 5/8 as implemented in the scheduler

```
// approximate_5by8.c

#include <stdio.h>
#include <math.h>

struct shift {
    int shift1;
    int shift2;
};

#define SCHED_DECAY_TICKS 32

static struct shift sched_decay_shifts[SCHED_DECAY_TICKS] = {
    {1, 1}, {1, 3}, {1, -3}, {2, -7}, {3, 5}, {3, -5}, {4, -8}, {5, 7},
    {5, -7}, {6, -10}, {7, 10}, {7, -9}, {8, -11}, {9, 12}, {9, -11}, {10, -13},
    {11,14}, {11,-13}, {12,-15}, {13,17}, {13,-15}, {14,-17}, {15,19}, {16,18},
    {16,-19}, {17,22}, {18,20}, {18,-20}, {19,26}, {20,22}, {20,-22}, {21,-27}
};

int
main(void)
{
    int    i, v, v0 = 10000000;
    double x5_8, y5_8;
    double const5_8 = (double)5/(double)8;
    struct shift *shiftp;

    for (i = 0; i < SCHED_DECAY_TICKS; i++) {
        shiftp = &sched_decay_shifts[i];
        v = v0;
        if (shiftp->shift2 > 0)
            v = (v >> shiftp->shift1) + (v >> shiftp->shift2);
        else
            v = (v >> shiftp->shift1) - (v >> -(shiftp->shift2));
        x5_8 = pow(const5_8, (double)i);
        y5_8 = (double)v/(double)v0;
        printf("%10.10f\t%10.10f\t%10.2f\n", x5_8, y5_8,
               ((x5_8 - y5_8)/x5_8) * 100.0);
    }

    return 0;
}
```

(continues)

FIGURE 7–52 Approximating multiplication by 5/8 as implemented in the scheduler
(continued)

```
$ gcc -Wall -o approximate_5by8 approximate_5by8.c
$ ./approximate_5by8
1.0000000000    1.0000000000         0.00
0.6250000000    0.6250000000         0.00
0.3906250000    0.3750000000         4.00
0.2441406250    0.2421875000         0.80
...
0.0000007523    0.0000007000         6.95
0.0000004702    0.0000004000        14.93
```

Note that it is not sufficient to make a thread responsible for decaying its processor usage. Threads with low priorities may continue to remain on the run queue without getting a chance to run because of higher-priority threads. In particular, these low-priority threads will be unable to raise their priorities by decaying their own usage—somebody else must do so on their behalf. The scheduler runs a dedicated kernel thread—thread_update_scan()—for this purpose.

```
// Pass #1 of thread run queue scanner
// Likely threads are referenced in thread_update_array[]
// This pass locks the run queues, but not the threads
//
static boolean_t
runq_scan(run_queue_t runq)
{
    ...
}


// Pass #2 of thread run queue scanner (invokes pass #1)
// A candidate thread may have its priority updated through update priority()
// This pass locks the thread, but not the run queue
//
static void
thread_update_scan(void)
{
    ...
}
```

thread_update_scan() is called from the scheduler tick function sched_tick_continue(), which periodically runs to perform scheduler-related bookkeeping functions. It consists of two logical passes. In the first pass, it iterates over the run queues, comparing the sched_stamp values of timesharing threads with sched_tick. This pass collects up to THREAD_UPDATE_SIZE (128) candidate threads in an array. The second pass iterates over this array's elements, calling `update_priority()` on timesharing threads that satisfy the following criteria.

- The thread is neither stopped nor requested to be stopped (the `TH_SUSP` bit in its state is not set).
- The thread is not queued for waiting (the `TH_WAIT` bit in its state is not set).
- The thread's `sched_stamp` is still not up to date with `sched_tick`.

7.4.3 Scheduling Policies

Mac OS X supports multiple scheduling policies, namely, `THREAD_STANDARD_POLICY` (timesharing), `THREAD_EXTENDED_POLICY`, `THREAD_PRECEDENCE_POLICY`, and `THREAD_TIME_CONSTRAINT_POLICY` (real time). The Mach routines `thread_policy_get()` and `thread_policy_set()` can be used to retrieve and modify, respectively, the scheduling policy of a thread. The Pthreads API supports retrieving and setting pthread scheduling policies and scheduling parameters through `pthread_getschedparam()` and `pthread_setschedparam()`, respectively. Scheduling policy information can also be specified at pthread creation time as pthread attributes. Note that the Pthreads API uses different policies, namely, `SCHED_FIFO` (first in, first out), `SCHED_RR` (round robin), and `SCHED_OTHER` (system-specific policy—maps to the default, timesharing policy on Mac OS X). In particular, the Pthreads API does not support specifying a real-time policy. Let us now look at each of the scheduling policies.

7.4.3.1 *THREAD_STANDARD_POLICY*

This is the standard scheduling policy and is the default for timesharing threads. Under this policy, threads running long-running computations are fairly assigned approximately equal processor resources. A count of timesharing threads is maintained for each processor set.

7.4.3.2 *THREAD_EXTENDED_POLICY*

This is an extended version of the standard policy. In this policy, a Boolean hint designates a thread as non-long-running (nontimesharing) or long-running (timesharing). In the latter case, this policy is identical to `THREAD_STANDARD_POLICY`. In the former case, the thread will run at a fixed priority, provided its processor usage does not exceed an unsafe limit, in which case the scheduler will temporarily demote it to being a timesharing thread through a fail-safe mechanism (see Section 7.4.3.4).

7.4.3.3 *THREAD_PRECEDENCE_POLICY*

This policy allows an *importance value*—a signed integer—to be associated with a thread, thus allowing threads within a task to be designated as more or less important relative to each other. Other aspects being equal (the same time constraint attributes, say), the more important thread in a task will be favored over a less important thread. Note that this policy can be used in conjunction with the other policies.

Let us look at an example of using THREAD_PRECEDENCE_POLICY. The program in Figure 7–53 creates two pthreads within a task. Both threads run a function called adder() that continually increments a counter provided to it as an argument. We set the scheduling policies of both threads to THREAD_PRECEDENCE_POLICY, with the respective importance values specified on the command line. The program runs for a few seconds, with the counters of both threads being incremented as the threads receive processing time. Before exiting, the program prints the valuse of both threads' counters. The valuse will be crude indcators of the respective amounts of processing time the two threads received.

FIGURE 7–53 Experimenting with the THREAD_PRECEDENCE_POLICY scheduling policy

```
// thread_precedence_policy.c

#include <stdio.h>
#include <unistd.h>
#include <stdlib.h>
#include <pthread.h>
#include <sys/param.h>
#include <mach/mach.h>
#include <mach/thread_policy.h>

#define PROGNAME "thread_precedence_policy"

void
usage(void)
{
    fprintf(stderr, "usage: %s <thread1 importance> <thread2 importance>\n"
                    "       where %d <= importance <= %d\n",
            PROGNAME, -MAXPRI, MAXPRI);
    exit(1);
}
```

(continues)

FIGURE 7–53 Experimenting with the `THREAD_PRECEDENCE_POLICY` scheduling policy *(continued)*

```c
void *
adder(void *arg)
{
    unsigned long long *ctr = (unsigned long long *)arg;
    sleep(1);
    while (1)
        (*ctr)++;

    return NULL;
}


int
main(int argc, char **argv)
{
    int                ret, imp1, imp2;
    kern_return_t      kr;
    pthread_t          t1, t2;
    unsigned long long ctr1 = 0, ctr2 = 0;

    thread_precedence_policy_data_t policy;

    if (argc != 3)
        usage();

    imp1 = atoi(argv[1]);
    imp2 = atoi(argv[2]);
    if ((abs(imp1) > MAXPRI) || (abs(imp2) > MAXPRI))
        usage();

    ret = pthread_create(&t1, (pthread_attr_t *)0, adder, (void *)&ctr1);
    ret = pthread_create(&t2, (pthread_attr_t *)0, adder, (void *)&ctr2);

    policy.importance = imp1;
    kr = thread_policy_set(pthread_mach_thread_np(t1),
                      THREAD_PRECEDENCE_POLICY,
                      (thread_policy_t)&policy,
                      THREAD_PRECEDENCE_POLICY_COUNT);

    policy.importance = imp2;
    kr = thread_policy_set(pthread_mach_thread_np(t2),
                      THREAD_PRECEDENCE_POLICY,
                      (thread_policy_t)&policy,
                      THREAD_PRECEDENCE_POLICY_COUNT);

    ret = pthread_detach(t1);
    ret = pthread_detach(t2);
```

(continues)

FIGURE 7–53 Experimenting with the `THREAD_PRECEDENCE_POLICY` scheduling policy *(continued)*

```
    sleep(10);

    printf("ctr1=%llu ctr2=%llu\n", ctr1, ctr2);

    exit(0);
}
```

```
$ gcc -Wall -o thread_precedence_policy thread_precedence_policy.c
$ ./thread_precedence_policy -127 -127
ctr1=953278876 ctr2=938172399
$ ./thread_precedence_policy -127 127
ctr1=173546131 ctr2=1201063747
```

7.4.3.4 *THREAD_TIME_CONSTRAINT_POLICY*

This is a real-time scheduling policy intended for threads with real-time constraints on their execution. Using this policy, a thread can specify to the scheduler that it needs a certain fraction of processor time, perhaps periodically. The scheduler will favor a real-time thread over all other threads, except perhaps other real-time threads. The policy can be applied to a thread using `thread_policy_set()` with the following policy-specific parameters: three integers (period, computation, and constraint) and a Boolean (preemptible). Each of the three integer parameters is specified in absolute-time units. A nonzero *period* value specifies the nominal periodicity in the computation—that is, the time between two consecutive processing arrivals. The *computation* value specifies the nominal time needed during a processing span. The *constraint* value specifies the maximum amount of real time that may elapse from the start of a processing span to the end of the computation. Note that the constraint value cannot be less than the computation value. The difference of the constraint and the computation values is the real-time latency. Finally, the *preemptible* parameter specifies whether the computation may be interrupted.

Note that the real-time policy does not require special privileges to be used. Therefore, it must be used with care, given that it raises a thread's priority above that of several kernel threads. For example, using a real-time thread may be beneficial if the thread has a time-critical deadline to meet and latency is an issue. However, if the thread consumes too much processor time, using the real-time policy can be counterproductive.

The scheduler includes a fail-safe mechanism for nontimesharing threads whose processor usage exceeds an unsafe threshold. When such a thread's quantum expires, it is demoted to being a timesharing thread, and its priority is set to DEPRESSPRI. However, in the case of a real-time thread, the scheduler remembers the thread's erstwhile real-time desires. After a safe release duration, the thread is promoted to being a real-time thread again, and its priority is set to BASEPRI_RTQUEUES.

> The maximum unsafe computation is defined as the product of the standard quantum and the max_unsafe_quanta constant. The default value of max_unsafe_quanta is MAX_UNSAFE_QUANTA, defined to be 800 in osfmk/kern/sched_prim.c. An alternate value can be provided through the unsafe boot-time argument.

The following are examples of the use of THREAD_TIME_CONSTRAINT_ POLICY:

- The dynamic_pager program
- Multimedia applications such as GarageBand, iTunes, MIDI Server, Quick-Time Player, and the Core Audio layer in general
- The I/O Kit's FireWire family
- The WindowServer program
- The IIDCAssistant program, which is part of the audio plug-in for Apple's iSight camera

You can use the lstasks program from Figure 7–21 to display the scheduling policy of a task's threads.

```
$ sudo ./lstasks -v
...
Task #70
  BSD process id (pid)   = 605 (QuickTime Player)
...
    thread 2/4 (0x16803) in task 70 (0x5803)
...
      scheduling policy         = TIME_CONSTRAINT
        period                  = 0
        computation             = 166650
        constraint              = 333301
        preemptible             = TRUE
  ...
```

The program in Figure 7–54 is a crude example of time-constrained processing. It creates a thread that performs a periodic computation that involves sleeping for a fixed duration followed by processing for a fixed duration. We use `mach_absolute_time()` to measure the approximate difference between the time the thread wished to sleep for and the actual sleeping time. If the difference is more than a predefined threshold, we increment an error count. If the program is run with no command-line arguments, it will not modify the thread's scheduling policy. If one or more command-line arguments *are* provided, the program will set the policy to `THREAD_TIME_CONSTRAINT_POLICY` using predefined parameters. Thus, we can compare the number of errors in the two cases. Moreover, we can run other programs to load the system. For example, we can run an infinite loop—say, through a command such as `perl -e 'while (1) {}'`.

FIGURE 7–54 Experimenting with the `THREAD_TIME_CONSTRAINT_POLICY` scheduling policy

```
// thread_time_constraint_policy.c

#include <stdio.h>
#include <unistd.h>
#include <stdlib.h>
#include <pthread.h>
#include <mach/mach.h>
#include <mach/mach_time.h>
#include <mach/thread_policy.h>

#define PROGNAME "thread_time_constraint_policy"

#define SLEEP_NS 50000000 // sleep for 50 ms

// if actual sleeping time differs from SLEEP_NS by more than this amount,
// count it as an error
#define ERROR_THRESH_NS ((double)50000) // 50 us

static double           abs2clock;
static unsigned long long nerrors = 0, nsamples = 0;
static struct timespec   rqt = { 0, SLEEP_NS };

// before exiting, print the information we collected
void
atexit_handler(void)
{
    printf("%llu errors in %llu samples\n", nerrors, nsamples);
}
```

(continues)

FIGURE 7–54 Experimenting with the THREAD_TIME_CONSTRAINT_POLICY scheduling policy *(continued)*

```
void *
timestamper(void *arg)
{
    int        ret;
    double     diff_ns;
    u_int64_t t1, t2, diff;

    while (1) {
        t1 = mach_absolute_time();   // take a high-resolution timestamp
        ret = nanosleep(&rqt, NULL); // sleep for SLEEP_NS seconds
        t2 = mach_absolute_time();   // take another high-resolution timestamp
        if (ret != 0)                // if sleeping failed, give up
            exit(1);
        diff = t2 - t1;              // how much did we sleep?

        // the "error" (in nanoseconds) in our sleeping time
        diff_ns = ((double)SLEEP_NS) - (double)diff * abs2clock;

        if (diff_ns < 0)
            diff_ns *= -1;

        if (diff_ns > ERROR_THRESH_NS)
            nerrors++;

        nsamples++;
    }

    return NULL;
}

int
main(int argc, char **argv)
{
    int             ret;
    kern_return_t   kr;
    pthread_t       t1;
    static double clock2abs;

    mach_timebase_info_data_t              tbinfo;
    thread_time_constraint_policy_data_t policy;

    ret = pthread_create(&t1, (pthread_attr_t *)0, timestamper, (void *)0);
    ret = atexit(atexit_handler);

    (void)mach_timebase_info(&tbinfo);
    abs2clock = ((double)tbinfo.numer / (double)tbinfo.denom);
```

(continues)

FIGURE 7–54 Experimenting with the `THREAD_TIME_CONSTRAINT_POLICY` scheduling policy *(continued)*

```
    // if any command-line argument is given, enable real-time
    if (argc > 1) {

        clock2abs = ((double)tbinfo.denom / (double)tbinfo.numer) * 1000000;

        policy.period      = 50 * clock2abs; // 50 ms periodicity
        policy.computation = 1 * clock2abs;  // 1 ms of work
        policy.constraint  = 2 * clock2abs;
        policy.preemptible = FALSE;

        kr = thread_policy_set(pthread_mach_thread_np(t1),
                        THREAD_TIME_CONSTRAINT_POLICY,
                        (thread_policy_t)&policy,
                        THREAD_TIME_CONSTRAINT_POLICY_COUNT);
        if (kr != KERN_SUCCESS) {
            mach_error("thread_policy_set:", kr);
            goto OUT;
        }
    }

    ret = pthread_detach(t1);

    printf("waiting 10 seconds...\n");
    sleep(10);

OUT:
    exit(0);
}


$ gcc -Wall -o thread_time_constraint thread_time_constraint.c
$ ./thread_time_constraint
waiting 10 seconds...
117 errors in 189 samples
$ ./thread_time_constraint enable_real_time
0 errors in 200 samples
```

7.4.3.5 Priority Recomputation on Policy Change

When `thread_policy_set()` is used to change a thread's scheduling policy, or to modify the parameters of an existing policy in effect, the kernel recomputes the thread's priority and importance values, subject to the thread's maximum and minimum priority limits. Figure 7–55 shows the relevant calculations.

FIGURE 7–55 Recomputing a thread's priority on a scheduling-policy change

```
// osfmk/kern/thread_policy.c

static void
thread_recompute_priority(thread_t thread)
{
    integer_t priority;

    if (thread->sched_mode & TH_MODE_REALTIME)
        priority = BASEPRI_RTQUEUES;          // real-time
    else {
        if (thread->importance > MAXPRI)      // very important thread
            priority = MAXPRI;
        else if (thread->importance < -MAXPRI) // very unimportant thread
            priority = -MAXPRI;
        else
            priority = thread->importance;

        priority += thread->task_priority;    // add base priority

        if (priority > thread->max_priority)  // clip to maximum allowed
            priority = thread->max_priority;
        else if (priority < MINPRI)           // clip to minimum possible
            priority = MINPRI;
    }

    // set the base priority of the thread and reset its scheduled priority
    set_priority(thread, priority);
}
```

7.4.3.6 Task Roles

As we saw earlier in this chapter, the task_policy_set() routine can be used to set the scheduling policy associated with a task. TASK_CATEGORY_POLICY is an example of a task policy flavor. It informs the kernel about the *role* of the task in the operating system. With this flavor, task_policy_set() can be used to designate a task's role. The following are examples of task roles in Mac OS X.

- TASK_UNSPECIFIED is the default role.
- TASK_FOREGROUND_APPLICATION is intended for a normal UI-based application meant to run in the foreground from the UI's standpoint. Assigning this role to a task sets its priority to BASEPRI_FOREGROUND (see Table 7–2). The task's maximum priority remains unchanged.

- `TASK_BACKGROUND_APPLICATION` is intended for a normal UI-based application meant to run in the background from the UI's standpoint. Assigning this role to a task sets its priority to `BASEPRI_BACKGROUND`. Again, the maximum priority is unaltered.

- `TASK_CONTROL_APPLICATION` can be assigned to at most one task at a time on a first-come first-serve basis. It designates the task as *the* UI-based control application. The `loginwindow` program normally uses this designation. Assigning this role is a privileged action that results in the task's priority being set to `BASEPRI_CONTROL` without affecting its maximum priority.

- `TASK_GRAPHICS_SERVER` should be assigned to the window management server—that is, the `WindowServer` program. Like `TASK_CONTROL_APPLICATION`, this role too is assignable—with privileged access—only to one task on a first-come first-serve basis. The task's priority and maximum priority are set to (`MAXPRI_RESERVED - 3`) and `MAXPRI_RESERVED`, respectively. The system may or may not use this role.

Note that roles are not inherited across tasks. Therefore, every task begins life with `TASK_UNSPECIFIED` as its role. We can use our `lstasks` program to examine the roles of various tasks in the system.

```
$ sudo ./lstasks -v
...
Task #21
  BSD process id (pid)    = 74 (loginwindow)
...
    role                  = CONTROL_APPLICATION
...
Task #29
  BSD process id (pid)    = 153 (Dock)
...
    role                  = BACKGROUND_APPLICATION
...
Task #31
  BSD process id (pid)    = 156 (Finder)
...
    role                  = BACKGROUND_APPLICATION
...
Task #45
  BSD process id (pid)    = 237 (Terminal)
...
    role                  = FOREGROUND_APPLICATION
...
```

7.5 The `execve()` System Call

The `execve()` system call is the only kernel-level mechanism available to user programs to execute another program. Other user-level program-launching functions are all built atop `execve()` [bsd/kern/kern_exec.c]. Figure 7–57 shows an overview of `execve()`'s operation.

   `execve()` initializes and partially populates an image parameter block (`struct image_params` [bsd/sys/imgact.h]), which acts as a container for passing around program parameters between functions called by `execve()`, while the latter is preparing to execute the given program. Other fields of this structure are set gradually. Figure 7–56 shows the contents of the `image_params` structure.

FIGURE 7–56 Structure for holding executable image parameters during the `execve()` system call

```
// bsd/sys/imgact.h

struct image_params {
     user_addr_t          ip_user_fname;// execve()'s first argument
     user_addr_t          ip_user_argv; // execve()'s second argument
     user_addr_t          ip_user_envv; // execve()'s third argument
     struct vnode         *ip_vp;        // executable file's vnode
     struct vnode_attr *ip_vattr;        // effective file attributes (at runtime)
     struct vnode_attr *ip_origvattr;    // original file attributes (at invocation)
     char                 *ip_vdata;     // file data (up to 1 page)
     int                  ip_flags;      // image flags
     int                  ip_argc;       // argument count
     char                 *ip_argv;      // argument vector beginning (kernel)
     int                  ip_envc;       // environment count
     char                 *ip_strings;   // base address for strings (kernel)
     char                 *ip_strendp;   // current end pointer (kernel)
     char                 *ip_strendargvp;   // end of argv/start of envp (kernel)
     int                  ip_strspace;   // remaining space
     user_size_t          ip_arch_offset;    // subfile offset in ip_vp
     user_size_t          ip_interp_name[IMG_SHSIZE]; // interpreter name
     char                 *ip_p_comm;       // optional alternative p->p_comm
     char                 *ip_tws_cache_name; // task working set cache
     struct vfs_context*ip_vfs_context;     // VFS context
     struct nameidata *ip_ndp;              // current nameidata
     thread_t             ip_vfork_thread;  // thread created, if vfork()
};
```

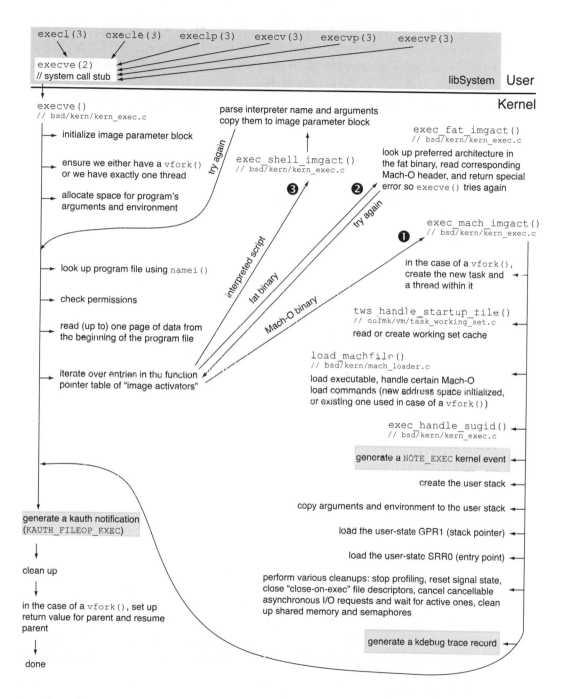

FIGURE 7–57 The operation of the `execve()` system call

execve() ensures that there is exactly one thread within the current task, unless it is an execve() preceded by a vfork(). Next, it allocates a block of pageable memory for holding its arguments and for reading the first page of the program executable. The size of this allocation is (NCARGS + PAGE_SIZE), where NCARGS is the maximum number of bytes allowed for execve()'s arguments.[19]

```
// bsd/sys/param.h
#define NCARGS ARG_MAX
```

```
// bsd/sys/syslimits.h
#define ARG_MAX (256 * 1024)
```

execve() saves a copy of its first argument—the program's path, which may be relative or absolute—at a specifically computed offset in this block. The argv[0] pointer points to this location. It then sets the ip_tws_cache_name field of the image parameter block to point to the filename component of the executable's path. This is used by the kernel's task working set (TWS) detection/caching mechanism, which we will discuss in Chapter 8. However, execve() does not perform this step if TWS is disabled (as determined by the app_profile global variable) or if the calling process is running chroot()'ed.

execve() now calls namei() [bsd/vfs/vfs_lookup.c] to convert the executable's path into a vnode. It then uses the vnode to perform a variety of permission checks on the executable file. To do so, it retrieves the following attributes of the vnode: the user and group IDs, the mode, the file system ID, the file ID (unique within the file system), and the data fork's size. The following are examples of the checks performed.

- Ensure that the vnode represents a regular file.
- Ensure that at least one execute bit is enabled on the file.
- Ensure that the data fork's size is nonzero.
- If the process is being traced, or if the file system has been mounted with the "nosuid" option, nullify the setuid (set-user-identifier) or setgid (set-group-identifier) bits should they be present.
- Call vnode_authorize() [bsd/vfs/vfs_subr.c], which calls kauth_authorize_action() [bsd/kern/kern_athorization.c] to authorize the requested action—in this case, KAUTH_VNODE_EXECUTE—with the kauth

---

19. As we will see in Chapter 8, an argument list longer than the maximum allowed size will result in an E2BIG error from the kernel.

authorization subsystem. (If the process is being traced, the KAUTH_VNODE_ READ action is also authorized, since traced executables must also be readable.)

- Ensure that the vnode is not opened for writing, and if it is, return an ETXTBSY error ("text file busy").

execve() then reads the first page of data from the executable into a buffer within the image parameter block, after which it iterates over the entries in the *image activator table* to allow a type-specific activator, or handler, to load the executable. The table contains activators for Mach-O binaries, fat binaries, and interpreter scripts.

// bsd/kern/kern_exec.c

```
struct execsw {
    int (* ex_imgact)(struct image_params *);
    const char *ex_name;
} execsw[] = {
    { exec_mach_imgact,   "Mach-o Binary"      },
    { exec_fat_imgact,    "Fat Binary"         },
    { exec_shell_imgact,  "Interpreter Script" },
    { NULL,               NULL                 }
};
```

Note that the activators are attempted in the order that they appear in the table—therefore, an executable is attempted as a Mach-O binary first and as an interpreter script last.

7.5.1 Mach-O Binaries

The exec_mach_imgact() [bsd/kern/kern_exec.c] activator handles Mach-O binaries. It is the most preferred activator, being the first entry in the activator table. Moreover, since the Mac OS X kernel supports only the Mach-O native executable format, activators for fat binaries and interpreter scripts eventually lead to exec_mach_imgact().

7.5.1.1 Preparations for the Execution of a Mach-O File

exec_mach_imgact() begins by performing the following actions.

- It ensures that the executable is either a 32-bit or a 64-bit Mach-O binary.
- If the current thread had performed a vfork() prior to calling execve()— as determined by the UT_VFORK bit being set in the uu_flag field of the

uthread structure—exec_mach_imgact() makes note of this by setting the vfexec variable to 1.

- If the Mach-O header is for a 64-bit binary, exec_mach_imgact() sets a flag indicating this fact in the image parameter block.

- It calls grade_binary() [bsd/dev/ppc/kern_machdev.c] to ensure that the process type and subtype specified in the Mach-O header are acceptable to the kernel—if not, an EBADARCH error ("Bad CPU type in executable") is returned.

- It copies into the kernel the arguments and environment variables that were passed to execve() from user space.

In the case of vfork(), the child process is using the parent's resources at this point—the parent is suspended. In particular, although vfork() would have created a BSD process structure for the child process, there is neither a corresponding Mach task nor a thread. exec_mach_imgact() now creates a task and a thread for a vfork()'ed child.

Next, exec_mach_imgact() calls task_set_64bit() [osfmk/kern/task.c] with a Boolean argument specifying whether the task is 64-bit or not. task_set_64bit() makes architecture-specific adjustments, some of which depend on the kernel version, to the task. For example, in the case of a 32-bit process, task_set_64bit() deallocates all memory that may have been allocated beyond the 32-bit address space (such as the 64-bit comm area). Since Mac OS X 10.4 does not support TWS for 64-bit programs, task_set_64bit() disables this optimization for a 64-bit task.

In the case of executables for which TWS is supported and the ip_tws_cache_name field in the image parameter block is not NULL, exec_mach_imgact() calls tws_handle_startup_file() [osfmk/vm/task_working_set.c]. The latter will attempt to read a per-user, per-application saved working set. If none exists, it will create one.

7.5.1.2 Loading the Mach-O File

exec_mach_imgact() calls load_machfile() [bsd/kern/mach_loader.c] to load the Mach-O file. It passes a pointer to a load_result_t structure to load_machfile()—the structure's fields will be populated on a successful return from load_machfile().

```
// bsd/kern/mach_loader.h

typedef struct _load_result {
    user_addr_t mach_header; // mapped user virtual address of Mach-O header
    user_addr_t entry_point; // thread's entry point (from SRR0 in thread state)
    user_addr_t user_stack;  // thread's stack (the default, or from GPR1 in
                             //                   thread state)
    int thread_count;        // number of thread states successfully loaded
    unsigned int
    /* boolean_t */ unixproc    : 1, // TRUE if there was an LC_UNIXTHREAD
                    dynlinker   : 1, // TRUE if dynamic linker was loaded
                    customstack : 1, // TRUE if thread state had custom stack
                                : 0;
} load_result_t;
```

load_machfile() first checks whether it needs to create a new virtual memory map[20] for the task. In the case of vfork(), a new map is not created at this point, since the map belonging to the task created by execve() is valid and appropriate. Otherwise, vm_map_create() [osfmk/vm/vm_map.c] is called to create a new map with the same lower and upper address bounds as in the parent's map. load_machfile() then calls parse_machfile() [bsd/kern/mach_loader.c] to process the load commands in the executable's Mach-O header. parse_machfile() allocates a kernel buffer and maps the load commands into it. Thereafter, it iterates over each load command, processing it if necessary. Note that two passes are made over the commands: The first pass processes commands the result of whose actions may be required by commands processed in the second pass. The kernel handles only the following load commands.

- LC_SEGMENT_64 maps a 64-bit segment into the given task address space, setting the initial and maximum virtual memory protection values specified in the load command (first pass).

- LC_SEGMENT is similar to LC_SEGMENT_64 but maps a 32-bit segment (first pass).

- LC_THREAD contains machine-specific data structures that specify the initial state of the thread, including its entry point (second pass).

- LC_UNIXTHREAD is similar to LC_THREAD but with somewhat different semantics; it is used for executables running as Unix processes (second pass).

- LC_LOAD_DYLINKER identifies the pathname of the dynamic linker—/usr/lib/dyld by default (second pass).

---

20. As we will see in Chapter 8, a virtual memory map (vm_map_t) contains mappings from valid regions of a task's address space to the corresponding virtual memory objects.

Standard Mac OS X Mach-O executables contain several LC_SEGMENT (or LC_SEGMENT_64, in the case of 64-bit executables) commands, one LC_UNIXTHREAD command, one LC_LOAD_DYLINKER command, and others that are processed only in user space. For example, a dynamically linked executable contains one or more LC_LOAD_DYLIB commands—one for each dynamically linked shared library it uses. The dynamic linker, which is a Mach-O executable of type MH_DYLINKER, contains an LC_THREAD command instead of an LC_UNIXTHREAD command.

parse_machfile() calls load_dylinker() [bsd/kern/mach_loader.c] to process the LC_LOAD_DYLINKER command. Since the dynamic linker is a Mach-O file, load_dylinker() also calls parse_machfile()—recursively. This results in the dynamic linker's entry point being determined as its LC_THREAD command is processed.

> In the case of a dynamically linked executable, it is the dynamic linker—and not the executable—that starts user-space execution. The dynamic linker loads the shared libraries that the program requires. It then retrieves the "main" function of the program executable—the SRR0 value from the LC_UNIXTHREAD command—and sets the main thread up for execution.

For regular executables (but not for the dynamic linker), parse_machfile() also maps system-wide shared regions, including the comm area, into the task's address space.

After parse_machfile() returns, load_machfile() performs the following steps if it earlier created a new map for the task (i.e., if this is *not* a vfork()'ed child).

- It shuts down the current task by calling task_halt() [osfmk/kern/task.c], which terminates all threads in the task except the current one. Moreover, task_halt() destroys all semaphores and lock sets owned by the task, removes all port references from the task's IPC space, and removes the existing entire virtual address range from the task's virtual memory map.

- It swaps the task's existing virtual memory map (cleaned in the previous step) with the new map created earlier.

- It calls vm_map_deallocate() [osfmk/vm/vm_map.c] to release a reference on the old map.

At this point, the child task has exactly one thread, even in the vfork() case, where a single-threaded task was explicitly created by execve(). load_machfile() now returns successfully to exec_mach_imgact().

7.5.1.3 *Handling Setuid and Setgid*

exec_mach_imgact() calls exec_handle_sugid() [bsd/kern/kern_exec.c] to perform special handling for setuid and setgid executables. exec_handle_sugid()'s operation includes the following.

- If the executable is setuid and the current user ID is not the same as the file owner's user ID, it disables kernel tracing for the process, unless the superuser enabled tracing. A similar action is performed for setgid executables.

- If the executable is setuid, the current process credential is updated with the effective user ID of the executable. A similar action is performed for setgid executables.

- It resets the task's kernel port by allocating a new one and destroying the old one. This is done to prevent an existing holder of rights to the old kernel port from controlling or accessing the task after its security status is elevated because of setuid or setgid.

- If one or more of the standard file descriptors 0 (standard input), 1 (standard output), and 2 (standard error) are not already in use, it creates a descriptor referencing /dev/null for each such descriptor. This is done to prevent a situation where an attacker can coerce a setuid or setgid program to open files on one of these descriptors. Note that exec_handle_sugid() caches a pointer to the /dev/null vnode on first use in a static variable.

- It calls kauth_cred_setsvuidgid() [bsd/kern/kern_credential.c] to update the process credential such that the effective user and group IDs become the saved user and group IDs, respectively.

7.5.1.4 *Execution Notification*

exec_mach_imgact() then posts a kernel event of type NOTE_EXEC on the kernel event queue of the process to notify that the process has transformed itself into a new process by calling execve(). Unless this is an execve() after a vfork(), a SIGTRAP (trace trap signal) is sent to the process if it is being traced.

7.5.1.5 Configuring the User Stack

exec_mach_imgact() now proceeds to create and populate the user stack for an executable—specifically one whose LC_UNIXTHREAD command was success-fully processed (as indicated by the unixproc field of the load_result struc-ture). This step is not performed for the dynamic linker, since it runs within the same thread and uses the same stack as the executable. In fact, as we noted ear-lier, the dynamic linker will gain control before the "main" function of the exe-cutable. exec_mach_imgact() calls create_unix_stack() [bsd/kern/kern_exec.c], which allocates a stack unless the executable uses a custom stack (as indicated by the customstack field of the load_result structure). Figure 7–58 shows the user stack's creation during execve()'s operation.

FIGURE 7–58 Creation of the user stack during the execve() system call

```
// bsd/kern/kern_exec.c

static int
exec_mach_imgact(struct image_params *imgp)
{
    ...
    load_return_t lret;
    load_result_t load_result;
    ...

    lret = load_machfile(imgp, mach_header, thread, map, clean_regions,
                         &load_result);
    ...

    if (load_result.unixproc &&
        create_unix_stack(get_task_map(task),
                        load_result.user_stack,
                        load_result.customstack, p)) {
        // error
    }
    ...
}

...
#define unix_stack_size(p) (p->p_rlimit[RLIMIT_STACK].rlim_cur)
...

static kern_return_t
create_unix_stack(vm_map_t map, user_addr_t user_stack, int customstack,
                struct proc *p)
```

(continues)

FIGURE 7–58 Creation of the user stack during the execve() system call *(continued)*

```
{
    mach_vm_size_t    size;
    mach_vm_offset_t addr;

    p->user_stack = user_stack;
    if (!customstack) {
        size = mach_vm_round_page(unix_stack_size(p));
        addr = mach_vm_trunc_page(user_stack - size);
        return (mach_vm_allocate(map, &addr, size,
                            VM_MAKE_TAG(VM_MEMORY_STACK) |
                            VM_FLAGS_FIXED));
    } else
        return (KERN_SUCCESS);
}
```

Now, user_stack represents one end of the stack: the end with the higher memory address, since the stack grows toward lower memory addresses. The other end of the stack is computed by taking the difference between user_stack and the stack's size. In the absence of a custom stack, user_stack is set to a default value (0xC0000000 for 32-bit and 0x7FFFF00000000 for 64-bit) when the LC_UNIXTHREAD command is processed. create_unix_stack() retrieves the stack size as determined by the RLIMIT_STACK resource limit, rounds up the size in terms of pages, rounds down the stack's address range in terms of pages, and allocates the stack in the task's address map. Note that the VM_FLAGS_FIXED flag is passed to mach_vm_allocate(), indicating that allocation must be at the specified address.

In contrast, a custom stack is specified in a Mach-O executable through a segment named __UNIXSTACK and is therefore initialized when the corresponding LC_SEGMENT command is processed. The -stack_addr and -stack_size arguments to ld—the static link editor—can be used to specify a custom stack at compile time.

Note in Figure 7–59 that for a stack whose size and starting point are 16KB and 0x70000, respectively, the __UNIXSTACK segment's starting address is 0x6c000—that is, 16KB less than 0x70000.

FIGURE 7–59 A Mach-O executable with a custom stack

```
// customstack.c

#include <stdio.h>
```

(continues)

FIGURE 7–59 A Mach-O executable with a custom stack *(continued)*

```
int
main(void)
{
    int var; // a stack variable
    printf("&var = %p\n", &var);
    return 0;
}


$ gcc -Wall -o customstack customstack.c -Wl,-stack_addr,0x60000 \
    -Wl,-stack_size,0x4000
$ ./customstack
&var = 0x5f998
$ gcc -Wall -o customstack customstack.c -Wl,-stack_addr,0x70000 \
    -Wl,-stack_size,0x4000
&var = 0x6f998
$ otool -l ./customstack
...
Load command 3
      cmd LC_SEGMENT
  cmdsize 56
  segname __UNIXSTACK
   vmaddr 0x0006c000
   vmsize 0x00004000
  fileoff 0
 filesize 0
  maxprot 0x00000007
 initprot 0x00000007
   nsects 0
    flags 0x4
...
```

Now that the user stack is initialized in both the custom and default cases, exec_mach_imgact() calls exec_copyout_strings() [bsd/kern/kern_exec.c] to arrange arguments and environment variables on the stack. Again, this step is performed only for a Mach-O executable with an LC_UNIXTHREAD load command. Moreover, the stack pointer is copied to the saved user-space GPR1 for the thread. Figure 7–60 shows the stack arrangement.

Note in Figure 7–60 that there is an additional element on the stack—a pointer to the Mach-O header of the executable—above the argument count (argc). In the case of dynamically linked executables, that is, those executables for which the dynlinker field of the load_result structure is true, exec_mach_act() copies this pointer out to the user stack and decrements the stack

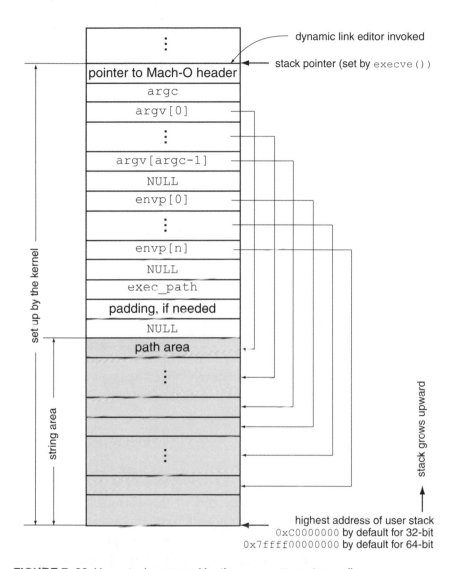

FIGURE 7–60 User stack arranged by the execve() system call

pointer by either 4 bytes (32-bit) or 8 bytes (64-bit). dyld uses this pointer. Moreover, before dyld jumps to the program's entry point, it adjusts the stack pointer and removes the argument so that the program never sees it.

We can also deduce from Figure 7–60 that a program executable's path can be retrieved within the program by using a suitable prototype, for example:

```
int
main(int argc, char **argv, char **envp, char **exec_path)
{
    // Our program executable's "true" path is contained in *exec_path
    // Depending on $PATH, *exec_path can be absolute or relative
    // Circumstances that alter argv[0] do not normally affect *exec_path

    ...
}
```

7.5.1.6 Finishing Up

`exec_mach_imgact()`'s final steps include the following.

- It sets the entry point for the thread by copying the `entry_point` field of the `load_result` structure to the saved user state SRR0.

- It stops profiling on the process.

- It calls `execsigs()` [bsd/kern/kern_sig.c] to reset signal state, which includes nullifying the alternate signal stack, if any.

- It calls `fdexec()` [bsd/kern/kern_descrip.c] to close those file descriptors that have the *close-on-exec* flag set.[21]

- It calls `_aio_exec()` [bsd/kern/kern_aio.c], which cancels any asynchronous I/O (AIO) requests on the process's "todo" work queue, and waits for requests that are already active to complete. Signaling is disabled for canceled or active AIO requests that complete.

- It calls `shmexec()` [bsd/kern/sysv_shm.c] to release references on System V shared memory segments.

- It calls `semexit()` [bsd/kern/sysv_sem.c] to release System V semaphores.

- It saves up to `MAXCOMLEN` (16) characters of the executable's name (or "command" name) in the `p_comm` array within the process structure. This information is used by the process accounting mechanism. Moreover, the `AFORK` flag is cleared in the `p_acflag` accounting-related field of the process structure. This flag is set during a `fork()` or a `vfork()` and indicates that a process has `fork()`'ed but not `execve()`'d.

- It generates a kdebug trace record.

---

21. A descriptor can be set to auto-close on `execve(2)` by calling `fcntl(2)` on it with the `F_SETFD` command.

- If the p_pflag field of the process structure has the P_PPWAIT flag set, it indicates that the parent is waiting for the child to exec or exit. If the flag is set (as it would be in the case of a vfork()), exec_mach_imgact() clears it and wakes up the parent.

On a successful return from exec_mach_imgact(), or any other image activator, execve() generates a kauth notification of type KAUTH_FILEOP_ EXEC. Finally, execve() frees the pathname buffer it used with namei(), releases the executable's vnode, frees the memory allocated for execve() arguments, and returns. In the case of an execve() after a vfork(), execve() sets up a return value for the calling thread and then resumes the thread.

7.5.2 Fat (Universal) Binaries

A fat binary contains Mach-O executables for multiple architectures. For example, a fat binary may encapsulate 32-bit PowerPC and 64-bit PowerPC executables. The exec_fat_imgact() [bsd/kern/kern_exec.c] activator handles fat binaries. Note that this activator is byte-order neutral. It performs the following actions.

- It ensures that the binary is fat by looking at its magic number.
- It looks up the preferred architecture, including its offset, in the fat file.
- It reads a page of data from the beginning of the desired architecture's executable within the fat file.
- It returns a special error that would cause execve() to retry execution using the encapsulated executable.

7.5.3 Interpreter Scripts

The exec_shell_imgact() [bsd/kern/kern_exec.c] activator handles interpreter scripts, which are often called *shell scripts* since the interpreter is typically a shell. An interpreter script is a text file whose content has # and ! as the first two characters, followed by a pathname to an interpreter, optionally followed by whitespace-separated arguments to the interpreter. There may be leading whitespace before the pathname. The #! sequence specifies to the kernel that the file is an interpreter script, whereas the interpreter name and the arguments are used as if they had been passed in an execve() invocation. However, the following points must be noted.

- The interpreter specification, including the #! characters, must be no more than 512 characters.

- An interpreter script must not redirect to another interpreter script—it will cause an ENOEXEC error ("Exec format error") if it does.

However, note that it *is* possible to execute plaintext shell scripts—that is, those that contain shell commands but do not begin with #!. Even in this case, the execution fails in the kernel and execve() returns an ENOEXEC error. The execvp(3) and execvP(3) library functions, which invoke the execve() system call, actually reattempt execution of the specified file if execve() returns ENOEXEC. In the second attempt, these functions use the standard shell (/bin/sh) as the executable, with the original file as the shell's first argument. We can see this behavior by attempting to execute a shell script containing no #! characters—first using execl(3), which should fail, and then using execvp(3), which should succeed in its second attempt.

```
$ cat /tmp/script.txt
echo "Hello"

$ chmod 755 /tmp/script.txt # ensure that it has execute permissions

$ cat execl.c
#include <stdio.h>
#include <unistd.h>

int
main(int argc, char **argv)
{
    int ret = execl(argv[1], argv[1], NULL);
    perror("execl");
    return ret;
}
$ gcc -Wall -o execl execl.c

$ ./execl /tmp/script.txt
execl: Exec format error

$ cat execvp.c
#include <stdio.h>
#include <unistd.h>

int
main(int argc, char **argv)
{
```

```
      int ret = execvp(argv[1], &(argv[1]));
      perror("execvp");
      return ret;
}
$ gcc -Wall -o execvp execvp.c

$ ./execvp /tmp/script.txt
Hello
```

`exec_shell_imgact()` parses the first line of the script to determine the interpreter name and arguments if any, copying the latter to the image parameter block. It returns a special error that causes `execve()` to retry execution: `execve()` looks up the interpreter's path using `namei()`, reads a page of data from the resultant vnode, and goes through the image activator table again. This time, however, the executable *must* be claimed by an activator other than `exec_shell_imgact()`.

Note that setuid or setgid interpreter scripts are *not permitted* by default. They can be enabled by setting the `kern.sugid_scripts` sysctl variable to 1. When this variable is set to 0 (the default), `exec_shell_imgact()` clears the setuid and setgid bits in the `ip_origvattr` (invocation file attributes) field of the image parameter block. Consequently, from `execve()`'s standpoint, the script is not setuid/setgid.

```
$ cat testsuid.sh
#! /bin/sh
/usr/bin/id -p
$ sudo chown root:wheel testsuid.sh
$ sudo chmod 4755 testsuid.sh
-rwsr-xr-x   1 root   wheel   23 Jul 30 20:52 testsuid.sh
$ sysctl kern.sugid_scripts
kern.sugid_scripts: 0
$ ./testsuid.sh
uid      amit
groups   amit appserveradm appserverusr admin
$ sudo sysctl -w kern.sugid_scripts=1
kern.sugid_scripts: 0 -> 1
$ ./testsuid.sh
uid      amit
euid     root
groups   amit appserveradm appserverusr admin
$ sudo sysctl -w kern.sugid_scripts=0
kern.sugid_scripts: 1 -> 0
```

7.6 Launching Applications

Users typically create new processes by launching applications through the graphical user interface—for example, through the Finder or the Dock. The Launch Services framework, which is a subframework of the Application Services umbrella framework, provides primary support for application launching. Launch Services allows programmatic opening of executables, documents,[22] and other entities either by file system references or by URL references. The framework provides functions such as the following.

- `LSOpenFSRef()` opens a file residing on a local or remote volume.
- `LSOpenFromRefSpec()`, which is a more general function than `LSOpenFSRef()`, is called by the latter.
- `LSOpenCFURLSpec()` opens a URL. Note that a URL could be a `file:` URL that refers to a file on a volume.
- `LSOpenFromURLSpec()`, which is a more general function than `LSOpenCFURLSpec()`, is called by the latter.

The Cocoa `NSWorkspace` class uses the Launch Services framework to launch applications. Launch Services eventually performs a `fork()` and an `execve()`.

7.6.1 Mapping Entities to Handlers

Applications can register themselves with Launch Services to advertise their ability to open documents of a certain type. Such ability can be specified by file extension, by URL scheme, and, more appropriately, through a generalized data identifier scheme called Uniform Type Identifiers (UTIs).[23] We will look at UTIs in the next section.

Typically, registration with Launch Services occurs automatically, without requiring any action from the user. For example, it could occur at the following times:

- When the system is booted

---

22. A document is launched by running the appropriate executable to handle the document.

23. Although UTI support was introduced in Mac OS X 10.3, comprehensive UTI support is available only beginning with Mac OS X 10.4.

- When a user logs in
- When the Finder locates a new application, such as on a newly mounted disk image—say, one that has been downloaded from the Internet

> When examining the output of the `ps` command, you can see that the parent of processes corresponding to GUI-based applications is the `WindowServer` program. When a user launches a GUI-based application through the Finder, Launch Services sends a message to `WindowServer`, which in turns calls `fork()` and `execve()` to run the requested application. You can use the `kdebug` program from Chapter 6 to monitor the invocation of `fork()` by `WindowServer`.

In particular, the `AppServices` startup item (`/System/Library/StartupItems/AppServices/AppServices`) runs the `lsregister` program—a support tool that resides within the Launch Services framework bundle—to load the Launch Services registration database. `lsregister` can also dump the contents of a registration database file—each user has a separate database stored as `/Library/Caches/com.apple.LaunchServices-*.csstore`. Figure 7-61 shows an example of using `lsregister`.

FIGURE 7–61 Dumping the Launch Services registration database

```
$ lsregister -dump
Checking data integrity......done.
Status: Database is seeded.
...
bundle id:          44808
    path:           /Applications/iWork/Keynote.app
    name:           Keynote
    identifier:     com.apple.iWork.Keynote
    version:        240
    mod date:       5/25/2005 19:26:46
    type code:      'APPL'
    creator code:   'keyn'
    sys version:    0
    flags:          apple-internal  relative-icon-path  ppc
    item flags:     container  package  application  extension-hidden  native-app
                    scriptable
    icon:           Contents/Resources/Keynote.icns
    executable:     Contents/MacOS/Keynote
    inode:          886080
    exec inode:     1581615
    container id:   32
```

(continues)

FIGURE 7–61 Dumping the Launch Services registration database *(continued)*

```
library:
library items:
-------------------------------------------------------
claim   id:          30072
        name:        Keynote Document
        role:        editor
        flags:       apple-internal  relative-icon-path  package
        icon:        Contents/Resources/KeyDocument.icns
        bindings:    .key, .boom, .k2
-------------------------------------------------------
claim   id:          30100
        name:        Keynote Theme
        role:        viewer
        flags:       apple-internal  relative-icon-path  package
        icon:        Contents/Resources/KeyTheme.icns
        bindings:    .kth, .bth, .kt2
...
```

Consider the situation when an application wants to handle a document or URL type that is already registered in the Launch Services database. Launch Services considers several aspects before selecting a candidate. A handler explicitly specified by the user takes the highest precedence. An application on the boot volume is preferred over applications on any other volumes—this is important to avoid running potentially malicious handlers from untrusted volumes. Similarly, an application on a local volume is preferred over those on remote volumes.

7.6.2 Uniform Type Identifiers

A Uniform Type Identifier (UTI) is a Core Foundation string—for example, "public.html" or "com.apple.quicktime-image"—that uniquely identifies an abstract type. Mac OS X uses UTIs to describe data types and file formats. In general, a UTI can be used to describe arbitrary type information about in-memory or on-disk entities, such as aliases, files, directories, frameworks, other bundles, and even in-transit data. Since UTIs provide a consistent mechanism for tagging data, services and applications should use UTIs to specify and recognize data formats that they support. The following are examples of using UTIs.

- Applications can use UTIs to register with Launch Services the document types they wish to handle. The UTI API is part of the Launch Services API.

- The Pasteboard Manager can use UTIs to specify flavors for items it holds, where a flavor identifies a particular data type. Each pasteboard item can be represented by one or more flavors, allowing different applications to retrieve the item's data in formats convenient to them.

- Navigation Services allows the use of UTIs for filtering file types.

A UTI string is syntactically similar to a bundle identifier. UTIs are written using a reverse DNS naming scheme, with certain top-level UTI domains being reserved for Apple's use.[24] For example, Apple declares types that it controls with identifiers in the com.apple domain. Public types—that is, those types that either are public standards or are not controlled by an organization—are declared with identifiers in the public domain. Third parties should use Internet domains they own for declaring their UTIs—for example, com.companyname. The use of a reverse DNS naming scheme ensures uniqueness without centralized arbitration.

> The Apple-reserved domain dyn is used for dynamic identifiers that are automatically created on the fly when a data type with no declared UTI is encountered. The creation of dyn UTIs is transparent to users. An example of a file whose content type is a dyn UTI is a .savedSearch file—these files correspond to Smart Folders and contain raw Spotlight queries.

The information property list file of /System/Library/CoreServices/CoreTypes.bundle contains specifications of various standard UTIs. For example, we can list the public types contained in that file as follows:

```
$ cd /System/Library/CoreServices/CoreTypes.bundle
$ awk '{ if (match ($1, /public\.[^<]*/)) { \
substr($1, RSTART, RLENGTH); } }' Info.plist | sort | uniq
public.3gpp
public.3gpp2
public.ada-source
...
public.camera-raw-image
public.case-insensitive-text
...
public.fortran-source
```

---

24. Such domains are outside the current IANA top-level Internet domain name space.

```
public.html
public.image
public.item
public.jpeg
...
```

The UTI mechanism supports multiple inheritance, allowing a UTI to conform to one or more other UTIs. For example, an instance of HTML content is also an instance of textual content. Therefore, the UTI for HTML content (`public.html`) conforms to the UTI for textual content (`public.text`). Moreover, textual content is, generically speaking, a stream of bytes. Therefore, `public.text` conforms to `public.data`. It also conforms to `public.content`, which is a UTI describing all content types. The `UTTypeConformsTo` key is used in a UTI's declaration to specify its conformance to a list of UTIs.

UTIs can be declared in the property list files of application bundles, Spotlight metadata importer bundles, Automator action bundles, and so on. Figure 7–62 shows an example of a UTI declaration—that of the `public.html` UTI. A bundle can export a UTI declaration using the `UTExportedTypeDeclarations` key, making that type available for use by other parties. Conversely, a bundle can import a UTI declaration through the `UTImportedTypeDeclarations` key, indicating that even though the bundle is not the owner of that type, it wishes to have the type made available on the system. If both imported and exported declarations for a UTI exist, the exported declaration takes precedence.

FIGURE 7–62 Example of a UTI declaration

```
<dict>
    <!-- one or more UTIs that this UTI conforms to -->
    <key>UTTypeConformsTo</key>
    <array>
        <string>public.text</string>
    </array>

    <!-- user-readable string describing this UTI; may be localized -->
    <key>UTTypeDescription</key>
    <string>HTML text</string>

    <!-- the UTI string -->
    <key>UTTypeIdentifier</key>
    <string>public.html</string>
```

(continues)

FIGURE 7–62 Example of a UTI declaration *(continued)*

```
<!-- icon to use when displaying items of this type -->
<key>UTTypeIconFile</key>
<string>SomeHTML.icns</string>

<!-- the URL of a reference document describing this type -->
<key>UTTypeReferenceURL</key>
<string>http://www.apple.com</string>

<!-- alternate identifier tags that match this type -->
<key>UTTypeTagSpecification</key>
<dict>
    <key>com.apple.nspboard-type</key>
    <string>Apple HTML pasteboard type</string>
    <key>com.apple.ostype</key>
    <string>HTML</string>
    <key>public.filename-extension</key>
    <array>
        <string>html</string>
        <string>htm</string>
        <string>shtml</string>
        <string>shtm</string>
    </array>
    <key>public.mime-type</key>
    <string>text/html</string>
</dict>
</dict>
```

Note that UTIs do not preclude other tagging methods. In fact, they are compatible with such methods. As shown in Figure 7–62, content of type HTML text (as specified by the UTTypeDescription key) can be identified by several tags (as specified by the UTTypeTagSpecification key): an NSPasteboard type, a four-character file type code, multiple file extensions, or a MIME type. Therefore, a UTI can unify alternative methods of type identification.

CHAPTER 8

Memory

Memory—specifically, physical memory—is a precious resource in a computer system. An integral feature of modern operating systems is *virtual memory* (VM), whose typical implementation provides an illusion of a large, contiguous virtual address space to each program without burdening the programmer with details such as which parts of the program are resident in physical memory at any given time, or where in physical memory the resident portions are located. Virtual memory is commonly implemented through *paging*: An address space is subdivided into fixed size *pages*. When resident, each virtual page is loaded into some portion of physical memory. This portion, essentially a physical slot for a logical page, is called a *page frame*.

8.1 Looking Back

Tom Kilburn, R. Bruce Payne, and David J. Howarth described the *Atlas supervisor* program in a 1961 paper.[1] A result of work that originated in the Computer Group

---

1. "The Atlas Supervisor," by Tom Kilburn, R. Bruce Payne, and David J. Howarth (*American Federation of Information Processing Societies Computer Conference* 20, 1961, pp. 279–294).

at Manchester University, the Atlas supervisor controlled the functioning of the Atlas computer system. When inaugurated in late 1962, Atlas was considered the most powerful computer in the world. It also had the earliest implementation of virtual memory—the so-called one-level storage system that decoupled *memory addresses* and *memory locations*. The core memory system of Atlas used a form of indirect addressing based on 512-word pages and page-address registers. When access to a memory address was made, a hardware unit (the *memory management unit*, or MMU) automatically attempted to locate the corresponding page in core memory (*primary memory*). If the page was not found in core memory, there was a nonequivalence interruption—a *page fault*, which resulted in the supervisor transferring data from a sector of drum store (*secondary memory*) to core memory. This process was referred to as *demand paging*. Moreover, the Atlas system provided per-page protection that allowed the supervisor to lock certain pages such that they became unavailable except when on interrupt control. A page replacement scheme was also used to move pages that were less likely to be used back to the drum store.

Within the next few years, virtual memory concepts were widely adopted, as major processor vendors incorporated virtual memory support in their processors. Most commercial operating systems of the 1960s and 1970s were capable of virtual memory.

8.1.1 Virtual Memory and UNIX

What can be considered as the Zeroth Edition of UNIX (late 1969) was not multiprogrammed—only one program could exist in memory at a time. It employed *swapping* as a form of memory management policy wherein entire *processes*, rather than individual pages, were transferred between physical memory and the swap device. Third Edition UNIX (February 1973) introduced multiprogramming, but it would not be until 3BSD (1979) that a UNIX-based system would be capable of paged virtual memory.

8.1.2 Virtual Memory and Personal Computing

Compared with UNIX, virtual memory would become part of personal computing much later, with personal computer software lagging behind the hardware by several years. Table 8–1 shows the time frames in which virtual memory (and multiprogramming) were introduced in personal computing.

TABLE 8–1 Virtual Memory and Multiprogramming in Personal Computing

Product	Date Introduced	Notes
Intel 80286	February 1, 1982	16-bit, segment-based memory management and protection
Motorola 68020	June 1984	32-bit, support for a paged MMU as a coprocessor chip—virtual memory possible with the latter
Intel 80386	October 17, 1985	32-bit, integrated MMU with support for paging and segmentation—virtual memory possible
Macintosh System 4.2	October 1987	Cooperative multitasking introduced with the optional MultiFinder
Macintosh System 7	May 13, 1991	MultiFinder made nonoptional, virtual memory support introduced
Microsoft Windows 3.1	April 6, 1992	Cooperative multitasking introduced, virtual memory support introduced
Microsoft Windows 95	August 24, 1995	Preemptive multitasking introduced (a Win32-only feature), virtual memory support enhanced

Thrashing

Early virtual memory implementations all suffered from *thrashing*—a severe loss of performance that occurred when a multiprogramming system was under heavy load. When thrashing, the system spent most of its time transferring data between primary and secondary memories. This problem was satisfactorily addressed by Peter J. Denning's *Working Set Principle*, using which the memory management subsystem could strive to keep each program's "most useful" pages resident to avoiding overcommitting.

8.1.3 Roots of the Mac OS X Virtual Memory Subsystem

We saw in Chapter 1 that the RIG and Accent operating systems were Mach's ancestors. One of Accent's prime goals was to use virtual memory to overcome RIG's limitations in the handling of large objects. Accent combined paged virtual memory and capability-based interprocess communication (IPC), allowing large IPC-based data transfers through copy-on-write (COW) memory mapping. The Accent kernel provided the abstraction of a *memory object*, which represented a data repository, and had a *backing store* such as a disk. Contents of disk blocks—

disk pages, whether they corresponded to an on-disk file or a paging partition—could be mapped into an address space.

Mach evolved from Accent as a system suited for general-purpose shared memory multiprocessors. Like Accent, Mach's VM subsystem was integrated with its IPC subsystem. However, Mach's implementation used simpler data structures, with a cleaner separation of machine-dependent and machine-independent components. Mach's VM architecture inspired several others. The VM subsystem of BSD Networking Release 2 (NET2) was derived from Mach. The 4.4BSD VM subsystem was based on Mach 2, with updates from Mach 2.5 and Mach 3. The 4.4BSD implementation was the basis for FreeBSD's VM subsystem. Moreover, Mach's VM architecture has several design similarities with that of SunOS/SVR4, which was independently designed around the same time as Mach.

The core of the Mac OS X VM architecture is a derivative of, and largely similar to, the Mach VM architecture. However, as the operating system has evolved and undergone various optimizations, several minor and a few major differences have appeared in its VM subsystem's implementation.

Virtual XYZ

It is worthwhile to somewhat deemphasize the "virtual" in virtual memory. As in a typical modern-day operating system, not just memory but all system resources are virtualized by the Mac OS X kernel. For example, threads execute in a virtual environment consisting of a virtual processor, with each thread having its own set of virtual processor registers. In that sense, *it's all virtual*.

8.2 An Overview of Mac OS X Memory Management

Besides the Mach-based core VM subsystem, memory management in Mac OS X encompasses several other mechanisms, some of which are not strictly parts of the VM subsystem but are closely related nonetheless.

Figure 8–1 shows an overview of key VM and VM-related components in Mac OS X. Let us briefly look at each of them in this section. The rest of the chapter discusses these components in detail.

- The Mach VM subsystem consists of the machine-dependent physical map (pmap) module and other, machine-independent modules for managing data

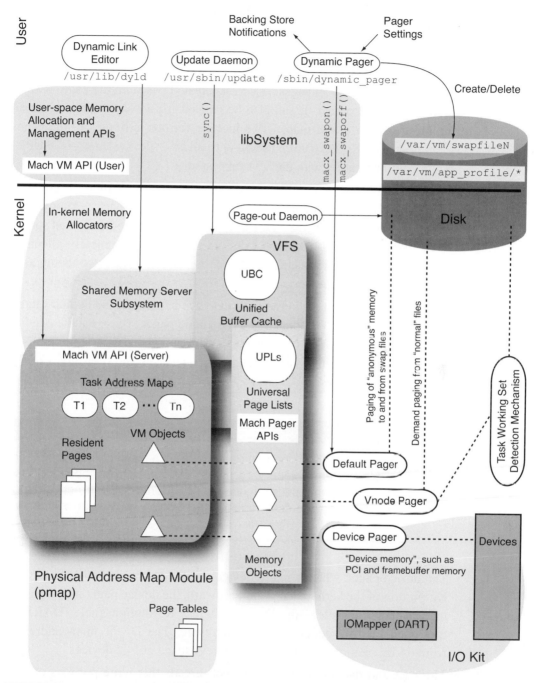

FIGURE 8–1 An overview of the Mac OS X memory subsystem

structures corresponding to abstractions such as virtual address space maps (VM maps), VM objects, named entries, and resident pages. The kernel exports several routines to user space as part of the Mach VM API.

- The kernel uses the universal page list (UPL) data structure to describe a bounded set of physical pages. A UPL is created based on the pages associated with a VM object. It can also be created for an object underlying an address range in a VM map. UPLs include various attributes of the pages they describe. Kernel subsystems—particularly file systems—use UPLs while communicating with the VM subsystem.

- The unified buffer cache (UBC) is a pool of pages for caching the contents of files and the anonymous portions of task address spaces. Anonymous memory is not backed by regular files, devices, or some other named source of memory—the most common example is that of dynamically allocated memory. The "unification" in the UBC comes from a single pool being used for file-backed and anonymous memory.

- The kernel includes three kernel-internal pagers, namely, the default (anonymous) pager, the device pager, and the vnode pager. These handle page-in and page-out operations over memory regions. The pagers communicate with the Mach VM subsystem using UPL interfaces and derivatives of the Mach pager interfaces.

Vnode

As we will see in Chapter 11, a vnode (virtual node) is a file-system-independent abstraction of a file system object, very much analogous to an abstract base class from which file-system-specific instances are derived. Each active file or directory (where "active" has context-dependent connotations) has an in-memory vnode.

- The device pager, which handles device memory, is implemented in the I/O Kit portion of the kernel. On 64-bit hardware, the device pager uses a part of the memory controller—the Device Address Resolution Table (DART)— that is enabled by default on such hardware. The DART maps addresses from 64-bit memory into the 32-bit address space of PCI devices.

- The page-out daemon is a set of kernel threads that write portions of task address spaces to disk as part of the paging operation in virtual memory. It examines the usage of resident pages and employs an LRU[2]-like scheme to page out those pages that have not been used for over a certain time.

- The `dynamic_pager` user-space program creates and deletes swap files for the kernel's use. The "pager" in its name notwithstanding, `dynamic_pager` does not perform any paging operations.

- The `update` user-space daemon periodically invokes the `sync()` system call to flush file system caches to disk.

- The task working set (TWS) detection subsystem maintains profiles of page-fault behaviors of tasks on a per-application basis. When an application causes a page fault, the kernel's page-fault-handling mechanism consults this subsystem to determine which additional pages, if any, should be paged in. Usually the additional pages are adjacent to those being faulted in. The goal is to improve performance by making resident—speculatively—the pages that may be needed soon.

- The kernel provides several memory allocation mechanisms, some of which are subsystem-specific wrappers around others. All such mechanisms eventually use the kernel's page-level allocator. User-space memory allocation schemes are built atop the Mach VM API.

- The Shared Memory Server subsystem is a kernel service that provides two globally shared memory regions: one for text (starting at user virtual address 0x9000_0000) and the other for data (starting at user virtual address 0xA000_0000). Both regions are 256MB in size. The text region is read-only and is completely shared between tasks. The data region is shared copy-on-write. The dynamic link editor (`dyld`) uses this mechanism to load shared libraries into task address spaces.

8.2.1 Reading Kernel Memory from User Space

Let us look at a couple of ways of reading kernel memory; these are useful in examining kernel data structures from user space.

8.2.1.1 dd and /dev/kmem

The Mac OS X kernel provides the /dev/kmem character device, which can be used to read kernel virtual memory from user space. The device driver for this

---

2. Least recently used.

pseudo-device disallows memory at addresses less than VM_MIN_KERNEL_ ADDRESS (4096) to be read—that is, the page at address 0 cannot be read.

Recall that we used the dd command in Chapter 7 to sample the sched_ tick kernel variable by reading from /dev/kmem. In this chapter, we will again read from this device to retrieve the contents of kernel data structures. Let us generalize our dd-based technique so we can read kernel memory at a given address or at the address of a given kernel symbol. Figure 8–2 shows a shell script that accepts a symbol name or an address in hexadecimal, attempts to read the corresponding kernel memory, and, if successful, displays the memory on the standard output. By default, the program pipes raw memory bytes through the hexdump program using hexdump's -x (hexadecimal output) option. If the -raw option is specified, the program prints raw memory on the standard output, which is desirable if you wish to pipe it through another program yourself.

FIGURE 8–2 A shell script for reading kernel virtual memory

```
#!/bin/sh
#
# readksym.sh

PROGNAME=readksym

if [ $# -lt 2 ]
then
      echo "usage: $PROGNAME <symbol>  <bytes to read> [hexdump option|-raw]"
      echo "        $PROGNAME <address> <bytes to read> [hexdump option|-raw]"
      exit 1
fi

SYMBOL=$1                   # first argument is a kernel symbol
SYMBOL_ADDR=$1             # or a kernel address in hexadecimal
IS_HEX=${SYMBOL_ADDR:0:2} # get the first two characters
NBYTES=$2                   # second argument is the number of bytes to read
HEXDUMP_OPTION=${3:--x}    # by default, we pass '-x' to hexdump
RAW="no"                    # by default, we don't print memory as "raw"

if [ ${HEXDUMP_OPTION:0:2} == "-r" ]
then
    RAW="yes" # raw... don't pipe through hexdump -- print as is
fi

KERN_SYMFILE=`sysctl -n kern.symfile | tr '\\' '/'` # typically /mach.sym
if [ X"$KERN_SYMFILE" == "X" ]
```

(continues)

FIGURE 8–2 A shell script for reading kernel virtual memory *(continued)*

```
then
    echo "failed to determine the kernel symbol file's name"
    exit 1
fi

if [ "$IS_HEX" != "0x" ]
then
    # use nm to determine the address of the kernel symbol
    SYMBOL_ADDR="0x`nm $KERN_SYMFILE | grep -w $SYMBOL | awk '{print $1}'`"
fi

if [ "$SYMBOL_ADDR" == "0x" ] # at this point, we should have an address
then
    echo "address of $SYMBOL not found in $KERN_SYMFILE"
    exit 1
fi

if [ ${HEXDUMP_OPTION:0:2} == " r" ] # raw... no hexdump
then
    dd if=/dev/kmem bs=1 count=$NBYTES iseek=$SYMBOL_ADDR of=/dev/stdout \
        2>/dev/null
else
    dd if=/dev/kmem bs=1 count=$NBYTES iseek=$SYMBOL_ADDR of=/dev/stdout \
        2>/dev/null | hexdump $HEXDUMP_OPTION
fi

exit 0


$ sudo ./readksym.sh 0x5000 8 -c # string seen only on the PowerPC
0000000   H   a   g   f   i   s   h
0000008
```

8.2.1.2 The `kvm(3)` Interface

Mac OS X also provides the kvm(3) interface for accessing kernel memory. It includes the following functions:

- kvm_read()—read from kernel memory
- kvm_write()—write to kernel memory
- kvm_getprocs(), kvm_getargv(), kvm_getenvv()—retrieve user process state
- kvm_nlist()—retrieve kernel symbol table names

Figure 8–3 shows an example of using the kvm(3) interface.

FIGURE 8–3 Using the kvm(3) interface to read kernel memory

// kvm_hagfish.c

```c
#include <stdio.h>
#include <stdlib.h>
#include <unistd.h>
#include <fcntl.h>
#include <kvm.h>

#define TARGET_ADDRESS  (u_long)0x5000
#define TARGET_NBYTES   (size_t)7
#define PROGNAME        "kvm_hagfish"

int
main(void)
{
    kvm_t *kd;
    char   buf[8] = { '\0' };

    kd = kvm_open(NULL,      // kernel executable; use default
                  NULL,      // kernel memory device; use default
                  NULL,      // swap device; use default
                  O_RDONLY,  // flags
                  PROGNAME); // error prefix string
    if (!kd)
        exit(1);


    if (kvm_read(kd, TARGET_ADDRESS, buf, TARGET_NBYTES) != TARGET_NBYTES)
        perror("kvm_read");
    else
        printf("%s\n", buf);

    kvm_close(kd);

    exit(0);
}


$ gcc -Wall -o kvm_hagfish kvm_hagfish.c # string seen only on the PowerPC
$ sudo ./kvm_hagfish
Hagfish
$
```

Raw Kernel Memory Access: Caveats

Exchanging information with the kernel by having raw access to its memory is unsatisfactory for several reasons. To begin with, a program must know the actual names, sizes, and formats of kernel structures. If these change across kernel versions, the program would need to be recompiled and perhaps even modified. Besides, it is cumbersome to access complicated data structures. Consider a linked list of deep structures—that is, structures with one or more fields that are pointers. To read such a list, a program must read each element individually and then must separately read the data referenced by the pointer fields. It would also be difficult for the kernel to guarantee the consistency of such information.

Moreover, the information sought by a user program must be either kernel-resident in its final form (i.e., the kernel must compute it), or it must be computed from its components by the program. The former requires the kernel to know about the various types of information user programs might need, precompute it, and store it. The latter does not guarantee consistency and requires additional hardcoded logic in the program.

Direct user-program access to all kernel memory may also be a security and stability concern, even though such access normally requires superuser privileges. It is difficult to both specify and enforce limits on the accessibility of certain parts of kernel memory. In particular, the kernel cannot do sanity checking of the data that is written to its raw memory.

Several approaches have been used in operating systems to address these issues. The `sysctl()` system call was introduced in 4.4BSD as a safe, reliable, and portable (across kernel versions) way to perform user-kernel data exchange. The Plan 9 operating system extended the file metaphor to export *services*—such as I/O devices, network interfaces, and the windowing system—as files. With these services, one could perform file I/O for most things that would require access to `/dev/kmem` on traditional systems. The `/proc` file system uses the file metaphor to provide both a view of currently running processes and an interface to control them. Linux extended the concept further by providing formatted I/O to files in `/proc`. For example, kernel parameters can be modified by writing strings to the appropriate files—the Linux kernel will parse, validate, and accept or reject the information. Newer versions of Linux provide `sysfs`, which is another in-memory file system used to export kernel data structures, their properties, and interconnections to user space.

8.2.2 Querying Physical Memory Size

The size of physical memory on a system can be programmatically determined through the `sysctl()` or `sysctlbyname()` functions. Figure 8–4 shows an example. Note that the retrieved size is the value of the `max_mem` kernel variable, which, as we saw in earlier chapters, can be artificially limited.

FIGURE 8–4 Determining the size of physical memory on a system

```c
// hw_memsize.c

#include <stdio.h>
#include <sys/sysctl.h>

int
main(void)
{
    int             ret;
    unsigned long long memsize;
    size_t          len = sizeof(memsize);

    if (!(ret = sysctlbyname("hw.memsize", &memsize, &len, NULL, 0)))
        printf("%lld MB\n", (memsize >> 20ULL));
    else
        perror("sysctlbyname");

    return ret;
}


$ gcc -Wall -o hw_memsize hw_memsize.c
$ ./hw_memsize
4096 MB
```

8.3 Mach VM

In this section, we will discuss the Mach VM architecture as it is implemented in the Mac OS X kernel. Mach's VM design has the following noteworthy aspects:

- A clean separation between machine-dependent and machine-independent parts. Only the latter part has complete VM-related information.
- Large, sparse virtual address spaces—one for each task, and fully shared by all threads within that task.
- Integration of memory management and interprocess communication. Mach provides IPC-based interfaces for working with task address spaces. These interfaces are especially flexible in allowing one task to manipulate the address space of another.
- Optimized virtual copy operations through symmetric or asymmetric copy-on-write (COW) algorithms.

- Flexible memory sharing between related or unrelated tasks, with support for copy-on-write, which is useful during `fork()` and during large IPC transfers. In particular, tasks can send parts of their address spaces to one another in IPC messages.

- Memory-mapped files.

- A variety of backing store types usable through multiple pagers. Although not supported in Mac OS X, Mach provides support for user-space pagers, wherein user programs can implement facilities such as encrypted virtual memory and distributed shared memory.

Figure 8–5 shows an overview of the relationships between the key components of Mach's VM architecture.

8.3.1 Overview

Each task's address space is represented in the kernel by an address map—a *VM map*, which contains a doubly linked list of memory regions and a machine-dependent physical map (*pmap*) structure. The pmap handles virtual-to-physical address translations. Each memory region—a *VM map entry*—represents a contiguous range of virtual addresses, all of which are currently mapped (valid) in the task. However, each range has its own protection and inheritance attributes, so even if an address is valid, the task may not be able to access it for one or more types of operations. Moreover, the VM map entries are ordered by address in the list. Each VM map entry has an associated *VM object*, which contains information about accessing the memory from its source. A VM object contains a list of resident pages, or *VM pages*. Each VM page is identified within the VM object by its offset from the start of the object. Now, some or all of the VM object's memory may not be resident in physical memory—it may be in a *backing store*, for example, a regular file, a swap file, or a hardware device. The VM object is backed[3] by a *memory object*, which, in the simplest sense, is a Mach port to which messages can be sent by the kernel to retrieve the missing data. The owner of a memory object is a *memory manager* (often called a *pager*). A pager is a specialized task (an in-kernel piece of code in Mac OS X) that supplies data to the kernel and receives modified data upon eviction.

---

3. A portion of a VM object can also be backed by another VM object, as we will see when we discuss Mach's copy-on-write mechanism.

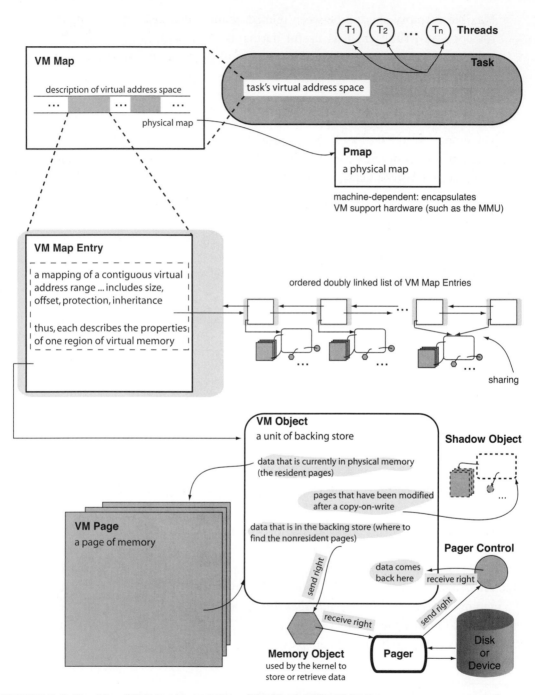

FIGURE 8–5 The Mac OS X implementation of the Mach VM architecture

Figure 8–6 is a more detailed version of Figure 8–5, showing a finer-grained view of the relationships between the VM subsystem data structures.

Let us now look at the important constituents of Mach's VM subsystem in detail.

8.3.2 Task Address Spaces

Each task has a virtual address space defining the set of valid virtual addresses that any thread within the task is allowed to reference. A 32-bit task has a 4GB virtual address space, whereas a 64-bit task's virtual address space is much larger—Mac OS X 10.4 provides a 64-bit user task with a 51-bit virtual address space, which amounts to over 2 petabytes[4] of virtual memory. For a typical task, its virtual address space is "large" in that it uses only a subset of the available virtual memory. At any given time, several subranges of a task's address space may be unused, leading to a typically sparsely populated virtual memory. It is, however, possible for special-purpose programs to have virtual memory requirements that exceed what a 32-bit address space can provide.

8.3.3 VM Maps

Each task's virtual address space is described by a VM map data structure (struct vm_map [osfmk/vm/vm_map.h]). The task structure's map field points to a vm_map structure.

> The task structure also contains information used by the task working set detection subsystem and the global shared memory subsystem. We will look at these subsystems in Sections 8.14 and 8.13, respectively.

A VM map is a collection of memory regions, or VM map entries, with each region being a virtually contiguous set of pages (a virtual range) with the same properties. Examples of these properties include the memory's source and attributes such as protection and inheritance. Each entry has a start address and an end address. The VM map points to an ordered doubly linked list of VM map entries.

---

4. A petabyte is approximately 10^{15} bytes.

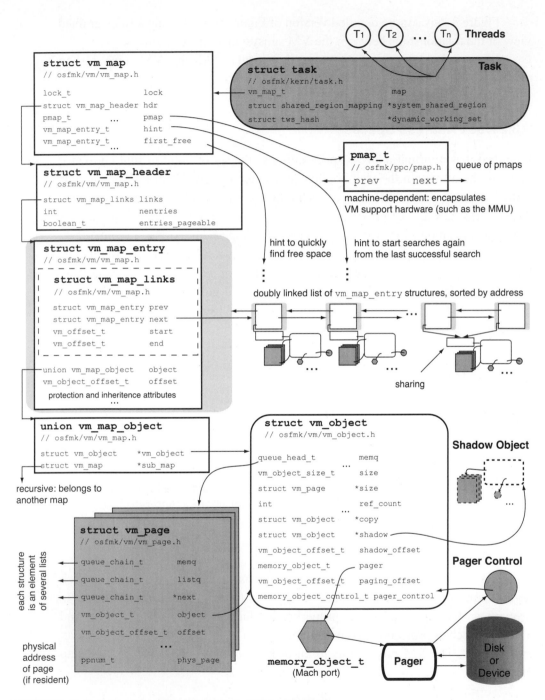

FIGURE 8–6 Details of the Mac OS X Mach VM architecture

8.3.4 VM Map Entries

A VM map entry is represented by a `vm_map_entry` structure (`struct vm_map_entry [osfmk/vm/vm_map.h]`). Since each entry represents a virtual memory range that is currently mapped in the task, the kernel searches the entry list at various times—in particular, while allocating memory. `vm_map_lookup_entry()` [`osfmk/vm/vm_map.c`] is used to find a VM map entry, if any, containing the specified address in the given VM map. The search algorithm is simple: The kernel searches the list linearly, either from the head of the list or from a hint that it previously saved after a successful lookup. The hint is maintained in the VM map, which also maintains a "free space" hint used to determine a free address quickly. If the given address cannot be found, `vm_map_lookup_entry()` returns the immediately preceding entry.

The kernel can split or merge VM map entries as necessary. For example, changing one or more attributes of a subset of a VM entry's pages will result in the entry being split into either two or three entries, depending on the offset of the modified page or pages. Other operations can lead to the merging of entries describing adjacent regions.

8.3.5 VM Objects

A task's memory can have several sources. For example, a shared library mapped into the task's address space represents memory whose source is the shared library file. We noted earlier that all pages in a single VM map entry have the same source. A VM object (`struct vm_object [osfmk/vm/vm_object.h]`) represents that source, with a VM map entry being the bridge between a VM object and a VM map. A VM object is conceptually a contiguous repository of data, some of which may be cached in resident memory, and the rest can be retrieved from the corresponding backing store. The entity in charge of transferring pages between physical memory and a backing store is called a *pager*, or more appropriately, a *memory manager*. In other words, a VM object is backed by a memory manager. As we will shortly see, when Mach uses copy-on-write optimizations, a VM object can be partially backed by another VM object.

> Although we will use the terms *pager* and *memory manager* synonymously, it must be noted that besides paging, a memory manager also plays an important role in maintaining consistency between the contents of the backing store and the contents of resident pages corresponding to a VM object. Sometimes a memory manager is also called a *data manager*.

8.3.5.1 *Contents of a VM Object*

A VM object contains a list of its resident pages, along with information about how to retrieve the pages that are not resident. Note that resident pages are not shared between VM objects—a given page exists within exactly one VM object. The list of resident page structures attached to a VM object is especially useful in releasing all pages associated with an object when it is destroyed.

A VM object data structure also contains properties such as the following:

- Object's size
- Number of references to the object
- Associated memory object (pager) and the offset into the pager
- Memory object control port
- Pointers to shadow and copy objects (see Section 8.3.7), if any
- "Copy strategy" that the kernel should use while copying the VM object's data
- Flag indicating whether the object is internal (and thus is created by the kernel and managed by the default pager)
- Flag indicating whether the object is temporary (and thus cannot be changed externally by a memory manager; in-memory changes to such an object are not reflected back to the memory manager)
- Flag indicating whether the object can persist (i.e., whether the kernel can keep the object's data cached, along with rights to the associated memory object) after all address map references to the object are deallocated

As shown in Figure 8–6, a memory object is implemented as a Mach port to which a pager owns receive rights.[5] When the kernel needs a VM object's pages to be brought into physical memory from the backing store, it communicates with the associated pager through the memory object port. The memory object control port, to which the kernel owns receive rights, is used to receive data from the pager.

With this knowledge, we can redescribe the bigger picture as follows: A VM map maps each valid region of a task's virtual address space to an offset within some memory object. For each memory object used in a VM map, the VM subsystem maintains a VM object.

---

5. We will discuss Mach port rights in Chapter 9.

8.3.5.2 Backing Stores

A backing store is a place for data to live when it is not resident. It can also be the source of the data, but not necessarily. In the case of a memory-mapped file, the backing store is the file itself. When the kernel needs to evict from physical memory a page that is backed by a file, it can simply discard the page unless the page has been modified while it was resident, in which case the change can be committed to the backing store.

Dynamically allocated memory, such as that obtained by calling `malloc(3)`, is anonymous in that it has no named source to begin with. When an anonymous memory page is used for the first time, Mach simply provides a physical page filled with zeros (hence, anonymous memory is also called *zero-filled memory*). In particular, there is no backing store initially associated with anonymous memory. When the kernel must evict such a page, it uses swap space as the backing store. Anonymous memory does not persist across system reboots. The corresponding VM objects, which are created by the kernel, are also called *internal* objects.

> When allocating anonymous memory, the kernel checks whether an existing VM map entry can be extended so that the kernel can avoid creating a new entry and a new VM object.

8.3.6 Pagers

A pager manipulates memory objects and pages. It owns the memory object port, which is used by the pager's clients (such as the kernel) as an interface to the memory object's pages, with operations for reading and writing those pages being part of the interface. The memory object is essentially a Mach port representation of the underlying backing storage[6]—it represents the nonresident state of the memory ranges backed by the memory object abstraction. The nonresident state (e.g., on-disk objects such as regular files and swap space) is essentially *secondary* memory that the kernel caches in *primary* (physical) memory.

As shown in Figure 8–1, Mac OS X provides three in-kernel pagers:

- The *default pager*, which transfers data between physical memory and swap space

---

6. Here's another way to look at this: A memory object is an object-oriented encapsulation of memory, implementing methods such as read and write.

- The *vnode pager*, which transfers data between physical memory and files
- The *device pager*, which is used for mapping special-purpose memory (such as framebuffer memory, PCI memory, or other physical addresses mapped to special hardware), with the necessary WIMG characteristics

> The letters in *WIMG* each specify a caching aspect, namely: write-through, caching-inhibited, memory coherency required, and guarded storage.

A pager may provide any number of memory objects, each of which represents one range of pages that the pager manages. Conversely, a task's address space may have any number of pagers managing separate pieces of it. Note that a pager is not directly involved in paging policies—it cannot alter the kernel's page replacement algorithm beyond setting memory object attributes.

8.3.6.1 External Pagers

The term *external memory manager* (or *external pager*) can be used to mean two things. In the first case, it refers to any pager other than the default—specifically, one that manages memory whose source is external to the kernel. Anonymous memory corresponds to internal objects, whereas memory-mapped files correspond to external objects. Therefore, the vnode pager would be termed as an external pager in this sense. This is the meaning we use in this chapter.

The other meaning refers to where the pager is implemented. If we designate an in-kernel pager as an internal pager, an external pager would be implemented as a specialized user task.

User-Space Pagers

User-space pagers allow flexibility in the types of backing stores that can be introduced without changing the kernel. For example, a pager can be written whose backing store is encrypted or compressed on disk. Similarly, distributed shared memory can be easily implemented via a user-space pager. Mac OS X does not support user-space pagers.

8.3.6.2 A Pager's Port

Whereas a memory object represents a source of data, the memory object's pager is the provider and manager of that data. When a portion of memory represented by a memory object is used by a client task, there are three parties primarily involved: the pager, the kernel, and the client task. As we will see in Section 8.6.1, a task directly or indirectly uses vm_map() (or its 64-bit variant) to map some or all of the memory object's memory into its address space. To do this, the caller of vm_map() must have send rights to the Mach port that represents the memory object. The pager owns this port and can therefore provide these rights to others.

A pager could advertise a service port to which clients could send messages to obtain memory objects. For example, a user-space pager could register its service port with the Bootstrap Server.[7] However, Mac OS X currently does not provide support for adding your own pagers. The three in-kernel pagers in Mac OS X have hardcoded ports. When pager-independent VM code needs to communicate with a pager, it determines the pager to call based on the value of the memory object passed, since the value must correspond to one of the known pagers.

```
kern_return_t
memory_object_init(memory_object_t            memory_object,
                   memory_object_control_t    memory_control,
                   memory_object_cluster_size_t memory_object_page_size)
{
    if (memory_object->pager = &vnode_pager_workaround)
       return vnode_pager_init(memory_object, memory_control,
                               memory_object_page_size);
    else if (memory_object->pager == &device_pager_workaround)
       return device_pager_init(memory_object, memory_control,
                                memory_object_page_size);
    else // default pager
       return dp_memory_object_init(memory_object, memory_control,
                                    memory_object_page_size);
}
```

The operation of a pager in the Mac OS X kernel uses a combination of the following: a subset of the original Mach pager interface, universal page lists (UPLs), and the unified buffer cache (UBC).

Note that the kernel implicitly provides the memory object for an internal pager—the calling task does not have to acquire send rights to one directly. For

7. We will discuss details of the Bootstrap Server in Section 9.4.

example, when a regular file is opened, the vnode pager's port is stashed into the UBC structure referenced from the vnode.

8.3.6.3 The Mach Pager Interface

Mach paging can be summarily described as follows: a client task obtains a memory object port directly or indirectly from a memory manager. It requests the kernel by calling `vm_map()` to map the memory object into its virtual address space. Thereafter, when the task attempts to access—read or write—a page from the newly mapped memory for the first time, a page-not-resident fault occurs. In handling the page fault, the kernel communicates with the memory manager by sending it a message requesting the missing data. The memory manager fetches the data from the backing store it is managing. Other types of page faults are handled as appropriate, with the kernel calling the memory manager and the latter responding asynchronously.

This is how the kernel uses physical memory as a cache for the contents of various memory objects. When the kernel needs to evict resident pages, it may—depending on the nature of the mapping—send "dirty" (modified while resident) pages to the memory manager.

When a client task is done using a mapped memory range, it can call `vm_deallocate()` to unmap that range. When all mappings of a memory object are gone, the object is terminated.

Figure 8–7 shows several messages (routines) that are part of the dialog between a memory manager and a kernel.[8] Let us look at some of these.

When a memory object is mapped for the first time, the kernel needs to notify the pager that it is using the object. It does so by sending a `memory_object_init()` message[9] to the pager. Regardless of where it is implemented, if you consider the pager as being logically external to the kernel, this is an *upcall* from the kernel to the pager. An external pager demultiplexes all messages it receives using the `memory_object_server()` routine.

```
kern_return_t
memory_object_init(memory_object_t            memory_object,
                   memory_object_control_t    memory_control,
                   memory_object_cluster_size_t memory_object_page_size);
```

---

8. We say "a kernel" because, pedantically speaking, a pager could be serving multiple kernels.

9. In Mac OS X, the "message" is simply a function call, not an IPC message.

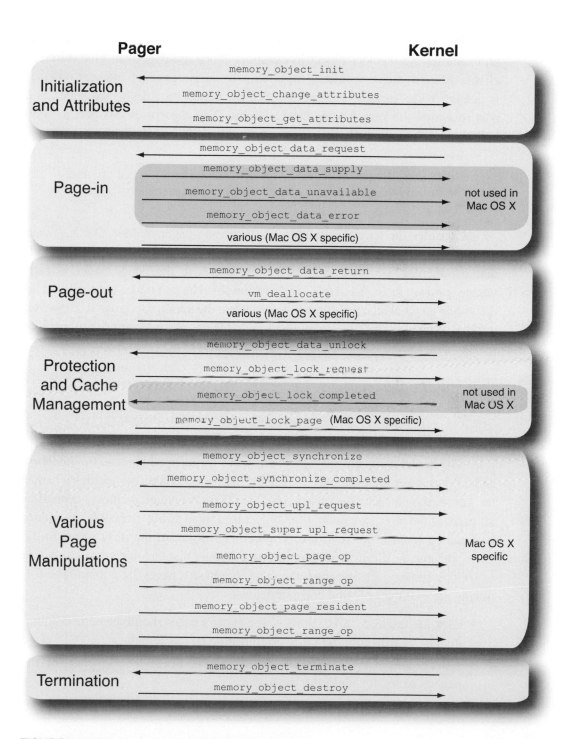

FIGURE 8–7 The Mach pager interface in Mac OS X

The `memory_object` argument to `memory_object_init()` is the port representing the memory object in question. Since the pager can give different clients different memory objects, the client tells the pager which memory object it is dealing with. `memory_control`, which the kernel provides to the pager, is a port to which the kernel holds receive rights. The pager uses this port to send messages to the kernel. Hence, it is also called the *pager reply port*.

> In Mach, a pager could be serving multiple kernels. In that case, there would be a separate control port for each kernel.

Consider the specific example of the vnode pager in Mac OS X. When `memory_object_init()` determines (using the hardcoded vnode pager port) that the memory object passed to it corresponds to the vnode pager, it calls `vnode_pager_init()` [osfmk/vm/bsd_vm.c]. The latter does not really set up the vnode pager, which was already set up when the vnode was created. However, `vnode_pager_init()` does call `memory_object_change_attributes()` to set the kernel's attributes for the memory object.

```
kern_return_t
memory_object_change_attributes(memory_object_control_t control,
                                memory_object_flavor_t  flavor,
                                memory_object_info_t    attributes,
                                mach_msg_type_number_t  count);
```

The kernel maintains per-object attributes for mapped objects. *Cacheability* and *copy strategy* are examples of such attributes. Cacheability specifies whether the kernel should cache the object (provided there is enough memory) even after all users of the object are gone. If an object is marked as not cacheable, it will not be retained when it is not in use: The kernel will return the dirty pages to the pager, reclaim the clean pages, and inform the pager that the object is no longer in use. Copy strategy specifies how the memory object's pages are copied. The following are examples of valid copy strategies.

- `MEMORY_OBJECT_COPY_NONE`—The pager's pages should be copied immediately, with no copy-on-write optimization by the kernel.
- `MEMORY_OBJECT_COPY_CALL`—If the kernel needs to copy any of the pager's pages, it should call the pager.

- MEMORY_OBJECT_COPY_DELAY—The pager promises not to change externally any of the data cached by the kernel, so the kernel is free to use an optimized copy-on-write strategy (see asymmetric copy-on-write in Section 8.3.7).

- MEMORY_OBJECT_COPY_TEMPORARY—This strategy acts like MEMORY_OBJECT_COPY_DELAY; additionally, the pager is not interested in seeing any changes from the kernel.

- MEMORY_OBJECT_COPY_SYMMETRIC—This strategy acts like MEMORY_OBJECT_COPY_TEMPORARY; additionally, the memory object will not be multiply mapped (see symmetric copy-on-write in Section 8.3.7).

The attributes can be retrieved through memory_object_get_attributes().

```
kern_return_t
memory_object_get_attributes(memory_object_control_t   control,
                             memory_object_flavor_t    flavor,
                             memory_object_info_t      attributes,
                             mach_msg_type_number_t   *count);
```

When a client task accesses a memory object page that is not resident, a page fault occurs. The kernel locates the appropriate VM object, which refers to the memory object. The kernel sends the pager a memory_object_data_request() message. The pager will typically provide the data, fetching it from the backing store.

```
kern_return_t
memory_object_data_request(memory_object_t            memory_object,
                           memory_object_offset_t     offset,
                           memory_object_cluster_size_t length,
                           vm_prot_t                  desired_access);
```

In Mach, the pager would respond to memory_object_data_request() by sending an asynchronous reply to the kernel: it would send a memory_object_data_supply() or memory_object_data_provided() message (depending on the Mach version) to the memory object control port. In Mac OS X, memory_object_data_request() explicitly calls one of the three pagers. In the case of the vnode pager, the kernel calls vnode_pager_data_request() [osfmk/vm/bsd_vm.c], which in turn calls vnode_pager_cluster_read() [osfmk/vm/bds_vm.c]. The latter causes data to be paged in by calling vnode_pagein() [bsd/vm/vnode_pager.c], which eventually calls the file-system-specific page-in operation.

> ### Paging Problems
>
> In Mach, the pager can also reply with a `memory_object_data_unavailable()` or `memory_object_data_error()` message. `memory_object_data_unavailable()` means that although the range within the memory object is valid, there is no data for it yet. This message notifies the kernel to return zero-filled pages for the range. Although the pager itself could create zero-filled pages and supply them through `memory_object_data_supply()`, the kernel's zero-fill code is likely to be more optimized. If a paging error—say, a bad disk sector—causes the pager to fail to retrieve data, the pager can respond with a `memory_object_data_error()` message.

When the kernel needs to reclaim memory and there are dirty pages for a memory object, the kernel can send those pages to the pager through `memory_object_data_return()`. In Mac OS X, the in-kernel page-out daemon does this.

```
kern_return_t
memory_object_data_return(memory_object_t          memory_object,
                          memory_object_offset_t   offset,
                          vm_size_t                size,
                          memory_object_offset_t  *resid_offset,
                          int                     *io_error,
                          boolean_t                dirty,
                          boolean_t                kernel_copy,
                          int                      upl_flags);
```

There is no explicit response to this message—the pager simply deallocates the pages from its address space so that the kernel can use the physical memory for other purposes. In Mac OS X, for the vnode pager, `memory_object_data_return()` calls `vnode_pager_data_return()` [osfmk/vm/bsd_vm.c], which in turn calls `vnode_pager_cluster_write()` [osfmk/vm/bsd_vm.c]. The latter causes data to be paged out by calling `vnode_pageout()` [bsd/vm/vnode_pager.c], which eventually calls the file-system-specific page-out operation.

A pager uses `memory_object_lock_request()` to control use of the (resident) data associated with the given memory object. The data is specified as the number of bytes (the `size` argument) starting at a given byte offset (the `offset` argument) within the memory object. `memory_object_lock_request()` sanity-checks its arguments and calls `vm_object_update()` [osfmk/vm/memory_object.c] on the associated VM object.

```
kern_return_t
memory_object_lock_request(memory_object_control_t control,
                           memory_object_offset_t  offset,
                           memory_object_size_t    size,
                           memory_object_offset_t *resid_offset,
                           int                    *io_errno,
                           memory_object_return_t  should_return,
                           int                     flags,
                           vm_prot_t               prot);
```

The `should_return` argument to `memory_object_lock_request()` is used to specify the data to be returned, if at all, to the memory manager. It can take the following values:

- `MEMORY_OBJECT_RETURN_NONE`—do not return any pages
- `MEMORY_OBJECT_RETURN_DIRTY`—return only dirty pages
- `MEMORY_OBJECT_RETURN_ALL`—return both dirty and precious pages
- `MEMORY_OBJECT_RETURN_ANYTHING`—return all resident pages

The `flags` argument specifies the operation to perform, if any, on the data. Valid operations are `MEMORY_OBJECT_DATA_FLUSH`, `MEMORY_OBJECT_DATA_NO_CHANGE`, `MEMORY_OBJECT_DATA_PURGE`, `MEMORY_OBJECT_COPY_SYNC`, `MEMORY_OBJECT_DATA_SYNC`, and `MEMORY_OBJECT_IO_SYNC`. Note that the combination of `should_return` and `flags` determines the fate of the data. For example, if `should_return` is `MEMORY_OBJECT_RETURN_NONE` and `flags` is `MEMORY_OBJECT_DATA_FLUSH`, the resident pages will be discarded.

The `prot` argument is used to restrict access to the given memory. Its value specifies the access that should be *disallowed*. The special value `VM_PROT_NO_CHANGE` is used when no change in protection is desired.

The kernel uses `memory_object_terminate()` to notify the pager that the object is no longer in use. The pager uses `memory_object_destroy()` to notify the kernel to shut down a memory object even if there are references to the associated VM object. This results in a call to `vm_object_destroy()` [osfmk/vm/vm_object.c]. In Mac OS X, `memory_object_destroy()` is called because of `vclean()` [bsd/vfs/vfs_subr.c], which cleans a vnode when it is being reclaimed.

```
kern_return_t
memory_object_terminate(memory_object_t memory_object);
```

```
kern_return_t
memory_object_destroy(memory_object_control_t control, kern_return_t reason);
```

8.3.7 Copy-on-Write

Copy-on-write (COW) is an optimization technique wherein a memory copy operation defers the copying of physical pages until one of the parties involved in the copy writes to that memory—until then, the physical pages are shared between the parties. As long as copied data is only read and not written to, copy-on-write saves both time and physical memory. Even when the data is written to, copy-on-write copies only the modified pages.

Note in Figure 8–6 that two of the VM entries are shown as pointing to the same VM object. This is how Mach implements *symmetric* copy-on-write sharing. Figure 8–8 shows the scheme. In a symmetric copy-on-write operation, the needs_copy bit is set in both the source and destination VM map entries. Both entries point to the same VM object, whose reference count is incremented. Moreover, all pages in the VM object are write-protected. At this point, both tasks access the same physical pages while reading from the shared memory. When such a page is written to by one of the tasks, a page protection fault occurs. The kernel does not modify the original VM object but creates a new VM object—a *shadow object* containing a copy of the faulting page—and gives it to the task that modified the page. The other pages, including the unmodified version of the page in question, remain in the original VM object, whose needs_copy bit remains set.

In Figure 8–8, when the destination task accesses a previously copy-on-write-shared page that it has already modified, the kernel will find that page in the shadow object. The remaining pages will not be found in the shadow object—the kernel will follow the pointer to the original object and find them there. Multiple copy-on-write operations can result in a shadow object being shadowed by another, leading to a *shadow chain*. The kernel attempts to collapse such chains when possible. In particular, if all pages in some VM object are shadowed by the parent object, the latter does not need to shadow the former any more—it can shadow the next VM object, if any, in the chain.

> The scheme is symmetric because its operation does not depend on which task—the source or the destination in the copy-on-write operation—modifies a shared page.

It is important to note that when a shadow object is created during a symmetric copy-on-write, no memory manager is recorded for it. The kernel will use swap space as the backing store, and the default pager as the memory manager, when it needs to page out anonymous memory. There is a problem, however, if an

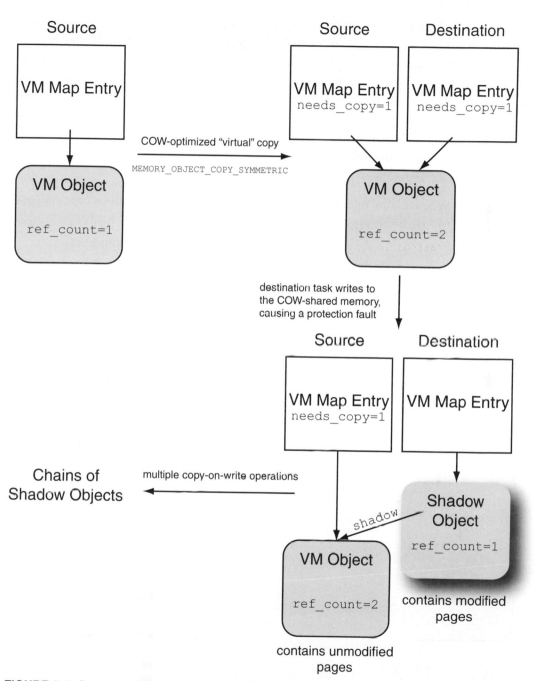

FIGURE 8–8 Symmetric copy-on-write using shadow objects

external memory manager—say, the vnode pager in the case of a memory-mapped file—backs the original VM object. The kernel cannot change the VM object because doing so would disconnect the file mapping. Since page modifications in a symmetric copy-on-write are seen only by shadow objects, the original VM object, which is connected to the memory manager, will never see those modifications. Mach solves this problem by using an *asymmetric* copy-on-write algorithm, in which the source party retains the original VM object and the kernel creates a new object for the destination. The asymmetric algorithm works as follows (see Figure 8–9).

- When a copy operation is performed, create a new object—a *copy object*—for use by the destination.
- Point the shadow field of the copy object to the original object.
- Point the copy field of the original object to the copy object.
- Mark the copy object as copy-on-write. Note that the original object is *not* marked copy-on-write in this case.
- Whenever a page is about to be modified in the source mapping, copy it to a new page first and push that page to the copy object.

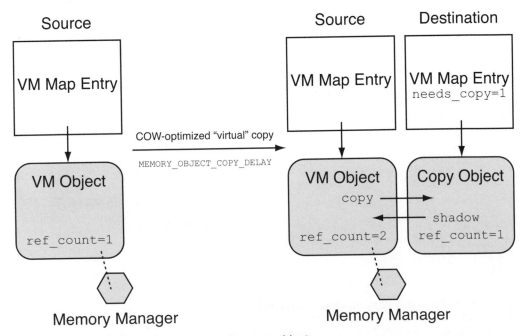

FIGURE 8–9 Asymmetric copy-on-write using copy objects

8.3.8 The Physical Map (Pmap)

A VM map also points to a physical map (pmap) data structure (`struct pmap` [`osfmk/ppc/pmap.h`]), which describes hardware-defined virtual-to-physical address translation mappings. Mach's pmap layer encapsulates the machine-dependent VM code—in particular, that for managing the MMU and the caches—and exports generic functions for use by the machine-independent layer. To understand the pmap layer's role in the system, let us look at examples of functions in the pmap interface.

> The Mac OS X kernel contains additional code outside of the pmap module—in `osfmk/ppc/mappings.c`—to maintain virtual-to-physical mappings on the PowerPC. This code acts as a bridge between the pmap layer and the underlying hardware, which is contrary to Mach's traditional encapsulation of *all* hardware-dependent code within the pmap layer.

8.3.8.1 The Pmap Interface

`pmap_map()` maps the virtual address range starting at `va` to the physical address range `spa` through `epa`, with the machine-independent protection value `prot`. This function is called during bootstrapping to map various ranges, such as those corresponding to the exception vectors, the kernel's text segment, and the kernel's data segment.

```
vm_offset_t
pmap_map(vm_offset_t va, vm_offset_t spa, vm_offset_t epa, vm_prot_t prot);
```

`pmap_map_physical()` and `pmap_map_iohole()` are special versions of `pmap_map()`. The former maps physical memory into the kernel's address map. The virtual address used for this mapping is `lgPMWvaddr`, the so-called *physical memory window*. `pmap_map_iohole()` takes a physical address and size and then maps an "I/O hole" in the physical memory window.

`pmap_create()` creates and returns a physical map, either by recovering one from the list of free pmaps or by allocating one from scratch.

```
pmap_t
pmap_create(vm_map_size_t size);
```

Besides the list of free pmaps (`free_pmap_list`), the kernel also maintains the following relevant data structures:

- A list of in-use pmaps (anchored by `kernel_pmap`, the kernel pmap).
- A list of physical addresses of in-use pmaps (anchored by `kernel_pmap_phys`).
- A pointer to a *cursor pmap* (`cursor_pmap`), which the kernel uses as the starting point while searching for free pmaps. `cursor_pmap` points to either the last pmap allocated or to the previous-to-last if it was removed from the in-use list of pmaps.

The kernel pmap is located in a 512-byte block in the V=R (virtual=real) area. Therefore, `kernel_pmap_phys` and `kernel_pmap` both point to the same location. Each address space is assigned an identifier that is unique within the system. The identifier is used to construct the 24-bit PowerPC virtual segment identifier (VSID). The number of active address spaces is limited by `maxAdrSp` (defined to be 16384 in `osfmk/ppc/pmap.h`).

`pmap_create()` is called during task creation, regardless of whether the child is inheriting the parent's memory or not. If no memory is being inherited, a "clean slate" address space is created for the child task; otherwise, each VM entry in the parent is examined to see if it needs to be shared, copied, or not inherited at all.

`pmap_destroy()` removes a reference to the given pmap. When the reference count reaches zero, the pmap is added to the list of free pmaps, which caches the first `free_pmap_max` (32) pmaps that are freed up. `pmap_destroy()` is called when a VM map is destroyed after the last reference to it goes away.

```
void
pmap_destroy(pmap_t pmap);
```

`pmap_reference()` increments the reference count of the given pmap by one.

```
void
pmap_reference(pmap_t pmap);
```

`pmap_enter()` creates a translation for the virtual address va to the physical page number pa in the given pmap with the protection prot.

```
void
pmap_enter(pmap_t          pmap,
           vm_map_offset_t  va,
           ppnum_t          pa,
           vm_prot_t        prot,
           unsigned int     flags,
           __unused boolean_t wired);
```

The flags argument can be used to specify particular attributes for the mapping—for example, to specify cache modes:

- VM_MEM_NOT_CACHEABLE (cache inhibited)
- VM_WIMG_WTHRU (write-through cache)
- VM_WIMG_WCOMB (write-combine cache)
- VM_WIMG_COPYBACK (copyback cache)

pmap_remove() unmaps all virtual addresses in the virtual address range determined by the given pmap and [sva, eva)—that is, inclusive of sva but exclusive of eva. If the pmap in question is a *nested* pmap, then pmap_remove() will not remove any mappings. A nested pmap is one that has been inserted into another pmap. The kernel uses nested pmaps to implement shared segments, which in turn are used by shared libraries and the commpage mechanism.

```
void
pmap_remove(pmap_t pmap, addr64_t sva, addr64_t eva);
```

pmap_page_protect() lowers the permissions for all mappings to a given page. In particular, if prot is VM_PROT_NONE, this function removes all mappings to the page.

```
void
pmap_page_protect(ppnum_t pa, vm_prot_t prot);
```

pmap_protect() changes the protection on all virtual addresses in the virtual address range determined by the given pmap and [sva, eva). If prot is VM_PROT_NONE, pmap_remove() is called on the virtual address range.

```
void
pmap_protect(pmap_t          pmap,
             vm_map_offset_t sva,
             vm_map_offset_t eva,
             vm_prot_t       prot);
```

pmap_clear_modify() clears the dirty bit for a machine-independent page starting at the given physical address. pmap_is_modified() checks whether the given physical page has been modified since the last call to pmap_clear_modify(). Similarly, pmap_clear_reference() and pmap_is_referenced() operate on the referenced bit of the given physical page.

```
void      pmap_clear_modify(ppnum pa);
boolean_t pmap_is_modified(register ppnum_t pa);
```

```
void       pmap_clear_reference(ppnum_t pa);
boolean_t pmap_is_referenced(ppnum_t pa);
```

pmap_switch() switches to a new pmap—that is, it changes to a new address space. It is called during a thread context switch (unless the two threads belong to the same task and therefore share the same address space).

```
void
pmap_switch(pmap_t pmap);
```

PMAP_ACTIVATE(pmap, thread, cpu) and PMAP_DEACTIVATE(pmap, thread, cpu) activate and deactivate, respectively, pmap for use by thread on cpu. Both these routines are defined to be null macros on the PowerPC.

8.4 Resident Memory

Mach divides an address space into pages, with the page size usually being the same as the native hardware page size, although Mach's design allows a larger virtual page size to be built from multiple physically contiguous hardware pages. Whereas programmer-visible memory is byte addressable, Mach virtual memory primitives operate only on pages. In fact, Mach will internally page-align memory offsets and round up the size of a memory range to the nearest page boundary. Moreover, the kernel's enforcement of memory protection is at the page level.

> It is possible that the native hardware supports multiple page sizes—for example, the PowerPC 970FX supports 4KB and 16MB page sizes. Mach can also support a virtual page size that is larger than the native hardware page size, in which case a larger virtual page will map to multiple contiguous physical pages. The kernel variable vm_page_shift contains the number of bits to shift right to convert a byte address into a page number. The library variable vm_page_size contains the page size being used by Mach. The hw.memsize sysctl variable also contains the page size.
>
> ```
> $ sudo ./readksym.sh _vm_page_shift 4 -d
> 0000000   00000    00012
> ```

8.4.1 The vm_page Structure

The valid portions of an address space correspond to valid virtual pages. Depending on a program's memory usage pattern and other factors, none, some, or even all of its virtual memory could be cached in physical memory through resident pages. A resident page structure (struct vm_page [osfmk/vm/vm_page.h]) corresponds to a page of physical memory and vice versa. It contains a pointer to the associated VM object and also records the offset into the object, along with information indicating whether the page is referenced, whether it has been modified, whether it is encrypted, and so on. Figure 8–10 shows an overview of how the vm_page structure is connected to other data structures. Note that the structure resides on several lists simultaneously.

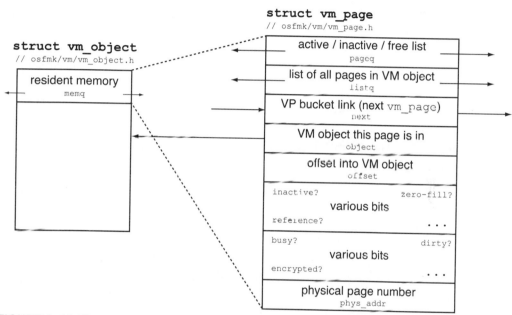

FIGURE 8–10 The structure of a resident page

8.4.2 Searching for Resident Pages

The kernel maintains a hash table of resident pages, with the next field of a vm_page structure chaining the page in the table. The hash table, also called the *virtual-to-physical* (VP) table, is used for looking up a resident page given a { VM object, offset } pair. The following are some of the functions used to access and manipulate the VP table.

```
vm_page_t
vm_page_lookup(vm_object_t object, vm_object_offset_t offset);
```

```
void
vm_page_insert(vm_page_t mem, vm_object_t object, vm_object_offset_t offset);

void
vm_page_remove(vm_page_t mem);
```

Object/offset pairs are distributed in the hash table using the following hash function (the `atop_64()` macro converts an address to a page):

```
H = vm_page_bucket_hash; // basic bucket hash (calculated during bootstrap)
M = vm_page_hash_mask;   // mask for hash function (calculated during bootstrap)

#define vm_page_hash(object, offset) \
    (((natural_t)((uint32_t)object * H) + ((uint32_t)atop_64(offset) ^ H)) & M)
```

Note that the lookup function uses a hint[10] recorded in the `memq_hint` field of the VM object. Before searching the hash table for the given object/offset pair, `vm_page_lookup()` [osfmk/vm/vm_resident.c] examines the resident page specified by the hint and, if necessary, also its next and previous pages. The kernel maintains counters that are incremented for each type of successful hint-based lookup. We can use the `readksym.sh` program to examine the values of these counters.

```
$ sudo readksym.sh _vm_page_lookup_hint 4 -d
0000000   00083   28675
...
$ sudo readksym.sh _vm_page_lookup_hint_next 4 -d
0000000   00337   03493
...
$ sudo readksym.sh _vm_page_lookup_hint_prev 4 -d
0000000   00020   48630
...
$ sudo readksym.sh _vm_page_lookup_hint_miss 4 -d
0000000   00041   04239
...
$
```

8.4.3 Resident Page Queues

A pageable resident page[11] resides on one of the following three paging queues through the `pageq` field of the `vm_page` structure.

---

10. There is also a version of the lookup function that does not use the VM object's hint—that version is used by the task-working-set-detection subsystem.

11. When a page is wired, it is removed from the paging queues.

- The *free queue* (vm_page_queue_free) contains free pages available for allocation immediately. A page on this queue has no mappings and does not contain useful data. When the kernel needs empty pages, say, during a page fault or during kernel memory allocation, it takes pages from this queue.

- The *inactive queue* (vm_page_queue_inactive) contains pages that are not referenced in any pmap but still have an object/offset page mapping. A page on this queue may be dirty. When the kernel needs to page out some memory, it evicts resident pages from the inactive list. There is a separate inactive memory queue for anonymous memory (vm_page_queue_zf), allowing the page-out daemon to assign a higher affinity to anonymous memory pages. This list is a first-in first-out (FIFO) list.

- The *active queue* (vm_page_queue_active) contains pages that are referenced in at least one pmap. This is also a FIFO list. It has an LRU-like ordering.

The top command can be used to display the amounts of memory currently distributed across the active, inactive, and free queues.

> Recall that we noted in Section 8.3.5.1 that a VM object can be persistent, in which case its pages are not freed when all its references go away. Such pages are placed on the inactive list. This is particularly useful for memory-mapped files.

8.4.4 Page Replacement

Since physical memory is a limited resource, the kernel must continually decide which pages should remain resident, which should be made resident, and which should be evicted from physical memory. The kernel uses a page replacement policy called *FIFO with Second Chance*, which approximates LRU behavior.

> A specific goal of page replacement is to maintain a balance between the active and inactive lists. The active list should ideally contain only the working sets of all programs.

The kernel manages the three aforementioned page queues using a set of page-out parameters that specify paging thresholds and other constraints. Page queue management includes the following specific operations.

- Move pages from the front of the active queue to the inactive queue.
- Clean dirty pages from the inactive queue.
- Move clean pages from the inactive queue to the free queue.

Since the active queue is a FIFO, the oldest pages are removed first. If an inactive page is referenced, it is moved back to the active queue. Thus, the pages on the inactive queue are eligible for a second chance of being referenced—if a page is referenced frequently enough, it will be prevented from moving to the free queue and therefore will not be reclaimed.

The so-called cleaning of dirty pages is performed by the *page-out daemon*, which consists of the following kernel threads:

- `vm_pageout_iothread_internal()` [`osfmk/vm/vm_pageout.c`]
- `vm_pageout_iothread_external()` [`osfmk/vm/vm_pageout.c`]
- `vm_pageout_garbage_collect()` [`osfmk/vm/vm_pageout.c`]

The "internal" and "external" threads both use the `vm_pageout_iothread_continue()` [`osfmk/vm/vm_pageout.c`] continuation, but they use separate page-out (laundry) queues: `vm_pageout_queue_internal` and `vm_pageout_queue_external`, respectively. `vm_pageout_iothread_continue()` services the given laundry queue, calling `memory_object_data_return()`—if necessary—to send data to the appropriate pager. `vm_pageout_garbage_collect()` frees excess kernel stacks and possibly triggers garbage collection in Mach's zone-based memory allocator module (see Section 8.16.3).

The page-out daemon also controls the rate at which dirty pages are sent to the pagers. In particular, the constant `VM_PAGE_LAUNDRY_MAX` (16) limits the maximum page-outs outstanding for the default pager. When the laundry count (the current count of laundry pages in queue or in flight) exceeds this threshold, the page-out daemon pauses to let the default pager catch up.

8.4.5 Physical Memory Bookkeeping

`vm_page_grab()` [`osfmk/vm/vm_resident.c`] is called to remove a page from the free list. If the number of free pages in the system (`vm_page_free_count`) is less than the number of reserved free pages (`vm_page_free_reserved`), this routine will not attempt to grab a page unless the current thread is a *VM-privileged* thread.

```
$ sudo readksym.sh _vm_page_free_count 4 -d
0000000    00001    60255
...
```

```
$ sudo readksym.sh _vm_page_free_reserved 4 -d
0000000    00000    00098
...
```

As shown in Figure 8–11, `vm_page_grab()` also checks the current values of free and inactive counters to determine whether it should wake up the page-out daemon.

FIGURE 8–11 Grabbing a page from the free list

```
// osfmk/vm/vm_resident.c

vm_page_t
vm_page_grab(void)
{
    register vm_page_t mem;

    mutex_lock(&vm_page_queue_free_lock);
    ...
    if ((vm_page_free_count < vm_page_free_reserved) &&
        !(current_thread()->options & TH_OPT_VMPRIV)) {
        mutex_unlock(&vm_page_queue_free_lock);
        mem = VM_PAGE_NULL;
        goto wakeup_pageout;
    }
    ...
    // try to grab a page from the free list
    ...
wakeup_pageout:

    if ((vm_page_free_count < vm_page_free_min) ||
        ((vm_page_free_count < vm_page_free_target) &&
        (vm_page_inactive_count < vm_page_inactive_target)))
        thread_wakeup((event_t) &vm_page_free_wanted);

    return mem;
}
```

Note in Figure 8–11 that `vm_page_grab()` also compares the current value of the free counter with `vm_page_inactive_target`. The latter specifies the minimum desired size of the inactive queue—it must be large enough so that pages on it get a sufficient chance of being referenced. The page-out daemon keeps updating `vm_page_inactive_target` according to the following formula:

```
vm_page_inactive_target =
    (vm_page_active_count + vm_page_inactive_count) * (1/3)
```

Similarly, `vm_page_free_target` specifies the minimum desired number of free pages. The page-out daemon, once started, continues running until `vm_page_free_count` is at least this number.

```
$ sudo readksym.sh _vm_page_inactive_target 4 -d
0000000   00003   44802
. . .
$ sudo readksym.sh _vm_page_active_count 4 -d
0000000   00001   60376
. . .
$ sudo readksym.sh _vm_page_inactive_count 4 -d
0000000   00009   04238
. . .
$ sudo readksym.sh _vm_page_free_target 4 -d
0000000   00000   09601
. . .
$ sudo readksym.sh _vm_page_free_count 4 -d
0000000   00000   11355
. . .
```

The `vm_page_free_reserved` global variable specifies the number of physical pages reserved for VM-privileged threads, which are marked by the `TH_OPT_VMPRIV` bit being set in the options field of the thread structure. Examples of such threads include the page-out daemon itself and the default pager. As shown in Figure 8–12, `vm_page_free_reserve()` allows the value of `vm_page_free_reserved` to be adjusted, which also results in `vm_page_free_target` being recomputed. For example, `thread_wire_internal()` [osfmk/kern/thread.c], which sets or clears the `TH_OPT_VMPRIV` option for a thread, calls `vm_page_free_reserve()` to increment or decrement the number of reserved pages.

FIGURE 8–12 Reserving physical memory

```
// osfmk/vm/vm_resident.c

unsigned int vm_page_free_target = 0;
unsigned int vm_page_free_min = 0;
unsigned int vm_page_inactive_target = 0;
unsigned int vm_page_free_reserved = 0;


// osfmk/vm/vm_pageout.c
```

(continues)

FIGURE 8–12 Reserving physical memory *(continued)*

```
#define VM_PAGE_LAUNDRY_MAX              16UL
...
#define VM_PAGE_FREE_TARGET(free)        (15 + (free) / 80)
#define VM_PAGE_FREE_MIN(free)           (10 + (free) / 100)
#define VM_PAGE_INACTIVE_TARGET(avail)   ((avail) * 1 / 3)
#define VM_PAGE_FREE_RESERVED(n)         ((6 * VM_PAGE_LAUNDRY_MAX) + (n))
...

void
vm_pageout(void)
{
    // page-out daemon startup
    vm_page_free_count_init = vm_page_free_count; // save current value
    ...
    if (vm_page_free_reserved < VM_PAGE_FREE_RESERVED(processor_count)) {
        vm_page_free_reserve((VM_PAGE_FREE_RESERVED(processor_count)) -
                             vm_page_free_reserved);
    } else
        vm_page_free_reserve(0);
    ...
}
...


void
vm_page_free_reserve(int pages)
{
    int free_after_reserve;

    vm_page_free_reserved += pages;

    // vm_page_free_count_init is initial value of vm_page_free_count
    // it was saved by the page-out daemon during bootstrap
    free_after_reserve = vm_page_free_count_init - vm_page_free_reserved;

    vm_page_free_min = vm_page_free_reserved +
                       VM_PAGE_FREE_MIN(free_after_reserve);

    vm_page_free_target = vm_page_free_reserved +
                          VM_PAGE_FREE_TARGET(free_after_reserve);

    if (vm_page_free_target < vm_page_free_min + 5)
        vm_page_free_target = vm_page_free_min + 5;
}
```

8.4.6 Page Faults

A page fault is the result of a task attempting to access data residing in a page that needs the kernel's intervention before it can be used by the task. There can be several reasons for a page fault, such as those listed here.

- An *invalid access*—The address is not mapped into the task's address space. This results in an `EXC_BAD_ACCESS` Mach exception with the specific exception code `KERN_INVALID_ADDRESS`. This exception is normally translated by the kernel to the `SIGSEGV` signal.

- A *nonresident page*—The task attempted to access a virtual page that is currently not entered in the task's pmap. If the page is truly not in physical memory and the data needs to be read (paged in) from secondary storage, the fault is classified as a "hard" page fault. The kernel contacts the pager managing the requested page, and the pager in turn accesses the associated backing store. If, however, the data exists in the cache, it is a "soft" page fault. In this case, the page must still be found in memory, and the appropriate page translations must still be set up.

- A *protection violation*—The task attempted to access the page with higher access than is permitted, for example. If the protection violation is correctable, the kernel will transparently handle the fault; otherwise, the exception will be reported to the task (normally as a `SIGBUS` signal). An example of the correctable type is a page fault that occurs when a task attempts to write to a page that was marked read-only because of a copy-on-write operation. An example of the latter type is a task attempting to write to the commpage.

The page-fault handler is implemented in `osfmk/vm/vm_fault.c`, with `vm_fault()` being the master entry point. Let us look at the sequence of steps involved in handling a typical page fault. As we saw in Table 5–1, a page fault or an erroneous data memory access on the PowerPC corresponds to a data access exception. To handle the exception, the kernel calls `trap()` [`osfmk/ppc/trap.c`] with the interrupt code set to `T_DATA_ACCESS`. `trap()` can handle this exception in several ways, depending on whether it occurred in the kernel or in user space, whether the kernel debugger is enabled, whether the faulting thread's `thread` structure contains a valid pointer to a "recover" function, and so on. In general, `trap()` will call `vm_fault()` to resolve the page fault. `vm_fault()` first searches the given VM map for the given virtual address. If successful, it finds a VM object, the offset into the object, and the associated protection value.

Next, it must be ensured that the page is resident. Either the page will be found in physical memory by looking up the virtual-to-physical hash table, or a new resident page will be allocated for the given object/offset pair and inserted into the hash table. In the latter case, the page must also be populated with data. If the VM object has a pager, the kernel will call `memory_object_data_request()` to request the pager to retrieve the data. Alternatively, if the VM object has a shadow, the kernel will traverse the shadow chain to look for the page. New pages corresponding to internal VM objects (anonymous memory) will be zero-filled. Moreover, if the VM object has an associated copy object and the page is being written, it will be pushed to the copy object if it hasn't already been.

Eventually, the page fault handler will enter the page into the task's pmap by calling `PMAP_ENTER()` `[osfmk/vm/pmap.h]`, which is a wrapper around `pmap_enter()`. Thereafter, the page is available to the task.

8.5 Virtual Memory Initialization during Bootstrap

We discussed several aspects of virtual memory initialization in Chapter 5. Since we have more context in this chapter, let us briefly revisit how the VM subsystem is brought up. Recall that on the PowerPC, `ppc_vm_init()` `[osfmk/ppc/ppc_vm_init.c]` performs hardware-specific initialization of the memory subsystem. In particular, it bootstraps the pmap module and enables address translation, kick-starting virtual memory and the use of page tables. Thereafter, higher-level bootstrap of the kernel is initiated. One of the first steps in this higher-level bootstrap is scheduler initialization, followed by initialization of the hardware-independent parts of the Mach VM subsystem. The latter is depicted in Figure 8–13, which is a more detailed version of the picture we saw in Chapter 5.

`ppc_vm_init()` `[osfmk/ppc/ppc_vm_init.c]` processes the physical memory bank information provided to the kernel by the bootloader and populates the `pmap_mem_regions` array for the pmap module. An element of this array is a `mem_region_t` data structure `[osfmk/ppc/mappings.c]`.

Note that although we say that Figure 8–13 shows a hardware-independent picture, the sequence of functions shown includes `pmap_init()` `[osfmk/ppc/pmap.c]`, which finishes the pmap module's initialization by calling `zinit()` to create a zone from which pmaps (`pmap_t`) are allocated. The function also initializes data structures for tracking free pmaps—specifically, a list of free pmaps, a count of pmaps on this list, and a simple lock.

8.6 The Mach VM User-Space Interface

Mach provides a powerful set of routines to user programs for manipulating task address spaces. Given the appropriate privileges, a task can perform operations on another task's address space identically to its own. All routines in the Mach VM user interface require the target task as an argument.[12] Therefore, the routines are uniform in how they are used, regardless of whether the target task is the caller's own task or another.

Since user address spaces have a one-to-one mapping with user tasks, there are no explicit routines to create or destroy an address space. When the first task (the kernel task) is created, the `map` field of its `task` structure is set to refer to the kernel map (`kernel_map`), which is created by `kmem_init()` [osfmk/vm/vm_kern.c] during VM subsystem initialization. For subsequent tasks, a virtual address space is created with the task and destroyed along with the task. We saw in Chapter 6 that the `task_create()` call takes a prototype task and an address space inheritance indicator as arguments. The initial contents of a newly created task's address map are determined from these arguments. In particular, the inheritance properties of the prototype task's address map determine which portions, if any, are inherited by the child task.

// osfmk/kern/task.c

```
kern_return_t
task_create_internal(task_t      parent_task,
                     boolean_t  inherit_memory,
                     task_t     *child_task)
{
    ...
    if (inherit_memory)
        new_task->map = vm_map_fork(parent_task->map);
    else
        new_task->map = vm_map_create(pmap_create(0),
                             (vm_map_offset_t)(VM_MIN_ADDRESS),
                             (vm_map_offset_t)(VM_MAX_ADDRESS), TRUE);
    ...
}
```

   `vm_map_fork()` [osfmk/vm/vm_map.c] first calls `pmap_create()` [osfmk/ppc/pmap.c] to create a new physical map and calls `vm_map_cre-ate()` [osfmk/vm/vm_map.c] to create an empty VM map with the newly cre-

---

12. Specifically, the target task is a send right to the control port of the target task.

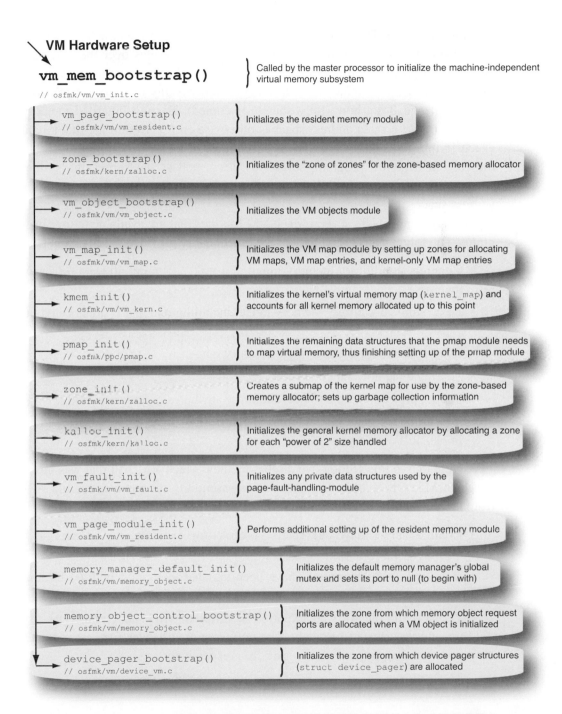

VM Hardware Setup

`vm_mem_bootstrap()`   Called by the master processor to initialize the machine-independent virtual memory subsystem

// osfmk/vm/vm_init.c

`vm_page_bootstrap()`   Initializes the resident memory module
// osfmk/vm/vm_resident.c

`zone_bootstrap()`   Initializes the "zone of zones" for the zone-based memory allocator
// osfmk/kern/zalloc.c

`vm_object_bootstrap()`   Initializes the VM objects module
// osfmk/vm/vm_object.c

`vm_map_init()`   Initializes the VM map module by setting up zones for allocating VM maps, VM map entries, and kernel-only VM map entries
// osfmk/vm/vm_map.c

`kmem_init()`   Initializes the kernel's virtual memory map (`kernel_map`) and accounts for all kernel memory allocated up to this point
// osfmk/vm/vm_kern.c

`pmap_init()`   Initializes the remaining data structures that the pmap module needs to map virtual memory, thus finishing setting up of the pmap module
// osfmk/ppc/pmap.c

`zone_init()`   Creates a submap of the kernel map for use by the zone-based memory allocator; sets up garbage collection information
// osfmk/kern/zalloc.c

`kalloc_init()`   Initializes the general kernel memory allocator by allocating a zone for each "power of 2" size handled
// osfmk/kern/kalloc.c

`vm_fault_init()`   Initializes any private data structures used by the page-fault-handling-module
// osfmk/vm/vm_fault.c

`vm_page_module_init()`   Performs additional setting up of the resident memory module
// osfmk/vm/vm_resident.c

`memory_manager_default_init()`   Initializes the default memory manager's global mutex and sets its port to null (to begin with)
// osfmk/vm/memory_object.c

`memory_object_control_bootstrap()`   Initializes the zone from which memory object request ports are allocated when a VM object is initialized
// osfmk/vm/memory_object.c

`device_pager_bootstrap()`   Initializes the zone from which device pager structures (`struct device_pager`) are allocated
// osfmk/vm/device_vm.c

FIGURE 8–13 Initialization of the hardware-independent part of the Mach VM subsystem

ated physical map. The minimum and maximum offsets of the new VM map are taken from the parent's map. `vm_map_fork()` then iterates over the VM map entries of the parent's address map, examining the inheritance property of each. These properties determine whether the child inherits any memory ranges from the parent, and if so, how (fully shared or copied). Barring inherited memory ranges, a newly created address space is otherwise empty. Before the first thread executes in a task, the task's address space must be populated appropriately. In the case of a typical program, several parties—such as the kernel, the system library, and the dynamic link editor—determine what to map into the task's address space.

Let us now look at several Mach VM routines that are available to user programs. The following is a summary of the functionality provided by these routines:

- Creating an arbitrary memory range in a task, including allocation of new memory

- Destroying an arbitrary memory range, including one that is unallocated, in a task

- Reading, writing, and copying a memory range

- Sharing a memory range

- Setting protection, inheritance, and other attributes of a memory range

- Preventing the pages in a memory range from being evicted by wiring them in physical memory

Note that in this section, we discuss the new Mach VM API that was introduced in Mac OS X 10.4. The new API is essentially the same as the old API from the programmer's standpoint, with the following key differences.

- Routine names have the `mach_` prefix—for example, `vm_allocate()` becomes `mach_vm_allocate()`.

- Data types used in routines have been updated to support both 64-bit and 32-bit tasks. Consequently, the new API can be used with any task.

- The new and old APIs are exported by different MIG subsystems[13]: `mach_vm` and `vm_map`, respectively. The corresponding header files are `<mach/mach_vm.h>` and `<mach/vm_map.h>`, respectively.

---

13. We will look at MIG subsystems in Chapter 9.

8.6.1 `mach_vm_map()`

`mach_vm_map()` is the fundamental user-visible Mach routine for establishing a new range of virtual memory in a task. It allows fine-grained specification of the properties of the virtual memory being mapped, which accounts for its large number of parameters.

```
kern_return_t
mach_vm_map(vm_map_t               target_task,
            mach_vm_address_t      *address,
            mach_vm_size_t         size,
            mach_vm_offset_t       mask,
            int                    flags,
            mem_entry_name_port_t  object,
            memory_object_offset_t offset,
            boolean_t              copy,
            vm_prot_t              cur_protection,
            vm_prot_t              max_protection,
            vm_inherit_t           inheritance);
```

Given the importance of `mach_vm_map()`, we will discuss each of its parameters. We will not do so for all Mach VM routines.

`target_task` specifies the task whose address space will be used for mapping. A user program specifies the control port of the target task as this argument, and indeed, the type `vm_map_t` is equivalent to `mach_port_t` in user space. Mach's IPC mechanism translates a `vm_map_t` to a pointer to the corresponding VM map structure in the kernel. We will discuss this translation in Section 9.6.2.

When `mach_vm_map()` returns successfully, it populates the `address` pointer with the location of the newly mapped memory in the target task's virtual address space. This is when the `VM_FLAGS_ANYWHERE` bit is set in the `flags` argument. If this bit is not set, then `address` contains a caller-specified virtual address for `mach_vm_map()` to use. If the memory cannot be mapped at that address (typically because there is not enough free contiguous virtual memory beginning at that location), `mach_vm_map()` will fail. If the user-specified address is not page-aligned, the kernel will *truncate* it.

`size` specifies the amount of memory to be mapped in bytes. It should be an integral number of pages; otherwise, the kernel will *round* it *up* appropriately.

The `mask` argument of `mach_vm_map()` specifies an alignment restriction on the kernel-chosen starting address. A bit that is set in `mask` will not be set in the address—that is, it will be masked out. For example, if `mask` is `0x00FF_FFFF`, the kernel-chosen address will be aligned on a 16MB boundary (the lower 24 bits of the address will be zero). This feature of `mach_vm_map()` can be used to emulate a virtual page size that is larger than the physical page size.

Caveat Regarding Offsets and Sizes

As we noted in Section 8.4, Mach VM API routines operate on page-aligned addresses and memory sizes that are integral multiples of the page size. In general, if a user-specified address is not the beginning of a page, the kernel truncates it—that is, the actual address used will be the beginning of the page in which the original address resides. Similarly, if a size-specifying argument contains a byte count that is not an integral number of pages, the kernel rounds the size up appropriately. The following macros are used for truncating and rounding offsets and sizes (note that rounding `0xFFFF_FFFF` pages yields the value 1):

```
// osfmk/mach/ppc/vm_param.h

#define PPC_PGBYTES 4096
#define PAGE_SIZE    PPC_PGBYTES
#define PAGE_MASK   (PAGE_SIZE - 1)

// osfmk/vm/vm_map.h

#define vm_map_trunc_page(x) ((vm_map_offset_t)(x) & ~((signed)PAGE_MASK))
#define vm_map_round_page(x) (((vm_map_offset_t)(x) + PAGE_MASK) & \
                              ~((signed)PAGE_MASK))
```

The following are examples of individual flags (bits) that can be set in the `flags` argument.

- `VM_FLAGS_FIXED`—This is used to specify that the new VM region should be allocated at the caller-provided address, if possible. `VM_FLAGS_FIXED` is defined to be the value `0x0`. Therefore, logically OR'ing this does not change the value of `flags`. It merely represents the absence of `VM_FLAGS_ANYWHERE`.

- `VM_FLAGS_ANYWHERE`—This is used to specify that the new VM region can be allocated anywhere in the address space.

- `VM_FLAGS_PURGABLE`—This is used to specify that a *purgable* VM object should be created for the new VM region. A purgable object has the special property that it can be put into a nonvolatile state in which its pages become eligible for reclamation without being paged out to the backing store.

- `VM_FLAGS_OVERWRITE`—This, when used along with `VM_FLAGS_FIXED`, is used to specify that the new VM region can replace existing VM regions if necessary.

object is the critical argument of mach_vm_map(). It must be a Mach port naming a memory object, which will provide backing for the range being mapped. As we saw earlier, a memory object represents a range of pages whose properties are controlled by a single pager. The kernel uses the memory object port to communicate with the pager. When mach_vm_map() is used to map some portion of a task's address space with a memory object, the latter's pages are accessible by the task. Note that the virtual address at which such a page range appears in a given task is task-dependent. However, a page has a fixed offset within its memory object—this offset is what a pager works with.

The following are some examples of memory objects used with mach_vm_map().

- When a Mach-O executable is loaded for execution by the execve() system call, the file is mapped into the address space of the target process through the vm_map() kernel function [osfmk/vm/vm_user.c], with the object argument referring to the vnode pager.

- If the object argument is the null memory object (MEMORY_OBJECT_NULL), or equivalently, MACH_PORT_NULL, mach_vm_map() uses the default pager, which provides initially zero-filled memory backed by the system's swap space. In this case, mach_vm_map() is equivalent to mach_vm_allocate() (see Section 8.6.3), albeit with more options for configuring the memory's properties.

- The object argument can be a *named entry* handle. A task creates a named entry from a given mapped portion of its address space by calling mach_make_memory_entry_64(), which returns a handle to the underlying VM object. The handle so obtained can be used as a shared memory object: The memory it represents can be mapped into another task's address space (or the same task's address space, for that matter). We will see an example of using mach_make_memory_entry_64() in Section 8.7.5.

> There is also mach_make_memory_entry(), which is a wrapper around mach_make_memory_entry_64(). The latter is not 64-bit-*only*, as its name suggests.

The offset argument specifies the beginning of the memory in the memory object. Along with size, this argument specifies the range of the memory to be mapped in the target task.

If `copy` is `TRUE`, the memory is copied (with copy-on-write optimization) from the memory object to the target task's virtual address space. This way, the target receives a private copy of the memory. Thereafter, any changes made by the task to that memory will *not* be sent to the pager. Conversely, the task will not see changes made by someone else. If `copy` is `FALSE`, the memory is directly mapped.

`cur_protection` specifies the initial *current protection* for the memory. The following individual protection bits can be set in a Mach VM protection value: `VM_PROT_READ`, `VM_PROT_WRITE`, and `VM_PROT_EXECUTE`. The values `VM_PROT_ALL` and `VM_PROT_NONE` represent all bits set (maximum access) and no bits set (all access disallowed), respectively. `max_protection` specifies the *maximum protection* for the memory.

Thus, each mapped region has a current protection and a maximum protection. Once the memory is mapped, the kernel will not allow the current to exceed the maximum. Both the current and maximum protection attributes can be subsequently changed using `mach_vm_protect()` (see Section 8.6.5), although note that the maximum protection can only be lowered—that is, made more restrictive.

`inheritance` specifies the mapped memory's initial inheritance attribute, which determines how the memory is inherited by a child task during a `fork()` operation. It can take the following values.

- `VM_INHERIT_NONE`—The range is undefined ("empty") in the child task.
- `VM_INHERIT_SHARE`—The range is shared between the parent and the child, allowing each to freely read from and write to the memory.
- `VM_INHERIT_COPY`—The range is copied (with copy-on-write and other, if any, optimizations) from the parent into the child.

The inheritance attribute can be later changed using `mach_vm_inherit()` (see Section 8.6.6).

8.6.2 `mach_vm_remap()`

`mach_vm_remap()` takes already mapped memory in a source task and maps it in the target task's address space, with allowance for specifying the new mapping's properties (as in the case of `mach_vm_map()`). You can achieve a similar effect by creating a named entry from a mapped range and then remapping it through `mach_vm_map()`. In that sense, `mach_vm_remap()` can be thought of as a "turnkey" routine for memory sharing. Note that the source and target tasks could be the same task.

```
kern_return_t
mach_vm_remap(vm_map_t            target_task,
              mach_vm_address_t *target_address,
              mach_vm_size_t      size,
              mach_vm_offset_t    mask,
              boolean_t           anywhere,
              vm_map_t            src_task,
              mach_vm_address_t   src_address,
              boolean_t           copy,
              vm_prot_t          *cur_protection,
              vm_prot_t          *max_protection,
              vm_inherit_t        inheritance);
```

The cur_protection and max_protection arguments return the protection attributes for the mapped region. If one or more subranges have differing protection attributes, the returned attributes are those of the range with the most restrictive protection.

8.6.3 mach_vm_allocate()

mach_vm_allocate() allocates a region of virtual memory in the target task. As noted earlier, its effect is similar to calling mach_vm_map() with a null memory object. It returns initially zero-filled, page-aligned memory. Like mach_vm_map(), it allows the caller to provide a specific address at which to allocate.

```
kern_return_t
mach_vm_allocate(vm_map_t            target_task,
                 mach_vm_address_t address,
                 mach_vm_size_t     size,
                 int                flags);
```

8.6.4 mach_vm_deallocate()

mach_vm_deallocate() invalidates the given range of virtual memory in the given address space.

```
kern_return_t
mach_vm_deallocate(vm_map_t            target_task,
                   mach_vm_address_t *address,
                   mach_vm_size_t     size);
```

It is important to realize that as used here, the terms *allocate* and *deallocate* subtly differ from how they are used in the context of a typical memory allocator (such as malloc(3)). A memory allocator usually *tracks* allocated memory—when you free allocated memory, the allocator will check that you are not freeing memory you did not allocate, or that you are not double-freeing memory. In contrast, mach_vm_deallocate() simply removes the given range—whether currently mapped or not—from the given address space.

When a task receives out-of-line memory in an IPC message, it should use mach_vm_deallocate() or vm_deallocate() to free that memory when it is not needed. Several Mach routines dynamically—and implicitly—allocate memory in the address space of the caller. Typical examples of such routines are those that populate variable-length arrays, such as process_set_tasks() and task_threads().

8.6.5 mach_vm_protect()

mach_vm_protect() sets the protection attribute for the given memory range in the given address space. The possible protection values are the same as those we saw in Section 8.6.1. If the set_maximum Boolean argument is TRUE, new_protection specifies the maximum protection; otherwise, it specifies the current protection. If the new maximum protection is more restrictive than the current protection, the latter is lowered to match the new maximum.

```
kern_return_t
mach_vm_protect(vm_map_t            target_task,
                mach_vm_address_t   address,
                mach_vm_size_t      size,
                boolean_t           set_maximum,
                vm_prot_t           new_protection);
```

8.6.6 mach_vm_inherit()

mach_vm_inherit() sets the inheritance attribute for the given memory range in the given address space. The possible inheritance values are the same as those we saw in Section 8.6.1.

```
kern_return_t
mach_vm_inherit(vm_map_t            target_task,
                mach_vm_address_t   address,
                mach_vm_size_t      size,
                vm_inherit_t        new_inheritance);
```

8.6.7 `mach_vm_read()`

`mach_vm_read()` transfers data from the given memory range in the given address space to *dynamically allocated memory* in the calling task. In other words, unlike most Mach VM API routines, `mach_vm_read()` implicitly uses the current address space as its destination. The source memory region must be mapped in the source address space. As with memory allocated dynamically in other contexts, it is the caller's responsibility to invalidate it when appropriate.

```
kern_return_t
mach_vm_read(vm_map_t                target_task,
            mach_vm_address_t        address,
            mach_vm_size_t           size,
            vm_offset_t              *data,
            mach_msg_type_number_t   *data_count);
```

The `mach_vm_read_overwrite()` variant reads into a caller-specified buffer. Yet another variant—`mach_vm_read_list()`—reads a list of memory ranges from the given map. The list of ranges is an array of `mach_vm_read_entry` structures [<mach/vm_region.h>]. The maximum size of this array is `VM_MAP_ENTRY_MAX` (256). Note that for each source address, memory is copied to the same address in the calling task.

```
kern_return_t
mach_vm_read_overwrite(vm_map_t             target_task,
                      mach_vm_address_t     address,
                      mach_vm_size_t        size,
                      mach_vm_address_t     data,
                      mach_vm_size_t        *out_size);

kern_return_t
mach_vm_read_list(vm_map_t                target_task,
                 mach_vm_read_entry_t     data_list,
                 natural_t                data_count);

struct mach_vm_read_entry {
    mach_vm_address_t address;
    mach_vm_size_t    size;
};

typedef struct mach_vm_read_entry mach_vm_read_entry_t[VM_MAP_ENTRY_MAX];
```

8.6.8 `mach_vm_write()`

`mach_vm_write()` copies data from a caller-specified buffer to the given memory region in the target address space. The destination memory range must already be allocated and writable from the caller's standpoint—in that sense, this is more precisely an *overwrite* call.

```
kern_return_t
mach_vm_write(vm_map_t              target_task,
              mach_vm_address_t     address,
              vm_offset_t           data,
              mach_msg_type_number_t data_count);
```

8.6.9 `mach_vm_copy()`

`mach_vm_copy()` copies one memory region to another within the same task. The source and destination regions must both already be allocated. Their protection attributes must permit reading and writing, respectively. Moreover, the two regions can overlap. `mach_vm_copy()` has the same effect as a `mach_vm_read()` followed by a `mach_vm_write()`.

```
kern_return_t
mach_vm_copy(vm_map_t              target_task,
             mach_vm_address_t source_address,
             mach_vm_size_t    count,
             mach_vm_address_t dest_address);
```

Comparing Mach VM Routines with Mach IPC Routines for Memory Transfer

Since large amounts of data—theoretically, entire address spaces—can be transferred through Mach IPC, it is interesting to note the difference between Mach VM routines and Mach IPC messaging when sending data from one task to another. In the case of a Mach VM routine such as `mach_vm_copy()` or `mach_vm_write()`, the calling task must have send rights to the control port of the target task. However, the target task does not have to participate in the transfer—it can be *passive*. In fact, it could even be suspended. In the case of Mach IPC, the sender must have send rights to a port that the receiving task has receive rights to. Additionally, the receiving task must actively receive the message. Moreover, Mach VM routines allow memory to be copied at a specific destination address in the target address space.

8.6.10 `mach_vm_wire()`

`mach_vm_wire()` alters the given memory region's pageability: If the `wired_access` argument is one of `VM_PROT_READ`, `VM_PROT_WRITE`, `VM_PROT_EXECUTE`, or a combination thereof, the region's pages are protected accordingly and wired in physical memory. If `wired_access` is `VM_PROT_NONE`, the pages are unwired. Since wiring pages is a privileged operation, `vm_wire()` requires send rights to the host's control port. The `host_get_host_priv_port()` routine, which itself requires superuser privileges, can be used to acquire these rights.

```
kern_return_t
mach_vm_wire(host_priv_t      host,
             vm_map_t         target_task,
             mach_vm_address_t address,
             mach_vm_size_t   size,
             vm_prot_t        wired_access);
```

> Unlike other Mach VM routines discussed so far, `mach_vm_wire()` is exported by the `host_priv` MIG subsystem.

8.6.11 `mach_vm_behavior_set()`

`mach_vm_behavior_set()` specifies the expected page reference behavior—the access pattern—for the given memory region. This information is used during page-fault handling to determine which pages, if any, to deactivate based on the memory access pattern.

```
kern_return_t
mach_vm_behavior_set(vm_map_t         target_task,
                     mach_vm_address_t address,
                     mach_vm_size_t   size,
                     vm_behavior_t    behavior);
```

The `behavior` argument can take the following values:

- `VM_BEHAVIOR_DEFAULT`—the default behavior for all nascent memory
- `VM_BEHAVIOR_RANDOM`—random access pattern
- `VM_BEHAVIOR_SEQUENTIAL`—sequential access (forward)
- `VM_BEHAVIOR_RSEQNTL`—sequential access (reverse)
- `VM_BEHAVIOR_WILLNEED`—will need these pages in the near future
- `VM_BEHAVIOR_DONTNEED`—will not need these pages in the near future

The kernel maps the VM_BEHAVIOR_WILLNEED and VM_BEHAVIOR_DONTNEED reference behavior specifications to the default behavior, which assumes a strong locality of reference.

> mach_vm_behavior_set() is analogous to the madvise() system call. In fact, the Mac OS X madvise() implementation is a simple wrapper around the in-kernel equivalent of mach_vm_behavior_set().

Since the expected reference behavior is applied to a memory range, the behavior setting is recorded as part of the VM map entry structure (struct vm_map_entry [osfmk/vm/vm_map.h]). Upon a page fault, the fault handler uses the behavior setting to determine which, if any, of the active pages are uninteresting enough to be deactivated. This mechanism also uses the sequential and last_alloc fields of the VM object structure (struct vm_object [osfmk/vm/vm_object.h]). The sequential field records the sequential access size, whereas last_alloc records the last allocation offset in that object.

If the reference behavior is VM_BEHAVIOR_RANDOM, the sequential access size is always kept as the page size, and no page is deactivated.

If the behavior is VM_BEHAVIOR_SEQUENTIAL, the page-fault handler examines the current and last allocation offsets to see if the access pattern is indeed sequential. If so, the sequential field is incremented by a page size, and the immediate last page is deactivated. If, however, the access is not sequential, the fault handler resets its recording by setting the sequential field to the page size. No page is deactivated in this case. The handling of VM_BEHAVIOR_RSEQNTL is similar, except the notion of sequential is reversed.

In the case of VM_BEHAVIOR_DEFAULT, the handler attempts to establish an access pattern based on the current and last offsets. If they are not consecutive (in units of a page), the access is deemed random, and no page is deactivated. If they are consecutive, whether increasing or decreasing, the handler increments the sequential field by a page size. If the pattern continues and the recorded sequential access size exceeds MAX_UPL_TRANSFER (256) pages, the page that is MAX_UPL_TRANSFER pages away (behind or forward, depending on the direction) is deactivated. While the recorded sequential access size remains less than MAX_UPL_TRANSFER, no page is deactivated. If, however, the pattern is broken, the sequential access size is reset to the page size.

> Page deactivation involves calling vm_page_deactivate() [osfmk/vm/vm_resident.c], which returns the page to the inactive queue.

8.6.12 `mach_vm_msync()`

`mach_vm_msync()` synchronizes the given memory range with its pager.

```
kern_return_t
mach_vm_msync(vm_map_t            target_task,
              mach_vm_address_t   address,
              mach_vm_size_t      size,
              vm_sync_t           sync_flags);
```

The `sync_flags` argument is the bitwise OR of synchronization bits defined in `<mach/vm_sync.h>`. The following are examples of valid combinations.

- `VM_SYNC_INVALIDATE` flushes pages in the given memory range, returning only precious pages to the pager and discarding dirty pages.

- If `VM_SYNC_ASYNCHRONOUS` is specified along with `VM_SYNC_INVALIDATE`, both dirty and precious pages are returned to the pager, but the call returns without waiting for the pages to reach the backing store.

- `VM_SYNC_SYNCHRONOUS` is similar to `VM_SYNC_ASYNCHRONOUS`, but the call does not return until the pages reach the backing store.

- When either `VM_SYNC_ASYNCHRONOUS` or `VM_SYNC_SYNCHRONOUS` is specified by itself, both dirty and precious pages are returned to the pager without flushing any pages.

- If `VM_SYNC_CONTIGUOUS` is specified, the call returns `KERN_INVALID_ADDRESS` if the specified memory range is not mapped in its entirety—that is, if the range has a hole in it. Nevertheless, the call still completes its work as it would have if `VM_SYNC_CONTIGUOUS` were not specified.

Precious Pages

A precious page is used when only one copy of its data is desired. There may not be a copy of a precious page's data both in the backing store and in memory. When a pager provides a precious page to the kernel, it means that the pager has not necessarily retained its own copy. When the kernel must evict such pages, they must be returned to the pager, even if they had not been modified while resident.

`mach_vm_msync()` is analogous to the `msync()` system call. In fact, the `msync()` implementation uses the in-kernel equivalent of `mach_vm_sync()`. POSIX.1 requires `msync()` to return an `ENOMEM` error if there are holes in the

region being synchronized. Therefore, msync() always sets the VM_SYNC_
CONTIGUOUS bit before calling the in-kernel version of mach_vm_msync(). If
the latter returns KERN_INVALID_ADDRESS, msync() translates the error to ENOMEM.

8.6.13 Statistics

System-wide VM statistics can be retrieved using the HOST_VM_INFO flavor of
the host_statistics() Mach routine. The vm_stat command-line program
also displays these statistics.

```
$ vm_stat
Mach Virtual Memory Statistics: (page size of 4096 bytes)
Pages free:                    144269.
Pages active:                  189526.
Pages inactive:                392812.
Pages wired down:               59825.
"Translation faults":        54697978.
Pages copy-on-write:           800440.
Pages zero filled:           38386710.
Pages reactivated:             160297.
Pageins:                        91327.
Pageouts:                        4335.
Object cache: 205675 hits of 378912 lookups (54% hit rate)
```

mach_vm_region() returns information about a memory region in the
given address space. The address argument specifies the location at which
mach_vm_region() starts to look for a valid region. The outbound values of
address and size specify the range of the region actually found. The flavor
argument specifies the type of information to retrieve, with info pointing to a
structure appropriate for the flavor being requested. For example, the VM_
REGION_BASIC_INFO flavor is used with a vm_region_basic_info structure.
The count argument specifies the size of the input buffer in units of natural_t.
For example, to retrieve information for the VM_REGION_BASIC_INFO flavor, the
size of the input buffer must be at least VM_REGION_BASIC_INFO_COUNT. The
outbound value of count specifies the size of the data filled in by the call.

```
kern_return_t
mach_vm_region(vm_map_t                 target_task,
               mach_vm_address_t        *address,
               mach_vm_size_t           *size,
               vm_region_flavor_t       flavor,
               vm_region_info_t         info,
               mach_msg_type_number_t   *info_count,
               mach_port_t              *object_name);
```

Note that a task should be suspended before `mach_vm_region()` is called on it, otherwise the results obtained may not provide a true picture of the task's VM situation.

The `mach_vm_region_recurse()` variant recurses into submap chains in the given task's address map. The `vmmap` command-line program uses both variants to retrieve information about the virtual memory regions allocated in the given process.

8.7 Using the Mach VM Interfaces

Let us now look at several examples of using Mach VM interface routines.

> The examples shown in this section use the new Mach VM API that we discussed in Section 8.6. The new API's implementation is transitional at the time of this writing. If you face problems while experimenting with it, you can resort to the `vm_*` routines. Moreover, the examples in this section can be compiled as either 64-bit or 32-bit programs. They are shown here as compiled for 64-bit.

8.7.1 Controlling Memory Inheritance

In this example, we will allocate two pages of memory using `mach_vm_allocate()`. We will call `mach_vm_inherit()` to set the inheritance attribute of one page to `VM_INHERIT_SHARE` and the other's to `VM_INHERIT_COPY`. We will then write some "marker" data to the two pages and call `fork()`. The parent will wait for the child to exit. The child will write its own marker data to the pages, which will cause the contents of the shared page to change in place, whereas the other page will be physically copied on being written. We will use the `VM_REGION_TOP_INFO` flavor of `mach_vm_region()` to inspect the VM objects corresponding to the two pages. Figure 8–14 shows the program.

> Note in Figure 8–14 that in this example, the program is being compiled as a 64-bit PowerPC executable, as specified by the `ppc64` architecture value. Since the Mach VM user interfaces are architecture-independent, the program will compile and run on all architectures supported by Mac OS X.

FIGURE 8–14 Controlling memory inheritance

```c
// vm_inherit.c

#include <stdio.h>
#include <sys/wait.h>
#include <stdlib.h>
#include <unistd.h>
#include <mach/mach.h>
#include <mach/mach_vm.h>

#define OUT_ON_MACH_ERROR(msg, retval) \
    if (kr != KERN_SUCCESS) { mach_error(msg ":" , kr); goto out; }

#define FIRST_UINT32(addr) (*((uint32_t *)addr))

static mach_vm_address_t page_shared; // fully shared
static mach_vm_address_t page_cow;    // shared copy-on-write

kern_return_t
get_object_id(mach_vm_address_t offset, int *obj_id, int *ref_count)
{
    kern_return_t    kr;
    mach_port_t      unused;
    mach_vm_size_t   size = (mach_vm_size_t)vm_page_size;
    mach_vm_address_t address = offset;

    vm_region_top_info_data_t info;
    mach_msg_type_number_t    count = VM_REGION_TOP_INFO_COUNT;

    kr = mach_vm_region(mach_task_self(), &address, &size, VM_REGION_TOP_INFO,
                        (vm_region_info_t)&info, &count, &unused);
    if (kr == KERN_SUCCESS) {
        *obj_id = info.obj_id;
        *ref_count = info.ref_count;
    }

    return kr;
}

void
peek_at_some_memory(const char *who, const char *msg)
{
    int obj_id, ref_count;
    kern_return_t kr;

    kr = get_object_id(page_shared, &obj_id, &ref_count);
    printf("%-12s%-8s-10x%-12x%-10d%s\n",
           who, "SHARED", FIRST_UINT32(page_shared), obj_id, ref_count, msg);
```

(continues)

FIGURE 8–14 Controlling memory inheritance *(continued)*

```
    kr = get_object_id(page_cow, &obj_id, &ref_count);
    printf("%-12s%-8s%-10x%-12x%-10d%s\n",
           who, "COW", FIRST_UINT32(page_cow), obj_id, ref_count, msg);
}

void
child_process(void)
{
    peek_at_some_memory("child", "before touching any memory");
    FIRST_UINT32(page_shared) = (unsigned int)0xFEEDF00D;
    FIRST_UINT32(page_cow)    = (unsigned int)0xBADDF00D;
    peek_at_some_memory("child", "after writing to memory");

    exit(0);
}

int
main(void)
{
    kern_return_t  kr;
    int            status;
    mach_port_t    mytask = mach_task_self();
    mach_vm_size_t size = (mach_vm_size_t)vm_page_size;

    kr = mach_vm_allocate(mytask, &page_shared, size, VM_FLAGS_ANYWHERE);
    OUT_ON_MACH_ERROR("vm_allocate", kr);

    kr = mach_vm_allocate(mytask, &page_cow, size, VM_FLAGS_ANYWHERE);
    OUT_ON_MACH_ERROR("vm_allocate", kr);

    kr = mach_vm_inherit(mytask, page_shared, size, VM_INHERIT_SHARE);
    OUT_ON_MACH_ERROR("vm_inherit(VM_INHERIT_SHARE)", kr);

    kr = mach_vm_inherit(mytask, page_cow, size, VM_INHERIT_COPY);
    OUT_ON_MACH_ERROR("vm_inherit(VM_INHERIT_COPY)", kr);

    FIRST_UINT32(page_shared) = (unsigned int)0xAAAAAAAA;
    FIRST_UINT32(page_cow)    = (unsigned int)0xBBBBBBBB;

    printf("%-12s%-8s%-10s%-12s%-10s%s\n",
           "Process", "Page", "Contents", "VM Object", "Refcount", "Event");

    peek_at_some_memory("parent", "before forking");

    if (fork() == 0)
        child_process(); // this will also exit the child
```

(continues)

FIGURE 8–14 Controlling memory inheritance *(continued)*

```
    wait(&status);

    peek_at_some_memory("parent", "after child is done");

out:
    mach_vm_deallocate(mytask, page_shared, size);
    mach_vm_deallocate(mytask, page_cow, size);

    exit(0);
}


$ gcc -arch ppc64 -Wall -o vm_inherit vm_inherit.c
$ ./vm_inherit
Process   Page     Contents  VM Object  Refcount  Event
parent    SHARED   aaaaaaaa  4fa4000    1         before forking
parent    COW      bbbbbbbb  5a93088    1         before forking
child     SHARED   aaaaaaaa  4fa4000    2         before touching any memory
child     COW      bbbbbbbb  5a93088    2         before touching any memory
child     SHARED   feedf00d  4fa4000    2         after writing to memory
child     COW      baddf00d  4ade198    1         after writing to memory
parent    SHARED   feedf00d  4fa4000    1         after child is done
parent    COW      bbbbbbbb  5a93088    1         after child is done
```

Note in the output shown in Figure 8–14 that the VM object corresponding to the copy-on-written page is different from the one before the child writes to the page.

8.7.2 Debugging the Mach VM Subsystem

The Mac OS X kernel provides powerful user-space interfaces for debugging the Mach VM and IPC subsystems. These interfaces provide access to a variety of kernel data structures that are normally not exposed to user space. However, the kernel must be recompiled in the DEBUG configuration to enable these interfaces. For example, the MACH_VM_DEBUG and MACH_IPC_DEBUG kernel-build-time configuration options enable the debugging routines for VM and IPC, respectively.

Let us consider an example—that of mach_vm_region_info(). This routine retrieves detailed information about a memory region: Given a memory address, it retrieves the contents of the corresponding VM map entry structure, along with the associated VM objects. We say "objects" because if there is a shadow chain, mach_vm_region_info() follows it.

```
kern_return_t
mach_vm_region_info(vm_map_t              map,
                    vm_offset_t           address,
                    vm_info_region_t      *regionp,
                    vm_info_object_array_t *objectsp,
                    mach_msg_type_number_t *objects_countp);
```

The `vm_info_region_t` structure [osfmk/mach_debug/vm_info.h] contains selected information from the VM map entry structure corresponding to `address` in the address space specified by `map`. On return, `objectsp` will point to an array containing `objects_countp` entries, each of which is a `vm_info_object_t` structure [osfmk/mach_debug/vm_info.h] containing information from a VM object.

Other routines in the VM debugging interface include the following:

- `mach_vm_region_info_64()`—provides a 64-bit version of `mach_vm_region_info()`

- `vm_mapped_pages_info()`—retrieves a list containing addresses of virtual pages mapped in a given task

- `host_virtual_physical_table_info()`—retrieves information about the host's virtual-to-physical table

8.7.3 Protecting Memory

The program in Figure 8–15 is a trivial example of using `mach_vm_protect()` to change the protection attribute of a given memory region. The program allocates a page of memory using `mach_vm_allocate()` and writes a string at an offset of 2048 bytes in the page. It then calls `mach_vm_protect()` to deny all access to the memory starting at the page's starting address, but it specifies a region length of only 4 bytes. We know that Mach will round the region size up to a page size, which means the program will not be able to access the string it wrote.

FIGURE 8–15 Protecting memory

`// vm_protect.c`

```c
#include <stdio.h>
#include <stdlib.h>
#include <mach/mach.h>
#include <mach/mach_vm.h>
```

(continues)

FIGURE 8–15 Protecting memory *(continued)*

```
#define OUT_ON_MACH_ERROR(msg, retval) \
    if (kr != KERN_SUCCESS) { mach_error(msg ":" , kr); goto out; }

int
main(int argc, char **argv)
{
    char              *ptr;
    kern_return_t     kr;
    mach_vm_address_t a_page = (mach_vm_address_t)0;
    mach_vm_size_t    a_size = (mach_vm_size_t)vm_page_size;

    kr = mach_vm_allocate(mach_task_self(), &a_page, a_size, VM_FLAGS_ANYWHERE);
    OUT_ON_MACH_ERROR("vm_allocate", kr);

    ptr = (char *)a_page + 2048;

    snprintf(ptr, (size_t)16, "Hello, Mach!");

    if (argc == 2) { // deny read access to a_page
        kr = mach_vm_protect(
                mach_task_self(),            // target address space
                (mach_vm_address_t)a_page,   // starting address of region
                (mach_vm_size_t)4,           // length of region in bytes
                FALSE,                       // set maximum?
                VM_PROT_NONE);               // deny all access
        OUT_ON_MACH_ERROR("vm_protect", kr);
    }

    printf("%s\n", ptr);

out:
    if (a_page)
        mach_vm_deallocate(mach_task_self(), a_page, a_size);

    exit(kr);
}


$ gcc -arch ppc64 -Wall -o vm_protect vm_protect.c
$ ./vm_protect
Hello, Mach!
$ ./vm_protect VM_PROT_NONE
zsh: bus error   ./vm_prot_none VM_PROT_NONE
```

8.7.4 Accessing Another Task's Memory

In this example, we will use `mach_vm_read()` and `mach_vm_write()` to manipulate the memory of one task from another. The target task will allocate a page of memory and fill it with the character A. It will then display its process ID and the newly allocated page's address and will go into a busy loop, exiting the loop when the first byte of the page changes to something other than A. The other program—the master—will read the target's memory, modify the first character to B, and write it back into the target's address space, which will cause the target to end its busy loop and exit.

Figure 8–16 shows the source for the target and master programs. Note that beginning with the x86-based Macintosh systems, the `task_for_pid()` call requires superuser privileges.

FIGURE 8–16 Accessing another task's memory

```
// vm_rw_target.c

#include <stdio.h>
#include <unistd.h>
#include <stdlib.h>
#include <mach/mach.h>
#include <mach/mach_vm.h>

#define SOME_CHAR 'A'

int
main()
{
    kern_return_t     kr;
    mach_vm_address_t address;
    mach_vm_size_t    size = (mach_vm_size_t)vm_page_size;

    // get a page of memory
    kr = mach_vm_allocate(mach_task_self(), &address, size, VM_FLAGS_ANYWHERE);
    if (kr != KERN_SUCCESS) {
        mach_error("vm_allocate:", kr);
        exit(1);
    }

    // color it with something
    memset((char *)address, SOME_CHAR, vm_page_size);

    // display the address so the master can read/write to it
    printf("pid=%d, address=%p\n", getpid(), (void *)address);
```

(continues)

FIGURE 8–16 Accessing another task's memory *(continued)*

```
    // wait until master writes to us
    while (*(char *)address == SOME_CHAR)
        ;

    mach_vm_deallocate(mach_task_self(), address, size);

    exit(0);
}


// vm_rw_master.c

#include <stdio.h>
#include <stdlib.h>
#include <mach/mach.h>
#include <mach/mach_vm.h>

#define PROGNAME "vm_rw_master"

#define EXIT_ON_MACH_ERROR(msg, retval) \
    if (kr != KERN_SUCCESS) { mach_error(msg ":" , kr); exit((retval)); }

int
main(int argc, char **argv)
{
    kern_return_t        kr;
    pid_t                pid;
    mach_port_t          target_task;
    mach_vm_address_t    address;
    mach_vm_size_t       size = (mach_vm_size_t)vm_page_size;
    vm_offset_t          local_address;
    mach_msg_type_number_t local_size = vm_page_size;

    if (argc != 3) {
        fprintf(stderr, "usage: %s <pid> <address in hex>\n", PROGNAME);
        exit(1);
    }

    pid = atoi(argv[1]);
    address = strtoul(argv[2], NULL, 16);

    kr = task_for_pid(mach_task_self(), pid, &target_task);
    EXIT_ON_MACH_ERROR("task_for_pid", kr);

    printf("reading address %p in target task\n", (void *)address);

    kr = mach_vm_read(target_task, address, size,  &local_address, &local_size);
    EXIT_ON_MACH_ERROR("vm_read", kr);
```

(continues)

FIGURE 8–16 Accessing another task's memory *(continued)*

```
// display some of the memory we read from the target task
printf("read %u bytes from address %p in target task, first byte=%c\n",
       local_size, (void *)address, *(char *)local_address);

// change some of the memory
*(char *)local_address = 'B';

// write it back to the target task
kr = mach_vm_write(target_task, address, local_address, local_size);
EXIT_ON_MACH_ERROR("vm_write", kr);

exit(0);
}
```

```
$ gcc -arch ppc64 -Wall -o vm_rw_target vm_rw_target.c
$ gcc -arch ppc64 -Wall -o vm_rw_master vm_rw_master.c
$ ./vm_rw_target
pid=3592, address=0x5000
        # another shell
        # will need superuser privileges on newer versions of Mac OS X
        $ ./vm_rw_master 3592 0x5000
        reading address 0x5000 in target task
        read 4096 bytes from address 0x5000 in target task, first byte-A
        $
$
```

8.7.5 Naming and Sharing Memory

We came across the mach_make_memory_entry_64() routine while discussing
mach_vm_map() in Section 8.6.1. In this example, we will write a program that
uses this routine to create a named entry corresponding to a given mapped portion
of its address space. Thereafter, the program will become a Mach server, waiting
for a client to send it a Mach IPC message, which it will respond to by sending
the named entry handle in a reply message. The client can then use the handle in
a mach_vm_map() call to map the associated memory into its address space.
When creating the named entry, the server will specify a permission value consisting of both VM_PROT_READ and VM_PROT_WRITE, allowing a client full read/
write shared access.

> The IPC concepts used in this example are discussed in Chapter 9.
> The example appears here because it is more of a VM example
> than an IPC example.

Figure 8–17 shows a common header file that both the client and server program sources will use.

FIGURE 8–17 Common header file for the shared memory client-server example

```
// shm_ipc_common.h

#ifndef _SHM_IPC_COMMON_H_
#define _SHM_IPC_COMMON_H_

#include <mach/mach.h>
#include <mach/mach_vm.h>
#include <servers/bootstrap.h>

#define SERVICE_NAME "com.osxbook.SHMServer"
#define SHM_MSG_ID   400

#define EXIT_ON_MACH_ERROR(msg, retval, success_retval) \
    if (kr != success_retval) { mach_error(msg ":" , kr); exit((retval)); }

// send-side version of the request message (as seen by the client)
typedef struct {
    mach_msg_header_t header;
} msg_format_request_t;

// receive-side version of the request message (as seen by the server)
typedef struct {
    mach_msg_header_t  header;
    mach_msg_trailer_t trailer;
} msg_format_request_r_t;

// send-side version of the response message (as seen by the server)
typedef struct {
    mach_msg_header_t           header;
    mach_msg_body_t             body;   // start of kernel processed data
    mach_msg_port_descriptor_t data;    // end of kernel processed data
} msg_format_response_t;

// receive-side version of the response message (as seen by the client)
typedef struct {
    mach_msg_header_t           header;
    mach_msg_body_t             body;   // start of kernel processed data
    mach_msg_port_descriptor_t data;    // end of kernel processed data
    mach_msg_trailer_t          trailer;
} msg_format_response_r_t;

#endif // _SHM_IPC_COMMON_H_
```

Figure 8–18 shows the source for the client. In the `mach_vm_map()` call, the client requests the kernel to map the memory object represented by the received named entry handle at any available location in its address space. Note that the client also writes a string (the program's first argument) to the string.

FIGURE 8–18 Source for the shared memory client

```c
// shm_ipc_client.c

#include <stdio.h>
#include <stdlib.h>
#include "shm_ipc_common.h"

int
main(int argc, char **argv)
{
    kern_return_t           kr;
    msg_format_request_t    send_msg;
    msg_format_response_r_t recv_msg;
    mach_msg_header_t        *send_hdr, *recv_hdr;
    mach_port_t             client_port, server_port, object_handle;

    // find the server
    kr = bootstrap_look_up(bootstrap_port, SERVICE_NAME, &server_port);
    EXIT_ON_MACH_ERROR("bootstrap_look_up", kr, BOOTSTRAP_SUCCESS);

    // allocate a port for receiving the server's reply
    kr = mach_port_allocate(mach_task_self(),       // our task is acquiring
                            MACH_PORT_RIGHT_RECEIVE, // a new receive right
                            &client_port);           // with this name
    EXIT_ON_MACH_ERROR("mach_port_allocate", kr, KERN_SUCCESS);

    // prepare and send a request message to the server
    send_hdr                 = &(send_msg.header);
    send_hdr->msgh_bits      = MACH_MSGH_BITS(MACH_MSG_TYPE_COPY_SEND, \
                                    MACH_MSG_TYPE_MAKE_SEND);
    send_hdr->msgh_size      = sizeof(send_msg);
    send_hdr->msgh_remote_port = server_port;
    send_hdr->msgh_local_port  = client_port;
    send_hdr->msgh_reserved  = 0;
    send_hdr->msgh_id        = SHM_MSG_ID;
    kr = mach_msg(send_hdr,              // message buffer
                  MACH_SEND_MSG,         // option indicating send
                  send_hdr->msgh_size,   // size of header + body
                  0,                     // receive limit
                  MACH_PORT_NULL,        // receive name
                  MACH_MSG_TIMEOUT_NONE, // no timeout, wait forever
                  MACH_PORT_NULL);       // no notification port
```

(continues)

FIGURE 8–18 Source for the shared memory client *(continued)*

```
EXIT_ON_MACH_ERROR("mach_msg(send)", kr, MACH_MSG_SUCCESS);

do {
    recv_hdr                  = &(recv_msg.header);
    recv_hdr->msgh_remote_port = server_port;
    recv_hdr->msgh_local_port  = client_port;
    recv_hdr->msgh_size        = sizeof(recv_msg);
    recv_msg.data.name         = 0;
    kr = mach_msg(recv_hdr,             // message buffer
                  MACH_RCV_MSG,         // option indicating receive
                  0,                    // send size
                  recv_hdr->msgh_size,  // size of header + body
                  client_port,          // receive name
                  MACH_MSG_TIMEOUT_NONE, // no timeout, wait forever
                  MACH_PORT_NULL);      // no notification port
    EXIT_ON_MACH_ERROR("mach_msg(rcv)", kr, MACH_MSG_SUCCESS);

    printf("recv_msg.data.name = %#08x\n", recv_msg.data.name);
    object_handle = recv_msg.data.name;

    { // map the specified memory object to a region of our address space

        mach_vm_size_t    size = vm_page_size;
        mach_vm_address_t address = 0;

        kr = mach_vm_map(
               mach_task_self(),               // target address space (us)
               (mach_vm_address_t *)&address,  // map it and tell us where
               (mach_vm_size_t)size,           // number of bytes to allocate
               (mach_vm_offset_t)0,            // address mask for alignment
               TRUE,                           // map it anywhere
               (mem_entry_name_port_t)object_handle, // the memory object
               (memory_object_offset_t)0,      // offset within memory object
               FALSE,                          // don't copy -- directly map
               VM_PROT_READ|VM_PROT_WRITE,     // current protection
               VM_PROT_READ|VM_PROT_WRITE,     // maximum protection
               VM_INHERIT_NONE);               // inheritance properties
        if (kr != KERN_SUCCESS)
            mach_error("vm_map", kr);
        else {
            // display the current contents of the memory
            printf("%s\n", (char *)address);
            if (argc == 2) { // write specified string to the memory
                printf("writing \"%s\" to shared memory\n", argv[1]);
                strncpy((char *)address, argv[1], (size_t)size);
                ((char *)address)[size - 1] = '\0';
            }
```

(continues)

FIGURE 8–18 Source for the shared memory client *(continued)*

```
                mach_vm_deallocate(mach_task_self(), address, size);
            }
        }
    } while (recv_hdr->msgh_id != SHM_MSG_ID);

    exit(0);
}
```

Figure 8–19 shows the source for the server. Since the named entry is represented by a Mach port, the server must send it specially: wrapped in a *port descriptor*, rather than passive, inline data. We will discuss such special IPC transfers in Section 9.5.5.

FIGURE 8–19 Source for the shared memory server

```c
// shm_ipc_server.c

#include <stdio.h>
#include <stdlib.h>
#include "shm_ipc_common.h"

int
main(void)
{
    char                    *ptr;
    kern_return_t           kr;
    mach_vm_address_t       address = 0;
    memory_object_size_t    size = (memory_object_size_t)vm_page_size;
    mach_port_t             object_handle = MACH_PORT_NULL;
    msg_format_request_r_t  recv_msg;
    msg_format_response_t   send_msg;
    mach_msg_header_t       *recv_hdr, *send_hdr;
    mach_port_t             server_port;

    kr = mach_vm_allocate(mach_task_self(), &address, size, VM_FLAGS_ANYWHERE);
    EXIT_ON_MACH_ERROR("vm_allocate", kr, KERN_SUCCESS);

    printf("memory allocated at %p\n", (void *)address);

    // Create a named entry corresponding to the given mapped portion of our
    // address space. We can then share this named entry with other tasks.
    kr = mach_make_memory_entry_64(
            (vm_map_t)mach_task_self(),           // target address map
            &size,                                // so many bytes
```

(continues)

FIGURE 8–19 Source for the shared memory server *(continued)*

```
            (memory_object_offset_t)address,          // at this address
            (vm_prot_t)(VM_PROT_READ|VM_PROT_WRITE),  // with these permissions
            (mem_entry_name_port_t *)&object_handle,  // outcoming object handle
            (mem_entry_name_port_t)NULL);             // parent handle
// ideally we should vm_deallocate() before we exit
EXIT_ON_MACH_ERROR("mach_make_memory_entry", kr, KERN_SUCCESS);

// put some data into the shared memory
ptr = (char *)address;
strcpy(ptr, "Hello, Mach!");

// become a Mach server
kr = bootstrap_create_service(bootstrap_port, SERVICE_NAME, &server_port);
EXIT_ON_MACH_ERROR("bootstrap_create_service", kr, BOOTSTRAP_SUCCESS);

kr = bootstrap_check_in(bootstrap_port, SERVICE_NAME, &server_port);
EXIT_ON_MACH_ERROR("bootstrap_check_in", kr, BOOTSTRAP_SUCCESS);

for (;;) { // server loop

    // receive a message
    recv_hdr                = &(recv_msg.header);
    recv_hdr->msgh_local_port = server_port;
    recv_hdr->msgh_size       = sizeof(recv_msg);
    kr = mach_msg(recv_hdr,               // message buffer
                MACH_RCV_MSG,             // option indicating service
                0,                        // send size
                recv_hdr->msgh_size,      // size of header + body
                server_port,              // receive name
                MACH_MSG_TIMEOUT_NONE,    // no timeout, wait forever
                MACH_PORT_NULL);          // no notification port
    EXIT_ON_MACH_ERROR("mach_msg(recv)", kr, KERN_SUCCESS);

    // send named entry object handle as the reply
    send_hdr                 = &(send_msg.header);
    send_hdr->msgh_bits      = MACH_MSGH_BITS_LOCAL(recv_hdr->msgh_bits);
    send_hdr->msgh_bits     |= MACH_MSGH_BITS_COMPLEX;
    send_hdr->msgh_size      = sizeof(send_msg);
    send_hdr->msgh_local_port = MACH_PORT_NULL;
    send_hdr->msgh_remote_port = recv_hdr->msgh_remote_port;
    send_hdr->msgh_id        = recv_hdr->msgh_id;
    send_msg.body.msgh_descriptor_count = 1;
    send_msg.data.name             = object_handle;
    send_msg.data.disposition      = MACH_MSG_TYPE_COPY_SEND;
    send_msg.data.type             = MACH_MSG_PORT_DESCRIPTOR;
    kr = mach_msg(send_hdr,               // message buffer
                MACH_SEND_MSG,            // option indicating send
```

(continues)

FIGURE 8–19 Source for the shared memory server *(continued)*

```
                        send_hdr->msgh_size,   // size of header + body
                        0,                     // receive limit
                        MACH_PORT_NULL,        // receive name
                        MACH_MSG_TIMEOUT_NONE, // no timeout, wait forever
                        MACH_PORT_NULL);       // no notification port
        EXIT_ON_MACH_ERROR("mach_msg(send)", kr, KERN_SUCCESS);
    }

    mach_port_deallocate(mach_task_self(), object_handle);
    mach_vm_deallocate(mach_task_self(), address, size);

    return kr;
}
```

Let us now test the shared memory client and server programs.

```
$ gcc -arch ppc64 -Wall -o shm_ipc_client shm_ipc_client.c
$ gcc -arch ppc64 -Wall -o shm_ipc_server shm_ipc_server.c
$ ./shm_ipc_server
memory allocated at 0x5000
        # another shell
        $ ./shm_ipc_client
        recv_msg.data.name = 0x001003
        Hello, Mach!
        $ ./shm_ipc_client abcdefgh
        recv_msg.data.name = 0x001003
        Hello, Mach!
        writing "abcdefgh" to shared memory
        $ ./shm_ipc_client
        recv_msg.data.name = 0x001003
        abcdefgh
        $
^C
$
```

8.8 Kernel and User Address Space Layouts

The Mac OS X kernel has a 32-bit virtual address space whether it runs on a 32-bit or 64-bit machine. Beginning with Mac OS X 10.4, it is possible to create 64-bit user programs, although very few user-space APIs are available in 64-bit versions.

On some systems, a portion of every user address space is reserved for use by the kernel. For example, on 32-bit Windows, a user process is given the lower

2GB[14] of its 4GB virtual address space for private use. The remaining 2GB is used by the operating system. Similarly, the Linux kernel divides a 4GB user address space into two parts. The operating system uses its portion by mapping the kernel into the address space of each process, which avoids the overhead of switching address spaces when the kernel needs to access a user virtual address space. However, there still needs to be a change in the privilege level.

This reduces the size of the available virtual address space for both the kernel and user. The benefit is that user virtual addresses can be directly accessed in the kernel. An operation such as a `copyout()` or `copyin()` can be implemented as a simple memory copy (although with a page-faulting caveat).

Mac OS X *does not* map the kernel into each user address space, and therefore each user/kernel transition (in either direction) requires an address space switch. Mac OS X does map a variety of library code and data into each task's address space, which reduces the amount of arbitrarily usable virtual memory available to the task.

Table 8–2 shows several VM-related limits known to the PowerPC version of the Mac OS X kernel. Many but not all of these limits are the same on the x86 version of Mac OS X.

TABLE 8–2 VM-Related System Limits

Mnemonic	Value	Notes
`VM_MAX_PAGE_ADDRESS`	`0x0007_FFFF_FFFF_F000` (PowerPC)	Highest possible page address. Mac OS X 10.4 provides 51 bits of user virtual memory on 64-bit hardware.
`MACH_VM_MIN_ADDRESS`	`0`	
`MACH_VM_MAX_ADDRESS`	`0x0007_FFFF_FFFF_F000` (PowerPC)	
`VM_MIN_ADDRESS` (32-bit)	`0`	
`VM_MAX_ADDRESS` (32-bit)	`0xFFFF_F000`	

(continues)

---

14. Certain versions of Windows allow the user address space size to be varied between 2GB and 3GB through a boot-time option.

TABLE 8–2 VM-Related System Limits *(Continued)*

Mnemonic	Value	Notes
USRSTACK (32-bit)	0xC000_0000	Default initial user stack pointer for a 32-bit process.
VM_MIN_ADDRESS (64-bit)	0	
VM_MAX_ADDRESS (64-bit)	0x7_FFFF_FFFF_F000	
USRSTACK64 (64-bit)	0x7_FFFF_0000_0000	Default initial user stack pointer for a 64-bit process.
VM_MIN_KERNEL_ADDRESS	0x0000_1000	Minimum kernel virtual address—does not include the first page, which contains the exception vectors and is mapped V=R.
VM_MAX_KERNEL_ADDRESS	0xDFFF_FFFF	Maximum kernel virtual address—does not include the last 512MB, which is used as the user memory window (see Table 8–3).
KERNEL_STACK_SIZE	16KB	The fixed size of a kernel thread's stack.
INTSTACK_SIZE	20KB	Interrupt stack size.

The Mac OS X kernel uses an optimization called the *user memory window*, which maps a portion of a user address space—on a per-thread basis—into the last 512MB of the kernel virtual address space. The kernel uses this mechanism during operations such as `copyin()`, `copyout()`, and `copypv()`. As shown in Table 8–2, the window starts at kernel virtual address `0xE000_0000`. Consequently, a user virtual address `addr` will be visible in the kernel at virtual address (`0xE000_0000 + addr`).

Let us now look at how the kernel and user virtual address spaces are laid out in Mac OS X. Tables 8–3 and 8–4 show the layouts of the kernel and user (32-bit) virtual address spaces, respectively, in Mac OS X 10.4.

Although virtual memory allows each task to theoretically use any virtual address in its virtual address space, in practice, a subset of each task's virtual address space is reserved for conventional or situational purposes. For example, the system maps code and data into predefined address ranges in every task's address space. Moreover, a task may be disallowed to access certain address

TABLE 8–3 Kernel Virtual Address Space Layout (32-bit PowerPC, Mac OS X 10.4)

Start	End	Notes
0x0000_0000	0x0000_4FFF	Exception vectors and low-memory code in osfmk/ppc/lowmem_vectors.s
0x0000_5000	0x0000_5FFF	Low-memory globals
0x0000_6000	0x0000_6FFF	Low-memory shared page used for low-level debugging
0x0000_7000	0x0000_DFFF	Boot processor interrupt and debug stacks
0x0000_E000	0x0FFF_FFFF	Kernel code and data
0x1000_0000		Physical memory window
	0xDFFF_FFFF	Highest kernel virtual address known to the VM subsystem
0xE000_0000	0xFFFF_FFFF	User memory window

TABLE 8–4 User Virtual Address Space Layout (32-bit, Mac OS X 10.4)

Start	End	Notes
0x0000_0000	0x0000_1000	So-called *zero page* (__PAGEZERO)—inaccessible by default so that dereferencing a NULL pointer (including small offsets from a NULL pointer) causes a protection fault
0x0000_1000	0x8FDF_FFFF	Application address range (about 2.3GB)
0x8FE0_0000	8x8FFF_FFFF	Space reserved exclusively for Apple system libraries; e.g., the dynamic linker's text segment, mapped starting at 0x8FE0_0000
0x9000_0000	0x9FFF_FFFF	Global shared text segment, reserved exclusively for Apple system libraries; e.g., the system library's text segment, mapped starting at 0x9000_0000
0xA000_0000	0xAFFF_FFFF	Global shared data segment, reserved exclusively for Apple system libraries; e.g., the system library's data segment, mapped starting at 0xA000_0000
0xB000_0000	0xBFFF_FFFF	Preferred address range for the application's main thread
0xC000_0000	0xEBFF_FFFF	Additional space available for third-party applications and framework code
0xF000_0000	0xFDFF_FFFF	Range preferred for use by additional thread stacks, although applications may use this range as necessary
0xFE00_0000	0xFFBF_FFFF	Range reserved for use by the pasteboard and other system services; not to be used by user programs

(continues)

TABLE 8–4 User Virtual Address Space Layout (32-bit, Mac OS X 10.4) *(Continued)*

Start	End	Notes
0xFFC0_0000	0xFFFD_FFFF	Range preferred for use by other system services, although applications may use this range as necessary
0xFFFE_0000	0xFFFF_7FFF	Range reserved for use by system services and not to be used by user programs; e.g., a portion of the address range starting at 0xFFFE_C000 is used by the Objective-C library as a commpage for optimizing message dispatch
0xFFFF_8000	0xFFFF_EFFF	System-shared commpage (seven pages)
0xFFFF_F000	0xFFFF_FFFF	Last page of a 32-bit address space; cannot be mapped by the Mach VM subsystem

ranges entirely. For example, every task is disallowed access to the first memory page by default. As a result, a 32-bit task, whose virtual address space is 4GB in size (corresponding to the range defined by 0 and 0xFFFF_FFFF as the lowest and highest virtual memory addresses, respectively), has only a subset of its address space to use for arbitrary purposes.

To sum up, the kernel does not take any part of a process's address space. The kernel and every user process get the full 4GB (32-bit) address space. Each transition from user to kernel (and back) requires an address space switch.

> The kernel supports setting a per-thread bit (ignoreZeroFault) that instructs the kernel to ignore a page fault because of the thread accessing page 0. This is useful in the case of certain ROM device drivers that access page 0 when they start. If the bit is set for the faulting thread and the faulting address is within the zeroth page, the trap handler simply continues. This technique is deprecated in recent versions of Mac OS X. It was used in earlier versions by the I/O Kit to temporarily allow a "native" driver to access page 0.

When there is a copy-in/copy-out, the code that eventually talks to the MMU handles the mapping between address spaces. The mapping's job is to translate a given address to a mapped address per the address space in use. The resultant address is then used in the copy operation.

Because of the address space switch (the kernel uses the entire 4GB address space), copy-in/copy-out operations, particularly on small amounts of memory, can be expensive. System calls become expensive as well.

8.9 Universal Page Lists (UPLs)

The kernel provides an abstraction called a universal page list (UPL), which can be thought of as a wrapper around a bounded set of pages.[15] A UPL describes a set of physical pages associated with some address range of a VM object. In particular, a UPL provides a snapshot of various properties of its pages, such as whether the pages are mapped, dirty, encrypted, busy (access-blocked), or correspond to I/O memory.

A UPL is internally created by upl_create() [osfmk/vm/vm_pageout.c], which allocates and initializes a UPL structure (struct upl [osfmk/vm/vm_pageout.h]). If the UPL is being created with the UPL_SET_INTERNAL control flag, all information about the UPL is contained in a single memory object, allowing convenient transportation of the UPL within the kernel. In the case of an internal UPL, upl_create() allocates additional memory to hold a upl_page_info structure [osfmk/mach/memory_object_types.h] for each page in the UPL. The maximum number of pages a UPL can handle is MAX_UPL_TRANSFER, which is defined to be 256—that is, 1MB of memory.

The primary clients of the UPL API include pagers, the file system layer, and the unified buffer cache (UBC). Clients of the UPL API do not call upl_create() directly when they need to create a UPL based on the contents of a VM object; instead, they call other, higher-level functions such as vm_object_upl_request(), vm_object_iopl_request(), and vm_map_get_upl(). The latter is useful when you do not have the VM object in question, since it looks up the underlying VM object given an address range in a VM map. However, this function returns a UPL only for the first VM object—if the requested range is not covered by the first VM object, the caller must make another call to retrieve another UPL, and so on.

Once a UPL has been modified, the changes can be committed or aborted through upl_commit() and upl_abort(), respectively. These functions operate on the entire UPL. A specific range of the UPL can be committed or aborted through upl_commit_range() and upl_abort_range(), respectively. The UBC functions ubc_upl_commit_range() and ubc_upl_abort_range() are wrappers around the UPL functions—they additionally deallocate the UPL if its associated VM object has no resident pages after the commit or abort, respectively.

---

15. A UPL can be considered as a Mach or BSD equivalent of an instance of the IOMemoryDescriptor class instance in the I/O Kit.

8.10 Unified Buffer Cache (UBC)

Historically, UNIX allocated a portion of physical memory to be used as the buffer cache. The goal was to improve performance by caching disk blocks in memory, therefore avoiding having to go to the disk while reading or writing data. Before the advent of unified buffer caching, a cached buffer was identified by a device number and a block number. Modern operating systems, including Mac OS X, use a unified approach wherein in-memory contents of files reside in the same namespace as regular memory.

The UBC conceptually exists in the BSD portion of the kernel. Each vnode corresponding to a regular file contains a reference to a ubc_info structure, which acts as a bridge between vnodes and the corresponding VM objects. Note that UBC information is not valid for system vnodes (marked as VSYSTEM), even if the vnode is otherwise regular. When a vnode is created—say, because of an open() system call—a ubc_info structure is allocated and initialized.

```
// bsd/sys/ubc_internal.h

struct ubc_info {
    memory_object_t          ui_pager;    // for example, the vnode pager
    memory_object_control_t  ui_control;  // pager control port
    long                     ui_flags;
    struct vnode             *ui_vnode;   // our vnode
    struct ucred             *ui_cred;    // credentials for NFS paging
    off_t                    ui_size;     // file size for vnode
    struct cl_readahead      *cl_rahead;  // cluster read-ahead context
    struct cl_writebehind    *cl_wbehind; // cluster write-behind context
};
```

```
// bsd/sys/vnode_internal.h

struct vnode {
    ...
    union {
        struct mount    *vu_mountedhere; // pointer to mounted vfs (VDIR)
        struct socket    *vu_socket;     // Unix IPC (VSOCK)
        struct specinfo *vu_specinfo;    // device (VCHR, VBLK)
        struct fifoinfo *vu_fifoinfo;    // fifo (VFIFO)
        struct ubc_info *vu_ubcinfo;     // regular file (VREG)
    } v_un;
    ...
};
```

The UBC's job is to cache file-backed and anonymous memory in physical memory using a greedy approach: It will attempt to consume all available physical memory. This is especially relevant for 32-bit processes on a 64-bit machine with more than 4GB of physical memory. Although no single 32-bit process can directly address more than 4GB of virtual memory, the larger physical memory benefits all processes as it amounts to a larger buffer cache. As we saw earlier, resident pages are evicted using an LRU-like page replacement policy. Recently used pages, say, corresponding to a file that was recently read, or memory that was recently allocated, are likely to be found in the buffer cache.

You can see the buffer cache at work by using the `fs_usage` utility. As we saw in Chapter 6, `fs_usage` uses the kernel's kdebug facility to perform fine-grained tracing of kernel events. The page-fault handler (`vm_fault()` [osfmk/vm/vm_fault.c]) creates trace records for various types of page faults.

```
// bsd/sys/kdebug.h

#define DBG_ZERO_FILL_FAULT   1
#define DBG_PAGEIN_FAULT      2
#define DBG_COW_FAULT         3
#define DBG_CACHE_HIT_FAULT   4
```

Specifically, a fault of type `DBG_CACHE_HIT_FAULT` means that the handler found the page in the UBC. A fault of type `DBG_PAGEIN_FAULT` means that the handler had to issue I/O for that page fault. `fs_usage` reports these two events as `CACHE_HIT` and `PAGE_IN`, respectively. Running `fs_usage` to report system-wide cache hits and page-ins should show that normally, many of the I/O requests are satisfied from the UBC.

```
$ sudo fs_usage -f cachehit
...
11:26:36  CACHE_HIT                                 0.000002   WindowServer
11:26:36  CACHE_HIT                                 0.000002   WindowServer
```

> Data caching can be disabled on a per-file basis by using the `F_NOCACHE` command with the `fcntl()` system call, which sets the `VNOCACHE_DATA` flag in the corresponding vnode. The cluster I/O layer examines this flag and performs I/O appropriately.

8.10.1 The UBC Interface

The UBC exports several routines for use by file systems. Figure 8–20 shows routines that operate on vnodes. For example, `ubc_setsize()`, which informs the UBC of a file size change, may be called when a file system's write routine extends the file. ubc_msync() can be used to flush out all dirty pages of an mmap()'ed vnode, for example:

```
int ret;
vnode_t vp;
off_t current_size;
...

current_size = ubc_getsize(vp);
if (current_size)
    ret = ubc_msync(vp,                          // vnode
                    (off_t)0,                    // beginning offset
                    current_size,                // ending offset
                    NULL,                        // residual offset
                    UBC_PUSHDIRTY | UBC_SYNC);   // flags
// UBC_PUSHDIRTY pushes any dirty pages in the given range to the backing store
// UBC_SYNC waits for the I/O generated by UBC_PUSHDIRTY to complete
```

Moreover, the UBC provides routines such as the following for working with UPLs.

- ubc_create_upl() creates a UPL given a vnode, offset, and size.
- ubc_upl_map() maps an entire UPL into an address space. ubc_upl_unmap() is the corresponding unmap function.
- ubc_upl_commit(), ubc_upl_commit_range(), ubc_upl_abort(), and ubc_upl_abort_range() are UBC wrappers around UPL functions for committing or aborting UPLs in their entirety or a range within.

FIGURE 8–20 Examples of exported UBC routines

```
// convert logical block number to file offset
off_t
ubc_blktooff(vnode_t vp, daddr64_t blkno);

// convert file offset to logical block number
daddr64_t
ubc_offtoblk(vnode_t vp, off_t offset);

// retrieve the file size
off_t
ubc_getsize(vnode_t vp);

// file size has changed
int
ubc_setsize(vnode_t vp, off_t new_size);
```

(continues)

FIGURE 8–20 Examples of exported UBC routines *(continued)*

```
// get credentials from the ubc_info structure
struct ucred *
ubc_getcred(vnode_t vp);

// set credentials in the ubc_info structure, but only if no credentials
// are currently set
int
ubc_setcred(vnode_t vp, struct proc *p);

// perform the clean/invalidate operation(s) specified by flags on the range
// specified by (start, end) in the memory object that backs this vnode
errno_t
ubc_msync(vnode_t vp, off_t start, off_t end, off_t *resid, int flags);

// ask the memory object that backs this vnode if any pages are resident
int
ubc_pages_resident(vnode_t vp);
```

8.10.2 The NFS Buffer Cache

Not all types of system caches are unified, and some cannot be unified. For example, file system metadata, which is not a part of the file from the user's standpoint, needs to be cached independently. Besides, performance-related reasons can make a private buffer cache more appealing in some circumstances, which is why the NFS implementation in the Mac OS X kernel uses a private buffer cache with an NFS-specific buffer structure (struct nfsbuf [bsd/nfs/nfsnode.h]).

> Mac OS X versions prior to 10.3 did not use a separate buffer cache for NFS.

NFS version 3 provides a new COMMIT operation that allows a client to ask the server to perform an *unstable write*, wherein data is written to the server, but the server is not required to verify that the data has been committed to stable storage. This way, the server can respond immediately to the client. Subsequently, the client can send a COMMIT request to commit the data to stable storage. Moreover, NFS version 3 provides a mechanism that allows a client to write the data to the server again if the server lost uncommitted data, perhaps because of a server reboot.

```
int
nfs_doio(struct nfsbuf *bp, kauth_cred_t cr, proc_t p)
{
    ...
    if (ISSET(bp->nb_flags, NB_WRITE)) { // we are doing a write
        ...
        if (/* a dirty range needs to be written out */) {
            ...
            error = nfs_writerpc(...);    // let this be an unstable write
            ...
            if (!error && iomode == NFSV3WRITE_UNSTABLE) {
                ...
                SET(bp->nb_flags, NB_NEEDCOMMIT);
                ...
            }
            ...
        }
        ...
    }
    ...
}
```

The regular buffer cache and cluster I/O mechanisms are not aware of the NFS-specific concept of unstable writes. In particular, once a client has completed an unstable write, the corresponding buffers in the NFS buffer cache are tagged as NB_NEEDCOMMIT.

NFS also uses its own asynchronous I/O daemon (nfsiod). The regular buffer laundry thread—bcleanbuf_thread() [bsd/vfs/vfs_bio.c]—is again not aware of unstable writes. While cleaning dirty NFS buffers, the laundry thread cannot help the NFS client code to coalesce COMMIT requests corresponding to multiple NB_NEEDCOMMIT buffers. Instead, it would remove one buffer at a time from the laundry queue and issue I/O for it. Consequently, NFS would have to send individual COMMIT requests, which would hurt performance and increase network traffic.

Another difference between the NFS and regular buffer caches is that the former explicitly supports buffers with multiple pages. The regular buffer cache provides a single bit (B_WASDIRTY) in the buf structure for marking a page that was found dirty in the cache. The nfsbuf structure provides up to 32 pages to be individually marked as clean or dirty. Larger NFS buffers help in improving NFS I/O performance.

```
// bsd/nfs/nfsnode.h

struct nfsbuf {
    ...
```

```
    u_int32_t nb_valid; // valid pages in the buffer
    u_int32_t nb_dirty; // dirty pages in the buffer
    ...
};

#define NBPGVALID(BP,P)     (((BP)->nb_valid >> (P)) & 0x1)
#define NBPGDIRTY(BP,P)     (((BP)->nb_dirty >> (P)) & 0x1)
#define NBPGVALID_SET(BP,P) ((BP)->nb_valid |= (1 << (P)))
#define NBPGDIRTY_SET(BP,P) ((BP)->nb_dirty |= (1 << (P)))
```

8.11 The Dynamic Pager Program

The dynamic pager program (/sbin/dynamic_pager) is a user-level process that creates and deletes backing store (swap) files in the designated directory /var/vm/. Notwithstanding its name, dynamic_pager is *not* a Mach pager and is not involved otherwise in actual paging operations. It is only a manager of swap space for use by the kernel.

By default, Mac OS X uses dynamically created, variable-size paging files instead of dedicated swap partitions. The kernel writes data to these paging files in groups of pages (clusters).

> dynamic_pager can be instructed—through the -S command-line option—to use a fixed size for the paging files.

In its typical mode of operation, dynamic_pager works with two byte limits: a high-water mark and a low-water mark. When there are fewer bytes free in the swap files than allowed by the high-water mark, dynamic_pager creates a new file and adds it to the swap pool by notifying the kernel. When there are more bytes free in the paging files than allowed by the low-water mark, the kernel sends a notification to dynamic_pager to trigger deletion of a swap file (only one swap file is deleted per notification). Note that the swap file being deleted is likely to have some paged-out pages in it—such pages are brought into the kernel and eventually paged out to another swap file. The high- and low-water marks can be specified to dynamic_pager through its -H and -L command-line options, respectively. If these limits are not explicitly specified, dynamic_pager calculates them when it starts. The startup script /etc/rc launches dynamic_pager, instructing it whether to encrypt the paging file data (the -E option) and specifying the path prefix of the swap files (/private/var/vm/swapfile by default).

> The free page level in the kernel must remain below the `maximum_pages_free` threshold for at least `PF_LATENCY` (10) intervals of `PF_INTERVAL` (3) seconds each before the kernel will send a notification for swap file deletion.

 # /etc/rc

```
...
if [ ${ENCRYPTSWAP:=-NO-} = "-YES-" ]; then
    encryptswap="-E"
else
    encryptswap=""
fi
/sbin/dynamic_pager ${encryptswap} -F ${swapdir}/swapfile
```

When it starts, `dynamic_pager` determines the high- and low-water marks and other limits based on command-line arguments, free file system space, installed physical memory, and built-in hard limits. Specifically, it establishes the following limits and rules.

- The absolute minimum and maximum swap file sizes are 64MB and 1GB, respectively.

- The maximum swap file size must not be greater than 12.5% of the free space available on the volume that contains the swap file. Moreover, the maximum swap file size must not be greater than the amount of physical memory on the system.

- At most, eight swap files can be created.

- The first two swap files have the same size: the minimum swap file size (64MB). Subsequent files double in size, up to the maximum swap file size.

- The default high-water mark is 40,000,000 bytes (approximately 38MB).

`dynamic_pager` uses the `macx_swapon()` system call [bsd/vm/dp_backing_store_file.c] to add a file to the backing store. The corresponding removal call is `macx_swapoff()`, which removes a file from the backing store. The files themselves are created and deleted from the file system by `dynamic_pager`. Note that `dynamic_pager` passes a swap file's *pathname*—rather than a file descriptor—to the kernel. The kernel (or rather, `dynamic_pager`'s thread running in the kernel) internally looks up the pathname through `namei()` to acquire the corresponding vnode.

`dynamic_pager` uses another system call—`macx_triggers()`—to enable or disable swap encryption and to set callbacks for high- and low-water marks.

```
kern_return_t
macx_triggers(int hi_water, int low_water, int flags, mach_port_t alert_port);
```

The kernel processes an invocation of macx_triggers() based on the flags argument as follows.

- If either SWAP_ENCRYPT_OFF or SWAP_ENCRYPT_ON is set in flags, the kernel instructs the default pager to disable or enable, respectively, swap encryption.

- If HI_WAT_ALERT is set and alert_port contains a valid port to which the caller (dynamic_pager) has receive rights, the kernel arranges for an IPC message to be sent to the port when available backing store space falls below the high-water mark.

- Similarly, if LO_WATER_ALERT is set, the kernel arranges for an IPC message to be sent to alert_port when available backing store space rises above the low-water mark.

Additionally, macx_triggers() elevates the calling thread's status as follows.

- It marks it as a nontimeshare thread.

- It sets the thread's importance to the maximum possible value.

- It designates the thread as a VM-privileged thread, which enables the thread to allocate memory from the reserved pool if necessary.

Mac OS X 10.4 supports encryption of the data written by the kernel to the swap files. This feature can be enabled through the "Use secure virtual memory" checkbox in the Security system preference pane. When enabled, the following line is written to /etc/hostconfig:

```
ENCRYPTSWAP=-YES-
```

As we saw earlier, /etc/rc parses /etc/hostconfig, and if the ENCRYPTSWAP variable is set to YES, dynamic_pager is launched with the -E option. The kernel uses a form of the AES encryption algorithm for encrypting swap file data.

Even without swap file encryption, the kernel prevents user-space programs from directly reading swap data by using a special implementation of the read() system call. The vn_read() and vn_rdwr_64() internal functions in the VFS layer check the vnode they are dealing with to see if it corresponds to a swap file.

If so, these functions call vn_read_swapfile() [bsd/vfs/vfs_vnops.c] instead of the usual internal read routine.

```
// bsd/vfs/vfs_vnops.c

...
    if (vp->v_flag & VSWAP) {
        // special case for swap files
        error = vn_read_swapfile(vp, uio);
    } else {
        error = VNOP_READ(vp, uio, ioflag, &context);
    }
...
```

vn_read_swapfile() reads zero-filled pages[16] instead of the actual contents of the file.

Mapping the Swap

It is not possible to map the pages in swap files to the tasks that were using them—the "user" is a VM object. As we have seen, a VM object can be shared between multiple tasks. Moreover, in the case of a copy object, there is no direct connection between any task and that copy object; the latter holds a reference to the original VM object. Normally, it is also not possible to determine which blocks in a swap file are currently being used to hold swapped-out pages. However, the kernel can be compiled with a feature called *Mach page map*, wherein the VM subsystem maintains a bitmap (called the *existence map*) for internal objects. The bitmap tracks which pages of the object are currently swapped out to the backing store—the trivial determination of whether the page corresponding to a given VM object/offset pair is available on the backing store can be used as an optimization during page-fault processing.

The existence map for a VM object can be printed through the object command in the built-in kernel debugger (KDB).

8.12 The Update Daemon

The update daemon (/usr/sbin/update) periodically flushes dirty file system buffers to disk by invoking the sync() system call. By default, the update daemon

---

16. The last byte of each page read is set to the newline character.

calls sync() once every 30 seconds, but an alternate interval can be specified as a command-line argument. Moreover, a separate power-save interval can be specified. When the system is on battery power and the disk is sleeping, the power-save interval is used instead of the normal interval.

> Flushing does not mean that the data is written to disk immediately—it is only queued for writing. The actual writing to disk typically happens at some time in the near future. The F_FULLSYNC file control operation can be used through the fcntl() system call to truly flush a file to disk.

The sync() system call iterates over the list of mounted file systems, calling sync_callback() [bsd/vfs/vfs_syscalls.c] on each file system. sync_callback() calls VFS_SYNC() [bsd/vfs/kpi_vfs.c], which calls the file-system-specific sync function through the appropriate file system function pointer table maintained by the VFS layer. For example, hfs_sync() [bsd/hfs/hfs_vfsops.c] is invoked in the case of the HFS Plus file system.

> A subtle caveat is that sync() does not flush a buffer that has been dirtied by writing to a memory-mapped file. The msync() system call must be used for that case.

8.13 System Shared Memory

The kernel provides a mechanism for system-wide memory sharing—the *Shared Memory Server* subsystem. Using this facility, both the kernel and user programs can share code and data among all tasks on the system. It is also possible to give one or more tasks private versions of the shared memory.

8.13.1 Applications of Shared Memory

In Chapter 6, we looked at the commpage area, which is a set of pages that are mapped (shared and read-only) into every task's virtual address space. The pages contain both code and data. As we saw in earlier chapters, during bootstrapping, the startup thread (kernel_bootstrap_thread() [osfmk/kern/startup.c]) calls commpage_populate() [osfmk/ppc/commpage/commpage.c] to populate the commpage arca. Figure 8–21 shows a summary of shared-memory-related initialization during bootstrapping.

FIGURE 8–21 System-wide shared memory setup during bootstrapping

```
// osfmk/kern/startup.c

static void
kernel_bootstrap_thread(void)
{
    ...
    shared_file_boot_time_init(ENV_DEFAULT_ROOT, cpu_type());
    ...
    commpage_populate();
    ...
}


// osfmk/vm/vm_shared_memory_server.c

void
shared_com_boot_time_init(void)
{
    ...
    // Create one commpage region for 32-bit and another for 64-bit
    ...
}

void
shared_file_boot_time_init(unsigned int fs_base, unsigned int system)
{
    // Allocate two 256MB regions for mapping into task spaces

    // The first region is the global shared text segment
    // Its base address is 0x9000_0000
    // This region is shared read-only by all tasks

    // The second region is the global shared data segment
    // Its base address is 0xA000_0000
    // This region is shared copy-on-write by all tasks

    // Create shared region mappings for the two regions
    // Each is a submap

    // Call shared_com_boot_time_init() to initialize the commpage area
    ...
}
```

The system library, which contains code to use the contents of the commpage area, places the commpage symbols in a special section called __commpage in its __DATA segment. Recall also that the last eight pages of a 32-bit virtual address space are reserved for the commpage area, of which the very last page is unmapped. We can use the vmmap utility to verify that the last submap is indeed the commpage area.

```
$ vmmap $$
...
==== Non-writable regions for process 24664
...
system   ffff8000-ffffa000 [  8K] r--/r-- SM=SHM  commpage [libSystem.B.dylib]
...
```

As shown in Figure 8–21, besides the commpage area, the kernel creates two 256MB submaps that are shared by all tasks. Mac OS X uses these submaps for supporting shared libraries. A shared library on Mac OS X can be compiled such that its read-only (__TEXT and __LINKEDIT[17]) and read-write (__DATA) segments are *split* and relocated at offsets relative to specific addresses. This *split-segment* dynamic linking is in contrast to the traditional case where the read-only and read-write portions are not separated into predefined, nonoverlapping address ranges.

> A split-segment dynamic shared library can be created by passing the -segs_read_only_addr and -segs_read_write_addr options to the static link editor (ld). Both options require a segment-aligned address as an argument, which becomes the starting address of the corresponding segments (read-only or read-write) in the library.

Now, a split-segment library can be mapped so that its text segment is completely shared between tasks—with a single physical map (i.e., the same page table entries)—whereas the data segment is shared copy-on-write. The predefined address ranges for the text and data segments of Apple-provided libraries are 0x9000_0000-0x9FFF_FFFF and 0xA000_0000-0xAFFF_FFFF, respectively. This way, a single mapping of a shared library can be used by multiple tasks. Note that programs cannot get write access to the global shared text segment by changing its protection: Calls such as vm_protect() and mprotect() eventu-

---

17. The __LINKEDIT segment contains raw data—such as symbols and strings—used by dyld.

ally call `vm_map_protect()` [`osfmk/vm/vm_map.c`], which will deny the protection change because the maximum protection value does not permit write access. If it is required to modify memory mapped in this range during runtime, an option is to use a debug version of the corresponding library, which will not be a split-segment library and as such will not map into the global shared regions.

> Split-segment libraries are meant to be implemented only by Apple. Therefore, the global shared text and data regions are reserved for Apple and must not be directly used by third-party software.

Let us consider the example of the system library. Its normal, nondebug version is a split-segment library with a preferred load address of `0x9000_0000` for its text segment.

> A library may not load at its preferred base address—the one it is prebound to—because an existing mapping may collide with the library's desired address range. If instructed by the caller, the Shared Memory Server subsystem can attempt to still load the library but at an alternative location—the library *slides* to a different base address.

```
$ otool -hv /usr/lib/libSystem.dylib
/usr/lib/libSystem.dylib:
Mach header
      magic cputype cpusubtype filetype ncmds sizeofcmds flags
   MH_MAGIC     PPC       ALL     DYLIB    10      2008 NOUNDEFS DYLDLINK PREBOUND
SPLIT_SEGS TWOLEVEL
$ otool -l /usr/lib/libSystem.dylib
/usr/lib/libSystem.dylib:
Load command 0
      cmd LC_SEGMENT
  cmdsize 872
  segname __TEXT
   vmaddr 0x90000000
...
Load command 1
      cmd LC_SEGMENT
  cmdsize 804
  segname __DATA
   vmaddr 0xa0000000
...
```

The debug version of the system library is not split-segment: It specifies `0x0000_0000` as the load address of its text segment.

```
$ otool -hv /usr/lib/libSystem_debug.dylib
/usr/lib/libSystem_debug.dylib:
Mach header
      magic cputype cpusubtype filetype ncmds sizeofcmds flags
   MH_MAGIC     PPC      ALL    DYLIB    9      2004 NOUNDEFS DYLDLINK TWOLEVEL
$ otool -l /usr/lib/libSystem_debug.dylib
/usr/lib/libSystem.B_debug.dylib:
Load command 0
      cmd LC_SEGMENT
  cmdsize 872
  segname __TEXT
   vmaddr 0x00000000
...
```

We can instruct `dyld` to load the debug versions of libraries (provided a library has a debug version available) by setting the value of the `DYLD_IMAGE_SUFFIX` environment variable to `_debug`. Let us verify the difference between the mappings of the split-segment and non-split-segment versions of the system library. Note that the current and maximum permissions of the text segment in the case of the split-segment library are `r-x` and `r-x`, respectively. The corresponding permissions for the debug version are `r-x` and `rwx`, respectively. Therefore, in the case of the debug version, a debugger can request write access to that memory—say, for inserting breakpoints.

```
$ vmmap $$
...
==== Non-writable regions for process 25928
...
__TEXT     90000000-901a7000 [ 1692K] r-x/r-x SM=COW  /usr/lib/libSystem.B.dylib
__LINKEDIT 901a7000-901fe000 [  348K] r--/r-- SM=COW  /usr/lib/libSystem.B.dylib
...
$ DYLD_IMAGE_SUFFIX=_debug /bin/zsh
$ vmmap $$
...
==== Non-writable regions for process 25934
...
__TEXT     01008000-0123b000 [2252K] r-x/rwx SM=COW /usr/lib/libSystem.B_debug.dylib
__LINKEDIT 0124e000-017dc000 [5688K] r--/rwx SM=COW /usr/lib/libSystem.B_debug.dylib
...
```

Using global shared regions for commonly used libraries (such as the system library, which is used by all normal programs) reduces the number of mappings maintained by the VM subsystem. In particular, shared regions facilitate prebinding since library contents are at known offsets.

8.13.2 Implementation of the Shared Memory Server Subsystem

The Shared Memory Server subsystem's implementation can be divided into a BSD front-end and a Mach back-end. The front-end provides a set of Apple-private system calls used by dyld. It is implemented in bsd/vm/vm_unix.c. The back-end, which is implemented in osfmk/vm/vm_shared_memory_server.c, hides Mach VM details and provides low-level shared memory functionality for use by the front-end.

The following system calls are exported by this subsystem:

- shared_region_make_private_np() (introduced in Mac OS X 10.4)
- shared_region_map_file_np() (introduced in Mac OS X 10.4)
- load_shared_file() (deprecated in Mac OS X 10.4)
- reset_shared_file() (deprecated in Mac OS X 10.4)
- new_system_shared_regions() (deprecated in Mac OS X 10.4)

8.13.2.1 *shared_region_make_private_np()*

shared_region_make_private_np() privatizes the current task's shared region, after which a file mapped into that region is seen only by threads in the current task. The call takes a set of address ranges as an argument. Except these explicitly specified ranges, all other mappings in the privatized "shared" region are deallocated, possibly creating holes in the region. dyld uses this call under circumstances in which a private mapping of a library is necessary or desired—say, because the shared region is full, because the split-segment library to be loaded conflicts with one that is already loaded (and the latter is not needed by the task), or because the DYLD_NEW_LOCAL_SHARED_REGIONS environment variable was set. dyld specifies the set of ranges not to deallocate based on the split-segment libraries used by the process so far.

DYLD_NEW_LOCAL_SHARED_REGIONS is useful when either additional or different libraries need to be loaded in a certain program and it is undesirable to pollute the globally shared submap.

Let us consider an example. Suppose you want to experiment with an alternate version of a split-segment system library you have. Assuming that the library file is located in /tmp/lib/, you can arrange for it to be loaded—say, for the zsh program—in a privatized "shared" region as follows:

```
$ DYLD_PRINT_SEGMENTS=1 DYLD_LIBRARY_PATH=/tmp/lib \
      DYLD_NEW_LOCAL_SHARED_REGIONS=1 /bin/zsh
```

```
dyld: making shared regions private
...
dyld: Mapping split-seg un-shared /usr/lib/libSystem.B.dylib
          __TEXT at 0x90000000->0x901A6FFF
          __DATA at 0xA0000000->0xA000AFFF
...
$ echo $$
26254
$ vmmap $$
...
__TEXT     90000000-901a7000 [ 1692K] r-x/r-x SM=COW  /tmp/lib/libSystem.B.dylib
__LINKEDIT 901a7000-901fe000 [  348K] r--/r-- SM=COW  /tmp/lib/libSystem.B.dylib
...
```

Note that all processes created from this shell will inherit the privacy of the shared regions—they will not share global shared submaps. We can modify our private copy of the system library to see this effect.

```
$ echo $$
26254
$ ls /var/vm/app_profile/
ls: app_profile: Permission denied
$ perl -pi -e 's#Permission denied#ABCDEFGHIJKLMNOPQ#g' /tmp/lib/libSystem.B.dylib
$ ls /var/vm/app_profile/
ls: app_profile: ABCDEFGHIJKLMNOPQ
```

8.13.2.2 `shared_region_map_file_np()`

`shared_region_map_file_np()` is used by `dyld` to map parts of a split-segment library in the global shared read-only and read-write regions. `dyld` parses the load commands in the library file and prepares an array of shared region mapping structures, each of which specifies the address, size, and protection values of a single mapping. It passes this array along with an open file descriptor for the library to `shared_region_map_file_np()`, which attempts to establish each of the requested mappings. `shared_region_map_file_np()` also takes as an argument a pointer to an address variable: If the pointer is non-NULL and the requested mappings cannot fit in the target address space as desired, the kernel will attempt to *slide* (move around) the mappings to make them fit. The resultant slide value is returned in the address variable. If the pointer is NULL instead, the call returns an error without attempting to slide.

```
struct shared_region_mapping_np {
    mach_vm_address_t address;
    mach_vm_size_t    size;
    mach_vm_offset_t  file_offset;
```

```
    vm_prot_t           max_prot;
    vm_prot_t           init_prot;
};
typedef struct shared_region_mapping_np sr_mapping_t;

int
shared_region_map_file_np(int            fd,
                          int            mapping_count,
                          sr_mapping_t *mappings,
                          uint64_t      *slide);
```

Note that a split-segment library file must reside on the root file system for it to be mapped into the system-wide global shared region (the *default* region). If the file resides on another file system, the kernel returns an EXDEV error ("Cross-device link") unless the calling task's shared region has been privatized by a prior call to shared_region_make_private_np().

shared_region_map_file_np() calls the back-end function map_shared_file() [osfmk/vm/vm_shared_memory_server.c] to perform the mappings. The back-end maintains a hash table of files loaded in the shared space. The hash function uses the relevant VM object's address. The actual mappings are handled by mach_vm_map() [osfmk/vm/vm_user.c].

> The two _np (nonportable) calls do not have stubs in the system segment library, whereas the other calls do. Mac OS X 10.4 is the first system version in which these two calls are implemented. The KERN_SHREG_PRIVATIZABLE sysctl can be used to determine whether shared regions can be privatized—that is, whether the shared_region_make_private_np() call is implemented. dyld uses this sysctl during its operation.

shared_region_make_private_np() calls clone_system_shared_regions() [bsd/vm/vm_unix.c] internal function to get a private copy of the current shared regions. clone_system_shared_regions() can either completely detach the cloned region from the old region, or it can create a *shadowed* clone and retain all mappings of the old region. In the latter case, if the back-end fails to locate something (a VM object) in the new region, it will also look in the old region. shared_region_make_private_np() uses this call to create a detached clone. The chroot() system call also uses it, but to create a shadowed clone.

8.13.2.3 `load_shared_file()`

`load_shared_file()` performs a similar role as `shared_region_map_file_np()` but has somewhat different semantics. Its arguments include an address in the caller's address space where the split-segment library is currently `mmap()`'d and an array of mapping structures (`struct sf_mapping`), each of which it attempts to load in the shared region.

```
// osfmk/mach/shared_memory_server.h

struct sf_mapping {
    vm_offset_t mapping_offset;
    vm_size_t   size;
    vm_offset_t file_offset;
    vm_prot_t   protection;
    vm_offset_t cksum;
};
typedef struct sf_mapping sf_mapping_t;

int
load_shared_file(char         *filename,
                 caddr_t       mmapped_file_address,
                 u_long        mmapped_file_size,
                 caddr_t      *base_address,
                 int           mapping_count,
                 sf_mapping_t *mappings,
                 int          *flags);
```

`load_shared_file()` can be passed the following flags to affect its behavior.

- `ALTERNATE_LOAD_SITE` instructs `load_shared_file()` to attempt to load the shared file in the alternate shared area, whose base is `SHARED_ALTERNATE_LOAD_BASE` (defined to be `0x0900_0000` in `osfmk/mach/shared_memory_server.h`).

- `NEW_LOCAL_SHARED_REGIONS` causes the existing system shared regions to be cloned through a call to `clone_system_shared_regions()`.

- `QUERY_IS_SYSTEM_REGION` can be passed in a null call to `load_shared_file()` to determine whether the system shared regions are being used. If so, the `SYSTEM_REGION_BACKED` bit is set in the outbound `flags` variable.

For each requested mapping, the sequence of actions performed by the back-end implementation of `load_shared_file()` includes the following:

- Calling `vm_allocate()` to reserve the desired address range

- Calling `vm_map_copyin()` to create a copy object for the specified region from the source address (the `mmap()`'d file)
- Using the copy object obtained in the previous step to copy over the target address range by a call to `vm_map_copy_overwrite()`
- Calling `vm_map_protect()` to set the maximum protection of the newly copied region
- Calling `vm_map_protect()` to set the current protection of the newly copied region

8.13.2.4 *reset_shared_file()*

Like `load_shared_file()`, `reset_shared_file()` takes a list of shared-file-mapping structures. For each mapping in the global shared data segment, it calls `vm_deallocate()` to deallocate that mapping and then calls `vm_map()` to create a fresh, copy-on-write mapping. In other words, this call discards any changes that the task may have made to its private copy of the library's data segment. Older versions of `dyld` used this call when they needed to remove a loaded split-segment library—say, because a bundle that loaded that library failed to load.

8.13.2.5 *new_system_shared_regions()*

`new_system_shared_regions()` calls `remove_all_shared_regions()` [osfmk/vm/vm_shared_memory_server.c] to disconnect all shared regions present in the default environment while marking the regions as stale. After this, new tasks will not have the old libraries mapped in their address spaces. `load_shared_file()` can be used to load new libraries into the new set of shared regions.

```
// osfmk/kern/task.c

kern_return_t
task_create_internal(task_parent_task, boolean_t inherit_memory, task_t *child_task)
{
    ...

    // increment the reference count of the parent's shared region
    shared_region_mapping_ref(parent_task->system_shared_region);

    new_task->system_shared_region = parent_task->system_shared_region;
    ...
}
```

8.13.3 The Loading of Shared Object Files by the Dynamic Linker

We have come across several aspects of Mach-O files in earlier chapters. We also noted that Apple does not support the creation of statically linked executables on Mac OS X. In fact, almost all executables that are part of Mac OS X are dynamically linked.

> The `otool` and `otool64` programs are examples of executables that are statically linked.

As we saw in Chapter 7, the `execve()` system call eventually hands over control to `dyld` while preparing to execute a dynamically linked Mach-O file. `dyld` processes several load commands found in the Mach-O file. In particular, `dyld` loads the shared libraries the program depends on. If the libraries depend on other libraries, `dyld` loads them too, and so on.

`dyld` was overhauled in Mac OS X 10.4. The following are important differences between the overhauled version and the older versions.

- The new `dyld` is an object-oriented program implemented in C++. Earlier versions had C-based procedural implementations.

- The new `dyld` uses `_shared_region_map_file_np()` and `_shared_region_make_private_np()` for handling split-segment dynamic shared libraries. Earlier versions used `load_shared_file()` and `reset_shared_file()`. However, the new `dyld` checks whether the newer `_np` APIs are provided by the current kernel—if not, it falls back to the older APIs.

- The new `dyld` itself implements the `NSObjectFileImage(3)` API. Before Mac OS X 10.4, this API was implemented in `libdyld`, which was a part of the system library. On Mac OS X 10.4, the latter still contains symbols for this API—the symbols resolve to `dyld`'s implementation of the API.

- The new `dyld` itself implements the `dlopen(3)` API, including the `dladdr()`, `dlclose()`, `dlerror()`, and `dlsym()` functions. Before Mac OS X 10.4, these functions were implemented in `libdyld`.

- The new `dyld` does not support a few environment variables supported by earlier versions and introduces several new ones. Table 8–5 shows some Mac OS X 10.4–specific `dyld` environment variables. Note that most variables are Boolean in nature—simply setting them to 1 will trigger their effect.

TABLE 8–5 Some `dyld` Environment Variables Introduced in Mac OS X 10.4

Variable	Description
DYLD_IGNORE_PREBINDING	If set, instructs `dyld` to do one of the following: not use prebinding at all (set to `all`), ignore prebinding only for applications (set to `app`), or use prebinding only for split-segment libraries (set to `nonsplit` or the empty string).
DYLD_PRINT_APIS	If set, `dyld` prints the name of each `dyld` API function called, along with the arguments passed to the function.
DYLD_PRINT_BINDINGS	If set, `dyld` prints information about each symbol it binds, whether it is an external relocation, a lazy symbol, or an indirect symbol pointer.
DYLD_PRINT_ENV	If set, `dyld` prints its environment vector.
DYLD_PRINT_INITIALIZERS	If set, `dyld` prints the address of each initializer function in each image it loads. Examples of such functions include C++ constructors, functions designated as library initialization routines through the static linker's `-init` option, and functions tagged as `__attribute__ ((constructor))`.
DYLD_PRINT_INTERPOSING	If set, `dyld` prints information about the old and new pointers (where "old" and "new" have the appropriate meanings in the context of interposing) if the interposing feature is enabled.
DYLD_PRINT_OPTS	If set, `dyld` prints its argument vector.
DYLD_PRINT_REBASINGS	If set, `dyld` prints names of the libraries that are "fixed up" by altering their base addresses.
DYLD_PRINT_SEGMENTS	If set, `dyld` prints information about each Mach-O segment it maps in.
DYLD_PRINT_STATISTICS	If set, `dyld` prints statistics about itself, such as a breakup of time that it spent performing its various operations.
DYLD_ROOT_PATH	A colon-separated list of directories, each of which will be used (in the given order) by `dyld` as a path prefix while searching for images.
DYLD_SHARED_REGION	If set, instructs `dyld` to use privatized shared region (set to `private`), avoid using shared region (set to `avoid`), or attempt to use shared region (set to `use`)—see Figure 8–23.
DYLD_SLIDE_AND_PACK_DYLIBS	If set, instructs `dyld` to privatize the shared region and map libraries—with sliding, if necessary—such that they are "packed" next to each other.

Figures 8–22 and 8–23 depict the operation of `dyld` while loading non-split-segment and split-segment Mach-O files, respectively.

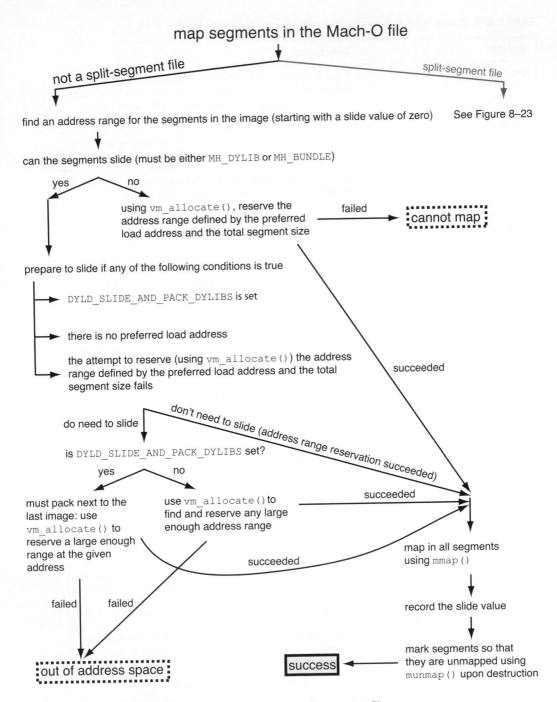

FIGURE 8–22 dyld's operation while loading a non-split-segment file

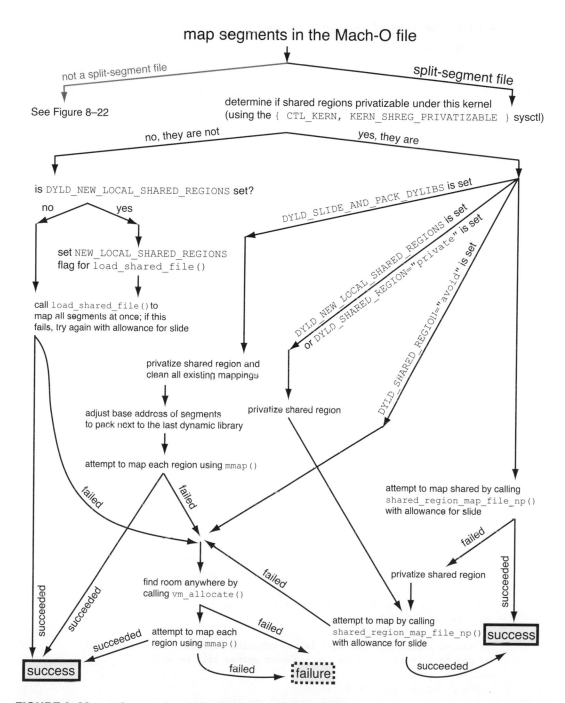

FIGURE 8-23 dyld's operation while loading a split-segment file

8.13.4 The Use of `shared_region_map_file_np()` by a System Application

Although all typical user applications benefit from the services of the Shared Memory Server subsystem, the corresponding APIs are reserved exclusively for Apple-provided applications, with `dyld` being the only client. Using these APIs can affect all applications on a system—potentially adversely. Therefore, third-party programs must not use these APIs, at least in products. With this caveat, let us look at an example of programmatically mapping a split-segment library into the global shared region. This example will help illustrate the actual working of this mechanism. Figure 8–24 shows the program.

FIGURE 8–24 Using `shared_region_map_file_np()`

```
// srmap.c
// maps a 32-bit, non-fat, dynamic shared library into the system shared region

#include <stdio.h>
#include <stdlib.h>
#include <unistd.h>
#include <limits.h>
#include <fcntl.h>
#include <sys/stat.h>
#include <sys/mman.h>
#include <sys/syscall.h>
#include <mach-o/loader.h>
#include <mach/shared_memory_server.h>

#define PROGNAME "srmap"

struct _shared_region_mapping_np {
    mach_vm_address_t address;
    mach_vm_size_t    size;
    mach_vm_offset_t  file_offset;
    vm_prot_t         max_prot;   // VM_PROT_{READ/WRITE/EXECUTE/COW/ZF}
    vm_prot_t         init_prot;  // VM_PROT_{READ/WRITE/EXECUTE/COW/ZF}
};
typedef struct _shared_region_mapping_np sr_mapping_t;
#define MAX_SEGMENTS 64

// shared_region_map_file_np() is not exported through libSystem in
// Mac OS X 10.4, so we use the indirect system call to call it
int
_shared_region_map_file_np(int fd,
                           unsigned int nregions,
                           sr_mapping_t regions[],
                           uint64_t *slide)
```

(continues)

FIGURE 8–24 Using `shared_region_map_file_np()` *(continued)*

```c
{
    return syscall(SYS_shared_region_map_file_np, fd, nregions, regions, slide);
}


int
main(int argc, char **argv)
{
    int                     fd, ret = 1;
    struct mach_header      *mh;            // pointer to the Mach-O header
    char                    *load_commands; // buffer for load commands
    uint32_t                ncmds;          // number of load commands
    struct load_command     *lc;            // a particular load command
    struct segment_command  *sc;            // a particular segment command
    uint64_t                vmaddr_slide;   // slide value from the kernel
    void                    *load_address = 0;   // for mmaping the Mach-O file
    unsigned                int entryIndex = 0;  // index into the mapping table
    sr_mapping_t            mappingTable[MAX_SEGMENTS], *entry;
    uintptr_t               base_address = (uintptr_t)ULONG_MAX;
    uint64_t                file_length;
    struct stat             sb;

    if (argc != 2) {
        fprintf(stderr, "usage: %s <library path>\n", PROGNAME);
        exit(1);
    }

    if ((fd = open(argv[1], O_RDONLY)) < 0) {
        perror("open");
        exit(1);
    }

    // determine the file's size
    if (fstat(fd, &sb))
        goto OUT;
    file_length = sb.st_size;

    // get a locally mapped copy of the file
    load_address = mmap(NULL, file_length, PROT_READ, MAP_FILE, fd, 0);
    if (load_address == ((void *)(-1)))
        goto OUT;

    // check out the Mach-O header
    mh = (struct mach_header *)load_address;

    if ((mh->magic != MH_MAGIC) && (mh->filetype != MH_DYLIB)) {
        fprintf(stderr, "%s is not a Mach-O dynamic shared library\n", argv[1]);
        goto OUT;
    }
```

(continues)

FIGURE 8–24 Using `shared_region_map_file_np()` *(continued)*

```
if (!(mh->flags & MH_SPLIT_SEGS)) {
    fprintf(stderr, "%s does not use split segments\n", argv[1]);
    goto OUT;
}

load_commands = (char *)((char *)load_address + sizeof(struct mach_header));
lc = (struct load_command *)load_commands;

// process all LC_SEGMENT commands and construct a mapping table
for (ncmds = mh->ncmds; ncmds > 0; ncmds--) {
    if (lc->cmd == LC_SEGMENT) {
        sc = (struct segment_command *)lc;

        // remember the starting address of the first segment (seg1addr)
        if (sc->vmaddr < base_address)
            base_address = sc->vmaddr;

        entry              = &mappingTable[entryIndex];
        entry->address     = sc->vmaddr;
        entry->size        = sc->filesize;
        entry->file_offset = sc->fileoff;

        entry->init_prot = VM_PROT_NONE;
        if (sc->initprot & VM_PROT_EXECUTE)
            entry->init_prot |= VM_PROT_EXECUTE;
        if (sc->initprot & VM_PROT_READ)
            entry->init_prot |= VM_PROT_READ;
        if (sc->initprot & VM_PROT_WRITE)
            entry->init_prot |= VM_PROT_WRITE | VM_PROT_COW;

        entry->max_prot = entry->init_prot;

        // check if the segment has a zero-fill area: if so, need a mapping
        if ((sc->initprot & VM_PROT_WRITE) && (sc->vmsize > sc->filesize)) {
            sr_mapping_t *zf_entry = &mappingTable[++entryIndex];
            zf_entry->address      = entry->address + sc->filesize;
            zf_entry->size         = sc->vmsize - sc->filesize;
            zf_entry->file_offset  = 0;
            zf_entry->init_prot    = entry->init_prot | \
                                        VM_PROT_COW | VM_PROT_ZF;
            zf_entry->max_prot     = zf_entry->init_prot;
        }
        entryIndex++;

    }
    // onto the next load command
    lc = (struct load_command *)((char *)lc + lc->cmdsize);
}
```

(continues)

FIGURE 8–24 Using `shared_region_map_file_np()` *(continued)*

```
    ret = _shared_region_map_file_np(fd,                // the file
                                     entryIndex,        // so many mappings
                                     mappingTable,      // the mappings
                                     &vmaddr_slide);    // OK to slide, let us know
    if (!ret) { // success
        printf("mapping succeeded: base = %#08lx, slide = %#llx\n",
               base_address, vmaddr_slide);
    }

OUT:
    close(fd);

    exit(ret);
}
```

We can test the program in Figure 8–24 by loading a trivial split-segment library in the global shared region. Figure 8–25 shows the test.

FIGURE 8–25 Loading a split-segment library in the global shared region

```
$ cat libhello.c
#include <stdio.h>

void
hello(void)
{
    printf("Hello, Shared World!\n");
}
$ gcc -Wall -dynamiclib -segs_read_only_addr 0x99000000 \
  -segs_read_write_addr 0xa9000000 -prebind -o /tmp/libhello.dylib libhello.c
$ otool -hv /tmp/libhello.dylib
/tmp/libhello.dylib:
Mach header
      magic cputype cpusubtype   filetype ncmds sizeofcmds      flags
   MH_MAGIC    PPC       ALL       DYLIB     8      924    NOUNDEFS DYLDLINK PREBOUND
SPLIT_SEGS TWOLEVEL
$ otool -l /tmp/libhello.dylib
/tmp/libhello.dylib:
Load command 0
      cmd LC_SEGMENT
  cmdsize 328
  segname __TEXT
   vmaddr 0x99000000
   vmsize 0x00001000
...
```

(continues)

FIGURE 8–25 Loading a split-segment library in the global shared region *(continued)*

```
Load command 1
        cmd LC_SEGMENT
    cmdsize 328
    segname __DATA
     vmaddr 0xa9000000
     vmsize 0x00001000
...
$ gcc -Wall -o srmap srmap.c
$ ./srmap /tmp/libhello.dylib
mapping succeeded: base = 0x99000000, slide = 0
$ cat test.c
#include <stdio.h>
#include <stdlib.h>
#include <limits.h>

#define PROGNAME "callfunc"

typedef void (*func_t)(void);

int
main(int argc, char **argv)
{
    unsigned long long addr;
    func_t func;

    if (argc != 2) {
        fprintf(stderr, "usage: %s <address in hexadecimal>\n", PROGNAME);
        exit(1);
    }

    addr = strtoull(argv[1], NULL, 16);
    if (!addr || (addr == ULLONG_MAX)) {
        perror("strtoull");
        exit(1);
    }

    func = (func_t)(uintptr_t)addr;
    func();

    return 0;
}
$ gcc -Wall -o test test.c
$ nm /tmp/libhello.dylib | grep _hello
99000f28 T _hello
$ ./test 0x99000f28
Hello, Shared World!
```

8.13.5 A Note on Prebinding

A prebound Mach-O executable contains an additional type of load command: LC_PREBOUND_DYLIB.[18] There is one such command for every shared library that the prebound executable links to. Figure 8–26 shows the structure of this load

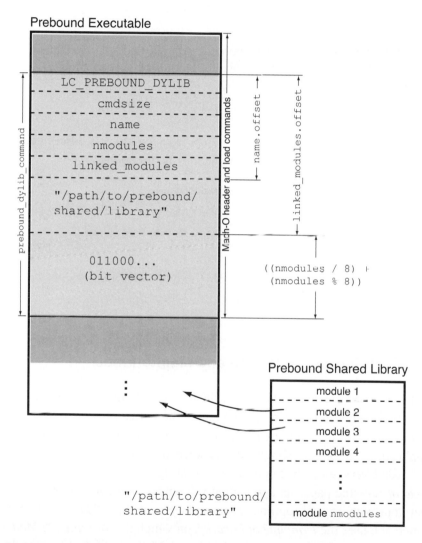

FIGURE 8–26 Structure of the LC_PREBOUND_DYLIB load command

---

18. A prebound executable can also have a prebinding checksum, which is present as a Mach-O load command of type LC_PREBIND_CKSUM.

command. The command is described by a `prebound_dylib_command` structure. The structure's `name` field refers to the prebound shared library's name. The `nmodules` field specifies the number of modules in the library—a single object file (a ".o") amounts to one module, and so does the *linkedit data*. The `linked_modules` field refers to a bit vector that contains a bit for each module in the library. If a module in the library is linked to a module in the executable, the bit corresponding to that library module is set in the vector.

> Since prebinding executables is deprecated beginning with Mac OS X 10.4, the static linker does not create prebound executables unless the environment variable `MACOSX_DEPLOYMENT_TARGET` is set to an earlier version of Mac OS X—for example, 10.3.

Note that although the generation of prebound executables is deprecated on Mac OS X 10.4, an Apple-provided executable may be prebound.

```
$ otool -hv /Applications/iTunes.app/Contents/MacOS/iTunes # PowerPC
/Applications/iTunes.app/Contents/MacOS/iTunes:
Mach header
      magic cputype cpusubtype  filetype ncmds sizeofcmds    flags
  MH_MAGIC    PPC       ALL     EXECUTE  115     14000  NOUNDEFS DYLDLINK PREBOUND
TWOLEVEL
$ otool -l /Applications/iTunes.app/Contents/MacOS/iTunes | \
    grep LC_PREBOUND_DYLIB | wc -l
90
```

8.14 Task Working Set Detection and Maintenance

The kernel uses physical memory as a cache for virtual memory. When new pages are to be brought in because of page faults, the kernel may need to decide which pages to reclaim from among those that are currently in physical memory. For an application, the kernel should ideally keep in memory those pages that would be needed very soon. In the utopian operating system, the kernel would know *ahead of time* the pages an application references as it runs. Several algorithms that approximate such optimal page replacement have been researched. Another approach uses the *Principle of Locality*, on which the *Working Set Model* is based. As described in the paper titled "Virtual Memory,"[19] *locality* can be

---

19. "Virtual Memory," by Peter J. Denning (*ACM Computing Surveys* 2:3, September 1970, pp. 153–189).

informally understood as a program's affinity for a subset of its pages, where this set of favored pages changes membership slowly. This gives rise to the *working set*—informally defined as the set of "most useful" pages for a program. The Working Set Principle establishes the rule that *a program may run if and only if its working set is in memory, and a page may not be removed if it is the member of a running program's working set*. Studies have shown that keeping a program's working set resident in physical memory typically allows it to run with acceptable performance—that is, without causing an unacceptable number of page faults.

8.14.1 The TWS Mechanism

The Mac OS X kernel includes an application-profiling mechanism that can construct per-user, per-application working set profiles, save the corresponding pages in a designated directory, and attempt to load them when the application is executed by that user. We will call this mechanism *TWS*, for task working set (the various functions and data structures in its implementation have the `tws` prefix in their names).

TWS is integrated with the kernel's page-fault-handling mechanism—it is called when there is a page fault. The first time an application is launched in a given user context, TWS captures the initial working set and stores it in a file in the `/var/vm/app_profile/` directory. Several aspects of the TWS scheme contribute to performance.

- The profile information is used during page-fault handling to determine whether any nearby pages should be brought in. Bringing more pages in than those corresponding to the immediate page fault leads to a single large request to the pager, avoiding multiple subsequent requests that would otherwise have to be made to bring in pages that are expected to be needed in the near future. This is relevant only for nonsequential pages, however, since sequential pages are brought in anyway because of cluster I/O.

- TWS captures and stores on disk an application's initial working set the first time the application is started by a particular user. This information is used for seeding (or preheating) the application's working set when it is launched again in the same user context. This way, the application's profile is built over time.

- The locality of memory references is often captured on disk, as on-disk files typically have good locality on HFS Plus volumes. Normally, the working sets can be read from disk with little seeking overheads.

8.14.2 TWS Implementation

Given a user with user ID U, TWS stores application profiles for that user as two files in /var/vm/app_profile/: #U_names and #U_data, where #U is the hexadecimal representation of U. The *names* file is a simple database that contains a header followed by profile elements, whereas the *data* file contains the actual working sets. The profile elements in the names file point to the working sets in the data file.

```
// bsd/vm/vm_unix.c

// header for the "names" file
struct profile_names_header {
        unsigned int    number_of_profiles;
        unsigned int    user_id;
        unsigned int    version;
        off_t           element_array;
        unsigned int    spare1;
        unsigned int    spare2;
        unsigned int    spare3;
};

// elements in the "names" file
struct profile_element {
        off_t           addr;
        vm_size_t       size;
        unsigned int    mod_date;
        unsigned int    inode;
        char name[12];
};
```

The kernel maintains a global profile cache data structure containing an array of global profiles, each of whose entries contains profile file information for one user.

```
// bsd/vm/vm_unix.c

// meta information for one user's profile
struct global_profile {
    struct vnode *names_vp;
    struct vnode *data_vp;
    vm_offset_t   buf_ptr;
    unsigned int  user;
    unsigned int  age;
    unsigned int  busy;
};
```

```
struct global_profile_cache {
    int max_ele;
    unsigned int age;
    struct global_profile profiles[3]; // up to 3 concurrent users
};

...

struct global_profile_cache global_user_profile_cache = {
    3,
    0,
    { NULL, NULL, 0, 0, 0, 0 },
    { NULL, NULL, 0, 0, 0, 0 },
    { NULL, NULL, 0, 0, 0, 0 }
};
```

Let us use the readksym.sh script to read the contents of global_user_profile_cache. We can see from the output shown in Figure 8–27 that the three global per-user slots are occupied by the user IDs 0x1f6 (502), 0, and 0x1f5 (501).

FIGURE 8–27 Reading the contents of the TWS subsystem's global user profile cache

```
$ sudo ./readksym.sh _global_user_profile_cache 128
0000000    0000    0003    0000    4815    053b    0c60    049a    dbdc
0000010    5da2    a000    0000    01f6    0000    47f9    0000    0000
0000020    040e    5ce4    0406    e4a4    5d5d    0000    0000    0000
0000030    0000    4814    0000    0000    045c    3738    045c    3840
0000040    5a74    d000    0000    01f5    0000    480c    0000    0000
0000050    0000    0001    040f    b7bc    03fa    9a00    04a5    f420
0000060    063b    3450    0472    4948    0442    96c0    0000    0000
0000070    0000    0000    0000    0000    0000    0000    0000    0000
```

Most of the TWS functionality is implemented in osfmk/vm/task_working_set.c and bsd/vm/vm_unix.c. The former uses functions implemented by the latter for dealing with profile files.

- prepare_profile_database() creates unique absolute pathnames to the names and data files for the given user ID. It is called by setuid() to prepare these files for the new user.

- bsd_search_page_cache_data_base() searches for an application's profile in the given names file.

- `bsd_open_page_cache_files()` attempts to either open or create the names and data files. If both files are present, they will be opened. If neither is present, both will be created. If only one is present, the attempt will fail.

- `bsd_close_page_cache_files()` decrements references on the names and data files for the given user profile.

- `bsd_read_page_cache_file()` first calls `bsd_open_page_cache_files()`, then looks for the given application's profile in the names file using `bsd_search_page_cache_data_base()`. If the profile is found, the function reads profile data from the data file into the given buffer.

- `bsd_write_page_cache_file()` writes to the names and data files.

As shown in Figure 8–6, the task structure's dynamic_working_set field is a pointer to a tws_hash structure [osfmk/vm/task_working_set.h]. This pointer is initialized during task creation—specifically by task_create_internal(), which calls task_working_set_create() [osfmk/vm/task_working_set.c]. Conversely, when the task is terminated, the working set is flushed (by task_terminate_internal()) and the corresponding hash entry is destroyed (by task_deallocate()).

```
// osfmk/kern/task.c

kern_return_t
task_create_internal(task_t      parent_task,
                      boolean_t   inherit_memory,
                      task_t      *child_task)
{
    ...
    new_task->dynamic_working_set = 0;
    task_working_set_create(new_task, TWS_SMALL_HASH_LINE_COUNT,
                            0, TWS_HASH_STYLE_DEFAULT);
    ...
}
```

task_working_set_create() calls tws_hash_create() [osfmk/vm/task_working_set.c] to allocate and initialize a tws_hash structure. As shown in Figure 8–28, execve() saves the executable's name for the TWS mechanism. Before a Mach-O executable is loaded, the Mach-O image activator calls tws_handle_startup_file() [osfmk/vm/task_working_set.c] to preheat the task if possible.

FIGURE 8–28 TWS-related processing during the `execve()` system call

```
// bsd/kern/kern_exec.c

int
execve(struct proc *p, struct execve_args *uap, register_t *retval)
{
    ...
    if (/* not chroot()'ed */ && /* application profiling enabled */) {
        // save the filename from the path passed to execve()
        // the TWS mechanism needs it to look up in the names file
        ...
    }
    ...
}

...


// image activator for Mach-O binaries
static int
exec_mach_imgact(struct image_params *imgp)
{
    ...
    if (/* we have a saved filename */) {
        tws_handle_startup_file(...);
    }

    vm_get_shared_region(task, &initial_region);
    ...

    // actually load the Mach-O file now
    ...
}
```

`tws_handle_startup_file()` first calls `bsd_read_page_cache_file()` [bsd/vm/vm_unix.c] to read the appropriate page cache file. If the read attempt succeeds, the existing profile is read by a call to `tws_read_startup_file()`. If the read attempt fails because no profile was found for the application, a new profile is created by calling `tws_write_startup_file()`, which in turn calls `task_working_set_create()`. The working set information is later written to disk by a call to `tws_send_startup_info()`, which calls `bsd_write_page_cache_file()`.

The rest (and most) of the TWS activity occurs during page-fault handling—the mechanism is specifically invoked on a page fault, which allows it to monitor the application's fault behavior. `vm_fault()` [osfmk/vm/vm_fault.c]—the page-fault handler—calls `vm_fault_tws_insert()` [osfmk/vm/vm_fault.c] to add page-fault information to the current task's working set. `vm_fault_tws_insert()` is provided with a VM object and an offset within it, using which it performs a hash lookup in the `tws_hash` data structure pointed to by the task's `dynamic_working_set` field. This way, it determines whether the object/offset pair needs to be inserted in the hash and whether doing so needs the cached working set to be expanded. Moreover, `vm_fault_tws_insert()` returns a Boolean value to its caller indicating whether the page cache files need to be written. If so, `vm_fault()` calls `tws_send_startup_info()` to write the files through an eventual call to `bsd_write_page_cache_file()`. `vm_fault()` may also call `vm_fault_page()` [osfmk/vm/vm_fault.c], which finds the resident page for the virtual memory specified by the given VM object and offset. In turn, `vm_fault_page()` may need to call the appropriate pager to retrieve the data. Before it issues a request to the pager, it calls `tws_build_cluster()` to add up to 64 pages from the working set to the request. This allows a single large request to be made to the pager.

8.15 Memory Allocation in User Space

There are several user-space and kernel-space memory allocation APIs in Mac OS X, although all such APIs are built atop a single low-level mechanism. In the kernel, memory is fundamentally allocated through a page-level allocator in the Mach VM subsystem. In user space, memory is fundamentally allocated through the Mach `vm_allocate()` API,[20] although user programs typically use application-environment-specific APIs for memory allocation. The system library provides `malloc()`, which is the preferred user-space memory allocation function. `malloc()` is implemented using the Mach API. Memory allocation APIs in Carbon and Core Foundation are implemented on top of `malloc()`. Besides malloc-based memory allocation, user programs can also use the stack-based `alloca(3)` memory allocator, which allocates temporary space in the runtime stack. The space is automatically reclaimed when the function returns.[21] The `alloca()` function is built into the C compiler on Mac OS X.

---

20. We will not distinguish between the 32-bit and 64-bit Mach VM APIs in this section.

21. The Mac OS X `alloca()` implementation frees the allocated memory not upon the function's return but during a subsequent invocation of the function.

Table 8–6 shows a sampling of ways in which memory can be allocated by user-space programs. Note that the list shown is not exhaustive—its purpose is to illustrate that a variety of APIs exist. Moreover, in many cases, you can use a function listed under a particular environment in other environments as well.

TABLE 8–6 Notable User-Level Memory Allocation Functions

Environment	Allocation	Deallocation
System library (Mach)	vm_allocate	vm_deallocate
System library	malloc	free
Carbon	NewPtr	DisposePtr
Carbon	NewHandle	DisposeHandle
Carbon Multiprocessing Services	MPAllocateAligned	MPFree
Cocoa	NSAllocateObject	NSDeallocateObject
Cocoa	[NSObject alloc]	[NSObject dealloc]
Core Foundation	CFAllocatorAllocate	CFAllocatorDeallocate
Open Transport	OTAllocInContext	OTFreeMem

8.15.1 A Historical Break

Historically, in UNIX the sbrk() and brk() system calls are used to dynamically change the amount of space allocated for the calling program's data segment. sbrk() is implemented but not supported by the Mac OS X kernel—*directly* invoking the system call will result in an ENOTSUP error being returned. brk() is not even implemented by the kernel. However, the system library implements both sbrk() and brk(). Whereas brk() always returns a value of -1, sbrk() simulates a program break region by using a 4MB memory area that it allocates through vm_allocate() on the first invocation of sbrk(). Subsequent invocations of sbrk() adjust the current break value within the simulated region. If the adjusted size falls outside the region, a value of -1 is returned.

```
// libSystem: mach/sbrk.c

static int          sbrk_needs_init = TRUE;
static vm_size_t    sbrk_region_size = 4*1024*1024;
static vm_address_t sbrk_curbrk;
```

```
caddr_t
sbrk(int size)
{
    kern_return_t ret;

    if (sbrk_needs_init) {
        sbrk_needs_init = FALSE;

        ret = vm_allocate(mach_task_self(), &sbrk_curbrk, sbrk_region_size,
                          VM_MAKE_TAG(VM_MEMORY_SBRK)|TRUE);
        ...
    }

    if (size <= 0)
        return((caddr_t)sbrk_curbrk);
    else if (size > sbrk_region_size)
        return((caddr_t)-1);
    sbrk_curbrk += size;
    sbrk_region_size -= size;
    return((caddr_t)(sbrk_curbrk - size));
}
```

Note the use of the `VM_MAKE_TAG` macro by `sbrk()`. The macro can be used to tag any `vm_allocate()` allocation, thereby indicating the purpose of that allocation. The available tag values are defined in `<mach/vm_statistics.h>`. Besides system-reserved tags, there are tags available that user programs can use for tagging application-specific allocations. The `vmmap` tool displays memory regions in a program along with the region types. For example, running `vmmap` with the process ID of the `WindowServer` program produces an output like the following.

```
$ sudo vmmap 71
...
REGION TYPE            [ VIRTUAL]
===========            [ =======]
Carbon                 [   4080K]
CoreGraphics           [ 271960K]
IOKit                  [ 139880K]
MALLOC                 [  46776K]
STACK GUARD            [     8K]
Stack                  [   9216K]
VM_ALLOCATE ?          [   7724K]
...
```

In a program that has called `sbrk()`, the 4MB region can be seen in the output of the `vmmap` command as a writable region labeled `SBRK`.

```
// sbrk.c

#include <stdio.h>
#include <stdlib.h>
#include <unistd.h>

int
main(void)
{
    char cmdbuf[32];
    sbrk(0);
    snprintf(cmdbuf, 32, "vmmap %d", getpid());
    return system(cmdbuf);
}
```

```
$ gcc -Wall -o sbrk sbrk.c
$ ./sbrk
...
SBRK                      [    4096K]
...
```

8.15.2 Memory Allocator Internals

The Mac OS X system library's malloc implementation uses an abstraction called a *malloc zone* (unrelated to the Mach zone allocator). Malloc zones are variable-size blocks of virtual memory from which malloc draws memory for its allocations. The system library creates a default malloc zone when the malloc package is initialized in a program, which occurs when the zone is accessed for the first time (e.g., during the program's first call to `malloc()` or `calloc()`).

A zone is analogous to a UNIX program's heap from the standpoint of memory allocation. The malloc implementation supports the creation of multiple zones. Although creating your own malloc zones is typically unnecessary, it may be useful in certain circumstances. Destroying a zone[22] frees all objects allocated from that zone; therefore, using a custom zone may improve performance if a large number of temporary objects need to be deallocated. Figure 8–29 shows the API exported by the malloc zone layer.

---

22. The default zone should not be destroyed.

FIGURE 8–29 The malloc zones API

```
// Retrieve a pointer to the default zone
malloc_zone_t *malloc_default_zone(void);

// Create a new malloc zone
malloc_zone_t *malloc_create_zone(vm_size_t start_size, unsigned flags);

// Destroy an existing zone, freeing everything allocated from that zone
void malloc_destroy_zone(malloc_zone_t *zone);

// Allocate memory from the given zone
void *malloc_zone_malloc(malloc_zone_t *zone, size_t size);

// Allocate cleared (zero-filled) memory from the given zone for num_items
// objects, each of which is size bytes large
void *malloc_zone_calloc(malloc_zone_t *zone, size_t num_items, size_t size);

// Allocate page-aligned, cleared (zero-filled) memory from the given zone
void *malloc_zone_valloc(malloc_zone_t *zone, size_t size);

// Free memory referred to by the given pointer in the given zone
void malloc_zone_free(malloc_zone_t *zone, void *ptr);

// Change the size of an existing allocation in the given zone
// The "existing" pointer can be NULL
void *malloc_zone_realloc(malloc_zone_t *zone, void *ptr, size_t size);

// Retrieve the zone, if any, corresponding to the given pointer
malloc_zone_t *malloc_zone_from_ptr(const void *ptr);

// Retrieve the actual size of the allocation corresponding to the given pointer
size_t malloc_size(const void *ptr);

// Batch Allocation
// Allocate num_requested blocks of memory, each size bytes, from the given zone
// The return value is the number of blocks being returned (could be less than
// num_requested, including zero if none could be allocated)
unsigned malloc_zone_batch_malloc(malloc_zone_t *zone, size_t size,
                                  void **results, unsigned num_requested);

// Batch Deallocation
// Free num allocations referred to in the to_be_freed array of pointers
void malloc_zone_batch_free(malloc_zone_t *zone, void **to_be_freed,
                            unsigned num);
```

Malloc Zones in Cocoa

The Cocoa API provides wrappers for several `malloc_zone_*` functions. For example, `NSCreateZone()` and `NSRecycleZone()` can be used to create and destroy, respectively, malloc zones. A malloc zone exists in Cocoa as an `NSZone` structure.

The `NSObject` class provides the `allocateWithZone:` method to create an instance of the receiving class with memory allocated from the specified zone.

The actual zone allocator is implemented in an independent module—separate from the malloc layer that consists of the programmer-visible malloc family of functions. The malloc layer uses well-defined functions exported by the zone layer, and in fact, the malloc front-end can support an alternate underlying allocator or even multiple allocators. Figure 8–30 shows an overview of the communication between the malloc layer and the zone allocator. The latter is called the *scalable zone allocator* because it uses allocation strategies that scale from very small to very large allocation sizes.

In the malloc layer, a malloc zone is represented by the `malloc_zone_t` structure, which is a substructure of the `szone_t` structure. The latter is visible only to the scalable zone layer. The malloc layer provides the `malloc_create_zone` function for creating zones. This function calls `create_scalable_zone()`, which creates a new scalable zone by allocating and initializing an `szone_t` structure. As part of this initialization, the scalable malloc layer populates the `malloc_zone_t` substructure, a pointer to which is returned to the malloc layer. Before returning, `malloc_create_zone()` calls `malloc_zone_register()`, which saves the `malloc_zone_t` pointer in a global array of malloc zones. Note that although the malloc layer directly calls `create_scalable_zone()`, it calls the other scalable zone functions only through the function pointers set up in the `malloc_zone_t` structure. As shown in Figure 8–30, the scalable zone layer provides standard malloc family functions, batch allocation and deallocation functions, and functions for introspection.

The scalable zone allocator categorizes memory allocation requests based on size into *tiny*, *small*, *large*, and *huge* requests. As shown in Figure 8–31, it maintains internal bookkeeping data structures for each of these categories. Tiny and small allocations are made from tiny and small regions, respectively. We earlier said that a zone is analogous to a program's heap. A specific tiny or small region can be regarded as a bounded subheap from which allocations falling within a certain size range are made.

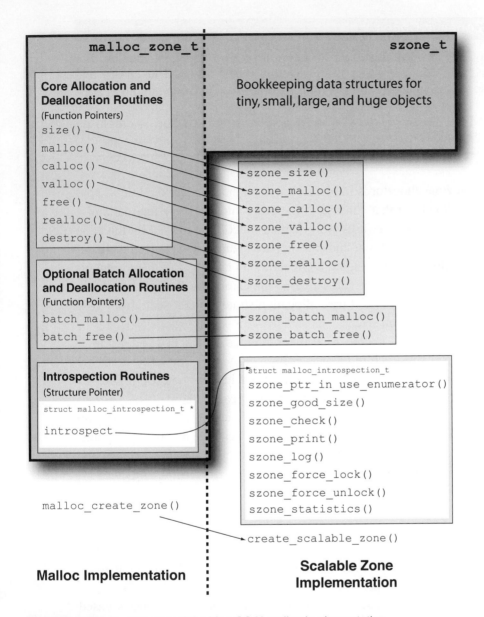

FIGURE 8–30 An overview of the Mac OS X malloc implementation

---

FIGURE 8–31 Scalable zone data structures

```
#define NUM_TINY_SLOTS           32
#define INITIAL_NUM_TINY_REGIONS  24
#define NUM_SMALL_SLOTS          32
#define INITIAL_NUM_SMALL_REGIONS 6
...

typedef struct {
    uintptr_t checksum;
    void      *previous;
    void      *next;
} free_list_t;

typedef struct {
    // Data structure for "compact" (small) pointers
    // Low bits represent number of pages, high bits represent address
    uintptr_t address_and_num_pages;
} compact_range_t;

typedef struct {
    vm_address_t address;
    vm_size_t    size;
} vm_range_t;

typedef void            *tiny_region_t;
typedef void            *small_region_t;
typedef compact_range_t large_entry_t;
typedef vm_range_t      huge_entry_t;

typedef struct {
    malloc_zone_t basic_zone; // This substructure is seen by the malloc layer
    ...

    // Regions for tiny objects
    unsigned        num_tiny_regions;
    tiny_region_t   *tiny_regions;
    void            *last_tiny_free;
    unsigned        tiny_bitmap; // Cache of the free lists
    free_list_t     *tiny_free_list[NUM_TINY_SLOTS]; // Free lists
    ...

    // Regions for small objects
    unsigned        num_small_regions;
    small_region_t  *small_regions;
    ...
    // Large objects
    unsigned        num_large_entries;
    large_entry_t   *large_entries; // Hashed by location
```

(continues)

FIGURE 8–31 Scalable zone data structures *(continued)*

```
// Huge objects
unsigned      num_huge_entries;
huge_entry_t  *huge_entries;
...

// Initial region list
tiny_region_t  initial_tiny_regions[INITIAL_NUM_TINY_REGIONS];
small_region_t initial_small_regions[INITIAL_NUM_SMALL_REGIONS];
} szone_t;
```

Table 8–7 shows the size ranges and the corresponding allocation quanta for the categories in the case of the 32-bit system library. Table 8–8 shows the numbers for the 64-bit version.

TABLE 8–7 Scalable Malloc Allocation Categories (32-bit)

Allocation Region	Region Size	Allocation Sizes	Allocation Quantum
Tiny	1MB	1–496 bytes	16 bytes
Small	8MB	497–15,359 bytes	512 bytes
Large	—	15,360–16,773,120 bytes	1 page (4096 bytes)
Huge	—	16,773,121 bytes and more	1 page (4096 bytes)

TABLE 8–8 Scalable Malloc Allocation Categories (64-bit)

Allocation Region	Region Size	Allocation Sizes	Allocation Quantum
Tiny	2MB	1–992 bytes	32 bytes
Small	16MB	993–15,359 bytes	1024 bytes
Large	—	15,360–16,773,120 bytes	1 page (4096 bytes)
Huge	—	16,773,121 bytes and more	1 page (4096 bytes)

The following are some noteworthy points about scalable malloc's allocation strategies.

- The maximum allocation size for a tiny request is 31 times the tiny allocation quantum—that is, 31×16 and 31×32 bytes for 32-bit and 64-bit, respectively.

- The minimum allocation size for a large request is 15×1024 bytes.
- The maximum allocation size for a large request is 4095 pages.
- Tiny requests are satisfied from tiny regions. Each such region is akin to a heap whose size is 1MB (32-bit) or 2MB (64-bit). Similarly, memory in the small range is allocated from small regions, each of which is akin to an 8MB heap.

Let us now look at the details of the individual strategies.

8.15.2.1 Tiny Allocations

Tiny allocations are made from *tiny regions*. The allocator divides a tiny region into equal-size pieces called *tiny quanta*. Each tiny quantum is TINY_QUANTUM bytes in size.

> TINY_QUANTUM is the minimum allocation size, regardless of the actual amount requested by the caller. For example, the amounts of memory actually allocated to satisfy allocation requests of one byte, TINY_QUANTUM bytes, and (TINY_QUANTUM+1) bytes are TINY_QUAN-TUM bytes, TINY_QUANTUM bytes, and 2×TINY_QUANTUM bytes, respectively.

The tiny region is laid out as a contiguous chunk of memory containing NUM_TINY_BLOCKS quanta. Immediately following the last quantum is a metadata area that has the following structure.

- At the beginning of the metadata is a *header bitmap* that contains one bit for each quantum in the tiny region. Thus, it contains NUM_TINY_BLOCKS bits.
- Following the header bitmap is a 32-bit pad word all of whose bits are set—that is, its value is 0xFFFF_FFFF.
- Following the pad word is an *in-use bitmap*. Like the header bitmap, this bitmap contains NUM_TINY_BLOCKS bits, one for each tiny quantum.
- Following the in-use bitmap is a 32-bit pad word that is not written to by the allocator.

Even though a tiny quantum's size is fixed, a tiny allocation can range from as small as 1 byte to as large as 31×TINY_QUANTUM. Allocations larger than a quantum will consist of multiple contiguous quanta. A set of such contiguous tiny quanta, whether allocated or free, is called a *tiny block*. The header and in-use bit-maps are used to maintain the notions of free and allocated blocks as follows.

- If a given quantum is the first quantum of a block in use, the corresponding bits in both the header bitmap and the in-use bitmap are 1.
- If a given quantum is part of a block in use (but is not the first quantum of that block), the corresponding bit in the header bitmap is 0, whereas the corresponding bit in the in-use bitmap is irrelevant.
- If a given quantum is the first quantum of a free block, the corresponding bits in the header and in-use bitmaps are 1 and 0, respectively.
- If a given quantum is part of a free block (but is not the first quantum of that block), the corresponding bits in both the header bitmap and the in-use bitmap are irrelevant.

When a pointer is freed, the corresponding block's header and in-use bits are appropriately modified. Moreover, information is written to the first few bytes of the pointed-to memory to convert that block into a free block. Free blocks are chained together in free lists. The allocator maintains 32 free lists for tiny region memory. Each list contains free blocks containing a particular number of quanta—the first list contains free blocks that are all one quantum in size, the second list contains free blocks that are all two quanta in size, and so on. Although the maximum allocation size contains 31 quanta, it is possible to have free blocks that are larger, since adjacent blocks can be coalesced. The last list holds these extra-large free blocks.

The structure of a free block is as follows:

- The first pointer-sized field contains a checksum computed by XOR'ing the free block's previous pointer, next pointer, and the constant CHECKSUM_ MAGIC (defined to be 0x357B).
- The next pointer-sized field contains a pointer to the previous free block, if any, in the chain. If there is no previous free block, this field contains a 0.
- The next pointer-sized field contains a pointer to the next free block, if any, in the chain. Again, the field is 0 if there is no next free block.
- The next field is an unsigned short value that specifies the free block's size in units of quanta.

Consider the free and allocated blocks shown in Figure 8–32. The free block starting at quantum q_i contains m quanta, whereas the allocated block starting at

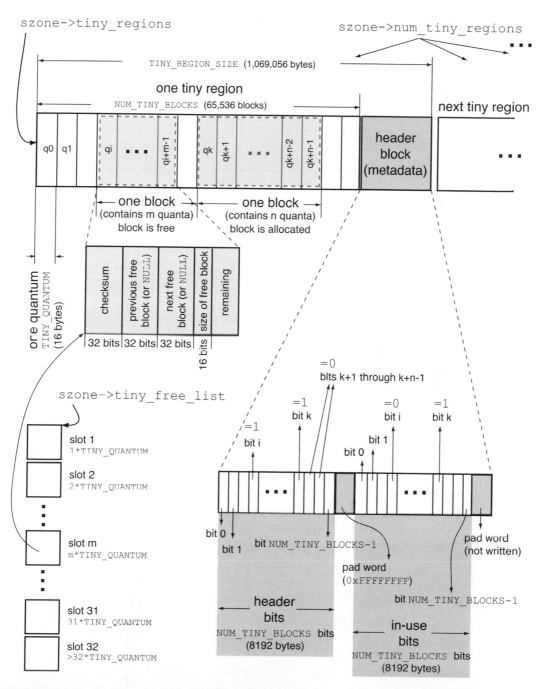

FIGURE 8–32 Internal bookkeeping of tiny allocations (32-bit)

quantum q_k contains n quanta. Bits i and k are both set in the header bitmap. However, only bit k is set in the in-use block.

Let us examine the working of the allocator by using the debugger on a simple program. Figure 8–33 shows a program that performs four tiny allocations. We will examine the allocator's state immediately after performing these allocations. Next, we will free the pointers and examine the state again. We will use a debugger watchpoint to stop execution of the program at the desired locations.

FIGURE 8–33 A program that performs tiny allocations

```
// test_malloc.c (32-bit)

#include <stdlib.h>

int watch = -1;

int
main(void)
{
    void *ptr1, *ptr2, *ptr3, *ptr4;

    ptr1 = malloc(490);  // 31 TINY_QUANTUMs
    ptr2 = malloc(491);  // 31 TINY_QUANTUMs
    ptr3 = malloc(492);  // 31 TINY_QUANTUMs
    ptr4 = malloc(493);  // 31 TINY_QUANTUMs
    watch = 1;           // breakpoint here

    free(ptr1);
    free(ptr3);
    watch = 2;           // breakpoint here

    free(ptr2);
    free(ptr4);
    watch = 3;           // breakpoint here

    return 0;
}
```

To examine the tiny region's metadata area, we first need to determine the area's base address. Given a pointer known to be allocated from a tiny region, we can determine the base address of that tiny region since the region is always aligned on a boundary defined by the product of NUM_TINY_BLOCKS and TINY_QUANTUM—that is, the total allocatable size of the tiny region. The allocator ensures this alignment when it allocates memory for the tiny region itself. Therefore, given a tiny region pointer p, the following formula will give us the tiny region's base address:

```
TINY_REGION_FOR_PTR(p) = p & ~((NUM_TINY_BLOCKS * TINY_QUANTUM) - 1)
```

Since we are dealing with a 32-bit program, we must use the 32-bit-specific values of `NUM_TINY_BLOCKS` and `TINY_QUANTUM`. As shown in Figure 8–32, these values are 65,536 and 16, respectively. Using these values, the product is calculated to be `0x100000`. Our formula then reduces to the following:

```
TINY_REGION_FOR_PTR(p) = p & 0xFFF00000
```

Given the tiny region's base address, we can readily compute the metadata area's base address, since the metadata area immediately follows the last tiny quantum. This means that the metadata area starts (`NUM_TINY_BLOCKS * TINY_QUANTUM`) bytes from the tiny region's base address, which gives us the following formula for the metadata area's base address:

```
TINY_REGION_END(p) = (p & 0xFFF00000) + 0x100000
```

The metadata area's base address is where the header bitmap is located. The location of the in-use bitmap can be calculated by adding `NUM_TINY_BLOCKS/8` bytes (the size of the header bitmap) and a further 4 bytes (the size of the pad word). We finally have the following expressions:

```
HEADER_BITMAP_32(p) = (p & 0xFFF00000) + 0x100000
INUSE_BITMAP_32(p)  = HEADER_BITMAP_32(p) + 0x2004
```

Now that we know how to calculate the addresses we wish to look at, let us compile and run the program shown in Figure 8–33.

```
$ gcc -Wall -g -o test_malloc test_malloc.c
$ gdb ./test_malloc
...
(gdb) watch watch
Hardware watchpoint 1: watch
(gdb) run
Starting program: /private/tmp/test_malloc
Reading symbols for shared libraries . done
Hardware watchpoint 1: watch

Old value = -1
New value = 1
main () at test_malloc.c:18
18              free(ptr1);
```

```
(gdb) where full
#0  main () at test_malloc.c:18
        ptr1 = (void *) 0x300120
        ptr2 = (void *) 0x300310
        ptr3 = (void *) 0x300500
        ptr4 = (void *) 0x3006f0
(gdb)
```

When the first watchpoint is hit, our program has performed the four tiny allocations. Given the pointer values and the formulas devised earlier, we see that for all four pointers, the tiny region's base address is 0x300000, the header bitmap is at address 0x400000, and the in-use bitmap is at address 0x400000+0x2004. Thus, the pointers are 0x120, 0x310, 0x500, and 0x6f0 bytes away, respectively, from the base address. We can divide these distances by TINY_QUANTUM—that is, 16—to get the starting quantum number for each pointer. The starting quanta are 18, 49, 80, and 111, with the first quantum being numbered 0. If we call the first bit in a bitmap as bit 0, we should examine bits 18, 49, 80, and 111 in both the header and in-use bitmaps.

```
(gdb) x/4x 0x400000
0x400000:       0x25920400      0x00000200      0x00000100      0x00800000
(gdb) x/4x 0x400000+0x2004
0x402004:       0x25920400      0x00000200      0x00000100      0x00800000
```

Indeed, each of the four bits is set in both the bitmaps. Note that while accessing a bit, the allocator first locates the byte that contains the bit. The leftmost byte is byte 0, the next byte to the right is byte 1, and so on. Within a byte, the lowest numbered bit is the rightmost one.

Let us continue the program, which will cause ptr1 and ptr3 to be freed before the next watchpoint is hit.

```
(gdb) cont
Continuing.
Hardware watchpoint 1: watch

Old value = 1
New value = 2
main () at test_malloc.c:22
22          free(ptr2);
```

At this point, we expect the header bitmap to remain unchanged, but bits 18 and 80—corresponding to ptr1 and ptr3—should have been cleared in the in-use bitmap.

```
(gdb) x/4x 0x400000
0x400000:        0x25920400     0x00000200     0x00000100     0x00800000
(gdb) x/4x 0x400000+0x2004
0x402004:        0x25920000     0x00000200     0x00000000     0x00800000
```

Moreover, the memory contents of `ptr1` and `ptr3` should have been populated to convert the corresponding blocks to free blocks.

```
(gdb) x/4x ptr1
0x300120:        0x0030307b     0x00300500     0x00000000     0x001f0000
(gdb) x/4x ptr3
0x300500:        0x0030345b     0x00000000     0x00300120     0x001f0000
```

Recall that the free block begins with a checksum, which is followed by pointers to previous and next free blocks, with a trailing unsigned short value specifying the size of the block in units of quanta. We see that the freed blocks are chained on the same free list—`ptr1`'s previous pointer points to `ptr3`, whereas `ptr3`'s next pointer points to `ptr1`. This is expected, as both blocks have the same number of quanta (0x1f, or 31). Moreover, we can verify that the two checksums are correct by XOR'ing the relevant pointers with the magic number we saw earlier (0x357B).

Let us continue the program again, which will free `ptr2` and `ptr4` before the next watchpoint is hit.

```
(gdb) cont
Continuing.
Hardware watchpoint 1: watch

Old value = 2
New value = 3
main () at test_malloc.c:26
26              return 0;
(gdb) x/4x 0x400000
0x400000:        0x25920400     0x00000200     0x00000000     0x00800000
(gdb) x/4x 0x400000+0x2004
0x402004:        0x25920000     0x00000200     0x00000000     0x00800000
(gdb) x/4x ptr2
0x300310:        0x00000000     0x00000000     0x00000000     0x00000000
(gdb) x/4x ptr4
0x3006f0:        0x00000000     0x00000000     0x00000000     0x00000000
(gdb)
```

We see that although `ptr2` and `ptr4` have been freed, the corresponding bits in both the header and in-use bitmaps are unchanged. Moreover, there is no free block information in the contents of `ptr2` and `ptr4`. This is so because the allocator has coalesced the four adjacent free blocks into a single big free block starting at `ptr1`. Examining `ptr1`'s contents should confirm this.

```
(gdb) x/4x ptr1
0x300120:        0x0000357b       0x00000000       0x00000000       0x007c0000
```

The free block at `ptr1` is now the only block on its free list, as both its previous and next pointers contain zeros. Moreover, the number of quanta in this free block is `0x7c` (124), which is as expected.

8.15.2.2 Small Allocations

Small allocations are handled in a manner conceptually similar to tiny allocations. Figure 8–34 shows the key data structures involved in small allocations. Besides the larger quantum size of a small region, the metadata area following the region is structured differently from the tiny region metadata area: Instead of the header and in-use bitmaps, the small region metadata area is an array of 16-bit quantities. The ith element of this array provides two pieces of information about the ith quantum in the small region. If the most significant bit of the array element is set, the corresponding quantum is the first quantum of a free block. The remaining 15 bits, which are nonzero only in a first quantum (whether of a free block or an allocated block), represent the number of quanta contained in the block. Like the set of tiny free lists, there are 32 small free lists, each of which is used for referring to free objects of the corresponding quantum size.

8.15.2.3 Large Allocations

Large allocations are described by `large_entry_t` structures. As shown in Figure 8–31, a `large_entry_t` structure is an alias for a `compact_range_t`, which contains a single field called `address_and_num_pages` that represents both an address (high bits) and the number of pages allocated at that address (low bits). Since the maximum large allocation is 4095 pages, the low 12 bits are used to specify the number of pages. Large allocations are performed through `vm_allocate()`, which always returns a page-aligned address—that is, the low 12 bits of the address are always zero. Therefore, it can be OR'ed with the number of pages to yield `address_and_num_pages` with no loss of information. The allocator tracks large entries by hashing their addresses in a table referenced by the `large_entries` field of the `szone_t` structure. An entry's hash index is its address modulo the total number of entries. If there is a hash collision, the index

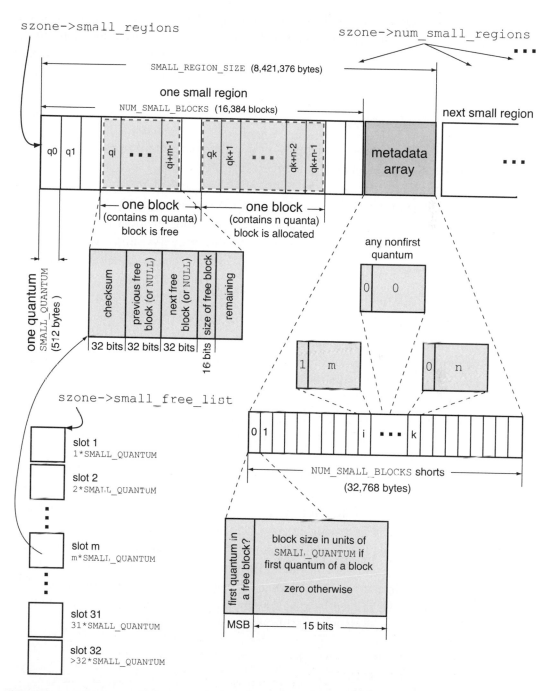

FIGURE 8–34 Internal bookkeeping of small malloc allocations (32-bit)

is incremented by one, and so on—when the index becomes equal to the size of the table, it wraps around to zero. If the number of large allocations in use becomes higher than approximately 25% of the number of entries in the hash table, the table's density is deemed too high, and the allocator grows the hash table.

8.15.2.4 Huge Allocations

Huge allocations have a relatively simpler bookkeeping. For each huge allocation, the allocator maintains a huge_entry_t structure. These structures are kept in the array referenced by the huge_entries field of the szone_t structure. Upon a huge entry allocation, which is performed through vm_allocate(), the allocator grows this array by internally allocating memory, copying the old entries to the grown array, and freeing the old array. As shown in Figure 8–31, huge_entry_t is an alias for vm_range_t, which contains an address and a size.

8.15.3 The `malloc()` Routine

The various malloc API functions, such as malloc() and free(), are simple wrappers around internal functions that in turn call the scalable zone functions through the function pointers in the malloc_zone_t structure corresponding to the default zone. To use any other zone than the default, the malloc_zone_* functions from Figure 8–29 must be used directly.

Figure 8–35 shows the processing of the malloc() library function, which simply calls malloc_zone_malloc(), with the return value from inline_malloc_default_zone() being the zone to allocate from. The inline function checks the value of the global variable malloc_num_zones to determine whether it is being called for the first time. If so, it first initializes the malloc package by creating a scalable zone, which will be used as the default malloc zone. It calls malloc_create_zone(), which first checks for the presence of several environment variables that affect malloc's behavior. These variables are documented in the malloc(3) manual page, and a summary of the available variables can be printed by running any program that uses malloc() with the MallocHelp environment variable set.

```
$ MallocHelp=1 /usr/bin/true
(10067) malloc: environment variables that can be set for debug:
- MallocLogFile <f> to create/append messages to file <f> instead of stderr
- MallocGuardEdges to add 2 guard pages for each large block
- MallocDoNotProtectPrelude to disable protection (when previous flag set)
- MallocDoNotProtectPostlude to disable protection (when previous flag set)
```

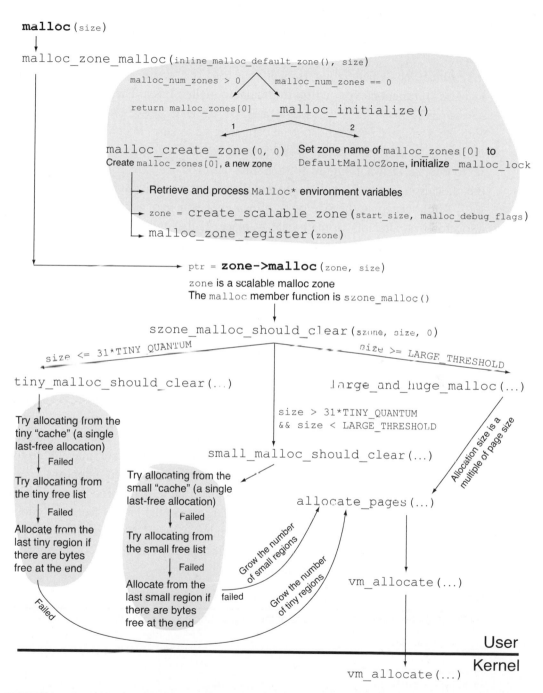

FIGURE 8–35 Processing of the `malloc()` function in the system library

```
...
- MallocBadFreeAbort <b> to abort on a bad free if <b> is non-zero
- MallocHelp - this help!
```

Once the default zone is available, `malloc_zone_malloc()` calls the `malloc()` function exported by the scalable malloc layer. The latter function—`szone_malloc()`—calls the `szone_malloc_should_clear()` internal function with the `cleared_request` Boolean parameter set to false. In contrast, the `szone_calloc()` function calls `szone_malloc_should_clear()` with `cleared_request` set to true. As shown in Figure 8–35, `szone_malloc_should_clear()` classifies the allocation request based on size and dispatches it to the appropriate handler.

While changing the size of an allocation because of a `realloc()` call, the allocator first attempts to reallocate in place. If that fails, a new buffer is allocated, into which the allocator copies the contents of the old buffer. If the old buffer had at least `VM_COPY_THRESHOLD` bytes (defined to be 40KB) of memory, the allocator uses `vm_copy()` for copying. If the old buffer had less memory, or if `vm_copy()` fails, the allocator uses `memcpy()`.

8.15.4 The Largest Single Allocation (32-bit)

Depending on a program's needs, it may be affected by the most amount of contiguous memory it can allocate. Given the size of a 64-bit virtual address space, a 64-bit program is highly unlikely to face this issue. However, a 32-bit address space is limited to 4GB of virtual memory, not all of which is available to the program. As we saw in Table 8–4, several virtual address ranges are unavailable for the program's use as the system uses these ranges for predefined mappings.

The program shown in Figure 8–36 can be used to determine the maximum size of a single allocation, which can be no larger than the largest free contiguous virtual address range. Note that the exact number is likely to differ across operating system versions and even across specific installations of the same version, although the difference may not be great.

FIGURE 8–36 Determining the size of the largest single `malloc()` allocation

```
// large_malloc.c

#include <stdio.h>
#include <stdlib.h>
#include <limits.h>
#include <mach/mach.h>
```

(continues)

FIGURE 8–36 Determining the size of the largest single `malloc()` allocation *(continued)*

```
#define PROGNAME "large_malloc"

int
main(int argc, char **argv)
{
    void *ptr;
    unsigned long long npages;

    if (argc != 2) {
        fprintf(stderr, "usage: %s <allocation size in pages>\n", PROGNAME);
        exit(1);
    }

    if ((npages = strtoull(argv[1], NULL, 10)) == ULLONG_MAX) {
        perror("strtoull");
        exit(1);
    }

    if ((ptr = malloc((size_t)(npages << vm_page_shift))) == NULL)
        perror("malloc");
    else
        free(ptr);

    exit(0);
}


$ gcc -Wall -o large_malloc large_malloc.c
$ ./large_malloc 577016
$ ./large_malloc 577017
large_malloc(786) malloc: *** vm_allocate(size=2363461632) failed (error code=3)
large_malloc(786) malloc: *** error: can't allocate region
large_malloc(786) malloc: *** set a breakpoint in szone_error to debug
malloc: Cannot allocate memory
```

As the output in Figure 8–36 shows, *on this particular system,* at the instant the program was run, a contiguous allocation is limited to 577,016 pages, or 2,363,457,536 bytes (approximately 2.2GB). Note that there still exist other, smaller free virtual address ranges, so the program could allocate a sum total that may be considerably larger than the single largest allocation. For example, on the system shown in Figure 8–36, allocating another 1GB (approximately) of memory through `malloc()` succeeds, after which several much smaller allocations can still be made before the process's virtual address space is exhausted.

8.15.5 The Largest Single Allocation (64-bit)

Let us see how much virtual memory we can allocate using mach_vm_allocate()
in a 64-bit task. Figure 8–37 shows a program that attempts to allocate the
amount of memory given as a command-line argument.

FIGURE 8–37 Allocating 2 petabytes of virtual memory

```c
// max_vm_allocate.c

#include <stdio.h>
#include <stdlib.h>
#include <limits.h>
#include <mach/mach.h>
#include <mach/mach_vm.h>

#define PROGNAME "max_vm_allocate"

int
main(int argc, char **argv)
{
    kern_return_t       kr;
    unsigned long long nbytes;
    mach_vm_address_t   address;

    if (argc != 2) {
        fprintf(stderr, "usage: %s <number of bytes>\n", PROGNAME);
        exit(1);
    }

    if ((nbytes = strtoull(argv[1], NULL, 10)) == ULLONG_MAX) {
        fprintf(stderr, "invalid number of bytes specified\n");
        exit(1);
    }

    kr = mach_vm_allocate(mach_task_self(), &address,
                        (mach_vm_size_t)nbytes, TRUE);
    if (kr == KERN_SUCCESS) {
        printf("allocated %llu bytes at %p\n", nbytes, (void *)address);
        mach_vm_deallocate(mach_task_self(), address, (mach_vm_size_t)nbytes);
    } else
        mach_error("mach_vm_allocate:", kr);

    exit(0);
}
```

(continues)

FIGURE 8–37 Allocating 2 petabytes of virtual memory *(continued)*

```
$ gcc -arch ppc64 -Wall -o max_vm_allocate max_vm_allocate.c
$ ./max_vm_allocate 2251793095786496
allocated 2251793095831552 bytes at 0x8feb0000
$ ./max_vm_allocate 2251793095786497
mach_vm_allocate: (os/kern) no space available
```

8.15.6 Enumerating All Pointers

The scalable zone implementation provides several functions for debugging and analysis. The malloc layer exports some of this functionality to user programs through functions such as malloc_zone_from_ptr(), malloc_zone_get_all_zones(), malloc_zone_print(), malloc_zone_print_ptr_info(), malloc_zone_statistics(), and malloc_zone_log(). Moreover, those scalable zone functions that have function pointers in the malloc_zone_t structure or the szone_t structure can also be called by a user program, although doing so would be a layering violation since the szone_t structure is meant to be opaque in the malloc layer.

Note that we cannot use printf(3) in our program since printf()'s implementation itself uses malloc(). We will use a custom printf()-like function—let us call it nomalloc_printf()—that does not use printf() and in turn does not use malloc(). Figure 8–38 shows the implementation of nomalloc_printf(). We will also use this function in other examples that follow.

FIGURE 8–38 Implementing a version of the printf() function without using malloc()

```
// nomalloc_printf.h

#ifndef _NOMALLOC_PRINTF_H
#define _NOMALLOC_PRINTF_H

#include <stdarg.h>

extern void _simple_vdprintf(int, const char *, va_list);

inline void
nomalloc_printf(const char *format, ...)
{
    va_list ap;
```

(continues)

FIGURE 8–38 Implementing a version of the `printf()` function without using `malloc()` *(continued)*

```
    va_start(ap, format);
    _simple_vdprintf(STDOUT_FILENO, format, ap);
    va_end(ap);
}

#endif
```

The program shown in Figure 8–39 calls a pointer enumeration function implemented by the scalable zone layer. The function is available to the malloc layer through the `enumerator` field of the `malloc_introspection_t` substructure within the `malloc_zone_t` structure. One of the arguments to the function is a pointer to a *recorder function*—a callback invoked for each allocated range encountered. The function also accepts a type mask that limits the enumeration to specific types of memory.

FIGURE 8–39 Enumerating all `malloc()`-allocated pointers in a program

```
// malloc_enumerate.c

#include <stdio.h>
#include <stdlib.h>
#include <unistd.h>
#include <limits.h>
#include <malloc/malloc.h>
#include <mach/mach.h>
#include "nomalloc_printf.h"

struct recorder_args {
    const char *label;
    unsigned type_mask;
} recorder_args[] = {
    { "Allocated pointers\n",            MALLOC_PTR_IN_USE_RANGE_TYPE    },
    { "\nRegions containing pointers\n", MALLOC_PTR_REGION_RANGE_TYPE    },
    { "\nInternal regions\n",            MALLOC_ADMIN_REGION_RANGE_TYPE },
};

void
my_vm_range_recorder(task_t task, void *context, unsigned type_mask,
                     vm_range_t *ranges, unsigned range_count)
{
    vm_range_t *r, *end;
```

(continues)

FIGURE 8–39 Enumerating all `malloc()`-allocated pointers in a program *(continued)*

```
    for (r = ranges, end = ranges + range_count; r < end; r++)
        nomalloc_printf("%16p    %u\n", r->address, r->size);
}

int
main(int argc, char **argv)
{
    int                 i;
    void                *ptr = NULL;
    unsigned long long  size;
    malloc_zone_t       *zone;

    if (!(zone = malloc_default_zone()))
        exit(1);

    if (argc == 2) { // allocate the requested size
        if ((size = strtoull(argv[1], NULL, 10)) == ULLONG_MAX) {
            fprintf(stderr, "invalid allocation size (%s)\n", argv[1]);
            exit(1);
        }

        if ((ptr = malloc((size_t)size)) == NULL) {
            perror("malloc");
            exit(1);
        }
    }

    for (i = 0; i < sizeof(recorder_args)/sizeof(struct recorder_args); i++) {
        nomalloc_printf("%s        address   bytes\n", recorder_args[i].label);
        zone->introspect->enumerator(mach_task_self(),         // task
                                     NULL,                     // context
                                     recorder_args[i].type_mask, // type
                                     (vm_address_t)zone,
                                     NULL,                     // reader
                                     my_vm_range_recorder);    // recorder
    }

    exit(0);
}


$ gcc -Wall -o malloc_enumerate malloc_enumerate.c
$ ./malloc_enumerate 8192
Allocated pointers
        address   bytes
        0x300000  32
        0x300020  48
```

(continues)

FIGURE 8–39 Enumerating all `malloc()`-allocated pointers in a program *(continued)*

```
        0x300050    64
        0x300090    48
        0x3000c0    48
        0x3000f0    48
        0x1800000   1024
        0x1800400   8192

Regions containing pointers
        address     bytes
        0x300000    1048576
        0x1800000   8388608

Internal regions
        address     bytes
        0x400000    20480
        0x300000    1048576
        0x2000000   32768
        0x1800000   8388608
```

8.15.7 Displaying Scalable Zone Statistics

The program shown in Figure 8–40 retrieves and displays statistics on the various types of malloc regions. In particular, you can use this program to see how the allocator classifies an allocation request as tiny, small, large, or huge based on the request's size.

FIGURE 8–40 Displaying scalable-zone statistics

```c
// scalable_zone_statistics.c

#include <stdio.h>
#include <stdlib.h>
#include <unistd.h>
#include <limits.h>
#include <malloc/malloc.h>
#include "nomalloc_printf.h"

#define PROGNAME "scalable_zone_statistics"

enum { TINY_REGION, SMALL_REGION, LARGE_REGION, HUGE_REGION };

extern boolean_t scalable_zone_statistics(malloc_zone_t *,
                                          malloc_statistics_t *, unsigned);
```

(continues)

FIGURE 8–40 Displaying scalable-zone statistics *(continued)*

```c
void
print_statistics(const char *label, malloc_statistics_t *stats)
{
    nomalloc_printf("%8s%16u%16lu%16lu", label, stats->blocks_in_use,
                    stats->size_in_use, stats->max_size_in_use);
    if (stats->size_allocated != -1)
        nomalloc_printf("%16lu\n", stats->size_allocated);
    else
        printf("%16s\n", "-");
}


int
main(int argc, char **argv)
{
    void                *ptr = NULL;
    unsigned long long   size;
    malloc_statistics_t  stats;
    malloc_zone_t       *zone;

    if (!(zone = malloc_default_zone()))
        exit(1);

    if (argc == 2) {
        if ((size = strtoull(argv[1], NULL, 10)) == ULLONG_MAX) {
            fprintf(stderr, "invalid allocation size (%s)\n", argv[1]);
            exit(1);
        }

        if ((ptr = malloc((size_t)size)) == NULL) {
            perror("malloc");
            exit(1);
        }
    }

    nomalloc_printf("%8s%16s%16s%16s%16s\n", "Region", "Blocks in use",
                    "Size in use", "Max size in use", "Size allocated");
    scalable_zone_statistics(zone, &stats, TINY_REGION);
    print_statistics("tiny", &stats);
    scalable_zone_statistics(zone, &stats, SMALL_REGION);
    print_statistics("small", &stats);
    scalable_zone_statistics(zone, &stats, LARGE_REGION);
    stats.size_allocated = -1;
    print_statistics("large", &stats);
    scalable_zone_statistics(zone, &stats, HUGE_REGION);
    stats.size_allocated = -1;
    print_statistics("huge", &stats);
```

(continues)

FIGURE 8–40 Displaying scalable-zone statistics *(continued)*

```
    if (ptr)
        free(ptr);

    exit(0);
}
```

```
$ gcc -Wall -o scalable_zone_statistics scalable_zone_statistics.c
$ ./scalable_zone_statistics 496
  Region   Blocks in use    Size in use Max size in use  Size allocated
    tiny              7             784           21264         1069056
    small             1               0           33792         8421376
    large             0               0               0               -
    huge              0               0               0               -
$ ./scalable_zone_statistics 497
  Region   Blocks in use    Size in use Max size in use  Size allocated
    tiny              6             288           20768         1069056
    small             2             512           34304         8421376
    large             0               0               0               -
    huge              0               0               0               -
$ ./scalable_zone_statistics 15360
  Region   Blocks in use    Size in use Max size in use  Size allocated
    tiny              6             288           20768         1069056
    small             2             512           34304         8421376
    large             1           16384           16384               -
    huge              0               0               0               -
$ ./scalable_zone_statistics 16777216
  Region   Blocks in use    Size in use Max size in use  Size allocated
    tiny              7             304           20784         1069056
    small             1               0           33792         8421376
    large             0               0               0               -
    huge              1        16777216        16777216               -
```

8.15.8 Logging Malloc Operations

The malloc implementation supports logging of malloc operations to help in the analysis of memory-related bugs. The `MallocStackLogging` environment variable can be set to cause the allocator to remember the function call stack at the time of each allocation. A variant—the `MallocStackLoggingNoCompact` environment variable—causes all allocations to be logged, regardless of their sizes or lifetimes. Mac OS X provides several tools for memory-related debugging, for example, `heap`, `leaks`, `malloc_history`, and `MallocDebug.app`.[23]

---

23. `MallocDebug.app` is part of the Apple Developer Tools package.

The malloc layer allows a custom malloc logger to be installed by setting the `malloc_logger` global function pointer. In fact, setting the aforementioned environment variables results in this pointer being set to an internal logger function. Figure 8–41 shows a program that implements its own malloc logging through this mechanism.

FIGURE 8–41 Logging malloc operations

`// malloc_log.c`

```
#include <stdio.h>
#include <stdlib.h>
#include <unistd.h>
#include <malloc/malloc.h>
#include "nomalloc_printf.h"

// defined in Libc/gen/malloc.c
#define MALLOC_LOG_TYPE_ALLOCATE     2
#define MALLOC_LOG_TYPE_DEALLOCATE   4
#define MALLOC_LOG_TYPE_HAS_ZONE     8
#define MALLOC_LOG_TYPE_CLEARED      64

#define MALLOC_OP_MALLOC    (MALLOC_LOG_TYPE_ALLOCATE|MALLOC_LOG_TYPE_HAS_ZONE)
#define MALLOC_OP_CALLOC    (MALLOC_OP_MALLOC|MALLOC_LOG_TYPE_CLEARED)
#define MALLOC_OP_REALLOC   (MALLOC_OP_MALLOC|MALLOC_LOG_TYPE_DEALLOCATE)
#define MALLOC_OP_FREE      (MALLOC_LOG_TYPE_DEALLOCATE|MALLOC_LOG_TYPE_HAS_ZONE)

typedef void (malloc_logger_t)(unsigned, unsigned, unsigned, unsigned, unsigned,
                               unsigned);

// declared in the Libc malloc implementation
extern malloc_logger_t *malloc_logger;

void
print_malloc_record(unsigned type, unsigned arg1, unsigned arg2, unsigned arg3,
                    unsigned result, unsigned num_hot_frames_to_skip)
{
    switch (type) {
    case MALLOC_OP_MALLOC: // malloc() or valloc()
    case MALLOC_OP_CALLOC:
        nomalloc_printf("%s : zone=%p, size=%u, pointer=%p\n",
                        (type == MALLOC_OP_MALLOC) ? "malloc" : "calloc",
                        arg1, arg2, result);
        break;

    case MALLOC_OP_REALLOC:
        nomalloc_printf("realloc: zone=%p, size=%u, old pointer=%p, "
                        "new pointer=%p\n", arg1, arg3, arg2, result);
        break;
```

(continues)

FIGURE 8–41 Logging malloc operations *(continued)*

```
    case MALLOC_OP_FREE:
        nomalloc_printf("free    : zone=%p, pointer=%p\n", arg1, arg2);
        break;
    }
}

void
do_some_allocations(void)
{
    void *m, *m_new, *c, *v, *m_z;
    malloc_zone_t *zone;

    m = malloc(1024);
    m_new = realloc(m, 8192);
    v = valloc(1024);
    c = calloc(4, 1024);

    free(m_new);
    free(c);
    free(v);

    zone = malloc_create_zone(16384, 0);
    m_z = malloc_zone_malloc(zone, 4096);
    malloc_zone_free(zone, m_z);
    malloc_destroy_zone(zone);
}

int
main(void)
{
    malloc_logger = print_malloc_record;
    do_some_allocations();

    return 0;
}
```

```
$ gcc -Wall -o malloc_log malloc_log.c
$ ./malloc_log
malloc : zone=0x1800000, size=1024, pointer=0x1800400
realloc: zone=0x1800000, size=8192, old pointer=0x1800400, new pointer=0x1800800
malloc : zone=0x1800000, size=1024, pointer=0x6000
calloc : zone=0x1800000, size=4096, pointer=0x1802a00
free    : zone=0x1800000, pointer=0x1800800
free    : zone=0x1800000, pointer=0x1802a00
free    : zone=0x1800000, pointer=0x6000
malloc : zone=0x2800000, size=4096, pointer=0x2800400
free    : zone=0x2800000, pointer=0x2800400
```

8.15.9 Intercepting the Malloc Layer

Since the malloc layer calls the allocator functions through function pointers, we can easily intercept invocations of these functions—say, for debugging or for experimenting with an alternate allocator. Specifically, we can retrieve a pointer to the default zone by calling `malloc_default_zone()`. We can then save the original function pointers from the `malloc_zone_t` structure and insert pointers to our own functions in the structure. Thereafter, we can call the original functions from our functions or provide an alternate allocator implementation altogether. Figure 8–42 shows an example of using such interception.

FIGURE 8–42 Intercepting the malloc layer

```
// malloc_intercept.c

#include <stdlib.h>
#include <unistd.h>
#include <malloc/malloc.h>
#include "nomalloc_printf.h"

void *(*system_malloc)(malloc_zone_t *zone, size_t size);
void (*system_free)(malloc_zone_t *zone, void *ptr);

void *
my_malloc(malloc_zone_t *zone, size_t size)
{
    void *ptr = system_malloc(zone, size);
    nomalloc_printf("%p = malloc(zone=%p, size=%lu)\n", ptr, zone, size);
    return ptr;
}

void
my_free(malloc_zone_t *zone, void *ptr)
{
    nomalloc_printf("free(zone=%p, ptr=%p)\n", zone, ptr);
    system_free(zone, ptr);
}

void
setup_intercept(void)
{
    malloc_zone_t *zone = malloc_default_zone();
    system_malloc = zone->malloc;
    system_free = zone->free;
    // ignoring atomicity/caching
    zone->malloc = my_malloc;
    zone->free = my_free;
}
```

(continues)

FIGURE 8–42 Intercepting the malloc layer *(continued)*

```
int
main(void)
{
    setup_intercept();
    free(malloc(1234));
    return 0;
}


$ gcc -Wall -o malloc_intercept malloc_intercept.c
$ ./malloc_intercept
0x1800400 = malloc(zone=0x1800000, size=1234)
free(zone=0x1800000, ptr=0x1800400)
```

8.16 Memory Allocation in the Kernel

Figure 8–43 shows an overview of kernel-level memory allocation functions in Mac OS X. The numerical labels are rough indicators of how low-level that group of functions is. For example, page-level allocation, which is labeled with the lowest number, is the lowest-level allocation mechanism, since it allocates memory directly from the list of free pages in the Mach VM subsystem.

Figure 8–44 shows an overview of kernel-level memory deallocation functions.

8.16.1 Page-Level Allocation

Page-level allocation is performed in the kernel by vm_page_alloc() [osfmk/ vm/vm_resident.c]. This function requires a VM object and an offset as arguments. It then attempts to allocate a page associated with the VM object/offset pair. The VM object can be the kernel VM object (kernel_object), or it can be a newly allocated VM object.

vm_page_alloc() first calls vm_page_grab() [osfmk/vm/vm_resident.c] to remove a page from the free list. If the free list is too small, vm_page_grab() fails, returning a VM_PAGE_NULL. However, if the requesting thread is a VM-privileged thread, vm_page_grab() consumes a page from the reserved pool. If there are no reserved pages available, vm_page_grab() waits for a page to become available.

If vm_page_grab() returns a valid page, vm_page_alloc() calls vm_ page_insert() [osfmk/vm/vm_resident.c] to insert the page into the hash

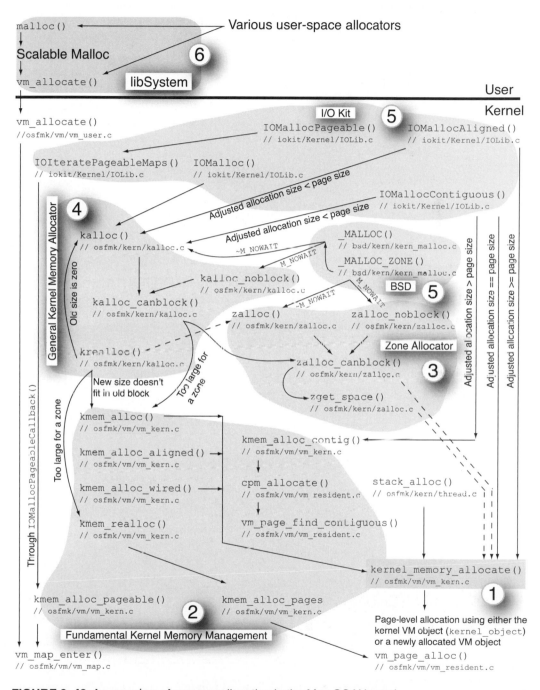

FIGURE 8–43 An overview of memory allocation in the Mac OS X kernel

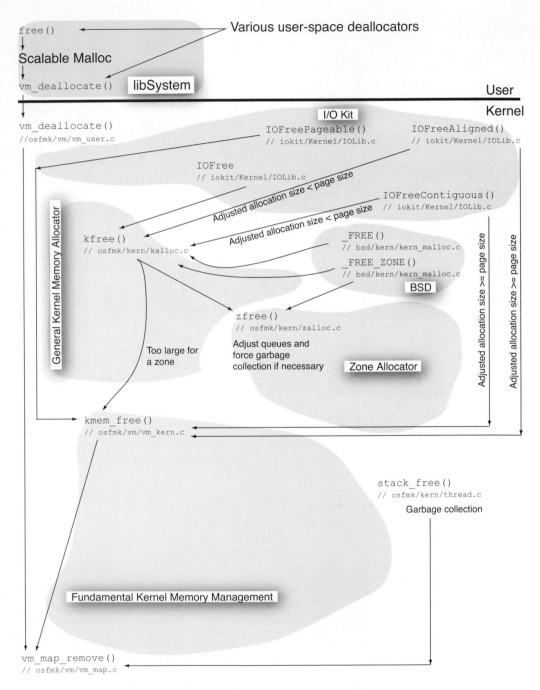

FIGURE 8–44 An overview of memory deallocation in the Mac OS X kernel

table that maps VM object/offset pairs to pages—that is, the virtual-to-physical (VP) table. The VM object's resident page count is also incremented.

`kernel_memory_allocate()` [`osfmk/vm/vm_kern.c`] is the master entry point for allocating kernel memory in that most but not all pathways to memory allocation go through this function.

```
kern_return_t
kernel_memory_allocate(
    vm_map_t      map,     // the VM map to allocate into
    vm_offset_t *addrp,    // pointer to start of new memory
    vm_size_t     size,    // size to allocate (rounded up to a page size multiple)
    vm_offset_t   mask,    // mask specifying a particular alignment
    int           flags);  // KMA_HERE, KMA_NOPAGEWAIT, KMA_KOBJECT
```

The flag bits are used as follows:

- If `KMA_HERE` is set, the address pointer contains the base address to use; otherwise, the caller doesn't care where the memory is allocated. For example, if the caller has a newly created submap that the caller knows is empty, the caller may want to allocate memory at the beginning of the map.

- If `KMA_NOPAGEWAIT` is set, the function does not wait for pages if memory is not available.

- If `KMA_KOBJECT` is set, the function uses the kernel VM object (`kernel_object`); otherwise, a new VM object is allocated.

`kernel_memory_allocate()` calls `vm_map_find_space()` [`osfmk/vm/vm_map.c`] to find and allocate a virtual address range in the VM map. A new VM map entry is initialized because of this. As shown in Figure 8–43, `kernel_memory_allocate()` calls `vm_page_alloc()` to allocate pages. If the VM object is newly allocated, it passes a zero offset to `vm_page_alloc()`. If the kernel object is being used, the offset is the difference of the address returned by `vm_map_find_space()` and the minimum kernel address (`VM_MIN_KERNEL_ADDRESS`, defined to be `0x1000` in `osfmk/mach/ppc/vm_param.h`).

8.16.2 `kmem_alloc`

The `kmem_alloc` family of functions is implemented in `osfmk/vm/vm_kern.c`. These functions are intended for use in the Mach portion of the kernel.

```
kern_return_t
kmem_alloc(vm_map_t map, vm_offset_t *addrp, vm_size_t size);
```

```
kern_return_t
kmem_alloc_wired(vm_map_t map, vm_offset_t *addrp, vm_size_t size);

kern_return_t
kmem_alloc_aligned(vm_map_t map, vm_offset_t *addrp, vm_size_t size);

kern_return_t
kmem_alloc_pageable(vm_map_t map, vm_offset_t *addrp, vm_size_t size);

kern_return_t
kmem_alloc_contig(vm_map_t map, vm_offset_t *addrp,
                  vm_size_t size, vm_offset_t mask, int flags);

kern_return_t
kmem_realloc(vm_map_t map, vm_offset_t oldaddr, vm_size_t oldsize,
             vm_offset_t *newaddrp, vm_size_t newsize);

void
kmem_free(vm_map_t map, vm_offset_t addr, vm_size_t size);
```

- kmem_alloc() simply forwards its arguments to kernel_memory_allocate() and also sets the latter's mask and flags parameters to 0 each.

- kmem_alloc_wired() simply forwards its arguments to kernel_memory_allocate() and also sets the latter's mask and flags parameters to 0 and KMA_KOBJECT, respectively. Consequently, memory is allocated in the kernel object—in either the kernel's map or a submap. The memory is not zero-filled.

- kmem_alloc_aligned() simply forwards its arguments to kernel_memory_allocate() after ensuring that the requested allocation size is a power of 2. Additionally, it sets the latter's flags parameter to KMA_KOBJECT and the mask parameter to (size -1), where size is the requested allocation size.

- kmem_alloc_pageable() allocates pageable kernel memory in the given address map. It only calls vm_map_enter() to allocate a range in the given VM map. In particular, it does not back the range with physical memory. The execve() system call implementation uses this function to allocate memory in the BSD pageable map (bsd_pageable_map) for execve() arguments.

- kmem_alloc_contig() allocates physically contiguous, wired kernel memory. The I/O Kit uses this function.

- kmem_realloc() reallocates wired kernel memory given a region that is already allocated using kmem_alloc().

- kmem_free() releases allocated kernel memory.

> Except `kmem_alloc_pageable()`, all `kmem_alloc` functions allocate wired memory.

8.16.3 The Mach Zone Allocator

The Mach zone allocator is a fast memory allocation mechanism with garbage collection. As shown in Figure 8–43, several allocation functions in the kernel directly or indirectly use the zone allocator.

A zone is a collection of fixed-size memory blocks that are accessible through an efficient interface for allocation and deallocation. The kernel typically creates a zone for each *class* of data structure to be managed. Examples of data structures for which the Mac OS X kernel creates individual zones include the following:

- Asynchronous I/O work queue entries (`struct aio_workq_entry`)
- Alarms (`struct alarm`) and timer data (`mk_timer_data_t`)
- Kernel audit records (`struct kaudit_record`)
- Kernel notifications (`struct knote`)
- Tasks (`struct task`), threads (`struct thread`), and uthreads (`struct uthread`)
- Pipes (`struct pipe`)
- Semaphores (`struct semaphores`)
- Buffer headers (`struct buf`) and metadata buffers
- Various protocol control blocks in the network stack
- Unified buffer cache "info" structures (`struct ubc_info`)
- Vnode pagers (`struct vnode_pager`) and device pagers (`struct device_pager`)
- Mach VM data structures, such as VM maps (`struct vm_map`), VM map entries (`struct vm_map_entry`), VM map copy objects (`struct vm_map_copy`), VM objects (`struct vm_object`), VM object hash entries (`struct vm_object_hash_entry`), and pages (`struct vm_page`)
- Mach IPC data structures, such as IPC spaces (`struct ipc_space`), IPC tree entries (`struct ipc_tree_entry`), ports (`struct ipc_port`), port sets (`struct ipc_pset`), and IPC messages (`ipc_kmsg_t`)

The `host_zone_info()` Mach routine retrieves information about Mach zones from the kernel. It returns an array of zone names and another array of zone_info structures [<mach_debug/zone_info.h>]. The zprint command-line program uses host_zone_info() to retrieve and display information about all zones in the kernel.

```
$ zprint
                         elem   cur    max   cur    max   cur alloc alloc
zone name                size   size   size  #elts  #elts inuse size count
-----------------------------------------------------------------------------
zones                      80    11K    12K    152    153    89   4K    51
vm.objects                136  6562K  8748K  49410  65867 39804   4K    30 C
vm.object.hash.entries      20   693K   768K  35496  39321 24754   4K   204 C
...
pmap_mappings              64 25861K 52479K 413789 839665272627   4K    64 C
kalloc.large            59229  2949K  4360K     51     75    51  57K     1
```

Note that zprint's output includes the size of an object in each zone (the elem size column). You can pipe zprint's output through the sort command to see that several zones have the same element sizes. A single physical page is never shared between two or more zones. In other words, all zone-allocated objects on a physical page will be of the same type.

```
$ zprint | sort +1 -n
...
alarms                   44     3K     4K     93     93     1   4K    93 C
kernel.map.entries       44  4151K  4152K  96628  96628  9582   4K    93
non-kernel.map.entries   44  1194K  1536K  27807  35746 18963   4K    93 C
semaphores               44    35K  1092K    837  25413   680   4K    93 C
vm.pages                 44 32834K     0K 764153      0763069   4K    93 C
...
```

A zone is described in the kernel by a zone structure (struct zone).

```
// osfmk/kern/zalloc.h

struct zone {
    int           count;          // number of elements used now
    vm_offset_t free_elements;
    decl_mutex_data(,lock);       // generic lock
    vm_size_t    cur_size;        // current memory utilization
    vm_size_t    max_size;        // how large this zone can grow
    vm_size_t    elem_size;       // size of an element
    vm_size_t    alloc_size;      // chunk size for more memory
    char         *zone_name;      // string describing the zone
    ...
    struct zone *next_zone;       // link for all-zones list
    ...
};
```

A new zone is initialized by calling `zinit()`, which returns a pointer to a newly created zone structure (zone_t). Various subsystems use `zinit()` to initialize the zones they need.

```
zone_t
zinit(vm_size_t   size,  // size of each object
      vm_size_t   max,   // maximum size in bytes the zone may reach
      vm_size_t   alloc, // allocation size
      const char *name); // a string that describes the objects in the zone
```

The allocation size specified in the `zinit()` call is the amount of memory to add to the zone each time the zone becomes empty—that is, when there are no free elements on the zone's free list. The allocation size is automatically rounded up to an integral number of pages. Note that zone structures are themselves allocated from a *zone of zones* (zone_zone). When the zone allocator is initialized during kernel bootstrap, it calls `zinit()` to initialize the zone of zones. `zinit()` treats this initialization specially: It calls `zget_space()` [osfmk/kern/zalloc.c] to allocate contiguous, nonpaged space through the master kernel memory allocator (`kernel_memory_allocate()` [osfmk/vm/vm_kern.c]). Other calls to `zinit()` allocate zone structures from the zone of zones through `zalloc()` [osfmk/kern/zalloc.c].

```
// osfmk/kern/zalloc.c

// zone data structures are themselves stored in a zone
zone_t zone_zone = ZONE_NULL;

zone_t
zinit(vm_size_t size, vm_size_t max, vm_size_t alloc, const char *name)
{
    zone_t z;

    if (zone_zone == ZONE_NULL) {
        if (zget_space(sizeof(struct_zone), (vm_offset_t *)&z)
            != KERN_SUCCESS)
                return(ZONE_NULL);
    } else
        z = (zone_t)zalloc(zone_zone);

    // initialize various fields of the newly allocated zone structure

    thread_call_setup(&z->call_async_alloc, zalloc_async, z);

    // add the zone structure to the end of the list of all zones

    return(z);
}
```

```
void
zone_bootstrap(void)
{
    ...
    // this is the first call to zinit()
    zone_zone = zinit(sizeof(struct zone), 128 * sizeof(struct zone),
                      sizeof(struct zone), "zones");
    // this zone's empty pages will not be garbage collected
    zone_change(zone_zone, Z_COLLECT, FALSE);
    ...
}
```

zinit() populates the various fields of a newly allocated zone structure. In particular, it sets the zone's current size to 0 and the zone's empty list to NULL. Therefore, at this point, the zone's memory pool is empty. Before returning, zinit() arranges for zalloc_async() [osfmk/kern/zalloc.c] to run by setting up a callout. zalloc_async() attempts to allocate a single element from the empty zone, because of which memory is allocated for the zone. zalloc_async() immediately frees the dummy allocation.

// osfmk/kern/zalloc.c

```
void
zalloc_async(thread_call_param_t p0, __unused thread_call_param_t p1)
{
    void *elt;

    elt = zalloc_canblock((zone_t)p0, TRUE);
    zfree((zone_t)p0, elt);
    lock_zone((zone_t)p0);
    ((zone_t)p0)->async_pending = FALSE;
    unlock_zone((zone_t)p0);
}
```

The zone allocator exports several functions for memory allocation, deallocation, and zone configuration. Figure 8–45 shows the important functions.

FIGURE 8–45 Zone allocator functions

```
// Allocate an element from the specified zone
void *zalloc(zone_t zone);

// Allocate an element from the specified zone without blocking
void *zalloc_noblock(zone_t zone);
```

(continues)

FIGURE 8–45 Zone allocator functions *(continued)*

```
// A special version of a nonblocking zalloc() that does not block
// even for locking the zone's mutex: It will return an element only
// if it can get it from the zone's free list
void *zget(zone_t zone);

// Free a zone element
void zfree(zone_t zone, void *elem);

// Add ("cram") the given memory to the given zone
void zcram(zone_t zone, void *newmem, vm_size_t size);

// Fill the zone with enough memory for at least the given number of elements
int zfill(zone_t zone, int nelem);

// Change zone parameters (must be called immediately after zinit())
void zone_change(zone_t zone, unsigned int item, boolean_t value);

// Preallocate wired memory for the given zone from zone_map, expanding the
// zone to the given size
void zprealloc(zone_t zone, vm_size_t size);

// Return a hint for the current number of free elements in the zone
integer_t zone_free_count(zone_t zone)
```

The zone_change() function allows the following Boolean flags to be modified for a zone.

- Z_EXHAUST—If this flag is true, the zone is exhaustible, and an allocation attempt simply returns if the zone is empty. This flag is false by default.

- Z_COLLECT—If this flag is true, the zone is collectable: Its empty pages are garbage collected. This flag is true by default.

- Z_EXPAND—If this flag is true, the zone is expandable: It can be grown by sending an IPC message. This flag is true by default.

- Z_FOREIGN—If this flag is true, the zone can contain foreign objects—that is, those objects that are not allocated through zalloc(). This flag is false by default.

The typical kernel usage of zalloc() is blocking—that is, the caller is willing to wait if memory is not available immediately. The zalloc_noblock() and zget() functions attempt to allocate memory with no allowance for blocking and therefore can return NULL if no memory is available.

As shown in Figure 8–43, the zone allocator eventually allocates memory through `kernel_memory_allocate()` [`osfmk/vm/vm_kern.c`]. If the system is low on available memory, this function returns `KERN_RESOURCE_SHORTAGE`, which causes the zone allocator to wait for a page to become available. However, if `kernel_memory_allocate()` fails because there is no more kernel virtual address space left, the zone allocator causes a kernel panic.

Freeing a zone element through `zfree()` [`osfmk/kern/zalloc.c`] causes the element to be added to the zone's free list and the zone's count of in-use elements to be decremented. A collectable zone's unused pages are periodically garbage collected.

During VM subsystem initialization, the kernel calls `zone_init()` [`osfmk/kern/zalloc.c`] to create a map for the zone allocator (`zone_map`) as a submap of the kernel map. `zone_init()` also sets up garbage collection information: It allocates wired memory for the *zone page table*—a linked list that contains one element, a `zone_page_table_entry` structure, for each page assigned to a zone.

```
// osfmk/kern/zalloc.c
```

```
struct zone_page_table_entry {
    struct zone_page_table_entry *link;
    short                        alloc_count;
    short                        collect_count;
};
```

The `alloc_count` field of the `zone_page_table_entry` structure is the total number of elements from that page assigned to the zone, whereas the `collect_count` field is the number of elements from that page on the zone's free list. Consider the following sequence of steps as an example of new memory being added to a zone.

- A caller invokes `zalloc()` to request memory. `zalloc()` is a wrapper around `zalloc_canblock()`, which it calls with the "can block" Boolean parameter (`canblock`) set to true.

- `zalloc_canblock()` attempts to remove an element from the zone's free list. If it succeeds, it returns; otherwise, the zone's free list is empty.

- `zalloc_canblock()` checks whether the zone is currently undergoing garbage collection. If so, it sets the zone structure's `waiting` bit field and goes to sleep. The garbage collector will wake it up, after which it can retry removing an element from the zone's free list.

- If allocation still doesn't succeed, `zalloc_canblock()` checks the zone structure's `doing_alloc` bit field to check whether someone else is allocating memory for the zone. If so, it goes to sleep again while setting the `waiting` bit field.

- If nobody else is allocating memory for the zone, `zalloc_canblock()` attempts to allocate memory for the zone by calling `kernel_memory_allocate()`. The size of this allocation is normally the zone's allocation size (the size structure's `alloc_size` field), but it can be just the size of a single element (rounded up to an integral number of pages) if the system is low on memory.

- On a successful return from `kernel_memory_allocate()`, `zalloc_canblock()` calls `zone_page_init()` on the new memory. For each page in the memory, `zone_page_init()` sets both the `alloc_count` and `collect_count` fields of the corresponding `zone_page_table_entry` structure to 0.

- `zalloc_canblock()` then calls `zcram()` on the new memory, which in turn calls `zone_page_alloc()` for each newly available element. `zone_page_alloc()` increments the appropriate `alloc_count` value by one for each element.

The zone garbage collector, `zone_gc()` [osfmk/kern/zalloc.c], is invoked by `consider_zone_gc()` [osfmk/kern/zalloc.c]. The latter ensures that garbage collection is performed at most once per minute, unless someone else has explicitly requested a garbage collection. The page-out daemon calls `consider_zone_gc()`.

> `zfree()` can request explicit garbage collection if the system is low on memory and the zone from which the element is being freed has an element size of a page size or more.

`zone_gc()` makes two passes on each collectable zone.[24] In the first pass, it calls `zone_page_collect()` [osfmk/kern/zalloc.c] on each free element. `zone_page_collect()` increments the appropriate `collect_count` value by one. In the second pass, it calls `zone_page_collectable()` on each element,

---

24. `zone_gc()` can skip a collectable zone if the zone has less than 10% of its elements free or if the amount of free memory in the zone is less than twice its allocation size.

which compares the `collect_count` and `alloc_count` values for that page. If the values are equal, the page can be reclaimed since all elements on that page are free. `zone_gc()` tracks such pages in a list of pages to be freed and eventually frees them by calling `kmem_free()`.

8.16.4 The Kalloc Family

The kalloc family of functions, implemented in `osfmk/kern/kalloc.c`, provides access to a fast general-purpose memory allocator built atop the zone allocator. `kalloc()` uses a 16MB submap (`kalloc_map`) of the kernel map from which it allocates its memory. The limited submap size avoids virtual memory fragmentation. `kalloc()` supports a set of allocation sizes, ranging from as little as `KALLOC_MINSIZE` bytes (16 bytes by default) to several kilobytes. Note that each size is a power of 2. When the allocator is initialized, it calls `zinit()` to create a zone for each allocation size that it handles. Each zone's name is set to reflect the zone's associated size, as shown in Figure 8–46. These are the so-called power-of-2 zones.

FIGURE 8–46 Printing sizes of kalloc zones supported in the kernel

```
$ zprint | grep kalloc
```

kalloc.16	16	484K	615K	30976	39366	26998	4K	256 C
kalloc.32	32	1452K	1458K	46464	46656	38240	4K	128 C
kalloc.64	64	2404K	2916K	38464	46656	24429	4K	64 C
kalloc.128	128	1172K	1728K	9376	13824	2987	4K	32 C
kalloc.256	256	692K	1024K	2768	4096	2449	4K	16 C
kalloc.512	512	916K	1152K	1832	2304	1437	4K	8 C
kalloc.1024	1024	804K	1024K	804	1024	702	4K	4 C
kalloc.2048	2048	1504K	2048K	752	1024	663	4K	2 C
kalloc.4096	4096	488K	4096K	122	1024	70	4K	1 C
kalloc.8192	8192	2824K	32768K	353	4096	307	8K	1 C
kalloc.large	60648	2842K	4360K	48	73	48	59K	1

Note that the zone named `kalloc.large` in the zprint output in Figure 8–46 is not real—it is a *fake* zone used for reporting on too-large-for-a-zone objects that were allocated through `kmem_alloc()`.

The kalloc family provides malloc-style functions, along with a version that attempts memory allocation without blocking.

```
void *
kalloc(vm_size_t size);
```

```
void *
kalloc_noblock(vm_size_t size);

void *
kalloc_canblock(vm_size_t size, boolean_t canblock);

void
krealloc(void **addrp, vm_size_t old_size, vm_size_t new_size,
         simple_lock_t lock);

void
kfree(void *data, vm_size_t size);
```

Both `kalloc()` and `kalloc_noblock()` are simple wrappers around `kalloc_canblock()`, which prefers to get memory through `zalloc_canblock()`, unless the allocation size is too large—`kalloc_max_prerounded` (8193 bytes by default or more). `krealloc()` uses `kmem_realloc()` if the existing allocation is already too large for a kalloc zone. If the new size is also too large, `krealloc()` uses `kmem_alloc()` to allocate new memory, copies existing data into it using `bcopy()`, and frees the old memory. If the new memory fits in a kalloc zone, `krealloc()` uses `zalloc()` to allocate new memory. It still must copy existing data and free the old memory, since there is no "zrealloc" function.

8.16.5 The OSMalloc Family

The file `osfmk/kern/kalloc.c` implements another family of memory allocation functions: the OSMalloc family.

```
OSMallocTag
OSMalloc_Tagalloc(const char *str, uint32_t flags);

void
OSMalloc_Tagfree(OSMallocTag tag);

void *
OSMalloc(uint32_t size, OSMallocTag tag);

void *
OSMalloc_nowait(uint32_t size, OSMallocTag tag);

void *
OSMalloc_noblock(uint32_t size, OSMallocTag tag);

void
OSFree(void *addr, uint32_t size, OSMallocTag tag);
```

The key aspect of these functions is their use of a tag structure, which encapsulates certain properties of allocations made with that tag.

```
#define OSMT_MAX_NAME 64

typedef struct _OSMallocTag_ {
    queue_chain_t OSMT_link;
    uint32_t      OSMT_refcnt;
    uint32_t      OSMT_state;
    uint32_t      OSMT_attr;
    char          OSMT_name[OSMT_MAX_NAME];
} *OSMallocTag;
```

Here is an example use of the OSMalloc functions:

```
#include <libkern/OSMalloc.h>

OSMallocTag my_tag;

void
my_init(void)
{
    my_tag = OSMalloc_Tagalloc("My Tag Name", OSMT_ATTR_PAGEABLE);
    ...
}

void
my_uninit(void)
{
    OSMalloc_Tagfree(my_tag);
}

void
some_function(...)
{
    void *p = OSMalloc(some_size, my_tag);
}
```

OSMalloc_Tagalloc() calls kalloc() to allocate a tag structure. The tag's name and attributes are set based on the arguments passed to OSMalloc_Tagalloc(). The tag's reference count is initialized to one, and the tag is placed on a global list of tags. Thereafter, memory is allocated using one of the OSMalloc allocation functions, which in turn uses one of kalloc(), kalloc_noblock(), or kmem_alloc_pageable() for the actual allocation. Each allocation increments the tag's reference count by one.

8.16.6 Memory Allocation in the I/O Kit

The I/O Kit provides its own interface for memory allocation in the kernel.

```
void *
IOMalloc(vm_size_t size);

void *
IOMallocPageable(vm_size_t size, vm_size_t alignment);

void *
IOMallocAligned(vm_size_t size, vm_size_t alignment);

void *
IOMallocContiguous(vm_size_t size, vm_size_t alignment,
                   IOPhysicalAddress *physicalAddress);

void
IOFree(void *address, vm_size_t size);

void
IOFreePageable(void *address, vm_size_t size);

void
IOFreeAligned(void *address, vm_size_t size);

void
IOFreeContiguous(void *address, vm_size_t size);
```

IOMalloc() allocates general-purpose, wired memory in the kernel map by simply calling kalloc(). Since kalloc() can block, IOMalloc() must not be called while holding a simple lock or from an interrupt context. Moreover, since kalloc() offers no alignment guarantees, IOMalloc() should not be called when a specific alignment is desired. Memory allocated through IOMalloc() is freed through IOFree(), which simply calls kfree(). The latter too can block.

Pageable memory with alignment restriction is allocated through IOMallocPageable(), whose alignment argument specifies the desired alignment in bytes. The I/O Kit maintains a bookkeeping data structure (gIOKitPageableSpace) for pageable memory.

```
// iokit/Kernel/IOLib.c

enum { kIOMaxPageableMaps    = 16 };
enum { kIOPageableMapSize    = 96 * 1024 * 1024 };
enum { kIOPageableMaxMapSize = 96 * 1024 * 1024 };
```

```
static struct {
    UInt32      count;
    UInt32      hint;
    IOMapData   maps[kIOMaxPageableMaps];
    lck_mtx_t *lock;
} gIOKitPageableSpace;
```

The `maps` array of `gIOKitPageableSpace` contains submaps allocated from the kernel map. During bootstrap, the I/O Kit initializes the first entry of this array by allocating a 96MB (`kIOPageableMapSize`) pageable map. `IOMallocPageable()` calls `IOIteratePageableMaps()`, which first attempts to allocate memory from an existing pageable map, failing which it fills the next slot—up to a maximum of `kIOPageableMaps` slots—of the `maps` array with a newly allocated map. The eventual memory allocation is done through `kmem_alloc_pageable()`. When such memory is freed through `IOFreePageable()`, the `maps` array is consulted to determine which map the address being freed belongs to, after which `kmem_free()` is called to actually free the memory.

Wired memory with alignment restriction is allocated through `IOMallocAligned()`, whose alignment argument specifies the desired alignment in bytes. If the adjusted allocation size (after accounting for the alignment) is equal to or more than the page size, `IOMallocAligned()` uses `kernel_memory_allocate()`; otherwise, it uses `kalloc()`. Correspondingly, the memory is freed through `kmem_free()` or `kfree()`.

`IOMallocContiguous()` allocates physically contiguous, wired, alignment-restricted memory in the kernel map. Optionally, this function returns the physical address of the allocated memory if a non-`NULL` pointer for holding the physical address is passed as an argument. When the adjusted allocation size is less than or equal to a page, physical contiguity is trivially present. In these two cases, `IOMallocContiguous()` uses `kalloc()` and `kernel_memory_allocate()`, respectively, for the underlying allocation. When multiple physical contiguous pages are requested, the allocation is handled by `kmem_alloc_contig()`. Like `vm_page_alloc()`, this function also causes memory allocation directly from the free list. It calls `kmem_alloc_contig()`, which in turn calls `vm_page_find_contiguous()` [osfmk/vm/vm_resident.c]. The latter traverses the free list, inserting free pages into a private sublist sorted on the physical address. As soon as a contiguous range large enough to fulfill the contiguous allocation request is detected in the sublist, the function allocates the corresponding pages and returns the remaining pages collected on the sublist to the free list. Because of the free list sorting, this function can take a substantial time to run when the free list is very large—for example, soon after bootstrapping on a system with a large amount of physical memory.

When the caller requests the newly allocated memory's physical address to be returned, `IOMallocContiguous()` first retrieves the corresponding physical page from the pmap layer by calling `pmap_find_phys()` [osfmk/ppc/pmap.c]. If the DART IOMMU[25] is present and active on the system, the address of this page is not returned as is. As we noted earlier, the DART translates I/O Kit-visible 32-bit "physical for I/O" addresses to 64-bit "true" physical addresses. Code running in the I/O Kit environment cannot even see the true physical address. In fact, even if such code attempted to use a 64-bit physical address, the DART would not be able to translate it, and an error would occur.

If the DART is active, `IOMallocContiguous()` calls it to allocate an appropriately sized I/O memory range—the address of this allocation is the "physical" address that is returned. Moreover, `IOMallocContiguous()` has to insert each "true" physical page into the I/O memory range by calling the DART's "insert" function. Since `IOFreeContiguous()` must call the DART to undo this work, `IOMallocContiguous()` saves the virtual address and the I/O address in an `_IOMallocContiguousEntry` structure. The I/O Kit maintains these structures in a linked list. When the memory is freed, the caller provides the virtual address, using which the I/O Kit can search for the I/O address on this linked list. Once the I/O address is found, the structure is removed from the list and the DART allocation is freed.

```
// iokit/Kernel/IOLib.c

struct _IOMallocContiguousEntry
{
    void           *virtual; // caller-visible virtual address
    ppnum_t         ioBase;  // caller-visible "physical" address
    queue_chain_t  link;     // chained to other contiguous entries
};
typedef struct _IOMallocContiguousEntry _IOMallocContiguousEntry;
```

8.16.7 Memory Allocation in the Kernel's BSD Portion

The BSD portion of the kernel provides `_MALLOC()` [bsd/kern/kern_malloc.c] and `_MALLOC_ZONE()` [bsd/kern/kern_malloc.c] for memory allocation.

---

25. We will discuss the DART in Section 10.3.

The header file `bsd/sys/malloc.h` defines the `MALLOC()` and `MALLOC_ZONE()` macros, which are trivial wrappers around `_MALLOC()` and `_MALLOC_ZONE()`, respectively.

```
void *
_MALLOC(size_t size, int type, int flags);

void
_FREE(void *addr, int type);

void *
_MALLOC_ZONE(size_t size, int type, int flags);

void
_FREE_ZONE(void *elem, size_t size, int type);
```

The BSD-specific allocator designates different types of memory with different numerical values, where the "memory type" (the `type` argument), which is specified by the caller, represents the purpose of the memory. For example, `M_FILEPROC` memory is used for open file structures, and `M_SOCKET` memory is used for socket structures. The various known types are defined in `bsd/sys/malloc.h`. The value `M_LAST` is one more than the last known type's value. This allocator is initialized during kernel bootstrap by a call to `kmeminit()` [bsd/kern/kern_malloc.c], which goes through a predefined array of `kmzones` structures (`struct kmzones [bsd/kern/kern_malloc.c]`). As shown in Figure 8–47, there is one `kmzones` structure for each type of memory supported by the BSD allocator.

FIGURE 8–47 Array of memory types supported by the BSD memory allocator

```
// bsd/kern/kern_malloc.c

char *memname[] = INITKMEMNAMES;

struct kmzones {
    size_t  kz_elemsize;
    void    *kz_zalloczone;
#define KMZ_CREATEZONE ((void *)-2)
#define KMZ_LOOKUPZONE ((void *)-1)
#define KMZ_MALLOC     ((void *)0)
#define KMZ_SHAREZONE  ((void *)1)
} kmzones[M_LAST] = {
#define SOS(sname)     sizeof (struct sname)
```

(continues)

FIGURE 8–47 Array of memory types supported by the BSD memory allocator *(continued)*

```
#define SOX(sname)      -1
    -1,          0,               /* 0 M_FREE       */
    MSIZE,       KMZ_CREATEZONE,  /* 1 M_MBUF       */
    0,           KMZ_MALLOC,      /* 2 M_DEVBUF     */
    SOS(socket), KMZ_CREATEZONE,  /* 3 M_SOCKET     */
    SOS(inpcb),  KMZ_LOOKUPZONE,  /* 4 M_PCB        */
    M_MBUF,      KMZ_SHAREZONE,   /* 5 M_RTABLE     */
    ...
SOS(unsafe_fsnode),KMZ_CREATEZONE, /* 102 M_UNSAFEFS */
#undef  SOS
#undef  SOX
};
...
```

Moreover, each type has a string name. These names are defined in `bsd/sys/malloc.h` in another array.

// bsd/sys/malloc.h

```
#define INITKMEMNAMES { \
        "free",         /* 0 M_FREE       */ \
        "mbuf",         /* 1 M_MBUF       */ \
        "devbuf",       /* 2 M_DEVBUF     */ \
        "socket",       /* 3 M_SOCKET     */ \
        "pcb",          /* 4 M_PCB        */ \
        "routetbl",     /* 5 M_RTABLE     */ \
        ...
        "kauth",        /* 100 M_KAUTH    */ \
        "dummynet",     /* 101 M_DUMMYNET */ \
        "unsafe_fsnode" /* 102 M_UNSAFEFS */ \
}
...
```

As `kmeminit()` iterates over the array of `kmzones`, it analyses each entry's `kz_elemsize` and `kz_zalloczone` fields. Entries with `kz_elemsize` values of -1 are skipped. For the other entries, if `kz_zalloczone` is `KMZ_CREATEZONE`, `kmeminit()` calls `zinit()` to initialize a zone using `kz_elemsize` as the size of an element of the zone, 1MB as the maximum memory to use, `PAGE_SIZE` as the allocation size, and the corresponding string in the `memname` array as the zone's name. The `kz_zalloczone` field is set to this newly initialized zone.

If `kz_zalloczone` is `KMZ_LOOKUPZONE`, `kmeminit()` calls `kalloc_zone()` to simply look up the kernel memory allocator (kalloc) zone with the appropriate allocation size. The `kz_zalloczone` field is set to the found zone or to `ZONE_NULL` if none is found.

If `kz_zalloczone` is `KMZ_SHAREZONE`, the entry shares the zone with the entry at index `kz_elemsize` in the kmzones array. For example, the kmzones entry for `M_RTABLE` shares the zone with the entry for `M_MBUF`. `kmeminit()` sets the `kz_zalloczone` and `kz_elemsize` fields of a `KMZ_SHAREZONE` entry to those of the "shared with" zone.

Thereafter, `_MALLOC_ZONE()` uses its type argument as an index into the kmzones array. If the specified type is greater than the last known type, there is a kernel panic. If the allocation request's size matches the `kz_elemsize` field of `kmzones[type]`, `_MALLOC_ZONE()` calls the Mach zone allocator to allocate from the zone pointed to by the `kz_zalloczone` field of `kmzones[type]`. If their sizes do not match, `_MALLOC_ZONE()` uses `kalloc()` or `kalloc_noblock()`, depending on whether the `M_NOWAIT` bit is clear or set, respectively, in the `flags` argument.

Similarly, `_MALLOC()` calls `kalloc()` or `kalloc_noblock()` to allocate memory. The `type` argument is not used, but if its value exceeds the last known BSD malloc type, `_MALLOC()` still causes a kernel panic. `_MALLOC()` uses a bookkeeping data structure of its own to track allocated memory. It adds the size of this data structure (`struct _mhead`) to the size of the incoming allocation request.

```
struct _mhead {
        size_t  mlen;   // used to record the length of allocated memory
        char    dat[0]; // this is returned by _MALLOC()
};
```

Moreover, if the `M_ZERO` bit is set in the `flags` argument, `_MALLOC` calls `bzero()` to zero-fill the memory.

8.16.8 Memory Allocation in libkern's C++ Environment

As we noted in Section 2.4.4, libkern defines `OSObject` as the root base class for the Mac OS X kernel. The `new` and `delete` operators for `OSObject` call `kalloc()` and `kfree()`, respectively.

```
// libkern/c++/OSObject.cpp

void *
OSObject::operator new(size_t size)
```

```
{
    void *mem - (void *)kalloc(size);
    ...
    return mem;
}

void
OSObject::operator delete(void *mem, size_t size)
{
    kfree((vm_offset_t)mem, size);
    ...
}
```

8.17 Memory-Mapped Files

Mac OS X provides the mmap() system call for mapping files, character devices, and POSIX shared memory descriptors into the caller's address space. Moreover, anonymous memory can be mapped by setting MAP_ANON in the flags argument to mmap().

```
void *
mmap(void *addr, size_t len, int prot, int flags, int fd, off_t offset);
```

When mmap() is used to map a regular file or anonymous memory, the mapping is backed by an on-disk object as follows.

- Anonymous memory is always backed by swap space.

- A regular file's mapping is backed by the file itself if MAP_SHARED was specified in the flags argument to mmap(). This means that any modifications made to the mapping are written to the original file when the corresponding pages are evicted.

- A regular file's mapping is backed by swap space if MAP_PRIVATE was specified in the flags argument. This means that any modifications made to the mapping are private.

Let us discuss the implementation of mmap() by looking at the sequence of operations that take place when a program maps a regular file. First, the program must acquire a file descriptor for the file in question. Figure 8–48 shows the relevant activity that occurs because of the open() system call. In this case, a preexisting regular file residing on an HFS Plus volume is being opened for the first time.

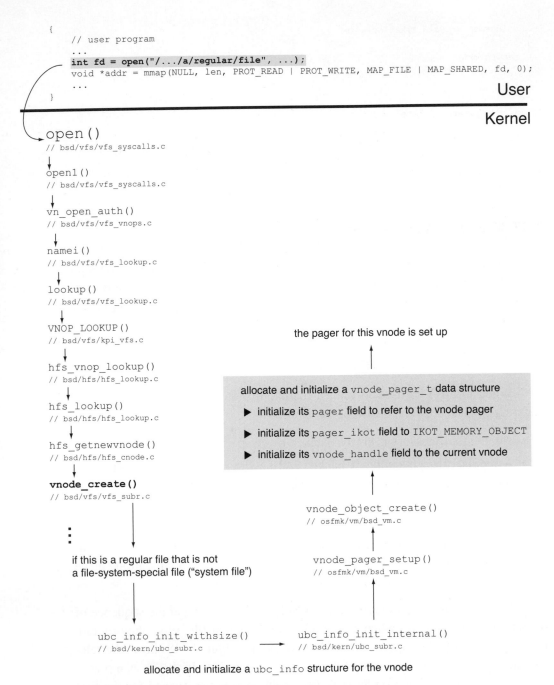

FIGURE 8–48 Setting up the vnode pager during the `open()` system call

The vnode structure (`struct vnode` [bsd/sys/vnode_internal.h]) corresponding to a regular file contains a pointer to a UBC information structure (`struct ubc_info` [bsd/sys/ubc_internal.h]). The `ubc_info` structure contains a pointer to the pager—in this case, the vnode pager, as represented by a `vnode_pager` structure (`struct vnode_pager` [osfmk/vm/bsd_vm.c]). Figure 8–49 shows how these structures are connected when the vnode is created.

Suppose a user program calls `mmap()` to map the file descriptor obtained in Figure 8–48. Figure 8–50 shows the ensuing kernel activity. `mmap()` calls `mach_vm_map()` [osfmk/vm/vm_user.c], which, in our case of a regular file, will call `vm_object_enter()` [osfmk/vm/vm_object.c]. Since no VM object will be associated with the given pager yet, `vm_object_enter()` will create a new VM object. Moreover, it will initialize the pager, which includes allocating a control port and passing it as an argument to `memory_object_init()`. Finally, the call to `vm_map_enter()` [osfmk/vm/vm_map.c] will result in a virtual address range being allocated in the task's virtual address space.

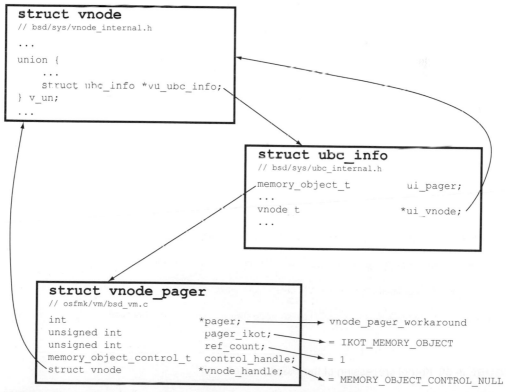

FIGURE 8–49 Setting up of the vnode pager for a newly created vnode

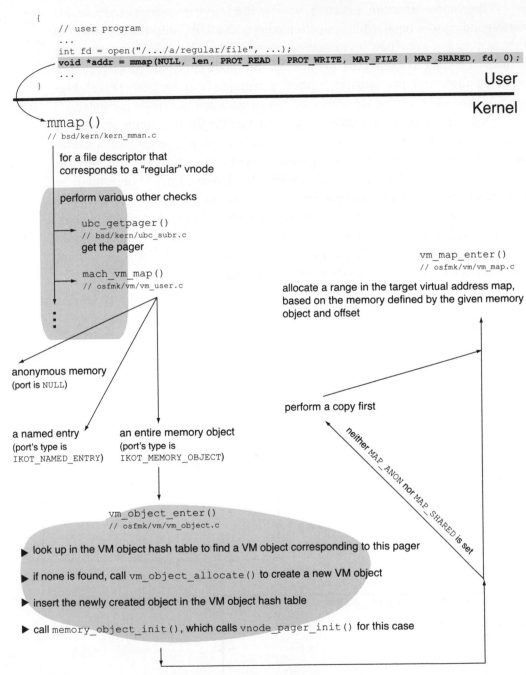

FIGURE 8–50 Kernel processing of the `mmap()` system call

When the program attempts to access an address of the mapped memory for reading, it will cause page-in activity if the corresponding page is not resident yet (to begin with, no pages will be resident). Since the program mapped the file with PROT_READ | PROT_WRITE as the protection value and MAP_SHARED specified in the flags, it will also eventually cause page-out activity if it modifies the mapped memory.

Figures 8–51 and 8–52 show an overview of the steps involved in a page-in operation, with the latter showing details of paging in from a vnode. Figures 8–53 and 8–54 show the analogous overview for a page-out operation.

8.18 64-bit Computing

When introduced in 1991, the MIPS R4000 was the world's first 64-bit processor. The term *64-bit* meant several things when applied to the R4000, for example:

- A 64-bit virtual address space (although the maximum user process size was limited to 40 bits on the R4000)
- A 64-bit system bus
- The 64-bit general-purpose (integer) registers
- A 64-bit ALU and a 64-bit on-chip FPU
- A 64-bit natural mode of operation, with support for 32-bit operation with integer registers acting as 32-bit registers

A processor is informally considered a 64-bit processor if it has 64-bit general-purpose registers and can support 64-bit (or at least "much more" than 32-bit) virtual memory. Moreover, the operating system must explicitly make use of the processor's 64-bit capabilities for 64-bit *computing* to materialize.

The introduction and evolution of 64-bit computing with Mac OS X can be summarized as follows:

- The G5 (PowerPC 970, specifically) was the first 64-bit processor to be used in a Macintosh computer.
- Mac OS X 10.3 was the first Apple operating system to support more than 4GB of physical memory on 64-bit hardware. User virtual address spaces were still 32-bit-only.
- Mac OS X 10.4 was the first Apple operating system to support 64-bit user virtual address spaces on 64-bit hardware.

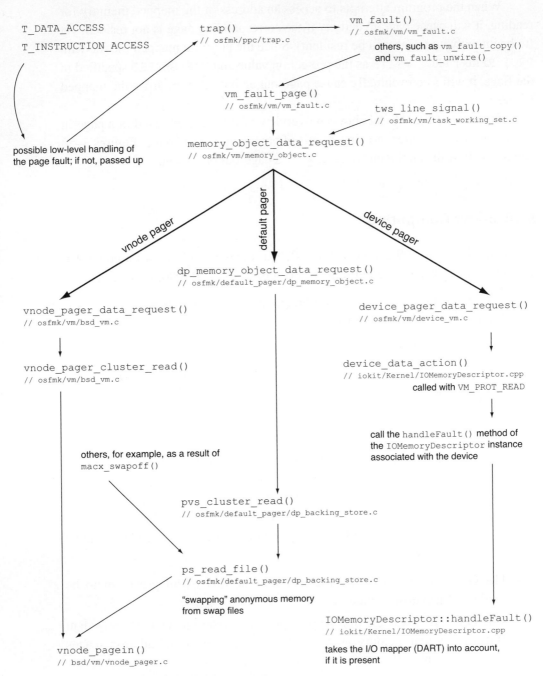

FIGURE 8–51 An overview of a page-in operation

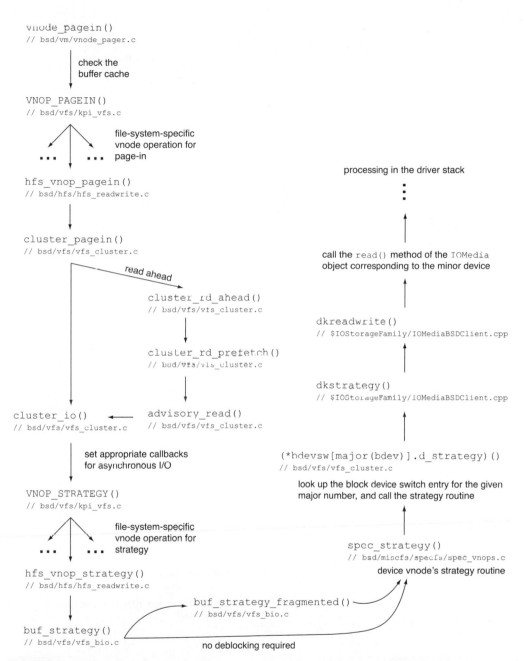

FIGURE 8–52 Paging in from a vnode

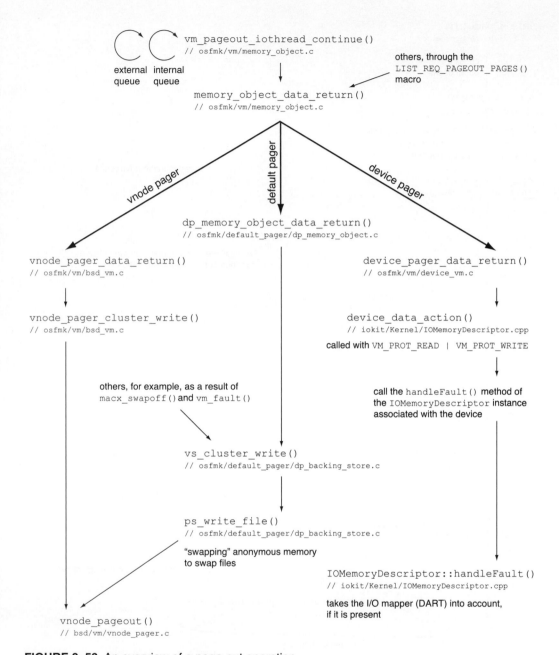

FIGURE 8–53 An overview of a page-out operation

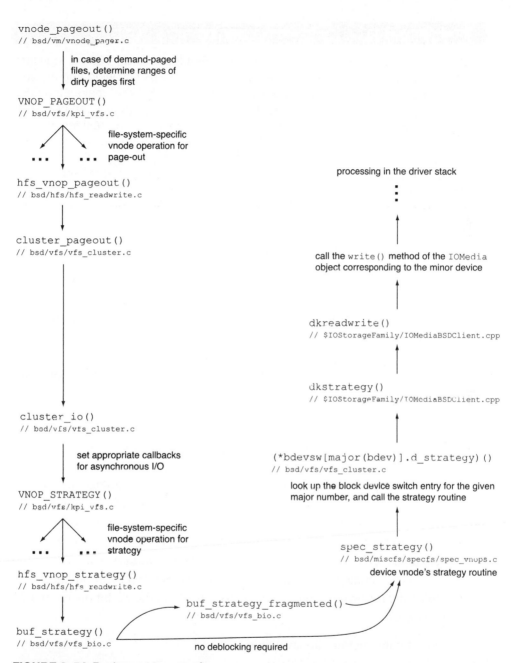

FIGURE 8–54 Paging out to a vnode

How Many Bits?

The G4, which is a 32-bit processor, contains 64-bit and even 128-bit registers. We saw in Chapter 3 that the floating-point registers are 64 bits wide and the vector registers are 128 bits wide on both the G4 and the G5. What makes the G5 a 64-bit processor is that it has 64-bit general-purpose registers, and it can use 64-bit virtual addressing. A 64-bit-wide C data type such as a long long resides in a single register when the G5 is operating as a 64-bit processor; however, on the G4 (or the G5 operating as a 32-bit processor), a long long is split into two 32-bit quantities, occupying two registers. Consequently, integer math and logical operations require more instructions and more registers.

8.18.1 Reasons for 64-bit Computing

Often 64-bit computing is (incorrectly) understood to be invariably conducive to performance. Although in some cases this may be true, usually only programs with very specific needs benefit from 64-bit computing. Whether a program performs better just by virtue of being 64-bit depends on whether the processor performs better in its 64-bit mode, perhaps because its 64-bit instructions operate on more data at the same time. Another, more important reason for justifying 64-bit computing is the substantially larger address space it provides. Let us look at some of these reasons in the context of Mac OS X on the G5.

8.18.1.1 32-bit Execution on 64-bit PowerPC

In general, 64-bit processors and operating systems allow simultaneous coexistence of 32-bit and 64-bit programs. However, architectures differ in how a 64-bit processor performs when in 32-bit mode. As we saw in Chapter 3, the PowerPC began life with a 64-bit architecture that had a 32-bit subset. When a 64-bit PowerPC implementation (such as the G5) operates in 32-bit *computation mode*, there is no great performance penalty as is the case with some other processor architectures. In particular, the following aspects are noteworthy about the 32-bit operation of a 64-bit PowerPC.

- All 64-bit instructions are available.
- All 64-bit registers are available.
- The processor's use of busses, caches, data paths, execution units, and other internal resources is the same regardless of the operating mode.

> The current computation mode is determined by bit 0—the SF (Sixty Four) bit—of the Machine State Register (MSR). The processor runs in 64-bit mode when this bit's value is 1.

However, there are important differences between the two computation modes.

- An effective address is treated as a 32-bit address in 32-bit mode. 32-bit load/store instructions ignore the upper 32 bits of memory addresses. Note that the address computations actually produce 64-bit addresses in 32-bit mode—the upper 32 bits are ignored as a software convention.

- Condition codes (such as carry, overflow, and zero bits) are set per 32-bit arithmetic in 32-bit mode.

- When branch conditional instructions test the Count Register (CTR), they use 32-bit conventions in 32-bit mode.

The available instructions, the number of available registers, and the width of these registers all remain the same in both 64-bit and 32-bit computation modes. In particular, you can perform hardware-optimized 64-bit integer arithmetic in 32-bit programs, albeit with some caveats. However, the 32-bit ABI will use the same conventions for passing parameters, saving nonvolatile registers, and returning values, regardless of which instructions are used. Consequently, using full 64-bit registers from a nonleaf function (one that calls at least one other function) in a 32-bit program is not safe.

Let us consider an example. The cntlzd instruction is a 64-bit-only instruction that counts the number of consecutive zero bits starting at bit 0 of its second operand, placing the count in the first operand. Consider the program shown in Figure 8–55. The main function causes this instruction to execute in two ways: first, by calling another function, and second, by using inline assembly.

FIGURE 8–55 Using a 64-bit-only instruction

```
; cntlzd.s
        .text
        .align 2
#ifndef __ppc64__
        .machine ppc970
#endif
        .globl _cntlzd
```

(continues)

FIGURE 8–55 Using a 64-bit-only instruction *(continued)*

```
_cntlzd:
        cntlzd  r3,r3
        blr

// cntlzd_main.c

#include <stdio.h>
#include <stdint.h>

extern uint64_t cntlzd(uint64_t in);

int
main(void)
{
    uint64_t out;
    uint64_t in = 0x4000000000000000LL;

    out = cntlzd(in);

    printf("%lld\n", out);

    __asm("cntlzd %0,%1\n"
        : "=r"(out)
        :  "r"(in)
    );

    printf("%lld\n", out);

    return 0;
}
```

We can attempt to compile the source shown in Figure 8–55 in several ways, as shown in Table 8–9.

Let us look at some examples of using the information in Table 8–9.

```
$ gcc -Wall -o cntlzd_32_32 cntlzd_main.c cntlzd.s
/var/tmp//ccozyb9N.s:38:cntlzd instruction is only for 64-bit implementations (not
allowed without -force_cpusubtype_ALL option)
cntlzd.s:6:cntlzd instruction is only for 64-bit implementations (not allowed with-
out -force_cpusubtype_ALL option)

$ gcc -Wall -force_cpusubtype_ALL -o cntlzd cntlzd_main.c cntlzd.s
$ ./cntlzd
141733920768
141733920768
```

TABLE 8–9 Compiling for a 64-bit PowerPC Target

Compiler Options	Description	Result
No special options	Compile normally, as a 32-bit program.	Will not compile.
`-force_cpu_subtype_ALL`	Compile as a 32-bit program, but force 64-bit instructions to be accepted by the compiler.	Will run only on 64-bit hardware, but both uses of `cntlzd` will produce undesirable results.
`-mpowerpc64 -mcpu=G5`	Compile as a 32-bit program, with explicit support for 64-bit instructions on 64-bit hardware.	Will run only on 64-bit hardware. The inline usage of `cntlzd` will produce the desired result, but the function call version will not, because `main()` will pass the 64-bit argument to `cntlzd()` as two 32-bit quantities in two GPRs.
`-arch ppc64`	Compile as a 64-bit program.	Will run only on 64-bit hardware and produce the desired result in both uses of `cntlzd`.

```
$ gcc -Wall -mpowerpc64 -mcpu=G5 -o cntlzd cntlzd_main.c cntlzd.s
$ ./cntlzd
141733920768
1

$ gcc -Wall -arch ppc64 -o cntlzd cntlzd_main.c cntlzd.s
$ ./cntlzd
1
1
```

Enabling 64-bit instructions in a 32-bit PowerPC program sets the CPU subtype in the Mach-O header to `ppc970`, which prevents `execve()` from running it on 32-bit hardware.

8.18.1.2 Need for Address Space

The need for more than 4GB of virtual address space is perhaps the most justifiable reason for 64-bit computing on the PowerPC. That said, even 32-bit Mac OS X programs can benefit from 64-bit hardware with more than 4GB of physical memory. Such systems are supported beginning with Mac OS X 10.3. A 32-bit program could use `mmap()` and `munmap()` to switch between multiple windows of disk-backed memory. The sum of all the window sizes could be larger than

4GB, even though the program would not be able to address more than 4GB of virtual memory at any given time. Since the Mac OS X buffer cache is greedy, it will consume all available physical memory, keeping as much data as possible resident, provided the file descriptors corresponding to the various mappings are kept open. This approach is tantamount to a program handling its own paging, whereas in the case of a 64-bit address space, the kernel would handle the paging.

This approach, although workable, is still a compromise. Depending on the specific needs of a memory-hungry program, the approach may be merely inconvenient, or it may be unacceptable.

8.18.1.3 Large-File Support

One aspect sometimes associated with 64-bit computing is large-file support—that is, the operating system's ability to use file offsets larger than 32 bits wide. A 32-bit signed offset can address only up to 2GB of data in a file. Besides support from the file system to house large files, you need larger offsets—say, 64 bits wide, for convenience—to use such files. However, large-file support *does not* require 64-bit hardware: Numbers larger than a hardware register can be synthesized using multiple registers on 32-bit hardware. Many operating systems, including Mac OS X, provide large-file support on 32-bit and 64-bit hardware alike.

The `off_t` data type, which is used by relevant system calls, is a 64-bit signed integer on Mac OS X, allowing file-system-related calls to handle 64-bit offsets in 32-bit programs. The `size_t` data type is defined to be an unsigned long integer, which is 32 or 64 bits wide, respectively, in the 32-bit and 64-bit environments.

8.18.2 Mac OS X 10.4: 64-bit User Address Spaces

The primary user-visible aspect of 64-bit computing in Mac OS X 10.4 is that you can have a user-space program with a 64-bit virtual address space, which allows the program to conveniently/concurrently use more than 4GB of virtual memory. The PowerPC version of Mac OS X explicitly supports binaries for two architectures: `ppc` and `ppc64`, with respective executable formats (Mach-O and Mach-O 64-bit). When a `ppc64` binary runs, the corresponding process can concurrently address more than 4GB of virtual memory.

> Both `ppc64` and `ppc` versions of an executable can be contained in a single file and executed transparently by using fat files. On 64-bit hardware, the `execve()` system call selects the `ppc64` executable from a fat file that contains both `ppc64` and `ppc` executables.

8.18.2.1 Data Model

The Mac OS X 64-bit environment uses the LP64 data model, as do most other 64-bit operating systems. The letters L and P in LP64 mean that the long and pointer data types are 64 bits wide. The integer data type remains 32 bits wide in this model. LP64 is also known as 4/8/8 for this reason. ILP64 (8/8/8) and LLP64 (4/4/8) are alternative models—the I in ILP64 represents the integer data type. Table 8–10 shows the models used by 64-bit versions of several operating systems. As seen in the table, the pointer data type is 64 bits wide in all models. In contrast, the 32-bit Mac OS X environment uses the ILP32 data model, in which the integer, long, and pointer data types all are 32 bits wide. In both the LP64 and ILP32 models, the following relationship holds:

```
sizeof(char) <= sizeof(short) <= sizeof(int) <= sizeof(long) <= sizeof(long long)
```

TABLE 8–10 A Sampling of Abstract Data Models in 64-bit-Capable Operating Systems

Operating System/Platform	Data Model
Mac OS X 10.4	LP64
AIX	LP64
Cray (various operating systems)	ILP64
Digital UNIX	LP64
HP-UX	LP64
IRIX	LP64
Linux	LP64
NetBSD (alpha, amd64, sparc64)	LP64
Solaris	LP64
Tru64	LP64
Windows	LLP64 (also known as P64)
z/OS	LP64

8.18.2.2 Implementation

Although Mac OS X 10.4 supports 64-bit user programs, the kernel is still 32-bit.[26] Although the kernel manages as much physical memory as the system can support, it does not directly address more than 4GB of physical memory concurrently. To achieve this, the kernel uses appropriately sized data structures to keep track of all memory, while itself using a 32-bit virtual address space with 32-bit kernel pointers. Similarly, device drivers and other kernel extensions remain 32-bit. Figure 8–56 shows a conceptual view of 64-bit support in Mac OS X 10.4.

The kernel uses `addr64_t`, defined to be a 64-bit unsigned integer, as the basic effective address type. An `addr64_t` is passed and returned as two adjacent 32-bit GPRs, regardless of the register width of the underlying processor. This data type is used in the kernel for common code that is used unchanged on 32-bit and 64-bit machines. For example, the pmap interface routines use `addr64_t` as the address data type. The kernel also uses the 64-bit long long data type (equivalent to `addr64_t`) for various VM subsystem entities. It internally converts between long long (or `addr64_t`) parameters and single 64-bit register values.

```
// osfmk/mach/memory_object_types.h

typedef unsigned long long memory_object_offset_t;
typedef unsigned long long memory_object_size_t;
```

```
// osfmk/mach/vm_types.h

typedef uint64_t vm_object_offset_t;
typedef uint64_t vm_object_size_t;
```

> Although the kernel's own virtual address space is 32-bit, the VM subsystem does run the processor in 64-bit computation mode for mapping certain VM-related data structures.

The kernel defines `ppnum_t`, the data type for the physical page number, to be a 32-bit unsigned integer. Consequently, there can be at most `UINT32_MAX` physical pages. For a page size of 4KB, this limits the physical address space to 16TB.

---

26. In fact, a given version of Mac OS uses the same kernel executable for all supported Apple computer models.

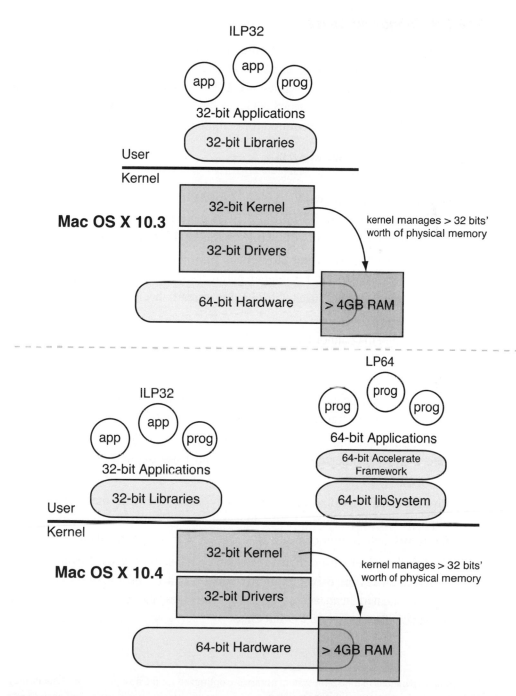

FIGURE 8–56 An overview of 64-bit support in Mac OS X

8.18.2.3 Usage and Caveats

In Mac OS X 10.4, 64-bit support is limited to C and C++ programs that only link against the system library (i.e., `libSystem.dylib` or `System.framework`),[27] which is available as a dual-architecture library. Additionally, the Accelerate framework (`Accelerate.framework`) is available in both 32-bit and 64-bit versions. GCC 4.0.0 or higher is required to compile 64-bit programs.

```
$ lipo -info /usr/lib/libSystem.dylib
Architectures in the fat file: /usr/lib/libSystem.dylib are: ppc ppc64
```

Key Mac OS X frameworks such as Carbon, Cocoa, Core Foundation, and the I/O Kit framework are 32-bit-only. Both generic and Mac OS X–specific migration issues must be dealt with while creating 64-bit programs.

- The 64-bit ABI has several differences from the 32-bit ABI, on which it is based. For example, 64-bit integer parameters are passed in a single GPR. The Pthreads library uses GPR13 for thread-specific data retrieved by `pthread_self()`.

- 64-bit programs cannot use 32-bit libraries or plug-ins and vice versa. Specifically, 32-bit and 64-bit code cannot be mixed in a single program, since the kernel tags an entire task as 32-bit or 64-bit.

- 64-bit programs cannot have native Mac OS X graphical user interfaces since the relevant frameworks are not available in 64-bit versions.

- Although 64-bit and 32-bit programs can share memory and can communicate with each other through IPC, they must use explicit data types while doing so.

- Programs that serialize binary data may want to ensure that the size and alignment of the serialized data does not change between 32-bit and 64-bit programs, unless only one type of program will access that data.

- An I/O Kit driver's user client (see Chapter 10) cannot be used from a 64-bit program unless the driver explicitly supports 64-bit user address spaces. A kernel extension can access physical addresses above 4GB by using the `IOMemoryDescriptor` I/O Kit class.

---

27. Certain operations in the 32-bit system library are optimized for the host processor—that is, they make use of 64-bit hardware if it is available.

The x86 version of Mac OS X 10.4 does not support 64-bit computing. As Apple adopts 64-bit x86 processors,[28] Mac OS X should regain 64-bit support. It is very likely that most, if not all, user libraries will have 64-bit equivalents in future versions of Mac OS X.

8.18.3 Why Not to Use 64-bit Executables

Especially in Mac OS X, 64-bit programs are not necessarily "better" just by being 64-bit. In fact, typical programs are likely to have poorer performance if compiled for 64-bit computing. The following are some reasons against using 64-bit executables on Mac OS X.

- The memory footprint of 64-bit programs is higher in general: They use larger pointers, stacks, and data sets. This potentially leads to more cache and TLB misses.

- 64-bit software support in Mac OS X 10.4 is nascent. The interfaces that have migrated to 64-bit are not mature, and most of the commonly used interfaces are still 32-bit.

- As we discussed earlier, some of the usual reasons for moving to 64-bit computing are not very compelling on the PowerPC.

- Certain PowerPC nuances can slow down 64-bit execution. For example, if a 32-bit signed integer is used as an array index, then, unless the integer is stored in a register, each access will require an extra `extsw` instruction to sign-extend the value.

8.18.4 The 64-bit "Scene"

As Table 8–10 indicates, there exist several 64-bit operating systems. For example, 64-bit Solaris has a fully 64-bit kernel with 64-bit drivers. Barring some obsolete libraries, Solaris system libraries have both 32-bit and 64-bit versions. Both types of applications can run concurrently. Similarly, the AIX 5L operating system for 64-bit POWER hardware has a fully 64-bit kernel. Again, drivers and other kernel extensions are also 64-bit, and both 32-bit and 64-bit user environments are supported concurrently. There is also a 32-bit AIX 5L kernel that supports

---

28. A likely first candidate is Intel's "Merom" 64-bit mobile processor.

64-bit applications on 64-bit hardware. However, the amount of physical memory it can support is limited (96GB) as compared to the 64-bit kernel.

Standards and 64-bit

The Single UNIX Specification, Version 2 (UNIX 98) included large-file support and removed architectural dependencies to allow 64-bit processing. APIs that were tied to 32-bit data types were cleaned up. For example, several functions were made large-file-aware, using `off_t` instead of `size_t`. Version 3 of the Single UNIX Specification (UNIX 03) revised, combined, and updated several standards, including the POSIX standard.

CHAPTER 9

Interprocess Communication

Complex programs, even those that are moderately so, are usually broken down into logically and functionally separate constituents, rather than being monolithic programs that do "everything." This allows for easier development, maintenance, and flexibility, as well as better comprehensibility of software. Although such division could be done in numerous ways, several of them formal and standardized, one general outcome is that on a typical operating system, there might be multiple entities performing related operations. Such entities often need to share information, synchronize, and otherwise communicate with each other. This chapter explores several means of information sharing and synchronization—*interprocess communication*—in Mac OS X.

9.1 Introduction

Running even the most trivial C program on Mac OS X leads to the invocation of dozens of system calls—as the runtime environment loads it, prepares it for execution, and executes it. Consider this simple example.

```
// empty.c

main()
{
}
```

```
$ gcc -o empty empty.c
$ ktrace ./empty
$ kdump | grep CALL | wc -l
49
```

Although our trivial program has an empty user-visible body, it still needs to be prepared by `dyld` so that the empty body can be executed. This preparation involves numerous steps, such as initializing Pthreads-related and Mach-related data structures for the new program. For example, `dyld` invokes a Mach trap to set the "self" value for the program's thread being run, initializes the special Mach ports in the application, and reserves the zeroth page so that it may not be allocated by the program. Consequently, there is a variety of communication between various bodies of user-space code and the kernel. Graphical interface systems make heavy use of communication between their components and with the rest of the system.

Nontrivial applications might comprise multiple threads—perhaps even multiple processes—that may need to communicate with each other in arbitrary ways, thus necessitating interfaces for such communication. Often, processes that are not part of the same program must communicate with each other too. The Unix command pipeline abstraction exemplifies such communication:

```
$ find . -type f | grep kernel | sort | head -5
```

It is worthwhile to question what qualifies as communication. In some cases, the line between communication and information sharing may be blurred. The Mac OS X `pbcopy` command-line utility is a Cocoa program that copies its standard output and places it in a pasteboard. It can handle ASCII data, Encapsulated PostScript (EPS), Rich Text Format (RTF), Portable Document Format (PDF), and so on. The `pbpaste` command removes data from a pasteboard and writes it to its standard output. These utilities allow command-line programs to communicate in a copy-and-paste way with other command-line or graphical programs. The following is a contrived (and expensive) way to print "Hello, World!" from the shell:

```
$ echo 'Hello, World!' | pbcopy
$ pbpaste
Hello, World!
```

For the purpose of this chapter, we understand interprocess communication (IPC) to be a well-defined mechanism—with a programming interface—for transferring information between two or more entities. Historically, the communicating entities were processes, hence the term *interprocess*. Since the early days of timesharing systems, a variety of computing resources have been associated with processes. IPC is also a means of sharing these resources. As we saw in Chapter 7, a runnable entity can take many forms in Mac OS X. Consequently, IPC can occur between any of these runnable entities—for example, threads in the same task, threads in different tasks, and threads in the kernel.

Depending on the type of IPC, communicating parties may require some form of synchronization for the IPC mechanism to operate correctly. For example, if multiple processes are sharing a file or a region of memory, they must synchronize with each other to ensure that shared information is not being modified and read simultaneously, as it could briefly be in an inconsistent state. In general, IPC might require and may consist of one or more of the following operations:

- Sharing of data
- Transfer of data
- Sharing of resources
- Synchronization between IPC participants
- Synchronous and asynchronous notifications
- Control operations, such as a debugger shepherding a target process

> The term *IPC* is often used synonymously with *message passing*, which could be thought of as one specific (and rather popular) IPC mechanism.

9.1.1 The Evolution of IPC

Early IPC mechanisms used files as the communication medium: an approach that did not work well owing to the slowness of disks and large windows for race conditions between programs. This was followed by shared memory approaches, wherein processes used commonly accessible regions of memory to implement ad hoc IPC and synchronization schemes. Eventually, IPC mechanisms became an abstraction provided by the operating system itself.

MULTICS IPC

Michael J. Spier and Elliott I. Organick described a general-purpose IPC facility in their 1969 paper titled "The MULTICS Interprocess Communication Facility."[1] A MULTICS process was defined as a "hardware-level" process whose address space was a collection of named segments, each with defined access, and over which a single execution point was free to fetch instructions and make data references. The MULTICS central supervisor program (the kernel) ensured that at most one execution point was ever awarded to an address space. With this definition of a process, MULTICS IPC was defined as an exchange of data communications among cooperating processes. This was achieved by an exchange of messages in a commonly accessible *mailbox*—a shared database whose identity was known to each IPC participant by common convention.

The MULTICS IPC facility was part of the central supervisor. It was one of the earliest examples of a completely generalized, modular interface available to programmers.

9.1.2 IPC in Mac OS X

Mac OS X provides a large number of IPC mechanisms, some with interfaces available at multiple layers of the system. The following are examples of IPC mechanisms/interfaces in Mac OS X:

- Mach IPC—the lowest-level IPC mechanism and the direct basis for many higher-level mechanisms
- Mach exceptions
- Unix signals
- Unnamed pipes
- Named pipes (fifos)
- XSI/System V IPC
- POSIX IPC
- Distributed Objects
- Apple Events

---

1. "The MULTICS Interprocess Communication Facility," by Michael J. Spier and Elliott I. Organick. In *Proceedings of the Second ACM Symposium on Operating Systems Principles* (Princeton, NJ: ACM, 1969, pp. 83–91).

- Various interfaces for sending and receiving notifications, such as `notify(3)` and `kqueue(2)`
- Core Foundation IPC mechanisms

> Note that the term *notification* is context-dependent. For example, Mach can send notifications when a Mach port is deleted or destroyed. The application environments provide interfaces for sending and receiving intraprocess and interprocess notifications.

Each of these mechanisms has certain benefits, shortcomings, and caveats. A programmer could need to use a particular mechanism, or perhaps even multiple mechanisms, based on the program's requirements and the system layer for which it is being targeted.

In the rest of this chapter, we will look at these IPC mechanisms. Those that are common across several platforms (such as System V IPC), and therefore abundantly documented elsewhere, will be discussed only briefly.

> An important IPC mechanism that we will *not* cover in this chapter is that provided by the ubiquitous BSD sockets. Similarly, we will also not discuss the older OpenTransport API, a subset of which is provided by Mac OS X as a compatibility library for legacy applications.

Since IPC usually goes hand in hand with synchronization, we will also look at the important synchronization mechanisms available on Mac OS X.

9.2 Mach IPC: An Overview

Mach provides a message-oriented, capability-based IPC facility that represents an evolution of similar approaches used by Mach's precursors, namely, Accent and RIG. Mach's IPC implementation uses the VM subsystem to efficiently transfer large amounts of data using copy-on-write optimizations. The Mac OS X kernel uses the general message primitive provided by Mach's IPC interface as a low-level building block. In particular, the Mach calls `mach_msg()` and `mach_msg_overwrite()` can be used for both sending and receiving messages (in that order), allowing RPC[2]-style interaction as a special case of IPC. This type of RPC is used for implementing several system services in Mac OS X.

---

2. Remote procedure call.

A Portly Look Back

David C. Walden's 1972 paper titled "A System for Interprocess Communication in a Resource Sharing Computer Network"[3] describes a set of operations enabling interprocess communication within a single timesharing system, but using techniques that could easily be generalized to permit communication between remote processes. Walden's description included an abstraction called a *port*, which he defined to be a particular data path to a process (a RECEIVE port) or from a process (a SEND port). All ports had associated unique identifiers called *port numbers*. The kernel maintained a table of port numbers associated with processes and *restart locations*. On completion of an IPC transmission, the kernel transferred the participant (sender or receiver) to a restart location, which was specified as part of a SEND or RECEIVE operation.

Although Walden's description was that of a hypothetical system, many parallels can be found in latter-day IPC mechanisms in systems like RIG, Accent, and Mach—including Mac OS X.

As we saw in Chapter 1, the Rochester's Intelligent Gateway (RIG) system, whose implementation began in 1975, used an IPC facility as the basic structuring tool. RIG's IPC facility used *ports* and *messages* as basic abstractions. A RIG port was a kernel-managed message queue, globally identified by a `<process number.port number>` pair of integers. A RIG message was a limited-size unit consisting of a header and some data.

The Accent system improved upon RIG's IPC by defining ports to be *capabilities* as well as communication objects and by using a larger address space along with copy-on-write techniques to handle large objects. An intermediary *Network Server* process could transparently extend Accent's IPC across the network.

A process was an address space and a single program counter in both RIG and Accent. Mach split the process abstraction into a task and a thread, with the task portion owning port access rights. The use of thread mechanisms to handle errors and certain asynchronous activities simplified Mach's IPC facility. Mach 3.0, from which the Mac OS X kernel's Mach component is derived, incorporated several performance- and functionality-related improvements to IPC.

The Mach IPC facility is built on two basic kernel abstractions: *ports* and *messages*, with messages passing between ports as the fundamental communication mechanism. A port is a multifaceted entity, whereas a message is an arbitrarily sized collection of data objects.

---

3. "A System for Interprocess Communication in a Resource Sharing Computer Network," by David C. Walden (*Communications of the ACM* 15:4, April 1972, pp. 221–230).

9.2.1 Mach Ports

Mach ports serve the following primary purposes in the operating system.

- A port is a communications channel—a kernel-protected, kernel-managed, and finite-length queue of messages. The most basic operations on a port are for *sending* and *receiving* messages. Sending to a port allows a task to place messages into the port's underlying queue. Receiving allows a task to retrieve messages from that queue, which holds incoming messages until the recipient removes them. When a queue corresponding to a port is full or empty, senders and receivers, respectively, are blocked in general.

- Ports are used to represent capabilities in that they themselves are protected by a capability mechanism to prevent arbitrary Mach tasks from accessing them. To access a port, a task must have a port capability, or *port right*, such as a *send right* or a *receive right*. The specific rights a task has to a port limit the set of operations the task may perform on that port. This allows Mach to prevent unauthorized tasks from accessing ports and, in particular, from manipulating objects associated with ports.

- Ports are used to represent resources, services, and facilities, thus providing object-style access to these abstractions. For example, Mach uses ports to represent abstractions such as hosts, tasks, threads, memory objects, clocks, timers, processors, and processor sets. Operations on such port-represented objects are performed by sending messages to their representative ports. The kernel, which typically holds the receive rights to such ports, receives and processes the messages. This is analogous to object-oriented method invocation.

A port's *name* can stand for several entities, such as a right for sending or receiving messages, a dead name, a port set, or nothing. In general, we refer to what a port name stands for as a *port right*, although the term *right* may seem unintuitive in some situations. We will discuss details of these concepts later in this chapter.

9.2.1.1 Ports for Communication

In its role as a communications channel, a Mach port resembles a BSD socket, but there are important differences, such as those listed here.

- Mach IPC, by design, is integrated with the virtual memory subsystem.
- Whereas sockets are primarily used for remote communication, Mach IPC is primarily used for (and optimized for) intramachine communication. However, Mach IPC, by design, can be transparently extended over the network.

- Mach IPC messages can carry typed content.
- In general, Mach IPC interfaces are more powerful and flexible than the socket interfaces.

> When we talk of a message being sent to a task, we mean that the message is sent to a port that the recipient task has receive rights to. The message is dequeued by a thread within the recipient task.

Integration of IPC with virtual memory allows messages to be mapped—copy-on-write, if possible and appropriate—into the receiving task's address space. In theory, a message could be as large as the size of a task's address space.

Although the Mach kernel itself does not include any explicit support for distributed IPC, communication can be transparently extended over the network by using external (user-level) tasks called *Network Servers*, which simply act as local proxies for remote tasks. A message sent to a remote port will be sent to a local Network Server, which is responsible for forwarding it to a Network Server on the remote destination machine. The participant tasks are unaware of these details, hence the transparency.

> Although the xnu kernel retains most of the semantics of Mach IPC, network-transparent Mach IPC is not used on Mac OS X.

9.2.1.2 *Port Rights*

The following specific port right types are defined on Mac OS X.

- `MACH_PORT_RIGHT_SEND`—A *send right* to a port implies that the right's holder can send messages to that port. Send rights are reference counted. If a thread acquires a send right that the task already holds, the right's reference count is incremented. Similarly, a right's reference count is decremented when a thread deallocates the right. This mechanism prevents race conditions involving premature deallocation of send rights, as the task will lose the send right only when the right's reference count becomes zero. Therefore, several threads in a multithreaded program can use such rights safely.
- `MACH_PORT_RIGHT_RECEIVE`—A *receive right* to a port implies that the right's holder can dequeue messages from that port. A port may have any

number of senders but *only one receiver*. Moreover, if a task has a receive right to a port, it automatically has a send right to it too.

- MACH_PORT_RIGHT_SEND_ONCE—A *send-once right* allows its holder to send only one message, after which the right is deleted. Send-once rights are used as reply ports, wherein a client can include a send-once right in a request message, and the server can use that right to send a reply. A send-once right always results in exactly one message being sent—even if it is destroyed, in which case a *send-once notification* is generated.

- MACH_PORT_RIGHT_PORT_SET—A *port set* name can be considered as a receive right encompassing multiple ports. A port set represents a group of ports to which the task has a receive right. In other words, a port set is a bucket of receive rights. It allows a task to receive a message, the first that is available, from any of the member ports of a set. The message identifies the specific port it was received on.

- MACH_PORT_RIGHT_DEAD_NAME—A *dead name* is not really a right; it represents a send or send-once right that has become invalid because the corresponding port was destroyed. As a send right transforms into a dead name on invalidation, its reference count also carries over to the dead name. Attempting to send a message to a dead name results in an error, which allows senders to realize that the port is destroyed. Dead names prevent the port names they take over from being reused prematurely.

> A port is considered to be destroyed when its receive right is deallocated. Although existing send or send-once rights will transform into dead names when this happens, existing messages in the ports queue are destroyed, and any associated out-of-line memory is freed.

The following are some noteworthy aspects of port rights.

- Rights are owned at the task level. For example, although the code to create a port executes in a thread, the associated rights are granted to the thread's task. Thereafter, any other thread within that task can use or manipulate the rights.

- The namespace for ports is per-task private—that is, a given port name is valid only within the IPC space of a task. This is analogous to per-task virtual address spaces.

- If a task holds both the send right and receive right for a port, the rights have the same name.

- No two send-once rights held by the task have the same name.

- Rights can be transferred through message passing. In particular, the frequent operation of gaining access to a port involves receiving a message containing a port right.

- After a task has sent a message containing one or more port rights, and before the message is dequeued by the receiver, the rights are held by the kernel. Since a receive right can be held by only one task at any time, there is the possibility of messages being sent to a port whose receive right is being transferred. In such a case, the kernel will enqueue the messages until the receiver task receives the rights and dequeues the messages.

9.2.1.3 *Ports as Objects*

The Mach IPC facility is a general-purpose object-reference mechanism that uses ports as protected access points. In semantic terms, the Mach kernel is a *server* that serves objects on various ports. This kernel server receives incoming messages, processes them by performing the requested operations, and, if required, sends a reply. This approach allows a more general and useful implementation of several operations that have been historically implemented as intraprocess function calls. For example, one Mach task can allocate a region of virtual memory in *another* task's address space—if permitted—by sending an appropriate message to the port representing the target task.

Note that the same model is used for accessing both user-level and kernel services. In either case, a task accesses the service by having one of its threads send messages to the service provider, which can be another user task or the kernel.

> Besides message passing, little Mach functionality is exposed through Mach traps. Most Mach services are provided through message-passing interfaces. User programs typically access these services by sending messages to the appropriate ports.

We saw earlier that ports are used to represent both tasks and threads. When a task creates another task or a thread, it automatically gets access to the newly created entity's port. Since port ownership is task-level, all per-thread ports in a task are accessible to all threads within that task. A thread can send messages to other threads within its task—say, to suspend or resume their execution. It follows that having access to a task's port implicitly provides access to all threads within that task. The converse does not hold, however: Having access to a thread's port does not give access to its containing task's port.

9.2.1.4 Mach Port Allocation

A user program can acquire a port right in several ways, examples of which we will see later in this chapter. A program creates a new port right through the mach_port_allocate family of routines, of which mach_port_allocate() is the simplest:

```
int
mach_port_allocate(ipc_space_t          task,  // task acquiring the port right
                   mach_port_right_t  right, // type of right to be created
                   mach_port_name_t   *name); // returns name for the new right
```

We will discuss details of port allocation in Section 9.3.5.

9.2.2 Mach IPC Messages

Mach IPC messages can be sent and received through the mach_msg family of functions. The fundamental IPC system call in Mac OS X is a trap called mach_msg_overwrite_trap() [osfmk/ipc/mach_msg.c], which can be used for sending a message, receiving a message, or both sending and receiving (in that order—an RPC) in a single call.

```
// osfmk/ipc/mach_msg.c

mach_msg_return_t
mach_msg_overwrite_trap(
     mach_msg_header_t  *snd_msg,   // message buffer to be sent
     mach_msg_option_t   option,    // bitwise OR of commands and modifiers
     mach_msg_size_t     send_size, // size of outgoing message buffer
     mach_msg_size_t     rcv_size,  // maximum size of receive buffer (rcv_msg)
     mach_port_name_t    rcv_name,  // port or port set to receive on
     mach_msg_timeout_t  timeout,   // timeout in milliseconds
     mach_port_name_t    notify,    // receive right for a notify port
     mach_msg_header_t  *rcv_msg,   // message buffer for receiving
     mach_msg_size_t     scatterlist_sz); // size of scatter list control info
```

The behavior of `mach_msg_overwrite_trap()` is controlled by setting the appropriate bits in the `option` argument. These bits determine what the call does and how it does it. Some bits cause the call to use one or more of the other arguments, which may be unused otherwise. The following are some examples of individual bits that can be set in `option`.

- `MACH_SEND_MSG`—If set, send a message.
- `MACH_RCV_MSG`—If set, receive a message.
- `MACH_SEND_TIMEOUT`—If set, the `timeout` argument specifies the timeout while sending.
- `MACH_RCV_TIMEOUT`—If set, `timeout` specifies the timeout while receiving.
- `MACH_SEND_INTERRUPT`—If set, the call returns `MACH_SEND_INTERRUPTED` if a software interrupt aborts the call; otherwise, an interrupted send is reattempted.
- `MACH_RCV_INTERRUPT`—This bit is similar to `MACH_SEND_INTERRUPT`, but for receiving.
- `MACH_RCV_LARGE`—If set, the kernel will not destroy a received message even if it is larger than the receive limit; this way, the receiver can reattempt to receive the message.

> The header file `osfmk/mach/message.h` contains the full set of modifiers that can be used with the `mach_msg` family of functions.

Another Mach trap, `mach_msg_trap()`, simply calls `mach_msg_overwrite_trap()` with zeros as the last two arguments—it uses the same buffer when the call is used for both sending and receiving, so the `rcv_msg` argument is not needed.

The `scatterlist_sz` argument is used when the receiver, while receiving an *out-of-line* message (see Section 9.5.5), wants the kernel not to dynamically allocate memory in the receiver's address space but to overwrite one or more pre-existing valid regions with the received data. In this case, the caller describes which regions to use through out-of-line descriptors in the ingoing `rcv_msg` argument, and `scatterlist_sz` specifies the size of this control information.

The system library provides user-level wrappers around the messaging traps (Figure 9–1). The wrappers handle possible restarting of the appropriate parts of IPC operations in the case of interruptions.

FIGURE 9–1 System library wrappers around Mach messaging traps

```
// system library

#define LIBMACH_OPTIONS (MACH_SEND_INTERRUPT|MACH_RCV_INTERRUPT)

mach_msg_return_t
mach_msg(msg, option, /* other arguments */)
{
    mach_msg_return_t mr;

    // try the trap
    mr = mach_msg_trap(msg, option &~ LIBMACH_OPTIONS, /* arguments */);
    if (mr == MACH_MSG_SUCCESS)
        return MACH_MSG_SUCCESS;

    // if send was interrupted, retry, unless instructed to return error
    if ((option & MACH_SEND_INTERRUPT) == 0)
        while (mr == MACH_SEND_INTERRUPTED)
            mr = mach_msg_trap(msg, option &~ LIBMACH_OPTIONS, /* arguments */);

    // if receive was interrupted, retry, unless instructed to return error
    if ((option & MACH_RCV_INTERRUPT) == 0)
        while (mr == MACH_RCV_INTERRUPTED)
            // leave out MACH_SEND_MSG: if we needed to send, we already have
            mr = mach_msg_trap(msg, option &~ (LIBMACH_OPTIONS|MACH_SEND_MSG),
                               /* arguments */);

    return mr;
}


mach_msg_return_t
mach_msg_overwrite(...)
{
    ...
    // use mach_msg_overwrite_trap()
    ...
}
```

User programs normally use mach_msg() or mach_msg_overwrite() to perform IPC operations. Variants such as mach_msg_receive() and mach_msg_send() are other wrappers around mach_msg().

The anatomy of a Mach message has evolved over time, but the basic layout consisting of a fixed-size header[4] and other variable-size data has remained unchanged. Mach messages in Mac OS X contain the following parts:

---

4. Note that unlike an Internet Protocol packet header, the send- and receive-side headers are not identical for a Mach IPC message.

- A fixed-size message header (`mach_msg_header_t`).

- A variable-size, possibly empty, body containing kernel and user data (`mach_msg_body_t`).

- A variable-size trailer—one of several types—containing message attributes appended by the kernel (`mach_msg_trailer_t`). A trailer is only relevant on the receive side.

A message can be either *simple* or *complex*. A simple message contains a header immediately followed by *untyped data*, whereas a complex message contains a structured message body. Figure 9–2 shows how the parts of a complex Mach message are laid out. The body consists of a descriptor count followed by that many descriptors, which are used to transfer out-of-line memory and port rights. Removing the body from this picture gives the layout of a simple message.

9.2.2.1 Message Header

The meanings of the message header fields are as follows.

- `msgh_bits` contains a bitmap describing the properties of the message. The `MACH_MSGH_BITS_LOCAL()` and `MACH_MSGH_BITS_REMOTE()` macros can be applied on this field to determine how the local port (`msgh_local_port`) and remote port (`msgh_remote_port`) fields will be interpreted. The `MACH_MSG_BITS()` macro combines the remote and local bits to yield a single value that can be used as `msgh_bits`. In particular, the presence of the `MACH_MSGH_BITS_COMPLEX` flag in `msgh_bits` marks the message as a complex message.

// osfmk/mach/message.h

```
#define MACH_MSGH_BITS(remote, local) ((remote | ((local) << 8))
```

- `msgh_size` is ignored while sending because the send size is provided as an explicit argument. In a received message, this field specifies the combined size, in bytes,[5] of the header and the body.

- `msgh_remote_port` specifies the destination port—a send or send-once right—while sending.

---

5. It is rather common for Mach routines to deal with sizes in units of `natural_t` instead of bytes. To avoid mysterious errors, be sure to verify the units that a given routine uses.

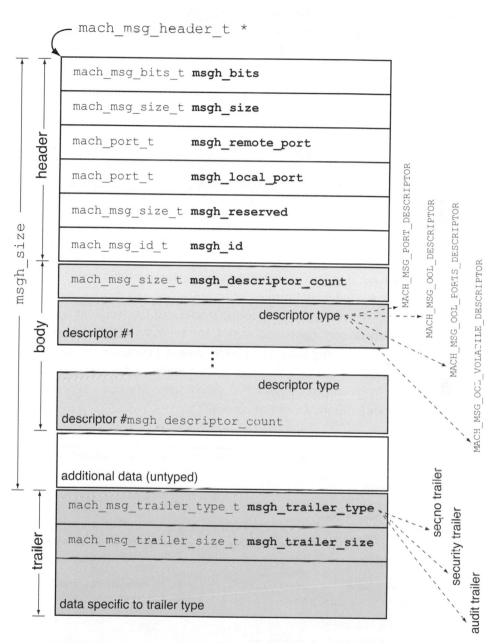

FIGURE 9–2 The layout of a complex Mach message

- `msgh_local_port` can be used to specify the reply port that the recipient will use to send a reply. It can be a valid send or send-once right but can also be `MACH_PORT_NULL` or `MACH_PORT_DEAD`.

- `msgh_id` contains an identifier that can be used to convey the meaning or format of the message, to be interpreted by the recipient. For example, a client can use this field to specify an operation to be performed by the server.

> The `msgh_remote_port` and `msgh_local_port` values are swapped (reversed with respect to the sender's view) in the message header seen by the recipient. Similarly, the bits in `msgh_bits` are also reversed.

9.2.2.2 Message Body

A nonempty message body may contain data that is *passive* (uninterpreted by the kernel), *active* (processed by the kernel), or both. Passive data resides inline in the message body and is meaningful only to the sender and the recipient. Examples of active data include port rights and out-of-line memory regions. Note that a message that carries anything but inline passive data is a complex message.

As noted earlier, a complex message body contains a descriptor count followed by that many descriptors. Figure 9–3 shows some descriptor types that are available for carrying different types of content.

FIGURE 9–3 Descriptors for sending ports and out-of-line memory in Mach IPC messages

```
// osfmk/mach/message.h

// for carrying a single port
typedef struct {
    mach_port_t                 name; // names the port whose right is being sent
    mach_msg_size_t             pad1;
    unsigned int                pad2        : 16;
    mach_msg_type_name_t        disposition : 8; // what to do with the right
    mach_msg_descriptor_type_t  type        : 8; // MACH_MSG_PORT_DESCRIPTOR
} mach_msg_port_descriptor_t;

// for carrying an out-of-line data array
typedef struct
{
    void                        *address; // address of the out-of-line memory
```
(continues)

FIGURE 9–3 Descriptors for sending ports and out-of-line memory in Mach IPC
messages *(continued)*

```
#if !defined(__LP64__)
    mach_msg_size_t               size;        // bytes in the out-of-line region
#endif
    boolean_t                     deallocate  : 8; // deallocate after sending?
    mach_msg_copy_options_t       copy        : 8; // how to copy?
    unsigned int                  pad1        : 8;
    mach_msg_descriptor_type_t type            : 8; // MACH_MSG_OOL_DESCRIPTOR
#if defined(__LP64__)
    mach_msg_size_t               size;        // bytes in the out-of-line region
#endif
} mach_msg_ool_descriptor_t;

// for carrying an out-of-line array of ports
typedef struct
{
    void                         *address; // address of the port name array
#if !defined(__LP64__)
    mach_msg_size_t               count;   // number of port names in the array
#endif
    boolean_t                     deallocate  : 8;
    mach_msg_copy_options_t       copy        : 8; // how to copy?
    mach_msg_type_name_t          disposition : 8; // what to do with the rights?
    mach_msg_descriptor_type_t type            : 8; // MACH_MSG_OOL_PORTS_DESCRIPTOR
#if defined(__LP64__)
    mach_msg_size_t               count;   // number of port names in the array
#endif
} mach_msg_ool_ports_descriptor_t;
```

A `mach_msg_port_descriptor_t` is used for passing a port right. Its
name field specifies the name of the port right being carried in the message,
whereas the `disposition` field specifies the IPC processing to be performed for
the right, based on which the kernel passes the appropriate right to the recipient.
The following are examples of disposition types.

- `MACH_MSG_TYPE_PORT_NONE`—The message carries neither a port name
  nor a port right.

- `MACH_MSG_TYPE_PORT_NAME`—The message carries only a port name and
  no rights. The kernel does not interpret the name.

- `MACH_MSG_TYPE_PORT_RECEIVE`—The message carries a receive right.

- `MACH_MSG_TYPE_PORT_SEND`—The message carries a send right.

- `MACH_MSG_TYPE_PORT_SEND_ONCE`—The message carries a send-once right.

A mach_msg_ool_descriptor_t is used for passing out-of-line memory. Its address field specifies the starting address of the memory in the sender's address space, whereas the size field specifies the memory's size in bytes. If the deallocate Boolean value is true, the set of pages containing the data will be deallocated in the sender's address space after the message is sent. The copy field is used by the sender to specify how the data is to be copied—either virtually (MACH_MSG_VIRTUAL_COPY) or physically (MACH_MSG_PHYSICAL_COPY). The recipient uses the copy field to specify whether to dynamically allocate space for the received out-of-line memory regions (MACH_RCV_ALLOCATE) or to write over existing specified regions of the receiver's address space (MACH_MSG_OVERWRITE). As far as possible, and unless explicitly overridden, memory transferred in this manner is shared copy-on-write between senders and recipients.

> Once a send call returns, the sender can modify the message buffer used in the send call without affecting the message contents. Similarly, the sender can also modify any out-of-line memory regions transferred.

A mach_msg_ool_ports_descriptor_t is used to pass an out-of-line array of ports. Note that such an array is always physically copied while being sent.

9.2.2.3 Message Trailer

A received Mach message contains a trailer after the message data. The trailer is aligned on a natural boundary. The msgh_size field in the received message header does not include the size of the received trailer. The trailer itself contains the trailer size in its msgh_trailer_size field.

The kernel may provide several trailer *formats*, and within each format, there can be multiple trailer *attributes*. Mac OS X 10.4 provides only one trailer format: MACH_MSG_TRAILER_FORMAT_0. This format provides the following attributes (in this order): a *sequence number*, a *security token*, and an *audit token*. During messaging, the receiver can request the kernel to append one or more of these attributes as part of the received trailer on a per-message basis. However, there is a caveat: To include a later attribute in the trailer, the receiver must accept all previous attributes, where the later/previous qualifiers are with respect to the aforementioned order. For example, including the audit token in the trailer will automatically include the security token and the sequence number. The following types are defined to represent valid combinations of trailer attributes:

- `mach_msg_trailer_t`—the simplest trailer; contains a `mach_msg_trailer_type_t` and a `mach_msg_trailer_size_t`, with no attributes
- `mach_msg_seqno_trailer_t`—also contains the sequence number (`mach_port_seqno_t`) of the message with respect to its port
- `mach_msg_security_trailer_t`—also contains the security token (`security_token_t`) of the task that sent the message
- `mach_msg_audit_trailer_t`—also contains an audit token (`audit_token_t`)

A security token is a structure containing the effective user and group IDs of the sending task (technically, of the associated BSD process). These are populated by the kernel securely and cannot be spoofed by the sender. An audit token is an opaque object that identifies the sender of a Mach message as a subject to the kernel's BSM auditing subsystem. It is also filled in securely by the kernel. Its contents can be interpreted using routines in the BSM library.

> A task inherits its security and audit tokens from the task that creates it. A task without a parent (i.e., the kernel task) has its security and audit tokens set to `KERNEL_SECURITY_TOKEN` and `KERNEL_AUDIT_TOKEN`, respectively. These are declared in `osfmk/ipc/mach_msg.c`. As the kernel evolves, it is likely that other types of tokens that include more comprehensive information could be supported.

Figure 9–4 shows an example of how to request the kernel to include the security token in the trailer of a received message.

FIGURE 9–4 Requesting the kernel to include the sender's security token in the message trailer

```
typedef struct { // simple message with only an integer as inline data
    mach_msg_header_t            header;
    int                          data;
    mach_msg_security_trailer_t trailer;
} msg_format_recv_t;
...

int
main(int argc, char **argv)
{
    kern_return_t       kr;
    msg_format_recv_t   recv_msg;
```

(continues)

FIGURE 9–4 Requesting the kernel to include the sender's security token in the message trailer *(continued)*

```
    msg_format_send_t  send_msg;
    mach_msg_header_t *recv_hdr, *send_hdr;
    mach_msg_option_t  options;
    ...

    options  = MACH_RCV_MSG | MACH_RCV_LARGE;
    options |= MACH_RCV_TRAILER_TYPE(MACH_MSG_TRAILER_FORMAT_0);
    // the following will include all trailer elements up to the specified one
    options |= MACH_RCV_TRAILER_ELEMENTS(MACH_RCV_TRAILER_SENDER);

    kr = mach_msg(recv_hdr, options, ...);
    ...
    printf("security token = %u %u\n",
           recv_msg.trailer.msgh_sender.val[0],  // sender's user ID
           recv_msg.trailer.msgh_sender.val[1]); // sender's group ID
    ...
}
```

The `MACH_RCV_TRAILER_ELEMENTS()` macro is used to encode the number of trailer elements desired—valid numbers are defined in `osfmk/mach/message.h`:

```
#define MACH_RCV_TRAILER_NULL    0 // mach_msg_trailer_t
#define MACH_RCV_TRAILER_SEQNO   1 // mach_msg_trailer_seqno_t
#define MACH_RCV_TRAILER_SENDER  2 // mach_msg_security_trailer_t
#define MACH_RCV_TRAILER_AUDIT   3 // mach_msg_audit_trailer_t
```

Note that the receive buffer must contain sufficient space to hold the requested trailer type.

> In a client-server system, both the client and the server can request the other party's security token to be appended to the incoming message trailer.

An Empty Message Sounds Much

Because of the trailer, the size of the smallest message you can send is different from the size of the smallest message you can receive. On the send side, an empty message consists of only the message header. The receiver must account for a trailer, so the smallest message that can be received consists of a header and the smallest trailer possible.

9.3 Mach IPC: The Mac OS X Implementation

The core of the IPC subsystem is implemented in files in the `osfmk/ipc/` directory in the kernel source tree. Moreover, the `osfmk/kern/ipc_*` set of files implements IPC support functions and IPC-related functions for kernel objects such as tasks and threads. Figure 9–5 shows an overview of Mach IPC implementation in Mac OS X. We will examine the pieces of this picture in the next few sections.

9.3.1 IPC Spaces

Each task has a private IPC *space*—a namespace for ports—that is represented by the `ipc_space` structure in the kernel. A task's IPC space defines its IPC capabilities.

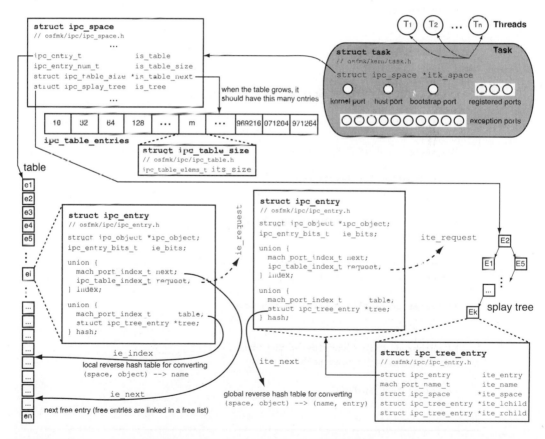

FIGURE 9–5 An overview of Mach IPC implementation in Mac OS X

Consequently, IPC operations such as send and receive consult this space. Similarly, IPC operations that manipulate a task's rights operate on the task's IPC space. Figure 9–6 shows the fields of the `ipc_space` structure.

FIGURE 9–6 The data structure for a task's IPC space

`// osfmk/ipc/ipc_space.h`

```
typedef natural_t ipc_space_refs_t;

struct ipc_space {
    decl_mutex_data(,is_ref_lock_data)
    ipc_space_refs_t is_references;

    decl_mutex_data(,is_lock_data)

    // is the space active?
    boolean_t is_active;

    // is the space growing?
    boolean_t is_growing;

    // table (array) of IPC entries
    ipc_entry_t is_table;

    // current table size
    ipc_entry_num_t is_table_size;

    // information for larger table
    struct ipc_table_size *is_table_next;

    // splay tree of IPC entries (can be NULL)
    struct ipc_splay_tree is_tree;

    // number of entries in the tree
    ipc_entry_num_t is_tree_total;

    // number of "small" entries in the tree
    ipc_entry_num_t is_tree_small;

    // number of hashed entries in the tree
    ipc_entry_num_t is_tree_hash;

    // for is_fast_space()
    boolean_t is_fast;
};
```

The IPC space encapsulates the knowledge necessary to translate between task-specific (local) port names and kernel-wide (global) port data structures. This translation is implemented using translation entries for port capabilities. Each capability is recorded in the kernel using an IPC entry data structure (`struct ipc_entry`). An IPC space always contains a *table* of IPC entries that is pointed to by the `is_table` field of the `ipc_space` structure. It can also contain a *splay tree*[6] of IPC entries, in which case the `is_tree` field will be non-`NULL`. Both these are per-task data structures.

The table holds "small" port rights, with each table entry (`struct ipc_entry`) consuming 16 bytes. If a port right is contained in the table, the right's name is an index into the table. The splay tree holds "large" port rights, with each tree entry (`struct ipc_tree_entry`) consuming 32 bytes.

Naturally Speaking

The integer type used to represent a port name is historically the native integer type for the machine. This type is called `natural_t` and is accessed by including `<mach/machine/vm_types.h>`, which in turn accesses it from `<mach/ppc/vm_types.h>` or `<mach/i386/vm_types.h>` on the PowerPC and x86 versions, respectively, of Mac OS X. With the introduction of the 64-bit Darwin ABI, several Mach data types (such as `vm_offset_t` and `vm_size_t`) have been scaled to be the same size as a pointer. However, `natural_t` is 32 bits in size regardless of the ABI.

9.3.1.1 IPC Entry Table

In general, port right names, which are integers (see Section 9.3.2), *do fit* in a table because the number of ports a typical task uses is small enough. As we will see shortly, Mach allows a task to rename a port. Moreover, ports can also be allocated using caller-specified names. This means a port name could represent an index that is out of bounds for the task's table. Such rights can be accommodated by overflowing them to the task's splay tree. To minimize memory consumption, the kernel dynamically adjusts the threshold at which entries are held in the splay tree. In fact, the table can also be grown in size. When the kernel does grow the table, it expands it to a new size that is specified (in units of number of table entries) by the `is_table_next` field of the `ipc_space` structure. As shown in Figure 9–5, the `is_table_next` field points to an `ipc_table_size` structure.

---

6. A splay tree is a space-efficient, self-adjusting binary search tree with (amortized) logarithmic time.

The kernel maintains an array called `ipc_table_entries` of such structures. This array, which is populated during the IPC subsystem's initialization, is simply a predefined sequence of table sizes.

Fast IPC Space

A *fast* IPC space is a special-case space that does not use a splay tree. It can be used only if port names are guaranteed to be within table bounds.

When a port right whose entry is in the table is deleted, the entry is placed on a free list of unused entries. The list is maintained within the table itself by chaining together unused entries through their `ie_next` fields. When the next port right is allocated, the last freed entry (if any) is used. The `ie_index` field implements an ordered hash table used for (reverse) translating an { IPC space, IPC object } pair to a name. This hash table uses open addressing with linear probing.

9.3.1.2 IPC Entry Splay Tree

As shown in Figure 9–5, an entry in the splay tree consists of an `ipc_entry` structure (the same as a table entry) along with the following additional fields: name, IPC space, and pointers to left and right children. The `ite_next` field implements a global open hash table used for (reverse) translating an { IPC space, IPC object } pair to a { name, IPC entry } pair.

9.3.2 The Anatomy of a Mach Port

A Mach port is represented in the kernel by a pointer to an `ipc_port` structure. The IPC entry structure's `ipc_object` field points to an `ipc_object` structure, which is logically superimposed on an `ipc_port` structure. Figure 9–7 shows an internal representation of the port data structure.

> From an object-oriented perspective, an `ipc_port` structure is a subclass of an `ipc_object` structure. Ports can be grouped into port sets in Mach, with the corresponding structure being an `ipc_pset` structure [osfmk/ipc/ipc_pset.h]. In such a case, a right will be represented in the kernel by passing a pointer to the `ipc_pset` structure in question (rather than an `ipc_port` structure). Another possibility is an `rpc_port` structure.

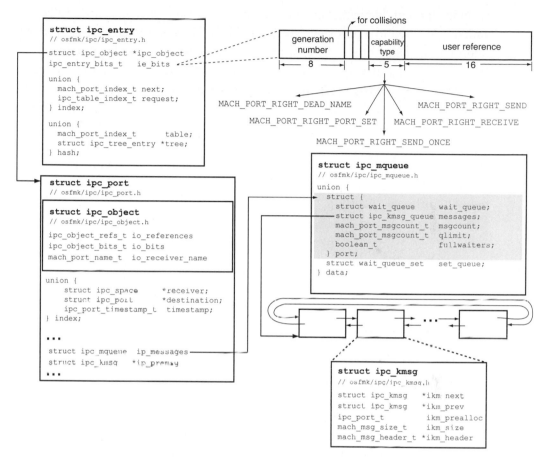

FIGURE 9–7 A view of the internal structure of a Mach port

The fields of an `ipc_port` structure include a pointer to the IPC space of the task holding the receive right, a pointer to the kernel object that the port represents, and various reference counts such as the make-send count, the number of send rights, and the number of send-once rights.

9.3.2.1 *What's in a Port's Name?*

It is important to realize the different between `mach_port_t` and `mach_port_name_t`: The two are treated the same in user space but not in the kernel. A port's name is relevant only in a particular namespace, corresponding to a task. A `mach_port_name_t` represents the local, namespace-specific identity of a port, without implying any associated rights. A `mach_port_t` represents a reference added or deleted to a port right. Such a reference is represented in user space by returning the name of the right (or many rights) that was altered within the task's IPC space, which is why it is the same as a `mach_port_name_t` in user space. Within the kernel, however, port rights are represented by passing a pointer to the appropriate port data structure (`ipc_port_t`). If a user program receives a `mach_port_name_t` from the kernel, it means that the kernel has not mapped any associated port rights—the name is simply the port's integer representation. When the kernel returns a `mach_port_t`, it maps the associated port rights to the recipient of the message. In both cases, the user program sees the same integer, but with different underlying semantics.

> The same port can exist with different names in multiple tasks. Conversely, the same port name can represent different ports in different tasks. It is important to note that knowing a port name in another task is not enough to use that port, since the kernel will evaluate the name in the caller's IPC space. For example, if you print a `mach_port_name_t` value in a program and then attempt to use the value in another task (one that does not have send rights to that port) to send a message, you will not succeed.

In a given port namespace, if there exist multiple rights for a given port, say, a send right and a receive right, the names for the various rights will coalesce into a single name. In other words, a single name can denote multiple rights. This is not so in the case of send-once rights, which are always named uniquely.

The `ie_bits` field of the `ipc_entry` structure holds the types of rights a given name represents. This bitmap is what allows a single name in an IPC space to represent multiple rights. The `IE_BITS_TYPE` macro is used to test the bit values.

```
// osfmk/mach/mach_port.h

typedef natural_t mach_port_right_t;

#define MACH_PORT_RIGHT_SEND      ((mach_port_right_t) 0)
#define MACH_PORT_RIGHT_RECEIVE   ((mach_port_right_t) 1)
#define MACH_PORT_RIGHT_SEND_ONCE ((mach_port_right_t) 2)
#define MACH_PORT_RIGHT_PORT_SET  ((mach_port_right_t) 3)
#define MACH_PORT_RIGHT_DEAD_NAME ((mach_port_right_t) 4)
#define MACH_PORT_RIGHT_NUMBER    ((mach_port_right_t) 5)

typedef natural_t        mach_port_type_t;
typedef mach_port_type_t *mach_port_type_array_t;
```

```
#define MACH_PORT_TYPE(right)                                              \
               ((mach_port_type_t)(((mach_port_type_t) 1)                  \
               << ((right) + ((mach_port_right_t) 16))))
```

```
#define MACH_PORT_TYPE_NONE       ((mach_port_type_t) 0L)
#define MACH_PORT_TYPE_SEND       MACH_PORT_TYPE(MACH_PORT_RIGHT_SEND)
#define MACH_PORT_TYPE_RECEIVE    MACH_PORT_TYPE(MACH_PORT_RIGHT_RECEIVE)
#define MACH_PORT_TYPE_SEND_ONCE  MACH_PORT_TYPE(MACH_PORT_RIGHT_SEND_ONCE)
#define MACH_PORT_TYPE_PORT_SET   MACH_PORT_TYPE(MACH_PORT_RIGHT_PORT_SET)
#define MACH_PORT_TYPE_DEAD_NAME  MACH_PORT_TYPE(MACH_PORT_RIGHT_DEAD_NAME)
```

> Before Mach 3.0, names of routines and data types in the IPC inter-
> face were not prefixed with `mach_` or `MACH_`. For example, instead of
> `mach_port_t`, there was `port_t`. The prefixes were added in Mach
> 3.0 to avoid any name conflicts between the old and the new Mach
> interfaces, even though the two are similar in many respects. This
> allows the same set of header files to export both interfaces and
> allows a program to mix interfaces, if necessary.

Although port names are commonly assigned by the kernel, a user program
can create a port right with a specific name—using the `mach_port_allocate_`
`name()` routine. A kernel-assigned `mach_port_name_t` value has two components: an *index* and a *generation number*.

// osfmk/mach/port.h

```
#define MACH_PORT_INDEX(name)      ((name) >> 8)
#define MACH_PORT_GEN(name)        (((name) & 0xff) << 24)
#define MACH_PORT_MAKE(index, gen) (((index) << 8) | (gen) >> 24)
```

If a user program needs to use port names for arbitrarily mapping them to
user data, it must use only the index part of the port name, which is why the layout of a `mach_port_name_t` is exposed to user space.

Renaming Ports

It is possible for a task to *rename* a port to a new name. Such renaming may be
useful if a program wishes to overload port names with some program-specific
meaning, say, the address of hash table entries, each of which has a one-to-one
correspondence with a port name. A task still cannot have multiple names for the
same port.

9.3.2.2 Validity of a Port Name

The kernel defines the value 0 to be the name of the *null* port (MACH_PORT_NULL). A null port is a legal port value that can be carried in messages to indicate the absence of any port or port rights. A *dead* port (MACH_PORT_DEAD) indicates that a port right was present but no longer is—that is, the right is dead. The numerical value of MACH_PORT_DEAD is a natural_t with all bits set. It is also a legal port value that can appear in a message. However, these two values do not represent *valid* ports. All remaining natural_t values are valid port values. The header file osfmk/mach/port.h contains several port-related definitions.

The code that manages IPC entries provides interfaces to look up an IPC object given its name in an IPC space and, conversely, to look up the name of an IPC object in a given IPC space. The former type of lookup, typically a <task, mach_port_name_t> → mach_port_t translation, is used while sending a message. The latter, typically a <task, mach_port_t> → mach_port_name_t translation, is used while receiving a message.

9.3.3 Tasks and IPC

Mach tasks and threads both begin life with certain sets of standard Mach ports (recall that we came across these ports in Chapter 7). Figure 9–8 shows the IPC-related data structures associated with a task. Besides the task's standard ports, the task structure also contains a pointer (itk_space) to the task's IPC space.

FIGURE 9–8 IPC-related data structures associated with a Mach task

```
// osfmk/mach/ppc/exception.h

#define EXC_TYPES_COUNT        10


// osfmk/mach/mach_param.h

#define TASK_PORT_REGISTER_MAX  3 // number of "registered" ports


// osfmk/kern/task.h

struct task {
    // task's lock
    decl_mutex_data(,lock)
    ...
```

(continues)

FIGURE 9–8 IPC-related data structures associated with a Mach task *(continued)*

```
// IPC lock
decl_mutex_data(,itk_lock_data)

// not a right -- ipc_receiver does not hold a reference for the space
// used for representing a kernel object of type IKOT_TASK
struct ipc_port *itk_self;

// "self" port -- a "naked" send right made from itk_self
// this is the task's kernel port (TASK_KERNEL_PORT)
struct ipc_port *itk_sself;

// "exception" ports -- a send right for each valid element
struct exception_action exc_actions[EXC_TYPES_COUNT];

// "host" port -- a send right
struct ipc_port *itk_host;

// "bootstrap" port -- a send right
struct ipc_port *itk_bootstrap;

// "registered" port -- a send right for each element
struct ipc_port *itk_registered[TASK_PORT_REGISTER_MAX];

// task's IPC space
struct ipc_space *itk_space;
...
};
```

The set of standard task ports includes the following:

- A *self port*—also known as the task's *kernel port*—represents the task itself. The kernel holds receive rights to this port. The self port is used by the task to invoke operations on itself. Other programs (such as debuggers) wishing to perform operations on a task also use this port.

- A set of *exception ports* includes one port for each type of exception supported by the kernel. The kernel sends a message to the task's appropriate exception port when an exception occurs in one of the task's threads. Note that exception ports also exist at the thread level (more specific than a task-level exception port) and the host level (less specific). As we will see in Section 9.7.2.1, the kernel attempts to send exception messages to the most specific port first. Exception ports are used for implementing both error-handling and debugging mechanisms.

- A *host port* represents the host on which the task is running.

- A *bootstrap port* is used to send messages to the *Bootstrap Server*, which is essentially a local name server for services accessible through Mach ports. Programs can contact the Bootstrap Server requesting the return of other system service ports.

- A set of well-known system ports are registered for a task—these are used by the runtime system to initialize the task. There can be at most TASK_PORT_REGISTER_MAX such ports. The mach_ports_register() routine can be used to register an array of send rights, with each right filling a slot in the itk_registered array in the task structure.

Host Special Ports

A host object is represented in the kernel by host_data_t, which is an alias for struct host [osfmk/kern/host.h]. This structure contains an array of host-level special ports and another array of host-level exception ports. The host special ports are *host port*, *host privileged port*, and *host security port*. These ports are used for exporting different interfaces to the host object.

The host port is used as an argument in "safe" Mach routines that retrieve unprivileged information about the host. Acquiring send rights to this port does not require the calling task to be privileged. The host privileged port, which can be acquired only by a privileged task, is used in privileged Mach routines, such as host_processors(), which retrieves a list of send rights representing all processors in the system. The host security port is used to change a given task's security token or to create a task with an explicit security token.

When the IPC subsystem is initialized, each host-level special port is set to represent a send right to the same port.

When a task is created, a new port is allocated in the kernel's IPC space. The task structure's itk_self field is set to the name of this port, whereas the itk_sself member contains a send right to this port. A new IPC space is created for the task and assigned to the task structure's itk_space field. The new task inherits the parent's registered, exception, host, and bootstrap ports, as the kernel creates naked[7] send rights for the child for each of these ports from the existing naked rights of the parent. As noted in Chapter 7, other than these ports, Mach ports are *not inherited* across task creation—that is, across the fork() system call.

---

7. A naked right exists only in the context of the kernel task. It is so named because such a right is not inserted into the port namespace of the kernel task—it exists in limbo.

As we saw in Chapter 5, `/sbin/launchd` is the first user-level program executed by the kernel. `launchd` is the ultimate parent of all user processes, analogous to the traditional `init` program on Unix systems. Moreover, `launchd` also acts as the Bootstrap Server.

> On Mac OS X versions prior to 10.4, the first user-level program executed by the kernel is `/sbin/mach_init`, which forks and runs `/sbin/init`. The `launchd` program subsumes the functionality of both `mach_init` and `init` in Mac OS X 10.4.

During its initialization, `launchd` allocates several Mach ports, one of which it sets as its bootstrap port by calling `task_set_bootstrap_port()`. This port (technically a *subset* of this port, with limited scope) is inherited by new tasks as they are created, allowing all programs to communicate with the Bootstrap Server.

> `task_set_bootstrap_port()` is a macro that resolves to a call to `task_set_special_port()` with `TASK_BOOTSTRAP_PORT` as an argument.

9.3.4 Threads and IPC

Figure 9–9 shows the IPC-related data structures associated with a thread. Like a task, a thread contains a self port and a set of exception ports used for error handling. Whereas a newly created task's exception ports are inherited from the parent, each of a thread's exception ports is initialized to the null port when the thread is created. Both task and thread exception ports can be programmatically changed later. If a thread exception port for an exception type is the null port, the kernel uses the next most specific port: the corresponding task-level exception port.

FIGURE 9–9 IPC-related data structures associated with a Mach thread

```
// osfmk/kern/thread.h

struct thread {
    ...
    struct ipc_kmsg_queue ith_messages;
```

(continues)

FIGURE 9–9 IPC-related data structures associated with a Mach thread *(continued)*

```
    // reply port -- for kernel RPCs
    mach_port_t ith_rpc_reply;
    ...

    // not a right -- ip_receiver does not hold a reference for the space
    // used for representing a kernel object of type IKOT_THREAD
    struct ipc_port *ith_self;

    // "self" port -- a "naked" send right made from ith_self
    // this is the thread's kernel port (THREAD_KERNEL_PORT)
    struct ipc_port *ith_sself;

    // "exception" ports -- a send right for each valid element
    struct exception_action exc_actions[EXC_TYPES_COUNT];
    ...
};
```

The `thread` structure's `ith_rpc_reply` field is used to hold the reply port for kernel RPCs. When the kernel needs to send a message to the thread and receives a reply (i.e., performs an RPC), it allocates a reply port if the current value of `ith_rpc_reply` is `IP_NULL`.

9.3.5 Port Allocation

Now that we are familiar with port-related data structures and the roles ports play, let us look at the important steps involved in the allocation of a port right. Figure 9–10 shows these steps.

Although `mach_port_allocate()` is typically used to allocate a port right, there exist more flexible variants such as `mach_port_allocate_name()` and `mach_port_allocate_qos()` that allow additional properties of the new right to be specified. All these routines are special cases of `mach_port_allocate_full()`, which is also available to user space.

```
typedef struct mach_port_qos {
    boolean_t name:1;      // caller-specified port name
    boolean_t prealloc:1;  // preallocate a message buffer
    boolean_t pad1:30;
    natural_t len;         // length of preallocated message buffer
} mach_port_qos_t;
```

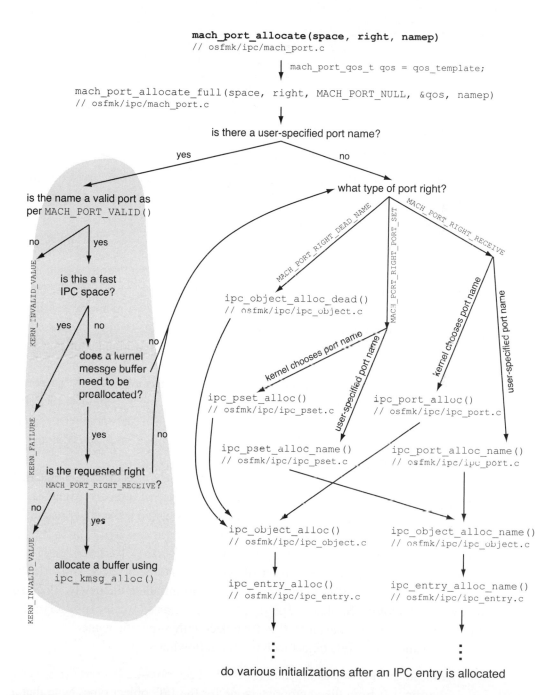

FIGURE 9–10 The allocation of a port right

```
kern_return_t
mach_port_allocate_full(
    ipc_space_t          space,   // target IPC space
    mach_port_right_t    right,   // type of right to be created
    mach_port_t          proto,   // subsystem (unused)
    mach_port_qos_t      *qosp,   // quality of service
    mach_port_name_t     *namep); // new port right's name in target IPC space
```

`mach_port_allocate_full()` creates one of three types of port rights based on the value passed as the `right` argument:

- A receive right (`MACH_PORT_RIGHT_RECEIVE`), which is the most common type of right created through this function
- An empty port set (`MACH_PORT_RIGHT_PORT_SET`)
- A dead name (`MACH_PORT_RIGHT_DEAD_NAME`) with one user reference

It is possible to create a port right with a caller-specified name, which must not already be in use for a port right in the target IPC space. Moreover, the target space must not be a fast IPC space. The caller can specify a name by passing a pointer to it in the `namep` argument and setting the `name` bit-field of the passed-in *quality of service* (QoS) structure. The latter is also used to designate the new port as a real-time port that requires QoS guarantees. The only manifestation of a QoS guarantee is that a message buffer is preallocated and associated with the port's internal data structure. The buffer's size is specified by the `len` field of the QoS structure. The kernel uses a port's preallocated buffer—if it has one—when sending messages from the kernel. This way, a sender of critical messages can avoid blocking on memory allocation.

As Figure 9–10 shows, `mach_port_allocate_full()` calls different internal "alloc" functions based on the type of right. In the case of a receive right, `ipc_port_alloc_name()` [osfmk/ipc/ipc_port.c] is called if the caller has mandated a specific name; otherwise, `ipc_port_alloc()` [osfmk/ipc/ipc_port.c] is called. `ipc_port_alloc()` calls `ipc_object_alloc()` [osfmk/ipc/ipc_object.c] to allocate an IPC object of type `IOT_PORT`. If successful, it calls `ipc_port_init()` [osfmk/ipc/ipc_port.c] to initialize the newly allocated port and then returns. Similarly, `ipc_port_alloc_name()` calls `ipc_object_alloc_name()` to allocate an `IOT_PORT` object with a specific name.

Allocation of an IPC object includes the following steps.

- Allocate an IPC object structure (`struct ipc_object` [osfmk/ipc/ipc_object.h]) from the appropriate zone for the IPC object type. Note that a pointer to this structure is the in-kernel representation of the port (`struct ipc_port` [`osfmk/ipc/ipc_port.h`]).

- Initialize the mutex within the IPC object structure.

- Allocate an IPC object entry structure (`struct ipc_entry` [`osfmk/ipc/ipc_entry.h`]). This operation first attempts to find a free entry in the given IPC space's table using the "first free" hint. If there are no free entries in the table, the table is grown. If the table is already being grown because of some other thread, the caller blocks until the growing finishes.

The `mach_port_names()` routine can be used to retrieve a list of ports, along with their types, in a given IPC space. Moreover, `mach_port_get_attributes()` returns various flavors of attribute information about a port. The program shown in Figure 9–11 lists details of port rights in a (BSD) task given its process ID. Note that the `mach_port_status` structure populated by `mach_port_get_attributes()` contains other fields besides those printed by our program.

FIGURE 9–11 Listing the Mach ports and their attributes in a given process

```
// lsports.c

#include <stdio.h>
#include <stdlib.h>
#include <mach/mach.h>

#define PROGNAME "lsports"

#define EXIT_ON_MACH_ERROR(msg, retval) \
    if (kr != KERN_SUCCESS) { mach_error(msg ":" , kr); exit((retval)); }

void
print_mach_port_type(mach_port_type_t type)
{
    if (type & MACH_PORT_TYPE_SEND)       { printf("SEND ");      }
    if (type & MACH_PORT_TYPE_RECEIVE)    { printf("RECEIVE ");   }
    if (type & MACH_PORT_TYPE_SEND_ONCE)  { printf("SEND_ONCE "); }
    if (type & MACH_PORT_TYPE_PORT_SET)   { printf("PORT_SET ");  }
    if (type & MACH_PORT_TYPE_DEAD_NAME)  { printf("DEAD NAME "); }
    if (type & MACH_PORT_TYPE_DNREQUEST)  { printf("DNREQUEST "); }
    printf("\n");
}

int
main(int argc, char **argv)
```

(continues)

FIGURE 9–11 Listing the Mach ports and their attributes in a given process *(continued)*

```
{
    int                      i;
    pid_t                    pid;
    kern_return_t            kr;
    mach_port_name_array_t   names;
    mach_port_type_array_t   types;
    mach_msg_type_number_t   ncount, tcount;
    mach_port_limits_t       port_limits;
    mach_port_status_t       port_status;
    mach_msg_type_number_t   port_info_count;
    task_t                   task;
    task_t                   mytask = mach_task_self();

    if (argc != 2) {
        fprintf(stderr, "usage: %s <pid>\n", PROGNAME);
        exit(1);
    }

    pid = atoi(argv[1]);
    kr = task_for_pid(mytask, (int)pid, &task);
    EXIT_ON_MACH_ERROR("task_for_pid", kr);

    // retrieve a list of the rights present in the given task's IPC space,
    // along with type information (no particular ordering)
    kr = mach_port_names(task, &names, &ncount, &types, &tcount);
    EXIT_ON_MACH_ERROR("mach_port_names", kr);

    printf("%8s %8s %8s %8s %8s task rights\n",
            "name", "q-limit", "seqno", "msgcount", "sorights");
    for (i = 0; i < ncount; i++) {
        printf("%08x ", names[i]);

        // get resource limits for the port
        port_info_count = MACH_PORT_LIMITS_INFO_COUNT;
        kr = mach_port_get_attributes(
                task,                              // the IPC space in question
                names[i],                          // task's name for the port
                MACH_PORT_LIMITS_INFO,             // information flavor desired
                (mach_port_info_t)&port_limits,    // outcoming information
                &port_info_count);                 // size returned
        if (kr == KERN_SUCCESS)
            printf("%8d ", port_limits.mpl_qlimit);
        else
            printf("%8s ", "-");

        // get miscellaneous information about associated rights and messages
        port_info_count = MACH_PORT_RECEIVE_STATUS_COUNT;
```

(continues)

FIGURE 9–11 Listing the Mach ports and their attributes in a given process *(continued)*

```
      kr = mach_port_get_attributes(task, names[i], MACH_PORT_RECEIVE_STATUS,
                                    (mach_port_info_t)&port_status,
                                    &port_info_count);
      if (kr == KERN_SUCCESS) {
          printf("%8d %8d %8d ",
                  port_status.mps_seqno,      // current sequence # for the port
                  port_status.mps_msgcount,   // # of messages currently queued
                  port_status.mps_sorights);  // # of send-once rights
      } else
          printf("%8s %8s %8s ", "-", "-", "-");
      print_mach_port_type(types[i]);
  }

  vm_deallocate(mytask, (vm_address_t)names, ncount*sizeof(mach_port_name_t));
  vm_deallocate(mytask, (vm_address_t)types, tcount*sizeof(mach_port_type_t));

  exit(0);
}


$ gcc -Wall -o lsports lsports.c
$ ./lsports $$ # superuser privileges required on newer versions of Mac OS X
    name q-limit    seqno msgcount sorights task rights
0000010f       5        0        0        0 RECEIVE
00000207       -        -        -        - SEND
00000307       -        -        -        - SEND
0000040f       5        0        0        0 RECEIVE
00000507       5       19        0        0 RECEIVE
0000060b       5        0        0        0 RECEIVE
0000070b       -        -        -        - SEND
00000807       -        -        -        - SEND
00000903       5        0        0        0 RECEIVE
00000a03       5       11        0        0 RECEIVE
00000b03       -        -        -        - SEND
00000c07       -        -        -        - SEND
00000d03       -        -        -        - SEND
00000e03       5       48        0        0 RECEIVE
00000f03       -        -        -        - SEND
```

9.3.6 Messaging Implementation

Let us look at how the kernel handles sending and receiving messages. Given that IPC underlies much of the functionality in Mach, messaging is a frequent operation in a Mach-based system. It is therefore not surprising that a Mach implementation, especially one used in a commercial system like Mac OS X, would be heavily optimized. The core kernel function involved in messaging—both sending and receiving—is the one that we came across earlier: `mach_msg_overwrite_trap()` [osfmk/ipc/mach_msg.c]. This function contains numerous special cases that attempt to improve performance in different situations.

One of the optimizations used is *handoff scheduling*. As we saw in Chapter 7, handoff scheduling involves direct transfer of processor control from one thread to another. A handoff may be performed both by senders and by receivers participating in RPCs. For example, if a server thread is currently blocked in a receive call, a client thread can hand off to the server thread and block itself while it waits for the reply. Similarly, when the server is ready to send a reply to the client, it will hand off to the waiting client thread and block itself as it waits for the next request. This way, it is also possible to avoid having to enqueue and dequeue messages, since a message can be directly transferred to the receiver.

Figure 9–12 shows a simplified overview—without any special cases—of the kernel processing involved in sending a message.

Mach message passing is reliable and order-preserving. Therefore, messages may not be lost and are always received in the order they were sent. However, the kernel delivers messages sent to send-once rights out of order and without taking into account the receiving port's queue length or how full it is. We noted earlier that the length of a port's message queue is finite. When a queue becomes full, several behaviors are possible, such as the following.

- The default behavior is to block new senders until there is room in the queue.
- If a sender uses the MACH_SEND_TIMEOUT option in its invocation of `mach_msg()` or `mach_msg_overwrite()`, the sender will block for at most the specified time. If the message still cannot be delivered after that time has passed, a MACH_SEND_TIMED_OUT error will be returned.
- If the message is being sent using a send-once right, the kernel will deliver the message despite the queue being full.

Various other error codes can be returned when sending a message fails. These fall in a few general categories, such as the following:

- Those that indicate that the send call did not perform any operation from the caller's standpoint, usually because one or more of the arguments (or their properties) were invalid—say, an invalid message header or an invalid destination port

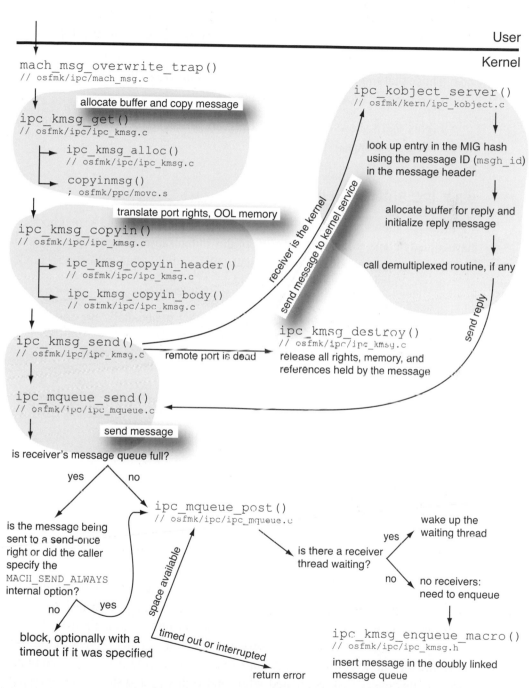

FIGURE 9–12 An overview of the kernel processing for sending a Mach IPC message

- Those that indicate that the message was partly or wholly destroyed—for example, because the out-of-line memory being sent was invalid or a port right being sent in the message was bogus

- Those that indicate that the message was returned to the sender because of a send timeout or a software interrupt

Figure 9–13 shows a simplified overview of the kernel processing involved in receiving a message.

9.3.7 IPC Subsystem Initialization

Figure 9–14 shows how the IPC subsystem is initialized when the kernel boots. We have already come across some aspects of this initialization, for example, the setting up of the host special ports. We will discuss MIG initialization in Section 9.6.3.2.

> `host_notify_init()` initializes a system-wide notification mechanism that allows user programs to request notifications on one of the host notification ports managed by Mach. Mac OS X 10.4 provides only one notification port as part of this mechanism: `HOST_NOTIFY_CALENDAR_CHANGE`. A program can use the `host_request_notification()` Mach routine to request the kernel to send it a message when the system's date or time changes. Mac OS X has numerous other notification mechanisms, most of which we will discuss in Section 9.16.

9.4 Name and Bootstrap Servers

Consider two programs communicating via Mach IPC—say, using the familiar client-server model. The server will have receive rights to a port, which is how it will receive request messages from a client. A client must possess send rights to such a port to send messages to the server. How does the client acquire these rights? A rather contrived and impractical way is that the server task creates the client task. As the client task's creator, the server task can manipulate the client task's port space. Specifically, the server task can insert send rights to the server port into the client's port space. A more reasonable alternative—one used in practice—is that every task is created with send rights to a system-wide server that acts as a trusted intermediary. Mach-based systems have such an intermediary: the *Network Message Server* (`netmsgserver`).

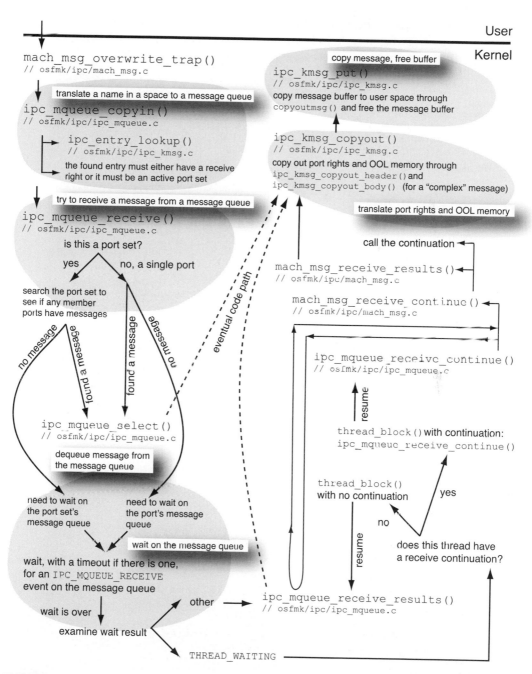

FIGURE 9–13 An overview of the kernel processing for receiving a Mach IPC message

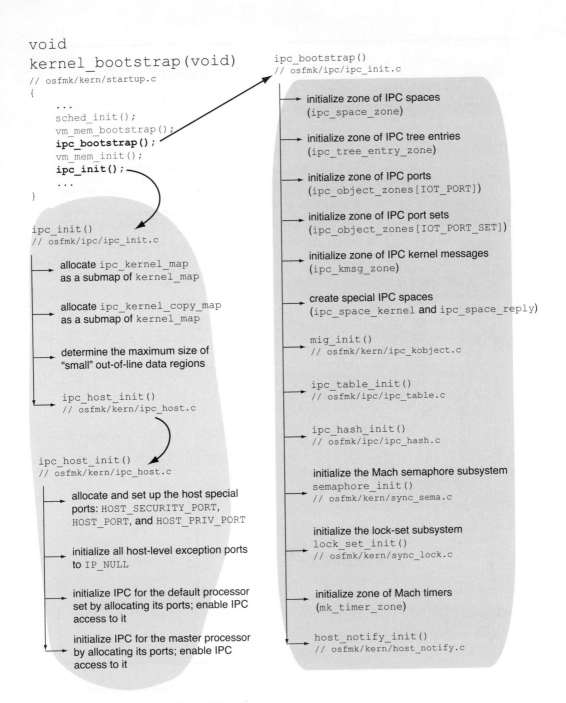

```
void
kernel_bootstrap(void)
// osfmk/kern/startup.c
{
    ...
    sched_init();
    vm_mem_bootstrap();
    ipc_bootstrap();
    vm_mem_init();
    ipc_init();
    ...
}
```

```
ipc_init()
// osfmk/ipc/ipc_init.c
```

→ allocate `ipc_kernel_map`
  as a submap of `kernel_map`

→ allocate `ipc_kernel_copy_map`
  as a submap of `kernel_map`

→ determine the maximum size of
  "small" out-of-line data regions

→ `ipc_host_init()`
  `// osfmk/kern/ipc_host.c`

```
ipc_host_init()
// osfmk/kern/ipc_host.c
```

→ allocate and set up the host special
  ports: `HOST_SECURITY_PORT`,
  `HOST_PORT`, and `HOST_PRIV_PORT`

→ initialize all host-level exception ports
  to `IP_NULL`

→ initialize IPC for the default processor
  set by allocating its ports; enable IPC
  access to it

→ initialize IPC for the master processor
  by allocating its ports; enable IPC
  access to it

```
ipc_bootstrap()
// osfmk/ipc/ipc_init.c
```

→ initialize zone of IPC spaces
  (`ipc_space_zone`)

→ initialize zone of IPC tree entries
  (`ipc_tree_entry_zone`)

→ initialize zone of IPC ports
  (`ipc_object_zones[IOT_PORT]`)

→ initialize zone of IPC port sets
  (`ipc_object_zones[IOT_PORT_SET]`)

→ initialize zone of IPC kernel messages
  (`ipc_kmsg_zone`)

→ create special IPC spaces
  (`ipc_space_kernel` and `ipc_space_reply`)

→ `mig_init()`
  `// osfmk/kern/ipc_kobject.c`

→ `ipc_table_init()`
  `// osfmk/ipc/ipc_table.c`

→ `ipc_hash_init()`
  `// osfmk/ipc/ipc_hash.c`

→ initialize the Mach semaphore subsystem
  `semaphore_init()`
  `// osfmk/kern/sync_sema.c`

→ initialize the lock-set subsystem
  `lock_set_init()`
  `// osfmk/kern/sync_lock.c`

→ initialize zone of Mach timers
  (`mk_timer_zone`)

→ `host_notify_init()`
  `// osfmk/kern/host_notify.c`

FIGURE 9–14 Initialization of the IPC subsystem

9.4.1 The Network Message Server

A Mach program desiring to receive messages on a port can publish the port through the `netmsgserver`. The publication process involves the server task registering the server port, along with an associated ASCII string name, with the `netmsgserver`. Since a client task will have send rights to a port that `netmsgserver` is listening on, it can send a lookup message containing the ASCII string associated with the desired service.

```
// ipc_common.h (shared between the client and the server)

#define SERVICE_NAME "com.osxbook.SomeService"

// ipc_server.c

#include "ipc_common.h"
...
kern_return_t kr;
port_t server_port;

server_port = mach_port_allocate(...);
...

kr = netname_check_in(name_server_port,
                      (netname_name_t)SERVICE_NAME,
                      mach_task_self(),
                      server_port);
...
```

The first argument to the `netname_check_in` call is the task's port to the *Network Name Server*. The global variable `name_server_port` represents send rights to the default system-wide name server. The second argument is the ASCII name of the service to be checked in. The third argument is a signature— typically a port to which the calling task has send rights. The signature is required later, when checking out (i.e., removing the port from the name server's namespace) the server port, which is the fourth argument.

```
...
kr = netname_check_out(name_server_port,
                       (netname_name_t)SERVICE_NAME,
                       mach_task_self());
...
```

Once a server task checks in a port successfully, a client can look it up using the ASCII name that the server used for it.

```
// ipc_client.c

#include "ipc_common.h"
...
kern_return_t kr;
port_t server_port;
...
kr = netname_look_up(name_server_port,
                     (netname_name_t)"*",
                     (netname_name_t)SERVICE_NAME,
                     &server_port);

...
```

The second argument is the host name whose Network Name Server is to be queried. An empty string represents the local host, whereas the `"*"` string specifies all hosts on the local network, resulting in a broadcast lookup.

> We noted earlier that the design of Mach's IPC allows for transparent extension to a distributed environment, even though the kernel does not have any explicit support for distributed IPC. Two programs residing on different machines can communicate using Mach IPC if both machines are running an intermediary user-level program that extends Mach IPC across a network. The `netmsgserver` transparently handles servers and clients residing on different machines. Whereas it communicates with tasks on the local machine using regular, local Mach IPC, it can communicate with other `netmsgserver` tasks on the network using arbitrary networking protocols, forwarding messages sent to local proxy ports to the appropriate remote `netmsgserver` tasks. Thus, the `netmsgserver` works both as a name server (allowing a network-wide name registration of ports) and a proxy server for distributed IPC (performing network-transparent message transfers). Mac OS X provides a conceptually similar facility called Distributed Objects (see Section 9.14) for use by Cocoa programs.

9.4.2 The Bootstrap Server

Mac OS X does not provide a `netmsgserver`, or rather, it doesn't provide a network-capable `netmsgserver`. It does provide a local name server—the *Bootstrap Server*—which allows tasks to publish ports that other tasks on the *same machine* can send messages to. The Bootstrap Server's functionality is provided by the bootstrap task, whose program encapsulation is the `launchd` program. Besides managing name-port bindings in its role as the Mach name server, the

Bootstrap Server also initiates certain (typically on-demand) system daemons—specifically those that have not been migrated to the higher-level server interface exported by `launchd`.

The need for a local name server arises from the fact that Mach port namespaces are local to tasks. Even though the kernel manages port structures, there is no kernel-wide global port namespace. Exporting services to clients through Mach ports would involve sharing of ports that provide access to these services. To achieve this, an external entity must act as the port name server, allowing service names and associated ports to be registered and looked up.

The Bootstrap Server was originally created by NeXT for its NEXTSTEP operating system.

9.4.2.1 The Bootstrap Port

Each task has a *bootstrap port* that it inherits from its parent task. The bootstrap port allows a task to access various system services. The Bootstrap Server provides its own service port to its descendant tasks via their bootstrap ports. Therefore, all direct descendants of the Bootstrap Server receive *privileged* bootstrap ports. It is possible for a parent task to change its bootstrap port while creating a task —say, to limit the set of services available to the child task. System services that execute untrusted tasks replace the Mach bootstrap task special port with a *subset port*. A task can retrieve its default bootstrap port by using `task_get_bootstrap_port()`.

9.4.2.2 The Bootstrap Context

The scope of the bootstrap task's lookup mechanism available to a subsequent task, as determined by the latter task's bootstrap port, is referred to as the task's *bootstrap context*. In other words, a task's bootstrap context determines which services (the corresponding ports, that is) the task can look up. There is a single top-level bootstrap context when Mac OS X boots: the *startup context*. `launchd` executes in this context, and so do early system services that rely on being able to look up various Mach ports. Subsequent, less privileged bootstrap contexts can be created by the system for running programs that may be untrusted. For example, when a user logs in, the bootstrap task creates a *login context*, which is a subset of the startup context. All of a user's processes are in the login context.

More Context on Contexts

In general, if a process was started in a user's login context, its children are automatically in the login context. Similarly, a process running in the startup context will spawn children that run in the startup context as well, unless the parent explicitly calls the Bootstrap Server to create a subset context. Recall from Chapter 5 the example of a user logging in both graphically (through `loginwindow.app`, at the console) and through SSH. When a user logs in by providing a username and password to `loginwindow.app`'s GUI (or automatically, if configured), a new login context is created for the user. Several user-specific services are present in the login context but not in the startup context. If the same user logs in at the console, by first providing `>console` as the username to `loginwindow.app` (which will cause it to exit, leading to `launchd` running a `getty` process on the console) and then typing his or her username and password, the user will be in the startup context. All programs in the chain of processes involved in the console login—`launchd`, `getty`, `login`, and the user's shell—remain in the startup context because `launchd` runs in the startup context, and the others do not create any subset context.

Similarly, the SSH daemon is launched at system boot time in the startup context. Therefore, logging in via SSH will put the user in the startup context. We will see an example in Section 9.4.3.1 of using the `bootstrap_info()` call to retrieve information about all known services in a context. This call does not return information on services that are defined only in subset contexts, unless the subset port is an ancestor of the bootstrap port (`bootstrap_port`). Consequently, running our service-listing program will show different results depending on how you are logged in.

9.4.2.3 Debugging the Bootstrap Server

When experimenting with the Bootstrap Server or `launchd` in general, you may find it worthwhile to configure `launchd` to log debugging messages. You can arrange for log messages from `launchd` to be written to a file by adjusting `launchd`'s log level and configuring the system log daemon (`syslogd`) not to ignore these messages. There are multiple ways to adjust `launchd`'s log level.

If you wish to debug `launchd` from the point where it starts, you should create a system-wide `launchd` configuration file (`/etc/launchd.conf`) with the following contents:

```
# /etc/launchd.conf
log level debug
```

When `launchd` starts, the contents of `launchd.conf` are run as subcommands through the `launchctl` program.

> Setting a log-level value of `debug` will cause `launchd` to generate a substantial amount of debugging output.

Alternatively, you can create a per-user `launchd` configuration file (`~/.launchd.conf`), which will apply the log-level change only to the per-user local scope.

Moreover, if you only wish to change `launchd`'s log level temporarily, you can run the `launchctl` program yourself.

`launchd` generates its log messages using the `syslog(3)` API. `syslogd` selects which messages to log based on rules specified in its configuration file (`/etc/syslog.conf`). The default rules do not include debugging or informational messages from `launchd`. You can temporarily log all `launchd` messages to a specific file by adding a rule such as the following to `/etc/syslog.conf`:

```
# /etc/syslog.conf

...
launchd.*     /var/log/launchd_debug.log
```

Thereafter, you must either send `syslogd` a hangup signal (`SIGHUP`) or restart it. In particular, you can examine `/var/log/launchd_debug.log` after system startup to see subset bootstrap contexts being created and disabled as users log in and log out.

```
Registered service 2307 bootstrap 1103: com.apple.SecurityServer
...
Service checkin attempt for service /usr/sbin/cupsd bootstrap 1103
bootstrap_check_in service /usr/sbin/cupsd unknown
received message on port 1103
Handled request.
Server create attempt: "/usr/sbin/cupsd -f" bootstrap 1103
adding new server "/usr/sbin/cupsd -f" with uid 0
Allocating port b503 for server /usr/sbin/cupsd -f
New server b503 in bootstrap 1103: "/usr/sbin/cupsd -f"
received message on port b503
Handled request.
Service creation attempt for service /usr/sbin/cupsd bootstrap b503
Created new service b603 in bootstrap 1103: /usr/sbin/cupsd
received message on port b503
Handled request.
Service checkin attempt for service /usr/sbin/cups
...
Subset create attempt: bootstrap 1103, requestor: ad07
Created bootstrap subset ac07 parent 1103 requestor ad07
...
Received dead name notification for bootstrap subset ac07 requestor port ad07
...
```

9.4.3 The Bootstrap Server API

Let us first look at examples of functions supported by the Mac OS X Bootstrap Server, after which we will see examples of communicating with the server using these functions.

bootstrap_create_server() defines a server that can be launched and relaunched by the Bootstrap Server in the context corresponding to bootstrap_ port.

```
kern_return_t
bootstrap_create_server(mach_port_t  bootstrap_port,
                        cmd_t        server_command,
                        integer_t    server_uid,
                        boolean_t    on_demand,
                        mach_port_t *server_port);
```

The on_demand argument determines the relaunching behavior as managed by launchd. If on_demand is true, launchd will relaunch a nonrunning server when any of the registered service ports is used for the first time. If on_demand is false, launchd will relaunch the server as soon as the server exits, regardless of whether any of its service ports are in use. The server task created because of relaunching has server_port as its bootstrap port. The server abstraction created by this call is automatically deleted when all of its associated services are deleted and the server program has exited.

Services associated with the server can be declared by calling bootstrap_ create_service(), with server_port (obtained by calling bootstrap_create_ server()) specified as the bootstrap port in that call.

```
kern_return_t
bootstrap_create_service(mach_port_t  bootstrap_port,
                         name_t       service_name,
                         mach_port_t *service_port);
```

bootstrap_create_service() creates a port and binds service_name to it. Send rights to the newly created port are returned in service_port. Later on, a service may call bootstrap_check_in() to check in the binding: In doing so, the caller will acquire receive rights for the bound port and the service will be made active. Thus, bootstrap_create_service() allows establishment of a name port binding before the backing service is even available. Lookups performed on bindings created by this mechanism return send rights to service_port, even if no service has checked in yet. If a caller uses such rights to send requests to the port, the messages will be queued until a server checks in.

```
kern_return_t
bootstrap_check_in(mach_port_t  bootstrap_port,
                   name_t          service_name,
                   mach_port_t *service_port);
```

`bootstrap_check_in()` returns the receive rights for the service named by `service_name`, thus making the service active. The service must already be defined in the bootstrap context by an earlier call to `bootstrap_create_service()`. When used in conjunction with `bootstrap_subset()`, `bootstrap_check_in()` can be used to create services that are available only to a subset of tasks. It is an error to attempt to check in an already active service.

`bootstrap_register()` registers a send right for the service port specified by `service_port`, with `service_name` specifying the service.

```
kern_return_t
bootstrap_register(mach_port_t bootstrap_port,
                   name_t          service_name,
                   mach_port_t service_port);
```

After a successful service registration, if a client looks up the service, the Bootstrap Server will provide send rights for the bound port to the client. Although you cannot register a service if an active binding already exists, you *can* register a service if an inactive binding exists. In the latter case, the existing service port, which the Bootstrap Server would have receive rights to, will be deallocated. In particular, if `service_port` is `MACH_PORT_NULL`, this can be used to undeclare (shut down) a declared service.

> Each service created by the Bootstrap Server has an associated *backup port*, which the Bootstrap Server uses to detect when a service is no longer being served. When this happens, the Bootstrap Server regains all rights to the named port. Clients can continue to perform successful lookups on the port while the Bootstrap Server has receive rights to the port. If a client wishes to determine whether the service is active or not, it must call `bootstrap_status()`. A restarting service that wishes to resume serving existing clients must first attempt to call `bootstrap_check_in()` to prevent the original port from being destroyed.

`bootstrap_look_up()` returns send rights for the service port of the service specified by `service_name`. A successful return means that the service must have been either declared or registered under this name, although it is not guaranteed to be active. `bootstrap_status()` can be used to check whether the service is active.

```
kern_return_t
bootstrap_look_up(mach_port_t     bootstrap_port,
                  name_service_t  service_name,
                  mach_port_t     *service_port);
```

`bootstrap_look_up_array()` returns send rights for the service ports of multiple services. The `service_names` array specifies the service names to look up, whereas the `service_ports` array contains the corresponding looked-up service ports. The Boolean out parameter `all_services_known` is true on return if *all* specified service names are known; it is false otherwise.

```
kern_return_t
bootstrap_look_up_array(mach_port_t     bootstrap_port,
                        name_array_t    service_names,
                        int             service_names_cnt,
                        port_array_t    *service_port,
                        int             *service_ports_cnt,
                        boolean_t       *all_services_known);
```

`bootstrap_status()` returns whether a service is known to users of the specified bootstrap port and whether a server is able to receive messages on an associated service port—that is, whether the service is active. Note that if a service is known but not active, then the Bootstrap Server has receive rights for the service port.

```
kern_return_t
bootstrap_status(mach_port_t          bootstrap_port,
                 name_t               service_name,
                 bootstrap_status_t   *service_active);
```

`bootstrap_info()` returns information about all services that are known, except those that are defined only in subset contexts—unless the subset port is an ancestor of `bootstrap_port`. The `service_names` array contains the names of all known services. The `server_names` array contains the names—if known—of the corresponding servers that provide the services. The `service_active` array contains a Boolean value for each name in the `service_names` array. This value is true for services that are receiving messages sent to their ports and false for the rest.

```
kern_return_t
bootstrap_info(port_t           bootstrap_port,
               name_array_t     *service_names,
```

```
int          *service_names_cnt,
name_array_t *server_names,
int          *server_names_cnt,
bool_array_t *service_active,
int          *service_active_cnt);
```

bootstrap_subset() returns a new port to be used as a *subset* bootstrap port. The new port is similar to bootstrap_port, but any ports dynamically registered by calling bootstrap_register() are available only to tasks using subset_port or its descendants.

```
kern_return_t
bootstrap_subset(mach_port_t  bootstrap_port,
                 mach_port_t  requestor_port,
                 mach_port_t *subset_port);
```

A lookup operation on subset_port will return not only ports registered with only subset_port but also ports registered with ancestors of subset_port. If the same service is registered with both subset_port and an ancestor port, a lookup for that service by a user of subset_port will fetch the subset_port version of the service. This way, services can be transparently customized for certain tasks without affecting the rest of the system, which can continue to use the default versions of the services in question. The lifespan of subset_port is determined by requestor_port; subset_port, its descendants, and any services advertised by these ports are all destroyed when requestor_port is destroyed.

bootstrap_parent() returns the parent bootstrap port of bootstrap_port, which is typically a bootstrap subset port. The calling task must have super-user privileges. For example, when called from a user login context, this function will return the bootstrap port corresponding to the startup context. When called from the startup context, the parent port returned is the same as the bootstrap port.

```
kern_return_t
bootstrap_parent(mach_port_t  bootstrap_port,
                 mach_port_t *parent_port);
```

> The /usr/libexec/StartupItemContext program can be used to run an executable in the startup context—that is, the context in which the Mac OS X startup items run. It works by calling bootstrap_parent() repeatedly until it has reached the startup (root) context. It then sets the port as its own bootstrap port, after which it can execute the requested program.

The automatic relaunching of servers by the Bootstrap Server is useful for creating crash-resistant servers. However, it is neither necessary nor advisable to create production servers by directly using the Bootstrap Server interface. Beginning with Mac OS X 10.4, the launch API,[8] as exported through `<launch.h>`, should be used. With this caveat, let us look at two examples of using the Bootstrap Server interface.

9.4.3.1 Displaying Information about All Known Services

In this example, we will use `bootstrap_info()` to retrieve a list of all known services that can be looked up in the bootstrap context associated with the given bootstrap port. Figure 9–15 shows the program.

FIGURE 9–15 Displaying information about all known services in a bootstrap context

```
// bootstrap_info.c

#include <stdio.h>
#include <stdlib.h>
#include <mach/mach.h>
#include <servers/bootstrap.h>

int
main(int argc, char **argv)
{
    kern_return_t           kr;
    name_array_t            service_names, server_names;
    bootstrap_status_array_t service_active;
    unsigned int            service_names_count, server_names_count;
    unsigned int            service_active_count, i;

    // We can use bootstrap_port, a global variable declared in a Mach header,
    // for the current task's bootstrap port. Alternatively, we can explicitly
    // retrieve the same send right by calling task_get_bootstrap_port(),
    // specifying mach_task_self() as the target task. This is how the system
    // library initializes the global variable.

    // launchd implements this routine
    kr = bootstrap_info(bootstrap_port,
                        &service_names,
                        &service_names_count,
                        &server_names,
```

(continues)

---

8. Section 5.10.1.2 provides an example of using the launch API.

FIGURE 9–15 Displaying information about all known services in a bootstrap context
(continued)

```
                    &server_names_count,
                    &service_active,
                    &service_active_count);
    if (kr != BOOTSTRAP_SUCCESS) {
        mach_error("bootstrap_info:", kr);
        exit(1);
    }

    printf("%s %-48s %s\n%s %-48s %s\n", "up?", "service name", "server cmd",
           "___", "_____", "_____");

    for (i = 0; i < service_names_count; i++)
        printf("%s %-48s %s\n",
                (service_active[i]) ? "1  " : "0  ", service_names[i],
                (server_names[i][0] == '\0') ? "-" : server_names[i]);

    // The service_names, server_names, and service_active arrays have been
    // vm_allocate()'d in our address space. Both "names" arrays are of type
    // name_array_t, which is an array of name_t elements. A name_t in turn
    // is a character string of length 128.
    //
    // As good programming practice, we should call vm_deallocate() to free up
    // such virtual memory when it is not needed anymore.

    (void)vm_deallocate(mach_task_self(), (vm_address_t)service_active,
                    service_active_count * sizeof(service_active[0]));

    (void)vm_deallocate(mach_task_self(), (vm_address_t)service_names,
                    service_names_count * sizeof(service_names[0]));

    (void)vm_deallocate(mach_task self(), (vm_address_t)server_names,
                    server_names_count * sizeof(server_names[0]));

    exit(0);
}



$ gcc -Wall -o bootstrap_info bootstrap_info.c
$ ./bootstrap_info
up? service name                                  server cmd

___ _____                                  _____
1   com.apple.KernelExtensionServer               -
...
1   com.apple.SystemConfiguration.configd         /usr/sbin/configd
...
1   com.apple.iChatAgent                          -
1   com.apple.audio.SystemSoundClient-561         -
1   com.apple.FontObjectsServer_258               -
```

You can run the `bootstrap_info` program in different bootstrap contexts to see the differences in the services that are accessible from those contexts. For example, the program's output will be different when run from a shell in an SSH login compared with running it from a normal, graphical login. Similarly, using `/usr/libexec/StartupItemContext` to run `bootstrap_info` will list services in the startup context.

9.4.3.2 Creating a Crash-Resistant Server

In this example, we will create a dummy server that will be crash resistant in that if it exits unexpectedly, it will be relaunched by the Bootstrap Server. We will also provide a way for our server to explicitly arrange for its shutdown if it really wishes to exit. The server will provide a service named `com.osxbook.DummySleeper` (the server does nothing but sleep). The server executable will reside as `/tmp/sleeperd`. The server will check for the existence of a flag file, `/tmp/sleeperd.off`; if it exists, the server will turn itself off by calling `bootstrap_register()` with a null port as the service port. Figure 9–16 shows the program.

FIGURE 9–16 A crash-resistant server

```
// bootstrap_server.c

#include <stdio.h>
#include <stdlib.h>
#include <sys/stat.h>
#include <unistd.h>
#include <asl.h>
#include <mach/mach.h>
#include <servers/bootstrap.h>

#define SERVICE_NAME          "com.osxbook.DummySleeper"
#define SERVICE_CMD           "/tmp/sleeperd"
#define SERVICE_SHUTDOWN_FILE SERVICE_CMD ".off"

static mach_port_t server_priv_port;
static aslmsg      logmsg;

// Note that asl_log() accepts the %m formatting character, which is
// replaced by the ASL facility with the error string corresponding to
// the errno variable's current value.
#define MY_ASL_LOG(fmt, ...) \
    asl_log(NULL, logmsg, ASL_LEVEL_ERR, fmt, ## __VA_ARGS__)
```

(continues)

FIGURE 9–16 A crash-resistant server *(continued)*

```
static kern_return_t
register_bootstrap_service(void)
{
    kern_return_t kr;
    mach_port_t    service_send_port, service_rcv_port;

    // Let us attempt to check in.... This routine will look up the service
    // by name and attempt to return receive rights to the service port.
    kr = bootstrap_check_in(bootstrap_port, (char *)SERVICE_NAME,
                            &service_rcv_port);
    if (kr == KERN_SUCCESS)
        server_priv_port = bootstrap_port;
    else if (kr == BOOTSTRAP_UNKNOWN_SERVICE) {

        // The service does not exist, so let us create it....

        kr = bootstrap_create_server(bootstrap_port,
                                     SERVICE_CMD,
                                     getuid(),        // server uid
                                     FALSE,           // not on-demand
                                     &server_priv_port);

        if (kr != KERN_SUCCESS)
            return kr;

        // We can now use server_priv_port to declare services associated
        // with this server by calling bootstrap_create_service() and passing
        // server_priv_port as the bootstrap port.

        // Create a service called SERVICE_NAME, and return send rights to
        // that port in service_send_port.
        kr = bootstrap_create_service(server_priv_port, (char *)SERVICE_NAME,
                                      &service_send_port);
        if (kr != KERN_SUCCESS) {
            mach_port_deallocate(mach_task_self(), server_priv_port);
            return kr;
        }

        // Check in and get receive rights to the service port of the service.
        kr = bootstrap_check_in(server_priv_port, (char *)SERVICE_NAME,
                                &service_rcv_port);
        if (kr != KERN_SUCCESS) {
            mach_port_deallocate(mach_task_self(), server_priv_port);
            mach_port_deallocate(mach_task_self(), service_send_port);
            return kr;
        }
    }
```

(continues)

FIGURE 9–16 A crash-resistant server *(continued)*

```
    // We are not a Mach port server, so we do not need this port. However,
    // we still will have a service with the Bootstrap Server, and so we
    // will be relaunched if we exit.
    mach_port_destroy(mach_task_self(), service_rcv_port);

    return kr;
}

static kern_return_t
unregister_bootstrap_service(void)
{
    return bootstrap_register(server_priv_port, (char *)SERVICE_NAME,
                              MACH_PORT_NULL);
}

int
main(void)
{
    kern_return_t kr;
    struct stat   statbuf;

    // Initialize a message for use with the Apple System Log (asl) facility.
    logmsg = asl_new(ASL_TYPE_MSG);
    asl_set(logmsg, "Facility", "Sleeper Daemon");

    // If the shutdown flag file exists, we are destroying the service;
    // otherwise, we are trying to be a server.
    if (stat(SERVICE_SHUTDOWN_FILE, &statbuf) == 0) {
        kr = unregister_bootstrap_service();
        MY_ASL_LOG("destroying service %s\n", SERVICE_NAME);
    } else {
        kr = register_bootstrap_service();
        MY_ASL_LOG("starting up service %s\n", SERVICE_NAME);
    }

    if (kr != KERN_SUCCESS) {
        // NB: When unregistering, we will get here if the unregister succeeded.
        mach_error("bootstrap_register", kr);
        exit(kr);
    }

    MY_ASL_LOG("server loop ready\n");

    while (1) // Dummy server loop.
        sleep(60);

    exit(0);
}
```

Note that the program also shows an example of using the Apple System Logger (ASL) facility. Beginning with Mac OS X 10.4, the `asl(3)` interface is available as a replacement for the `syslog(3)` logging interface. Besides logging, the ASL facility provides functions for querying logged messages. Section 10.8.3 contains an overview of logging in Mac OS X. Our server logs a few messages at the `ASL_LEVEL_ERR` log level. These messages will be written to both `/var/log/system.log` and `/var/log/asl.log`. Moreover, if `launchd`'s debugging output is enabled (as described in Section 9.4.2.3), you will see detailed log messages corresponding to the Bootstrap Server calls made by our program.

```
$ gcc -Wall -o /tmp/sleeperd bootstrap_server.c
$ /tmp/sleeperd
```

Apple System Logger (ASL)

The ASL facility allows structured log messages that consist of string-based key-value dictionaries. The facility provides several predefined keys, such as for priority level, process ID, time, and message sender. An application can extend the message dictionary by defining its own keys. Moreover, applications need not be concerned about the whereabouts of log files—ASL stores messages in a single data store. The ASL interface includes functions for constructing queries and searching for log messages based on those queries.

Beginning with Mac OS X 10.4, the `syslogd` program is the ASL daemon, although it provides backward compatibility with previous `syslogd` implementations. ASL also supports message filtering both in the client library and in `syslogd`.

Since our server does not fork and performs no operation other than sleeping, it will hang on running. We can examine the `launchd` log at this point to see the relevant messages, which are shown annotated, with prefixes removed, in Figure 9–17.

FIGURE 9–17 `launchd` debug messages corresponding to a Mach server's initialization

```
# server -> bootstrap_check_in()
Service checkin attempt for service com.osxbook.DummySleeper bootstrap 5103
bootstrap_check_in service com.osxbook.DummySleeper unknown
received message on port 5103
...
# server -> bootstrap_create_server()
Server create attempt: "/tmp/sleeperd" bootstrap 5103
adding new server "/tmp/sleeperd" with uid 501
```

(continues)

FIGURE 9–17 `launchd` debug messages corresponding to a Mach server's initialization *(continued)*

```
Allocating port f70f for server /tmp/sleeperd
New server f70f in bootstrap 5103: "/tmp/sleeperd"
...
# server -> bootstrap_create_service()
Service creation attempt for service com.osxbook.DummySleeper bootstrap f70f
Created new service c19f in bootstrap 5103: com.osxbook.DummySleeper
...
# server -> bootstrap_check_in()
Service checkin attempt for service com.osxbook.DummySleeper bootstrap f70f
Checkin service com.osxbook.DummySleeper for bootstrap 5103
Check-in service c19f in bootstrap 5103: com.osxbook.DummySleeper
...
# server -> mach_port_destroy()
received destroyed notification for service com.osxbook.DummySleeper
Service f797 bootstrap 5103 backed up: com.osxbook.DummySleeper
...
```

Let us kill the server by sending it the interrupt signal—that is, by typing **ctrl-c** in the shell from which we executed `/tmp/sleeperd`. We can then verify that the server was indeed relaunched.

```
^C
$ ps -ax | grep sleeperd
2364  ?? Ss   0:00.01 /tmp/sleeperd
```

Let us examine `launchd`'s log again (Figure 9–18).

FIGURE 9–18 `launchd` debug messages corresponding to a Mach server's relaunch

```
...
# server died; will be relaunched
server /tmp/sleeperd dropped server port
Allocating port f627 for server /tmp/sleeperd
Launched server f627 in bootstrap 5103 uid 501: "/tmp/sleeperd": [pid 2364]
received message on port f627
# server-> bootstrap_check_in()
Service checkin attempt for service com.osxbook.DummySleeper bootstrap f627
Checkin service com.osxbook.DummySleeper for bootstrap 5103
Check-in service f797 in bootstrap 5103: com.osxbook.DummySleeper
...
# server -> mach_port_destroy()
Received destroyed notification for service com.osxbook.DummySleeper
Service f797 bootstrap 5103 backed up: com.osxbook.DummySleeper
...
```

We can see that certain log messages are different from when we executed /tmp/sleeperd for the first time. In the first case, both a new server and a new service were created. In this case, when launchd respawns the server, the server's first attempt to call bootstrap_check_in() succeeds because the *service* already exists.

Now, even if we kill the server process by sending it SIGKILL, launchd will relaunch it. We can cause the server to terminate permanently by creating the /tmp/sleeperd.off file.

```
$ touch /tmp/sleeperd.off
$ kill -TERM 2344
$ ps -ax | grep sleeperd
$
```

The log messages will show that launchd relaunched our server even this time. However, instead of calling bootstrap_check_in(), the server calls bootstrap_register() with MACH_PORT_NULL specified as the service port, which makes the service unavailable.

```
...
# server died
received message on port f627
server /tmp/sleeperd dropped server port
received message on port f03
Notified dead name c1ab
Received task death notification for server /tmp/sleeperd
waitpid: cmd = /tmp/sleeperd: No child processes
# launchd is attempting to relaunch
Allocating port f62b for server /tmp/sleeperd
Launched server f62b in bootstrap 5103 uid 501: "/tmp/sleeperd": [pid 2380]
...
# server -> bootstrap_register(..., MACH_PORT_NULL)
server /tmp/sleeperd dropped server port
received message on port f03
Notified dead name f84f
# server -> exit()
Received task death notification for server /tmp/sleeperd
waitpid: cmd = /tmp/sleeperd: No child processes
Deleting server /tmp/sleeperd
Declared service com.osxbook.DummySleeper now unavailable
...
```

9.5 Using Mach IPC

We will now look at some examples of using Mach IPC. Besides serving as programming examples, these will also help illustrate the working of several interesting aspects of Mach IPC, for example, out-of-line transfers, interposition of port rights, port sets, and dead names.

9.5.1 A Simple Client-Server Example

In this client-server example, the client will send an integer value as inline data in a Mach message to the server, which will compute the factorial of the integer and send the result in a reply message to the client. We will use this example to demonstrate how to send and receive Mach messages. The next few examples assume familiarity with this example.

Figure 9–19 shows the common header file shared between the client and the server. Note the data type for send and receive buffers: We account for a message trailer on the receive side.

FIGURE 9–19 Common header file for the simple IPC client-server example

```
// simple_ipc_common.h

#ifndef _SIMPLE_IPC_COMMON_H_
#define _SIMPLE_IPC_COMMON_H_

#include <mach/mach.h>
#include <servers/bootstrap.h>

#define SERVICE_NAME    "com.osxbook.FactorialServer"
#define DEFAULT_MSG_ID 400

#define EXIT_ON_MACH_ERROR(msg, retval, success_retval) \
    if (kr != success_retval) { mach_error(msg ":" , kr); exit((retval)); }

typedef struct {
    mach_msg_header_t header;
    int               data;
} msg_format_send_t;

typedef struct {
    mach_msg_header_t  header;
    int                data;
    mach_msg_trailer_t trailer;
} msg_format_recv_t;

#endif // _SIMPLE_IPC_COMMON_H_
```

Figure 9–20 shows the code for the simple IPC server. To become a Mach server that provides a named service, our program creates and checks in that service. After that, it goes into the idiomatic server loop consisting of the *receive message*, *process message*, and *send reply* operations.

FIGURE 9–20 Source for the simple IPC server

```
// simple_ipc_server.c

#include <stdio.h>
#include <stdlib.h>
#include "simple_ipc_common.h"

int
factorial(int n)
{
    if (n < 1)
        return 1;
    else return n * factorial(n - 1);
}

int
main(int argc, char **argv)
{
    kern_return_t        kr;
    msg_format_recv_t    recv_msg;
    msg_format_send_t    send_msg;
    mach_msg_header_t *recv_hdr, *send_hdr;
    mach_port_t          server_port;

    kr = bootstrap_create_service(bootstrap_port, SERVICE_NAME, &server_port);
    EXIT_ON_MACH_ERROR("bootstrap_create_service", kr, BOOTSTRAP_SUCCESS);

    kr = bootstrap_check_in(bootstrap_port, SERVICE_NAME, &server_port);
    EXIT_ON_MACH_ERROR("bootstrap_check_in", kr, BOOTSTRAP_SUCCESS);

    printf("server_port = %d\n", server_port);

    for (;;) { // server loop

        // receive message
        recv_hdr                  = &(recv_msg.header);
        recv_hdr->msgh_local_port = server_port;
        recv_hdr->msgh_size       = sizeof(recv_msg);
        kr = mach_msg(recv_hdr,                  // message buffer
                      MACH_RCV_MSG,              // option indicating receive
                      0,                         // send size
```

(continues)

FIGURE 9–20 Source for the simple IPC server *(continued)*

```
                        recv_hdr->msgh_size,    // size of header + body
                        server_port,            // receive name
                        MACH_MSG_TIMEOUT_NONE,  // no timeout, wait forever
                        MACH_PORT_NULL);        // no notification port
        EXIT_ON_MACH_ERROR("mach_msg(recv)", kr, MACH_MSG_SUCCESS);

        printf("recv data = %d, id = %d, local_port = %d, remote_port = %d\n",
                recv_msg.data, recv_hdr->msgh_id,
                recv_hdr->msgh_local_port, recv_hdr->msgh_remote_port);

        // process message and prepare reply
        send_hdr                    = &(send_msg.header);
        send_hdr->msgh_bits         = MACH_MSGH_BITS_LOCAL(recv_hdr->msgh_bits);
        send_hdr->msgh_size         = sizeof(send_msg);
        send_hdr->msgh_local_port   = MACH_PORT_NULL;
        send_hdr->msgh_remote_port  = recv_hdr->msgh_remote_port;
        send_hdr->msgh_id           = recv_hdr->msgh_id;
        send_msg.data               = factorial(recv_msg.data);

        // send message
        kr = mach_msg(send_hdr,                 // message buffer
                        MACH_SEND_MSG,          // option indicating send
                        send_hdr->msgh_size,    // size of header + body
                        0,                      // receive limit
                        MACH_PORT_NULL,         // receive name
                        MACH_MSG_TIMEOUT_NONE,  // no timeout, wait forever
                        MACH_PORT_NULL);        // no notification port
        EXIT_ON_MACH_ERROR("mach_msg(send)", kr, MACH_MSG_SUCCESS);

        printf("reply sent\n");
    }

    exit(0);
}
```

Figure 9–21 shows the source for the simple IPC client. Note that we use the MACH_MSGH_BITS() macro to set the value of the msgh_bits field in the request message. The value of the remote bits is MACH_MSG_TYPE_COPY_SEND, which means the message carries a caller-provided send right (server_port). The value of the local bits is MACH_MSG_TYPE_MAKE_SEND, which means that a send right is created from the caller-supplied receive right (client_port) and carried in the message.

FIGURE 9–21 Source for the simple IPC client

```c
// simple_ipc_client.c

#include <stdio.h>
#include <stdlib.h>
#include "simple_ipc_common.h"

int
main(int argc, char **argv)
{
    kern_return_t       kr;
    msg_format_recv_t   recv_msg;
    msg_format_send_t   send_msg;
    mach_msg_header_t *recv_hdr, *send_hdr;
    mach_port_t         client_port, server_port;

    kr = bootstrap_look_up(bootstrap_port, SERVICE_NAME, &server_port);
    EXIT_ON_MACH_ERROR("bootstrap_look_up", kr, BOOTSTRAP_SUCCESS);

    kr = mach_port_allocate(mach_task_self(),        // our task is acquiring
                        MACH_PORT_RIGHT_RECEIVE, // a new receive right
                        &client_port);           // with this name
    EXIT_ON_MACH_ERROR("mach_port_allocate", kr, KERN_SUCCESS);

    printf("client_port = %d, server_port = %d\n", client_port, server_port);

    // prepare request
    send_hdr                  = &(send_msg.header);
    send_hdr->msgh_bits       = MACH_MSGH_BITS(MACH_MSG_TYPE_COPY_SEND, \
                                               MACH_MSG_TYPE_MAKE_SEND);
    send_hdr->msgh_size       = sizeof(send_msg);
    send_hdr->msgh_remote_port = server_port;
    send_hdr->msgh_local_port = client_port;
    send_hdr->msgh_reserved   = 0;
    send_hdr->msgh_id         = DEFAULT_MSG_ID;
    send_msg.data             = 0;

    if (argc == 2)
        send_msg.data = atoi(argv[1]);
    if ((send_msg.data < 1) || (send_msg.data > 20))
        send_msg.data = 1; // some sane default value

    // send request
    kr = mach_msg(send_hdr,                   // message buffer
                  MACH_SEND_MSG,              // option indicating send
                  send_hdr->msgh_size,        // size of header + body
                  0,                          // receive limit
                  MACH_PORT_NULL,             // receive name
                  MACH_MSG_TIMEOUT_NONE,      // no timeout, wait forever
```

(continues)

FIGURE 9–21 Source for the simple IPC client *(continued)*

```
                        MACH_PORT_NULL);          // no notification port
    EXIT_ON_MACH_ERROR("mach_msg(send)", kr, MACH_MSG_SUCCESS);

    do { // receive reply
        recv_hdr                    = &(recv_msg.header);
        recv_hdr->msgh_remote_port = server_port;
        recv_hdr->msgh_local_port  = client_port;
        recv_hdr->msgh_size        = sizeof(recv_msg);

        kr = mach_msg(recv_hdr,              // message buffer
                      MACH_RCV_MSG,          // option indicating receive
                      0,                     // send size
                      recv_hdr->msgh_size,   // size of header + body
                      client_port,           // receive name
                      MACH_MSG_TIMEOUT_NONE, // no timeout, wait forever
                      MACH_PORT_NULL);       // no notification port
        EXIT_ON_MACH_ERROR("mach_msg(recv)", kr, MACH_MSG_SUCCESS);

        printf("%d\n", recv_msg.data);

    } while (recv_hdr->msgh_id != DEFAULT_MSG_ID);

    exit(0);
}
```

Let us now test the simple IPC client-server example.

```
$ gcc -Wall -o simple_ipc_server simple_ipc_server.c
$ gcc -Wall -o simple_ipc_client simple_ipc_client.c
$ ./simple_ipc_server
server_port = 3079
                    # another shell
                    $ ./simple_ipc_client 10
recv data = 10, id = 400, local_port = 3079, remote_port = 3843
reply sent
                    client_port = 3843, server_port = 3079
                    3628800
```

9.5.2 Dead Names

We came across the concept of *dead names* earlier in this chapter. When a port is destroyed, its receive right is deallocated,[9] causing the port's send rights to

---

9. When a port dies, all messages in its queue are destroyed.

become invalid and turn into dead names. Dead names inherit references from the erstwhile send rights. Only when a dead name loses all its references does the port name become available for reuse. The `mach_msg` routines return an error when sending to a dead name. This way, a program can realize that a right it holds is dead and can then deallocate the dead name.

Moreover, if the server wishes to be notified of a client's death earlier, it can use `mach_port_request_notification()` to request the kernel to send it a *dead-name notification* for the client's send-once right reply port. Conversely, if a server dies during an RPC, any send-once rights held by the server will be deallocated. Recall that send-once rights always result in a message. In this case, the kernel will use the send-once rights to send a notification message to the client.

```
kern_return_t
mach_port_request_notification(

    // task holding the right in question
    ipc_space_t          task,

    // name for the right in the task's IPC space
    mach_port_name_t     name,

    // type of notification desired
    mach_msg_id_t        variant,

    // used for avoiding race conditions for some notification types
    mach_port_mscount_t  sync,

    // send-once right to which notification will be sent
    mach_port_send_once_t  notify,

    // MACH_MSG_TYPE_MAKE_SEND_ONCE or MACH_MSG_TYPE_MOVE_SEND_ONCE
    mach_msg_type_name_t   notify_right_type,

    // previously registered send-once right
    mach_port_send_once_t *previousp);
```

Table 9–1 shows the values that can be passed as the `variant` argument to `mach_port_request_notification()`.

9.5.3 Port Sets

Mach allows ports to be grouped into port sets. A port set represents a queue that is a combination of the queues of its constituent ports. Listening on a port set is equivalent to listening on all members of the set concurrently—analogous to the

TABLE 9–1 Notifications That Can Be Requested from the Kernel

Notification Type	Description
MACH_NOTIFY_PORT_DELETED	A send or send-once right was deleted.
MACH_NOTIFY_PORT_DESTROYED	A receive right was (would have been) destroyed; instead of actually being destroyed, the right is sent in the notification.
MACH_NOTIFY_NO_SENDERS	A receive right has no existing send rights; this can be used for garbage collection of receive rights.
MACH_NOTIFY_SEND_ONCE	An existing send-once right died.
MACH_NOTIFY_DEAD_NAME	A send or send-once right died and became a dead name.

select() system call. Specifically, a port set can be used by a thread to receive messages sent to any of the member ports. The receiving task knows which port the message was sent to because that information is specified in the message.

A given port may belong to at most one port set at a time. Moreover, while a port is a member of a port set, that port cannot be used to receive messages other than through the port set. The name of a port set is on par with the name of a port—both reside in the same namespace. However, unlike a port's name, a port set's name cannot be transferred in a message.

Figure 9–22 shows the skeleton for a server (based on our example from Section 9.5.1) that provides two services. It places the server ports for both services into a single port set, which it then uses to receive request messages.

FIGURE 9–22 Using a port set to receive request messages destined for multiple services

```
// port_set_ipc_server.c
...

int
main(int argc, char **argv)
{
    ...
    mach_port_t        server_portset, server1_port, server2_port;

    // allocate a port set
    kr = mach_port_allocate(mach_task_self(), MACH_PORT_RIGHT_PORT_SET,
                       &server_portset);

    // first service
    kr = bootstrap_create_service(bootstrap_port, SERVICE1_NAME, &server1_port);
    ...
```

(continues)

FIGURE 9–22 Using a port set to receive request messages destined for multiple services
(continued)

```
    kr = bootstrap_check_in(bootstrap_port, SERVICE1_NAME, &server1_port);
    ...

    // second service
    kr = bootstrap_create_service(bootstrap_port, SERVICE2_NAME, &server2_port);
    ...
    kr = bootstrap_check_in(bootstrap_port, SERVICE2_NAME, &server2_port);
    ...

    // move right to the port set
    kr = mach_port_move_member(mach_task_self(), server1_port, server_portset);
    ...

    // move right to the port set
    kr = mach_port_move_member(mach_task_self(), server2_port, server_portset);
    ...

    for (;;) {

        // receive message on the port set
        kr = mach_msg(recv_hdr, ..., server_portset, ...);
        ...

        // determine target service and process
        if (recv_hdr->msgh_local_port == server1_port) {
            // processing for the first service
        } else if (recv_hdr->msgh_local_port == server2_port) {
            // processing for the second service
        } else {
            // unexpected!
        }

        // send reply
    }
    ...
}
```

9.5.4 Interposition

Port rights can be added to or removed from a target task's IPC space—even
without involving the target task. In particular, port rights can be *interposed*,
which allows a task to transparently intercept messages sent to or sent by another
task. This is how the `netmsgserver` program provides network transparency.

Another example is that of a debugger that can intercept all messages sent through a send right. Specifically, the debugger extracts a task's send right and inserts a send right for another port that the debugger owns. The `mach_port_extract_right()` and `mach_port_insert_right()` routines are used for this purpose. Thereafter, the debugger will receive messages sent by the task—it can examine and forward these messages to the extracted send right.

Figure 9–23 shows a program that demonstrates the use of `mach_port_insert_right()`. The program forks, after which the child task suspends itself. The parent acquires send rights to the host privileged port and calls `mach_port_insert_right()` to insert these rights into the child, giving the rights a specific name that is unused in the child's IPC space—say, `0x1234`. It then resumes the child, which uses the send rights named by `0x1234` to retrieve the number of processors on the system. Note that the parent process requires superuser privileges in this case, but the child process, which actually uses the host privileged port, does not.

FIGURE 9–23 Inserting port rights into an IPC space

```
// interpose.c

#include <stdio.h>
#include <unistd.h>
#include <mach/mach.h>

#define OUT_ON_MACH_ERROR(msg, retval) \
    if (kr != KERN_SUCCESS) { mach_error(msg ":" , kr); goto out; }

void
print_processor_count(host_priv_t host_priv)
{
    kern_return_t          kr;
    natural_t              processor_count = 0;
    processor_port_array_t processor_list;

    kr = host_processors(host_priv, &processor_list, &processor_count);
    if (kr == KERN_SUCCESS)
        printf("%d processors\n", processor_count);
    else
        mach_error("host_processors:", kr);
}

void
childproc()
```

(continues)

FIGURE 9–23 Inserting port rights into an IPC space *(continued)*

```
{
    printf("child suspending...\n");
    (void)task_suspend(mach_task_self());
    printf("child attempting to retrieve processor count...\n");
    print_processor_count(0x1234);
}

void
parentproc(pid_t child)
{
    kern_return_t kr;
    task_t        child_task;
    host_priv_t   host_priv;

    // kludge: give child some time to run and suspend itself
    sleep(1);

    kr = task_for_pid(mach_task_self(), child, &child_task);
    OUT_ON_MACH_ERROR("task_for_pid", kr);

    kr = host_get_host_priv_port(mach_host_self(), &host_priv);
    OUT_ON_MACH_ERROR("host_get_host_priv_port", kr);

    kr = mach_port_insert_right(child_task, 0x1234, host_priv,
                                MACH_MSG_TYPE_MOVE_SEND);
    if (kr != KERN_SUCCESS)
        mach_error("mach_port_insert_right:", kr);

out:
    printf("resuming child...\n");
    (void)task_resume(child_task);
}

int
main(void)
{
    pid_t pid = fork();

    if (pid == 0)
        childproc();
    else if (pid > 0)
        parentproc(pid);
    else
        return 1;

    return 0;
}
```

(continues)

FIGURE 9–23 Inserting port rights into an IPC space *(continued)*

```
$ gcc -Wall -o interpose interpose.c
$ sudo ./interpose
child suspending...
resuming child...
child attempting to retrieve processor count...
2 processors
```

9.5.5 Transferring Out-of-Line Memory and Port Rights

When transferring large amounts of data, a sender can include the address of a memory region (rather than the entire data inline) in its address space as part of the message. This is called an *out-of-line (OOL) transfer*. On the receive side, the out-of-line region is mapped by the kernel to a hitherto unused portion of the receiver's address space. In particular, the sender and the receiver share the region thus transferred as copy-on-write. Moreover, the sender can set the *deallocate bit* in the out-of-line data's type descriptor to have the kernel automatically deallocate the region from the sender's address space. In this case, copy-on-write will not be used—the kernel will instead move the region.

Figure 9–24 shows partial source for a simple OOL memory server. When the server receives a message from a client, it sends a character string as OOL memory back to the client. The program is based on the simple IPC client-server example from Section 9.5.1, with the following differences.

- The request message from the client has an empty body in this case—it is used only as a trigger.

- The response message from the server contains an OOL descriptor for memory. The server initializes various fields of this descriptor before sending it.

- The server must mark the response message as a complex message by setting MACH_MSGH_BITS_COMPLEX in the msgh_bits field of the outgoing message.

The client code remains almost the same, except that the client uses the updated request and response message buffer structures. When the client receives the server's response, the address field of the out-of-line descriptor will contain the address of the string in the client's virtual address space.

FIGURE 9–24 Sending out-of-line memory in an IPC message

```c
// ool_memory_ipc_common.h

#ifndef _OOL_MEMORY_IPC_COMMON_H_
#define _OOL_MEMORY_IPC_COMMON_H_

...
#define SERVICE_NAME    "com.osxbook.OOLStringServer"
...

typedef struct {
    mach_msg_header_t header;
} msg_format_request_t;

typedef struct {
    mach_msg_header_t  header;
    mach_msg_trailer_t trailer;
} msg_format_request_r_t;

typedef struct {
    mach_msg_header_t           header;
    mach_msg_body_t             body; // start of kernel-processed data
    mach_msg_ool_descriptor_t   data; // end of kernel-processed data
    mach_msg_type_number_t      count;
} msg_format_response_t;

typedef struct {
    mach_msg_header_t           header;
    mach_msg_body_t             body; // start of kernel-processed data
    mach_msg_ool_descriptor_t   data; // end of kernel-processed data
    mach_msg_type_number_t      count;
    mach_msg_trailer_t          trailer;
} msg_format_response_r_t;

#endif // _OOL_MEMORY_IPC_COMMON_H_


// ool_memory_ipc_server.c

...
#include "ool_memory_ipc_common.h"

// string we will send as OOL memory
const char *string = "abcdefghijklmnopqrstuvwxyz";

int
main(int argc, char **argv)
{
    ...
```

(continues)

FIGURE 9–24 Sending out-of-line memory in an IPC message *(continued)*

```
msg_format_request_r_t recv_msg;
msg_format_response_t  send_msg;
...
for (;;) { // server loop

    // receive request
    ...

    // prepare response
    send_hdr                    = &(send_msg.header);
    send_hdr->msgh_bits         = MACH_MSGH_BITS_LOCAL(recv_hdr->msgh_bits);
    send_hdr->msgh_bits        |= MACH_MSGH_BITS_COMPLEX;
    send_hdr->msgh_size         = sizeof(send_msg);
    send_hdr->msgh_local_port   = MACH_PORT_NULL;
    send_hdr->msgh_remote_port  = recv_hdr->msgh_remote_port;
    send_hdr->msgh_id           = recv_hdr->msgh_id;

    send_msg.body.msgh_descriptor_count = 1;
    send_msg.data.address           = (void *)string;
    send_msg.data.size              = strlen(string) + 1;
    send_msg.data.deallocate        = FALSE;
    send_msg.data.copy              = MACH_MSG_VIRTUAL_COPY;
    send_msg.data.type              = MACH_MSG_OOL_DESCRIPTOR;
    send_msg.count                  = send_msg.data.size;

    // send response
    ...

}

exit(0);
}
```

We could modify the example in Figure 9–24 to send port rights instead of out-of-line memory in an IPC message. The kernel provides both inline and out-of-line descriptors for sending port rights, although a message carrying a port right is always complex. Figure 9–25 shows another adaptation of our client-server example that acquires send rights to the host privileged port and sends them to a client. The client can then use these rights, which appear in the name field of the received port descriptor, just as if it had acquired these rights normally (say, by calling host_get_host_priv_port()).

FIGURE 9–25 Sending port rights in an IPC message

```
// ool_port_ipc_common.h

#ifndef _OOL_PORT_IPC_COMMON_H_
#define _OOL_PORT_IPC_COMMON_H_

...
#define SERVICE_NAME    "com.osxbook.ProcessorInfoServer"
...
typedef struct {
    mach_msg_header_t           header;
    mach_msg_body_t             body; // start of kernel-processed data
    mach_msg_port_descriptor_t  data; // end of kernel-processed data
} msg_format_response_t;

typedef struct {
    mach_msg_header_t           header;
    mach_msg_body_t             body; // start of kernel-processed data
    mach_msg_port_descriptor_t  data; // end of kernel-processed data
    mach_msg_trailer_t          trailer;
} msg_format_response_r_t;

#endif // _OOL_PORT_IPC_COMMON_H_


// ool_port_ipc_server.c

int
main(int argc, char **argv)
{
    ...
    host_priv_t                 host_priv;
    ...

    // acquire send rights to the host privileged port in host_priv
    ...

    for (;;) { // server loop

        // receive request
        ...

        // prepare response
        send_hdr                    = &(send_msg.header);
        send_hdr->msgh_bits         = MACH_MSGH_BITS_LOCAL(recv_hdr->msgh_bits);
        send_hdr->msgh_bits        |= MACH_MSGH_BITS_COMPLEX;
        send_hdr->msgh_size         = sizeof(send_msg);
        send_hdr->msgh_local_port   = MACH_PORT_NULL;
```

(continues)

FIGURE 9–25 Sending port rights in an IPC message *(continued)*

```
        send_hdr->msgh_remote_port = recv_hdr->msgh_remote_port;
        send_hdr->msgh_id          = recv_hdr->msgh_id;

        send_msg.body.msgh_descriptor_count = 1;
        send_msg.data.name               = host_priv;
        send_msg.data.disposition        = MACH_MSG_TYPE_COPY_SEND;
        send_msg.data.type               = MACH_MSG_PORT_DESCRIPTOR;

        // send response
        ...
    }

    exit(0);
}
```

9.6 MIG

Informally speaking, the phrase *remote procedure call* (RPC) denotes a mechanism that allows programs to call procedures transparently with respect to the procedures' locations. In other words, using RPC, a program can call a remote procedure, which may reside within another program or even within a program on another computer.

The Remote Past of RPC

Jim E. White described an alternative approach to network-based resource sharing in a paper (RFC 707) in 1975.[10] White's approach was based on having a framework that required a common command/response discipline that was independent of any specific network application. His paper described what was perhaps the first formal RPC mechanism. Instead of reimplementing the network runtime environment as part of every application, the programmer could execute a procedure with the specified arguments on a remote machine, much like a usual (local) procedure call. Numerous RPC systems have been built since White's paper, such as Xerox Courier (1981), Sun RPC (1985), and OSF Distributed Computing Environment (DCE, 1991). Examples of relatively recent systems include XML RPC and Simple Object Access Protocol (SOAP).

---

10. "A High-Level Framework for Network-Based Resource Sharing" (RFC 707), by Jim E. White (The Internet Engineering Task Force, December 1975).

Most RPC systems include tools that ease the programmer's job by taking care of repetitive, tedious, and mechanical aspects of RPC programming. For example, Sun RPC provides the `rpcgen` program, which compiles an RPC specification file to generate C language code that can be linked with other C code explicitly written by the programmer. The specification file—a `.x` file—defines server procedures, their arguments, and their results.

Mach Interface Generator (MIG) is a tool[11] that generates RPC code for client-server-style Mach IPC from specification files. Since typical IPC programs perform similar operations of preparing, sending, receiving, unpacking, and demultiplexing messages, MIG is able to automatically generate code for these operations based on programmer-provided specifications of message passing and procedure call interfaces. Automated code generation also promotes consistency and reduces the likelihood of programming errors. Besides, if the programmer wishes to change the *interface*, only the appropriate specification file needs to be modified.

A Ma(t)ch Made . . .

MIG originally implemented a subset of a language called *Matchmaker*, which was also intended for specifying and automating the generation of IPC interfaces. Matchmaker was meant to be multilingual: It generated C, Pascal, and Lisp code at different times during its evolution. In fact, the syntax of MIG declarations still resembles Pascal syntax, although MIG generates only C code.

Depending on the specific RPC system, tools similar to MIG may or may not hide features of the underlying IPC layer from the programmer—however, MIG does *not*.

9.6.1 MIG Specification Files

A MIG specification file conventionally has the `.defs` extension. MIG processes a `.defs` file to generate the following three files:

- A *header file* for inclusion by client code
- A *user-interface module* to be linked with client code—contains functions for sending request messages to the server and receiving replies

---

11. Another term for tools such as MIG is *stub generators*—MIG generates client stubs for Mach IPC.

- A *server-interface module* to be linked with server code—contains functions for receiving requests from the client, for calling the appropriate server function (programmer-provided) based on the contents of the request message, and for sending reply messages

A MIG specification file contains the following types of sections, not all of which are mandatory:

- Subsystem identifier
- Serverdemux declaration
- Type specifications
- Import declarations
- Operation descriptions
- Options declarations

A MIG "subsystem" is a collective name for a client, the server called by the client, and the set of operations exported by the server. The subsystem keyword names the MIG subsystem specified by the file. MIG use this identifier as a prefix in the names of the code files it generates.

```
subsystem          system-name          message-base-id ;
```

The subsystem keyword is followed by the ASCII name (e.g., foo) of the subsystem being defined. message-base-id is the integer base value used as the IPC message identifier (the msgh_id field in the message header) of the first operation in the specification file. In other words, this value is the base beginning with which operations are numbered sequentially. message-base-id may be arbitrarily chosen. However, if the same program serves multiple interfaces, then each interface must have a unique identifier so that the server can unambiguously determine the operations invoked.

> When MIG creates a reply message corresponding to a request message, the reply identifier is conventionally the sum of the request identifier and the number 100.

The serverdemux declaration section can be used to specify an alternative name for the server demultiplexing routine in the server-interface module. The demultiplexing routine examines the request message, calling the appropriate subsystem routine based on the msgh_id value in the message header. If the value is out of bounds for the subsystem, the demultiplexing routine returns an error. The default name for this routine is `<system-name>_server`, where `<system-name>` is the name specified through the `subsystem` statement.

```
serverdemux    somethingelse_server ;
```

The type specifications section is used for defining data types corresponding to parameters of the calls exported by the user-interface module. MIG supports declarations for types such as simple, structured, pointer, and polymorphic.

```
/*
 * Simple Types
 * type type-name = type-description;
 */
type int           = MACH_MSG_TYPE_INTEGER_32;
type kern_return_t = int;
type some_string   = (MACH_MSG_TYPE_STRING, 8*128);

/*
 * Structured and Pointer Types
 * type type-name = array [size] of type-description;
 * type type-name = array [*:maxsize] of type-description;
 * struct [size] of type-description;
 * type type-name = ^ type-description;
 */
type thread_ids    = array[16] of MACH_MSG_TYPE_INTEGER_32;
type a_structure   = struct[16] of array[8] of int;
type ool_array     = ^ array[] of MACH_MSG_TYPE_INTEGER_32;
type intptr        = ^ MACH_MSG_TYPE_INTEGER_32;
type input_string  = array[*:64] of char;
```

A polymorphic type is used to specify an argument whose exact type is not determined until runtime—a client must specify the type information as an auxiliary argument at runtime. MIG automatically includes an additional argument to accommodate this. Consider the following simple definition file:

```
/* foo.defs */

subsystem foo 500

#include <mach/std_types.defs>
#include <mach/mach_types.defs>

type my_poly_t = polymorphic;

routine foo_func(
        server : mach_port_t;
        arg    : my_poly_t);
```

The MIG-generated code for `foo_func()` has the following prototype:

```
kern_return_t
foo_func(mach_port_t          server,
         my_poly_t            arg,
         mach_msg_type_name_t argPoly);
```

A type declaration can optionally contain information specifying procedures for *translating* or *deallocating* types. Translation allows a type to be seen differently by the user- and server-interface modules. A deallocation specification allows a destructor function to be specified. In Section 9.6.2 we will see an example involving translation and deallocation specifications.

Import declarations are used to include header files in MIG-generated modules. MIG can be directed to include such headers in both the user- and server-interface modules, or in only one of the two.

```
/*
 * import header-file;
 * uimport header-file;
 * simport header-file;
 */
import "foo.h";          /* imported in both modules */
uimport <stdlib.h>;      /* only in user-interface module */
simport <stdio.h>;       /* only in server-interface module */
```

The operations section contains specifications for one or more types of IPC operations. The specification includes a keyword for the kind of operation being described, the name of the operation, and the names and types of its arguments. When MIG compiles the specification file, it generates client and server stubs for each operation. A client stub resides in the user-interface module. Its job is to package and send the message corresponding to a procedure call invocation in the client program. The server stub resides in the server-interface module. It unpacks received messages and calls the programmer's server code that implements the operation.

Operation types supported by MIG include `Routine`, `SimpleRoutine`, `Procedure`, `SimpleProcedure`, and `Function`. Table 9–2 shows the characteristics of these types.

The following is an example of an operation specification:

```
routine vm_allocate(
                target_task     : vm_task_entry_t;
        inout   address         : vm_address_t;
                size            : vm_size_t;
                flags           : int);
```

TABLE 9–2 Operation Types Supported by MIG

Operation Type	Reply Received?	Error Returned?
`Routine`	Yes	Yes, a `kern_return_t` return value specifying whether the operation was successfully completed
`SimpleRoutine`	No	Yes, the return value from Mach's message-sending primitive
`Procedure`	Yes	No
`SimpleProcedure`	No	No
`Function`	Yes	No error code returned, but a value from the server function is returned

A parameter specification contains a name and a type and may optionally be adorned by one of the keywords `in`, `out`, or `inout`, representing that the argument is only sent to the server, is sent by the server on its way out, or both, respectively.

> In the operations section, the `skip` keyword causes MIG to skip assignment of the next operation ID, resulting in a hole in the sequence of operation IDs. This can be useful to preserve compatibility as interfaces evolve.

The options declarations section is used for specifying special-purpose or global options that affect the generated code. The following are examples of options:

- `WaitTime`—used for specifying the maximum time in milliseconds that the user-interface code will wait for receiving a reply from the server
- `MsgType`—used for setting the message type (e.g., to mark messages as being encrypted)
- `UserPrefix`—used for specifying a string that will be a prefix of client-side function names that call IPC operations
- `ServerPrefix`—used for specifying a string that will be a prefix of server-side function names that implement IPC operations
- `Rcsid`—used for specifying a string that will cause static string variables called `Sys_server_rcsid` and `Sys_user_rcsid` to be declared in the server and user modules, respectively, with their constant values each being the specified string

Numerous examples of MIG specification files exist in `/usr/include/mach/` and its subdirectories.

9.6.2 Using MIG to Create a Client-Server System

Let us use MIG to create a simple client-server system. A MIG server is a Mach task that provides services to its clients using a MIG-generated RPC interface. Our MIG server will serve two routines: one to calculate the length of a string sent by the client and another to calculate the factorial of a number sent by the client. In our example, the client will send the string inline, and the server will send only simple integers. Recall that when an interface call returns out-of-line data, it is the caller's responsibility to deallocate the memory by calling `vm_deallocate()`. For example, we could add another operation to our interface, say, one that reverses the string sent by the client and returns the reversed string by allocating memory for it in the caller's address space.

We call our MIG server the *Miscellaneous Server*. Its source consists of the following four files:

- A header file containing useful definitions and prototypes used by both the client and the server (`misc_types.h`)
- The MIG specification file (`misc.defs`)
- Setup and main loop for the server (`server.c`)
- Demonstration of the interface (`client.c`)

Figure 9–26 shows the common header file. We define two new data types: `input_string_t`, which is a character array 64 elements in size, and `xput_number_t`, which is another name for an integer.

FIGURE 9–26 Common header file for the Miscellaneous Server and its client

```
// misc_types.h

#ifndef _MISC_TYPES_H_
#define _MISC_TYPES_H_

#include <stdio.h>
#include <stdlib.h>
#include <string.h>
```

(continues)

FIGURE 9–26 Common header file for the Miscellaneous Server and its client *(continued)*

```
#include <mach/mach.h>
#include <servers/bootstrap.h>

// The server port will be registered under this name.
#define MIG_MISC_SERVICE "MIG-miscservice"

// Data representations
typedef char input_string_t[64];
typedef int  xput_number_t;

typedef struct {
    mach_msg_header_t head;

    // The following fields do not represent the actual layout of the request
    // and reply messages that MIG will use. However, a request or reply
    // message will not be larger in size than the sum of the sizes of these
    // fields. We need the size to put an upper bound on the size of an
    // incoming message in a mach_msg() call.
    NDR_record_t NDR;
    union {
        input_string_t string;
        xput_number_t  number;
    } data;
    kern_return_t      RetCode;
    mach_msg_trailer_t trailer;
} msg_misc_t;

xput_number_t misc_translate_int_to_xput_number_t(int);
int           misc_translate_xput_number_t_to_int(xput_number_t);
void          misc_remove_reference(xput_number_t);
kern_return_t string_length(mach_port_t, input_string_t, xput_number_t *);
kern_return_t factorial(mach_port_t, xput_number_t, xput_number_t *);

#endif // _MISC_TYPES_H_
```

Figure 9–27 shows the specification file. Note the type specification of xput_number_t. Each MIG type can have up to three corresponding C types: a type for the user-interface module (specified by the CUserType option), a type for the server module (specified by the CServerType option), and a translated type for internal use by server routines. The CType option can be used in place of CUserType and CServerType if both types are the same. In our case, the CType option specifies the C data type for the MIG type xput_number_t.

FIGURE 9–27 MIG specification file for the Miscellaneous Server

```
/*
 * A "Miscellaneous" Mach Server
 */


/*
 * File:    misc.defs
 * Purpose: Miscellaneous Server subsystem definitions
 */


/*
 * Subsystem identifier
 */
Subsystem misc 500;


/*
 * Type declarations
 */
#include <mach/std_types.defs>
#include <mach/mach_types.defs>

type input_string_t = array[64] of char;
type xput_number_t  = int
        CType    : int
        InTran   : xput_number_t misc_translate_int_to_xput_number_t(int)
        OutTran  : int misc_translate_xput_number_t_to_int(xput_number_t)
        Destructor : misc_remove_reference(xput_number_t)
    ;


/*
 * Import declarations
 */
import "misc_types.h";


/*
 * Operation descriptions
 */


/* This should be operation #500 */
routine string_length(
                    server_port : mach_port_t;
                in instring    : input_string_t;
                out len        : xput_number_t);


/* Create some holes in operation sequence */
Skip;
Skip;
Skip;
```

(continues)

FIGURE 9–27 MIG specification file for the Miscellaneous Server *(continued)*

```
/* This should be operation #504, as there are three Skip's */
routine factorial(
                server_port : mach_port_t;
        in num          : xput_number_t;
        out fac         : xput_number_t);

/*
 * Option declarations
 */
ServerPrefix Server_;
UserPrefix   Client_;
```

We use the `InTran`, `OutTran`, and `Destructor` options to specify procedures that we will provide for translation and deallocation. Translation is useful when a type must be seen differently by the server and the client. In our example, we want the type in question to be an `xput_number_t` for the server and an `int` for the client. We use `InTran` to specify `misc_translate_int_to_xput_number_t()` as the incoming translation routine for the type. Similarly, `misc_translate_xput_number_t_to_int()` is the outgoing translation routine. Since `xput_number_t` is actually just another name for an `int` in our case, our translation functions are trivial: They simply print a message.

> Real-life translation functions can be arbitrarily complex. The kernel makes heavy use of translation functions. See Section 9.6.3 for an example.

We also use the `Destructor` option to specify a deallocation function that MIG will call at the appropriate time.

Figure 9–28 shows the source for the server.

FIGURE 9–28 Programmer-provided source for the Miscellaneous Server

```
// server.c

#include "misc_types.h"

static mach_port_t server_port;

extern boolean_t misc_server(mach_msg_header_t *inhdr,
                             mach_msg_header_t *outhdr);
```

(continues)

FIGURE 9–28 Programmer-provided source for the Miscellaneous Server *(continued)*

```
void
server_setup(void)
{
    kern_return_t kr;

    if ((kr = bootstrap_create_service(bootstrap_port, MIG_MISC_SERVICE,
                                       &server_port)) != BOOTSTRAP_SUCCESS) {
        mach_error("bootstrap_create_service:", kr);
        exit(1);
    }

    if ((kr = bootstrap_check_in(bootstrap_port, MIG_MISC_SERVICE,
                                 &server_port)) != BOOTSTRAP_SUCCESS) {
        mach_port_deallocate(mach_task_self(), server_port);
        mach_error("bootstrap_check_in:", kr);
        exit(1);
    }
}


void
server_loop(void)
{
    mach_msg_server(misc_server,            // call the server-interface module
                    sizeof(msg_misc_t),     // maximum receive size
                    server_port,            // port to receive on
                    MACH_MSG_TIMEOUT_NONE); // options
}


// InTran
xput_number_t
misc_translate_int_to_xput_number_t(int param)
{
    printf("misc_translate_incoming(%d)\n", param);
    return (xput_number_t)param;
}


// OutTran
int
misc_translate_xput_number_t_to_int(xput_number_t param)
{
    printf("misc_translate_outgoing(%d)\n", (int)param);
    return (int)param;
}


// Destructor
void
misc_remove_reference(xput_number_t param)
```

(continues)

FIGURE 9–28 Programmer-provided source for the Miscellaneous Server *(continued)*

```
{
    printf("misc_remove_reference(%d)\n", (int)param);
}


// an operation that we export
kern_return_t
string_length(mach_port_t    server_port,
              input_string_t  instring,
              xput_number_t   *len)
{
    char *in = (char *)instring;

    if (!in || !len)
        return KERN_INVALID_ADDRESS;

    *len = 0;

    while (*in++)
        (*len)++;

    return KERN_SUCCESS;
}


// an operation that we export
kern_return_t
factorial(mach_port_t server_port, xput_number_t num, xput_number_t *fac)
{
    int i;

    if (!fac)
        return KERN_INVALID_ADDRESS;

    *fac = 1;

    for (i = 2; i <= num, i++)
        *fac *= i;

    return KERN_SUCCESS;
}

int
main(void)
{
    server_setup();
    server_loop();
    exit(0);
}
```

Figure 9–29 shows the programmer-provided source for the client we will use to call the Miscellaneous Server interface routines.

FIGURE 9–29 A client for accessing the services provided by the Miscellaneous Server

```
// client.c

#include "misc_types.h"

#define INPUT_STRING "Hello, MIG!"
#define INPUT_NUMBER 5

int
main(int argc, char **argv)
{
    kern_return_t kr;
    mach_port_t   server_port;
    int           len, fac;

    // look up the service to find the server's port
    if ((kr = bootstrap_look_up(bootstrap_port, MIG_MISC_SERVICE,
                                &server_port)) != BOOTSTRAP_SUCCESS) {
        mach_error("bootstrap_look_up:", kr);
        exit(1);
    }

    // call a procedure
    if ((kr = string_length(server_port, INPUT_STRING, &len)) != KERN_SUCCESS)
        mach_error("string_length:", kr);
    else
        printf("length of \"%s\" is %d\n", INPUT_STRING, len);

    // call another procedure
    if ((kr = factorial(server_port, INPUT_NUMBER, &fac)) != KERN_SUCCESS)
        mach_error("factorial:", kr);
    else
        printf("factorial of %d is %d\n", INPUT_NUMBER, fac);

    mach_port_deallocate(mach_task_self(), server_port);

    exit(0);
}
```

Next, we must run the `mig` program on the specification file. As noted earlier, doing so will give us a header file (`misc.h`), a user-interface module (`miscUser.c`), and a server-interface module (`miscServer.c`). As Figure 9–30 shows, we compile and link together `client.c` and `miscUser.c` to yield the client program. Similarly, `server.c` and `miscServer.c` yield the server program.

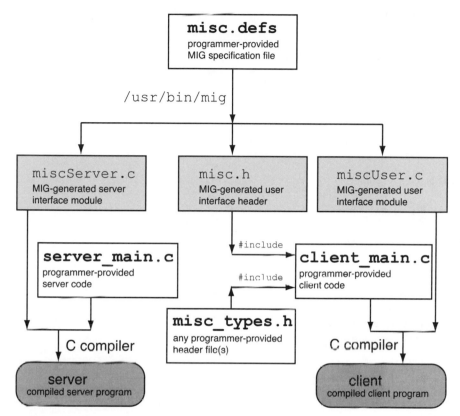

FIGURE 9–30 Creating a MIG-based client and server system

```
$ ls -m
client.c, misc.defs, misc_types.h, server.c
$ mig -v misc.defs
Subsystem misc: base = 500

Type int8_t = (9, 8)

Type uint8_t = (9, 8)
...

Type input_string_t = array [64] of (8, 8)

Type xput_number_t = (2, 32)
        CUserType:      int
        CServerType:    int
        InTran:         xput_number_t misc_translate_int_to_xput_number_t(int)
        OutTran:        int misc_translate_xput_number_t_to_int(xput_number_t)
        Destructor:     misc_remove_reference(xput_number_t)
```

```
Import "misc_types.h"

Routine (0) string_length(
        RequestPort     server_port: mach_port_t
        In              instring: input_string
        Out             len: xput_number)

Routine (4) factorial(
        RequestPort     server_port: mach_port_t
        In              num: xput_number
        Out             fac: xput_number)


ServerPrefix Server_

UserPrefix Client_

Writing misc.h ... done.
Writing miscUser.c ... done.
Writing miscServer.c ... done.
$ ls -m
client.c, misc.defs, misc.h, miscServer.c, miscUser.c,
misc_types.h, server.c
$ gcc -Wall -o server server.c miscServer.c
$ gcc -Wall -o client client.c miscUser.c
$ ./server
```

Once the server is running, we can also use our `bootstrap_info` program to verify that our service's name (`MIG-miscservice`, as defined in `misc_types.h`) is listed.

```
$ bootstrap_info
...
1   MIG-miscservice
$ ./client
length of "Hello, MIG!" is 11
factorial of 5 is 120
```

Figure 9–31 shows the sequence of actions that occur when the client calls the server's `string_length()` operation.

9.6.3 MIG in the Kernel

MIG is used to implement most Mach system calls. Several system calls, such as task-related, IPC-related, and VM-related calls, take a target task as one of their arguments. MIG translates the task argument in each case depending on the ker-

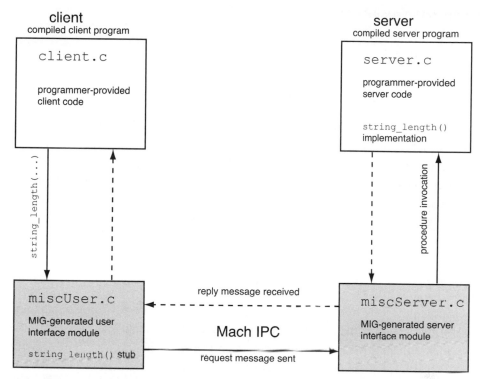

FIGURE 9–31 Invocation of Miscellaneous Server routines by a client

nel-facing data type. For example, a Mach thread is seen as a port name in user space, but inside the kernel, MIG calls `convert_port_to_thread()` [osfmk/ kern/ipc_tt.c] to translate an incoming thread port name to a pointer to the kernel object represented by the port—a `thread` structure.

```
/* osfmk/mach/mach_types.defs */

type thread_t = mach_port_t
#if     KERNEL_SERVER
            intran:     thread_t convert_port_to_thread(mach_port_t)
            outtran:    mach_port_t convert_thread_to_port(thread_t)
            destructor: thread_deallocate(thread_t)
#endif  /* KERNEL_SERVER */
```

Note the KERNEL_SERVER conditional directive. The Mac OS X kernel uses it, and a related directive KERNEL_USER, in MIG specification files to specify the KernelServer and KernelUser subsystem modifiers.

```
/* osfmk/mach/task.defs */

subsystem
#if KERNEL_SERVER
    KernelServer
#endif /* KERNEL_SERVER */
    task 3400;
```

The subsystem modifiers instruct MIG to generate alternate code for the user and server modules for special environments. For example, when a MIG server routine resides in the kernel, it is said to be in the `KernelServer` environment. Although the routine will have the same prototype as it would without the `KernelServer` modifier, the latter changes how MIG performs type translation. A `mach_port_t` type is automatically converted to the kernel type `ipc_port_t` on the `KernelServer` subsystem's server side.

9.6.3.1 Interfaces to Kernel Objects

Mach not only uses ports to represent several types of kernel objects but also exports interfaces to these objects through Mach IPC. Such interfaces are also implemented using MIG. User programs can use these interfaces either directly via Mach IPC or, as is typically the case, by calling standard library functions. When the system library is compiled, it links in user-interface modules corresponding to several kernel object MIG definition files. The library build process runs `mig` on the definition files to generate the interface modules.

> Examples of kernel object types include thread, task, host, processor, processor set, memory object, semaphore, lock set, and clock. A complete list of defined kernel object types is in `osfmk/kern/ipc_kobject.h`.

9.6.3.2 MIG Initialization in the Kernel

The kernel maintains a `mig_subsystem` structure [`osfmk/mach/mig.h`] for the MIG subsystem corresponding to each type of kernel object. As the IPC subsystem is initialized during kernel startup, the MIG initialization function—`mig_init()` [`osfmk/kern/ipc_kobject.c`]—iterates over each subsystem, populating a global hash table of MIG routines. Figure 9–32 shows an excerpt from this process.

FIGURE 9–32 Initialization of MIG subsystems during kernel bootstrap

// osfmk/mach/mig.h

```c
typedef struct mig_subsystem {
    mig_server_routine_t     server;      // pointer to demux routine
    mach_msg_id_t            start;       // minimum routine number
    mach_msg_id_t            end;         // maximum routine number + 1
    mach_msg_size_t          maxsize;     // maximum reply message size
    vm_address_t             reserved;    // reserved for MIG use
    mig_routine_descriptor   routine[1];  // routine descriptor array
} *mig_subsystem_t;
```

// osfmk/kern/ipc_kobject.c

```c
typedef struct {
    mach_msg_id_t   num;
    mig_routine_t   routine;
    int             size;
#if MACH_COUNTERS
    mach_counter_t callcount;
#endif
} mig_hash_t;

#define MAX_MIG_ENTRIES 1024
mig_hash_t mig_buckets[MAX_MIG_ENTRIES];

const struct mig_subsystem* mig_e[] = {
    (const struct mig_subsystem *)&mach_vm_subsystem,
    (const struct mig_subsystem *)&mach_port_subsystem,
    (const struct mig_subsystem *)&mach_host_subsystem,
    ...
    (const struct mig_subsystem *)&is_iokit_subsystem),
    ...
};

void
mig_init(void)
{
    unsigned int i, n = sizeof(mig_e)/sizeof(const struct mig_subsystem *);
    int howmany;
    mach_msg_id_t j, pos, nentry, range;

    for (i = 0; i < n; i++) { // for each mig_e[i]
        range = mig_e[i]->end - mig_e[i]->start;
        ...
        for (j = 0; j < range; j++) { // for each routine[j] in mig_e[i]
            ...
            // populate mig_buckets hash table with routines
        }
    }
}
```

9.7 Mach Exceptions

Exceptions are synchronous interruptions to the normal flow of program control caused by the program itself. The following are examples of reasons why exceptions can occur:

- Attempting to access nonexistent memory
- Attempting to access memory that violates address-space protection
- Failing to execute an instruction because of an illegal or undefined opcode or operand
- Producing an arithmetic error such as division by zero, overflow, or underflow
- Executing an instruction intended to support emulation
- Hitting a debugger-installed breakpoint or other exceptions related to debugging, tracing, and error detection
- Executing the system call instruction

Some exceptions do not represent abnormal conditions in that they are part of the normal functioning of the operating system. Examples of such exceptions include page faults and system calls. As we saw in Chapters 3 and 6, a Mac OS X program invokes a system call through the sc instruction, which causes a hardware exception. A system call exception is handled differently from other types by the operating system. The operating system also handles page faults transparently to user programs.

Several other types of exceptions must either be reported to user programs or otherwise require explicit handling. These include exceptions that may be deliberately caused by programs, such as by a debugger using hardware breakpoint and trace facilities.

> The deliberate use of exceptions can be classified into categories such as error handling, debugging, and emulation/virtualization.

Mach provides an IPC-based exception-handling facility wherein exceptions are converted to messages. When an exception occurs, a message containing information about the exception—such as the exception type, the thread that caused it, and the thread's containing task—is sent to an *exception port*. The reply to this message, which the thread waits for, indicates whether the exception was successfully handled by an exception handler. Exceptions are system-level primitives in Mach.

Sets of exception ports—one port per exception type—are maintained at the host, task, and thread levels (Figure 9–33). When an exception message is to be delivered, the kernel attempts to deliver it to the most specific port first. If either the delivery or the processing of that message fails, the kernel attempts the next most specific port. Thus, the order is thread, task, and host. Typically, the delivery of an exception message fails at a given level because there is no exception handler registered at that level. Similarly, processing of the message fails because the handler returned an error.

FIGURE 9–33 Exception ports at the host, task, and thread levels

```
// osfmk/kern/exception.h

struct exception_action {
    struct ipc_port      *port;     // exception port
    thread_state_flavor_t flavor;   // state flavor to send
    exception_behavior_t  behavior; // exception type to raise
};


// osfmk/kern/host.h

struct host {
    ...
    struct exception_action exc_actions[EXC_TYPES_COUNT];
    ...
};


// osfmk/kern/task.h

struct task {
    ...
    struct exception_action exc_actions[EXC_TYPES_COUNT];
    ...
};


// osfmk/kern/thread.h

struct thread {
    ...
    struct exception_action exc_actions[EXC_TYPES_COUNT];
    ...
};
```

As we saw earlier, by default, the thread-level exception ports are all set to the null port, and the task-level exception ports are inherited during `fork()`. Figure 9–34 shows the initialization of exception handling during bootstrap. In particular, the *Unix exception handler* is also initialized here. This handler translates several types of Mach exceptions to Unix signals. We discuss this mechanism in Section 9.8.8.

FIGURE 9–34 Initialization of exception handling during kernel bootstrap

```
// bsd/kern/bsd_init.c

void
bsdinit_task(void)
{
    struct proc     *p = current_proc();
    struct uthread *ut;
    kern_return_t   kr;
    thread_act_t    th_act;
    ...

    // initialize the Unix exception handler
    ux_handler_init();

    th_act = current_thread();

    // the various exception masks are defined in osfmk/mach/exception_types.h
    (void)host_set_exception_ports(host_priv_self(),
                        EXC_MASK_ALL & ~(EXC_MASK_SYSCALL |
                        EXC_MASK_MACH_SYSCALL | EXC_MASK_RPC_ALERT),
                        ux_exception_port, EXCEPTION_DEFAULT, 0);

    (void)task_set_exception_ports(get_threadtask(th_act),
                        EXC_MASK_ALL & ~(EXC_MASK_SYSCALL |
                        EXC_MASK_MACH_SYSCALL | EXC_MASK_RPC_ALERT),
                        ux_exception_port, EXCEPTION_DEFAULT, 0);

    ...
    // initiate loading of launchd
}
```

> Note that one or more exception ports at any level can be retrieved or set through `<level>_get_exception_ports()` and `<level>_set_exception_ports()`, respectively, where `<level>` is one of host, task, or thread.

9.7.1 Programmer-Visible Aspects of Mach's Exception-Handling Facility

A Mach exception handler is a recipient of exception messages. It runs in its own thread. Although it could be in the same task as the excepting thread, it often is in another task, such as a debugger. A more appropriate name for an excepting thread—the one in which the exception occurs—is the *victim thread*. The thread running the exception handler is called the *handler thread*. A thread attains handler status for a task or a thread by acquiring receive rights to an exception port of that task or thread. For example, if a thread wants to be the exception handler for a task, it can call `task_set_exception_ports()` to register one of its ports as one of the task's exception ports. A single port can be used to receive multiple types of exception messages, depending on the arguments to `<level>_set_exception_ports()`.

```
kern_return_t
task_set_exception_ports(task_t                  task,
                exception_mask_t        exception_types,
                mach_port_t             exception_port,
                exception_behavior_t    behavior,
                thread_state_flavor_t   flavor);

kern_return_t
task_get_exception_ports(task_t                      task,
                exception_mask_t            exception_types,
                exception_mask_array_t      old_masks,
                exception_handler_array_t   old_handlers,
                exception_behavior_array_t  old_behaviors,
                exception_flavor_array_t    old_flavors);
```

Let us look at the parameters of `task_set_exception_ports()` first. `exception_types` is the bitwise OR of the exception type bits for which the port is being set. Table 9–3 shows the machine-independent exception types defined on Mac OS X. An exception message contains additional, machine-dependent information corresponding to the machine-independent exception type. For example, if an `EXC_BAD_ACCESS` exception occurs because of unaligned access on the PowerPC, machine-dependent information will include an exception code of `EXC_PPC_UNALIGNED` and an exception subcode whose value will be the contents of the Data Access Register (DAR). Table 9–6 in Section 9.7.2 shows the codes and subcodes corresponding to several Mach exceptions. The machine-dependent codes are defined in `osfmk/mach/ppc/exception.h` and `osfmk/mach/i386/exception.h`.

TABLE 9–3 Machine-Independent Mach Exceptions

Exception	Notes
EXC_BAD_ACCESS	Could not access memory
EXC_BAD_INSTRUCTION	Illegal or undefined instruction or operand
EXC_ARITHMETIC	Arithmetic exception (such as a division by zero)
EXC_EMULATION	Emulation support instruction encountered
EXC_SOFTWARE	Software-generated exception (such as a floating-point assist)
EXC_BREAKPOINT	Trace or breakpoint
EXC_SYSCALL	Unix system call
EXC_MACH_SYSCALL	Mach system call
EXC_RPC_ALERT	RPC alert (actually used during performance monitoring, not for RPC)

The `behavior` argument to `task_set_exception_ports()` specifies the type of exception message that should be sent when the exception occurs. Table 9–4 shows the machine-independent exception behaviors defined on Mac OS X.

TABLE 9–4 Machine-Independent Mach Exception Behaviors

Behavior	Notes
EXCEPTION_DEFAULT	Send a `catch_exception_raise` message including the thread identity.
EXCEPTION_STATE	Send a `catch_exception_raise_state` message including the thread state.
EXCEPTION_STATE_IDENTITY	Send a `catch_exception_raise_state_identity` message including the thread identity and state.

The `flavor` argument specifies the type of thread state to be sent with the exception message. Table 9–5 shows the machine-dependent[12] (PowerPC) thread state types on Mac OS X. If no thread state is desired along with the exception

---

12. The machine-dependent thread states for PowerPC and x86 are defined in `osfmk/mach/ppc/thread_status.h` and `osfmk/mach/i386/thread_status.h`, respectively.

message, the flavor THREAD_STATE_NONE can be used. Note that regardless of whether thread state is sent in an exception message, the exception handler can use thread_get_state() and thread_set_state() to retrieve and set, respectively, the victim thread's machine-dependent state.

TABLE 9–5 Machine-Dependent (PowerPC) Mach Thread States

Type	Notes
PPC_THREAD_STATE	Contains 32-bit GPRs, CR, CTR, LR, SRR0, SRR1, VRSAVE, and XER
PPC_FLOAT_STATE	Contains FPRs and FPSCR
PPC_EXCEPTION_STATE	Contains DAR, DSISR, and a value specifying the PowerPC exception that was taken
PPC_VECTOR_STATE	Contains VRs, VSCR, and a validity bitmap indicating the VRs that have been saved
PPC_THREAD_STATE64	Is the 64-bit version of PPC_THREAD_STATE
PPC_EXCEPTION_STATE64	Is the 64-bit version of PPC_EXCEPTION_STATE

Let us see what happens when an exception occurs in a thread. The kernel suspends the victim thread and sends an IPC message to the appropriate exception port. The victim remains suspended in the kernel until a reply is received. A thread within any task with receive rights to the exception port may retrieve the message. Such a thread—the exception handler for that message—calls exc_server() to handle the message. exc_server() is a MIG-generated server-handling function available in the system library. It performs the necessary argument handling for the kernel message, decodes the message, and calls one of the following programmer-provided functions: catch_exception_raise(), catch_exception_raise_identity(), or catch_exception_raise_state_identity(). As shown in Table 9–4, the behavior specified when the exception port was registered determines which of these functions will be called by exc_server(). All three functions are meant to handle the exception and return a value that determines what the kernel does next with the victim thread. In particular, if a catch_exception_raise function returns KERN_SUCCESS, exc_server() prepares a return message to be sent to the kernel that causes the thread to continue execution from the point of the exception. For example, if the exception was not fatal and the catch_exception_raise function fixed the problem—perhaps by modifying the thread's state—it may be desirable for the thread to continue. A `catch_exception_raise` function may use a variety of thread functions to affect the course of actions, for example, `thread_abort()`, `thread_suspend()`, `thread_resume()`, `thread_set_state()`, and so on. If KERN_SUCCESS is not returned, the kernel will send the exception message to the next-level exception handler.

```
boolean_t
exc_server(mach_msg_header_t request_msg, mach_msg_header_t reply_msg);

kern_return_t
catch_exception_raise(mach_port_t              exception_port,
                      mach_port_t              thread,
                      mach_port_t              task,
                      exception_type_t         exception,
                      exception_data_t         code,
                      mach_msg_type_number_t   code_count);
```

```
// osfmk/mach/exception_types.h

typedef integer_t *exception_data_t;
```

```
// osfmk/mach/exc.defs

type exception_data_t          = array[*:2] of integer_t;
type exception_type_t          = int;
```

> `thread_set_state()` allows the state of the victim thread to be crafted as desired. In particular, the resumption point of the thread can be modified.

9.7.2 The Mach Exception-Handling Chain

As we saw in Chapter 6, the low-level trap handler calls `trap()` [osfmk/ppc/trap.c] to perform higher-level trap processing, passing it the trap number, the saved state, and the contents of the DSISR and DAR registers (if applicable). `trap()` deals with several types of exceptions: preemptions, page faults, performance-monitoring exceptions, software-generated ASTs, and so on. Exceptions that are known to the Mach exception-handling facility are passed up to Mach by calling `doexception()` [osfmk/ppc/trap.c]. Table 9–6 shows how low-level traps are translated to Mach exception data. `doexception()` calls exception_ `triage()` [`osfmk/kern/exception.c`], which attempts to make an upcall to the thread's exception server. Figure 9–35 shows the important kernel functions involved in exception delivery.

TABLE 9–6 Traps and Corresponding Mach Exception Data

Trap Identifier	Mach Exception	Exception Code	Exception Subcode
T_ALTIVEC_ASSIST	EXC_ARITHMETIC	EXC_PPC_ALTIVECASSIST	Saved SRR0
T_DATA_ACCESS	EXC_BAD_ACCESS	Computed	DAR
T_INSTRUCTION_ACCESS	EXC_BAD_ACCESS	Computed	Saved SRR0
T_INSTRUCTION_BKPT	EXC_BREAKPOINT	EXC_PPC_TRACE	Saved SRR0
T_PROGRAM	EXC_ARITHMETIC	EXC_ARITHMETIC	Saved FPSCR
T_PROGRAM	EXC_BAD_INSTRUCTION	EXC_PPC_UNIPL_INST	Saved SRR0
T_PROGRAM	EXC_BAD_INSTRUCTION	EXC_PPC_PRIVINST	Saved SRR0
T_PROGRAM	EXC_BREAKPOINT	EXC_PPC_BREAKPOINT	Saved SRR0
T_PROGRAM	EXC_SOFTWARE	EXC_PPC_TRAP	Saved SRR0

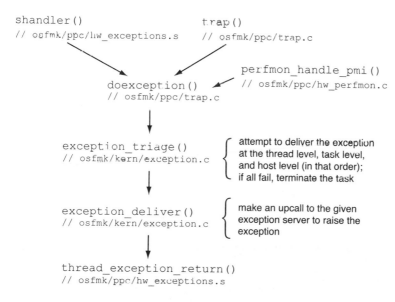

FIGURE 9–35 Kernel functions involved in Mach exception delivery

```
// osfmk/ppc/trap.c

void
doexception(int exc, int code, int sub)
{
    exception_data_type_t codes[EXCEPTION_CODE_MAX];

    codes[0] = code;
    codes[1] = sub;
    exception_triage(exc, codes, 2);
}
```

9.7.2.1 Delivering Exceptions

`exception_triage()` is so called because it first attempts to raise the exception at the thread level, failing which it attempts the task and host levels, in that order. Raising an exception involves calling `exception_deliver()` [osfmk/kern/exception.c], which calls one of the following MIG routines, depending on the exception behavior: `exception_raise()`, `exception_raise_state()`, or `exception_raise_state_identity()`. The exception is caught by the handler calling one of the `catch_exception_raise` functions we saw in Section 9.7.1.

If the exception remains unhandled at all levels, `exception_triage()` attempts to call the built-in kernel debugger if it is available. If all these attempts fail, the task is terminated. Figure 9–36 shows an excerpt from the relevant code in the kernel.

FIGURE 9–36 Delivery of Mach exceptions

```
// osfmk/kern/exception.c

// Current thread caught an exception; make an upcall to the exception server
void
exception_triage(exception_type_t       exception,
                 exception_data_t       code,
                 mach_msg_type_number_t codeCnt)
{
    ...

    // Try to raise the exception at the thread level
    thread = current_thread();
    mutex  = mutex_addr(thread->mutex);
    excp   = &thread->exc_actions[exception];
    exception_deliver(exception, code, codeCnt, excp, mutex);
```

(continues)

FIGURE 9–36 Delivery of Mach exceptions *(continued)*

```
    // We're still here, so delivery must have failed
    // Try to raise the exception at the task level
    task  = current_task();
    mutex = mutex_addr(task->lock);
    excp  = &task->exc_actions[exception];
    exception_deliver(exception, code, codeCnt, excp, mutex);

    // Still failed; try at the host level
    host_priv = host_priv_self();
    mutex     = mutex_addr(host_priv->lock);
    excp      = &host_priv->exc_actions[exception];
    exception_deliver(exception, code, codeCnt, excp, mutex);

#if MACH_KDB
    // If KDB is enabled, debug the exception with KDB
#endif

    // All failed; terminate the task
    ...
}
```

9.7.2.2 Unresolved Kernel Traps

If there is an exception that neither maps to a Mach exception nor can be dealt with otherwise, it leads to an *unresolved kernel trap*. For example, if `trap()` encounters an unexpected trap number—say, one that should have been handled earlier in the overall exception-handling chain, or one that is fatal in the kernel—it calls `unresolved_kernel_trap()` [osfmk/ppc/trap.c], which dumps debugging information on the screen and then either calls the debugger or panics the system (Figure 9–37).

FIGURE 9–37 Processing of unresolved kernel traps

```
// osfmk/ppc/trap.c

void
unresolved_kernel_trap(int              trapno,
                       struct savearea *ssp,
                       unsigned int     dsisr,
                       addr64_t         dar,
                       char            *message)
```

(continues)

FIGURE 9–37 Processing of unresolved kernel traps *(continued)*

```
{
    ...
    kdb_printf("\n\nUnresolved kernel trap(cpu %d): %s DAR=0x%016llX PC=%016llX\n",
            cpu_number(), trap_name, dar, ssp->save_ssr0);

    // this comes from osfmk/ppc/model_dep.c
    print_backtrace(ssp);

    ...
    draw_panic_dialog();

    if (panicDebugging)
        (void *)Call_Debugger(trapno, ssp);
    panic(message);
}


// osfmk/console/panic_dialog.c

void
draw_panic_dialog(void)
{
    ...
    if (!panicDialogDrawn && panicDialogDesired) {
        if (!logPanicDataToScreen) {
            ...
            // dim the screen 50% before putting up the panic dialog
            dim_screen();

            // set up to draw background box and draw panic dialog
            ...
            panic_blit_rect(...);

            // display the MAC address and the IP address, but only if the
            // machine is attachable, to avoid end-user confusion
            if (panicDebugging) {
                ...
                // blit the digits for MAC address and IP address
                ...
            }
        }
    }

    panicDialogDrawn = TRUE;
    panicDialogDesired = FALSE;
}
```

9.7.3 Example: A Mach Exception Handler

Let us see a programming example to understand the working of a Mach exception handler. In our program, we will allocate a Mach port and set it as the exception port of the program's main thread. We will be interested only in illegal instruction exceptions, so we will specify EXC_MASK_BAD_INSTRUCTION as the exception mask value when calling thread_set_exception_ports(). Moreover, we will ask for the default exception behavior, with no exception state, to be sent along with the message.

Then, we will create another thread to run the exception handler. This second thread will receive exception messages on the main thread's exception port. Once a message arrives, it will call exc_server(). We will then deliberately cause an exception to occur by trying to execute noninstruction data. Since we asked for the default behavior, exc_server() will call catch_exception_raise(). In our implementation of catch_exception_raise(), we will call thread_get_state() to retrieve the victim thread's machine state. We will modify the SRR0 value to contain the address of a function that will simply print a message, thereby causing the victim thread to die gracefully. We will use thread_set_state() to set the modified state, after which we will return KERN_SUCCESS from catch_exception_raise(). When the consequent reply is sent to the kernel, it will continue the thread.

Perhaps the most critical piece of information we need to write an exception handler is the format of the exception message that will be sent to us by the kernel. The implementation of ux_handler() [bsd/uxkern/ux_exception.c] provides this information. We call our exception message's data type exc_msg_t. Note that we use a large trailing pad. The NDR field contains a Network Data Representation (NDR) record [osfmk/mach/ndr.h] that we will not deal with.

Figure 9–38 shows the program. It can be trivially ported to the x86 version of Mac OS X.

FIGURE 9–38 An exception handler for "fixing" illegal instructions

```
// exception.c

#include <stdio.h>
#include <stdlib.h>
#include <unistd.h>
#include <pthread.h>
#include <mach/mach.h>
```

(continues)

FIGURE 9-38 An exception handler for "fixing" illegal instructions *(continued)*

```c
// exception message we will receive from the kernel
typedef struct exc_msg {
    mach_msg_header_t            Head;
    mach_msg_body_t             msgh_body; // start of kernel-processed data
    mach_msg_port_descriptor_t  thread;    // victim thread
    mach_msg_port_descriptor_t  task;      // end of kernel-processed data
    NDR_record_t                NDR;       // see osfmk/mach/ndr.h
    exception_type_t            exception;
    mach_msg_type_number_t      codeCnt;   // number of elements in code[]
    exception_data_t            code;      // an array of integer_t
    char                        pad[512];  // for avoiding MACH_MSG_RCV_TOO_LARGE
} exc_msg_t;

// reply message we will send to the kernel
typedef struct rep_msg {
    mach_msg_header_t           Head;
    NDR_record_t                NDR;       // see osfmk/mach/ndr.h
    kern_return_t               RetCode;   // indicates to the kernel what to do
} reply_msg_t;

// exception handling
mach_port_t exception_port;
void exception_handler(void);
extern boolean_t exc_server(mach_msg_header_t *request,
                            mach_msg_header_t *reply);

// demonstration function and associates
typedef void    (* funcptr_t)(void);
funcptr_t       function_with_bad_instruction;
kern_return_t   repair_instruction(mach_port_t victim);
void            graceful_dead(void);

// support macros for pretty printing
#define L_MARGIN "%-21s: "
#define FuncPutsN(msg)    printf(L_MARGIN "%s", __FUNCTION__, msg)
#define FuncPuts(msg)     printf(L_MARGIN "%s\n", __FUNCTION__, msg)
#define FuncPutsIDs(msg)  printf(L_MARGIN "%s (task %#lx, thread %#lx)\n", \
                                  __FUNCTION__, msg, (long)mach_task_self(), \
                                  (long)pthread_mach_thread_np(pthread_self()));


#define EXIT_ON_MACH_ERROR(msg, retval) \
    if (kr != KERN_SUCCESS) { mach_error(msg ":" , kr); exit((retval)); }

#define OUT_ON_MACH_ERROR(msg, retval) \
    if (kr != KERN_SUCCESS) { mach_error(msg ":" , kr); goto out; }

int
main(int argc, char **argv)
```

(continues)

FIGURE 9–38 An exception handler for "fixing" illegal instructions *(continued)*

```
{
    kern_return_t kr;
    pthread_t      exception_thread;
    mach_port_t    mytask = mach_task_self();
    mach_port_t    mythread = mach_thread_self();

    FuncPutsIDs("starting up");

    // create a receive right
    kr = mach_port_allocate(mytask, MACH_PORT_RIGHT_RECEIVE, &exception_port);
    EXIT_ON_MACH_ERROR("mach_port_allocate", kr);

    // insert a send right: we will now have combined receive/send rights
    kr = mach_port_insert_right(mytask, exception_port, exception_port,
                        MACH_MSG_TYPE_MAKE_SEND);
    OUT_ON_MACH_ERROR("mach_port_insert_right", kr);

    kr = thread_set_exception_ports(mythread,            // target thread
                            EXC_MASK_BAD_INSTRUCTION,    // exception types
                            exception_port,              // the port
                            EXCEPTION_DEFAULT,           // behavior
                            THREAD_STATE_NONE);          // flavor
    OUT_ON_MACH_ERROR("thread_set_exception_ports", kr);

    if ((pthread_create(&exception_thread, (pthread_attr_t *)0,
                    (void *(*)(void *))exception_handler, (void *)0))) {
        perror("pthread_create");
        goto out;
    }

    FuncPuts("about to dispatch exception_handler pthread");
    pthread_detach(exception_thread);

    // some random bad address for code, but otherwise a valid address
    function_with_bad_instruction = (funcptr_t)exception_thread;

    FuncPuts("about to call function_with_bad_instruction");
    function_with_bad_instruction();
    FuncPuts("after function_with_bad_instruction");

out:
    mach_port_deallocate(mytask, mythread);
    if (exception_port)
        mach_port_deallocate(mytask, exception_port);

    return 0;
}
```

(continues)

FIGURE 9–38 An exception handler for "fixing" illegal instructions *(continued)*

```
void
exception_handler(void)
{
    kern_return_t kr;
    exc_msg_t     msg_recv;
    reply_msg_t   msg_resp;

    FuncPutsIDs("beginning");

    msg_recv.Head.msgh_local_port = exception_port;
    msg_recv.Head.msgh_size = sizeof(msg_recv);

    kr = mach_msg(&(msg_recv.Head),          // message
                MACH_RCV_MSG|MACH_RCV_LARGE, // options
                0,                           // send size (irrelevant here)
                sizeof(msg_recv),            // receive limit
                exception_port,              // port for receiving
                MACH_MSG_TIMEOUT_NONE,       // no timeout
                MACH_PORT_NULL);             // notify port (irrelevant here)
    EXIT_ON_MACH_ERROR("mach_msg_receive", kr);

    FuncPuts("received message");
    FuncPutsN("victim thread is ");
    printf("%#lx\n", (long)msg_recv.thread.name);
    FuncPutsN("victim thread's task is ");
    printf("%#lx\n", (long)msg_recv.task.name);

    FuncPuts("calling exc_server");
    exc_server(&msg_recv.Head, &msg_resp.Head);
    // now msg_resp.RetCode contains return value of catch_exception_raise()

    FuncPuts("sending reply");
    kr = mach_msg(&(msg_resp.Head),          // message
                MACH_SEND_MSG,               // options
                msg_resp.Head.msgh_size,     // send size
                0,                           // receive limit (irrelevant here)
                MACH_PORT_NULL,              // port for receiving (none)
                MACH_MSG_TIMEOUT_NONE,       // no timeout
                MACH_PORT_NULL);             // notify port (we don't want one)
    EXIT_ON_MACH_ERROR("mach_msg_send", kr);

    pthread_exit((void *)0);
}

kern_return_t
catch_exception_raise(mach_port_t          port,
                    mach_port_t          victim,
```

(continues)

FIGURE 9–38 An exception handler for "fixing" illegal instructions *(continued)*

```
                mach_port_t           task,
                exception_type_t      exception,
                exception_data_t      code,
                mach_msg_type_number_t code_count)
{
    FuncPutsIDs("beginning");

    if (exception != EXC_BAD_INSTRUCTION) {
        // this should not happen, but we should forward an exception that we
        // were not expecting... here, we simply bail out
        exit(-1);
    }

    return repair_instruction(victim);
}

kern_return_t
repair_instruction(mach_port_t victim)
{
    kern_return_t      kr;
    unsigned int       count;
    ppc_thread_state_t state;

    FuncPutsIDs("fixing instruction");

    count = MACHINE_THREAD_STATE_COUNT;
    kr = thread_get_state(victim,                 // target thread
                    MACHINE_THREAD_STATE,         // flavor of state to get
                    (thread_state_t)&state,       // state information
                    &count);                      // in/out size
    EXIT_ON_MACH_ERROR("thread_get_state", kr);

    // SRR0 is used to save the address of the instruction at which execution
    // continues when rfid executes at the end of an exception handler routine
    state.srr0 = (vm_address_t)graceful_dead;

    kr = thread_set_state(victim,                 // target thread
                    MACHINE_THREAD_STATE,         // flavor of state to set
                    (thread_state_t)&state,       // state information
                    MACHINE_THREAD_STATE_COUNT);  // in size
    EXIT_ON_MACH_ERROR("thread_set_state", kr);

    return KERN_SUCCESS;
}

void
graceful_dead(void)
```

(continues)

FIGURE 9–38 An exception handler for "fixing" illegal instructions *(continued)*

```
{
    FuncPutsIDs("dying graceful death");
}
```

```
$ gcc -Wall -o exception exception.c
$ ./exception
main                 : starting up (task 0x807, thread 0xd03)
main                 : about to dispatch exception_handler pthread
main                 : about to call function_with_bad_instruction
exception_handler    : beginning (task 0x807, thread 0xf03)
exception_handler    : received message
exception_handler    : victim thread is 0xd03
exception_handler    : victim thread's task is 0x807
exception_handler    : calling exc_server
catch_exception_raise: beginning (task 0x807, thread 0xf03)
repair_instruction   : fixing instruction (task 0x807, thread 0xf03)
exception_handler    : sending reply
graceful_dead        : dying graceful death (task 0x807, thread 0xd03)
main                 : after function_with_bad_instruction
```

The use of exc_server() in Figure 9–38 is a typical example of Mach server programming. Other such server functions can be used to replace repetitive code for receiving and sending messages. For example, mach_msg_server() is a generic server function whose arguments include a port (receive rights) and a pointer to a message demultiplexing function. It runs the following loop internally: receive a request message, call the demultiplexer with request and reply buffers, and possibly send a reply message based on the demultiplexer's return value.

```
mach_msg_return_t
mach_msg_server(boolean_t        (*demux)(mach_msg_header_t *,
                                          mach_msg_header_t *),
                mach_msg_size_t   max_size,
                mach_port_t       rcv_name,
                mach_msg_options_t options);
```

mach_msg_server_once() is a variant that processes only one request and then returns to the user. In fact, we can replace the entire implementation of exception_handler() in Figure 9–38 with the following code, using exc_server() as the demultiplexing function.

```
void
exception_handler(void)
```

```
{
    (void)mach_msg_server_once(exc_server,              // demultiplexing function
                               sizeof(exc_msg_t),       // maximum receive size
                               exception_port,          // port for receiving
                               MACH_MSG_TIMEOUT_NONE);  // options, if any
    pthread_exit((void *)0);
}
```

9.8 Signals

Besides Mach exception handling, Mac OS X provides Unix-style signals as
well, with the latter built atop the former.

Old Signals Are Hard to `kill()`

Early versions of UNIX used signals primarily to provide a mechanism for a process to be terminated, interrupted, or diverted—because of an error in its own
operation or due to an action of another process. For example, if a user wanted to
terminate a runaway process, the `kill` command could be used to send the process a kill signal.

Third Edition UNIX (1973) had twelve signals, all of which exist in Mac OS X—
most with the same names. The Third Edition signals were: SIGHUP, SIGINT,
SIGQIT, SIGINS, SIGTRC, SIGIOT, SIGEMT, SIGFPT, SIGKIL, SIGBUS, SIGSEG, and
SIGSYS.

Over time, signals were increasingly used for purposes besides error handling—for example, as a facility for IPC and synchronization. In particular, the
advent of job control in shells was a contributing factor to the widespread use of
signals. In modern Unix systems, exceptions are only one class of events that
result in the generation of signals. Various other synchronous and asynchronous
events result in signals, for example:

- Explicit generation of a signal by calling `kill(2)` or `killpg(2)`
- Change in the status of a child process
- Terminal interrupts
- Job control operations by interactive shells
- Expiration of timers
- Miscellaneous notifications, such as a process exceeding its CPU resource
  limit or file size limit (say, while writing a file)

An implementation of the signal mechanism involves two well-defined phases: *signal generation* and *signal delivery.* Signal generation is the occurrence of an event that warrants a signal. Signal delivery is the invocation of the signal's disposition—that is, the carrying out of the associated signal action. Each signal has a default action, which can be one of the following on Mac OS X.

- *Terminate*—Abnormally terminate the process, with the termination occurring as if _exit() had been called, with the only difference being that wait() and waitpid() receive status values that indicate the abnormal termination.

- *Dump core*—Abnormally terminate the process, but also create a core file.

- *Stop*—Suspend the process.

- *Continue*—Resume the process if it is stopped; otherwise, ignore the signal.

- *Ignore*—Don't do anything (discard the signal).

A signal can have its default action be overridden by a user-specified handler. The sigaction() system call can be used to assign signal actions, which can be specified as SIG_DFL (use the default action), SIG_IGN (ignore the signal), or a pointer to a signal handler function (catch the signal). A signal can also be blocked, wherein it remains pending until it is unblocked or the corresponding signal action is set to SIG_IGN. The sigprop array [bsd/sys/signalvar.h] categorizes the known signals and their default actions.

```
// bsd/sys/signalvar.h

#define SA_KILL    0x01 // terminates process by default
#define SA_CORE    0x02 // ditto and dumps core
#define SA_STOP    0x04 // suspend process
#define SA_TTYSTOP 0x08 // ditto, from tty
#define SA_IGNORE  0x10 // ignore by default
#define SA_CONT    0x20 // continue if suspended

int sigprop[NSIG + 1] = {
    0,                  // unused
    SA_KILL,            // SIGHUP
    SA_KILL,            // SIGINT
    SA_KILL|SA_CORE,    // SIGQUIT
    ...
    SA_KILL,            // SIGUSR1
    SA_KILL,            // SIGUSR2
};
```

The following exceptional cases should be noted about blocking, catching, and ignoring signals.

- SIGKILL and SIGSTOP cannot be blocked, caught, or ignored.
- If a SIGCONT (the "continue" signal) is sent to a process that is stopped, the process is continued even if SIGCONT is blocked or ignored.

> The signal(3) man page provides a list of supported signals and their default actions.

The Mach exception-handling facility was designed to address several problems with the prevailing signal mechanisms in Unix systems. As Unix systems have evolved, the design and implementation of signal mechanisms have improved too. Let us look at some aspects of signals in the context of Mac OS X.

9.8.1 Reliability

Early signal implementations were unreliable in that a signal's action was reset to the default action whenever that signal was caught. If there were two or more successive occurrences of the same signal, there was a race condition as the kernel would reset the signal handler, and before the program could reinstall the user-defined handler, the default action would be invoked. Since the default action of many signals is to terminate the process, this was a severe problem. POSIX.1 included a reliable signal mechanism based on the signal mechanisms in 4.2BSD and 4.3BSD. The new mechanism requires the use of the newer sigaction(2) interface instead of the older signal(3) interface. Mac OS X provides both interfaces, although signal(3) is implemented in the system library as a wrapper call to sigaction(2).

9.8.2 The Number of Signals

Although the number of signal types available in Unix systems has increased over the years, often there are hard upper bounds because of the data types that kernels use to represent signal types. Mac OS X uses a 32-bit unsigned integer to represent a signal number, allowing a maximum of 32 signals. Mac OS X 10.4 has 31 signals.

One Can Never Have Too Many Signals

The Mac OS X signal implementation is derived from FreeBSD's, which also uses a 32-bit quantity to represent a signal. Recent versions of FreeBSD have 32 signals. AIX and recent versions of Solaris support more than 32 signals. Solaris can accommodate more than 32 signals by using an array of unsigned long values to represent the data type for the signal bitmap. In general, it is nontrivial to add new signals to an existing implementation.

9.8.3 Application-Defined Signals

POSIX.1 provides two application-defined signals, SIGUSR1 and SIGUSR2, which can be used by the programmer for arbitrary purposes—for example, as a rudimentary IPC mechanism.

Signals and IPC

A process can send a signal to itself, another process, or a group of processes by using the kill(2) or killpg(2) calls. Signals do not amount to a powerful or efficient mechanism for general-purpose IPC. Besides the limit on the number of signals, it is not possible to communicate arbitrary types and amounts of data using signals. Moreover, signal delivery is usually more expensive than dedicated IPC mechanisms.

Mac OS X 10.4 *does not* support real-time signals, which were originally defined as part of the Real-time Signals Extension in POSIX.4. Real-time signals are application-defined signals and can vary in number—ranging from SIGRTMIN to SIGRTMAX—across systems that provide them. Other characteristics distinguish real-time signals from regular signals. For example, real-time signals are delivered in a guaranteed order: Multiple simultaneously pending real-time signals of the same type are delivered in the order they were sent, whereas simultaneously pending real-time signals of different types are delivered in the order of their signal numbers (lowest numbered first).

9.8.4 Signal-Based Notification of Asynchronous I/O

Mac OS X provides the asynchronous I/O (AIO) family of functions, also defined as part of POSIX.4. When an asynchronous event (such as a completed read or write) occurs, a program can receive a notification through one of the following mechanisms:

- SIGEV_NONE—no notification delivered
- SIGEV_SIGNAL—notification through signal generation (delivery depends on whether the implementation supports the Real-time Signals Extension)
- SIGEV_THREAD—notification function called to perform notification (intended for multithreaded programs)

Mac OS X 10.4 supports only SIGEV_NONE and SIGEV_SIGNAL. Figure 9–39 shows a contrived program that uses the lio_listio() system call to submit an asynchronous read operation, while requesting notification of read completion through the SIGUSR1 signal. Multiple—up to AIO_LISTIO_MAX (16)—read or write operations can be submitted in a single call through lio_listio().

FIGURE 9–39 Signal notification of asynchronous I/O completion

```c
// aio_read.c

#include <stdio.h>
#include <fcntl.h>
#include <stdlib.h>
#include <sys/types.h>
#include <signal.h>
#include <aio.h>

#define PROGNAME "aio_read"

#define AIO_BUFSIZE 4096
#define AIOCB_CONST struct aiocb *const*

static void
SIGUSR1_handler(int signo __unused)
{
    printf("SIGUSR1_handler\n");
}

int
main(int argc, char **argv)
{
    int             fd;
    struct aiocb    *aiocbs[1], aiocb;
    struct sigaction  act;
    char            buf[AIO_BUFSIZE];
```

(continues)

FIGURE 9–39 Signal notification of asynchronous I/O completion *(continued)*

```
if (argc != 2) {
    fprintf(stderr, "usage: %s <file path>\n", PROGNAME);
    exit(1);
}

if ((fd = open(argv[1], O_RDONLY)) < 0) {
    perror("open");
    exit(1);
}

aiocbs[0] = &aiocb;

aiocb.aio_fildes = fd;
aiocb.aio_offset = (off_t)0;
aiocb.aio_buf    = buf;
aiocb.aio_nbytes = AIO_BUFSIZE;

// not used on Mac OS X
aiocb.aio_reqprio = 0;

// we want to be notified via a signal when the asynchronous I/O finishes
// SIGEV_THREAD (notification via callback) is not supported on Mac OS X
aiocb.aio_sigevent.sigev_notify = SIGEV_SIGNAL;

// send this signal when done: must be valid (except SIGKILL or SIGSTOP)
aiocb.aio_sigevent.sigev_signo = SIGUSR1;

// ignored on Mac OS X
aiocb.aio_sigevent.sigev_value.sival_int = 0;
aiocb.aio_sigevent.sigev_notify_function = (void(*)(union sigval))0;
aiocb.aio_sigevent.sigev_notify_attributes = (pthread_attr_t *)0;

aiocb.aio_lio_opcode = LIO_READ;

// set up a handler for SIGUSR1
act.sa_handler = SIGUSR1_handler;
sigemptyset(&(act.sa_mask));
act.sa_flags = 0;
sigaction(SIGUSR1, &act, NULL);

// initiates a list of I/O requests specified by a list of aiocb structures
if (lio_listio(LIO_NOWAIT, (AIOCB_CONST)aiocbs, 1, &(aiocb.aio_sigevent)))
    perror("lio_listio");
else {
    printf("asynchronous read issued...\n");
```

(continues)

FIGURE 9–39 Signal notification of asynchronous I/O completion *(continued)*

```
        // quite contrived, since we could have used LIO_WAIT with lio_listio()
        // anyway, the I/O might already be done by the time we call this
        aio_suspend((const AIOCB_CONST)aiocbs, 1, (const struct timespec *)0);
    }

    return 0;
}


$ gcc -Wall -o aio_read aio_read.c
SIGUSR1_handler
asynchronous read issued...
```

9.8.5 Signals and Multithreading

The signal mechanism does not lend itself well to a multithreaded environment. Traditional signal semantics require exceptions to be handled serially, which is problematic when a multithreaded application generates exception signals. For example, if several threads hit breakpoints while debugging a multithreaded application, only one breakpoint can be reported to the debugger, which will therefore not have access to the entire state of the process. Modern-day operating systems have to deal with several common and system-specific problems in their signal implementations. A representative multithreaded signal implementation in a modern Unix system has *per-thread signal masks*, allowing threads to block signals independently of other threads in the same process. Mac OS X provides the pthread_sigmask() system call to examine or change (or both) the calling thread's signal mask.

If a signal is generated because of a trap, such as an illegal instruction or an arithmetic exception (i.e., the signal is *synchronous*), it is sent to the thread that caused the trap. Others (typically *asynchronous* signals) are delivered to the first thread that is not blocking the signal. Note that signals such as SIGKILL, SIGSTOP, and SIGTERM affect the entire process.

9.8.6 Signal Actions

A signal action can be carried out only by the process (technically, a thread within that process) to which the signal was delivered. Unlike Mach exceptions, which can be handled by any thread in any task (with prior arrangement), no process can execute a signal handler on another process's behalf. This is problematic when the complete register context of an exception is desirable or the exception may have corrupted the resources of the victim process. Debuggers have been historically difficult to implement on Unix systems because of limitations in prevailing signal mechanisms.

POSIX.1 allows a process to declare a signal to have its handler execute on an alternate stack, which can be defined and examined using `sigaltstack(2)`. When changing a signal action through `sigaction(2)`, the `sa_flags` field of the `sigaction` structure can have the `SA_ONSTACK` flag set to cause delivery of the signal in question on the alternate stack, provided an alternate stack has been declared with `sigaltstack()`.

```
int
sigaltstack(const struct sigaltstack *newss, struct sigaltstack *oldss);

// bsd/sys/signal.h

struct sigaltstack {
    user_addr_t ss_sp;    // signal stack base
    user_size_t ss_size;  // signal stack length
    int  ss_flags;        // SA_DISABLE and/or SA_ONSTACK
};

#define SS_ONSTACK   0x0001  // take signal on signal stack
#define SS_DISABLE   0x0004  // disable taking signals on alternate stack
#define MINSIGSTKSZ 32768    // (32KB) minimum allowable stack
#define SIGSTKSZ    131072   // (128KB) recommended stack size
```

If the signal handler needs exception context, the kernel must explicitly save the context and pass it to the handler for examination. For example, POSIX.1 stipulates that the signal-catching function (handler) for a signal will be entered differently based on whether the `SA_SIGINFO` flag is set for the signal or not.

```
// SA_SIGINFO is cleared for this signal (no context passed)
void sig_handler(int signo);

// SA_SIGINFO is set for this signal (context passed)
void sig_handler(int signo, siginfo_t *info, void *context);
```

The `siginfo_t` structure on a system must at least contain the signal number, the cause of the signal, and the signal value.

```
// bsd/sys/signal.h
```

```
// kernel representation of siginfo_t
typedef struct __user_siginfo {
        int              si_signo;   // signal number
        int              si_errno;   // errno association
        int              si_code;    // signal code
        pid_t            si_pid;      // sending process
        uid_t            si_uid;      // sender's real user ID
        int              si_status;  // exit value
        user_addr_t      si_addr;     // faulting instruction
        union user_sigval si_value;  // signal value
        user_long_t      si_band;     // band event for SIGPOLL
        user_ulong_t     pad[7];      // reserved
} user_siginfo_t;
```

When a signal handler is invoked, the current user context is saved and a new context is created. The context argument to sig_handler() can be cast to a pointer to an object of type ucontext_t. It refers to the receiving process's user context that was interrupted when the signal was delivered. The ucontext_t structure contains a data structure of type mcontext_t, which represents the machine-specific register state of the context.

```
// kernel representation of 64-bit ucontext_t
struct user_ucontext64 {
    // SA_ONSTACK set?
    int                  uc_onstack;

    // set of signals that are blocked when this context is active
    sigset_t             uc_sigmask;

    // stack used by this context
    struct user_sigaltstack uc_stack;

    // pointer to the context that is resumed when this context returns
    user_addr_t          uc_link;

    // size of the machine-specific representation of the saved context
    user_size_t          uc_mcsize;

    // machine-specific representation of the saved context
    user_addr_t          uc_mcontext64;
};
```

```
// kernel representation of 64-bit PowerPC mcontext_t
struct mcontext64 {                    // size_in_units_of_natural_t =
    struct ppc_exception_state64 es;   // PPC_EXCEPTION_STATE64_COUNT +
    struct ppc_thread_state64    ss;   // PPC_THREAD_STATE64_COUNT +
    struct ppc_float_state       fs;   // PPC_FLOAT_STATE_COUNT +
    struct ppc_vector_state      vs;   // PPC_VECTOR_STATE_COUNT
};
```

The type and the amount of context made available to a signal handler depend on the operating system and the hardware—the context is not guaranteed against corruption.

> Mac OS X does not provide the POSIX `getcontext()` and `setcontext()` functions for retrieving and setting, respectively, the current user context of the calling thread. As we saw earlier, `thread_get_state()` and `thread_set_state()` are used for this purpose. Other related functions such as `makecontext()` and `swapcontext()` are also not available on Mac OS X. In any case, the `getcontext()` and `setcontext()` routines have been marked as obsolescent in SUSv3[13] and can be replaced using POSIX thread functions.

9.8.7 Signal Generation and Delivery

The `kill()` system call, which is used to send a signal to one or more processes, is invoked with two arguments: a process ID (pid) and a signal number. It sends the specified signal (provided that the caller's credentials permit it) to one or more processes based on whether the given pid is positive, 0, -1, or otherwise negative. The details of `kill()`'s behavior are described in the `kill(2)` man page. The `killpg()` system call sends the given signal to the given process group. For a certain combination of its arguments, `kill()` is equivalent to `killpg()`. The implementations of both system calls on Mac OS X use the `psignal()` internal function [bsd/kern/kern_sig.c] to send the signal. `psignal()` is a simple wrapper around `psignal_lock()` [bsd/kern/kern_sig.c]. If the signal has an associated action, `psignal_lock()` adds the signal to the set of pending signals for the process. Figure 9–40 shows the important functions that are part of the signal mechanism in the kernel.

`psignal_lock()` calls `get_signalthread()` [bsd/kern/kern_sig.c] to select a thread for signal delivery. `get_signalthread()` examines the threads within the process, normally selecting the first thread that is not blocking the signal. Sending signals to the first thread allows single-threaded programs to be linked with multithreaded libraries. If `get_signalthread()` returns successfully,

---

13. Single UNIX Specification, Version 3.

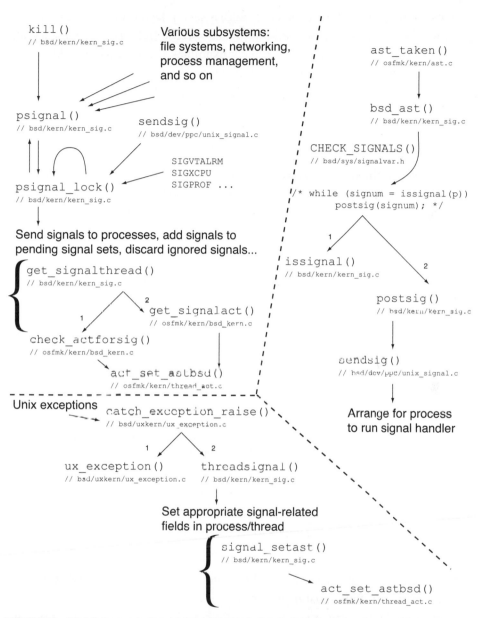

FIGURE 9–40 Implementation of the signal mechanism in the kernel

a specific asynchronous system trap (AST_BSD) is set for the thread. `psignal_lock()` then processes the signal, performing signal-specific actions as necessary and allowed. In particular, `psignal_lock()` examines the following fields of the uthread structure, possibly modifying `uu_siglist` and `uu_sigwait`:

- `uu_siglist`—signals pending for the thread
- `uu_sigwait`—signals for `sigwait(2)` on this thread
- `uu_sigmask`—signal mask for the thread

Before the thread returns to user space from the kernel (after a system call or trap), the kernel checks the thread for pending BSD ASTs. If it finds any, the kernel calls `bsd_ast()` [bsd/kern/kern_sig.c] on the thread.

// bsd/kern/kern_sig.c

```
void
bsd_ast(thread_t thr_act)
{
    ...
    if (CHECK_SIGNALS(p, current_thread(), ut)) {
        while ((signum = issignal(p)))
            postsig(signum);
    }
    ...
}
```

> `psignal_lock()` does not send signals to the kernel task, zombie processes, or a process that has invoked the `reboot()` system call.

The `CHECK_SIGNALS()` macro [bsd/sys/signalvar.h] ensures that the thread is active (not terminated) and then calls the `SHOULDissignal()` macro to determine whether there are signals to be delivered based on the following quick checks.

- There must be at least one signal pending—that is, the uthread structure's `uu_siglist` field must be nonzero.
- The thread may be blocking one or more signals, as specified by the uthread structure's `uu_sigmask` field being nonzero. Note that there is also a per-process signal mask, which is deprecated.
- The process may be ignoring one or more signals, as specified by the proc structure's p_sigignore field.

- The signals contained in the `sigcantmask` global bitmap—`SIGKILL` and `SIGSTOP`—cannot be masked.

- If the process is being traced, even blocked and ignored signals will be delivered so that the debugger can know about them.

When called in a loop, `issignal()` [bsd/kern/kern_sig.c] keeps returning a signal number if the current process has received a signal that should be caught, should cause termination of the process, or should interrupt the current system call. `issignal()` performs a variety of processing depending on the type of the signal, whether the signal is masked, whether the signal has the default action, and so on. For example, if the process has a pending `SIGSTOP` with the default action, `issignal()` processes the signal immediately and clears the signal. No signal number is returned in this case. Signals that have actions (including the default action of terminating the process) are returned and are processed by `postsig()` [bsd/kern/kern_sig.c].

`postsig()` either terminates the process if the default action warrants so or calls `sendsig()` [bsd/dev/ppc/unix_signal.c] to arrange for the process to run a signal handler. This arrangement primarily involves population of `ucontext` and `mcontext` structures (32-bit or 64-bit, as appropriate) that contain the context information required by the handler to run within the thread in user space. The context is copied to user space and various registers are set up, including `SRR0`, which contains the address at which the handler will start execution. Finally, `postsig()` calls `thread_setstatus()` [osfmk/kern/thread_act.c] to set the thread's machine state. `thread_setstatus()` is a trivial wrapper around the `thread_set_state()` Mach routine.

9.8.8 Mach Exceptions and Unix Signals Living Together

When the kernel starts up, `bsdinit_task()` [bsd/kern/bsd_init.c] calls `ux_handler_init()` [bsd/uxkern/ux_exception.c] to initialize the Unix exception handler. `ux_handler_init()` starts a kernel thread that runs `ux_handler()` [bsd/uxkern/ux_exception.c]—an internal kernel exception handler that provides Unix compatibility by converting Mach exception messages to Unix signals. `ux_handler()` allocates a port set for receiving messages and then allocates an exception port within the set. The global name for this port is contained in `ux_exception_port`. The exception ports of both the host and the BSD init task (that would eventually run `launchd`) are set to `ux_exception_port`. Since `launchd` is the ultimate ancestor of all Unix processes, and task exception ports are inherited across fork(), most exceptions that have signal analogs are converted to signals by default.

The message-handling loop of ux_handler() is the typical Mach exception handler loop: An exception message is received, exc_server() is called, and a reply message is sent. If there is an error in receiving a message because it is too large, the message is ignored. Any other error in message reception results in a kernel panic. The corresponding call to catch_exception_raise() causes an exception to be converted to a Unix signal and code by calling ux_exception() [bsd/uxkern/ux_exception.c]. Finally, the resultant signal is sent to the appropriate thread.

```
// bsd/uxkern/ux_exception.c

kern_return_t
catch_exception_raise(...)
{
    ...
    if (th_act != THR_ACT_NULL) {

        ut = get_bsdthread_info(th_act);

        // convert {Mach exception, code, subcode} to {Unix signal, uu_code}
        ux_exception(exception, code[0], code[1], &ux_signal, &ucode);

        // send signal
        if (ux_signal != 0)
            threadsignal(th_act, signal, ucode);

        thread_deallocate(th_act);
    }
    ...
}
```

ux_exception() first calls machine_exception() [bsd/dev/ppc/unix_signal.c] to attempt a machine-dependent translation of the given Mach exception and code to a Unix signal and code. The translation is as follows:

- { EXC_BAD_INSTRUCTION, code } is translated to { SIGILL, code }.
- { EXC_ARITHMETIC, code } is translated to { SIGFPE, code }.
- { EXC_PPC_SOFTWARE, EXC_PPC_TRAP } is translated to { SIGTRAP, EXC_PPC_TRAP }.

If machine_exception() fails to translate a Mach exception, ux_exception() itself translates exceptions as shown in Table 9–7.

TABLE 9–7 Translation of Mach Exceptions to Unix Signals

Mach Exception	Mach Exception Code	Unix Signal
EXC_ARITHMETIC	—	SIGFPE
EXC_BAD_ACCESS	KERN_INVALID_ADDRESS	SIGSEGV
EXC_BAD_ACCESS	—	SIGBUS
EXC_BAD_INSTRUCTION	—	SIGILL
EXC_BREAKPOINT	—	SIGTRAP
EXC_EMULATION	—	SIGEMT
EXC_SOFTWARE	EXC_UNIX_ABORT	SIGABRT
EXC_SOFTWARE	EXC_UNIX_BAD_PIPE	SIGPIPE
EXC_SOFTWARE	EXC_UNIX_BAD_SYSCALL	SIGSYS
EXC_SOFTWARE	EXC_SOFT_SIGNAL	SIGKILL

The difference between SIGBUS and SIGSEGV must be carefully noted. Both correspond to a bad memory access, but for different reasons. A SIGBUS (bus error) occurs when the memory is valid in that it is mapped, but the victim is not allowed to access it. Accessing page 0, which is normally mapped into each address space with all access to it disallowed, will result in a SIGBUS. In contrast, a SIGSEGV (segmentation fault) occurs when the memory address is invalid in that it is not even mapped.

The automatic conversion of Mach exceptions to signals does not preclude user-level handling of the Mach exceptions underlying those signals. If there exists a task-level or thread-level exception handler, it will receive the exception message instead of ux_handler(). Thereafter, the user's handler can handle the exception entirely, performing any cleanup or corrective actions, or it may forward the initial exception message to ux_handler(), which would cause the exception to be converted to a signal after all. This is what the GNU debugger (GDB) does.

Moreover, instead of forwarding the initial exception message, a user's exception handler can also send a new message to ux_handler(). This would require send rights to ux_exception_port, which is the original task exception port before the task-level or thread-level exception handler is installed by the user. A rather convoluted way of sending a software signal to a process would be to package and send the relevant information in a Mach exception message. (The exception type, code, and subcode would be EXC_SOFTWARE, EXC_SOFT_SIGNAL, and the signal number, respectively.)

9.8.9 Exceptions, Signals, and Debugging

Even though signal mechanisms in modern Unix systems have greatly improved, the relative cleanliness of Mach's exception-handling mechanism is still evident, especially when it comes to debugging. Since exceptions are essentially queued messages, a debugger can receive and record all exceptions that have occurred in a program since it was last examined. Multiple excepting threads can remain suspended until the debugger has dequeued and examined all exception messages. Such examination may include retrieving the victim's entire exception context. These features allow a debugger to determine a program's state more precisely than traditional signal semantics would allow.

Moreover, an exception handler runs in its own thread, which may be in the same task or in a different task altogether. Therefore, exception handlers do not require the victim thread's resources to run. Even though Mac OS X does not support distributed Mach IPC, Mach's design does not preclude exception handlers from running on a different host.

We saw that exception handlers can be designated in a fine-grained manner, as each exception type can have its own handler, which may further be per-thread or per-task. It is worthwhile to note that a thread-level exception handler is typically suitable for error handling, whereas a task-level handler is typically suitable for debugging. Task-level handlers also have the debugger-friendly property that they remain in effect across a fork() because task-level exception ports are inherited by the child process.

9.8.10 The ptrace() System Call

Mac OS X provides the ptrace() system call for process tracing and debugging, although certain ptrace() requests that are supported on FreeBSD are not implemented on Mac OS X, for example, PT_READ_I, PT_READ_D, PT_WRITE_I, PT_WRITE_D, PT_GETREGS, PT_SETREGS, and several others. Operations equivalent to those missing from the Mac OS X implementation of ptrace() can be typically performed through Mach-specific routines. For example, reading or writing program memory can be done through Mach VM routines.[14] Similarly, thread registers can be read or written through Mach thread routines.

Moreover, `ptrace()` on Mac OS X provides certain requests that are specific to Mac OS X, such as those listed here.

- `PT_SIGEXC`—Deliver signals as Mach exceptions.
- `PT_ATTACHEXC`—Attach to a running process and also apply the effects of `PT_SIGEXC` to it.
- `PT_THUPDATE`—Send a signal to the given Mach thread.

If `PT_SIGEXC` is applied to a process, when there is a signal to be delivered, `issignal()` [bsd/dkern/kern_sig.c] calls `do_bsdexception()` [bsd/kern/kern_sig.c] to generate a Mach exception message instead. The exception's type, code, and subcode are `EXC_SOFTWARE`, `EXC_SOFT_SIGNAL`, and the signal number, respectively. `do_bsdexception()`, which is analogous to the `doexception()` function we saw in Section 9.7.2, calls `bsd_exception()` [osfmk/kern/exception.c]. The latter calls one of the `exception_raise` functions.

9.9 Pipes

Ever since pipes were introduced in Third Edition UNIX (1973), they have been an integral feature of Unix systems. The Unix program-stream redirection facility uses pipes. Therefore, Unix shells use pipes extensively. Mac OS X provides the `pipe()` system call, which allocates and returns a pair of file descriptors: The first is the *read end*, and the second is the *write end*. The two descriptors can provide an I/O stream between two processes, thus serving as an IPC channel. However, pipes have several limitations, some of which may be rather severe for certain applications.

- Pipes are possible only between related processes—that is, those with a common ancestor.
- The kernel buffer corresponding to a pipe consumes kernel memory.
- Pipes support only untyped byte streams.
- Historically, pipes have allowed only unidirectional data flow. The Single UNIX Specification allows but does not require full-duplex pipes.

---

14. Note, however, that the Mach VM routines are not optimal for operating on small amounts of data.

- Only writes below PIPE_BUF bytes in size are guaranteed to be atomic. PIPE_BUF is 512 bytes on Mac OS X. The fpathconf() system call can be used to retrieve the value of PIPE_BUF given a pipe descriptor.

- You can use pipes only for local (non-networked) communication.

Bidirectional Pipes

Not all of the shortcomings with pipes are universal. Certain operating systems—for example, FreeBSD and Solaris—implement bidirectional pipes, wherein the pair of descriptors returned by the pipe system call is such that data written to one can be read on the other. Although the Mac OS X pipe implementation is based on FreeBSD's, Mac OS X 10.4 does not provide bidirectional pipes.

Moreover, it is possible to send a pipe descriptor to another, unrelated process through file descriptor passing, which is supported on Mac OS X. We will see an example of descriptor passing in Section 9.11.

Pipes are also called *unnamed pipes*, since there also exist *named pipes* (see Section 9.10). The kernel's internal file descriptor type for a pipe descriptor is DTYPE_PIPE. Descriptors for other IPC mechanisms, such as sockets, POSIX semaphores, and POSIX shared memory, have their own descriptor types. Table 9–8 shows the various descriptor types used in the kernel.

TABLE 9–8 File Descriptor Types Used in the Kernel

Descriptor Type	Notes
DTYPE_VNODE	File
DTYPE_SOCKET	Socket-based communication end point
DTYPE_PSXSHM	POSIX shared memory
DTYPE_PSXSEM	POSIX semaphore
DTYPE_KQUEUE	Kqueue
DTYPE_PIPE	Pipe
DTYPE_FSEVENTS	File system event notification descriptor

9.10 Named Pipes (Fifos)

A named pipe—also called a *fifo*—is an abstraction that provides the functionality of an unnamed pipe but uses the file system namespace to represent the pipe, allowing readers and writers to open the fifo file like a regular file. A fifo can be created using the mkfifo() system call or through the mkfifo command-line program.

If a fifo is opened for reading, the open() call will block if there are no writers—that is, if somebody else does not have the fifo open for writing. Conversely, if a fifo is opened for writing, the open() will block if there are no readers. It is possible to open a fifo in nonblocking mode by specifying the O_NONBLOCK flag in the open() call. A nonblocking open for reading will return immediately, with a valid file descriptor, even if there are no writers. A nonblocking open for writing, however, will return immediately with an ENXIO error if there are no readers.

The Mac OS X implementation of fifos internally uses local (Unix Domain) stream sockets—that is, sockets of type SOCK_STREAM in the AF_LOCAL domain.

Although a fifo has physical existence on a file system, it must be different from a regular file for the kernel to treat it as a communication channel with properties that regular files do not have. This is indeed the case: Fifos are conceptually similar to block or character special files in how the file system treats them. Consider a fifo on an HFS Plus volume. The mkfifo() system call simply calls the create operation exported by the HFS Plus file system, additionally setting the type of the vnode as VFIFO. The file type is stored as part of the BSD information structure (struct HFSPlusBSDInfo), which in turn is part of the on-disk file metadata. Thereafter, whenever the fifo file is being looked up (typically for opening), the corresponding vnode's file system operations table pointer is switched by HFS Plus to point to another table, some (but not all) of whose operations are that of the *fifo file system* (fifofs).

> Block and character devices on HFS Plus are handled similarly, except the *special file system* (specfs) is used instead of fifofs. We will see more of fifofs and specfs in Chapter 11. Chapter 12 is entirely dedicated to HFS Plus.

This way, opening a fifo file results in fifo_open() [bsd/miscfs/fifofs/fifo_vnops.c] being called. On the first open of a fifo, fifo_open() creates two AF_LOCAL stream sockets: one for reading and the other for writing. Similarly, several other system calls, in particular read() and write(), eventually resolve to fifofs functions.

9.11 File Descriptor Passing

On a Unix system, a file descriptor is an integer that represents an open file in a process.[15] Each file descriptor is an index into the process's kernel-resident file descriptor table. The descriptor is local to the process in that it is meaningful only in the process that acquired the descriptor—say, by opening a file. In particular, a process A cannot access a file that is open in another process B by simply using the value of the descriptor representing that file in B.

Many Unix systems support sending file descriptors from one process to another, unrelated process over an AF_LOCAL socket. Mac OS X also provides this IPC mechanism. Figure 9–41 shows details of the program-visible message buffer data structure involved in sending one or more file descriptors through the sendmsg() system call.

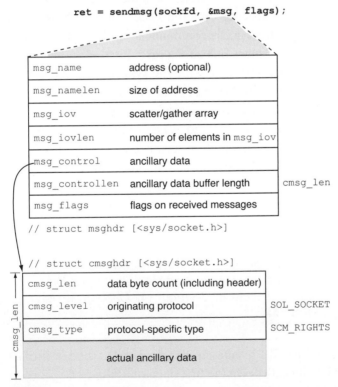

FIGURE 9–41 Program-visible data structures involved in file descriptor passing

---

15. Section 11.5 discusses the kernel handling of file descriptors.

The msghdr structure encapsulates several parameters to sendmsg() and recvmsg(). It can contain a pointer to a *control buffer*, which is ancillary data laid out as a control message structure consisting of a header (struct cmsghdr) and data (immediately following the header). In our case, the data is a file descriptor. Note that we have shown the msg_control field to point to a control buffer with one control message. In theory, the buffer could contain multiple control messages, with msg_controllen adjusted accordingly. The control buffer would then be a sequence of cmsghdr structures, each containing its length. The Mac OS X implementation supports only one control message per control buffer.

Protocol processing for sendmsg() [bsd/kern/uipc_syscalls.c] eventually results in a call to uipc_send() [bsd/kern/uipc_usrreq.c], which is passed a pointer to a control mbuf if the original call to sendmsg() contained a valid control buffer pointer. If so, uipc_send() calls unp_internalize() [bsd/kern/uipc_usrreq.c] to *internalize* the ancillary data—it iterates over the list of file descriptors in the buffer and converts each to its corresponding file structure (struct fileglob [bsd/sys/file_internal.h]). unp_internalize() requires that the cmsg_level and cmsg_type fields be set to SOL_SOCKET and SCM_RIGHTS, respectively. SCM_RIGHTS specifies that the control message data contains access rights.

When such a message is received, the list of file structures is *externalized* by a call to unp_externalize() [bsd/kern/uipc_usrreq.c]; for each file structure, a local file descriptor in the receiving process is consumed to represent an open file. After a successful recvmsg(), the receiver can use such file descriptors normally.

> File descriptor passing has many conceptual parallels with passing port rights in a Mach IPC message.

Let us look at a programming example of descriptor passing. We will write a descriptor-passing server that serves a given file over an AF_LOCAL socket connection. A client will connect to this server, receive the file descriptor, and then use the descriptor to read the file. The socket's address and the format of the control message are specified in a common header file that will be shared between server and client implementations. Figures 9-42, 9-43, and 9-44 show the common header file, the server's implementation, and the client's implementation.

FIGURE 9–42 Common header file for the descriptor-passing client-server implementation

```
// fd_common.h

#ifndef _FD_COMMON_H_
#define _FD_COMMON_H_

#include <stdio.h>
#include <fcntl.h>
#include <string.h>
#include <unistd.h>
#include <stdlib.h>
#include <sys/types.h>
#include <sys/socket.h>
#include <sys/un.h>

#define SERVER_NAME "/tmp/.fdserver"

typedef union {
    struct cmsghdr cmsghdr;
    u_char         msg_control[CMSG_SPACE(sizeof(int))];
} cmsghdr_msg_control_t;

#endif // _FD_COMMON_H_
```

FIGURE 9–43 Implementation of the descriptor-passing server

```
// fd_sender.c

#include "fd_common.h"

int setup_server(const char *name);
int send_fd_using_sockfd(int fd, int sockfd);

int
setup_server(const char *name)
{
    int sockfd, len;
    struct sockaddr_un server_unix_addr;

    if ((sockfd = socket(AF_LOCAL, SOCK_STREAM, 0)) < 0) {
        perror("socket");
        return sockfd;
    }

    unlink(name);
```

(continues)

FIGURE 9–43 Implementation of the descriptor-passing server *(continued)*

```
    bzero((char *)&server_unix_addr, sizeof(server_unix_addr));
    server_unix_addr.sun_family = AF_LOCAL;
    strcpy(server_unix_addr.sun_path, name);
    len = strlen(name) + 1;
    len += sizeof(server_unix_addr.sun_family);

    if (bind(sockfd, (struct sockaddr *)&server_unix_addr, len) < 0) {
        close(sockfd);
        return -1;
    }

    return sockfd;
}

int
send_fd_using_sockfd(int fd, int sockfd)
{
    ssize_t               ret;
    struct iovec          iovec[1];
    struct msghdr         msg;
    struct cmsghdr        *cmsghdrp;
    cmsghdr_msg_control_t cmsghdr_msg_control;

    iovec[0].iov_base = "";
    iovec[0].iov_len = 1;

    msg.msg_name = (caddr_t)0;  // address (optional)
    msg.msg_namelen = 0;        // size of address
    msg.msg_iov = iovec;        // scatter/gather array
    msg.msg_iovlen = 1;         // members in msg.msg_iov
    msg.msg_control = cmsghdr_msg_control.msg_control;  // ancillary data
    // ancillary data buffer length
    msg.msg_controllen = sizeof(cmsghdr_msg_control.msg_control);
    msg.msg_flags = 0;          // flags on received message

    // CMSG_FIRSTHDR() returns a pointer to the first cmsghdr structure in
    // the ancillary data associated with the given msghdr structure
    cmsghdrp = CMSG_FIRSTHDR(&msg);

    cmsghdrp->cmsg_len = CMSG_LEN(sizeof(int));  // data byte count
    cmsghdrp->cmsg_level = SOL_SOCKET;           // originating protocol
    cmsghdrp->cmsg_type = SCM_RIGHTS;            // protocol-specified type

    // CMSG_DATA() returns a pointer to the data array associated with
    // the cmsghdr structure pointed to by cmsghdrp
    *((int *)CMSG_DATA(cmsghdrp)) = fd;
```

(continues)

FIGURE 9–43 Implementation of the descriptor-passing server *(continued)*

```c
    if ((ret = sendmsg(sockfd, &msg, 0)) < 0) {
        perror("sendmsg");
        return ret;
    }

    return 0;
}

int
main(int argc, char **argv)
{
    int             fd, sockfd;
    int             csockfd;
    socklen_t       len;
    struct sockaddr_un client_unix_addr;

    if (argc != 2) {
        fprintf(stderr, "usage: %s <file path>\n", argv[0]);
        exit(1);
    }

    if ((sockfd = setup_server(SERVER_NAME)) < 0) {
        fprintf(stderr, "failed to set up server\n");
        exit(1);
    }

    if ((fd = open(argv[1], O_RDONLY)) < 0) {
        perror("open");
        close(sockfd);
        exit(1);
    }

    listen(sockfd, 0);

    for (;;) {
        len = sizeof(client_unix_addr);
        csockfd = accept(sockfd, (struct sockaddr *)&client_unix_addr, &len);
        if (csockfd < 0) {
            perror("accept");
            close(sockfd);
            exit(1);
        }

        if ((send_fd_using_sockfd(fd, csockfd) < 0))
            fprintf(stderr, "failed to send file descriptor (fd = %d)\n", fd);
        else
            fprintf(stderr, "file descriptor sent (fd = %d)\n", fd);
```

(continues)

FIGURE 9–43 Implementation of the descriptor-passing server *(continued)*

```
        close(sockfd);
        close(csockfd);
        break;
    }

    exit(0);
}
```

FIGURE 9–44 Implementation of the descriptor-passing client

// **fd_receiver.c**

```
#include "fd_common.h"

int receive_fd_using_sockfd(int *fd, int sockfd);

int
receive_fd_using_sockfd(int *fd, int sockfd)
{
    ssize_t                 ret;
    u_char                  c;
    int                     errcond = 0;
    struct iovec            iovec[1];
    struct msghdr           msg;
    struct cmsghdr          *cmsghdrp;
    cmsghdr_msg_control_t   cmsghdr_msg_control;

    iovec[0].iov_base = &c;
    iovec[0].iov_len = 1;

    msg.msg_name = (caddr_t)0;
    msg.msg_namelen = 0;
    msg.msg_iov = iovec;
    msg.msg_iovlen = 1;
    msg.msg_control = cmsghdr_msg_control.msg_control;
    msg.msg_controllen = sizeof(cmsghdr_msg_control.msg_control);
    msg.msg_flags = 0;

    if ((ret = recvmsg(sockfd, &msg, 0)) <= 0) {
        perror("recvmsg");
        return ret;
    }

    cmsghdrp = CMSG_FIRSTHDR(&msg);
```

(continues)

FIGURE 9–44 Implementation of the descriptor-passing client *(continued)*

```c
    if (cmsghdrp == NULL) {
        *fd = -1;
        return ret;
    }

    if (cmsghdrp->cmsg_len != CMSG_LEN(sizeof(int)))
        errcond++;

    if (cmsghdrp->cmsg_level != SOL_SOCKET)
        errcond++;

    if (cmsghdrp->cmsg_type != SCM_RIGHTS)
        errcond++;

    if (errcond) {
        fprintf(stderr, "%d errors in received message\n", errcond);
        *fd = -1;
    } else
        *fd = *((int *)CMSG_DATA(cmsghdrp));

    return ret;
}

int
main(int argc, char **argv)
{
    char                buf[512];
    int                 fd = -1, sockfd, len, ret;
    struct sockaddr_un server_unix_addr;

    bzero((char *)&server_unix_addr, sizeof(server_unix_addr));
    strcpy(server_unix_addr.sun_path, SERVER_NAME);
    server_unix_addr.sun_family = AF_LOCAL;
    len = strlen(SERVER_NAME) + 1;
    len += sizeof(server_unix_addr.sun_family);

    if ((sockfd = socket(AF_LOCAL, SOCK_STREAM, 0)) < 0) {
        perror("socket");
        exit(1);
    }

    if (connect(sockfd, (struct sockaddr *)&server_unix_addr, len) < 0) {
        perror("connect");
        close(sockfd);
        exit(1);
    }
```

(continues)

FIGURE 9-44 Implementation of the descriptor-passing client *(continued)*

```
ret = receive_fd_using_sockfd(&fd, sockfd);

if ((ret < 0) || (fd < 0)) {
    fprintf(stderr, "failed to receive file descriptor\n");
    close(sockfd);
    exit(1);
}

printf("received file descriptor (fd = %d)\n", fd);
if ((ret = read(fd, buf, 512)) > 0)
    write(1, buf, ret);

exit(0);
}
```

Let us now test our descriptor-passing client and server.

```
$ gcc -Wall -o fd_sender fd_sender.c
$ gcc -Wall -o fd_receiver fd_receiver.c
$ echo "Hello, Descriptor" > /tmp/message.txt
$ ./fd_sender /tmp/message.txt
...
        $ ./fd_receiver # from another shell prompt
        received file descriptor (fd = 10)
        Hello, Descriptor
```

9.12 XSI IPC

The Single UNIX Specification defines a set of IPC interfaces as part of the X/Open System Interface (XSI) extensions. The XSI IPC interfaces are essentially the same as the (erstwhile) System V IPC interfaces, which have been widely supported across most Unix systems, even though they were not part of any standard for a long time. Mac OS X provides system calls for the System V IPC mechanisms, namely, message queues, semaphores, and shared memory.

> XSI is a superset of the mandatory requirements for conformance to POSIX.1.

9.13 POSIX IPC

The POSIX 1003.1b-1993 (POSIX93) standard introduced a set of IPC interfaces as part of the POSIX Real-time Extensions. Collectively known as POSIX IPC, these interfaces define functions for message queues, semaphores, and shared memory. The POSIX IPC functions are rather different from their XSI counterparts.

> Mac OS X 10.4 does not provide POSIX message queues. It does, however, provide the POSIX semaphore and shared memory interfaces.

In contrast to XSI IPC, which uses keys as IPC identifiers, POSIX IPC uses string names for IPC objects. The Single UNIX Specification specifies several things about IPC names but leaves several other things unspecified and therefore open to implementation-specific behavior, as shown in the following examples.

- It is unspecified whether an IPC name appears in the file system. Mac OS X does not require the name to be present in the file system, and if it is, its presence does not affect the behavior of POSIX IPC calls.

- Mac OS X allows an IPC name to be at most 31 characters long (including the terminating NUL character).

- If an IPC name begins with the slash character, any caller of an IPC open function (such as sem_open() or shm_open()) with the same name refers to the same IPC object, as long as that name has not been removed.

- If an IPC name does not begin with the slash character, the effect is implementation-defined. Mac OS X treats this case identically to the case when the name does begin with a slash character.

- The interpretation of slash characters other than the leading slash character in a name is implementation-defined. Mac OS X treats a slash character in an IPC name as any other character. In particular, unlike file system pathnames, it does not canonicalize multiple slash characters. For example, the following IPC names are valid and different on Mac OS X: ipcobject, /ipcobject, //ipcobject, and /ipcobject/.

9.13.1 POSIX Semaphores

A named POSIX semaphore is created using sem_open() and deleted using sem_unlink(). sem_open() is also used to connect the calling process to an existing semaphore. sem_close() closes an open semaphore. These functions resemble the open(), unlink(), and close() functions for files. In fact, like open(), sem_open() accepts the O_CREAT and O_EXCL flags to determine whether the named object is only being accessed or also being created. However, instead of integer-based file descriptors, the semaphore functions deal with pointers to sem_t structures.

POSIX semaphores are counting semaphores: A lock operation on a semaphore decrements its value by one, whereas an unlock operation increments its value by one. In the simplest sense, a POSIX semaphore is an integer variable that is accessed through two atomic operations: sem_wait() and sem_post(). Given an open semaphore, sem_wait() and sem_post() perform lock and unlock operations, respectively, on the semaphore. If the semaphore value is zero when sem_wait() is called, the caller blocks. Such blocking can be interrupted by a signal.

Figure 9–45 shows the source for the following four simple programs, which demonstrate the working of POSIX semaphores on Mac OS X.

- sem_create creates a named semaphore if it does not already exist.
- sem_unlink deletes an existing named semaphore.
- sem_post unlocks an existing named semaphore.
- sem_wait locks an existing named semaphore, blocking until it can do so.

The programs all include a common header file (sem_common.h).

FIGURE 9–45 Working with POSIX semaphores

```
// sem_common.h

#ifndef _SEM_COMMON_H_
#define _SEM_COMMON_H_

#include <stdio.h>
#include <stdlib.h>
#include <semaphore.h>

#define CHECK_ARGS(count, msg) {                              \
    if (argc != count) {                                      \
        fprintf(stderr, "usage: %s " msg "\n", PROGNAME);     \
        exit(1);                                              \
    }                                                         \
}
#endif


// sem_create.c

#include "sem_common.h"
```

(continues)

FIGURE 9–45 Working with POSIX semaphores *(continued)*

```c
#define PROGNAME "sem_create"

int
main(int argc, char **argv)
{
    int    val;
    sem_t *sem;

    CHECK_ARGS(3, "<path> <value>");

    val = atoi(argv[2]);

    sem = sem_open(argv[1], O_CREAT | O_EXCL, 0644, val);
    if (sem == (sem_t *)SEM_FAILED) {
        perror("sem_open");
        exit(1);
    }

    sem_close(sem);

    exit(0);
}

// sem_unlink.c

#include "sem_common.h"

#define PROGNAME "sem_unlink"

int
main(int argc, char **argv)
{
    int ret = 0;

    CHECK_ARGS(2, "<path>");

    if ((ret = sem_unlink(argv[1])) < 0)
        perror("sem_unlink");

    exit(ret);
}

// sem_post.c

#include "sem_common.h"

#define PROGNAME "sem_post"
```

(continues)

FIGURE 9–45 Working with POSIX semaphores *(continued)*

```c
int
main(int argc, char **argv)
{
    int    ret = 0;
    sem_t *sem;

    CHECK_ARGS(2, "<path>");

    sem = sem_open(argv[1], 0);
    if (sem == (sem_t *)SEM_FAILED) {
        perror("sem_open");
        exit(1);
    }

    if ((ret = sem_post(sem)) < 0)
        perror("sem_post");

    sem_close(sem);

    exit(ret);
}

// sem_wait.c

#include "sem_common.h"

#define PROGNAME "sem_wait"

int
main(int argc, char **argv)
{
    int    ret = 0;
    sem_t *sem;

    CHECK_ARGS(2, "<path>");

    sem = sem_open(argv[1], 0);
    if (sem == (sem_t *)SEM_FAILED) {
        perror("sem_open");
        exit(1);
    }

    if ((ret = sem_wait(sem)) < 0)
        perror("sem_wait");

    printf("successful\n");

    sem_close(sem);

    exit(ret);
}
```

We can test the programs by using `sem_create` to create a semaphore with some initial count, say, 2. We should then be able to call `sem_wait` on that semaphore twice without blocking. The third call would block and can be unblocked by calling `sem_post` once. Finally, we can delete the semaphore using `sem_unlink`.

```
$ gcc -Wall -o sem_create sem_create.c
...
$ ./sem_create /semaphore 2
$ ./sem_create /semaphore 2
sem_open: File exists
$ ./sem_wait /semaphore
successful
$ ./sem_wait /semaphore
successful
$ ./sem_wait /semaphore        # blocks
                               # another shell prompt
                               $ ./sem_post /semaphore
successful
$ ./sem_unlink /semaphore
$ ./sem_wait /semaphore
sem_open: No such file or directory
```

Besides named POSIX semaphores, there also exist *unnamed* POSIX semaphores, which can be initialized and destroyed by calling `sem_init()` and `sem_destroy()`, respectively. These two system calls are *not* supported on Mac OS X 10.4.

> Named POSIX semaphores are implemented atop Mach semaphores, which we will discuss in Section 9.18.5.

9.13.2 POSIX Shared Memory

A named POSIX shared memory segment can be created using `shm_open()`, which is also used to open an existing segment—similar to using `sem_open()`. An existing segment can be deleted using `shm_unlink()`.

`shm_open()` returns a file descriptor that can be mapped into memory through the `mmap()` system call. Once access to the memory is no longer needed, it can be unmapped through `munmap()`, and the descriptor can be closed through `close()`. Thus, POSIX shared memory objects resemble memory-mapped files. Note that the initial size of a newly created segment is zero. A specific size can be set using `ftruncate()`. Information about an existing segment can be retrieved by calling `fstat()` on the file descriptor obtained from `shm_open()`.

Figure 9–46 shows the source for the following three simple programs, which demonstrate the working of POSIX shared memory on Mac OS X.

- `shm_create` creates a named shared memory segment and copies a given string to it.
- `shm_info` displays information about an existing segment.
- `shm_unlink` deletes an existing segment.

The programs all include a common header file (`shm_common.h`).

FIGURE 9–46 Working with POSIX shared memory

```c
// shm_common.h

#ifndef _SHM_COMMON_H_
#define _SHM_COMMON_H_

#include <stdio.h>
#include <stdlib.h>
#include <unistd.h>
#include <fcntl.h>
#include <sys/mman.h>

#define CHECK_ARGS(count, msg) {                            \
    if (argc != count) {                                    \
        fprintf(stderr, "usage: %s " msg "\n", PROGNAME);   \
        exit(1);                                            \
    }                                                       \
}
#endif

// shm_create.c

#include "shm_common.h"
#include <string.h>

#define PROGNAME "shm_create"

int
main(int argc, char **argv)
{
    char    *p;
    int     shm_fd;
    size_t  len;

    CHECK_ARGS(3, "<path> <shared string>");
```

(continues)

FIGURE 9–46 Working with POSIX shared memory *(continued)*

```
    if ((shm_fd = shm_open(argv[1], O_CREAT | O_EXCL | O_RDWR, S_IRWXU)) < 0) {
        perror("shm_open");
        exit(1);
    }

    len = strlen(argv[2]) + 1;
    ftruncate(shm_fd, len);
    if (!(p = mmap(NULL, len, PROT_READ | PROT_WRITE, MAP_SHARED, shm_fd, 0))) {
        perror("mmap");
        shm_unlink(argv[1]);
        exit(1);
    }

    // copy the user-provided data into the shared memory
    snprintf(p, len + 1, "%s", argv[2]);
    munmap(p, len);

    close(shm_fd);

    exit(0);
}

// shm_info.c

#include "shm_common.h"
#include <sys/stat.h>
#include <pwd.h>
#include <grp.h>

#define PROGNAME "shm_info"

void
print_stat_info(char *name, struct stat *sb)
{
    struct passwd *passwd;
    struct group  *group;
    char           filemode[11 + 1];

    passwd = getpwuid(sb->st_uid);
    group = getgrgid(sb->st_gid);
    strmode(sb->st_mode, filemode);

    printf("%s  ", filemode);

    if (passwd)
        printf("%s  ", passwd->pw_name);
    else
        printf("%d  ", sb->st_uid);
```

(continues)

FIGURE 9–46 Working with POSIX shared memory *(continued)*

```c
    if (group)
        printf("%s  ", group->gr_name);
    else
        printf("%d  ", sb->st_gid);

    printf("%u %s\n", (unsigned int)sb->st_size, name);
}

int
main(int argc, char **argv)
{
    char        *p;
    int          shm_fd;
    struct stat  sb;

    CHECK_ARGS(2, "<path>");

    if ((shm_fd = shm_open(argv[1], 0)) < 0) {
        perror("shm_open");
        exit(1);
    }

    if (fstat(shm_fd, &sb)) {
        perror("fstat");
        exit(1);
    }

    print_stat_info(argv[1], &sb);

    p = mmap(NULL, sb.st_size, PROT_READ, MAP_SHARED, shm_fd, 0);
    printf("Contents: %s\n", p);
    munmap(p, sb.st_size);

    close(shm_fd);

    exit(0);
}

// shm_unlink.c

#include "shm_common.h"

#define PROGNAME "shm_unlink"

int
main(int argc, char **argv)
{
    int ret = 0;
```

(continues)

FIGURE 9–46 Working with POSIX shared memory *(continued)*

```
    CHECK_ARGS(2, "<path>");

    if ((ret = shm_unlink(argv[1])))
        perror("shm_unlink");

    exit(ret);
}
```

```
$ gcc -Wall -o shm_create shm_create.c
$ gcc -Wall -o shm_info shm_info.c
$ gcc -Wall -o shm_unlink shm_unlink.c
$ ./shm_create /shm "what the world wants is character"
$ ./shm_info /shm
rwx------  amit  amit  4096 /shm
Contents: what the world wants is character
$ ./shm_unlink /shm
$ ./shm_info /shm
shm_open: No such file or directory
```

9.14 Distributed Objects

The Objective-C runtime environment provides an IPC mechanism called *Distributed Objects* that allows one application to call a remote object, which could be in another application, in a different thread in the same application, or even in an application running on another computer. In other words, Distributed Objects supports intramachine or intermachine remote messaging.

Distributed Objects makes it rather simple to make a remote object locally available, although the usual distributed computing caveats related to latency, performance, and reliability still apply. Let us look at a client-server system implemented using Distributed Objects.

In our system, the server object (DOServer) will implement the ClientProtocol Objective-C protocol, whose methods will be called by the client as follows.

- (void)helloFromClient:(id)client—The client calls this method to "say hello" to the server.
- (void)setA:(float)arg—The client calls this method to set the value of the server variable A to the given floating-point value.
- (void)setB:(float)arg—The client calls this method to set the value of the server variable B to the given floating-point value.

- (float)getSum—The client calls this method to retrieve the sum of server variables A and B.

The client object (DOClient) will implement a single method as part of the ServerProtocol Objective-C protocol. This method—whoAreYou—will be called from the server's implementation of the helloFromClient method. This is to demonstrate that both the client and the server can remotely call each other's methods.

Objective-C Protocols

An Objective-C formal protocol is a list of method declarations not attached to a class definition. The methods can be implemented by any class, which is then said to *adopt* the protocol. In a class declaration, a comma-separated list of adopted protocols can be specified within angled brackets after the superclass specification.

```
@interface class_name : superclass_name <protocol1, protocol2, ...>
```

A remote object's implementation advertises the messages it responds to in a formal Objective-C protocol. In our example, the DOClient class adopts the ServerProtocol protocol, whereas DOServer adopts the ClientProtocol protocol.

The server will create an instance of the NSConnection class for receiving client requests on a well-known (to our client) TCP port. It will then call the setRootObject method of NSConnection to attach the server object to the connection. Thereafter, the object will be available to other processes through the connection. This is referred to as *vending an object*.

> Note that although we use sockets for communication, Distributed Objects can use other communication mechanisms too, such as Mach ports. Moreover, remote messaging can be synchronous, blocking the sender until a reply is received, or it can be asynchronous, in which case no reply is desired.

The client will begin by establishing a connection to the server—again, an instance of the NSConnection class. It will then call the rootProxy method of NSConnection to retrieve the proxy for the root object of the server end of the connection. This way, the client will have a *proxy object*—an instance of the NSDistantObject class—in its address space representing the vended object in the server's address space. Thereafter, the client can send messages to the proxy object with reasonable transparency—as if it were the real object. Figure 9–47 shows the working of our client and server.

In Objective-C, a local object's methods are invoked by sending the appropriate messages to the object. In Figure 9–47, when a method of the remote object is invoked, the Objective-C message goes to the NSDistantObject instance, which renders the message static by turning it into an instance of the NSInvocation class. The latter is a container for carrying all constituents of a message—such as target, selector, arguments, return value, and data types of the arguments and the return value. The NSConnection instance encodes the NSInvocation object into a low-level, platform-independent form—NSPortMessage—that contains a local port, a remote port, a message ID, and an array of encoded data components. The encoded data is eventually transmitted across the connection. The reverse process occurs on the server: When the NSPortMessage is received by

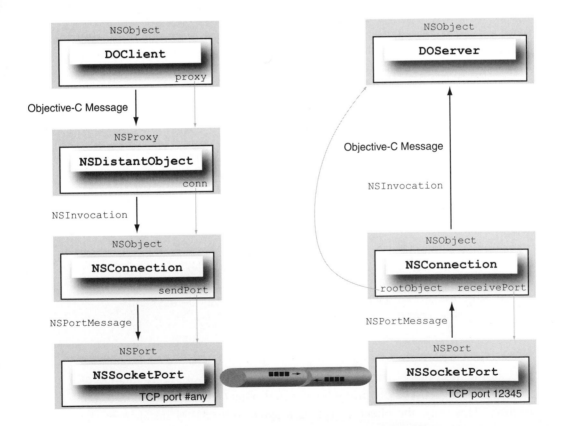

FIGURE 9–47 Communication in a Distributed Objects client-server system

the server, it is decoded and given to NSConnection as an NSPortMessage. NSConnection converts the NSPortMessage to an NSInvocation and finally sends the corresponding message, along with arguments, to the target (the vended object). This is referred to as *dispatching the NSInvocation*.

Our implementation of the client-server system consists of a common header file (do_common.h, shown in Figure 9–48), the server source (do_server.m, shown in Figure 9–49), and the client source (do_client.m, shown in Figure 9–50).

FIGURE 9–48 Common header file for the Distributed Objects client-server example

```
// do_common.h

#import <Foundation/Foundation.h>
#include <sys/socket.h>

#define DO_DEMO_PORT 12345
#define DO_DEMO_HOST "localhost"

@protocol ClientProtocol

- (void)setA:(float)arg;
- (void)setB:(float)arg;
- (float)getSum;
- (void)helloFromClient:(id)client;

@end

@protocol ServerProtocol

- (bycopy NSString *)whoAreYou;

@end
```

FIGURE 9–49 Server source for the Distributed Objects client-server example

```
// do_server.m

#import "do_common.h"

@interface DOServer : NSObject <ClientProtocol>
{
    float a;
    float b;
}
@end
```

(continues)

FIGURE 9–49 Server source for the Distributed Objects client-server example *(continued)*

```
// server

@implementation DOServer

- (id)init
{
    [super init];
    a = 0;
    b = 0;
    return self;
}

- (void)dealloc
{
    [super dealloc];
}

- (void)helloFromClient:(in byref id<ServerProtocol>)client
{
    NSLog([client whoAreYou]);
}

- (oneway void)setA:(in bycopy float)arg
{
    a = arg;
}

- (oneway void)setB:(in bycopy float)arg
{
    b = arg;
}

- (float)getSum
{
    return (float)(a + b);
}

@end

// server main program

int
main(int argc, char **argv)
{
    NSSocketPort *port;
    NSConnection *connection;
```

(continues)

FIGURE 9–49 Server source for the Distributed Objects client-server example *(continued)*

```
    NSAutoreleasePool *pool = [[NSAutoreleasePool alloc] init];
    NSRunLoop *runloop = [NSRunLoop currentRunLoop];
    DOServer *server = [[DOServer alloc] init];

NS_DURING
    port = [[NSSocketPort alloc] initWithTCPPort:DO_DEMO_PORT];
NS_HANDLER
    NSLog(@"failed to initialize TCP port.");
    exit(1);
NS_ENDHANDLER

    connection = [NSConnection connectionWithReceivePort:port sendPort:nil];
    [port release];
    // vend the object
    [connection setRootObject:server];
    [server release];
    [runloop run];
    [connection release];
    [pool release];

    exit(0);
}
```

FIGURE 9–50 Client source for the Distributed Objects client-server example

```
// do_client.m

#import "do_common.h"

@interface DOClient : NSObject <ServerProtocol>
{
    id proxy;
}

- (NSString *)whoAreYou;
- (void)cleanup;
- (void)connect;
- (void)doTest;

@end

// client

@implementation DOClient
```

(continues)

FIGURE 9–50 Client source for the Distributed Objects client-server example *(continued)*

```objc
- (void)dealloc
{
    [self cleanup];
    [super dealloc];
}


- (void)cleanup
{
    if (proxy) {
        NSConnection *connection = [proxy connectionForProxy];
        [connection invalidate];
        [proxy release];
        proxy = nil;
    }
}


- (NSString *)whoAreYou
{
    return @"I am a DO client.";
}


- (void)connect
{
    NSSocketPort *port;
    NSConnection *connection;

    port = [[NSSocketPort alloc] initRemoteWithTCPPort:DO_DEMO_PORT
                                        host:@DO_DEMO_HOST];
    connection = [NSConnection connectionWithReceivePort:nil sendPort:port];
    [connection setReplyTimeout:5];
    [connection setRequestTimeout:5];
    [port release];
NS_DURING
    proxy = [[connection rootProxy] retain];
    [proxy setProtocolForProxy:@protocol(ClientProtocol)];
    [proxy helloFromClient:self];
NS_HANDLER
    [self cleanup];
NS_ENDHANDLER
}


- (void)doTest
{
    [proxy setA:4.0];
    [proxy setB:9.0];
    float result = [proxy getSum];
    NSLog(@"%f", result);
}
```

(continues)

FIGURE 9–50 Client source for the Distributed Objects client-server example *(continued)*

```
@end

// client main program

int
main(int argc, char **argv)
{
    NSAutoreleasePool *pool = [[NSAutoreleasePool alloc] init];
    DOClient *client = [[DOClient alloc] init];
    [client connect];
    [client doTest];
    [client release];
    [pool release];

    exit(0);
}
```

Let us now test the Distributed Objects client-server system.

```
$ gcc -Wall -o do_server do_server.m -framework Foundation
$ gcc -Wall -o do_client do_client.m -framework Foundation
$ ./do_server
    # another shell prompt
    $ ./do_client
    ... do_client[4741] 13.000000
... do_server[4740] I am a DO client.
```

Note that we use the NS_DURING, NS_HANDLER, and NS_ENDHANDLER macros in our client and server implementations. These demarcate an exception-handling domain and a local exception handler. Specifically, if an exception is raised in the section of code between NS_DURING and NS_HANDLER, the section of code between NS_HANDLER and NS_ENDHANDLER is given a chance to handle the exception. Figure 9–51 shows a code excerpt with the expanded forms of these macros.

FIGURE 9–51 Exception-handling macros in the Foundation framework

```
NS_DURING      {
NS_DURING          NSHandler2 _localHandler;
NS_DURING          _NSAddHandler2(&_localHandler);
NS_DURING          if (!_NSSETJMP(_localHandler._state, 0)) {
                       // section of code
                       ...
```

(continues)

FIGURE 9–51 Exception-handling macros in the Foundation framework *(continued)*

```
NS_HANDLER              _NSRemoveHandler2(&_localHandler);
NS_HANDLER          } else {
NS_HANDLER              NSException *localException =
NS_HANDLER                  _NSExceptionObjectFromHandler2(&_localHandler);
                        // local exception-handler code
                    ...
NS_ENDHANDLER           localException = nil;
NS_ENDHANDLER       }
NS_ENDHANDLER }
```

9.15 Apple Events

Mac OS X includes a system-wide user-level IPC mechanism called *Apple Events*. An *Apple Event* is a message capable of encapsulating arbitrarily complex data and operations. The Apple Events mechanism provides the framework for transporting and dispatching these messages. Apple Events communication can be intraprocess or interprocess, including between processes on different networked computers. In general, one entity can request information or services from another entity by exchanging Apple Events.

AppleScript is the preferred scripting system on Mac OS X, providing direct control of applications and of many parts of the system. You can use the AppleScript scripting language to write programs (or AppleScripts) to automate operations and exchange data with or send commands to applications. Since AppleScript uses Apple Events to communicate with applications, the applications must be able to understand such messages and perform the requested operations—that is, the applications must be *scriptable*. The Mac OS X Cocoa and Carbon frameworks provide support for creating scriptable applications.[16] Most GUI-based Mac OS X applications support at least some basic Apple Events, such as the ones used by the Finder for launching an application and providing a list of documents for it to open.

AppleScript has a syntax similar to natural language. Consider the example shown in Figure 9–52.

---

16. Java applications, although typically not scriptable, can be made scriptable to some extent without including native code.

FIGURE 9–52 AppleScript program to speak the system version

```
-- osversion.scpt
tell application "Finder"
    -- get "raw" version
    set version_data to system attribute "sysv"

    -- get the 'r' in MN.m.r, where MN=major, m=minor, r=revision
    set revision to ((version_data mod 16) as string)

    -- get the 'm' in MN.m.r
    set version_data to version_data div 16
    set minor to ((version_data mod 16) as string)

    -- get the 'N' in MN.m.r
    set version_data to version_data div 16
    set major to ((version_data mod 16) as string)
    -- get the 'M' in MN.m.r
    set version_data to version_data div 16
    set major to ((version_data mod 16) as string) & major

    -- paste it all together
    set os_version to major & "." & minor & "." & revision
    set message to "This is Mac OSX " & os_version

    say message
    return os_version
end tell
```

Mac OS X provides a standard, extensible mechanism called the *Open Scripting Architecture* (OSA), which can be used to implement and use Apple Events–based IPC in any language.[17] AppleScript is the only OSA language provided by Apple. The osalang command-line tool lists all installed OSA languages.

```
$ osalang -l
ascr appl cgxervdh  AppleScript
scpt appl cgxervdh  Generic Scripting System
```

The first column in osalang's output is the component subtype, followed by the manufacturer, capability flags, and the language name. Each letter (unless it is the - character) in the capability flags string indicates whether a particular group of optional routines is supported. For example, c means that compilation of scripts is supported, whereas r means that recording scripts is supported. The

---

17. There exist third-party implementations for other languages such as JavaScript.

Generic Scripting System entry is a pseudo-entry that transparently supports all installed OSA scripting systems.

You can use the `osascript` command-line tool to execute AppleScripts—or scripts written in any installed OSA language. Let us run our sample script from Figure 9–52 using `osascript`.

```
$ osascript osversion.scpt
10.4.6
```

This will result in several Apple Events being sent and received. The Finder will be instructed to retrieve the Mac OS X system version, which will be stored in the `version_data` variable. A human-friendly version string and a message announcing the version will be constructed, after which the Finder will run the `say` AppleScript command to convert the announcement string to speech.

If you wish to see internals of the Apple Events generated because of running your AppleScript, you can run it with one or more AppleScript debugging environment variables set. For example, setting each of the `AEDebugVerbose`, `AEDebugReceives`, and `AEDebugSends` environment variables to 1 will print an excruciatingly detailed trace of Apple Events being sent and received.

```
$ AEDebugVerbose=1 AEDebugSends=1 AEDebugReceives=1 osascript osversion.scpt
AE2000 (2185): Sending an event:
------oo start of event oo------
{ 1 } 'aevt':  ascr/gdut (ppc ){
         return id: 143196160 (0x8890000)
     transaction id: 0 (0x0)
  interaction level: 64 (0x40)
     reply required: 1 (0x1)
             remote: 0 (0x0)
  target:
    { 2 } 'psn ':  8 bytes {
      { 0x0, 0x2 } (osascript)
    }
  optional attributes:
   < empty record >
  event data:
    { 1 } 'aevt':  - 0 items {
    }
}
...
{ 1 } 'aevt':  - 0 items {
    }
}

------oo  end of event  oo------
10.4.6
```

The AppleScript Studio application (included with Xcode) can be used to rapidly develop complex AppleScripts, including those with user-interface elements. You can also compile your textual Apple-Scripts into stand-alone application bundles.

Let us look at some more examples of using Apple Events, including how to generate and send Apple Events in C programs.

9.15.1 Tiling Application Windows Using Apple Events in AppleScript

This example is an AppleScript program called `NTerminal.scpt`, which communicates with the Mac OS X Terminal application (`Terminal.app`) and instructs it to open and tile a given number of windows. Running `NTerminal.scpt` will launch `Terminal.app` if it is not already running. Then, a given number of Terminal windows—as specified through the `desiredWindowsTotal` variable—will be opened. If there are already `desiredWindowsTotal` or more windows open, no further Terminal windows will be opened. Finally, `NTerminal.scpt` will tile `desiredWindowsTotal` windows in a grid, with `desiredWindowsPerRow` windows per row.

Note that the script is naïve—it does not handle varying window sizes that would lead to complex arrangements. Moreover, its real-life utility is superfluous, since `Terminal.app` already supports saving window arrangements in `.term` files for subsequent restoration.

Figure 9–53 shows the `NTerminal.scpt` program. You can adjust the `desiredWindowsTotal` and `desiredWindowsPerRow` parameters based on the size of the display screen.

FIGURE 9–53 AppleScript program for opening and tiling Terminal application windows

```
-- NTerminal.scpt

tell application "Terminal"

    launch

    -- Configurable parameters
    set desiredWindowsTotal to 4
    set desiredWindowsPerRow to 2
```

(continues)

FIGURE 9–53 AppleScript program for opening and tiling Terminal application windows *(continued)*

```
-- Ensure we have N Terminal windows: open new ones if there aren't enough
set i to (count windows)
repeat
    if i >= desiredWindowsTotal
        exit repeat
    end if
    do script with command "echo Terminal " & i
    set i to i + 1
end repeat

-- Adjust window positions
set i to 1
set j to 0
set { x0, y0 } to { 0, 0 }
set listOfWindows to windows

repeat
    if i > desiredWindowsTotal then
        exit repeat
    end if
    tell item i of listOfWindows
        set { x1, y1, x2, y2 } to bounds
        set newBounds to { x0, y0, x0 + x2 - x1, y0 + y2 - y1 }
        set bounds to newBounds
        set j to j + 1
        set { x1, y0, x0, y1 } to bounds
        if j = desiredWindowsPerRow then -- Move to the next row
            set x0 to 0
            set y0 to y1
            set j to 0
        end if
    end tell
    set i to i + 1
end repeat
end tell
```

9.15.2 Building and Sending an Apple Event in a C Program

In this example, we "manually" craft and send Apple Events to the Finder. We will send two types of events: one that will cause the Finder to open the given document using the preferred application for the document's type and another that will cause the Finder to reveal the given document in a Finder window.

We will use the `AEBuild` family of functions to construct in-memory Apple Event structures, which can be sent to other applications through the `AESend()` function. While constructing Apple Events using the `AEBuild` functions, we use an event description language that employs C-style formatting strings to describe events. The `AEBuild` functions parse the programmer-provided strings to yield event descriptors, simplifying an otherwise painful process wherein we would have to construct such event descriptors incrementally.

An event descriptor record is an arbitrarily ordered group of name-value pairs, where each name is a four-letter type code, and the corresponding value is a valid descriptor. The name and value within a name-value pair are separated by a colon, whereas multiple name-value pairs are separated by commas.

Let us compile and run the program shown in Figure 9–54.

FIGURE 9–54 Sending Apple Events to the Finder from a C program

```
// AEFinderEvents.c

#include <Carbon/Carbon.h>

OSStatus
AEFinderEventBuildAndSend(const char    *path,
                          AEEventClass  eventClass,
                          AEEventID     eventID)
{
    OSStatus     err = noErr;
    FSRef        fsRef;
    AliasHandle  fsAlias;
    AppleEvent   eventToSend = { typeNull, nil };
    AppleEvent   eventReply  = { typeNull, nil };
    AEBuildError eventBuildError;
    const OSType finderSignature = 'MACS';

    if ((err = FSPathMakeRef((unsigned char *)path, &fsRef, NULL)) != noErr) {
        fprintf(stderr, "Failed to get FSRef from path (%s)\n", path);
        return err;
    }

    if ((err = FSNewAliasMinimal(&fsRef, &fsAlias)) != noErr) {
        fprintf(stderr, "Failed to create alias for path (%s)\n", path);
        return err;
    }

    err = AEBuildAppleEvent(
            eventClass,            // Event class for the resulting event
            eventID,               // Event ID for the resulting event
```

(continues)

FIGURE 9–54 Sending Apple Events to the Finder from a C program *(continued)*

```
                typeApplSignature,        // Address type for next two parameters
                &finderSignature,         // Finder signature (pointer to address)
                sizeof(OSType),           // Size of Finder signature
                kAutoGenerateReturnID,    // Return ID for the created event
                kAnyTransactionID,        // Transaction ID for this event
                &eventToSend,             // Pointer to location for storing result
                &eventBuildError,         // Pointer to error structure
                "'----':alis(@@)",        // AEBuild format string describing the
                                          // AppleEvent record to be created

            fsAlias
        );
    if (err != noErr) {
        fprintf(stderr, "Failed to build Apple Event (error %d)\n", (int)err);
        return err;
    }


    err = AESend(&eventToSend,
                &eventReply,
                kAEWaitReply,         // Send mode (wait for reply)
                kAENormalPriority,
                kNoTimeOut,
                nil,                  // No pointer to idle function
                nil);                 // No pointer to filter function


    if (err != noErr)
        fprintf(stderr, "Failed to send Apple Event (error %d)\n", (int)err);

    // Dispose of the send/reply descs
    AEDisposeDesc(&eventToSend);
    AEDisposeDesc(&eventReply);


    return err;
}


int
main(int argc, char **argv)
{
    switch (argc) {
    case 2:
        (void)AEFinderEventBuildAndSend(argv[1], kCoreEventClass,
                                        kAEOpenDocuments);
        break;

    case 3:
        (void)AEFinderEventBuildAndSend(argv[2], kAEMiscStandards,
                                        kAEMakeObjectsVisible);
        break;
```

(continues)

FIGURE 9–54 Sending Apple Events to the Finder from a C program *(continued)*

```
default:
    fprintf(stderr, "usage: %s [-r] <path>\n", argv[0]);
    exit(1);
    break;
}

exit(0);
}
```

When run with only the pathname to a file or directory, the program will cause the Finder to open that file system object—similar to using the /usr/bin/open command. A file will be opened with the preferred application for that file type, whereas a directory will be opened by virtue of its contents being shown in a new Finder window. When the -r option is provided to the program, it will reveal the file system object—that is, a file or directory will be shown in a Finder window with the corresponding icon selected. Note that a directory's contents will not be shown in this case.

```
$ gcc -Wall -o AEFinderEvents AEFinderEvents.c -framework Carbon
$ ./AEFinderEvents -r /tmp/
...
$ echo hello > /tmp/file.txt
$ ./AEFinderEvents /tmp/file.txt
...
```

> The open command is built atop the AppKit framework's NSWorkspace class, which in turn uses the Launch Services framework.

9.15.3 Causing the System to Sleep by Sending an Apple Event

In this example, we will create and send a kAESleep Apple Event to the *system process*, causing the system to go to sleep. The loginwindow program is the system process, although we do not refer to the system process by name or process ID in our program—we use the special process serial number { 0, kSystemProcess } to specify the target of the Apple Event.

```
// sleeper.c

#include <Carbon/Carbon.h>

int
main(void)
```

```
{
    OSStatus            osErr = noErr;
    AEAddressDesc       target;
    ProcessSerialNumber systemProcessPSN;
    AppleEvent          eventToSend, eventToReceive;

    // Initialize some data structures
    eventToSend.descriptorType    = 0;
    eventToSend.dataHandle        = NULL;
    eventToReceive.descriptorType = 0;
    eventToReceive.dataHandle     = NULL;
    systemProcessPSN.highLongOfPSN = 0;
    systemProcessPSN.lowLongOfPSN  = kSystemProcess;

    // Create a new descriptor record for target
    osErr = AECreateDesc(typeProcessSerialNumber,  // descriptor type
                         &systemProcessPSN,         // data for new descriptor
                         sizeof(systemProcessPSN),  // length in bytes
                         &target);                  // new descriptor returned
    if (osErr != noErr) {
        fprintf(stderr, "*** failed to create descriptor for target\n");
        exit(osErr);
    }

    // Create a new Apple Event that we will send
    osErr = AECreateAppleEvent(
                kCoreEventClass,        // class of Apple Event
                kAESleep,               // event ID
                &target,                // target for event
                kAutoGenerateReturnID,  // use auto ID unique to current session
                kAnyTransactionID,      // we are not doing an event sequence
                &eventToSend);          // pointer for result
    if (osErr != noErr) {
        fprintf(stderr, "*** failed to create new Apple Event\n");
        exit(osErr);
    }

    // Send the Apple Event
    osErr = AESend(&eventToSend,
                   &eventToReceive,     // reply
                   kAENoReply,          // send mode
                   kAENormalPriority,   // send priority
                   kAEDefaultTimeout,   // timeout in ticks
                   NULL,                // idle function pointer
                   NULL);               // filter function pointer
    if (osErr != noErr) {
        fprintf(stderr, "*** failed to send Apple Event\n");
        exit(osErr);
    }

    // Deallocate memory used by the descriptor
    AEDisposeDesc(&eventToReceive);
```

```
    exit(0);
}
```

```
$ gcc -Wall -o sleeper sleeper.c -framework Carbon
$ ./sleeper # make sure you mean to do this!
```

9.16 Notifications

In simple terms, a notification is a message sent by one entity to another to inform the latter of an event's occurrence. The following are some general aspects of notifications and notification mechanisms in the context of Mac OS X.

- Notifications can be intraprocess, interprocess, or even between the kernel and a user process. A single notification can also be broadcast to multiple parties. Mac OS X provides several user-level and kernel-level notification mechanisms.

- There are several ways notification messages can be transmitted, for example, using Mach IPC, signals, shared memory, and so on. A single notification API may offer multiple delivery mechanisms.

- In a typical interprocess notification mechanism, one party programmatically registers a request with a (usually) centralized notification broker. The registration includes details of the types of events the caller is interested in knowing about. Mac OS X frameworks refer to such an interested party as an *observer*.

- A notification may be generated because an event of interest occurred, or it may be programmatically posted (fabricated) by a *poster*. Depending on program logic, the observer and poster may be the same process.

Let us look at some important notification mechanisms in Mac OS X. Some of these are general-purpose notification mechanisms, allowing programs to exchange arbitrary information, whereas others are special-purpose mechanisms that support only specific types of notifications.

9.16.1 Foundation Notifications

The Foundation framework provides the `NSNotificationCenter` and `NSDistributedNotificationCenter` classes for intraprocess and interprocess notifications, respectively. Both these classes use the abstraction of a notification broker—the *notification center*. The default notification center for either class can be accessed through the `defaultCenter` class method.

Each process has a default process-local NSNotificationCenter object that is automatically created. The class provides instance methods for adding observers, removing observers, and posting notifications. A single notification is represented as an NSNotification object, which consists of a name, an object, and an optional dictionary that can contain arbitrary associated data.

The NSDistributedNotificationCenter class is similar in concept and provides similar methods. Since its scope is system-wide, it requires a different broker—the distributed notification daemon (/usr/sbin/distnoted) provides the relevant services. distnoted is automatically started during system bootstrap.

Let us look at an example of using distributed notifications in an Objective-C program. The example consists of two programs: an observer and a poster. The poster takes a name-value pair of strings and calls the postNotificationName:object: selector. The latter creates an NSNotification object, associates the given name and value with it, and posts it to the distributed notification center. Figure 9–55 shows the source for the poster.

FIGURE 9–55 A program for posting distributed notifications (NSNotification)

// NSNotificationPoster.m

```
#import <AppKit/AppKit.h>

#define PROGNAME "NSNotificationPoster"

int
main(int argc, char **argv)
{
    if (argc != 3) {
        fprintf(stderr, "usage: %s <some name> <some value>\n", PROGNAME);
        exit(1);
    }

    NSAutoreleasePool *pool = [[NSAutoreleasePool alloc] init];

    NSString *someName = [NSString stringWithCString:argv[1]
                                       encoding:NSASCIIStringEncoding];
    NSString *someValue = [NSString stringWithCString:argv[2]
                                        encoding:NSASCIIStringEncoding];

    NSNotificationCenter *dnc = [NSDistributedNotificationCenter defaultCenter];
    [dnc postNotificationName:someName object:someValue];

    [pool release];

    exit(0);
}
```

The observer communicates with the distributed notification center to register its interest in all distributed notifications, after which it simply runs in a loop, printing the name and value of each notification as it arrives. Figure 9–56 shows the source for the observer.

FIGURE 9–56 A program for observing distributed notifications (NSNotification)

```
// NSNotificationObserver.m

#import <AppKit/AppKit.h>

@interface DummyNotificationHandler : NSObject
{
    NSNotificationCenter *dnc;
}

- (void)defaultNotificationHandler:(NSNotification *)notification;

@end

@implementation DummyNotificationHandler

- (id)init
{
    [super init];
    dnc = [NSDistributedNotificationCenter defaultCenter];
    [dnc addObserver:self
            selector:@selector(defaultNotificationHandler:)
                name:nil
              object:nil];
    return self;
}

- (void)dealloc
{
    [dnc removeObserver:self name:nil object:nil];
    [super dealloc];
}

- (void)defaultNotificationHandler:(NSNotification *)notification
{
    NSLog(@"name=%@ value=%@", [notification name], [notification object]);
}

@end

int
main(int argc, char **argv)
```

(continues)

FIGURE 9–56 A program for observing distributed notifications (NSNotification)
(continued)

```
{
    NSAutoreleasePool *pool = [[NSAutoreleasePool alloc] init];
    NSRunLoop *runloop = [NSRunLoop currentRunLoop];
    [[DummyNotificationHandler alloc] init];
    [runloop run];
    [pool release];
    exit(0);
}
```

Let us test the programs by first running the observer and then posting a few notifications through the poster.

```
$ gcc -Wall -o observer NSNotificationObserver.m -framework Foundation
$ gcc -Wall -o poster NSNotificationPoster.m -framework Foundation
$ ./observer
    # another shell prompt
    $ ./poster system mach
2005-09-17 20:39:10.093 observer[4284] name=system value=mach
```

> Note that since the observer program specified the notification name and identifying object as nil while adding the DummyNotification-Handler class instance as an observer, it will receive all other system-wide notifications that distnoted broadcasts.

9.16.2 The notify(3) API

Mac OS X provides a stateless, system-wide notification system whose services are available to user programs through the notify(3) API. The mechanism is implemented as a client-server system. The notification server (/usr/sbin/notifyd) provides a system-wide notification center. It is one of the daemons started during a normal bootstrap of the system. The client API, which is implemented as part of the system library, uses Mach IPC to communicate with the server.

A notify(3) notification is associated with a null-terminated, UTF-8-encoded string name in a namespace shared system-wide by all clients of the system. Although a notification name can be arbitrary, Apple recommends using reverse DNS naming conventions. The names prefixed by com.apple. are reserved for Apple's use, whereas the names prefixed by self. should be used by a program for process-local notifications.

A client can post a notification for a given name by calling the `notify_post()` function, which takes a single argument: the notification's name.

A client can monitor a given name for notifications. Moreover, the client can specify the mechanism through which the system should deliver the notification to the client. Supported delivery mechanisms are as follows: sending a specified *signal*, writing to a *file descriptor*, sending a message to a *Mach port*, and updating a *shared memory* location. Clients can register for these mechanisms by calling `notify_register_signal()`, `notify_register_file_descriptor()`, `notify_register_mach_port()`, and `notify_register_check()`, respectively. Each registration function provides the caller with a token and, if necessary, a mechanism-specific object such as a Mach port or a file descriptor, which the client will use to receive the notification. The token can be used with the `notify_check()` call to check whether any notifications have been posted for the associated name. It is also used with the `notify_cancel()` call to cancel the notification and free any associated resources.

Let us look at an example of posting and receiving notifications using the `notify(3)` API. Figure 9–57 shows a common header file in which we define names for our notifications. We use a common prefix, followed by one of `descriptor`, `mach_port`, or `signal`, indicating the delivery mechanism we will specify when registering for each name.

FIGURE 9–57 Common header file for defining notification names

```
// notify_common.h

#ifndef _NOTIFY_COMMON_H_
#define _NOTIFY_COMMON_H_

#include <stdio.h>
#include <unistd.h>
#include <stdlib.h>
#include <notify.h>

#define PREFIX "com.osxbook.notification."
#define NOTIFICATION_BY_FILE_DESCRIPTOR PREFIX "descriptor"
#define NOTIFICATION_BY_MACH_PORT       PREFIX "mach_port"
#define NOTIFICATION_BY_SIGNAL          PREFIX "signal"

#define NOTIFICATION_CANCEL             PREFIX "cancel"

#endif
```

Figure 9–58 shows the program we will use to post notifications. Note that posting is independent of the delivery mechanism—you always use `notify_post()` to explicitly post a notification, regardless of how it is delivered.

FIGURE 9–58 Program for posting `notify(3)` notifications

```
// notify_producer.c

#include "notify_common.h"

#define PROGNAME "notify_producer"

int
usage(void)
{
    fprintf(stderr, "usage: %s -c|-f|-p|-s\n", PROGNAME);
    return 1;
}

int
main(int argc, char **argv)
{
    int   ch, options = 0;
    char *name;

    if (argc != 2)
        return usage();

    while ((ch = getopt(argc, argv, "cfps")) != -1) {
        switch (ch) {
        case 'c':
            name = NOTIFICATION_CANCEL;
            break;
        case 'f':
            name = NOTIFICATION_BY_FILE_DESCRIPTOR;
            break;
        case 'p':
            name = NOTIFICATION_BY_MACH_PORT;
            break;
        case 's':
            name = NOTIFICATION_BY_SIGNAL;
            break;
        default:
            return usage();
            break;
        }
        options++;
    }
```

(continues)

```
    if (options == 1)
        return (int)notify_post(name);
    else
        return usage();
}
```

Let us now write the consumer program for receiving notifications produced by the program in Figure 9–58. We will register for four specific notifications, one to be delivered through a signal, another to be delivered through a file descriptor, and two to be delivered through Mach messages. One of the latter will be used as a cancellation trigger—it will cause the program to cancel all registrations and exit. Figure 9–59 shows the consumer program.

FIGURE 9–59 Receiving notifications through multiple mechanisms

```
// notify_consumer.c

#include "notify_common.h"
#include <pthread.h>
#include <mach/mach.h>
#include <signal.h>

void sighandler_USR1(int s);
void cancel_all_notifications(void);
static int token_fd = -1, token_mach_port = -1, token_signal = -1;
static int token_mach_port_cancel = -1;

void *
consumer_file_descriptor(void *arg)
{
    int      status;
    int fd, check;

    status = notify_register_file_descriptor(NOTIFICATION_BY_FILE_DESCRIPTOR,
                                             &fd, 0, &token_fd);
    if (status != NOTIFY_STATUS_OK) {
        perror("notify_register_file_descriptor");
        return (void *)status;
    }

    while (1) {
        if ((status = read(fd, &check, sizeof(check))) < 0)
            return (void *)status; // perhaps the notification was canceled
        if (check == token_fd)
            printf("file descriptor: received notification\n");
```

(continues)

FIGURE 9–59 Receiving notifications through multiple mechanisms *(continued)*

```
        else
            printf("file descriptor: spurious notification?\n");
    }

    return (void *)0;
}

void *
consumer_mach_port(void *arg)
{
    int             status;
    kern_return_t   kr;
    mach_msg_header_t msg;
    mach_port_t     notify_port;

    status = notify_register_mach_port(NOTIFICATION_BY_MACH_PORT, &notify_port,
                                    0, &token_mach_port);
    if (status != NOTIFY_STATUS_OK) {
        perror("notify_register_mach_port");
        return (void *)status;
    }

    // to support cancellation of all notifications and exiting, we register
    // a second notification here, but reuse the Mach port allocated above
    status = notify_register_mach_port(NOTIFICATION_CANCEL, &notify_port,
                                    NOTIFY_REUSE, &token_mach_port_cancel);
    if (status != NOTIFY_STATUS_OK) {
        perror("notify_register_mach_port");
        mach_port_deallocate(mach_task_self(), notify_port);
        return (void *)status;
    }

    while (1) {
        kr = mach_msg(&msg,                     // message buffer
                    MACH_RCV_MSG,               // option
                    0,                          // send size
                    MACH_MSG_SIZE_MAX,          // receive limit
                    notify_port,                // receive name
                    MACH_MSG_TIMEOUT_NONE,      // timeout
                    MACH_PORT_NULL);            // cancel/receive notification
        if (kr != MACH_MSG_SUCCESS)
            mach_error("mach_msg(MACH_RCV_MSG)", kr);

        if (msg.msgh_id == token_mach_port)
            printf("Mach port: received notification\n");
        else if (msg.msgh_id == token_mach_port_cancel) {
            cancel_all_notifications();
```

(continues)

FIGURE 9–59 Receiving notifications through multiple mechanisms *(continued)*

```
            printf("canceling all notifications and exiting\n");
            exit(0);
        } else
            printf("Mach port: spurious notification?\n");
    }

    return (void *)0;
}

void
sighandler_USR1(int s)
{
    int status, check;

    status = notify_check(token_signal, &check);
    if ((status == NOTIFY_STATUS_OK) && (check != 0))
        printf("signal: received notification\n");
    else
        printf("signal: spurious signal?\n");
}

void *
consumer_signal(void *arg)
{
    int status, check;

    // set up signal handler
    signal(SIGUSR1, sighandler_USR1);

    status = notify_register_signal(NOTIFICATION_BY_SIGNAL, SIGUSR1,
                                    &token_signal);
    if (status != NOTIFY_STATUS_OK) {
        perror("notify_register_signal");
        return (void *)status;
    }

    // since notify_check() always sets check to 'true' when it is called for
    // the first time, we make a dummy call here
    (void)notify_check(token_signal, &check);

    while (1) {
        // just sleep for a day
        sleep(86400);
    }

    return (void *)0;
}
```

(continues)

FIGURE 9–59 Receiving notifications through multiple mechanisms *(continued)*

```
void
cancel_all_notifications(void)
{
    if (token_fd != -1)
        notify_cancel(token_fd);
    if (token_mach_port != -1)
        notify_cancel(token_mach_port);
    if (token_signal != -1)
        notify_cancel(token_signal);
}

int
main(int argc, char **argv)
{
    int ret;
    pthread_t pthread_fd, pthread_mach_port;

    if ((ret = pthread_create(&pthread_fd, (const pthread_attr_t *)0,
                            consumer_file_descriptor, (void *)0)))

        goto out;

    if ((ret = pthread_create(&pthread_mach_port, (const pthread_attr_t *)0,
                            consumer_mach_port, (void *)0)))

        goto out;

    if (consumer_signal((void *)0) != (void *)0)
        goto out;

out:
    cancel_all_notifications();

    return 0;
}
```

```
$ gcc -Wall -o notify_consumer notify_consumer.c
$ gcc -Wall -o notify_producer notify_producer.c
$ ./notification_consumer
    # another shell prompt
    $ ./notify_producer -f
file descriptor: received notification
    $ ./notify_producer -p
Mach port: received notification
    $ ./notify_producer -s
signal: received notification
    $ killall -USR1 notify_consumer
signal: spurious signal?
    $ ./notify_producer -c
canceling all notifications and exiting
$
```

Once you have a token after registering for a notification, you can also use the token to monitor a file pathname by calling `notify_monitor_file()`, whose arguments include a token and a pathname. Thereafter, in addition to notifications explicitly posted through `notify_post()`, the system will deliver a notification each time the pathname is modified. Note that the pathname does not have to exist when you call `notify_monitor_file()`—if it doesn't exist, the first notification will correspond to the file's creation. We can add the code shown in Figure 9–60 (the highlighted portion) to the `consumer_mach_port()` function in Figure 9–59 to make the program exit whenever a given path—say, `/tmp/notify.cancel`—is modified.

FIGURE 9–60 Monitoring a file through `notify(3)`

```
void *
consumer_mach_port(void *arg)
{
    ...
    status = notify_register_mach_port(NOTIFICATION_CANCEL, &notify_port,
                                       NOTIFY_REUSE, &token_mach_port_cancel);
    if (status != NOTIFY_STATUS_OK) {
        perror("notify_register_mach_port");
        mach_port_deallocate(mach_task_self(), notify_port);
        return (void *)status;
    }

    status = notify_monitor_file(token_mach_port_cancel, "/tmp/notify.cancel");
    if (status != NOTIFY_STATUS_OK) {
        perror("notify_monitor_file");
        mach_port_deallocate(mach_task_self(), notify_port);
        return (void *)status;
    }

    while (1) {
        ...
    }
    ...
}
```

9.16.3 Kernel Event Notification Mechanism (`kqueue(2)`)

Mac OS X provides a FreeBSD-derived mechanism called *kqueue* for kernel event notification. The mechanism gets its name from the `kqueue` data structure (`struct kqueue` [`bsd/sys/eventvar.h`]), which represents a kernel queue of events.

A program uses this mechanism through the kqueue() and kevent() system calls. kqueue() creates a new kernel event queue and returns a file descriptor. Specific operations performed by kqueue() in the kernel include the following:

- Create a new open file structure (struct fileproc [bsd/sys/file_internal.h]) and allocate a file descriptor, which the calling process uses to refer to the open file.

- Allocate and initialize a kqueue data structure (struct kqueue [bsd/sys/eventvar.h]).

- Set the file structure's f_flag field to (FREAD | FWRITE) to specify that the file is open for both reading and writing.

- Set the file structure's f_type (descriptor type) field to DTYPE_KQUEUE to specify that the descriptor references a kqueue.

- Set the file structure's f_ops field (file operations table) to point to the kqueueops global structure variable [bsd/kern/kern_event.c].

- Set the file structure's f_data field (private data) to point to the newly allocated kqueue structure.

kevent() is used both for registering events with a kernel queue (given the corresponding descriptor) and for retrieving any pending events. An event is represented by a kevent structure [bsd/sys/event.h].

```
struct kevent {
    uintptr_t  ident;   // identifier for this event
    short      filter;  // filter for event
    u_short    flags;   // action flags for kqueue
    u_int      fflags;  // filter flag value
    intptr_t   data;    // filter data value
    void       *udata;  // opaque user data identifier
};
```

> Kernel events are generated by various parts of the kernel calling kqueue functions to add *kernel notes* (struct knote [bsd/sys/event.h]). The proc structure's p_klist field is a list of attached kernel notes.

A caller can populate a kevent structure and invoke kevent() to request to be notified when that event occurs. The kevent structure's filter field specifies the kernel filter to be used to process the event. The ident field is interpreted by the kernel based on the filter. For example, the filter can be EVFILT_

PROC, which means the caller is interested in process-related events, such as the process exiting or forking. In this case, the `ident` field specifies a process ID. Table 9–9 shows the system-defined filters and corresponding identifier types.

TABLE 9–9 Kqueue Filters

Filter	Identifier	Examples of Events
EVFILT_FS	—	File system being mounted or unmounted, NFS server not responding, free space falling below the minimum threshold on an HFS Plus file system
EVFILT_PROC	A process ID	Process performing a fork, exec, or exit operation
EVFILT_READ	A file descriptor	Data available to read
EVFILT_SIGNAL	A signal number	Specified signal delivered to the process
EVFILT_TIMER	An interval	Timer expired
EVFILT_VNODE	A file descriptor	Vnode operations such as deletion, rename, content change, attribute change, link count change, and so on
EVFILT_WRITE	A file descriptor	Possibility of data to be written

The `flags` field specifies one or more actions to perform, such as adding the specified event to the kqueue (EV_ADD) or removing the event from the kqueue (EV_DELETE). The `fflags` field is used to specify one or more filter-specific events that should be monitored. For example, if the exit and fork operations are to be monitored for a process using the EVFILT_PROC filter, the `fflags` field should contain the bitwise OR of NOTE_EXIT and NOTE_FORK.

The `data` field contains filter-specific data, if any. For example, for the EVFILT_SIGNAL filter, data will contain the number of times the signal has occurred since the last call to kevent().

The `udata` field optionally contains user-defined data that is not interpreted by the kernel.

The EV_SET macro can be used to populate a `kevent` structure.

Figure 9–61 shows a program that uses the EVFILT_VNODE filter to watch for events on a given file.

FIGURE 9–61 Using the `kqueue()` and `kevent()` system calls to watch for file events

```
// kq_fwatch.c

#include <stdio.h>
#include <stdlib.h>
#include <sys/fcntl.h>
#include <sys/event.h>
#include <unistd.h>

#define PROGNAME "kq_fwatch"

typedef struct {
    u_int        event;
    const char *description;
} VnEventDescriptions_t;

VnEventDescriptions_t VnEventDescriptions[] = {
    { NOTE_ATTRIB, "attributes changed"                    },
    { NOTE_DELETE, "deleted"                               },
    { NOTE_EXTEND, "extended"                              },
    { NOTE_LINK,   "link count changed"                    },
    { NOTE_RENAME, "renamed"                               },
    { NOTE_REVOKE, "access revoked or file system unmounted" },
    { NOTE_WRITE,  "written"                               },
};
#define N_EVENTS (sizeof(VnEventDescriptions)/sizeof(VnEventDescriptions_t))

int
process_events(struct kevent *kl)
{
    int i, ret = 0;

    for (i = 0; i < N_EVENTS; i++)
        if (VnEventDescriptions[i].event & kl->fflags)
            printf("%s\n", VnEventDescriptions[i].description);

    if (kl->fflags & NOTE_DELETE) // stop when the file is gone
        ret = -1;

    return ret;
}

int
main(int argc, char **argv)
{
    int fd, ret = -1, kqfd = -1;
    struct kevent changelist;

    if (argc != 2) {
        fprintf(stderr, "usage: %s <file to watch>\n", PROGNAME);
        exit(1);
    }
```

(continues)

FIGURE 9–61 Using the `kqueue()` and `kevent()` system calls to watch for file events
(continued)

```
    // create a new kernel event queue (not inherited across fork())
    if ((kqfd = kqueue()) < 0) {
        perror("kqueue");
        exit(1);
    }

    if ((fd = open(argv[1], O_RDONLY)) < 0) {
        perror("open");
        exit(1);
    }

#define NOTE_ALL NOTE_ATTRIB |\
                 NOTE_DELETE |\
                 NOTE_EXTEND |\
                 NOTE_LINK   |\
                 NOTE_RENAME |\
                 NOTE_REVOKE |\
                 NOTE_WRITE
    EV_SET(&changelist, fd, EVFILT_VNODE, EV_ADD | EV_CLEAR, NOTE_ALL, 0, NULL);
    // the following kevent() call is for registering events
    ret = kevent(kqfd,         // kqueue file descriptor
                 &changelist,  // array of kevent structures
                 1,            // number of entries in the changelist array
                 NULL,         // array of kevent structures (for receiving)
                 0,            // number of entries in the above array
                 NULL);        // timeout
    if (ret < 0) {
        perror("kqueue");
        goto out;
    }

    do {
        // the following kevent() call is for receiving events
        // we recycle the changelist from the previous call
        if ((ret = kevent(kqfd, NULL, 0, &changelist, 1, NULL)) == -1) {
            perror("kevent");
            goto out;
        }

        // kevent() returns the number of events placed in the receive list
        if (ret != 0)
            ret = process_events(&changelist);

    } while (!ret);

out:
    if (kqfd >= 0)
        close(kqfd);
```

(continues)

FIGURE 9–61 Using the `kqueue()` and `kevent()` system calls to watch for file events *(continued)*

```
    exit(ret);
}


$ gcc -Wall -o kq_fwatch kq_fwatch.c
$ touch /tmp/file.txt
$ ./kq_fwatch /tmp/file.txt
        # another shell prompt
        $ touch /tmp/file.txt
attributes changed
        $ echo hello > /tmp/file.txt
attributes changed
written
        $ sync /tmp/file.txt
attributes changed
        $ ln /tmp/file.txt /tmp/file2.txt
attributes changed
link count changed
        $ rm /tmp/file2.txt
deleted
```

> The Finder uses the kqueue mechanism to learn about changes made to a directory that is being displayed in a Finder window, with the Desktop being a special case of a Finder window. This allows the Finder to update the directory's view.

9.16.4 Core Foundation Notifications

Core Foundation notifications are discussed in Section 9.17.1. We mention them here for completeness.

9.16.5 Fsevents

Mac OS X 10.4 introduced an in-kernel notification mechanism called *fsevents* that can inform user-space subscribers of volume-level file system changes as they occur. The Spotlight search system uses this mechanism. We will discuss fsevents in Chapter 11.

9.16.6 Kauth

Kauth (kernel authorization) is a kernel subsystem introduced in Mac OS X 10.4 that provides a kernel programming interface (KPI) using which loadable kernel code can participate in authorization decisions in the kernel. It can also be used as a notification mechanism. We will discuss kauth in Chapter 11.

9.17 Core Foundation IPC

Core Foundation is an important Mac OS X framework that provides fundamental data types and several essential services, including a variety of IPC mechanisms.

9.17.1 Notifications

The Core Foundation (CF) framework provides the `CFNotificationCenter` data type, which, along with its associated functions, can be used for sending and receiving intraprocess and interprocess notifications. A CF notification is a message consisting of the following three elements:

- A notification name (a `CFStringRef`), which must be non-NULL.
- An object identifier, which can either be NULL or point to a value that identifies the object that posted the notification. For distributed (interprocess) notifications, the identifier must be a string (a `CFStringRef`).
- A dictionary, which can either be NULL or contain arbitrary information that further describes the notification. For distributed notifications, the dictionary can contain only property list objects.

The CF notification API supports the following three types of notification centers (a process can have at most one of each type): *local center*, *distributed center*, and *Darwin notify center*. The local center is process-local, and the other two are for distributed notifications. The distributed center provides access to `distnoted` (see Section 9.16.1), whereas the Darwin notify center provides access to `notifyd` (see Section 9.16.2). A reference to any of these centers is obtained by calling the appropriate `CFNotificationCenterGet*` function, which returns a `CFNotificationCenterRef` data type.

```
// distributed notification center (/usr/sbin/notifyd)
CFNotificationCenterRef CFNotificationCenterGetDarwinNotifyCenter(void);
```

```
// distributed notification center (/usr/sbin/distnoted)
CFNotificationCenterRef CFNotificationCenterGetDistributedCenter(void);

// process-local notification center
CFNotificationCenterRef CFNotificationCenterGetLocalCenter(void);
```

Once you have a reference to a notification center, you can add an observer, remove an observer, or post notifications. The same set of functions is used to perform these operations regardless of the notification center type. Figure 9–62 shows a program that posts notifications to the distributed center.

FIGURE 9–62 A program for posting Core Foundation distributed notifications

```
// CFNotificationPoster.c

#include <CoreFoundation/CoreFoundation.h>

#define PROGNAME "cfposter"

int
main(int argc, char **argv)
{
    CFStringRef             name, object;
    CFNotificationCenterRef distributedCenter;
    CFStringEncoding        encoding = kCFStringEncodingASCII;

    if (argc != 3) {
        fprintf(stderr, "usage: %s <name string> <value string>\n", PROGNAME);
        exit(1);
    }

    name = CFStringCreateWithCString(kCFAllocatorDefault, argv[1], encoding);
    object = CFStringCreateWithCString(kCFAllocatorDefault, argv[2], encoding);

    distributedCenter = CFNotificationCenterGetDistributedCenter();
    CFNotificationCenterPostNotification(
        distributedCenter, // the notification center to use
        name,              // name of the notification to post
        object,            // optional object identifier
        NULL,              // optional dictionary of "user" information
        false);            // deliver immediately (if true) or respect the
                           // suspension behaviors of observers (if false)

    CFRelease(name);
    CFRelease(object);

    exit(0);
}
```

Figure 9–63 shows a program that registers an observer of all distributed notifications, after which it runs in a loop, printing information about each received notification. When it receives a notification named `cancel`, it removes the observer and terminates the loop. Note that the observer program uses the concept of a *run loop*, which is discussed in Section 9.17.2.

FIGURE 9–63 A program for observing Core Foundation distributed notifications

```c
// CFNotificationObserver.c

#include <CoreFoundation/CoreFoundation.h>

void
genericCallback(CFNotificationCenterRef  center,
                void                     *observer,
                CFStringRef               name,
                const void               *object,
                CFDictionaryRef           userInfo)
{
    if (!CFStringCompare(name, CFSTR("cancel"), kCFCompareCaseInsensitive)) {
        CFNotificationCenterRemoveObserver(center, observer, NULL, NULL);
        CFRunLoopStop(CFRunLoopGetCurrent());
    }

    printf("Received notification ==>\n");
    CFShow(center), CFShow(name), CFShow(object), CFShow(userInfo);
}

int
main(void)
{
    CFNotificationCenterRef distributedCenter;
    CFStringRef             observer = CFSTR("A CF Observer");

    distributedCenter = CFNotificationCenterGetDistributedCenter();
    CFNotificationCenterAddObserver(
        distributedCenter, // the notification center to use
        observer,          // an arbitrary observer-identifier
        genericCallback,   // callback to call when a notification is posted
        NULL,              // optional notification name to filter notifications
        NULL,              // optional object identifier to filter notifications
        CFNotificationSuspensionBehaviorDrop); // suspension behavior

    CFRunLoopRun();

    // not reached
    exit(0);
}
```

Let us now test the poster and observer programs from Figures 9–62 and 9–63, respectively.

```
$ gcc -Wall -o cfposter CFNotificationPoster.c -framework CoreFoundation
$ gcc -Wall -o cfobserver CFNotificationObserver.c -framework CoreFoundation
$ ./cfobserver
        # another shell prompt
        $ ./cfposter system mach
Received notification ==>
<CFNotificationCenter 0x300980 [0xa0728150]>
system
mach
(null)
        $ ./cfposter cancel junk
Received notification ==>
<CFNotificationCenter 0x300980 [0xa0728150]>
cancel
junk
(null)
$
```

As we noted in Section 9.16.1, an observer of all distributed notifications will receive notifications from other posters. If you let the cfobserver program run for some time, you will see a variety of notifications being sent by different parts of the operating system.

```
...
Received notification ==>
<CFNotificationCenter 0x300980 [0xa0728150]>
com.apple.carbon.core.DirectoryNotification
/.vol/234881027/244950
(null)
...
Received notification ==>
<CFNotificationCenter 0x300980 [0xa0728150]>
com.apple.screensaver.willstop
(null)
(null)
...
Received notification ==>
<CFNotificationCenter 0x300980 [0xa0728150]>
com.apple.Cookies.Synced
448
(null)
...
```

The object identifier `448` in the notification named `com.apple.`
`Cookies.Synced` is the process ID of the Safari application. The
iTunes application is a poster of interesting notifications that contain
dictionaries with detailed song information—such as details of a
new song as it starts to play.

9.17.2 The Run Loop

A run loop is an event loop that monitors sources of input to a task, and when an
input source becomes ready for processing (i.e., the source has some activity), the
run loop dispatches control to all entities that have registered interest in the
sources. Examples of such input sources include user-input devices, network connections, timer events, and asynchronous callbacks.

A `CFRunLoop` is an opaque Core Foundation object that provides
the run-loop abstraction. Carbon and Cocoa both use `CFRunLoop`
as a building block to implement higher-level event loops. For example, the `NSRunLoop` class in Cocoa is implemented atop `CFRunLoop`.

The following points are noteworthy about run loops.

- An event-driven application enters its main run loop after initializing.

- Each thread has exactly *one* run loop, which is automatically created by
  Core Foundation. A thread's run loop cannot be created or destroyed programmatically.

- An input source object is placed into (registered in) a run loop by calling the
  appropriate `CFRunLoopAdd*` function for that input source. Then, the run
  loop is typically run. If there are no events, the run loop blocks. When an
  event occurs because of an input source, the run loop wakes up and calls any
  callback functions that may be registered for that source.

- Run-loop event sources are grouped into sets called *modes*, where a mode
  restricts which event sources the run loop will monitor. A run loop can run in
  several modes. In each mode, a run loop monitors a particular set of objects.
  Examples of modes include `NSModalPanelRunLoopMode` (used when waiting
  for input from a modal panel) and `NSEventTrackingRunLoopMode` (used
  in event-tracking loops). The default mode—`kCFRunLoopDefaultMode`—
  is used for monitoring objects while the thread is idle.

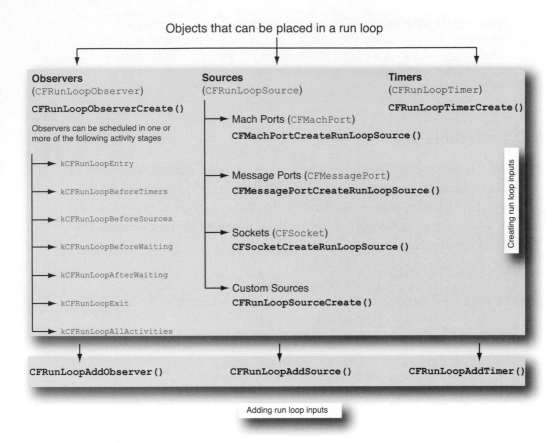

FIGURE 9–64 Creating and adding run-loop input sources

Figure 9–64 shows the types of objects that can be placed into a run loop, the functions used for creating the objects, and the functions used for adding them to a run loop.

9.17.2.1 Run-Loop Observers

A run-loop observer (CFRunLoopObserver) is a run-loop input source that generates events at one or more specified locations, or activity stages, within the run loop. The stages of interest are specified as the bitwise OR of individual stage identifiers when the observer is created. For example, the kCFRunLoopEntry stage represents the entrance of the run loop—it will be hit each time the run loop starts running as a result of either CFRunLoopRun() or CFRunLoopRunInMode().

> Note that the term *observer* is somewhat confusing in that so far we have used the term to refer to entities that *receive* notifications; here, an observer generates notifications, although it is observing the run loop's activities in doing so.

9.17.2.2 Run-Loop Sources

A run-loop source (CFRunLoopSource) abstracts an underlying source of events, such as a Mach port (CFMachPort), a message port (CFMessagePort), or a network socket (CFSocket). The arrival of a message on one of these communication end points is an asynchronous event that represents input to a run loop. Core Foundation also allows custom input sources to be created.

Given an underlying primitive type supported by Core Foundation as an input source, a CFRunLoopSource object must be created before the source can be added to a run loop. For example, given a CFSocket, the CFSocketCreate-RunLoopSource() function returns a reference to a CFRunLoopSource, which can then be added to a run loop using CFRunLoopAddSource().

Let us look at some properties of the input sources provided by Core Foundation.

CFMachPort

A CFMachPort is a wrapper around a native Mach port, but it allows the port to be used only for receiving messages—Core Foundation does not provide a function for sending messages. However, CFMachPortGetPort() retrieves the underlying native Mach port, which can then be used with the Mach APIs to send messages. Conversely, CFMachPortCreateWithPort() creates a CFMachPort from an existing native Mach port. If an existing port is not being used, CFMachPortCreate() can be used to create both a CFMachPort and the underlying native port. Both creation functions accept as an argument a callback function, which is called when a message arrives on the port. The callback is passed a pointer to the raw message—specifically, the mach_msg_header_t structure. CFMachPortSetInvalidation-CallBack() can be used to set another callback function that would be invoked when the port is invalidated.

CFMessagePort

A CFMessagePort is a wrapper around *two* native Mach ports—unlike a CFMachPort, a CFMessagePort supports bidirectional communication. Like a

CFMachPort, it can be used only for local (non-networked) intraprocess or inter-process communication since Mac OS X does not provide network-transparent Mach IPC.

In a typical use of CFMessagePort, a process creates a local port through CFMessagePortCreateLocal(), specifying a string name with which to register the port. The name can also be set later or changed by using CFMessagePort-SetName(). Thereafter, another process can call CFMessagePortCreateRemote() with the same string name to create a CFMessagePort that is connected to the remote (to this process) port.

Let us look at an example of using a CFMessagePort. Figure 9–65 shows a server that creates a CFMessagePort and advertises its name. The server then creates a run-loop source from the port and adds it to the main run loop. On receiving a message, the only service the server provides is printing the contents of the message—no reply is sent.

FIGURE 9–65 A CFMessagePort server

```
// CFMessagePortServer.c

#include <CoreFoundation/CoreFoundation.h>

#define LOCAL_NAME "com.osxbook.CFMessagePort.server"

CFDataRef
localPortCallBack(CFMessagePortRef local, SInt32 msgid, CFDataRef data,
                  void *info)
{
    printf("message received\n");
    CFShow(data);
    return NULL;
}

int
main(void)
{
    CFMessagePortRef   localPort;
    CFRunLoopSourceRef runLoopSource;

    localPort = CFMessagePortCreateLocal(
                    kCFAllocatorDefault, // allocator
                    CFSTR(LOCAL_NAME),   // name for registering the port
                    localPortCallBack,   // call this when message received
                    NULL,                // contextual information
                    NULL);               // free "info" field of context?
```

(continues)

FIGURE 9–65 A CFMessagePort server *(continued)*

```
    if (localPort == NULL) {
        fprintf(stderr, "*** CFMessagePortCreateLocal\n");
        exit(1);
    }

    runLoopSource = CFMessagePortCreateRunLoopSource(
                        kCFAllocatorDefault, // allocator
                        localPort, // create run-loop source for this port
                        0);          // priority index
    CFRunLoopAddSource(CFRunLoopGetCurrent(), runLoopSource,
                        kCFRunLoopCommonModes);
    CFRunLoopRun();

    CFRelease(runLoopSource);
    CFRelease(localPort);

    exit(0);
}
```

Figure 9–66 shows the source for a client of the CFMessagePort server. The client uses the remote port's name (shared between the client and the server) to create a connection and sends a few bytes of data to the server.

FIGURE 9–66 A CFMessagePort client

```
// CFMessagePortClient.c

#include <CoreFoundation/CoreFoundation.h>

#define REMOTE_NAME "com.osxbook.CFMessagePort.server"

int
main(void)
{
    SInt32           status;
    CFMessagePortRef remotePort;
    CFDataRef        sendData;
    const UInt8      bytes[] = { 1, 2, 3, 4 };

    sendData = CFDataCreate(kCFAllocatorDefault, bytes,
                            sizeof(bytes)/sizeof(UInt8));
    if (sendData == NULL) {
        fprintf(stderr, "*** CFDataCreate\n");
        exit(1);
    }
```

(continues)

FIGURE 9–66 A `CFMessagePort` client *(continued)*

```
    remotePort = CFMessagePortCreateRemote(kCFAllocatorDefault,
                                        CFSTR(REMOTE_NAME));
    if (remotePort == NULL) {
        CFRelease(sendData);
        fprintf(stderr, "*** CFMessagePortCreateRemote\n");
        exit(1);
    }

    status = CFMessagePortSendRequest(
                remotePort,      // message port to which data should be sent
                (SInt32)0x1234,  // msgid, an arbitrary integer value
                sendData,        // data
                5.0,             // send timeout
                5.0,             // receive timeout
                NULL,            // reply mode (no reply expected or desired)
                NULL);           // reply data

    if (status != kCFMessagePortSuccess)
        fprintf(stderr, "*** CFMessagePortSendRequest: error %ld.\n", status);
    else
        printf("message sent\n");

    CFRelease(sendData);
    CFRelease(remotePort);

    exit(0);
}
```

Let us now test the `CFMessagePort` server and client programs.

```
$ gcc -Wall -o client CFMessagePortClient.c -framework CoreFoundation
$ gcc -Wall -o server CFMessagePortServer.c -framework CoreFoundation
$ ./server
        # another shell prompt
        $ ./client
        message sent
message received
<CFData 0x300990 [0xa0728150]>{length = 4, capacity = 4, bytes = 0x01020304}
```

CFSocket

A `CFSocket` is conceptually similar to a `CFMessagePort` with the key difference being that BSD sockets are used as the underlying communication channel. A `CFSocket` can be created in several ways: from scratch, from an existing native socket, or even from a native socket that is already connected.

A CFSocket supports callbacks for several types of socket activity, for example, when there is data to read (kCFSocketReadCallBack), when the socket is writable (kCFSocketWriteCallBack), when an explicitly back-grounded connection attempt finishes (kCFSocketConnectCallBack), and so on.

Figure 9–67 shows a client program that uses a CFSocket to connect to a well-known time server and retrieves the current time.

FIGURE 9–67 A CFSocket client

```
// CFSocketTimeClient.c

#include <CoreFoundation/CoreFoundation.h>
#include <netdb.h>

#define REMOTE_HOST "time.nist.gov"

void
dataCallBack(CFSocketRef s, CFSocketCallBackType callBackType,
             CFDataRef address, const void *data, void *info)
{
    if (data) {
        CFShow((CFDataRef)data);
        printf("%s", CFDataGetBytePtr((CFDataRef)data));
    }
}

int
main(int argc, char **argv)
{
    CFSocketRef           timeSocket;
    CFSocketSignature     timeSignature;
    struct sockaddr_in    remote_addr;
    struct hostent        *host;
    CFDataRef             address;
    CFOptionFlags         callBackTypes;
    CFRunLoopSourceRef    source;
    CFRunLoopRef          loop;
    struct servent        *service;

    if (!(host = gethostbyname(REMOTE_HOST))) {
        perror("gethostbyname");
        exit(1);
    }

    if (!(service = getservbyname("daytime", "tcp"))) {
        perror("getservbyname");
        exit(1);
    }
```

(continues)

FIGURE 9–67 A CFSocket client *(continued)*

```
remote_addr.sin_family = AF_INET;
remote_addr.sin_port = htons(service->s_port);
bcopy(host->h_addr, &(remote_addr.sin_addr.s_addr), host->h_length);

// a CFSocketSignature structure fully specifies a CFSocket's
// communication protocol and connection address
timeSignature.protocolFamily = PF_INET;
timeSignature.socketType    = SOCK_STREAM;
timeSignature.protocol      = IPPROTO_TCP;
address = CFDataCreate(kCFAllocatorDefault, (UInt8 *)&remote_addr,
                       sizeof(remote_addr));
timeSignature.address = address;

// this is a variant of the read callback (kCFSocketReadCallBack): it
// reads incoming data in the background and gives it to us packaged
// as a CFData by invoking our callback
callBackTypes = kCFSocketDataCallBack;

timeSocket = CFSocketCreateConnectedToSocketSignature(
                kCFAllocatorDefault, // allocator to use
                &timeSignature,      // address and protocol
                callBackTypes,       // activity type we are interested in
                dataCallBack,        // call this function
                NULL,                // context
                10.0);               // timeout (in seconds)

source = CFSocketCreateRunLoopSource(kCFAllocatorDefault, timeSocket, 0);
loop = CFRunLoopGetCurrent();
CFRunLoopAddSource(loop, source, kCFRunLoopDefaultMode);
CFRunLoopRun();

CFRelease(source);
CFRelease(timeSocket);
CFRelease(address);

exit(0);
}


$ gcc -Wall -o timeclient CFSocketTimeClient.c -framework CoreFoundation
$ ./timeclient
<CFData 0x500fb0 [0xa0728150]>{length = 51, capacity = 51, bytes =
0x0a3533363332 2030352d30392d313920 ... 49535429202a200a}

53632 05-09-19 04:21:43 50 0 0 510.7 UTC(NIST) *
<CFData 0x500b40 [0xa0728150]>{length = 0, capacity = 16, bytes = 0x}
```

CFRunLoopTimer

A CFRunLoopTimer is a special case of a run-loop source that can be set to fire at some time in the future, either periodically or one time only. In the latter case, the timer is automatically invalidated. A CFRunLoopTimer is created using CFRunLoopTimerCreate(), which takes a callback function as an argument. The timer can then be added to a run loop.

> A run loop must be running to be able to process a timer. A timer can only be added to one run loop at a time, although it can be in multiple modes in that run loop.

Figure 9–68 shows a program that creates a periodic timer, adds it to the main run loop, and sets the run loop running for a given time. While the run loop is running, the timer gets processed and the associated callback is invoked.

FIGURE 9–68 Using a CFRunLoopTimer

```
// CFRunLoopTimerDemo.c

#include <CoreFoundation/CoreFoundation.h>
#include <unistd.h>

void timerCallBack(CFRunLoopTimerRef timer, void *info);

void
timerCallBack(CFRunLoopTimerRef timer, void *info)
{
    CFShow(timer);
}

int
main(int argc, char **argv)
{
    CFRunLoopTimerRef runLoopTimer = CFRunLoopTimerCreate(
        kCFAllocatorDefault,              // allocator
        CFAbsoluteTimeGetCurrent() + 2.0, // fire date (now + 2 seconds)
        1.0,            // fire interval (0 or -ve means a one-shot timer)
        0,              // flags (ignored)
        0,              // order (ignored)
        timerCallBack,  // called when the timer fires
        NULL);          // context
```

(continues)

FIGURE 9–68 Using a `CFRunLoopTimer` *(continued)*

```
CFRunLoopAddTimer(CFRunLoopGetCurrent(),  // the run loop to use
                  runLoopTimer,            // the run-loop timer to add
                  kCFRunLoopDefaultMode);  // add timer to this mode

CFRunLoopRunInMode(kCFRunLoopDefaultMode,  // run it in this mode
                   4.0,      // run it for this long
                   false);   // exit after processing one source?

printf("Run Loop stopped\n");

// sleep for a bit to show that the timer is not processed any more
sleep(4);

CFRunLoopTimerInvalidate(runLoopTimer);
CFRelease(runLoopTimer);

exit(0);
}
```

```
$ gcc -Wall -o timerdemo CFRunLoopTimerDemo.c -framework CoreFoundation
$ ./timerdemo
<CFRunLoopTimer ...>{locked = No, valid = Yes, interval = 1, next fire date =
148797186, order = 0, callout = 0x28ec, context = <CFRunLoopTimer context 0x0>}
<CFRunLoopTimer ...>{locked = No, valid = Yes, interval = 1, next fire date =
148797187, order = 0, callout = 0x28ec, context = <CFRunLoopTimer context 0x0>}
<CFRunLoopTimer ...>{locked = No, valid = Yes, interval = 1, next fire date =
148797188, order = 0, callout = 0x28ec, context = <CFRunLoopTimer context 0x0>}
Run Loop stopped
$
```

9.18 Synchronization

Mac OS X provides several synchronization mechanisms, two of which we have already come across in this chapter, namely, POSIX and System V semaphores. Figure 9–69 shows the important kernel-level and user-level synchronization mechanisms. Frameworks such as Core Foundation and Foundation provide their own wrappers around some of the mechanisms shown in Figure 9–69.

In general, a synchronization mechanism is based on a hardware implementation of a multiprocessor lock. Depending on a specific locking mechanism's semantics, along with the lock's associated storage, there may be additional data structures, such as a queue of threads waiting for the lock.

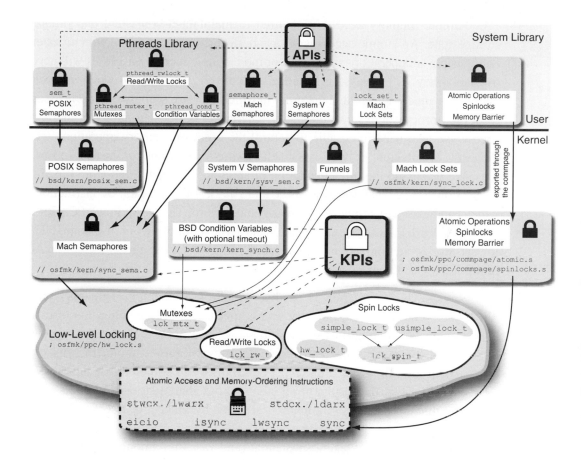

FIGURE 9–69 An overview of Mac OS X synchronization mechanisms

Typical operations required to implement some form of synchronization include atomic *compare-and-store* (also called *test-and-set*) and *compare-and-swap*. For example, given a hardware implementation of the test-and-set operation, we can treat a word of storage as a simple lock. We initialize the word to 0 (unlocked) and define the *lock* operation as a successful test-and-set operation that sets the word's value to 1. Conversely, the *unlock* operation sets the word's value to 0. A test-and-set operation also returns the old value, so the thread attempting to acquire a lock will know if it succeeded. If the lock acquisition attempt failed, what the thread does depends on the nature of the locking mechanism. Two obvious options are that the thread keeps trying actively and that the thread sleeps.

Atomic memory access is required to maintain a consistent and ordered storage state. An atomic access is always performed in its entirety, with no externally visible suboperations. Thus, two or more atomic memory accesses will never overlap—they will always be serialized. Moreover, the order in which memory operations are completed and the order in which they are seen by other processors (in a multiprocessor system) do matter. Therefore, besides atomicity of memory access, we also need to be able to control the order of memory operations. The PowerPC architecture provides special hardware instructions for these purposes.

We discussed the implementation of an atomic compare-and-store function in Section 3.5.2. That function used the `lwarx/stwcx.` pair of instructions, which can be used to atomically write a memory word. The 64-bit PowerPC 970FX also provides `ldarx/stdcx.` to atomically write a double-word of memory. The lowest-level synchronization mechanisms in Mac OS X use these instructions as building blocks. Other relevant PowerPC instructions are the following:

- `sync`—This instruction is used to synchronize memory with respect to other processors and memory access mechanisms. Executing this instruction ensures that all instructions that appear before it are (effectively) completed before the sync instruction completes. Moreover, no instructions that appear after the `sync` are executed until the `sync` completes. It can be used to ensure that the results of all stores into a shared storage location—say, one that corresponds to a mutex—are seen by other processors before performing a store to unlock that mutex. The `sync` instruction is rather heavy-duty in that it may take a substantial (and variable) amount of time to execute. The `eieio` instruction is often a better alternative.

- `eieio`—The `eieio` (*enforce-in-order-execution-of-I/O*) instruction is similar to `sync` but enforces a weaker ordering—it may itself complete before memory accesses caused by instructions that appear before it have completed with respect to main memory. However, it does ensure that the accesses have completed before any instructions that appear after the `eieio` instruction can access main memory. Thus, `eieio` can be used to enforce memory ordering without stalling dispatch of further instructions.

- `lwsync`—This is a lightweight version of `sync` available on the 970FX, on which it is faster than `eieio`. It cannot, however, be used in place of `eieio` under all circumstances.

- `isync`—This instruction ensures that all instructions before it have completed before it itself completes. Until `isync` completes, the processor does not initiate any instructions that appear after the `isync`. Moreover, when `isync` completes, any prefetched instructions are discarded. Note that `isync` waits only for the preceding instructions to complete—not for the completion of any memory accesses caused by the preceding instructions. `isync` does not affect any other processor or another processor's caches.

With the understanding that the atomic access and memory-ordering instructions are directly or indirectly used as primitives in all Mac OS X synchronization mechanisms, let us look at some of the individual mechanisms shown in Figure 9–69.

9.18.1 Interfaces for Atomic Operations

The system library provides functions for performing a variety of atomic operations, ordering memory accesses through a memory barrier, and using spinlocks. These functions are actually implemented in the kernel but made available to user space through the commpage mechanism. The implementations reside in `osfmk/ppc/commpage/atomic.s` and `osfmk/ppc/commpage/spinlock.s`.

9.18.2 Low-Level Locking

The Mach portion of the kernel provides the following primary types of low-level locks (or lock protocols) that can be held by threads[18]:

- Spinlocks (or simple locks)
- Mutexes
- Read/write locks

9.18.2.1 Spinlocks

A spinlock is a simple locking primitive: It protects a shared resource by making the lock-holder thread busy-wait, or "spin" (in a tight loop). Since a thread holding a spinlock causes a processor to be tied up, it is important not to hold such locks for too long. In general, if a resource is accessed only briefly, it is a likely candidate for protection through a spinlock. Moreover, the use of a spinlock is different on a multiprocessor system compared with a uniprocessor system. On the former, a thread could busy-wait on one processor while the holder of a spinlock

---

18. A lock holder in Mach is always a thread.

uses the protected resource on another processor. On a uniprocessor, a tight loop—if not preempted—will spin forever, since the holder of the lock will never get a chance to run and free the lock!

Mach uses simple locks to protect most of the kernel data structures. It provides three flavors of spinlocks: *hw_lock* (hw_lock_t), *usimple* (usimple_lock_t), and *simple* (lck_spin_t). Only the latter is exported to loadable kernel extensions.

An hw_lock is the lowest-level locking abstraction provided by the kernel. The following primary functions are exported by this lock package:

```
void          hw_lock_init(hw_lock_t);                    [osfmk/ppc/hw_lock.s]
void          hw_lock_lock(hw_lock_t);                    [osfmk/ppc/hw_lock.s]
void          hw_lock_unlock(hw_lock_t);                  [osfmk/ppc/hw_lock.s]
unsigned int  hw_lock_to(hw_lock_t, unsigned int);        [osfmk/ppc/hw_lock.s]
unsigned int  hw_lock_try(hw_lock_t);                     [osfmk/ppc/hw_lock.s]
unsigned int  hw_lock_held(hw_lock_t);                    [osfmk/ppc/hw_lock.s]
```

The hw_lock_t data type is declared in osfmk/ppc/hw_lock_types.h.

```
// osfmk/ppc/hw_lock_types.h

struct hslock {
    int lock_data;
};
typedef struct hslock hw_lock_data_t, *hw_lock_t;
```

A lock attempt for an hw_lock lock can be made—through hw_lock_to()—with a timeout value specified as a number of ticks of the Timebase Register. The lock spins for up to the duration of the timeout. The locking function even disables interruptions for up to 128 ticks of the Timebase Register.

The usimple variant (the "u" stands for uniprocessor) has two implementations: a portable C implementation [osfmk/ppc/locks_ppc.c] built atop hw_lock and an assembly-language implementation [osfmk/ppc/hw_lock.s]. The portable implementation also supports interfaces for debugging and statistics gathering. Unlike a simple lock, which disappears on a uniprocessor, a usimple lock provides actual locking on a uniprocessor. Acquiring a usimple lock returns with preemption disabled, whereas releasing a usimple lock reenables preemption.

The simple lock variant is the primary spin-locking mechanism in Mac OS X for multiprocessor systems. The following primary functions are exported by this lock package:

```
lck_spin_t *lck_spin_alloc_init(lck_grp_t *grp, lck_attr_t *attr);
void         lck_spin_free(lck_spin_t *lck, lck_grp_t *grp);
void         lck_spin_init(lck_spin_t *lck, lck_grp_t *grp, lck_attr_t *attr);
void         lck_spin_destroy(lck_spin_t *lck, lck_grp_t *grp);
```

```
void          lck_spin_lock(lck_spin_t *lck);
void          lck_spin_unlock(lck_spin_t *lck);

wait_result_t lck_spin_sleep(lck_spin_t         *lck,
                             lck_sleep_action_t  lck_sleep_action,
                             event_t             event,
                             wait_interrupt_t    interruptible);
wait_result_t lck_spin_sleep_deadline(lck_spin_t         *lck,
                                      lck_sleep_action_t  lck_sleep_action,
                                      event_t             event,
                                      wait_interrupt_t    interruptible,
                                      uint64_t            deadline);
```

> When preemption is disabled, the holder of a spinlock must not—
> directly or indirectly—acquire a blocking lock (such as a mutex or a
> semaphore). Doing so will result in a kernel panic.

9.18.2.2 Mutexes

Mach mutexes are blocking mutual-exclusion locks. If a thread attempts to
acquire a mutex that is currently locked, it will relinquish the processor and sleep
until the mutex is available. In doing so, the thread will also give up any scheduling time quantum that it may have remaining. Although a thread is permitted to
block[19] while holding a Mach mutex, the mutexes are not recursive: If a thread
attempts to acquire a mutex that it already holds, it will cause a kernel panic.

The mutex package exports the following functions, whose prototypes are
listed in osfmk/kern/locks.h:

```
lck_mtx_t     lck_mtx_alloc_init(lck_grp_t *grp, lck_attr_t *attr);
void          lck_mtx_free(lck_mtx_t *lck, lck_grp_t *grp);
void          lck_mtx_init(lck_mtx_t *lck, lck_grp_t *grp, lck_attr_t *attr);
void          lck_mtx_destroy(lck_mtx_t *lck, lck_grp_t *grp);

void          lck_mtx_lock(lck_mtx_t *lck);
void          lck_mtx_unlock(lck_mtx_t *lck);

wait_result_t lck_mtx_assert(lck_mtx_t *lck, int type);
wait_result_t lck_mtx_sleep(lck_mtx_t          *lck,
                            lck_sleep_action_t  lck_sleep_action,
                            event_t             event,
                            wait_interrupt_t    interruptible);
```

---

19. The safety of blocking still depends on whether blocking is allowed in the given context and
whether the code is written correctly.

```
wait_result_t lck_mtx_sleep_deadline(lck_mtx_t          *lck,
                              lck_sleep_action_t  lck_sleep_action,
                              event_t             event,
                              wait_interrupt_t    interruptible
                              uint64_t            deadline);
```

The mutex package is implemented in osfmk/ppc/locks_ppc.c, osfmk/ppc/hw_lock.s, and osfmk/kern/locks.c. The lck_mtx_t data type is declared in osfmk/ppc/locks.h.

9.18.2.3 Read/Write Locks

Mach read/write locks are blocking synchronization locks that permit multiple simultaneous readers or a single writer. Before a writer can acquire the lock for writing, it must wait until all readers have released the lock. Moreover, if a writer is already waiting on a lock, a new reader attempting to get the read lock will block until the writer has acquired and released the lock. It is possible to downgrade (write → read) or upgrade (read → write) a lock. A read-to-write upgrade is favored over a new writer.

The read/write locks package exports the following functions, whose prototypes are listed in osfmk/kern/locks.h:

```
lck_rw_t *lck_rw_alloc_init(lck_grp_t *grp, lck_attr_t *attr);
void      lck_rw_free(lck_rw_t *lck, lck_grp_t *grp);
void      lck_rw_init(lck_rw_t *lck, lck_grp_t *grp, lck_attr_t *attr);
void      lck_rw_destroy(lck_rw_t *lck, lck_grp_t *grp);

void      lck_rw_lock(lck_rw_t *lck, lck_rw_type_t lck_rw_type);
void      lck_rw_unlock(lck_rw_t *lck, lck_rw_type_t lck_rw_type);
void      lck_rw_lock_shared(lck_rw_t *lck);
void      lck_rw_unlock_shared(lck_rw_t *lck);
void      lck_rw_lock_exclusive(lck_rw_t *lck);
void      lck_rw_unlock_exclusive(lck_rw_t *lck);

wait_result_t lck_rw_sleep(lck_rw_t           *lck,
                          lck_sleep_action_t  lck_sleep_action,
                          event_t             event,
                          wait_interrupt_t    interruptible);
wait_result_t lck_rw_sleep_deadline(lck_rw_t           *lck,
                              lck_sleep_action_t  lck_sleep_action,
                              event_t             event,
                              wait_interrupt_t    interruptible,
                              uint64_t            deadline);
```

The implementation of the read/write locks package is split across the same files as those of the mutex package.

9.18.2.4 Lock Groups and Attributes

As we saw in the previous three sections, spinlocks, mutexes, and read/write locks all provide similar interfaces. In particular, the functions in these interfaces deal with lock groups (lck_grp_t) and lock attributes (lck_attr_t). A lock group is a container for one or more locks—that is, it names a set of locks. It is allocated separately, after which it can be used to group together locks—say, based on the purpose the locks are used for. Every lock belongs to exactly one group.

Lock attributes are flags—a collection of bits—that qualify a lock. Examples of lock attributes are LCK_ATTR_NONE (no attributes specified) and LCK_ATTR_DEBUG (lock debugging enabled). A lock group also has its own attributes (lck_grp_attr_t). Figure 9–70 shows an example of using the lock interfaces.

FIGURE 9–70 Using locks in the kernel

```
lck_grp_attr_t *my_lock_group_attr; // lock group attributes
lck_grp_t      *my_lock_group       // lock group
lck_attr_t     *my_lock_attr        // lock attributes
lck_mtx_t      *my_mutex;

void
my_init_locking() // set up locks
{
    ...
    // allocate lock group attributes and the lock group
    my_lock_group_attr = lck_grp_attr_alloc_init();
    my_lock_group = lck_grp_alloc_init("my-mutexes", my_lock_group_attr);

    my_lock_attr = lck_attr_alloc_init(); // allocate lock attribute
    lck_attr_setdebug(my_lock_attr);      // enable lock debugging

    my_mutex = lck_mtx_alloc_init(my_lock_group, my_lock_attr);
    ...
}

void
my_fini_locking() // tear down locks
{
    lck_mtx_free(my_mutex, my_lock_group);
    lck_attr_free(my_lock_attr);
    lck_grp_free(my_lock_group);
    lck_grp_attr_free(my_lock_group_attr);
}
```

9.18.3 BSD Condition Variables

The BSD portion of the kernel implements the `msleep()`, `wakeup()`, and `wakeup_one()` functions [`bsd/kern/kern_synch.c`], which provide the semantics of condition variables, with an additional feature that a timeout value can be specified.

9.18.4 Mach Lock Sets

Mach provides an interface for creating and using lock sets, where a set contains one or more *ulocks*. The contents of a ulock data structure (`struct ulock` [`osfmk/kern/sync_lock.h`]) include a mutex and a wait queue of blocked threads. Figure 9–71 shows examples of routines in the lock set interface.

FIGURE 9–71 The Mach lock set interface

```
// create a lock set with nlocks ulocks
kern_return_t
lock_set_create(task_t task, lock_t lock_set, int nlocks, int policy);

// destroy lock set and all of its associated locks
// any blocked threads will unblock and receive KERN_LOCK_SET_DESTROYED
kern_return_t
lock_set_destroy(task_t task, lock_set_t lock_set);

// acquire access rights to the given lock in the lock set
kern_return_t
lock_acquire(lock_set_t lock_set, int lock_id);

// release access rights to the given lock in the lock set
kern_return_t
lock_release(lock_set_t lock_set, int lock_id);

// hand off ownership of lock to an anonymous accepting thread
kern_return_t
lock_handoff(lock_set_t lock_set, int lock_id);

// accept an ownership handoff from an anonymous sending thread
// caller will block if nobody is waiting to hand off the lock
// at most one thread can wait to accept handoff of a given lock
kern_return_t
lock_handoff_accept(lock_set_t lock_set, int lock_id);

// mark the internal state of the lock as stable
// the state destabilizes when a lock-holder thread terminates
kern_return_t
lock_make_stable(lock_set_t lock_set, int lock_id);
```

9.18.5 Mach Semaphores

Besides the POSIX and System V semaphore interfaces that we have seen earlier, there is another semaphore interface available in user space—Mach semaphores. In fact, POSIX semaphores in Mac OS X are implemented atop Mach semaphores. Other parts of the kernel that use Mach semaphores include the IOCommandQueue, IOService, and IOGraphics classes in the I/O Kit.

A Mach semaphore is represented as a Mach port (semaphore_t) that names a kernel object of type IKOT_SEMAPHORE. The corresponding kernel structure is struct semaphore [osfmk/kern/sync_sema.h]. A new Mach semaphore is obtained by calling semaphore_create(), which returns with a send right naming the new semaphore.

```
kern_return_t
semaphore_create(task_t task, semaphore_t *semaphore, int policy, int value);
```

The value argument to semaphore_create() specifies the initial value of the semaphore count, whereas the policy argument specifies the policy (e.g., SYNC_POLICY_FIFO) the kernel will use to select a thread to wake up from among multiple threads that are blocked on the semaphore.

Given a semaphore, semaphore_wait() decrements the semaphore count, blocking if the count is negative after decrementing. semaphore_signal() increments the semaphore count, scheduling a waiting thread to execute if the new count becomes non-negative. semaphore_signal_all() can be used to wake up all threads blocked on a semaphore, while resetting the semaphore count to zero. Finally, semaphore_signal_thread() can be used to signal a specific thread.

Figure 9–72 shows a program that demonstrates the use of Mach semaphores. The main thread creates two semaphores—both with an initial value of 0—and three threads. It calls semaphore_wait() three times on one of the semaphores. Each thread calls semaphore_signal() on this semaphore as its first operation. Therefore, the main thread blocks until all three threads are ready. Each thread then calls semaphore_wait() on the other semaphore. Since the latter's value is 0, all threads will block. The main thread first wakes up a specific thread using semaphore_signal_thread() and then wakes up the remaining two threads using semaphore_signal_all().

FIGURE 9-72 Using Mach semaphores

// mach_semaphore.c

```
#include <stdio.h>
#include <unistd.h>
#include <stdlib.h>
#include <pthread.h>
#include <mach/mach.h>

#define OUT_ON_MACH_ERROR(msg, retval) \
    if (kr != KERN_SUCCESS) { mach_error(msg ":" , kr); goto out; }

#define PTHID() (unsigned long)(pthread_self())

#define SEMAPHORE_WAIT(s, n) \
    { int i; for (i = 0; i < (n); i++) { semaphore_wait((s)); } }

void *
start_routine(void *semaphores)
{
    semaphore_t *sem = (semaphore_t *)semaphores;

    semaphore_signal(sem[1]);
    printf("thread: %lx about to decrement semaphore count\n", PTHID());
    semaphore_wait(sem[0]);
    printf("thread: %lx succeeded in decrementing semaphore count\n", PTHID());
    semaphore_signal(sem[1]);
    return (void *)0;
}

int
main(void)
{
    pthread_t      pthread1, pthread2, pthread3;
    semaphore_t    sem[2] = { 0 };
    kern_return_t kr;

    setbuf(stdout, NULL);

    kr = semaphore_create(mach_task_self(), &sem[0], SYNC_POLICY_FIFO, 0);
    OUT_ON_MACH_ERROR("semaphore_create", kr);

    kr = semaphore_create(mach_task_self(), &sem[1], SYNC_POLICY_FIFO, 0);
    OUT_ON_MACH_ERROR("semaphore_create", kr);

    (void)pthread_create(&pthread1, (const pthread_attr_t *)0,
                         start_routine, (void *)sem);
    printf("created thread1=%lx\n", (unsigned long)pthread1);
```

(continues)

FIGURE 9–72 Using Mach semaphores *(continued)*

```
    (void)pthread_create(&pthread2, (const pthread_attr_t *)0,
                         start_routine, (void *)sem);
    printf("created thread2=%lx\n", (unsigned long)pthread2);

    (void)pthread_create(&pthread3, (const pthread_attr_t *)0,
                         start_routine, (void *)sem);
    printf("created thread3=%lx\n", (unsigned long)pthread3);

    // wait until all three threads are ready
    SEMAPHORE_WAIT(sem[1], 3);

    printf("main: about to signal thread3\n");
    semaphore_signal_thread(sem[0], pthread_mach_thread_np(pthread3));

    // wait for thread3 to sem_signal()
    semaphore_wait(sem[1]);

    printf("main: about to signal all threads\n");
    semaphore_signal_all(sem[0]);

    // wait for thread1 and thread2 to sem_signal()
    SEMAPHORE_WAIT(sem[1], 2);

out:
    if (sem[0])
        semaphore_destroy(mach_task_self(), sem[0]);
    if (sem[1])
        semaphore_destroy(mach_task_self(), sem[1]);

    exit(kr);
}



$ gcc -Wall -o mach_semaphore mach_semaphore.c
$ ./mach_semaphore
created thread1=1800400
created thread2=1800800
created thread3=1800c00
thread: 1800400 about to decrement semaphore count
thread: 1800800 about to decrement semaphore count
thread: 1800c00 about to decrement semaphore count
main: about to signal thread3
thread: 1800c00 succeeded in decrementing semaphore count
main: about to signal all threads
thread: 1800400 succeeded in decrementing semaphore count
thread: 1800800 succeeded in decrementing semaphore count
```

Figure 9–73 shows the kernel data structure associated with a Mach semaphore. Note that the semaphore lock, which exists within the wait queue structure, is an `hw_lock_t` spinlock.

FIGURE 9–73 Internal structure of a Mach semaphore

```
// osfmk/kern/sync_sema.h

typedef struct semaphore {
    queue_chain_t    task_link;    // chain of semaphores owned by a task
    struct wait_queue wait_queue;  // queue of blocked threads and lock
    task_t           owner;        // task that owns semaphore
    ipc_port_t       port;         // semaphore port
    int              ref_count;    // reference count
    int              count;        // current count value
    boolean_t        active;       // active status
} Semaphore;


// osfmk/mach/mach_types.h
typedef struct semaphore *semaphore_t;


// osfmk/kern/wait_queue.h
typedef struct wait_queue {
    unsigned int     wq_type    : 16,  // the only public field
                     wq_fifo    : 1,   // FIFO wakeup policy
                     wq_isrepost: 1,   // is waitq preposted?
                                : 0;
    hw_lock_data_t   wq_interlock;     // interlock
    queue_data_t     wq_queue;         // queue of elements
} WaitQueue;
```

9.18.6 Pthreads Synchronization Interfaces

The Pthreads library provides functions for using mutexes, condition variables, and read/write locks. The internal structures of these abstractions are as follows:

- A Pthreads mutex includes two Mach semaphores, a spinlock, and other data.
- A Pthreads condition variable internally includes a Mach semaphore, a Pthreads mutex, a spinlock, and other data.
- A Pthreads read/write lock internally includes a pair of Pthreads condition variables, a Pthreads mutex, and other data.

The Pthreads library uses the spinlock implementation that the kernel makes available through the commpage mechanism.

9.18.7 Locking in the I/O Kit

The I/O Kit is the object-oriented driver subsystem of the xnu kernel. It provides synchronization primitives that are simple wrappers around the Mach primitives discussed in this chapter.

- `IOSimpleLock` is a wrapper around Mach spinlocks (specifically, `lck_spin_t`). When used to synchronize between interrupt context and thread context, an `IOSimpleLock` should be locked with interrupts disabled. The I/O Kit provides `IOSimpleLockLockDisableInterrupt` as a metafunction that performs both operations. It also provides the corresponding inverse function, `IOSimpleLockUnlockEnableInterrupt`.

- `IOLock` is a wrapper around Mach mutexes (`lck_mtx_t`).

- `IORecursiveLock` is also a wrapper around Mach mutexes, along with a reference counter that allows one thread to lock it more than once (recursively). Note that if another thread is holding the recursive mutex, an attempt to lock it would still block.

- `IORWLock` is a wrapper around Mach read/write locks (`lck_rw_t`).

Besides these, the I/O Kit supports a more sophisticated construct, the `IOWorkLoop`, which provides both implicit and explicit synchronization, among an extensive array of other features. We will discuss the `IOWorkLoop` and the I/O Kit in general in Chapter 10.

9.18.8 Funnels

The xnu kernel provides a synchronization abstraction called *funnels* to serialize access to the BSD portion of the kernel. In the simplest terms, an xnu funnel is a giant mutex with the special property that it gets automatically unlocked when the holding thread sleeps. Funnels were heavily used in the kernel before Mac OS X 10.4—for example, in file systems and system call processing. Mac OS X 10.4 replaced the use of funnels with finer-grained locking in many but not all instances—the kernel still provides funnels for backward compatibility and uses them in some portions that are not performance-critical.

Let us look at the background of funnels and how they are used in Mac OS X.

9.18.8.1 History

Funnels originated in the Digital UNIX operating system as a mechanism to help implement SMP-safe device drivers. A Digital UNIX funnel allowed device drivers to force execution onto a single processor. Therefore, a funneled device driver saw a single-processor environment even on an SMP system. There was no locking of resources or code blocks—SMP resource protection was achieved as a side effect of an entire subsystem always running on a single processor. A device driver could be funneled by setting the d_funnel member of its device switch table entry data structure to the value DEV_FUNNEL. Using funnels degraded SMP performance, but then, no locking mechanism is without tradeoffs in preemption latency and performance. An important caveat in using Digital UNIX funnels was that a funneled driver's resources had to be self-contained if they were to be protected by the funnel. If the driver shared resources with the kernel or with another driver, you still had to use another locking mechanism to protect the integrity of those resources. Moreover, the kernel had only one funnel, which was tied to the primary processor.

> Digital UNIX funnels were a poor man's way of making a driver SMP-safe transitionally, while the developer worked on making the driver really SMP-safe.

9.18.8.2 Funnels in Mac OS X

We have seen that the xnu kernel is a combination of a few very different components. In particular, Mac OS X file system and networking support comes largely from the kernel's BSD portion. In the traditional BSD architecture, the kernel is logically divided into a *top half* and a *bottom half*. When a user thread makes a system call, the top half runs either until it is done or until it is blocked, which can occur when the kernel is waiting on a resource. The bottom half is invoked to handle hardware interrupts—it runs synchronously with respect to the interrupt source. Since hardware interrupts have higher priority than threads in the top half, a thread in the top half cannot assume that it will not be preempted by the lower half. Historically, the top half synchronizes with the bottom half by disabling interrupts. Some newer BSD-flavored kernels use mutexes to protect data structures that both halves may try to access concurrently.

Mac OS X's bottom half is not executed in the context of a hardware interrupt, as an interrupt would simply cause an I/O Kit work-loop thread in the kernel to wake up, which would actually run the bottom half. This means that disabling interrupts is no longer a viable synchronization approach because the top and bottom halves in xnu could be running concurrently—as threads on different processors in a multiprocessor system. In such situations where access to the BSD portion of xnu must be serialized, Mac OS X—depending on the kernel version—uses funnels as a cooperative serialization mechanism.

Phasing Out Funnels

xnu funnels are implemented differently from Digital UNIX funnels. Notably, there can be multiple funnels and they can run on any processor, not just the primary processor. However, a thread holding a funnel on one processor cannot take that funnel on another processor in an SMP system. Another way of looking at this is that any code that runs under a funnel becomes implicitly single-threaded.

Nevertheless, the reason for the existence of funnels on Mac OS X is similar to that on Digital UNIX—that is, to provide a transitional mechanism for making the xnu kernel SMP-safe. With the evolution of Mac OS X, components of xnu are being rewritten using finer-grained locking with reasonably bounded latencies, thus phasing out dependencies on funnels.

An xnu funnel is built on top of a Mach mutex, as shown in Figure 9–74.

FIGURE 9–74 The structure of a Mac OS X funnel

```
// osfmk/kern/thread.h

struct funnel_lock {
    int         fnl_type;        // funnel type
    lck_mtx_t *fnl_mutex;        // underlying mutex for the funnel
    void      *fnl_mtxholder;    // thread (last) holding mutex
    void      *fnl_mtxrelease;   // thread (last) releasing mutex
    lck_mtx_t *fnl_oldmutex;     // mutex before collapsing split funnel
};

typedef struct funnel_lock funnel_t;
```

Even though a funnel is built on a mutex, there is an important difference in how funnels and mutexes are used: If a thread holding a mutex is blocked (say, in a memory allocation operation), the mutex will still be held. However, the scheduler will release a thread's funnel on descheduling and reacquire it when the thread is rescheduled. Another thread can enter the critical section protected by the funnel in this window. Therefore, any critical state that was being protected by the funnel is *not* guaranteed to be preserved while the thread is blocked. The thread must ensure that such state is protected—perhaps through other locking mechanisms. Consequently, the programmer must be careful while using potentially blocking operations in kernel code.

Before Mac OS X 10.4, there were two funnels in xnu: the *kernel* funnel (kernel_flock) and the *network* funnel (network_flock). Mac OS X 10.4 has only the kernel funnel. When Mach initializes the BSD subsystem at boot time, the first operation performed is allocation of these funnels. The rationale behind having two funnels was that the networking subsystem and the rest of the BSD kernel (file system, process management, device management, and so on) are not likely to contend for the same resources. Hence, one funnel for networking and one for everything else is likely to benefit SMP performance. The kernel funnel ensures that only one thread runs inside the BSD portion of xnu at a time.

> Funnels affect only the BSD portion of the kernel. Other components, such as Mach and the I/O Kit, use their own locking and synchronization mechanisms.

In Mac OS X 10.4, the file system and the networking subsystem use fine-grained locks, as shown in these examples.

- The domain structure (struct domain [bsd/sys/domain.h]) now contains a mutex.
- The protocol switch structure (structure protosw [bsd/sys/protosw.h]) provides locking hooks, namely, pr_lock(), pr_unlock(), and pr_getlock().
- The vnode structure (struct vnode [bsd/sys/vnode_internal.h]) contains a mutex.

If a file system is thread- and preemption-safe, this capability (including others, such as whether the file system is 64-bit-safe) is maintained as part of the configuration information within a mount structure (struct mount [bsd/sys/mount_internal.h]). When a vnode corresponding to a file on this file system is created, the v_unsafefs field of the vnode structure inherits this capability as a Boolean value. Thereafter, the file system layer uses the THREAD_SAFE_FS macro to determine whether a given vnode belongs to a reentrant file system.

```
// bsd/vfs/kpi_vfs.c

#define THREAD_SAFE_FS(VP) ((VP)->v_unsafefs ? 0 : 1)
```

If a file system is not reentrant, the VNOP (vnode operation) and VFS interfaces take the kernel funnel before calling the file system's operations. Figure 9–75 shows an overview of the relevant kernel code for a VNOP call.

FIGURE 9–75 Automatic funnel use in a thread-unsafe file system

`// bsd/vfs/kpi_vfs.c`

```
errno_t
VNOP_OPEN(vnode_t vp, int mode, vfs_context_t context)
{
    int _err;
    struct vnop_open_args a;
    int thread_safe;
    int funnel_state = 0;
    ...
    thread_safe = THREAD_SAFE_FS(vp);

    if (!thread_safe) {
        // take the funnel
        funnel_state = thread_funnel_set(kernel_flock, TRUE);
        ...
    }

    // call the file system entry point for open
    err = (*vp->v_op[vnop_open_desc.vdesc_offset])(&a);

    if (!thread_safe) {
        ...
        // drop the funnel
        (void)thread_funnel_set(kernel_flock, funnel_state);
        ...
    }
    ...
}
```

To determine whether a given file system is thread- and preemption-safe, the VFS interfaces check the `vfc_threadsafe` field of the `vfstable` structure [bsd/sys/mount_internal.h] within the mount structure [bsd/sys/mount_internal.h] for that file system.

`// bsd/vfs/kpi_vfs.c`

```
int
VFS_START(struct mount *mp, int flags, vfs_context_t context)
{
    int thread_safe;
    ...
    thread_safe = mp->mnt_vtable->vfc_threadsafe;
    ...
}
```

A file system can (indirectly) set the `vfc_threadsafe` field by passing the appropriate flags (`VFS_TBLTHREADSAFE` or `VFS_TBLFSNODELOCK`) to the `vfs_fsadd()` function [`bsd/vfs/kpi_vfs.c`], which adds a new file system to the kernel.

Certain parts of the Mac OS X 10.4 kernel, such as the audit subsystem [`bsd/kern/kern_audit.c`], the vnode disk driver [`bsd/dev/vn/vn.c`], and the console driver [`bsd/dev/ppc/cons.c`], expressly use funnels.

A thread can hold only one funnel at a time. If the `thread_funnel_set()` function detects that a thread is trying to hold multiple funnels concurrently, it will panic the system. The pre-10.4 funnel implementation provides a function for *merging* two funnels (`thread_funnel_merge()`), which can merge two funnels into a single funnel. There is no function to get the two original funnels back from a merged funnel.

> In contrast to a merged funnel, the multiple-funnel scheme that is normally used may be called a *split-funnel* scheme. It is possible to disable this scheme (in pre-10.4 kernels) and have both funnel locks point to the same funnel by using the `dfnl=1` boot-time argument.

Before Mac OS X 10.4, a network file system was a likely candidate for needing to hold both the kernel and network funnels concurrently. xnu's NFS implementation made heavy use of `thread_funnel_switch()` to switch between the two funnels. This function was called with two funnels, an old one and a new one, as arguments, where the old funnel must be held by the calling thread.

```
boolean_t thread_funnel_switch(int oldfnl, int newfnl);
...
thread_funnel_switch(KERNEL_FUNNEL, NETWORK_FUNNEL);
```

Funnels can also be acquired as part of BSD system call entry. As we saw in Chapter 6, a BSD system call table entry in xnu has a member indicating the funnel type to acquire when entering the kernel.

```
// bsd/sys/sysent.h

struct sysent {
    ...
    int8_t  sy_funnel; // funnel type
    ...
} sysent[];
```

The sysent array is initialized in `bsd/kern/init_sysent.c`. Since Mac OS X 10.4 has only the kernel funnel, a system call that takes this funnel on entry will have the `sy_funnel` field of its sysent entry set to KERNEL_FUNNEL.

```
// bsd/kern/init_sysent.c

__private_extern__ struct sysent sysent[] = {
    ...
    { ..., KERNEL_FUNNEL, (sy_call_t *)exit, ... },
    { ..., KERNEL_FUNNEL, (sy_call_t *)fork, ...},
    ...
    { ..., KERNEL_FUNNEL, (sy_call_t *)ptrace, ...},
    ...
};
```

> Only certain BSD system calls (most of them in pre-10.4 systems, fewer in 10.4) take funnels by default. In both Mac OS X 10.4 and earlier versions, Mach system calls, or system calls related to the I/O Kit, do *not* take a funnel as they enter the kernel. That said, an I/O Kit driver can take a funnel if it really must. For example, if a driver is bent on invoking certain file system operations using BSD functions within the kernel, it must take the kernel funnel on pre-10.4 systems. I/O Kit work-loop threads do make upcalls into the BSD kernel—for example, to deliver network packets or to complete disk I/O requests. Such a thread in a pre-10.4 kernel will acquire the appropriate funnel before calling the BSD functions. In many cases, the underlying driver family handles funnel-related details. For example, in the case of a USB networking driver, the `IONetworkingFamily` hides the details of using funnels.

It was said earlier that a thread's funnel is automatically released if the thread sleeps in the kernel. A funnel state is maintained for each thread in the `funnel_state` field of the `thread` structure. When the scheduler switches to a new thread, it checks the funnel state of the old thread. If it is TH_FN_OWNED (i.e., the thread owns the funnel pointed to by the `funnel_lock` member of the `thread` structure), the thread's funnel state is set to TH_FN_REFUNNEL, which marks the funnel to be reacquired on dispatch. After this, the thread's funnel is released. Conversely, if the new thread's `funnel_state` field is TH_FN_REFUNNEL, the funnel pointed to by the `funnel_lock` field will be acquired, and `funnel_state` will be set to TH_FN_OWNED.

9.18.9 SPLs

In traditional BSD kernels, a critical section makes a *set-priority-level* (SPL) call to block interrupt routines at (and below) a given priority level, for example:

```
// raise priority level to block network protocol processing
// return the current value
s = splnet();

// do network-related operations
...

// reset priority level to the previous (saved) value
splx(s);
```

The usual repertoire of SPL functions alone would not be sufficient for synchronization on Mac OS X for reasons discussed earlier. Although xnu implements these functions, they are all null implementations on Mac OS X 10.4. On earlier versions, they are still null operations, but they also ensure that the calling thread is running under a funnel (causing a panic otherwise).

```
// bsd/kern/spl.c (Mac OS X 10.3)

...
unsigned
splnet(void)
{
    if (thread_funnel_get() == THR_FUNNEL_NULL)
        panic("%s not under funnel", "splnet()");
    return(0);
}
...
```

```
// bsd/kern/spl.c (Mac OS X 10.4)

...
unsigned
splnet(void)
{
    return(0);
}
...
```

9.18.10 Advisory-Mode File Locking

Mac OS X provides several interfaces for *advisory-mode* locking of files, both in their entirety and as byte ranges. Figure 9–76 shows an overview of file locking

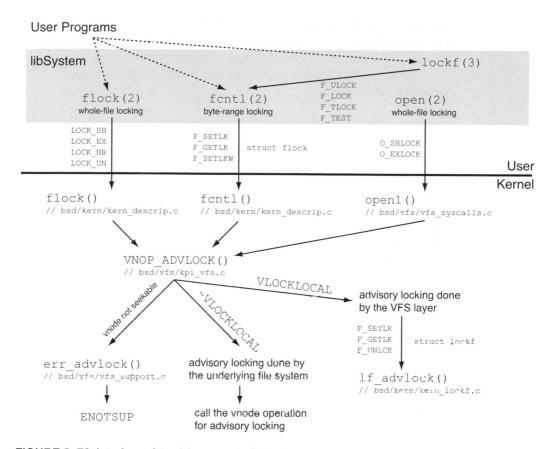

FIGURE 9–76 Interfaces for advisory-mode file locking

through the `lockf()` library function, the `flock()` system call, and the `fcntl()` system call.

```
// to lock, specify operation as either LOCK_SH (shared) or LOCK_EX (exclusive)
// additionally, bitwise OR operation with LOCK_NB to not block when locking
// to unlock, specify operation as LOCK_UN
int flock(int fd, int operation);

// cmd is one of F_GETLK, F_SETLK, or F_SETLKW
// arg is a pointer to a flock structure
int fcntl(int fd, int cmd, int arg);

// function is one of F_ULOCK, F_TEST, F_TLOCK, or F_TEST
// size specifies the number of bytes to lock, starting from the current offset
int lockf(int fd, int function, off_t size);
```

> The term *advisory* in *advisory-mode locking* means that all pro-
> cesses accessing a shared file must cooperate and use the advi-
> sory locking mechanism before reading from or writing to the file. If
> a process accesses such a file without using advisory locking,
> inconsistencies may result.

As shown in Figure 9–76, all three interfaces lead to the same locking
mechanism in the kernel. The kernel provides a file-system-independent locking
implementation in the VFS layer. This is referred to as the *local lock* implementation. Alternatively, a file system can implement its own advisory locking. Given a
vnode, `VNOP_ADVLOCK()` decides whether to use local locking or to call the file
system's advisory locking operation based on the `VLOCKLOCAL` flag on the vnode.
This flag, in turn, depends on the `MNTK_LOCK_LOCAL` flag of the file system. If a
file system wants the VFS layer to handle advisory locking, it can call the `vfs_`
`setlocklocal()` function [`bsd/vfs/vfs_subr.c`] in its mount operation to
set the `MNTK_LOCK_LOCAL` flag.

The local lock implementation uses the `lockf` structure [`bsd/sys/`
`lockf.h`] to represent a byte-range advisory lock. The `vnode` structure contains
a list of advisory locks for the file. The list is sorted on the starting offset of the
lock.

CHAPTER 10

Extending the Kernel

T he line between RISC and CISC microprocessors has been growing fuzzier
over the years, particularly as the focus of microprocessor companies has
shifted to microarchitecture. It is common to see companies attempting to optimize superscalar, out-of-order execution. In other words, modern RISC processors have become more CISC-like and vice versa. An equally interesting
evolutionary circle can be observed in kernel design: "technically monolithic"
kernels have evolved to contain enough modularity and flexibility to offer many
of the benefits provided by microkernels.

10.1 A Driver down the Memory Lane

In commercial operating systems, the majority of third-party kernel programming
pertains to *device drivers*. A driver can be informally defined as a flow of control—
say, a thread—that manages one or more devices. Given the variety of operating
systems and device driver models in existence, the control flow could be in the
kernel or in user space, and the device could be a physical device or a software

(pseudo) device. From an implementation standpoint, a device driver in a typical modern Unix system is a software component that groups functions corresponding to one or more related devices. It is common for device drivers to be dynamically loadable modules that can be unloaded when not used, in order to lower resource consumption. It is also usually possible to compile a device driver into the kernel, if necessary.

10.1.1 Driver Programming Considered Difficult

Historically, it has been considered rather difficult to write device drivers for an operating system. One reason was that many operating systems did not have well-defined driver architectures. This has improved, as most modern systems have driver architectures and environments that emphasize modularity and, to varying degrees, code reuse. Another reason, which continues to remain valid, is that drivers typically execute in the kernel environment, which is inherently more complex and fragile than user space. The Mac OS X driver architecture is especially helpful in this regard, since it supports versatile mechanisms to access devices from user space. In particular, the architecture supports user-space drivers. For example, devices such as keyboards, mice, printers, scanners, digital still cameras, and digital videocameras can be driven by user-space programs on Mac OS X.

10.1.2 Good Inheritance

The Mac OS X driver architecture is implemented by the I/O Kit, which is a descendent of NEXTSTEP's Driver Kit. The latter was a package of object-oriented software and tools that helped the programmer write device drivers in a modular fashion. The Driver Kit's goal was to make writing and debugging drivers almost as easy as writing and debugging regular NEXTSTEP applications. It aimed to generalize the software involved in drivers, so that writing them would require less time and effort. The underlying observation was that although drivers may drive vastly different devices, they still have several common aspects and requirements. The Driver Kit treated drivers as essential components of the I/O subsystem, since peripherals required for various types of I/O in a computer system were also driven by drivers. Moreover, drivers for loosely related devices might be very close to each other in implementation. The commonalities could be offered as libraries for use by driver developers. The Driver Kit used Objective-C as its programming language.

10.1.3 Everything Is a File

Typical Unix systems provide a file-system-based user interface to devices—a user-space process addresses a device through *device special files* (or simply *device files*) that conventionally reside in the /dev/ directory. Older systems had a static /dev/, wherein the constituent device files were explicitly created or deleted, and device major numbers were statically assigned. Newer systems, including Mac OS X, manage devices more dynamically. For example, the Mac OS X device file system allows device files to be dynamically created or deleted and major numbers to be automatically assigned on device file creation.

The device files in the earliest versions of UNIX were hardcoded into the kernel. For example, /dev/rk0 and /dev/rrk0 were the block and character devices, respectively, representing the first moving-head RK disk drive attached to the system. /dev/mem mapped the core memory of the computer into a file. It was possible to patch the running system using a debugger on /dev/mem. When such a file was read from or written to, the underlying device was activated—that is, the corresponding kernel-resident functions were invoked. Besides data I/O, control operations could also be performed on device files.

The basic concepts of device files have remained largely the same as UNIX and its derivatives have evolved. Mac OS X provides device files for storage devices,[1] serial devices, pseudo-terminals, and several pseudo-devices.

10.1.4 There Is More to Extending the Kernel Than Driving Devices

Besides device drivers, several other types of code can extend the kernel. Loadable kernel components on Mac OS X include file systems, file system authorization modules (see Section 11.10), storage device filters, BSD-style sysctl variables, and network extensions. Beginning with version 10.4, Mac OS X provides stable kernel programming interfaces (KPIs) for these various types of kernel components.

10.2 The I/O Kit

The I/O Kit is a collection of several pieces of kernel-level and user-level software that together constitute a simplified driver development mechanism for

---

1. As we will see in Section 11.3, storage-related Unix-style devices on Mac OS X are implemented by the I/O Kit.

many types of devices. It provides a layered runtime architecture in which various pieces of software and hardware have dynamic relationships. Besides being a foundation for device drivers, the I/O Kit also coordinates the use of device drivers. Features of the I/O Kit include the following.

- It presents an abstract view of the system's hardware to higher layers of Mac OS X. In this sense, one of the I/O Kit's jobs is to act as a hardware abstraction layer (HAL). In particular, it provides an approximation of the hardware hierarchy by representing it in software: Each type of device or service is abstracted by an I/O Kit C++ class, and each real-life instance of that device or service is represented by an instance of the corresponding C++ class.

- It incorporates an in-memory database called the I/O Registry for tracking live (instantiated) objects and another database called the I/O Catalog for tracking all I/O Kit classes available on a system, including uninstantiated ones.

- It facilitates code reuse and promotes stability by encapsulating common functionality and behavior shared among various driver types (or *driver families*) and specific drivers. In particular, the I/O Kit exports a unified object-oriented programming interface. Certain types of devices can be driven by user-space drivers. Examples of such devices include cameras, printers, and scanners. Specifically, the connection protocols of these devices—such as USB and FireWire—are handled by kernel-resident I/O Kit families, but device-specific higher-level aspects are handled in user space.

- In general, the I/O Kit provides a variety of services for accessing and manipulating devices from user space. These services are available to user programs through the I/O Kit framework (`IOKit.framework`).

- Besides helping to avoid duplicating common functionality across drivers, the I/O Kit shields the programmer—to some extent—from having to know details of kernel internals. For example, the I/O Kit abstracts Mach-level details of virtual memory and threading—it provides simpler wrappers as part of its programming interface.

- It supports automatic configuration, or *Plug-and-Play*. Device drivers can be automatically loaded and unloaded as appropriate.

- It provides interfaces for driver stacking, wherein new services can be instantiated based on existing services.

Code reuse is not always possible as the I/O Kit may have limited or no support for some types of devices. Hardware quirks and subtleties may mean that apparently similar cases must be handled separately.

Figure 10–1 shows an overview of the important components and features of the I/O Kit.

Note that whereas a user-space program using the I/O Kit links against `IOKit.framework`, a kernel-space program, such as a device driver, uses the Kernel framework (`Kernel.framework`) during its build stage. `Kernel.framework` does not contain any libraries; it provides only kernel header files. In other words, a driver does not link against `Kernel.framework`—it links against the kernel itself.

10.2.1 Embedded C++

Unlike its predecessor, the Driver Kit, which used Objective-C, the I/O Kit uses a restricted subset of C++ as its programming language— it is implemented in and is programmed by using *embedded C++* (EC++).[2] The EC++ specification includes a minimum language specification, which is a proper subset of C++, a library specification, and a style guide. The library is more than a typical embedded C library but less than a full-fledged C++ library. Important C++ features omitted from EC++ are the following:

- Exceptions
- Templates
- Multiple inheritance and virtual base classes
- Namespaces
- Runtime type identification (RTTI)

Note that the I/O Kit does implement its own minimal runtime typing system.

---

2. The EC++ Technical Committee was formed in Japan in late 1995, with the goal of providing an open standard for the language and encouraging commercial products that support the standard.

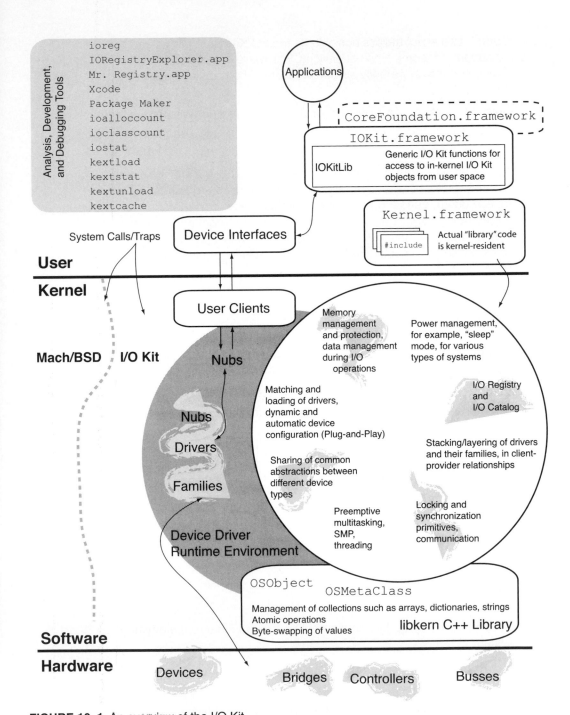

FIGURE 10–1 An overview of the I/O Kit

10.2.2 I/O Kit Class Hierarchy

The various parts of the I/O Kit are implemented using building blocks from the kernel-resident libkern C++ library. Figure 10–2 shows the high-level class hierarchy of the I/O Kit.

The *General OS Classes* category includes OSObject, which is the kernel's root base class. Besides device drivers, these OS classes are available to all kernel code.

The *General I/O Kit Classes* category includes IORegistryEntry and its subclass, IOService. The former is the root class of the I/O Kit hierarchy. It allows I/O Kit objects to appear in the I/O Registry and manages their "personalities." In particular, an I/O Kit driver's attach() and detach() methods are used for connecting to the I/O Registry.

The *Family Superclasses* category includes I/O Kit families for several device types. IOService is the direct or indirect superclass of most I/O Kit Family Superclasses—typically, at least one important class in each family inherits from IOService. In turn, most drivers are instances of a subclass of a class in an I/O Kit family. A driver's lifecycle within the I/O Kit's dynamic runtime environment is captured by IOService—specifically, by its virtual functions. Examples of interfaces defined by IOService include functions for the following purposes:

- Initializing and terminating driver objects
- Attaching and detaching driver objects to the I/O Registry
- Probing hardware to match drivers to devices
- Instantiating drivers based on the existence of their providers
- Managing power
- Mapping and accessing device memory
- Notifying interested parties of changes in the states of services
- Registering, unregistering, enabling, and triggering device interrupts

The I/O Kit's main architectural abstractions are *families*, *drivers*, and *nubs*.

10.2.3 I/O Kit Families

An I/O Kit family is a set of classes and associated code that implement abstractions common to devices of a particular category. From a packaging standpoint, a family may include kernel extensions, libraries, header files, documentation,

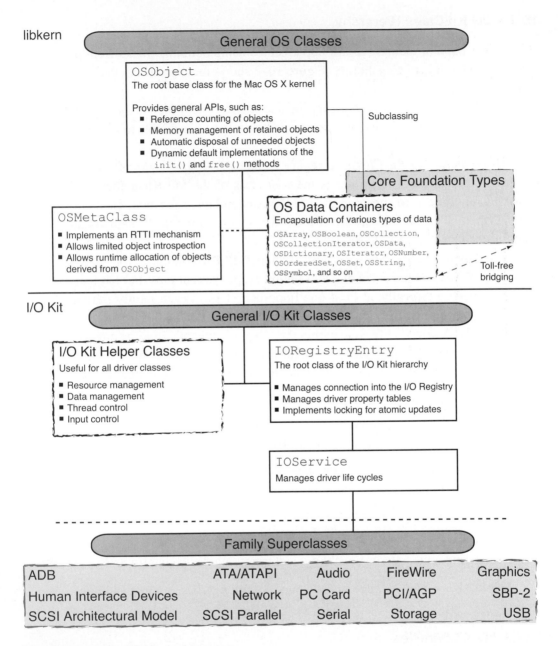

FIGURE 10–2 The I/O Kit class hierarchy

example code, test modules, test harnesses, and so on. Typically, the kernel components of a family can be dynamically loaded into the kernel as needed. The purpose of a family is to allow the driver programmer to focus on device-specific issues, rather than reimplementing frequently used abstractions, which the family implements and provides as a library. In other words, given the specific needs of a particular device, its driver can be constructed by extending the appropriate family.

> In some cases, the services a driver requires may be directly provided by the `IOService` class—that is, the driver may not have a specific family.

Families exist for storage devices, human-interface devices, network devices and services, bus protocols, and others. Examples of Apple-provided I/O Kit families include the following:

- Apple Desktop Bus (ADB)
- ATA and ATAPI
- Audio
- FireWire
- Graphics
- Human Interface Device (HID)
- Network
- PC Card
- PCI and AGP
- Serial Bus Protocol 2 (SBP-2)
- SCSI Parallel and SCSI Architecture Model
- Serial
- Storage
- USB

> Device/service types for which no families exist include tape drives, telephony services, and digital imaging devices.

10.2.4 I/O Kit Drivers

A driver is an I/O Kit object that manages a specific piece of hardware. It is usually an abstraction around a particular device or a bus. I/O Kit drivers have dependencies on one or more families and perhaps on other types of kernel extensions. These dependencies are enumerated by the driver in an XML-formatted property list file (`Info.plist`), which is part of the driver's packaging as a Mac OS X bundle. A driver is dynamically loaded into the kernel, and so are the driver's non-kernel-resident dependencies,[3] which must be loaded before the driver.

> The default locations for drivers are the `Library/Extensions/` directories in Mac OS X file system domains. Apple-provided drivers reside in `/System/Library/Extensions/`.

When a driver belongs to a family, the driver's class typically inherits from some class in the family. This way, all drivers that inherit from a given family acquire the family's instance variables and common behaviors. A family may need to call methods in a driver that inherits from it, in which case the driver implements the methods.

When the system starts to boot, a logical chain of devices and services involved in I/O connections is initialized, starting with the main logic board (hardware) and the corresponding driver (software). This chain grows incrementally, as busses are scanned, devices attached to them are discovered, matching drivers are found, and stacks of providers and clients are constructed. In such a layered stack, each layer is a *client* of the layer below it and a *provider* of services to the layer above it. From an implementation standpoint, a typical driver conceptually sits between two families in a stack of C++ objects that represent family instances. The driver inherits from a class in the top family and uses the services provided by the bottom family.

10.2.5 Nubs

A nub is an I/O Kit object representing a controllable entity—specifically, a device or a logical service. It is a logical connection point and communication channel that bridges two drivers and, in turn, the drivers' families. Besides pro-

---

3. A driver can also depend on built-in kernel components.

viding access to the entity it represents, a nub provides functionality such as arbitration, matching of drivers to devices, and power management. In contrast to a nub, an actual driver manages specific hardware, with which it communicates through the nub.

Examples of entities represented by nubs include disks, disk partitions, emulated SCSI peripheral devices, keyboards, and graphics adapters.

> A driver may publish a nub for each individual device or service it controls or may even act as its own nub—that is, a nub can also be a driver.

A nub's most important function is driver matching: On discovering a new device, the nub attempts to find one or more drivers that match that specific hardware device. We will discuss driver matching in Section 10.2.11.

Although we differentiate between nubs and drivers, they are both classified as *driver objects*, with the IOService class being the eventual superclass of all driver classes. Moreover, a family usually makes available a class that describes a nub and another class that member drivers use in their implementations. A nub is always registered in the I/O Registry—the registration initiates driver matching. In contrast, it is possible for a driver to be *attached* but not registered in the I/O Registry. An attached-but-unregistered object is not directly found through I/O Kit lookup functions but must be indirectly looked up by first finding a registered parent or child, after which a parent/child traversal function is used to reach the unregistered object.

10.2.6 General I/O Kit Classes

As shown in Figure 10–2, General I/O Kit Classes include IORegistryEntry, IOService, and a variety of helper classes. IORegistryEntry is the base class for all I/O Registry objects, whereas IOService is the base class for most I/O Kit families and drivers. Other fundamental I/O Kit classes include IORegistryIterator and IOCatalogue. The former implements an iterator object for traversing (recursively, if desired) the I/O Registry. IOCatalogue implements the in-kernel database containing all I/O Kit driver personalities.

The helper class category primarily includes two types of classes: those that provide memory-related operations, including management of memory involved in I/O transfers, and those that are useful for synchronization and serialization of access.

10.2.6.1 Classes for Memory-Related Operations

The following classes provide memory-related operations.

- `IOMemoryDescriptor` is an abstract base class used for representing a buffer or range of memory, where the memory could be physical or virtual.

- `IOBufferMemoryDescriptor` is a type of memory descriptor that also allocates its memory when it is created.

- `IOMultiMemoryDescriptor` is a type of memory descriptor that encapsulates an ordered list of multiple `IOMemoryDescriptor` instances, which together represent a single contiguous memory buffer.

- `IODeviceMemory` is a subclass of `IOMemoryDescriptor` that describes a single range of device physical memory.

- `IOMemoryMap` is an abstract base class that provides methods for memory-mapping a range of memory described by an `IOMemoryDescriptor`.

- `IOMemoryCursor` implements the mechanism for generating a scatter/gather list of physical segments from a memory descriptor. The generation is based on the nature of the target hardware. During the initialization of an instance of `IOMemoryCursor`, a pointer to a *segment function* is provided by the caller. Each invocation of the segment function outputs a single physical segment.

- `IOBigMemoryCursor` is a subclass of `IOMemoryCursor` that generates physical segments in the big-endian byte order.

- `IOLittleMemoryCursor` is a subclass of `IOMemoryCursor` that generates physical segments in the little-endian byte order.

- `IONaturalMemoryCursor` is a subclass of `IOMemoryCursor` that generates physical segments in the processor's natural byte order.

- `IODBDMAMemoryCursor` is a subclass of `IOMemoryCursor` that generates a vector of descriptor-based DMA (DBDMA) descriptors.

- `IORangeAllocator` implements a range-based memory allocator. A new instance of the class is created with either an empty free list or a free list that contains a single initial fragment.

10.2.6.2 Classes for Synchronization and Serialization of Access

The following classes assist with synchronization and serialization of access.

- `IOWorkLoop` is a thread of control that helps drivers protect resources from concurrent or reentrant access. For example, a work loop can be used to serialize invocations of functions that access critical resources. A single work loop can have multiple registered event sources, each of which has an associated action.

- `IOEventSource` is an abstract superclass representing a work-loop event source.

- `IOTimerEventSource` is a work-loop event source that implements a simple timer.

- `IOInterruptEventSource` is a work-loop event source for delivering interrupts to a driver in a single-threaded manner. In contrast to conventional primary interrupts, `IOInterruptEventSource` delivers secondary or deferred interrupts.

- `IOFilterInterruptEventSource` is a version of `IOInterruptEventSource` that first calls the driver—in primary interrupt context—to determine whether the interrupt should be scheduled on the driver's work loop.

- `IOCommandGate` inherits from `IOEventSource` and provides a lightweight mechanism for executing an action in a single-threaded manner (with respect to all other work-loop event sources).

- `IOCommand` is an abstract base class that represents an I/O command passed from a device driver to a controller. Controller command classes such as `IOATACommand`, `IOFWCommand`, and `IOUSBCommand` inherit from `IOCommand`.

- `IOCommandPool` implements a pool of commands that inherit from `IOCommand`. It supports extracting commands from the pool and returning commands to the pool in a serialized manner.

10.2.6.3 Miscellaneous Classes

The I/O Kit also contains the following miscellaneous classes.

- `IONotifier` is an abstract base class used for implementing `IOService` notification requests. It provides methods for enabling, disabling, and removing notification requests.

- `IOPMpriv` encapsulates private power management instance variables for `IOService` objects.

- `IOPMprot` encapsulates protected power management instance variables for `IOService` objects.

- `IOKernelDebugger` acts as a kernel debugger nub, interfacing with the Kernel Debugging Protocol (KDP) module and dispatching KDP requests to the debugger device, which is typically a subclass of `IOEthernetController`.

- `IOUserClient` is used to implement a mechanism for communicating between in-kernel I/O Kit objects and user-space programs.

- `IODataQueue` implements a queue that can be used for passing arbitrary, variable-size data from the kernel to a user task. The queue instance can also notify the user task of data availability.

10.2.7 The Work Loop

The I/O Kit's work-loop abstraction, which is implemented by the `IOWorkLoop` class, provides a synchronization and serialization mechanism to drivers. An `IOWorkLoop` instance is essentially a thread of control. A key feature of the class is that one or more *event sources* can be added to it. Each event represents work to be done by the loop, hence the name. Examples of events are command requests, interrupts, and timers. In general, a source can represent any event that should awaken a driver's work loop to perform some work. Each event source has an associated action, the execution of which manifests the concept of work. `IOWorkLoop` incorporates internal locking to ensure that only one unit of work is being processed at a time in a given instance of the class—all event sources acquire the work loop's mutex (or close the work-loop gate) before executing the associated callbacks. Therefore, it is guaranteed that only one action can execute at a time in a work loop. In this sense, the `IOWorkLoop` class provides the semantics of a master lock for a given driver stack. In the case of interrupts, the work loop's thread acts as the context thread for secondary interrupts (a secondary interrupt is a deferred version of a primary interrupt).

A driver does not usually need to create its own `IOWorkLoop` instance. It can use its provider's work loop, which can be retrieved using the `getWorkLoop()` method of the `IOService` object representing the provider. If the driver does have a current work loop, `getWorkLoop()` will return that; otherwise, it will walk up the provider chain, calling itself recursively until it finds a valid work loop.

As Figure 10–3 shows, an `IOWorkLoop`'s main function—`threadMain()`—consists of three distinct loops: an outermost semaphore clear-and-wait loop, a middle loop that terminates when there is no more work, and an inner loop that traverses the chain of events looking for work. An event source indicates that there is more work to be done through the `checkForWork()` method implemented by a subclass of `IOEventSource`. `checkForWork()` is supposed to check the internal state of the subclass and also call out to the action. If there is more work, the middle loop repeats. Note that the `openGate()` and `closeGate()`

methods are simple wrappers around `IORecursiveLockUnlock()` and `IORecursiveLockLock()`, respectively, with the recursive mutex lock being a protected member of the class.

FIGURE 10–3 The main function of the `IOWorkLoop` class

```
// iokit/Kernel/IOWorkLoop.cpp

void
IOWorkLoop::threadMain()
{
    ...
    // OUTER LOOP
    for (;;) {
        ...
        closeGate();
        if (ISSETP(&fFlags, kLoopTerminate))
            goto exitThread;

        // MIDDLE LOOP
        do {
            workToDo = more = false;
            // INNER LOOP
            // look at all registered event sources
            for (IOEventSource *event = eventChain; event;
                 event = event->getNext()) {
                ...
                // check if there is any work to do for this source
                // a subclass of IOEventSource may or may not do work here
                more |= event->checkForWork();
                ...
            }
        } while (more);
        ...
        openGate();
        ...
        if (workToDo)
            continue;
        else
            break;
    }

exitThread:
    workThread = 0;
    free();
    IOExitThread();
}
```

Let us look at an example of using `IOWorkLoop` in a hypothetical driver—let us call it `SomeDummyDriver`—that uses `IOWorkLoop` with two event sources: an interrupt and a command gate. In its `start()` method, the driver first creates and initializes its own work loop by calling the `IOWorkLoop` class' `workLoop()` method. In most cases, a driver higher up in a driver stack could use its provider's work loop.

The driver creates an `IOInterruptEventSource` object. In this example, the provider's `IOService` represents the source of interrupts, as specified by the last argument to `interruptEventSource()`. If this argument is `NULL`, the event source assumes that its `interruptOccurred()` method will be called by the client somehow. Next, the driver adds the interrupt event source to be monitored by the work loop. It then calls the work loop's `enableAllInterrupts()` method, which calls the `enable()` method in all interrupt event sources.

The driver also creates an `IOCommandGate` object, which inherits from `IOEventSource`, for single-threaded execution of commands, with `commandGateHandler()`—a static function—being the designated action for the command gate. `commandGateHandler()` ensures that the object type passed to it is an instance of `SomeDummyDriver` and dispatches commands based on its first argument. Actions that are performed through the `runCommand()` or `runAction()` methods of `IOCommandGate` are guaranteed to be executed in a single-threaded manner.

Figure 10–4 shows the relevant portions of code from `SomeDummyDriver`.

FIGURE 10–4 Using `IOWorkLoop` in a driver

```
// SomeDummyDriver.h

class SomeDummyDriver : public SomeSuperClass
{
    OSDeclareDefaultStructors(SomeDummyDriver)

private:
    ...
    IOWorkLoop            *workLoop;
    IOCommandGate         *commandGate;
    IOInterruptEventSource *intSource;
    ...
    static void handleInterrupt(OSObject *owner, IOInterruptEventSource *src,
                                int count);

    static IOReturn commandGateHandler(OSObject *owner, void *arg0,
                                       void *arg1, void *arg2, void *arg3);

    ...
```

(continues)

FIGURE 10–4 Using `IOWorkLoop` in a driver *(continued)*

```
    typedef enum {
        someCommand      = 1,
        someOtherCommand = 2,
        ...
    };

protected:
    ...

public:
    ...
    virtual void free(void);
    virtual bool start(IOService *provider);
    virtual bool free(void);
    ...
    IOreturn somePublicMethod_Gated(/* argument list */);
};

bool
SomeDummyDriver::start(IOService *provider)
{
    if (!super::start(provider))
        return false;

    workLoop = IOWorkLoop::workLoop(); // Could also use provider->getWorkLoop()
    ...
    intSource = IOInterruptEventSource::interruptEventSource(

                    this,
                    // Handler to call when an interrupt occurs
                    (IOInterruptEventAction)&handleInterrupt,
                    // The IOService that represents the interrupt source
                    provider);
    ...
    workLoop->addEventSource(intSource);
    ...
    workLoop->enableAllInterrupts();
    ...
    commandGate = IOCommandGate::commandGate(
                    this, // Owning client of the new command gate
                    commandGateHandler); // Action
    ...
    workLoop->addEventSource(commandGate);
}

void
SomeDummyDriver::free(void)
```

(continues)

FIGURE 10–4 Using `IOWorkLoop` in a driver *(continued)*

```
{
    ...
    if (workLoop) {

        if (intSource) {
            workLoop->removeEventSource(intSource);
            intSource->release();
            intSource = 0;
        }

        if (commandGate) {
            workLoop->removeEventSource(commandGate);
            commandGate->release();
            commandGate = 0;
        }

        workLoop->release(); // Since we created it
    }
    ...
    super::free();
}

/* static */ void
SomeDummyDriver::handleInterrupt(OSObject             *owner,
                                 IOInterruptEventSource *src,
                                 int                    count)
{
    // Process the "secondary" interrupt
}

/* static */ IOReturn
SomeDummyDriver::commandGateHandler(OSObject *owner,
                                    void     *arg0,
                                    void     *arg1,
                                    void     *arg2,
                                    void     *arg3)
{
    IOReturn ret;

    SomeDummyDriver *xThis = OSDynamicCast(SomeDummyDriver, owner);
    if (xThis == NULL)
        return kIOReturnError;
    else {
        // Use arg0 through arg3 to process the command. For example, arg0
        // could be a command identifier, and the rest could be arguments
        // to that command.
        switch ((int)arg0) {
```

(continues)

FIGURE 10–4 Using `IOWorkLoop` in a driver *(continued)*

```
        case someCommand:
            ret = xThis->somePublicMethod_Gated(/* argument list */);
            ...
            break;

        case someOtherCommand:
            ...
            break;
        ...
        }
    return ret;
}


IOReturn
SomeDummyDriver::somePublicMethod_Gated(/* argument list */)
{
    // Calls the current action in a single-threaded manner
    return commandGate->runCommand(/* argument list */);
}
```

10.2.8 The I/O Registry

The I/O Registry can be seen as an information hub between the kernel and user spaces. It is a kernel-resident, in-memory database that is both constructed and maintained dynamically. Its contents include the set of live I/O Kit objects—such as families, nubs, and drivers—in a running system. On discovering new hardware, whether at boot time or at some point in a running system, the I/O Kit attempts to find a matching driver for the hardware and load it. If the driver is loaded successfully, the I/O Registry is updated to reflect the newly added or updated provider-client relationships between driver objects. The I/O Registry also tracks various other types of information, such as that related to power management and the state of a network controller. Consequently, the I/O Registry changes in various scenarios—for example, when a system wakes up from sleep.

The I/O Registry is structured as an inverted tree, each of whose nodes is an object ultimately derived from the `IORegistryEntry` class. The tree's root node corresponds to the system's main logic board. A stack of I/O Kit objects can be visualized as a branch in the tree. A typical node in the tree represents a driver object, with each node having one or more properties, which can be of various types and in turn are represented by various data types such as numbers, strings, lists, and dictionaries. A node's properties may have multiple sources, with a typical source being the driver's personality, which could be seen as a set of key-value pairs describing the driver. Properties may also represent configurable information, statistics, or arbitrary driver state.

> There can be nodes in the I/O Registry that are contrary to the definition of a tree. For example, in the case of a RAID disk controller, several disks appear as one logical volume, with the consequence that some nodes have multiple parents.

The two-dimensional tree structure of the I/O Kit is projected onto multiple conceptual *I/O Kit planes*, such as the ones listed here.

- *The Service plane* (`IOService`), the most general plane, captures the relationships of all I/O Kit objects to their ancestors.
- *The Device Tree plane* (`IODeviceTree`) captures the hierarchy of the Open Firmware device tree.
- *The Power plane* (`IOPower`) captures the dependencies between I/O Kit objects with respect to power. It is possible to determine, by traversing the connections in this plane, how power flows from one node to another (say, from a provider to a client). In particular, the effects of turning a given device's power on or off can also be visualized.
- *The FireWire plane* (`IOFireWire`) captures the hierarchy of FireWire devices.
- *The USB plane* (`IOUSB`) captures the hierarchy of USB devices.

The sets of branches and nodes in different I/O Kit planes are not identical because each plane is a representation of different provider-client relationships between I/O Kit objects. Even though all I/O Registry objects exist on all planes, only connections that exist in a particular plane's definition are expressed in that plane.

> The I/O Registry can be examined through the command-line program `ioreg` or by using graphical tools such as `IORegistry-Explorer.app` (part of Apple Developer Tools) and `Mr. Registry.app` (part of the FireWire SDK).

10.2.9 The I/O Catalog

Whereas the I/O Registry maintains the collection of objects active in the running system, the I/O Catalog maintains the collection of available drivers—it is an in-kernel dynamic database containing *all* I/O Kit driver personalities. The `IOService` class uses this resource when matching devices to their associated drivers. In particular, on discovering a device, a nub consults the I/O Catalog to retrieve the list of all drivers belonging to the device's family. The `IOCatalogue` class provides methods for initializing the catalog, adding drivers, removing drivers, finding drivers based on caller-provided information, and so on.

During bootstrapping, the I/O Catalog is initialized from a list of built-in catalog entries. The list is represented by the `gIOKernelConfigTables` string [`iokit/KernelConfigTables.cpp`], which holds the built-in drivers' serialized information. Table 10–1 shows the members of the list. Much of the I/O Catalog's functionality is implemented in `libsa/catalogue.cpp`.

TABLE 10–1 Initial Entries in the I/O Catalog

IOClass	IOProviderClass	IONameMatch
IOPanicPlatform	IOPlatformExpertDevice	—
AppleCPU	IOPlatformDevice	cpu
AppleNMI	AppleMacIODevice	programmer-switch
AppleNVRAM	AppleMacIODevice	nvram

> `IOPanicPlatform` represents a catch-all Platform Expert that matches if no legitimate `IOPlatformDevice` matches. The start routine of this class causes a kernel panic with a message indicating that no driver for the unknown platform could be found.

10.2.10 I/O Kit Initialization

We discussed I/O Kit initialization in Section 5.6. As shown in Figure 5–14, the bulk of I/O Kit initialization is performed by `StartIOKit()` [`iokit/Kernel/IOStartIOKit.cpp`]. `OSlibkernInit()` [`libkern/c++/OSRuntime.cpp`] initializes a `kmod_info` structure (Figure 10–5). The kernel variable that corresponds to this instance of the `kmod_info` structure is also called `kmod_info`.

This instance is used to represent the kernel as a fictitious library kernel-module whose name is __kernel__. The module's starting address is set to the kernel's Mach-O header. As with normal kernel extensions, OSRuntimeInitializeCPP() [libkern/c++/OSRuntime.cpp] is called to initialize the C++ runtime. The OSBoolean class is also initialized by OSlibkernInit().

FIGURE 10–5 The kmod_info structure

// osfmk/mach/kmod.h

```
typedef struct kmod_info {
    struct kmod_info    *next;
    int                 info_version;
    int                 id;
    char                name[KMOD_MAX_NAME];
    char                version[KMOD_MAX_NAME];
    int                 reference_count;  // number of references to this kmod
    kmod_reference_t    *reference_list;  // references made by this kmod
    vm_address_t        address;          // starting address
    vm_size_t           size;             // total size
    vm_size_t           hdr_size;         // unwired header size
    kmod_start_func_t   *start;           // module start entry point
    kmod_stop_func_t    *stop;            // module termination entry point
} kmod_info_t;
```

StartIOKit() also initializes key I/O Kit classes by calling their initialize() methods, such as the following.

- IORegistryEntry::initialize() sets up the I/O Registry by creating its root node (called Root) and initializing relevant data structures such as locks and an OSDictionary object to hold I/O Kit planes.

- IOService::initialize() initializes I/O Kit planes (such as the Service and Power planes) and creates various global I/O Kit data structures such as keys, locks, dictionaries, and lists.

- As we saw earlier, the IOCatalogue class implements an in-kernel database for driver personalities. An IOCatalogue instance is published as a resource used by IOService to match devices to their associated drivers. A typical matching process involves a caller providing a matching dictionary containing key-value pairs on which to base the matching. The number and type of keys determine how specific or generic a result will be and whether there will be a match at all. IOCatalogue::initialize() uses gIOKernelConfigTables, which is a serialized OSArray of OSDictionary data types, to initialize the I/O Catalog with personalities corresponding to a few built-in drivers, such as those shown in Table 10–1.

- `IOMemoryDescriptor::initialize()` allocates a recursive lock used by the `IOMemoryDescriptor` class, which is an abstract base class that defines common methods for describing both physical and virtual memory. An `IOMemoryDescriptor` is specified as one or more physical or virtual address ranges corresponding to a memory buffer or memory range. The initialization function also creates an I/O Registry property (`IOMaximumMappedIOByteCount`) representing the maximum amount of memory that can be wired using the `wireVirtual()` method.

`StartIOKit()` finally creates an instance of the `IOPlatformExpertDevice` class as the system's root nub. As we have seen earlier, the Platform Expert is a motherboard-specific driver object that knows the type of platform the system is running on. The root nub's initialization allocates the I/O Kit device tree, initializes the Device Tree plane, and creates an instance of the `IOWorkLoop` class. The `model` property of the root nub specifies a particular type and version of Apple computer, such as the following:

- MacBookProM,N (the x86-based MacBook Pro line)
- PowerBookM,N (the PowerBook and iBook lines)
- PowerMacM,N (the PowerMac line)
- RackMacM,N (the Xserve line)

M represents the major revision, whereas N represents the minor revision.

The root nub instance is then published for matching. The matching process begins with the `IOService` class method `startMatching()`, which invokes the `doServiceMatch()` method synchronously or asynchronously, as indicated by the caller.

`IOPlatformExpertDevice` is a provider to a system architecture–specific driver, such as `MacRISC4PE` (systems based on the G5 processor, the U3 memory controller, and the K2 I/O controller) or `MacRISC2PE` (systems based on G3 and G4 processors, the UniNorth memory controller, and the KeyLargo I/O controller).

10.2.11 Driver Matching in the I/O Kit

The process of finding a suitable driver for a device attached to the system is called *driver matching*. This process is performed every time a system boots but can also be performed later if a device is attached to a running system.

Each driver's property list file defines one or more of the driver's *personalities*, which are sets of properties specified as key-value pairs. These properties are used to determine whether the driver can drive a particular device. At the nub's behest, the I/O Kit finds and loads candidate drivers. Next, it incrementally narrows the search for the most suitable driver. A typical search has the following stages of matching:

- *Class matching*, during which drivers are ruled out based on their class being inappropriate with respect to the provider service (the nub)

- *Passive matching*, during which drivers are ruled out based on device-specific properties contained in driver personalities, with respect to the properties specific to the provider's family

- *Active matching*, during which drivers in the pared-down list of candidates are actively probed by calling each driver's `probe()` method, passing it a reference to the nub it is being matched against

Before active matching begins, the list of candidate drivers is ordered by the initial *probe score* of each driver. The probe score signifies confidence in the drivability of the device by the driver. A driver personality can specify an initial score using the `IOProbeScore` key. For each candidate driver, the I/O Kit instantiates the driver's *principal class* and calls its `init()` method. The principal class is the one specified by the `IOClass` key in the driver's personality. Next, the I/O Kit attaches the new instance to the provider by calling the `attach()` method. If the driver implements the `probe()` method, the I/O Kit calls it. In this method, a driver can communicate with the device to verify whether it can drive the device and possibly modify the probe score. Once the `probe()` method returns (or if there is no `probe()` implementation), the I/O Kit detaches the driver by calling the `detach()` method and moves to the next candidate driver.

After the probing phase, the probe scores of candidate drivers that could be successfully probed are considered in decreasing order. The drivers are first grouped into categories based on the `IOMatchCategory` optional key in driver personalities. Drivers that do not specify this key are all considered to belong to the same category. At most one driver in each category can be started on a given provider. For each category, the driver with the highest probe score is attached (again, through the `attach()` method) and started (through the `start()` method). A copy of the driver's personality is placed in the I/O Registry. If the driver starts successfully, the remaining drivers in the category are discarded; otherwise, the failed driver's class instance is freed and the candidate with the next highest probe score is considered.

> If a driver has multiple personalities, each personality is treated as a separate driver from the standpoint of the matching process. In other words, a driver containing multiple matching dictionaries can apply to multiple devices.

10.3 DART

With the advent of the 64-bit G5-based computers that support more than 4GB of physical memory, Mac OS X had to incorporate support for 64-bit memory addressing.[4] However, the PCI and PCI-X busses on the G5 still employ 32-bit addressing. This causes *physical addresses* (64-bit) to be different from *I/O addresses* (32-bit) on the G5.

> As we saw in Chapter 8, even with support for 64-bit user address spaces, the kernel's address space, including the I/O Kit's runtime environment, remains 32-bit in Mac OS X.

As we noted in Section 3.3.3.2, besides the standard memory management unit (MMU), G5-based Apple computers use an additional MMU for I/O addresses. This *Device Address Resolution Table* (DART) creates mappings between linear addresses and physical addresses. It is implemented as an application-specific integrated circuit (ASIC) that physically resides in the North Bridge. It translates memory accesses from HyperTransport/PCI devices. In particular, it provides dynamic DMA mapping support, and all DMA accesses are channeled through it.

The DART translates only memory accesses that fall in the range 0GB through 2GB, that is, 31 bits of memory; thus, HyperTransport/PCI devices cannot access more than 2GB of memory at a time. In other words, the DART supports up to 2GB of I/O data in some stage of transfer at any given time. The translated physical addresses are 36 bits wide. The DART driver manages the

---

4. It is possible for a computer system based on a 32-bit processor to support more than 4GB of physical memory.

2GB I/O space using power-of-2-sized zones, with the smallest zone size being 16KB, which, consequently, is the lower bound on the size of an allocation. The driver limits the size of a single allocation to be at most half the total size of the space. Therefore, a single mapping can be at most 1GB in size.

> The `AppleMacRiscPCI` kernel extension implements the DART driver. The `AppleDART` class inherits from the `IOMapper` class, which in turn inherits from `IOService`.

Given its allocation algorithm, the DART driver is likely to return contiguous I/O memory for most allocations, even though the underlying physical memory may be fragmented. In general, the driver of the device in question will see the memory as contiguous and is likely to have improved performance for DMA transfers. This is why the DART is enabled even on G5-based systems with less than 2GB of physical memory.

A device driver is not required to directly interface with the DART or to even know of its existence. If a driver uses `IOMemoryDescriptor` objects for accessing and manipulating memory, the I/O Kit automatically sets up the DART. If a driver performs DMA on a G5-based system, it *must* use `IOMemoryDescriptor` and thus will implicitly use the DART. Moreover, before DMA can be initiated for an `IOMemoryDescriptor` object, its `prepare()` method must be called to prepare the associated memory for an I/O transfer. On the G5, this preparation converts the system's 64-bit addresses to 32-bit addresses for DMA, including creation of entries in the DART. Additionally, the preparation may page in memory and wire it down for the duration of the transfer. The `complete()` method of `IOMemoryDescriptor` must be called to complete the processing of memory after the I/O transfer finishes. As a general rule, a driver must call `prepare()` on all `IOMemoryDescriptor` objects before using them,[5] whether it is for DMA or programmed I/O (PIO). The `getPhysicalSegment()` method of `IOMemoryDescriptor` is relevant for DMA, since it breaks a memory descriptor into its physically contiguous segments. Progammed I/O can be performed by calling the `readBytes()` and `writeBytes()` methods of `IOMemoryDescriptor`.

---

5. In some cases, if a memory descriptor describes wired memory, preparation may be automatic.

As we saw in Section 8.16.6, the I/O Kit's `IOMallocContiguous()` function implicitly prepares the physically contiguous memory it returns. Although it is possible to obtain the physical address of the allocated memory from `IOMallocContiguous()`, that address is not the actual physical address but the DART'ed (translated) physical address.[6] The I/O Kit does not expose the real physical address to the programmer. If a real address were nevertheless presented to the I/O Kit by a driver, the operation would fail because the DART would be unable to handle the translation.

10.4 Dynamically Extending the Kernel

The Mac OS X kernel is extensible through dynamically loadable components called kernel extensions, or simply *kexts*. A kext is loaded into the kernel either by the kernel's built-in loader (during early stages of bootstrapping) or by the user-level daemon `kextd`, which loads kexts when requested by user processes or the kernel. On being loaded, a kext resides in the kernel's address space, executing in privileged mode as part of the kernel. Numerous I/O Kit device drivers and device families are implemented as kexts. Besides device drivers, kexts also exist for loadable file systems and networking components. In general, a kext can contain arbitrary code—say, common code that may be accessed from multiple other kexts. Such a kext would be akin to a loadable in-kernel library.

10.4.1 The Structure of a Kernel Extension

A kext is a type of bundle, much like an application bundle. A kext bundle's folder has a `.kext` extension.[7] Note that the extension is not merely conventional—it is required by the Mac OS X tools that deal with kernel extensions. A kext bundle must contain an information property list file (`Info.plist`) in its `Contents/` subdirectory. The property list specifies the kext's contents, configuration, and dependencies in an XML-formatted dictionary of key-value pairs. When a kext is loaded into the kernel, the contents of its `Info.plist` are converted to kernel data structures for in-memory storage.[8] A kext bundle normally

---

6. A corollary is that DMA addresses are always less than 2GB on Mac OS X.

7. The Finder treats a kext bundle as a single, indivisible entity.

8. Many of these data structures are analogs of Core Foundation data structures, such as dictionaries, arrays, strings, and numbers.

also contains at least one kernel extension binary, which is a Mach-O executable. It can optionally contain resources such as helper programs and icons in its `Resources/` subdirectory. Moreover, a kext bundle can contain other kext bundles as plug-ins.

> It is possible to have a valid kext bundle without any executables. The `Info.plist` file of such a kext may reference another kext in order to alter the characteristics of the latter. For example, `ICAClassicNotSeizeDriver.kext` does not contain an executable, but it holds several driver personalities that refer to `AppleUSBMerge-Nub.kext`, which is a plug-in kext within `IOUSBFamily.kext`.

Kernel-loadable binaries contained within kexts are statically linked, relocatable Mach-O binaries called kernel modules, or *kmods*. In other words, a kext is a structured folder containing one or more kmods along with mandatory metadata and optional resources. Figure 10–6 shows the structure of a simple kext bundle.

FIGURE 10–6 The contents of a simple kernel extension bundle

```
DummyKEXT.kext/
DummyKEXT.kext/Contents/
DummyKEXT.kext/Contents/Info.plist
DummyKEXT.kext/Contents/MacOS/
DummyKEXT.kext/Contents/MacOS/DummyKEXT
DummyKEXT.kext/Contents/Resources/
DummyKEXT.kext/Contents/Resources/English.lproj/
DummyKEXT.kext/Contents/Resources/English.lproj/InfoPlist.strings
```

> It is important to note that even though a kmod is a statically linked Mach-O object file, nontrivial kmods usually have unresolved external references that are resolved when the kext is dynamically loaded into the kernel.

10.4.2 Creation of Kernel Extensions

Although most driver kexts are created using only I/O Kit interfaces, a kext may—depending on its purpose and nature—interact with the BSD and Mach portions of the kernel. In any case, loading and linking of kexts is always handled by the I/O Kit. The preferred and most convenient way to create a kernel extension is by using one of the kernel extension project templates in Xcode. In fact, other than for a contrived reason, it would be rather pointless to compile a kmod and package it into a kernel extension manually—say, using a hand-generated makefile. Xcode hides several details (such as variable definitions, compiler and linker flags, and other rules for compiling and linking kernel extensions) from the programmer. Two kernel extension templates are available in Xcode: one for *generic kernel extensions* and one for *I/O Kit drivers*. A primary difference between them is that an I/O Kit driver is implemented in C++, whereas a generic kernel extension is implemented in C. It is also possible to create a library kext containing reusable code that can be used by multiple other kexts.

> Definitions and rules for various types of Xcode projects reside in the `/Developer/Makefiles/` directory.

Figure 10–7 shows an excerpt from the build output of a Universal kernel extension—an I/O Kit driver—containing kmods for the PowerPC and x86 architectures. The path to the build directory, which is normally a subdirectory called `build` in the kernel extension's Xcode project directory, has been replaced by `$BUILDDIR` in the output shown.

FIGURE 10–7 Excerpt from the build output of a Universal kernel extension

```
/usr/bin/gcc-4.0 -x c++ -arch ppc -pipe -Wno-trigraphs -fasm-blocks Os -Wreturn-type
-Wunused-variable -fmessage-length=0 -fapple-kext -mtune=G5 -Wno-invalid-offsetof
-I$BUILDDIR/DummyDriver.build/Release/DummyDriver.build/DummyDriver.hmap
-F$BUILDDIR/Release -I$BUILDDIR/Release/include -I/System/Library/Frameworks/
Kernel.framework/PrivateHeaders -I/System/Library/Frameworks/Kernel.framework/Headers
-I$BUILDDIR/DummyDriver.build/Release/DummyDriver.build/DerivedSources -fno-common
-nostdinc -fno-builtin -finline -fno-keep-inline-functions -force_cpusubtype_ALL
-fno-exceptions -msoft-float -static -mlong-branch -fno-rtti -fcheck-new -DKERNEL
-DKERNEL_PRIVATE -DDRIVER_PRIVATE -DAPPLE -DNeXT -isysroot /Developer/SDKs/
MacOSX10.4u.sdk -c /tmp/DummyDriver/DummyDriver.cpp -o $BUILDDIR/DummyDriver.build/
Release/DummyDriver.build/Objects-normal/ppc/DummyDriver.o
...
/usr/bin/g++-4.0 -o $BUILDDIR/DummyDriver.build/Release/DummyDriver.build/Objects-
normal/ppc/DummyDriver -L$BUILDDIR/Release -F$BUILDDIR/Release -filelist $BUILDDIR/
DummyDriver.build/Release/DummyDriver.build/Objects-normal/ppc/
DummyDriver.LinkFileList -arch ppc -static -nostdlib -r -lkmodc++ $BUILDDIR/
DummyDriver.build/Release/DummyDriver.build/Objects-normal/ppc/DummyDriver_info.o
-lkmod -lcc_kext
-lcpp_kext -isysroot /Developer/SDKs/MacOSX10.4u.sdk
...
```

(continues)

FIGURE 10–7 Excerpt from the build output of a Universal kernel extension *(continued)*

```
/usr/bin/lipo -create $BUILDDIR/DummyDriver.build/Release/DummyDriver.build/
Objects-normal/ppc/DummyDriver $BUILDDIR/DummyDriver.build/Release/
DummyDriver.build/Objects-normal/i386/DummyDriver -output $BUILDDIR/Release/
DummyDriver.kext/Contents/MacOS/DummyDriver
...
```

> Note that the Kernel framework (`Kernel.framework`), which is referenced by the compiler in the output shown in Figure 10–7, provides only kernel headers—it does not contain any libraries.

We see in Figure 10–7 that the kmod being compiled is linked with several libraries and an object file called `<kmod>_info.o`, where `<kmod>` is the kmod's name—`DummyDriver` in our example. These entities serve the following purposes.

- `libkmodc++.a` and `libkmod.a` both reside in `/usr/lib/` and contain the runtime startup and shutdown routines for C++ and C, respectively.

- `<kmod>_info.c`, the source file corresponding to the object file `<kmod>_info.o`, is generated during the kernel module's compilation. The combination of `libkmodc++.a`, `libkmod.a`, and `<kmod>_info.o` provides conceptually similar functionality as a user-space language runtime initialization object file (such as `crt0.o`).

- `libcc_kext.a` is a specially compiled version of the GCC library (`libgcc.a`) that provides runtime support routines for code that runs in the kernel environment. Note that many standard `libgcc` routines are not supported in the kernel.

- `libcpp_kext.a` is a minimal C++ library—a stripped-down version of `libstdc++.a`. Its purpose is similar to `libcc_kext.a`.

The order of arguments in the linker command line is instrumental in differentiating between the compilation of C++-based and C-based kmods. As shown in Figure 10–7, the order of object files and libraries in the linker command line is as follows:

```
...DummyDriver.LinkFileList ... -lkmodc++ ...DummyDriver_info.o -lkmod ...
```

The file `DummyDriver.LinkFileList` contains the pathnames of the kmod's object files. If the kmod uses C++, the compiler will add references in object files to undefined symbols called `.constructors_used` and `.destructors_used`.

In the case of a kmod that does not use C++, the references to these symbols will not be present. Let us see how these symbols affect linking by examining the implementations of `libkmodc++.a` and `libkmod.a`, which are shown in Figures 10–8 and 10–10, respectively.

FIGURE 10–8 Implementation of `libkmodc++.a`

```
// libkmodc++.a: cplus_start.c

asm(".constructors_used = 0");
asm(".private_extern .constructors_used");


// defined in <kmod>_info.c
extern kmod_start_func_t *_realmain;


// defined in libkern/c++/OSRuntime.cpp
extern kern_return_t OSRuntimeInitializeCPP(kmod_info_t *ki, void *data);


__private_extern__ kern_return_t _start(kmod_info_t *ki, void *data)
{
    kern_return_t res = OSRuntimeInitializeCPP(ki, data);

    if (!res && _realmain)
        res = (*_realmain)(ki, data);

    return res;
}


// libkmodc++.a: cplus_stop.c

asm(".destructors_used = 0");
asm(".private_extern .destructors_used");


// defined in libkern/c++/OSRuntime.cpp
extern kern_return_t OSRuntimeFinalizeCPP(kmod_info_t *ki, void *data);


// defined in <kmod>_info.c
extern kmod_stop_func_t *_antimain;


__private_extern__ kern_return_t _stop(kmod_info_t *ki, void *data)
{
    kern_return_t res = OSRuntimeFinalizeCPP(ki, data);

    if (!res && _antimain)
        res = (*_antimain)(ki, data);

    return res;
}
```

Since libkmodc++.a exports the .constructors_used and .destructors_used symbols, it will be used to resolve references to these symbols in the case of a C++ kmod object file. As a side effect, the symbols _start and _stop will also come from libkmodc++.a. The <kmod>_info.c file uses these symbols to populate a kmod_info data structure (struct kmod [osfmk/mach/kmod.h]) to describe the kernel module. The kmod_info structure contains the starting address of the kernel module in its address field. Since the module is a Mach-O binary, the binary's Mach-O header is located at this address.

Juxtaposing the information in Figures 10–8 and 10–9, we see that the start and stop routines of an I/O Kit driver kmod will come from libkmodc++.a. Moreover, these routines will run OSRuntimeInitializeCPP() and OSRuntime-FinalizeCPP(), respectively. Since the _realmain and _antimain function pointers are both set to NULL in <kmod>_info.c, the start and stop routines will not invoke the corresponding functions.

FIGURE 10–9 Declaration of the kmod_info structure for an I/O Kit driver kernel module

```
// <kmod>_info.c for an I/O Kit driver (C++)
...
// the KMOD_EXPLICIT_DECL() macro is defined in osfmk/mach/kmod.h
KMOD_EXPLICIT_DECL(com.osxbook.driver.DummyDriver, "1.0.0d1", _start, _stop)
__private_extern__ kmod_start_func_t *_realmain = 0;
__private_extern__ kmod_stop_func_t *_antimain = 0;
...
```

> In the case of a C++ kext, a particular virtual function may be overridden by another subclass at runtime. Since this cannot be determined at compile time, virtual function calls in a C++ kext are dispatched through the vtable. Depending on the kext ABI of the running system and the kext ABI of a given kext, the loading mechanism can patch vtables to maintain ABI compatibility.

OSRuntimeInitializeCPP() calls the preModLoad() member function of OSMetaClass, passing it the module's name as the argument. preModLoad() prepares the runtime system for loading a new module, including taking a lock for the duration of the loading. OSRuntimeInitializeCPP() then scans the module's Mach-O header, seeking segments with sections named __constructor. If any such sections are found, the constructors within them are invoked. If this process fails, OSRuntimeInitializeCPP() calls the destructors (that is, sections named __destructor) for those segments that had their constructors successfully invoked. Eventually, OSRuntimeInitializeCPP() calls the postModLoad() member function of OSMetaClass. postModLoad() performs various book-keeping functions and releases the lock that was taken by preModLoad().

OSRuntimeFinalizeCPP() is called when a module is unloaded. It ensures that no objects represented by OSMetaClass and associated with the module being unloaded have any instances. It does this by checking all meta-classes associated with the module's string name and examining their instance counts. If there are outstanding instances, the unload attempt fails. The actual unloading operation is performed by OSRuntimeUnloadCPP(), the call to which is surrounded by preModLoad() and postModLoad(). OSRuntimeUnloadCPP() iterates over the module's segments, examining them for sections named __destructor and, if any are found, calling the corresponding destructor functions.

Next, let us see how libkmod.a (Figure 10–10) is used in the implementation of a C-only kmod.

FIGURE 10–10 Implementation of libkmod.a

```
// libkmod.a: c_start.c

// defined in <kmod>_info.c
extern kmod_start_func_t *_realmain;

__private_extern__ kern_return_t _start(kmod_info_t *ki, void *data)
{
    if (_realmain)
        return (*_realmain)(ki, data);
    else
        return KERN_SUCCESS;
}


// libkmod.a: c_stop.c

// defined in <kmod>_info.c
extern kmod_stop_func_t *_antimain;

__private_extern__ kern_return_t _stop(kmod_info_t *ki, void *data)
{
    if (_antimain)
        return (*_antimain)(ki, data);
    else
        return KERN_SUCCESS;
}
```

In the case of a C-only kmod object file, which will not contain unresolved references to `.constructors_used` and `.destructors_used`, `libkmodc++.a` will not be used. The `_start` and `_stop` symbols referenced in `<kmod>_info.c` will come from the next library that contains these symbols—that is, `libkmod.a`. As Figure 10–11 shows, the `<kmod>_info.c` file of such a kernel module will set `_realmain` and `_antimain` to point to the module's start and stop entry points, respectively.

FIGURE 10–11 Declaration of the `kmod_info` structure for a generic kernel module

```
// <kmod>_info.c for a generic kernel module (C-only)
...
// the KMOD_EXPLICIT_DECL() macro is defined in osfmk/mach/kmod.h
KMOD_EXPLICIT_DECL(com.osxbook.driver.DummyKExt, "1.0.0d1", _start, _stop)
__private_extern__ kmod_start_func_t *_realmain = DummyKExtStart;
__private_extern__ kmod_stop_func_t *_antimain = DummyKExtStart;
...
```

In other words, although every kmod has start and stop entry points, they can be implemented by the programmer only in the case of a generic kernel module. In the case of an I/O Kit driver, these entry points are unavailable to the programmer because they correspond to the C++ runtime initialization and termination routines. It follows that these two types of loadable entities cannot be implemented within the same kext.

10.4.3 Management of Kernel Extensions

The functionality for working with kernel extensions is implemented across several Darwin packages, such as `xnu`, `IOKitUser`, `kext_tools`, `cctools`, and `extenTools`. The following are the primary command-line programs available for managing kernel extensions.

- `kextd` loads kexts on demand.
- `kextload` loads kexts, validates them to ensure that they can be loaded by other mechanisms, and generates debugging symbols.
- `kextunload` unloads code associated with a kext, terminating and unregistering I/O Kit objects, if any, associated with the kext.
- `kextstat` displays the status of currently loaded kexts.

- `kextcache` creates or updates kext caches.
- `mkextunpack` extracts the contents of a multikext (mkext) archive.

`kextd`, the kernel extension daemon, is the focal point of much of the activity that occurs when kexts are loaded or unloaded in a normally running system. During the early stages of bootstrapping, `kextd` is not yet available. The libsa support library in the kernel handles kernel extensions during early boot. Normally, libsa's code is removed from the kernel when `kextd` starts running. If you boot Mac OS X in verbose mode, you will see a "Jettisoning kernel linker" message printed by the kernel. `kextd` sends a message to the I/O Kit to get rid of the in-kernel linker. In response, the I/O Kit invokes destructors for the kernel's __KLD and __LINKEDIT segments and deallocates their memory. The memory set up by BootX is also freed. `kextd` can be instructed (via the `-j` option) not to jettison the kernel linker. This allows the kernel to continue handling all load requests. In this case, `kextd` exits with a zero status if there is no other error. Bootable optical discs can use this option in startup scripts, along with an mkext cache, to accelerate booting. For example, as we saw in Section 5.10.4, Apple's Mac OS X installer disc runs `kextd` with the `-j` option in `/etc/rc.cdrom`.

`kextd` registers `com.apple.KernelExtensionServer` as its service name with the Bootstrap Server. It processes signals, kernel requests, and client requests (in that order) in its run loop. `kextd` and command-line tools such as `kextload` and `kextunload` use the `KXKextManager` interface for manipulating kernel extensions. `KXKextManager` is implemented as part of the I/O Kit framework (`IOKit.framework`). Figure 10–12 shows an overview of `kextd`'s role in the system.

When `kextd` starts running, it calls `KXKextManagerCreate()` to create an instance of `KXKextManager` and initializes it by calling `KXKextManagerInit()`. The latter creates data structures such as a list of kext repositories, a dictionary of all potentially loadable kexts, and a list of kexts with missing dependencies.

10.4.4 Automatic Loading of Kernel Extensions

If a `kext` is to be loaded every time the system boots, it must be placed in the `/System/Library/Extensions/` directory. All contents of the kext bundle must have the owner and group as `root` and `wheel`, respectively. Moreover, all directories and files in the kext bundle must have mode bit values of `0755` and `0644`, respectively. The system maintains a cache of installed kexts, along with their information dictionaries, to speed up boot time. It updates this cache when it

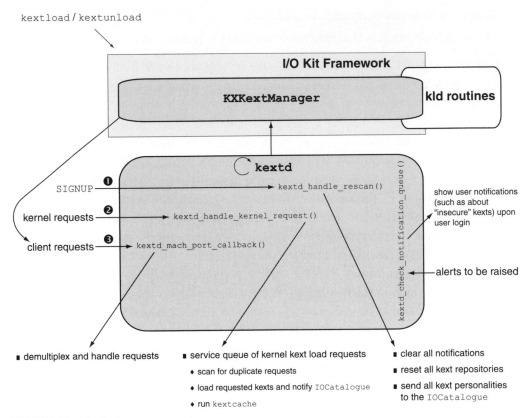

FIGURE 10–12 Kext management

detects any change to the /System/Library/Extensions/ directory. If an installer installs an extension as a plug-in of another, however, only a subdirectory of /System/Library/Extensions/ is updated, and the automatic cache update is not triggered. In such a case, the installer must explicitly touch /System/Library/Extensions/ to ensure that the caches are recreated to include the newly installed kext.

A kext can be declared as a boot-time kext by setting the OSBundleRequired property in its Info.plist file. The valid values this property can take include Root (required to mount root), Local-Root (required to mount root on locally attached storage), Network-Root (required to mount root on network-attached storage), Safe Boot (required even in safe-mode boot), and Console (required to provide character console support—that is, for single-user mode).

Although a driver kext can be explicitly loaded with `kextload`, it is preferable to restart the system to ensure reliable matching so the driver can be considered for all potential devices it can drive. In the case of a running system, if a driver is already managing a given device, another driver will not be able to manage the device in question.

10.5 Communicating with the Kernel

User programs communicate with kernel components frequently through system calls. Besides traditional system calls, Mac OS X provides other mechanisms to allow user programs to have a more direct communication with kernel components—in particular, for low-level access to hardware.

One of the mechanisms is the I/O Kit *Device Interface* mechanism. A device interface is a user-space entity (say, a library) that user programs can call to access a device. Communication from user programs goes through the device interface to a kernel-resident *user client*, which in turn dispatches it to the device. From the kernel's standpoint, the user client is a driver whose class derives from `IOService`. Each user client instance represents a user-kernel connection. Note that user clients are not supported by all drivers.

A device interface is a plug-in interface conforming to the Core Foundation plug-in model.

Through the I/O Kit Device Interface mechanism, user programs can communicate with a driver or nub in the kernel and can therefore access devices, manipulate their properties, and use the associated I/O Kit services. As is typical of finding I/O Registry objects, a user program creates a *matching dictionary* containing one or more properties of the device it wishes to access using the Device Interface mechanism. For example, a match criterion could seek all FireWire mass-storage devices. This process is termed *device matching*. We saw in Section 10.2.11 that driver matching is performed by the I/O Kit during bootstrapping and results in the population of the I/O Registry. In contrast, device matching results in the I/O Registry being searched for objects that already exist (corresponding to drivers that are already loaded).

> An application communicating with a device through its device inter-
> face can be seen as a user-space driver for that device.

Specification of matching criteria involves providing key-value pairs that identify one or more devices or services—say, by describing some of their properties. The key-value pairs are encapsulated in a matching dictionary, which is essentially a reference to a Core Foundation CFMutableDictionary object. The I/O Kit framework provides functions such as IOServiceMatching(), IOServiceNameMatching(), IOOpenFirmwarePathMatching(), and IOBSDNameMatching() to create matching dictionaries. Given a matching dictionary, devices can be looked up in the I/O Registry using functions such as IOServiceGetMatchingService(), IOService-GetMatchingServices(), and IOServiceAddMatchingNotification(). The latter also installs a notification request of new IOService objects that match. When one of these functions is called, the I/O Kit compares the values in the provided matching dictionary against the properties of nodes in the I/O Registry.

> The I/O Kit defines several keys that can be used in matching dictio-
> naries. Additional, family-specific keys are usually available in
> device families.

After finding a device, a program communicates with it using functions from the I/O Kit framework. Functions that communicate with the I/O Kit require the *I/O Kit master port*, which can be retrieved by using IOMasterPort(). Alternatively, the constant kIOMasterPortDefault can be specified to cause the I/O Kit framework to look up the default master port.

Another user-kernel communication mechanism is available through device files, which are rather ubiquitous on Unix-style systems. The I/O Kit automatically supports the device file mechanism for mass-storage and serial communications devices. On discovering such a device, besides configuring the usual stack of appropriate drivers, the I/O Kit creates an instance of a user client object—an IOMediaBSDClient or IOSerialBSDClient. The user client instance calls on the device file system (devfs) module to create the appropriate device file nodes. Since devfs is normally mounted under the /dev/ directory, these device nodes are visible within that directory—for example, /dev/disk0 and /dev/cu.modem.

Similar to the case of a device interface, the kernel-resident user client in this case sits between the kernel entity representing the device and the user-space program that uses the /dev node to access the device.

> The name of the `/dev` node corresponding to a device can be retrieved from the I/O Kit using device matching functions. The node's path is a property in the I/O Registry.

10.6 Creating Kernel Extensions

In this section, we will discuss how kernel extensions are created and loaded. Note that Apple urges third-party programmers to avoid programming in the kernel unless absolutely necessary. A legitimate reason for a device driver to reside in the kernel is if it handles a primary interrupt or if its primary client is kernel resident.

10.6.1 A Generic Kernel Extension

Let us create a trivial kext—one that implements only the start and stop entry points. Once we can compile and load the kext, we will extend it to implement a couple of sysctl entries. We will call our kext `DummySysctl`.

We begin with an Xcode project instantiated from the template for generic kernel extensions. Since sysctl implementation is a BSD-only endeavor, we need to specify our kext's dependency on the BSD KPI. We will use the kernel version of the `printf()` function to print messages in our kext. Therefore, we need libkern, which provides `printf()`. The key contents of the kext's `Info.plist` file are as follows:

```
...
<plist version="1.0">
<dict>
      ...
    <key>CFBundleExecutable</key>
    <string>DummySysctl</string>
    <key>CFBundleIdentifier</key>
    <string>com.osxbook.kext.DummySysctl</string>
    ...
    <key>OSBundleLibraries</key>
    <dict>
        <key>com.apple.kpi.bsd</key>
        <string>8.0.0</string>
        <key>com.apple.kpi.libkern</key>
        <string>8.0.0</string>
    </dict>
</dict>
</plist>
```

At least certain values in the stock `Info.plist` file generated by Xcode must be modified or added before the compiled kext can be successfully loaded. The `CFBundleIdentifier` key should be set to a reverse-DNS-style name for the kext. The `OSBundleLibraries` key is used to enumerate a kext's dependencies. This key's value is a dictionary—specifically, an `OSDictionary`—that has been serialized into the XML property list format. It may contain an empty dictionary. Beginning with Mac OS X 10.4, a kext can declare dependencies either on new-style kernel programming interfaces (KPIs) or on compatibility interfaces. KPI dependencies are specified through `com.apple.kpi.*` identifiers, whereas the others are specified through `com.apple.kernel.*` identifiers. The former start from version 8.0.0 (Mac OS X 10.4 and newer), whereas the latter end at version 7.9.9 (Mac OS X 10.3 and older). The `kextstat` command can be used to list the interfaces available in the current kernel—the interfaces correspond to the "fake" kexts that represent built-in kernel components such as Mach, BSD, libkern, and the I/O Kit.

> A kext can also declare a dependency on a specific version of the entire kernel by using the `com.apple.kernel` identifier. Although this approach would provide the kext access to all available kernel interfaces, including internal ones, it is not recommended because Apple does not guarantee binary compatibility across kernel versions to such kexts.

```
$ kextstat | egrep -e 'com.apple.(kernel|kpi)'
    1    1 0x0        0x0        0x0        com.apple.kernel (8.6.0)
    2   11 0x0        0x0        0x0        com.apple.kpi.bsd (8.6.0)
    3   12 0x0        0x0        0x0        com.apple.kpi.iokit (8.6.0)
    4   12 0x0        0x0        0x0        com.apple.kpi.libkern (8.6.0)
    5   12 0x0        0x0        0x0        com.apple.kpi.mach (8.6.0)
    6   10 0x0        0x0        0x0        com.apple.kpi.unsupported (8.6.0)
   11   60 0x0        0x0        0x0        com.apple.kernel.6.0 (7.9.9)
   12    1 0x0        0x0        0x0        com.apple.kernel.bsd (7.9.9)
   13    1 0x0        0x0        0x0        com.apple.kernel.iokit (7.9.9)
   14    1 0x0        0x0        0x0        com.apple.kernel.libkern (7.9.9)
   15    1 0x0        0x0        0x0        com.apple.kernel.mach (7.9.9)
```

You can view the list of symbols corresponding to a KPI identifier by running nm on the corresponding "pseudo-extension"—the various pseudo-extensions reside as plug-ins within the System kext.

```
$ cd /System/Library/Extensions/System.kext/PlugIns
$ ls
AppleNMI.kext                    IOSystemManagement.kext
```

```
ApplePlatformFamily.kext        Libkern.kext
BSDKernel.kext                  Libkern6.0.kext
BSDKernel6.0.kext               Mach.kext
IOKit.kext                      Mach6.0.kext
IOKit6.0.kext                   System6.0.kext
IONVRAMFamily.kext              Unsupported.kext
$ nm BSDKernel.kext/BSDKernel
...
        U _vnode_iterate
        U _vnode_lookup
        U _vnode_mount
...
```

Besides core kernel components, kexts can depend on various I/O Kit families by using identifiers such as `com.apple.iokit.IOGraphicsFamily`, `com.apple.iokit.IONetworkingFamily`, `com.apple.iokit.IOPCIFamily`, and `com.apple.iokit.IOStorageFamily`.

Figure 10–13 shows the source for the kext. The start function is called when the kext is loaded, and the stop function is called when it is unloaded. Xcode inserts skeletal implementations of these functions in the automatically generated C file for the Generic Kernel Extension project template. We have added a `printf()` statement to both functions.

FIGURE 10–13 Source for the `DummySysctl` kernel extension

```
// DummySysctl.c

#include <mach/mach_types.h>

kern_return_t
DummySysctl_start(kmod_info_t *ki, void *d)
{
    printf("DummySysctl_start\n");
    return KERN_SUCCESS;
}

kern_return_t
DummySysctl_stop(kmod_info_t *ki, void *d)
{
    printf("DummySysctl_stop\n");
    return KERN_SUCCESS;
}
```

Let us now compile the kext. The benefits of Xcode are most evident in the compilation stage, since a manual compilation would need to specify the appropriate combination of compiler arguments, environment variables, linker arguments, and so on. Note that it is possible to initiate an Xcode build from the command line using the `xcodebuild` program. On successful compilation, the target kext bundle is created in a subdirectory of the `build/` directory within the Xcode project directory.

```
$ xcodebuild -list
Information about project "DummySysctl":
    Targets:
        DummySysctl (Active)

    Build Configurations:
        Debug (Active)
        Release

    If no build configuration is specified "Release" is used.
$ xcodebuild -configuration Debug -target DummySysctl
=== BUILDING NATIVE TARGET DummySysctl WITH CONFIGURATION Debug ===
...
** BUILD SUCCEEDED **
$ ls build/Debug
DummySysctl.kext
```

Since loading a kext requires the kext bundle's contents to have `root` and `wheel` as the owner and group, respectively, a typical compile-test-debug cycle would involve copying the kext bundle from the build directory to a temporary location—say, to `/tmp/`—and using the `chown` command on the copy. As we noted earlier, besides ownership, the modifiability of objects within the bundle also matters—the bundle's contents must not be writable by any user except root.

```
$ sudo rm -rf /tmp/DummySysctl.kext    # remove any old bundles
$ cp -pr build/DummySysctl.kext /tmp/  # copy newly compiled bundle to /tmp
$ sudo chown -R root:wheel /tmp/DummySysctl.kext
```

We can use `kextload` to load the kext manually.

```
$ sudo kextload -v /tmp/DummySysctl.kext
kextload: extension /tmp/DummySysctl.kext appears to be valid
kextload: loading extension /tmp/DummySysctl.kext
kextload: sending 1 personality to the kernel
kextload: /tmp/DummySysctl.kext loaded successfully
```

If the kext fails to load, the `-t` (test) option of `kextload` may provide information about possible problems. For example, suppose we specified an unavailable version of a dependency—say, version `7.9.9` for `com.apple.kpi.libkern`—then the `-t` option would be helpful in identifying the cause of the problem.

```
$ sudo kextload -v /tmp/DummySysctl.kext
kextload: extension /tmp/DummySysctl.kext appears to be valid
kextload: loading extension /tmp/DummySysctl.kext
kextload: cannot resolve dependencies for kernel extension /tmp/DummySysctl.kext
$ sudo sysctl -v -t /tmp/DummySysctl.kext
...
kernel extension /tmp/DummySysctl.kext has problems:
...
Missing dependencies
{
    "com.apple.kpi.libkern" =
        "A valid compatible version of this dependency cannot be found"
}
```

> When the -t option is specified, kextload neither loads the kext
> nor sends its personality to the kernel. It only performs a series of
> tests on the kext and determines whether it is loadable. The tests
> include validation, authentication, and dependency resolution.

Besides dependency resolution failures, other reasons for a kext's failure to load include incorrect file permissions, a flawed bundle structure, a missing CFBundleIdentifier property in the kext's Info.plist file, and a missing or syntactically invalid Info.plist file.

We can use the kextstat command to check whether our kext is currently loaded in the kernel.

```
$ kextstat
Index Refs Address    Size    Wired   Name (Version)              <Linked Against>
1      1 0x0          0x0     0x0     com.apple.kernel (8.6.0)
2     11 0x0          0x0     0x0     com.apple.kpi.bsd (8.6.0)
3     12 0x0          0x0     0x0     com.apple.kpi.iokit (8.6.0)
4     12 0x0          0x0     0x0     com.apple.kpi.libkern (8.6.0)
...
133    0 0x5cbca000 0x2000  0x1000  com.osxbook.kext.DummySysctl (1.0.0d1) <4 2>
```

The value 133 in the kextstat output indicates the index at which the kext is loaded. The kernel uses these indices for tracking interkext dependencies. The second value, which is 0 in our case, shows the number of references to this kext. A nonzero reference indicates that one or more kexts are using this kext. The next value, 0x5cbca000, is the kext's load address in the kernel's virtual address space. The next two values, 0x2000 and 0x1000, represent the amounts (in bytes) of kernel memory and wired kernel memory, respectively, used by the kext. The final value in the column is a list of indices of all other kexts that this kext references. We see that `DummySysctl` references two kexts: the ones loaded at indices 4 (`com.apple.kpi.libkern`) and 2 (`com.apple.kpi.bsd`).

We can unload the kext manually by using the `kextunload` command.

```
$ sudo kextunload -v /tmp/DummySysctl.kext
kextunload: unload kext /tmp/DummySysctl.kext succeeded
```

> In a deployment scenario, one does not have to run `kextload` or `kextunload` manually—kexts are loaded automatically when they are needed and unloaded when they are not being used.

The output from the `printf()` statements we inserted in our kext should appear in `/var/log/system.log`.

```
$ grep DummySysctl_ /var/log/system.log
Mar  14 17:32:48 g5x4 kernel[0]: DummySysctl_start
Mar  14 17:34:48 g5x4 kernel[0]: DummySysctl_stop
```

10.6.2 Implementing Sysctl Variables Using a Generic Kext

Let us extend our generic kext from Section 10.6.1 to implement a sysctl node with two variables: an integer and a string. We will call the new node `osxbook`, and it will have the following properties.

- It will be a subcategory of the existing top-level sysctl node called `debug`. In other words, the new node's MIB-style name would be `debug.osxbook`.

- One of its two children will be called `uint32`, which will hold a 32-bit unsigned integer. The integer's value will be readable or writable by any user.

- The second of its children will be called `string`, which will hold a string up to 16 characters in length (including the terminating NUL character). The string's value will be readable by anyone but writable only by the root user.

When our sysctl kext is loaded, the kernel's sysctl hierarchy would look like the one shown in Figure 10–14, with possibly other top-level categories depending on the kernel version.

The most general way to create a sysctl variable is to use the `SYSCTL_PROC()` macro, which allows a handler function to be specified for the sysctl. The handler is called when the variable is accessed for reading or writing. There exist data-type-specific macros such as `SYSCTL_UINT()` for unsigned integers and `SYSCTL_STRING()` for strings. The sysctls defined using these macros are served

```
├─ debug
│   ├─ . . .
│   ├─ osxbook
│   └─ . . .  ├─ uint32
│             └─ string
├─ hw
│   └─ . . .
├─ kern
│   └─ . . .
├─ net
│   └─ . . .
├─ user
│   └─ . . .
├─ vfs
│   └─ . . .
└─ vm
    └─ . . .
```

FIGURE 10–14 The kernel's sysctl hierarchy

by predefined type-specific functions such as `sysctl_handle_int()` and `sysctl_handle_string()`. We will use `SYSCTL_PROC()` to define our sysctl variables, with our own handler functions, although we will simply call the pre-defined handlers from our handlers. Figure 10–15 shows the updated contents of `DummySysctl.c`. Note that we register the three sysctl entries—`debug.osxbook`, `debug.osxbook.uint32`, and `debug.osxbook.string`—in the kext's start routine and unregister them in the stop routine.

FIGURE 10–15 Implementing sysctl nodes

```c
// DummySysctl.c

#include <sys/systm.h>
#include <sys/types.h>
#include <sys/sysctl.h>

static u_int32_t k_uint32 = 0;        // the contents of debug.osxbook.uint32
static u_int8_t k_string[16] = { 0 }; // the contents of debug.osxbook.string

// Construct a node (debug.osxbook) from which other sysctl objects can hang.
SYSCTL_NODE(_debug,        // our parent
            OID_AUTO,      // automatically assign us an object ID
            osxbook,       // our name
            CTLFLAG_RW,    // we will be creating children, therefore, read/write
            0,             // handler function (none needed)
            "demo sysctl hierarchy");
```

(continues)

FIGURE 10–15 Implementing sysctl nodes *(continued)*

```
// Prototypes for read/write handling functions for our sysctl nodes.
static int sysctl_osxbook_uint32 SYSCTL_HANDLER_ARGS;
static int sysctl_osxbook_string SYSCTL_HANDLER_ARGS;

// We can directly use SYSCTL_INT(), in which case sysctl_handle_int()
// will be assigned as the handling function. We use SYSCTL_PROC() and
// specify our own handler sysctl_osxbook_uint32().
//
SYSCTL_PROC(
    _debug_osxbook,                    // our parent
    OID_AUTO,                          // automatically assign us an object ID
    uint32,                            // our name
    (CTLTYPE_INT |                     // type flag
     CTLFLAG_RW | CTLFLAG_ANYBODY),    // access flags (read/write by anybody)
    &k_uint32,                         // location of our data
    0,                                 // argument passed to our handler
    sysctl_osxbook_uint32,             // our handler function
    "IU",                              // our data type (unsigned integer)
    "32-bit unsigned integer"          // our description
);

// We can directly use SYSCTL_STRING(), in which case sysctl_handle_string()
// will be assigned as the handling function. We use SYSCTL_PROC() and
// specify our own handler sysctl_osxbook_string().
//
SYSCTL_PROC(
    _debug_osxbook,                    // our parent
    OID_AUTO,                          // automatically assign us an object ID
    string,                            // our name
    (CTLTYPE_STRING | CTLFLAG_RW),     // type and access flags (write only by root)
    &k_string,                         // location of our data
    16,                                // maximum allowable length of the string
    sysctl_osxbook_string,             // our handler function
    "A",                               // our data type (string)
    "16-byte string"                   // our description
);

static int
sysctl_osxbook_uint32 SYSCTL_HANDLER_ARGS
{
    // Do some processing of our own, if necessary.
    return sysctl_handle_int(oidp, oidp->oid_arg1, oidp->oid_arg2, req);
}

static int
sysctl_osxbook_string SYSCTL_HANDLER_ARGS
{
```

(continues)

FIGURE 10–15 Implementing sysctl nodes *(continued)*

```
        // Do some processing of our own, if necessary.
        return sysctl_handle_string(oidp, oidp->oid_arg1, oidp->oid_arg2, req);
}

kern_return_t
DummySysctl_start(kmod_info_t *ki, void *d)
{
        // Register our sysctl entries.
        sysctl_register_oid(&sysctl__debug_osxbook);
        sysctl_register_oid(&sysctl__debug_osxbook_uint32);
        sysctl_register_oid(&sysctl__debug_osxbook_string);

        return KERN_SUCCESS;
}


kern_return_t
DummySysctl_stop(kmod_info_t *ki, void *d)
{
        // Unregister our sysctl entries.
        sysctl_unregister_oid(&sysctl__debug_osxbook_string);
        sysctl_unregister_oid(&sysctl__debug_osxbook_uint32);
        sysctl_unregister_oid(&sysctl__debug_osxbook);

        return KERN_SUCCESS;
}
```

Let us compile and load the kext to test it. Once it is loaded, the `sysctl` command can be used to get and set the values of our sysctl variables.

```
$ sysctl debug
...
debug.osxbook.uint32: 0
debug.osxbook.string:
$ sysctl -w debug.osxbook.uint32=64
debug.osxbook.uint32: 0 -> 64
$ sysctl debug.osxbook.uint32
debug.osxbook.uint32: 64
$ sysctl -w debug.osxbook.string=kernel
debug.osxbook.string:
sysctl: debug.osxbook.string: Operation not permitted
$ sudo sysctl -w debug.osxbook.string=kernel
debug.osxbook.string:   -> kernel
$ sysctl debug.osxbook.string
debug.osxbook.string: kernel
```

10.6.3 I/O Kit Device Driver Kext

As we saw in Section 10.4.2, an I/O Kit driver is a kext that uses C++ in its implementation—it runs in the kernel's C++ runtime environment provided by the I/O Kit. The `Info.plist` file of an I/O Kit driver kext contains one or more driver personality dictionaries. Moreover, unlike a generic kext, the driver implementor does not provide start/stop routines for the kext because, as we saw earlier, these routines are used as hooks to initialize/terminate the C++ runtime. However, an I/O Kit driver has several other entry points. Depending on the type and nature of the driver, many of these entry points can be optional or mandatory. The following are examples of I/O Kit driver entry points.

- `init()`—During active matching, the I/O Kit loads a candidate driver's code and creates an instance of the driver's principal class, which is specified in the driver's personality. The first method called on each instance of the driver's class is `init()`, which may be semantically seen as a constructor and may allocate resources needed by the instance. It is passed a dictionary object containing the matching properties from the selected driver personality. A driver may or may not override the `init()` method. If it does, it must call the superclass's `init()` as the first action.

- `free()`—The `free()` method is called when the driver is unloaded. It should free any resources allocated by `init()`. If `init()` calls the superclass's `init()`, `free()` must make a corresponding call to the superclass's `free()`. Note that unlike the start and stop entry points of a kmod, `init()` and `free()` are called once for each instance of the driver's class.

- `probe()`—This method is called to probe the hardware to determine whether the driver is suited for that hardware. It must leave the hardware in a sane state after it has finished probing. It takes as arguments the driver's provider and a pointer to a *probe score*—a signed 32-bit integer initialized to the value of the `IOProbeScore` key in the driver's personality, or to zero if the personality does not contain this key. The I/O Kit gives the driver with the highest probe score the first opportunity to drive the hardware.

- `start()`—This is the actual starting point of the driver's lifecycle. Here the driver advertises its services and publishes any nubs. If `start()` returns successfully, it means that the device hardware has been initialized and is ready for operation. Thereafter, the I/O Kit will not consider any remaining candidate driver instances.

- `stop()`—This method represents the end point of the driver's lifecycle. Here the driver unpublishes any nubs and stops providing its services.

- attach()—This method attaches the driver (an IOService client) to a provider (nub) through registration in the I/O Registry. In other words, when called in a driver, it enters the driver in the I/O Registry as a child of the provider in the Service plane.

- detach()—This method detaches the driver from a nub.

Let us implement an I/O Kit driver kext by starting with the IOKit Driver Xcode template. We will call our driver DummyDriver. Xcode will generate a header file (DummyDriver.h), a C++ source file (DummyDriver.cpp), and an Info.plist file, besides other project-related files. As we will see, it takes somewhat more work to create a trivial I/O Kit driver than a trivial generic kext.

Figure 10–16 shows the key contents of the driver's property list file.

FIGURE 10–16 An I/O Kit driver's personality and dependencies

```
...
<dict>
...
    <key>IOKitPersonalities</key>
    <dict>
        <key>DummyPersonality_0</key>
        <dict>
            <key>CFBundleIdentifier</key>
            <string>com.osxbook.driver.DummyDriver</string>
            <key>IOClass</key>
            <string>com_osxbook_driver_DummyDriver</string>
            <key>IOKitDebug</key>
            <integer>65535</integer>
            <key>IOMatchCategory</key>
            <string>DummyDriver</string>
            <key>IOProviderClass</key>
            <string>IOResources</string>
            <key>IOResourceMatch</key>
            <string>IOKit</string>
        </dict>
    </dict>
    <key>OSBundleLibraries</key>
    <dict>
        <key>com.apple.kpi.iokit</key>
        <string>8.0.0</string>
        <key>com.apple.kpi.libkern</key>
        <string>8.0.0</string>
    </dict>
</dict>
</plist>
```

As in the case of `DummySysctl`, we identify our driver kext using a reverse-DNS-style name. The `IOKitPersonalities` property, which is an array of personality dictionaries, contains properties for matching and loading the driver. Our driver contains only one personality called `DummyPersonality_0`.

The `IOClass` key in the personality specifies the name of the driver's primary class, based on the driver kext's bundle identifier for uniformity. Note, however, that the name of the driver class cannot contain dots. Therefore, we translate dots to underscores while naming our driver's class.

`DummyDriver` neither controls any hardware nor implements any real functionality. In order for it to load and match successfully, we specify its `IOProviderClass` property as `IOResources`, which is a special nub that can be matched against any driver. Note that it is possible for real drivers that do not attach to any hardware to match against `IOResources`. The BootCache kext (`BootCache.kext`)[9] is an example—it operates within the Mach and BSD portions of the kernel but implements minimal glue code for the I/O Kit. It also specifies `IOResources` as its provider class. Figure 10–17 shows the personality specification from the BootCache kext's `Info.plist` file.

FIGURE 10–17 The driver personality of the BootCache kernel extension

```
...
    <key>IOKitPersonalities</key>
    <dict>
        <key>BootCache</key>
        <dict>
            <key>CFBundleIdentifier</key>
            <string>com.apple.BootCache</string>
            <key>IOClass</key>
            <string>com_apple_BootCache</string>
            <key>IOMatchCategory</key>
            <string>BootCache</string>
            <key>IOProviderClass</key>
            <string>IOResources</string>
            <key>IOResourceMatch</key>
            <string>IOKit</string>
        </dict>
    </dict>
...
```

---

9. We discussed BootCache in Section 4.14.

IOMatchCategory is a special property that allows multiple drivers to match a single nub. Examples of kexts whose driver personalities specify this property include AppleRAID, IOFireWireFamily, IOGraphicsFamily, IOSerialFamily, IOStorageFamily, and IOUSBFamily. Note that a kext that specifies an IOResourceMatch property is eligible for loading after the subsystem named by the value of IOResourceMatch has been published as available.

The iPod Driver

The iPod driver kext (iPodDriver.kext) is an example of a driver containing multiple personalities. Figure 10–18 shows an excerpt from the iPod driver's Info.plist file.

FIGURE 10–18 An excerpt from the iPod driver's property list file

```
...
    <key>IOKitPersonalities</key>
    <dict>

        <key>iPodDriver</key>
        <dict>
            <key>CFBundleIdentifier</key>
            <string>com.apple.driver.iPodDriver</string>
            <key>IOClass</key>
            <string>com_apple_driver_iPod</string>
            <key>IOProviderClass</key>
            <string>IOSCSIPeripheralDeviceNub</string>
            <key>Peripheral Device Type</key>
            <integer>14</integer>
            <key>Product Identification</key>
            <string>iPod</string>
            <key>Vendor Identification</key>
            <string>Apple</string>
        </dict>

        <key>iPodDriverIniter</key>
        <dict>
            <key>CFBundleIdentifier</key>
            <string>com.apple.iokit.SCSITaskUserClient</string>
            <key>IOClass</key>
            <string>SCSITaskUserClientIniter</string>
            ...
            <key>IOProviderClass</key>
            <string>com_apple_driver_iPodNub</string>
            ...
        </dict>

    </dict>
...
```

The base class for most I/O Kit families and drivers is `IOService`. We will also subclass `IOService` to implement `com_osxbook_driver_DummyDriver`. Our driver's source references two macros that are defined by the I/O Kit.

- `OSDeclareDefaultStructors()` declares C++ constructors and is conventionally inserted as the first element of the class declaration in a driver header file.

- `OSDefineMetaClassAndStructors()`, which is used in the driver's class implementation, defines the constructors and destructors, implements the `OSMetaClass` allocation member function for the class, and supplies the metaclass RTTI information for the RTTI system.

> In general, all subclasses of `OSObject` use these macros or variants of them.

We implement several class methods in our dummy driver to examine when and in which order they are called. However, we need not implement any logic in these methods—we can simply log a message and forward the invocation to the corresponding superclass method.

Figure 10–19 shows the contents of `DummyDriver.h`.

FIGURE 10–19 Header file for the `DummyDriver` I/O Kit driver

```
// DummyDriver.h

#include <IOKit/IOService.h>

class com_osxbook_driver_DummyDriver : public IOService
{
    OSDeclareDefaultStructors(com_osxbook_driver_DummyDriver)

public:
    virtual bool      init(OSDictionary *dictionary = 0);
    virtual void      free(void);

    virtual bool      attach(IOService *provider);
    virtual IOService *probe(IOService *provider, SInt32 *score);
    virtual void      detach(IOService *provider);

    virtual bool      start(IOService *provider);
    virtual void      stop(IOService *provider);
};
```

Figure 10–20 shows the contents of DummyDriver.cpp. Note how the OSDefineMetaClassAndStructors() macro is used: The first argument is the literal name of the driver's class (the same as the value of the IOClass property in the personality), and the second argument is the literal name of the driver's superclass.

FIGURE 10–20 Implementation of the DummyDriver I/O Kit driver's class

```
// DummyDriver.cpp

#include <IOKit/IOLib.h>
#include "DummyDriver.h"
#define super IOService

OSDefineMetaClassAndStructors(com_osxbook_driver_DummyDriver, IOService)

bool
com_osxbook_driver_DummyDriver::init(OSDictionary *dict)
{
    bool result = super::init(dict);
    IOLog("init\n");
    return result;
}

void
com_osxbook_driver_DummyDriver::free(void)
{
    IOLog("free\n");
    super::free();
}

IOService *
com_osxbook_driver_DummyDriver::probe(IOService *provider, SInt32 *score)
{
    IOService *result = super::probe(provider, score);
    IOLog("probe\n");
    return result;
}

bool
com_osxbook_driver_DummyDriver::start(IOService *provider)
{
    bool result = super::start(provider);
    IOLog("start\n");
    return result;
}

void
com_osxbook_driver_DummyDriver::stop(IOService *provider)
```

(continues)

FIGURE 10–20 Implementation of the `DummyDriver` I/O Kit driver's class *(continued)*

```
{
    IOLog("stop\n");
    super::stop(provider);
}

bool
com_osxbook_driver_DummyDriver::attach(IOService *provider)
{
    bool result = super::attach(provider);
    IOLog("attach\n");
    return result;
}

void
com_osxbook_driver_DummyDriver::detach(IOService *provider)
{
    IOLog("detach\n");
    super::detach(provider);
}
```

Let us load the driver manually using `kextload` and unload it using `kextunload`.

```
$ sudo kextload -v DummyDriver.kext
kextload: extension DummyDriver.kext appears to be valid
kextload: notice: extension DummyDriver.kext has debug properties set
kextload: loading extension DummyDriver.kext
kextload: DummyDriver.kext loaded successfully
kextload: loading personalities named:
kextload:     DummyPersonality_0
kextload: sending 1 personality to the kernel
kextload: matching started for DummyDriver.kext
$ sudo kextunload -v /tmp/DummyDriver.kext
kextunload: unload kext /tmp/DummyDriver.kext succeeded
```

We can now look in `/var/log/system.log` for messages logged by `DummyDriver`. The following excerpt from the log shows the sequence in which the I/O Kit calls the driver's methods.

```
init               # kextload
    attach
            probe
    detach

    attach
            start
```

```
        . . .
        stop    # kextunload
    detach
free
```

We see active matching in action as the I/O Kit calls `attach()`, `probe()`, and `detach()`, in that order. Since our `probe()` implementation returns success, the I/O Kit proceeds to start the driver. Had we returned a failure from `probe()`, the next method to be called would have been `free()`.

Figure 10–21 shows a more general view of how the I/O Kit calls driver methods in a driver's lifecycle.

While debugging an I/O Kit driver, it is possible to only load the kext and defer the matching phase. The `-l` option instructs `kextload` not to start the matching process. Moreover, the `-s` option can be used to instruct `kextload` to create symbol

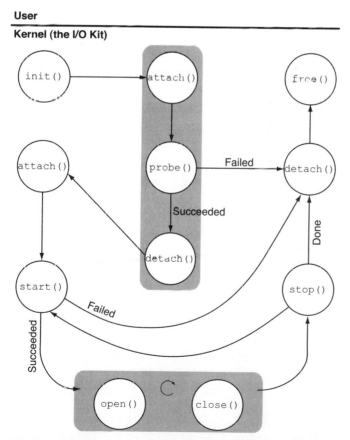

User

Kernel (the I/O Kit)

FIGURE 10–21 The sequence of I/O Kit driver methods called in a driver's lifecycle

files for the kext and its dependencies.[10] This allows the programmer to set up the debugger before initiating the matching process, which can be performed later using the -m option of kextload. If the matching succeeds, the driver will be started eventually. Section 10.8.4 provides an example of this debugging approach.

Providing User-Space Information to an I/O Kit Driver

A driver kext can retrieve information from the kext's property list file, which provides a load-time mechanism for providing information to a driver from user space. However, there is an important caveat: Because kext property lists are normally cached, modifying a property list will take effect only when the caches are updated.

Drivers can access user-space memory by creating an IOMemoryDescriptor instance based on a virtual address in a given task and then preparing and mapping the descriptor.

The user client interface is a convenient mechanism—provided the driver in question supports it—for exchanging arbitrary information between a driver and a user program.

Some drivers implement the setProperty() method, which allows user programs to set properties of I/O Registry entry objects through I/O Kit library functions, namely, IORegistryEntrySetCFProperty() and IORegistryEntrySetCFProperties().

10.7 A Programming Tour of the I/O Kit's Functionality

In this section, we will look at a variety of examples of programmatic interaction with the I/O Kit, both from user space and within the kernel.

10.7.1 Rotating a Framebuffer

The IOServiceRequestProbe() function in the I/O Kit framework can be used to request a bus to be rescanned for family-specific device changes. The function takes two arguments: an IOService object to be used to request the scan and an options mask that is interpreted by the object's family. In this example, we will use IOServiceRequestProbe() to rotate the framebuffer corresponding to a display (that is, the displayed desktop) in its entirety. We will use CGDisplayIOServicePort() to retrieve the I/O Kit service port of the display—the port represents the IOService object of interest. The options mask is

---

10. When a kext is loaded, its symbols are relocated.

constructed based on the desired angle of rotation. Figure 10–22 shows how a user-program invocation of IOServiceRequestProbe() is communicated to the appropriate family—IOGraphics in this case.

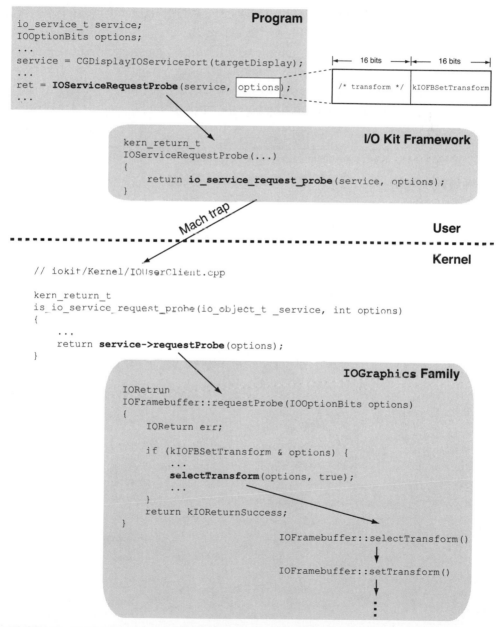

FIGURE 10–22 Processing involved in user-program-induced framebuffer rotation

As Figure 10–22 shows, the 32-bit options mask value for framebuffer rotation (and in general, for a supported framebuffer transform) consists of the constant kIOFBSetTransform in its lower 16 bits and an encoding of the desired transform in the upper 16 bits. For example, the constants kIOScaleRotate90, kIOScaleRotate180, and kIOScaleRotate270 rotate the framebuffer by 90, 180, and 270 degrees, respectively, while scaling it appropriately.

The program shown in Figure 10–23 rotates the specified display by the given angle, which must be a multiple of 90 degrees. The target display is specified to the program by the display's unique ID assigned by the Quartz layer. The program's -l option can be used to list the display ID and resolution of each online display. Moreover, specifying 0 as the display ID rotates the main display.

FIGURE 10–23 Programmatically rotating a framebuffer

```c
// fb-rotate.c

#include <getopt.h>
#include <IOKit/graphics/IOGraphicsLib.h>
#include <ApplicationServices/ApplicationServices.h>

#define PROGNAME "fb-rotate"
#define MAX_DISPLAYS 16

// kIOFBSetTransform comes from <IOKit/graphics/IOGraphicsTypesPrivate.h>
// in the source for the IOGraphics family
enum {
    kIOFBSetTransform = 0x00000400,
};

void
usage(void)
{
    fprintf(stderr, "usage: %s -l\n"
                    "       %s -d <display ID> -r <0|90|180|270>\n",
                    PROGNAME, PROGNAME);
    exit(1);
}

void
listDisplays(void)
{
    CGDisplayErr      dErr;
    CGDisplayCount    displayCount, i;
    CGDirectDisplayID mainDisplay;
    CGDisplayCount    maxDisplays = MAX_DISPLAYS;
    CGDirectDisplayID onlineDisplays[MAX_DISPLAYS];
```

(continues)

FIGURE 10–23 Programmatically rotating a framebuffer *(continued)*

```
    mainDisplay = CGMainDisplayID();

    dErr = CGGetOnlineDisplayList(maxDisplays, onlineDisplays, &displayCount);
    if (dErr != kCGErrorSuccess) {
        fprintf(stderr, "CGGetOnlineDisplayList: error %d.\n", dErr);
        exit(1);
    }

    printf("Display ID        Resolution\n");
    for (i = 0; i < displayCount; i++) {
        CGDirectDisplayID dID = onlineDisplays[i];
        printf("%-16p %lux%lu %32s", dID,
               CGDisplayPixelsWide(dID), CGDisplayPixelsHigh(dID),
               (dID == mainDisplay) ? "[main display]\n" : "\n");
    }

    exit(0);
}

IOOptionBits
angle2options(long angle)
{
    static IOOptionBits anglebits[] = {
                (kIOFBSetTransform | (kIOScaleRotate0)   << 16),
                (kIOFBSetTransform | (kIOScaleRotate90)  << 16),
                (kIOFBSetTransform | (kIOScaleRotate180) << 16),
                (kIOFBSetTransform | (kIOScaleRotate270) << 16)
            };

    if ((angle % 90) != 0) // Map arbitrary angles to a rotation reset
        return anglebits[0];

    return anglebits[(angle / 90) % 4];
}

int
main(int argc, char **argv)
{
    int  i;
    long angle = 0;

    io_service_t      service;
    CGDisplayErr      dErr;
    CGDirectDisplayID targetDisplay = 0;
    IOOptionBits      options;

    while ((i = getopt(argc, argv, "d:lr:")) != -1) {
        switch (i) {
```

(continues)

FIGURE 10–23 Programmatically rotating a framebuffer *(continued)*

```
        case 'd':
            targetDisplay = (CGDirectDisplayID)strtol(optarg, NULL, 16);
            if (targetDisplay == 0)
                targetDisplay = CGMainDisplayID();
            break;
        case 'l':
            listDisplays();
            break;
        case 'r':
            angle = strtol(optarg, NULL, 10);
            break;
        default:
            break;
        }
    }

    if (targetDisplay == 0)
        usage();

    options = angle2options(angle);

    // Get the I/O Kit service port of the target display
    // Since the port is owned by the graphics system, we should not destroy it
    service = CGDisplayIOServicePort(targetDisplay);

    // We will get an error if the target display doesn't support the
    // kIOFBSetTransform option for IOServiceRequestProbe()
    dErr = IOServiceRequestProbe(service, options);
    if (dErr != kCGErrorSuccess) {
        fprintf(stderr, "IOServiceRequestProbe: error %d\n", dErr);
        exit(1);
    }

    exit(0);
}


$ gcc -Wall -o fb-rotate fb-rotate.c -framework IOKit \
    -framework ApplicationServices
$ ./fb-rotate -l
Display ID      Resolution
0x4248edd       1920x1200                    [main display]
0x74880f18      1600x1200
$ ./fb-rotate -d 0x4248edd -r 90 # rotates given display by 90 degrees
$ ./fb-rotate -d 0x4248edd -r 0  # restores to original
```

10.7.2 Accessing Framebuffer Memory

We saw how to access the contents of framebuffer memory through the diagnostics system call interface in Section 6.8.8.2. The Quartz Services function `CGDisplayBaseAddress()` returns the base address of a display's framebuffer. Given this address, the framebuffer memory can be read or written using the `read()` and `write()` system calls, respectively.

Quartz Services

As we saw in Chapter 2, the majority of what constitutes the windowing and graphics system of Mac OS X is collectively referred to as Quartz. The Quartz Services API provides a set of low-level window server features. In particular, display hardware can be accessed and manipulated through this API.

Figure 10–24 shows a program that dumps the entire contents of a given display's framebuffer to a file. It assumes 32 bits per pixel. The contents can be converted to a viewable image using the same approach as in the screenshot-capturing example from Section 6.8.8.2. Note that the program uses the `list-Displays()` function from Figure 10–23.

FIGURE 10–24 Accessing framebuffer memory

```
// fb-dump.c

#include <getopt.h>
#include <IOKit/graphics/IOGraphicsLib.h>
#include <ApplicationServices/ApplicationServices.h>

#define PROCNAME          "fb-dump"
#define DUMPFILE_TMPDIR    "/tmp/"
#define DUMPFILE_TEMPLATE "fb-dump.XXXXXX"

...

int
main(int argc, char * argv[])
{
    int     i, saveFD = -1;
    char    template[] = DUMPFILE_TMPDIR DUMPFILE_TEMPLATE;
    uint32_t width, height, rowBytes, rowUInt32s, *screen;

    CGDirectDisplayID targetDisplay = 0;
```

(continues)

FIGURE 10–24 Accessing framebuffer memory *(continued)*

```
// populate targetDisplay as in Figure 10-23
// use listDisplays() from Figure 10-23

...

screen = (uint32_t *)CGDisplayBaseAddress(targetDisplay);
rowBytes = CGDisplayBytesPerRow(targetDisplay);
rowUInt32s = rowBytes / 4;
width = CGDisplayPixelsWide(targetDisplay);
height = CGDisplayPixelsHigh(targetDisplay);

if ((saveFD = mkstemp(template)) < 0) {
    perror("mkstemps");
    exit(1);
}

for (i = 0; i < height; i++)
    write(saveFD, screen + i * rowUInt32s, width * sizeof(uint32_t));

close(saveFD);

exit(0);
}
```

10.7.3 Retrieving the List of Firmware Variables

In this example, we will contact the I/O Kit to retrieve and display the list of firmware variables. As we saw in Section 4.10.3, the `options` device in the Open Firmware device tree contains NVRAM-resident system configuration variables. The contents of this device are available in the I/O Registry as the properties of the entry called `options` in the Device Tree plane. Similarly, on EFI-based Macintosh systems, EFI NVRAM variables are available through the `options` property. We can use `IORegistryEntryFromPath()` to look up the registry entry given its path. Once we have the entry, we can use `IORegistryEntryCreate-CFProperties()` to construct a Core Foundation dictionary from the entry's properties. The program shown in Figure 10–25 performs these steps. Additionally, it displays an XML representation of the dictionary's contents.

FIGURE 10–25 Retrieving the list of firmware variables from the I/O Registry

```c
// lsfirmware.c

#include <unistd.h>
#include <IOKit/IOKitLib.h>
#include <CoreFoundation/CoreFoundation.h>

#define PROGNAME "lsfirmware"

void
printDictionaryAsXML(CFDictionaryRef dict)
{
    CFDataRef xml = CFPropertyListCreateXMLData(kCFAllocatorDefault,
                                                (CFPropertyListRef)dict);
    if (xml) {
        write(STDOUT_FILENO, CFDataGetBytePtr(xml), CFDataGetLength(xml));
        CFRelease(xml);
    }
}

int
main(void)
{
    io_registry_entry_t    options;
    CFMutableDictionaryRef optionsDict;
    kern_return_t          kr = KERN_FAILURE;

    options = IORegistryEntryFromPath(kIOMasterPortDefault,
                                      kIODeviceTreePlane ":/options");
    if (options) {
        kr = IORegistryEntryCreateCFProperties(options, &optionsDict, 0, 0);
        if (kr == KERN_SUCCESS) {
            printDictionaryAsXML(optionsDict);
            CFRelease(optionsDict);
        }
        IOObjectRelease(options);
    }

    if (kr != KERN_SUCCESS)
        fprintf(stderr, "failed to retrieve firmware variables\n");

    exit(kr);
}
```

```
$ gcc -Wall -o lsfirmware lsfirmware.c -framework IOKit \
    -framework CoreFoundation
$ ./lsfirmware # PowerPC
```

(continues)

FIGURE 10–25 Retrieving the list of firmware variables from the I/O Registry *(continued)*

```
...
        <key>boot-command</key>
        <string>mac-boot</string>
        <key>boot-device</key>
        <string>hd:,\\:tbxi</string>
...
$ ./lsfirmware # x86
...
        <key>SystemAudioVolume</key>
        <data>
        cg==
        </data>
        <key>efi-boot-device</key>
        <data>
...
```

10.7.4 Retrieving Information about Loaded Kernel Extensions

We can retrieve information about loaded kernel extensions—a list of kmod_
info_t structures—using the kmod_get_info() routine that is part of the
Mach host interface. Figure 10–26 shows a program that retrieves and displays
this information.

FIGURE 10–26 Retrieving information about loaded kernel extensions

```c
// lskmod.c

#include <stdio.h>
#include <mach/mach.h>

int
main(void)
{
    kern_return_t            kr;
    kmod_info_array_t        kmods;
    mach_msg_type_number_t   kmodBytes = 0;
    int                      kmodCount = 0;
    kmod_info_t              *kmodp;
    mach_port_t              host_port = mach_host_self();

    kr = kmod_get_info(host_port, (void *)&kmods, &kmodBytes);
    (void)mach_port_deallocate(mach_task_self(), host_port);
```

(continues)

FIGURE 10–26 Retrieving information about loaded kernel extensions *(continued)*

```
    if (kr != KERN_SUCCESS) {
        mach_error("kmod_get_info:", kr);
        return kr;
    }


    for (kmodp = (kmod_info_t *)kmods; kmodp->next; kmodp++, kmodCount++) {
        printf("%5d %4d %-10p %-10p %-10p %s (%s)\n",
                kmodp->id,
                kmodp->reference_count,
                (void *)kmodp->address,
                (void *)kmodp->size,
                (void *)(kmodp->size - kmodp->hdr_size),
                kmodp->name,
                kmodp->version);
    }


    vm_deallocate(mach_task_self(), (vm_address_t)kmods, kmodBytes);


    return kr;
}



$ gcc -Wall -o lskmod lskmod.c
$ ./lskmod
...
   27    0 0x761000  0x5000    0x4000    com.apple.driver.AppleRTC (1.0.2)
   26    0 0x86a000  0x3000    0x2000    com.apple.driver.AppleHPET (1.0.0d1)
   25    0 0x7f6000  0x4000    0x3000    com.apple.driver.AppleACPIButtons (1.0.3)
   24    0 0x7fa000  0x4000    0x3000    com.apple.driver.AppleSMBIOS (1.0.7)
...
```

10.7.5 Retrieving Accelerometer Data from the Sudden Motion Sensor

Apple added a feature called the *Sudden Motion Sensor* (SMS)[11] to the Power-Book line of computers in early 2005.[12] Eventually, the feature was added to all Apple notebook computers. The sensor is used as part of a mechanism for attempting to prevent data loss by parking the heads of an active disk drive after detecting a sudden motion.

---

11. The SMS is also called the Mobile Motion Module or the Apple Motion Sensor (AMS).

12. IBM had been offering a conceptually identical feature in ThinkPad notebooks before Apple introduced the SMS. The ThinkPad sensor can be programmatically accessed as well.

The Background behind the Sudden Motion Sensor

In modern disk drives, the "flying height" between a platter and a head is very small. This increases the possibility of a disturbed head colliding with a platter. Modern drives support parking their heads in a safe position under various circumstances. In particular, heads are automatically parked when the system is powered off or is asleep. SMS adds the ability to park the heads in the event of an accidental drop, strong vibrations, or other accelerated movement. The mechanism works by using a tri-axis accelerometer to detect sudden motion. When the threshold for emergency action is reached—say, because of a shock or free fall—an interrupt is generated. In processing this interrupt, the SMS driver (such as `IOI2CMotionSensor.kext`, `PMUMotionSensor.kext`, or `SMCMotionSensor.kext`) may send a "park" command to the disk drive, thereby reducing the possibility of damage to the drive on impact. Conversely, when the SMS detects that the computer is once again level and not under acceleration, it unlocks the drive heads so that the system can continue to use the disk normally.

On some models, the accelerometer is an integrated feature of the main logic board—specifically, an Inter-Integrated Circuit (I^2C) device[13] that is not tied to a specific disk drive. Typically, such an accelerometer uses a silicon sensor based on integrated microelectromechanical systems (iMEMS) technology. Acceleration or inclination causes an electrical property (say, capacitance) of the sensor to be altered. The sensor's interface can then translate these tiny changes to present them as acceleration readings.

It is interesting to note that depending on your working environment, the default sensitivity of the SMS may be too aggressive. For example, loud music—perhaps music with rather high bass and the consequential vibrations—can activate SMS undesirably. If the computer in question is itself involved in the generation or recording of such music, this may cause unacceptable interruptions. The mechanism can be disabled using the `pmset` power management configuration utility.

The SMS driver implements an I/O Kit user client, which allows several types of operations to be performed from user space, such as:

- Querying miscellaneous information such as vendor, version, and status
- Retrieving and setting sensitivity

---

13. Philips developed the I^2C bus in the early 1980s. I^2C is a multimaster control bus using which various ICs in a system can communicate with each other. It uses only two control lines and has a software-defined protocol.

- Resetting the hardware
- Retrieving orientation values

The orientation values consist of a triplet (x, y, z) that is related to the acceleration vector acting on the computer. The individual components of this vector change when external acceleration is applied to the computer (such as in a sideways sudden motion) or when the computer is rotated (thereby changing the angle of the gravity vector). Note the following points regarding the vector's components.

- The value of x is zero when the computer's bottom is parallel to the ground and it is not under lateral acceleration along its long edge. Rotating the computer's base around an axis parallel to its short edge changes the value of x.
- The value of y is zero when the computer's bottom is parallel to the ground and it is not under lateral acceleration along its short edge. Rotating the computer's base around an axis parallel to its long edge changes the value of y.
- The value of z changes when the computer is rotated such that its bottom does not remain in the horizontal plane.
- A perfectly calibrated SMS accelerometer would read (0, 0, 0) when the computer is in free fall in a vacuum.

In practice, an SMS unit may not be calibrated perfectly, and different units may have different calibrations. For example, the x and y values reported by the SMS hardware may not be zeros when the computer is parallel to the ground. Moreover, depending on the surroundings and the configured sensitivity of the hardware, minor fluctuations may be seen even when there is no perceptible movement of the computer.

Let us now see how to retrieve orientation data by communicating with the SMS driver. To invoke a user client method, we need to know the method's identifier and the types of its parameters.

```
$ cd /System/Library/Extensions/IOI2CMotionSensor.kext/Contents/MacOS
$ nm IOI2CMotionSensor | c++filt
...
00003934 T IOI2CMotionSensor::getOrientationUC(paramStruct*, paramStruct*,
                                    unsigned long, unsigned long*)
...
```

Since the getOrientationUC() method is exported by the user client, its address—0x3934 in this case—must also appear in the array of IOExternal-Method structures within the driver executable. The position of the structure within the array will give us the index of the method, whereas the structure's contents will indicate the sizes of the structures we need to provide while calling the method.

```
// iokit/IOKit/IOUserClient.h

struct IOExternalMethod {
    IOService     *object;
    IOMethod      func;
    IOOptionBits  flags;
    IOByteCount   count0;
    IOByteCount   count1;
};
```

Figure 10–27 shows the contents of the `IOExternalMethod` structure corresponding to `getOrientationUC()`. The index of this particular structure in the method array can be different based on the driver version. Although not shown in the figure, in this case (version 1.0.3 of both `IOI2CMotionSensor` and `PMUMotionSensor`), the index is 21. The index is 5 for `SMCMotionSensor`.

```
$ hexdump IOI2CMotionSensor
...
0005580 0000 38a4 0000 0003 0000 003c 0000 003c
0005590 0000 0000 0000 ffff 0000 3934 0000 0003
00055a0 0000 003c 0000 003c 0000 0000 0000 ffff
00055b0 0000 3ad8 0000 0003 0000 003c 0000 003c
...

count0          count1          func                flags
// 60 bytes    // 60 bytes    // getOrientationUC()  // kIOUCStructIStructO
```

FIGURE 10–27 Relevant contents of the `IOExternalMethod` structure corresponding to `getOrientationUC()`

Note in Figure 10–27 that the value of `flags` is `kIOUCStructIStructO`, which means that the method has one structure input parameter and one structure output parameter. The `count0` and `count1` values, which are 60 bytes each (40 bytes for `SMCMotionSensor`), represent the sizes of the input and output structures, respectively. We can invoke such a method using the `IOConnectMethod-StructureIStructureO()` function from the I/O Kit framework, which provides this function and other similar functions (such as `IOConnectMethod-ScalarIStructure0()`) to pass untyped data across the user-kernel boundary.

```
kern_return_t
IOConnectMethodStructureIStructure0(
    io_connect_t connect,           // acquired by calling IOServiceOpen()
    unsigned int index,             // index for kernel-resident method
    IOItemCount  structureInputSize, // size of the input struct parameter
    IOByteCount *structureOutputSize, // size of the output structure (out)
    void        *inputStructure,    // pointer to the input structure
    void        *ouputStructure);   // pointer to the output structure
```

In this case, we are interested only in the output structure, the first three bytes of which contain the x, y, and z values.[14] We can define the output structure as follows:

```
typedef struct {
    char x;
    char y;
    char z;
    // filler space to make size of the structure at least 60 bytes
    pad[57];
} SuddenMotionSensorData_t;
```

First, we need to create a connection to the appropriate `IOService` instance. Figure 10–28 shows the function that looks up the service and requests a connection to it.

FIGURE 10–28 Opening a connection to the motion sensor service object

```
static io_connect_t dataPort = 0;

kern_return_t
sms_initialize(void)
{
    kern_return_t   kr;
    CFDictionaryRef classToMatch;
    io_service_t    service;

    // create a matching dictionary given the class name, which depends on
    // hardware: "IOI2CMotionSensor", "PMUMotionSensor", "SMCMotionSensor" ...
    classToMatch = IOServiceMatching(kTargetIOKitClassName);
```

(continues)

---

14. Note that these values are not raw acceleration values—they have been processed before we receive them. Nevertheless, they will change in direct correspondence to the computer's movement.

FIGURE 10–28 Opening a connection to the motion sensor service object *(continued)*

```
// look up the IOService object (must already be registered)
service = IOServiceGetMatchingService(kIOMasterPortDefault, classToMatch);
if (!service)
    return KERN_FAILURE;

// create a connection to the IOService object
kr = IOServiceOpen(service,         // the IOService object
                   mach_task_self(), // the task requesting the connection
                   0,                // type of connection
                   &dataPort);      // connection handle


IOObjectRelease(service);

return kr;
}
```

> Note that for this section's technique to work on a particular model of an SMS-equipped Apple computer, the I/O Service class name, the user client method index, and the sizes of the input/output parameters must be appropriate for the SMS driver being used on that computer.

Given a connection handle to the IOService instance, we can invoke the getOrientationUC() method as shown in Figure 10–29.

FIGURE 10–29 Invoking a user client method given an IOService connection handle

```
static const int getOrientationUC_methodID = 21;

kern_return_t
sms_getOrientation(MotionSensorData_t *data)
{
    kern_return_t       kr;
    IOByteCount         size = 60;
    MotionSensorData_t unused_struct_in = { 0 };

    kr = IOConnectMethodStructureIStructureO(dataPort,
                                             getOrientationUC_methodID,
                                             size,
                                             &size,
                                             &unused_struct_in,
                                             data);
    return kr;
}
```

Note that the orientation data received from the SMS driver can be used to map the physical tilting of the computer to mouse or keyboard input events. Such mapping can be readily used for purposes such as human input for games, multi-directional scrolling, and panning across large maps.

10.7.6 Listing PCI Devices

Since the I/O Registry maintains information about all devices in the system, it is rather straightforward to look up specific devices and their properties based on a variety of search criteria. Figure 10–30 shows a program that lists all PCI devices in the system, along with the path of each device in the Service plane.

FIGURE 10–30 Listing PCI devices in the system

```
// lspci.c

#include <stdio.h>
#include <IOKit/IOKitLib.h>

int
main(void)
{
    kern_return_t kr;
    io_iterator_t pciDeviceList;
    io_service_t  pciDevice;
    io_name_t     deviceName;
    io_string_t   devicePath;

    // get an iterator for all PCI devices
    if (IOServiceGetMatchingServices(kIOMasterPortDefault,
                                     IOServiceMatching("IOPCIDevice"),
                                     &pciDeviceList) != KERN_SUCCESS)
        return 1;

    while ((pciDevice = IOIteratorNext(pciDeviceList))) {

        kr = IORegistryEntryGetName(pciDevice, deviceName);
        if (kr != KERN_SUCCESS)
            goto next;

        kr = IORegistryEntryGetPath(pciDevice, kIOServicePlane, devicePath);
        if (kr != KERN_SUCCESS)
            goto next;
```

(continues)

FIGURE 10–30 Listing PCI devices in the system *(continued)*

```
        // don't print the plane name prefix in the device path
        printf("%s (%s)\n", &devicePath[9], deviceName);

next:
        IOObjectRelease(pciDevice);
    }

    return kr;
}


$ gcc -Wall -o lspci lspci.c -framework IOKit -framework CoreFoundation
$ ./lspci # PowerPC
:/MacRISC4PE/pci@0,f0000000/AppleMacRiscAGP/ATY,WhelkParent@10 (ATY,WhelkParent)
:/MacRISC4PE/ht@0,f2000000/AppleMacRiscHT/pci@1 (pci)
...
:/MacRISC4PE/ht@0,f2000000/AppleMacRiscHT/pci@4/IOPCI2PCIBridge/usb@B,2 (usb)
:/MacRISC4PE/ht@0,f2000000/AppleMacRiscHT/pci@5 (pci)
:/MacRISC4PE/ht@0,f2000000/AppleMacRiscHT/pci@5/IOPCI2PCIBridge/ata-6@D (ata-6)
...
$ ./lspci # x86
:/AppleACPIPlatformExpert/PCI0@0/AppleACPIPCI/GFX0@2 (GFX0)
:/AppleACPIPlatformExpert/PCI0@0/AppleACPIPCI/HDEF@1B (HDEF)
...
```

10.7.7 Retrieving the Computer's Serial Number and Model Information

The program shown in Figure 10–31 communicates with the I/O Registry to retrieve the computer's serial number and model information, both of which are maintained as properties of the I/O Registry entry corresponding to the Platform Expert.

FIGURE 10–31 Retrieving the computer's serial number and model information

```
// lsunitinfo.c

#include <IOKit/IOKitLib.h>
#include <CoreFoundation/CoreFoundation.h>

int
main(void)
```

(continues)

FIGURE 10–31 Retrieving the computer's serial number and model information *(continued)*

```
{
    kern_return_t kr;
    io_service_t  pexpert;
    CFStringRef   serial, model;

    // get the Platform Expert object
    pexpert = IOServiceGetMatchingService(kIOMasterPortDefault,
                IOServiceMatching("IOPlatformExpertDevice"));
    if (!pexpert)
        return KERN_FAILURE;

    serial = IORegistryEntryCreateCFProperty(
                pexpert, CFSTR(kIOPlatformSerialNumberKey),
                kCFAllocatorDefault,kNilOptions);
    if (serial) {
        // note that this will go to stderr
        CFShow(serial);
        CFRelease(serial);
    }

    model = IORegistryEntryCreateCFProperty(
                pexpert, CFSTR("model"), kCFAllocatorDefault, kNilOptions);
    if (model) {
        printf("%s\n", CFDataGetBytePtr((CFDataRef)model));
        CFRelease(model);
    }

    if (pexpert)
        IOObjectRelease(pexpert);

    return kr;
}


$ gcc -Wall -o lsunitinfo lsunitinfo.c -framework IOKit -framework CoreFoundation
$ ./lsunitinfo
G84XXXXXXPS
PowerMac7,3
```

10.7.8 Retrieving Temperature Sensor Readings

As power and thermal management have become integral parts of computer system design, it is common to find several types of hardware sensors in a modern computer system. Depending on the model, an Apple computer may contain temperature sensors, voltage and current sensors, fan speed sensors, and so on. In certain types of systems, such as MacRISC4-based systems, the concept of a *platform plug-in* is used along with the Platform Expert. Whereas the Platform Expert is specific to system *architecture*, a platform plug-in is specific to a particular *platform*, which depends on the motherboard and usually changes more frequently than system architecture. In particular, the plug-in usually performs thermal management, which includes monitoring the various sensors and, based on their values, controlling processor and fan speeds. The available platform plug-ins reside within the `AppleMacRISC4PE` kernel extension bundle.

```
$ cd /System/Library/Extensions/AppleMacRISC4PE.kext/Contents/PlugIns
$ ls
IOPlatformPluginFamily.kext        PowerMac12_1_ThermalProfile.kext
MacRISC4_PlatformPlugin.kext       PowerMac7_2_PlatformPlugin.kext
PBG4_PlatformPlugin.kext           PowerMac8_1_ThermalProfile.kext
PBG4_ThermalProfile.kext           PowerMac9_1_ThermalProfile.kext
PowerMac11_2_PlatformPlugin.kext   RackMac3_1_PlatformPlugin.kext
PowerMac11_2_ThermalProfile.kext   SMU_Neo2_PlatformPlugin.kext
PowerMac12_1_PlatformPlugin.kext
```

If a system uses a platform plug-in, the properties (including current values) of all hardware sensors in the system are available in the I/O Registry as the `IOHWSensors` property of the system-specific platform plug-in class, which inherits from `IOPlatformPlugin`. A sensor is abstracted in the platform plug-in by an instance of the `IOPlatformSensor` class. Each hardware sensor's driver is an `IOHWSensor` object.

We can retrieve the readings of temperature sensors in a system either by looking up the `IOHWSensors` property of the platform plug-in (if there is one) or by looking up each `IOHWSensor` object whose type is `temperature`. The latter approach is more generic because it will work even if a system has no platform plug-in. Figure 10–32 shows a program that uses this approach to display the locations and values of temperature sensors in a system.

FIGURE 10–32 Retrieving temperature sensor readings

```
// lstemperature.c

#include <unistd.h>
#include <IOKit/IOKitLib.h>
#include <CoreFoundation/CoreFoundation.h>

#define kIOPPluginCurrentValueKey "current-value" // current measured value
#define kIOPPluginLocationKey     "location"      // readable description
```

(continues)

FIGURE 10–32 Retrieving temperature sensor readings *(continued)*

```c
#define kIOPPluginTypeKey       "type"          // sensor/control type
#define kIOPPluginTypeTempSensor "temperature"  // desired type value

// macro to convert sensor temperature format (16.16) to integer (Celsius)
#define SENSOR_TEMP_FMT_C(x) (double)((x) >> 16)

// macro to convert sensor temperature format (16.16) to integer (Fahrenheit)
#define SENSOR_TEMP_FMT_F(x) \
    (double)((((double)((x) >> 16) * (double)9) / (double)5 + (double)32)

void
printTemperatureSensor(const void *sensorDict, CFStringEncoding encoding)
{
    SInt32       currentValue;
    CFNumberRef  sensorValue;
    CFStringRef  sensorType, sensorLocation;

    if (!CFDictionaryGetValueIfPresent((CFDictionaryRef)sensorDict,
                                       CFSTR(kIOPPluginTypeKey),
                                       (void *)&sensorType))
        return;

    if (CFStringCompare(sensorType, CFSTR(kIOPPluginTypeTempSensor), 0) !=
                    kCFCompareEqualTo) // we handle only temperature sensors
        return;

    sensorLocation = CFDictionaryGetValue((CFDictionaryRef)sensorDict,
                                          CFSTR(kIOPPluginLocationKey));

    sensorValue = CFDictionaryGetValue((CFDictionaryRef)sensorDict,
                                       CFSTR(kIOPPluginCurrentValueKey));
    (void)CFNumberGetValue(sensorValue, kCFNumberSInt32Type,
                           (void *)&currentValue);

    printf("%24s %7.1f C %9.1f F\n",
           // see documentation for CFStringGetCStringPtr() caveat
           CFStringGetCStringPtr(sensorLocation, encoding),
           SENSOR_TEMP_FMT_C(currentValue),
           SENSOR_TEMP_FMT_F(currentValue));
}

int
main(void)
{
    kern_return_t       kr;
    io_iterator_t       io_hw_sensors;
    io_service_t        io_hw_sensor;
    CFMutableDictionaryRef sensor_properties;
    CFStringEncoding    systemEncoding = CFStringGetSystemEncoding();
```

(continues)

FIGURE 10–32 Retrieving temperature sensor readings *(continued)*

```
    kr = IOServiceGetMatchingServices(kIOMasterPortDefault,
            IOServiceNameMatching("IOHWSensor"), &io_hw_sensors);

    while ((io_hw_sensor = IOIteratorNext(io_hw_sensors))) {
        kr = IORegistryEntryCreateCFProperties(io_hw_sensor, &sensor_properties,
                kCFAllocatorDefault, kNilOptions);
        if (kr == KERN_SUCCESS)
            printTemperatureSensor(sensor_properties, systemEncoding);

        CFRelease(sensor_properties);
        IOObjectRelease(io_hw_sensor);
    }

    IOObjectRelease(io_hw_sensors);

    exit(kr);
}


$ gcc -Wall -o lstemperature lstemperature.c -framework IOKit \
    -framework CoreFoundation
$ sudo hwprefs machine_type # Power Mac G5 Dual 2.5 GHz
PowerMac7,3
$ ./lstemperature
            DRIVE BAY     25.0 C      77.0 F
             BACKSIDE     44.0 C     111.2 F
          U3 HEATSINK     68.0 C     154.4 F
     CPU A AD7417 AMB     49.0 C     120.2 F
     CPU B AD7417 AMB     47.0 C     116.6 F
$ sudo hwprefs machine_type # Xserve G5 Dual 2.0 GHz
RackMac3,1
$ ./lstemperature
     SYS CTRLR AMBIENT    35.0 C      95.0 F
    SYS CTRLR INTERNAL    47.0 C     116.6 F
      CPU A AD7417 AMB    28.0 C      82.4 F
      CPU B AD7417 AMB    27.0 C      80.6 F
             PCI SLOTS    26.0 C      78.8 F
            CPU A INLET   19.0 C      66.2 F
            CPU B INLET   20.0 C      68.0 F
```

The `IOHWControls` property of the platform plug-in contains, among other things, the current RPM readings of the fans in the system. The same information can also be obtained from the `control-info` property of the `AppleFCU` class instance, which represents a fan control unit. The fan control unit driver publishes `control-info` as an array containing data on all controls it is responsible for.

10.7.9 Retrieving MAC Addresses of Ethernet Interfaces

Figure 10–33 shows a program that retrieves the MAC addresses of all Ethernet interfaces in the system. It iterates over the list of all instances of the `IOEthernetInterface` class, whose parent class—an instance of `IOEthernetController`—contains the MAC address as one of its properties (`kIOMACAddress`, which is defined as `IOMACAddress`). Note that an `IOEthernetInterface` instance contains various other interesting aspects of the network interface, such as its BSD name, information about active packet filters, and several types of statistics.

FIGURE 10–33 Retrieving the MAC addresses of Ethernet interfaces in the system

```
// lsmacaddr.c

#include <IOKit/IOKitLib.h>
#include <IOKit/network/IOEthernetInterface.h>
#include <IOKit/network/IOEthernetController.h>
#include <CoreFoundation/CoreFoundation.h>

typedef UInt8 MACAddress_t[kIOEthernetAddressSize];

void
printMACAddress(MACAddress_t MACAddress)
{
    int i;

    for (i = 0; i < kIOEthernetAddressSize - 1; i++)
        printf("%02x:", MACAddress[i]);

    printf("%x\n", MACAddress[i]);
}

int
main(void)
{
    kern_return_t          kr;
    CFMutableDictionaryRef classToMatch;
    io_iterator_t          ethernet_interfaces;
    io_object_t            ethernet_interface, ethernet_controller;
    CFTypeRef              MACAddressAsCFData;

    classToMatch = IOServiceMatching(kIOEthernetInterfaceClass);
    kr = IOServiceGetMatchingServices(kIOMasterPortDefault, classToMatch,
                               &ethernet_interfaces);
    if (kr != KERN_SUCCESS)
        return kr;
```

(continues)

FIGURE 10–33 Retrieving the MAC addresses of Ethernet interfaces in the system *(continued)*

```
    while ((ethernet_interface = IOIteratorNext(ethernet_interfaces))) {

        kr = IORegistryEntryGetParentEntry(ethernet_interface, kIOServicePlane,
                                    &ethernet_controller);
        if (kr != KERN_SUCCESS)
            goto next;

        MACAddressAsCFData = IORegistryEntryCreateCFProperty(
                            ethernet_controller,
                            CFSTR(kIOMACAddress),
                            kCFAllocatorDefault, 0);
        if (MACAddressAsCFData) {
            MACAddress_t address;
            CFDataGetBytes(MACAddressAsCFData,
                        CFRangeMake(0, kIOEthernetAddressSize), address);
            CFRelease(MACAddressAsCFData);
            printMACAddress(address);
        }
        IOObjectRelease(ethernet_controller);
next:
        IOObjectRelease(ethernet_interface);
    }
    IOObjectRelease(ethernet_interfaces);

    return kr;
}


$ gcc -Wall -o lsmacaddr lsmacaddr.c -framework IOKit \
    -framework CoreFoundation
$ ./lsmacaddr
00:0d:xx:xx:xx:xx
00:0d:xx:xx:xx:xx
```

10.7.10 Implementing an Encrypted Disk Filter Scheme

In this example, we will create a mass-storage filter scheme driver that implements transparent encryption at the device level. The driver will facilitate encrypted volumes wherein all data (both user data and file system data) will be encrypted on the storage medium, but mounting such a volume will allow us to access it normally. We will assume familiarity with the concepts described in Apple's technical document titled "Mass Storage Device Driver Programming

Guide." As discussed in this document, a filter scheme driver inherits from the `IOStorage` class and logically sits between two media objects, each of which is an instance of the `IOMedia` class. The driver allows mapping of one or more media objects to one or more different media objects. Our encryption filter is an example of a one-to-one mapping. A partition scheme driver maps one media object (say, representing a whole disk) to many media objects (each representing a partition on the disk). Conversely, a RAID scheme maps multiple media objects (RAID members) to a single media object.

An important consideration while writing a filter scheme driver is the specification of a media object's properties that the filter driver will match against. The set of target properties is specified in the filter scheme driver's personality. Examples of `IOMedia` properties include whether the media is ejectable, whether it is writable, the media's preferred block size in bytes, the media's entire size in bytes, the media's BSD device node name, and the media's content description (or *content hint*, as specified when the media object was created). In this example, we will arrange for our filter scheme driver to match all `IOMedia` objects whose content description is `osxbook_HFS`—this way, it will not inadvertently match existing volumes. To test the driver, we will explicitly create a volume on a disk image.

Let us call our driver `SimpleCryptoDisk`. We will begin with an Xcode project template for I/O Kit drivers. Figure 10–34 shows the personality and dependency specifications from the driver's `Info.plist` file. Note that the personality includes a content-hint string.

FIGURE 10–34 Personality and dependency list for the `SimpleCryptoDisk` I/O Kit driver

```
...
<key>IOKitPersonalities</key>
<dict>
        <key>SimpleCryptoDisk</key>
        <dict>
                <key>CFBundleIdentifier</key>
                <string>com.osxbook.driver.SimpleCryptoDisk</string>
                <key>Content Hint</key>
                <string>osxbook_HFS</string>
                <key>IOClass</key>
                <string>com_osxbook_driver_SimpleCryptoDisk</string>
                <key>IOMatchCategory</key>
                <string>IOStorage</string>
                <key>IOProviderClass</key>
                <string>IOMedia</string>
        </dict>
</dict>
<key>OSBundleLibraries</key>
```

(continues)

FIGURE 10–34 Personality and dependency list for the `SimpleCryptoDisk` I/O Kit driver *(continued)*

```
        <dict>
                <key>com.apple.iokit.IOStorageFamily</key>
                <string>1.5</string>
                <key>com.apple.kpi.iokit</key>
                <string>8.0.0</string>
                <key>com.apple.kpi.libkern</key>
                <string>8.0.0</string>
        </dict>
</dict>
</plist>
```

Since the data is to be stored encrypted on disk, we will need to implement a `read()` method that performs decryption and a `write()` method that performs encryption. Both these methods are asynchronous—when the I/O completes, the caller must be notified using the specified completion action. As we will shortly see, the asynchrony somewhat complicates the implementation of these methods because our driver must substitute its own completion action in place of the caller's actions, which it must eventually invoke. Figure 10–35 shows the header file (`SimpleCryptoDisk.h`) for the driver.

FIGURE 10–35 Header file for the `SimpleCryptoDisk` I/O Kit driver

```
// SimpleCryptoDisk.h

#include <IOKit/storage/IOMedia.h>
#include <IOKit/storage/IOStorage.h>

class com_osxbook_driver_SimpleCryptoDisk : public IOStorage {

    OSDeclareDefaultStructors(com_osxbook_driver_SimpleCryptoDisk)

protected:
        IOMedia * _filteredMedia;

        virtual void free(void);

        virtual bool handleOpen(IOService    *client,
                                IOOptionBits  options,
                                void         *access);

        virtual bool handleIsOpen(const IOService *client) const;
        virtual void handleClose(IOService *client, IOOptionBits options);
```

(continues)

FIGURE 10–35 Header file for the `SimpleCryptoDisk` I/O Kit driver *(continued)*

```
public:
        virtual bool init(OSDictionary *properties = 0);
        virtual bool start(IOService *provider);

        virtual void read(IOService          *client,
                          UInt64              byteStart,
                          IOMemoryDescriptor *buffer,
                          IOStorageCompletion completion);

        virtual void write(IOService          *client,
                           UInt64              byteStart,
                           IOMemoryDescriptor *buffer,
                           IOStorageCompletion completion);

        virtual IOReturn synchronizeCache(IOService *client);
        virtual IOMedia *getProvider() const;
};
```

Figure 10–36 shows the driver's source (`SimpleCryptoDisk.cpp`). Besides relatively trivial method implementations that simply forward the invocation to the provider's methods, we implement the following important methods and functions.

- `com_osxbook_driver_SimpleCryptoDisk::start()` initializes and publishes a new media object. Note that our filter scheme driver matches against a content hint of `osxbook_HFS` but publishes a media object with a content hint of `Apple_HFS`.

- `com_osxbook_driver_SimpleCryptoDisk::read()` reads data from storage. Once the I/O finishes, the driver postprocesses the data read by decrypting it. We use a structure of type `SimpleCryptoDiskContext` to hold the context, including the caller's completion routine, for a read or write operation.

- `com_osxbook_driver_SimpleCryptoDisk::write()` writes data to storage. The driver preprocesses the data to encrypt it.

- `fixBufferUserRead()` is the encryption routine, where encryption is simply a logical NOT operation.

- `fixBufferUserWrite()` is the decryption routine, where decryption is again a logical NOT operation.

- `SCDReadWriteCompletion()` is the driver's completion routine. We replace the caller's completion routine for both reads and writes. It is clear that we cannot decrypt until a read completes. In the case of writes, we do not encrypt the caller's data buffer in place—we allocate a new data buffer for encryption and wrap it in two IOMemoryDescriptor instances: one with a direction of kIODirectionIn (used while encrypting) and another with a direction of kIODirectionOut (passed to the provider's write() method).

FIGURE 10–36 Source for the SimpleCryptoDisk I/O Kit driver

```
// SimpleCryptoDisk.cpp

#include <IOKit/assert.h>
#include <IOKit/IOLib.h>
#include "SimpleCryptoDisk.h"

#define super IOStorage

OSDefineMetaClassAndStructors(com_osxbook_driver_SimpleCryptoDisk, IOStorage)

// Context structure for our read/write completion routines
typedef struct {
    IOMemoryDescriptor *buffer;
    IOMemoryDescriptor *bufferRO;
    IOMemoryDescriptor *bufferWO;
    void               *memory;
    vm_size_t           size;
    IOStorageCompletion completion;
} SimpleCryptoDiskContext;

// Internal functions
static void fixBufferUserRead(IOMemoryDescriptor *buffer);
static void fixBufferUserWrite(IOMemoryDescriptor *bufferR,
                               IOMemoryDescriptor *bufferW);
static void SCDReadWriteCompletion(void *target, void *parameter,
                                   IOReturn status, UInt64 actualByteCount);

bool
com_osxbook_driver_SimpleCryptoDisk::init(OSDictionary *properties)
{
    if (super::init(properties) == false)
        return false;

    _filteredMedia = 0;

    return true;
}
```

(continues)

FIGURE 10–36 Source for the `SimpleCryptoDisk` I/O Kit driver *(continued)*

```
void
com_osxbook_driver_SimpleCryptoDisk::free(void)
{
    if (_filteredMedia)
        _filteredMedia->release();

    super::free();
}

bool
com_osxbook_driver_SimpleCryptoDisk::start(IOService *provider)
{
    IOMedia *media = (IOMedia *)provider;

    assert(media);

    if (super::start(provider) == false)
        return false;

    IOMedia *newMedia = new IOMedia;
    if (!newMedia)
        return false;

    if (!newMedia->init(
            0,                                 // media offset in bytes
            media->getSize(),                  // media size in bytes
            media->getPreferredBlockSize(),    // natural block size in bytes
            media->isEjectable(),              // is media ejectable?
            false,                             // is it the whole disk?
            media->isWritable(),               // is media writable?
            "Apple_HFS")) {                    // hint of media's contents
        newMedia->release();
        newMedia = 0;
        return false;
    }

    UInt32 partitionID = 1;
    char name[32];

    // Set a name for this partition.
    sprintf(name, "osxbook_HFS %ld", partitionID);
    newMedia->setName(name);

    // Set a location value (partition #) for this partition.
    char location[32];
    sprintf(location, "%ld", partitionID);
    newMedia->setLocation(location);
```

(continues)

FIGURE 10–36 Source for the `SimpleCryptoDisk` I/O Kit driver *(continued)*

```
    _filteredMedia = newMedia;
    newMedia->attach(this);
    newMedia->registerService();

    return true;
}

bool
com_osxbook_driver_SimpleCryptoDisk::handleOpen(IOService    *client,
                                                IOOptionBits options,
                                                void         *argument)
{
    return getProvider()->open(this, options, (IOStorageAccess)argument);
}

bool
com_osxbook_driver_SimpleCryptoDisk::handleIsOpen(const IOService *client) const
{
    return getProvider()->isOpen(this);
}

void
com_osxbook_driver_SimpleCryptoDisk::handleClose(IOService    *client,
                                                 IOOptionBits options)
{
    getProvider()->close(this, options);
}

IOReturn
com_osxbook_driver_SimpleCryptoDisk::synchronizeCache(IOService *client)
{
    return getProvider()->synchronizeCache(this);
}

IOMedia *
com_osxbook_driver_SimpleCryptoDisk::getProvider(void) const
{
    return (IOMedia *)IOService::getProvider();
}

void
com_osxbook_driver_SimpleCryptoDisk::read(IOService            *client,
                                          UInt64               byteStart,
                                          IOMemoryDescriptor   *buffer,
                                          IOStorageCompletion  completion)
{
    SimpleCryptoDiskContext *context =
        (SimpleCryptoDiskContext *)IOMalloc(sizeof(SimpleCryptoDiskContext));
```

(continues)

FIGURE 10–36 Source for the `SimpleCryptoDisk` I/O Kit driver *(continued)*

```
    context->buffer      = buffer;
    context->bufferRO    = NULL;
    context->bufferWO    = NULL;
    context->memory      = NULL;
    context->size        = (vm_size_t)0;

    // Save original completion function and insert our own.
    context->completion  = completion;
    completion.action    = (IOStorageCompletionAction)&SCDReadWriteCompletion;
    completion.target    = (void *)this;
    completion.parameter = (void *)context;

    // Hand over to the provider.
    return getProvider()->read(this, byteStart, buffer, completion);
}


void
com_osxbook_driver_SimpleCryptoDisk::write(IOService          *client,
                                           UInt64             byteStart,
                                           IOMemoryDescriptor *buffer,
                                           IOStorageCompletion completion)
{
    // The buffer passed to this function would have been created with a
    // direction of kIODirectionOut. We need a new buffer that is created
    // with a direction of kIODirectionIn to store the modified contents
    // of the original buffer.

    // Determine the original buffer's length.
    IOByteCount length = buffer->getLength();

    // Allocate memory for a new (temporary) buffer. Note that we would be
    // passing this modified buffer (instead of the original) to our
    // provider's write function. We need a kIODirectionOut "pointer",
    // a new memory descriptor referring to the same memory, that we shall
    // pass to the provider's write function.
    void *memory = IOMalloc(length);

    // We use this descriptor to modify contents of the original buffer.
    IOMemoryDescriptor *bufferWO =
        IOMemoryDescriptor::withAddress(memory, length, kIODirectionIn);

    // We use this descriptor as the buffer argument in the provider's write().
    IOMemoryDescriptor *bufferRO =
        IOMemoryDescriptor::withSubRange(bufferWO, 0, length, kIODirectionOut);

    SimpleCryptoDiskContext *context =
        (SimpleCryptoDiskContext *)IOMalloc(sizeof(SimpleCryptoDiskContext));
```

(continues)

FIGURE 10–36 Source for the `SimpleCryptoDisk` I/O Kit driver *(continued)*

```
    context->buffer      = buffer;
    context->bufferRO    = bufferRO;
    context->bufferWO    = bufferWO;
    context->memory      = memory;
    context->size        = (vm_size_t)length;

    // Save the original completion function and insert our own.
    context->completion  = completion;
    completion.action    = (IOStorageCompletionAction)&SCDReadWriteCompletion;
    completion.target    = (void *)this;
    completion.parameter = (void *)context;

    // Fix buffer contents (apply simple "encryption").
    fixBufferUserWrite(buffer, bufferWO);

    // Hand over to the provider.
    return getProvider()->write(this, byteStart, bufferRO, completion);
}

static void
fixBufferUserRead(IOMemoryDescriptor *buffer)
{
    IOByteCount i, j;
    IOByteCount length, count;
    UInt64      byteBlock[64];

    assert(buffer);

    length = buffer->getLength();
    assert(!(length % 512));
    length /= 512;

    buffer->prepare(kIODirectionOutIn);

    for (i = 0; i < length; i++) {
        count = buffer->readBytes(i * 512, (UInt8 *)byteBlock, 512);
        for (j = 0; j < 64; j++)
            byteBlock[j] = ~(byteBlock[j]);
        count = buffer->writeBytes(i * 512, (UInt8 *)byteBlock, 512);
    }

    buffer->complete();

    return;
}

static void
fixBufferUserWrite(IOMemoryDescriptor *bufferR, IOMemoryDescriptor *bufferW)
```

(continues)

FIGURE 10–36 Source for the `SimpleCryptoDisk` I/O Kit driver *(continued)*

```
{
    IOByteCount i, j;
    IOByteCount length, count;
    UInt64      byteBlock[64];

    assert(bufferR);
    assert(bufferW);

    length = bufferR->getLength();
    assert(!(length % 512));
    length /= 512;

    bufferR->prepare(kIODirectionOut);
    bufferW->prepare(kIODirectionIn);

    for (i = 0; i < length; i++) {
        count = bufferR->readBytes(i * 512, (UInt8 *)byteBlock, 512);
        for (j = 0; j < 64; j++)
            byteBlock[j] = ~(byteBlock[j]);
        count = bufferW->writeBytes(i * 512, (UInt8 *)byteBlock, 512);
    }

    bufferW->complete();
    bufferR->complete();

    return;
}


static void
SCDReadWriteCompletion(void    *target,
                       void    *parameter,
                       IOReturn status,
                       UInt64   actualByteCount)
{
    SimpleCryptoDiskContext *context = (SimpleCryptoDiskContext *)parameter;

    if (context->bufferWO == NULL) { // this was a read

        // Fix buffer contents (apply simple "decryption").
        fixBufferUserRead(context->buffer);

    } else { // This was a write.

        // Release temporary memory descriptors and free memory that we had
        // allocated in the write call.
        (context->bufferRO)->release();
        (context->bufferWO)->release();
        IOFree(context->memory, context->size);
    }
```

(continues)

FIGURE 10–36 Source for the `SimpleCryptoDisk` I/O Kit driver *(continued)*

```
// Retrieve the original completion routine.
IOStorageCompletion completion = context->completion;

IOFree(context, sizeof(SimpleCryptoDiskContext));

// Run the original completion routine, if any.
if (completion.action)
    (*completion.action)(completion.target, completion.parameter, status,
                         actualByteCount);
}
```

To test the `SimpleCryptoDisk` driver, we will create a disk image with a partition type of `osxbook_HFS`. We will also create a regular disk image so we can highlight the difference between encrypted and cleartext storage. Let us create a regular disk image first (Figure 10–37).

FIGURE 10–37 Reading the contents of cleartext storage directly from the storage medium

```
$ hdiutil create -size 32m -fs HFS+ -volname Clear /tmp/clear.dmg
...
created: /private/tmp/clear.dmg
$ open /tmp/clear.dmg # mount the volume contained in clear.dmg
$ echo "Secret Message" > /Volumes/Clear/file.txt
$ hdiutil detach /Volumes/Clear # unmount the volume
...
$ strings /tmp/clear.dmg
...
Secret Message
...
```

> The use of the `hdiutil` command-line program to create and manipulate disk images is discussed in Chapter 11.

As Figure 10–37 shows, we can see the contents of the text file we created on a cleartext volume by accessing the raw storage medium. Let us attempt to do the same in the case of an encrypted disk (Figure 10–38).

FIGURE 10–38 Using encrypted storage with the `SimpleCryptoDisk` filter scheme driver

```
$ hdiutil create -size 32m -partitionType osxbook_HFS /tmp/crypto.dmg
...
created: /private/tmp/crypto.dmg
$ sudo kextload -v SimpleCryptoDisk.kext
kextload: extension SimpleCryptoDisk.kext appears to be valid
kextload: loading extension SimpleCryptoDisk.kext
kextload: SimpleCryptoDisk.kext loaded successfully
kextload: loading personalities named:
kextload:     SimpleCryptoDisk
kextload: sending 1 personality to the kernel
kextload: matching started for SimpleCryptoDisk.kext
$ hdiutil attach -nomount /tmp/crypto.dmg
/dev/disk10                Apple_partition_scheme
/dev/disk10s1             Apple_partition_map
/dev/disk10s2             osxbook_HFS
/dev/disk10s2s1           Apple_HFS
$ newfs_hfs -v Crypto /dev/rdisk10s2s1
Initialized /dev/rdisk10s2s1 as a 32 MB HFS Plus Volume
$ hdiutil detach disk10
...
"disk10" ejected.
$ open /tmp/crypto.dmg
$ echo "Secret Message" > /Volumes/Crypto/file.txt
$ cat /Volumes/Crypto/file.txt
Secret Message
$ hdiutil detach /Volumes/Crypto
$ strings /tmp/crypto.dmg
# the cleartext message is not seen
```

> An experimental use of a filter scheme driver could be to analyze patterns of block reads and writes.

10.8 Debugging

Casually speaking, debugging can be defined as the process of finding and fixing defects, or bugs,[15] in an object of interest, which could be a piece of software, firmware, or hardware. In this section, we will look at several areas related to kernel debugging.

---

15. A real-life bug—a moth—caused program malfunction in the Harvard Mark I computer and gained the distinction of being the first computer bug.

10.8.1 Kernel Panics

When there is a kernel panic, the kernel takes different actions depending on whether kernel debugging is enabled or not. By default, kernel debugging is disabled, in which case the kernel displays a panic user interface that instructs the user to restart the computer. We saw in Section 5.6 how to customize and test this user interface. Various kernel-debugging options can be enabled by setting the appropriate bits in the kernel's `debug` boot-time argument. Table 4–13 lists details of this argument. A typical setting of `debug` is `0x144`, which is the bitwise OR of `DB_LOG_PI_SCRN` (disables the panic user interface), `DB_ARP` (allows the kernel debugger nub to use ARP), and `DB_NMI` (enables support for NMI generation). With this setting, the kernel dumps kernel panic information on the screen and waits for a debugger connection. Figure 10–39 shows an example of a kernel panic dump, along with the functions involved in generating the dump. The panic corresponds to a `NULL` pointer being dereferenced in the kernel.

> The file `osfmk/kern/debug.c` contains definitions of several panic-related data structures and variables, such as `panicstr`, `panic_lock`, `paniccpu`, `panicDebugging`, `debug_mode`, `logPanicDataToScreen`, and `debug_buf`. It also implements the platform-independent `panic()` routine, which calls the platform-dependent routine `Debugger()` [`osfmk/ppc/model_dep.c`].

As we saw in Section 4.11.1.1, if kernel debugging *is* disabled, information about the last kernel panic—if there was one—is saved in a special NVRAM partition, provided there is sufficient space in the NVRAM. The panic information represents the contents of the `debug_buf` global buffer. Even though a page of memory is allocated for the latter, only up to 2040 bytes of its contents are saved to NVRAM,[16] or transmitted to another computer, by `Debugger()`. On rebooting, the contents of the panic log are available as an NVRAM property called `aapl,panic-info`, which is read-only from the user's standpoint. The property is created when Open Firmware variables are initialized in the IONVRAM module [`iokit/Kernel/IONVRAM.cpp`]. Additionally, the NVRAM panic partition is marked for clearing.

---

16. The kernel attempts to apply rudimentary compression on the panic log. Therefore, the saved panic information may contain more information than the same number of bytes in the debug buffer.

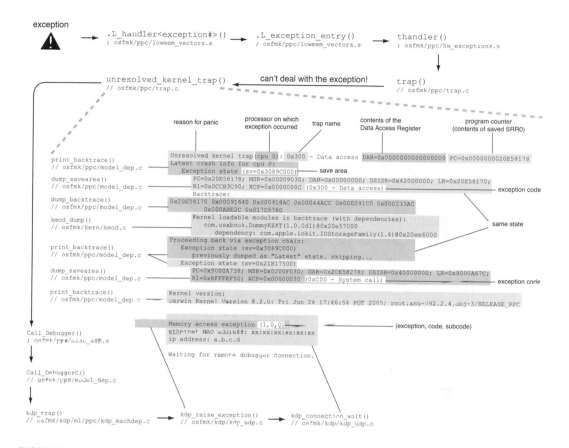

FIGURE 10–39 Dissection of a kernel panic dump

> Once the kernel panics, a driver cannot automatically reboot the system because the kernel does not run driver threads after a panic. However, the Xserve hardware watchdog timer can be used to trigger a reboot.

During bootstrapping, the crash reporter daemon (/usr/libexec/crashreporterd) is launched by the CrashReporter startup item. crashreporterd calls a helper tool (/usr/libexec/crashdump) to read the contents of aapl,panic-info and dump them to the panic log file (/Library/Logs/panic.log). The raw contents can also be viewed using the nvram command-line program:

```
$ nvram -p aapl,panic-info
aapl,panic-info %e1%87v%9cj1%f0%ea%81%82%0cxvl%cb%c9%03%0f...
```

Note that the contents of aapl,panic-info are the same as what would have been displayed on-screen if kernel-debugging were enabled.

> On Old World Macintosh computers, the NVRAM may not have enough space to store the panic information. On such computers, no panic log will be dumped on rebooting after a panic.

10.8.2 Remote Core Dumps

The Mac OS X kernel supports remote core dumping wherein one Mac OS X system can send core dumps to another system, with the latter running the remote kernel core dump server (/usr/libexec/kdumpd)—also called the *panic server*. kdumpd is derived from the BSD tftp program.[17] It listens on UDP port number 1069, which is hardcoded in the implementation of the Kernel Debugging Protocol (KDP). It should be executed as a low-privilege user such as "nobody." The directory for storing received core files is specified to kdumpd as an argument.

> A single panic server can receive core dump files and panic logs from multiple systems.

The core dump filename sent by a target kernel uses the string "core-<kernel-version>-<ip>-<abstime>" as the template, where <ip> is the IP address of the sender in dotted-decimal format and <abstime> is the hexadecimal representation of the lower 32 bits of the absolute time value (as reported by mach_absolute_time()). Note that the kernel can send both core dump files and panic logs to kdumpd. The following is an example of the message printed by a target machine while sending a core dump file to kdumpd:

```
Entering system dump routine
Attempting connection to panic server configured at IP 10.0.0.1
Routing via router MAC address xx:xx:xx:xx:xx:xx
Kernel map size is 725536768
Sending write request for core-xnu-792-10.0.0.2-4104e078
```

---

17. It is possible to run kdumpd on a system other than Mac OS X.

To enable sending core dumps to a panic server, the latter's IP address is specified through the _panicd_ip boot-time argument to the target kernel. Moreover, the appropriate bits of the debug argument must be set—in particular, the DB_KERN_DUMP_ON_PANIC (0x400) bit must be set to trigger a core dump on panic. Additionally, DB_KERN_DUMP_ON_NMI (0x800) can be set to trigger a core dump on an NMI without inducing a kernel panic.

```
$ sudo nvram boot-args="-v debug=0xd44 panicd_ip=10.0.0.1"
```

There are certain caveats in transmitting core dumps to the panic server, such as the following.

- The system running kdumpd must have a static IP address.

- In its current implementation, remote core dumping is inherently insecure in that kernel memory is transmitted over the network.

- There must be sufficient free disk space on the system running kdumpd to accommodate the incoming core dump.

10.8.3 Logging

Logging is an integral part of software debugging, whether it is kernel-level or user-level software. The Mac OS X kernel provides several mechanisms that kernel extensions can use to log messages. The Mac OS X system log facility, Apple System Logger (ASL), supports several methods of dispatching log messages. Figure 10–40 shows an overview of logging in Mac OS X.

The following are the primary logging functions available in the kernel.

- IOLog() is the preferred logging function in the I/O Kit. It generates a message that is destined for the system log file and possibly for the console. It is a wrapper around _doprnt() [osfmk/kern/printf.c]. IOLog() is not synchronous normally, which means it is possible to miss log messages in the case of a kernel panic. However, setting the kIOLogSynchronous bit (0x00200000) in the io boot-time argument makes the console output synchronous. The file iokit/IOKit/IOKitDebug.h enumerates several other bits that can be set in the io argument to enable specific types of I/O Kit log messages.

- printf() is similar to IOLog() but can be used from outside the I/O Kit. It is another wrapper around _doprnt(), but it also surrounds the call to _doprnt() by disable_preemption() and enable_preemption().

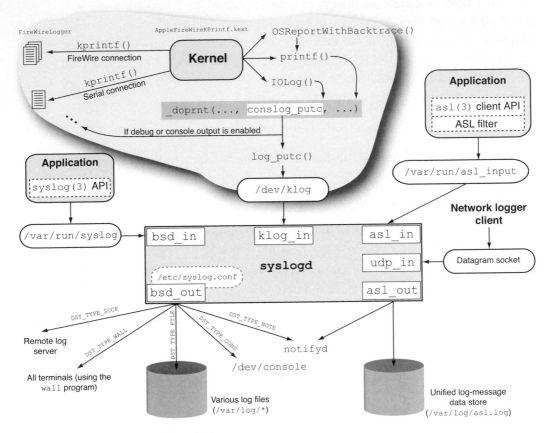

FIGURE 10–40 Logging in Mac OS X

- `OSReportWithBacktrace()` calls `OSBacktrace()` [libkern/gen/ OSDebug.cpp] to generate a stack backtrace and prints it using `printf()`. It also calls `kmod_dump_log()` [osfmk/kern/kmod.c] to print loadable kernel modules—along with their dependencies—associated with the backtrace.

- `kprintf()` is a synchronous logging function whose output must be enabled by setting the `DB_KPRT` (0x8) bit in the `debug` boot-time argument. Its output can be sent across a serial connection (provided a native serial port is available) or a FireWire connection. The latter requires the `AppleFireWireKPrintf` kernel extension on the system generating the messages and the `FireWireLogger` program on the system used for viewing the messages.[18]

---

18. `AppleFireWireKPrintf.kext` and `FireWireLogger` are available as parts of Apple's FireWire SDK.

conslog_putc() [osfmk/kern/printf.c] calls log_putc() [bsd/kern/subr_log.c] to append messages to a global message buffer—a msgbuf structure that we came across in Section 5.3.3.

```
// bsd/sys/msgbuf.h

#define MSG_BSIZE        (4096 - 3 * sizeof(long))
struct  msgbuf {
#define MSG_MAGIC        0x063061
        long    msg_magic;
        long    msg_bufx;               // write pointer
        long    msg_bufr;               // read pointer
        char    msg_bufc[MSG_BSIZE];    // circular buffer
};
```

The user-space system log daemon (/usr/sbin/syslogd) retrieves log messages from the kernel by reading from the kernel log device /dev/klog. During file system initialization, the device file system layer (devfs) is initialized. As part of devfs initialization, several built-in BSD-style devices, including /dev/klog, are initialized. The device-switch structure (struct cdevsw) of /dev/klog contains logopen(), logread(), and logselect() [bsd/kern/subr_log.c] as the open, read, and select functions, respectively. syslogd uses the select() system call to see if the log device is ready for reading. As shown in Figure 10–41, the kernel periodically wakes up the thread waiting on the log device by calling klogwakeup().

FIGURE 10–41 Periodic delivery of log messages to readers of the log device

```
// bsd/kern/bsd_init.c

void
bsd_init()
{
    ...
    // hz is 100 by default
    timeout((void (*)(void *))lightning_bolt, 0, hz);
    ...
}

void
lightning_bolt()
{
    ...
    timeout(lightning_bolt, 0, hz);
```

(continues)

FIGURE 10–41 Periodic delivery of log messages to readers of the log device *(continued)*

```
    klogwakeup();
    ...
}

// bsd/kern/subr_log.c

void
logwakeup()
{
    ...
    // wake up threads in select()
    selwakeup(...);
    ...
}

void
klogwakeup()
{
    if (_logentrypend) {
        _logentrypend = 0;
        logwakeup();
    }
}
```

> The `logopen()` function ensures that only one thread can open the log device at a time.

10.8.4 Debugging by Using GDB

As we discussed in Section 6.8.1, Mac OS X supports two-machine kernel debugging using GDB over an Ethernet or FireWire connection. Consider the case of Ethernet-based debugging. We saw earlier that a network driver that supports such debugging provides polled-mode implementations of functions to transmit and receive packets—`sendPacket()` and `receivePacket()`, respectively. The `IONetworkController` class provides the `attachDebuggerClient()` method to allocate an `IOKernelDebugger` object and attach it as a client, leading to the creation of a debugger client nub. The `IOKernelDebugger` instance calls a KDP-layer function—`kdp_register_send_receive()` [osfmk/kdp/kdp_udp.c]—to register internal transmit and receive dispatcher functions, which in turn call the polled-mode methods when the debugger is active. Thereafter, the KDP module can send and receive protocol packets. Figure 10–42 shows a portion of the I/O Kit stack relevant to Ethernet- and FireWire-based debugging.

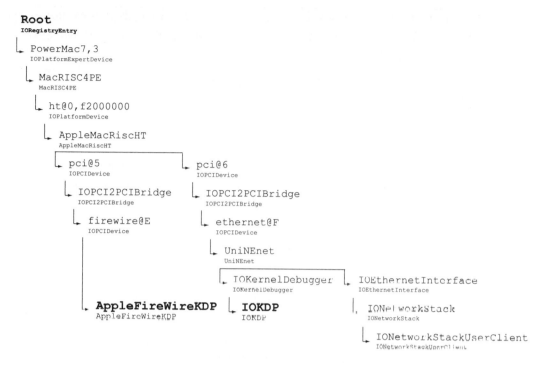

FIGURE 10–42 Objects that implement target-side KDP

A network controller can have at most one debugger client.

Apple provides a package called *Kernel Debug Kit* that contains debug versions of the Mac OS X kernel and several I/O Kit family kernel extensions. The executables in this kit are meant for remote debugging using GDB—they contain full symbolic information. Note, however, that the kernel contained in the kit is a *release* kernel—that is, it is compiled in the RELEASE_xxx configuration, rather than the DEBUG_xxx configuration.

There are several ways to cause a kernel to stop normal execution and wait for a remote GDB connection. A kernel panic is one, but it is possible to invoke the debugger by generating an NMI and even by calling a function. As listed in Table 4–13, the debug boot-time argument can be set to the following values to cause the kernel to wait for debugger connection on an NMI:

- DB_NMI
- DB_NMI | DB_KERN_DUMP_ON_NMI | DB_DBG_POST_CORE

You can programmatically enter the debugger from a kernel extension by calling the `PE_enter_debugger()` function. One approach to performing two-machine debugging of an I/O Kit driver involves calling `PE_enter_debugger()` from the driver's `start` method. The driver is loaded—but not started—by calling `kextload` with the `-l` option. The `-s` option is specified to generate the symbol files for the driver and its dependencies. These are then available to the debugging machine. Thereafter, matching can be initiated for the driver by calling `kextload` with the `-m` option, which this will cause the target kernel to wait for a remote debugger connection. The debugging machine can then attach to it.

Let us modify our `DummyDriver` example by adding a call to `PE_enter_debugger("Entering  Debugger")` in its `start` method. Recall that the `OSBundleLibraries` key of the driver lists `com.apple.kernel.iokit` as a dependency.

```
$ sudo kextload -s /tmp -vl /tmp/DummyDriver.kext
kextload: extension DummyDriver.kext appears to be valid
kextload: notice: extension DummyDriver.kext has debug properties set
kextload: loading extension DummyDriver.kext
kextload: writing symbol file /tmp/com.apple.kernel.iokit.sym
kextload: writing symbol file /tmp/com.osxbook.driver.DummyDriver.sym
kextload: DummyDriver.kext loaded successfully
```

The driver is now loaded but not started. After transferring the symbol files to the debugging machine, we can start the loaded driver:

```
$ sudo kextload -m DummyDriver.kext
```

If the panic user interface is disabled, the target machine will display a text message. Let us assume that the target machine's IP address and Ethernet address are `10.0.0.2` and `aa:bb:cc:dd:ee:ff`, respectively.

```
Debugger(DummyDriver: we are entering the debugger)
ethernet MAC address: aa:bb:cc:dd:ee:ff
ip address: 10.0.0.2

Waiting for remote debugger connection.
```

Now we can prepare and launch the debugger from the debugging machine.

```
$ sudo arp -s 10.0.0.2 aa:bb:cc:dd:ee:ff
$ gdb /path/to/copy/of/target/machines/mach_kernel
...
(gdb) source /path/to/kgmacros
Loading Kernel GDB Macros Package. Try "help kgm" for more info.
(gdb) add-symbol-file /tmp/com.osxbook.driver.DummyDriver.sym
```

```
add symbol table from ...? (y or n) y
Reading symbols from ... done.
...
(gdb) target remote-kdp
(gdb) attach 10.0.0.2
Connected.
[switching to process 3]
...
(gdb) where
...
(gdb) continue
```

10.8.5 Debugging by Using KDB

As we discussed in Section 6.8.2, the Mac OS X kernel also supports a built-in kernel debugger called KDB, which is more suitable for low-level kernel debugging. In some cases, KDB may be the only kernel-debugging option—say, if you need to debug a kernel component before an Ethernet or FireWire connection can be operational. KDB requires a native serial port—such as the one in an Xserve—that the kernel can operate by polling, without requiring additional drivers. In particular, PCI- or USB-based serial port adapters will not work with KDB.

Unlike the KDP shim for Ethernet debugging, KDB support is not compiled into the default kernel. It is also not available as a loadable kernel extension as in the case of FireWire-based debugging. To use KDB, the kernel must be compiled in the debug configuration.

```
$ cd /path/to/xnu/source
$ make exporthdrs && KERNEL_CONFIGS=DEBUG all
...
$ ls BUILD/obj/DEBUG_PPC/mach_kernel
mach_kernel
...
$ sudo cp BUILD/obj/DEBUG_PPC/mach_kernel /mach_kernel.debug
$ sudo chown root:wheel /mach_kernel.debug
$ sudo chmod 644 /mach_kernel.debug
```

A convenient way to boot an alternate kernel is to set the boot-file Open Firmware variable appropriately.

```
$ mount
...
/dev/disk0s3 on / (local, journaled)
$ ls /mach_kernel*
/mach_kernel            /mach_kernel.debug
$ nvram boot-file
```

```
boot-file
$ sudo nvram boot-file='hd:3,mach_kernel.debug'
```

Moreover, the DB_KDB (0x10) bit must be set in the debug boot-time argument to use KDB as the default debugger, for example:

```
$ sudo nvram boot-args="-v debug=0x11c"
```

The value 0x11c is the logical OR of DB_NMI, DB_KPRT, DB_KDB, and DB_LOG_PI_SCRN.

Let us look at a sample KDB session to get a flavor of its functionality. Figure 10–43 shows how the two machines involved are connected. The debugging machine has a USB-to-serial adapter, through which it connects to the native serial port of an Xserve, which is the target machine. We assume that /dev/tty.usb is the serial terminal device node created by the adapter's driver. We use the minicom serial communications program, but in general, any such program can be used.

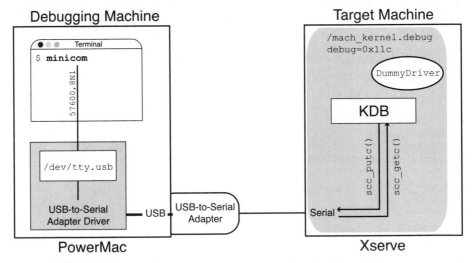

FIGURE 10–43 A KDB setup

Tables 10–2, 10–3, and 10–4 list most of the commands available in KDB. Several commands take one or more arguments, as well as optional modifiers that are specified using the slash character. Assuming that our DummyDriver kernel extension called PE_enter_debugger("Hello, KDB!"), a KDB session would be initiated as follows:

```
...
kmod_create: com.osxbook.driver.DummyDriver (id 100), 2 pages loaded at 0x0
Matching service count = 1
...
init
attach
com_osxbook_driver_DummyDriver::probe(IOResources)
probe
detach
com_osxbook_driver_DummyDriver::start(IOResources) <1>
attach
start
Debugger(Hello, KDB!)
Stopped at   _Debugger+228:       tweq r3,r3
db{0}>
```

Thereafter, KDB commands are entered at the db prompt. As shown in Table 10–2, KDB provides commands that act on specific kernel objects and addresses, as well as commands that act globally—say, on all tasks.

```
db{0}> dc 0x5000 # the address 0x5000 (PowerPC) contains the characters "Hagfish "
0000000000005000   Hagf ish  .... .... .9.. .... .... .6.$
0000000000005020   .... .... .... .... .... .... .... ....
...
db{0}> search /1 0x5000 0x48616765 # search for "Hage"

no memory is assigned to src address 0000c000
db{0}> search /1 0x5000 0x48616766 # search for "Hagf"
0x5000:
```

KDB commands are especially suited for examining Mach data structures.

```
db{0}> show task        # show current task
  0 (01BCCD58): 41 threads:
            0 (003C2638)  W N (_vm_pageout_continue) _vm_page free_wanted
            1 (01BD691C)  R    (_idle_thread)
            2 (01BD6588)  W N (_sched_tick_continue) _sched_tick_thread
            ...
           39 (0280FACC)  W N  _clock_delay_until
           40 (028941F4)  R
db{0}> show vmtask       # show VM information for current task
id    task       map     pmap   virtual   rss pg rss mem  wir pg wir mem
 0 01bccd58 00e3fe50 003a1000  796236K   14857  59428K       0      0K
db{0}> show map 0xe3fe50 # show details of VM map
task map 00E3FE50
  prev = 00F862A8  next = 00F98FD4  start = 0000000000001000  end = 00000000DFF0
  nentries = 00000588, !entries_pageable
...
```

KDB commands are also useful for viewing system-wide information and statistics.

```
db{0}> show runq          # show run queue information
PROCESSOR SET 41b800
PRI  TASK.ACTIVATION
 63: 41.1 44.4
 31: 5.0
db{0}> dk                 # show information about kernel extensions
info      addr      start   - end       name ver
...
2F739E44  2F738000  2F739000 - 2F73A000: com.osxbook.driver.DummyDriver, 11
...
01BC1780  00000000  00000000 - 00000000: com.apple.kpi.bsd, 8.2.0
01BC1890  00000000  00000000 - 00000000: com.apple.kernel, 8.2.0
db{0}> show system        # show scheduling and VM statistics
Scheduling Statistics:
  Thread invocations:  csw 115458 same 7585
  Thread block:  calls 202781
  Idle thread:        handoff 146906 block 0 no_dispatch 0
  Sched thread blocks:  0

VM Statistics:
  pages:
    activ 13344  inact 21024  free  210689   wire  17087  gobbl    0
  target:    min    2569  inact   586  free   3190   resrv    98
  pause:
  Pageout Statistics:
    active    0  inactv    0
    nolock    0  avoid     0  busy      0  absent    0
    used      0  clean     0  dirty     0
    laundry_pages_freed 0
```

TABLE 10–2 KDB Commands

Command	Description
break	Set breakpoint, along with a skip count.
call	Call function at the given address.
cm	Verify the consistency of virtual-to-real mappings and the page table entry group (PTEG) hash table.
cond	Set condition on breakpoint.
continue, c	Continue execution.
cp	Verify the consistency of the pmap skip-list data structures.

(continues)

TABLE 10–2 KDB Commands *(Continued)*

Command	Description
cpu	Switch to another CPU.
dc	Starting at a given address, print 256 bytes as characters.
delete, d	Delete breakpoint.
dh	Given a virtual address and an address space number (explicitly specified or the last entered space), display the corresponding page table entry group (PTEG) and PTEG control area (PCA) data structures.
di	Display information about the I/O Kit Device Tree and Service planes.
dk	Display information about loaded kernel extensions.
dl	Starting at a given address, display 256 bytes of information, printing a long at a time.
dm	Given a virtual address and an address space number (explicitly specified or the last entered space), display the corresponding virtual-to-real translation information.
dmacro	Delete a debugger macro.
dp	Display all in-use pmaps in the system.
dr	Starting at a given real address, display 256 bytes of real memory.
ds	Iterate over all threads in all tasks, printing the associated save areas.
dv	Starting at a given virtual address, display 256 bytes of virtual memory in the address space specified by the given address space number.
dwatch	Delete watchpoint.
dx	Display the contents of registers other than general-purpose registers.
gdb	Continue execution and switch to GDB.
lt	Display the contents of the low-level trace table, starting either at the given entry address (if any) or at the most current entry.
macro	Define a debugger macro.
match	Continue execution until matching return.
print	Use for formatted printing.
reboot	Reboot the system.
search	Search for a given char, short, or long value in memory, starting at a given address.

(continues)

TABLE 10–2 KDB Commands *(Continued)*

Command	Description
set	Set the value of a debugger variable.
show	Display various types of information (see Tables 10–3 and 10–4).
step, s	Single-step execution.
trace	Display stack traces of one or all threads.
until	Trace and print execution until call or return.
watch	Set watchpoint.
write, w	Write to memory.
x, examine	Print data at a given address for examination. Sets the "next" and "previous" address values for use by xb and xf.
xb	Examine data in backward direction.
xf	Examine data in forward direction.

TABLE 10–3 KDB show all Commands

Command	Description
show all spaces	Print IPC space information for all tasks in the system.
show all tasks	Print information about all tasks, including information about all threads in each task.
show all zones	Print information about all zones being managed by the Mach zone-based allocator.
show all vmtask	Print VM information for all tasks in the system.

TABLE 10–4 KDB show Commands

Command	Description
show act	Display information about the given activation (thread_t) or the current activation.
show breaks	List all breakpoints.
show copy	Display information about a VM copy object (vm_map_copy_t).

(continues)

TABLE 10–4 KDB show Commands *(Continued)*

Command	Description
show ipc_port	Display information about all IPC ports in the task containing the given thread or the current thread.
show kmsg	Display information about an IPC message kernel buffer (ipc_kmsg_t).
show lock	Display information about the given read/write lock (lock_t).
show macro	Display the expanded version of the given user macro.
show map	Display information about the given VM map (vm_map_t).
show msg	Display information about an IPC message header (mach_msg_header_t).
show mutex_lock	Display information about the given mutex (mutex_t).
show object	Display information about the given VM object (vm_object_t).
show page	Display information about the given resident page (vm_page_t).
show port	Display information about the given IPC port (ipc_port_t).
show pset	Display information about the given port set (ipc_pset_t).
show registers	Display contents of registers in a given thread (if one is specified) or in the default thread (if one is set).
show runq	Display run queue information.
show simple_lock	Display information about the given simple lock (simple_lock_t).
show space	Display information about the IPC space (ipc_space_t) associated with the given task or the current task.
show system	Display scheduling and virtual memory statistics.
show task	Display information about the given task or the current task.
show tr	Display events in the KDB trace buffer (if available).
show variables	Display values of one or more debugger variables.
show vmtask	Display VM information about the given task or the task containing the default thread (if one is set).
show watches	List all watchpoints.
show zone	Display information about the given Mach zone-based allocator zone (struct zone).

10.8.6 Miscellaneous Debugging Tools

Mac OS X provides several programs such as the following that are useful while analyzing, profiling, or debugging kernel extensions.

- `Shark.app` (part of the CHUD package) is a powerful tool for performance understanding and optimization. It can profile the entire operating system— that is, the kernel, kernel extensions, and applications—to produce detailed profiles of hardware and software performance events. Section 2.13.4.2 enumerates various other tools available in the CHUD package.

- A kext's memory usage can be tracked using a combination of `kextstat`, `ioalloccount`, and `ioclasscount`. As we saw earlier, `kextstat` shows the amount of memory, including wired memory, allocated for each loaded kext. `ioalloccount` displays the total amount of memory allocated through I/O Kit memory allocators and also the memory consumed by I/O Kit object instances. `ioclasscount` displays the instance counts of one or more I/O Kit classes.

- The `iostat` command can be used to display kernel-level I/O statistics for disk devices.

- The `latency` command can be used to monitor scheduling and interrupt latency—for example, to see if a thread is causing interrupts to be blocked for too long.

- `ioreg`, `IORegistryExplorer.app`, and `Mr. Registry.app` can be used to search and browse the I/O Registry.

10.8.7 Stabs

Mac OS X uses the GNU C compiler (GCC) suite for compiling C, C++, and Objective-C source. When the compiler is passed the `-g` option, it produces additional debugging information in the Mach-O output. This debugging information can then be used by both KDB and GDB. By default, the popular *stabs* format is used on Mac OS X to represent information that describes a program to a debugger. Originally used for the `pdx` Pascal debugger, stabs began as a set of special symbols within an "a.out" executable. It has since been adopted widely and has been encapsulated into several other file formats.

The word *stabs* is derived from *symbol table*. Stabs describe various features of the program source, such as source filenames and line numbers, function names, function parameters, variable types, and variable scopes. The information is emitted through a set of assembler directives called *stab directives* (or simply stabs). The assembler uses the stabs information while populating the symbol table and the string table of object files. The linker consolidates one or more object files into a final executable. Thereafter, a debugger can examine the stabs in the executable to glean debugging information.

Consider a simple C function such as the one shown in Figure 10–44.

FIGURE 10–44 A simple C function

```
01:     // func.c
02:     unsigned int
03:     func(unsigned int x, unsigned int y)
04:     {
05:         unsigned int sum;
06:         int negative;
07:
08:         sum = x + y;
09:         negative = -1 * sum;
10:
11:         return sum;
12:     }
```

Let us compile the function shown in Figure 10–44 first without any debugging options and then with debugging turned on. We will save the intermediate assembly output for the latter compilation so that we can examine the stabs encodings generated.

```
$ gcc -Wall -c -o func_nondebug.o func.c
$ gcc -Wall -g -c -o func_debug.o func.c
$ gcc -Wall -g -S -o func_debug.s func.c
$ ls func*
func.c          func_debug.o    func_debug.s    func_nondebug.o
```

Let us use nm to display the symbol tables of the object files obtained. Note that we will use nm with the -a option, which displays all symbol table entries, including those inserted for use by debuggers.

```
$ nm -a func_nondebug.o
00000000 T _func
```

We see that the nondebug version of the object file has only one symbol: _func. This makes sense, since func.c contains only one function, func(), which does not call any external functions.

```
$ nm -a func_debug.o
00000044 - 01 0000 RBRAC
00000000 - 01 0000 LBRAC
00000044 - 01 0000   SO
00000000 - 01 0000 BNSYM
00000000 - 01 0004 SLINE
00000014 - 01 0008 SLINE
00000024 - 01 0009 SLINE
00000030 - 01 000b SLINE
00000034 - 01 000c SLINE
00000044 - 01 0000 ENSYM
00000044 - 00 0000   FUN
00000000 - 01 0002   SO /tmp/
00000000 T _func
00000000 - 01 0002   SO func.c
00000000 - 01 0004   FUN func:F(0,1)
00000000 - 00 0000   OPT gcc2_compiled.
00000000 - 00 0000  LSYM int:t(0,2)=r(0,2);-2147483648;2147483647;
00000018 - 00 0006  LSYM negative:(0,2)
0000001c - 00 0005  LSYM sum:(0,1)
00000000 - 00 0000  LSYM unsigned int:t(0,1)=r(0,1);0;037777777777;
00000058 - 00 0003  PSYM x:p(0,1)
0000005c - 00 0003  PSYM y:p(0,1)
```

In contrast, the debug version of the object file has several other symbols besides _func. These additional symbols are stabs that encode the program's structure. Let us look at the assembly file (func_debug.s) corresponding to the debug compilation and analyze the stabs to understand their purpose. Figure 10–45 shows the assembly file's contents, with the stabs information highlighted.

FIGURE 10–45 Stabs-encoded debugging information in an assembly file

```
$ cat func_debug.s
.section __TEXT,__text,regular,pure_instructions
        .section __TEXT,__picsymbolstub1,symbol_stubs,pure_instructions,32
        .machine ppc
        .stabs  "/tmp/",100,0,2,Ltext0
        .stabs  "func.c",100,0,2,Ltext0
        .text
Ltext0:
        .stabs  "gcc2_compiled.",60,0,0,0
        .align 2
        .globl _func
_func:
        .stabd  46,0,0
        .stabd  68,0,4
        stmw r30,-8(r1)
```

(continues)

FIGURE 10–45 Stabs-encoded debugging information in an assembly file *(continued)*

```
        stwu r1,-64(r1)
        mr r30,r1
        stw r3,88(r30)
        stw r4,92(r30)
        .stabd  68,0,8
        lwz r2,88(r30)
        lwz r0,92(r30)
        add r0,r2,r0
        stw r0,28(r30)
        .stabd  68,0,9
        lwz r0,28(r30)
        neg r0,r0
        stw r0,24(r30)
        .stabd  68,0,11
        lwz r0,28(r30)
        .stabd  68,0,12
        mr r3,r0
        lwz r1,0(r1)
        lmw r30,-8(r1)
        blr
        .stabs   "func:F(0,1)",36,0,4,_func
        .stabs   "unsigned int:t(0,1)=r(0,1);0;037777777777;",128,0,0,0
        .stabs   "x:p(0,1)",160,0,3,88
        .stabs   "y:p(0,1)",160,0,3,92
        .stabs   "sum:(0,1)",128,0,5,28
        .stabs   "negative:(0,2)",128,0,6,24
        .stabs   "int:t(0,2)=r(0,2);-2147483648;2147483647;",128,0,0,0
        .stabn   192,0,0,_func
        .stabn   224,0,0,Lscope0
Lscope0:
        .stabs   "",36,0,0,Lscope0-_func
        .stabd   78,0,0
        .stabs   "",100,0,0,Letext0
Letext0:
        .subsections_via_symbols
```

As Figure 10–45 shows, stabs assembler directives generated by GCC fall in three main classes on Mac OS X: `.stabs` (string), `.stabn` (number), and `.stabd` (dot). These classes have the following formats:

```
.stabs   "string",type,other,desc,value

.stabn   type,other,desc,value

.stabd   type,other,desc
```

For each class, the `type` field contains a number that provides basic information about the stab type. If the number does not correspond to a valid stab type, the symbol is not treated as a stab. The other fields in a stab are interpreted based on the stab type. For example, the `string` field of the `.stabs` directive has the format `"name:symbol-descriptor type-information"`, where the fields have the following meanings.

- The `name` field names the symbol represented by the stab. It can be omitted for unnamed objects.
- `symbol-descriptor` describes the kind of symbol represented by the stab.
- `type-information` either refers by number to a type that has already been defined or defines a new type.

A new type definition may refer to previously defined types by number. Whereas the type number is a single number on some implementations, it is a `(file-number, filetype-number)` pair on others, including Mac OS X. A `file-number` value starts from 0 and is incremented for each distinct source file in the compilation. A `filetype-number` value starts from 1 and is incremented for each distinct type in that file.

In the example shown in Figure 10–45, we see the following stab types (in the order that they appear): 100, 60, 46, 68, 36, 128, 160, 192, 224, and 78. Table 10–5 shows the meanings of these symbols. Note that a given programming language may have certain stab types specific to it.

TABLE 10–5 Stab Symbol Types Used in the Example from Figure 10–45

Symbol Number	Symbol Name	Description
36 (0x24)	N_FUN	Function name
46 (0x2E)	N_BNSYM	Begin nsect symbol
60 (0x3C)	N_OPT	Debugger options
68 (0x44)	N_SLINE	Line number in text segment
78 (0x4E)	N_ENSYM	End nsect symbol
100 (0x64)	N_SO	Path and name of source file
128 (0x80)	N_LSYM	Stack variable or type
160 (0xA0)	N_PSYM	Parameter variable
192 (0xC0)	N_LBRAC	Beginning of a lexical block
224 (0xE0)	N_RBRAC	End of a lexical block

Let us analyze some of the stab directives to understand how the scheme works.

```
.stabs  "/tmp/",100,0,2,Ltext0
.stabs  "func.c",100,0,2,Ltext0
```

Stab type 100 (N_SO) specifies the paths and names of source files. The symbol's value in this case—Ltext0—represents the start address of the text section that comes from the given file.

```
.stabs  "gcc2_compiled.",60,0,0,0
```

Stab type 60 (N_OPT) specifies debugger options. In this case, "gcc2_compiled" is defined to allow GDB to detect that GCC compiled this file.

```
.stabd  68,0,4
...
.stabd  68,0,8
...
.stabd  68,0,9
...
.stabd  68,0,11
...
.stabd  68,0,12
```

Stab type 68 (N_SLINE) represents the start of a source line. In this case, we have stabs for line numbers 4, 8, 9, 11, and 12—the other line numbers in func.c do not contain active code.

```
.stabs  "unsigned int:t(0,1)=r(0,1);0;037777777777;",128,0,0,0
...
.stabs  "int:t(0,2)=r(0,2);-2147483648;2147483647;",128,0,0,0
```

Stab type 128 (N_LSYM) is used both for variables allocated on the stack and for giving names to types. In this case, the stab names the C type unsigned int. The t symbol descriptor is followed by the type number (0,1), thus associating unsigned int with type number (0,1). The r type descriptor defines a type as a subrange of another type. Here, it (circularly) defines (0,1) as a subrange of (0,1), with the lower and upper bounds being 0 and the octal number 0037777777777 (that is, 0xFFFF_FFFF), respectively. Similarly, the type (0,2)— the second type number in the file—represents the C type int, with upper and lower bounds being 2147483647 (2^{31}) and -2147483648 (-2^{31}), respectively.

```
.stabs  "func:F(0,1)=r(0,1);0000000000000;0037777777777;",36,0,4,_func
```

Stab type 36 (N_FUN) describes a function. In this example, the function's name is func. The F symbol descriptor identifies it as a global function. The type information that follows F represents the return type of the function—(0,1), or unsigned int, in this case. The stab's value—_func—specifies the start of the function. Note that the stab describing a function immediately follows the function's code.

```
.stabs  "x:p(0,1)",160,0,3,88
.stabs  "y:p(0,1)",160,0,3,92
```

Stab type 160 (N_PSYM) is used to represent the formal parameters of a function. The p symbol descriptor specifies a parameter passed on the stack. Recall from our discussion of C calling conventions for the PowerPC in Chapter 3 that even though the first few arguments are normally passed in registers, there is always space reserved for them in the caller's stack, where the callee saves them after it is called. In this example, we have two parameters named x and y. The type number following p—(0,1)—denotes the parameter's type. The desc field is 3 for both x and y, indicating that the parameters are on source line number 3. The value field, which is 88 and 92 for x and y, respectively, represents the offset (from the frame pointer) used to locate the parameter.

```
.stabs  "sum:(0,1)",128,0,5,32
```

This stab corresponds to the variable named sum, whose type is (0,1). The variable is at source line number 5. Its offset from the frame pointer is 32 bytes.

```
.stabn  192,0,0,_func
.stabn  224,0,0,Lscope0
```

Stab types 192 (N_LBRAC) and 224 (N_RBRAC) correspond to the left and right brace, respectively—they represent the program's block structure. The value fields refer to assembly labels surrounding the scope that is described by the N_LBRAC/N_RBRAC pair.

```
.stabs  "",36,0,0,Lscope0-_func
```

This is an N_FUN stab with an empty string as the function name and Lscope0-_func as its value. The purpose of such a stab is to indicate the address of the end of a function. In this case, the stab marks the end of _func.

```
.stabs  "",100,0,0,Letext0
```

This is an N_SO stab with an empty string as the filename and Lextext0 as the value. Similar in purpose to an N_FUN stab with an empty string, this stab marks the end of the source file.

CHAPTER 11

File Systems

A file system is an operating system component that provides an abstract view of data on a storage device. At the user-visible level, a file system's contents are usually organized hierarchically into files and directories (or folders—we will use the terms *directory* and *folder* synonymously in this chapter and the next). A file system's storage device is often persistent, but it is possible—and useful—to have file systems on nonpersistent devices such as physical memory.

11.1 Disks and Partitions

A common medium for storing user data is a hard[1] disk drive. The storage space on a disk is divided at the hardware level into fundamental units called *sectors*. In a typical hard drive, each sector holds 512 bytes[2] of user data. A sector may also

---

1. Given that it uses rigid platters, a hard disk was originally so called to distinguish it from a floppy disk.

2. In contrast with disk drives, optical drives commonly use a sector size of 2KB.

hold some additional data used internally by the drive—such as data for error correction and synchronization. A disk may also have some number of spare sectors that are not exposed through its interface. If a regular sector goes bad, the disk can attempt to transparently replace it with a spare one. Modern drives deprecate the geometric Cylinder-Head-Sector (CHS) addressing model for accessing a sector. The preferred model is Logical Block Addressing (LBA), in which addressable storage on a drive appears as a linear sequence of sectors.

The program in Figure 11–1 uses disk I/O control (ioctl) operations to retrieve and display basic information about a disk device on Mac OS X.

FIGURE 11–1 Using ioctl operations to display information about a disk device

```
// diskinfo.c

#include <stdio.h>
#include <fcntl.h>
#include <unistd.h>
#include <stdlib.h>
#include <sys/disk.h>

#define PROGNAME "diskinfo"

void
cleanup(char *errmsg, int retval)
{
    perror(errmsg);
    exit(retval);
}

#define TRY_IOCTL(fd, request, argp) \
    if ((ret = ioctl(fd, request, argp)) < 0) { \
        close(fd); cleanup("ioctl", ret); \
    }

int
main(int argc, char **argv)
{
    int        fd, ret;
    u_int32_t blockSize;
    u_int64_t blockCount;
    u_int64_t maxBlockRead;
    u_int64_t maxBlockWrite;
    u_int64_t capacity1000, capacity1024;

    dk_firmware_path_t fwPath;
```

(continues)

FIGURE 11–1 Using ioctl operations to display information about a disk device *(continued)*

```
    if (argc != 2) {
        fprintf(stderr, "usage: %s <raw disk>\n", PROGNAME);
        exit(1);
    }

    if ((fd = open(argv[1], O_RDONLY, 0)) < 0)
        cleanup("open", 1);

    TRY_IOCTL(fd, DKIOCGETFIRMWAREPATH, &fwPath);
    TRY_IOCTL(fd, DKIOCGETBLOCKSIZE, &blockSize);
    TRY_IOCTL(fd, DKIOCGETBLOCKCOUNT, &blockCount);
    TRY_IOCTL(fd, DKIOCGETMAXBLOCKCOUNTREAD, &maxBlockRead);
    TRY_IOCTL(fd, DKIOCGETMAXBLOCKCOUNTWRITE, &maxBlockWrite);

    close(fd);

    capacity1024  = (blockCount * blockSize) / (1ULL << 30ULL);
    capacity1000  = (blockCount * blockSize) / (1000ULL * 1000ULL * 1000ULL);
    printf("%-20s = %s\n", "Device", argv[1]);
    printf("%-20s = %s\n", "Firmware Path", fwPath.path);
    printf("%-20s = %llu GB / %llu GiB\n", "Capacity",
            capacity1000, capacity1024);
    printf("%-20s = %u bytes\n", "Block Size", blockSize);
    printf("%-20s = %llu\n", "Block Count", blockCount);
    printf("%-20s = { read = %llu blocks, write = %llu blocks }\n",
            "Maximum Request Size", maxBlockRead, maxBlockWrite);

    exit(0);
}
```

```
$ gcc -Wall -o diskinfo diskinfo.c
$ sudo ./diskinfo /dev/rdisk0
Device               = /dev/rdisk0
Firmware Path        = first-boot/@0:0
Capacity             = 250 GB / 232 GiB
Block Size           = 512 bytes
Block Count          = 488397168
Maximum Request Size = { read = 2048 blocks, write = 2048 blocks }
```

The two capacity numbers listed in Figure 11–1 are calculated using the metric and computer definitions of the *giga* prefix. The metric definition (1 gigabyte = 10^9 bytes; abbreviated as GB) leads to a larger capacity than a traditional computer science definition (1 gigabyte = 2^{30} bytes; abbreviated as GiB).

A disk may be logically divided into one or more *partitions*, which are sets of contiguous blocks that can be thought of as subdisks. A partition may contain an instance of a *file system*. Such an instance—a *volume*—is essentially a structured file residing on the partition. Besides user data, its contents include data structures that facilitate organization, retrieval, modification, access control, and sharing of the user data, while hiding the disk's physical structure from the user. A volume has its own block size that is usually a multiple of the disk block size.

The `mount` command, when invoked without any arguments, prints the list of currently mounted file systems. Let us determine the partition that corresponds to the root file system.[3]

```
$ mount
/dev/disk0s10 on / (local, journaled)
...
```

In this case, the root file system is on the tenth partition—or *slice*—of `disk0`. This system uses the Apple partitioning scheme (see Section 11.1.1), and therefore, the partition table for `disk0` can be viewed using the `pdisk` command, which is a partition table editor for this scheme.

FIGURE 11–2 Listing a disk's partitions

```
$ sudo pdisk /dev/rdisk0 -dump
Partition map (with 512 byte blocks) on '/dev/rdisk0'
 #:                type name              length   base    ( size )
 1: Apple_partition_map Apple                 63 @ 1
 2:      Apple_Driver43*Macintosh             56 @ 64
 3:      Apple_Driver43*Macintosh             56 @ 120
 4:    Apple_Driver_ATA*Macintosh             56 @ 176
 5:    Apple_Driver_ATA*Macintosh             56 @ 232
 6:     Apple_FWDriver Macintosh             512 @ 288
 7: Apple_Driver_IOKit Macintosh             512 @ 800
 8:        Apple_Patches Patch Partition     512 @ 1312
 9:            Apple_Free                  262144 @ 1824     (128.0M)
10:         Apple_HFS Apple_HFS_Untitled_1 24901840 @ 263968  ( 11.9G)
11:            Apple_Free                      16 @ 25165808
```

```
Device block size=512, Number of Blocks=25165824 (12.0G)
...
```

---

3. You can retrieve information about mounted file systems programmatically by calling the `get-mntinfo()` library function.

Raw Devices

/dev/rdisk0 is the raw device corresponding to disk0. A disk or disk slice can be accessed through either its *block* device (such as /dev/disk0 or /dev/disk0s9) or the corresponding *character* device (such as /dev/rdisk0 or /dev/rdisk0s9). When data is read from or written to a disk's block device, it goes through the operating system's buffer cache. In contrast, with a character device, data transfers are *raw*—without the involvement of the buffer cache. I/O to raw disk devices requires that the size of an I/O request be a multiple of the disk's block size and the request's offset to be aligned to the block size.

Many systems have historically provided raw devices so that programs for partitioning disks, creating file systems, and repairing existing file systems can do their job without invalidating the buffer cache. An application may also wish to implement its own buffering for the data it reads directly from disk into memory, in which case it is wasteful to have the data cached by the system as well. Using the raw interface to modify data that is already present in the buffer cache could lead to undesirable results. It can also be argued that raw devices are unnecessary because low-level file system utilities are rarely run. Moreover, mmap() is an alternative to reading directly from raw devices.

Sometimes a block device is referred to as a *cooked* device in contrast to a raw device.

A similar list of disk0's partitions can be obtained using the diskutil command.

```
$ diskutil list disk0
/dev/disk0
   #:                     type name              size       identifier
   0: Apple_partition_scheme                    *12.0 GB   disk0
   1:     Apple_partition_map                    31.5 KB   disk0s1
...
   8:         Apple_Patches                     256.0 KB   disk0s8
   9:         Apple_HFS Macintosh HD            11.9 GB    disk0s10
```

11.1.1 The Apple Partitioning Scheme

The disk in Figure 11–2 uses the *Apple partitioning scheme*, with a specific partition layout called UNIVERSAL HD, which includes several legacy partitions. Let us analyze the pdisk output for disk0.

- There are 11 partitions on this disk.

- The first partition (disk0s1) is the *partition map* that contains partitioning-related metadata. The metadata consists of *partition map entries*, each of which describes one partition. The map is 63 blocks in size, with each block being 512 bytes.

- Partition numbers 2 (disk0s2) through 7 (disk0s7) are Mac OS 9 *driver partitions*. Historically, block device drivers could be loaded from several places: the ROM, a USB or FireWire device, or a special partition on a fixed disk. To support multiple operating systems or other features, a disk may have one or more device drivers installed—each in its own partition. The partitions named Apple_Driver43 in this example contain SCSI Manager 4.3. Note that neither Mac OS X nor the Classic environment uses these Mac OS 9 drivers.

- Partition number 8 (disk0s8) is a *patch partition*—a metadata partition that can contain patches to be applied to the system before it can boot.

- Partition number 9 consists of free space—a partition whose type is Apple_Free.

- Partition number 10 (disk0s10) is a *data partition*. In this example, the disk has only one data partition that contains an HFS Plus (or HFS) file system.

- The trailing free space constitutes the last partition.

> A variant partition layout called UNIVERSAL CD would have partitions containing ATAPI drivers and SCSI Manager for CD.

Figure 11–3 shows details of the Apple partitioning scheme. Although the disk shown in this case has a simpler layout, with no patch or driver partitions, the on-disk data structures follow similar logic regardless of the number and types of partitions.

The first physical block's first two bytes are set to 0x4552 ('ER'), which is the Apple partitioning scheme signature. The next two bytes represent the disk's physical block size. The total number of blocks on the disk is contained in the next four bytes. We can use the dd command to examine the contents of these bytes for disk0.

```
$ sudo dd if=/dev/disk0 of=/dev/stdout bs=8 count=1 2>/dev/null | hexdump
0000000 4552 0200 0180 0000
...
```

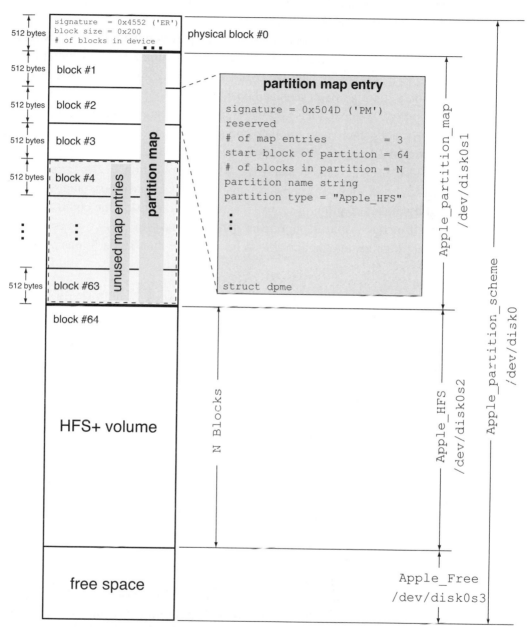

FIGURE 11–3 A disk partitioned using the Apple partitioning scheme

We see that the block size is 0x200 (512), and that the disk has 0x1800000 (25165824) 512-byte blocks.

The next 63 512-byte blocks constitute the partition map. Each block represents a single partition map entry that describes a partition. Each map entry contains 0x504D ('PM') as its first two bytes, followed by information that includes the partition's starting offset, size, and type.

The pdisk command lets you view, edit, and create Apple partitions—both interactively and otherwise. Another command-line tool, diskutil, uses the Mac OS X Disk Management framework to let you modify, verify, and repair disks. You can also use the GUI-based Disk Utility application (/Applications/Utilities/Disk Utility.app) to manage disks, partitions, and volumes. Disk Utility allows creation of up to 16 partitions on a disk. One could create as many partitions as would fit in a given partition map—say, using pdisk. However, some programs may not be able to handle more than 16 partitions properly.

11.1.2 PC-Style Partitioning

In contrast with the Apple partitioning scheme, PC partitions may be primary, extended, or logical, with at most four primary partitions allowed on a disk. The first 512-byte sector of a PC disk, the *master boot record* (MBR), has its space divided as follows: 446 bytes for bootstrap code, 64 bytes for four partition table entries of 16 bytes each, and 2 bytes for a signature. Therefore, the size of a PC partition table is rather limited, which in turn limits the number of primary partitions. However, one of the primary partitions may be an *extended partition*. An arbitrary number of logical partitions can be defined within an extended partition. The Mac OS X command-line program fdisk can be used to create and manipulate PC-style partitions.

11.1.3 GUID-Based Partitioning

We discussed GUID-based partitioning in Section 4.16.4.4 in the context of the Extensible Firmware Interface (EFI). x86-based Macintosh computers use the GUID-based scheme instead of the Apple partitioning scheme. In particular, although x86-based Macintosh computers support the Apple partitioning scheme, they can boot only from a volume partitioned using the GUID-based scheme.

Figure 4–23 shows the structure of a GPT-partitioned disk. The gpt command-line program can be used on Mac OS X to initialize a disk with a GUID

Partition Table (GPT) and to manipulate partitions within it. Section 11.4.4 provides an example of using gpt. The diskutil command also works with GPT disks.

```
$ diskutil list disk0 # GPT disk
/dev/disk0
   #:                      type name          size       identifier
   0:  GUID_partition_scheme               *93.2 GB   disk0
   1:                       EFI             200.0 MB   disk0s1
   2:          Apple_HFS Mini HD            92.8 GB    disk0s2
```

11.2 Disk Arbitration

The Mac OS X *Disk Arbitration* subsystem manages disks and disk images. It consists of the disk arbitration daemon (diskarbitrationd) and a framework (DiskArbitration.framework). diskarbitrationd is the central authority for disk management. Its duties include the following:

- Processing newly appearing disks to possibly mount any volumes on them
- Notifying its clients of the appearance or disappearance of disks and volumes
- Acting as the arbiter for the claiming and unclaiming of disks by its clients

Figure 11–4 shows a simplified overview of the interactions in the Disk Arbitration subsystem. diskarbitrationd registers for several types of notifications to learn of the appearance and disappearance of disks, unmounting of file systems, and configuration changes. Based on these notifications, it performs actions such as automatic mounting of an incoming disk device's volumes under the default mount point folder (/Volumes/).

The Disk Arbitration API provided by the Disk Arbitration framework can be used to access and manipulate disk objects, which are abstractions of disk devices. The following are examples of this API's functions:

- DADiskMount()—mount the volume at the given disk object
- DADiskUnmount()—unmount the volume at the given disk object
- DADiskEject()—eject the given disk object
- DADiskRename()—rename the volume at the given disk object
- DADiskSetOptions()—set or clear disk options
- DADiskGetOptions()—get disk options

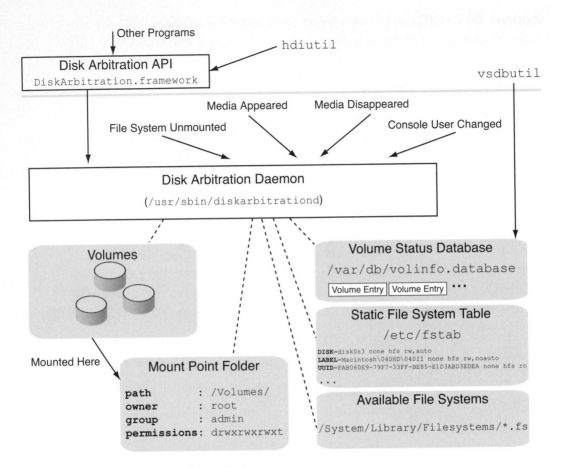

FIGURE 11–4 An overview of disk arbitration

- `DADiskCopyDescription()`—retrieve a disk object's latest description, as maintained by `diskarbitrationd`
- `DADiskClaim()`—claim the given disk object for exclusive use
- `DADiskUnclaim()`—release claim on the given disk object

All `DADisk*` functions operate on a *disk object*, which can be created by calling `DADiskCreateFromBSDName()` or `DADiskCreateFromIOMedia()`. The former accepts a disk's BSD device name, whereas the latter accepts an I/O Kit media object.

Client programs can also register several types of callbacks with Disk Arbitration. In particular, clients can use approval callbacks to participate in the approval or denial of operations such as mounting, unmounting, and ejecting of disk devices. The callback registration functions are all of the form `DARegisterDisk` `<type>Callback()`, where `<type>` can be `Appeared`, `Disappeared`, `Description-` `Changed`, `Peek`, `MountApproval`, `UnmountApproval`, or `EjectApproval`.

The Volume Status Database

Mac OS X uses volume UUIDs to track the status of on-disk permissions on removable volumes. The volume status database (vsdb), which is stored in `/var/` `db/volinfo.database`, maintains this information. The `vsdbutil` command-line program can be used to enable or disable permissions on a volume. Besides updating the vsdb entry of the given volume, `vsdbutil` executes the `mount` command with the `-u` option to change the status of the corresponding mounted file system.

Let us now look at some examples of working with disk devices using the Disk Arbitration framework. We will also see an example of how to receive device appearance and disappearance notifications directly from the I/O Kit.

11.2.1 Retrieving a Disk's Description

The program shown in Figure 11–5 calls `DACopyDiskDescription()` to obtain and display the description of the given BSD device (or `/dev/disk0`, if none was specified).

FIGURE 11–5 Using Disk Arbitration to obtain a disk's description

```
// diskarb_info.c

#include <unistd.h>
#include <DiskArbitration/DiskArbitration.h>

#define DEFAULT_DISK_NAME "/dev/disk0"

int
printDictionaryAsXML(CFDictionaryRef dict)
{
    CFDataRef xml = CFPropertyListCreateXMLData(kCFAllocatorDefault,
                                     (CFPropertyListRef)dict);
```

(continues)

FIGURE 11–5 Using Disk Arbitration to obtain a disk's description *(continued)*

```
    if (!xml)
        return -1;

    write(STDOUT_FILENO, CFDataGetBytePtr(xml), CFDataGetLength(xml));
    CFRelease(xml);

    return 0;
}

#define OUT_ON_NULL(ptr, msg) \
    if (!ptr) { fprintf(stderr, "%s\n", msg); goto out; }

int
main(int argc, char **argv)
{
    int              ret       = -1;
    DASessionRef     session   = NULL;
    DADiskRef        disk      = NULL;
    CFDictionaryRef  diskInfo  = NULL;
    char             *diskName = DEFAULT_DISK_NAME;

    // create a new Disk Arbitration session
    session = DASessionCreate(kCFAllocatorDefault);
    OUT_ON_NULL(session, "failed to create Disk Arbitration session");

    if (argc == 2)
        diskName = argv[1];

    // create a new disk object from the given BSD device name
    disk = DADiskCreateFromBSDName(kCFAllocatorDefault, session, diskName);
    OUT_ON_NULL(disk, "failed to create disk object");

    // obtain disk's description
    diskInfo = DADiskCopyDescription(disk);
    OUT_ON_NULL(diskInfo, "failed to retrieve disk description");

    ret = printDictionaryAsXML(diskInfo);

out:
    if (diskInfo)
        CFRelease(diskInfo);
    if (disk)
        CFRelease(disk);
    if (session)
        CFRelease(session);

    exit(ret);
}
```

(continues)

FIGURE 11–5 Using Disk Arbitration to obtain a disk's description *(continued)*

```
$ gcc -Wall -o diskarb_info diskarb_info.c \
    -framework DiskArbitration -framework CoreFoundation
$ ./diskarb_info
...
<dict>
        <key>DAAppearanceTime</key>
        <real>151748243.60000801</real>
        <key>DABusName</key>
        <string>k2-sata</string>
        <key>DABusPath</key>
        <string>IODeviceTree:sata/k2-sata@1</string>
        <key>DADeviceInternal</key>
        <true/>
        ...
        <key>DADeviceProtocol</key>
        <string>ATA</string>
        <key>DADeviceRevision</key>
        <string>V360A63A</string>
        <key>DADeviceUnit</key>
        <integer>0</integer>
        ...
```

11.2.2 Participating in Disk Mounting Decisions

The program in Figure 11–6 registers a mount-approval callback with Disk Arbitration. Thereafter, when a device is to be mounted, the callback function can either allow the mount to proceed by returning NULL or cause it to fail by returning a reference to a *dissenter object* (DADissenterRef). Our example runs for a limited time, after which it deregisters the callback. While the program is running, Disk Arbitration will not be permitted to mount any disk devices.[4]

FIGURE 11–6 Expressing dissent against a mount operation

```
// dissent_mount.c

#include <DiskArbitration/DiskArbitration.h>

#define OUT_ON_NULL(ptr, msg) \
    if (!ptr) { fprintf(stderr, "%s\n", msg); goto out; }
```

(continues)

---

4. It will still be possible to mount devices manually—by running the mount command, for example.

FIGURE 11–6 Expressing dissent against a mount operation *(continued)*

```
DADissenterRef
mountApprovalCallback(DADiskRef disk, void *context)
{
    DADissenterRef dissenter = DADissenterCreate(kCFAllocatorDefault,
                                                 kDAReturnNotPermitted,
                                                 CFSTR("mount disallowed"));
    printf("%s: mount disallowed\n", DADiskGetBSDName(disk));
    return dissenter;
}


int
main(void)
{
    DAApprovalSessionRef session = DAApprovalSessionCreate(kCFAllocatorDefault);
    OUT_ON_NULL(session, "failed to create Disk Arbitration session");

    DARegisterDiskMountApprovalCallback(session,
                                        NULL,  // matches all disk objects
                                        mountApprovalCallback,
                                        NULL); // context

    DAApprovalSessionScheduleWithRunLoop(session, CFRunLoopGetCurrent(),
                                         kCFRunLoopDefaultMode);

    CFRunLoopRunInMode(kCFRunLoopDefaultMode, 30 /* seconds */, false);

    DAApprovalSessionUnscheduleFromRunLoop(session, CFRunLoopGetCurrent(),
                                           kCFRunLoopDefaultMode);

    DAUnregisterApprovalCallback(session, mountApprovalCallback, NULL);

out:
    if (session)
        CFRelease(session);

    exit(0);
}



$ gcc -Wall -o dissent_mount dissent_mount.c \
    -framework DiskArbitration -framework CoreFoundation
$ ./dissent_mount
        # another shell
        $ open /tmp/somediskimage.dmg
disk10s2: mount disallowed
...
```

11.2.3 Receiving Media Notifications from the I/O Kit

The program in Figure 11–7 requests the I/O Kit to send it notifications when removable storage devices appear or disappear. More precisely, *appearance* means that the IOService matching the given matching dictionary has had all relevant drivers probed and started. Similarly, *disappearance* means that the IOService has terminated. Our example's matching dictionary looks for all IOMedia objects. Optionally, we could refine the dictionary by adding other key-value pairs using CFDictionaryAddValue(). For example, the following will limit matching to only whole media devices (and not partitions):

```
...
CFDictionaryAddValue(match, CFSTR(kIOMediaWholeKey), kCFBooleanTrue);
...
```

A notification we receive will provide us an iterator (io_iterator_t) containing one or more I/O Registry entries (io_registry_entry_t), each corresponding to a device. We will fetch and display the properties of each device.

FIGURE 11–7 Monitoring the appearance and disappearance of storage devices

```c
// mediamon.c

#include <unistd.h>
#include <IOKit/IOKitLib.h>
#include <IOKit/storage/IOMedia.h>
#include <CoreFoundation/CoreFoundation.h>

int
printDictionaryAsXML(CFDictionaryRef dict)
{
    CFDataRef xml = CFPropertyListCreateXMLData(kCFAllocatorDefault,
                                          (CFPropertyListRef)dict);
    if (!xml)
        return -1;

    write(STDOUT_FILENO, CFDataGetBytePtr(xml), CFDataGetLength(xml));
    CFRelease(xml);

    return 0;
}

void
matchingCallback(void *refcon, io_iterator_t deviceList)
```

(continues)

FIGURE 11–7 Monitoring the appearance and disappearance of storage devices *(continued)*

```c
{
    kern_return_t       kr;
    CFDictionaryRef     properties;
    io_registry_entry_t device;

    // Iterate over each device in this notification.
    while ((device = IOIteratorNext(deviceList))) {

        // Populate a dictionary with device's properties.
        kr = IORegistryEntryCreateCFProperties(
                device, (CFMutableDictionaryRef *)&properties,
                kCFAllocatorDefault, kNilOptions);

        if (kr == KERN_SUCCESS)
            printDictionaryAsXML(properties);

        if (properties)
            CFRelease(properties);

        if (device)
            IOObjectRelease(device);
    }
}


int
main(void)
{
    CFMutableDictionaryRef match;
    IONotificationPortRef  notifyPort;
    CFRunLoopSourceRef     notificationRunLoopSource;
    io_iterator_t          notificationIn, notificationOut;

    // Create a matching dictionary for all IOMedia objects.
    if (!(match = IOServiceMatching("IOMedia"))) {
        fprintf(stderr, "*** failed to create matching dictionary.\n");
        exit(1);
    }

    // Create a notification object for receiving I/O Kit notifications.
    notifyPort = IONotificationPortCreate(kIOMasterPortDefault);

    // Get a CFRunLoopSource that we will use to listen for notifications.
    notificationRunLoopSource = IONotificationPortGetRunLoopSource(notifyPort);

    // Add the CFRunLoopSource to the default mode of our current run loop.
    CFRunLoopAddSource(CFRunLoopGetCurrent(), notificationRunLoopSource,
                        kCFRunLoopDefaultMode);
```

(continues)

FIGURE 11–7 Monitoring the appearance and disappearance of storage devices *(continued)*

```
// One reference of the matching dictionary will be consumed when we install
// a notification request. Since we need to install two such requests (one
// for ejectable media coming in and another for it going out), we need
// to increment the reference count on our matching dictionary.
CFRetain(match);

// Install notification request for matching objects coming in.
// Note that this will also look up already existing objects.
IOServiceAddMatchingNotification(
    notifyPort,            // notification port reference
    kIOMatchedNotification, // notification type
    match,                 // matching dictionary
    matchingCallback,      // this is called when notification fires
    NULL,                  // reference constant
    &notificationIn);      // iterator handle

// Install notification request for matching objects going out.
IOServiceAddMatchingNotification(
    notifyPort,
    kIOTerminatedNotification,
    match,
    matchingCallback,
    NULL,
    &notificationOut);

// Invoke callbacks explicitly to empty the iterators/arm the notifications.
matchingCallback(0, notificationIn);
matchingCallback(0, notificationOut);

CFRunLoopRun(); // run

exit(0);
}



$ gcc -Wall -o mediamon mediamon.c -framework IOKit -framework CoreFoundation
$ ./mediamon
        # some disk is attached, probed for volumes, and a volume is mounted
...
<dict>
        <key>BSD Major</key>
        <integer>14</integer>
        <key>BSD Minor</key>
        <integer>3</integer>
        <key>BSD Name</key>
        <string>disk0s3</string>
...
```

11.3 The Implementation of Disk Devices

Although the file system layer in the Mac OS X kernel sees storage devices as BSD devices, the I/O Kit ultimately drives these devices. Figure 11–8 shows the relevant portion of the I/O Kit stack on a system with two serial ATA (SATA) disks.

The `IOATABlockStorageDriver` is a client of the I/O Kit ATA family and a member of the storage family. In the I/O Kit, the actual storage on a storage device is represented by an I/O Media object (`IOMedia`), an instance of which can abstract several types of random access devices—both real and virtual—such as the following:

- Whole disks
- Disk partitions
- Disk supersets (e.g., RAID volumes)

> Apple's implementation of software RAID (`AppleRAID`) combines multiple block devices to construct an I/O Kit storage stack yielding a single virtual device. When I/O is performed to the virtual device, the RAID implementation calculates the offsets on the specific physical devices to which the I/O must be dispatched.

An I/O Media object acts as a channel for all I/O that goes to the storage underlying it. As we saw in Chapter 10, Mac OS X also supports I/O Media Filter objects, which are subclasses of `IOMedia` and can be inserted between I/O Media objects and their clients, thereby routing all I/O through the filter object as well.

The `IOMediaBSDClient` class, which is implemented as part of the `IOStorageFamily` I/O Kit family, is the entity in charge of making storage devices appear as BSD-style block and character devices. In particular, as disks and partitions appear in the I/O Kit, `IOMediaBSDClient` calls the device file system (devfs) to dynamically add the corresponding block and character device nodes. Similarly, when a device is removed, `IOMediaBSDClient` calls devfs to remove the corresponding BSD nodes. The block and character device function tables—the traditional Unix-style `bdevsw` and `cdevsw` structures—are also part of the `IOMediaBSDClient` implementation (Figure 11–9).

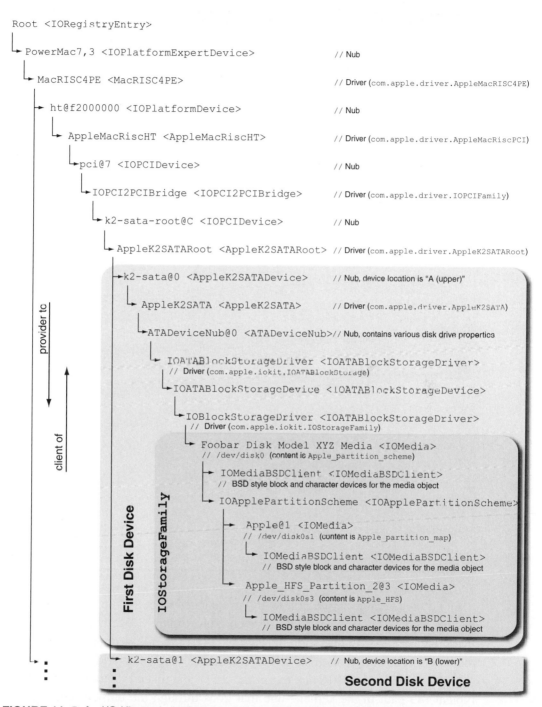

FIGURE 11–8 An I/O Kit stack depicting a disk device and its partitions

FIGURE 11–9 The Mac OS X block and character device switch structures

```
// IOMediaBSDClient.cpp
...
static struct bdevsw bdevswFunctions =
{
    /* d_open     */ dkopen,
    /* d_close    */ dkclose,
    /* d_strategy */ dkstrategy,
    /* d_ioctl    */ dkioctl_bdev,
    /* d_dump     */ eno_dump,
    /* d_psize    */ dksize,
    /* d_type     */ D_DISK
};

static struct cdevsw cdevswFunctions =
{
    /* d_open     */ dkopen,
    /* d_close    */ dkclose,
    /* d_read     */ dkread,
    /* d_write    */ dkwrite,
    /* d_ioctl    */ dkioctl,
    ...
};
...
// Implementations of the dk* functions

void
dkstrategy(buf_t bp)
{
    dkreadwrite(bp, DKTYPE_BUF);
}
...
int
dkreadwrite(dkr_t dkr, dkrtype_t dkrtype)
{
    // I/O Kit-specific implementation
}
...
```

Let us see an example of how I/O propagates from the file system to a disk device. Figure 11–10 is partially derived from Figure 8–52, which showed an overview of a page-in operation. In Figure 11–10, we follow the path of a typical read request destined for an HFS Plus volume residing on an ATA device.

Note in Figure 11–10 that cluster_io() and related routines represent the typical I/O path in the kernel—one that goes through the unified buffer cache.

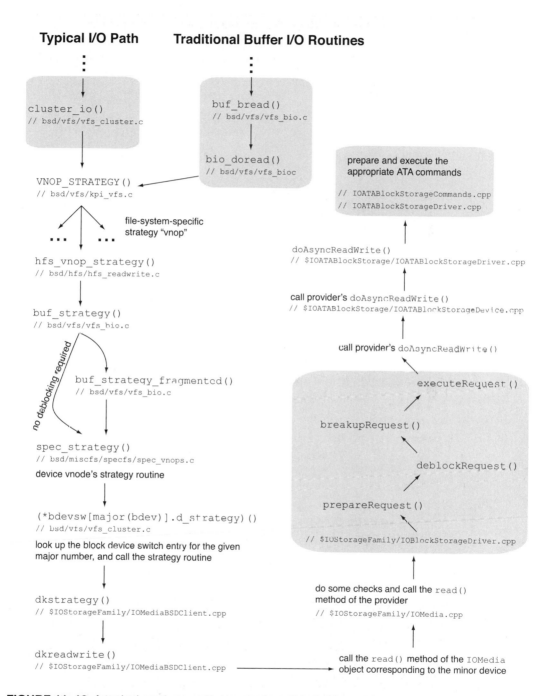

FIGURE 11–10 A typical read request's journey to a disk device

Although not shown in the figure, before issuing the I/O through the file system's strategy routine, `cluster_io()` calls the file system's `VNOP_BLOCKMAP()` operation to map file offsets to disk offsets. Eventually, the strategy routine of the block device—`dkstrategy()`—is called. `dkstrategy()` calls `dkreadwrite()`, which sends the I/O down the I/O Kit stack. In this example, the device is an ATA device. When the I/O eventually reaches the `IOBlockStorageDriver` class, the latter will choose the appropriate ATA commands and flags to perform the actual transfer.

> Note that Mac OS X does not use explicit disk scheduling. In particular, I/O requests are not explicitly reordered, although the non–I/O Kit parts of the kernel may defer a request in order to combine several requests into a single large request.

11.4 Disk Images

Exploring and experimenting with disks and file systems is a potentially risky activity in that a mistake might lead to catastrophic data loss. A safer and more convenient alternative is to work with virtual disks—or *disk images*—rather than physical disks. In the simplest terms, a disk image is a file containing what would normally reside on a physical storage device. Given the appropriate support from the operating system, virtual disks behave just like their physical counterparts. The following are some examples of using virtual disks.

- You could read raw data from a floppy disk and save it to a file—say, using the `dd` command on Unix or `RAWRITE.EXE` on Windows. The file so obtained is a block-by-block image of the physical floppy disk. It could be written back to another, similar physical disk to yield a sector-by-sector copy of the original. This process could be used to obtain a disk image from an optical disk, a hard disk partition, or even an entire hard disk.

- Many operating systems allow regular files to be accessed as virtual disk device nodes. These virtual disks may be used like regular disks: You can partition them, use them for swapping, and create file systems on them. Examples include Linux "loop" devices, the Solaris `lofi` driver, and BSD's vnode pseudo disk (`vn`) driver.

- Virtualizers and emulators typically use disk images for running guest operating systems.

- A disk image could be compressed or encrypted. Mac OS X's File Vault feature employs an encrypted disk image to provide an encrypted home directory for a user.

Thus, disk images are useful for archives, software distribution, emulation, virtualization, and so on. They are well suited for file system experimentation because they allow you to perform potentially dangerous operations without having to worry about loss of precious data.

11.4.1 Using the `hdiutil` Program

Apple has used disk images for a long time, primarily for software distribution. The Mac OS X Disk Images framework (`System/Library/PrivateFrameworks/DiskImages.framework`) is a private framework that provides comprehensive support for disk images. The `hdiutil` command-line program, which we will frequently use in this chapter and the next, is a versatile tool to access this framework's functionality.

> **Warning:** If you try disk-image-based examples on your computer, be warned that you must be careful about the device node names you use. The I/O Kit dynamically assigns names such as `/dev/disk1` and `/dev/disk1s2` to devices depending on the number of disks—whether real or virtual—currently attached. Therefore, if you have multiple real disks attached to your computer, `disk1` is likely to refer to a real disk on your system. We will use fictitious disk numbers that start from 10 in our examples—that is, `disk10`, `disk11`, and so on. Please note and use the dynamic names assigned to virtual disks on *your* system.

The following `hdiutil` command line creates a file (`/tmp/hfsj.dmg`) containing a 32MB disk image. It also partitions the resultant virtual disk using the Apple partitioning scheme and creates a journaled HFS Plus file system on the data partition. The resultant volume's name is `HFSJ`.

```
$ hdiutil create -size 32m -fs HFSJ -volname HFSJ -verbose /tmp/hfsj.dmg
Initializing...
Creating...
...
DIBackingStoreCreateWithCFURL: creator returned 0
DIDiskImageCreateWithCFURL: creator returned 0
DI_kextWaitQuiet: about to call IOServiceWaitQuiet...
```

```
DI_kextWaitQuiet: IOServiceWaitQuiet took 0.000013 seconds
Formatting...
Initialized /dev/rdisk10s2 as a 32 MB HFS Plus volume with a 8192k journal
Finishing...
created: /tmp/hfsj.dmg
hdiutil: create: returning 0
```

> Using the `-debug` option instead of `-verbose` causes `hdiutil` to print excruciatingly detailed progress information. Normally, we will not use either of these two options.

We can mount a disk image in several ways. Double-clicking a disk image's icon in the Finder or opening it with the `open` command-line utility launches `/System/Library/CoreServices/DiskImageMounter.app` to handle the mounting. Alternatively, `hdiutil` can be used to attach the image to the system as a device. `hdiutil`, along with a helper program (`diskimages-helper`), communicates with `diskarbitrationd` to attempt to mount the volumes contained on the disk.

```
$ hdiutil attach /tmp/hfsj.dmg
/dev/disk10          Apple_partition_scheme
/dev/disk10s1        Apple_partition_map
/dev/disk10s2        Apple_HFS                        /Volumes/HFSJ
```

> `diskimages-helper` resides in the `Resources` directory of the Disk Images framework.

The disk image appears as a virtual disk with `/dev/disk10` being its block device node. The `pdisk` utility can dump partition information from this disk just as in the case of a real disk.

```
$ pdisk /dev/rdisk10 -dump
Partition map (with 512 byte blocks) on '/dev/rdisk10'
 #:                type name          length   base    ( size )
 1: Apple_partition_map Apple            63 @ 1
 2:          Apple_HFS disk image    65456 @ 64     ( 32.0M)
 3:         Apple_Free               16 @ 65520

Device block size=512, Number of Blocks=65536 (32.0M)
```

Detaching a disk unmounts and ejects it.

```
$ hdiutil detach disk10
"disk10" unmounted.
"disk10" ejected.
```

By default, hdiutil uses a disk image format called *Universal Disk Image Format* (UDIF). Moreover, the default partition layout contains a partition map with space for 63 map entries, a single data partition of type Apple_HFS, and a trailing free partition containing 16 blocks. This layout is called *Single Partition UDIF* (SPUD). hdiutil also supports other partition layouts, for example:

```
$ hdiutil create -size 32m -volname HFSJ_UCD \
    -fs HFSJ -layout "UNIVERSAL CD" /tmp/hfsj_ucd.dmg
...
$ hdiutil attach /tmp/hfsj_ucd.dmg
/dev/disk10                 Apple_partition_scheme
/dev/disk10s1               Apple_partition_map
/dev/disk10s2               Apple_Driver43
/dev/disk10s3               Apple_Driver43_CD
/dev/disk10s5               Apple_Driver_ATAPI
/dev/disk10s6               Apple_Driver_ATAPI
/dev/disk10s7               Apple_Patches
/dev/disk10s9               Apple_HFS
```

In particular, a partition layout of type NONE creates an image with no partition map.

```
$ hdiutil create -size 32m -volname HFSJ_NONE \
    -fs HFSJ -layout NONE /tmp/hfsj_none.dmg
...
$ hdiutil attach /tmp/hfsj none.dmg
...
/dev/disk11
```

Note that a single device entry is listed when the image is attached—*there are no slices*. pdisk will not dump partition information in the absence of a partition map, but hdiutil's pmap verb can be used instead.

```
$ hdiutil pmap /dev/rdisk11
Partition List
## Dev_____ Type_____ Name_____ Start___ Size____ End_____
-1 disk11      Apple_HFS            Single Volume          0    65536    65535
Legend
     - ... extended entry
     + ... converted entry

Type 128 partition map detected.
Block0.blockSize 0x0200
NativeBlockSize  0x0200
...
```

11.4.2 RAM Disks

A memory-backed virtual disk device can be created using `hdiutil` as follows:

```
$ hdiutil attach -nomount ram://1024
/dev/disk10
```

Given `ram://N` as the device argument, `hdiutil` creates a RAM disk with N sectors, each 512 bytes. As with disk-backed disk images, we can partition a RAM disk, create file systems on it, and so on.

```
$ newfs_hfs -v RAMDisk /dev/rdisk10
Initialized /dev/rdisk10 as a 512 KB HFS Plus volume
$ mkdir /tmp/RAMDisk
$ mount_hfs /dev/disk10 /tmp/RAMDisk
$ df /tmp/RAMDisk
File system 512-blocks Used Avail Capacity  Mounted on
/dev/disk10       1024 152   872     15%    /private/tmp/RAMDisk
```

Detaching a RAM disk frees any physical memory associated with it.

```
$ umount /tmp/RAMDisk
$ hdiutil detach disk10
```

> `hdiutil` and the Disk Images framework have several other interesting features, such as the ability to use disk images specified with HTTP URLs, support for encrypted disk images, and support for *shadowing*, wherein all writes to an image are redirected to a shadow file (when a read occurs, blocks in the shadow file have precedence).

11.4.3 The BSD Vnode Disk Driver

As we have seen, `hdiutil` automatically attaches a virtual device node under `/dev` to a disk image file and prints the dynamically assigned device name. Mac OS X provides another mechanism, the BSD vnode disk driver, which allows files to be treated as disks by attaching them to specific "vn" device nodes. The `/usr/libexec/vndevice` command-line program is used to control this mechanism.

```
$ hdiutil create -size 32m -volname HFSJ_VN \
    -fs HFSJ -layout NONE /tmp/hfsj_vn.dmg
...
$ sudo /usr/libexec/vndevice attach /dev/vn0 /tmp/hfsj_vn.dmg
$ mkdir /tmp/mnt
```

```
$ sudo mount -t hfs /dev/vn0 /tmp/mnt
$ df -k /tmp/mnt
Filesystem 1K-blocks Used Avail Capacity  Mounted on
/dev/vn0      32768 8720 24048   27%    /private/tmp/mnt
$ sudo umount /tmp/mnt
$ sudo /usr/libexec/vndevice detach /dev/vn0
```

11.4.4 Creating a Virtual Disk from Scratch

Although we will mostly use hdiutil to create disk images with automatically constructed partition layouts and file systems, it is instructive to look at an example that starts with a "blank disk." The latter is simply a zero-filled file—say, one created using the mkfile program.

```
$ mkfile 64m blankhd.dmg
```

So far, we have seen that attaching a disk image using hdiutil also mounts the volumes within the image. We can instruct hdiutil to only attach the image and not mount any volumes, thereby giving us block and character devices to use as we please.

```
$ hdiutil attach -nomount /tmp/blankhd.dmg
/dev/disk10
```

Since this disk has no partitions yet, nor even a partition scheme, pdisk will not display any partition information for it. We can initialize a partition map using pdisk.

```
$ pdisk /dev/rdisk10 -dump
pdisk: No valid block 1 on '/dev/rdisk10'
$ pdisk /dev/rdisk10 -initialize
$ pdisk /dev/rdisk10 -dump

Partition map (with 512 byte blocks) on '/dev/rdisk10'
 #:                 type name   length    base   ( size )
 1: Apple_partition_map Apple      63 @ 1
 2:          Apple_Free Extra 131008 @ 64      ( 64.0M)

Device block size=512, Number of Blocks=131072 (64.0M)
...
```

As we saw earlier, in the Apple partitioning scheme, a disk partition map entry is 512 bytes in size. Our partition map occupies 63 blocks, each 512 bytes. Therefore, it has room for 63 map entries. Since the first entry is used for the partition map itself, we have room for as many as 62 new partition map entries, or

61, if the last entry is used for any trailing free space. Let us use, say, 31 of them[5] to create partitions, even though it is rather uncommon to actually *need* so many partitions. The following shell script attempts to create 31 partitions, assigning 1MB of disk space to each.

```
#! /bin/zsh
# usage: createpartitions.zsh <raw device>

DISK=$1
base=64
foreach pnum ({1..31})
    pdisk $DISK -createPartition Partition_$pnum Apple_HFS $base 2048
    base=$[base + 2048]
end
```

Let us run the script with the name of our blank disk's raw device node as an argument. Note that pdisk prints the number of the map entry it uses while creating a partition.

```
$ ./createpartitions.zsh /dev/rdisk10
2
3
...
31
32
$ pdisk /dev/rdisk10 -dump

Partition map (with 512 byte blocks) on '/dev/rdisk10'
 #:                   type name          length   base   ( size )
 1: Apple_partition_map Apple              63 @ 1
 2:          Apple_HFS Partition_1       2048 @ 64      ( 1.0M)
 3:          Apple_HFS Partition_2       2048 @ 2112    ( 1.0M)
 4:          Apple_HFS Partition_3       2048 @ 4160    ( 1.0M)
...
32:          Apple_HFS Partition_31      2048 @ 61504   ( 1.0M)
33:         Apple_Free Extra            67520 @ 63552   ( 33.0M)
...
```

We can now create file systems on each of the Apple_HFS data partitions. Note that at this point, the block and character device nodes corresponding to each partition will already exist in the /dev directory.

```
#! /bin/zsh
# usage: newfs_hfs.zsh <raw device>
```

---

5. The Mac OS X 10.4 kernel panics if all 61 entries are used.

```
DISK-$1
foreach slicenum ({2..32}) # first data partition is on the second slice
    fsnum=$[slicenum - 1]
    newfs_hfs -v HFS$fsnum "$DISK"s$slicenum
end
```

Again, we run our script with the virtual disk's raw device as an argument.

```
$ ./newfs_hfs.zsh /dev/rdisk10
Initialized /dev/rdisk10s2 as a 1024 KB HFS Plus volume
Initialized /dev/rdisk10s3 as a 1024 KB HFS Plus volume
...
Initialized /dev/rdisk10s31 as a 1024 KB HFS Plus volume
Initialized /dev/rdisk10s32 as a 1024 KB HFS Plus volume
$ hdiutil detach disk10
$ open /tmp/blankhd.dmg
...
```

At this point, all 31 volumes should be mounted under /Volumes. Detaching the disk will unmount all of them.

Let us also look at an example of creating GUID-based partitions using the gpt command. We will assume that we already have a blank disk image attached, with /dev/rdisk10 being its raw device node.

```
$ gpt show /dev/rdisk10 # we have nothing on this 64MB disk
start    size  index   contents
      0  131072
$ gpt create /dev/rdisk10 # create a new (empty) GPT
$ gpt show /dev/rdisk10
   start   size  index  contents
       0      1         PMBR
       1      1         Pri GPT header
       2     32         Pri GPT table
      34 131005
  131039     32         Sec GPT table
  131071      1         Sec GPT header
$ gpt add -s 1024 -t hfs /dev/rdisk10 # add a new partition
$ gpt show /dev/rdisk10
   start   size  index  contents
       0      1         PMBR
       1      1         Pri GPT header
       2     32         Pri GPT table
      34   1024      1  GPT part - 48465300-0000-11AA-AA11-00306543ECAC
    1058 129981
  131039     32         Sec GPT table
  131071      1         Sec GPT header
$ gpt add -i 8 -s 1024 -t ufs /dev/rdisk10 # add at index 8
$ gpt show /dev/rdisk10
    ...
```

```
    34    1024    1  GPT part - 48465300-0000-11AA-AA11-00306543ECAC
  1058    1024    8  GPT part - 55465300-0000-11AA-AA11-00306543ECAC
   . . .
```

11.5 Files and File Descriptors

At the system call level, Mac OS X represents open files in a process by using integral *file descriptors*, each of which is an index into the process's file descriptor table in the kernel. When a user program uses a file descriptor in a system call, the kernel uses the file descriptor to find the corresponding file data structure, which in turn contains information—such as a function-pointer table—using which I/O can be performed on the file. This scenario is conceptually the same across Unix and Unix-like systems. However, the specific data structures involved are often different. Figure 11–11 shows the primary file-related kernel data structures in Mac OS X.

Let us assume there is a file descriptor called `fd` in a process with ID `pid`. Each process structure (`struct proc`) contains a pointer (`p_fd`) to a `filedesc` structure, which holds information about the process's open files. In particular, it contains pointers to two arrays: an array of `fileproc` structures (`fd_ofiles`) and an array of open file flags (`fd_ofileflags`). In the case of our file descriptor `fd`, the elements with index `fd` in both these arrays will correspond to the file `fd` represents. If a descriptor is released (because it has no remaining references), that index in both arrays becomes free. The `fd_freefile` field of the `filedesc` structure is used to store a hint that the kernel uses while searching for a free file descriptor.

As Figure 11–11 shows, each entry of the `fd_ofiles` array is a `fileproc` structure. This structure has a `fileglob` substructure whose `fg_ops` and `fg_data` fields point to data structures whose contents depend on the file descriptor's type. Besides files, the kernel uses file descriptors to represent several types of entities, which are listed in Table 11–1. Figure 11–11 assumes that `fd` corresponds to a file. Therefore, `fg_ops` points to a table of vnode operations[6] (the global data structure vnops), whereas `fg_data` points to a vnode structure. If the descriptor represented a socket instead, `fg_ops` would point to a table of socket operations, and `fg_data` would point to a `socket` structure.

---

6. There are far more vnode operations than are contained in a `fileops` structure, which is more relevant for "nonfile" file descriptors—vnode operations can be accessed through the vnode structure itself.

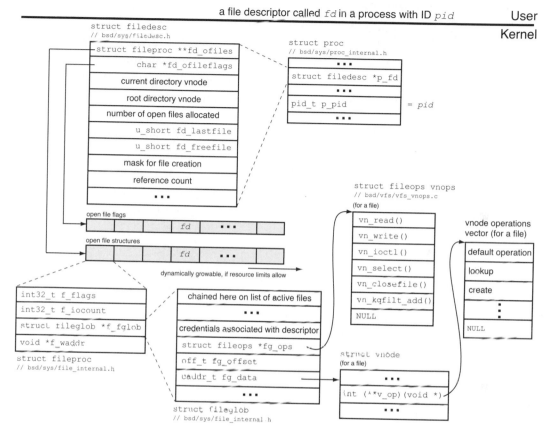

FIGURE 11–11 How a file descriptor leads to a file in Mac OS X

TABLE 11–1 Types of File Descriptors in Mac OS X

File Type	`fg_data` Points to an Instance of This Structure	`fg_ops` Points to This Operation Table
DTYPE_VNODE	struct vnode	vnops
DTYPE_SOCKET	struct socket	socketops
DTYPE_PSXSHM	struct pshmnode	pshmops
DTYPE_PSXSEM	struct psemnode	psemops
DTYPE_KQUEUE	struct kqueue	kqueueops
DTYPE_PIPE	struct pipe	pipeops
DTYPE_FSEVENTS	struct fsevent_handle	fsevents_ops

11.6 The VFS Layer

Mac OS X provides a virtual file system interface—the vnode/vfs layer—often referred to simply as the *VFS layer*. First implemented by Sun Microsystems, the vnode/vfs concept is widely used by modern operating systems to allow multiple file systems to coexist in a clean and maintainable manner. A *vnode* (virtual node) is an in-kernel representation of a file, whereas a *vfs* (virtual file system) represents a file system. The VFS layer sits between the file-system-independent and file-system-dependent code in the kernel, thereby abstracting file system differences from the rest of the kernel, which uses VFS-layer functions to perform I/O—regardless of the underlying file systems. Beginning with Mac OS X 10.4, a VFS kernel programming interface (KPI) is implemented in `bsd/vfs/kpi_vfs.c`.

> The Mac OS X VFS is derived from FreeBSD's VFS, although there are numerous—usually minor in concept—differences. An area of major difference is the file system layer's integration with virtual memory. The unified buffer cache (UBC) on Mac OS X is integrated with Mach's virtual memory layer. As we saw in Chapter 8, the `ubc_info` structure associates Mac OS X vnodes with the corresponding virtual memory objects.

Figure 11–12 shows a simplistic visualization of the vnode/vfs layer. In object-oriented parlance, the vfs is akin to an *abstract base class* from which specific file system instances such as HFS Plus and UFS are derived. Continuing with the analogy, the vfs "class" contains several pure virtual functions that are defined by the derived classes. The `vfsops` structure [`bsd/sys/mount.h`] acts as a function-pointer table for these functions, which include the following (listed in the order they appear in the structure):

- `vfs_mount()`—implements the `mount()` system call
- `vfs_start()`—called by the `mount()` system call to perform any operations that the file system wishes to perform after a successful mount operation
- `vfs_unmount()`—implements the `unmount()` system call
- `vfs_root()`—retrieves the root vnode of the file system
- `vfs_quotactl()`—implements the `quotactl()` system call (handles quota operations on the file system)
- `vfs_getattr()`—populates a `vfs_attr` structure with file system attributes

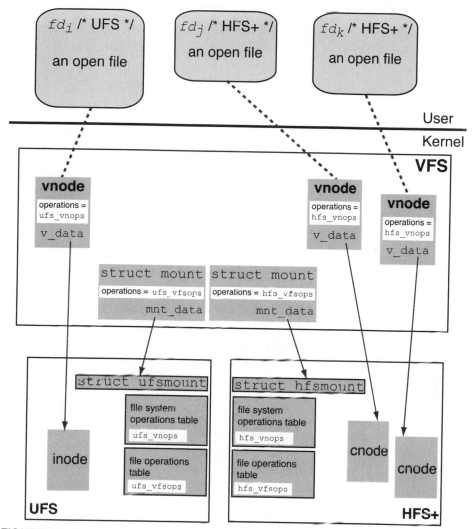

FIGURE 11–12 An overview of the vnode/vfs layer's role in the operating system

- `vfs_statfs()`—implements the `statfs()` system call (retrieves file system statistics by populating a `statfs` structure)
- `vfs_sync()`—synchronizes in-memory dirty data with the on-disk data
- `vfs_vget()`—retrieves an existing file system object given its ID—for example, the catalog node ID in the case of HFS Plus (see Chapter 12)
- `vfs_fhtovp()`—translates a file handle to a vnode; used by the NFS server

- `vfs_init()`—performs one-time initialization of the file system
- `vfs_sysctl()`—handles file-system-level sysctl operations specific to this file system, for example, enabling or disabling the journal on an HFS Plus volume
- `vfs_setattr()`—sets file system attributes, if any can be set, for example, the volume name in the case of HFS Plus

Similarly, a vnode is an abstract base class from which files residing on various file systems are conceptually derived. A vnode contains all the information that the file-system-independent layer of the kernel needs. Just as the vfs has a set of virtual functions, a vnode too has a (larger) set of functions representing vnode operations. Normally, all vnodes representing files on a given file system *type* share the same function-pointer table.

As Figure 11–12 shows, a `mount` structure represents an instance of a mounted file system. Besides a pointer to the vfs operations table, the mount structure also contains a pointer (`mnt_data`) to instance-specific private data—which is private in that it is opaque to the file-system-independent code. For example, in the case of HFS Plus, `mnt_data` points to an `hfsmount` structure, which we will discuss in Chapter 12. Similarly, a vnode contains a private data pointer (`v_data`) that points to a file-system-specific per-file structure—for example, the `cnode` and `inode` structures in the case of HFS Plus and UFS, respectively.

Because of the arrangement shown in Figure 11–12, the code outside of the VFS layer usually need not worry about file system differences. Incoming file and file system operations are routed through the `vnode` and `mount` structures, respectively, to the appropriate file systems.

> Technically, code outside the VFS layer should see the `vnode` and `mount` structures as opaque handles. The kernel uses `vnode_t` and `mount_t`, respectively, as the corresponding opaque types.

Figure 11–13 shows a more detailed view of key vnode/vfs data structures. The `mountlist` global variable is the head of a list of `mount` structures—one per mounted file system. Each `mount` structure has a list of associated vnodes—multiple lists, actually (the `mnt_workerqueue` and `mnt_newvnodes` lists are used when iterating over all vnodes in the file system). Note that the details shown correspond to a mounted HFS Plus file system.

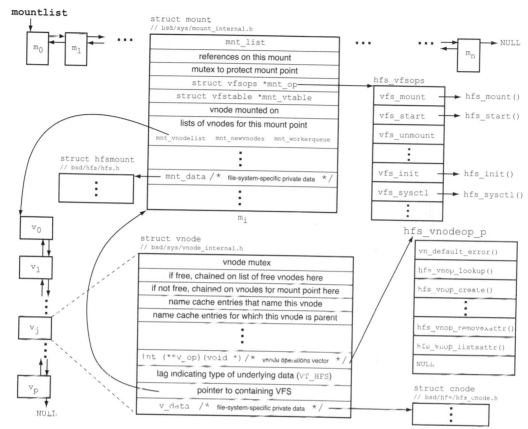

FIGURE 11–13 A mounted file system and its vnodes

The kernel maintains an in-memory `vfstable` structure ([bsd/sys/ mount_internal.h]) for each file system type supported. The global variable `vfsconf` points to a list of these structures. When there is a mount request, the kernel searches this list to identify the appropriate file system. Figure 11–14 shows an overview of the `vfsconf` list, which is declared in `bsd/vfs/vfs_ conf.c`.

There also exists a user-visible `vfsconf` *structure* (not a list), which contains a subset of the information contained in the corresponding `vfstable` structure. The `CTL_VFS→VFS_CONF` sysctl operation can be used to retrieve the `vfsconf` structure for a given file system type. The program in Figure 11–15 retrieves and displays information about all file system types supported by the running kernel.

struct vfstable ***vfsconf**

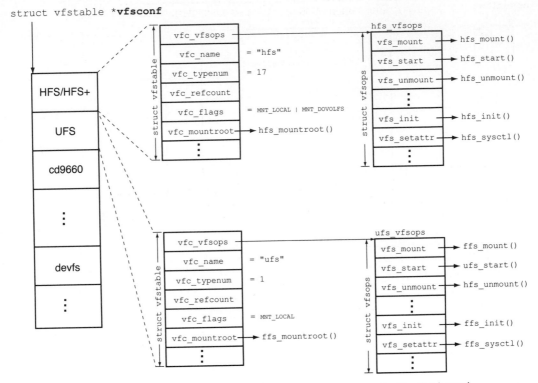

FIGURE 11–14 Configuration information for file system types supported by the kernel

---

FIGURE 11–15 Displaying information about all available file system types

```
// lsvfsconf.c

#include <stdio.h>
#include <stdlib.h>
#include <sys/mount.h>
#include <sys/sysctl.h>
#include <sys/errno.h>

void
print_flags(int f)
{
    if (f & MNT_LOCAL)      // file system is stored locally
        printf("local ");
    if (f & MNT_DOVOLFS)   // supports volfs
        printf("volfs ");
    printf("\n");
}
```

(continues)

FIGURE 11–15 Displaying information about all available file system types *(continued)*

```c
int
main(void)
{
    int     i, ret, val;
    size_t len;
    int     mib[4];

    struct vfsconf vfsconf;

    mib[0] = CTL_VFS;

    mib[1] = VFS_NUMMNTOPS; // retrieve number of mount/unmount operations
    len = sizeof(int);
    if ((ret = sysctl(mib, 2, &val, &len, NULL, 0)) < 0)
        goto out;
    printf("%d mount/unmount operations across all VFSs\n\n", val);

    mib[1] = VFS_GENERIC;
    mib[2] = VFS_MAXTYPENUM; // retrieve highest defined file system type
    len = sizeof(int);
    if ((ret = sysctl(mib, 3, &val, &len, NULL, 0)) < 0)
        goto out;

    mib[2] = VFS_CONF; // retrieve vfsconf for each type
    len = sizeof(vfsconf);
    printf("name            typenum refcount mountroot next      flags\n");
    printf("----            ------- -------- --------- ----      -----\n");
    for (i = 0; i < val; i++) {
        mib[3] = i;
        if ((ret = sysctl(mib, 4, &vfsconf, &len, NULL, 0)) != 0) {
            if (errno != ENOTSUP) // if error is ENOTSUP, let us ignore it
                goto out;
        } else {
            printf("%-11s %-7d %-8d %#09lx %#08lx ",
                    vfsconf.vfc_name, vfsconf.vfc_typenum, vfsconf.vfc_refcount,
                    (unsigned long)vfsconf.vfc_mountroot,
                    (unsigned long)vfsconf.vfc_next);
            print_flags(vfsconf.vfc_flags);
        }
    }

out:
    if (ret)
        perror("sysctl");

    exit(ret);
}
```

(continues)

FIGURE 11–15 Displaying information about all available file system types *(continued)*

```
$ gcc -Wall -o lsvfsconf lsvfsconf.c
$ ./lsvfsconf
14 mount/unmount operations across all VFSs

name        typenum refcount mountroot next       flags
----        ------- -------- --------- ----       -----
ufs         1       0        0x020d5e8 0x367158 local
nfs         2       4        0x01efcfc 0x3671e8
fdesc       7       1        000000000 0x367278
cd9660      14      0        0x0112d90 0x3671a0 local
union       15      0        000000000 0x367230
hfs         17      2        0x022bcac 0x367110 local, volfs
volfs       18      1        000000000 0x3672c0
devfs       19      1        000000000 00000000
```

Note that the program output in Figure 11–15 would contain additional file system types if new file systems (such as MS-DOS and NTFS) were dynamically loaded into the kernel.

The `vnode` structure is declared in `bsd/sys/vnode_internal.h`—its internals are private to the VFS layer, although the VFS KPI provides several functions to access and manipulate `vnode` structures. `vnode_internal.h` also declares the `vnodeop_desc` structure, an instance of which describes a single vnode operation such as "lookup," "create," and "open." The file `bsd/vfs/vnode_if.c` contains the declaration of a `vnodeop_desc` structure for each vnode operation known to the VFS layer, as shown in this example.

```
struct vnodeop_desc vnop_mknod_desc = {

    0, // offset in the operations vector (initialized by vfs_op_init())

    "vnop_mknod", // a human-readable name -- for debugging

    0 | VDESC_VP0_WILLRELE | VDESC_VPP_WILLRELE, // flags

    // various offsets used by the nullfs bypass routine (unused in Mac OS X)
    ...
};
```

> The shell script `bsd/vfs/vnode_if.sh` parses an input file (`bsd/vfs/vnode_if.src`) to automatically generate `bsd/vfs/vnode_if.c` and `bsd/sys/vnode_if.h`. The input file contains a specification of each vnode operation descriptor.

A `vnodeop_desc` structure is referred to by a `vnodeopv_entry_desc` [bsd/sys/vnode.h] structure, which represents a single entry in a vector of vnode operations.

// bsd/sys/vnode.h

```
struct vnodeopv_entry_desc {
    struct vnodeop_desc *opve_op;  // which operation this is
    int (*opve_impl)(void *);      // code implementing this operation
};
```

The `vnodeopv_desc` structure [bsd/sys/vnode.h] describes a vector of vnode operations—it contains a pointer to a null-terminated list of `vnodeopv_entry_desc` structures.

// bsd/sys/vnode.h

```
struct vnodeopv_desc {
    int (***opv_desc_vector_p)(void *);
    struct vnodeopv_entry_desc *opv_desc_ops;
};
```

Figure 11–16 shows how vnode operation data structures are maintained in the VFS layer. There is a `vnodeopv_desc` for each supported file system. The file `bsd/vfs/vfs_conf.c` declares a list of `vnodeopv_desc` structures for built-in file systems.

FIGURE 11–16 Vnode operations vectors in the VFS layer

// bsd/vfs/vfs_conf.c

```
extern struct vnodeopv_desc ffs_vnodeop_opv_desc;
...
extern struct vnodeopv_desc hfs_vnodeop_opv_desc;
extern struct vnodeopv_desc hfs_specop_opv_desc;
extern struct vnodeopv_desc hfs_fifoop_opv_desc;
...

struct vnodeopv_desc *vfs_opv_descs[] = {
    &ffs_vnodeop_opv_desc,
    ...
    &hfs_vnodeop_opv_desc,
    &hfs_specop_opv_desc,
    &hfs_fifoop_opv_desc,
    ...
    NULL
};
```

Typically, each `vnodeopv_desc` is declared in a file-system-specific file. For example, `bsd/hfs/hfs_vnops.c` declares `hfs_vnodeop_opv_desc`.

```
// bsd/hfs/hfs_vnops.c

struct vnodeopv_desc hfs_vnodeop_opv_desc =
    { &hfs_vnodeop_p, hfs_vnodeop_entries };
```

`hfs_vnodeop_entries`—a null-terminated list of `vnodeopv_entry_` `desc` structures—is declared in `bsd/hfs/hfs_vnops.c` as well.

```
// bsd/hfs/hfs_vnops.c

#define VOPFUNC int (*)(void *)

struct vnodeopv_entry_desc hfs_vnodeop_entries[] = {

    { &vnop_default_desc,  (VOPFUNC)vn_default_error },    // default
    { &vnop_lookup_desc,   (VOPFUNC)hfs_vnop_lookup },     // lookup
    { &vnop_create_desc,   (VOPFUNC)hfs_vnop_create },     // create
    { &vnop_mknod_desc,    (VOPFUNC)hfs_vnop_mknod  },     // mknod

    ...
    { NULL, (VOPFUNC)NULL }
};
```

During bootstrapping, `bsd_init()` [`bsd/kern/bsd_init.c`] calls `vfsinit()` [`bsd/vfs/vfs_init.c`] to initialize the VFS layer. Section 5.7.2 enumerates the important operations performed by `vfsinit()`. It calls `vfs_op_init()` [`bsd/vfs/vfs_init.c`] to set known vnode operation vectors to an initial state.

```
// bsd/vfs/vfs_init.c

void
vfs_op_init()
{
    int i;

    // Initialize each vnode operation vector to NULL
    // struct vnodeopv_desc *vfs_opv_descs[]
    for (i = 0; vfs_opv_descs[i]; i++)
        *(vfs_opv_descs[i]->opv_desc_vector_p) = NULL;

    // Initialize the offset value in each vnode operation descriptor
    // struct vnodeop_desc *vfs_op_descs[]
    for (vfs_opv_numops = 0, i = 0, vfs_op_descs[i]; i++) {
        vfs_op_descs[i]->vdesc_offset = vfs_opv_numops;
        vfs_opv_numops++;
    }
}
```

Next, `vfsinit()` calls `vfs_opv_init()` [bsd/vfs/vfs_init.c] to populate the operations vectors. `vfs_opv_init()` iterates over each element of `vfs_opv_descs`, checking whether the `opv_desc_vector_p` field of each entry points to a NULL—if so, it allocates the vector before populating it. Figure 11–17 shows the operation of `vfs_opv_init()`.

FIGURE 11–17 Initialization of vnode operations vectors during bootstrap

```
// bsd/vfs/vfs_init.c

void
vfs_opv_init()
{
    int i, j, k;
    int (***opv_desc_vector_p)(void *);
    int (**opv_desc_vector)(void *);
    struct vnodeopv_entry_desc *opve_descp;

    for (i = 0; vfs_opv_descs[i]; i++) {

        opv_desc_vector_p = vfs_opv_descs[i]->opv_desc_vector_p;

        if (*opv_desc_vector_p == NULL) {

            // allocate and zero out *opv_desc_vector_p
            ...
        }

        opv_desc_vector = *opv_desc_vector_p;

        for (j = 0; vfs_opv_descs[i]->opv_desc_ops[j].opve_op; j++) {

            opve_descp = &(vfs_opv_descs[i]->opv_desc_ops[j]);

            // sanity-check operation offset (panic if it is 0 for an
            // operation other than the default operation)

            // populate the entry
            opv_desc_vector[opve_descp->opve_op->vdesc_offset] =
                    opve_descp->opve_impl;
        }
    }

    // replace unpopulated routines with defaults
    ...
}
```

> Figure 11–16 shows an interesting feature of the FreeBSD-derived VFS layer: There can be multiple vnode operations vectors for a given `vnodeopv_desc`.

11.7 File System Types

Early Macintosh systems used the Macintosh File System (MFS)—a flat file system in which all files were stored in a single directory. The software presented an illusory hierarchical view that *showed* nested folders. MFS was designed for floppy disks, not for high-capacity storage media such as hard disks and CD-ROMs. The Hierarchical File System (HFS) was introduced with the Macintosh Plus as a file system with "true" hierarchy, although it differed from a traditional Unix file system in that the hierarchical structure was entirely maintained in a central catalog. HFS was the primary file system format used until Mac OS 8.1, when HFS Plus replaced it.

> Each MFS volume contained a folder called `Empty Folder` at its root level. Renaming this folder created a new folder, with a replacement `Empty Folder` appearing as a side effect.

It is common for modern operating systems to support several file systems—Linux supports dozens! Mac OS X also supports a number of file systems. Because of the number of sources Mac OS X draws from, it has multiple file system APIs: Carbon File Manager, `NSFileManager` and family (Cocoa), and BSD system calls. Figure 11–18 shows how these APIs are layered in the system.

The file systems available on Mac OS X can be categorized as follows.

- *Local file systems* are those that use locally attached storage. Mac OS X supports HFS Plus, HFS, ISO 9660, MS-DOS, NTFS, UDF, and UFS.

- *Network file systems* are those that allow files residing on one computer to appear locally on another computer, provided the two computers are connected over a network. Mac OS X supports the Apple Filing Protocol (AFP), FTP file system, NFS, SMB/CIFS, and the WebDAV file system.

- *Pseudo file systems* are those typically used for providing file-like views of nonfile information. Some others are used as special file system layers. In

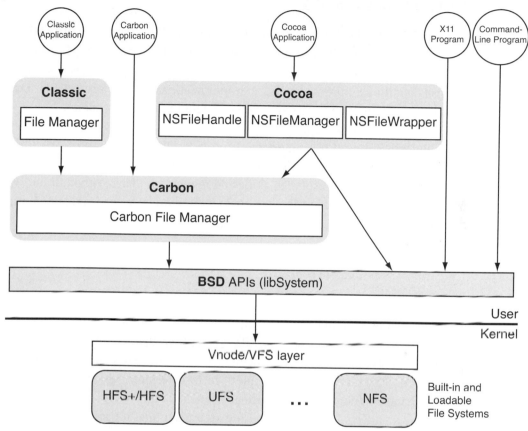

FIGURE 11–18 Mac OS X file system APIs

general, pseudo file systems do not have persistent backing stores.[7] Mac OS X supports cddafs, deadfs, devfs, fdesc, specfs, fifofs, synthfs, union, and volfs.

> Another Apple-provided file system for Mac OS X is the Apple Clus-
> ter File System (ACFS)—a shared SAN file system that underlies
> the Xsan product (see Section 2.15.2).

Let us briefly look at each of these file systems.

---

7. cddafs provides a file system view of nonfile information that is persistent.

11.7.1 HFS Plus and HFS

The Mac OS Extended file system (another name for HFS Plus, or simply HFS+) is the preferred, default, and most feature-rich file system on Mac OS X. Although it is architecturally similar to its predecessor, HFS, it has undergone numerous additions, improvements, and optimizations to be a respectable modern-day file system. We will discuss HFS+ in detail in the next chapter.

When HFS was introduced, it was quite innovative in how it lent support to the Macintosh graphical user interface. It provided the abstraction of two forks, the data fork and the resource fork, with the latter allowing structured storage of GUI-related (and other) resources alongside regular file data. Although the two forks were parts of the same file, they could be individually accessed and manipulated. The following are examples of resources:

- `'ICON'`—an icon
- `'CODE'`—executable code
- `'STR'`—program strings

Besides the data and resource forks, HFS provides for additional per-file information, such as a four-character file type, a four-character creator code, and attributes such as those specifying whether the file is locked, is invisible, or has a custom icon. This allowed the user interface to determine which application to launch to handle a file when the user double-clicked on its icon.

HFS also differs from traditional file systems in that it uses a B-Tree-based catalog file to store the file system's hierarchical structure, rather than explicitly storing directories on disk. In order to locate the contents of a fork, HFS records up to the first three *extents*—that is, { starting block, block count } pairs—in the corresponding file record in the catalog file. If a fork is fragmented enough to have more than three extents, the remaining extents overflow to another B-Tree-based file: the extents overflow file. As we will see in Chapter 12, HFS+ retains the basic design of HFS.

Both HFS and HFS+ use the colon character (:) as a path separator—it is not a valid filename character. They also do not have the notion of a filename extension.

11.7.2 ISO 9660

ISO 9660 is a system-independent file system for read-only data CDs. Apple has its own set of ISO 9660 extensions. Moreover, Mac HFS+/ISO 9660 hybrid discs contain both a valid HFS+ and a valid ISO 9660 file system. Both file systems can be read on Mac OS X, whereas on non-Apple systems, you would typically be able to read only the ISO 9660 data. This does not mean there is redundant data on the disc—usually, the data that needs to be accessed from both Mac OS X and other operating systems is stored on the ISO 9660 volume and is *aliased* on the HFS+ volume. Consider the following example, where we create a hybrid ISO image containing two files, each visible from only a single file system.

```
$ hdiutil makehybrid -o /tmp/hybrid.iso . -hfs -iso -hfs-volume-name HFS \
    -iso-volume-name ISO -hide-hfs iso.txt -hide-iso hfs.txt
Creating hybrid image...
...
$ hdiutil attach -nomount /tmp/hybrid.iso
/dev/disk10              Apple_partition_scheme
/dev/disk10s1           Apple_partition_map
/dev/disk10s2           Apple_HFS
$ hdiutil pmap /dev/rdisk10
Partition List
## Dev_____ Type__  _____ Name_____ Start___ Size____ End____
 0 disk10s1  Apple_partition_map Apple              1       63       63
-1            Apple_ISO           ISO               64       24       87
 1 disk10s2  Apple_HFS           DiscRecording 3.0  88       36      123
Legend
     - ... extended entry
     + ... converted entry
...
```

If we explicitly mount the hybrid volume's ISO 9660 file system, we will not see the HFS+-only file hfs.txt on it. If we mount it as an HFS+ volume, we will see only hfs.txt on it.

```
$ mkdir /tmp/iso
$ mount -t cd9660 /dev/disk10 /tmp/iso
$ ls /tmp/iso
ISO.TXT
$ umount /tmp/iso
$ hdiutil detach disk10
...
$ open /tmp/hybrid.iso
...
$ ls /Volumes/HFS
hfs.txt
```

> Apple's ISO 9660 implementation stores a resource fork as an *associated file*, which it names by adding the ._ prefix to the containing file's name.

11.7.3 MS-DOS

Mac OS X includes support for the FAT12, FAT16, and FAT32 variants of the MS-DOS file system. The file system is not compiled into the kernel but is present as a loadable kernel extension (/System/Library/Extensions/ msdosfs.kext). When an MS-DOS volume is being mounted, the mount_ msdos command attempts to load the kernel extension if it is not already loaded.

hdiutil supports writing an MS-DOS file system to a disk image.

```
$ hdiutil create -size 32m -fs MS-DOS -volname MS-DOS /tmp/ms-dos.dmg
$ hdiutil attach /tmp/ms-dos.dmg
/dev/disk10                                          /Volumes/MS-DOS
$ hdiutil pmap /dev/rdisk10
## Dev_____ Type_____ Name_____ Start___ Size____ End_____
-1 disk10    MS-DOS              Single Volume         0    65536    65535
...
```

The Mac OS X MS-DOS file system implementation supports symbolic links by storing link-target information in a specially formatted text file that is exactly 1067 bytes in size. Figure 11–19 shows the contents of a symbolic link file symlink.txt whose link target is specified as a relative path target.txt.

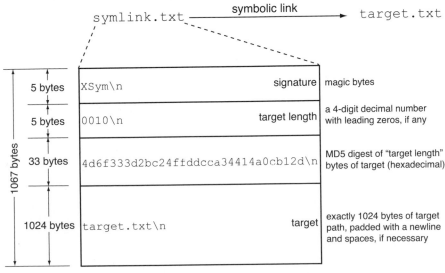

FIGURE 11–19 Structure of a symbolic link on the MS-DOS file system on Mac OS X

You can synthesize your own symbolic link by simply writing the appropriate information to a file[8]—the MD5 digest of the link-target path can be generated using a command such as the following.

```
$ echo -n target.txt | md5
4d6f333d2bc24ffddcca34414a0cb12d
```

11.7.4 NTFS

Mac OS X includes *read-only* support for NTFS. The NTFS file system driver (`/System/Library/Extensions/ntfs.kext`) is based on the FreeBSD NTFS driver. As with the MS-DOS file system, NTFS it is not compiled into the kernel but is loaded by the `mount_ntfs` program when required.

11.7.5 UDF

Universal Disk Format (UDF) is the file system used by DVD-ROM discs (including DVD-video and DVD-audio discs) and many CD-R/RW packet-writing programs. It is implemented as a kernel extension (`/System/Library/Extensions/udf.kext`) that is loaded by the `mount_udf` program when required. Mac OS X 10.4 supports the "normal" flavor of the UDF 1.5 specification.

11.7.6 UFS

Darwin's implementation of UFS is similar to that on FreeBSD, but they are not entirely compatible because the Darwin implementation is always big-endian (as was NEXTSTEP's)—even on little-endian hardware. Technically, UFS is BSD's Unix file system layer that is independent of the underlying file system implementation. The part that deals with on-disk structures is based on the Berkeley Fast File System (FFS). We will use the term *UFS* to represent the combination of UFS and FFS.

UFS does not provide some features that HFS+ provides—for example, it does not support multiple forks, (native) extended attributes, and aliases. However, resource forks and extended attributes can be used on UFS through emulation.

---

8. You may need to unmount and remount the volume; the file system initially might not recognize the file as a symbolic link because of caching.

For example, when a file (named, say, `file.txt`) with a nonzero resource fork is copied to a UFS volume, it is split into two files: `file.txt` (containing the data fork) and `._file.txt` (containing the resource fork). Copying such a file to an HFS+ volume will populate both forks in the destination file.

UFS2

Newer versions of FreeBSD include UFS2, a redesigned version of UFS (or UFS1, as it is now called). UFS2 provides numerous improvements over UFS1, such as the following: 64-bit block pointers, 64-bit time fields for access and modification times, support for a per-file "birth time" field, support for extended attributes, and dynamically allocated inodes. As in the case of HFS+, UFS2 extended attributes are used for implementing access control lists (ACLs). They are also used for data labeling in FreeBSD's mandatory access control (MAC) framework.

Unlike HFS+, UFS is always case-sensitive. It also supports sparse files—or files with "holes"—which HFS+ does not. If a file contains a relatively large amount of zero data (as compared to its size), it is efficiently represented as a sparse file. On a file system with sparse file support, you can create a physically empty file with a nonzero size. In other words, the file would contain virtual disk blocks. When such a file is read, the kernel returns zero-filled memory in place of the virtual disk blocks. When a portion of a sparse file is written, the file system manages the sparse and nonsparse data. A good example of the utility of sparse files is in an emulator (such as Virtual PC) that uses large disk images as virtual disks belonging to guest operating systems. If the emulator is not to allocate physical storage until necessary, either it must use sparse files or it must simulate the sparseness itself—above the file system. The latter is likely to result in a fragmented disk image.

> Even though HFS+ does not support sparse files, it supports deferred zeroing of file blocks that have never been written. Meanwhile, the kernel will return zero-filled pages when such blocks are read.

Let us compare the behavior of HFS+ and UFS when we attempt to create an empty file with a nonzero size that exceeds the file system's capacity. We will create two disk images, each 16MB in size, but one containing an HFS+ file system and the other containing a UFS file system. Note that `hdiutil` supports writing a UFS file system to a disk image. Next, we will use the `mkfile` command to attempt to create 32MB sparse files on both volumes.

```
$ hdiutil create -size 16m -fs HFS -volname HFS hfs.dmg
...
$ hdiutil create -size 16m -fs UFS -volname UFS ufs.dmg
...
$ open hfs.dmg
$ open ufs.dmg

$ cd /Volumes/HFS
$ df -k .
Filesystem    1K-blocks Used Avail Capacity  Mounted on
/dev/disk10s2    16337  261 16076    2%    /Volumes/HFS
$ mkfile -nv 32m bigfile
mkfile: (bigfile removed) Write Error: No space left on device

$ cd /Volumes/UFS
$ df -k .
Filesystem    1K-blocks Used Avail Capacity  Mounted on
/dev/disk11s2    15783   15 14979    0%    /Volumes/UFS
$ mkfile -nv 32m bigfile
bigfile 33554432 bytes
$ ls -lh bigfile
-rw-------  1 amit  amit        32M Oct 22 11:40 bigfile
$ df -k .
Filesystem    1K blocks Used Avail Capacity  Mounted on
/dev/disk11s2    15783   27 14967    0%    /Volumes/UFS
```

> Although Mac OS X supports UFS as a root file system, the operating system's features are best integrated with HFS+. Therefore, HFS+ is recommended as the primary file system.

11.7.7 AFP

The Apple Filing Protocol (AFP) is a protocol for file sharing over the network. It was the primary file-sharing protocol in Mac OS 9 and was extensively used by AppleShare servers and clients. It still is the default protocol for sharing files between Mac OS X systems. In general, any file system that supports Unix semantics can be shared over AFP. In particular, besides HFS+ mounts, AFP can be used to export NFS and UFS mounts.

The Mac OS X implementation of AFP is contained in a loadable kernel extension (`/System/Library/Filesystems/AppleShare/afpfs.kext`).

> The `/Systems/Library/Filesystems/AppleShare/` directory also contains the `asp_atp.kext` and `asp_tcp.kext` kernel extensions. These implement the Apple Session Protocol (ASP) over AppleTalk and TCP, respectively. ASP is a session-layer protocol that allows a client to establish a session with a server and send commands to the latter.

When an application on an AFP client computer accesses a remote file residing on an AFP file server, the native file system layer sends the requests to the AFP translator, which translates and sends the requests to the server. Not all AFP-related communication goes through the translator, however. There are AFP commands with no native file system equivalents—for example, commands for user authentication. Such commands may be sent directly to the AFP server while bypassing the translator.

Unlike traditional NFS, which is stateless, AFP is session based. An AFP server shares one or more volumes, which AFP clients can access during sessions. An AFP session begins when an AFP client authenticates with an AFP server using a *User Authentication Method* (UAM). AFP supports multiple UAMs such as the following:

- No User Authentication
- Cleartext Password
- Random Number Exchange
- Two-Way Random Number Exchange
- Diffie-Hellman Exchange
- Diffie-Hellman Exchange 2
- Kerberos
- Reconnect

> The Reconnect UAM is intended for use by a client for reconnecting a session that was disrupted—say, due to a network outage. Note also that AFP supports tunneling with SSH as an option.

AFP has another, less secure level of access control, wherein each volume made available through AFP may have a fixed-length eight-character password associated with it. It also provides Unix-style access privileges, with support for owner and group privileges for searching, reading, and writing.

AFP versions older than 3.0 do not support file permissions. If both the AFP client and server support AFP 3.x, BSD file permissions are sent as-is (untranslated) over the connection. If only the client or the server is using AFP 2.x, permissions have slightly different semantics. For example, when dealing with folders, the 3.x party (server or client) maps between BSD's read, write, and execute bits to AFP's *See Files*, *See Folders*, and *Make Changes* analogs. Note that a process with an effective user ID (UID) of 0 cannot use AFP to access data over the network.

Mac OS X uses a user-space AFP daemon (/usr/sbin/AppleFileServer), which is launched when you select the Personal File Sharing checkbox under System Preferences → Sharing. The AFP server provides synchronization rules to facilitate sane simultaneous-file access. In particular, AFP has the notion of a *deny mode*—an application opening a file fork can use this mode to specify privileges that should be denied to other applications that open the same fork.

AFP commands can be grouped under the following functional categories:

- Login commands
- Volume commands
- Directory commands
- File commands
- Combined directory and file commands
- Fork commands
- Desktop database commands

11.7.8 FTP

The mount_ftp command makes a directory residing on an FTP server locally visible, thus providing an FTP file system.

```
$ mount_ftp ftp://user:password@host/directory/path local-mount-point
```

Mac OS X includes a private framework called URLMount that allows AFP, FTP, HTTP (WebDAV), NFS, and SMB URLs to be mounted. The directory /System/Library/Filesystems/URLMount/ contains .URLMounter plug-in bundles for each of these URL types.

The FTP file system is implemented as a user process that is both an FTP client and a local NFS server—it uses NFS to export the FTP view, which is then mounted by the Mac OS X built-in NFS client. You can use the `nfsstat` program to monitor client-side NFS activity caused by accessing an instance of the FTP file system.

```
$ mkdir /tmp/ftp
$ mount -t ftp ftp://anonymous@sunsite.unc.edu/pub /tmp/ftp
$ ls /tmp/ftp
Linux                   electronic-publications micro
X11                     gnu                     mirrors
academic                historic-linux          multimedia
archives                languages               packages
docs                    linux                   solaris
$ nfsstat
Rpc Counts:
  Getattr   Setattr    Lookup  Readlink      Read     Write    Create    Remove
       12         0        19         1         0         0         0         0
   Rename      Link   Symlink     Mkdir     Rmdir   Readdir  RdirPlus    Access
        0         0         3         0         0         1         0         0
    Mknod    Fsstat    Fsinfo  PathConf    Commit
        0         8         0         0         0
Rpc Info:
 TimedOut  Invalid X Replies   Retries  Requests
        0         0         0         3        44
...
```

> Even in the absence of any explicit NFS mounts, `nfsstat` will normally report NFS activity because the `automount` daemon, which is started by default on Mac OS X, also uses the local NFS server approach used by the FTP file system.

11.7.9 NFS

Mac OS X derives its NFS client and server support from FreeBSD. The implementation conforms to NFS version 3 and includes the NQNFS extensions. As we saw in Section 8.10.2, the Mac OS X kernel uses a separate buffer cache for NFS.

Mac OS X also includes the usual supporting daemons for NFS, namely, the following.

- `rpc.lockd` implements the Network Lock Management protocol.
- `rpc.statd` implements the Status Monitor protocol.
- `nfsiod` is the local asynchronous NFS I/O server.

Not Quite NFS (NQNFS)

NQNFS adds procedures to NFS to make the protocol stateful, which is a departure from the original NFS design. The NFS server maintains states of open and cached files on clients. NQNFS uses leases to facilitate server recovery of client state in the case of a crash. The leases are short term but are extended on use.

11.7.10 SMB/CIFS

Server Message Block (SMB) is a widely used protocol for sharing a variety of resources over a network. Examples of SMB-shareable resources include files, printers, serial ports, and named pipes. SMB has been around since the early 1980s. Microsoft and other vendors helped evolve an enhanced version of SMB—the Common Internet File System (CIFS). Mac OS X provides support for SMB/CIFS through *Samba*, a popular Open Source SMB server that is available for numerous platforms.

11.7.11 WebDAV

Web-based Distributed Authoring and Versioning (WebDAV) is an extension of the ubiquitous Hypertext Transfer Protocol (HTTP) that allows collaborative file management on the web. For example, using WebDAV, you can create and edit content remotely by connecting to a WebDAV-enabled web server. Given the URL to a WebDAV-enabled directory, the mount_webdav command can mount the remote directory as a locally visible file system. In particular, since a .Mac account's iDisk is available through WebDAV, it can also be mounted this way.

```
$ mkdir /tmp/idisk
$ mount_webdav http://idisk.mac.com/<member name>/ /tmp/idisk
... # a graphical authentication dialog should be displayed
$ ls /tmp/idisk
About your iDisk.rtf     Movies            Sites
Backup                   Music             Software
Documents                Pictures
Library                  Public
```

Mac OS X also supports secure WebDAV, in which Kerberos and the HTTPS protocol can be used while accessing WebDAV volumes.

The Mac OS X WebDAV file system implementation uses a hybrid approach that involves a user-space daemon (implemented within mount_webdav) and a loadable file system kernel extension (/System/Library/Extensions/ webdav_fs.kext). Figure 11–20 shows an overview of this implementation.

Most of the actual work is performed by the user-space daemon. As Figure 11–20 shows, the file system kernel extension communicates with the daemon using an AF_LOCAL socket, which the daemon provides to the kernel as a mount() system call argument. The various vnode operations in the kernel-resident WebDAV code simply redirect I/O requests to the daemon, which services the requests by performing the appropriate network transfers. The daemon also uses a local temporary cache directory.[9] Note that the daemon does not actually send file data to the kernel—once the data of interest has been downloaded to a cache file, the kernel reads it directly from the file. This setup may be thought of as a special form of file system stacking.

11.7.12 cddafs

The cdda[10] file system is used to make the tracks of an audio compact disc appear as AIFF files. The implementation consists of a mounting utility (mount_cddafs) and a loadable file system kernel extension (/System/Library/Extensions/cddafs.kext). The mount utility attempts to determine the album name and the names of the audio tracks on the disc. If it fails, "Audio CD" and "<track number> Audio Track" are used as the album and track names, respectively. The mount utility uses the mount() system call to pass these names to the cddafs kernel extension, which creates a file system view from the audio tracks on the disc. Each track's filename has the format <track number> <track name>.aiff, whereas the album name is used as the volume's name. The kernel extension also creates an in-memory file called .TOC.plist, which appears in the root directory along with the track files and contains XML-formatted table-of-contents data for the disc.

```
$ cat /Volumes/Joshua Tree/.TOC.plist
...
<key>Sessions</key>
    <array>
        <dict>
            <key>First Track</key>
```

---

9. The files in this directory are unlinked by the daemon while they are open; therefore, they are "invisible."

10. CD-DA stands for Compact Disc Digital Audio.

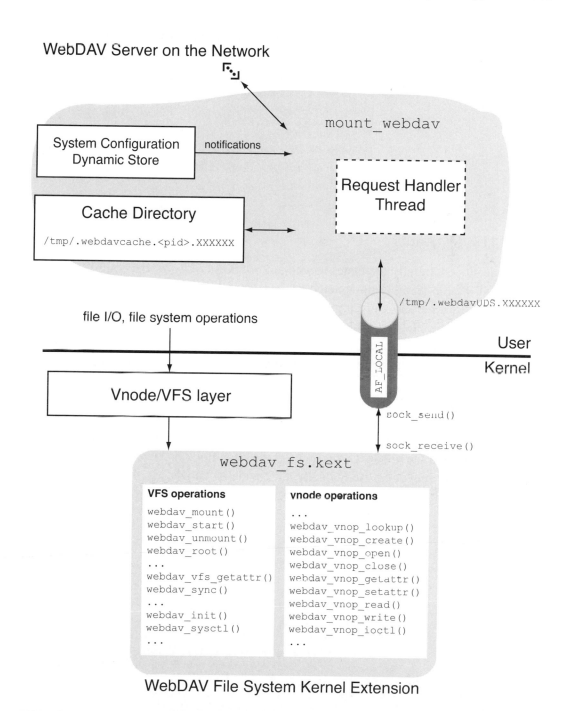

FIGURE 11–20 Implementation of the WebDAV file system

```
                        <integer>1</integer>
                        <key>Last Track</key>
                        <integer>11</integer>
                        <key>Leadout Block</key>
                        <integer>226180</integer>
                        <key>Session Number</key>
                        <integer>1</integer>
                        <key>Session Type</key>
                        <integer>0</integer>
                        <key>Track Array</key>
                        <array>
```

...

11.7.13 deadfs

deadfs essentially facilitates revocation of access—say, to the controlling terminal or to a forcibly unmounted file system. The revoke() system call, which revokes access to a given pathname by invalidating all open file descriptors that refer to the file, also causes the corresponding vnode to be dissociated from the underlying file system. Thereafter, the vnode is associated with deadfs. The launchd program uses revoke() to prepare a controlling terminal while starting a session.

The VFS layer (see Section 11.6) uses the vclean() function [bsd/vfs/vfs_subr.c] to dissociate the underlying file system from a vnode—it removes the vnode from any mount list it might be on, purges the name-cache entry associated with the vnode, cleans any associated buffers, and eventually reclaims the vnode for recycling. Additionally, the vnode is "moved" to the *dead* file system (deadfs). Its vnode operations vector is also set to that of the dead file system.

```
// bsd/vfs/vfs_subr.c

static void
vclean(vnode_t vp, int flags, proc_t p)
{
    ...
    if (VNOP_RECLAIM(vp, &context))
        panic("vclean: cannot reclaim");
    ...
    vp->v_mount = dead_mountp; // move to the dead file system
    vp->v_op = dead_vnodeop_p; // vnode operations vector of the dead file system
    vp->v_tag = VT_NON;
    vp->v_data = NULL;
    ...
}
```

Most operations in deadfs return an error, with a few exceptions, such as those listed here.

- `close()` trivially succeeds.
- `fsync()` trivially succeeds.
- `read()` returns end-of-file for character devices but an `EIO` error for all others.

11.7.14 devfs

The device file system (devfs) provides access to the kernel's device namespace in the global file system namespace. It allows device entries to be dynamically added and removed. In particular, the I/O Kit's `IOStorageFamily` uses devfs functions to add and remove block and character nodes corresponding to media devices as they are attached and detached, respectively.

devfs is allocated, initialized, and mounted from within the Mac OS X kernel during BSD initialization. The kernel mounts it on the `/dev/` directory by default. Additional instances of it can be mounted later, from user space, using the `mount_devfs` program.

```
$ mkdir /tmp/dev
$ mount_devfs devfs /tmp/dev
$ ls /tmp/dev
bpf0                    ptyte                    ttyr4
bpf1                    ptytf                    ttyr5
...
$ umount /tmp/dev
```

During bootstrapping, VFS initialization iterates over each built-in file system, calling the file system's initialization function, which is `devfs_init()` [bsd/miscfs/devfs/devfs_vfsops.c] in the case of devfs. Shortly afterward, the kernel mounts devfs. `devfs_init()` creates device entries for the following devices: `console`, `tty`, `mem`, `kmem`, `null`, `zero`, and `klog`.

> devfs redirects most of its vnode operations to specfs (see Section 11.7.16).

11.7.15 fdesc

The fdesc file system, which is conventionally mounted on /dev/fd/, provides a list of all active file descriptors in the calling process.[11] For example, if a process has descriptor number n open, then the following two function calls will be equivalent:

```
int fd;
...
fd = open("/dev/fd/n", ...); /* case 1 */
fd = dup(n);                  /* case 2 */
```

In Mac OS X versions older than 10.4, the /etc/rc startup script mounts the fdesc file system as a union mount on /dev/. Beginning with Mac OS X 10.4, fdesc is mounted by launchd instead.

```
// launchd.c
...
if (mount("fdesc", "/dev", MNT_UNION, NULL) == 1)
    ...
```

Note that the mount point in launchd's invocation of the mount() system call invocation is /dev/ (and not /dev/fd/). The fd/ directory is maintained by the fdesc file system as one of the entries in its root directory. Besides fd/, it also maintains three symbolic links: stdin, stdout, and stderr. The targets of these links are fd/0, fd/1, and fd/2, respectively. Like devfs, there can be multiple instances of fdesc.

```
$ mkdir /tmp/fdesc
$ mount_fdesc fdesc /tmp/fdesc
$ ls -l /tmp/fdesc
total 4
dr-xr-xr-x  2 root  wheel  512 Oct 23 18:33 fd
lr--r--r--  1 root  wheel    4 Oct 23 18:33 stderr -> fd/2
lr--r--r--  1 root  wheel    4 Oct 23 18:33 stdin -> fd/0
lr--r--r--  1 root  wheel    4 Oct 23 18:33 stdout -> fd/1
```

> The functionality of fdesc is similar to Linux's /proc/self/fd/ directory, which allows a process to access its own open file descriptors. Linux systems also have /dev/fd/ symbolically linked to /proc/self/fd/.

---

11. A process can access only its own open file descriptors using the fdesc file system.

11.7.16 specfs and fifofs

Devices (the so-called special files) and named pipes (fifos) can reside on any file system that can house such files. Although the host file system maintains the names and attributes of special files, it cannot easily handle the operations that are performed on such files. In fact, many operations that are relevant for regular files may not even make sense for special files. Moreover, multiple special files with the same major and minor numbers may exist with different pathnames on a file system, or even on different file systems. It must be ensured that each of these files—essentially a device alias—unambiguously refers to the same underlying device. A related issue is that of multiple buffering, where the buffer cache could hold more than one buffer for the same block on a device.

Ideally, accesses to device files should be directly mapped to their underlying devices—that is, to the respective device drivers. It would be unreasonable to require each file system type to include explicit support for special file operations. The specfs layer, which was introduced in SVR4, provides a solution to this problem: It implements special-file vnode operations that can be used by any file system. Consider the example of a block or character special file on an HFS+ volume. When HFS+ needs a new vnode, say, during a lookup operation, it calls hfs_getnewvnode() [bsd/hfs/hfs_cnode.c]. The latter checks whether it is a fifo or a special file. If so, it arranges for the vnode to be created with a vnode operations table other than the one for HFS+: hfs_fifoop_p and hfs_specop_p redirect appropriate operations to fifofs and specfs, respectively.

```
// bsd/hfs/hfs_cnode.c

int
hfs_getnewvnode(struct hfsmount *hfsmp, ...)
{
    ...
        if (vtype == VFIFO )
                vfsp.vnfs_vops = hfs_fifoop_p;      // a fifo
        else if (vtype == VBLK || vtype == VCHR)
                vfsp.vnfs_vops = hfs_specop_p;      // a special file
        else
                vfsp.vnfs_vops = hfs_vnodeop_p;     // use HFS+ vnode operations
        ...
        if ((retval = vnode_create(VNCREATE_FLAVOR, VCREATESIZE, &vfsp, ...))) {
    ...
}
```

Note that both fifofs and specfs are file system *layers*—not file systems. In particular, they cannot be mounted, unmounted, or seen by users.

11.7.17 synthfs

synthfs is an in-memory file system that provides a namespace for creation of arbitrary directory trees. Therefore, it can be used for *synthesizing* mount points—say, while booting from a read-only device that may not have a spare directory for use as a mount point. Besides directories, synthfs also allows creation of symbolic links (but not files).

> Although synthfs source is part of the xnu source, the default Mac OS X kernel does not include synthfs as a compiled-in file system. In the case of such a kernel, you must first compile synthfs.

Let us look at an example of using synthfs. Suppose you have a read-only file system mounted on /Volumes/ReadOnly/, and you wish to synthesize a directory tree within /Volumes/ReadOnly/mnt/, where mnt/ is an existing subdirectory. You can do so by mounting an instance of synthfs on top of /Volumes/ReadOnly/mnt/. Thereafter, you can create directories and symbolic links within the mnt/ subdirectory.

```
$ lsvfs # ensure that synthfs is available
Filesystem                          Refs Flags
-------------------------------- ----- ---------------
ufs                                    0 local
...
synthfs                                0
$ ls -F /Volumes/ReadOnly # a read-only volume
mnt/ root/ boot/ ...
$ ls -F /Volumes/ReadOnly/mnt # subdirectory of interest
$ sudo mkdir /Volumes/ReadOnly/mnt/MyDir # cannot create a new directory
mkdir: /Volumes/ReadOnly/mnt: No such file or directory
$ mount_synthfs synthfs /Volumes/ReadOnly/mnt # mount synthfs
$ mount
...
<synthfs> on /Volumes/ReadOnly/mnt (nodev, suid, mounted by amit)
$ sudo mkdir /Volumes/ReadOnly/mnt/MyDir # try again
$ ls -F /Volumes/ReadOnly/mnt # now a directory can be created
MyDir/
$ umount /Volumes/ReadOnly/mnt # cannot unmount synthfs because of MyDir/
umount: unmount(/Volumes/ReadOnly/mnt): Resource busy
$ sudo rmdir /Volumes/ReadOnly/mnt/MyDir # remove MyDir/
$ umount /Volumes/ReadOnly/mnt # now synthfs can be unmounted
$
```

Note that if it is required to keep a synthfs mount point's existing contents visible, you can mount synthfs with the union option (see Section 11.7.18).

11.7.18 union

The *null mount* file system (nullfs) is a stackable file system in 4.4BSD. It allows mounting of one part of the file system in a different location. This can be used to join multiple directories into a new directory tree. Thus, file system hierarchies on various disks can be presented as one directory tree. Moreover, subtrees of a writable file system can be made read-only. Mac OS X does not use nullfs, but it does provide the *union mount* file system, which conceptually extends nullfs by not hiding the files in the "mounted on" directory—rather, it *merges* the two directories (and their trees) into a single view. In a union mount, duplicate names are suppressed. Given a name, a lookup locates the logically topmost entity with that name. Let us look at a sequence of commands that will illustrate the basic concepts behind union mounting.

First, we create two disk images with HFS+ file systems and attach them.

```
$ hdiutil create -size 16m -layout NONE -fs HFS+ \
    -volname Volume1 /tmp/Volume1.dmg
...
$ hdiutil create -size 16m -layout NONE -fs HFS+ \
    -volname Volume2 /tmp/Volume2.dmg
...
$ hdiutil attach -nomount /tmp/Volume1.img
/dev/disk10             Apple_HFS
$ hdiutil attach -nomount /tmp/Volume2.img
/dev/disk11             Apple_HFS
```

Next, we mount both images and create files on them: Volume1 will contain one file (a.txt), whereas Volume2 will contain two files (a.txt and b.txt).

```
$ mkdir /tmp/union

$ mount -t hfs /dev/disk10 /tmp/union
$ echo 1 > /tmp/union/a.txt
$ umount /dev/disk10

$ mount -t hfs /dev/disk11 /tmp/union
$ echo 2 > /tmp/union/a.txt
$ echo 2 > /tmp/union/b.txt
$ umount /dev/disk11
```

Let us now union-mount both file systems by specifying the union option to the mount command.

```
$ mount -t hfs -o union /dev/disk10 /tmp/union
$ mount -t hfs -o union /dev/disk11 /tmp/union
```

Since `Volume2` was mounted on top of `Volume1`, a filename that exists in both—`a.txt` in our case—will be suppressed in the latter. In other words, we will access the file on the logically topmost volume.

```
$ ls /tmp/union        # contents will be union of Volume1 and Volume2
a.txt b.txt
$ cat /tmp/union/a.txt # this should come from Volume2 (the top volume)
2
$ umount /dev/disk11   # let us unmount Volume2
$ ls /tmp/union        # we should only see the contents of Volume1
a.txt
$ cat /tmp/union/a.txt # this should now come from Volume1
1
$ umount /dev/disk10
```

We can also union-mount the volumes in the opposite order and verify whether doing so causes `a.txt` to come from `Volume1` instead.

```
$ mount -t hfs -o union /dev/disk11 /tmp/union
$ mount -t hfs -o union /dev/disk10 /tmp/union
$ ls /tmp/union
a.txt    b.txt
$ cat /tmp/union/a.txt
1
```

If we wrote to `a.txt` now, it would modify only the top volume (`Volume1`). The file `b.txt` appears in the union but is present only in the bottom volume. Let us see what happens if we write to `b.txt`.

```
$ cat /tmp/union/b.txt
2
$ echo 1 > /tmp/union/b.txt
$ cat /tmp/union/b.txt
1
$ umount /dev/disk10s2      # unmount top volume (Volume1)
$ cat /tmp/union/b.txt      # check contents of b.txt in Volume2
2
```

We see that the bottom volume's `b.txt` is unchanged. Our writing to `b.txt` resulted in its creation as well, because it did not exist in the union layer we were writing to. If we delete a file that exists in the top two layers, the file in the topmost layer is deleted, and the one from the layer below shows up.

```
$ mount -t hfs -o union /dev/disk10 /tmp/union
$ cat /tmp/union/b.txt
1
```

```
$ rm /tmp/union/b.txt
$ cat /tmp/union/b.txt
2
```

> The /etc/rc startup script on the Mac OS X installer disc uses union mounting to mount RAM disks on top of directories that the installation process is likely to write to, such as /Volumes, /var/tmp, and /var/run.

11.7.19 volfs

The *volume ID* file system (volfs) is a virtual file system that exists over the VFS of another file system. It serves the needs of two different Mac OS X APIs: the POSIX API and the Carbon File Manager API. Whereas the POSIX API uses Unix-style pathnames, the Carbon API specifies a file system object by a triplet consisting of a volume ID, a containing folder ID, and a node name. volfs makes it possible to use the Carbon API atop a Unix-style file system.

By default, volfs is mounted on the /.vol directory. Each mounted volume is represented by a subdirectory under /.vol, provided the volume's file system supports volfs. HFS+ and HFS support volfs, whereas UFS does not.

> In Mac OS X versions prior to 10.4, volfs is mounted by /etc/rc during system startup. Beginning with Mac OS X 10.4, it is mounted by launchd.

```
$ mount
/dev/disk1s3 on / (local, journaled)
devfs on /dev (local)
fdesc on /dev (union)
<volfs> on /.vol
...
$ ls -li /.vol
total 0
234881029 dr-xr-xr-x   2 root  wheel  64 Oct 23 18:33 234881029
```

/.vol in this example contains only one entry, which corresponds to the root volume. In general, reading directory entries at the topmost level in a volfs instance will return a list of all mounted volumes that support volfs. Each directory's name is the decimal representation of the corresponding device number (dev_t). Given a device's major and minor numbers, the value of `dev_t` can be constructed using the `makedev()` macro.

```
// <sys/types.h>
#define makedev(x,y)    ((dev_t)(((x) << 24) | (y)))
```

Let us compute the device number of the disk in our current example and verify that its volfs entry indeed has that name.

```
$ ls -l /dev/disk1s3
brw-r-----   1 root  operator   14,   5 Oct 23 18:33 /dev/disk1s3
$ perl -e 'my $x = (14 << 24) | 5; print "$x\n"'
234881029
```

If we know a file's ID and the volume ID of its containing volume, we can access the file through volfs. As we will see in Chapter 12, a file's inode number (as reported by `ls -i`) is its HFS+ file ID in most cases. Consider a file, say, /mach_kernel:

```
$ ls -li /mach_kernel
2150438 -rw-r--r--   1 root   wheel   4308960 Jul  2 22:28 /mach_kernel
$ ls -li /.vol/234881029/2150438
2150438 -rw-r--r--   1 root   wheel   4308960 Jul  2 22:28 /.vol/234881029/2150438
```

Similarly, all files and directories within the root file system are accessible using their file IDs through volfs. However, note that volfs vnodes exist only for the root of each volume—that is, the volfs hierarchy has only two levels. Reading directory entries within a /.vol subdirectory will return only the . and .. entries. In other words, you cannot enumerate the contents of a file system through volfs—you must know the ID of the target file system object to access it through volfs.

```
$ ls -lid /usr
11061 drwxr-xr-x   11 root   wheel   374 May 11 19:18 /usr
$ ls -las /.vol/234881029/usr
ls: /.vol/234881029/usr: No such file or directory
$ ls -las /.vol/234881029/11061
total 0
0 drwxr-xr-x    11 root   wheel     374 May 11 19:18 .
0 drwxrwxr-t    39 root   admin    1428 Oct 23 18:33 ..
0 drwxr-xr-x     8 root   wheel     272 Mar 27  2005 X11R6
0 drwxr-xr-x   736 root   wheel   25024 Oct 24 15:00 bin
...
```

The /proc File System

Mac OS X does not provide the /proc file system. It does provide alternative interfaces such as sysctl(3) and the obsoleted kvm(3). The sysctl(3) interface provides read and write access to a management information base (MIB) whose contents are various categories of kernel information, such as information related to file systems, virtual memory, networking, and debugging. As we saw in Chapter 8, the kvm(3) interface provides access to raw kernel memory.

11.8 Spotlight

As the capacities of commonly available storage devices continue to grow, we find it possible to store staggering amounts of information on personal computer systems. Besides, new information is continually being generated. Unfortunately, such information is merely "bytes" unless there are powerful and efficient ways to present it to humans. In particular, one must be able to search such information. By the arrival of the twenty-first century, searching had established itself as one of the most pervasive computing technologies in the context of the Internet. In comparison, typical search mechanisms in operating systems remained primitive.

Although a single computer system is nowhere near the Internet in terms of the amount of information it contains, it is still a daunting task for users to search for information "manually." There are several reasons why it is difficult.

- Traditional file system organization, although hierarchical in nature, still requires the *user* to classify and organize information. Furthermore, as existing information is updated and new information is added, the user must incorporate such changes in the file organization. If multiple views into the data are required, they must be painfully constructed—say, through symbolic links or by replicating data. Even then, such views will be *static*.

- There are simply too many files. As more computer users adopt mostly digital lifestyles, wherein music, pictures, and movies reside on their systems along with traditional data, the average number of files on a representative personal computer will continue to grow.

- Historically, users have worked with very little file system metadata: primarily, filenames, sizes, and modification times. Even though typical file systems store additional metadata, it is mostly for storage bookkeeping— such data is neither intuitive nor very useful for everyday searching. Data particularly useful for flexible searching is often the user data *within* files (such as the text within a text document) or is best provided as additional file-specific metadata (such as an image's dimensions and color model). Traditional file systems also do not allow users to add their own metadata to files.

- In situations where several applications access or manipulate the same information, it would be beneficial for both application developers and users to have such applications share information. Although means for sharing data abound in computing, traditional APIs are rather limited in their support for sharing typed information, even on a given platform.

Memex

When Vannevar Bush was the Director of the Office of Scientific Research and Development in the United States, he published an article that described, among several visionary insights and observations, a hypothetical device Bush had conceived many years earlier—the memex.[12] The memex was a mechanized private file and library—a supplement to human memory. It would store a vast amount of information and allow for rapid searching of its contents. Bush envisioned that a user could store books, letters, records, and any other arbitrary information on the memex, whose storage capacity would be large enough. The information could be textual or graphic.

Mac OS X 10.4 introduced *Spotlight*—a system for extracting (or harvesting), storing, indexing, and querying metadata. It provides an integrated system-wide service for searching and indexing.

11.8.1 Spotlight's Architecture

Spotlight is a collection of both kernel- and user-level mechanisms. It can be divided into the following primary constituents:

- The fsevents change notification mechanism
- A per-volume metadata store
- A per-volume content index
- The Spotlight server (mds)

---

12. "As We May Think," by Vannevar Bush (*Atlantic Monthly* 176:1, July 1945, pp. 101–108).

- The mdimport and mdsync helper programs (which have symbolic links to them, mdimportserver and mdsyncserver, respectively)
- A suite of metadata importer plug-ins
- Programming interfaces, with the Metadata framework (a subframework of the Core Services umbrella framework) providing low-level access to Spotlight's functionality
- End-user interfaces, including both command-line and graphical interfaces

Figure 11–21 shows how various parts of Spotlight interact with each other.

The fsevents mechanism is an in-kernel notification system with a subscription interface for informing user-space subscribers of file system changes as they occur. Spotlight relies on this mechanism to keep its information current—it

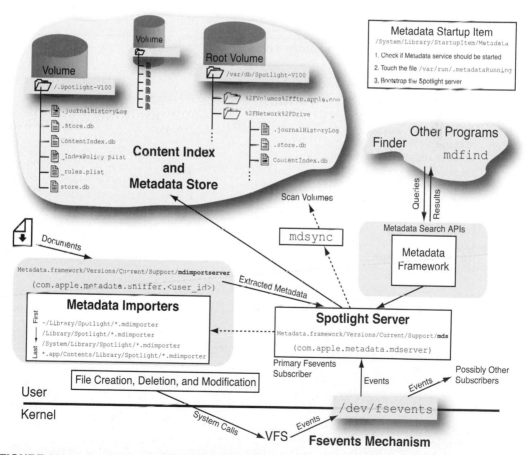

FIGURE 11–21 Architecture of the Spotlight system

updates a volume's metadata store and content index if file system objects are added, deleted, or modified. We will discuss fsevents in Section 11.8.2.

On a volume with Spotlight indexing enabled, the /.Spotlight-V100 directory contains the volume's content index (ContentIndex.db), metadata store (store.db), and other related files. The content index is built atop Apple's Search Kit technology, which provides a framework for searching and indexing text in multiple languages. The metadata store uses a specially designed database in which each file, along with its metadata attributes, is represented as an MDItem object, which is a Core Foundation–compliant object that encapsulates the metadata. The MDItemCreate() function from the Metadata framework can be used to instantiate an MDItem object corresponding to a given pathname. Thereafter, one or more attributes can be retrieved or set[13] in the MDItem by calling other Metadata framework functions. Figure 11–22 shows a program that retrieves or sets an individual attribute of the MDItem associated with a given pathname.

FIGURE 11–22 Retrieving and setting an *MDItem* attribute

```
// mditem.c

#include <getopt.h>
#include <CoreServices/CoreServices.h>

#define PROGNAME "mditem"
#define RELEASE_IF_NOT_NULL(ref) { if (ref) { CFRelease(ref); } }
#define EXIT_ON_NULL(ref)        { if (!ref) { goto out; } }

void MDItemSetAttribute(MDItemRef item, CFStringRef name, CFTypeRef value);

usage(void)
{
    fprintf(stderr, "Set or get metadata. Usage:\n\n\
    %s -g <attribute-name> <filename>                    # get\n\
    %s -s <attribute-name>=<attribute-value> <filename> # set\n",
    PROGNAME, PROGNAME);
}

int
main(int argc, char **argv)
{
    int            ch, ret = -1;
    MDItemRef      item = NULL;
```

(continues)

---

13. In Mac OS X 10.4, the functions for setting MDItem attributes are not part of the public API.

FIGURE 11–22 Retrieving and setting an *MDItem* attribute *(continued)*

```
CFStringRef        filePath = NULL, attrName = NULL;
CFTypeRef          attrValue = NULL;
char               *valuep;
CFStringEncoding   encoding = CFStringGetSystemEncoding();

if (argc != 4) {
    usage();
    goto out;
}

filePath = CFStringCreateWithCString(kCFAllocatorDefault,
                                 argv[argc - 1], encoding);
EXIT_ON_NULL(filePath);
argc--;

item = MDItemCreate(kCFAllocatorDefault, filePath);
EXIT_ON_NULL(item);

while ((ch = getopt(argc, argv, "g:s:")) != -1) {
    switch (ch) {
    case 'g':
        attrName = CFStringCreateWithCString(kCFAllocatorDefault,
                                        optarg, encoding);
        EXIT_ON_NULL(attrName);
        attrValue = MDItemCopyAttribute(item, attrName);
        EXIT_ON_NULL(attrValue);
        CFShow(attrValue);
        break;

    case 's':
        if (!(valuep = strchr(argv[optind - 1], '='))) {
            usage();
            goto out;
        }

        *valuep++ = '\0';
        attrName = CFStringCreateWithCString(kCFAllocatorDefault,
                                        optarg, encoding);
        EXIT_ON_NULL(attrName);
        attrValue = CFStringCreateWithCString(kCFAllocatorDefault,
                                        valuep, encoding);
        EXIT_ON_NULL(attrValue);
        (void)MDItemSetAttribute(item, attrName, attrValue);
        break;

    default:
        usage();
        break;
```

(continues)

FIGURE 11–22 Retrieving and setting an *MDItem* attribute *(continued)*

```
        }
    }

out:
    RELEASE_IF_NOT_NULL(attrName);
    RELEASE_IF_NOT_NULL(attrValue);
    RELEASE_IF_NOT_NULL(filePath);
    RELEASE_IF_NOT_NULL(item);

    exit(ret);
}


$ gcc -Wall -o mditem mditem.c -framework CoreServices
$ ./mditem -g kMDItemKind ~/Desktop
Folder
$ ./mditem -g kMDItemContentType ~/Desktop
public.folder
```

From a programming standpoint, an MDItem is a dictionary containing a unique abstract key, along with a value, for each metadata attribute associated with the file system object. Mac OS X provides a large number of predefined keys encompassing several types of metadata. As we will see in Section 11.8.3, we can enumerate all keys known to Spotlight by using the mdimport command-line program.

The Spotlight server—that is, the metadata server (mds)—is the primary daemon in the Spotlight subsystem. Its duties include receiving change notifications through the fsevents interface, managing the metadata store, and serving Spotlight queries. Spotlight uses a set of specialized plug-in bundles called metadata importers for extracting metadata from different types of documents, with each importer handling one or more specific document types. The mdimport program acts as a harness for running these importers. It can also be used to explicitly import metadata from a set of files. The Spotlight server also uses mdimport—specifically, a symbolic link to it (mdimportserver)—for this purpose. An importer returns metadata for a file as a set of key-value pairs, which Spotlight adds to the volume's metadata store.

Custom metadata importers must be careful in defining what constitutes metadata. Although an importer can technically store any type of information in the metadata store by simply providing it to Spotlight, storing information that is unlikely to be useful in searching (for example, thumbnails or arbitrary binary data) will be counterproductive. The Search Kit may be a better alternative for application-specific indexing. Mac OS X applications such as Address Book, Help Viewer, System Preferences, and Xcode use the Search Kit for efficient searching of application-specific information.

Spotlight versus BFS

Spotlight is sometimes compared to the metadata-indexing functionality offered by BFS—the native file system in BeOS.[14] BFS was a 64-bit journaled file system that provided native support for extended attributes. A file could have an arbitrary number of attributes that were actually stored as files within a special, internal directory associated with the file. Moreover, BFS maintained indexes for standard file system attributes (such as name and size). It also provided interfaces that could be used to create indexes for other attributes. The indexes were stored in a hidden directory that was otherwise a normal directory. The query syntax of the BFS query engine was largely identical to Spotlight's. As with Spotlight, a query could be *live* in that it could continue to report any changes to the query results.

As we will see in Chapter 12, HFS+ provides native support for extended attributes. In that light, the combination of Spotlight and HFS+ might appear similar to BFS. However, there are several important differences.

Perhaps the most important point to note is that as implemented in Mac OS X 10.4, Spotlight does not use the support for native extended attributes in HFS+. All harvested metadata—whether extracted from on-disk file structures or provided explicitly by the user (corresponding to the Spotlight Comments area in the Finder's information pane for a file or folder)—is stored externally. In particular, Spotlight itself does not modify or add any metadata, including extended attributes, to files.

In the case of BFS, the creation of indexes occurred in the file system itself. In contrast, Spotlight builds and maintains indexes entirely in user space, although it depends on the fsevents kernel-level mechanism for timely notification of file system changes.

Purely based on theoretical grounds, the BFS approach appears more optimal. However, Spotlight has the benefit of being independent of the file system—for example, it works on HFS+, UFS, MS-DOS, and even AFP volumes. Since the metadata store and the content index need not reside on the volume they are for, Spotlight can even be made to work on a read-only volume.

---

14. The comparison is especially interesting since the same engineer played key roles in the design and implementation of both BFS and Spotlight.

11.8.2 The Fsevents Mechanism

The fsevents mechanism provides the basis for Spotlight's live updating. The kernel exports the mechanism to user space through a pseudo-device (/dev/fsevents). A program interested in learning about file system changes—a *watcher* in fsevents parlance—can subscribe to the mechanism by accessing this device. Specifically, a watcher opens /dev/fsevents and *clones* the resultant descriptor using a special ioctl operation (FSEVENTS_CLONE).

> The Spotlight server is the primary subscriber of the fsevents mechanism.

The ioctl call requires a pointer to an fsevent_clone_args structure as argument. The event_list field of this structure points to an array containing up to FSE_MAX_EVENTS elements, each of which is an int8_t value indicating the watcher's interest in the event with the corresponding index. If the value is FSE_REPORT, it means the kernel should report that event type to the watcher. If the value is FSE_IGNORE, the watcher is not interested in that event type. Table 11–2 lists the various event types. If the array has fewer elements than the maxi-

TABLE 11–2 Event Types Supported by the Fsevents Mechanism

Event Index	Event Type	Description
0	FSE_CREATE_FILE	A file was created.
1	FSE_DELETE	A file or a folder was deleted.
2	FSE_STAT_CHANGED	A change was made to the stat structure—for example, an object's permissions were changed.
3	FSE_RENAME	A file or folder was renamed.
4	FSE_CONTENT_MODIFIED	A file's content was modified—specifically, a file that is being closed was written to while it was open.
5	FSE_EXCHANGE	The contents of two files were swapped through the exchangedata() system call.
6	FSE_FINDER_INFO_CHANGED	A file or folder's Finder information was changed—for example, the Finder label color was changed.
7	FSE_CREATE_DIR	A folder was created.
8	FSE_CHOWN	A file system object's ownership was changed.

mum number of event types, the watcher is implicitly disinterested in the remaining types. The `event_queue_depth` field of the `fsevent_clone_args` structure specifies the size of the per-watcher event queue (expressed as the number of events) that the kernel should allocate. This size is limited by MAX_KFS_EVENTS (2048).

> As we will shortly see, the elements of a per-watcher event queue are not the events themselves but pointers to `kfs_event` structures, which are reference-counted structures that contain the actual event data. In other words, all watchers share a single event buffer in the kernel.

```
int ret, fd, clonefd;
int8_t event_list[] = { /* FSE_REPORT or FSE_IGNORE for each event type */ }
struct fsevent_clone_args fca;
...
fd = open("/dev/fsevents", O_RDONLY);
...

fca.event_list        = event_list;
fca.num_events        = sizeof(event_list)/sizeof(int8_t);
fca.event_queue_depth = /* desired size of event queue in the kernel */
fca.fd                = &clonefd;

ret = ioctl(fd, FSEVENTS_CLONE, (char *)&fca);
...
```

Once the FSEVENTS_CLONE ioctl returns successfully, the program can close the original descriptor and read from the cloned descriptor. Note that if a watcher is interested in knowing about file system changes only on one or more specific devices, it can specify its devices of interest by using the FSEVENTS_DEVICE_FILTER ioctl on the cloned /dev/fsevents descriptor. By default, fsevents assumes that a watcher is interested in all devices.

A read call on the cloned descriptor will block until the kernel has file system changes to report. When such a read call returns successfully, the data read would contain one or more events, each encapsulated in a `kfs_event` structure. The latter contains an array of event arguments, each of which is a structure of type `kfs_event_arg_t`, containing variable-size argument data. Table 11–3 shows the various possible argument types. The argument array is always terminated by the special argument type FSE_ARG_DONE.

TABLE 11–3 Argument Types Contained in Events Reported by the Fsevents Mechanism

Event Type	Description
FSE_ARG_VNODE	A vnode pointer
FSE_ARG_STRING	A string pointer
FSE_ARG_PATH	A full pathname
FSE_ARG_INT32	A 32-bit integer
FSE_ARG_INT64	A 64-bit integer
FSE_ARG_RAW	A void pointer
FSE_ARG_INO	An inode number
FSE_ARG_UID	A user ID
FSE_ARG_DEV	A file system identifier (the first component of an fsid_t) or a device identifier (a dev_t)
FSE_ARG_MODE	A 32-bit number containing a file mode
FSE_ARG_GID	A group ID
FSE_ARG_FINFO	An argument used internally by the kernel to hold an object's device information, inode number, file mode, user ID, and group ID—translated to a sequence of individual arguments for user space
FSE_ARG_DONE	A special type (with value 0xb33f) that marks the end of a given event's argument list

```
typedef struct kfs_event_arg {
    u_int16_t       type; // argument type
    u_int16_t       len;  // size of argument data that follows this field
    ...                   // argument data
} kfs_event_arg_t;

typedef struct kfs_event {
    int32_t         type; // event type
    pid_t           pid;  // pid of the process that performed the operation
    kfs_event_arg_t args[KFS_NUM_ARGS]; // event arguments
} kfs_event;
```

Figure 11–23 shows an overview of the fsevents mechanism's implementation in the kernel. There is an fs_event_watcher structure for each subscribed watcher. The event_list field of this structure points to an array of event types. The array contains values that the watcher specified while cloning the device. The devices_to_watch field, if non-NULL, points to a list of devices the watcher is

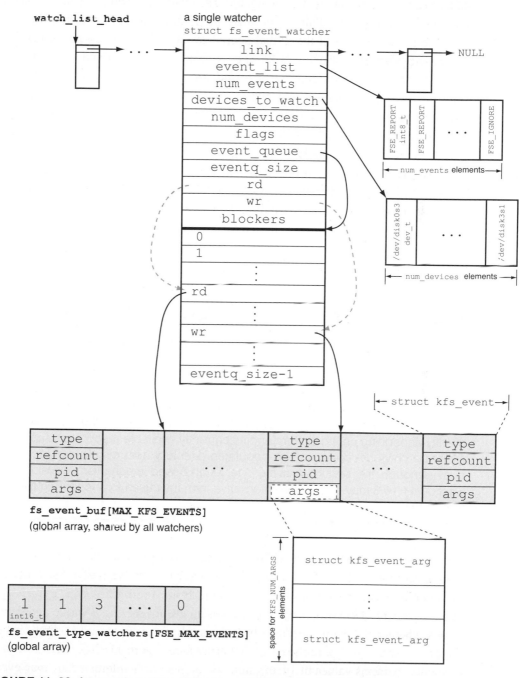

FIGURE 11–23 An overview of the fsevents mechanism's implementation

interested in. Immediately following the `fs_event_watcher` structure is the watcher's event queue—that is, an array of pointers to `kfs_event` structures, with the latter residing in the global shared event buffer (`fs_event_buf`). The `fs_event_watcher` structure's `rd` and `wr` fields act as read and write cursors, respectively. While adding an event to the watcher, if it is found that the write cursor has wrapped around and caught up with the read cursor, it means the watcher has dropped one or more events. The kernel reports dropping of events as a special event of type `FSE_EVENTS_DROPPED`, which has no arguments (except `FSE_ARG_DONE`) and contains a fake process ID of zero.

Events can also be dropped because the `fs_event_buf` global shared buffer is full, which can happen because of a slow watcher. This is a more serious condition from Spotlight's standpoint. In this case, the kernel must discard an existing event to make space for the new event being added, which means at least one watcher will not see the discarded event. To simplify implementation, the kernel delivers an `FSE_EVENTS_DROPPED` event to all watchers.

Dropped Events and Spotlight

Since events dropped from the global shared event buffer affect all subscribers, a slow subscriber can adversely affect the primary subscriber—that is, the Spotlight server. If Spotlight misses any events, it may need to scan the entire volume looking for changes that it missed.

A typical scenario in which a subscriber's slowness will manifest itself is one involving heavy file system activity, where the meaning of "heavy" may vary greatly depending on the system and its currently available resources. Unpacking a giant archive or copying a well-populated directory hierarchy is likely to cause heavy-enough file system activity. The kauth-based mechanism developed in Section 11.10.3 may be a better alternative in many cases for monitoring file system activity.

Figure 11–24 shows how events are added to the global shared event buffer. Various functions in the VFS layer call `add_fsevent()` [bsd/vfs/vfs_fsevents.c] to generate events based on the return value from `need_fsevent(type, vp)` [bsd/vfs/vfs_fsevents.c], which takes an event type and a vnode and determines whether the event needs to be generated. `need_fsevent()` first checks the `fs_event_type_watchers` global array (see Figure 11–23), each of whose elements maintains a count of the number of watchers interested in that event type. If `fs_event_type_watchers[type]` is zero, it means that an event

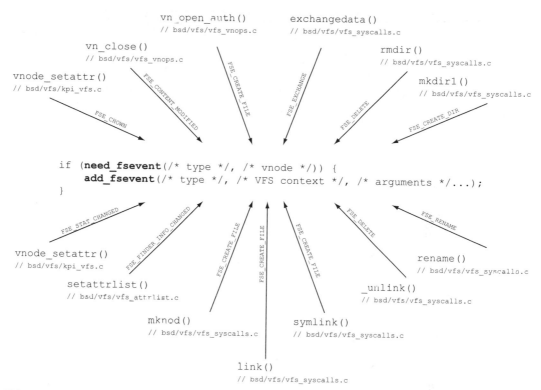

FIGURE 11–24 Event generation in the fsevents mechanism

whose type is type need not be generated, since there are no watchers interested. Fsevents uses this array as a quick check mechanism to bail out early. Next, need_fsevent() checks each watcher to see if at least one watcher wants the event type to be reported *and* is interested in the device the vnode belongs to. If there is no such watcher, the event need not be generated.

add_fsevent() expands certain kernel-internal event arguments into multiple user-visible arguments. For example, both FSE_ARG_VNODE and the kernel-only argument FSE_ARG_FINFO cause FSE_ARG_DEV, FSE_ARG_INO, FSE_ARG_MODE, FSE_ARG_UID, and FSE_ARG_GUID to be appended to the event's argument list.

We will now write a program—let us call it fslogger—that subscribes to the fsevents mechanism and displays the change notifications as they arrive from the kernel. The program will process the argument list of each event, enhance it in certain cases (e.g., by determining human-friendly names corresponding to process, user, and group identifiers), and display the result. Figure 11–25 shows the source for fslogger.

FIGURE 11–25 A file system change logger based on the fsevents mechanism

```c
// fslogger.c

#include <stdio.h>
#include <string.h>
#include <fcntl.h>
#include <stdlib.h>
#include <unistd.h>
#include <sys/ioctl.h>
#include <sys/types.h>
#include <sys/sysctl.h>
#include <sys/fsevents.h>
#include <pwd.h>
#include <grp.h>


#define PROGNAME "fslogger"


#define DEV_FSEVENTS      "/dev/fsevents" // the fsevents pseudo-device
#define FSEVENT_BUFSIZ    131072          // buffer for reading from the device
#define EVENT_QUEUE_SIZE  2048            // limited by MAX_KFS_EVENTS

// an event argument
typedef struct kfs_event_arg {
    u_int16_t  type;          // argument type
    u_int16_t  len;           // size of argument data that follows this field
    union {
        struct vnode *vp;
        char         *str;
        void         *ptr;
        int32_t       int32;
        dev_t         dev;
        ino_t         ino;
        int32_t       mode;
        uid_t         uid;
        gid_t         gid;
    } data;
} kfs_event_arg_t;


#define KFS_NUM_ARGS  FSE_MAX_ARGS

// an event
typedef struct kfs_event {
    int32_t          type; // event type
    pid_t            pid;  // pid of the process that performed the operation
    kfs_event_arg_t args[KFS_NUM_ARGS]; // event arguments
} kfs_event;

// event names
static const char *kfseNames[] = {
```

(continues)

FIGURE 11–25 A file system change logger based on the fsevents mechanism *(continued)*

```
    "FSE_CREATE_FILE",
    "FSE_DELETE",
    "FSE_STAT_CHANGED",
    "FSE_RENAME",
    "FSE_CONTENT_MODIFIED",
    "FSE_EXCHANGE",
    "FSE_FINDER_INFO_CHANGED",
    "FSE_CREATE_DIR",
    "FSE_CHOWN",
};

// argument names
static const char *kfseArgNames[] = {
    "FSE_ARG_UNKNOWN", "FSE_ARG_VNODE", "FSE_ARG_STRING", "FSE_ARGPATH",
    "FSE_ARG_INT32",   "FSE_ARG_INT64", "FSE_ARG_RAW",    "FSE_ARG_INO",
    "FSE_ARG_UID",     "FSE_ARG_DEV",   "FSE_ARG_MODE",   "FSE_ARG_GID",
    "FSE_ARG_FINFO",
};

// for pretty-printing of vnode types
enum vtype {
    VNON, VREG, VDIR, VBLK, VCHR, VLNK, VSOCK, VFIFO, VBAD, VSTR, VCPLX
};

enum vtype iftovt_tab[] = {
    VNON, VFIFO, VCHR, VNON, VDIR,  VNON, VBLK, VNON,
    VREG, VNON,  VLNK, VNON, VSOCK, VNON, VNON, VBAD,
};

static const char *vtypeNames[] = {
    "VNON",  "VREG",  "VDIR", "VBLK", "VCHR", "VLNK",
    "VSOCK", "VFIFO", "VBAD", "VSTR", "VCPLX",
};
#define VTYPE_MAX (sizeof(vtypeNames)/sizeof(char *))

static char *
get_proc_name(pid_t pid)
{
    size_t      len = sizeof(struct kinfo_proc);
    static int  name[] = { CTL_KERN, KERN_PROC, KERN_PROC_PID, 0 };
    static struct kinfo_proc kp;

    name[3] = pid;

    kp.kp_proc.p_comm[0] = '\0';
    if (sysctl((int *)name, sizeof(name)/sizeof(*name), &kp, &len, NULL, 0))
        return "?";
```

(continues)

FIGURE 11–25 A file system change logger based on the fsevents mechanism *(continued)*

```c
    if (kp.kp_proc.p_comm[0] == '\0')
        return "exited?";

    return kp.kp_proc.p_comm;
}

int
main(int argc, char **argv)
{
    int32_t arg_id;
    int     fd, clonefd = -1;
    int     i, j, eoff, off, ret;

    kfs_event_arg_t *kea;
    struct          fsevent_clone_args fca;
    char            buffer[FSEVENT_BUFSIZ];
    struct passwd   *p;
    struct group    *g;
    mode_t          va_mode;
    u_int32_t       va_type;
    u_int32_t       is_fse_arg_vnode = 0;
    char            fileModeString[11 + 1];
    int8_t          event_list[] = { // action to take for each event
                        FSE_REPORT,   // FSE_CREATE_FILE
                        FSE_REPORT,   // FSE_DELETE
                        FSE_REPORT,   // FSE_STAT_CHANGED
                        FSE_REPORT,   // FSE_RENAME
                        FSE_REPORT,   // FSE_CONTENT_MODIFIED
                        FSE_REPORT,   // FSE_EXCHANGE
                        FSE_REPORT,   // FSE_FINDER_INFO_CHANGED
                        FSE_REPORT,   // FSE_CREATE_DIR
                        FSE_REPORT,   // FSE_CHOWN
                    };

    if (argc != 1) {
        fprintf(stderr, "%s accepts no arguments. It must be run as root.\n",
                PROGNAME);
        exit(1);
    }

    if (geteuid() != 0) {
        fprintf(stderr, "You must be root to run %s. Try again using 'sudo'.\n",
                PROGNAME);
        exit(1);
    }

    setbuf(stdout, NULL);

    if ((fd = open(DEV_FSEVENTS, O_RDONLY)) < 0) {
        perror("open");
```

(continues)

FIGURE 11–25 A file system change logger based on the fsevents mechanism *(continued)*

```
        exit(1);
    }

    fca.event_list = (int8_t *)event_list;
    fca.num_events = sizeof(event_list)/sizeof(int8_t);
    fca.event_queue_depth = EVENT_QUEUE_SIZE;
    fca.fd = &clonefd;
    if ((ret = ioctl(fd, FSEVENTS_CLONE, (char *)&fca)) < 0) {
        perror("ioctl");
        close(fd);
        exit(1);
    }

    close(fd);
    printf("fsevents device cloned (fd %d)\nfslogger ready\n", clonefd);

    while (1) { // event-processing loop

        if ((ret = read(clonefd, buffer, FSEVENT_BUFSIZ)) > 0)
            printf("=> received %d bytes\n", ret);

        off = 0;

        while (off < ret) { // process one or more events received

            struct kfs_event *kfse = (struct kfs_event *)((char *)buffer + off);

            off += sizeof(int32_t) + sizeof(pid_t); // type + pid

            if (kfse->type == FSE_EVENTS_DROPPED) { // special event
                printf("# Event\n");
                printf("  %-14s = %s\n", "type", "EVENTS DROPPED");
                printf("  %-14s = %d\n", "pid", kfse->pid);
                off += sizeof(u_int16_t); // FSE_ARG_DONE: sizeof(type)
                continue;
            }

            if ((kfse->type < FSE_MAX_EVENTS) && (kfse->type >= -1)) {
                printf("# Event\n");
                printf("  %-14s = %s\n", "type", kfseNames[kfse->type]);
            } else { // should never happen
                printf("This may be a program bug (type = %d).\n", kfse->type);
                exit(1);
            }

            printf("  %-14s = %d (%s)\n", "pid", kfse->pid,
                    get_proc_name(kfse->pid));
            printf("  # Details\n    # %-14s%4s  %s\n", "type", "len", "data");
```

(continues)

FIGURE 11–25 A file system change logger based on the fsevents mechanism *(continued)*

```c
kea = kfse->args;
i = 0;

while ((off < ret) && (i <= FSE_MAX_ARGS)) { // process arguments

    i++;

    if (kea->type == FSE_ARG_DONE) { // no more arguments
        printf("    %s (%#x)\n", "FSE_ARG_DONE", kea->type);
        off += sizeof(u_int16_t);
        break;
    }

    eoff = sizeof(kea->type) + sizeof(kea->len) + kea->len;
    off += eoff;

    arg_id = (kea->type > FSE_MAX_ARGS) ? 0 : kea->type;
    printf("    %-16s%4hd  ", kfseArgNames[arg_id], kea->len);

    switch (kea->type) { // handle based on argument type

    case FSE_ARG_VNODE:  // a vnode (string) pointer
        is_fse_arg_vnode = 1;
        printf("%-6s = %s\n", "path", (char *)&(kea->data.vp));
        break;

    case FSE_ARG_STRING: // a string pointer
        printf("%-6s = %s\n", "string", (char *)&(kea->data.str));
        break;

    case FSE_ARG_INT32:
        printf("%-6s = %d\n", "int32", kea->data.int32);
        break;

    case FSE_ARG_RAW: // a void pointer
        printf("%-6s = ", "ptr");
        for (j = 0; j < kea->len; j++)
            printf("%02x ", ((char *)kea->data.ptr)[j]);
        printf("\n");
        break;

    case FSE_ARG_INO: // an inode number
        printf("%-6s = %d\n", "ino", kea->data.ino);
        break;

    case FSE_ARG_UID: // a user ID
        p = getpwuid(kea->data.uid);
        printf("%-6s = %d (%s)\n", "uid", kea->data.uid,
               (p) ? p->pw_name : "?");
        break;
```

(continues)

FIGURE 11–25 A file system change logger based on the fsevents mechanism *(continued)*

```
            case FSE_ARG_DEV: // a file system ID or a device number
                if (is_fse_arg_vnode) {
                    printf("%-6s = %#08x\n", "fsid", kea->data.dev);
                    is_fse_arg_vnode = 0;
                } else {
                    printf("%-6s = %#08x (major %u, minor %u)\n",
                            "dev", kea->data.dev,
                            major(kea->data.dev), minor(kea->data.dev));
                }
                break;

            case FSE_ARG_MODE: // a combination of file mode and file type
                va_mode = (kea->data.mode & 0x0000ffff);
                va_type = (kea->data.mode & 0xfffff000);
                strmode(va_mode, fileModeString);
                va_type = iftovt_tab[(va_type & S_IFMT) >> 12];
                printf("%-6s = %s (%#08x, vnode type %s)\n", "mode",
                        fileModeString, kea->data.mode,
                        (va_type < VTYPE_MAX) ?  vtypeNames[va_type] : "?");
                break;

            case FSE_ARG_GID: // a group ID
                g = getgrgid(kea->data.gid);
                printf("%-6s = %d (%s)\n", "gid", kea->data.gid,
                        (g) ? g->gr_name : "?");
                break;

            default:
                printf("%-6s = ?\n", "unknown");
                break;
            }

            kea = (kfs_event_arg_t *)((char *)kea + eoff); // next
        } // for each argument
      } // for each event
    } // forever

    close(clonefd);

    exit(0);
}
```

Since `fslogger.c` includes `bsd/sys/fsevents.h`, a kernel-only header file, you need the kernel source to compile `fslogger`.

```
$ gcc -Wall -I /path/to/xnu/bsd/ -o fslogger fslogger.c
$ sudo ./fslogger
fsevents device cloned (fd 5)
fslogger ready
...
        # another shell
        $ touch /tmp/file.txt
=> received 76 bytes
# Event
  type          = FSE_CREATE_FILE
  pid           = 5838 (touch)
  # Details
    # type        len  data
    FSE_ARG_VNODE  22  path  = /private/tmp/file.txt
    FSE_ARG_DEV     4  fsid  = 0xe000005
    FSE_ARG_INO     4  ino   = 3431141
    FSE_ARG_MODE    4  mode  = -rw-r--r--  (0x0081a4, vnode type VREG)
    FSE_ARG_UID     4  uid   = 501 (amit)
    FSE_ARG_GID     4  gid   = 0 (wheel)
    FSE_ARG_DONE (0xb33f)
        $ chmod 600 /tmp/file.txt
=> received 76 bytes
# Event
  type          = FSE_STAT_CHANGED
  pid           = 5840 (chmod)
  # Details
    # type        len  data
    FSE_ARG_VNODE  22  path  = /private/tmp/file.txt
    FSE_ARG_DEV     4  fsid  = 0xe000005
    FSE_ARG_INO     4  ino   = 3431141
    FSE_ARG_MODE    4  mode  = -rw-------  (0x008180, vnode type VREG)
    FSE_ARG_UID     4  uid   = 501 (amit)
    FSE_ARG_GID     4  gid   = 0 (wheel)
    FSE_ARG_DONE (0xb33f)
...
```

11.8.3 Importing Metadata

Spotlight metadata includes both conventional file system metadata and other metadata that resides within files. The latter must be explicitly extracted (or harvested) from files. The extraction process must deal with different file formats and must choose what to use as metadata. For example, a metadata extractor for text files may first have to deal with multiple text encodings. Next, it may construct a list of textual keywords—perhaps even a full content index—based on the file's content. Given that there are simply too many file formats, Spotlight uses a suite of *metadata importers* for metadata extraction, distributing work among

individual plug-ins, each of which handles one or more specific types of documents. Mac OS X includes importer plug-ins for several common document
types. The `mdimport` command-line program can be used to display the list of
installed Spotlight importers.

```
$ mdimport -L
...
    "/System/Library/Spotlight/Image.mdimporter",
    "/System/Library/Spotlight/Audio.mdimporter",
    "/System/Library/Spotlight/Font.mdimporter",
    "/System/Library/Spotlight/PS.mdimporter",
...
    "/System/Library/Spotlight/Chat.mdimporter",
    "/System/Library/Spotlight/SystemPrefs.mdimporter",
    "/System/Library/Spotlight/iCal.mdimporter"
)
```

> In a given Mac OS X file system domain, Spotlight plug-ins reside in
> the `Library/Spotlight/` directory. An application bundle can also
> contain importer plug-ins for the application's document types.

An importer plug-in claims document types it wishes to handle by specifying their content types in its bundle's `Info.plist` file.

```
$ cat /System/Library/Spotlight/Image.mdimporter/Contents/Info.plist
...
                        <key>LSItemContentTypes</key>
                        <array>
                                <string>public.jpeg</string>
                                <string>public.tiff</string>
                                <string>public.png</string>
                                ...
                                <string>com.adobe.raw-image</string>
                                <string>com.adobe.photoshop-image</string>
                        </array>
...
```

You can also use the `lsregister` support tool from the Launch Services
framework to dump the contents of the global Launch Services database and
therefore view the document types claimed by a metadata importer.

Mac OS X provides a simple interface for implementing metadata importer
plug-ins. An importer plug-in bundle must implement the `GetMetadataForFile()`
function, which should read the given file, extract metadata from it, and populate
the provided dictionary with the appropriate attribute key-value pairs.

> If multiple importer plug-ins claim a document type, Spotlight will choose the one that matches a given document's UTI most closely. In any case, Spotlight will run only one metadata importer for a given file.

```
Boolean
GetMetaDataForFile(
    void                    *thisInterface, // the CFPlugin object that is called
    CFMutableDictionaryRef  attributes,     // to be populated with metadata
    CFStringRef             contentTypeUTI, // the file's content type
    CFStringRef             pathToFile);    // the full path to the file
```

It is possible for an importer to be called to harvest metadata from a large number of files—say, if a volume's metadata store is being regenerated or being created for the first time. Therefore, importers should use minimal computing resources. It is also a good idea for an importer to perform file I/O that bypasses the buffer cache; this way, the buffer cache will not be polluted because of the one-time reads generated by the importer.

> Unbuffered I/O can be enabled on a per-file level using the F_NOCACHE file control operation with the `fcntl()` system call. The Carbon File Manager API provides the `noCacheMask` constant to request that the data in a given read or write request not be cached.

Once the metadata store is populated for a volume, file system changes will typically be incorporated practically immediately by Spotlight, courtesy of the fsevents mechanism. However, it is possible for Spotlight to miss change notifications. The metadata store can become out of date in other situations as well—for example, if the volume is written by an older version of Mac OS X or by another operating system. In such cases, Spotlight will need to run the indexing process to bring the store up to date. Note that Spotlight does not serve queries while the indexing process is running, although the volume can be written normally during this time, and the resultant file system changes *will* be captured by the indexing process as it runs.

> The Spotlight server does not index temporary files residing in the `/tmp` directory. It also does not index any directory whose name contains the `.noindex` or `.build` suffixes—Xcode uses the latter type for storing files (other than targets) generated during a project build.

11.8.4 Querying Spotlight

Spotlight provides several ways for end users and programmers to query files and folders based on several types of metadata: importer-harvested metadata, conventional file system metadata, and file content (in the case of files whose content has been indexed by Spotlight). The Mac OS X user interface integrates Spotlight querying in the menu bar and the Finder. For example, a Spotlight search can be initiated by clicking on the Spotlight icon in the menu bar and typing a search string. Clicking on Show All in the list of search results—if any—brings up the dedicated Spotlight search window. Programs can also launch the search window to display results of searching for a given string. Figure 11–26 shows an example.

FIGURE 11–26 Programmatically launching the Spotlight search window

```
// spotlightit.c

#include <Carbon/Carbon.h>

#define PROGNAME "spotlightit"

int
main(int argc, char **argv)
{
    OSStatus status;
    CFStringRef searchString;

    if (argc != 2) {
        fprintf(stderr, "usage: %s <search string>\n", PROGNAME);
        return 1;
    }

    searchString = CFStringCreateWithCString(kCFAllocatorDefault, argv[1],
                                             kCFStringEncodingUTF8);
    status = HISearchWindowShow(searchString, kNilOptions);
    CFRelease(searchString);

    return (int)status;
}


$ gcc -Wall -o spotlightit spotlightit.c -framework Carbon
$ ./spotlightit "my query string"
...
```

The MDQuery API is the primary interface for programmatically querying the Spotlight metadata store. It is a low-level procedural interface based on the MDQuery object, which is a Core Foundation–compliant object.

Cocoa and Spotlight

Mac OS X also provides an Objective-C-based API for accessing the Spotlight metadata store. The `NSMetadataQuery` class, which supports Cocoa bindings, provides methods for creating a query, setting the search scope, setting query attributes, running the query, and retrieving query results. It is a higher-level object-oriented wrapper[15] around the MDQuery API. The `NSMetadataItem` class encapsulates a file's associated metadata. Other relevant classes are `NSMetadataQuery-AttributeValueTuple` and `NSMetadataQueryResultGroup`.

A single query expression is of the following form:

```
metadata_attribute_name operator "value"[modifier]
```

`metadata_attribute_name` is the name of an attribute known to Spotlight—it can be a built-in attribute or one defined by a third-party metadata importer. The `mdimport` command can be used to enumerate all attributes available in the user's context.[16]

```
$ mdimport -A
...
'kMDItemAuthors'        'Authors'         'Authors of this item'
'kMDItemBitsPerSample'  'Bits per sample' 'Number of bits per sample'
'kMDItemCity'           'City'            'City of the item'
...
'kMDItemCopyright'      'Copyright'       'Copyright information about this item'
...
'kMDItemURL'            'Url'             'Url of this item'
'kMDItemVersion'        'Version'         'Version number of this item'
'kMDItemVideoBitRate'   'Video bit rate'  'Bit rate of the video in the media'
...
```

> Note that the predefined metadata attributes include both generic (such as `kMDItemVersion`) and format-specific (such as `kMDItemVideoBitRate`) attributes.

`operator` can be one of the standard comparison operators, namely, `==`, `!=`, `<`, `>`, `<=`, and `>=`.

---

15. `NSMetadataQuery` does not support synchronous queries in Mac OS X 10.4. Moreover, as query results are collected, it provides only minimal feedback through notifications.

16. If a metadata importer is installed locally in a user's home directory, any attributes it defines will not be seen by other users.

value is the attribute's value, with any single- or double-quote characters escaped using the backslash character. An asterisk in a value string is treated as a wildcard character. value can be optionally followed by a modifier consisting of one or more of the following characters.

- c specifies case-insensitive comparison.
- d specifies that diacritical marks should be ignored in the comparison.
- w specifies word-based comparison, with the definition of a "word" including transitions from lowercase to uppercase (e.g., "process"wc will match "GetProcessInfo")

Multiple query expressions can be combined using the && and || logical operators. Moreover, parentheses can be used for grouping.

Figure 11–27 shows an overview of a representative use of the MDQuery API. Note that a query normally runs in two phases. The initial phase is a results-gathering phase, wherein the metadata store is searched for files that match the given query. During this phase, progress notifications are sent to the caller depending on the values of the query's batching parameters, which can be configured using MDQueryBatchingParams(). Once the initial phase has finished, another notification is sent to the caller. Thereafter, the query continues to run if it has been configured for live updates, in which case the caller will be notified if the query's results change because of files being created, deleted, or modified.

FIGURE 11–27 Pseudocode for creating and running a Spotlight query using the *MDQuery* interface

```
void
notificationCallback(...)
{
    if (notificationType == kMDQueryProgressNotification) {

        // Query's result list has changed during the initial
        // result-gathering phase

    } else if (notificationType == kMDQueryDidFinishNotification) {

        // Query has finished with the initial result-gathering phase
        // Disable updates by calling MDQueryDisableUpdates()
        // Process results
        // Reenable updates by calling MDQueryEnableUpdates()

    } else if (notificationType == kMDQueryDidUpdateNotification) {
```

(continues)

FIGURE 11–27 Pseudocode for creating and running a Spotlight query using the *MDQuery* interface *(continued)*

```
            // Query's result list has changed during the live-update phase
        }
    }


int
main(...)
{
    // Compose query string (a CFStringRef) to represent search expression

    // Create MDQueryRef from query string by calling MDQueryCreate()

    // Register notification callback with the process-local notification center

    // Optionally set batching parameters by calling MDQuerySetBatchingParameters()

    // Optionally set the search scope by calling MDQuerySetSearchScope()

    // Optionally set callback functions for one or more of the following:
    //      * Creating the result objects of the query
    //      * Creating the value objects of the query
    //      * Sorting the results of the query

    // Execute the query and start the run loop
}
```

Let us write a program that uses the MDQuery API to execute a raw query and displays the results. The Finder's Smart Folders feature works by saving the corresponding search specification as a raw query in an XML file with a .savedSearch extension. When such a file is opened, the Finder displays the results of the query within. We will include support in our program for listing the contents of a smart folder—that is, we will parse the XML file to retrieve the raw query.

Figure 11–28 shows the program—it is based on the template from Figure 11–27.

> Technically, the program in Figure 11–28 does not necessarily list the contents of a smart folder—it only executes the raw query corresponding to the smart folder. The folder's contents will be different from the query's result if the XML file contains additional search criteria—say, for limiting search results to the user's home directory. We can extend the program to apply such criteria if it exists.

FIGURE 11–28 A program for executing raw Spotlight queries

```
// lsmdquery.c

#include <unistd.h>
#include <sys/stat.h>
#include <CoreServices/CoreServices.h>

#define PROGNAME "lsmdquery"

void
exit_usage(void)
{
    fprintf(stderr, "usage: %s -f <smart folder path>\n"
                    "       %s -q <query string>\n", PROGNAME, PROGNAME);
    exit(1);
}

void
printDictionaryAsXML(CFDictionaryRef dict)
{
    CFDataRef xml = CFPropertyListCreateXMLData(kCFAllocatorDefault,
                                                (CFPropertyListRef)dict);
    if (!xml)
        return;

    write(STDOUT_FILENO, CFDataGetBytePtr(xml), (size_t)CFDataGetLength(xml));
    CFRelease(xml);
}

void
notificationCallback(CFNotificationCenterRef  center,
                     void                    *observer,
                     CFStringRef              name,
                     const void              *object,
                     CFDictionaryRef          userInfo)
{
    CFDictionaryRef attributes;
    CFArrayRef      attributeNames;
    CFIndex         idx, count;
    MDItemRef       itemRef = NULL;
    MDQueryRef      queryRef = (MDQueryRef)object;

    if (CFStringCompare(name, kMDQueryDidFinishNotification, 0)
            == kCFCompareEqualTo) { // gathered results
        // disable updates, process results, and reenable updates
        MDQueryDisableUpdates(queryRef);
        count = MDQueryGetResultCount(queryRef);
        if (count > 0) {
            for (idx = 0; idx < count; idx++) {
                itemRef = (MDItemRef)MDQueryGetResultAtIndex(queryRef, idx);
```

(continues)

FIGURE 11–28 A program for executing raw Spotlight queries *(continued)*

```
                attributeNames = MDItemCopyAttributeNames(itemRef);
                attributes = MDItemCopyAttributes(itemRef, attributeNames);
                printDictionaryAsXML(attributes);
                CFRelease(attributes);
                CFRelease(attributeNames);
            }
            printf("\n%ld results total\n", count);
        }
        MDQueryEnableUpdates(queryRef);
    } else if (CFStringCompare(name, kMDQueryDidUpdateNotification, 0)
                == kCFCompareEqualTo) { // live update
        CFShow(name), CFShow(object), CFShow(userInfo);
    }
    // ignore kMDQueryProgressNotification
}


CFStringRef
ExtractRawQueryFromSmartFolder(const char *folderpath)
{
    int                 fd, ret;
    struct stat         sb;
    UInt8               *bufp;
    CFMutableDataRef    xmlData  = NULL;
    CFPropertyListRef   pList    = NULL;
    CFStringRef         rawQuery = NULL, errorString = NULL;

    if ((fd = open(folderpath, O_RDONLY)) < 0) {
        perror("open");
        return NULL;
    }

    if ((ret = fstat(fd, &sb)) < 0) {
        perror("fstat");
        goto out;
    }

    if (sb.st_size <= 0) {
        fprintf(stderr, "no data in smart folder (%s)?\n", folderpath);
        goto out;
    }

    xmlData = CFDataCreateMutable(kCFAllocatorDefault, (CFIndex)sb.st_size);
    if (xmlData == NULL) {
        fprintf(stderr, "CFDataCreateMutable() failed\n");
        goto out;
    }
    CFDataIncreaseLength(xmlData, (CFIndex)sb.st_size);
```

(continues)

FIGURE 11-28 A program for executing raw Spotlight queries *(continued)*

```
        bufp = CFDataGetMutableBytePtr(xmlData);
        if (bufp == NULL) {
            fprintf(stderr, "CFDataGetMutableBytePtr() failed\n");
            goto out;
        }
        ret = read(fd, (void *)bufp, (size_t)sb.st_size);

        pList = CFPropertyListCreateFromXMLData(kCFAllocatorDefault,
                                      xmlData,
                                      kCFPropertyListImmutable,
                                      &errorString);
        if (pList == NULL) {
            fprintf(stderr, "CFPropertyListCreateFromXMLData() failed (%s)\n",
                    CFStringGetCStringPtr(errorString, kCFStringEncodingASCII));
            CFRelease(errorString);
            goto out;
        }

        rawQuery = CFDictionaryGetValue(pList, CFSTR("RawQuery"));
        CFRetain(rawQuery);
        if (rawQuery == NULL) {
            fprintf(stderr, "failed to retrieve query from smart folder\n");
            goto out;
        }

out:
    close(fd);

    if (pList)
        CFRelease(pList);
    if (xmlData)
        CFRclease(xmlData);

    return rawQuery;
}

int
main(int argc, char **argv)
{
    int                     i;
    CFStringRef             rawQuery = NULL;
    MDQueryRef              queryRef;
    Boolean                 result;
    CFNotificationCenterRef localCenter;
    MDQueryBatchingParams   batchingParams;

    while ((i = getopt(argc, argv, "f:q:")) != -1) {
        switch (i) {
```

(continues)

FIGURE 11–28 A program for executing raw Spotlight queries *(continued)*

```
        case 'f':
            rawQuery = ExtractRawQueryFromSmartFolder(optarg);
            break;
        case 'q':
            rawQuery = CFStringCreateWithCString(kCFAllocatorDefault, optarg,
                                                CFStringGetSystemEncoding());
            break;

        default:
            exit_usage();
            break;
        }
    }

    if (!rawQuery)
        exit_usage();

    queryRef = MDQueryCreate(kCFAllocatorDefault, rawQuery, NULL, NULL);
    if (queryRef == NULL)
        goto out;

    if (!(localCenter = CFNotificationCenterGetLocalCenter())) {
        fprintf(stderr, "failed to access local notification center\n");
        goto out;
    }

    CFNotificationCenterAddObserver(
        localCenter,            // process-local center
        NULL,                   // observer
        notificationCallback,   // to process query finish/update notifications
        NULL,                   // observe all notifications
        (void *)queryRef,       // observe notifications for this object
        CFNotificationSuspensionBehaviorDeliverImmediately);

    // maximum number of results that can accumulate and the maximum number
    // of milliseconds that can pass before various notifications are sent
    batchingParams.first_max_num    = 1000; // first progress notification
    batchingParams.first_max_ms     = 1000;
    batchingParams.progress_max_num = 1000; // additional progress notifications
    batchingParams.progress_max_ms  = 1000;
    batchingParams.update_max_num   = 1;    // update notification
    batchingParams.update_max_ms    = 1000;
    MDQuerySetBatchingParameters(queryRef, batchingParams);

    // go execute the query
    if ((result = MDQueryExecute(queryRef, kMDQueryWantsUpdates)) == TRUE)
        CFRunLoopRun();
```

(continues)

FIGURE 11–28 A program for executing raw Spotlight queries *(continued)*

```
out:
    CFRelease(rawQuery);
    if (queryRef)
        CFRelease(queryRef);

    exit(0);
}
```

```
$ gcc -Wall -o lsmdquery lsmdquery.c -framework CoreServices
$ ./lsmdquery -f ~/Desktop/AllPDFs.savedSearch # assuming this smart folder exists
...
        <key>kMDItemFSName</key>
        <string>gimpprint.pdf</string>
        <key>kMDItemFSNodeCount</key>
        <integer>0</integer>
        <key>kMDItemFSOwnerGroupID</key>
        <integer>501</integer>
...
```

11.8.5 Spotlight Command-Line Tools

Mac OS X provides a set of command-line programs for accessing Spotlight's functionality. Let us look at a summary of these tools.

mdutil is used to manage the Spotlight metadata store for a given volume. In particular, it can enable or disable Spotlight indexing on a volume, including volumes corresponding to disk images and external disks.

mdimport can be used to explicitly trigger importing of file hierarchies into the metadata store. It is also useful for displaying information about the Spotlight system.

- The -A option lists all metadata attributes, along with their localized names and descriptions, known to Spotlight.

- The -X option prints the metadata schema for the built-in UTI types.

- The -L option displays a list of installed metadata importers.

mdcheckschema is used to validate the given schema file—typically one belonging to a metadata importer.

mdfind searches the metadata store given a query string, which can be either a plain string or a raw query expression. Moreover, mdfind can be instructed through its `-onlyin` option to limit the search to a given directory. If the `-live` option is specified, `mdfind` continues running in live-update mode, printing the updated number of files that match the query.

`mdls` retrieves and displays all metadata attributes for the given file.

11.8.6 Overcoming Granularity Limitations

An important aspect of Spotlight is that it works at the *file* level—that is, the results of Spotlight queries are files, not locations or records within files. For example, even if a database has a Spotlight importer that can extract per-record information from the database's on-disk files, all queries that refer to records in a given file will result in a reference to that file. This is problematic for applications that do not store their searchable information as individual files. The Safari web browser, the Address Book application, and the iCal application are good examples.

- Safari stores its bookmarks in a single property list file (`~/Library/Safari/Bookmarks.plist`).

- Address Book stores its data in a single data file (`~/Library/Application Support/AddressBook/AddressBook.data`). It also uses two Search Kit index files (`ABPerson.skIndexInverted` and `ABSubscribedPerson.skIndexInverted`).

- iCal maintains a directory for each calendar (`~/Library/Application Support/iCal/Sources/<UUID>.calendar`). Within each such directory, it maintains an index file for calendar events.

Nevertheless, Safari bookmarks, Address Book contacts, and iCal events appear in Spotlight search results as clickable entities. This is made possible by storing individual files for each of these entities and indexing *these files* instead of the monolithic index or data files.

```
$ ls ~/Library/Caches/Metadata/Safari/
...
A182FB56-AE27-11D9-A9B1-000D932C9040.webbookmark
A182FC00-AE27-11D9-A9B1-000D932C9040.webbookmark
...
$ ls ~/Library/Caches/com.apple.AddressBook/MetaData/
...
6F67C0E4-F19B-4D81-82F2-F527F45D6C74:ABPerson.abcdp
80C4CD5C-F9AE-4667-85D2-999461B8E0B4:ABPerson.abcdp
...
$ ls ~/Library/Caches/Metadata/iCal/<UUID>/
```

```
...
49C9A25D-52A3-46A7-BAAC-C33D8DC56C36%2F-.icalevent
940DE117-47DB-495C-84C6-47AF2D68664F%2F-.icalevent
...
```

The corresponding UTIs for the `.webbookmark`, `.abcdp`, and `.icalevent` files are `com.apple.safari.bookmark`, `com.apple.addressbook.person`, and `com.apple.ical.bookmark`, respectively. The UTIs are claimed by the respective applications. Therefore, when such a file appears in Spotlight results, clicking on the result item launches the appropriate application.

Note, however, that unlike normal search results, we do not see the *filename* of an Address Book contact in the Spotlight result list. The same holds for Safari bookmarks and iCal events. This is because the files in question have a special metadata attribute named `kMDItemDisplayName`, which is set by the metadata importers to user-friendly values such as contact names and bookmark titles. You can see the filenames if you search for these entities using the `mdfind` command-line program.

```
$ mdfind 'kMDItemContentType == com.apple.addressbook.person && kMDItemDisplayName
== "Amit Singh"'
/Users/amit/Library/Caches/com.apple.AddressBook/Metadata/<UUID>;ABPerson.abcdp
$ mdls /Users/amit/Library/Caches/com.apple.AddressBook/Metadata/<UUID>:
ABPerson.abcdp
...
kMDItemDisplayName                = "Amit Singh"
...
kMDItemKind                       = "Address Book Person Data"
...
kMDItemTitle                      = "Amit Singh"
```

11.9 Access Control Lists

An access control list (ACL) is an ordered list of access control entries (ACEs). ACLs represent a popular implementation approach[17] to the access control mechanism based on the *Access Matrix* model. In this model, we have the following entities:

- *Objects*, which are resources (such as files) that must be accessed in a protected manner

---

17. Another common approach is the one using *capability lists*.

- *Subjects*, which are active entities (such as user processes) that access objects
- *Rights*, which represent operations (such as read, write, and delete) on objects

An ACL enumerates through its ACEs which objects may or may not access a particular object for one or more rights. As we will see in Section 11.10, ACLs are evaluated by the *kauth* subsystem in the kernel. Evaluation begins at the first ACE in the list, which may theoretically contain any number of ACEs. The request is denied if an ACE denies any of the requested rights; the remaining ACEs, if any, are not considered. Conversely, the request is granted if all requested rights are satisfied by the ACEs evaluated so far—again, the remaining ACEs are not considered.

> The Mac OS X `chmod` command can be used to insert or delete an ACE at a specific position in an ACL.

The Mac OS X ACL implementation requires extended attributes to be supported in the file system. As we will see in Chapter 12, HFS+, which has native support for extended attributes, stores an ACL as the attribute data of a special attribute named `com.apple.system.Security`. Before ACLs can be used on an HFS+ volume, they must be enabled on the volume—either through the `fsaclctl` command-line program or, programmatically, by using the `HFS_SET-ACLSTATE` file system control operation.

```
...
int      ret;
char     volume_path[...];
u_int32_t aclstate = 1; // 1 enables, 0 disables
...

// HFS_SETACLSTATE is defined in bsd/hfs/hfs_fsctl.h
ret = fsctl(volume_path, HFS_SETACLSTATE, (void *)aclstate, 0);
...
```

The system library implements the POSIX.1e ACL security API, which is documented in the `acl(3)` manual page. Figure 11–29 shows a program that—given a file (or folder) pathname—uses the `acl(3)` API to create an ACL, add an entry to it that denies deletion of that file to the calling user, and associate the ACL with the file.

FIGURE 11–29 A program to create and set an ACL

```
// aclset.c

#include <stdio.h>
#include <stdlib.h>
#include <unistd.h>
#include <sys/acl.h>
#include <membership.h>

#define PROGNAME "aclset"

#define EXIT_ON_ERROR(msg, retval) if (retval) { perror(msg); exit((retval)); }

int
main(int argc, char **argv)
{
    int         ret, acl_count = 4;
    acl_t       acl;
    acl_entry_t acl_entry;
    acl_permset_t acl_permset;
    acl_perm_t  acl_perm;
    uuid_t      uu;

    if (argc != 2) {
        fprintf(stderr, "usage: %s <file>\n", PROGNAME);
        exit(1);
    }

    // translate Unix user ID to UUID
    ret = mbr_uid_to_uuid(getuid(), uu);
    EXIT_ON_ERROR("mbr_uid_to_uuid", ret);

    // allocate and initialize working storage for an ACL with acl_count entries
    if ((acl = acl_init(acl_count)) == (acl_t)NULL) {
        perror("acl_init");
        exit(1);
    }

    // create a new ACL entry in the given ACL
    ret = acl_create_entry(&acl, &acl_entry);
    EXIT_ON_ERROR("acl_create_entry", ret);

    // retrieve descriptor to the permission set in the given ACL entry
    ret = acl_get_permset(acl_entry, &acl_permset);
    EXIT_ON_ERROR("acl_get_permset", ret);

    // a permission
    acl_perm = ACL_DELETE;
```

(continues)

FIGURE 11–29 A program to create and set an ACL *(continued)*

```
    // add the permission to the given permission set
    ret = acl_add_perm(acl_permset, acl_perm);
    EXIT_ON_ERROR("acl_add_perm", ret);

    // set the permissions of the given ACL entry to those contained in this set
    ret = acl_set_permset(acl_entry, acl_permset);
    EXIT_ON_ERROR("acl_set_permset", ret);

    // set the tag type (we want to deny delete permissions)
    ret = acl_set_tag_type(acl_entry,  ACL_EXTENDED_DENY);
    EXIT_ON_ERROR("acl_set_tag_type", ret);

    // set qualifier (in the case of ACL_EXTENDED_DENY, this should be a uuid_t)
    ret = acl_set_qualifier(acl_entry, (const void *)uu);
    EXIT_ON_ERROR("acl_set_qualifier", ret);

    // associate the ACL with the file
    ret = acl_set_file(argv[1], ACL_TYPE_EXTENDED, acl);
    EXIT_ON_ERROR("acl_set_file", ret);

    // free ACL working space
    ret = acl_free((void *)acl);
    EXIT_ON_ERROR("acl_free", ret);

    exit(0);
}


$ gcc -Wall -o aclset aclset.c
$ touch /tmp/file.txt
$ ls -le /tmp/file.txt
-rw-r--r-- + 1 amit   wheel   0 Oct 22 01:49 /tmp/file.txt
 0: user:amit deny delete
$ rm /tmp/file.txt
rm: /tmp/file.txt: Permission denied
$ sudo rm /tmp/file.txt
$
```

Figure 11–29 illustrates numerous steps involved in manipulating ACLs. However, you can achieve the same effect as the program with a single chmod command line:

```
$ chmod +a '<username> deny delete' <pathname>
```

The acl_set_file() function, which is implemented in the system library, internally uses an extended version of the chmod() system call to set the ACL. Given an ACL, it performs the following operations:

- Creates a file security descriptor object (filesec_t) by calling filesec_init()

- Adds the ACL to the security descriptor by calling filesec_set_security()

- Calls chmodx_np() with the security descriptor as an argument (note that np stands for nonportable—chmodx_np() invokes the extended chmod() system call)

Besides chmod(), several other system calls were extended in Mac OS X 10.4 to add support for ACLs—for example, there are extended versions of open(), umask(), stat(), lstat(), fstat(), fchmod(), mkfifo(), and mkdir(). The following code excerpt shows how the program from Figure 11–29 might be modified to create a file with an ACL.

```
...
// assuming the ACL has been set up at this point

// create a file security object
filesec = filesec_init();

// set the ACL as the file security object's property
filesec_set_property(filesec, FILESEC_ACL, &acl);

if ((fd = openx_np(argv[1], O_CREAT | O_RDWR | O_EXCL, filesec)) < 0)
    perror("openx_np");
else
    close(fd);

filesec_free(filesec);
...
```

11.10 The Kauth Authorization Subsystem

Beginning with Mac OS X 10.4, the kernel uses a flexible and extensible subsystem called *kauth* for handling file-system-related authorizations. The following are some of kauth's noteworthy features.

- It encapsulates the evaluation of access control lists (ACLs). When the VFS layer determines that a vnode has an associated ACL, it calls kauth to determine whether the given credential has the requested rights for the vnode in light of the given ACL.

- It is not limited to file system authorizations. It can be used to implement authorization decision makers for arbitrary types of operations in the kernel.

The kauth kernel programming interface (KPI) allows third-party programmers to load such decision makers for existing or new scenarios, as we will shortly see.

- It can be used as a notification mechanism for informing interested parties about file system operations. The prime example of an application that would use such functionality is that of an antivirus file scanner. Moreover, kauth can be used to implement a fine-grained file system activity monitor for reporting vnode-level operations. We will write such a monitor later in Section 11.10.3.

11.10.1 Kauth Concepts

Figure 11–30 shows the fundamental abstractions in kauth. A *scope* is an authorization domain—an area within which an *action* performed by an *actor* is to be authorized. An actor is identified by an associated *credential*. Code executing in the kernel makes an authorization request to kauth, providing it a scope, a credential, an action, and scope- or action-specific arguments. Each scope has a default *listener* callback and possibly other registered listeners. Kauth calls *each* listener in the scope while authorizing a request. A listener examines the available information and makes an authorization decision.

11.10.1.1 Scopes and Actions

A kauth scope groups together a set of actions. For example, operations pertaining to the VFS layer are in one scope, whereas process-related operations are in another scope. A scope is identified by a string, which is conventionally in reverse DNS format. The kernel has several built-in scopes, each with a set of predefined actions, such as those listed here.

- `KAUTH_SCOPE_GENERIC` authorizes whether the actor has superuser privileges.
- `KAUTH_SCOPE_PROCESS` authorizes whether the current process can signal or trace another process.
- `KAUTH_SCOPE_VNODE` authorizes operations on vnodes.
- `KAUTH_SCOPE_FILEOP` is a special scope that is used not for authorization but as a notification mechanism. A listener in this scope is called when certain file system operations occur, but the "decision" returned by the listener is ignored.

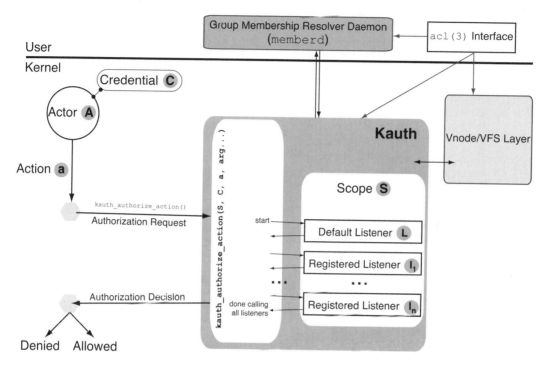

FIGURE 11-30 An overview of the kauth mechanism

> Depending on the scope, an action may represent an individual operation, or it may be a bit-field representing multiple operations. The vnode scope uses bit-fields—for example, a single authorization request may include both read and write operations.

Figure 11–31 shows the kernel's built-in scopes along with their reverse DNS names, actions, and default listener callbacks.

Figure 11–31 also shows a third-party scope. Although it may not normally be necessary, new scopes can be registered with kauth through kauth_register_scope().

```
kauth_scope_t
kauth_register_scope(
    const char                *identifier, // the scope identifier string
    kauth_scope_callback_t    callback,    // default listener callback for scope
    void                      *data);      // cookie passed to the callback

void
kauth_deregister_scope(kauth_scope_t scope);
```

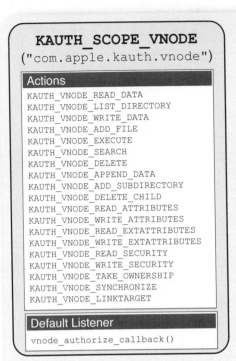

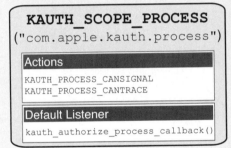

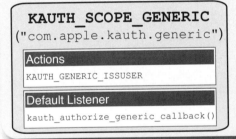

Built-in Scopes

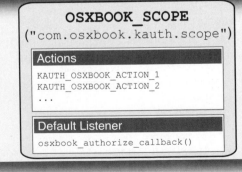

Third-Party Scopes

FIGURE 11–31 Kauth scopes and actions

11.10.1.2 Listeners and Authorization Decisions

A listener can return one of three values as its authorization decision: KAUTH_RESULT_ALLOW, KAUTH_RESULT_DENY, or KAUTH_RESULT_DEFER. The latter means that the listener neither allows nor denies the request—it is simply deferring the decision to other listeners. The following points regarding listeners must be noted.

- The default listener for a scope is established when the scope is registered. It is possible for a scope to have no default listener—KAUTH_SCOPE_FILEOP is an example of such a scope. When this is the case, kauth proceeds as if there were a default listener that always returned KAUTH_RESULT_DEFER as its decision.

- Kauth always calls all listeners for each request. The default listener is always the first to be called.

- Only the default listener can allow a request. If any subsequent listeners return KAUTH_RESULT_ALLOW, kauth ignores their return values. In other words, any listener other than the default listener can only be *more restrictive*.

- If there is no default listener for a scope, and all other listeners—if any— have returned KAUTH_RESULT_DEFER, the request is denied.

Additional listeners can be installed for a given scope through kauth_listen_scope(). Note that it is possible to install a listener for a scope that is not registered. The kernel maintains a list of such dangling listeners. Every time a new scope is registered, the kernel checks this list. If any listeners are found waiting for the scope being registered, they are moved to the new scope. Conversely, when a scope is deregistered, all its installed listeners are moved to the list of dangling listeners.

```
typedef int (* kauth_scope_callback_t)(
    kauth_cred_t    _credential,  // the actor's credentials
    void            *_idata,       // cookie
    kauth_action_t  _action,       // requested action
    uintptr_t       _arg0,         // scope-/action-specific argument
    uintptr_t       _arg1,         // scope-/action-specific argument
    uintptr_t       _arg2,         // scope-/action-specific argument
    uintptr_t       _arg3);        // scope-/action-specific argument

kauth_listener_t
kauth_listen_scope(
    const char              *identifier, // the scope identifier string
    kauth_scope_callback_t  callback,    // callback function for the listener
    void                    *idata);     // cookie passed to the callback

void
kauth_unlisten_scope(kauth_listener_t listener);
```

11.10.2 Implementation

As Figure 11–32 shows, the kernel maintains a list (a *tail queue*, specifically) of registered scopes, with each scope being represented by a kauth_scope structure [bsd/kern/kern_authorization.c]. Each scope includes a pointer to the default listener callback function and a list of other listeners—if any—installed in the scope.

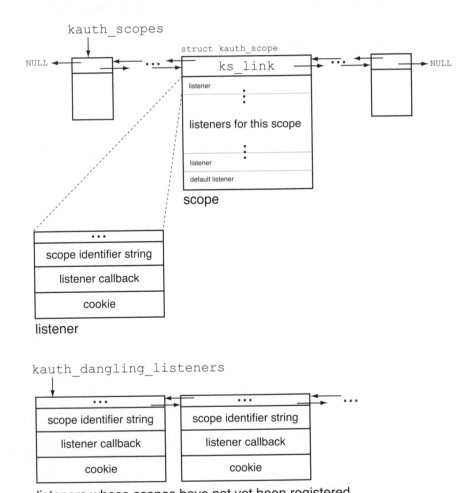

FIGURE 11–32 An overview of the scope and listener data structures in the kauth mechanism

The kauth subsystem is initialized when `bsd_init()` [bsd/kern/bsd_init.c] calls `kauth_init()` [bsd/kern/kern_authorization.c]—before the first BSD process is created. `kauth_init()` performs the following actions.

- It initializes the lists of scopes and dangling listeners.

- It initializes synchronization data structures.

- It calls `kauth_cred_init()` [bsd/kern/kern_credentials.c] to allocate the credential hash table and associated data structures. The kauth implementation provides several kernel functions for working with credentials.

- It calls `kauth_identity_init()` [bsd/kern/kern_credential.c] and `kauth_groups_init()` to initialize identity and group membership data structures, respectively.

- It calls `kauth_scope_init()` [bsd/kern/kern_credential.c] to register the process, generic, and file operation scopes. The vnode scope is initialized during initialization of the VFS layer, when `bsd_init()` calls `vfsinit()` [bsd/vfs/vfs_init.c].

- It calls `kauth_resolver_init()` [bsd/kern/kern_credential.c] to initialize work queues, mutex, and sequence number[18] for the external resolver mechanism that the kernel uses to communicate with the user-space group membership resolution daemon (`memberd`).

Group Membership Resolution Daemon

A user ID in Mac OS X can be a member of an arbitrary number of groups. Moreover, groups can be nested. In particular, it is not necessary that the list of all groups corresponding to a user ID be available in the kernel. Therefore, the kernel uses `memberd` as an external (out-of-kernel) identity resolver.

`memberd` invokes the special system call `identitysvc()` to register itself as the external resolver. Thereafter, it serves the kernel by using `identitysvc()` to fetch work, resolving identities using Open Directory calls, and informing the kernel of completed work—again, through `identitysvc()`. User programs can also access `memberd`'s services through Membership API calls.

The majority of authorization activity in the kernel occurs in the vnode scope. As Figure 11–33 shows, the VFS layer, specific file systems, and system calls such as `execve()` and `mmap()` call the kauth subsystem through the

---

18. The sequence number is initialized to `31337`.

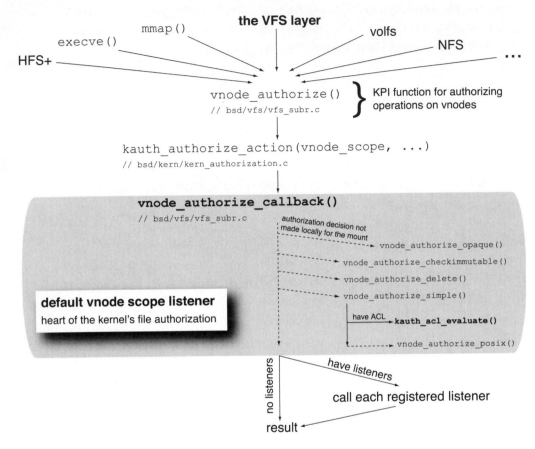

FIGURE 11–33 Authorization in the vnode scope

vnode_authorize() function. The default listener for the vnode scope—
vnode_authorize_callback()—performs numerous checks, depending on
factors such as the type of mount, the identity of the actor, and the presence of an
ACL. The following are examples of checks performed by vnode_authorize_
callback().

- It checks whether the file system is mounted in a manner that warrants
  denial of the request without further tests—for example, a read-only file
  system (MNT_READONLY) cannot be written to, and files residing on a
  "noexec" file system (MNT_NOEXEC) cannot be executed.

- It calls vnode_authorize_opaque() if the file system is mounted with
  the indication that authorization decisions are not to be made locally. NFS is

an example. Such opaque file systems may handle authorization during an actual request or may implement a reliable `access()` operation. Depending on the value returned by `vnode_authorize_opaque()`, `vnode_authorize_callback()` can return immediately or continue with further checks.

- It ensures that if a file is being modified, it is mutable.

- Unless the provided VFS context corresponds to the superuser, `vnode_authorize_callback()` uses file attributes to determine whether the requested access is allowed.[19] Depending on the specific request, this may result in a call to `vnode_authorize_simple()`, which calls the kauth subsystem to evaluate the ACL, if any, associated with the vnode.

11.10.3 A Vnode-Level File System Activity Monitor

Now that we are familiar with the kauth KPI, let us use the knowledge to implement a listener for the vnode scope. We will not use the listener to participate in authorization decisions. Our listener will always return `KAUTH_RESULT_DEFER` as its "decision," which will defer every request to other listeners. However, for each request, it will package the vnode information received into a data structure, placing the latter on a shared memory queue that is accessible from a user-space program. We will also write a program that retrieves information from this queue and displays details of the corresponding vnode operations. Figure 11–34 shows the arrangement.

> Examining file system activity in detail can be an effective learning tool for understanding system behavior. Unlike the `fslogger` program (Figure 11–25), which reports only file system modifications, the activity monitor we discuss in this section reports most file system accesses.[20]

The kernel portion of our activity monitor is contained within a kernel extension called `VnodeWatcher.kext`, which implements an I/O Kit driver and an I/O Kit user client. When the user client starts, it allocates an `IODataQueue` object for passing data from the kernel to user space. When a user-space program

---

19. The superuser is denied execute access to a file unless at least one execute bit is set on the file.

20. In some cases, the kernel may use cached results of certain file system operations. If so, subsequent invocations of these operations will not be visible to kauth.

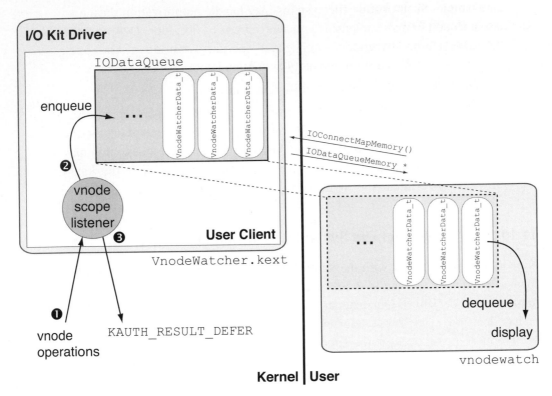

FIGURE 11–34 The design of a simple vnode-level file system activity monitor

calls its `open()` method, the user client registers a kauth listener for the vnode scope. Thereafter, the program performs the following operations:

- Calls `IODataQueueAllocateNotificationPort()` to allocate a Mach port to receive notifications about availability of data on the queue
- Calls `IOConnectSetNotificationPort()` to set the port as the notification port
- Calls `IOConnectMapMemory()` to map the shared memory corresponding to the queue into its address space
- Loops waiting for data to be available on the queue, calling `IODataQueueDequeue()` to dequeue the next available entry on the queue and displaying the dequeued entry

When the user program exits, dies, or calls the user client's `close()` method, the kauth listener is deregistered.

Let us look at the kernel-side source first. Figure 11–35 shows the header file that is shared between the kernel extension and the user-space program. We only implement the start() method of the I/O Kit driver class—we use it to publish the "VnodeWatcher" service. Note that we will treat a predefined filename (/private/tmp/VnodeWatcher.log) specially by ignoring all vnode operations on it. This way, we can use it as a log file without causing its own file system activity to be reported by the monitor.

FIGURE 11–35 Common header file for the vnode-level file system activity monitor

```
// VnodeWatcher.h

#include <sys/param.h>
#include <sys/kauth.h>
#include <sys/vnode.h>

typedef struct {
    UInt32        pid;
    UInt32        action;
    enum vtype    v_type;
    enum vtagtype v_tag;;
    char          p_comm[MAXCOMLEN + 1];
    char          path[MAXPATHLEN];
} VnodeWatcherData_t;

enum {
    kt_kVnodeWatcherUserClientOpen,
    kt_kVnodeWatcherUserClientClose,
    kt_kVnodeWatcherUserClientNMethods,
    kt_kStopListeningToMessages = 0xff,
};

#define VNW_LOG_FILE "/private/tmp/VnodeWatcher.log"

#ifdef KERNEL

#include <IOKit/IOService.h>
#include <IOKit/IOUserClient.h>
#include <IOKit/IODataQueue.h>
#include <sys/types.h>
#include <sys/kauth.h>

// the I/O Kit driver class
class com_osxbook_driver_VnodeWatcher : public IOService
{
    OSDeclareDefaultStructors(com_osxbook_driver_VnodeWatcher)
```

(continues)

FIGURE 11–35 Common header file for the vnode-level file system activity monitor *(continued)*

```
public:
    virtual bool start(IOService *provider);
};


enum { kt_kMaximumEventsToHold = 512 };

// the user client class
class com_osxbook_driver_VnodeWatcherUserClient : public IOUserClient
{
    OSDeclareDefaultStructors(com_osxbook_driver_VnodeWatcherUserClient)

private:
    task_t                              fClient;
    com_osxbook_driver_VnodeWatcher *fProvider;
    IODataQueue                        *fDataQueue;
    IOMemoryDescriptor                 *fSharedMemory;
    kauth_listener_t                    fListener;

public:
    virtual bool      start(IOService *provider);
    virtual void      stop(IOService *provider);
    virtual IOReturn open(void);
    virtual IOReturn clientClose(void);
    virtual IOReturn close(void);
    virtual bool      terminate(IOOptionBits options);
    virtual IOReturn startLogging(void);
    virtual IOReturn stopLogging(void);

    virtual bool      initWithTask(
                          task_t owningTask, void *securityID, UInt32 type);
    virtual IOReturn registerNotificationPort(
                          mach_port_t port, UInt32 type, UInt32 refCon);

    virtual IOReturn clientMemoryForType(UInt32 type, IOOptionBits *options,
                                          IOMemoryDescriptor **memory);
    virtual IOExternalMethod *getTargetAndMethodForIndex(IOService **target,
                                                          UInt32 index);
};

#endif // KERNEL
```

Figure 11–36 shows the contents of VnodeWatcher.cpp, which implement both the driver and the user client. The following points are noteworthy.

- The listener function—my_vnode_authorize_callback()—adds information about the process name, vnode type, and vnode tag[21] to the information packet placed on the shared queue. Moreover, the listener calls vn_getpath() to build the pathname associated with the vnode.

- The listener keeps track of the number of times it is invoked by using a counter whose value it atomically adjusts. In Mac OS X 10.4, when a listener is deregistered through kauth_unlisten_scope(), the latter can return even though one or more threads executing the listener may still not have returned. Therefore, any state shared by the listener must not be destroyed until all such threads have returned.

- The user client allows only one user-space program at a time to use the monitoring service. Moreover, the listener is registered only when a client program is attached, even though the kernel extension may remain loaded.

> vn_getpath() is also used by the fcntl() system call's F_GETPATH command, which retrieves the complete path corresponding to a given file descriptor. It is important to note that this mechanism is not foolproof. For example, if an open file is deleted, the path reported by vn_getpath() will be stale.

FIGURE 11–36 Source for the vnode-level file system activity monitor kernel extension

```
// VnodeWatcher.cpp

#include <IOKit/IOLib.h>
#include <IOKit/IODataQueueShared.h>
#include <sys/proc.h>
#include "VnodeWatcher.h"

#define super IOService
OSDefineMetaClassAndStructors(com_osxbook_driver_VnodeWatcher, IOService)

static char   *gLogFilePath = NULL;
static size_t  gLogFilePathLen = 0;
static SInt32  gListenerInvocations = 0;

bool
com_osxbook_driver_VnodeWatcher::start(IOService *provider)
```

(continues)

---

21. A tag type indicates the file system type the vnode is associated with.

FIGURE 11–36 Source for the vnode-level file system activity monitor kernel extension *(continued)*

```
{
    if (!super::start(provider))
        return false;

    gLogFilePath = VNW_LOG_FILE;
    gLogFilePathLen = strlen(gLogFilePath) + 1;

    registerService();

    return true;
}

#undef super
#define super IOUserClient
OSDefineMetaClassAndStructors(
    com_osxbook_driver_VnodeWatcherUserClient, IOUserClient)

static const IOExternalMethod sMethods[kt_kVnodeWatcherUserClientNMethods] =
{
    {
        NULL,
        (IOMethod)&com_osxbook_driver_VnodeWatcherUserClient::open,
        kIOUCScalarIScalarO,
        0,
        0
    },
    {
        NULL,
        (IOMethod)&com_osxbook_driver_VnodeWatcherUserClient::close,
        kIOUCScalarIScalarO,
        0,
        0
    },
};

static int
my_vnode_authorize_callback(
    kauth_cred_t    credential,  // reference to the actor's credentials
    void            *idata,      // cookie supplied when listener is registered
    kauth_action_t  action,      // requested action
    uintptr_t       arg0,        // the VFS context
    uintptr_t       arg1,        // the vnode in question
    uintptr_t       arg2,        // parent vnode, or NULL
    uintptr_t       arg3)        // pointer to an errno value
{
    UInt32 size;
```

(continues)

FIGURE 11–36 Source for the vnode-level file system activity monitor kernel extension *(continued)*

```
    VnodeWatcherData_t data;
    int name_len = MAXPATHLEN;

    (void)OSIncrementAtomic(&gListenerInvocations); // enter the listener

    data.pid = vfs_context_pid((vfs_context_t)arg0);
    proc_name(data.pid, data.p_comm, MAXCOMLEN + 1);
    data.action = action;
    data.v_type = vnode_vtype((vnode_t)arg1);
    data.v_tag = (enum vtagtype)vnode_tag((vnode_t)arg1);

    size = sizeof(data) - sizeof(data.path);

    if (vn_getpath((vnode_t)arg1, data.path, &name_len) == 0)
        size += name_len;
    else {
        data.path[0] = '\0';
        size += 1;
    }

    if ((name_len != gLogFilePathLen) ||
        memcmp(data.path, gLogFilePath, gLogFilePathLen)) { // skip log file
        IODataQueue *q = OSDynamicCast(IODataQueue, (OSObject *)idata);
        q->enqueue(&data, size);
    }

    (void)OSDecrementAtomic(&gListenerInvocations); // leave the listener

    return KAUTH_RESULT_DEFER; // defer decision to other listeners
}

#define c_o_d_VUC com_osxbook_driver_VnodeWatcherUserClient

bool
c_o_d_VUC::start(IOService *provider)
{
    fProvider = OSDynamicCast(com_osxbook_driver_VnodeWatcher, provider);
    if (!fProvider)
        return false;

    if (!super::start(provider))
        return false;

    fDataQueue = IODataQueue::withCapacity(
                     (sizeof(VnodeWatcherData_t)) * kt_kMaximumEventsToHold +
                     DATA_QUEUE_ENTRY_HEADER_SIZE);
```

(continues)

FIGURE 11–36 Source for the vnode-level file system activity monitor kernel extension
(continued)

```
    if (!fDataQueue)
        return kIOReturnNoMemory;

    fSharedMemory = fDataQueue->getMemoryDescriptor();
    if (!fSharedMemory) {
        fDataQueue->release();
        fDataQueue = NULL;
        return kIOReturnVMError;
    }

    return true;
}


void
c_o_d_VUC::stop(IOService *provider)
{
    if (fDataQueue) {
        UInt8 message = kt_kStopListeningToMessages;
        fDataQueue->enqueue(&message, sizeof(message));
    }

    if (fSharedMemory) {
        fSharedMemory->release();
        fSharedMemory = NULL;
    }

    if (fDataQueue) {
        fDataQueue->release();
        fDataQueue = NULL;
    }

    super::stop(provider);
}


IOReturn
c_o_d_VUC::open(void)
{
    if (isInactive())
        return kIOReturnNotAttached;

    if (!fProvider->open(this))
        return kIOReturnExclusiveAccess; // only one user client allowed

    return startLogging();
}
```

(continues)

FIGURE 11–36 Source for the vnode-level file system activity monitor kernel extension *(continued)*

```
IOReturn
c_o_d_VUC::clientClose(void)
{
    (void)close();
    (void)terminate(0);

    fClient = NULL;
    fProvider = NULL;

    return kIOReturnSuccess;
}


IOReturn
c_o_d_VUC::close(void)
{
    if (!fProvider)
        return kIOReturnNotAttached;

    if (fProvider->isOpen(this))
        fProvider->close(this);

    return kIOReturnSuccess;
}


bool
c_o_d_VUC::terminate(IOOptionBits options)
{
    // if somebody does a kextunload while a client is attached
    if (fProvider && fProvider->isOpen(this))
        fProvider->close(this);

    (void)stopLogging();

    return super::terminate(options);
}


IOReturn
c_o_d_VUC::startLogging(void)
{

    fListener = kauth_listen_scope(              // register our listener
                KAUTH_SCOPE_VNODE,               // for the vnode scope
                my_vnode_authorize_callback,     // using this callback
                (void *)fDataQueue);             // give this cookie to callback
```

(continues)

FIGURE 11–36 Source for the vnode-level file system activity monitor kernel extension *(continued)*

```
    if (fListener == NULL)
        return kIOReturnInternalError;

    return kIOReturnSuccess;
}

IOReturn
c_o_d_VUC::stopLogging(void)
{
    if (fListener != NULL) {
        kauth_unlisten_scope(fListener); // unregister our listener
        fListener = NULL;
    }

    do { // wait for any existing listener invocations to return
        struct timespec ts = { 1, 0 }; // one second
        (void)msleep(&gListenerInvocations,      // wait channel
                    NULL,                         // mutex
                    PUSER,                        // priority
                    "c_o_d_VUC::stopLogging()",   // wait message
                    &ts);                         // sleep interval
    } while (gListenerInvocations > 0);

    return kIOReturnSuccess;
}

bool
c_o_d_VUC::initWithTask(task_t owningTask, void *securityID, UInt32 type)
{
    if (!super::initWithTask(owningTask, securityID , type))
        return false;

    if (!owningTask)
        return false;

    fClient = owningTask;
    fProvider = NULL;
    fDataQueue = NULL;
    fSharedMemory = NULL;

    return true;
}

IOReturn
c_o_d_VUC::registerNotificationPort(mach_port_t port, UInt32 type, UInt32 ref)
{
```

(continues)

FIGURE 11–36 Source for the vnode-level file system activity monitor kernel extension
(continued)

```
    if ((!fDataQueue) || (port == MACH_PORT_NULL))
        return kIOReturnError;

    fDataQueue->setNotificationPort(port);

    return kIOReturnSuccess;
}


IOReturn
c_o_d_VUC::clientMemoryForType(UInt32 type, IOOptionBits *options,
                                IOMemoryDescriptor **memory)
{
    *memory = NULL;
    *options = 0;

    if (type == kIODefaultMemoryType) {
        if (!fSharedMemory)
            return kIOReturnNoMemory;
        fSharedMemory->retain(); // client will decrement this reference
        *memory = fSharedMemory;
        return kIOReturnSuccess;
    }

    // unknown memory type
    return kIOReturnNoMemory;
}


IOExternalMethod *
c_o_d_VUC::getTargetAndMethodForIndex(IOService **target, UInt32 index)
{
    if (index >= (UInt32)kt_kVnodeWatcherUserClientNMethods)
        return NULL;

    switch (index) {
    case kt_kVnodeWatcherUserClientOpen:
    case kt_kVnodeWatcherUserClientClose:
        *target = this;
        break;

    default:
        *target = fProvider;
        break;
    }

    return (IOExternalMethod *)&sMethods[index];
}
```

The sources in Figures 11–35 and 11–36 can be used in an Xcode project of type "IOKit Driver," with the following I/O Kit personality in the kernel extension's `Info.plist` file.

```
...
<key>IOKitPersonalities</key>
<dict>
    <key>VnodeWatcher</key>
    <dict>
        <key>CFBundleIdentifier</key>
        <string>com.osxbook.driver.VnodeWatcher</string>
        <key>IOClass</key>
        <string>com_osxbook_driver_VnodeWatcher</string>
        <key>IOProviderClass</key>
        <string>IOResources</string>
        <key>IOResourceMatch</key>
        <string>IOKit</string>
        <key>IOUserClientClass</key>
        <string>com_osxbook_driver_VnodeWatcherUserClient</string>
        </dict>
</dict>
...
```

Finally, let us look at the source for the user program (Figure 11–37). It is a reasonably lightweight client in that it does not perform much processing itself— it merely displays the information contained in the queue while printing descriptive names of action bits that are set in the reported vnode operation.

FIGURE 11–37 Source for the user-space retrieval program for the vnode-level file system activity monitor

```
// vnodewatch.c

#include <IOKit/IOKitLib.h>
#include <IOKit/IODataQueueShared.h>
#include <IOKit/IODataQueueClient.h>

#include <mach/mach.h>
#include <pthread.h>
#include <stdio.h>
#include <stdlib.h>
#include <sys/types.h>
#include <sys/acl.h>

#include "VnodeWatcher.h"
```

(continues)

FIGURE 11–37 Source for the user-space retrieval program for the vnode-level file system activity monitor *(continued)*

```c
#define PROGNAME "vnodewatch"
#define VNODE_WATCHER_IOKIT_CLASS "com_osxbook_driver_VnodeWatcher"

#define printIfAction(action, name) \
    { if (action & KAUTH_VNODE_##name) { printf("%s ", #name); } }

void
action_print(UInt32 action, int isdir)
{
    printf("{ ");

    if (isdir)
        goto dir;

    printIfAction(action, READ_DATA);    // read contents of file
    printIfAction(action, WRITE_DATA);   // write contents of file
    printIfAction(action, EXECUTE);      // execute contents of file
    printIfAction(action, APPEND_DATA);  // append to contents of file
    goto common;

dir:
    printIfAction(action, LIST_DIRECTORY);   // enumerate directory contents
    printIfAction(action, ADD_FILE);         // add file to directory
    printIfAction(action, SEARCH);           // look up specific directory item
    printIfAction(action, ADD_SUBDIRECTORY); // add subdirectory in directory
    printIfAction(action, DELETE_CHILD);     // delete an item in directory

common:
    printIfAction(action, DELETE);           // delete a file system object
    printIfAction(action, READ_ATTRIBUTES);  // read standard attributes
    printIfAction(action, WRITE_ATTRIBUTES); // write standard attributes
    printIfAction(action, READ_EXTATTRIBUTES);  // read extended attributes
    printIfAction(action, WRITE_EXTATTRIBUTES); // write extended attributes
    printIfAction(action, READ_SECURITY);    // read ACL
    printIfAction(action, WRITE_SECURITY);   // write ACL
    printIfAction(action, TAKE_OWNERSHIP);   // change ownership
    // printIfAction(action, SYNCHRONIZE);   // unused
    printIfAction(action, LINKTARGET);       // create a new hard link
    printIfAction(action, CHECKIMMUTABLE);   // check for immutability

    printIfAction(action, ACCESS);           // special flag
    printIfAction(action, NOIMMUTABLE);      // special flag

    printf("}\n");
}
```

(continues)

FIGURE 11–37 Source for the user-space retrieval program for the vnode-level file system activity monitor *(continued)*

```
const char *
vtype_name(enum vtype vtype)
{
    static const char *vtype_names[] = {
        "VNON",  "VREG",  "VDIR", "VBLK", "VCHR", "VLNK",
        "VSOCK", "VFIFO", "VBAD", "VSTR", "VCPLX",
    };

    return vtype_names[vtype];
}


const char *
vtag_name(enum vtagtype vtag)
{
    static const char *vtag_names[] = {
        "VT_NON",   "VT_UFS",   "VT_NFS",    "VT_MFS",     "VT_MSDOSFS",
        "VT_LFS",   "VT_LOFS",  "VT_FDESC",  "VT_PORTAL",  "VT_NULL",
        "VT_UMAP",  "VT_KERNFS", "VT_PROCFS", "VT_AFS",    "VT_ISOFS",
        "VT_UNION", "VT_HFS",   "VT_VOLFS",  "VT_DEVFS",   "VT_WEBDAV",
        "VT_UDF",   "VT_AFP",   "VT_CDDA",   "VT_CIFS",    "VT_OTHER",
    };

    return vtag_names[vtag];
}


static IOReturn
vnodeNotificationHandler(io_connect_t connection)
{
    kern_return_t        kr;
    VnodeWatcherData_t   vdata;
    UInt32               dataSize;
    IODataQueueMemory    *queueMappedMemory;
    vm_size_t            queueMappedMemorySize;
    vm_address_t         address = nil;
    vm_size_t            size = 0;
    unsigned int         msgType = 1; // family-defined port type (arbitrary)
    mach_port_t          recvPort;

    // allocate a Mach port to receive notifications from the IODataQueue
    if (!(recvPort = IODataQueueAllocateNotificationPort())) {
        fprintf(stderr, "%s: failed to allocate notification port\n", PROGNAME);
        return kIOReturnError;
    }

    // this will call registerNotificationPort() inside our user client class
    kr = IOConnectSetNotificationPort(connection, msgType, recvPort, 0);
```

(continues)

FIGURE 11–37 Source for the user-space retrieval program for the vnode-level file system activity monitor *(continued)*

```
    if (kr != kIOReturnSuccess) {
        fprintf(stderr, "%s: failed to register notification port (%d)\n",
                PROGNAME, kr);
        mach_port_destroy(mach_task_self(), recvPort);
        return kr;
    }


    // this will call clientMemoryForType() inside our user client class
    kr = IOConnectMapMemory(connection, kIODefaultMemoryType,
                            mach_task_self(), &address, &size, kIOMapAnywhere);
    if (kr != kIOReturnSuccess) {
        fprintf(stderr, "%s: failed to map memory (%d)\n", PROGNAME, kr);
        mach_port_destroy(mach_task_self(), recvPort);
        return kr;
    }


    queueMappedMemory = (IODataQueueMemory *)address;
    queueMappedMemorySize = size;

    while (IODataQueueWaitForAvailableData(queueMappedMemory, recvPort) ==
           kIOReturnSuccess) {
        while (IODataQueueDataAvailable(queueMappedMemory)) {
            dataSize = sizeof(vdata);
            kr = IODataQueueDequeue(queueMappedMemory, &vdata, &dataSize);
            if (kr == kIOReturnSuccess) {

                if (*(UInt8 *)&vdata == kt_kStopListeningToMessages)
                    goto exit;

                printf("\"%s\" %s %s %lu(%s) ",
                       vdata.path,
                       vtype_name(vdata.v_type),
                       vtag_name(vdata.v_tag),
                       vdata.pid,
                       vdata.p_comm);
                action_print(vdata.action, (vdata.v_type & VDIR));
            } else
                fprintf(stderr, "*** error in receiving data (%d)\n", kr);
        }
    }

exit:

    kr = IOConnectUnmapMemory(connection, kIODefaultMemoryType,
                              mach_task_self(), address);
    if (kr != kIOReturnSuccess)
        fprintf(stderr, "%s: failed to unmap memory (%d)\n", PROGNAME, kr);
```

(continues)

FIGURE 11–37 Source for the user-space retrieval program for the vnode-level file system activity monitor *(continued)*

```
        mach_port_destroy(mach_task_self(), recvPort);

        return kr;
}

#define PRINT_ERROR_AND_RETURN(msg, ret) \
        { fprintf(stderr, "%s: %s\n", PROGNAME, msg); return ret; }

int
main(int argc, char **argv)
{
        kern_return_t    kr;
        int              ret;
        io_iterator_t    iterator;
        io_service_t     serviceObject;
        CFDictionaryRef  classToMatch;
        pthread_t        dataQueueThread;
        io_connect_t     connection;

        setbuf(stdout, NULL);

        if (!(classToMatch = IOServiceMatching(VNODE_WATCHER_IOKIT_CLASS)))
            PRINT_ERROR_AND_RETURN("failed to create matching dictionary", -1);

        kr = IOServiceGetMatchingServices(kIOMasterPortDefault, classToMatch,
                                          &iterator);
        if (kr != kIOReturnSuccess)
            PRINT_ERROR_AND_RETURN("failed to retrieve matching services", -1);

        serviceObject = IOIteratorNext(iterator);
        IOObjectRelease(iterator);
        if (!serviceObject)
            PRINT_ERROR_AND_RETURN("VnodeWatcher service not found", -1);

        kr = IOServiceOpen(serviceObject, mach_task_self(), 0, &connection);
        IOObjectRelease(serviceObject);
        if (kr != kIOReturnSuccess)
            PRINT_ERROR_AND_RETURN("failed to open VnodeWatcher service", kr);

        kr = IOConnectMethodScalarIScalarO(connection,
                                           kt_kVnodeWatcherUserClientOpen, 0, 0);
        if (kr != KERN_SUCCESS) {
            (void)IOServiceClose(connection);
            PRINT_ERROR_AND_RETURN("VnodeWatcher service is busy", kr);
        }
```

(continues)

FIGURE 11–37 Source for the user-space retrieval program for the vnode-level file system activity monitor *(continued)*

```
    ret = pthread_create(&dataQueueThread, (pthread_attr_t *)0,
                         (void *)vnodeNotificationHandler, (void *)connection);
    if (ret)
        perror("pthread_create");
    else
        pthread_join(dataQueueThread, (void **)&kr);

    (void)IOServiceClose(connection);

    return 0;
}
```

Let us now test the programs we have created in this section. We will assume that the compiled kernel extension bundle resides as /tmp/VnodeWatcher.kext.

```
$ gcc -Wall -o vnodewatch vnodewatch.c -framework IOKit
$ sudo kextload -v /tmp/VnodeWatcher.kext
kextload: extension /tmp/VnodeWatcher.kext appears to be valid
kextload: loading extension /tmp/VnodeWatcher.kext
kextload: /tmp/VnodeWatcher.kext loaded successfully
kextload: loading personalities named:
kextload:       VnodeWatcher
kextload: sending 1 personality to the kernel
kextload: matching started for /tmp/VnodeWatcher.kext
$ ./vnodewatch
...
"/Users/amit/Desktop/hello.txt" VREG VT_HFS 3898(mdimport) { READ_DATA }
"/Users/amit/Desktop/hello.txt" VREG VT_HFS 3898(mdimport) { READ_ATTRIBUTES }
"/Users/amit/Desktop/hello.txt" VREG VT_HFS 3898(mdimport) { READ_ATTRIBUTES }
"/" VDIR VT_HFS 189(mds) { SEARCH }
"/.vol" VDIR VT_VOLFS 189(mds) { SEARCH }
"/Users/amit/Desktop" VDIR VT_HFS 189(mds) { SEARCH }
...
```

CHAPTER 12

The HFS Plus File System

T he HFS Plus file system (or simply HFS+) is the preferred and default volume format on Mac OS X. The term *HFS* stands for *Hierarchical File System*, which replaced the flat Macintosh File System (MFS) used in early Macintosh operating systems. HFS remained the primary volume format for Macintosh systems before Mac OS 8.1, which was the first Apple operating system to support HFS+. Also called the *Mac OS X Extended* volume format, HFS+ is architecturally similar to HFS but provides several important benefits over the latter.[1] Moreover, HFS+ itself has evolved greatly since its inception—not so much in fundamental architecture but in its implementation. In this chapter, we will discuss features and implementation details of HFS+ in Mac OS X.

---

1. Two of the major limitations in HFS were that it was largely single threaded and that it supported only 16-bit allocation blocks.

Looking Back

Apple filed a patent for the Macintosh Hierarchical File System (U.S. Patent Number 4,945,475) in late 1989. The patent was granted in mid-1990. The original HFS was implemented using two B-Tree data structures: the Catalog B-Tree and the Extents B-Tree. As we will see in this chapter, HFS+ uses both of these B-Trees. Lisa OS—the operating system for Apple's Lisa computer (1983)—used a hierarchical file system before the Macintosh. Indeed, the HFS volume format benefited from work done on the Lisa's file system.

As we noted in Chapter 11, one hallmark of HFS was that it lent support to the graphical user interface by providing a separate data stream in a file—the *resource fork*—for storing application icons, resources, and other auxiliary data independently of the file's "main" data.

Noteworthy features of HFS+ include the following:

- Support for files up to 2^{63} bytes in size
- Unicode-based file/directory name encoding, with support for names containing up to 255 16-bit Unicode characters[2]
- A B+ Tree (the *Catalog B-Tree*) for storing the file system's hierarchical structure, allowing tree-based indexing
- Extent-based allocation of storage space using 32-bit allocation block numbers, with delayed allocation of physical blocks
- A B+ Tree (the *Extents Overflow B-Tree*) for recording files' "overflow" extents (the ninth and subsequent—for files with more than eight extents)
- Multiple byte-streams (or forks) per file, with two predefined forks and an arbitrary number of other, named forks that are stored in a separate B-Tree (see next item).
- A B+ Tree (the *Attributes B-Tree*) for storing arbitrary metadata[3] per file, thus providing native support for extended file system attributes (the names of which are Unicode strings up to 128 16-bit Unicode characters in length)
- Metadata journaling through the kernel's VFS-level journaling mechanism
- Multiple mechanisms to allow one file system object to refer to another: aliases, hard links, and symbolic links

---

2. HFS+ stores Unicode characters in canonical, fully decomposed form.

3. The size of the data associated with a single extended attribute is limited to slightly less than 4KB in Mac OS X 10.4.

- An adaptive clustering scheme called *Hot File Clustering* for improving the performance of small, frequently accessed files

- Dynamic relocation of small fragmented files—based on several conditions—to promote file contiguity

- Native support for access control lists (ACLs), with ACLs being stored as extended attributes

- Unix-style file permissions

- BSD-style file flags, allowing files to be designated as append-only, immutable, undeletable, and so on

- Support for volume-level user and group quotas

- Provision for storing Finder information in a file system object's metadata, allowing per-file maintenance of properties such as file-extension hiding and color-coded labels

- Support for the `searchfs()` system call, which searches a volume for file system objects matching the given criteria (e.g., object name, Finder information, and modification date)

- Provision for storing multiple timestamps per file system object, including an explicit creation date

- Support for case sensitivity (although by default, HFS+ is case-*preserving* but not case-sensitive)

- The dedicated Startup file, whose location is stored at a fixed offset in the volume header (allowing it to be found without having to know details of the volume format) and which can be used by a non–Mac OS X operating system to boot from an HFS+ volume

- Support for byte-range and whole-file advisory locking[4]

> HFS+ does not support sparse files. However, it does support deferred zeroing of ranges of a file that have never been written. Such ranges are marked invalid until they are physically written—for example, because of a sync operation.

We will discuss most of these features in this chapter.

---

4. HFS+ does not implement locking—it uses the locking implemented in the kernel's VFS layer.

12.1 Analysis Tools

Let us first look at some tools and sources of information that will be useful in understanding the implementation and operation of HFS+.

12.1.1 HFSDebug

We will use `hfsdebug`, a command-line file system debugger, as a companion program to this chapter.[5] The term *debugger* is somewhat of a misnomer because a key feature (rather, a limitation) of `hfsdebug` is that it *always* operates on an HFS+ volume in read-only mode. It also does not allow for interactive debugging. Nevertheless, it is meant as a useful tool for exploring HFS+ internals, since it allows you to browse, inspect, and analyze various aspects of the file system. It has the following primary features.

- It displays raw details of data structures associated with the volume as a whole. Examples of such data structures are the volume header, the master directory block (in the case of an HFS+ volume embedded in an HFS wrapper), the journal files, and the on-disk B-Trees, namely, the Catalog file, the Extents Overflow file, the Attributes file, and the Hot Files B-Tree. We will discuss each of these data structures in this chapter.

- It displays raw details of data structures associated with individual file system objects such as files, directories, aliases, symbolic links, and hard links. Examples of such data structures include standard attributes, extended attributes (including ACLs), and file extents. `hfsdebug` supports looking up a file system object in multiple ways, namely, using its catalog node ID (typically—but not always, as we will see—the same as the inode number reported by the POSIX API), using a Carbon-style specification consisting of the object's node name and the catalog node ID of its parent, or using the object's POSIX path.

- It calculates various types of volume statistics, for example, a summary of the numbers and types of file system objects present on a volume, the space used by these objects, special cases such as invisible and empty files, the top *N* files ordered by size or degree of fragmentation, and details of hot files.

---

5. I created `hfsdebug` to explore the working of HFS+ and to quantify fragmentation in HFS+ volumes. `hfsdebug` is available for download on this book's accompanying web site (www.osxbook.com).

- It displays details of all fragmented files on a volume.
- It displays locations and sizes of all free extents on a volume.

> hfsdebug supports only the HFS+ volume format—the older HFS format is not supported. However, it does handle HFS+ variants such as journaled HFS+, embedded HFS+, and case-sensitive HFS+ (HFSX).

Since much of the raw information displayed by hfsdebug is not available through a standard programming interface, hfsdebug works by directly accessing the character device associated with a volume. This means several things.

- You will require superuser access to use hfsdebug on volumes whose character devices are accessible only to the superuser.[6] This is the case for the root volume.
- You can use hfsdebug even on a mounted HFS+ volume.
- Since hfsdebug does not access a volume through the volume's associated block device or through some higher-level API, its operation does not interfere with the buffer cache.
- Unlike a block device, which allows I/O to be performed at arbitrary byte offsets, character device I/O must be performed in units of the device's sector size, with I/O offsets being aligned on a sector boundary.
- hfsdebug is oblivious of the nature of the underlying storage medium, which could be a disk drive, an optical disc, or a virtual disk such as a disk image.

Finally, hfsdebug can also display the contents of the in-memory HFS+-specific mount structure corresponding to a mounted HFS+ volume. This data resides in the kernel as an hfsmount structure [bsd/hfs/hfs.h], a pointer to which is held in the mnt_data field of the mount structure [bsd/sys/mount_internal.h] corresponding to that mount instance. hfsdebug uses the Mach VM interface to retrieve this data. We are interested in the hfsmount structure because some of its relevant constituents have no on-disk counterparts.

---

6. When you run hfsdebug as the superuser (via the sudo command, say), it drops its privileges once it has completed the privileged operations it needs to perform.

12.1.2 Interface for Retrieving File System Attributes

HFS+ supports the `getattrlist()` system call, which allows retrieval of several types of file system attributes. The complementary system call, `setattrlist()`, allows those attributes that are modifiable to be set programmatically. Note that these two system calls are standard vnode operations in the Mac OS X VFS layer—Apple-provided file systems typically implement these operations. The attributes accessible through these calls are divided into the following *attribute groups*:

- Common attribute group (`ATTR_CMN_*`)—attributes applicable to any type of file system objects, for example, `ATTR_CMN_NAME`, `ATTR_CMN_OBJTYPE`, and `ATTR_CMN_OWNERID`
- Volume attribute group (`ATTR_VOL_*`)—for example, `ATTR_VOL_FSTYPE`, `ATTR_VOL_SIZE`, `ATTR_VOL_SPACEFREE`, and `ATTR_VOL_FILECOUNT`
- Directory attribute group (`ATTR_DIR_*`)—for example, `ATTR_DIR_LINKCOUNT` and `ATTR_DIR_ENTRYCOUNT`
- File attribute group (`ATTR_FILE_*`)—for example, `ATTR_FILE_TOTALSIZE`, `ATTR_FILE_FILETYPE`, and `ATTR_FILE_FORKCOUNT`
- Fork attribute group (`ATTR_FORK_*`)—attributes applicable to data or resource forks, for example, `ATTR_FORK_TOTALSIZE` and `ATTR_FORK_ALLOCSIZE`

Besides attributes, `getattrlist()` can also be used to retrieve *volume capabilities*, which specify what features and interfaces (from among a predefined list of features and another list of interfaces) a given volume supports. We will see an example of using `getattrlist()` in Section 12.11.

12.1.3 Mac OS X Command-Line Tools

In Chapter 11, we came across several file-system-related command-line tools available on Mac OS X. In particular, we used the `hdiutil` program to manipulate disk images. Besides its typical use, `hdiutil` can print information about the given HFS+ or HFS volume when used with the `hfsanalyze` option.

```
$ sudo hdiutil hfsanalyze /dev/rdisk0s3
0x00000000131173B6 (319910838) sectors total
0x131173B0 (319910832) partition blocks
native block size: 0200
HFS Plus
...
```

12.1.4 HFS+ Source and Technical Note TN1150

To make the most out of the discussion in this chapter, it would be valuable to have access to the Mac OS X kernel source. The following parts of the kernel source tree are particularly relevant to this chapter:

- `bsd/hfs/`—the core HFS+ implementation
- `bsd/hfs/hfs_format.h`—declarations of fundamental HFS+ data structures
- `bsd/vfs/vfs_journal.*`—implementation of the file-system-independent journaling mechanism

It is also recommended that you have a copy of Apple's Technical Note TN1150 ("HFS Plus Volume Format"), since it contains information that we refer to (but don't always cover) in this chapter.

12.2 Fundamental Concepts

Before we look at details of HFS+, let us familiarize ourselves with some fundamental terminology and data structures.

12.2.1 Volumes

In Chapter 11, we defined a *file system* as a scheme for arranging data on a storage medium, with a *volume* being an instance of a file system. An HFS+ volume may span an entire disk or it may use only a portion—that is, a *slice* or a *partition*—of a disk. HFS+ volumes can also span multiple disks or partitions, although such spanning is at the device level and thus is not specific to HFS+, which will still see a single logical volume. Figure 12-1 shows a conceptual view of a disk containing two HFS+ volumes.

12.2.2 Allocation Blocks

Space on an HFS+ volume is allocated to files in fundamental units called *allocation blocks*. For any given volume, its allocation block size is a multiple of the storage medium's *sector size* (i.e., the hardware-addressable block size). Common sector sizes for disk drives and optical drives are 512 bytes and 2KB, respectively. In

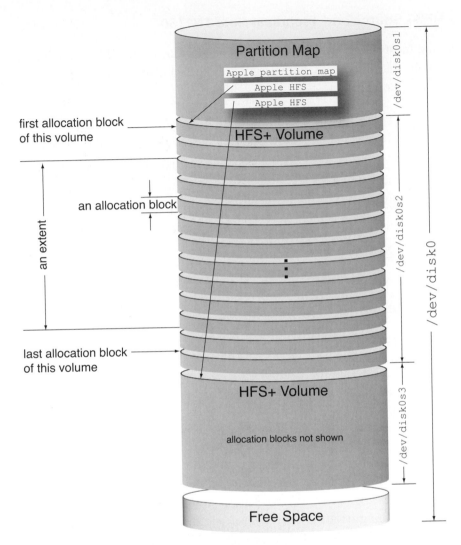

FIGURE 12–1 A disk containing two HFS+ volumes

contrast, the default (and optimal, for the Mac OS X implementation of HFS+) allocation block size is 4KB.

As shown in Figure 12–1, the storage on an HFS+ volume is divided into some number of equal-size allocation blocks. The blocks are conceptually numbered sequentially. The file system implementation addresses volume contents using allocation block numbers, which are 32-bit quantities represented by the u_int32_t data type in the kernel.

> Unlike HFS+, HFS supports only 16-bit allocation block numbers. Therefore, the total space on an HFS volume can be divided into at most 2^{16} (65,536) allocation blocks. Note that the file system will allocate space in multiples of the allocation block size regardless of the space that is actually used. Consider a somewhat contrived example: If you use the HFS volume format on a 100GB disk, the allocation block size will be 1,638,400 bytes. In other words, the file system will allocate 1.6MB even for a 1-byte file.

The allocation block size is a fundamental property of a given volume. You can choose an allocation block size other than the default when you construct a new HFS+ file system—say, using the `newfs_hfs` command-line program. The following rules apply when choosing an alternate allocation block size.

- It must be a power of 2.

- It should be a multiple of the sector size of the storage device, with the smallest legal value being the sector size itself. Thus, for an HFS+ volume on a disk drive, an allocation block must be no smaller than 512 bytes.

- `newfs_hfs` will not accept an allocation block size larger than `MAXBSIZE`, which is defined to be 1MB in `<sys/param.h>`. This is not a file system limitation, however, and if you really must, you *can* have a larger allocation block size by using another program (or a modified version of `newfs_hfs`) to construct the file system.

It is possible for the capacity of a volume to not be a multiple of its allocation block size. In such a case, there will be trailing space on the volume that would not be covered by any allocation block.

Fragments

An allocation block cannot be shared (split) between two files or even between forks of the same file. BSD's UFS (including the Mac OS X implementation) employs another unit of allocation besides a block: a *fragment*. A fragment is a fraction of a block that allows a block to be shared between files. When a volume contains a large number of small files, such sharing leads to more efficient use of space, but at the cost of more complicated logic in the file system.

12.2.3 Extents

An *extent* is a range of contiguous allocation blocks. It is represented in HFS+ by the *extent descriptor* data structure (struct HFSPlusExtentDescriptor [bsd/hfs/hfs_format.h]). An extent descriptor contains a pair of numbers: the allocation block number where the range starts and the number of allocation blocks in the range. For example, the extent descriptor { 100, 10 } represents a sequence of 10 consecutive allocation blocks, beginning at block number 100 on the volume.

```
struct HFSPlusExtentDescriptor {
    u_int32_t startBlock; // first allocation block in the extent
    u_int32_t blockCount; // number of allocation blocks in the extent
};
typedef struct HFSPlusExtentDescriptor HFSPlusExtentDescriptor;

typedef HFSPlusExtentDescriptor HFSPlusExtentRecord[8];
```

An eight-element array of HFS+ extent descriptors constitutes an *extent record*.[7] HFS+ uses an extent record as an inline extent list for a file's contents—that is, up to the first eight extents of a file (specifically, a file fork; see the next section) are stored as part of the file's basic metadata. For a file that has more than eight extents, HFS+ maintains one or more additional extent records, but they are not kept inline in the metadata.

12.2.4 File Forks

A file is traditionally equivalent to a single stream of bytes. HFS+ supports multiple byte-streams per file, with two special streams that are always present, although one or both may be empty (zero-size). These are the *data fork* and the *resource fork*. Each fork is a distinct part of the file and may be perceived as a file in itself. A fork is represented in HFS+ by the HFSPlusForkData structure [bsd/hfs/hfs_format.h].

```
struct HFSPlusForkData {
    u_int64_t        logicalSize; // fork's logical size in bytes
    u_int32_t        clumpSize;   // fork's clump size in bytes
    u_int32_t        totalBlocks; // total blocks used by this fork
    HFSPlusExtentRecord extents;    // initial set of extents
};
typedef struct HFSPlusForkData HFSPlusForkData;
```

---

7. More precisely, it should be called an *extents* record, since it contains multiple extents. However, we will call it an extent record based on the data structure's name.

Both forks have their own `HFSPlusForkData` structures (and therefore, extent records) that are stored along with the file's standard metadata.

The traditional view of a file maps to its data fork. Most files on a typical Mac OS X installation have only the data fork—their resource forks are empty.

> The Launch Services framework accesses a file's resource fork to retrieve the path to the application to use to open that file, provided such an application has been specified for that particular file—say, through the "Open with" section of the Finder's information window.

Another noteworthy aspect of the data and resource forks is that their names cannot be changed. Any additional byte-streams created have Unicode names. These named streams can have arbitrary contents, although an HFS+ implementation may limit the amount of data a named stream can hold.

Beginning with Mac OS X 10.4, named streams are used to provide native support for extended attributes, which in turn are used to provide native support for access control lists.

12.2.5 Clumps

Whereas an allocation block is a fixed-size group (for a given volume) of contiguous sectors, a *clump* is a fixed-size group of contiguous allocation blocks. Although every clump is an extent, not every extent is a clump. When allocating space to a fork, an HFS+ implementation *may* do so in terms of clumps—rather than individual allocation blocks—to avoid external fragmentation.

HFS+ has a provision for default clump sizes for the volume as a whole, for each B-Tree, for all data forks, and for all file forks. Note in Section 12.2.4 that the `HFSPlusForkData` structure has a field called `clumpSize`. Although this field could be used to support per-fork clump size specifications, HFS+ implementations with support for Hot File Clustering use this field to record the number of allocation blocks read from that fork.

12.2.6 B-Trees

HFS+ uses B-Trees to implement its critical indexing data structures that make it possible to locate both file content and metadata residing on a volume.

The Popularity of B-Trees

B-Trees were discovered by Rudolf Bayer and Edward M. McCreight in 1970.[8] They were subsequently described in a 1972 paper titled "Organization and Maintenance of Large Ordered Indexes."[9] Since then, B-Trees have been immensely popular and successful as an efficient and scalable external index mechanism. B-Tree variants, especially B+ Trees, are widely used in relational databases, file systems, and other storage-based applications. Microsoft's NTFS also uses B+ Trees for its catalog.

A B-Tree is a generalization of a balanced binary search tree. Whereas a binary tree has a branching factor of two, a B-Tree can have an arbitrarily large branching factor. This is achieved by having very large tree nodes. A B-Tree node may be thought of as an encapsulation of many levels of a binary tree. Having a very large branching factor leads to very low tree height, which is the essence of B-Trees: They are exceptionally suited for cases where the tree structure resides on an expensive-to-access storage medium, such as a disk drive. The lower the height, the fewer the number of disk accesses required to perform a B-Tree search. B-Trees offer guaranteed worst-case performance for common tree operations such as insertion, retrieval, and deletion of records. The operations can be implemented using reasonably simple algorithms, which are extensively covered in computing literature.

> We will not discuss the theory behind B-Trees in this chapter. Please refer to an algorithms textbook for further details on B-Trees.

12.2.6.1 B+ Trees in HFS+

HFS+ specifically uses a variant of *B+ Trees*, which themselves are B-Tree variants. In a B+ Tree, all data resides in leaf (external) nodes, with index (internal) nodes containing only keys and pointers to subtrees. Consequently, index and leaf

---

8. The authors never disclosed what the "B" in B-Trees stands for. A few plausible explanations are often cited: "balanced," "broad," "Bayer," and "Boeing." The latter is in the picture because the authors worked at Boeing Scientific Research Labs at that time.

9. "Organization and Maintenance of Large Ordered Indexes," by Rudolf Bayer and Edward M. McCreight (*Acta Informatica 1*, 1972, pp. 173–189).

nodes can have different formats and sizes. Moreover, the leaf nodes, which are all at the same (lowest) level in the balanced tree,[10] are chained together from left to right in a linked list to form a *sequence set*. Whereas the index nodes allow random searching, the list of leaf nodes can be used for sequential access to the data. Note that since data corresponding to a key can be found only in a leaf node, a B+ Tree search—starting from the root node—always ends at a leaf node.

The HFS+ implementation of B+ Trees differs from the standard definition in one notable respect. In a B+ Tree, an index node I containing N keys has $N + 1$ pointers—one to each of its $N + 1$ children. In particular, the first (leftmost) pointer points to the child (subtree) containing keys that are less than the first key of node I. This way, node I serves as an $(N + 1)$-way decision point while searching, with each pointer leading to the next level in the search based on which of the $N + 1$ ranges, if any, the search key falls in. The B+ Trees used in HFS+ do not have the leftmost pointer in their index nodes—that is, for an index node I, there is no leftmost subtree containing keys that are less than the first key of I. This means each index node with N keys has N pointers.

Hereafter, we will use the term *B-Tree* to refer to the HFS+ implementation of B+ Trees.

Although HFS+ uses several B-Trees, with differing key and data formats, all its trees share the same basic structure. In fact, all HFS+ B-Trees can be accessed and manipulated using mostly the same set of functions—only certain operations (such as key comparison) require code specific to tree content. The following are common characteristics of HFS+ B-Trees.

- Each B-Tree is implemented as a special file that is neither visible to the user nor accessible through any standard file system interface. Unlike regular files, which have two predefined forks, a special file has only one fork for holding its contents. The Hot File Clustering B-Tree is an exception, however. Although it is a system file, it is implemented as a regular file that is user-visible and has two predefined forks (the resource fork is empty).

> An HFS+ system file is designated as such by the `CD_ISMETA` bit being set in the `cd_flags` field of the in-memory *catalog node descriptor* corresponding to that file.

- The total space in a B-Tree file is conceptually divided into equal-size *nodes*. Each B-Tree has a fixed node size that must be a power of 2, ranging

---

10. In other words, all paths to leaf nodes have the exact same length in a balanced B-Tree.

from 512 bytes to 32,768 bytes. The node size is determined when the volume is created and cannot be changed—at least using standard utilities—without reformatting the volume. Moreover, each HFS+ B-Tree also has some initial size that is determined based on the size of the volume being created.

- Nodes are numbered sequentially starting from zero. Therefore, the offset of a node numbered N in a given B-Tree is obtained by multiplying N with the tree's node size. A node number is represented as a 32-bit unsigned integer.

- Each B-Tree has a single *header node* (of type `kBTHeaderNode`) that is the first node in the tree.

- Each B-Tree has zero or more *map nodes* (of type `kBTMapNode`) that are essentially allocation bitmaps used for tracking which tree nodes are in use and which are free. The first part of the allocation bitmap resides in the header node, so one or more map nodes are required only if the entire bitmap doesn't fit in the header node.

- Each B-Tree has zero or more *index nodes* (of type `kBTIndexNode`) that contain keyed pointer records leading to other index nodes or a leaf node. Index nodes are also called *internal nodes*.

- Each B-Tree has one or more *leaf nodes* (of type `kBTLeafNode`) that contain keyed records holding the actual data associated with the keys.

- All node types can hold variable-length records.

12.2.6.2 Nodes

Figure 12–2 shows the structure of a generic B-Tree node. Note that the nodes are only logically contiguous—like any other file, a B-Tree may or may not be physically contiguous on disk.

The node structure shown in Figure 12–2 is shared by all node types. There is a node descriptor (`struct BTNodeDescriptor [bsd/hfs/hfs_format.h]`) at the beginning of each node. The `bLink` and `fLink` fields of this structure chain together nodes of a particular type (indicated by the `kind` field) in the tree. Immediately following the node descriptor is the *records segment* that contains the node's records. Since node records can be of varying lengths, the latter part of the node contains a list of 16-bit offsets, each being a record's offset from the beginning of the node. The last entry in the offset list is the offset to the unused space in the node—that is, the space immediately following the records segment and before the offset list. Note that if there is no free space left, there still is a free space offset entry—it points to its own offset in that case.

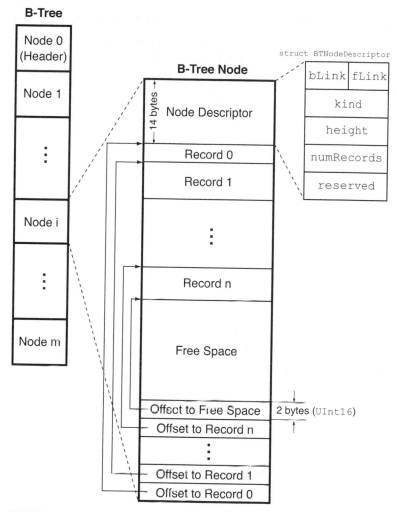

FIGURE 12–2 The structure of an HFS+ B-Tree node

Figure 12–3 shows the structure of a B-Tree header node. The header node has exactly three records, namely, the following:

- The *header record* contains general information about the B-Tree, such as the tree's node size, its depth,[11] the number of the root node (if any), the number of leaf records in the tree, and the total number of nodes.

---

11. A tree's depth is the same as its height. We say *depth* because we visualize the B-Tree's structure as growing downward.

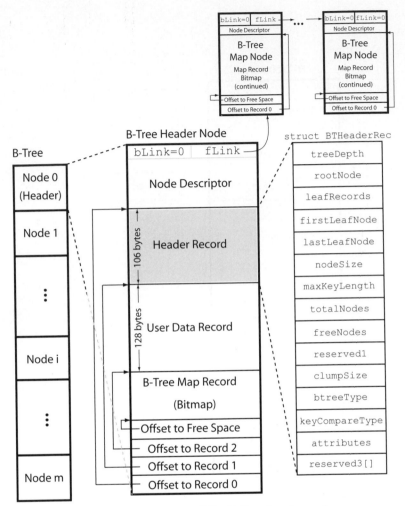

FIGURE 12–3 The structure of an HFS+ B-Tree header node

- The *user data record* provides 128 bytes of space for storing arbitrary information associated with the tree. Of all the HFS+ B-Trees, only the Hot File Clustering B-Tree uses this area.

- The *map record* contains a bitmap, each of whose bits indicates whether a node in the tree is in use or not.

As we noted earlier, a tree may have more nodes than can be represented by the header node's map record, whose size depends on the node size. The sum of the sizes of the node descriptor (14 bytes), the header record (106 bytes), the user data record (128 bytes), and the offset entries (4 × 2 bytes) is 256 bytes, leaving the remaining space for the map record. If additional space is required, the tree uses map nodes to house the extension of the bitmap. If a tree has one or more map nodes, the header node's `fLink` field will contain the number of the next map node. The first map node's `fLink` field will contain the next map node's number, if any, and so on, with the last map node's `fLink` field being set to zero. The `bLink` fields of all map nodes, and that of the header node, are always set to zero.

12.2.6.3 Records

Whereas the header and map nodes of a B-Tree contain administrative information for the tree itself, the index and leaf nodes contain file system information, where the type of information depends on the specific B-Tree in question. Nevertheless, the records in index and leaf nodes have the same general structure, which is shown in Figure 12–4.

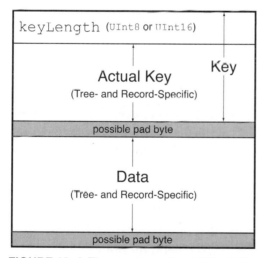

FIGURE 12–4 The structure of an HFS+ B-Tree record

At the beginning of the record is a key length (`keyLength`), which is stored using either one or two bytes, depending on whether the `attributes` field in the B-Tree's header node has the `kBTBigKeysMask` bit clear or set, respectively. Immediately following the key length is the actual key. The key length may or may not represent the actual key length, which is determined as follows.

- In the case of a leaf node, `keyLength` represents the actual key length.

- In the case of an index node, `keyLength` represents the actual key length if the `kBTVariableIndexKeysMask` bit is set in the header node's `attributes` field.

- If the `kBTVariableIndexKeysMask` bit is not set in the header node's `attributes` field, the actual key length is the constant value contained in the header node's `maxKeyLength` field.

As shown in Figure 12–4, a record's data may be preceded and succeeded by single pad bytes. Record data is required to be aligned on a two-byte boundary and to have a size that is an even number of bytes. If the combined size of the key length and the actual key is such that the data would start on an odd-numbered byte, a pad byte is inserted before the data. Similarly, if the data's size is an odd number of bytes, a pad byte is inserted after the data.

Index and leaf nodes contain only index and leaf records, respectively. Since these are B+ Trees, the actual data is stored only in leaf nodes. An index record's data is merely a node number—a pointer to another index node or a leaf node. In other words, index nodes together constitute an index for arbitrarily searching the data stored in leaf nodes.

12.2.6.4 Searching

A fundamental operation involved in B-Tree access and manipulation is *key comparison*. An important property of a B-Tree node is that all records within the node are stored such that their keys are in increasing order. For simple keys, say, integers, comparison could be as trivial as numerical comparison. Complex keys—such as those used in HFS+ B-Trees—have several components and therefore require more complicated comparison operations. Typically, the various components of a complex key are assigned precedence values. When two keys of a given type are compared, the individual components are compared in decreasing order of precedence. If an individual comparison results in equality, the overall comparison operation moves to the next component. This process continues until there is an inequality or until all components are exhausted, in which case the keys are deemed equal.

Figure 12–5 shows a hypothetical B-Tree that uses fixed-size integral keys. The tree's height is 3. In general, leaf nodes, all of which are at the same level and therefore have the same height, are assigned 1 as their height. An index node immediately above the leaf node has 2 as its height, and so on. The index node

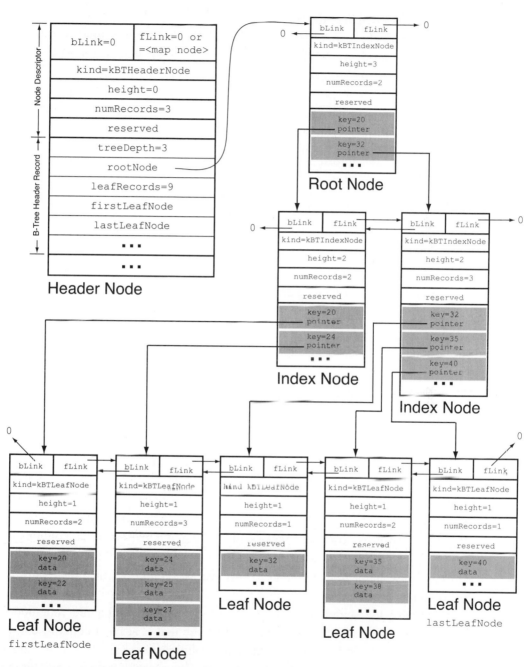

FIGURE 12–5 The contents of a hypothetical HFS+ B-Tree

with the highest height is the root node, a reference to which is maintained in the header node. Each node's height is contained in the `height` field of the node descriptor. The header node's `height` field is always set to zero, but its `treeDepth` field contains the tree's depth, which is the same as the root node's height.

> In an empty tree, there is no root node. Moreover, a root node does not have to be an index node. If all records are contained within a single node, that node is both the root node and the solitary leaf node.

The following are noteworthy observations about the tree shown in Figure 12–5.

- All nodes with a given height are chained together in a noncircular, doubly linked list through the `fLink` and `bLink` fields of their respective node descriptors. In a given chain, the `bLink` field of the first node and the `fLink` field of the last node are both set to zero.
- The header record in the header node contains node numbers of the root node, the first leaf node, and the last leaf node.
- Within a node, records are stored in increasing order of their keys.
- At any given height, all keys in a node are less than all keys in the node after it in the same-level chain. As a corollary, the first node in the chain contains the smallest keys and the last node contains the largest keys.

Let us see how data corresponding to a given key—the *search key*—can be searched for in this tree. The search always begins at the root node, which can always be found by examining the header record. The latter is at a fixed location within the tree, and the tree itself is assumed to be at a known location. Thereafter, the search proceeds downward, eventually ending at a leaf node that contains the search key, unless the key does not exist in the tree. In particular, the search algorithm used by HFS+ *does not back up*—it accesses a node at most once during a given search operation.

Suppose the search key is 38. We begin by examining the root node's records, with the goal of finding the greatest key that is at most equal to but not greater than the search key. In this case, we would choose 32, which is the greatest key in the root node but is still less than 38. The record's data is a pointer that leads us to an index node that is one level down in the B-Tree. This node has three records. Again, we search for the record with the largest key that does not exceed the search key: we choose 35. The corresponding pointer leads us to a leaf node. The search key matches the key of the first record in the leaf node. Therefore, the search is successful.

> A B-Tree search is analogous to a binary search, except that at each decision point, we decide between multiple paths instead of two paths. Searches *within* a node can be performed using any algorithm, with binary search and linear search (for small nodes) being common alternatives. The HFS+ implementation uses binary search.

For all leaf nodes to be at the same level, a B-Tree must be balanced. There exist several techniques to balance a B-Tree. HFS+ uses the *left-rotate* and *left-split* operations to maintain a balanced tree. Intuitively speaking, existing records are moved to the left and new records are inserted at the rightmost points in the tree.

12.3 The Structure of an HFS+ Volume

Figure 12–6 shows the structure of a representative HFS+ volume. Besides regular files and directories, an HFS+ volume contains (or may contain, since some are optional) the following entities.

- *Reserved areas* appear at the beginning and end of the volume.
- The *volume header* contains a variety of information about the volume, including the locations of the volume's other key data structures.
- The *alternate volume header* is a copy of the volume header. It is located near the end of the volume.
- The *Catalog B-Tree* stores the basic metadata for files and directories, including the first extent record (i.e., up to the first eight extents) for each file. The file system's hierarchical structure is also captured in the Catalog B-Tree through records that store parent-child relationships between file system objects.
- The *Extents Overflow B-Tree* stores overflow (additional) extent records of files that have more than eight extents.
- The *Attributes B-Tree* stores extended attributes for files and directories.
- The *Allocation file* is a bitmap containing a bit for each allocation block, indicating whether the block is in use or not.

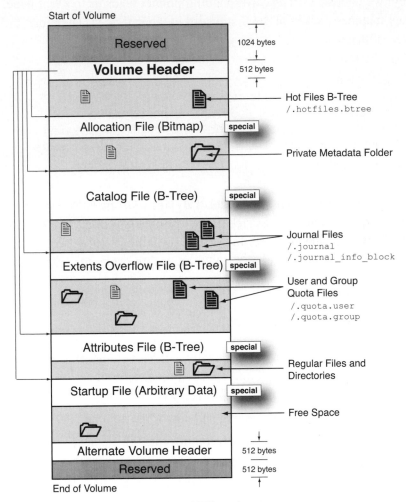

Start of Volume

Reserved — 1024 bytes

Volume Header — 512 bytes

Hot Files B-Tree
`/.hotfiles.btree`

Allocation File (Bitmap) `special`

Private Metadata Folder

Catalog File (B-Tree) `special`

Journal Files
`/.journal`
`/.journal_info_block`

Extents Overflow File (B-Tree) `special`

User and Group
Quota Files
`/.quota.user`
`/.quota.group`

Attributes File (B-Tree) `special`

Regular Files and
Directories

Startup File (Arbitrary Data) `special`

Free Space

Alternate Volume Header — 512 bytes

Reserved — 512 bytes

End of Volume

FIGURE 12–6 The structure of an HFS+ volume

- The *private metadata folder* is used for implementing hard links and for storing files that are deleted while they are open (`/\xC0\x80\xC0\x80\xC0\x80\xC0\x80HFS+ Private Data`).

- The *Hot Files B-Tree* is used by the built-in Hot File Clustering optimization mechanism for recording information about frequently accessed files (`/.hotfiles.btree`).

- The *Startup file* is meant to contain arbitrary information that an operating system might use to boot from an HFS+ volume.

- *Journal files* are used to hold information about the file system journal (`/.journal_info_block`) and the contents of the journal itself (`/.journal`).
- *Quota files* are used to hold information pertaining to volume-level user quotas (`/.quota.user`) and group quotas (`/.quota.group`).

In the rest of this chapter, we will explore the implementation and working of HFS+ by using `hfsdebug` to examine various aspects of the file system.

12.4 Reserved Areas

The first two logical sectors (1024 bytes) and the last logical sector (512 bytes) of a volume are reserved. Although Mac OS X does not use these areas, they were used by earlier Mac OS versions.

The 1024-byte reserved area at the beginning of a volume was used as *boot blocks*. These blocks contained information necessary to boot the system, including the entry point to the boot code and names of several critical files, for example:

- System file (typically `System`)
- Shell file (typically `Finder`)
- First debugger installed during startup (typically `Macsbug`)
- Second debugger installed during startup (typically `Disassembler`)
- File containing the startup screen (`StartUpScreen`)
- System scrap file (`Clipboard`)

The boot blocks also contained configurable system parameters such as the maximum number of open files allowed, the fraction of physical memory to be used for the system heap, and the number of event queue entries to allocate.

The 512-byte reserved area at the end of a volume was used by Apple during system manufacturing.

12.5 The Volume Header

The most critical structure of an HFS+ volume is the 512-byte *volume header*, which is stored at a 1024-byte offset from the start of the volume—immediately after the first reserved area. The information contained in the volume header includes locations of various other important data structures. Unlike the volume header, these other structures do not have a predefined, fixed location—the volume header serves as a starting point for the operating system (or other entities, such as a disk utility) while accessing the volume.

A copy of the volume header—the *alternate volume header*—is stored at a 1024-byte offset from the end of the volume, immediately before the last reserved area. Disk and file system repair utilities typically make use of this copy.

12.5.1 Viewing the Volume Header

Let us use `hfsdebug` to display the volume header of an HFS+ volume, which we will first create using `hdiutil`. The following `hdiutil` command line creates a disk image containing a 32MB journaled HFS+ volume, with the volume name being HFSJ. We can then mount the volume using either the `hdiutil` or `open` command-line programs.

```
$ hdiutil create -size 32m -fs HFSJ -volname HFSJ /tmp/hfsj.dmg
...
created: /tmp/hfsj.dmg
$ hdiutil mount /tmp/hfsj.dmg
/dev/disk10                 Apple_partition_scheme
/dev/disk10s1               Apple_partition_map
/dev/disk10s2               Apple_HFS                       /Volumes/HFSJ
```

As Figure 12–7 shows, the volume header contains the extents of the HFS+ B-Trees and of other special files.

FIGURE 12–7 The contents of an HFS+ volume header

```
$ hfsdebug -d /dev/rdisk10s2 -v
# HFS Plus Volume
  Volume size        = 32728 KB/31.96 MB/0.03 GB
# HFS Plus Volume Header
  signature          = 0x482b (H+)
  version            = 0x4
  lastMountedVersion = 0x4846534a (HFSJ)
  attributes         = 00000000000000000010000000000000
                     . kHFSVolumeJournaled (volume has a journal)
  journalInfoBlock   = 0x2
  createDate         = Sun Oct  9 19:24:50 2005
  modifyDate         = Sun Oct  9 19:28:36 2005
  backupDate         = Fri Jan  1 00:00:00 1904
  checkedDate        = Sun Oct  9 19:24:50 2005
  fileCount          = 3
```

(continues)

FIGURE 12–7 The contents of an HFS+ volume header *(continued)*

```
folderCount          = 3 /* not including the root folder */
blockSize            = 4096
totalBlocks          = 8182
freeBlocks           = 6002
nextAllocation       = 2807
rsrcClumpSize        = 65536
dataClumpSize        = 65536
nextCatalogID        = 22
writeCount           = 3
encodingsBitmap      = 00000000000000000000000000000000
                       00000000000000000000000000000001
                         . MacRoman
# Finder Info
...
# Allocation Bitmap File
...
# Extents Overflow File
logicalSize          = 258048 bytes
totalBlocks          = 63
clumpSize            - 258048 bytes
extents              =   startBlock    blockCount     % of file
                            0x803          0x3f         100.00 %
                       63 allocation blocks in 1 extents total.
                       63.00 allocation blocks per extent on an average.
# Catalog File
...
# Attributes File
logicalSize          = 0 bytes
# Startup File
logicalSize          = 0 bytes
```

Note in Figure 12–7 that the volume header's `signature` field contains the two characters H+. If this were a case-sensitive volume, this field would contain HX. Similarly, the `version` field would contain the value 5 (instead of 4) for a case-sensitive volume.

While mounting an HFS+ volume, an HFS+ implementation is required to identify itself by setting the `lastMountedVersion` field in the volume header. This way, an implementation can detect whether there might be a problem because of an earlier mount (e.g., if a journaled volume was mounted without journaling). Examples of values contained in the `lastMountedVersion` field include 8.10 (mounted on Mac OS 8.1 through 9.2.2), 10.0 (mounted nonjournaled), HFSJ (mounted journaled), fsck (mounted by fsck), and registered creator codes (mounted by a third party represented by the creator code).

The `hfsdebug` output in Figure 12–7 includes several dates. HFS+ dates are stored as 32-bit unsigned integers containing the number of seconds since midnight, January 1, 1904, GMT.[12] The volume creation date, however, is stored as local time instead of GMT. Since Unix-style dates are represented as the number of seconds since midnight, January 1, 1970, UTC, one must convert HFS+ dates to Unix-style dates before calling functions such as `gmtime()` and `localtime()`.

> Note that the backup date shown in Figure 12–7 is January 1, 1904. This is because the corresponding date integer contains a zero— that is, it has not been set, say, by a backup utility.

The HFS+ volume header's information in Figure 12–7 indicates that there are three files and three folders[13] (in addition to the root folder) on the newly created volume. Let us account for these files and folders, while noting that some are created not along with the file system but when the volume is mounted in the Desktop environment. (See the sidebar "Disk Arbitration.")

On a volume without user home directories (typically a nonboot volume), the per-user trash folders, which are used for storing files that have been dragged to the trash, are named `.Trashes/<uid>`, with `<uid>` being the numerical user ID of a user.

```
% id
uid=501(amit) gid=501(amit) groups=501(amit) ...
% sudo ls -l /Volumes/HFSJ/.Trashes
total 0
drwx------  2 amit  amit    68 19 Apr 00:58 501
```

> On a boot volume, the per-user trash folders are in the respective home directories (`~/.Trash`).

Thus, two folders are accounted for: `.Trashes` and `.Trashes/501`. These two folders will not exist if you mount our newly created volume manually—say, using the `mount_hfs` program from the command line.

---

12. The date integer would overflow after 6:28:15 GMT on February 6, 2040.

13. We will treat the terms *folder* and *directory* as synonymous in the context of HFS+.

Disk Arbitration

As we saw in Chapter 11, the Disk Arbitration daemon (diskarbitrationd) is in charge of mounting volumes as disks, disk images, and removable media devices appear.

Volumes are mounted by diskarbitrationd under the /Volumes directory. Each such volume appears in this directory by either its actual name or a modification of its name. Such modification may be required for two reasons. First, if an HFS+ volume's name contains a / character, diskarbitrationd translates it to a : character, since /, although a valid HFS+ pathname character, can be only a path separator in BSD pathnames. Note that regardless of which /Volumes subdirectory a volume is mounted on, the volume name that appears on the Desktop, along with the volume's icon, is unchanged.

Secondly, it is possible for two or more volumes to have the same name. Suppose you mount four volumes, each named HFSDisk. Even though their Desktop icons will all have the label HFSDisk, they will appear under /Volumes with automatically assigned suffixes—for example, as HFSDisk, HFSDisk 1, HFSDisk 2, and HFSDisk 3.

The third folder is the invisible *private metadata folder*, which is used internally by the file system and is created during volume creation. We discuss this private folder when we discuss hard links (Section 12.8.6). Note that the . (current directory) and .. (parent directory) directory entries do not reside physically on disk on an HFS+ volume—they are simulated by the HFS+ implementation.

We can verify the number and names of the folders on this volume by using hfsdebug to print the *folder thread* records in the volume's Catalog B-Tree.

```
% hfsdebug -b catalog -l folderthread -d /dev/rdisk10s2
# Folder Thread Record
  parentID           = 1
  nodeName           = HFSJ
# Folder Thread Record
  parentID           = 2
  nodeName           = %00%00%00%00HFS+ Private Data
# Folder Thread Record
  parentID           = 2
  nodeName           = .Trashes
# Folder Thread Record
  parentID           = 17
  nodeName           = 501
```

Two of the three files on this volume are the invisible journal files: / . journal and / . journal_info_block. The third file is / . DS_Store,[14] which, again, will not exist if you manually mount the newly created volume in our example. We can verify the names of these files by using hfsdebug to print the *file thread* records in the Catalog B-Tree.

```
$ hfsdebug -b catalog -l filethread -d /dev/rdisk10s2
# File Thread Record
  parentID              = 2
  nodeName              = .journal
# File Thread Record
  parentID              = 2
  nodeName              = .journal_info_block
# File Thread Record
  parentID              = 2
  nodeName              = .DS_Store
```

We will discuss file and folder thread records in greater detail in Section 12.7.2.

The volume header also includes an array (the finderInfo field) containing eight 32-bit values, whose meanings are listed in Table 12–1.

TABLE 12–1 Contents of the finderInfo Array in the HFS+ Volume Header

Element at Index	Description
0	If the volume contains a bootable system (typically the one specified by finderInfo[3] or finderInfo[5]), this entry contains its directory ID, and 0 otherwise.
1	If the volume is bootable, this entry contains the parent directory ID of the startup application (such as the Finder); ignored on the PowerPC version of Mac OS X.
2	This entry may contain the ID of a directory that should be opened in the Finder as the volume is mounted.
3	If the volume contains a bootable Mac OS 9 (or 8) system folder, this entry contains its directory ID, and 0 otherwise.
4	This entry is reserved.

(continues)

---

14. This is a file used by the Finder for caching information about a directory's contents.

TABLE 12–1 Contents of the `finderInfo` Array in the HFS+ Volume Header *(Continued)*

5	If the volume contains a bootable Mac OS X system, this entry contains the directory ID of the "system" folder (by default, the folder containing the bootloader–that is, the `BootX` or `boot.efi` files), and 0 otherwise.
6	This is the upper half of a unique 64-bit volume identifier.
7	This is the lower half of the volume identifier.

Since several elements of the volume header's `finderInfo` array are related to booting, it would be more interesting to look at the volume header on a boot volume. When no volume or device is explicitly specified, `hfsdebug` operates on the root volume (Figure 12–8), which normally is also the boot volume.

FIGURE 12–8 Finder information contained in the volume header of a boot volume

```
$ sudo hfsdebug -v
...
# Finder Info
      # Bootable system blessed folder ID
      finderInfo[0] = 0xcf5 (Macintosh HD:/System/Library/CoreServices)
      # Parent folder ID of the startup application
      finderInfo[1] = 0
      # Open folder ID
      finderInfo[2] = 0
      # Mac OS 9 blessed folder ID
      finderInfo[3] = 0xd6533 (Macintosh HD:/System Folder)
      # Reserved
      finderInfo[4] = 0
      # Mac OS X blessed folder ID
      finderInfo[5] = 0xcf5 (Macintosh HD:/System/Library/CoreServices)
      # VSDB volume identifier (64-bit)
      finderInfo[6] = 0x79a955b7
      finderInfo[7] = 0xe0610f64
      # File System Boot UUID
              UUID = B229E7FA-E0BA-345A-891C-80321D53EE4B
...
```

As Figure 12–8 shows, the volume contains both a bootable Mac OS X system and a bootable Mac OS 9 system, with `finderInfo[5]` and `finderInfo[3]` containing the respective system folder IDs. In the case of Mac OS X, the "system" folder is the one containing BootX—that is, `/System/Library/CoreServices`. The Boot UUID string shown is not part of `finderInfo`—it is constructed by hfsdebug (and by BootX during bootstrapping)—from the 64-bit volume identifier contained in the last two elements of finderInfo.

As listed in Table 12–1, if finderInfo[2] contains a folder ID, the Finder will open a window displaying that directory when the volume is mounted. Let us verify this. We can use hdiutil to create an image with a designated "auto-open" folder.

```
$ mkdir /tmp/auto-open
$ mkdir /tmp/auto-open/directory
$ echo Hello > /tmp/auto-open/directory/ReadMe.txt
$ hdiutil makehybrid -hfs -hfs-openfolder /tmp/auto-open/directory \
        -o /tmp/auto-open.dmg /tmp/auto-open
Creating hybrid image...
...
$ hdiutil mount /tmp/auto-open.dmg
...
/dev/disk10s2       Apple_HFS               /Volumes/auto-open
```

As the volume is mounted, a Finder window should open displaying the folder named directory on the volume. Moreover, finderInfo[2] should be equal to the catalog node ID of directory.

```
$ hfsdebug -V /Volumes/auto-open -v
...
      # Open folder ID
      finderInfo[2] = 0x10 (auto-open:/directory)
...
$ ls -di /Volumes/auto-open/directory
16 /Volumes/auto-open/directory
```

12.5.2 Viewing a Volume Control Block

When an HFS+ volume is mounted, an in-kernel block of memory called a *volume control block* (VCB) holds most of the volume header's information, along with other, dynamic information about the volume. The VCB is represented by the hfsmount structure in the kernel. Given a mounted HFS+ volume, hfsdebug can retrieve the corresponding hfsmount structure's contents from kernel memory.

```
$ sudo hfsdebug -m
  Volume name                = Macintosh HD (volfs_id  = 234881028)
  block device number        = { major=14, minor=4 }
  HFS+ flags                 = 00000000000000000000000010001100
                               + HFS_WRITEABLE_MEDIA
                               + HFS_CLEANED_ORPHANS
                               + HFS_METADATA_ZONE
```

```
    default owner                           = { uid=99, gid=99 }
...
    free allocation blocks                  = 0x86fe4f
    start block for next allocation search  = 0x2065a66
    next unused catalog node ID             = 3251700
    file system write count                 = 61643383
    free block reserve                      = 64000
    blocks on loan for delayed allocations  = 0
...
```

We will revisit the hfsmount structure later in this chapter.

12.6 The HFS Wrapper

An HFS+ volume may be *embedded* in an HFS wrapper. After the introduction of HFS+ with Mac OS 8.1, Apple had to ensure that computers with no HFS+ support in ROM were able to boot Mac OS 8.1 and newer systems from an HFS+ volume. The solution Apple used was to wrap the HFS+ volume so that it appeared as an HFS volume to the ROM. The System file residing on the HFS volume would only contain code to find the offset of the embedded HFS+ volume, mount it, and perform the actual boot using the System file on the HFS+ volume.

In HFS-embedded HFS+ volumes, the HFS+ volume header does not reside at a 1024-byte offset from the beginning of the volume—the HFS *master directory block* (MDB) does. The MDB is the HFS analog of the volume header. It contains enough information so that the HFS+ volume header's location can be computed. There is also an alternate MDB that is analogous to the alternate volume header.

Let us create an embedded HFS+ volume and examine its contents.

```
% hdiutil create -size 16m -layout NONE /tmp/hfswrapper.dmg
...
created: /tmp/hfswrapper.dmg
% hdiutil attach -nomount /tmp/hfswrapper.dmg
...
/dev/disk10
```

> Note the device node path (/dev/disk10 in this example) printed by hdiutil. Make sure you use the correct device path; otherwise, you may destroy existing data on a volume.

The -w option to newfs_hfs adds an HFS wrapper around the HFS+ file system that newfs_hfs creates. Similarly, the -w option to mount_hfs causes the wrapper volume to be mounted instead of the embedded HFS+ volume.

```
% newfs_hfs -w -v HFSWrapper /dev/rdisk10
Initialized /dev/rdisk10 as a 16 MB HFS Plus Volume
% mkdir /tmp/mnt
% mount_hfs -w /dev/disk10 /tmp/mnt
% ls -l /tmp/mnt
total 64
-rwxr-xr-x  1 amit   wheel   4096 17 Apr 17:40 Desktop DB
-rwxr-xr-x  1 amit   wheel      0 17 Apr 17:40 Desktop DF
-rwxr-xr-x  1 amit   wheel      0 17 Apr 17:40 Finder
-rwxr-xr-x  1 amit   wheel   1781 17 Apr 17:40 ReadMe
-rwxr-xr-x  1 amit   wheel      0 17 Apr 17:40 System
```

The wrapper volume is created with five files in its root directory. The System file's data fork is empty, but its resource fork contains boot code. The Finder file has both forks empty. All files are marked invisible except ReadMe. When such a volume is used on a system with no HFS+ support (e.g., a system earlier than Mac OS 8.1), the user would see a volume with only the ReadMe file on it. The file explains why the user cannot see any files on the volume and the steps needed to access them.

Figure 12–9 shows the layout of an HFS wrapper volume containing an embedded HFS+ volume.

Let us unmount the wrapper volume and mount the HFS+ volume within it. Unless explicitly instructed to mount the wrapper volume, Mac OS X will mount the embedded HFS+ volume.

```
$ umount /tmp/mnt
$ hdiutil detach disk10
"disk10" unmounted.
"disk10" ejected.
$ open /tmp/hfswrapper.dmg
$ mount
...
/dev/disk10 on /Volumes/HFSWrapper  (local, nodev, suid, mounted by amit)
```

When used to display the volume header of an embedded HFS+ volume, hfsdebug also displays the contents of the MDB (Figure 12–10).

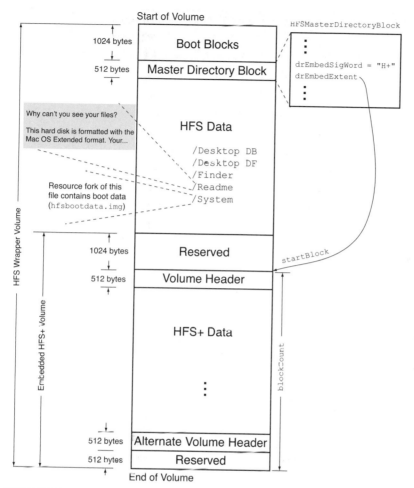

Start of Volume

HFSMasterDirectoryBlock

⋮

drEmbedSigWord = "H+"
drEmbedExtent

⋮

FIGURE 12–9 An HFS wrapper volume containing an embedded HFS+ volume

FIGURE 12–10 The contents of a master directory block

```
$ sudo hfsdebug -d /dev/rdisk10 -v
HFS Plus Volume with HFS Wrapper
  Embedded offset      = 88 bytes
  Wrapper volume size  = 16376.00 KB/15.99 MB/0.02 GB
  Embedded volume size = 16336.00 KB/15.95 MB/0.02 GB
# HFS Wrapper Master Directory Block
  drSigWord            = $4244 (BD)
  drCrDate             = Sun Oct  9 18:17:08 2005
  drLsMod              = Sun Oct  9 18:17:08 2005
  drAtrb               = 1000001100000000
                       . kHFSVolumeUnmounted (volume was successfully unmounted)
```

(continues)

FIGURE 12–10 The contents of a master directory block *(continued)*

```
                          . kHFSVolumeSparedBlocks (volume has bad blocks spared)
                          . kHFSVolumeSoftwareLock (volume is locked by software)
    drNmFls          = 5
    drVBMSt          = 0x3 (3)
    drAllocPtr       = 0 (0)
    drNmAlBlks       = 4094
    drAlBlkSiz       = 4096 bytes
    drClpSiz         = 4096
    drAlBlSt         = 0x8 (8)
    drNxtCNID        = 21
    drFreeBks        = 0
    drVN             = HFSWrapper (10 characters)
    drVolBkUp        = Fri Jan  1 00:00:00 1904
    drVSeqNum        = 0
    drWrCnt          = 3
    drXTClpSiz       = 4096
    drNmRtDirs       = 0
    drFilCnt         = 5
    drDirCnt         = 0
    EmbedSigWord     = $482B (H+)
    # Finder Info
    drFndrInfo   [0] = 0x2
    drFndrInfo   [1] = 0
    drFndrInfo   [2] = 0
    drFndrInfo   [3] = 0
    drFndrInfo   [4] = 0x656e6300
    drFndrInfo   [5] = 0
    drFndrInfo   [6] = 0x8a0d0159
    drFndrInfo   [7] = 0xf39492fd
    drEmbedExtent    = start   count
                       0x000a 0x0ff4
    drXTFlSize       = 4096 blocks
    drXTExtRec       = start   count
                       0x0000 0x0001
                       0x0000 0x0000
                       0x0000 0x0000
    drCTFlSize       = 4096 blocks
    drCTExtRec       = start   count
                       0x0001 0x0001
                       0x0000 0x0000
                       0x0000 0x0000
# HFS Plus Volume Header
...
  fileCount          = 1
  folderCount        = 3 /* not including the root folder */
  blockSize          = 4096
  totalBlocks        = 4084
  freeBlocks         = 4017
...
```

Figure 12–10 shows that the embedded signature field (EmbedSigWord) contains H+ to indicate the presence of an embedded volume. Note that the wrapper volume has no free blocks, as is indicated by the MDB's drFreeBks field. This is because from the HFS volume's standpoint, all space is already allocated—it is used by the embedded volume. Moreover, the embedded volume's space is actually marked as "bad" in the HFS volume, as indicated by the kHFSVolumeSparedBlocks bit being set in the MDB's drAtrb field. This prevents the embedded volume's space from being recovered or otherwise used in any way. The MDB's drNmFls field is 5, indicating that the wrapper volume contains 5 files.

12.7 Special Files

The HFS+ volume header contains a fork-data structure (HFSPlusForkData) for each of the five special files tagged as "special" in Figure 12–6—three B-Trees, a bitmap, and an optional Startup file. Since a fork-data structure contains the fork's total size and the initial set of the file's extents, these files can all be accessed starting from the volume header. An HFS+ implementation reads the volume header and the appropriate special files to provide access to the user data (i.e., files, folders, and attributes) contained on a volume.

The special files are not user-visible. They also do not contribute to the file count maintained in the volume header.

> An important point to note about the special files is that besides being free to reside at any available locations on the volume, they need not be contiguous. Moreover, all special files, *except* the Extents Overflow file, can grow beyond eight extents, in which case the "overflowing" extents will be stored in the Extents Overflow file.

12.7.1 The Allocation File

The Allocation file tracks whether an allocation block is in use. It is simply a bitmap, containing a bit for each allocation block on the volume. If a given block is either holding user data or assigned to a file system data structure, the corresponding bit is set in the Allocation file. Thus, each byte in this file tracks eight allocation blocks.

Note that being a file, the Allocation file itself consumes an integral number of allocation blocks. One of its nice properties is that it can be grown or shrunk, allowing flexibility in manipulation of a volume's space. This also means that the last allocation block assigned to the Allocation file may have unused bits—such bits must be explicitly set to zero by the HFS+ implementation.

> We saw in Section 12.4 that an HFS+ volume has two reserved areas: the first 1024 bytes and the last 512 bytes. The 512-byte volume header and the 512-byte alternate volume header are adjacent—after and before, respectively—to these two areas. The allocation blocks that encompass the reserved areas and the two volume headers must be marked as used in the Allocation file. Moreover, if the volume size is not an integral multiple of the allocation block size, there will be some trailing space that will not have a corresponding bit in the Allocation file. Even in this case, the alternate volume header is stored at a 1024-byte offset from the end of the volume—that is, possibly in the unaccounted-for area. Nevertheless, HFS+ will still consider the last *Allocation-file-tracked* 1024 bytes as used and will mark the corresponding allocation block (or blocks) as allocated.

12.7.1.1 *Viewing the Contents of the Allocation File*

We can use hfsdebug to view—indirectly—the contents of the Allocation file. We say "indirectly" because hfsdebug can examine the Allocation file and enumerate all free extents on a volume. Thus, the Allocation file bits corresponding to the extents that hfsdebug lists are all clear, whereas the remaining bits are all set.

```
$ sudo hfsdebug -0
# Free Contiguous      Starting @      Ending @       Space
            16           0x60c7         0x60d6     64.00 KB
            16          0x1d6d7        0x1d6e6     64.00 KB
            16          0x1f8e7        0x1f8f6     64.00 KB
            32          0x23cf7        0x23d16    128.00 KB
        130182          0x25f67        0x45bec    508.52 MB
...
           644        0x2180d00      0x2180f83      2.52 MB
       4857584        0x2180f85      0x2622e74     18.53 GB

Allocation block size  = 4096 bytes
Allocation blocks total = 39988854 (0x2622e76)
Allocation blocks free  = 8825849 (0x86abf9)
```

12.7.1.2 The Roving Next-Allocation Pointer

For each mounted HFS+ volume, the kernel maintains a roving pointer—an allocation block number as a hint—that is used as a starting point while searching for free allocation blocks in many (but not all) cases. The pointer is held in the nextAllocation field of the hfsmount structure. An allocation operation that uses the pointer also updates it.

```
$ sudo hfsdebug -m
...
  free allocation blocks                = 0x86d12b
  start block for next allocation search = 0x20555ea
  next unused catalog node ID           = 3256261
...
$ echo hello > /tmp/newfile.txt
$ sudo hfsdebug -m
...
  free allocation blocks                = 0x86d123
  start block for next allocation search = 0x20555eb
  next unused catalog node ID           = 3256262
...
$ sudo hfsdebug /tmp/newfile.txt
...
# Catalog File Record
  type             = file
  file ID          = 3256261
...
  # Data Fork
...
  extents          =    startBlock   blockCount    % of file
                         0x20555eb        0x1       100.00 %
                    1 allocation blocks in 1 extents total.
...
```

You can also set the value of nextAllocation for a given volume. The HFS_CHANGE_NEXT_ALLOCATION request of the fsctl() system call can be used to do so. Figure 12–11 shows a program that sets nextAllocation for the given volume path.

FIGURE 12–11 Hinting to the file system where to look for free space on a volume

```
// hfs_change_next_allocation.c

#include <stdio.h>
#include <unistd.h>
#include <stdlib.h>
#include <sys/ioctl.h>
```

(continues)

FIGURE 12–11 Hinting to the file system where to look for free space on a volume
(continued)

```
// ensure that the following match the definitions in bsd/hfs/hfs_fsctl.h
// for the current kernel version, or include that header file directly
#define HFSIOC_CHANGE_NEXT_ALLOCATION  _IOWR('h', 3, u_int32_t)
#define HFS_CHANGE_NEXT_ALLOCATION  IOCBASECMD(HFSIOC_CHANGE_NEXT_ALLOCATION)


#define PROGNAME "hfs_change_next_allocation"

int
main(int argc, char **argv)
{
    int ret = -1;
    u_int32_t block_number, new_block_number;

    if (argc != 3) {
        fprintf(stderr, "usage: %s <volume path> <hexadecimal block number>\n",
                PROGNAME);
        exit(1);
    }

    block_number = strtoul(argv[2], NULL, 16);
    new_block_number = block_number;

    ret = fsctl(argv[1], HFS_CHANGE_NEXT_ALLOCATION, (void *)block_number, 0);
    if (ret)
        perror("fsctl");
    else
        printf("start block for next allocation search changed to %#x\n",
                new_block_number);

    exit(ret);
}
```

Let us test the program shown in Figure 12–11 on a new HFS+ disk image
(Figure 12–12).

FIGURE 12–12 Examining allocation block consumption on a volume

```
$ hdiutil create -size 32m -fs HFSJ -volname HFSHint /tmp/hfshint.dmg
...
created: /tmp/hfshint.dmg
$ open /tmp/hfshint.dmg
$ sudo hfsdebug -V /Volumes/HFSHint -m
...
  start block for next allocation search  = 0xaf7
```

(continues)

FIGURE 12–12 Examining allocation block consumption on a volume *(continued)*

```
...
$ hfsdebug -V /Volumes/HFSHint -0
# Free Contiguous        Starting @      Ending @     Space
            630            0x881          0xaf6      2.46 MB
           5372            0xaf9          0x1ff4    20.98 MB

Allocation block size   = 4096 bytes
Allocation blocks total = 8182 (0x1ff6)
Allocation blocks free  = 6002 (0x1772)
$ echo hello > /Volumes/HFSHint/file.txt
$ hfsdebug /Volumes/HFSHint/file.txt
...
   extents              =   startBlock   blockCount    % of file
                            0xaf9          0x1         100.00 %
                    1 allocation blocks in 1 extents total.
...
$ hfsdebug -V /Volumes/HFSHint -0
# Free Contiguous        Starting @      Ending @     Space
            630            0x881          0xaf6      2.46 MB
           5371            0xafa          0x1ff4    20.98 MB

Allocation block size   = 4096 bytes
Allocation blocks total = 8182 (0x1ff6)
Allocation blocks free  = 6001 (0x1771)
$ sudo hfsdebug -V /Volumes/HFSHint -m
...
   start block for next allocation search  = 0xaf9
...
$
```

Since allocation blocks 0xafa through 0x1ff4 are free on the volume shown in Figure 12–12, let us use the program from Figure 12–11 to set the nextAllocation value to 0xbbb. We can then create a file and see if the file starts at that allocation block.

```
$ gcc -Wall -o hfs_change_next_allocation hfs_change_next_allocation.c
$ ./hfs_change_next_allocation /Volumes/HFSHint 0xbbb
start block for next allocation search changed to 0xbbb
$ echo hello > /Volumes/HFSHint/anotherfile.txt
$ hfsdebug /Volumes/HFSHint/anotherfile.txt
...
   extents              =   startBlock   blockCount    % of file
                            0xbbb          0x1         100.00 %
                    1 allocation blocks in 1 extents total.
...
```

12.7.2 The Catalog File

The Catalog file describes the hierarchy of files and folders on a volume. It acts both as a container for holding vital information for all files and folders on a volume and as their catalog. HFS+ stores file and folder names as Unicode strings represented by `HFSUniStr255` structures, which consist of a length and a 255-element double-byte Unicode character array.

```
// bsd/hfs/hfs_format.h

struct HFSUniStr255 {
    u_int16_t length;          // number of Unicode characters in this name
    u_int16_t unicode[255];    // Unicode characters
                               // (fully decomposed, in canonical order)
};
```

Each file or folder on the volume is identified by a unique *catalog node ID* (CNID) in the Catalog file. The CNID is assigned at file creation time. In particular, HFS+ does not use an inode table. A folder's CNID (directory ID) and a file's CNID (file ID) are reported[15] as their respective inode numbers when queried through a Unix-based interface such as the `stat()` system call.

> On traditional Unix file systems, an *index node*, or *inode*, is an object describing the internal representation of a file. Each file or directory object has a unique on-disk inode that contains the object's metadata and the locations of the object's blocks.

As noted earlier, the Catalog file is organized as a B-Tree to allow for quick and efficient searching. Its fundamental structure is the same as we discussed in Section 12.2.6. However, the formats of the keys and the data stored in its records are specific to it.

Each user file has two leaf records in the Catalog file: a *file* record and a *file thread* record. Similarly, each folder has two leaf records: a *folder* record and a *folder thread* record. The purposes of these records are as follows.

- A file record (`struct HFSPlusCatalogFile` [bsd/hfs/hfs_format.h]) contains standard (as opposed to extended) file metadata, which includes the file's CNID, various timestamps, Unix-style permissions, Finder information, and the initial extents of the file's data and resource forks.

---

15. Hard links are an exception to this behavior. See Section 12.8.6.

- A folder record (struct HFSPlusCatalogFolder [bsd/hfs/hfs_format.h]) contains standard folder metadata, most of which is identical to file metadata, except that a folder has no data or resource forks. Each folder has a *valence* value representing the number of children (*not* descendants) the folder has—that is, the sum of the numbers of files and immediate subdirectories within the folder.

- Both file thread and folder thread records are represented by an HFSPlus-CatalogThread structure [bsd/hfs/hfs_format.h], whose recordType field indicates the thread record's type. A thread record contains the name and parent CNID of the catalog node it represents. Thread records represent the hierarchical structure of the file system by *threading together* the relative organization of files and folders.

> In traditional Unix file systems, directories are explicitly stored on disk. Storing the hierarchical structure in a B-Tree has several performance benefits, but not without cost—for example, the Catalog B-Tree must be locked, sometimes exclusively, for several file system operations.

Let us see how a file might be accessed given its identifying information. Depending on the programming interface it uses, a user program can specify the file system object it wishes to access on a given volume in several ways:

- The target's Unix-style relative or absolute pathname
- The target's CNID
- The target's node name and the CNID of its parent folder

> The volume file system—normally mounted under /.vol—allows files and folders on an HFS+ volume to be looked up by their CNIDs. As we saw in Chapter 11, the /.vol directory contains a subdirectory for each mounted volume that supports the volume file system. The subdirectory names are the same as the respective volume IDs.

Pathname lookups are broken down into component-wise lookup operations in the kernel. Recently looked up names are cached[16] so that the namei() function

---

16. Resource fork names are not cached.

does not have to go all the way down to the file system on every lookup. At the catalog-level, tree searches are either one-step or two-step, depending on how the search key is populated. A Catalog B-Tree key is represented by the `HFSPlus-CatalogKey` structure.

`// bsd/hfs/hfs_format.h`

```
struct HFSPlusCatalogKey {
    u_int16_t    keyLength;

    // parent folder's CNID for file and folder records;
    // node's own CNID for thread records
    u_int32_t    parentID;

    // node's Unicode name for file and folder records;
    // empty string for thread records
    HFSUniStr255 nodeName;
};
```

Figure 12–13 shows an overview of how the Catalog B-Tree is searched. If we begin with only the CNID of the target object, a two-step search is required. The search key is prepared as follows: The `parentID` field of the `HFSPlusCatalogKey` structure is set to the target's CNID, and the `nodeName` field is set to the empty string. A B-Tree lookup performed with such a key yields the target's thread record (if it exists). The contents of the thread record—the target's node name and its parent's CNID—are what we require to perform a one-step search. A second lookup will yield an `HFSPlusCatalogFile` or `HFSPlusCatalogFolder` record, depending on whether the target is a file or a folder, respectively. When comparing two catalog keys, their `parentID` fields are compared first and the `nodeName` fields are compared next.

Figure 12–14 shows an overall picture of how a file might be accessed by an HFS+ implementation. Suppose we wish to read a file. We will start at the volume header (1), which will provide us with the extents of the Catalog file (2). We will search the Catalog B-Tree to find the desired file record (3), which will contain the file's metadata and initial extents (4). Given the latter, we can seek the appropriate disk sectors and read the file data (5). If the file has more than eight extents, we will have to perform one or more additional lookups in the Extents Overflow file.

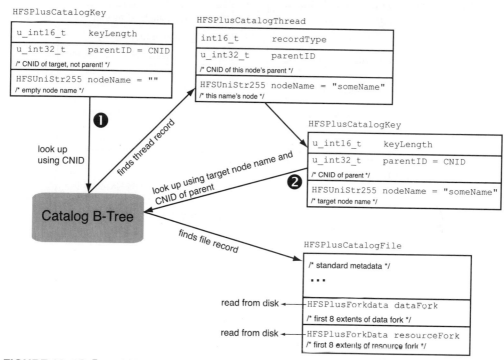

FIGURE 12–13 Searching in the Catalog B-Tree

12.7.2.1 Catalog Node IDs

As noted earlier, each file and folder on an HFS+ volume—including the special files—is assigned a unique CNID, which is implemented as a 32-bit unsigned integer. Apple reserves the first 16 CNIDs for its own use. Table 12–2 shows how these CNIDs are used.

> The next unused CNID is maintained in both the volume header (as the nextCatalogID field) and the hfsmount structure (as the vcb-NxtCNID field).

The first CNID available for user files and folders is 16. In practice, it will be assigned to a file or a folder created before the user begins to access the volume—for example, a journal file.

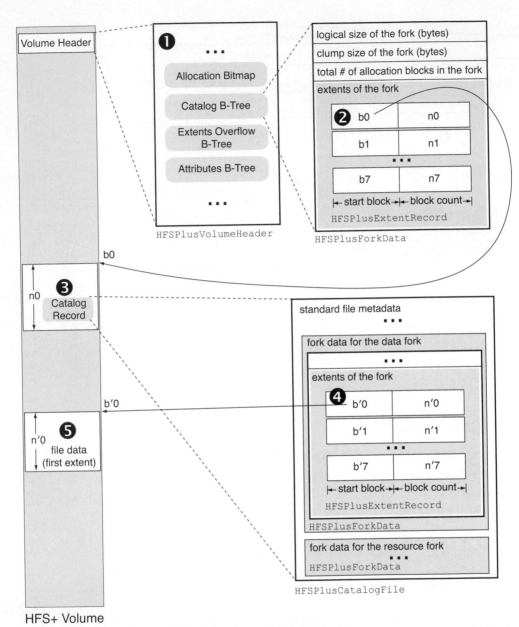

HFS+ Volume

FIGURE 12–14 An overview of accessing a file's contents

An interesting property of HFS+ is that it allows a Unix pathname of a file system object to be determined from its inode number. With the exception of hard links, an object's CNID is used as its inode number from the standpoint of the Unix APIs. Since a thread record connects an object to its parent, a complete pathname can be constructed by repeatedly looking up thread records until we reach the root. Note that we say "a pathname" and not "the pathname" because a Unix-visible inode number may have more than one referring pathname if the file's link count is greater than one—that is, if it has several hard links.[17]

TABLE 12–2 Standard CNID Assignments on HFS+ Volumes

CNID	Assignment
0	Invalid CNID—never used for a file system object.
1	Represents the parent ID of the root folder (for the purpose of B-Tree lookups).
2	Root folder's ID (similar to the Unix convention of using 2 as the inode number for a file system's root directory).
3	The Extents Overflow file's ID.
4	The Catalog file's ID.
5	Used as the ID of a hypothetical file (the Bad Blocks file) that owns allocation blocks containing bad sectors. The Bad Blocks file does not have any catalog records—all its extents are in the Extents Overflow file.
6	The Allocation file's ID.
7	The Startup file's ID.
8	The Attributes file's ID.
9	Unused/reserved.
10	Unused/reserved.
11	Unused/reserved.
12	Unused/reserved.
13	Unused/reserved.
14	Used as the ID of a temporary Catalog file while the file system is being repaired.
15	Used temporarily during an invocation of the `exchangedata()` system call, which performs an atomic swap of the fork data in two files.

---

17. As is normally the case on file systems that support hard links, HFS+ does not permit hard links to directories.

hfsdebug supports the previously mentioned methods of looking up a file system object, for example:

```
$ sudo hfsdebug -c 16 # look up by CNID
<Catalog B-Tree node = 9309 (sector 0x32c88)>
  path                 = Macintosh HD:/.journal
# Catalog File Record
  type                 = file
  file ID              = 16
...
$ sudo hfsdebug -F 2:.journal # look up by node name and parent's CNID
<Catalog B-Tree node = 9309 (sector 0x32c88)>
  path                 = Macintosh HD:/.journal
...
```

The Carbon File Manager provides the PBResolveFileIDRefSync() function to retrieve the node name and parent CNID of a file system object given its CNID. The program shown in Figure 12–15 prints the Unix pathname of a file or folder—given its CNID—residing on the default (root) volume. It continues to find the name of each component of the given pathname until the parent ID of a given component is the same as that of the component.

FIGURE 12–15 Using the Carbon File Manager API to convert a CNID to a Unix pathname

```c
// cnid2path.c

#include <stdio.h>
#include <sys/param.h>
#include <Carbon/Carbon.h>

typedef struct { // this is returned by PBResolveFileIDRefSync()
    unsigned char length;
    unsigned char characters[255];
} HFSStr255;

int
main(int argc, char **argv)
{
    FIDParam   pb;
    OSStatus   result;
    long       tmpSrcDirID;
    int        len = MAXPATHLEN - 1;
    char       path[MAXPATHLEN] = { '\0' };
    char       *cursor = (char *)(path + (MAXPATHLEN - 1));
    char       *upath;
    HFSStr255 *p, pbuf;
```

(continues)

FIGURE 12–15 Using the Carbon File Manager API to convert a CNID to a Unix pathname *(continued)*

```
    if (argc != 2) {
        fprintf(stderr, "usage: %s <CNID>\n", argv[0]);
        exit(1);
    }

    tmpSrcDirID = atoi(argv[1]);

    pb.ioVRefNum = 0;    // no volume reference number -- use default
    pb.ioSrcDirID = -1; // parent directory ID -- we don't know it yet

    while (1) {

        pb.ioNamePtr = (StringPtr)&pbuf; // a pointer to a pathname
        pb.ioFileID = tmpSrcDirID;         // the given CNID
        if ((result = PBResolveFileIDRefSync((HParmBlkPtr)&pb)) < 0)
            return result;

        if ((pb.ioSrcDirID == tmpSrcDirID) || (len <= 0)) {
            cursor++;
            break;
        }

        p = (HFSStr255 *)&pbuf;
        cursor -= (p->length);
        memcpy(cursor, p->characters, p->length);
        *--cursor = '/';
        len -= (1 + p->length);

        tmpSrcDirID = pb.ioSrcDirID;
    }

    if ((upath = strchr(cursor, '/')) != NULL) {
        *upath = '\0';
        upath++;
    } else
        upath = "";

    printf("%s:/%s\n", cursor, upath);

    return 0;
}
```

```
$ gcc -Wall -o cnid2path cnid2path.c -framework Carbon
$ ls -i /mach_kernel
2150438 /mach_kernel
$ ./cnid2path 2150438
Macintosh HD:/mach_kernel
```

12.7.2.2 *Examining the Catalog B-Tree*

We can use hfsdebug to examine the header node of the Catalog B-Tree (Figure 12–16) and to list one or more types of records contained in the tree's leaf nodes.

FIGURE 12–16 The contents of a Catalog B-Tree's header node

```
$ sudo hfsdebug -v
...
  fileCount           = 1447728
  folderCount         = 148872 /* not including the root folder */
...
$ sudo hfsdebug -b catalog
# HFS+ Catalog B-Tree
# B-Tree Node Descriptor
  fLink               = 60928
  bLink               = 0
  kind                = 1 (kBTHeaderNode)
  height              = 0
  numRecords          = 3
  reserved            = 0
# B-Tree Header Record
  treeDepth           = 4
  rootNode            = 38030
  leafRecords         = 3193202
  firstLeafNode       = 9309
  lastLeafNode        = 71671
  nodeSize            = 8192 bytes
  maxKeyLength        = 516 bytes
  totalNodes          = 73984
  freeNodes           = 2098
  reserved1           = 0
  clumpSize           = 35651584 (ignored)
  btreeType           = 0 (kHFSBTreeType)
  keyCompareType      = 0xcf (kHFSCaseFolding, case-insensitive)
  attributes          = 00000000000000000000000000000110
                        . kBTBigKeys (keyLength is UInt16)
                        . kBTVariableIndexKeys
```

The volume whose Catalog B-Tree's header node is shown in Figure 12–16 contains over 3 million leaf nodes. We can verify that the precise number is equal to exactly twice the sum of the volume's file and folder counts, with the folder count being one more than what's displayed (to account for the root folder). Of particular interest is the tree's depth—only 4. The node size of 8KB is the default for volumes greater than 1GB in size.[18]

12.7.3 The Extents Overflow File

Depending on the amount and contiguity of free space available on a volume, allocation of storage to a file fork may be physically noncontiguous. In other words, a fork's logically contiguous content may be divided into multiple contiguous segments, or extents. We earlier defined an extent descriptor as a pair of numbers representing a contiguous range of allocation blocks belonging to a fork, and an extent record as an array of eight extent descriptors. A file record in the catalog has space for holding an extent record each for the file's data and resource forks. If a fork has more than eight fragments, its remaining extents are stored in the leaf nodes of the Extents Overflow file.

Unlike the Catalog B-Tree, which has multiple types of leaf records, the Extents Overflow B-Tree has only one, consisting of a single `HFSPlusExtentRecord` structure. The key format is represented by the `HFSPlusExtentKey` structure, which consists of a fork type (`forkType`), a CNID (`fileID`), and a starting allocation block number (`startBlock`). Whereas the Catalog B-Tree uses variable-length keys, the Extents Overflow keys are fixed-size. Figure 12–17 shows the data types used in the key format. When comparing two Extents Overflow B-Tree keys, their `fileID` fields are compared first, followed by the `forkType` fields, and finally the `startBlock` fields.

12.7.3.1 Examining Fragmentation

We can use `hfsdebug` to display all fragmented file forks on a volume. Fragmentation in file systems has traditionally been an important factor that affects performance negatively. Modern file systems are usually less prone to fragmentation than their ancestors are. Numerous algorithms and schemes have been incorporated into file systems to reduce fragmentation and, in some cases, even *undo* existing fragmentation—the Mac OS X HFS+ implementation is an example of the latter. Nevertheless, fragmentation is still a cause for concern for both the designers and the users of file systems.

---

18. The default catalog B-Tree node size is 4KB for volumes less than 1GB in size.

What Is Fragmentation?

In a typical scenario, an operating system uses a disk drive in a mode where the drive's storage space appears as a logically contiguous sequence of blocks. The drive performs read-ahead operations and supports large-size I/O requests for contiguous blocks. The performance of modern drives is higher when I/O requests have a larger size. More contiguity in file allocation allows for larger I/O requests (plus any CPU overheads may be amortized), leading to better sequential I/O performance. Therefore, it is desirable for data to be contiguous on disk. It is somewhat subjective and context-dependent to define fragmentation, especially since it can exist in several forms, such as those listed here.

- *User-level data fragmentation*—Even if a file is contiguous on disk, it may contain information that is not contiguous at the user level. For example, a word processor document may be contiguous on disk but not in how the word processor reads it. It is both difficult and not worthwhile to quantify or deal with such fragmentation because it depends on the application in question, the file format, and other hard-to-control factors. We will not discuss this kind of fragmentation here.

- *Internal fragmentation*—We alluded to internal fragmentation in Section 12.2.2. Both the allocation block size and the storage medium's sector size are much larger than a byte-stream's fundamental unit of storage consumption: a byte. On a volume with 4KB allocation blocks, a 1-byte file would "use" 4KB of on-disk storage. Thus, 4095 bytes would be wasted until the file's size grows. Such wastage is referred to as internal fragmentation.

- *External fragmentation*—External fragmentation is what people usually mean when they refer to fragmentation. A file is externally fragmented if not all its contents reside in contiguous blocks at the volume level. We can consider a fragment to be synonymous with an HFS+ extent. In other words, an unfragmented file has exactly one extent. Each additional extent introduces one discontinuity in the file.

Since an HFS+ file can have a data fork, a resource fork, and an arbitrary number of named forks (see Section 12.7.4), each of which is an on-disk stream of bytes, it is easier to talk about a fork's fragmentation rather than a file's fragmentation. Moreover, since a data or resource fork's first eight extent descriptors are resident in the file's Catalog file record, we can classify the fragmentation of these forks as mild (at least two and at most eight extents) or severe (more than eight extents).

HFSPlusExtentKey

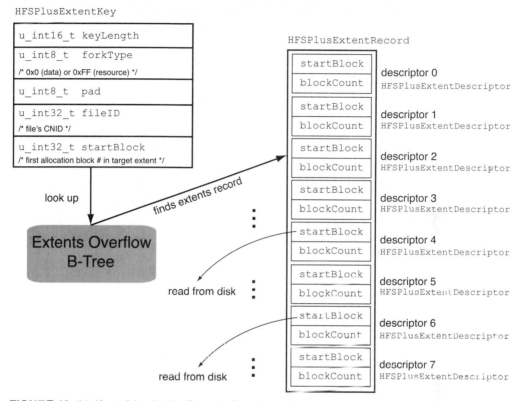

FIGURE 12–17 Searching in the Extents Overflow B-Tree

We can use hfsdebug to obtain summarized usage statistics for a volume. The information printed includes the total sizes of all the data and resource forks on the volume, along with the amounts of storage actually allocated. The difference between allocated storage and actual usage quantifies internal fragmentation.

```
$ sudo hfsdebug -s
# Volume Summary Information
    files                       = 1448399
    folders                     = 149187
    aliases                     = 10
    hard links                  = 6010
    symbolic links              = 13037
    invisible files             = 737
    empty files                 = 10095
  # Data Forks
    non-zero data forks         = 1437152
    fragmented data forks       = 2804
```

```
    allocation blocks used         = 31022304
    allocated storage              = 127067357184 bytes
                                      (124089216.00 KB/121180.88 MB/118.34 GB)
    actual usage                   = 123375522741 bytes
                                      (120483908.93 KB/117660.07 MB/114.90 GB)
    total extent records           = 1437773
    total extent descriptors       = 1446845
    overflow extent records        = 621
    overflow extent descriptors    = 4817
 # Resource Forks
    non-zero resource forks        = 11570
    fragmented resource forks      = 650
    allocation blocks used         = 158884
    allocated storage              = 650788864 bytes
                                      (635536.00 KB/620.64 MB/0.61 GB)
    actual usage                   = 615347452 bytes
                                      (600925.25 KB/586.84 MB/0.57 GB)
    total extent records           = 11570
    total extent descriptors       = 12234
    overflow extent records        = 0
    overflow extent descriptors    = 0
```

```
10418 files have content in both their data and resource forks.
```

We can also use hfsdebug to examine the fragmented forks in more detail. When run with the -f option, hfsdebug lists all forks with more than one extent on the volume. For each fork, the output consists of the following information:

- The owning file's CNID
- The fork's type
- A map of the fork's layout on disk (e.g., the string ":10:20:30:" for a fork that has three extents containing 10, 20, and 30 blocks, respectively)
- The size of the fork in bytes
- The fork's total number of allocation blocks
- The fork's total number of extents
- The fork's average blocks per extent
- The owning file's Unix pathname

```
$ sudo hfsdebug -f
# Volume Fragmentation Details
cnid=877872 fork=data map=:265:11:6:3:2:2:8: bytes=1213026 blocks=297 extents=7
avg=42.43 blks/ext path=Macintosh HD:/Desktop DF
cnid=329243 fork=data map=:256:27: bytes=1155108 blocks=283 extents=2 avg=141.50
blks/ext path=Macintosh HD:/%00%00%00%00HFS+ Private Data/iNode329243
...
```

12.7.3.2 Examining the Extents Overflow B-Tree

Figure 12–18 shows the output for the header node of the Extents Overflow B-Tree on the volume from Figure 12–16.

FIGURE 12–18 The contents of an Extents Overflow B-Tree's header node

```
$ sudo hfsdebug -b extents
# HFS+ Overflow Extents B-Tree
# B-Tree Node Descriptor
  fLink                 = 0
  bLink                 = 0
  kind                  = 1 (kBTHeaderNode)
  height                = 0
  numRecords            = 3
  reserved              = 0
# B-Tree Header Record
  treeDepth             = 2
  rootNode              = 3
  leafRecords           = 617
  firstLeafNode         = 13
  lastLeafNode          = 17
  nodeSize              = 4096 bytes
  maxKeyLength          = 10 bytes
  totalNodes            = 2048
  freeNodes             = 2030
  reserved1             = 0
  clumpSize             = 8388608 (ignored)
  btreeType             = 0 (kHFSBTreeType)
  keyCompareType        = 0 (unspecified/default)
  attributes            = 00000000000000000000000000000010
                        . kBTBigKeys (keyLength is UInt16)
```

Figure 12–18 shows that there are 617 leaf records in the tree. We can list all the leaf records to determine the number of files that have more than eight extents. As shown here, there are 37 such files in our example.

```
$ sudo hfsdebug -b extents -l any
# Extent Record
  keyLength             = 10
  forkType              = 0
  pad                   = 0
  fileID                = 118928
  startBlock            = 0x175 (373)
  path                  = Macintosh HD:/.Spotlight-V100/store.db
                              0x180dc7          0x50
                              0x180f3e          0x10
```

```
                                0x180f9d          0x40
                                0x1810ee          0x80
                                0x191a33          0xf0
                                0x1961dc          0x10
                                0x19646d          0x10
                                0x19648d          0x10
# Extent Record
  keyLength            = 10
^C
$ sudo hfsdebug -b extents -l any | grep fileID | sort | uniq | wc -l
37
```

12.7.4 The Attributes File

The Attributes file is a B-Tree that allows the implementation of *named forks*. A named fork is simply another byte-stream—similar to the data and resource forks. However, it can be associated with either a file or a folder, which can have any number of associated named forks. Beginning with Mac OS X 10.4, named forks are used to implement extended attributes for files and folders. In turn, the support for access control lists (ACLs) in Mac OS X 10.4 uses extended attributes for storing ACL data attached to files and folders. Each extended attribute is a name-value pair: The name is a Unicode string and the corresponding value is arbitrary data. As with node names in the Catalog B-Tree, the Unicode characters in attribute names are stored fully decomposed and in canonical order. Attribute data can have its own extents, so, in theory, attributes can be arbitrarily large. However, Mac OS X 10.4 supports only *inline* attributes, which can fit within a single B-Tree node while maintaining any structural overheads and other requirements for B-Tree nodes. In other words, inline attributes do not require any initial or overflow extents for their storage.

> A B-Tree node must be large enough that if it were an index node, it would contain at least two keys of maximum size. This means space must be reserved for at least three record offsets. Each node also has a node descriptor. Given that the default node size for the Attributes B-Tree is 8KB, the kernel calculates the maximum inline attribute size as 3802 bytes.

Figure 12–19 shows the key and record formats used in the Attributes B-Tree. The key format is represented by an `HFSPlusAttrKey` structure, which includes

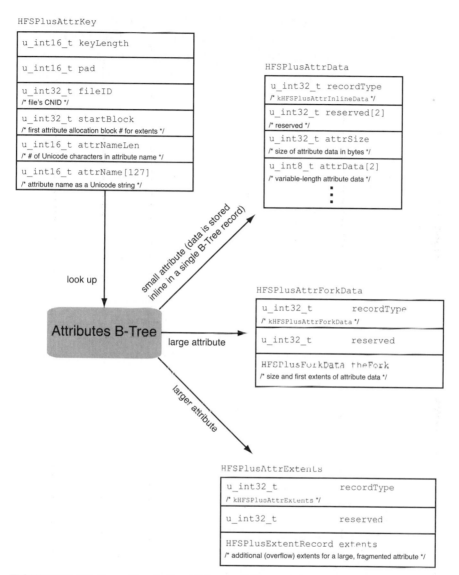

FIGURE 12–19 Searching in the Attributes B-Tree

a CNID (`fileID`), a starting allocation block number (`startBlock`) for attributes with extents, and a Unicode name (`attrName`) for the attribute.

When comparing two Attributes B-Tree keys, their `fileID` fields are compared first, followed by the `attrName` fields, and finally the `startBlock` fields. Figure 12–19 shows that there can be three types of records in the Attributes B-Tree. The one represented by an `HFSPlusAttrData` structure holds inline attribute data. The other two are used for larger attributes that require their extents to be tracked. `HFSPlusAttrForkData` includes an `HFSPlusForkData` structure—that is, up to eight initial extents. If an attribute's on-disk data is more fragmented, it will require one or more `HFSPlusAttrExtents` records, each of which will track an additional eight extents.

12.7.4.1 *Working with Extended Attributes*

Extended attributes of HFS+ file system objects are manipulated through the BSD system calls `setxattr()`, `getxattr()`, `listxattr()`, and `removexattr()`, all of which operate on pathnames.[19] These system calls also have variants—with an `f` prefix in their names—that operate on open file descriptors.

There is a single, global namespace for attributes. Although attribute names can be arbitrary, Apple recommends using a reverse-DNS-style naming scheme. Examples of attributes commonly employed by the operating system include the following:

- `system.extendedsecurity`—a volume attribute held by the parent of the root folder (i.e., CNID 1) of a volume on which ACLs are enabled
- `com.apple.diskimages.recentcksum`—an attribute used by Apple's Disk Images framework for storing the checksum of the disk image file to which the attribute applies
- `com.apple.system.Security`—an attribute used for ACLs
- `com.apple.system.*`—protected system attributes
- `com.apple.FinderInfo`—a fake attribute mapped to a file or folder's Finder information (fake in that it is not actually stored in the Attributes B-Tree)
- `com.apple.ResourceFork`—a fake attribute mapped to a file's resource fork

The program shown in Figure 12–20 sets and retrieves extended attributes for the given pathname.

---

19. In Mac OS X 10.4, no other application environment besides BSD has interfaces for manipulating extended attributes.

FIGURE 12–20 Programmatically setting an extended attribute

```c
// xattr.c

#include <stdio.h>
#include <string.h>
#include <unistd.h>
#include <stdlib.h>
#include <sys/xattr.h>

#define PROGNAME "xattr"

void
usage()
{
    fprintf(stderr, "\
Set or remove extended attributes. Usage:\n\n\
    %s -s <attribute-name>=<attribute-value> <filename> # set\n\
    %s -r <attribute-name> <filename>                   # remove\n\n\
    Notes: <attribute-name> must not contain a '=' character\n\
           <filename> must be the last argument\n", PROGNAME, PROGNAME);
    exit(1);
}

int
main(int argc, char **argv)
{
    size_t      size;
    u_int32_t   position = 0;
    int         ch, ret, options = XATTR_NOFOLLOW;
    char        *path = NULL, *name = NULL, *value = NULL;

    if (argc != 4)
        usage();

    path = argv[argc - 1];
    argc--;

    while ((ch = getopt(argc, argv, "r:s:")) != -1) {
        switch (ch) {
        case 'r':
            if (ret = removexattr(path, optarg, options))
                perror("removexattr");
            break;

        case 's':
            name = optarg;
            if ((value = strchr(optarg, '=')) == NULL)
                usage();
```

(continues)

FIGURE 12–20 Programmatically setting an extended attribute *(continued)*

```
            *value = '\0';
            value++;
            size = strlen(value) + 1;
            if (ret = setxattr(path, name, value, size, position, options))
                perror("setxattr");
            break;

        default:
            usage();
        }
    }

    exit(ret);
}


$ gcc -Wall -o xattr xattr.c
$ touch /tmp/file.txt
$ ./xattr -s com.osxbook.importance=none /tmp/file.txt
$ sudo hfsdebug /tmp/file.txt
# Attributes
  <Attributes B-Tree node = 1 (sector 0x18f4758)>
  # Attribute Key
  keyLength          = 66
  pad                = 0
  fileID             = 3325378
  startBlock         = 0
  attrNameLen        = 27
  attrName           = com.osxbook.importance
  # Inline Data
  recordType         = 0x10
  reserved[0]        = 0
  reserved[1]        = 0
  attrSize           = 5 bytes
  attrData           = 6e 6f 6e 65 00
                          n  o  n  e
```

Note that HFS+ only *stores* extended attributes—it does not index them. In particular, it does not participate in search operations performed by the Spotlight search mechanism (see Section 11.8), which uses external index files, not extended attributes, to store metadata.

12.7.4.2 Examining the Attributes B-Tree

Unlike the Catalog and Extents Overflow B-Trees, the Attributes B-Tree is not a mandatory constituent of an HFS+ volume. Even if an HFS+ implementation supports extended attributes and ACLs, an attached HFS+ volume may have a zero-length Attributes file if no file system object on that volume has ever used these features. If this is the case, the volume's Attributes file will be created when a setxattr() operation is attempted on one of the volume's files or folders, or when ACLs are enabled for the volume.

```
$ hdiutil create -size 32m -fs HFSJ -volname HFSAttr /tmp/hfsattr.dmg
$ open /tmp/hfsattr.dmg
$ hfsdebug -V /Volumes/HFSAttr -v
...
# Attributes File
  logicalSize         = 0 bytes
...
$ fsaclctl -p /Volumes/HFSAttr
Access control lists are not supported or currently disabled on /Volumes/HFSAttr.
$ sudo fsaclctl -p /Volumes/HFSAttr -e
$ fsaclctl -p /Volumes/HFSAttr
Access control lists are supported on /Volumes/HFSAttr.
$ hfsdebug -V /Volumes/HFSAttr -v
...
# Attributes File
  logicalSize         = 1048576 bytes
  totalBlocks         = 256
  clumpSize           = 1048576 bytes
  extents             =    startBlock   blockCount     % of file
                              0xaf9        0x100       100.00 %
                      256 allocation blocks in 1 extents total.
                      256.00 allocation blocks per extent on an average.
...
```

We can create an ACL entry for a file and use hfsdebug to display the corresponding Attributes B-Tree record, which will illustrate how ACLs are stored as extended attributes on an HFS+ volume.

```
$ touch /Volumes/HFSAttr/file.txt
$ chmod +a 'amit allow read' /Volumes/HFSAttr/file.txt
$ hfsdebug /Volumes/HFSAttr/file.txt
# Attributes
  <Attributes B-Tree node = 1 (sector 0x57d8)>
  # Attribute Key
  keyLength           = 62
  pad                 = 0
  fileID              = 22
```

```
startBlock           = 0
attrNameLen          = 25
attrName             = com.apple.system.Security
# Inline Data
recordType           = 0x10
reserved[0]          = 0
reserved[1]          = 0
attrSize             = 68 bytes
attrData             = 01 2c c1 6d 00 00 00 00 00 00 00 00 00 00 00 00
                           ,    m

...

    # File Security Information
    fsec_magic           = 0x12cc16d
    fsec_owner           = 0 0 0 0 0 0 0 0 0 0 0 0 0 0 0 0
    fsec_group           = 0 0 0 0 0 0 0 0 0 0 0 0 0 0 0 0
    # ACL Record
    acl_entrycount       = 1
    acl_flags            = 0
      # ACL Entry
      ace_applicable     = 53 25 a9 39 2f 3f 49 35 b0 e4 7e f4 71 23 64 e9
        user             = amit
        uid              = 501
        group            = amit
        gid              = 501
      ace_flags          = 00000000000000000000000000000001 (0x000001)
                           . KAUTH_ACE_PERMIT
      ace_rights         = 00000000000000000000000000000010 (0x000002)
                           . KAUTH_VNODE_READ_DATA
```

12.7.5 The Startup File

HFS+ supports an optional Startup file that can contain arbitrary information—
such as a secondary bootloader—for use while booting the system. Since the
location of the Startup file is at a well-known offset in the volume header, it helps
a system without built-in HFS+ support (in ROM, say) to boot from an HFS+ volume. A Startup file is used for booting Mac OS X from an HFS+ volume on an
Old World machine. Other hardware compatibility issues aside, the machine is
likely to have booting problems because of its older Open Firmware. The firmware may not support HFS+. Moreover, it will be programmed to execute the
Mac OS ROM instead of BootX. One solution involves storing the XCOFF version of BootX in the Startup file and creating an HFS wrapper volume containing
a special "system" file that *patches* Open Firmware such that the firmware does
not execute the Mac OS ROM—instead, it loads BootX from the Startup file.

12.8 Examining HFS+ Features

In this section, we will look at several standard HFS+ features, such as case sensitivity, journaling, hard links, symbolic links, and aliases.

12.8.1 Case Sensitivity

By default, HFS+ is a case-preserving, case-insensitive file system, whereas traditional Unix file systems are case-sensitive. The case insensitivity of HFS+ might be undesirable in certain situations. Suppose you have an archive containing files called Makefile and makefile in the same directory:

```
$ tar -tf archive.tar
Makefile
makefile
```

If we extract these files on an HFS+ volume, the second file to be extracted would overwrite the first:

```
$ tar -xvf archive.tar
Makefile
makefile
$ ls *akefile
makefile
```

> The default case insensitivity of HFS+ applies only to file and folder names. Extended attribute names are always case-sensitive.

HFSX was introduced with Mac OS X 10.3 as an extension to HFS+ for supporting case-sensitive file and folder names. You can create a case-sensitive HFS+ file system by passing the -s option to newfs_hfs. HFSX disk images can be created using hdiutil.

```
$ hdiutil create -size 32m -fs HFSX -volname HFSX /tmp/hfsx.dmg
...
created: /tmp/hfsx.dmg
$ open /tmp/hfsx.dmg
$ hfsdebug -V /Volumes/HFSX -v
...
# HFS Plus Volume
  Volume size          = 32728 KB/31.96 MB/0.03 GB
# HFS Plus Volume Header
  signature            = 0x4858 (HX)
```

```
    version              = 0x5
    ...
$
```

Note the differences from a case-insensitive HFS+ volume: The volume signature is HX instead of H+, and the version is 5 instead of 4. A signature value of HX is still stored as H+ in memory and therefore is not flushed to disk.

The case sensitivity of a volume is also recorded in the `keyCompareType` field of the Catalog B-Tree. If this field's value is 0xbc, binary comparison (case-sensitive) is used to compare names. If the field's value is 0xcf, case folding is performed while comparing names. Note that `keyCompareType` is always 0xbc in the Attributes B-Tree and is irrelevant in the Extents Overflow B-Tree.

```
$ sudo hfsdebug -b catalog # root volume, should be case-insensitive by default
...
keyCompareType          = 0xcf (kHFSCaseFolding, case-insensitive)
...
$ hfsdebug -V /Volumes/HFSX -b catalog # case-sensitive volume
...
keyCompareType          = 0xbc (kHFSBinaryCompare, case-sensitive)
...
```

12.8.2 Filename Encodings

HFS+ uses Unicode for encoding names of files, folders, and extended attributes. As we saw in Section 12.7.2, file and folder names are represented by the HFSUniStr255 structure, which consists of a 16-bit length followed by up to 255 double-byte Unicode characters. HFS+ stores Unicode characters *fully decomposed*, with the composing characters being in *canonical order*. When strings containing such characters are exchanged between HFS+ and user space, they are encoded by the kernel as ASCII-compatible UTF-8 bytes (see Figure 12–21). hfsdebug can be used to view the Unicode characters stored on disk corresponding to a node name.

```
$ /bin/zsh
$ cd /tmp
$ touch `echo '\xe0\xa4\x85\xe0\xa4\xae\xe0\xa4\xbf\xe0\xa4\xa4'` # UTF-8
$ ls -wi # -w forces raw printing of non-ASCII characters
...
3364139 अमित # Terminal.app can display the name
$ sudo hfsdebug -c 3364139 # the UTF-8-encoded name can also be used here
  <Catalog B-Tree node = 68829 (sector 0x11b588)>
  path                 = Macintosh HD:/private/tmp/%0905%092e%093f%0924
...
```

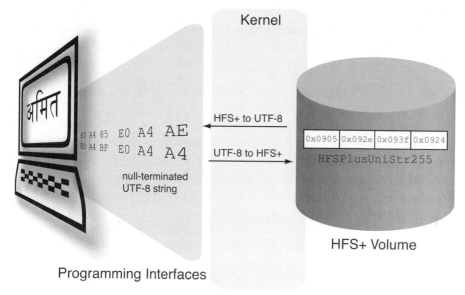

FIGURE 12–21 Unicode filenames in Mac OS X

HFS+ uses the : character as a path separator, whereas the Unix APIs use the / character. Since : cannot appear in an HFS+ node name, HFS+ translates any : characters that may appear in a user-provided node name (through a Unix API function, say) to / when storing them to disk. Conversely, when encoding an HFS+ Unicode string as a UTF-8 string for a Unix function, any / characters are translated to : characters.

UTF-8

Unicode is an encoding scheme that maps characters to integers. It is meant to contain characters for all known languages and various categories of symbols. Such a huge character set requires multiple bytes to be represented. Traditionally, operating systems have used single-byte characters. A convenient representation of Unicode on such systems is UTF-8, which is an 8-bit, variable-length encoding scheme. UTF-8 encodes each 7-bit ASCII character as itself in a single byte, whereas non-ASCII characters are encoded as multibyte sequences, with the high-order bits of the first byte indicating the number of bytes that follow. Moreover, UTF-8 preserves the C convention of null-terminated strings.

UTF-8 was created by Ken Thompson and Rob Pike. It was first implemented on Plan 9.

Older Mac OS APIs use file system names consisting of characters encoded using localization-specific Apple-only text encodings—for example, MacDevanagari, MacGreek, MacJapanese, and MacRoman. For the benefit of these APIs, file and folder records in the Catalog B-Tree contain a hint (the textEncoding field) for name conversions between Unicode and older text encodings. The various conversion tables are loadable, with the exception of tables for conversion between HFS MacRoman and Unicode—these are built into the kernel. The volume header contains a 64-bit encoding bitmap (the encodingsBitmap field) for recording encodings used on the volume. Based on this bitmap, the appropriate encoding tables—if available—may be loaded by an implementation when a volume is mounted. The directory /System/Library/Filesystems/hfs.fs/ Encodings/ contains loadable encodings.

12.8.3 Permissions

HFS+ provides Unix-style file system permissions. Both the HFSPlusCatalogFile and HFSPlusCatalogFolder structures include an HFSPlusBSDInfo structure that encapsulates information related to ownership, permissions, and file type.

```
struct HFSPlusBSDInfo {
    // owner ID 99 ("unknown") is treated as the user ID of the calling
    // process (substituted on the fly)
    u_int32_t ownerID;

    // group ID 99 ("unknown") is treated as the owner ID of the calling
    // process (substituted on the fly)
    u_int32_t groupID;

    // superuser-changeable BSD flags, see chflags(2)
    u_int8_t  adminFlags;

    // owner-changeable BSD flags, see chflags(2)
    u_int8_t ownerFlags;

    // file type and permission bits
    u_int16_t fileMode;

    union {
        // indirect inode number for hard links
        u_int32_t iNodeNum;

        // links that refer to this indirect node
        u_int32_t linkCount;
```

```
        // device number for block/character devices
        u_int32_t rawDevice;
    } special;
};
```

12.8.3.1 Manipulating Volume-Level Ownership Rights

Although permissions are mandatory on a root volume, they can be deactivated
on a nonroot HFS+ volume.

```
$ hdiutil create -size 32m -fs HFSJ -volname HFSPerms /tmp/hfsperms.dmg
...
$ open /tmp/hfsperms.dmg
$ touch /Volumes/HFSPerms/file.txt
$ chmod 600 /Volumes/HFSPerms/file.txt
$ sudo chown root:wheel /Volumes/HFSPerms/file.txt
$ ls -l /Volumes/HFSPerms
total 0
-rw-------   1 root  wheel  0 Oct 15 10:55 file.txt
$ mount -u -o noperm /Volumes/HFSPerms
$ ls -l /Volumes/HFSPerms
total 0
-rw------   1 amit  amit  0 Oct 11 10:55 file.txt
```

Disabling permissions essentially assigns the ownership of the volume's
files and folders to a single user ID—the so-called replacement user ID. The
replacement user ID can be explicitly specified; otherwise, the kernel will use
UNKNOWNUID, the unknown user's ID (99). UNKNOWNUID has the special property
that it matches any user ID when IDs are being compared for ownership rights
determination.

The replacement is purely behavioral. Each file system object retains its
original owner ID. The hfsmount structure holds the replacement ID in memory.

```
$ hfsdebug /Volumes/HFSPerms/file.txt
...
  # BSD Info
  ownerID            = 0 (root)
  groupID            = 0 (wheel)
...
$ sudo hfsdebug -V /Volumes/HFSPerms -m
...
  HFS+ flags                   = 00000000000000000000000000001110
                                 + HFS_UNKNOWN_PERMS
                                 + HFS_WRITEABLE_MEDIA
                                 + HFS_CLEANED_ORPHANS
  default owner                = { uid=99, gid=99 }
...
```

Note that the term *permissions* really means ownership in this context—the file mode bits are still honored.

```
$ chmod 000 /Volumes/HFSPerms/file.txt
$ cat /Volumes/HFSPerms/file.txt
cat: /Volumes/HFSPerms/file.txt: Permission denied
```

Figure 12–22 shows the algorithm that the Mac OS X HFS+ implementation uses to determine whether a given process has ownership rights to a file system object.

12.8.3.2 Repairing Permissions

Applications written using older APIs may disregard (and possibly even clobber) Unix-style permissions. Therefore, a permissions-unaware or misbehaving application can corrupt on-disk permissions if it is run with enough privileges. Mac OS X supports the concept of repairing permissions to address this problem.

Permissions are usually repaired only on a boot volume. The Mac OS X installer uses a *bill of materials* for each package it installs. A bill-of-materials (*bom*) file contains a listing of all files within a directory, along with metadata for each file. In particular, it contains each file's Unix permissions. Bom files for installed packages are located within the package metadata[20] found in /Library/ Receipts/. Tools that repair permissions use these bom files to determine the original permissions.

Let us create a disk image with some files, create a bom file for the disk image, corrupt a file's permissions, and then repair permissions on the volume. Note that we need to make the disk image look like a boot volume to the programs we will use in this experiment.

First we create a disk image, mount it, and ensure that permissions are enabled.

```
$ hdiutil create -size 32m -fs HFSJ -volname HFSPR /tmp/hfspr.dmg
...
$ open /tmp/hfspr.dmg
$ mount -u -o perm /Volumes/HFSPR
```

---

20. For a given package, this metadata is also known as its *package receipt*.

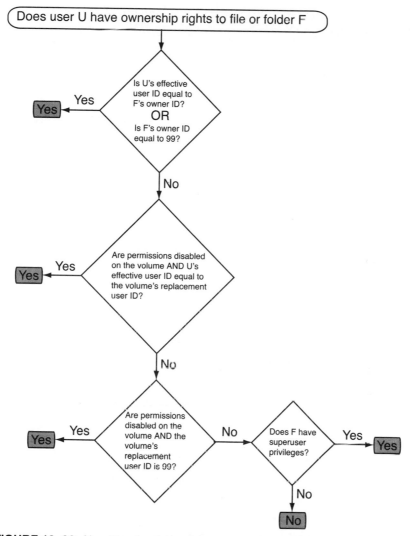

FIGURE 12–22 Algorithm for determining ownership rights to a file system object

Next we add certain files to the volume so that the permissions repair tool
will run on it.

```
$ mkdir -p /Volumes/HFSPR/System/Library/CoreServices
$ mkdir -p /Volumes/HFSPR/Library/Receipts/BaseSystem.pkg/Contents
$ cp /System/Library/CoreServices/SystemVersion.plist \
        /Volumes/HFSPR/System/Library/CoreServices/
```

Then we create a file whose permissions we will repair. We also set the file's permissions to some initial value.

```
$ touch /Volumes/HFSPR/somefile.txt
$ chmod 400 /Volumes/HFSPR/somefile.txt
```

Next we create a bom file for the disk image. Note that during creation of the bom file, the existing permissions on somefile.txt will be picked up as the correct ones.

```
$ cd /Volumes/HFSPR/Library/Receipts/BaseSystem.pkg/Contents/
$ sudo mkbom /Volumes/HFSPR Archive.bom
```

Finally we change the permissions on somefile.txt and run diskutil to repair the volume's permissions.

```
$ chmod 444 /Volumes/HFSPR/somefile.txt
$ sudo diskutil repairPermissions /Volumes/HFSPR
Started verify/repair permissions on disk disk10s2 HFSPR
Determining correct file permissions.
Permissions differ on ./somefile.txt, should be -r-------- , they are -r--r--r--
Owner and group corrected on ./somefile.txt
Permissions corrected on ./somefile.txt
The privileges have been verified or repaired on the selected volume
Verify/repair finished permissions on disk disk10s2 HFSPR
$ ls -l /Volumes/HFSPR/somefile.txt
-r--------   1 amit  amit  0 Oct 16 12:27 /Volumes/HFSPR/somefile.txt
```

12.8.4 Journaling

HFS+ supports *journaling* of metadata, including volume data structures, wherein metadata-related file system changes are recorded to a log file (the *journal*) that is implemented as a circular on-disk buffer.[21] The primary purpose of a journal is to ensure file system consistency in the case of failure. Certain file system operations are semantically atomic but may result in considerable I/O internally. For example, creating a file, which involves adding the file's thread and file records to the Catalog B-Tree, will cause one or more disk blocks to be written. If the tree needs balancing, several more blocks will be written. If a failure occurs before all changes have been committed to physical storage, the file system will be in an inconsistent state—perhaps even irrecoverably so. Journaling allows

---

21. Since the journaling mechanism first writes intended changes to the journal file and then to the actual destination blocks (typically in the buffer cache), it is said to perform *write-ahead journaling*.

related modifications to be grouped into *transactions* that are recorded in a journal file. Then related modifications can be committed to their final destinations in a transactional manner—either all of them or none at all. Journaling makes it easier and significantly faster to repair the volume after a crash, because only a small amount of information—that contained in the journal—needs to be examined. Without a journal, the entire volume would typically need to be scanned by fsck_hfs for inconsistencies.

> Since writes to files occur independently of the journal, which strives only to keep the metadata consistent, journaling cannot guarantee consistency *between* a file's metadata and its user data.

Syncing Fully

The journal implementation uses the DKIOCSYNCHRONIZECACHE ioctl operation to flush media state to the drive. This ioctl is also used to implement the F_FULLFSYNC fcntl(2) command, which performs a similar flush operation. More precisely, the flush operation is *attempted*—it may or may not succeed, depending on whether the underlying device supports and honors the corresponding hardware command. Figure 12–23 shows how an F_FULLFSYNC request on an HFS+ file is propagated from user space to an ATA device that supports the FLUSH CACHE command.

Journaling was retrofitted into HFS+ by introducing a VFS-level journaling layer in the kernel [bsd/vfs/vfs_journal.c]. This layer exports an interface that can be used by any file system to incorporate a journal. Figure 12–24 shows an overview of the journaling interface and its use by HFS+. Note that from the journal's standpoint, modifications are performed in units of *journal block size*, which must be specified when the journal is created. HFS+ uses the physical block size (typically 512 bytes for disks) as the journal block size. When HFS+ needs to modify one or more blocks as part of an operation, it starts a journal transaction to encapsulate related changes. Modification of each block is indicated separately to the journal. When all blocks in the transactions have been modified, the file system ends the transaction. When the volume is cleanly unmounted, the transactions recorded in the journal are committed by copying modified blocks from the journal file to their actual on-disk locations, which are also recorded in the journal.

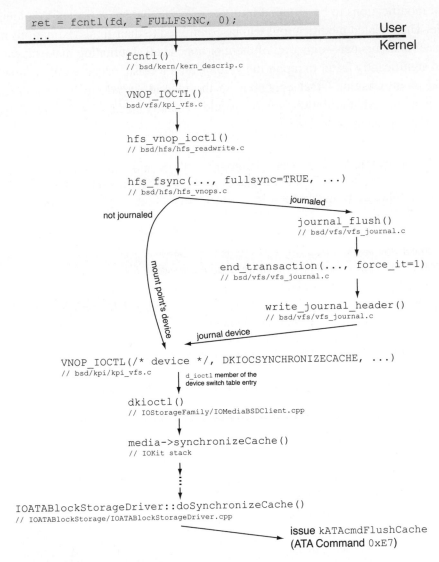

FIGURE 12–23 Processing of the `F_FULLFSYNC` file control operation

When a journaled volume is mounted, HFS+ checks the `lastMountedVersion` field of the volume header to determine whether the last mount was performed by a journaling-aware implementation, in which case the field would contain `HFSJ`, as we saw earlier. If that is the case, and the journal contains uncommitted transactions (because of an unclean shutdown, say), HFS+ will commit transactions recorded in the journal before the volume is available—that is, the journal will be *replayed*.

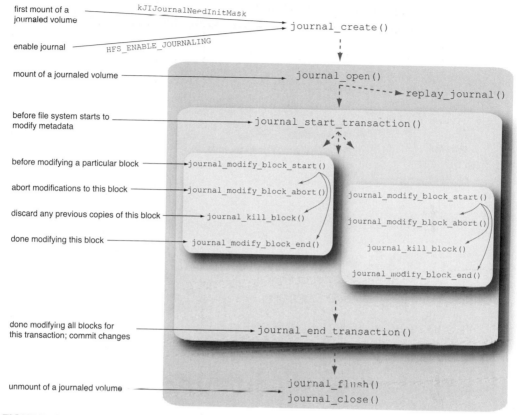

FIGURE 12–24 The VFS-layer journaling interface in Mac OS X

The volume header on a journaled HFS+ volume contains the location of a data structure called the *journal info block*, which in turn contains the location and size of the journal proper. The latter consists of a header and a circular buffer. Both the info block and the journal are stored as files: `.journal_info_block` and `.journal`, respectively. Both these files are contiguous (occupying exactly one extent each). They are normally neither visible nor directly accessible through the file system APIs. The invisibility is implemented inside the kernel, as the file system's catalog-level lookup routine returns an ENOENT error if the file's CNID matches that of one of the journal files. The journal files may be seen, if they exist, through an EFI or Open Firmware shell, for example:

```
0 > dir hd:\
...
 8388608 10/ 7/ 3  2:11:34          .journal
    4096 10/ 7/ 3  2:11:34          .journal_info_block
...
```

hfsdebug can also retrieve information about the journal files. We specify a journal file to it by providing its name and the CNID of its parent (the root folder).

```
$ sudo hfsdebug -F 2:.journal
<Catalog B-Tree node = 9309 (sector 0x32c88)>
  path                   = Macintosh HD:/.journal
# Catalog File Record
  type                   = file
  file ID                = 16
...
  extents                =    startBlock   blockCount     % of file
                                   0x4c7       0x1000       100.00 %
                           4096 allocation blocks in 1 extents total.
                           4096.00 allocation blocks per extent on an average.

...
```

Figure 12–25 shows the structures of the journal files.

We can use hfsdebug to view the contents of the .journal_info_block file and the journal header.

```
$ sudo hfsdebug -j
# HFS+ Journal
# Journal Info Block
  flags                  = 00000000000000000000000000000001
                           . Journal resides on local volume itself.
  device_signature       =
...
  offset                 = 5009408 bytes
  size                   = 16777216 bytes
  reserved               =
...
# Journal Header
  magic                  = 0x4a4e4c78
  endian                 = 0x12345678
  start                  = 15369216 bytes
  end                    = 677376 bytes
  size                   = 16777216 bytes
  blhdr_size             = 16384 bytes
  checksum               = 0x8787407e
  jhdr_size              = 512 bytes
```

With reference to Figure 12–25, the structure of a transaction is as follows. Each transaction consists of one or more block lists. Each block list begins with a block_list_header structure, followed by two or more block_info structures, and finally followed by the actual block data—one chunk for each block_info structure *except the first*.

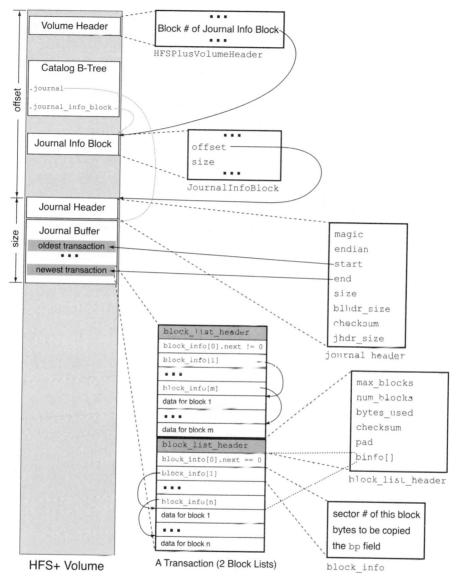

FIGURE 12–25 An overview of the file-system-independent journal used by HFS+

```
typedef struct block_info {
    off_t       bnum;   // sector number where data in this block is to be written
    size_t      bsize;  // number of bytes to be copied from journal buffer to bnum
    struct buf *bp;     // used as "next" when on disk
} block_info;
```

The first `block_info` structure connects two consecutive block lists as part of the same transaction. If the first structure's `bp` field is 0, the current block list is the last in the current transaction. If the `bp` field is not 0, then the transaction continues on to the next block list.

12.8.4.1 Enabling or Disabling Journaling on a Volume

The `diskutil` program can be used to enable or disable journaling on a mounted HFS+ volume. The `hfs.util` program (/System/Library/Filesystems/ hfs.fs/hfs.util) can also be used for this purpose and to display the size and location of the journal file.

```
$ /System/Library/Filesystems/hfs.fs/hfs.util -I "/Volumes/Macintosh HD"
/Volumes/Macintosh HD : journal size 16384 k at offset 0x4c7000
```

The following sysctl operations, defined in `bsd/hfs/hfs_mount.h`, allow programmatic manipulation of the journal:

- `HFS_ENABLE_JOURNALING`
- `HFS_DISABLE_JOURNALING`
- `HFS_GET_JOURNAL_INFO`

12.8.4.2 Observing the Journal's Operation

Let us now use `hfsdebug` to view the contents of the journal buffer and relate them to specific file system operations. We will create a fresh disk image for this purpose.

```
$ hdiutil create -size 32m -fs HFSJ -volname HFSJ /tmp/hfsj.dmg
...
$ open /tmp/hfsj.dmg
$ hfsdebug -V /Volumes/HFSJ -J
# HFS+ Journal
# Journal Buffer

# begin transaction
  # Block List Header
  max_blocks         = 1023
  num_blocks         = 5
  bytes_used         = 29184
  checksum           = 0xfdfd8386
  pad                = 0
  binfo[0].bp        = 0
     block_info[  1] { bnum 0x0000000000004218 bsize  4096 bytes bp 0x5208ed90 }
```

```
   block_info[  2] { bnum 0x0000000000004210 bsize  4096 bytes bp 0x52147860 }
   block_info[  3] { bnum 0x0000000000000002 bsize   512 bytes bp 0x5208d440 }
   block_info[  4] { bnum 0x0000000000000008 bsize  4096 bytes bp 0x520ea6e0 }
#end transaction

Summary: 5 blocks using 29184 bytes in 1 block lists.
```

We see that the newly mounted volume has several modified blocks recorded in the journal. Recall that the journal is using disk sectors for blocks. block_info[3]'s target sector is 2, which is the volume header. As we saw earlier, the disk arbitration daemon would have created the .Trashes folder when we mounted the newly created volume. The modifications to the Catalog B-Tree and the Allocation file must also be part of the journal records. Let us verify this.

```
$ hfsdebug -V /Volumes/HFSJ -v
...
  blockSize              = 4096 bytes
...
# Allocation Bitmap File
  logicalSize            = 4096 bytes
  totalBlocks            = 1
  clumpSize              = 4096 bytes
  extents                =    startBlock    blockCount    % of file
                                  0x1           0x1       100.00 %
...
# Catalog File
  logicalSize            = 258048 bytes
  totalBlocks            = 63
  clumpSize              = 258048 bytes
  extents                =    startBlock    blockCount    % of file
                                  0x842        0x3f        100.00 %
...
```

The Allocation file is entirely contained within allocation block number 1—that is, it starts at sector 8 and is 4096 bytes in size. Therefore, block_info[4] corresponds to the Allocation file.

block_info[1] and block_info[2] correspond to allocation block numbers 0x843 and 0x842, respectively. (We simply divide the sector numbers by 8, since a 4KB allocation block contains 8 512-byte sectors.) Both these allocation blocks belong to the Catalog file. Since allocation block 0x842 (sector 0x4210) is also the beginning of the Catalog file, it is the location of the tree's header node. hfsdebug displays the sector number where a given Catalog file record's tree node is located. Let us use it to display this information for the .Trashes folder.

```
$ hfsdebug -V /Volumes/HFSJ/.Trashes
<Catalog B-Tree node = 1 (sector 0x4218)>
  path                    = HFSJ:/.Trashes
# Catalog Folder Record
...
```

Thus, all records in the journal are accounted for.

12.8.5 Quotas

HFS+ supports volume-level quotas based on user and group IDs. It theoretically supports quotas based on other criteria, since the in-memory catalog-node structure (struct cnode [bsd/hfs/hfs_cnode.h]) contains an *array* of disk quota usage records (struct dquot [bsd/sys/quota.h]). The array contains two elements in Mac OS X 10.4, one for user quotas and one for group quotas. The corresponding quota filenames are .quota.user and .quota.group. These files reside in the file system's root directory. Each file contains a header followed by a hash table of structures specifying various quota limits and usage values for user or group IDs. These IDs are hashed to yield offsets into the quota hash tables.

We can enable user (group) quotas on a volume by creating an empty mount options file named .quota.ops.user (.quota.ops.group) in the volume's root directory. The presence of this file would cause user (group) quotas to be enabled at mount time, provided a .quota.user (.quota.group) file also exists. The latter file is created by running the quotacheck program.

Let us create an HFS+ disk image and enable quotas on it. By default, a Mac OS X client installation does not have quotas enabled. You can use the quota or repquota commands to view quota information for a file system.

```
$ sudo repquota -a
$ hdiutil create -size 32m -fs HFSJ -volname HFSQ /tmp/hfsq.dmg
$ open /tmp/hfsq.dmg
$ mount -u -o perm,uid=99 /Volumes/HFSQ
$ sudo touch /Volumes/HFSQ/.quota.ops.user /Volumes/HFSQ/.quota.ops.group
$ sudo quotacheck -ug /Volumes/HFSQ
quotacheck: creating quota file /Volumes/HFSQ/.quota.user
quotacheck: creating quota file /Volumes/HFSQ/.quota.group
```

We can now turn quotas on using the quotaon command.

```
$ sudo quotaon -ug /Volumes/HFSQ
$ sudo repquota -u /Volumes/HFSQ
```

		1K Block limits			File limits			
User		used	soft	hard	grace	used	soft	hard	grace
amit	--	8	0	0		4	0	0	

We see that the user has already consumed a few inodes (because of `.DS_Store` and such). We can edit a user's quota values using the `edquota` command, which will launch the text editor specified by the `EDITOR` environment variable (or `vi`, if `EDITOR` is not set).

```
$ sudo edquota -u amit
Quotas for user amit:
/Volumes/HFSQ: 1K blocks in use: 8, limits (soft = 0, hard = 0)
        inodes in use: 4, limits (soft = 4, hard = 4)
```

We change the `soft` and `hard` limits and save the file, after which there is a limit on the total number of files and folders the user can have on this volume.

```
$ sudo repquota -u /Volumes/HFSQ
                    1K Block limits                  File limits
User            used      soft      hard  grace   used  soft  hard  grace
amit      -+      8         0         0            4     4     4
```

`repquota` reports the updated quota limits for user `amit`. Let us attempt to exceed this limit.

```
$ touch /Volumes/HFSQ/file.txt
touch: /Volumes/HFSQ/file.txt: Disc quota exceeded
```

12.8.6 Hard Links

On typical Unix file systems, each file has an associated *link count* representing the number of physical references to it. Suppose a file `foo` has a link count of 1. If you make a *hard link* `bar` to it (using the `ln` command or the `link()` system call), the following statements will apply to the two files.

- `foo` and `bar` are two different pathnames—with corresponding directory entries—that refer to the same physical file on disk. The links are equivalent in all respects. The `stat()` system call will return the same inode numbers for `foo` and `bar`.

- The link count of the file becomes 2. Since `foo` and `bar` are equivalent, the link counts of both files will be reported as 2.

- If you remove either `foo` or `bar`, the link count will decrease by 1. As long as the link count is greater than 0, the physical file will not be deleted.

We can consider a hard link to be simply another directory entry for an existing file. Normally, only files are allowed to have hard links, as hard links to folders can create cycles in the folder hierarchy—with highly undesirable results. Hard links may also not span across file systems.

> Early versions of UNIX allowed the superuser to create a hard link to a directory.

Hard links to a file on HFS+ are conceptually similar to those on Unix systems: They represent multiple directory entries referring to common file content. The Mac OS X implementation of HFS+ hard links uses a special *hard-link file* for each directory entry. The common file content is stored in another special file: the *indirect-node file*.

> The `linkCount` field in the `HFSPlusBSDInfo` structure, which we saw in Section 12.8.3, holds the link count for a file. A folder also has a link count that represents the number of its directory entries. However, a folder's `HFSPlusBSDInfo` structure does not hold the folder's link count in its `linkCount` field—the `valence` field of the `HFSPlusCatalogFolder` structure does. A folder's link count value, as reported by the Unix APIs, is two more than the on-disk value because of the . and .. directory entries, which are dummy entries on HFS+.

A hard-link file has a file type `hlnk` and a creator code `hfs+`. It is otherwise an ordinary file in the Catalog B-Tree. All indirect-node files are stored in the *private metadata folder*, which resides in the file system's root directory. When an HFS+ volume is mounted, the kernel checks for the existence of this folder, creating it if it doesn't exist. Several measures such as the following are taken to make the metadata folder tamper-resistant.

- Its name is four null characters (NUL) followed by the string "HFS+ Private Data".
- Its permissions are set to 000 by default—that is, no read, write, or execute access to anyone.
- It is set to be invisible in the Finder through the `kIsInvisible` Finder flag.
- Its `kNameLocked` Finder flag is set so that it cannot be renamed, nor can its icon be changed, from the Finder.
- Its icon location is set to (22460, 22460) in its Finder information.

The folder may be seen[22] from Open Firmware, where it sorts last in the output of the `dir` command.

```
0 > dir hd:\
...
   10/ 7/ 3  2: 7:21   %00%00%00%00HFS+%20Private%20Data
```

`hfsdebug` can be used to display the properties of this folder and those of its contents (Figure 12–26 shows an example). Since the folder is created before user files are created, it will typically have a low CNID. Given that the first user-available CNID is 16, the metadata folder is likely to have the CNID 18 on a journaled volume, since CNIDs 16 and 17 would have been taken by the two journal files.

FIGURE 12–26 Examining the HFS+ private metadata folder and hard-link creation

```
$ hdiutil create -size 32m -fs HFSJ -volname HFSLink /tmp/hfslink.dmg
$ open /tmp/hfslink.dmg
$ hfsdebug -V /Volumes/HFSLink -c 18
  <Catalog B-Tree node = 1 (sector 0x4218)>
  path                   = HFSLink:/%00%00%00%00HFS+ Private Data
# Catalog Folder Record
...
  # BSD Info
  ownerID                = 0 (root)
  groupID                = 0 (wheel)
  adminFlags             = 00000000
  ownerFlags             = 00000000
  fileMode               = d---------
...
  frFlags                = 0101000000000000
                           . kNameLocked
                           . kIsInvisible
  frLocation             = (v = 22460, h = 22460)
...
$ cd /Volumes/HFSLink
$ touch file.txt
$ ls -i file.txt # note the inode number
22 file.txt
$ ln file.txt link.txt
$ sudo hfsdebug link.txt
  <Catalog B-Tree node = 1 (sector 0x4218)>
  path                   = HFSLink:/link.txt
```

(continues)

---

22. However, the folder is *not* visible from an EFI shell.

FIGURE 12–26 Examining the HFS+ private metadata folder and hard-link creation *(continued)*

```
# Catalog File Record
  type                    = file (hard link)
  file ID                 = 24
  flags                   = 0000000000000010
                          . File has a thread record in the catalog.
...
  # BSD Info
  ownerID                 = 0 (root)
  groupID                 = 0 (wheel)
  adminFlags              = 00000000
  ownerFlags              = 00000000
  fileMode                = ----------
  iNodeNum                = 22 (link reference number)
...
  # Finder Info
  fdType                  = 0x686c6e6b (hlnk)
  fdCreator               = 0x6866732b (hfs+)
...
$ ls -l link.txt
-rw-r--r--   2 amit  amit  0 Oct 12 05:12 link.txt
```

It is also possible for the superuser to change directory to the private metadata folder (from a shell, say), provided its pathname is passed to the cd command *appropriately*. The problem is that the folder's name begins with NUL characters, which terminate C-style strings. We can use the NUL character's UTF-8 representation, which is the following byte sequence: 0xe2, 0x90, 0x80.

```
$ sudo /bin/zsh
# cd /Volumes/HFSLink
# cd "`echo '\xE2\x90\x80\xE2\x90\x80\xE2\x90\x80\xE2\x90\x80HFS+ Private Data'`"
# ls -l
iNode22
```

We see that the metadata folder on our example volume contains a single file named iNode22. We also see that 22 is the link reference number reported for the hard-link file (link.txt) we created in Figure 12–26—iNode22 is the indirect-node file for the hard link in question. An interesting observation is that the ownership and file mode details for link.txt in Figure 12–26 do not match between hfsdebug and the ls command. This is because link.txt is a kernel-owned reference to iNode22, which holds the original contents (along with the original ownership and file mode information) of the hard link's target `file.txt`. In fact, `file.txt` is also a hard-link file now and has properties similar to those of `link.txt`.

```
$ cd /Volumes/HFSLink
$ hfsdebug file.txt
...
# Catalog File Record
  type                 = file (hard link)
  indirect node file   = HFSLink:/%00%00%00%00HFS+ Private Data/iNode22
  file ID              = 23
...
```

> HFS+ indirect-node files are always named iNode<LRN>, where
> <LRN> is a *link reference number* represented in decimal. Link reference numbers are randomly generated. They are unique on a given
> volume but are unrelated to CNIDs.

Note that the CNIDs of `file.txt` and `link.txt` are 23 and 24, respectively. Since hard-link semantics require that all hard links to a given file have the same inode numbers, in this case, HFS+ does not report the hard-link files' CNIDs as their respective inode numbers. Instead, it reports the indirect-node file's CNID, which is the same as the original CNID of `file.txt`, as the inode numbers of both hard-link files.

```
$ ls -i file.txt link.txt
22 file.txt    22 link.txt
```

We can now summarize the process of hard-link creation on HFS+ as follows. When the first hard link is created to a file, its link count goes from 1 to 2. Moreover, the file's content is moved to the private metadata folder as an indirect-node file, which retains the CNID and other properties of the original file. Two new entries are created in the catalog: one for the original pathname and the other for the newly created hard link. The "original" notwithstanding, both are brand-new entries—hard-link files—that serve as references to the indirect-node file. Both have the file type `hlnk` and the creator code `hfs+`. Although they have their own CNIDs that are unrelated to the original file's CNID, the `stat()` system call still reports the latter as the inode number of each hard-link file. When a user accesses a hard-link file, HFS+ automatically follows it so that the user actually accesses the indirect-node file.

12.8.7 Unlinking Open Files

Whereas Carbon semantics prohibit deletion of open files, POSIX semantics do not. HFS+ supports both behaviors: The delete() and unlink() system calls provide Carbon and POSIX semantics, respectively. The private metadata folder is used to store files that are unlinked while they are still open, or busy. Such files are renamed and moved to the metadata folder, where they are stored temporarily—at least until they are closed. If the busy file being unlinked has multiple nonzero forks, any forks that are not busy are truncated.

We can observe this behavior by listing the contents of the private metadata folder after using the rm command to remove a busy file—say, one that we are viewing using the less command. Figure 12–27 shows this experiment.

FIGURE 12–27 Use of the private metadata folder for storing unlinked busy files

```
$ sudo /bin/zsh
# cd /Volumes/HFSLink
# cd "`echo '\xE2\x90\x80\xE2\x90\x80\xE2\x90\x80\xE2\x90\x80HFS+ Private Data'`"
# echo hello > /Volumes/HFSLink/busyunlink.txt
# hfsdebug /Volumes/HFSLink/busyunlink.txt
...
  file ID           = 27
...
  extents           =    startBlock    blockCount    % of file
                           0xaf9           0x1        100.00 %
...
# less /Volumes/HFSLink/busyunlink.txt
hello
/Volumes/HFSLink/busyunlink.txt lines 1-1/1 (END)
^z
zsh: suspended  less /Volumes/HFSLink/busyunlink.txt
# rm /Volumes/HFSUnlink/busyunlink.txt
# ls
iNode22 temp27
# cat temp27
hello
# hfsdebug temp27
...
  file ID           = 27
...
  extents           =    startBlock    blockCount    % of file
                           0xaf9           0x1        100.00 %
...
```

As seen in Figure 12–27, a temporary file appears in the private metadata folder after a busy file is unlinked. The file is a moved version of the original file, with any nonbusy forks truncated.

> It is possible for the "temp" files in the private metadata folder to persist across a reboot if the volume was not cleanly unmounted. Such files are called *orphaned* files. They are removed when the volume is mounted next.

12.8.8 Symbolic Links

A symbolic link (or *symlink*) is a file system entity that refers to another file or folder by relative or absolute pathname. The following are some important properties of symbolic links.

- Unlike the case of a hard link, a symbolic link's target may reside on a different file system or may not even exist.

- Unlike HFS+ aliases (see Section 12.8.9), if a symbolic link's target is renamed or deleted, the symbolic link is not updated in any way—it is broken.

- Most file operations on a symbolic link are forwarded to its target. Some system calls have special versions that operate on symbolic links themselves, rather than their targets.

- The ownership and file mode of a symbolic link file are unrelated to its target. Although a symbolic link's ownership can be changed through the lchown() system call, there is no analogous call to change the file mode of a symbolic link.

- Symbolic links can easily lead to cycles, for example:

```
$ ln -s a b
$ ln -s b a
$ cat a
cat: a: Too many levels of symbolic links
```

HFS+ implements symbolic links as normal files whose data forks contain the UTF-8-encoded pathnames of their targets. A symbolic link file's resource fork is empty. Moreover, the file's type and creator code are slnk and rhap, respectively.

```
$ cd /Volumes/HFSLink
$ echo hello > target.txt
$ ln -s target.txt symlink.txt
```

```
$ hfsdebug symlink.txt
...
# Catalog File Record
  type                 = file (symbolic link)
  linkTarget           = target.txt
...
  # Finder Info
  fdType               = 0x736c6e6b (slnk)
  fdCreator            = 0x72686170 (rhap)
...
```

You can even synthesize your own symbolic links manually by simply setting the file type and creator code of a file. If the file contains a valid pathname, it will be a working symbolic link.

```
$ cd /tmp
$ echo hello > target.txt
$ echo -n /tmp/target.txt > symlink.txt
$ ls -l /tmp/symlink.txt
-rw-r--r--   1 amit   wheel  15 Oct 12 07:25 /tmp/symlink.txt
$ /Developer/Tools/SetFile -t slnk -c rhap /tmp/symlink.txt
$ ls -l /tmp/symlink.txt
lrwxr-xr-x   1 amit   wheel  15 Oct 12 07:25 /tmp/symlink.txt -> /tmp/target.txt
$ cat /tmp/symlink.txt
hello
```

> The `SetFile` program is part of Apple Developer Tools. Alternatively, you can set a file's type and creator code by setting the `com.apple.FinderInfo` pseudo extended attribute or by using the `FSSetCatalogInfo()` Carbon function.

12.8.9 Aliases

Aliases, which are supported by both HFS and HFS+, are lightweight references to files and folders. An alias has semantics similar to that of a symbolic link, except that it fares better when the link target is moved: It has the special property that moving its target on the volume does not break the alias, whereas a symbolic link would break if its target were moved.

The resource fork of an alias file is used to track the alias target by storing both the pathname and the CNID of the target. The CNID works as a unique, persistent identity that will not change when the target is moved. When an alias is accessed, it can withstand the staleness of one of the two references (pathname or unique identity). If one of the two is wrong in that the target cannot be found using it, the alias is updated with the correct one (using which the target *could* be found). This feature is the reason why it is possible to rename applications or move them to different places on a volume without breaking their Dock shortcuts.

An alias is described by an *alias-record* data structure. An alias's target may be a file, directory, or volume. Besides the target's location, an alias record contains some other information such as creation date, file type, creator code, and possibly volume mounting information.

> To make use of aliases, an application must use either the Carbon API or the Cocoa API—aliases are not available through the Unix API. On the other hand, although the Finder presents aliases and symbolic links similarly to the user, it allows creation of aliases only through its user interface. Symbolic links must be created by using the ln command or programmatically through the Unix API.

Figure 12–28 shows a Python program that resolves an alias and prints the pathname of its target.

FIGURE 12–28 A Python program to resolve an alias

```python
#! /usr/bin/python
# ResolveAlias.py

import sys
import Carbon.File

def main():

    if len(sys.argv) != 2:
        sys.stderr.write("usage: ResolveAlias <alias path>\n")
        return 1

    try:
        fsspec, isfolder, aliased = \
            Carbon.File.ResolveAliasFile(sys.argv[1], 0)
    except:
        raise "No such file or directory."

    print fsspec.as_pathname()

    return 0
```

(continues)

FIGURE 12–28 A Python program to resolve an alias *(continued)*

```
if __name__ == "__main__":
    sys.exit(main())
```

```
$ ResolveAlias.py "/User Guides And Information"
/Library/Documentation/User Guides And Information.localized
```

12.8.10 Resource Forks

Historically, resource forks on HFS and HFS+ file systems have been used to hold resources. For an application, resources might include custom icons, menus, dialog boxes, the application's executable code and runtime memory requirements, license information, and arbitrary key-value pairs. For a document, resources might include fonts and icons used by the document, preview pictures, preferences, and window locations to use while opening the document. A resource fork is usually *structured* in that there is a map describing resources that follow it. There are practical limits on the number of resources you could put in a resource fork. In contrast, a data fork is unstructured—it simply contains the file's data bytes.

By default, the Unix API on Mac OS X accesses a file's data fork. It is, however, possible to access a resource fork through the Unix API by using the special suffix /..namedfork/rsrc after the file's pathname.

```
$ cd /System/Library/CoreServices/
$ ls -l System
-rw-r--r--   1 root   wheel   0 Mar 20   2005 System
$ ls -l System/..namedfork/rsrc
504 -rw-r--r--   1 root   wheel   256031 Mar 20   2005 System/rsrc
```

> The shortened suffix /rsrc can also be used to access the resource fork, although it is deemed a legacy suffix and is deprecated in Mac OS X 10.4.

An HFS+ file with multiple nonzero forks is not a single stream of bytes and is therefore incompatible with most other file systems. Care must be taken while transferring HFS+ files to other file systems. Before Mac OS X 10.4, most standard Unix utilities on Mac OS X either didn't handle multiple forks at all or handled them poorly. Mac OS X 10.4 has better command-line support for multiple forks—standard tools such as cp, mv, and tar handle multiple forks and extended attributes, including when the destination file system does not support these features. These programs rely on the copyfile() function, whose purpose is to create faithful copies of HFS+ file system objects. copyfile() simulates multiple forks on certain file systems that do not support them. It does so by using two files for each file: one containing the data fork and the other containing the resource fork and attributes, flattened and concatenated. The second file's name is the prefix ._ followed by the first file's name. This scheme of storing multiple forks is known as the *AppleDouble* format.

> The SplitFork command can be used to convert a two-fork file into AppleDouble format. Conversely, the FixupResourceForks command can be used to combine AppleDouble files into two-fork resource files.

/usr/bin/ditto can be used to copy files and directories while preserving resource forks and other metadata. If the destination file system does not have native support for multiple forks, ditto will store this data in additional files. ditto can also be used to create PKZip archives with flattened resource forks, in which case it will keep resource forks and other metadata in a directory called __MACOSX within the PKZip archive.

```
$ cd /tmp
$ touch file
$ echo 1234 > file/..namedfork/rsrc
$ ls -l file
-rw-r--r--  1 amit  wheel  0 24 Apr 15:56 file
$ ls -l file/..namedfork/rsrc
-rw-r--r--  1 amit  wheel  5 24 Apr 15:56 file/..namedfork/rsrc
$ ditto -c -k -sequesterRsrc file file.zip
$ unzip file.zip
Archive:  file.zip
 extracting: file
   creating: __MACOSX/
  inflating: __MACOSX/._file
$ cat __MACOSX/._file
       2 R1234
```

The original file can be recreated from the PKZip archive using ditto.

```
% rm -rf file __MACOSX
% ditto -x -k -sequesterRsrc file.zip .
% ls -l file
```

```
-rw-r--r--  1 amit  wheel  0 24 Apr 15:56 file
% ls -l file/rsrc
-rw-r--r--  1 amit  wheel  5 24 Apr 15:56 file/rsrc
```

12.9 Optimizations

The Mac OS X HFS+ implementation contains adaptive optimizations to improve performance and reduce fragmentation. We will look at these optimizations in this section.

12.9.1 On-the-Fly Defragmentation

When a user file is opened on an HFS+ volume, the kernel checks whether the file is qualified for on-the-fly defragmentation. All of the following conditions must be met for the file to be eligible.

- The file system is not read-only.
- The file system is journaled.
- The file is a regular file.
- The file is not already open.
- The file fork being accessed is nonzero and no more than 20MB in size.
- The fork is fragmented into eight or more extents.
- The system has been up for more than three minutes (to ensure that bootstrapping has finished).

If all the preceding conditions are satisfied, the file is relocated by calling `hfs_relocate()` [bsd/hfs/hfs_readwrite.c], which attempts to find contiguous allocation blocks for the file. A successful relocation results in a defragmented file. Let us see this mechanism in action by creating a fragmented file and causing its relocation. We will use a somewhat unsavory method to create our fragmented file. Recall that we wrote a program (`hfs_change_next_allocation`, shown earlier in Figure 12–11) to provide a hint to the kernel regarding the location of the next allocation block search. We will use that program to our advantage in the following algorithm to create the file we desire.

1. Start with a small file *F*.
2. Use `hfsdebug` to determine the location of *F*'s last extent.

3. Use `hfs_change_next_allocation` to set the next allocation pointer immediately after *F* ends.

4. Create a nonempty dummy file *d*. This should consume the allocation block immediately after *F*'s last allocation block.

5. Append an allocation block's worth of data to *F*. Since *F* cannot grow contiguously any more, it will require another extent to house the newly written data.

6. Delete the dummy file *d*.

7. If *F* has eight extents, we are done; otherwise, go back to step 2.

Figure 12–29 shows a Perl program that implements the algorithm.

FIGURE 12–29 A Perl program to create a file with eight fragments on an HFS+ volume

```perl
#! /usr/bin/perl -w

my $FOUR_KB  = "4" x 4096;
my $BINDIR   = "/usr/local/bin";
my $HFSDEBUG = "$BINDIR/hfsdebug";
my $HFS_CHANGE_NEXT_ALLOCATION = "$BINDIR/hfs_change_next_allocation";

sub
usage()
{
    die "usage: $0 <volume>\n\twhere <volume> must not be the root volume\n";
}

(-x $HFSDEBUG && -x $HFS_CHANGE_NEXT_ALLOCATION) or die "$0: missing tools\n";
($#ARGV == 0) or usage();
my $volume = $ARGV[0];
my @sb = stat($volume);
((-d $volume) && @sb && ($sb[0] != (stat("/"))[0])) or usage();
my $file = "$volume/fragmented.$$";
(! -e $file) or die "$0: file $file already exists\n";

`echo -n $FOUR_KB > "$file"`; # create a file
(-e "$file") or die "$0: failed to create file ($file)\n";

WHILE_LOOP: while (1) {

    my @out = `$HFSDEBUG "$file" | grep -B 1 'allocation blocks'`;

    $out[0] =~ /^\s+([^\s]+)\s+([^\s]+)..*$/;
    my $lastStartBlock = $1; # starting block of the file's last extent
    my $lastBlockCount = $2; # number of blocks in the last extent
```

(continues)

FIGURE 12–29 A Perl program to create a file with eight fragments on an HFS+ volume *(continued)*

```
    $out[1] =~ /[\s*\d+] allocation blocks in (\d+) extents total.*/;
    my $nExtents = $1;          # number of extents the file currently has
    if ($nExtents >= 8) {       # do we already have 8 or more extents?
        print "\ncreated $file with $nExtents extents\n";
        last WHILE_LOOP;
    }

    # set volume's next allocation pointer to the block right after our file
    my $conflict = sprintf("0x%x", hex($lastStartBlock) + hex($lastBlockCount));
    `$HFS_CHANGE_NEXT_ALLOCATION $volume $conflict`;

    print "start=$lastStartBlock count=$lastBlockCount extents=$nExtents ".
          "conflict=$conflict\n";

    `echo hello > "$volume/dummy.txt"`;  # create dummy file to consume space
    `echo -n $FOUR_KB >> "$file"`;       # extend our file to cause discontiguity
    `rm "$volume/dummy.txt"`;            # remove the dummy file
} # WHILE_LOOP

exit(0);
```

Now that we have the means of creating a file that should be eligible for on-the-fly defragmentation, let us test the feature on a disk image.

```
$ hdiutil create -size 32m -fs HFSJ -volname HFSFrag /tmp/hfsfrag.dmg
...
$ open /tmp/hfsfrag.dmg
$ ./mkfrag.pl /Volumes/HFSFrag
start=0xaf9 count=0x1 extents=1 conflict=0xafa
start=0xafb count=0x1 extents=2 conflict=0xafc
start=0xafd count=0x1 extents=3 conflict=0xafe
start=0xaff count=0x1 extents=4 conflict=0xb00
start=0xb01 count=0x1 extents=5 conflict=0xb02
start=0xb03 count=0x1 extents=6 conflict=0xb04
start=0xb05 count=0x1 extents=7 conflict=0xb06

created /Volumes/HFSFrag/fragmented.2189 with 8 extents
$ hfsdebug /Volumes/HFSFrag/fragmented.2189
...
  extents           =    startBlock   blockCount    % of file
                             0xaf9         0x1        12.50 %
                             0xafb         0x1        12.50 %
                             0xafd         0x1        12.50 %
                             0xaff         0x1        12.50 %
                             0xb01         0x1        12.50 %
                             0xb03         0x1        12.50 %
```

```
                  0xb05              0x1         12.50 %
                  0xb07              0x1         12.50 %
            8 allocation blocks in 8 extents total.
  ...
$ cat /Volumes/HFSFrag/fragmented.2189 > /dev/null # open the file
$ hfsdebug /Volumes/HFSFrag/fragmented.12219
  ...
    extents                =   startBlock    blockCount      % of file
                  0x1b06              0x8        100.00 %
            8 allocation blocks in 1 extents total.
  ...
```

We see that opening a fragmented file that is eligible for on-the-fly defragmentation indeed caused relocation of the file to a single extent.

12.9.2 The Metadata Zone

The HFS+ implementation in Mac OS X 10.3 introduced an allocation policy that reserves space for several volume metadata structures, placing them next to each other—if possible—in an area near the beginning of the volume. This area is called the *metadata allocation zone*. Unless disk space is scarce, the HFS+ allocator will not consume space from the metadata zone for normal file allocations. Similarly, unless the metadata zone is exhausted, HFS+ will allocate space for metadata from within the zone. Thus, various types of metadata are likely to be physically adjacent and have higher contiguity in general—if so, the consequent reduction in seek times will improve file system performance. The policy is enabled for a volume at runtime when the volume is mounted. The volume must be journaled and at least 10GB in size. The hfsmount structure stores runtime details of the metadata zone. We can use hfsdebug to view these details.

```
$ sudo hfsdebug -V /Volumes/HFSFrag -m # metadata zone should not be enabled
  ...
# Metadata Zone
  metadata zone start block            = 0
  metadata zone end block              = 0
  hotfile start block                  = 0
  hotfile end block                    = 0
  hotfile free blocks                  = 0
  hotfile maximum blocks               = 0
  overflow maximum blocks              = 0
  catalog maximum blocks               = 0
  ...
$ sudo hfsdebug -m # metadata zone should be enabled for the root volume
  ...
```

```
# Metadata Zone
    metadata zone start block           = 0x1
    metadata zone end block             = 0x67fff
    hotfile start block                 = 0x45bed
    hotfile end block                   = 0x67fff
    hotfile free blocks                 = 0x1ebaa
    hotfile maximum blocks              = 0x22413
    overflow maximum blocks             = 0x800
    catalog maximum blocks              = 0x43f27
...
```

Figure 12–30 shows a representative layout of the metadata zone. Note that a given volume may not have all shown constituents in use—for example, quotas are typically not enabled on Mac OS X systems, so there will be no quota files. The last part of the metadata zone is used for an optimization called *Hot File Clustering* and is therefore called the *Hot File area*.

12.9.3 Hot File Clustering

Hot File Clustering (HFC) is an adaptive, multistage clustering scheme based on the premise that frequently accessed files are small both in *number* and in *size*.

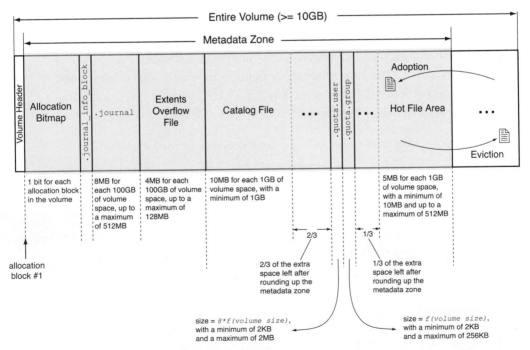

FIGURE 12–30 Layout of the HFS+ metadata zone

Such files are termed *hot files* in the context of HFC. As part of HFC, Apple's HFS+ implementation performs the following operations to improve performance while accessing hot files.

- It keeps track of blocks read from file forks to identify candidate hot files.
- After a predetermined recording period, it analyzes the list of candidate hot files to determine those that should be moved to the Hot File area within the latter part of the metadata zone.
- If necessary, it evicts existing files from the Hot File area to make space for newer and hotter files.
- It moves selected hot files to the Hot File area, allocating contiguous space for them as they are moved.

HFC records each file's *temperature*, which is defined as the ratio of the number of bytes read from that file during the recording period to the file's size. Thus, the more frequently a file is accessed, the higher its temperature. HFS+ uses the `clumpSize` field of the `HFSPlusForkData` structure to record the amount of data read from a fork.[23]

12.9.3.1 Hot File Clustering Stages

At any given time, HFC on a volume can be in one of the following stages.

- `HFC_DISABLED`—HFC is currently disabled, typically because the volume is not a root volume. HFC also enters this stage if the volume was unmounted while HFC was in its recording stage.
- `HFC_IDLE`—HFC is waiting to start recording. This stage is entered after HFC is initialized during mount. It can also be entered from the evaluation and adoption stages.
- `HFC_BUSY`—This is a temporary stage that HFC remains in while performing work to transition from one stage to another.
- `HFC_RECORDING`—HFC is recording file temperatures.
- `HFC_EVALUATION`—HFC has stopped recording file temperatures and is now processing the list of newly recorded hot files to determine whether to adopt new files or to evict old files before adopting.

---

23. HFC stores the number of allocation blocks read—rather than the number of bytes read—in the `clumpSize` field, which is a 32-bit number.

- `HFC_EVICTION`—HFC is relocating colder and older files to reclaim space in the Hot File area.

- `HFC_ADOPTION`—HFC is relocating hotter and newer files to the Hot File area.

Figure 12–31 shows a state diagram showing the transitions between various HFC stages. If the current stage is adoption, eviction, idle, or recording, the transition to the next stage is triggered as a side effect of a sync operation on the volume.

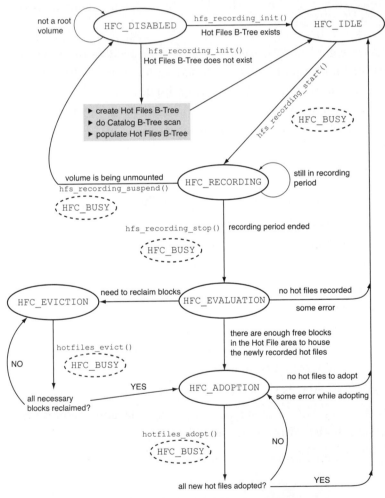

FIGURE 12–31 Transitions between Hot File Clustering stages

12.9.3.2 *The Hot Files B-Tree*

HFC uses a B-Tree file—the *Hot Files B-Tree*—for tracking hot files or, specifically, file forks. Unlike the other HFS+ special files, this tree's extents are not recorded in the volume header. It is an on-disk file that the kernel accesses by its pathname (/.hotfiles.btree).

```
$ ls -l /.hotfiles.btree
640 -rw-------  1 root  wheel  327680 Oct  7 05:25 /.hotfiles.btree
```

The Hot Files B-Tree is similar to the Catalog B-Tree in that each fork being tracked has a thread record and a Hot File record. Figure 12–32 shows the key format used by the Hot Files B-Tree. Given a file's CNID and fork type, the thread record for that fork can be looked up by setting the search key's temperature field to the special value HFC_LOOKUPTAG (0xFFFFFFFF). A Hot File thread record's data is a 32-bit unsigned integer that represents the fork's temperature. If no thread record can be found, HFC is not tracking that fork as a hot file. By including the fork's temperature in the search key, the corresponding Hot File record can be looked up. The data for this record is also a 32-bit unsigned integer, but it has no relevance to HFC. It contains one of two values for debugging purposes: either the first four bytes of the file's UTF-8-encoded Unicode name or the ASCII string "????".

hfsdebug can display details and contents (leaf records) of the Hot Files B-Tree. Note that unlike other HFS+ B-Trees, this B-Tree contains a user data record in its header node. The record holds a HotFilesInfo structure [bsd/hfs/hfs_hotfiles.h].

```
$ sudo hfsdebug -b hotfile
# HFS+ Hot File Clustering (HFC) B-Tree
...
# User Data Record
  magic             = 0XFF28FF26
  version           = 1
  duration          = 216000 seconds
...
  timeleft          = 42710 seconds
  threshold         = 24
  maxfileblks       = 2560 blocks
  maxfilecnt        = 1000
  tag               = CLUSTERED HOT FILES B-TREE
```

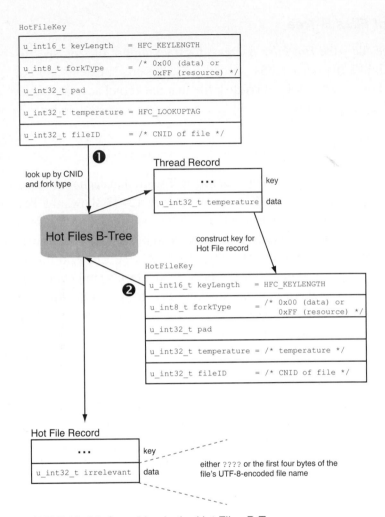

FIGURE 12–32 Searching in the Hot Files B-Tree

12.9.3.3 The Working of Hot File Clustering

Let us now look at details of some key HFC operations while referring to Figure 12–31. A typical starting point is the HFC_DISABLED stage, which a volume is considered to be in after it is unmounted.

When a volume is mounted, hfs_recording_init() ensures that it is a root volume, disabling HFC otherwise. Next, if the Hot Files B-Tree already exists, HFC transitions to the idle stage; otherwise, hfs_recording_init() creates a B-Tree and initiates a scan of the Catalog B-Tree. During this scan, HFC

> A volume's current HFC stage is contained in the `hfc_stage` field of the `hfsmount` structure, which is initially zero-filled. The numerical value of `HFC_DISABLED` is zero as well. Therefore, HFC is implicitly disabled at the start for every volume.

examines each leaf record in the catalog, performing the following operations for each file record.

- It ignores resource forks[24] and empty data forks.
- It ignores files whose extents are all outside of the Hot File area.
- It skips over the two journal files, `/.journal_info_block` and `/.journal`.
- It adds a thread record and a Hot File record to the Hot Files B-Tree for the remaining files, all of which will have at least one block within the Hot File area. The initial data values for the thread and Hot File records are `HFC_MINIMUM_TEMPERATURE` and the number `0x3f3f3f3f`, respectively.

After the Catalog B-Tree scan is complete, `hfs_recording_init()` places HFC in the idle stage. The transition to the next stage—the recording stage—occurs when `hfs_hotfilesync()` calls `hfs_recording_start()`.

> A sync operation results in a call to `hfs_hotfilesync()`, which is responsible for calling the appropriate functions when the current stage is one of `HFC_ADOPTION`, `HFC_EVICTION`, `HFC_IDLE`, or `HFC_RECORDING`. A sync operation normally occurs because of the update daemon invoking the `sync()` system call periodically.

For HFC to record file temperatures on a volume, several conditions must hold.

- The volume must not be read-only.
- The volume must be journaled.
- The volume's `hfsmount` structure must indicate that the metadata zone has been established for the volume.
- The number of free allocation blocks on the volume must be at least twice the total number of Hot File area blocks possible.

Table 12–3 shows various other constraints that HFC uses.

---

24. In Mac OS X 10.4, HFC works only on data forks.

TABLE 12–3 Constraints Used by Hot File Clustering

Name	Value	Notes
HFC_BLKSPERSYNC	300	The maximum number of allocation blocks that can be moved—whether for eviction or adoption—during a single sync-triggered HFC operation. Adoption does not move only parts of a file; therefore, this effectively limits the size of a hot file to 1.2MB for the default allocation block size of 4KB.
HFC_FILESPERSYNC	50	The maximum number of files that can be moved during adoption or eviction.
HFC_DEFAULT_DURATION	60 hours	The default temperature-recording duration.
HFC_DEFAULT_FILE_COUNT	1000	The default number of hot files to track.
HFC_MAXIMUM_FILE_COUNT	5000	The upper limit on the number of hot files to track.
HFC_MAXIMUM_FILESIZE	10MB	The upper limit on the size of files to track during recording. Files larger than this will not be tracked.
HFC_MINIMUM_TEMPERATURE	24	The threshold temperature for residency in the Hot File area.

hfs_recording_start() allocates memory for data structures used during recording. In particular, an instance of the hotfile_data_t structure [bsd/hfs/hfs_hotfiles.c] is used as an anchor for a *runtime recording list* of hotfile_entry_t structures [bsd/hfs/hfs_hotfiles.c]. The hfc_recdata field of the hfsmount structure refers to the hotfile_data_t structure.

```
typedef struct hotfile_entry {

    struct hotfile_entry *left;
    struct hotfile_entry *right;

    u_int32_t  fileid;
    u_int32_t  temperature;
    u_int32_t  blocks;

} hotfile_entry_t;
```

During the recording stage, read operations accumulate the number of bytes read for each file, whereas write operations reset such a count to zero (specifically, a file whose size is changing is not a desirable Hot File candidate). Moreover, even during read operations, the bytes-read count for a file will be *initialized* to the I/O count of the current read operation—rather than being added cumulatively—if the file's access time is older than the start of the current recording period.

When an active vnode[25] becomes inactive, the HFS+ reclaim operation, `hfs_vnop_reclaim()`, calls `hfs_addhotfile()` to add the file—if appropriate—to the runtime recording list. A vnode must satisfy several criteria to be added to the list, such as the following.

- It must be either a regular file or a symbolic link.
- It must not be a system file.
- It must not be a resource fork.
- It must have a nonzero size that is less than the maximum hot file size.
- It must have an access time newer than the start of the current recording period.
- It must have its temperature above the threshold.

If a file on the runtime recording list becomes active, it is removed from the list by `hfs_getnewvnode()` [bsd/hfs/hfs_cnode.c] through a call to `hfs_removehotfile()`. Active vnodes are examined separately once the recording period has ended.

After the recording period ends, the next sync-triggered call to `hfs_hotfilesync()` will invoke `hfs_recording_stop()`, which first calls `hotfiles_collect()` to add all active hot files to the recording list. `hotfiles_collect()` iterates over each active vnode associated with the volume's mount point and calls `hfs_addhotfile_internal()`—the back-end of `hfs_hotfile()`—to update the recording list.

Once `hotfiles_collect()` returns, `hfs_recording_stop()` moves to the evaluation stage, during which it performs the following operations.

- It ages the existing records (only the coldest 50%) in the Hot Files B-Tree by halving their temperatures, while limiting the lowest possible temperature to 4.
- It sorts the runtime recording list entries by temperature.
- It identifies the list entries that are already in the Hot Files B-Tree. For each such entry, its B-Tree information is updated, after which the entry is invalidated in the list. This operation results in a refined list of hot files eligible for adoption.

---

25. Technically, a catalog node (cnode).

At this point, the next HFC stage will be set as either adoption or eviction, depending on whether the free space available in the Hot File area is more or less, respectively, than the total space required by all hot files ready for adoption.

If the current stage is `HFC_EVICTION`, the next sync will trigger the invocation of `hotfiles_evict()`, which attempts to reclaim space by moving files out of the Hot File area by calling `hfs_relocate()`. It begins with the coldest files but may end up evicting all files depending on the space that must be reclaimed. However, as listed in Table 12–3, only up to `HFC_BLKSPERSYNC` allocation blocks—corresponding to no more than `HFC_FILESPERSYNC` files—can be moved during a single HFC eviction or adoption. If `hotfiles_evict()` is unable to finish its work before hitting these constraints, HFC remains in the eviction stage and will continue when the next sync occurs. Once eviction finishes, HFC moves to the adoption stage, which is handled by `hotfiles_adopt()`. Adoption is similar to eviction—it is also performed through `hfs_relocate()` and is subject to the same transfer constraints.

After adoption, HFC moves to the idle stage, from where it will enter the next recording period.

12.10 Miscellaneous Features

In this section, we will look at sundry HFS+ features.

12.10.1 Special System Calls

Noteworthy system calls supported by HFS+ include the following.

- `exchangedata()` is used for exchanging the data and resource forks of the files referenced by two pathnames. File attributes and extended attributes, including ACLs, are not exchanged, although modification times *are* exchanged. The call is atomic in that neither of the two files will be seen in an inconsistent state by any process. After the exchange is complete, all open file descriptors for the original file follow the swapped data. The primary purpose of `exchangedata()` is to provide applications that do not edit files in place (for safety) a way to save changes, without modifying the CNID of the original file. This way, CNID-based references to the original file will not break.

- `getattrlist()` and `setattrlist()` are used for retrieving and setting, respectively, attributes of file system objects, including volumes (see Section 12.11).

- `getdirentriesattr()` is used for retrieving file system attributes for items in a given directory. This call is essentially a combination of `getdirentries(2)` and `getattrlist(2)`. Note that `getdirentries(2)` is the system call invoked by `readdir(3)`.

- `searchfs()` is used for searching the file system based on a variety of criteria.[26]

12.10.2 Freezing and Thawing a Volume

HFS+ provides the file control operations `F_FREEZE_FS` and `F_THAW_FS` for freezing and thawing, respectively, a journaled mounted volume. Freezing allows a superuser process to lock down a file system by stopping file system operations. In processing a freeze request, the kernel performs the following operations on the file system corresponding to the given file descriptor.

- It iterates over all vnodes of the mounted file system and waits for any pending write operations to finish.[27]

- It flushes the journal.

- It acquires the global volume lock exclusively. This prevents the `hfs_start_transaction()` function [bsd/hfs/hfs_vfsutils.c] from acquiring this lock. Therefore, any file system functions that call `hfs_start_transaction()`—directly or indirectly—will wait for the lock to be released.

- It waits for any pending writes to finish on vnodes for the Extents Overflow file, the Catalog file, the Attributes file, and the volume device.

- It records the identity of the calling process in the `hfs_freezing_proc` field of the `hfsmount` structure.

Thawing releases the global volume lock. A frozen volume can be thawed only by the process that froze it.

The `fsck_hfs` program uses `F_FREEZE_FS` and `F_THAW_FS` to support "live" testing (the `-l` option) of a mounted file system.

---

26. The `searchfs(2)` man page provides details of using this system call.
27. The waiting period uses a timeout of 10 ms.

12.10.3 Extending and Shrinking a Volume

HFS+ has built-in support for growing or shrinking a mounted journaled file system. The `hfs_extendfs()` and `hfs_truncatefs()` kernel-internal functions, both of which are implemented in `bsd/hfs/hfs_vfsops.c`, provide this functionality. The functionality can be accessed from user space through the `HFS_RESIZE_VOLUME` command of `fsctl(2)` or the `HFS_EXTEND_FS` operation through `sysctl(3)`, for example:

```
int ret, options = 0;
u_int64_t newsize; // initialize this to the new size of the file system
...
ret = fsctl(mounted_volume_path, HFS_RESIZE_VOLUME, &newsize, options);
```

12.10.4 Volume Notifications

HFS+ generates a volume notification through `hfs_generate_volume_notifications()` [bsd/hfs/hfs_notifications.c] when free space on a volume falls below a warning limit. Another notification is generated when the volume's free space rises above a minimal desired limit. Both limits are stored in the hfsmount structure as the `hfs_freespace_notify_warninglimit` and `hfs_freespace_notify_desiredlevel` fields, respectively. The `BlockAllocate()` and `BlockDeallocate()` low-level functions in `bsd/hfs/hfscommon/Misc/VolumeAllocation.c` call the notification function every time they are invoked, allowing notifications to be generated if the current allocation or deallocation operation caused the free space situation to change with respect to the limits.

We can view VFS notifications (including the HFS+ notifications mentioned in this section) by using the program shown in Figure 12–33. The `KernelEventAgent` program (`/usr/sbin/KernelEventAgent`) receives these notifications and logs them to the system log file.

FIGURE 12–33 Viewing VFS event notifications using kqueue/kevent

```
// kq_vfswatch.c

#include <stdio.h>
#include <stdlib.h>
#include <sys/event.h>
#include <sys/mount.h>
#include <unistd.h>
```

(continues)

FIGURE 12–33 Viewing VFS event notifications using kqueue/kevent *(continued)*

```c
#define PROGNAME "kq_vfswatch"

struct VfsEventDescriptions{
    u_int       event;
    const char *description;
} VfsEventDescriptions[] = {
    { VQ_NOTRESP,      "server is down"                                    },
    { VQ_NEEDAUTH,     "server needs authentication"                       },
    { VQ_LOWDISK,      "disk space is low"                                 },
    { VQ_MOUNT,        "file system mounted"                               },
    { VQ_UNMOUNT,      "file system unmounted"                             },
    { VQ_DEAD,         "file system is dead (needs force unmount)"         },
    { VQ_ASSIST,       "file system needs assistance from external program" },
    { VQ_NOTRESPLOCK,  "server locked down"                                },
    { VQ_UPDATE,       "file system information has changed"               },
};
#define NEVENTS sizeof(VfsEventDescriptions)/sizeof(struct VfsEventDescriptions)

int
process_events(struct kevent *kl)
{
    int i, ret = 0;

    printf("notification received\n");
    for (i = 0; i < NEVENTS; i++)
        if (VfsEventDescriptions[i].event & kl->fflags)
            printf("\t %s\n", VfsEventDescriptions[i].description);

    return ret;
}

#define OUT_ON_ERROR(msg, ret) { if (ret < 0) { perror(msg); goto out; } }

int
main(int argc, char **argv)
{
    int ret = -1, kqfd = -1;
    struct kevent changelist;

    ret = kqfd = kqueue();
    OUT_ON_ERROR("kqueue", ret);

    EV_SET(&changelist, 0, EVFILT_FS, EV_ADD, 0, 0, NULL);
    ret = kevent(kqfd, &changelist, 1, NULL, 0, NULL);
    OUT_ON_ERROR("kqueue", ret);

    while (1) {
        ret = kevent(kqfd, NULL, 0, &changelist, 1, NULL);
        OUT_ON_ERROR("kevent", ret);
```

(continues)

FIGURE 12–33 Viewing VFS event notifications using kqueue/kevent *(continued)*

```
        if (ret > 0)
            ret = process_events(&changelist);
    }

out:
    if (kqfd >= 0)
        close(kqfd);

    exit(ret);
}
```

```
$ gcc -Wall -o kq_vfswatch kq_vfswatch.c
$ ./kq_vfswatch
        # another shell
        $ hdiutil create -size 32m -fs HFSJ -volname HFSJ /tmp/hfsj.dmg
        ...
        $ open /tmp/hfsj.dmg
notification received
        + file system mounted
        $ dd if=/dev/zero of=/Volumes/HFSJ/data bs=4096
        dd: /Volumes/HFSJ/data: No space left on device
        ...
notification received
        + disk space is low
        $ mount -u -o,perm /Volumes/HFSJ
notification received
        + file system information has changed
        $ umount /Volumes/HFSJ
notification received
        + file system unmounted
```

> `hfs_generate_volume_notifications()` calls `vfs_event_signal()` [bsd/vfs/vfs_subr.c] to generate a kqueue notification. Several HFS+ internal operations also use the kqueue mechanism to generate notifications when file system objects are modified. This allows interested user-space parties—the prime example being the Finder—to learn about these changes.

12.10.5 Support for Sparse Devices

HFS+ allows the device underlying a file system to be sparse. Apple's Disk Images framework uses this feature to support sparse disk images—it uses the

HFS_SETBACKINGSTOREINFO control operation to inform the kernel of the backing store file system. Sparse disk images can be created using hdiutil, either by specifying SPARSE as the disk image type or by providing a disk image name that contains the .sparseimage suffix. Let us look at an example.

```
$ hdiutil create -size 128m -fs HFSJ -volname HFSSparse /tmp/hfsj.sparseimage
created: /tmp/hfsj.sparseimage
$ ls -lh /tmp/hfsj.sparseimage
-rw-r--r--   1 amit   wheel        12M Oct 13 18:48 /tmp/hfsj.sparseimage
$ open /tmp/hfsj.sparseimage
```

We see that even though the volume's capacity is 128MB, the sparse disk image currently occupies only 12MB. It will be dynamically grown, up to the volume's capacity, when necessary.

12.11 Comparing Mac OS X File Systems

Now that we have looked at details of HFS+ and overviews of commonly available file systems on Mac OS X (in Chapter 11), let us compare key features and interfaces supported by all these file systems. We will use the getattrlist() system call to display a given volume's capabilities.

```
int
getattrlist(
     const char      *path,        // path of a file system object on the volume
     struct attrlist *attrList,    // a populated attribute list structure
     void            *attrBuf,     // buffer for receiving attributes
     size_t          attrBufSize,  // size of the buffer
     unsigned long   options);     // any options
```

The call returns attributes in a caller-provided buffer whose format depends on the specific attribute or attributes being retrieved. However, the buffer always begins with an unsigned long value that specifies the size of the returned attributes (including this size value) in bytes. In the case of volume attributes, the size value is followed by a vol_capabilities_attr_t data structure, which consists of two arrays of bitmaps: the *valid array* and the *capabilities array*. We will deal with only two elements of each array: the one at index VOL_CAPABILITIES_FORMAT (which contains information about volume format features) and the other at index VOL_CAPABILITIES_INTERFACES (which contains information about interfaces provided by the volume format). If a bit is set in a valid bitmap, it means the volume format implementation recognizes that bit. If the same bit is also set in the corresponding `capabilities` bitmap, it means the volume provides that capability.

```
typedef u_int32_t vol_capabilities_set_t[4];

#define VOL_CAPABILITIES_FORMAT      0
#define VOL_CAPABILITIES_INTERFACES  1
#define VOL_CAPABILITIES_RESERVED1   2
#define VOL_CAPABILITIES_RESERVED2   3

typedef struct vol_capabilities_attr {
    vol_capabilities_set_t capabilities;
    vol_capabilities_set_t valid;
} vol_capabilities_attr_t;
```

Figure 12–34 shows the source for a program that retrieves and displays a volume's capabilities—both features and interfaces.

FIGURE 12–34 Querying a volume's capabilities

```
// getattrlist_volinfo.c

#include <stdio.h>
#include <stdlib.h>
#include <unistd.h>
#include <sys/attr.h>

#define PROGNAME "getattrlist_volinfo"

// getattrlist() returns volume capabilities in this attribute buffer format
typedef struct {
    unsigned long           size;
    vol_capabilities_attr_t attributes;
} volinfo_buf_t;

// for pretty-printing convenience
typedef struct {
    u_int32_t   bits;
    const char *name;
} bits_name_t;

#define BITS_NAME(bits) { bits, #bits }

// map feature availability bits to names
bits_name_t vol_capabilities_format[] = {
    BITS_NAME(VOL_CAP_FMT_2TB_FILESIZE),
    BITS_NAME(VOL_CAP_FMT_CASE_PRESERVING),
```

(continues)

FIGURE 12–34 Querying a volume's capabilities *(continued)*

```
    BITS_NAME(VOL_CAP_FMT_CASE_SENSITIVE),
    BITS_NAME(VOL_CAP_FMT_FAST_STATFS),
    BITS_NAME(VOL_CAP_FMT_HARDLINKS),
    BITS_NAME(VOL_CAP_FMT_JOURNAL),
    BITS_NAME(VOL_CAP_FMT_JOURNAL_ACTIVE),
    BITS_NAME(VOL_CAP_FMT_NO_ROOT_TIMES),
    BITS_NAME(VOL_CAP_FMT_PERSISTENTOBJECTIDS),
    BITS_NAME(VOL_CAP_FMT_SYMBOLICLINKS),
    BITS_NAME(VOL_CAP_FMT_SPARSE_FILES),
    BITS_NAME(VOL_CAP_FMT_ZERO_RUNS),
};
#define VOL_CAP_FMT_SZ (sizeof(vol_capabilities_format)/sizeof(bits_name_t))

// map interface availability bits to names
bits_name_t vol_capabilities_interfaces[] = {
    BITS_NAME(VOL_CAP_INT_ADVLOCK),
    BITS_NAME(VOL_CAP_INT_ALLOCATE),
    BITS_NAME(VOL_CAP_INT_ATTRLIST),
    BITS_NAME(VOL_CAP_INT_COPYFILE),
    BITS_NAME(VOL_CAP_INT_EXCHANGEDATA),
    BITS_NAME(VOL_CAP_INT_EXTENDED_SECURITY),
    BITS_NAME(VOL_CAP_INT_FLOCK),
    BITS_NAME(VOL_CAP_INT_NFSEXPORT),
    BITS_NAME(VOL_CAP_INT_READDIRATTR),
    BITS_NAME(VOL_CAP_INT_SEARCHFS),
    BITS_NAME(VOL_CAP_INT_USERACCESS),
    BITS_NAME(VOL_CAP_INT_VOL_RENAME),
};
#define VOL_CAP_INT_SZ (sizeof(vol_capabilities_interfaces)/sizeof(bits_name_t))

void
print_volume_capabilities(volinfo_buf_t *volinfo_buf,
                          bits_name_t   *bits_names,
                          ssize_t        size,
                          u_int32_t      index)
{
    u_int32_t capabilities = volinfo_buf->attributes.capabilities[index];
    u_int32_t valid        = volinfo_buf->attributes.valid[index];
    int i;

    for (i = 0; i < size; i++)
        if ((bits_names[i].bits & valid) && (bits_names[i].bits & capabilities))
            printf("%s\n", bits_names[i].name);
    printf("\n");
}


int
main(int argc, char **argv)
```

(continues)

FIGURE 12–34 Querying a volume's capabilities *(continued)*

```
{
    volinfo_buf_t    volinfo_buf;
    struct attrlist attrlist;

    if (argc != 2) {
        fprintf(stderr, "usage: %s <volume path>\n", PROGNAME);
        exit(1);
    }

    // populate the ingoing attribute list structure
    attrlist.bitmapcount = ATTR_BIT_MAP_COUNT;    // always set to this constant
    attrlist.reserved   = 0;                      // reserved field zeroed
    attrlist.commonattr = 0;                      // we don't want ATTR_CMN_*
    attrlist.volattr    = ATTR_VOL_CAPABILITIES;  // we want these attributes
    attrlist.dirattr    = 0;                      // we don't want ATTR_DIR_*
    attrlist.fileattr   = 0;                      // we don't want ATTR_FILE_*
    attrlist.forkattr   = 0;                      // we don't want ATTR_FORK_*

    if (getattrlist(argv[1], &attrlist, &volinfo_buf, sizeof(volinfo_buf), 0)) {
        perror("getattrlist");
        exit(1);
    }

    print_volume_capabilities(&volinfo_buf,
                              (bits_name_t *)&vol_capabilities_format,
                              VOL_CAP_FMT_SZ, VOL_CAPABILITIES_FORMAT);

    print_volume_capabilities(&volinfo_buf,
                              (bits_name_t *)&vol_capabilities_interfaces,
                              VOL_CAP_INT_SZ, VOL_CAPABILITIES_INTERFACES);

    exit(0);
}


$ gcc -Wall -o getattrlist_volinfo getattrlist_volinfo.c
$ getattrlist_volinfo / # an HFS+ volume
VOL_CAP_FMT_2TB_FILESIZE
VOL_CAP_FMT_CASE_PRESERVING
VOL_CAP_FMT_FAST_STATFS
VOL_CAP_FMT_HARDLINKS
VOL_CAP_FMT_JOURNAL
VOL_CAP_FMT_JOURNAL_ACTIVE
VOL_CAP_FMT_PERSISTENTOBJECTIDS
VOL_CAP_FMT_SYMBOLICLINKS

VOL_CAP_INT_ADVLOCK
VOL_CAP_INT_ALLOCATE
```

(continues)

FIGURE 12–34 Querying a volume's capabilities *(continued)*

```
VOL_CAP_INT_ATTRLIST
VOL_CAP_INT_EXCHANGEDATA
VOL_CAP_INT_EXTENDED_SECURITY
VOL_CAP_INT_FLOCK
VOL_CAP_INT_NFSEXPORT
VOL_CAP_INT_READDIRATTR
VOL_CAP_INT_SEARCHFS
VOL_CAP_INT_VOL_RENAME

$
```

The program output in Figure 12–33 shows the volume capabilities supported by an HFS+ volume on Mac OS X. Let us look at the meanings of the various feature and interface bits that may be reported by getattrlist() for a volume. The following is an overview of the feature bits.

- VOL_CAP_FMT_2TB_FILESIZE supports a maximum file size of *at least* 2TB, provided sufficient storage is available.

- VOL_CAP_FMT_CASE_PRESERVING preserves the case of a file system object name when writing the name to disk but otherwise does not use case sensitivity. In particular, name comparisons are case-insensitive.

- VOL_CAP_FMT_CASE_SENSITIVE uses case sensitivity at all times when dealing with file system object names.

- VOL_CAP_FMT_FAST_STATFS provides a statfs() system call implementation that is fast enough to not require caching of its results by higher layers of the operating system. Typically, a volume format with this capability will provide its own caching of statfs() data. If this capability is missing, the information must typically be retrieved from the storage medium (which could be across the network) every time statfs() is called.

- VOL_CAP_FMT_HARDLINKS natively supports hard links.

- VOL_CAP_FMT_JOURNAL supports journaling, although journaling may not be enabled.

- VOL_CAP_FMT_JOURNAL_ACTIVE indicates that the volume has journaling enabled. This is not really a capability bit but a status bit.

- VOL_CAP_FMT_NO_ROOT_TIMES does not store times for the root directory reliably.

- VOL_CAP_FMT_PERSISTENTOBJECTIDS has persistent object identifiers that can be used for looking up file system objects. As we saw in Section 11.7.19, Mac OS X provides the volume file system (volfs) for performing such lookups on volumes that support this capability.

- VOL_CAP_FMT_SPARSE_FILES supports files with "holes"—that is, the logical size of a file can be greater than the sum of the physical blocks it occupies on disk (see also Section 11.7.6). Specifically, blocks that have never been written are not allocated on disk, leading to space savings and possibly better performance for such files (if the file system would otherwise explicitly zero-fill the unused blocks on disk; see VOL_CAP_FMT_ ZERO_RUNS).

- VOL_CAP_FMT_SYMBOLICLINKS natively supports symbolic links. Note that although FAT32 does not support symbolic links natively, the Mac OS X implementation of FAT32 emulates symbolic links using regular files.

- VOL_CAP_FMT_ZERO_RUNS indicates that the volume can dynamically substitute zeroes while reading a file's blocks that have been allocated but never written. Normally, such blocks are zero-filled on the disk by the file system. This capability is similar to sparse files in that there will be no I/O for the unwritten parts of a file, but it is dissimilar in that the corresponding blocks will still be allocated on disk.

Table 12–4 shows which features are supported by commonly used volume formats on Mac OS X.

The following is an overview of the interface bits that may be reported by getattrlist() for a volume.

- VOL_CAP_INT_ADVLOCK provides POSIX-style byte-range, advisory-mode locking. As we saw in Section 9.18.10, the Mac OS X VFS layer provides an implementation of advisory locking, which a local file system may choose to use. Alternatively, a file system can implement locking itself or may not support locking at all. As Table 12–5 shows, HFS+, HFS, and UFS use VFS-layer locking, whereas FAT32 and SMB implement their own. In the case of NFS, locking is courtesy of the lock daemon.

- VOL_CAP_INT_ALLOCATE implements the F_PREALLOCATE file control operation, which allows the caller to preallocate storage space for a given file.

- VOL_CAP_INT_ATTRLIST implements the setattrlist() and getattrlist() system calls.

TABLE 12–4 Features Supported by Common Volume Formats on Mac OS X

Feature	HFS+	UFS	HFS	NTFS	FAT32	AFP	SMB	NFS	WebDAV
2TB_FILESIZE	✔					✔		✔	
CASE_PRESERVING	✔	✔	✔	✔	✔			✔	
CASE_SENSITIVE	✔ (HFSX)	✔							
FAST_STATFS	✔	✔	✔	✔	✔	✔	✔		✔
HARDLINKS	✔	✔		✔				✔	
JOURNAL	✔								
NO_ROOT_TIMES					✔		✔		
PERSISTENTOBJECTIDS	✔		✔			✔			
SPARSE_FILES		✔		✔					
SYMBOLICLINKS	✔	✔				✔	✔	✔	
ZERO_RUNS									

TABLE 12–5 Interfaces Supported by Common File System Implementations on Mac OS X

Interface	HFS+	UFS	HFS	FAT32	AFP	SMB	NFS
ADVLOCK	✔ (VFS)	✔ (VFS)	✔ (VFS)	✔		✔	✔ (lock daemon)
ALLOCATE	✔		✔				
ATTRLIST	✔		✔		✔		
COPYFILE					✔		
EXCHANGEDATA	✔		✔		✔		
EXTENDED_SECURITY	✔						
FLOCK	✔ (VFS)	✔ (VFS)	✔ (VFS)	✔		✔	✔ (lock daemon)
NFSEXPORT	✔	✔	✔				
READDIRATTR	✔		✔		✔		
SEARCHFS	✔		✔		✔		
USERACCESS							
VOL_RENAME	✔	✔	✔				

- VOL_CAP_INT_COPYFILE implements the copyfile() system call. Originally meant for the Apple Filing Protocol (AFP), copyfile() is used to copy a file system object along with some or all of its metadata, such as ACLs and other extended attributes. Note that the system library provides a user-space implementation of a copyfile() function that does not use the system call. The function also flattens out metadata into external files on volumes that do not support that metadata natively.

- VOL_CAP_INT_EXCHANGEDATA implements the exchangedata() system call.

- VOL_CAP_INT_EXTENDED_SECURITY implements extended security (i.e., ACLs).

- VOL_CAP_INT_FLOCK provides whole-file, advisory-mode locking through the flock(2) system call. The note about VFS-level locking in the description of VOL_CAP_INT_ADVLOCK also applies here.

- VOL_CAP_INT_NFSEXPORT indicates that the volume allows its contents to be exported via NFS.

- VOL_CAP_INT_READDIRATTR implements the readdirattr() system call.

- VOL_CAP_INT_SEARCHFS implements the searchfs() system call.

- VOL_CAP_INT_USERACCESS is obsolete in Mac OS X 10.4.

- VOL_CAP_INT_VOL_RENAME indicates that the volume name can be changed through the setattrlist() system call.

12.12 Comparing HFS+ and NTFS

It is interesting to compare features of HFS+ with those of NTFS, the native file system format for Microsoft Windows. In general, NTFS is a more sophisticated file system in terms of built-in features.[28] Table 12–6 compares some noteworthy aspects of these two file systems.

---

28. In this section, we talk only about features that are available in the version of NTFS that is current at the time of this writing. Upcoming NTFS features such as Transactional NTFS (TxF) are not included in the comparison. Moreover, it is very likely that a new file system is on the horizon for Mac OS X.

TABLE 12–6 A Comparison of HFS+ and NTFS

Feature/Aspect	HFS+	NTFS
Allocation unit	Allocation block (32-bit).	Cluster (64-bit, but limited by Windows to 32 bits).
Minimum allocation unit size	512 bytes (must be integral multiple of sector size).	512 bytes (must be integral multiple of sector size).
Default allocation unit size	4KB.	4KB (for volumes larger than 2GB).
Maximum volume size	8 exabytes.	16 exabytes (the theoretical maximum; Windows limits the maximum volume size to 256TB, with 32-bit clusters).
Maximum file size	8 exabytes.	16 exabytes (the theoretical maximum; Windows limits the maximum file size to 16TB).
Redundant storage of file-system-critical data	Yes. An alternate volume header is stored on the next-to-last sector.	Yes. A mirror of the master file table is stored immediately following the original.
Filenames	A filename can have up to 255 Unicode characters. Mac OS X uses UTF-8 encoding.	A filename can have up to 255 Unicode characters. Windows uses UTF-16 encoding.
Case sensitivity	HFS+ is case-insensitive and case-preserving by default; it has a case-sensitive variant (HFSX).	NTFS supports case sensitivity, but the Win32 environment doesn't. The default system setting for name comparison is case-insensitive.
Metadata journaling	Yes, through a VFS-level journaling layer.	Yes, the journal is NTFS-specific.
Multiple data streams	Yes: two inline streams (the data and resource forks), and an arbitrary number of named streams. A named stream is limited to 3802 bytes on Mac OS X 10.4.	Yes: one unnamed stream (the default) and an arbitrary number of named streams. The latter have their own sizes and locks.
Permissions	Yes.	Yes.
Access control lists	Yes.	Yes.
Extended attributes	Yes.	Yes.
File-system-level search	Yes, through the `searchfs()` system call.	No.
Dedicated Startup file	Yes.	Yes (the `$Boot` file).

(continues)

TABLE 12–6 A Comparison of HFS+ and NTFS *(Continued)*

Feature/Aspect	HFS+	NTFS
Hard links	Yes.	Yes.
Symbolic links	Yes, with Unix semantics.	Yes, but semantics differ from Unix. NTFS provides reparse points, using which Unix-like semantics can be implemented.
Support for resilient "shortcuts"	Yes, through aliases.	Yes, but requires the link-tracking system service.
Volume quotas	Yes, per-user and per-group quotas.	Yes, per-user quotas.
Support for sparse files	No.	Yes.
Built-in compression	No.	Yes.
Built-in encryption	No.	Yes, through the Encrypting File System (EFS) facility that provides application-transparent encryption.
Built-in change logging	No.	Yes, through the Change Journal mechanism.
Support for fault-tolerant volumes	No.	Yes.
Reserved area for metadata	Yes, the metadata zone.	Yes, the MFT Zone.
Built-in support for tracking file access and relocating frequently used files	Yes, adaptive Hot File Clustering.	No.
Support for live resizing	Yes, through the `HFS_RESIZE_VOLUME` control operation. This support is experimental in Mac OS X 10.4 and requires a journaled volume. It can extend or shrink a mounted file system if several conditions are satisfied.	Yes, through the `FSCTL_EXTEND_VOLUME` control operation.
Support for "freezing" the file system	Yes, through the `F_FREEZE_FS` and `F_THAW_FS` control operations.	Yes, through volume shadow copying.
Support for "full" sync	Yes. The `F_FULLFSYNC` control operation asks the storage driver to flush all buffered data to the physical storage device.	No.

(continues)

TABLE 12–6 A Comparison of HFS+ and NTFS *(Continued)*

Feature/Aspect	HFS+	NTFS
Support for bulk querying of access permissions	Yes. The `HFS_BULKACCESS` control operation can determine, in a single system call, whether the given user has access to a set of files.	No.
User control of the next allocation location	Yes. The `HFS_CHANGE_NEXT_ ALLOCATION` control operation allows the user to specify which block the file system should attempt to allocate from next.	—
Read-only support	Yes.	Yes.

This concludes our exploration of Mac OS X internals—well, at least as far as this book's chapters are concerned. I hope the book has given you enough background and tools so that you can now continue the journey on your own. *Happy Exploring!*

APPENDIX A

Mac OS X on x86-Based Macintosh Computers

We discussed details of several x86-related features of Mac OS X in earlier chapters. In this appendix, we will briefly highlight the key differences between the x86-based and PowerPC-based versions of Mac OS X. It must be noted that despite the differences, most of the operating system is independent of the processor architecture.

A.1 Hardware Differences

Besides the difference in processors, x86-based and PowerPC-based Macintosh computers have several other architectural differences. Programs such as `ioreg`, `hwprefs`,[1] `sysctl`, `hostinfo`, `machine`, and `system_profiler` can be used to glean hardware-related information under Mac OS X. It is beyond the scope of this appendix to go into the details of hardware differences.

---

1. `hwprefs` is a part of the CHUD Tools package.

```
$ hostinfo # x86
...
Kernel configured for up to 2 processors.
...
Processor type: i486 (Intel 80486)
Processors active: 0 1
...
Primary memory available: 1.00 gigabytes
...
Load average: 0.02, Mach factor 1.97

$ hostinfo # PowerPC
...
Kernel configured for up to 2 processors.
...
Processor type: ppc970 (PowerPC 970)
Processors active: 0 1
...
Primary memory available: 4.00 gigabytes
...
Load average: 0.02, Mach factor 1.96
```

Table A–1 shows the results of running `hwprefs` with various arguments on the two platforms. (The x86 machine is a Mac mini Core Duo, whereas the PowerPC machine is a dual 2.5GHz Power Mac G5.) `hwprefs` also has processor-specific options, such as `ht` on the x86 and `cpu_hwprefetch` on the PowerPC.

There also now exist several machine-dependent sysctl nodes.

```
$ sysctl machdep
machdep.cpu.vendor: GenuineIntel
machdep.cpu.brand_string: Genuine Intel(R) CPU    1300  @ 1.66GHz
machdep.cpu.model_string: Unknown Intel P6 family
...
```

TABLE A–1 Running `hwprefs` on the x86 and PowerPC Versions of Mac OS X

Command	Sample Output on x86	Sample Output on PowerPC
`hwprefs machine_type`	Macmini1,1	PowerMac7,1
`hwprefs cpu_type`	Intel Core Duo	970FX v3.0
`hwprefs memctl_type`	Intel 945 v0	U3 Heavy 1.1 v5
`hwprefs ioctl_type`	ICH7-M v0	K2 v96
`hwprefs os_type`	Mac OS X 10.4.6 (8I1119)	Mac OS X 10.4.6 (8I127)

A.2 Firmware and Booting

We saw in earlier chapters (in particular, Section 4.16) that the x86-based Macintosh computers use the Extensible Firmware Interface (EFI) as their firmware, whereas Open Firmware is used on the PowerPC. While booting, like Open Firmware, EFI examines the volume headers of available HFS+ volumes. A bootable (blessed) volume's header contains information about the Mac OS X bootloader. As Figure A–1 shows, the `bless` command can be used to display this information.

FIGURE A–1 Using the *bless* command to view boot-related information in the volume header

```
$ bless -info / # x86-based Macintosh
finderinfo[0]: 3050 => Blessed System Folder is /System/Library/CoreServices
finderinfo[1]: 6484 => Blessed System File is /System/Library/CoreServices/boot.efi
...

$ bless -info / # PowerpPC-based Macintosh
finderinfo[0]: 3317 => Blessed System Folder is /System/Library/CoreServices
finderinfo[1]:    0 => No Startup App folder (ignored anyway)
...
```

Figure A–1 shows that in the case of an x86-based Macintosh, the volume header contains the path to `boot.efi`, which is the bootloader. `boot.efi`, a PE32 executable image, is a special EFI application whose job is similar to that of BootX on Open Firmware machines.

```
$ cd /System/Library/CoreServices
$ ls -l BootX boot.efi
-rw-r--r--   1 root   wheel   170180 Mar  17 07:48 BootX
-rw-r--r--   1 root   wheel   134302 Mar  17 07:48 boot.efi
```

You can cause EFI to run an alternate bootloader by recording the latter's pathname in the volume header using `bless`.

```
$ bless --folder /SomeVolume/SomeDirectory/ \
    --file /SomeVolume/SomeDirectory/SomeEFIProgram.efi
```

The Apple EFI Runtime kernel extension (`AppleEFIRuntime.kext`) provides access to EFI runtime services, which, as we saw in Chapter 4, are available even after EFI boot services have been terminated. `AppleEFIRuntime.kext` contains `AppleEFINVRAM.kext` as a plug-in extension. Like Open Firmware, the EFI NVRAM is used to store user-defined variables and other special-purpose variables (e.g., `aapl,panic-info`, which holds kernel-panic information). Again, as in the case of Open Firmware, the `nvram` command can be used to access these variables from Mac OS X.

The global kernel variables `gPEEFISystemTable` and `gPEEFIRuntime-Services` contain pointers to the EFI System Table (the `EFI_SYSTEM_TABLE` data structure) and the EFI Runtime Services (the `EFI_RUNTIME_SERVICES` data structure), respectively. The `<pexpert/i386/efi.h>` header in the Kernel framework contains definitions of these and other EFI-related data structures.

```
$ nvram -p
efi-boot-device-data %02%01...
SystemAudioVolume    %ff
efi-boot-device      <array ID="0">...
boot-args            0x0
aapl,panic-info      ...
```

A.3 Partitioning

As we noted in Section 11.1.3, x86-based Macintosh computers do not use the Apple partitioning scheme (also called Apple Partition Map, or APM)—they use the GUID Partition Table (GPT) scheme, which is defined by EFI. Specifically, internal drives use GPT, whereas external drives use APM by default. We discussed GPT in Section 4.16.4.4. We also saw an example of working with GPT partitions using the `gpt` command in Section 11.4.4. We can use `gpt`—and other commands such as `diskutil` and `hdiutil`—to display partitioning-related information about a volume, say, the root volume. Figure A–2 shows an example.

FIGURE A–2 Using command-line tools to display partitioning-related information

```
$ mount
/dev/disk0s2 on / (local, journaled)
$ sudo gpt -r show /dev/rdisk0
      start       size  index  contents
          0          1         PMBR
          1          1         Pri GPT header
          2         32         Pri GPT table
         34          6
         40     409600      1  GPT part - C12A7328-F81F-11D2-BA4B-00A0C93EC93B
     409640  311909984      2  GPT part - 48465300-0000-11AA-AA11-00306543ECAC
```
(continues)

FIGURE A–2 Using command-line tools to display partitioning-related information *(continued)*

```
   312319624       262151
   312581775           32        Sec GPT table
   312581807            1        Sec GPT header
$ diskutil info disk0
...
   Partition Type:       GUID_partition_scheme
   Media Type:           Generic
   Protocol:             SATA
...
$ sudo hdiutil pmap /dev/rdisk0
...
```

We see in Figure A–2 that the disk has two partitions, the second of which (disk0s2) is the root volume. The first partition, which is about 200MB (409600 512-byte blocks) in size, is a FAT32 partition that could be used by EFI as a dedicated on-disk system partition (see Section 4.16.4.4). You can normally mount this partition from Mac OS X.

```
$ mkdir /tmp/efi
$ sudo mount_msdos /dev/disk0s1 /tmp/efi
kextload: /System/Library/Extensions/msdosfs.kext loaded successfully
$ df -k /tmp/efi
Filesystem    1K-blocks Used  Avail Capacity  Mounted on
/dev/disk0s1    201609     0 201608     0%    /private/tmp/efi
```

A.4 Universal Binaries

We discussed the structure of a Universal Binary in Chapter 2. In the x86 version of Mac OS X, almost all[2] Mach-O executables—including the kernel—are Universal Binaries.

> Even with a Universal installation of the entire operating system, for such an installation to boot on both the PowerPC and x86 platforms, the respective firmware implementations will have to understand the partitioning scheme in use.

---

2. The executable that corresponds to Rosetta is not Universal—it is x86-only.

```
$ file /mach_kernel
/mach_kernel: Mach-O universal binary with 2 architectures
/mach_kernel (for architecture ppc):    Mach-O executable ppc
/mach_kernel (for architecture i386):    Mach-O executable i386
$ lipo -thin ppc /mach_kernel -output /tmp/mach_kernel.ppc
$ lipo -thin i386 /mach_kernel -output /tmp/mach_kernel.i386
$ ls -l /tmp/mach_kernel.*
-rw-r-----  1 amit  wheel  4023856 Feb  4 17:30 /tmp/mach_kernel.i386
-rw-r-----  1 amit  wheel  4332672 Feb  4 17:30 /tmp/mach_kernel.ppc
```

Note that the x86 kernel is somewhat smaller than the PowerPC kernel. Let us look at another example—that of the system library.

```
...
-rw-r-----  1 amit  wheel  1873472 Feb  4 17:30 /tmp/libSystem.B.dylib.i386
-rw-r-----  1 amit  wheel  2216288 Feb  4 17:30 /tmp/libSystem.B.dylib.ppc
```

Again, we see that the x86 version of the system library is somewhat smaller. In general, x86 binaries are smaller than PowerPC binaries. One reason is that the latter has a fixed instruction size (4 bytes, with 4-byte alignment), whereas the x86 has variable-size instructions (ranging from 1 byte to over 10 bytes). Figure A–3 shows a simple experiment to compare the size of an "empty" C program's executables when the program is compiled for x86, PowerPC, and 64-bit PowerPC.

FIGURE A–3 Compiling an "empty" C program on the x86, PowerPC, and 64-bit PowerPC

```
$ cat empty.c
main() {}
$ gcc -arch i386 -o empty-i386 empty.c
$ gcc -arch ppc -o empty-ppc empty.c
$ gcc -arch ppc64 -o empty-ppc64 empty.c
$ ls -l empty-*
-rwxr-xr-x  1 amit  wheel  14692 Feb  4 17:33 empty-i386
-rwxr-xr-x  1 amit  wheel  17448 Feb  4 17:33 empty-ppc
-rwxr-xr-x  1 amit  wheel  14838 Feb  4 17:33 empty-ppc64
```

A.5 Rosetta

We briefly discussed Rosetta in Section 2.11.9. Rosetta is a binary translation process that allows unmodified PowerPC executables to run on x86-based Macintosh computers. Rosetta's implementation consists of a program (/usr/libexec/oah/translate), a daemon (/usr/libexec/oah/translated), a collection of library/framework shims (/usr/libexec/oah/Shims/*), and support in the kernel, which has explicit knowledge of the translate program.

```
$ sysctl kern.exec.archhandler.powerpc # read-only variable
kern.exec.archhandler.powerpc: /usr/libexec/oah/translate
$ strings /mach_kernel
...
/usr/libexec/oah/translate
...
```

The translate program can also be used from the command line to run programs under Rosetta. Figure A–4 shows the source for a program that can be run both natively and under Rosetta to highlight the byte-ordering difference (see Section A.6) between the PowerPC and x86 platforms.

FIGURE A–4 Running a program both natively and under Rosetta

```
// endian.c

#include <stdio.h>

int
main(void)
{
    int i = 0xaabbccdd;
    char *c = (char *)&i;

    printf("%hhx %hhx %hhx %hhx\n", c[0], c[1], c[2], c[3]);

    return 0;
}


$ gcc -Wall -arch i386 -arch ppc -o endian endian.c
$ time ./endian # native (little-endian)
dd cc bb aa
./endian  0.00s user 0.00s system 77% cpu 0.004 total
$ time /usr/libexec/oah/translate ./endian # under Rosetta (big-endian)
aa bb cc dd
/usr/libexec/oah/translate ./endian  0.01s user 0.08s system 97% cpu 0.089 total
```

Rather than directly using translate, Universal binaries can be forced to run under Rosetta through several more appropriate means, such as the following.

- Set the "Open using Rosetta" option in the Info window of an application. This adds an entry to the LSPrefsFatApplications dictionary in the per-user com.apple.LaunchServices.plist file.

- Add the key named `LSPrefersPPC`, with its value being `true`, in the `Info.plist` file of an application.

- Use the `sysctlbyname()` library function in a program to set the value of the sysctl named `sysctl.proc_exec_affinity` to `CPU_TYPE_POWERPC`. Thereafter, a Universal binary launched through `fork()` and `exec()` will cause the PowerPC version to run.

Whereas Rosetta has support for AltiVec, it does not support executables that require a G5 processor (which means it also does not support 64-bit PowerPC executables).

Note that Rosetta reports a PowerPC G4 processor to programs. Running the `host_info` program from Figure 6–1 under Rosetta will show the following:

```
...
cpu ppc7400 (PowerPC 7400, type=0x12 subtype=0xa threadtype=0x0
...
```

A.6 Byte Ordering

The byte-ordering difference between the x86 and PowerPC platforms, along with the resultant caveats and handling approaches, are discussed in detail in Apple's documentation. A noteworthy point is that the HFS+ file system uses big-endian ordering for storing multibyte integer values.

> The PowerPC version of `hfsdebug`, the accompanying program to Chapter 12, can also be used on x86-based computers, courtesy of Rosetta. Note that on the x86, `hfsdebug` has to explicitly swap the journal data it reads from disk.

A.7 Miscellaneous Changes

Finally, let us look at a few miscellaneous system-level changes introduced in the x86 version of Mac OS X.

A.7.1 No Dual-Mapped Kernel Address Space

The kernel is not mapped into the address space of each task—it has its own 4GB address space. As we saw earlier, this is also the case with the PowerPC version of Mac OS X. Previous versions of Darwin/x86 (including the prototype x86-based Apple machines) *did* map the kernel into each user address space. An important reason for the change is the need to support video drivers for graphics cards with large amounts of physical memory. In a system with such a card (perhaps even multiple cards), if the driver wishes to map the entire memory of the card(s), a limited kernel address space would be problematic.

A.7.2 Nonexecutable Stack

The processors used in the x86-based Macintosh computers support a per-page nonexecutable bit, which can be used to implement a nonexecutable stack. The latter is one approach to countering the stack overflow class of security attacks. The approach can be generalized to making any kind of buffers nonexecutable, so that even if an attacker manages to introduce rogue code into a program's address space, it simply cannot be executed. This bit is enabled on the x86 version of Mac OS X. The program shown in Figure A–5 attempts to "execute" the stack, which contains illegal instructions (all zeros). The program will fail with an illegal instruction error on the PowerPC. In contrast, on the x86, access to the memory would be disallowed for execution, and the program would fail with a bus error.

FIGURE A–5 Testing a nonexecutable stack on the x86 version of Mac OS X

```
// runstack.c
#include <sys/types.h>

typedef void (* funcp_t)(void);

int
main(void)
{
    funcp_t funcp;
    uint32_t stackarray[] = { 0 };

    funcp = (funcp_t)stackarray;
    funcp();

    return 0;
}


$ gcc -Wall -o runstack runstack.c
```

(continues)

FIGURE A–5 Testing a nonexecutable stack on the x86 version of Mac OS X *(continued)*

```
$ machine
ppc970
$ ./runstack
zsh: illegal hardware instruction  ./runstack

$ machine
i486
$ ./runstack
Bus error
```

Note, however, that a program can programmatically change a page's protection value to allow for execution. For example, the vm_protect() Mach call (see Chapter 8 for details) can be used for this purpose.

```
// stackarray not executable
...
vm_protect(mach_task_self(), stackarray, 4, FALSE, VM_PROT_ALL);
// stackarray executable now
...
```

A.7.3 Thread Creation

In Section 7.3.1.2, we saw an example (Figure 7–20) of creating a Mach thread within an existing task. Thread creation on x86 is largely identical, except that setup of the thread's initial state is x86-specific. Figure A–6 shows an excerpt from the x86 version of the my_thread_setup() function from Figure 7–20.

FIGURE A–6 Setting up a newly created thread's state on the x86 version of Mac OS X

```
void
my_thread_setup(thread_t th)
{
    kern_return_t           kr;
    mach_msg_type_number_t count;
    i386_thread_state_t    state = { 0 };
    uintptr_t              *stack = threadStack;

    ...
    count = i386_THREAD_STATE_COUNT;
    kr = thread_get_state(th, i386_THREAD_STATE,
                          (thread_state_t)&state, &count);

    ...
```

(continues)

FIGURE A–6 Setting up a newly created thread's state on the x86 version of Mac OS X *(continued)*

```
    //// setup of machine-dependent thread state

    // stack (grows from high memory to low memory)
    stack += PAGE_SIZE;
    // arrange arguments, if any, while ensuring 16-byte stack alignment
    *--stack = 0;
    state.esp = (uintptr_t)stack;

    // where to begin execution
    state.eip = (unsigned int)my_thread_routine;

    kr = thread_set_state(th, i386_THREAD_STATE, (thread_state_t)&state,
                          i386_THREAD_STATE_COUNT);
    ...
}
```

A.7.4 System Calls

When we discussed PowerPC system call processing in Chapter 6, we saw that in order to invoke a system call, the call number is passed in GPR0, and the `sc` instruction is executed. On the x86, the system call number is passed in the EAX register, and the `sysenter` instruction is used to enter the system call. Figure A–7 shows an assembly-language excerpt for invoking a system call.

FIGURE A–7 Invoking a system call on the x86 version of Mac OS X

```
movl     $N,%eax ; we are invoking system call number N
...
popl     %edx
movl     %esp,%ecx
sysenter
...
```

A.7.5 No `/dev/mem` or `/dev/kmem`

Beginning with the first x86 version of Mac OS X, the `/dev/mem` and `/dev/kmem` devices are no longer available. Consequently, interfaces such as `kvm(3)` are also not available. Rather than accessing raw kernel memory, user programs are now expected to use only published interfaces—such as the I/O Kit user library and the sysctl interface—to access kernel information.

This book's accompanying web site (www.osxbook.com) provides information about writing a kernel extension that provides /dev/kmem's functionality.

A.7.6 A New I/O Kit Plane

The I/O Registry has a new plane—the *ACPI plane* (IOACPIPlane)—on the x86 version of Mac OS X. The ACPI plane's root node, called acpi, is an instance of the IOPlatformExpertDevice class.

> Advanced Configuration and Power Interface (ACPI) exists as an interface for allowing the operating system to direct configuration and power management on the computer.

```
$ ioreg -p IOACPIPlane -w 0
+-o acpi  <class IOPlatformExpertDevice, ...>
   +-o CPU0@0  <class IOACPIPlatformDevice, ...>
   +-o CPU1@1  <class IOACPIPlatformDevice, ...>
   +-o _SB  <class IOACPIPlatformDevice, ...>
    +-o PWRB  <class IOACPIPlatformDevice, ...>
    +-o PCI0@0  <class IOACPIPlatformDevice, ...>
     +-o PDRC  <class IOACPIPlatformDevice, ...>
     +-o GFX0@20000  <class IOACPIPlatformDevice, ...>
     | +-o VGA@300  <class IOACPIPlatformDevice, ...>
     | +-o TV@200  <class IOACPIPlatformDevice, ...>
     +-o HDEF@1b0000  <class IOACPIPlatformDevice, ...>
     ...
     +-o SATA@1f0002  <class IOACPIPlatformDevice, ...>
     | +-o PRID@0  <class IOACPIPlatformDevice, ...>
     | | +-o P_D0@0  <class IOACPIPlatformDevice, ...>
     | | +-o P_D1@1  <class IOACPIPlatformDevice, ...>
     | +-o SECD@1  <class IOACPIPlatformDevice, ...>
     |   +-o S_D0@0  <class IOACPIPlatformDevice, ...>
     |   +-o S_D1@1  <class IOACPIPlatformDevice, ...>
     +-o SBUS@1f0003  <class IOACPIPlatformDevice, ...>
```

Index

W

inform**IT**

www.informit.com

YOUR GUIDE TO IT REFERENCE

Articles

Keep your edge with thousands of free articles, in-depth features, interviews, and IT reference recommen-dations – all written by experts you know and trust.

Online Books

Answers in an instant from **InformIT Online Book's** 600+ fully searchable on line books. For a limited time, you can get your first 14 days **free**.

POWERED BY
Safari
TECH BOOKS ONLINE®

Catalog

Review online sample chapters, author biographies and customer rankings and choose exactly the right book from a selection of over 5,000 titles.